Assessing Special Students

THIRD
EDITION

Assessing Special Students

James A. McLoughlin and Rena B. Lewis

University of Louisville   San Diego State University

Merrill, an Imprint of
Macmillan Publishing Company
New York

Collier Macmillan Canada, Inc.
Toronto

Maxwell Macmillan International Publishing Group
New York   Oxford   Singapore   Sydney

Cover art: Jodi McGlaughlin

This book was set in Univers and Meridien.

Administrative Editor: Ann Castel
Production Editor: Carol Sykes
Art Coordinator: Jim Hubbard
Cover Designer: Brian Deep
Photo Editor: Gail Meese

Photo credits: Andy Brunk/Merrill, pp. 1, 71, 256, 452;
Lloyd Lemmerman/Merrill, pp. 3, 184, 557; Gale
Zucker, pp. 27, 407; Merrill, p. 46; Jean Greenwald,
pp. 48, 370; Paul Conklin, p. 97; courtesy Apple
Computer, Inc., p. 131; Bruce Johnson/Merrill, pp. 146,
222; Kevin Fitzsimons/Merrill, pp. 148, 293, 450, 518;
Celia Drake/Merrill, pp. 291, 335; David Strickler, p.
481; Jo Hall/Merrill, p. 502; Michael Siluk, p. 516; and
Larry Hammill/Merrill, p. 588.

Library of Congress Catalog Card Number: 89–62392
International Standard Book Number: 0–675–21116–6
Printed in the United States of America
2 3 4 5 6 7 8 9 — 94 93 92 91 90

For our parents: Kathleen and Peter McLoughlin
Margaret and Willard Bishopp

Preface

Assessment is at the center of all good teaching, and this book is designed to provide a clear, comprehensive guide to the assessment of students with mild handicaps. This book will give you both an understanding of the assessment process and the concrete, practical skills necessary to assess special students successfully so that you can teach them well. To structure the process, we offer an assessment question model and we have developed the concept of the Individualized Assessment Plan (IAP). Our basis for the assessment questions and suggested procedures is a combination of good professional practice and legal mandates. This functional approach allows you sufficient flexibility to explore the areas and types of assessment in which you are particularly interested. In accordance with our belief that educators need useful information, we maintain a strong educational orientation toward assessment.

This is the third edition of *Assessing Special Students,* and it reflects many changes in professional thought and practice. A new chapter on the use of computers has been added to provide information on the ways technological tools can assist teachers in the assessment process. Curriculum-based assessment is featured as one of the important strategies for informal assessment, and new information is provided on the design, construction, and interpretation of classroom probes and quizzes. The chapter on early childhood assessment includes coverage of new legislation (PL 99–457) and family assessment, and the chapter on career and vocational assessment has been expanded to include information on college assessment and postsecondary concerns. New issues, trends, and ideas are discussed throughout; for example, decision-making models in assess-ment and litigation concerning assessment are discussed in the last chapter. Throughout the book we have maintained our interest in nonbiased assessment of culturally and ethnically diverse students, and Chapter 14 focuses on assessment of students who speak nonstandard English or languages other than English.

This third edition has been thoroughly updated, and it features many new tests and procedures, several of which are revised editions of measures covered in previous editions. Among the new instruments discussed are the following:

- □ *Peabody Individual Achievement Test–Revised*
- □ *Woodcock-Johnson Psycho-Educational Battery Revised, Tests of Cognitive Ability* and *Tests of Achievement*
- □ *Auditory Discrimination Test* (2nd edition)
- □ *Detroit Tests of Learning Aptitude–Primary*
- □ *Test of Gross Motor Development*
- □ *Revised Behavior Problem Checklist*
- □ *The Instructional Environment Scale*
- □ *Woodcock Reading Mastery Tests–Revised*
- □ *Gray Oral Reading Tests–Revised*
- □ *Test of Reading Comprehension* (revised edition)
- □ *Analytical Reading Inventory* (4th edition)
- □ *KeyMath Revised: A Diagnostic Inventory of Essential Mathematics*
- □ *Test of Written Spelling–2*
- □ *Test of Written Language–2*
- □ *Test of Adolescent Language–2*
- □ *Test of Language Development–2, Primary* and *Intermediate*
- □ *Clinical Evaluation of Language Fundamentals– Revised*
- □ *Boehm Test of Basic Concepts–Revised*

☐ *Metropolitan Readiness Tests–Revised*
☐ *BRIGANCE® K & 1 Screen*
☐ *Social and Prevocational Information Battery–Revised*
☐ *APTICOM® Aptitude Test Battery*

Our goal in this book is to provide you with a foundation for understanding the assessment process and with the skills necessary for carrying out meaningful assessments. The chief strength of this text remains its balanced coverage of formal and informal assessment. Critiques of the strengths and weaknesses of formal tests and informal procedures help you select the tools that will supply the information you need.

We have chosen to speak about popular assessment procedures as well as less well known, but distinctive, measures. Popular instruments are discussed in some depth, not necessarily because they are always the best techniques, but because they reflect current practice. On the other hand, information about less well known tests and techniques is provided to acquaint you with promising procedures. With this comprehensive coverage, you will find out not only what is currently being done (and how well) but also what needs to be changed and how to do that.

In addition, we provide the connection between gathering assessment information and using it to make decisions. There are regular reminders to consider assessment data in relation to the classroom setting and suggestions for making sense out of all the information gathered. This process is described in the context of a team approach to educational assessment but with particular emphasis on the role of the special education teacher.

To make our book a more practical classroom resource, we have included several useful case reports, sample test profiles, checklists, and illustrations. Also, information boxes throughout the chapters summarize the important characteristics of tests discussed in depth. We have tried to give you a feel for the procedures you will use in assessment and to critique and relate them to one another so that you can better understand how to use them. Each chapter begins with a brief topical outline of its contents and ends with a Study Guide containing factual review questions, applied activities, and discussion questions focusing on critical issues addressed in the chapter.

We would like to express our appreciation to the many people who have supported us in the development of this third edition. Reviewers of the manuscript who offered helpful advice were Martin Agran, Utah State University; Libby G. Cohen, University of Southern Maine; John M. Dodd, Eastern Montana College; Janice Ferguson, Western Kentucky University; Robert G. Harrington, University of Kansas—Lawrence; Alfred Hirshoren, St. John's University; Robert E. Lang, Valparaiso University; Barbara Lowenthal, Northeastern Illinois University; Terry M. McLeod, North Georgia College; Sam Minner, Murray State University; Scott Sparks, Ohio University; Carol Swift, Oakland University; and Don Walker, University of Virginia. Thanks to them all. We appreciate our editors, Vicki Knight and Carol Sykes, for their insightful, considerate, and generous encouragement throughout this project. We also wish to thank the many publishers and agencies who permitted us to reproduce their material.

Graduate students Shelley Thomas and Lisa Lallo, of the University of Louisville, helped with library research and the appendixes and indexes. Deirdre Jordan, doctoral student at San Diego State University, updated the Instructor's Manual for this edition and prepared questions for the computerized test bank. We especially appreciate the typing of Vicki Bowen, from the University of Louisville School of Education. Most of all, special thanks to our spouses, JoAnn and Jim, and to our boys, Sean, Tim, and Dylan, for carrying on when we went off to write and being there for us when we returned.

We hope that our efforts to clarify and explain the educational assessment of mildly handicapped students prove useful to you. We invite your personal written response.

Contents

ix

Nature of Educational Assessment

Educational assessments are performed for many reasons, and there are many types of formal and informal assessment procedures. Chapter 1 provides an overview of the assessment techniques used today. As the section on history of assessment points out, formal tests must be complemented with informal assessment strategies. Many issues are involved in our current practices, and a brief discussion of major ones will prepare you for suggested solutions throughout this book. Also, educational assessment of special students is carried out by a team. In Chapter 1, the roles of team members are explained, and their activities in making decisions about eligibility for special services and the design of instructional programs are described.

Chapter 1 also stresses the systematic nature of educational assessment, explaining how to use a set of assessment questions to select appropriate data-collection procedures. We need to know what to assess in major areas, what types of data are needed, what procedures can be used to gather those data, and how the data will be applied. A suggested sequence for activities, including how to draw relationships among various types of assessment information, should be helpful in organizing assessment results for the design of appropriate instructional programs. For now, it is important to focus on the types of assessment data required, not specific tests and informal techniques. Furthermore, the limitation of academic assessment considerations to school skills in this section does not mean that the needs of very young or adolescent students are overlooked; those assessment procedures are treated separately in Chapters 18 and 19.

Chapter 2 takes you step by step through an educational assessment. The suggested procedures are based on good practice and the requirements of Public Law (PL) 94−142, as well as the assessment question model described earlier. We begin to identify and refer students after efforts to solve their problems by classroom modifications. The rights of students' parents to be informed and involved are evident at this point and throughout the process.

Of particular note in Chapter 2 is the Individualized Assessment Plan (IAP), one way to organize your thinking about the assessment and to actualize the assessment question model. Given a plan to conduct the assessment, you can proceed with the collection of information and its interpretation. A particularly important phase of any assessment is when results are reported and used to make educational decisions. The development of the Individualized Education Program (IEP) is also briefly described here because many examples of both IAPs and IEPs appear throughout this text. The full assessment cycle is complete when we monitor and evaluate the student's progress. Thus, Chapter 2 provides an overview of the total process, the elements of which are treated in detail in later chapters.

1

The Definition of Assessment

All educators assess their students. They use informal methods, gathering daily information through worksheets, questions, and quizzes. Formally, they may regularly administer standardized tests to determine a student's performance level. They use these data for various administrative and instructional decisions.

Educators of handicapped students, or special educators, particularly need a wide variety of information about their students. Regular education is designed to meet the needs of average learners, whereas special education services are designed to meet the individual needs of students with more severe school performance problems. Their instructional plans must be highly individualized, which means that their teachers must have precise information about what the students need in instructional terms. And that is where assessment comes in.

DEFINITION

Educational assessment of handicapped students is the systematic process of gathering educationally relevant information to make legal and instructional decisions about the provision of special services. The special educator pursues information that relates to the everyday concerns of the classroom. However, educational assessment is also part of an interdisciplinary effort to understand the handicapped student's learning problems. It is performed in conjunction with the work of other professionals, such as physicians, speech-language clinicians, and physical therapists.

Educational assessment focuses mainly on the many areas of learning in school, as well as any other factors affecting school achievement. Academic, language, and social skills are examined. Environmental factors may also be considered, along with analyzing the student's observable and measurable learning behavior and learning strategies.

Educational assessment extends beyond school into areas of early childhood development and adulthood. The development of infants and young children in language, motor areas, cognition, social-emotional behavior, and other skills are analyzed both individually and collectively for their impact upon one another. The transition of adolescents from the world of school into the adult world of work, careers, higher education, and other adult issues requires careful scrutiny.

Educational assessment, testing, and diagnosis are related, but not synonymous. *Testing* elicits the responses of students to questions under structured conditions. Depending upon how structured the test is, the results of testing may include a variety of scores, a list of acquired skills, and so on. Testing is only one of many strategies used in educational assessment to gather information about the special student.

Diagnosis is a term borrowed from the medical profession, and used in that context, refers to the effort to establish the cause of an illness and to describe the appropriate treatment. The condition is generally categorized with a label such as "autism," and the label implies the treatment. In contrast, educational assessment does not set out to establish causes, assign labels to the handicapped student, or determine remediation (treatment) based on the label. If the student is labeled as "handicapped" in a certain way, the label is only given to document eligibility for certain kinds of services and is not necessarily an indication of a cause of the learning problem. Furthermore, educational assessment organizes programs for exceptional students on the basis of demonstrated skill deficits, rather than global syndromes or labels. Programs are based on needed services, rather than the type of handicap. In other words, special educators use assessment to determine that Jim has special needs in the area of reading, rather than to say he is "dyslexic."

HISTORICAL PERSPECTIVE

Educational assessment of exceptional students has developed considerably over the past 80 years. It has been influenced by trends in many fields and shaped by many forces.

While the measurement of personality and other psychological factors was a topic of study in the 19th century, the work of Alfred Binet and others led to the major development of assessment techniques during the first part of this century. Assessments were developed to meet a variety of needs, including the screening of handicapped students in public schools and the evaluation of military personnel and potential employees. These early efforts became the prototypes for many current group and individual tests in psychology and education.

The controversy over the nature of intelligence has affected assessment practices used with handicapped students. One debate centers around whether intelligence is one entity or is made up of a set of factors. Some tests attempt to measure a variety of factors that comprise intelligence; these factors are then analyzed to identify individual strengths and weaknesses within the global characteristic of intelligence.

Another cause for lively discussion has been the question of whether intelligence is changeable. Most professionals consider intelligence a product of the interaction between people and their environment and, therefore, subject to change. Educational assessment of handicapped students now incorporates procedures that analyze the environment, as well as the person's abilities.

The field of medicine has had a profound effect on the development of educational assessment procedures. For many years, special education assessment practices used a medical model. An assessment merely yielded a diagnostic label, such as "mental retardation." It was assumed that a "retarded" person would always remain that way, with no remedial action available in the classroom. Considerable progress has been made toward the development of an assessment model more relevant to educational concerns.

Work in other fields is also being applied toward assessment in special education. Tests of perception study an exceptional student's processing of information through various senses, such as vision or hearing. Psychoeducational test batteries combine the analysis of psychological and educational factors. Applications of behavioral psychology have resulted in the use of many systems for behavioral observations of the student's environment, including a special interest in the curriculum and tasks with which the special student must deal. Other forms of informal assessment like interviewing have been borrowed and adapted from other fields, such as anthropology and sociology.

After World War II, services for the handicapped grew tremendously, with a subsequent growth in assessment procedures, particularly tests. Individual tests were developed in all academic areas— and in language, social skills, and vocational skills— with the help of commercial companies. In addi-

tion, special educators and other professionals created informal procedures directly related to classroom needs. Criterion-referenced testing played a major role in linking assessment and instructional programming.

Unfortunately, many abuses of assessment accompanied growth. Invalid and unreliable measures were used, sometimes administered by untrained individuals. Some assessments were too narrow in nature; some discriminated on the basis of the student's language, cultural background, or sex. Results were used inappropriately, with students erroneously labeled "handicapped." Handicapped students' and their parents' rights to due process under law were violated.

In 1975, PL 94–142 greatly influenced and improved the content and procedures of assessment. The law mandates a set of due process procedures as well as assessment guidelines to correct the problems. Handicapped students must be adequately assessed by a team and an Individualized Education Program (IEP) developed. State departments of education must meet federal standards to receive funding for handicapped student programs. PL 99–457 sets similar standards for infant and early childhood assessment.

Current trends in the kinds of services and teaching methods used with exceptional students have also been influential in the development of assessment procedures. Services for students with many different kinds of handicapping conditions require precise assessment procedures, particularly with mildly handicapped children. A particular challenge has been creating culture-fair procedures to assess minority students suspected of having a handicap.

In addition, current efforts to mainstream special students create a need for regular teachers to have procedures to observe and assess these students. Educators of exceptional students are held accountable for ongoing evaluation of learning; they need to monitor student progress more frequently, with less time and expense than standardized tests. Indeed, dissatisfaction with standardized tests has created a demand for other kinds of assessment procedures. The growth of criterion-referenced assessment reflects this effort to clarify the relationship between assessment and instruction. Assessment information can be generated to develop goals and objectives in instruction. Applications of computer technology, in terms of data gathering, storage, and use, also shape the assessment process.

In summary, we can describe educational assessment today in the following terms:

1. Assessment is tailored to the individual needs of each exceptional student.
2. Assessment data are used to make legal and instructional decisions concerning handicapped students.
3. Assessment identifies educationally relevant information, such as instructional goals and objectives.
4. The learning environment is evaluated as well as the student's response to questions and tasks.
5. A variety of procedures are used in assessment, not only standardized tests.
6. Assessment is characterized by a team approach, and the special educator is an important member of that team.
7. Professionals use nondiscriminatory assessment procedures.
8. Instructional programs are continuously evaluated or monitored.
9. Procedures are available to attend to the assessment needs of preschool children and the career-vocational needs of older students and adults.
10. New tests and other procedures to assess academic, language, and other skill areas continue to be developed.
11. Computer technology is being harnessed to facilitate test administration and scoring and the interpretation and reporting of assessment data.

PURPOSES

Educational assessment of handicapped students has many specific purposes. Assessment is used throughout every phase of a student's program. From the first indication of a learning problem to its successful remediation, the special educator systematically gathers information to aid in decision making. In general, this information is used to document eligibility for services for the handicapped and to plan an Individualized Education Program (IEP). In particular, the five main purposes for educational assessment are screening, determining eligibility, planning a program, monitoring student progress, and evaluating a program.

First, screening is performed to identify students who may have severe learning problems. In screening, the assessment procedures used must be as efficient, time-effective, and reliable as possible. The lower performers may be observed, and their academic performance and social behavior may be rated by teachers. Parents may be consulted to determine whether they feel a learning problem exists. The student's current instructional environment must be examined and alternate strategies attempted to accommodate the student's academic and behavioral needs. If the information and results of classroom modifications suggest a persistent learning problem, the student is referred for testing.

Second, educational assessment is performed to establish whether a student qualifies for special education and to determine whether the child has a school performance problem related to a handicap. To receive special services, students must meet eligibility requirements established by their state departments of education, based upon PL 94–142 and PL 99–457. A student's intellectual, academic, sensory, and other abilities are analyzed to establish the severity of any disability. If the student's performance and other data meet the standards, the student is eligible for special services. In addition, the school may receive federal and state government support to help pay for the provision of services.

Assessment at this level is more in-depth than that done for screening. Individual tests are given in major areas of school achievement, in social skill development, in intelligence, and in other related areas. Useful information is collected in various settings and from a variety of sources.

Third, the data from the educational assessment are used to plan an IEP. Annual goals and short-term objectives are chosen on the basis of a prioritized list of needs. The IEP indicates who will accomplish these goals and objectives with the student, as well as in what setting and for how long the service will be offered. The plan also outlines the duties of special and regular educators and support personnel.

The fourth reason for assessment is to monitor the progress of the exceptional student during the program. Information is gathered about the immediate effects of instruction. A variety of procedures document the level and kind of achievement of stated goals and objectives. Of particular interest is any information used to make program modifications. Informal assessment procedures and a blend of assessment and teaching are particularly helpful at this level, along with daily direct measurement and charting.

The fifth purpose for educational assessment is program evaluation. PL 94–142 requires at least an annual review of all IEPs for handicapped students. The staff and parents examine the results of the program over the past year and decide if the special services should be continued as is, modified, or discontinued. In addition to data from the continuous program monitoring, this annual review requires information about any changes in performance. Both standardized and informal techniques are used.

KINDS OF ASSESSMENT PROCEDURES

Many types of assessment procedures are available, requiring varying degrees of expertise. Several of these strategies will be employed in any complete educational assessment. Some combination may be used in the initial assessment, or they can be used individually to monitor program success.

Formal Strategies

Formal tests are structured assessment procedures with specific guidelines for administration, scoring, and interpretation of results. Norm-referenced tests compare a student's performance to that of a normative group. These tests may be group or individually administered and are available for most academic subjects as well as other areas of learning. Their use is limited to students who are very similar to the group used as a norm in compiling the test scores. The directions for administration, scoring, and interpretation of the tests are usually very explicit. The results may be expressed with a variety of quantitative scores, such as grade equivalents, standard scores, and percentile ranks. Information about the test's statistical validity and reliability is usually presented in the manual. The results from norm-referenced

tests are used in a number of ways, including documentation of eligibility for special education and related services and identification of general strengths and weaknesses in school learning.

An assessment may be administered to a group of individuals or to one person. Group procedures usually penalize exceptional students. Such procedures are generally not recommended for this population because they require skills in reading, ability to follow directions, and so forth, that the handicapped student may not have. Thus, the tests may serve merely to screen, that is, to identify those students who may be handicapped. However, group tests do take much less time to administer than most individual tests.

The two types of group tests most frequently encountered are achievement and aptitude tests. Students take these tests at regular intervals. Some of the major group achievement tests are the *California Achievement Tests* (1985, 1986, 1987), *Comprehensive Tests of Basic Skills* (1981, 1982, 1983, 1984, 1985, 1987), the *Metropolitan Achievement Tests* (6th ed.) (Prescott, Balow, Hogan, & Farr, 1985, 1986, 1987), and the *Stanford Achievement Tests* (7th ed.) (Gardner, Rudman, Karlsen, & Merwin, 1982, 1983, 1984, 1986, 1987). These and other tests are used for screening, grouping, and evaluating student progress, and measuring curriculum effectiveness. For the handicapped student, they mainly serve to screen achievement in the areas measured. Because they are group administered, there is little opportunity to do careful analysis.

Some of the major group aptitude tests are the *Test of Cognitive Skills* (1981), the *Otis-Lennon School Ability Test* (Otis & Lennon, 1979, 1982), and the *Cognitive Abilities Test* (Thorndike & Hagen, 1986). These require reading and other basic skills and serve to screen and identify students with learning problems. Exceptional students are also apt to have relatively low performance on these kinds of tests.

There are also many individual achievement and aptitude tests available. Individual and group tests described in this textbook are listed in the Test Index. As will be discussed throughout this text, popularity is no guarantee of technical adequacy. Commonly administered individual achievement tests include the *Wide Range Achievement Test– Revised,* or *WRAT–R* (Jastak & Wilkinson, 1984), and the *Peabody Individual Achievement Test–Revised,* or *PIAT–R* (Markwardt, 1989). These tests contain items in the basic skill areas of oral reading, spelling, and arithmetic. The *PIAT–R* offers a more comprehensive view of these skills and measures spelling and arithmetic skills differently from the *WRAT–R*. The *Woodcock-Johnson Psycho-Educational Battery–Revised,* or *Woodcock-Johnson–R* (Woodcock & Johnson, 1989), covers basic skills and content area subjects as well as cognitive abilities.

Individually administered tests supply many opportunities to probe skills and to observe the student under special conditions. For example, reading is measured with an oral response on both the *WRAT–R* and *PIAT–R*. Various cues and prompts not available in group assessment are supplied, making these tests more useful with students with learning problems. Also, other individual tests can be used for an in-depth probe of each academic area if necessary. For example, the *Woodcock Reading Mastery Tests–Revised* (Woodcock, 1987) are more detailed than either the *PIAT–R* or *WRAT–R*.

The same features are evident in individual aptitude tests. The major individual aptitude test used with school-aged individuals is the *Wechsler Intelligence Scale for Children–Revised,* or the *WISC–R* (Wechsler, 1974). The *WISC–R* contains a combination of verbal and visual-motor tasks. Different subtests of learning ability, using various measures of reasoning and problem solving are included. The *Woodcock-Johnson–R* (Woodcock & Johnson, 1989) also offers cognitive abilities tests, as does the *Kaufman Assessment Battery for Children* (Kaufman & Kaufman, 1983). In most states, one of these measures must be given to obtain special services for the handicapped.

A number of individual measures assess areas such as adaptive behavior, specific learning abilities, and classroom behavior. In addition, a variety of tests provide information about the student's status in the acquisition of reading, mathematics, and written language skills, as well as oral language development.

Informal Strategies

A variety of informal procedures are used in educational assessment to determine current levels of performance, document student progress, and/or direct instructional changes. A distinction is often made between the formal procedures just described and these less formal techniques.

Formal procedures usually are standardized, normative tests. Administration, scoring, and interpretation procedures are clearly delineated. Formal tests yield many different kinds of scores, the majority of which provide information about a student's standing in relation to other students.

Informal procedures usually are less structured or structured differently from standardized tests. Inventories, such as the traditional Friday spelling quiz or an arithmetic worksheet, fit into this category. There is an element of subjectivity in the administration, scoring (if they are scored), and interpretation. Some are easy to administer but difficult to design; furthermore, interpretation is often difficult because of a lack of guidelines.

Although informal procedures lack the kinds of scores yielded by standardized tests, their results are relevant to instruction, because data are expressed in instructional terms. Informal assessment tools vary in how directly they measure student performances and instructional conditions. Some directly involve the student, whereas others rely on informants.

There are many types of informal assessment procedures: observations, curriculum-based assessment, work sample analyses, task analyses, informal inventories, criterion-referenced tests, and so on. *Observations* are used to study the exceptional student in the learning environment over a period of time in order to describe patterns of behavior. Classroom behavior, interactions with peers and teachers, and other observable factors may be studied. The procedure can be used with any type of student for any purpose, but it is most often used to assess social skills.

Tester requirements vary, depending upon how systematically the observations are conducted. The results are usually the number and nature of the student's classroom behaviors; they are frequently represented in graph form. The quality of these observations depends upon such factors as how precisely the problem behavior is defined, how the data are gathered, and so forth. The information can be used to compose goals and objectives for instruction in the observed skill.

Curriculum-based assessment is a way to establish a student's instructional needs in relationship to the requirements of the actual curriculum being used (Tucker, 1985). Student skills are matched to those required by the curriculum. The instructional levels and rates of learning the material must be established (Hargis, 1987). The component skills of the curriculum are identified, appropriate informal tests of each one are administered to the student, and instructional objectives are stated to guide necessary instruction (Blankenship, 1985). The process is performed in conjunction with the instructional process and serves as a basis for evaluation and modification of the curriculum for the individual student.

Work sample analysis is used to study the correct and incorrect responses made in a student's work. Work samples can be taken in any subject and for any student. Knowledge of typical errors is required to use this strategy. The results are the number, types, and patterns of frequently made errors and successes. Because of the clear connection to the curriculum, the potential usefulness of the data is high. A teacher can use the information to establish goals and identify ways to modify instruction.

Task analysis is used to identify the main components of a task and to arrange the necessary skills in an appropriate instructional sequence. The procedure can be used with any student and can apply to any task. Task analysis becomes more difficult as the complexity of the task increases. The teacher who develops a task analysis must have an excellent grasp of the nature of the curriculum, tasks, and skill hierarchies. The results are a list of task components and of necessary skills stated in teachable terms. The teacher will know the parts of the task the student has mastered, along with those needing more instruction. The quality of the procedure depends on the teacher's expertise. The meaning and educational implications are clear and direct, and the results can be used to determine instructional objectives.

Inventories examine how a student performs within a specific curriculum or with instructional material. They can be developed for a wide variety of skills in the classroom and are often based on skill hierarchies. Because inventories are not standardized, they apply only to students in a particular class or a specific curriculum. They can be teacher-constructed or commercially available. The results are used to identify specific skills requiring instruction. However, interpretation of the full significance of missed items is difficult. There may be a certain degree of subjectivity involved or inadequacy in test design.

Criterion-referenced tests, or CRTs, compare a student's performance to a specified level of mastery or achievement. They are available in most academic areas or can be constructed by a teacher, and they are appropriate for students learning specific skills. CRTs may be group or individually administered. Tester requirements are different from NRT ones. The results are expressed in terms of skills mastered or not mastered at a certain level of proficiency; sometimes scores are available. The quality of criterion-referenced tests is relatively difficult to establish. They are useful in designing instructional programs because they supply information suggesting specific classroom goals and objectives. However, they tend to be time-consuming and tedious to administer.

CRTs differ from the norm-referenced tests (NRTs) described earlier. NRTs are used to compare an individual's performance to that of peers through a variety of scores and offer an overview of general strengths and weaknesses in a skill area. For example, an NRT would indicate that a student's oral reading skills were significantly lower than those of classmates, whereas his or her mathematics skills were not. The more specific CRTs can be used to analyze weak areas in more detail; for example, the *BRIGANCE® Diagnostic Inventory of Basic Skills* (Brigance, 1977) focuses on specific skill areas such as phonics and outlines the extent of mastery. CRTs are thus of more assistance in program planning and monitoring of progress.

Diagnostic teaching is another informal form of assessment used to evaluate the differential impact of two instructional techniques. An educator systematically monitors the effects of a teaching strategy on student performance and compares it to the impact of another technique. Diagnostic teaching is a powerful form of classroom research and evaluation.

Checklists and *rating scales* gather information in a variety of structured formats. They often obtain data not readily found with other techniques. They may be used by professionals, parents, or students with any subject matter. Checklists and rating scales may be formal in design or constructed by the teacher. They may yield descriptive or quantitative data, depending on format. The quality of the data depends on such factors as precision of design and the veracity and judgment of the user. They can be difficult to interpret because of the lack of guidelines, but can supply useful information for instructional programming.

Interviews and *questionnaires* gather information not otherwise easily accessible. For example, parents may be interviewed and/or asked to complete a questionnaire concerning their child's developmental, academic, and social history. Teachers' observations and professionals' judgments can also be valuable. The use of informants is advisable when children are too young to respond themselves, when others have exclusive access to information by virtue of experience and opportunity, or when one needs a broader perspective on the learning problems.

There are no restrictions on who can be interviewed or who can complete a questionnaire. If the interview or questionnaire is loosely structured, the user must be experienced in interpreting the results. The results are descriptive data, the quality of which depends heavily upon the knowledge of the person being interviewed or completing the form. Ease of interpretation generally depends upon the clarity of purpose and the degree of structure supplied.

A form of interviewing used frequently with students is the clinical interview, which is performed when a student is engaged in a task. The student is encouraged to verbalize his or her strategies to complete the assignment. The interviewer asks leading questions and probes significant statements. The goal is to identify the student's procedures and correct the faulty strategies.

In addition to interviews and questionnaires, a number of assessment tools rely on parent informants. The *BRIGANCE® Diagnostic Inventory of Early Development* (Brigance, 1978) is a CRT for the young child in areas such as language and motor development; parents are frequently asked to confirm a child's particular skill. The *Vineland Adaptive Behavior Scales* (Sparrow, Balla, & Cicchetti, 1984) and the *Adaptive Behavior Inventory*

for Children (Mercer & Lewis, 1977a) are procedures that rely on adults familiar with the students.

SPECIAL STUDENTS

Special educational assessment involves students referred to as handicapped by PL 94–142, that is,

those children evaluated as being mentally retarded, hard of hearing, deaf, speech impaired, visually handicapped, seriously emotionally disturbed, orthopedically impaired, other health impaired, deaf-blind, multi-handicapped, or as having specific learning disabilities, who because of those impairments need special education and related services. (PL 94–142, §121a.5)

Students qualifying for these services must receive a free and appropriate education from special educators and other professionals.

In this book, the needs of students with three of these handicaps are emphasized. As Table 1–1 indicates, the federal law recognizes the need for special services for the mentally retarded, emotionally disturbed, and learning disabled, along with other exceptional students. The mildly or educable mentally retarded, mildly emotionally disturbed or behavior disordered, and learning disabled students comprise the largest group of all handicapped students, about 7% of the total school-age population, and are frequently found in regular classrooms. From an educational perspective, these students share many common psychological, academic, and social problems requiring assessment. In educational terms, they are more alike than different.

Hallahan, Kauffman, and Lloyd (1985) consider the major distinction among the mentally retarded, emotionally disturbed, and learning disabled to be the frequency of particular problems. The area of primary concern for retarded students is general intellectual functioning and adaptive behavior; for the emotionally disturbed, emotional and social development; and for the learning disabled, academic and language disorders. Although mildly handicapped students may have problems in any of these areas, each handicap is characterized by its own set of frequently occurring problems.

The educational assessment strategies described in this book are particularly applicable to mildly handicapped students. Many of these procedures may also be used for students with other exceptionalities; however, educational assess-

TABLE 1–1
Mild handicapping conditions

Mental Retardation	Significantly subaverage general intellectual functioning existing concurrently with deficits in adaptive behavior and manifested during the developmental period, which adversely affects a child's educational performance. [PL 94–142, §121a.5b(4)]
Seriously Emotionally Disturbed	(i) The term means a condition exhibiting one or more of the following characteristics over a long period of time and to a marked degree, which adversely affects educational performance: (A) An inability to learn which cannot be explained by intellectual, sensory, or health factors; (B) An inability to build or maintain satisfactory interpersonal relationships with peers and teachers; (C) Inappropriate types of behavior or feelings under normal circumstances; (D) A general pervasive mood of unhappiness or depression; or (E) A tendency to develop physical symptoms or fears associated with personal or school problems. (ii) The term includes children who are schizophrenic. The term does not include children who are socially maladjusted, unless it is determined that they are seriously emotionally disturbed. [PL 94–142, §121a.5b(8); as amended in *Federal Register,* 1981, *46,* 3866]
Specific Learning Disabilities	A disorder in one or more of the basic psychological processes involved in understanding or in using language, spoken or written, which may manifest itself in an imperfect ability to listen, think, speak, read, write, spell, or to do mathematical calculations. The term includes such conditions as perceptual handicaps, brain injury, minimal brain dysfunction, dyslexia, and developmental aphasia. The term does not include children who have learning problems which are primarily the result of visual, hearing, or motor handicaps, of mental retardation, or of environmental, cultural, or economic disadvantage. [PL 94–142, §121a.5b(9)]

ment for the severely handicapped and for students with sensory and physical handicaps requires special considerations beyond the scope of this book. Throughout this book, we will use the terms *exceptional, handicapped, mildly handicapped,* and *special* interchangeably.

This book focuses on the school-aged student with classroom-related learning problems. Special programs for the preschool handicapped and for young adults with disabilities are currently being developed. Specific procedures used with the very young exceptional child are discussed in Chapter 18 and with the handicapped adolescent and adult in Chapter 19.

TEAM APPROACH

Important educational decisions about handicapped students are made by a team, rather than a single educator. The team approach brings together individuals from different disciplines who contribute their expertise and make complex decisions. The team may be composed of parents and other individuals representing education, special education, psychology, speech pathology, and medicine. Each team member gathers data about the student and interprets it from a professional perspective, sharing it with the team. The team then analyzes all contributions and attempts to render the most appropriate educational decision.

The team approach is not new to education, but it has gained impetus in recent years. PL 94–142 explicitly requires that teams rather than individuals make the following decisions:

1. Evaluation of students for placement in special education and related services
2. Formulation of Individualized Education Programs (IEPs)

3. Evaluation of IEPs
4. Reevaluation of special education placement

The membership of educational decision-making teams varies. Different purposes require different numbers of team members and the representation of different disciplines. For example, the team that assesses a student for eligibility for special services is likely to have more members than the team responsible for formulating the IEP for the same student. The needs of the student also influence team membership. A student with several severe handicaps is likely to require a larger team representing more disciplines than a student with a mild handicap.

Many individuals participate in educational teams. These participants make important contributions to the assessment and planning activities of the team. The special educator plays a significant role in combining their input into a unified profile of the student's needs.

School Personnel

Teachers, whether regular or special education, who are directly involved with the student on a day-to-day basis are necessary team members. Teachers are able to provide information on all aspects of student development, especially academic performance and social and emotional status.

Regular classroom teachers provide valuable information about students' social skills in dealing with their peers. They can describe the kinds of instructional programs and procedures used in the classroom. Their assessment procedures often consist of group-administered achievement tests, informal tests, and inventories. Consequently, they can describe how well the handicapped student is responding to group instruction, compared to non-handicapped classroom peers. This information is particularly useful in considering whether the regular classroom is the best instructional environment for the student.

Special educators offer information about student performance under specialized conditions. Their assessment procedures are generally more individualized; they gather formal and informal data about academic, language, and behavioral problems. This information, when combined with data from the regular classroom teachers, allows a comparison of student performance. Regular and special educators can determine the needs best met in the regular classroom, along with those requiring special education services.

Special educators may be involved early in the referral process when school-based teams are screening for students with problems and determining whether their learning and behavioral difficulties are easily remediated or whether they require further study. Special educators may perform classroom observations or consult with regular classroom teachers about possible remedial activities. Their time commitment to this process varies depending on their role descriptions. Those with classroom instructional responsibilities generally do less than those serving on district assessment teams or as consultants. Special educators tend to spend more time in performing assessments related to planning individualized instructional programs and evaluating them. These assessments are generally done during the school day, as part of the instructional program. In some cases, special educators are released from classroom duties to perform individualized testing and observations.

School administrators on educational decision-making teams may include building principals, directors of special education, or other supervisory personnel. Building principals are often included to involve them in the education of handicapped students and thereby enlist their cooperation. Special education administrators are able to share their knowledge about the programs available in the school district or division. Administrators provide information about administrative options and particular students they know.

Parents and Students

The intent of PL 94–142 is to involve the parents of the handicapped students and the students themselves, when appropriate, in the educational decision-making process. Parents have much to contribute to the team. They are completely familiar with the child's behavior and have acted as the child's teacher in the parenting role.

Like educators, parents provide information on many aspects of the student's development. They give details on the student's past health and developmental history and social and emotional behavior in the home, neighborhood, and community. They can be interviewed and can complete case history forms. If appropriate, they can be observed at home while interacting with their child, or taught to gather informal observations about home behavior. Besides being mandated by PL 94–142, parental participation on the team maximizes the chance that parents will support and become involved with the program.

The student can also provide information about all aspects of development. Students can relate their feelings, attitudes, goals, and aspirations. Student interviews often yield useful information.

School Support Personnel

Psychologists and speech-language clinicians often support regular and special educators, and they are frequently members of educational decision-making teams. Psychologists assess the student to determine eligibility for special education programs as well as gather related data. The school psychologist is usually responsible for giving and interpreting tests to determine general intelligence level.

Psychological reports address concerns about level of ability and/or expectancy for the student, status of specific skills involved in learning, and emotional and behavioral status. When combined with the results of the academic report from teachers, psychological reports allow the team to compare a student's actual classroom achievement with some indications of potential ability as well as learning strategy. In planning a program for the student, psychologists can assist in establishing reasonable goals and levels of expected performance, as well as possible student reactions to different learning conditions.

Speech-language pathologists are involved in assessment and instruction of handicapped students with speech and/or language disabilities. They are responsible for evaluating the communication skills of the student, referring children to other specialists, providing services, and counseling others working with the child.

Their assessment procedures are both formal and informal; they frequently solicit input from educators about a student's classroom speech and language performance. Special educators may screen for speech and language problems and supply their referral data to speech-language pathologists. Furthermore, knowledge of speech and language problems helps the team understand academic and behavioral problems with speech or language components. In planning the IEP, speech-language specialists specify goals for the student and indicate how others can cooperate. For some handicapped students, speech-language instruction is the only special service received; for others, it accompanies other programs such as special classes or resource room services.

Medical Personnel

Medical information about the student is obtained from the student's physician, the school nurse, and other medical specialists. This information may include results of vision and hearing screenings, as well as the current physical status of the student.

All students should be screened for possible vision and hearing impairments. This screening is generally carried out by the school nurse, who then refers students with possible problems to appropriate specialists. The results of screening and any subsequent evaluations are reported to the team by the school nurse. Of particular interest to the team is how vision and hearing problems affect assessment performance and subsequent programming.

The school nurse or physician may also report information about any relevant health problems, conditions, or diseases. Pediatricians, neurologists, psychiatrists, and other physicians may be involved. Also of interest is whether the student is currently receiving any medical treatment, such as drug therapy. All medical information should be reported so the educational implications are clear. Data from assessments and classroom performance must be considered by the team in light of any medical problems.

Social/Career Needs Personnel

Social workers and counselors provide information about the social and emotional status and career-vocational planning of the student. Social work services in schools include preparing a social or developmental history, conducting group and individual counseling with the child and family, working with problems in a child's living situation that affect adjustment in school, and mobilizing school and community resources.

The assessment procedures used by social workers include interviews and home visits. Data gathered regarding a student's background, home life, and values can help the team interpret other assessment data. Social workers may also assist team members, particularly parents, in identifying goals and strategies for action at home and in the community.

Counselors also help in the area of emotional development. Counseling services, according to PL 94–142, may be provided by a variety of professionals including social workers, psychologists, guidance counselors, and vocational rehabilitation counselors. Counselors use both formal and informal procedures and concentrate on the emotional and behavioral problems of the student, and sometimes of other family members, along with career and vocational areas. Because of their in-depth involvement, counselors can add emotional and career-vocational dimensions to the student profile. Data from counseling may indicate the need for specific goals or shape decisions about placement or instructional strategies, such as peer tutoring and vocational training.

Motor Development Personnel

Information about the motor development of the student may be obtained from adaptive physical education teachers, physical therapists, and occupational therapists. In addition, the school nurse or a physician, such as an orthopedic surgeon, may also contribute medical information about motor disabilities.

The adaptive physical education teacher is involved with the instruction of handicapped students requiring special physical education programs, and he or she can provide information about the student's motor abilities. Teachers, psychologists, and others may also have input about the student's gross and fine motor behavior. In some cases, motor disabilities may be related to other kinds of problems, such as difficulty in writing words. Adaptive physical education teachers specify goals for the student and assist team members in programming for motor needs.

Physical and occupational therapists also contribute information. Some authors distinguish between physical therapists, who are concerned with gross motor development, and occupational therapists, who work with fine motor development. Both kinds of therapists use specialized assess-

ment procedures; their data may be supplemented by results of interviews or experiences of other team members.

Along with reporting on curriculum related to vocational/career development, teachers can provide information on behavior and demands in motor skills. Parents may also have useful data. The IEP contains goals in all these areas if necessary and allows the therapists to suggest strategies useful in the development of better motor coordination or realistic career goals.

Other Personnel

Occasionally, team members other than those just described are needed to present important information about the student. Tutors or paraprofessional aides working closely with the student may provide insight into strengths and weaknesses. Members of the community, such as employers or supervisors, may be able to give the team a better understanding of realistic vocational goals. Other family members such as grandparents can sometimes supplement input from the parents and student.

The purpose of the team approach is to assemble all the information necessary for educational decision making through members' combined expertise. The team may involve only educators and the parents, or it may extend to all the disciplines. A team is made up of only necessary members. Teams generally require representatives from only some of the disciplines; only in rare cases would all the disciplines participate. The team should be kept as small as possible to make parents feel comfortable and encourage their participation.

PL 94–142 requires that team decisions take into account several areas of student functioning, if those areas are pertinent to the educational needs of the student. Table 1–2 lists several possible areas of concern and the team members who are the primary sources of information for each area. Although certain members take primary responsibility for information in certain areas, any team member may provide additional information.

A natural differentiation in contribution to decision making appears related to professional role and training. The relative contributions of professionals vary during the process. The most influential team members seem to be those

TABLE 1–2
Primary source of information about student functioning

Team member					TYPE OF INFORMATION			
	Health	Vision and hearing	Social and emotional status	General intelligence	Academic performance	Communicative status	Motor abilities	Vocational career factors
Educators			*		*	*		*
Parents	*		*			*	*	*
Student			*		*			*
Psychologist			*	*	*			
Speech-language clinician						*		
Medical personnel	*	*					*	
Social worker			*					
Counselors								
Vocational rehabilitation counselor								*
Adaptive physical education teacher								
Physical therapist							*	*
Occupational therapist								

responsible for gathering actual test data (Ysseldyke, Algozzine, & Epps, 1983). There is no single structured form of deliberation or decision-making model in use, a fact that is related to the lack of consistency in definitions of exceptional conditions and in the use of measurement procedures. In fact, observations of some teams during their deliberations indicate considerable subjectivity (Ysseldyke, Algozzine, Regan, & McGue, 1981).

Team members also tend to emphasize some variables more than others when making decisions, such as comparisons of strengths and weaknesses or comparisons of intelligence and academic achievement scores (Valus, 1986). It is unclear, however, whether one type of data consistently dominates team discussions, because each student represents a unique case. Overall, a team, rather than an individual, approach to making decisions about eligibility and instructional planning seems preferable because it enhances reliability (Pfeiffer & Naglieri, 1983).

This book is written from the perspective of the special educator. Although many of the assessment procedures described here can be used by other professionals, the special educator is the team member responsible for handicapped students and trained to perform many of the necessary assessment and remedial activities. Having the dual responsibilities of assessment and instruction, the special educator is in a unique position to maintain an educational focus and relevance in the assessment of special students.

CRITICAL ISSUES

Many major issues face the field of educational assessment of exceptional students. And many of the areas of assessment are subject to criticism. These controversies are dealt with throughout the text, but a brief overview is provided here.

Professionals define and conduct educational assessment in various ways. Current practices do not seem cost-effective (Ysseldyke & Algozzine, 1982) and reflect little consensus in terms of choice of procedures (Ysseldyke, Algozzine, Regan, Potter, Richey & Thurlow, 1980). Tests meant for one purpose are used for others.

The technical quality of some popular tests has been a critical issue, particularly in relation to the psychological processing tests used in learning disabilities. The lack of expertise demonstrated by some examiners in administering, scoring, and interpreting tests (McLoughlin, 1985b) has been of equal concern. The use of clinical judgment has also been questioned (Davis & Shepard, 1983). Curriculum-based assessment has been advocated as the necessary correction for the limitations of standardized testing and current placement procedures (Tucker, 1985).

Such faults naturally lead to charges of discriminatory practices in assessment of exceptional students. Student and parent due process rights are not always observed, and the ethical issues, such as data confidentiality, continue to be critical. Incidental data (sex, race, socioeconomic status) may receive more attention than the critical variables of performance (Ysseldyke et al., 1981). Efforts to observe the rights of minority students and other groups are not yet totally successful. The role of bilingualism in assessment continues to be of pressing concern.

Studies of the workings of the all-important assessment team have not shown positive results. Participation has been weak by all concerned parties, particularly parents. The interdynamics of the situation suggest dominance by certain groups (Poland, Thurlow, Ysseldyke, & Mirkin, 1982). Compliance with due process procedures does not always occur, and there is evidence of role confusion and professional competition (Yoshida, 1984). The actual meetings studied seemed to lack structure and purpose, contributing to lower quality decision making (Ysseldyke, Thurlow, Graden, Wesson, Algozzine, & Deno, 1983). Concern about subjectivity in decisions about eligibility has encouraged some state departments of education to adopt discrepancy formulas as a factor in placing students in special education services, especially for learning disabilities (Wallace & McLoughlin, 1988).

No aspect of educational assessment escapes criticism, and each one merits considerable attention. As each facet of this process is described in this text, these same issues are considered in more detail. We hope the approaches and strategies described will help service providers address each of these issues.

EDUCATIONAL ASSESSMENT QUESTIONS

One way of overcoming these problems is to develop structure and purpose for the educational assessment process. The key to formulating such a format is learning how to ask the necessary questions and use them to guide the choice of procedures. Interpretation then becomes an integrated process.

The assessment process consists of five phases.

1. During a prereferral stage data are gathered to substantiate the nature of the student's problem and to clarify whether some effort has been made to correct obvious reasons for the difficulty.
2. The student's eligibility for specific special education services is studied by matching the student's learning profile to that set forth by federal and state guidelines.
3. An in-depth assessment is performed to identify strengths and weaknesses in critical basic skills and other areas for inclusion in an appropriate course of action.
4. An IEP is planned to include priority goals for an intervention program.
5. The program is monitored and evaluated on a regular basis.

As illustrated in Figure 1–1, these phases of the assessment process can be conceptualized as a series of assessment questions. In fact, the assessment of exceptional children has three main considerations. When expressed in questions, they are (a) Is there a school performance problem? (b) Is it related to a handicapping condition? and (c) What are the student's educational needs? To answer these questions, many specific issues must be addressed. The questions parallel the purposes of assessment described earlier, beginning with identification of mildly handicapped students and progressing through program evaluation. Figure 1–1 provides a step-by-step process of conducting an educational assessment.

Is There a School Performance Problem?

Students must be having difficulty performing in school to be eligible for special education and related services. Their deficit areas and the severity of the problems must be documented. The information needed includes current levels of performance in both academic skills and social behavior.

The procedures used to describe school learning include an examination of the results of group achievement tests, grades, and other school history data. This information is frequently maintained in the student's records. Teacher input is also gathered through referral forms. Referral information is most useful when the student's problems are stated precisely, indicating strengths as well as weaknesses; when teachers avoid making inferences about a student's behavior and describe what the student actually does; when supportive documentation of the learning problem, such as current test scores and methods and materials, is provided; and when teachers supply accurate information. A referral with these characteristics presents a preliminary profile of a student's learning problem. Of particular value are descriptions and results of educational strategies used with the student.

Another useful procedure for gathering initial data is to have teachers and others complete checklists or rating scales. These can cover both academic and social skills. An example of one such measure is the *Pupil Rating Scale–Revised* (Myklebust, 1981).

Parent interviews and other efforts to gather data about the student's medical, educational, and social development are also important. One device used to collect information systematically from parents is the case history form in Appendix A. Parents can be asked to supply information on family background; physical, psychological, and social history; and educational experiences.

Information from parents, the student, siblings, physicians, and peers can help establish the nature of learning problems. Physical, psychological, social, and cultural factors may be significant variables in school difficulties.

Several classroom assessment procedures can also be used to determine whether a learning problem exists. Systematic behavioral observations may identify a pattern of events affecting the student's achievement. Teachers may see a pattern of difficulty when they systematically analyze classroom activities and subsequent student responses. The curriculum itself may serve as the

FIGURE 1–1
The assessment question model

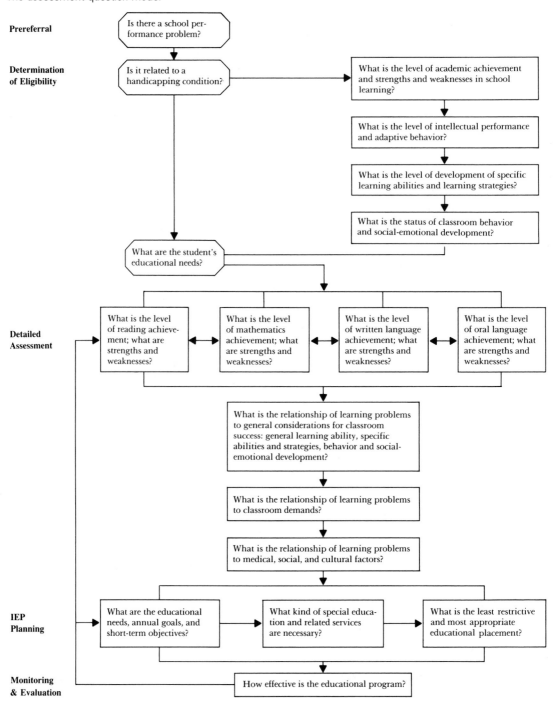

Prereferral

Is there a school performance problem?

Determination of Eligibility

Is it related to a handicapping condition?

What is the level of academic achievement and strengths and weaknesses in school learning?

What is the level of intellectual performance and adaptive behavior?

What is the level of development of specific learning abilities and learning strategies?

What is the status of classroom behavior and social-emotional development?

What are the student's educational needs?

Detailed Assessment

What is the level of reading achievement; what are strengths and weaknesses?

What is the level of mathematics achievement; what are strengths and weaknesses?

What is the level of written language achievement; what are strengths and weaknesses?

What is the level of oral language achievement; what are strengths and weaknesses?

What is the relationship of learning problems to general considerations for classroom success: general learning ability, specific abilities and strategies, behavior and social-emotional development?

What is the relationship of learning problems to classroom demands?

What is the relationship of learning problems to medical, social, and cultural factors?

IEP Planning

What are the educational needs, annual goals, and short-term objectives?

What kind of special education and related services are necessary?

What is the least restrictive and most appropriate educational placement?

Monitoring & Evaluation

How effective is the educational program?

18

framework for assessment, as the student's proficiency in component skills and performance at different levels are examined.

Based on this information, teachers may make instructional and environmental modifications and note an immediate change in the student's school performance. In this way, any student with temporary or situational learning problems will be identified, and further concern and assessment can be avoided. Students who do not respond to these efforts and whose learning difficulties are clearly documented are then referred for in-depth assessment. The outcome of the questioning is the identification of general problem areas, an assessment of their approximate severity, and a clear indication of the need for further assessment.

Is the School Performance Problem Related to a Handicapping Condition?

Students with learning problems qualify for special education and related services only if they meet the criteria for a handicapping condition as set forth in federal, state, and local guidelines. The information needed usually includes an indication of a severe deficit in intellectual, academic, and/or behavioral development. Depending on the specific disability, one of these factors may be stressed.

In most states, the student's performance must be below average on individual measures of general intellectual functioning, academic performance, and adaptive behavior to establish him or her as eligible for services for the mentally retarded. In order to be eligible for learning disability services, performance in at least one specific learning ability or strategy and in at least one area of educational academic performance must be significantly different from the norm. Emotionally disturbed students are eligible only when performance is average or above on a measure of general intellectual functioning, but below average in at least one area of behavior and perhaps in at least one area of academic performance.

The procedures used to gather these data are varied. Normative information concerning intellectual functioning and academics is required to establish a student's handicap in comparison to other students. Tests and other scales yielding comparative scores are valuable. Formulas and other procedures may be applied to assist in judging the severity of disabilities.

Interviews with parents and others help answer questions about social skills. A number of published scales can be used for this purpose. Systematic behavioral observations and rating scales are appropriate informal procedures for analyzing behavior problems.

The team looks at several general areas, regardless of the specific academic problem, when evaluating exceptional students. The answers to the following questions help team members make legal decisions about the presence of a handicapping condition and its relationship to the school performance problem.

What is the level of academic achievement; what are strengths and weaknesses in school learning? The information needed here is an individual assessment of school performance in comparison to other students. Preliminary screening has already indicated possible learning problems. Strengths and weaknesses are now specified by using individual formal and informal procedures. These data are used to direct more in-depth assessment if needed, as well as to partially establish a basis for eligibility. Individual norm-referenced tests, such as the *Peabody Individual Achievement Test–Revised* (Markwardt, 1989), indicate an overall level of achievement and can be used in making decisions about degree of deficit. Informal procedures, such as interviews, classroom observations, and analysis of assignments, permit confirmation and description of the deficits. An informal analysis of incorrect responses on a formal test may indicate specific aspects of the problem. An academic assessment should identify global areas of deficit for further assessment and indicate the more severe problem areas.

What are the levels of intellectual functioning and adaptive behavior? The combination of these two issues helps predict classroom success. Intellectual functioning involves a composite of skills related to thinking, problem solving, and general academic aptitude. Adaptive behavior involves the ability to exist in and cope with environments other than the school classroom. Included are self-help skills, communication, and social and interpersonal skills.

Normative data are needed in each area. The team must decide how students compare to their peers and whether their scores fall within average ranges. This information must be related to academic and other performance data before making final judgments.

Procedures used for measuring intellectual functioning include norm-referenced standardized tests, such as the *Wechsler Intelligence Scale for Children–Revised* (Wechsler, 1974), systematic observations, and interviews. The results are one indication of learning expectancy. Other indicators are chronological age and grade level.

Both formal and informal procedures are appropriate for measuring adaptive behavior. The numerous published adaptive behavior rating scales include the *Adaptive Behavior Inventory for Children* (Mercer & Lewis, 1977a). Parents and others familiar with the out-of-school behavior are interviewed using these scales. School and home observations and examination of cultural practices contribute to a clearer understanding of functional skills.

The outcomes are normative statements about the levels of functioning and behavior needed to perform in school, at home, and in the community. The results indicate whether students are markedly different from their peers in global cognitive skills and functional abilities. This information is useful in making decisions concerning eligibility for services for the mildly handicapped and in designing the IEP.

What is the level of development of specific learning abilities and strategies? Specific learning abilities are generally considered prerequisites for school success. They underlie academic and other areas of development. Attention, perception, and memory are considered specific features of readiness for school. Furthermore, a variety of other specific strategies represent approaches to learning.

Formal procedures for the evaluation of specific learning abilities include the *Illinois Test of Psycholinguistic Abilities* (Kirk, McCarthy, & Kirk, 1968). There are also many informal techniques available. Some measures, such as the *Motor-Free Visual Perception Test* (Colarusso & Hammill, 1972) and the *Auditory Discrimination Test* (2nd ed.) (Reynolds, 1987; Wepman, 1975), assess one specific area of functioning. However, tests of specific abilities have been heavily criticized for poor technical quality and irrelevance to educa-

tional matters (Arter & Jenkins, 1979; Hammill & Larsen, 1974a, 1974b).

Specific learning strategies, such as organizational skills, must be studied informally or by drawing from parts of formal tests. Useful informal procedures include making observations, noting how students approach different kinds of learning tasks, and interviewing teachers and others. This assessment indicates the current status of the student's learning abilities as well as his or her learning strategies, and can be used to understand academic and social disabilities. In addition, eligibility requirements for services in specific learning disabilities often require documentation of problems.

What is the status of classroom behavior and social-emotional development? Evaluators assess the student's classroom behavior, including major behavior problems, interaction with teachers and peers, and the influences of other physical and curricular environments. Does the student have the necessary social and behavioral skills to learn well in a classroom setting?

Information gathered includes both normative and descriptive data. For eligibility decisions, especially for services in behavior disorders, a severe deficit in one or more major aspects of behavior must be documented. Specific behaviors and environmental factors must be identified to design remedial instructional programs.

Assessment procedures include formal rating scales and a variety of informal techniques. Rating scales completed by parents, teachers, and others can indicate whether behavior at school and elsewhere seems significantly inappropriate. For example, with the *Behavior Rating Profile* (Brown & Hammill, 1983a), parents, teachers, and students rate student behavior; these ratings permit a comparison of their perceptions. Such ratings help screen for possible problem behaviors that require further assessment.

Systematic behavioral observations allow analysis of specific behaviors. Particular attention must be given to the conditions under which a problem behavior occurs and the consequences of the behavior. Other procedures include using sociograms, analyzing interactions with teachers and peers, and relating behavior to medical and psychological problems.

This assessment indicates whether a student can successfully learn in the current environment. A secondary outcome is information about the nature of the specific problem, such as disruptive behavior.

These four considerations define the nature of students' learning problems. Specific deficits in the major skill areas need to be clarified further.

What Are the Student's Educational Needs?

Once the broad parameters of the learning problem are established, academically based questions should be considered. The four major academic skills taught in school are reading, mathematics, and oral/written language. Handicapped students frequently have difficulties with basic skills in these areas, and their deficits impede the learning of content subjects such as science and history. The needed information in all areas is the same: (a) an indication of current level of performance and whether the achievement is below average compared to other students; (b) specific strengths and weaknesses; (c) a list of mastered and unmastered skills; and (d) the relationship of skills in one area to deficits in others, such as the influence of reading upon mathematics.

What is the level of reading achievement; what are strengths and weaknesses?
The three main areas to be assessed in reading are word recognition, reading comprehension, and the use of reading skills to learn other material. Formal tests generating normative scores establish the current level of reading performance. For example, the *Woodcock Reading Mastery Tests–Revised* (Woodcock, 1987) measure identification of letters, oral reading of real and nonsense words, knowledge of word meanings, and comprehension of passages. The results, reported through a variety of scores, supply an indication of reading problems by identifying strengths and weaknesses across areas of reading.

Informal reading inventories are often administered to further assess possible weakness in major reading skills and related factors. For example, the *Analytical Reading Inventory* (Woods & Moe, 1989), the *Classroom Reading Inventory* (Silvaroli, 1986), and the *New Sucher–Allred Reading Placement Inventory* (Sucher & Allred, 1981) use oral reading of passages to assess a variety of required skills, including decoding and comprehension. The *Test of Reading Comprehension* (rev. ed.) (Brown, Hammill, & Wiederholt, 1986) measures sequencing events in a story as well as use of the reading skills in learning mathematics, science, and social studies.

Criterion-referenced tests are useful in identifying a specific list of mastered and unmastered reading skills. The *BRIGANCE® Diagnostic Inventory of Basic Skills* (Brigance, 1977) measures oral reading, comprehension, and study skills. Other useful procedures include teacher-made checklists, analyses of reading errors and materials, and observations of students during reading lessons.

What is the level of mathematics achievement; what are strengths and weaknesses?
The main mathematics areas of assessment are computation, problem-solving, and application skills. The *KeyMath Revised* (Connolly, 1988) is a formal test providing information about levels of mathematics performance and allowing for a comparison of strengths and weaknesses.

Criterion-referenced tests, such as the *BRIGANCE® Diagnostic Inventory of Basic Skills* (Brigance, 1977), identify mastered and unmastered skills. Task analyses of classroom assignments may also pinpoint skill deficits. A classroom assignment can be examined for error patterns; an analysis of methods and materials may also be revealing.

What is the level of oral language development; what are strengths and weaknesses?
The major areas to be assessed in oral language are comprehension and use of semantics, syntax, morphology, phonology, and pragmatics. A preliminary screening for oral language skills is useful in pinpointing specific areas needing assessment. For example, the *Test of Language Development– 2, Primary* (Newcomer & Hammill, 1988) samples the comprehension and production of various dimensions of language. This standardized test indicates levels of language development as well as strengths and weaknesses. Standardized tests for many specific areas of language include the *Northwestern Syntax Screening Test* (Lee, 1971), which measures comprehension and use of grammar.

Informally, language samples and classroom observations can identify specific aspects of the language problems. Lists of language skills arranged in a hierarchy can be used to specify language deficits. *System Fore* (Bagai & Bagai, 1979), for example, offers a list of skills in major areas of language, along with a set of informal probes. This assessment produces a statement about strengths, weaknesses, and current levels of language performance. Specific skill deficits are identified for instruction.

What is the level of written language development; what are strengths and weaknesses?

The main areas to be assessed are spelling, handwriting, and composition skills. A screening test can identify the level of performance in each area and deficits needing more assessment. For example, the *Test of Written Language–2* (Hammill & Larsen, 1988) samples story writing, punctuation and capitalization, vocabulary, and spelling. More specific tests include the *Test of Written Spelling–2* (Larsen & Hammill, 1986), which can be used to examine written skills in spelling various types of words. Task analysis and analysis of written products are informal procedures to identify more specific aspects of written language deficits.

The outcomes of these academic assessments yield a clear statement of the student's levels of performance, strengths, and weaknesses. Results should be examined further to determine how task demands influence students' performance. For example, a student may do well in written computation, but poorly in mental computation. Thus, it is useful to include different types of tests of the same skill in the assessment. The learning strategies of a student will become more apparent if he or she performs differently based on task demands.

After these assessments are completed, we should ask how deficits in one or more of these areas influence each other. For example, poor oral reading skills may be related to spelling deficits. These relationships may suggest some common factors to a problem and may become a basis for sequencing remedial programs or otherwise coordinating instruction.

Noting Interrelationships

The results of one or more tests or informal techniques only begin to answer the key assessment questions. Data must be related to factors central to classroom success and demands, along with medical, social, and cultural needs.

What is the relationship of learning problems to general considerations for classroom success?

A school performance problem must be examined in the context of general academic achievement; the academic deficit may be a specific disability or part of a pattern. The level of intellectual functioning and adaptive behavior may, to some extent, indicate whether academic deficits are commensurate with the student's general abilities. For some students, low levels of academic performance correlate with low intellectual and/or adaptive behavior skills. Relating specific findings to an overall profile of achievement and ability helps maintain a perspective of the whole child.

Another consideration is whether academic problems are accompanied by specific learning disabilities in acquiring and using information or learning strategies. Problems in specific learning abilities can interfere with the acquisition of reading, mathematics, and other subjects. For example, problems in discriminating sounds or with memory may be related to a difficulty in learning the sounds of letters. By relating findings about academic deficits to specific learning deficits, the team may determine that a student uses an inappropriate learning strategy or lacks certain prerequisite skills.

Academic deficits should be considered in the general context of necessary conditions for learning. The student's ability to function socially and respond to the general instructional demands of the classroom must be clarified so effective instructional programs can be designed. For example, the academic program for a student with a behavioral problem may be designed differently from that for a student with another kind of deficit.

What is the relationship of learning problems to classroom demands?

A student's academic deficits and learning traits should also be considered in the context of the instructional tasks, methods, and materials used in the classroom, as well as in the physical environment. Task analysis can be used to study the instructional tasks to see if the student has specific components needed to master each deficit skill. Task analysis will also show if the task structure is causing the student problems. Modifications in task features can be identified, resulting in improved performance. Such comparisons may also involve information about the student's specific learning abilities. The demands of instructional tasks are compared to disabilities in both academic skills and specific learning abilities/strategies.

Teaching procedures and classroom conditions are also examined through observations, interviews, and material analysis. The student's learning abilities and disabilities can be compared to the classroom learning conditions using this information. Possible assessment questions include the following:

1. What are the features of instructional materials—what kind of prerequisite skills, pace, and objectives do they require? Do they meet the learning needs of the student? Bleil (1975), Brown (1975), and Affleck, Lowenbraun, and Archer (1980) suggest ways to evaluate materials.
2. What are the procedures used by the teacher? Does he or she use modeling, prompting, or reinforcement? Are the techniques appropriate for the needs and learning style of this student? Classroom observational systems and teacher interviews can help answer this question.
3. Are the physical surroundings (lighting, heating, work space, noise level) conducive to learning? Are they appropriate for the student's needs? Smith, Neisworth, and Greer (1978) suggest ways to study the physical environment.

This information will help the team avoid mismatches between learning conditions and student needs. Poor student performance in a certain skill area may be directly related to inappropriate learning conditions. If this is the case, then the problem lies with the environment instead of the student's ability to learn. Environmental modifications become a priority, and these data can guide the changes.

What is the relationship of learning problems to medical, social, and cultural factors? Medical, social, and cultural factors may affect student performance. Medical correlates to learning include general health, vision, hearing, and motor development. Important social factors may include number and age of siblings, the value the family places on schooling, emphasis on literacy at home, and provisions for doing homework. Other social

background data are age of peers and favorite pastimes. Cultural correlates are linguistic differences, forms of communication, and cultural perceptions of school learning.

As indicated earlier, much of this information can be gathered if parents and others are interviewed and/or if they complete developmental and social histories. Home visits, observations in the neighborhood and playground, sociograms, and other informal techniques are used. Team input is imperative in this assessment area, as are consultations with physicians, social workers, and others who have worked or are familiar with the student. Copies of medical records and other information should be reviewed when necessary.

These factors sometimes provide explanations for the learning problem. Inappropriate action can sometimes be avoided if these dimensions are considered; however, usually additional aspects of a student's learning problem are discovered. For example, poor vision may partially explain a reading disability; both remedial education and corrective lenses may be necessary. Or if a student performs at an extremely low level of intellectual functioning and adaptive behavior and a severe hearing loss is discovered, all assessment results must be reinterpreted.

Noting interrelationships helps integrate all information. By putting the specifics of the assessment in context, it helps the team decide what to do. In addition, all dimensions of the individual must be looked at before choosing goals and developing programs. An academic deficit may be considered less extreme if the student's general ability to learn is low, if he or she is inattentive in class, if the tasks in the classroom have an inappropriate response requirement, or if the student has a hearing loss. Noting interrelationships produces a clearer understanding of educational needs and accompanying problems.

Making Instructional Decisions

The team of involved professionals and the student's parents (and perhaps the student) are now ready to develop an appropriate educational plan. For students with disabilities, the three main educational considerations are (a) the annual goals and short-term objectives of such a program, (b) the type of special education and/or related services required, and (c) the least restrictive and most appropriate learning environment. These factors are also the core of the Individualized Education Program (IEP) designed by the team.

What are the educational needs, annual goals, and short-term objectives? The outcome of this aspect of the assessment process is a list of priority goals and specific objectives. First, any academic and other deficits noted through formal and informal assessment are identified. Second, the team must decide whether the deficits constitute valid educational needs. The team developing the IEP must consider the student's age, grade placement, other handicapping conditions, the student's desires and priorities, parental desires and priorities, and cultural background. For example, certain academic deficits, such as knowledge of short vowel sounds, may not be a priority educational need for a 17-year-old student concerned about employability.

Third, the student's educational needs are prioritized and stated in general annual goals that direct the program. Short-term objectives indicate more specific aspects of the educational program. They are designed by drawing upon the results of criterion-referenced testing, task analysis, and so forth, and represent intermediate steps the student must take to accomplish the goals.

What kinds of special education and related services are required? The regulations and guidelines set forth by individual state departments of education, as well as local practices, must be consulted in deciding eligibility for special services.

Furthermore, the student may also qualify for related services, such as speech therapy, physical therapy, or counseling. The student's program goals will dictate the types of special education and related services provided. In many states, programs are organized by handicapping conditions: the learning disabled, the mildly mentally handicapped, and the emotionally disturbed or behavior disordered.

What is the least restrictive and most appropriate educational placement? The number, nature, and severity of the student's educational needs are studied; the personnel qualified to offer the required services are identified. The team then examines the appropriateness of different service arrangements, choosing the best delivery model. A continuum of services are available, ranging from the regular classroom with support aid to residential settings.

Evaluation

Part of the IEP is a plan of the evaluation design for its mandated annual review. The specific question to ask is, "How effective is the educational program?" To answer that question, one must gather data concerning the accomplishment of goals and objectives, the effectiveness of teaching strategies, and current levels of performance. The outcome of this assessment indicates the impact and appropriateness of the IEP. This information can be used to direct further assessment, modify goals and objectives, reconsider the need for special services, and reexamine the service delivery model being used.

STUDY GUIDE

Review Questions

1. Define educational assessment.
2. Educational assessment, testing, and diagnosis are synonymous. (True or False)
3. What are the five main purposes of educational assessment?
4. Match the type of assessment in Column A with descriptions in Column B.

Column A		*Column B*
a. Norm-referenced tests	_____	Establish student proficiency according to levels of curriculum and component skill requirements
b. Criterion-referenced tests	_____	Used to gather information from parents about a student's background
c. Informal inventories	_____	A list of sight words used in a reading lesson or a sheet of one-digit addition problems

d. Work sample analysis   _____ A graph of the number of times a student speaks out of turn during a lesson

e. Task analysis   _____ A test of vocabulary that indicates how well a student compares to others of similar age

f. Observation   _____ Used by teachers and parents to rate a student in motor and language development

g. Checklists and rating scales   _____ A test of reading three-syllable words with 90% accuracy

h. Interviews and questionnaires   _____ A teacher finds a student consistently forgets to carry the digit in addition on the math worksheet

i. Curriculum-based assessment   _____ A teacher identifies the skills needed to copy and sequence numbers from the board

5. Major individual achievement tests are the *WISC–R* and *Stanford–Binet Intelligence Scale.* (True or False)

6. Norm-referenced tests may report a student's performance in grade or age levels. (True or False)

7. Criterion-referenced tests report a student's mastery skill level. (True or False)

8. One difference between formal and informal tests is the use of standardization and norms. (True or False)

9. A reading test is *not* an aptitude or ability test. (True or False)

10. The only useful respondent or informant in educational assessment is the student. (True or False)

11. Match the assessment area in Column A with the appropriate test in Column B.

Column A	*Column B*
a. Achievement	_____ *Auditory Discrimination Test*
b. Intellectual performance	_____ *Woodcock Reading Mastery Tests–Revised*
c. Specific learning abilities	_____ *ENRIGHT™ Diagnostic Inventory of Basic Arithmetic Skills*
d. Classroom behavior	_____ *Wechsler Intelligence Scale for Children–Revised*
e. Reading	_____ *Test of Written Spelling–2*
f. Arithmetic	_____ *Burks' Behavior Rating Scale*
g. Spoken language	_____ *Northwestern Syntax Screening Test*
h. Written language	_____ *Peabody Individual Achievement Test–Revised*

12. A team approach is always necessary in educational assessment of exceptional students. (True or False)

13. Match the team member in Column A with the type of information provided in Column B.

Column A	*Column B*
a. Parent	_E_ Vision and hearing
b. Adaptive physical education teacher	_A_ Past health and developmental history
c. School psychologist	_C_ General intelligence
d. Educator	_D_ Academic performance
e. School nurse	_F_ Communication status
f. Speech-language clinician	_B_ Motor abilities

14. Group assessment is particularly appropriate for the handicapped. (True or False)

15. Only tests are used in an assessment. (True or False)

16. PL 94–142 requires a comprehensive assessment of the handicapped. (True or False)

17. What are the three main assessment questions?

Activities

1. Interview professionals engaged in educational assessment of the handicapped, especially special educators. Ask them how they define and go about assessment.

2. Interview classroom teachers of students with learning problems. Find out what kind of information they expect from assessments. Which procedures discussed in the chapter seem most appropriate?

3. Obtain a copy of a test listed in the Test Index. Using the distinctions in the chapter, how would you describe it?

4. Interview a school psychologist and a counselor. Ask them to describe their relationship with special educators on the assessment team.

5. Interview several members of a school assessment team. Ask each to describe the advantages and disadvantages of the team approach.

Discussion Questions

1. Discuss why there is a need for different types of assessment procedures. What problems could arise if only certain kinds are used? Why would professionals tend to use the same kinds again and again?

2. Discuss potential conflicts among team members. Who would have opposing interests? Why? How would they reconcile their differences?

3. How would you react to current research that indicates a lack of structure in the assessment process and suggests discriminatory practices and inefficiency? Discuss the implications for current practitioners.

2

Steps in Educational Assessment

Decisions to Be Made
Steps in Assessment

As discussed in Chapter 1, the reasons for an assessment influence the content and extent of the process. The procedures are implemented to decide if the student's school performance merits in-depth diagnostic study, if the student's educational needs warrant extraordinary services, how the services should be organized in a plan, and whether the program is effective and merits continuation. Some of these considerations are legal decisions and others are instructional.

DECISIONS TO BE MADE

Legal Decisions

The determination of eligibility for special services and the reevaluation of eligibility are essentially legal decisions. Their purpose is to certify that a student is handicapped to allow allocation of funds, resources, and personnel. These decisions basically concern who will receive instruction in special education services.

Each exceptional condition is defined by PL 94–142, PL 99–457 for early childhood education, and PL 98–524 for vocational education, and in state laws and regulations. The kind of information needed is guided in part by these definitions. However, as seen by the definitions for the mildly handicapping conditions, found in Chapter 1, it can be difficult to see the immediate direction that assessment must take. Therefore, state guidelines generally supply more specific suggestions, although these guidelines usually stop short of naming particular tests. What does become clear is the essential information needed and the specific assessment team members required. Some state guidelines supply a procedure, such as a cutoff point, to assist the team in deciding eligibility. But

often the decisions are left to the professional judgment of team members. Considerable expertise is needed to put legal definitions into operation.

In determining eligibility of mildly handicapped students, most states require at least two types of assessment information: (a) *general intellectual level* determined by measures of both adaptive behavior and intellectual functioning, and (b) *academic performance*. Table 2–1 indicates points of special concern in the cases of these disabilities.

The mildly handicapping conditions require the expertise and cooperation of many team members. A major or significant discrepancy between expected and actual performance in academic and language skills must be established to document learning disabilities (Wallace & McLoughlin, 1988). Teachers and psychologists compare assessment data to document the difference between actual performance on academic/language measures and indicators of ability on psychological measures. Physicians, parents, and other team members must show that the student is not primarily handicapped by other problems, such as hearing and vision disorders, or lack of an opportunity to learn. Teachers, psychologists, neurologists, and speech-language clinicians may be involved in establishing a specific problem in acquiring and using information and effective learning strategies.

There are many similarities in the team activities required to decide eligibility for mental retardation services. Educators, psychologists, and others must show that the student has poor school achievement (achievement not commensurate with grade or age expectations) and a significantly reduced or depressed rate of learning. Data from academic and psychological assessment aid in this decision, as well as input from the student's parents about developmental history. Problems in the

TABLE 2–1
Comparison of eligibility for mildly handicapping conditions

	Mild Retardation	Learning Disabilities	Behavior Disorders
General intellectual functioning	Below average	Average or above	Average or above
Educational performance	Below average in most areas	Low or below average in at least one area	Low or below average in at least one area
Index of handicap	Low or below average in adaptive behavior and most other areas	Low or below average in at least one area of specific learning ability or strategy	Low or below average in at least one area of behavior

adaptive behavior needed to function independently at school and home must be specified. Testing by educators and psychologists, parental responses to interviews, and social work reports all contribute the needed data. Physicians also help to establish levels of physical development and possible medical problems.

Team cooperation is again needed to establish emotional disturbance. In addition to the areas already mentioned, the social and emotional behavior of the student is of particular interest. Educators, psychologists, and parents must describe the student's behavioral problems. Rating scales, interviews, and systematic observations are typically used to gather necessary documentation. Psychiatrists and other medical specialists may be called upon to establish the nature and severity of the student's emotional problems.

All eligibility decisions rely heavily on the results of norm-referenced standardized tests, because the assessment requires the comparison of a student's performance with that of other students. Salvia and Ysseldyke (1988) maintain that, "when appropriately administered, scored, and interpreted, norm-referenced devices can serve to protect children from haphazard and capricious decision-making" (p. 524). Guidelines for interpreting standardized test results for eligibility decisions are presented in Chapter 4.

However, informal assessment procedures are equally significant. Checklists, interviews, rating scales, observations, and criterion-referenced tests offer necessary documentation that standardized test procedures cannot or only partially provide. The team approach to making legal decisions establishes the importance of both the members and their use of assessment procedures.

Instructional Decisions

An Individualized Education Program (IEP) must be written when a student has been declared eligible for special education services, before services are provided. The IEP includes a statement of the student's current functioning levels and plans for an individualized curriculum, implementation of services, and evaluation of student progress. Instructional decisions are made in formulating and evaluating a student's program. Basically, they concern what to teach and how to teach it, providing the individual with a uniquely designed program.

Instructional decisions are made by teams and by the individuals responsible for implementation of the program.

The main elements of the instructional decision-making process are accomplished at a meeting. Elements include examining the assessment data to establish current levels of performance, strengths, and weaknesses; defining the goals and other features of the student's program; and agreeing on a suitable evaluation plan for the program's effectiveness. These IEP meetings should include only a small number of people directly involved with the student. Parents are then encouraged to become active in instructional decision making. Also, the teachers and therapists directly responsible for implementing the IEP can communicate with parents and student.

The team uses the results of norm-referenced standardized tests and informal assessment procedures in formulating the specific curriculum areas of the IEP. Standardized test results help the team isolate and prioritize the IEP curriculum areas. Informal assessment procedures, such as observations, criterion-referenced tests, and checklists, pinpoint the student's specific skill levels. The reporting systems of assessment procedures vary, requiring team effort to develop an understandable profile of the student's strengths and weaknesses. For example, a description of language ability may require input from educators and psychologists, in addition to the speech-language clinician.

The IEP team focuses on the areas where the student experiences difficulty, addressing deficits in relevant functional skills. The assessment results from standardized tests screen out adequate achievement areas. The IEP should present a prioritized list of deficit curriculum areas to be addressed. For many students, it may be possible to state several goals. If this is the case, the team needs to decide which goals are most crucial and therefore focus instructional efforts. The parents and the student should have a major voice in the selection of IEP curricular goals (Roos, 1985).

STEPS IN ASSESSMENT

Current assessment practices for exceptional students are regulated by a combination of federal and state laws and professionals' beliefs about "good" practices. The steps shown in Table 2–2

TABLE 2–2

Steps in educational assessment

Steps	Process	Outcome
Screening/ prereferral	The team uses common traits, observes students, examines existing test scores and grades, and provides instructional changes.	The student is identified as having a possible handicapping condition related to school performance problems or in developmental areas.
Referral	After efforts to remediate the problems, the faculty decide they need more information and question whether the student may be eligible for special education services.	The student is referred to special education for assessment, and his or her parents are informed.
Design of the Individualized Assessment Plan	The concerns about the student are arranged into questions that focus the assessment; the team develops a plan to coordinate their efforts.	Stated assessment questions are used to guide the assessment. The procedures, personnel, and timeline are designated.
Parental permission for assessment	Parents are informed of the need for an assessment, the nature of the testing, and their rights.	Parents agree, in writing, to the assessment.
Administration, scoring, and interpretation	Over a suitable time period, team members test the student, observe in the classroom, conduct interviews, etc.	The appropriate formal and informal diagnostic instruments are used by the assessment team.
Reporting results	Assessment results are compiled, discussed, and integrated into an intelligible profile of strengths and weaknesses; they are explained to parents.	The assessment data are interpreted and discussed with the student's parents and other team members.
Deciding eligibility for special education	Test data and other information are used to address established guidelines for receiving special education services.	The team examines the student's needs and assessment data in relationship to eligibility criteria.
Design of the Individualized Education Plan	The team organizes priority needs of the student and develops a coordinated plan of improvement.	The team establishes goals and objectives of the student's program, including the amount of time in the least restrictive environment and a timeline for program evaluation.
Parental agreement to the IEP	Parents participate in the development of an appropriate educational plan, establishing goals and ways to accomplish and evaluate them.	The student's parents indicate their agreement with all elements of the IEP, including placement in special education.

are generally followed in an assessment incorporating legal requirements, common practices, and useful strategies. This sequence helps answer the main assessment questions on special education eligibility and instructional needs. Later in this chapter the case of William, a 7-year-old with behavior disorders, illustrates this process.

The assessment process is strongly influenced by federal, state, and local procedures. PL 94–142 guarantees a free and appropriate public education for all handicapped individuals between ages 3 and 21. All states must offer free special education

services to school-aged students; however, preschool and postsecondary special education is required only in those states providing these services to all public school students. Now, PL 99–457 mandates assessment and interventions for infants and preschoolers and their families.

PL 94–142 mandates many of the particulars involved in meeting the needs of exceptional students. A large part of the law and its subsequent regulations concerns assessment. The gathering, interpretation, and use of data concerning exceptional students are regulated stringently. This guarantees use of a valid basis in making decisions and protects the due process rights of students and parents. In terms of assessment, PL 94–142 specifies the following: identification of the handicapped, procedural safeguards, nondiscriminatory assessment, placement in the least restrictive environment, confidentiality of information, and the development of the IEP. States must conform to these regulations to receive federal aid for education of handicapped students.

PL 94–142 has established due process procedures to insure the rights of exceptional persons and their parents. Turnbull, Strickland, and Brantley (1982) define due process as "a procedure which seeks to insure the fairness of educational decisions and the accountability of both the professionals and parents making these decisions" (p. 10). Due process protects the consumers of the assessment process—for example, informing parents of the need to test a child and involving them in making decisions based on the data.

However, such regulations are often general and permit state and local educational agencies to develop specific procedures. Local school districts must decide how they will organize the assessment process—what they will use for nomenclature and forms, and so on. Such flexibility results in considerable procedural variations within a state and in the development of many sound but nonmandated strategies.

Screening/Prereferral

According to PL 94–142, state education agencies are responsible for identifying, locating, and evaluating all handicapped students. The state department works with public and private schools and other agencies to screen student populations.

Screening and identification take many forms. Both mass media and printed literature are used to make the general public, especially parents, aware of the needs of exceptional people (McLoughlin, Edge, Strenecky, & Petrosko, 1981). The symptoms of handicaps and the available services in the state or region are stressed.

A school district or other agency must choose reliable, but time-saving, procedures to identify the most needy students. Generally, the screening program includes a variety of procedures. Teachers and other personnel are alerted to signs of various exceptionalities. Lists of warning signs are distrib-

uted, and teachers are informed of the referral process. Teachers may be asked periodically to complete checklists or rating forms that help identify suspected students. Students may be observed in the classroom, and school records may be consulted, especially the results of group testing and report cards.

Classroom teachers are also expected to modify the instructional and environmental demands on the student to identify obvious causative factors for problems. Individual schools often have child study teams that coordinate these activities. However, when the teacher's information and the results of modifications continue to indicate the possibility of a handicapping condition, students are referred for further assessment. They can also be referred by parents, tutors, physicians, or anyone else concerned.

Referral

Once a student is formally referred for special education assessment, a chain of events is set in motion. School districts usually have an individual or team that receives referrals from schools in the district (Figure 2–1) or, in the case of new students, from other agencies or individuals. A team forms and processes the referral by alerting the student's parents and by gathering all available data.

PL 94–142 requires that parents be informed of any referral *in writing*. They must also know whenever any testing for possible special education program changes will take place. Figure 2–2 shows how one school district alerts parents. Parents have the right to participate in the assessment and in subsequent decisions about the child's program. They must give their permission for assessment and should receive an explanation of the results and any proposed action. They can ask for an independent evaluation, inspect all school records, and request a due process hearing whenever they disagree with a proposed action, such as placement in special education.

Handicapped students have the right to be represented in assessment and other matters. When no parents or guardian can be identified, when their whereabouts are unknown, or when the student is a ward of the state, the state can assign a surrogate parent. The person chosen must be qualified to serve the best interests of the child. He or she represents the student in all the matters

FIGURE 2–1
Student referral form

Name: <u>William Bruce</u>   School: <u>Starlight Elementary</u>   Parent/Guardian:
                                                                                                                             <u>Mrs. Jean Bruce</u>

Birthdate: <u>6/15/82</u>   C.A. <u>7–5</u>   Teacher: <u>Mrs. Sharon Lake</u>   Address: <u>1214 E. Walnut</u>

Date of Referral: <u>11/17/89</u>   Grade: <u> 2 </u>   Phone: <u>555-2101</u>

Home Language: <u>English</u>

<u>Reason for referral:</u> Math skills are below grade level. William is also hyperactive and does not do his work. He very seldom responds in group situations and is kind of a loner. I'm concerned about his math skills and social adjustment.

<u>Describe program and materials used with student in the classroom:</u> Lately William has been using the manipulative materials in the math center with some success. I have tried some math drill games, but William gets tense and seems confused. I have offered him playtime if he gets his work done.

<u>Areas of strength:</u> William is intelligent and well-spoken. On a one-to-one basis he is a joy. He enjoys drawing and painting and is very interested in cars.

<u>Math-Text and Skill Level:</u> Greater Omaha TRA Achievement Test (arithmetic) given 9/24/89 grade placement score = 1.0. Errors in reading numbers and writing answers were noted.

<u>Reading-Text and Skill Level:</u> Merryweather Reader-Kentucky Reading Test, Lower Primary (9/19/89) score = 2.4. Comprehension skills are average.

<u>Social Adjustment:</u> William is new in our school this year. He does not seem to have many friends and usually plays alone at recess or stands watching a group of kids. He responds well to adult attention, but cannot relate well to peers. He fights, bites, kicks, and shouts insults.

<u>Health:</u> Generally good, although William frequently appears tired and listless. Vision and hearing are normal.

<u>Parent's Cooperation:</u> William's mother seems very concerned about his school performance and says she would like to help; but she is working on shifts and does not see William when he comes home from school. The father is not in the home, and a divorce is imminent.

<u>Other agencies involved with child:</u> None at present. I have suggested to Mrs. Bruce that she contact Big Brother.

Note. From Humboldt-Del Norte Master Plan Project, Eureka, CA: Humboldt County Office of Education. Adapted by permission.

mentioned here and cannot be employed by the school district.

A plan for an assessment must also be developed to provide direction and coordinate the activities of assessment personnel. This plan must be comprehensive and individualized. The process looks like the following, after the screening and referral steps.

William

William Bruce is a 7-year-old black student in the second grade. His teacher is concerned about his behavior and school achievement. On the group achievement tests administered to all the students, William performed average in reading but below average in mathematics. He cannot remember his computational facts from one day to the next. Also, William's classroom behavior is disruptive; he is attending to instructions less frequently and does not complete assignments.

Earlier in the school year, William's teacher was given a referral form indicating signs of learning problems, as well as the information required to request an assessment. This alerted her to his possible special needs; she sought help from the child study team. With their assistance, she examined the task demands and environmental conditions in the classroom. The pace of lessons was made slower, with provision of more visual cues and prompts. William could use classroom centers if he completed assignments and was less disruptive. However, these strategies had only minimal effects on his problem behaviors.

William's parents are undergoing a divorce, and he lives with his mother, who is also concerned about his school problems and home behavior. His unwillingness to practice his math facts or do what he is told upsets her. Because she wonders if something is wrong with him, she agrees with his teacher's recommendation for further study. William's teacher has decided to refer him for assessment, and his mother is informed.

Design of the Individualized Assessment Plan

Educational assessment of handicapped students must be systematic. A plan of action helps assessment proceed purposefully. In this text, that plan is called the Individualized Assessment Plan (IAP). Although it is not a legal requirement, it helps meet each student's unique needs and individu-alize the assessment process. Standard assessment batteries are neither appropriate nor useful for this. Furthermore, the assessment design must be prepared in relationship to the total process of serving handicapped students. The assessment is linked to decisions concerning instructional design, placement, and other facets of the educational program; the IAP must reflect the requirements of these other phases. Particular care must be taken to maintain educational relevance.

An IAP describes the steps and procedures in the assessment. As part of the total IAP, the assessment must reflect the reason for referral and must yield systematically organized data.

The IAP primarily concentrates on relating other areas of assessment to educational matters. The three main dimensions of educational concern are (a) the student's skills and abilities, (b) the curriculum and the tasks he or she is having difficulty with, and (c) the learning environment. However, the IAP can also reflect the student's physical, social, and cultural characteristics. These correlates may better explain a student's educational needs. For example, a student may have a severe reading disability partially due to a vision disorder.

FIGURE 2–2
Initial parent contact letter to inform parents of referral

Date: 12/1/89

Dear Ms. Bruce:

In order for the educational program to be effective for each child, it is important that school personnel and parents work together as a team. A part of this teamwork is two-way communication.

We would share our concern regarding William's educational progress at this time, and we invite you to confer with us to exchange information that may be helpful to us and your child. With your help we can better evaluate the educational needs of your child and hopefully plan the most appropriate educational program. It is possible that your child may be found to need some special educational service. The specific reasons for referral for testing are academic and behavioral problems in the classroom.

Please contact us at 555-6993 as soon as possible to plan for a mutually convenient personal conference. Your cooperation is appreciated.

Sincerely,

Anna Smith

Anna Smith
Chairperson
Child Study Team
Starlight Elementary School

Note. From Fayette County Public Schools Regulations, Lexington, KY: Fayette County Public Schools. Adapted by permission.

An IAP can be developed by using a set of questions that direct the choice of assessment procedures. The overall structure was described in Chapter 1 (see Figure 1–1). The questions are arranged from general to specific, producing increasingly detailed data. By organizing the IAP with a set of assessment questions, the team can prevent the waste of precious time, energy, and resources. A vague, general question such as, "What's the student's learning problem?" usually leads to an unfocused assessment and ambiguous results. More precise questions help insure that needed data will be gathered. For example, the question, "What is the student's current level of performance in oral reading and specific mastered and unmastered word attack skills?" provides direction and suggests the choice of certain tests and procedures and the exclusion of others. In this case, a standardized test of oral reading skills yielding an index of reading proficiency and a criterion-referenced test of word attack skills may be appropriate.

The IAP may employ formal and/or informal procedures, depending upon the question. The questions may concern any subject matter area; they may relate to academic subjects (reading), social-emotional concerns (self-concept), or the physical environment of the classroom (seating plan). The type of data needed may dictate both the procedure and the particular kind of result. For example, norm-referenced tests may answer a question about level of proficiency, but they do not describe specific skill deficits. A parent interview, rather than a formal test, would be used to gather data about a student's medical and family backgrounds. Other criteria for the selection of formal and informal procedures are described in Chapter 3.

PL 94–142 makes several specific provisions for evaluation. Before receiving special education services, a multidisciplinary team must assess the student to determine eligibility for special education services. Thereafter, a reevaluation must take place at least every 3 years or more frequently if conditions warrant or at the parent's or teacher's request. The multidisciplinary team includes at least one teacher or other specialist with knowledge of the suspected disability area. Also, the team making decisions about placement must include other persons familiar with the student, the meaning of the evaluation data, and the placement options.

The IAP reflects the team nature of the assessment process. Depending on the needs of the student, both educational and other dimensions may be studied. The diversity among professional team members may also result in the inclusion of many different kinds of assessment procedures. No matter who is on the team, however, the IAP must maintain an educational focus and place related noneducational assessments in the appropriate context.

The following specific considerations should guide the design of the IAP and choice of assessment procedures:

1. Use procedures that gather the kind of information needed and yield useful results, such as normative scores or a specific list of mastered and unmastered skills.
2. Use procedures of the highest technical quality.
3. Consider the procedures in the context of a team effort. Avoid duplication, and specify roles of various team members. For example, one professional may screen for potential problems in hearing so the student can be referred to another professional, such as an audiologist.
4. Choose more in-depth, specific assessments only for identified problem areas.
5. Validate assessments by confirming results in the student's actual learning environment.
6. Select multifaceted procedures, accounting for the assessment of three main dimensions: the student, the learning tasks, and the learning environment.
7. Arrange the procedures from general to specific and relate them to one another. Thus, finer and finer levels of information can be gathered.

These policies influence both the content and process of assessment. They are quality controls to assess students accurately, fully, and fairly. Decisions affecting educational and other programs are based upon these results. Students must not be misdiagnosed as having a disability based on inaccurate procedures.

An example of William's IAP is provided in Figure 2–3. After identifying the assessment questions, the team chooses tests or other procedures to gather the data. They cooperatively agree on scheduling and role assignment aspects.

The IAP can also be used to structure other types of assessments and evaluations. As de-

FIGURE 2–3

Individualized Assessment Plan

Reason for Referral: Disruptive classroom behavior, interpersonal problems, and math underachievement.

For: William Bruce	2	7–5	12/20/89	Ms. Smith
Student's Name	Grade	Age	Date	Coordinator

Assessment Question	Assessment Procedures	Person Responsible	Date/Time
What is the student's level of intellectual functioning?	Wechsler Intelligence Scale for Children–Revised	Ms. Paine (school psychologist)	1/12/90 9:00 a.m.
What is the student's level of adaptive behavior?	AAMD Adaptive Behavior Scale–School Edition	Ms. Paine (school psychologist) with mother	1/12/90 2:00 p.m.
What is the overall level of academic achievement?	Woodcock-Johnson Psycho-Educational Battery–Revised	Ms. Knox (resource teacher)	1/14/90 9:00 a.m.
What is the level of math achievement?	KeyMath Revised	Ms. Knox (resource teacher)	1/15/90 9:00 a.m.
What is the level of oral language development?	Test of Language Development–2, Primary	Ms. Thompson (speech-language pathologist)	1/15/90 10:00 a.m.
What is the status of classroom behavior?	Behavior Rating Profile	Ms. Knox (resource teacher)	1/15/90 11:00 a.m.
	Sociogram, behavioral observation	Ms. Paine (school psychologist)	30 minutes each day for the week of 1/12/90–1/16/90 at different times

For Parental Use: I am aware of the need for testing William and the procedures to be used. I give my approval.

Jean Bruce
Parent's Signature

12/22/89
Date

scribed later, educators and others have many occasions to evaluate the student's progress and the program's effectiveness. The IAP can be used at these points, too.

Parental Permission for Assessment

Once the goals for an assessment and the procedures to be used become clear, parental permission must be obtained before testing may begin. Parents must give their written permission for the initial assessment for a possible handicapping condition. The written notice must be given a reasonable time before the school proposes to do the assessment, and it must include an explanation of the various procedural safeguards, a clear explanation of the reason for assessment, and a description of the procedures to be used. The IAP illustrated in Figure 2–3 can be used for this purpose with a place for William's mother to sign.

PL 94–142 has some additional stipulations. The request for permission and all related communications with parents must be clearly presented to them, with documentation that this step was taken. All communication must be written in the native language of the parents. Forms may be translated, or if parents are illiterate, the written material can be read to them and their signature or mark requested.

Administration, Scoring, and Interpretation of the Assessment

General guidelines for using various assessment techniques are described and discussed in Chapters 4 and 5. Manuals accompanying formal standardized tests also contain specific instructions. Informal procedures, such as interviews and observations, are also governed by principles of good practice. Many of the points previously made about PL 94–142 regulations are also applicable to the administration, scoring, and interpretation of tests and other techniques. This profile of William illustrates the assessment process up to this point.

William

William's mother, upon request, has given her written permission for an assessment plan. The special educator administers a series of individual tests related to reading and mathematical achievement. The tests measure several different aspects of academic performance in many ways. For example, William's ability to solve addition problems is assessed both by a paper-and-pencil computation test and by a test that requires William to add in his head. Also, both William's oral and silent reading skills are assessed, not only in word recognition but also in comprehension. The speech-language pathologist also tests William's understanding and use of oral language.

William and his teacher are observed in the regular classroom; a structured checklist is used for this form of assessment. Samples of his seatwork are studied, with classroom conditions noted. William's teacher and his mother are also interviewed to help the assessment team understand his classroom and home environments.

Meanwhile, other professionals gather vital information. The school psychologist administers

intellectual performance tests and other measures of development. William's attitude toward schoolwork and preferences in recreation and playmates are noted. Physicians examine William's physical condition, especially looking for vision and hearing problems and possible physical factors related to his hyperactivity.

Reporting Results

The team members prepare and then share the results of their individual assessments. Scores and other data are only meaningful when combined into a full student profile, as illustrated in Figure 2–4. Each participant should attend a postassessment conference to report and discuss the results. Key figures at this meeting are the student's parents and perhaps the student.

Parents of assessed students must have the results reported to them, whether or not the student is ultimately found to be eligible for special education services. The results are presented at a meeting with the professionals involved in the assessment; parents are to serve as active team members. Parents must be clearly told if the student has a handicap and is eligible for special education services. If so, the components of an Individualized Education Program (IEP) are developed.

PL 94–142 also specifies that parents must be informed of their right to have access to all school records concerning their child's identification, assessment, and placement in special education. Frequently, parents wish to examine the records to better understand the school's basis for concern. A school system must respond promptly to such a request, in no more than 45 days.

If the parents have any questions about information in the records, the school system must also supply an explanation. If the parents feel statements in the records are inaccurate or misleading, or violate the child's rights to privacy, they can ask the school system to amend them. The school system must then respond within a reasonable amount of time. If the school refuses the parents' request, it must inform the parents and advise them of their right to a hearing.

Furthermore, these records are maintained by strict regulations of confidentiality. Parents must be informed of the procedures to store, disclose

FIGURE 2–4
Student performance profile

Area	Source	RESULTS			Strength	Weakness
		Above Average	Average	Below Average		
Intelligence	*WISC–R*		X		Visual skills	Verbal skills
Adaptive behavior	*AAMD*		X			
Academics						
Reading	*Woodcock– Johnson–R*		X		Decoding	Comprehension
Written language	*Woodcock– Johnson–R*		X		Copying, spelling	
Math	*Woodcock– Johnson–R* *KeyMath Revised*			X		Written & mental computation; problem solving
Oral language	*TOLD–2, Primary*		X		Phonology, vocabulary	Grammar
Classroom behavior	Observations *Behavior Rating Profile*			X		Hyperactive, disruptive, abusive; poor work habits

to another person, retain, or destroy any records concerning the child. Parents must give their permission before information concerning their child is given to anyone not authorized within the school system. Anyone other than the parents and authorized school personnel examining the records must list their name, the date, and intent.

When the school system no longer needs the information for educational purposes, it must inform the parents. At their request, the records may be destroyed or kept permanently. Otherwise, only a limited set of information, such as the student's name, address, and grades, is retained.

By law, the school system must provide information about where parents can obtain an independent educational evaluation, if requested. The parents have the right to an independent evaluation at public expense if they disagree with the school system's evaluation and the school system does not or cannot substantiate its own evaluation. If parents initiate an evaluation, the results must be considered by the school system in making any decision about special education services and may be presented at any hearing on the matter.

The principles that guide reporting assessment results are described in Chapter 15. Techniques for effective involvement of parents at these postassessment conferences are covered in Chapter 17.

Deciding Eligibility

The team often decides at the postassessment conference whether the student has a handicapping condition and is eligible for special education services. This legal decision is made by comparing the student's assessment results to the criteria for eligibility in that state or area of the country.

As indicated earlier, eligibility for mildly handicapped students centers around assessment questions of ability, academic achievement, and social behavior. The team must apply any available state guidelines specifying the use of formulas or cutoffs to measure the degree of impairment. Also, the professionals and parents may need to document the performance of certain assessment activities, such as classroom observation, to support their decisions. If the student meets all the criteria and all procedures have been performed as required, the student is designated as having a handicapping condition; that is, learning disabilities, mild mental retardation, or emotional disturbance. The following profile describes William's case at this step of decision making as the team prepares to design an appropriate program.

William

William's mother attends the conference after the assessment is completed. The results of the testing are described by the team members. William's intellectual performance and adaptive behavior are described as average for his age. Although his reading and writing skills are considered acceptable for his grade level, William has specific deficits in computation skills and application. His completion of arithmetic assignments is occasional and sloppy.

The behavioral profile of William's social adjustment is particularly poor. His teachers consider him disruptive and hard to motivate, and William's mother also reports difficulties. Classroom observations reveal a pattern of verbal outbursts, negative remarks, physical threats made to peers, and out-of-seat behavior. The team has concluded that William has a variety of behavior disorders and is eligible for special education. An Individualized Education Program must be designed to remedy the behavioral and academic problems.

Design of the Individualized Education Program

The team now turns its attention to instructional matters and designs an Individualized Education Program for the student. The participants at the IEP conference are a school system representative to supervise the proceedings; the student's teacher or teachers; one or both parents; the student, if appropriate; and a member of the team that performed the assessment or someone knowledgeable about the procedures used and the results obtained. The teacher may be a regular classroom teacher, special educator, or speech-language pathologist, depending upon the nature of the student's educational needs. The parents particularly must be encouraged to attend and participate in designing the IEP in the following ways:

1. Parents must be notified in advance of the purpose, time, location, and participants for the meeting. The meeting should be scheduled at a mutually agreed-upon time and place.
2. If the parents cannot attend, other means of communication (for example, conference telephone calls) should be used.
3. If parents do not attend in spite of requests, records of all efforts to encourage their presence must be kept.
4. At the meeting, every effort must be made to insure that parents understand the proceedings. This may involve the use of interpreters. (Techniques to stimulate parental participation at this point are discussed in Chapter 17.)
5. Parents must receive a copy of the IEP at their request. It should be in their native language.

Professionals and parents make decisions about the IEP based on the data gathered in the assessment. Although assessment results can be reported in many ways and used for a variety of purposes, the IEP offers a common format for the plans of all exceptional students. The IEP is to contain the following basic features:

(a) A statement of the child's present levels of educational performance;
(b) A statement of annual goals, including short-term instructional objectives;
(c) A statement of the specific special education and related services to be provided to the child, and the extent to which the child will be able to participate in regular educational programs;
(d) The projected dates for initiation of services and the anticipated duration of the services; and
(e) Appropriate objective criteria and evaluation procedures and schedules for determining, on at least an annual basis, whether the short term instructional objectives are being achieved. (PL 94–142, §121a.346).

The IEP meeting must occur within 30 calendar days of a determination that the student is handicapped and in need of special services. The IEP must be developed before the student begins to receive special services and must be implemented without any undue delay after the meeting. Furthermore, a similar meeting must be held at least annually to reexamine the appropriateness of the IEP and revise it if necessary.

The team needs many kinds of assessment data to develop the components of the IEP. The full array of educational assessment procedures described in Chapter 1 may be used to make these program decisions. As illustrated in the sample IEP in Figure 2–5, all of the following components are required elements in William's IEP. However, school districts and other educational agencies vary in how they describe these components of the IEP. For example, the specific special education and related services may not be designated by the types of personnel and their names. Broader designations of services would suffice.

Current performance level. The first step in writing an IEP is to specify the student's current levels of educational performance. The IEP team reviews the information gathered by the assessment team and collects more information if necessary. The team then chooses the specific curriculum areas for the IEP and describes current levels of performance for each (Turnbull, Strickland, & Brantley, 1982). In William's case, his performance is average and in keeping with his abilities, except in the areas of classroom behavior and arithmetic.

Annual goals. The IEP team considers the student's current levels of educational performance, strengths, and weaknesses in setting annual goals for each curriculum area. Teachers, therapists, and other team members abstract the priority goals from the assessment data. Useful assessment information includes the student's current rate of educational progress and history. Annual goals should be stated so the rate of student progress required by the goals is commensurate with ability. Results of the psychological report and input from educators, parents, and others who have worked with the student are particularly useful in projecting these expectation levels. The findings of physicians and mental health specialists may influence the number and nature of the goals chosen. For example, a student's general health, vision, or hearing may be such that limits must be put on demands at school and at home.

Annual goals are usually general, but the degree of specificity in these goal statements seems to vary with each locale. Some examples of commonly used goals include the following:

□ Improve oral reading ability
□ Increase reading comprehension to the 2.5 grade level
□ Joe will be prompt in reporting to class and beginning work
□ Assist him in computing and writing the sum of a one-digit and a two-digit number

Each student's goals must be prioritized. The most severe deficits noted in the assessment are the first concerns. Second, the priorities of the student, parents, teachers, and others must be considered. Third, the age of the student may be a factor; for example, the handicapped adolescent may need vocational preparation more than training in basic skills. As illustrated in the sample IEP in Figure 2–5, William's annual goals are to decrease a variety of inappropriate behaviors, increase independent task completion, and improve computational skills and their use.

Short-term objectives. The IEP team attempts to bridge the gap between the student's current levels and the projected goals with short-term instructional objectives. Task analysis breaks down the annual goals into teachable subcomponents or objectives. Curriculum guides and other published sources may also be used to locate instructional objectives.

Team members can draw upon their own experience with the student to suggest more specific objectives to attain a goal. Parents are often aware of opportunities for additional practice at home and in the community. Classroom teachers, vocational teachers, and specialists may assist by pinpointing necessary objectives. As shown in the sample IEP, the objectives can involve activities at home as well as in school. William's annual goals in the area of behavior call for activities by teachers and his parent as well as services from the school counselor.

Type of education program and/or related services. When goals and objectives are stated, the IEP team decides on the type of special education and related services required. In addition,

FIGURE 2–5
Sample IEP

Child's Name: William Bruce   Birthdate: 6/15/82   Grade: 2.5

School: Starlight   Date Referred: 11/17/89   Date Tested: 1/15/90

CURRENT LEVELS OF PERFORMANCE (STRENGTHS & WEAKNESSES)

William is average in terms of intelligence and adaptive behavior. He is developing appropriately in all academic areas except arithmetic. Functioning on the early first-grade level, William cannot add or subtract 2-digit numbers, nor use number lines or other aids. He is particularly deficient in mental computation and problem solving.

However, it is William's social skills that are particularly underdeveloped. He is disruptive in class and verbally and physically threatens his peers. He cannot work independently and rarely finishes his work. He is very active, out of his seat frequently and making attention-getting noises.

LONG-TERM GOALS

Area: Behavior

1. To decrease out-of-seat behavior and verbal outbursts

2. To decrease verbal and physical abuse of peers

3. To increase independent management and assignment completion

4. To improve ability to follow directions and be responsible

SHORT-TERM OBJECTIVES

Area: Behavior

1. Given a suitable behavior management program, William will remain in his seat and speak when spoken to or after raising his hand.

2. Same as #1.

3. Same as #1.

4a. Given a joint behavior program between home and school, William will follow directions and take care of his personal things.

b. William will see the school counselor twice a week for an hour to discuss his behavior and feelings.

Area: Mathematics

1. To improve addition and subtraction of 2-digit numbers

2. To improve mental computation without the aid of fingers, number lines, and so on

3. To apply computation skills in solving word problems

Area: Mathematics

1. Given manipulative objects (e.g., cuisenaire rods), William will calculate 2-digit addition and subtraction problems on paper.

2. Given no arithmetic aids, William will calculate 1- and 2-digit addition and subtraction problems in his head and give verbal answers.

3. Given problems from the computer program "Mind Benders," William will identify the needed computation procedure, perform it on paper correctly, and check his answer on the computer.

RESPONSIBLE PERSONNEL

Behavior Goals: Mrs. Lake (second grade teacher), Mrs. Smith (special education teacher consultant), Mrs. Bruce (William's mother), and Mr. Philips (school counselor).

Arithmetic Goals: Mrs. Lake (second grade teacher) and Mrs. Smith (special education teacher consultant).

PLACEMENT RECOMMENDATION

William will remain in the regular classroom. His second grade teacher will receive the support of the special education teacher consultant for designing and implementing the behavioral and academic programs. William will visit with the counselor twice a week for an hour.

TIMELINE

Program starts 2/1/90 and continues until review on 6/6/90.

EVALUATION

Charts will be maintained for behavioral goals; teacher, parent, and child interviews will also be used. For the arithmetic area, the *KeyMath Revised* and *BRIGANCE® Diagnostic Inventory of Basic Skills* will be readministered in May, 1990.

Committee Members:	Member Name	Signature
Parent	Jean Bruce	*Jean Bruce*
Special education consultant teacher	Anna Smith	*Anna Smith*
Second-grade teacher	Sharon Lake	*Sharon Lake*
Counselor	Sidney Philips	*Sidney Philips*

For Parent Use: I agree with this plan and grant permission for my child to receive special education services.

Jean Bruce   1/27/90
Signature   Date

the team determines how much the student will participate in the regular classroom.

Although IEPs vary in how they indicate services, the IEP may designate the special educators that provide the services. In addition, classroom teachers are frequently involved in the program for mildly handicapped students in the regular classroom. Counselors, speech-language pathologists, and other specialists are also designated when appropriate.

The team makes these designations cooperatively to coordinate the assignment of responsibilities. In the case of mildly handicapped students, regular classroom teachers and special educators specify their areas of mutual responsibility. In William's case, a special education teacher consultant will be assigned to his second-grade teacher, and the counselor will also see William regularly.

Placement in the least restrictive environment. The team must also address the issue of least restrictive placement. To the maximum extent appropriate, handicapped students must be educated in the same classroom as their nonhandicapped peers. However, each model for delivery of special services has pros and cons. From the point of view of time in the regular classroom, the teacher-consultant and itinerant models are the better options. However, the specific student's needs and other considerations may move the IEP team to choose a more restrictive model. What makes the process of choosing how to deliver services particularly valid is that a team of involved and informed individuals, including parents and the students themselves, discuss the issue based on the student's needs and family preferences. For example, as illustrated in the sample IEP, William will not need to leave the regular classroom except to visit the counselor for 2 hours a week. A teacher-consultant will come into his classroom and assist his teacher or him as needed. William's mother will also help accomplish some objectives.

Beginning and ending dates. A timeline must also be established by the IEP team, designating beginning and ending dates. The whole team should discuss the features of a student's program that may depend on one another. Teachers, therapists, and others must judge when they will begin work on certain goals and how long the instruction or therapy may take. Everyone on the team should synchronize their efforts to accomplish the goals by the designated time. William's IEP meeting was held in late January, at the beginning of the new term. His services begin immediately in February 1990 and will continue until the school year's end.

Evaluation criteria and annual review. The IEP team must also set up a plan for evaluation of student progress that includes a schedule. The team members with the responsibility for accomplishing the IEP goals describe the procedures to be used for the evaluation. The evaluation plan will serve to guide both ongoing monitoring of the program and the annual review. As discussed in Chapter 16, special arrangements for grading, minimum competency testing, and graduation will be specified for some students.

All the assessment procedures discussed in Chapter 1 can be used to gather data for this evaluation and review. Two elements of evaluation, formative and summative, are involved. *Formative* evaluation is ongoing; it is performed while the IEP is being implemented and measures student progress toward accomplishing the goals and objectives. Direct and frequent measures of the program are imperative (Howell, Kaplan, & O'Connell, 1979). Formative procedures include the use of criterion-referenced testing, daily behavioral observations, and logs. This ongoing evaluation supplies information for the immediate revision of the instructional procedures, if necessary.

Summative evaluation is performed after the IEP is implemented and demonstrates the effects of the program. Norm-referenced tests, criterion-referenced tests, interviews with students and parents, and observations may all be used. Different kinds of data are needed to make decisions about program continuation, revision, or termination. Comparative data from norm-referenced tests as well as continually gathered data may be necessary to confirm a student's continued eligibility for special education.

Involved professionals, the student's parents, and the student (if appropriate) will use the evaluation data to decide whether to continue, modify, or terminate the special program. Data are examined to determine if the goals and objectives set forth in the IEP have been accomplished. If they have been achieved and no further special education needs are apparent, the student's program is terminated. However, if the goals and objectives have not been totally accomplished or if additional ones need to be achieved, then the IEP is revised and the student continues to receive special services. Although the school system is responsible for offering these services, PL 94–142 does not necessarily hold it accountable if the student falls short of goals and objectives. However, the school system must document that every effort has been made to achieve them. If the student does not achieve as expected, the parents may request any necessary revisions of the IEP; for example, they may request an increase in the amount of special education services.

This evaluation requirement also determines whether handicapped students continue to need the special education and related specialized services that may isolate them from normal peers. Review is intended to prevent endless placement in special education and to guarantee that students who leave the regular classroom for special services return as soon as possible. Furthermore, the annual review is an effort to maintain a sense of direction in the student's program. As illustrated in the sample IEP in Figure 2–5, William's teachers and parent will reevaluate the IEP in June 1990. His behavior will be monitored regularly, and post-testing of arithmetic skills will be performed.

Parental Agreement to the IEP

The student's parents are asked to approve the IEP and the placement of their child in special education by signing the IEP or another form (Figure 2–5). PL 94–142 grants them a number of rights and options. They have the right to approve or disapprove placement in services for exceptional conditions, such as mild mental retardation or specific learning disabilities. They must also decide whether to approve placement in a certain type of service, such as a special class or a resource room. If the parents disagree with professional recommendations, they are entitled to an impartial due process hearing. But if the parents refuse to agree to the special placement, the school district can also request a hearing.

Parents must sign the IEP and grant permission to place the child in services for handicapped students. The area of exceptionality is specified. All regulations for prior notice, clarity and appro-

priateness of communication, and documented effort to inform and solicit parental consent govern this activity. When parents and the school system cannot agree upon the initial assessment findings for placement, the nature of the placement in special education, or any other aspect, PL 94–142 provides for an impartial due process hearing. The parents and the school system may first attempt to use mediation to solve their differences. However, if this fails, an impartial hearing officer is appointed from a list of qualified individuals.

For the purpose of these hearings, the parents and/or the school system can be advised by legal counsel or other qualified advisors. In fact, the school system must inform parents of the availability of free or low-cost legal services. At the hearing, parents and their counsel can present evidence, confront and cross-examine, and call witnesses. All evidence to be presented must be disclosed to the parents at least 5 days before the hearing. Parents may also request a verbatim recording of the hearing.

The decision of this impartial hearing is final, unless the parents and/or the school district wish to appeal to the state department of education. In that case, the state department of education reviews the hearing according to federal guidelines and makes a decision. If the parents and/or the school system are not satisfied, they can take civil action. Such action can also be taken at any time.

The law sets up timelines governing the expediency of conducting both the impartial hearing and the state department review. During this period, the student remains in the current educational placement, unless both the parents and the school system agree otherwise.

William

William's mother agrees with the various components of the IEP, along with the provision of a special education program for her son. She is pleased with the education program she and the team have put together. The goals cover William's needs in social adjustment, as well as remediation in arithmetic. William's mother indicates her interest in conducting a joint behavior management program because she feels it will help her manage William at home. However, due to her work and other demands on her time, including William's 2-year-old sister, she will not be able to help William with homework. She is confident that once her divorce from William's father is settled, much of William's confusion will disappear. She hopes the school counselor can help William adjust, too. William's mother signs the IEP and gives her permission to special education placement. She is relieved that William will not be out of his classroom for a long period of time and that his intellectual abilities are on a level with those of his peers. She hopes William improves by the time they meet again to review the program in June.

Assessment involves the systematic gathering of information according to an individually designed assessment plan, or IAP. A variety of formal and informal assessment tools are used to accomplish the plan. The next three chapters describe procedures for the selection and use of both standardized tests and informal assessments, as well as strategies for applying results in educational decision making.

STUDY GUIDE

Review Questions

1. Define due process.
2. Parents must be notified in writing if their child has been referred for special testing. (True or False)
3. Parents must be informed of their rights. (True or False)
4. Parents must give their written consent for testing for special education placement. (True or False)
5. Parents can seek an independent evaluation. (True or False)
6. Parents can examine only those areas of their child's school records designated by the schools. (True or False)
7. Parents must be informed of the evaluation results. (True or False)
8. Parents must give their approval for placement in special education. (True or False)
9. Parents who disagree with recommendations have a right to a due process hearing by an impartial hearing officer. (True or False)
10. The IAP may employ formal and informal procedures. (True or False)
11. The IAP's content depends on the purpose of the assessment. (True or False)
12. The team nature of assessment affects the design of an IAP. (True or False)
13. Surrogate parents can represent handicapped children if their parents are unavailable. (True or False)
14. What are three provisions of PL 94–142 against discriminatory practices in assessment?
15. What are the main components of the IEP required by PL 94–142?
16. Only standardized tests can be used to develop an IEP. (True or False)
17. Exceptional students are to be educated with their normal peers to the "maximum extent appropriate." (True or False)
18. What are three ways to deliver services to exceptional students?
19. The least restrictive learning environment is the most appropriate. (True or False)
20. The IEP must be reviewed at least annually. (True or False)
21. Evaluation data about the IEP may only be gathered at the end of the program. (True or False)
22. Match the required IEP features in Column A and examples of each in Column B.

Column A	*Column B*
a. Current level of functioning	_____ The IEP will be reviewed on June 1, 1990. Criterion-referenced tests and behavioral observations will be used to evaluate progress.
b. Annual goals	_____ Deborah will be placed in a learning disabilities program and will receive speech therapy.

c. Short-term objectives _____ In oral reading, Deborah must learn to read three-letter words with short vowels accurately.

d. Type of special education and related services _____ Deborah's program will begin September 1, 1989 and end June 1, 1990.

e. Extent of time in the regular classroom _____ Deborah will be with the resource teacher for 2 hours a day and with the speech therapist 1 hour weekly. Otherwise she will be in the regular classroom.

f. Beginning and ending dates _____ Deborah's strengths are in social skills, motor development, and auditory comprehension. However, she has significant problems in oral reading and arithmetic. Her articulation skills are also below average.

g. Review schedule and procedures _____ To increase Deborah's oral reading skills; to improve her computational and problem-solving skills; to increase the intelligibility of her speech.

Activities

1. Examine a copy of an IEP. Does it contain the seven components mandated by PL 94–142?
2. Compare IEPs from two school systems or perhaps two states. Do they meet the requirements of PL 94–142 in different ways?
3. Examine the forms and procedures used by a school district to comply with due process safeguards.
4. Interview parents who have recently had their child assessed for special education. Were their rights honored? How?
5. Interview a local special educator, school psychologist, or other person who performs school assessments. What kind of procedures are used?

Discussion Questions

1. "A goal of an educational assessment is to find out how exceptional students learn, as well as how much they know." What does this mean?
2. Discuss your state department of education's regulations and guidelines for deciding eligibility for serving the mildly handicapped. What kind of information is required? Are any assessment procedures recommended? Are criteria set forth, such as ranges of performance?
3. What is the importance of the prereferral phase in which teachers attempt curricular modifications?
4. Is it as important to develop an Individualized Assessment Plan as an Individualized Education Program?

PART
TWO

Technical Aspects

Professionals engaged in special education assessment must possess a range of technical skills. This section is designed to provide you with knowledge about the technical aspects of assessment. You will also have the opportunity to learn about and practice skills needed to select and use assessment techniques and, when necessary, to design and modify them.

Chapter 3 presents specific criteria for evaluating and selecting formal and informal procedures. The appropriateness of a procedure depends upon its relevance, accuracy, and usefulness. Accuracy is related to a measure's technical adequacy, and in this chapter you will learn how to evaluate technical aspects of tests such as norms, reliability, validity, and the types of test scores offered. Also, measures must be examined to insure choices that are not biased or discriminatory. An evaluation form is provided at the end of this chapter to assist you in reviewing tests and other assessment procedures.

How do you use these procedures and make sense out of the results? Chapter 4 discusses the basics of standardized testing. The steps to prepare the tester, testing environment, and the student and to actually administer tests are described, including observation of the student during testing. The process of converting test results into various types of scores is outlined. Interpretation is based upon the scores obtained and the student's behavior during testing; results are reported in a variety of ways, including a system of score ranges. Two additional aspects of standardized testing are discussed: (a) test modifications for informal analysis and (b) the prevention of discriminatory practices.

Chapter 5 describes the design, use, and interpretation of the companion assessment procedures to standardized tests: informal assessment strategies. Observation, analysis of student work samples, and task analysis permit the professional to focus on environmental factors that may influence the learning problem. When the classroom performance of the student is the concern, curriculum-based measures such as inventories, classroom quizzes, and criterion-referenced tests are the assessment methods of choice. Of particular usefulness are diagnostic probes and diagnostic teaching, techniques that merge assessment and instruction. Gathering information from others is another important aspect of informal assessment; various techniques are suggested for questioning students, teachers, parents, and others. And as with formal testing, concerns about bias in informal assessment and the need for interpretation of data in a nondiscriminatory manner are discussed.

Chapter 6 focuses on the use of computers as tools in the assessment process. Technology can assist in the selection of appropriate assessment strategies by providing access to information sources. Some tests have been adapted so that they are actually administered by computer, although this application is as yet rarely used in special education. More common are software programs for scoring tests, writing reports, managing assessment data, and generating IEPs. Chapter 6 provides several examples of these uses and a listing of the test-scoring programs currently available. Computers can also contribute to informal assessment by providing data on student performance and assisting the teacher in analysis of those data.

3

Selection of Assessment Tools

Assessment is an information-gathering activity. Its purpose is to provide answers to important educational questions, whether these concern identification and placement, instructional planning, or monitoring of student progress and program effectiveness. The assessment process begins with careful planning, and one of the most critical preparatory steps is selection of appropriate tools.

The tools selected for assessment influence the success of the data-gathering process. Inaccurate measures produce useless and potentially harmful information; tools that are inappropriate, even if their results are accurate, fail to provide the type of information necessary to assist educational decision making.

The appropriateness of an assessment tool depends upon the context in which it will be used. Although poor-quality measures yielding inaccurate results are never appropriate, most tools provide information useful for some purposes, for some students, in some situations. In judging the worth of a measure or strategy, the professional first assures its technical adequacy and then determines its value for the particular assessment task.

Criticism of special education assessment practices in the 1960s and early 1970s centered around the inappropriate use of assessment tools, specifically the misuse of standardized intelligence tests with students from cultural and linguistic minorities. Leaders such as Lloyd Dunn (1968) charged that special classes for the mentally retarded contained disproportionate numbers of minority children. Researchers such as Jane Mercer (1973) attributed this overrepresentation to reliance on a single test score, the IQ, for placement decisions. The appropriateness of standard intelligence measures for the minority population was challenged in the courts. *Diana v. State Board of Education* (1970) questioned the use of English language IQ tests with children whose home language was Spanish, and *Larry P. v. Riles* (1972, 1979, 1984) sought to establish the discriminatory nature of dominant culture intelligence measures for ethnic minority students.

Although some controversies surrounding testing continue, assessment practices today are much improved. One major impetus for this change was the enactment of state and federal laws setting forth specific guidelines for special education assessment and placement.

CRITERIA FOR THE SELECTION OF ASSESSMENT TOOLS

One purpose of PL 94–142, the Education for All Handicapped Children Act of 1975, was the establishment of a set of procedures to guard against inappropriate assessment and placement practices. As Table 3–1 suggests, this law provides safeguards to prevent recurrence of past abuses. Although appropriate assessment procedures are mandated by PL 94–142, its regulations, and the state laws resulting from it, actual practice may fall short of intended goals. However, special education laws do attempt to describe an exemplary system for assessment of handicapped students.

Legal Guidelines for Assessment

The regulations for PL 94–142 provide specific guidelines for the evaluation and placement of handicapped individuals in special education programs. This law focuses on the use of assessment information for legal decisions, that is, decisions about identification and determination of eligibility for special education services. This type of information has implications for long-range instructional decisions such as those associated with design of the Individualized Education Program (IEP). However, laws such as PL 94–142 do not attempt to regulate classroom assessment and the day-to-day instructional decisions practitioners face.

PL 94–142 includes several guidelines for the selection of assessment tools and the conduct of the assessment process. They are described in the following sections.

Assessment is nondiscriminatory. PL 94–142 expressly forbids three types of discrimination. First, assessment tools must be free of racial and cultural bias. Tests and other procedures must be selected on this basis, and care must be taken to prevent the intrusion of bias into test administration. Second, if a student's native language is not English, every effort must be made to provide assessment tools in the student's language. This mandate extends not only to individuals who speak languages other than English but also to those whose mode of communication is not spoken language. For example, hearing impaired students communicating through sign language should be assessed in sign language. However, according to

TABLE 3-1
Safeguards of PL 94–142 against assessment abuses

Past Abuses	Safeguards
Students evaluated for special education without notice to parents or parental consent	Prior written notice must be given to parents before evaluation; parents must give consent before evaluation [121a.504][a]
Culturally biased tests used in evaluation	Tests must be selected and administered so that they are not racially or culturally discriminatory [121a.530]
Non-English-speaking students assessed in English	Tests must be provided and administered in the child's native language or other mode of communication, if feasible [121a.532]
Tests administered by untrained or poorly trained personnel	Trained professionals must administer tests according to the test instructions [121a.532]
Poor-quality assessment instruments used for evaluation	Tests must have been validated for the specific purpose for which they are used [121a.532]
Tests used that penalized handicapped individuals	Tests must be selected so that they do not discriminate against the individual on the basis of handicap (unless their purpose is the identification of the handicapping condition) [121a.532]
Placement in services for the retarded based solely on IQ scores	No one procedure may be used as the sole criterion for determination of the educational program [121a.532]; tests selected for use in evaluation must include not merely those that yield a single general IQ score [121a.532]
Placement decisions made without a complete evaluation of the individual	Individuals must be assessed in all areas related to the suspected disability (e.g., health, vision, hearing, social and emotional status, general intelligence, academic performance, communicative status, motor ability) [121a.532]; information from a variety of sources (aptitude and achievement tests, teacher recommendations, physical condition, social and cultural background, adaptive behavior) must be documented and carefully considered [121a.533]

[a]*The numbers in brackets refer to sections of the Code of Federal Regulations; 45 CFR Part 121a contains regulations promulgated under the Education of the Handicapped Act (PL 91–320), as amended by the Education of All Handicapped Children Act (PL 94–142).*

Note. From "Assessing Retarded Development" by R. B. Lewis, in *Mental Retardation* (p. 36) by P. T. Cegelka and H. J. Prehm (Eds.), 1982, Columbus, OH: Merrill. Copyright 1982 by Bell & Howell Company. Reprinted by permission.

PL 94–142, because appropriate assessment tools are not available in all languages, assessment may proceed if testing in the native language is clearly not feasible. Third, assessment tools must not discriminate on the basis of handicapping condition. Unless the purpose of assessment is to study the disability, tests and other procedures should bypass the student's problem. For instance, if the purpose of assessment is to study spelling achievement, the student with impaired motor skills should not be required to write his or her answers.

Assessment focuses on educational needs.
The major purpose of assessment is to determine educational needs. Although the presence of a handicapping condition must be established to support eligibility for special education services, simply identifying a student as mentally retarded or learning disabled is insufficient. Attention must also be directed to the specific educational needs resulting from the disability.

Assessment is comprehensive and multidisciplinary. All important areas of student performance must be studied. Although intelligence tests may be used, they must be accompanied by other measures that assess educational needs. The results of a single measure must never be the sole basis for placement in special education. The assessment must be so comprehensive that no important area of performance is neglected; several sources should be consulted for information about the student. Health, vision, hearing, social and emotional status, general intelligence, academic performance, communicative status, and motor abilities may be considered, if these are areas of potential need for the student under assessment. The assessment must also be multidisciplinary. The team must consist of professionals representing several disciplines, including at least one person knowledgeable about the student's suspected disability.

Assessment tools are technically adequate and administered by trained professionals.

Assessment devices must be good measurement tools that have been validated for the specific purpose for which they will be used. They must display adequate technical quality to insure accurate results. If the goal is study of reading achievement, the instrument chosen must be a valid measure of reading achievement. Assessment must also be conducted by trained professionals. The administration, scoring, and interpretation rules specified in the measure's manual must be scrupulously followed.

Rights of handicapped students and their parents are protected during assessment.

Throughout the assessment process, safeguards protect the rights of handicapped individuals and their parents or guardians. As Chapter 2 discussed, parents must be notified when a student is referred for assessment; they must receive information about their rights; and they must give informed consent before assessment begins. No student may be placed in special education without a comprehensive assessment that includes evaluation of his or her educational needs. The student's progress in special education must be evaluated at least annually and a complete reevaluation conducted at least every 3 years. Parents may review school records that concern their child's identification, assessment, and placement in special education; they also have the right to an explanation

of the assessment results. In addition, parents participate as members of the IEP team and assist in the development of their child's educational program.

Professional Guidelines

There are several sources of guidance in the selection of assessment tools in addition to legal requirements. A major resource is *Standards for Educational and Psychological Testing* (1985), prepared by a joint committee of the American Educational Research Association, American Psychological Association, and the National Council on Measurement in Education. This guide for test users and producers contains standards for tests, manuals, and reports; it also includes standards for reports of research on reliability and validity and standards for the use of tests.

Catalogues of test publishers, test manuals, and other information provided by producers of assessment tools may also aid in the selection process. Test catalogues provide an overview of available instruments, particularly newer ones, and often include brief descriptions of each measure. However, the more detailed information needed for selection decisions can be found in test manuals. Manuals should discuss important characteristics of the instrument including purpose, the procedures used for development, and data on psychometric quality. Not all manuals are complete, and few seek to emphasize the weak points of the measure, so the buyer must beware.

The *Mental Measurements Yearbook* series offers assistance in the evaluation of specific measures. Issued periodically, these references contain reviews of commercially available psychological, educational, and vocational tests. The most recent edition, the *Ninth Mental Measurements Yearbook* (Mitchell, 1985), includes information about more than 1,400 measures. A supplement was published in 1988 (Conoley, Kramer, & Mitchell), and beginning in 1989, a new *Mental Measurements Yearbook* will be issued every 2 years, with supplements in alternating years. *Tests in Print III* (Mitchell, 1983) provides a bibliography of published tests. Other volumes in the series include *Intelligence Tests and Reviews, Reading Tests and Reviews,* and *Mathematics Tests and Reviews,* all by Buros (1975). Another resource is *A Consumer's Guide to Tests in Print* (Hammill,

Brown, & Bryant, 1989). This guide contains reviewers' ratings of the technical characteristics of 148 individually administered tests commonly used for special education purposes.

Professional journals are the best source for research relating to assessment and for critical reviews of newly developed assessment tools. *Diagnostique,* published by the Council for Educational Diagnostic Services of the Council for Exceptional Children (CEC), focuses on special education assessment. Other journals that often contain articles about assessment tools and their use in special education are *Exceptional Children, Journal of Special Education,* and *Remedial and Special Education,* as well as those journals that address specific handicapping conditions (e.g., *Journal of Learning Disabilities, Behavioral Disorders, Education and Training in Mental Retardation*).

Evaluation Criteria

Whether a multidisciplinary team is faced with choosing the tools for eligibility assessment or a classroom teacher is searching for a measure to evaluate academic progress, the task is the same: selection of the most accurate, effective, and efficient means of data collection. The tools for assessment must be the most appropriate available. The questions that follow provide a structure for the evaluation of assessment tools.

Does the tool fit the purpose of assessment? A technically excellent assessment device is useless if it does not provide the particular information needed to answer an assessment question. Because the type of tool needed is related to the purpose of the assessment, the ways in which assessment information will be used must be clear. If the goal is to answer questions about a student's standing in relation to his or her peers, then norm-referenced measures are appropriate. If questions concern classroom behaviors, observational strategies are indicated; for questions about mastery of specific academic skills, the most valuable information sources may be criterion-referenced tests, informal inventories, classroom quizzes, and teacher checklists.

The form in which assessment results appear is also important. Sometimes comparative scores such as percentile ranks or standard scores are

necessary; for other purposes, a simple frequency count of the number of times a student performs a particular behavior will suffice.

Other considerations are the content and scope of the measure: the specific achievement, aptitude, or attitude areas that are assessed. If the goal is study of a student's reading abilities, a test of mathematics skills is obviously inappropriate. Less apparent is the choice between a global achievement test designed to screen for problems in reading and other academic subjects and a diagnostic reading test that assesses decoding, structural analysis, comprehension, and vocabulary skills. Before it is possible to select the most appropriate tool, the purpose of the assessment must be clearly understood.

Is the tool appropriate for the student? The assessment instrument or strategy must fit the student's needs and abilities. If norm-referenced measures are used, the student's characteristics must be consistent with those of the norm group with which the test was standardized. The age or grade of the student is also important, because test norms are generally arranged by chronological age or grade in school. For instance, if a 5-year-old is administered a test normed with 6- to 12-year-olds, it is impossible to convert his or her responses to norm-referenced test scores.

With any type of measure, the assessment tasks must be compatible with the skills of the student. No student should be asked to attempt tasks clearly beyond his or her current functioning level. In addition to the content and difficulty level of the assessment task, other important skill considerations are

- *Presentation mode,* or the method by which the test task is presented to the student. Is the student required to listen, read, look at figures or pictures, attend to a demonstration?
- *Response mode,* or the method by which the student must answer the question or perform the specified task. Must the student speak, make a check or darken a square, write words or sentences, point to the correct response?
- *Group versus individual administration,* or whether the student takes part in assessment as one of a group or as the only participant.
- *Time factors* such as the length of the assessment, particularly as it relates to the student's

attention span, and whether the student is required to respond under timed conditions.

Tools should capitalize on the student's strengths rather than penalize weaknesses. Individual measures are more appropriate for students with difficulty maintaining attention during group testing. Students who write poorly should be assessed with measures that allow oral responses, unless the purpose of assessment is the study of writing skills. The assessment device should not discriminate against the student on the basis of race, culture, language, gender, or handicapping condition.

Is the tool appropriate for the tester? The assessment device must match the skills of the professional using it. No tool should be selected unless adequately trained personnel are available to take responsibility for administration of the measure, scoring of student responses, and interpretation of results. In untrained hands, even the best instrument can produce erroneous information.

Is the tool technically adequate? Before confidence can be placed in the results of an assessment tool, its quality must be demonstrated. The techniques used to construct the measure must be sound, it must produce reliable data, and it must show validity. Information on the measurement characteristics of norm-referenced standardized measures is generally presented in the test manual or a technical supplement. The same types of information may be available for less formal measures such as rating scales, criterion-referenced tests, checklists, and inventories. However, in many cases, the technical quality of informal instruments remains unknown. Although some technical considerations may not be relevant for certain types of informal measures (for example, standardization procedures in the case of unstandardized instruments), an assessment tool's reliability and validity and the methods used in its construction are always important.

Is the tool an efficient data-collection mechanism? An efficient device produces the needed information with minimum expenditure of time and effort. Administration, preparation by the tester, scoring of assessment results, and interpretation of data are all factors to consider. Ease of use also

influences efficiency; more difficult procedures typically take longer and introduce greater possibility of error. Measures are considered effective and efficient when their results are worth the time and effort of both student and professional.

If no available measure is appropriate for a particular assessment task, several options remain open. Two or more existing measures may be combined to produce a tool sufficiently comprehensive to collect the needed information. Or an instrument or data-collection strategy can be modified to fit the purposes of assessment and the characteristics of the student. However, when adaptations are made in procedures for standardized tests, test norms can no longer be used. Such measures should be considered informal and their results interpreted cautiously. Another alternative is to construct a new assessment tool that satisfies the demands of the situation. This solution is not simple and should be reserved for cases in which modification of available measures is clearly unacceptable. Devising a new assessment tool is time-consuming, and unless technical adequacy of the new device can be demonstrated, its quality remains unknown.

In many assessment situations, a professional or team puts together an assessment battery—a collection of tools designed to answer several assessment questions. For instance, in determining whether a student is eligible for special education, the team may pose a series of questions necessitating the use of many types of assessment strategies. In selecting the measures for an assessment battery, these principles should be followed:

1. The assessment battery must be comprehensive and complete, but unnecessary duplication should be avoided.
2. An attempt should be made to select measures that include a variety of different activities.
3. In selecting the tools for an initial assessment, measures to substantiate the reasons for referral should be included.
4. In general, results of group measures should be used only as screening information.
5. If two procedures appear equally appropriate, the more efficient one should be selected.
6. If possible, only measures with known technical adequacy should be included in the battery.

EVALUATING TECHNICAL QUALITY

Technical quality refers to the adequacy of an assessment tool as a measurement device. Four major characteristics of an instrument are considered in the evaluation of technical quality: reliability, validity, measurement error, and, for norm-referenced and criterion-referenced measures, the reference group or standard against which a student's performance is compared. Before describing procedures for evaluating these characteristics, we will introduce some terminology used in the study of measurement.

Measurement Terminology

Everyone is familiar with common units of measurement—inches, centimeters, miles, pounds, pints, liters, and degrees. Each represents a scale for quantifying some physical property such as distance, weight, or temperature. Educational assessment is less precise because it deals with human, rather than physical, properties; the goal is the quantification of psychological dimensions such as aptitude, attitude, and achievement.

There are four types of measurement scales: nominal, ordinal, interval, and ratio scales.

Nominal. A nominal scale is divided into categories. For example, the students in a classroom could be categorized on the basis of hair color and sorted into blondes, brunettes, and redheads. In nominal measurement, no values are assigned to categories; categories are simply different from one another. Because of this, it is impossible to add, subtract, multiply, or divide this type of information. This restricts the ways in which nominal scales can be statistically analyzed.

Ordinal. Persons or other subjects of study are placed in sequence in an ordinal scale. In the classroom, the teacher might rank students according to their artistic ability: Maria, the class artist, is ranked first; then Henry, a skilled cartoonist; then Susette, a fair painter; and so forth. Ordinal scales only place individuals in position relative to one another; no assumption can be made about the distance between individuals. From the teacher's ranking of the class, we know Maria is more artistic than either Henry or Susette, but we do not know how much more. Maria may be just a little more proficient than Henry, or she

may be six times more talented. Like nominal data, ordinal data cannot be arithmetically manipulated.

Interval. With interval scales, there are equal intervals between the units of measurement, and the scale begins at an arbitrary starting point. A quiz, for example, would yield interval data; John might earn a score of 10, Sally 8, Rose 6, and Harvey 5. Individuals can be ordered according to their scores; in addition, the distance between scores can be discussed. The distance between John's score of 10 and Sally's score of 8 is the same as the distance between Sally's score of 8 and Rose's score of 6. However, interval scales do not begin with a true zero; if a student earns a score of zero on a classroom quiz, it does not mean that he or she has zero information about the subject assessed. Thus, it is impossible to multiply or divide interval data; one cannot say that John's score of 10 represents two times as much knowledge as Harvey's score of 5. Despite this, most common statistical techniques are appropriate for interval data. Many psychological variables measured in educational assessment are arranged on interval scales.

Ratio. A ratio scale begins with a true zero and has equal intervals between units of measurement. These scales are considered the most sophisticated. They allow all arithmetic operations including multiplication and division, and any type of statistical procedure can be used. Unfortunately, few variables of interest in educational assessment are arranged on ratio scales; those that are include physical properties such as height and weight and also some physiological measures.

Descriptive statistics assist in summarizing information from all types of scales. Measures of central tendency describe a set or distribution of data with one index that represents the entire set. For example, instead of listing the exam scores of all 35 members of a class, the class mode, median, or mean can be computed. The *mode* is the most common value among a set of values, the score that occurs most frequently. The *median* is the middle score in a set of scores; one half of the scores are higher than the median score and one half are lower. The *mean* is the arithmetic average of the scores and is computed by adding all scores together and dividing by the number of scores. If data are nominal, the only measure of central tendency that can be used is the mode. With ordinal data, the median is appropriate, as is the mode. Interval data allow the calculation of all three measures. For most interval data, the mean is the most accurate descriptor of central tendency. However, the median is a better choice if the distribution contains extreme scores.

Measures of variability are another type of descriptive statistic. Their purpose is description of the spread or dispersion of a distribution. Sets of scores, even those with identical means and medians, can differ in variability. One set might have scores clustering around the mean (e.g., 59, 60, 61) whereas another might have scattered scores (e.g., 40, 60, 80). The *range* can be used to describe scatter; it is the distance between the highest and lowest scores in the distribution. With interval data, a better estimate of variability is *standard deviation*. The standard deviation takes each score's relationship to the mean into account; the higher the standard deviation, the more variability within a set of scores. The computational formula for standard deviation (σ) is:

$$\sigma = \sqrt{\frac{\Sigma X^2 - \frac{(\Sigma X)^2}{N}}{N}}$$

where Σ signifies the addition operation, X the test scores, and N the number of cases. To determine ΣX^2, each score is squared, then the squares are added. To determine $(\Sigma X)^2$, the scores are first added, then the total sum is squared.

A third type of descriptive statistic is measures of *correlation*. These express the degree of relationship between two sets of scores. If two measures are highly correlated, the scores from one measure can be used to predict performance on the other. Several measures of correlation are available, but the most common is the Pearson product moment correlation coefficient. The Pearson *r*, as it is often called, is appropriate for interval data. Correlation coefficients range in value from -1.00 to $+1.00$. A coefficient of 0 indicates no relationship between two sets of scores. A coefficient of $+1.00$ indicates a perfect positive correlation; individuals with the highest scores in the first set of scores also achieved the highest scores in the second set. A perfect negative correlation

is represented by a coefficient of -1.00; in this case, the persons with the highest scores in the first data set obtained the lowest scores in the second.

Correlational techniques are frequently used to analyze the technical adequacy of assessment tools, particularly in the study of reliability and validity. Because of this, professionals should be able to interpret correlational data. The direction of a correlation coefficient refers to whether it is positive or negative; magnitude is the size of the coefficient. However, a correlation coefficient of .73 does *not* mean 73% of a perfect relationship between sets of scores. To determine the usefulness of the correlation coefficient, the coefficient of determination is computed; this is simply the square of the correlation coefficient. Thus, if the Pearson *r* is either $-.70$ or $+.70$, the coefficient of determination is 49% (.70 $\times$ .70 = .49 or 49%). This percentage indicates the degree to which one set of scores can be used to predict the other. As Ary, Jacobs, and Razavieh (1985) explain, "If we find a correlation of $+.80$ between achievement and intelligence, 64 percent of the variance in achievement is associated with variance in intelligence test scores" (p. 126).

Test Norms and Other Standards of Comparison

Some types of assessment tools compare an individual's performance with an outside reference or standard. With norm-referenced tests, the standard is the performance of a norm group, and with criterion-referenced tests, the standard is a curricular goal. For a tool to be appropriate for assessment, its standard of comparison must fit the purpose of assessment and the needs and characteristics of the student.

A norm group serves as the outside reference for norm-referenced tests. The test is administered to a large number of individuals selected to represent the types of persons with whom the test will be used. For instance, for a measure of beginning reading skills, the norm group might be a representative sample of first and second graders. Test norms are then derived from the performance of persons in the norm group. If results are to have meaning for a particular student, the norm group must be an appropriate standard against which to evaluate the student's performance. Factors to consider in determining the appropriateness of test norms are

1. *Age, grade, and gender of norm group members.* These characteristics must match the characteristics of the student. Many of the psychological variables of interest in educational assessment differ by gender and across age groups and grade levels. Thus, it is incorrect to administer a test to a student beyond the age or grade of the norms and then use the closest age or grade group to estimate results. Likewise, if the variable to be measured is related to gender, a test normed only with males is not appropriate for female students.

2. *Method of selection.* Norm groups are samples intended to represent some population of interest. Because randomly selected samples are most likely to approximate the characteristics of a population, norm groups obtained through this method are preferable. Samples selected only because of their accessibility to the test producer are unsatisfactory.

3. *Representativeness of the norm group.* A representative sample includes members from all important segments of the population. If the goal were to construct a national norm group representative of American schoolchildren, it would be unsuitable to select only 6-year-olds or females. Important population characteristics in test construction are age, gender, geographic region (e.g., the Eastern Seaboard, the South, the Midwest), location of residence (rural, urban, suburban), ethnicity, and some index of socioeconomic status. Variables pertinent to school populations are grade, school placement (regular versus special education), type of handicapping condition, and language or languages spoken.

4. *Size of the norm group.* Generally, larger samples produce more accurate results. If the norm group is divided into age or grade levels for which separate norms are provided, the size of these subgroups should also be considered.

5. *Recency of test norms.* Test norms should reflect current standards of student performance. Norms established with first graders in 1970 may be a poor index for evaluating the first graders of 1990. Both test norms and test content should be periodically updated for subject areas that change over time.

It has been suggested that the norm groups of all tests used for special education purposes should include individuals identified as handicapped (Fuchs, Fuchs, Benowitz, & Barringer, 1987). This makes sense if the purpose of assessment is to compare a student's performance to that of the total school population, handicapped and nonhandicapped alike. However, because in eligibility decisions it is necessary to determine whether achievement problems exist, the appropriate standard of comparison is the performance of students placed in regular education classrooms. Norm groups drawn from regular classrooms will likely include mainstreamed students with mild handicaps, and test manuals should describe the characteristics of these students as fully as possible.

Criterion-referenced tests and other informal devices also provide a standard against which student performance can be compared. These measures determine whether students have mastered specific skills; they compare a student's performance to the desired curricular goal rather than to the performance of other students. Again, the appropriateness of the standard must be evaluated. Just as norm groups may not approximate the characteristics of a student, the content of a published criterion-referenced measure may not represent the student's current skill repertoire or the curriculum taught in the student's classroom. Even if a measure has been developed for curriculum-based assessment in a specific district, it may not reflect current instruction in all schools and classrooms within that district.

The manual accompanying the measure is the best source of information about test norms and other standards of comparison. Test producers are expected to provide a complete manual that describes the purpose of the measure, how it was constructed, characteristics of the norm group or other standard, and results of reliability and validity studies. However, not all manuals include these components.

Reliability

Reliability refers to consistency. In everyday language, a reliable person is one who can be counted on. A reliable assessment tool produces consistent results. For example, if a reliable test were to be administered several times to the same individual, the person's scores would remain stable and would not randomly fluctuate. Reliability, as defined by Anastasi (1988), is "the consistency of scores obtained by the same persons when reexamined with the same test on different occasions, or with different sets of equivalent items, or under other variable examining conditions" (p. 109).

Correlational techniques are the most usual methods for studying reliability. Although there are no set rules for determining if a correlation coefficient is of adequate magnitude, it appears logical to set .80 as a minimum. If two sets of scores are related at this level, the coefficient of determination is 64%, meaning that approximately two thirds of the variance in the first set of scores is associated with the variance in the second. Explanation of this proportion of the variance should be regarded as a minimum standard. Salvia and Ysseldyke (1988) recommend a minimum level of .60 for group data used for administrative purposes, .80 for individual data that influence screening decisions, and .90 for individual data considered for important decisions such as placement in special education.

There are several types of reliability. *Test-retest reliability* refers to the consistency of a measure from one administration to another. This is typically studied with some segment of the norm group; the measure is administered once during norming and then again to the same group of individuals after a brief period, perhaps a few weeks. *Equivalent-forms reliability* is of interest when there is more than one form of the same measure and these forms are designed to be used interchangeably. To determine if different forms of the same measure produce consistent results, all forms are administered to the same group and results are correlated.

Split-half reliability concerns a measure's internal consistency and is studied with one form of a measure and one group. After administration, the measure is divided in half (for instance, into odd-numbered and even-numbered items), and the scores from each half are correlated. The Kuder–Richardson procedures provide another approach to the study of internal consistency. Instead of splitting an instrument in half and comparing one half to the other, these methods consider the equivalence of all items and produce an estimate of interitem consistency.

The last major type of reliability is scorer reliability, also called *interrater* or *interobserver reliability*. This type is concerned with the consistency among persons who evaluate the performance of the individual being assessed; it is most important when scoring standards are subject to interpretation. If two different professionals rate a student's responses to test items, their ratings should be consistent.

Perhaps the most typical assessment situation in which scorer reliability is a factor is in the use of observational techniques. When two observers collect data on the same student, they must insure consistency. To calculate interobserver reliability, observation records are compared to determine the number of times observers agreed and disagreed on their ratings of behavior. The percentage of agreement is then computed with the formula

$$\% \text{ of Agreement} = \frac{\text{Number of Agreements}}{\text{Number of Agreements} + \text{Number of Disagreements}} \times 100$$

The minimum acceptable rate of agreement between observers is 80% (Cooper, Heron, & Heward, 1987; Sulzer-Azaroff & Mayer, 1977).

Validity

Validity refers to whether an assessment tool actually measures what it purports to measure. If a test claims to assess skill in driving a car but includes only multiple-choice questions on the parts of an engine, it is clearly invalid. Also, measurement tools can be valid for one purpose but not for another. For example, a test may be a valid method of screening for academic difficulties but not for differentiating between types of reading problems. According to the legal guidelines for assessment in PL 94–142, assessment tools used with handicapped students must be validated for the specific purpose for which they are used. Thus, studies of a measure's validity should include handicapped individuals as subjects if that measure is to be used for special education purposes (Fuchs et al., 1987).

Validity is related to reliability. No measure can be considered valid if it produces inconsistent results. Valid instruments are reliable instruments, although a measure can lack validity and still be reliable. Validity is concerned with the content of the measure and whether that content enables the measure to perform its intended function.

Content validity is defined as "the extent to which the instrument represents the content of interest" (Ary et al., 1985, p. 214). Content validity, an important consideration in the evaluation of any measure, is particularly critical with criterion-referenced tests, inventories, and other informal instruments that compare student performance to curricular standards. Determination of a measure's content validity is a matter of judgment rather than statistical analysis. Factors to consider are

☐ What content area does the measure claim to assess? What are the boundaries of that area?
☐ Does the measure attempt to assess the entire universe of content, or does it include only a sampling from that universe?
☐ If the measure assesses only a portion of the content universe, is the sample a representative one? Is it complete? Are all important elements included?
☐ What types of tasks are used to assess content? Are these appropriate for the skill or knowledge being assessed?

The content validity of an assessment tool must be evaluated in relation to the assessment task. Even if an instrument does an adequate job of measuring the content area, it may be inappropriate for a particular student or the specific question guiding the assessment.

Another type of validity is *criterion-related validity*. The instrument is validated in terms of some outside criterion. For example, a new test of academic achievement might be validated against an existing achievement test, school grades, or teacher ratings of academic performance. This assumes, of course, that the criterion chosen is itself a valid measure of the content area.

There are two types of criterion-related validity, predictive and concurrent. *Predictive validity* refers to a measure's ability to predict future performance. It is studied by administering the measure in question to a group of individuals and then, sometime in the future, administering the criterion measure to the same group. For example, the predictive validity of a school readiness test could

be established by administering it at the start of kindergarten, then correlating its results with teacher ratings of academic performance at the end of first grade. *Concurrent validity* is concerned with a measure's relationship to some current criterion. It is studied by administering both the measure in question and the criterion measure to the same group at the same time. For example, the concurrent validity of a new algebra test could be established by correlating its results with student grades in algebra.

The correlation coefficients resulting from the study of criterion-related validity are examined to determine their direction and magnitude. As a general rule, the greater the magnitude of a positive correlation between a measure and its criterion, the more support for that measure's validity. Unlike the study of reliability, there are no set rules for judging whether a validity coefficient is of adequate magnitude. At minimum, however, the correlation should be statistically significant (Anastasi, 1988). That is, there should be reason to believe that the relationship between the two measures is not simply due to chance. Information about statistical significance should be provided in the test's manual or technical report; statistical significance cannot be determined by inspecting the correlation coefficient's magnitude.

In evaluating criterion-related validity, the appropriateness of the criterion measure must be considered. If a test of reading skills is under study, another reading test should be selected as the criterion, not a test of general aptitude. The criterion should address and be a valid measure of the content of interest. According to Ary et al. (1985), appropriate criterion measures are relevant to the content area, reliable, and free from bias.

A third type of validity is *construct validity*, or the degree to which an instrument measures the theoretical construct it intends to measure. Many assessment devices claim to measure constructs such as intelligence, visual perception, and auditory processing. Theoretical constructs are not directly observable; they must be inferred from observed behaviors. The construct validity of a measure can be studied with correlational techniques. For example, if a new test of construct X is found to relate to an established measure of construct X, the validity of the new test is supported. Other methods of determining construct validity include factor analysis, investigation of age differentiation for measures of developmental constructs, and validation by experimental intervention (Anastasi, 1988).

Measurement Error

Error intrudes into any measurement system, and assessment is no exception. If a test, even the most reliable and valid one, were to be administered twice to the same student by the same examiner, the scores obtained would likely differ— even if testing conditions were identical, the test was administered and scored correctly each time, and the student had not acquired new skills from one administration to the next. Test scores and other assessment results are observed scores made up of two parts—a hypothetical true score and an error component. The less error in an observed score, the more precise the measurement tool.

Although measurement error is inevitable, it can be quantified by a statistic called the *standard error of measurement*. The standard error of measurement can be determined if the standard deviation and reliability of the measure are known. Most manuals for norm-referenced tests provide information on standard error, or it can be calculated with the formula

$$SE_m = \sigma \sqrt{1 - r}$$

in which SE_m represents standard error of measurement, σ the standard deviation, and r reliability.

Measurement error is related to both the variability of scores and reliability. As variability increases, so does error. However, as reliability increases, error decreases. Thus, to reduce measurement error, professionals should select instruments with low variability and high reliability.

The standard error of measurement is an indicator of the technical quality of an assessment tool and assists with interpretation of results. As explained in the next chapter, standard error is used to construct confidence intervals around observed scores. This allows a student's performance to be reported as a range of scores where it is highly probable the true score lies, rather than as a single score known to include both the true score and error.

TEST SCORES AND OTHER ASSESSMENT RESULTS

Another consideration in the selection of assessment tools is the type of results needed to answer the assessment questions. Assessment data must be in a form that allows their use in educational decisions. With informal measures, comparing a student's performance to curricular goals or classroom behavioral expectations can produce very simple data such as the number of skills mastered or the number of inappropriate behaviors observed. Sometimes, that is the type of information needed. At other times, the more sophisticated results of norm-referenced tests are necessary to answer the assessment questions.

Results of Informal Measures

Most informal assessment results are straightforward, easy to understand, and descriptive in nature. Frequency counts are a typical example; they simply report the number of occurrences of a behavior. For example, findings from informal inventories are often expressed as the number of questions, problems, or items answered correctly. Frequency data are easily converted to percentages. If a student answers 8 out of 10 items correctly on a classroom quiz, the percentage correct is 80. Informal assessments also yield duration data. Duration refers to time elapsed; if a student begins work on an assignment at 9:00 a.m. and completes it at 9:25 a.m., the duration of this activity is 25 minutes.

Frequency counts and percentages are interval data that can be manipulated by addition or subtraction. A student's performance can be compared by examining the difference between the number or percentage correct on each occasion. For example, a student may answer 20 out of 45 questions correctly at the beginning of September but improve to 35 out of 45 correct by the end of October; this represents an increase of 15 questions. Duration data are ratio data; time scales have true zeros and may be added, subtracted, multiplied, or divided. Thus, it is correct to say duration has doubled if a student increases the time spent on homework each evening from 30 minutes to 1 hour.

Some informal measures produce nominal data. Criterion-referenced tests, for example, may yield categorical findings. The student's performance on many criterion-referenced measures is classified either as demonstrating or failing to demonstrate skill mastery; no other descriptive information is provided. Checklists also produce a form of categorical data. If a teacher checks all items that describe a student's typical classroom behavior, in effect each item is classified as either representative or not representative of the student's typical behavior.

Other informal assessments provide ordinal data. Rating scales list a set of descriptions in some logical order—"The spelling performance of this student is (a) below grade level, (b) at grade level, (c) above grade level." The task is to select the most appropriate description. Rating instruments are considered ordinal scales unless they are Likert-type. Likert-type scales appear to be divided into equal intervals. For instance, a student may be asked to express degree of agreement with the statement "My favorite school subject is science" by selecting one of the following options:

1	2	3	4	5
Strongly Disagree	Disagree	Neutral	Agree	Strongly Agree

Likert-type scales are generally assumed to produce interval data.

Some informal measures are described as age-referenced or grade-referenced. For example, a developmental checklist that presents skills in the order in which they are usually acquired may pro-vide age standards for each skill. Or an informal inventory may be referenced to the subject matter of specific grade levels; it may include first grade spelling words, second grade spelling words, and so forth. Such measures usually are not norm-referenced. If age or grade standards are derived from some source other than the performance of a norm group, the way in which these standards were determined must be carefully evaluated.

Age and grade ratings are ordinal data. Such scales place skills, traits, or other characteristics into some order; however, distances between points on these scales do not represent equal intervals. As with nominal scales, data from ordinal scales cannot be treated arithmetically.

Table 3–2 presents several informal assessment tools, their typical results, and the type of data they produce. This information can assist in selecting the most appropriate informal measure for an assessment purpose. If the assessment question demands numerical information, a measure yielding interval or ratio data is needed. Examples of numerical questions are "How many sight words can Sue Ellen read?" and "How much time does John take to complete his biology assignment?" Nominal scales are indicated if the assessment question is concerned with classification. Examples of categorical questions are "Has Yvonne mastered basic number facts?" and "Can Erin type 40 words per minute with no errors?" Ordinal scales fill the gap between numerical and categorical data; they provide descriptive infor-

TABLE 3–2
Results available from informal measures

Type of Measure	Typical Results	Type of Data
Criterion-referenced test	Pass/fail; the skill is mastered or not mastered	Nominal
Classroom quiz	Number or percentage correct	Interval
Inventory	Number or percentage correct	Interval
	Age or grade rating	Ordinal
Observation	Number of occurrences of a behavior	Interval
	Duration of a behavior	Ratio
Checklist	Yes/no; the description is appropriate or inappropriate	Nominal
Rating scale	Verbal description (e.g., "usually punctual")	Ordinal
	A numerical rating with Likert-type scales	Interval
Work sample analysis	Number or percentage correct and/or incorrect	Interval
Interview or questionnaire	Verbal description, if questions open-ended; otherwise, results similar to checklists and rating scales	Varies

mation and answer questions about relative standing. Examples are, "Is Louis considered to be one of the more industrious students in his class?" and "How would Joan's handwriting be characterized: neat and legible, messy but still legible, or illegible?"

Norm-Referenced Test Scores

The results of norm-referenced tests take many forms: age and grade equivalents, percentile ranks, stanines, standard scores, and so forth. The raw score is common to all norm-referenced measures. Raw scores are similar to scores on classroom quizzes. They are not related to the performance of a norm group, and they are used only to obtain other scores. In most cases, raw scores are an index of the number of test items answered correctly. They must be converted to derived scores before a student's test performance can be compared to a norm group.

Age and grade equivalents. Many norm-referenced measures provide age and/or grade equivalents. These derived scores express test performance in terms of the familiar units of chronological age or grade in school. For example, a student may receive an age score of 7 years, 6 months on a test of spoken language or a grade score of 4.5 on a reading achievement test. Of all norm-referenced scores, age and grade equivalents appear to be the easiest to understand and interpret, but they are quite complicated and therefore subject to misinterpretation.

Age and grade scores are derived from the performance of the norm group. For example, if the third graders in the norm group earn an average raw score of 20, a grade equivalent of 3 is assigned to raw score 20. Anyone who achieves a raw score of 20 on this test will earn a grade equivalent of 3. Decimal grade equivalents (e.g., 3.1, 3.2, 3.3, and so forth) are usually derived by interpolation of data already available, rather than by testing separate groups of students or the same group at successive intervals. Also, the range of grade equivalents in test norms may exceed the range of grades of individuals within the norm group. For example, if a test was normed with only fourth, fifth, and sixth graders, its grade equivalent scores may extend below fourth grade and above sixth grade. If the average performance of grade 6 students is a raw score of 40, a grade equivalent

of 9.5 may be assigned to a raw score of 48. Such scores are obtained by extrapolation; the known scores of sixth graders within the norm group are extended to produce estimates of how students in higher grades would have performed, had they taken the test.

Age and grade equivalents are ordinal data. Although an equal-interval time scale underlies chronological age and grade in school, there is not a one-to-one correspondence between time and skill mastery. The gain in achievement from grade 1.0 to grade 1.5 in reading is much greater than the gain from grade 10.0 to grade 10.5; the intervals do not represent equal units of measurement.

The deceptive simplicity of age and grade equivalents leads to their misinterpretation. Thus, professionals should select norm-referenced measures that offer other types of derived scores, either in addition to or instead of age and grade equivalents. This viewpoint is supported by the International Reading Association (1981) in its resolution on the misuse of grade equivalents. This resolution calls upon test publishers to eliminate grade equivalents and urges practitioners to stop using grade equivalents to report test performance. According to the International Reading Association,

One of the most serious misuses of tests is the reliance on a grade equivalent as an indicator of absolute performance, when a grade equivalent should be interpreted as an indicator of a test-taker's performance in relation to the performance of other test-takers used to norm the test.

Percentile ranks. Another type of derived score is the percentile rank. The percentile rank for a particular raw score indicates the percentage of individuals within the norm group who achieved this raw score or a lower one. If a raw score of 40 corresponds to a percentile rank of 62, this means that 62% of the norm group earned raw scores of 40 or less. A student whose raw score converts to the 62nd percentile can be said to perform at a level equal to or greater than that of 62% of the norm group and at a level lower than that of the remaining 38% of the norm group.

Usually, tests provide separate tables of percentile rank norms for different age or grade levels. One table may list norms for students age 6–0 to 6–11, another for students age 7–0 to 7–11, and so forth. This allows more precise description of student performance. For example, it may be possible to say that a 12-year-old performed at the 75th percentile when compared with age 12 students in the norm group.

Percentile ranks are relatively easy to understand as long as they are not confused with percentages. A percentile rank refers to a percentage of persons; percentage correct refers to a percentage of test items. A student may answer only 50% of the items on a test correctly but perform at the 99th percentile for his or her age. Percentile rank data indicate relative position within the norm group. Salvia and Ysseldyke (1988) prefer percentile ranks to other derived scores because "percentiles tell us nothing more than what any norm-referenced derived score can tell us—namely an individual's relative standing in a group" (p. 93).

Standard scores.   Standard scores are available on many norm-referenced measures. These derived scores transform raw scores to a new scale with a set mean and standard deviation. Standard scores are useful for comparing the performance of the same individual on two different measures, as long as the raw score distributions of the measures are similar. They also provide a standard scale for reporting norms for various age or grade groups within the total standardization sample.

Standard score distributions can be constructed using any mean or standard deviation; the values are arbitrary. The z score is one type of standard score, and its distribution has a mean of 0 and a standard deviation of 1. Many norm-referenced tests set the mean of the standard score distribution at 100 and the standard deviation at 15.

Examples are the *Wechsler Intelligence Scale for Children–Revised* (Wechsler, 1974) and the *Wide Range Achievement Test–Revised* (Jastak & Wilkinson, 1984). On these tests, if a student's raw score converts to a standard score of 100, the student performed at the mean. A standard score of 115 indicates performance one standard deviation above the mean, and a standard score of 85 indicates performance one standard deviation below the mean.

The values selected for the mean and standard deviation of standard score distributions vary from measure to measure and sometimes between different parts of the same measure. For example, measures that provide two sets of standard scores—one for overall test performance and the other for performance on individual subtests—may use two separate score distributions to differentiate the scores. An example is the *Wechsler Intelligence Scale for Children–Revised*. Its total test scores, called IQ scores, have a mean of 100 and a standard deviation of 15. In contrast, the standard scores for the individual subtests, called scaled scores, have a mean of 10 and a standard deviation of 3. The term *scaled score* is frequently used to refer to subtest standard scores.

Separate standard score norms may be provided by age or grade. However, whatever the distribution for a particular standard score, the same scale is used for all students taking the test. A standard score mean of 100 is used to indicate average performance, whatever the student's age or grade. Thus, a 6-year-old would earn a standard score of 100 if his or her raw score equaled the mean of the 6-year-old segment of the norm group,

FIGURE 3–1
Normal distribution

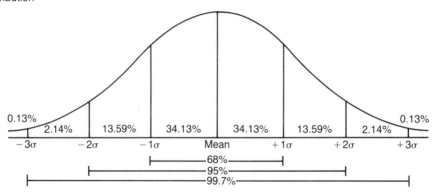

and a 12-year-old would earn a standard score of 100 if his or her raw score equaled the mean of the 12-year-old segment of the norm group.

Comparison of standard scores from one test to another makes sense only if the raw score distributions of the two measures are similar. One way to insure similarity is to select measures with raw score distributions that are normal or have been normalized by the test producer. As Figure 3–1 shows, most scores in a normal distribution are found in the middle and a few at the extremes. When a distribution is normal, it is possible to determine the exact percentage of cases that fall within any portion of the curve. The majority of cases fall in the center portion; 68% of the scores of a normally distributed measure occur in the range from one standard deviation below the mean to one standard deviation above—that is, from -1 to $+1$ standard deviations. Approximately 14% of the scores fall between -1 and -2 standard deviations, with the same percentage found between $+1$ and $+2$ standard deviations; thus, the

range from -2 to $+2$ standard deviations includes 95% of the cases. When the range is extended to include from -3 to $+3$ standard deviations, it accounts for 99.7% of the cases.

Standard scores based on normal distributions have special characteristics. They allow a student's performance to be related to the mean and standard deviation of the norm group, and they can be directly converted into percentile ranks. Figure 3–2 presents this relationship. If a student scores one standard deviation above the mean on a measure that is normally distributed, the percentile rank of that score is 84. A score equal to the mean earns a percentile rank of 50, and if a score lies one standard deviation below the mean, its percentile rank is 16. Thus, test performance can be described in relation to the mean and to a percentage of the norm group. With a measure in which the mean is 100, the standard deviation is 15, and scores are normally distributed, a standard score of 70 indicates performance that is (a) two standard deviations below the mean of the norm group and (b)

FIGURE 3–2

Relationships among different types of scores in a normal distribution

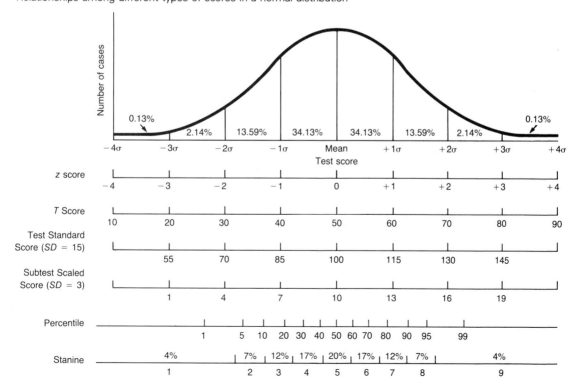

equal to or greater than the performance of 2% of the norm group. Because they provide these two types of information, normalized standard scores are particularly useful in the interpretation of norm-referenced test results.

Stanines.   Stanines are another type of derived score. The stanine distribution is divided into nine segments or standard nines, each of which is .5 standard deviations in width. Figure 3–2 illustrates the relationship between stanines, percentile ranks, and other standard scores. It also lists the percentage of cases expected to fall within each stanine if raw scores are normally distributed. Because stanines represent a range of performance rather than a specific score, the data they provide are less precise than that from standard scores.

It is apparent that norm-referenced measures offer a variety of different scores, and the types available from a particular measure should be considered as part of the selection process. In general, if the purpose of assessment is to compare a student's performance to that of a norm group, the most informative type of score is the normalized standard score. However, the same information can be obtained from a measure that is not normally distributed if it provides both standard scores and percentile ranks. Whenever possible, tests that offer only age or grade equivalents should be avoided. If age or grade scores are used, they should be accompanied by either percentile ranks, standard scores, or both.

PROMOTING NONBIASED ASSESSMENT

Oakland (1980) points out that the potential for bias is not limited to the selection, administration, and interpretation of assessment devices. Bias can enter at any point in the special education process: prior to assessment in referral, screening, and the selection of assessment tools; during assessment in the utilization of data-collection strategies and in relation to student and examiner characteristics; and after assessment in placement, program planning, and reevaluation. Nevertheless, a major concern in the prevention of bias is the selection of appropriate assessment tools.

Issues in Assessment of Minority Group Students

Much of the controversy surrounding special education in the past was due to the inappropriate use of standardized tests with students from minority cultures. Laosa (1977) summarizes one major objection to standardized testing for minority group students.

Standardized tests are biased and unfair to persons from cultural and sociocultural minorities since most tests reflect largely white, middle-class values and attitudes and they do not reflect the experiences and the linguistic, cognitive, and other cultural styles and values of minority group persons. (p. 10)

This is a validity concern. With students who do not speak English, it is obvious that an achievement test written in English is an invalid measure of academic performance. Although cultural differences are sometimes less clear, it is equally discriminatory to assess minority culture students with measures that are based upon the values, beliefs, and cultural heritage of the dominant American culture.

The problems associated with assessment of minority students have stimulated a number of proposed solutions, although no solution has been accepted universally. Several of the proposals for reducing bias in assessment are described in the paragraphs that follow.

Translation of measures into languages other than English.   For the assessment of students whose primary language is not English, it is recommended that tests and test directions be translated into the student's home language. Many of the standardized tests commonly used in special education assessment have been translated into Spanish. Several approaches have been used, including translating from English into Spanish and then back again to discover significant discrepancies.

However, translating a measure from one language to another does not eliminate the possibility of bias. The translation must not only preserve the literal and cultural meaning of the original but also the difficulty level of each test item. The measure must also be renormed with an appropriate standardization sample. If a Spanish-language version of a test is intended for use in the United States, norming it with a sample of students from Mexico

City is very likely inappropriate. A related concern is regional differences. The Spanish spoken by students in Texas may be quite different from that of New York or Miami.

Use of interpreters.   Another strategy for the assessment of non-English-speaking students is the use of interpreters. The professional conducting the assessment can act as an interpreter, or another professional or even a member of the community could be asked to assist. This practice is not recommended. Spontaneous translations of test instructions and items are likely to include inaccuracies and, like any departure from the test's standardization conditions, they make the use of test norms impossible. Nonetheless, tests and other assessment tools are not available in all languages, and it is sometimes necessary to rely on interpreters.

Culture-fair tests.   One of the methods proposed to combat cultural bias is the development of culture-free and culture-fair measures. These measures attempt to minimize factors that may depress the performance of minority group students: for example, high verbal demands, timed tasks, and emphasis on school learning. One of the first efforts to produce such measures was Cattell's *Culture Fair Intelligence Tests* (Cattell, 1950; Cattell & Cattell, 1960, 1963, 1977). The *Leiter International Performance Scale* (Leiter, 1948) and other nonverbal measures of intelligence are also considered by some to be culture-fair tests.

However, many studies indicate that culture-fair measures may be just as discriminatory as the culturally biased verbal tests they were designed to replace (Gonzales, 1982). Even nonverbal measures require some degree of verbal mediation as the student thinks about the test questions and how to respond. According to Gonzales, a culturally fair measure must meet the following criteria:

1. The same predictions can be made from the results across cultures or given populations.
2. Language and reading are kept to a minimum.
3. Adequate representation of the target population is in the norming.
4. Subjects should not be penalized by time factors.
5. Target populations must have the opportunity to learn the material.
6. Item content must be familiar to all groups. (p. 385)

Culture-specific measures.   Another strategy is the development of measures that relate directly to a minority culture. A major example is the *Black Intelligence Test of Cultural Homogeneity* (Williams, 1972). This 100-item multiple-choice test assesses knowledge of the black experience. According to Samuda (1975), "When applied to white subjects, the test becomes a measure of their sensitivity and responsiveness to the black culture" (p. 145). Although culture-specific measures can promote understanding of minority cultures, they may not solve bias problems. Culture-specific measures are often not transportable from one region of the country to another. In addition, their predictive validity may be less than adequate (Duffey, Salvia, Tucker, & Ysseldyke, 1981).

Separate norms for minority group students. An alternative to culture-specific measures is the construction of separate norms for minority and dominant culture students. However, this practice would further encourage separation of these two groups (Alley & Foster, 1978). Gonzales (1982) recommends that separate local norms be established for minority students only when their cultural and linguistic characteristics are significantly different from those of the dominant culture, as with some groups of American Indian students.

Pluralistic assessment.   Another proposed solution is to include a broad range of skills in assessment to provide a pluralistic perspective that accounts for the minority culture's strengths and preferences. An example is Mercer's assessment system, the *System of Multicultural Pluralistic Assessment (SOMPA)* (Mercer & Lewis, 1977b), which is described in Chapter 8. In the *SOMPA*, traditional assessment procedures are supplemented with sociocultural data so the minority student's performance can be viewed within the perspective of his or her own culture. Although the *SOMPA* has successfully reduced the number of minority students in classes for the mildly retarded (Gonzales, 1982), professionals are concerned about its ability to accurately predict a minority student's likelihood of success in a dominant culture school (Oakland, 1979).

Modification of test administration procedures.   Test administration procedures can be altered in an attempt to improve the performance of minority group students. For example, students could be allowed unlimited time to perform tasks that usually have strict time limits. When administration procedures are altered, however, norm-referenced tests become informal procedures. Such modifications prevent the use of the test's norms and invalidate the comparative power of standardized tests. It may be useful to administer a test under standard conditions and then repeat administration with modified procedures.

A related strategy is to train minority students in test-taking skills (Duffey et al., 1982). If students are unfamiliar with testing procedures or certain assessment tasks, lack of preparation may hinder their performance. For example, many group tests require students to write responses on separate answer sheets. Preparing students by providing practice activities may help make them less anxious about testing and increase their ability to cope with test tasks.

Replacement of standardized tests with informal procedures. A more controversial proposal is to replace standardized measures with informal procedures such as criterion-referenced tests. Criterion-referenced tests evaluate a student's performance without reference to the performance of other students. Furthermore, criterion-referenced tests provide direction for instruction based upon the minority student's needs.

The fact that an assessment tool is informal, however, does not mean that it is nondiscriminatory. Criterion-referenced tests and other informal tools can be subjective (Laosa, 1977), and their results can be interpreted in a biased manner. In addition, replacement of standardized testing with informal assessment would be expensive in terms of time, personnel, and resources (Duffey et al., 1981).

Moratorium on standardized testing. The most controversial alternative is the abolition of standardized testing. The Association of Black Psychologists and the National Education Association have called for a moratorium on psychological testing of disadvantaged and minority students, and other groups have made similar recommendations (Oakland & Laosa, 1977). In California, a recent order in the *Larry P. v. Riles* court case (1972, 1979, 1984) resulted in a complete prohibi-

tion against the use of IQ tests with black students for any special education purpose whatsoever.

However, a total ban on standardized testing could have adverse consequences for minority students with special needs (Gonzales, 1982). Special education assessment would take more time, thereby delaying the provision of needed services. Also, professionals would be forced to rely on informal procedures that are open to charges of subjectivity and technical inadequacy. In addition, professionals would continue to remain susceptible to influence by irrelevant student traits such as gender, race, and socioeconomic status. According to Duffey and others (1981), the real bias against minority students comes in the *use* of assessment data, not from the instruments themselves. Standardized tests cannot prevent this type of bias, but carefully selected tests can provide professionals with objective information about a student's standing relative to other students.

Guidelines for the Selection of Nondiscriminatory Assessment Tools

By law, assessment devices and procedures must be nondiscriminatory. One difficulty in implementing this requirement is the lack of agreement about what constitutes nondiscriminatory assessment. Alley and Foster (1978) describe a nondiscriminatory measure as "one which results in similar performance distributions across cultural groups" (p. 3). Under this definition, all groups would need to perform equally well on a measure, with similar means and similar variability. However, the relative performance of groups is only one criterion (Lambert, 1981b). Other concerns are the instrument's predictive validity, factor analytic structure, and the variance in item scores.

Another major impediment to nondiscriminatory assessment is the scarcity of appropriate assessment tools for minority populations. There is little agreement about which norm-referenced tests are nondiscriminatory; few measures are available in languages other than English, and most of these are in Spanish.

However, the potentiality for bias can be minimized if assessment tools are carefully evaluated and selected. With norm-referenced measures, it is important to determine if the norm group is representative of the race, culture, and gender of the student. It is also necessary to consider how many of the individuals in the norm group have

FIGURE 3–3
Guide for the evaluation of assessment tools

include copy of Reviews & years written

sense of trend or change?

How easy is it to give? score?

understand manual?

norms table
technical manual
administrance

Name of measure _____

Author(s) _____ Date _____

Publisher _____ Cost _____

DESCRIPTION OF THE MEASURE

1. Purpose(s) of the measure, as stated in the manual

2. Type of measure (e.g., norm-referenced test, inventory, checklist)

3. Content area(s) assessed (descriptions of each area and, if applicable, a list of subtests)

4. Student requirements
   a. Language
   b. Presentation mode
   c. Response mode
   d. Group or individual administration
   e. Time factors

5. Tester requirements
   a. Necessary training
   b. Administration time and other time requirements
   c. Ease of use

6. Test norms or other standards
   a. Type of reference (i.e., norm group or curricular goals)
   b. If applicable, characteristics of norm group
      (1) Age, grade, and gender
      (2) Method of selection
      (3) Representativeness
      (4) Size
      (5) Recency of norms
   c. If applicable, description of curricular standards
      (1) Content domain
      (2) Representativeness of item pool
      (3) Completeness of item pool
      (4) Appropriateness of tasks

7. Reliability
   a. Test-retest reliability
   b. Equivalent-form reliability
   c. Internal consistency
   d. Scorer reliability

   increasing reliability with age or grade

   ex. 9 out of 10 subtests are adequate reliability the range of

8. Validity
   a. Content validity
   b. Criterion-related validity (predictive and/or concurrent)
   c. Construct validity

9. Results
   a. Type(s) of scores or other results
   b. Standard error of measurement

10. Other comments

CONSIDERATIONS IN NONBIASED ASSESSMENT

1. Is the norm group or other standard of comparison appropriate for the student in terms of race, culture, and gender?

2. Are test items free from cultural bias?

3. Is the language of the measure appropriate for the student?

4. Does the measure bypass the limitations imposed by the handicapping condition?

CONCLUSIONS

1. Does the tool fit the purpose of assessment?

2. Is the tool appropriate for the student?

3. Is the tool appropriate for the tester?

4. Is the tool technically adequate?

5. Is the tool an efficient data-collection mechanism?

Standard & supplemental batteries of achievement

Summarize test reviews

characteristics similar to the student. Although a norm group may accurately represent the general population by including the proper proportion of minority individuals, the total number of such individuals may be very small. Some tests avoid this difficulty by using several norm groups of approximately equal size; separate norms are offered by gender, ethnic group, or some other population variable.

Another step in evaluation is the review of test items for cultural bias. If items demand an experiential background inconsistent with that of the student, the student will probably perform poorly. There are many examples of test items that illustrate cultural bias. Williams (1974), as cited by Alley and Foster (1978), suggests that culture influences how a person responds to the test question "When is Washington's birthday?" If the person thinks of George Washington, the answer is February 22; if he or she thinks of Booker T., the answer is April 5. Another example is the following:

The mountain boy who names the seasons of the year as "deer season, trout season, and bear season;" the desert child who responds "hot, rainy, and chilly;" the teenage Vietnamese refugee who answers "football, basketball, and baseball"—are these students less correct than their middle class American counterparts who reply "summer, fall, winter, and spring"? (Lynch & Lewis, 1987, p. 403)

Because norm-referenced tests have been the most criticized, they are associated with the issue of nonbiased assessment. Professionals today are aware of the ways these tests can be misused, so they attempt to select nondiscriminatory measures. However, other types of assessment tools can also be biased. The informal nature of an instrument or strategy is no guarantee that it is nondiscriminatory. Bailey and Harbin (1980) point out that "many of the discriminatory aspects of norm referenced measures, such as wording or content, can be found in criterion referenced measures as well" (p. 593).

Identifying appropriate assessment tools for students whose communication mode is not English poses special problems. No difficulties arise *if* the student speaks only one language, *if* technically adequate tools are available in that language, and *if* a professional who is fluent in the language has the assessment expertise necessary for the use of these tools. Unfortunately, this is seldom the case.

A final consideration is the handicap of the student. Unless the purpose of assessment is exploration of the handicapping condition, the tools for assessment should minimize the effects of the disability. If a student's academic disability is in the skill area of reading, measures in which the tester presents questions orally or through demonstration are most appropriate. Other characteristics sometimes associated with handicapping conditions are short attention span, impulsivity, poor self-concept, and expectation for failure. These factors should be considered in selecting assessment procedures.

The evaluation guide in Figure 3–3 can be used to review and critique norm-referenced tests and other assessment tools. It summarizes the important factors in selecting measures that produce nonbiased, accurate, and useful results.

STUDY GUIDE

Review Questions

1. Tell whether each of the following statements about the selection of tools for assessment is true or false.

   T F **a.** If the assessment procedure is appropriate for the age, grade, and ability level of the student, then its technical quality is not a consideration.

   T F **b.** Trained professionals must be available to administer, score, and interpret the assessment.

   T F **c.** Assessment devices must be selected and administered so they are not racially or culturally discriminatory.

   T F **d.** The regulations for PL 94–142 provide a recommended list of tests and other procedures for use in special education assessment.

2. Assessment must be nondiscriminatory and must focus on the student's _____ needs.

3. Several descriptive statistics can be used to summarize information. Which would be the best statistic to report the central tendency of a set of test scores expressed as percentages?
   _____ a. mode
   _____ b. standard deviation
   _____ c. mean
   _____ d. range

4. Which of the following descriptive statistics describes the relationship between two sets of scores?
   _____ a. median
   _____ b. correlation coefficient
   _____ c. standard deviation
   _____ d. percentile rank

5. With norm-referenced tests, one factor that should be considered in evaluation is the appropriateness of the norm group. List three aspects of the norm group that should be examined.

6. Reliability and validity also influence technical adequacy. Which of these statements about test quality is true?
   _____ a. Reliability refers to consistency.
   _____ b. Validity refers to whether a test measures what it purports to measure.
   _____ c. Correlational techniques are the most usual way of studying reliability.
   _____ d. Valid tests are reliable, although a test may be reliable without being valid.
   _____ e. All of these statements are true.

7. Match the terms in Column A with the best explanation in Column B.

Column A	*Column B*
a. Test-retest reliability	_____ The test items appear to assess the skill areas the test is designed to measure
b. Predictive validity	_____ Current test results are related to future results on a criterion measure
c. Alternate-form reliability	_____ Current test results are related to future results on the same test
d. Content validity	_____ The results from one form of the test are related to the results from a second form
e. Concurrent validity	_____ Current test results are related to current results on a criterion measure

8. The statistic used to quantify the measurement error present in a test score is called the _____ .

9. Tests and informal procedures produce many different types of results. Determine if these statements about assessment results are true or false.
   T F a. Results of informal measures such as inventories are often expressed as frequency counts (for example, the number of items the student answers correctly).
   T F b. Age and grade equivalents are useful scores because they are easy to understand and are rarely misinterpreted.
   T F c. Percentile ranks are comparative scores that allow the student's performance to be contrasted with the performance of age or grade peers in the norm group.
   T F d. When standard scores are based on a normal distribution, they are easily converted into percentile ranks, stanines, and other types of standard scores.

10. Many suggestions have been made for reducing the potential for bias in assessment. For example, if students speak languages other than English, measures can be translated into the student's language or interpreters can be used to assist with administration. List four other strategies for reducing bias in assessment.

Activities

1. Obtain copies of the manual for two or three norm-referenced standardized tests. Examine each manual to see how it treats the question of technical adequacy. Is the norm group adequately described? Are studies of the test's reliability reported? Is there support for test validity?

2. Figure 3–3 is a guide for the evaluation of assessment tools. Use this guide to critique a norm-referenced test or an informal assessment device.

3. One concern in the selection of assessment tools is the types of tasks that students are expected to perform. Analyze the assessment tasks on a measure such as the *Wide Range Achievement Test–Revised* or the *Peabody Individual Achievement Test–Revised.* Consider presentation mode, response mode, group versus individual administration, and time factors.

4. Locate a review of a new test or assessment procedure in a professional journal such as *Diagnostique* or *Remedial and Special Education.* Read the review and write a brief summary of its major points.

5. Read Oakland's (1980) article on "Nonbiased Assessment of Minority Group Children." This article discusses several potential sources of bias in the assessment process, including the selection of inappropriate procedures. Identify five ways in which bias can be introduced into assessment, and discuss how each can be prevented.

Discussion Questions

1. One major impetus for the passage of PL 94–142, the Education for All Handicapped Children Act, was concern over misuse of standardized tests with minority group students. Using Table 3–1 as a guide, discuss several inappropriate assessment practices of the past and explain the current legal safeguards to prevent the recurrence of these practices.

2. On norm-referenced tests, the standard of comparison against which a student's performance is evaluated is the performance of age or grade peers in the norm group. Explain the standard of comparison for informal assessment tools such as classroom quizzes, inventories, and criterion-referenced tests.

3. When professionals select a tool for assessment, they consider not only the technical quality of the measurement device but also the particular purpose for which it will be used. Tell why a technically poor measure is never an appropriate assessment tool. Then give an example of a situation in which a technically adequate measure is inappropriate because it does not fit the purpose of the assessment.

4. Grade equivalents are available on many tests, although there are many criticisms of this type of score. Describe the advantages and disadvantages of grade scores, giving your opinion on the International Reading Association's recommendation that grade equivalents be eliminated from standardized tests.

5. One suggestion for reducing bias in assessment is to replace standardized tests with informal procedures. Discuss the merits of this. Take into account the meaning of assessment bias and the possibilities for bias in informal assessment.

4

Standardized Tests

Tests are the best-known type of assessment measures. They are part of the school experience from the early grades to the college classroom. No one passes through the educational system without taking a weekly quiz, a test at the end of a unit, or a final exam. Tests range from informal measures devised by teachers for classroom use to very structured instruments known as norm-referenced standardized tests. These formal tests are also a regular feature of education, whether they are achievement tests administered at intervals throughout the grades, aptitude measures used for college admission, or individual tests used in special education.

In standardized testing, test tasks are presented under standard conditions so the student's performance can be contrasted to the performance of a norm group. The resulting data are comparative; the student's level of functioning is described in relation to typical or average performance. This type of information is necessary in screening and determination of eligibility, where the goal is selection of students whose performance is so divergent from that of others that special attention is warranted. Results also help professionals to plan instruction by identifying curriculum areas where students fail to perform as well as their peers and, in evaluation, to document changes in performance relative to age and grade level expectations.

Norm-referenced tests must be administered and scored in strict accordance with the standard conditions described in the test manual. If the conditions under which the test was normed are not duplicated, then the student's performance cannot be compared to the performance of the norm group. At the same time, the tester must ensure the full and active participation of the student. Because tests elicit only a sample of behavior, test performance must be an accurate representation of the student's capabilities. These concerns are as old as the history of standardized testing. Terman and Merrill pointed out in 1937

Three requirements must be satisfied: (1) the standard procedures must be followed; (2) the child's best efforts must be enlisted by the establishment and maintenance of adequate rapport; and (3) the responses must be correctly scored. It can hardly be said that any one of the three is more important than the others, for all are absolutely essential. (p. 52)

PREPARATION FOR TESTING

Testing does not begin immediately after an appropriate measure has been selected. The tester (that is, the professional responsible for test administration) must first ensure that he or she is adequately prepared to administer and score the test. Then, the testing environment is readied, and the student is carefully introduced to the testing experience.

Preparation of the Tester

Most standardized tests are designed for use by trained testers, professionals who have mastered the skills of test administration and scoring. Preparation programs for professionals such as special educators typically include training in assessment, with supervised practice in the use of standardized measures. As Anastasi (1988) notes

For individual testing, supervised training in the administration of the particular test is usually essential. Depending upon the nature of the test and the type of persons to be examined, such training may require from a few demonstration and practice sessions to over a year of instruction. (p. 34).

Tests differ in the amount of training needed to guarantee valid administration. Some measures, such as individual intelligence tests, require extensive preparation; in many states, school psychologists and psychometrists are the only school personnel licensed to administer them. Other tests, such as the achievement tests used by special educators, presume that the tester is knowledgeable about and trained in standardized testing procedures but holds no special license or certification. For example, some manuals say that the test can be administered by persons properly prepared by training and/or self-study.

It is the professional responsibility of the tester to administer only those tests he or she is trained for or, after extensive study, similar tests. Measures administered by untrained testers produce highly questionable results that must be considered invalid. Incorrect administration may also render a test invalid for future use with a student if, for example, an inexperienced tester reveals the correct answers. Practice is necessary but not sufficient in learning new tests; the tester must receive feedback on the accuracy of his or her performance. No new test should be considered learned until the tester's administration and scoring skills have been checked by a qualified professional; it is too easy to make mistakes and allow them to become habits.

Preparation of the Testing Environment

The testing environment consists of the room where the test is administered, the seating arrangements, the testing equipment, and the participants. This environment can influence test performance. Think, for example, of trying to concentrate on an important examination in a stifling hot or noisy room. The tester should make every effort to create a comfortable testing environment.

The testing room should be just large enough to accommodate the testing procedures. Unless gross motor tasks such as running are part of the test, an office-sized room provides sufficient space. Large rooms such as classrooms are not recommended because they often contain distractions. The room's lighting, temperature, and ventilation should be adequate. Light from windows should not shine in the eyes of tester or student. Nonglare lighting is best, particularly when test materials are printed on shiny pages. Test administration should not be attempted in rooms with inadequate lighting, extremes of temperature, or poor ventilation.

The testing room should be in a quiet location, away from the playground, gymnasium, cafeteria, and music room. A constant noise source, such as an air conditioner, is permissible as long as it does not interfere with communication between the tester and student. The room should be free of visual distractions such as colorful bulletin boards, posters, and other attention-drawing stimuli; windows with interesting views should be curtained or masked. The goal is to make the test the most interesting aspect of the room.

The room should be secured so people cannot walk in and interrupt. The tester can post a notice on the door stating that testing is in progress; persons who use the room can be informed it will be occupied. Despite these precautions, interruptions such as a fire drill or other emergency may occur.

It is often impossible to find an ideal testing room, particularly with the time and space constraints in most public schools. Fortunately, valid tests can be given in less than ideal conditions as long as the tester is sensitive to the behavior of the student. The student is observed carefully, and if noise or other environmental factors appear to interfere with concentration, testing is immediately discontinued. The testing environment checklist in Figure 4–1 can assist the tester in evaluating the adequacy of the room and other important factors.

Testing should not be attempted if seating arrangements are inadequate: if the student or tester must stand, if chairs are so low or high as to affect vision, if no work surface is available, or if the work surface is very small or not level. Ideal seats are comfortable, straight-backed chairs. Chairs should be of correct size, so that the student's feet comfortably touch the floor; chairs should not swivel. Chairs with attached desks or work surfaces are unsuitable. They offer too little space for test materials, do not allow the tester to sit close to the student, and, if slanted, permit test materials to slide onto the floor.

A table is the most appropriate work surface. The tester and student should be able to sit and write comfortably at the table. Rectangular or square tables are preferred; the surface should be large enough to hold necessary materials, yet narrow enough for the tester to reach across to the student's side. Many standardized tests are designed so the tester can sit across the table from the student; this arrangement facilitates the observation of student behavior and discourages the student from attempting to view the test manual and scoresheet. Other tests require that students sit across the corner of the table from the tester.

The tester should gather all materials needed for administration (the examiner's manual, pencils and paper, and so forth) and place these in the testing room before the start of the test. Once administration has begun, if the tester discovers a vital piece of equipment missing, testing should be discontinued at a logical breaking point (such as between subtests), and the missing item obtained.

Most tests include stimulus material to be shown to the student, an examiner's manual for the tester, and score sheets or student record booklets. Other equipment may be furnished as part of the test kit, or the tester may need to obtain materials from the classroom. Generally, testers provide writing implements for themselves and the student. Several sharpened pencils of the

FIGURE 4–1
Testing environment checklist

	Optimal	Adequate	Poor
The Room			
Size	☐	☐	☐
Lighting	☐	☐	☐
Temperature/ventilation	☐	☐	☐
Noise level	☐	☐	☐
Freedom from distractions	☐	☐	☐
Freedom from interruptions	☐	☐	☐
Seating			
Chairs	☐	☐	☐
Table	☐	☐	☐
Arrangement	☐	☐	☐

	Available	Not Applicable	Not Available
Equipment			
Test materials	☐	☐	☐
Writing implements	☐	☐	☐
Timing device	☐	☐	☐

	Optimal	Adequate	Poor
Arrangement	☐	☐	☐

	Present	
Participants		
Student	☐	
Tester	☐	
Other(s)	☐	Explain: _____
		_____

Summary

The testing environment was adequate for administration of a valid test.   ☐

The testing environment was not adequate for administration
of a valid test because _____   ☐

size and type used by the student in the classroom should be available; these may have erasers if not prohibited by the test manual. The tester will also need several pencils with erasers. Some tests require precise timing of student responses. If timing must be accurate to the second, appropriate devices include a stopwatch, a digital watch with output in seconds, or a clock or watch with a second hand; if minutes must be timed, a wristwatch or clock will suffice. Timing devices should be silent so they do not distract the student.

When the materials are arranged, the test kit is placed near the tester, either on the floor or a separate chair. Materials are then transferred to the table as needed. All distracting materials should be removed from the student's view and reach. No extraneous items such as books or toys should clutter the table.

There should be no one in the testing room but the tester and the student. However, a parent may need to accompany a young child into the room to help acclimate the child to the new environment. Parents or others should leave the room before test administration begins; observation is best done through a one-way glass, if available. If for some reason parents must remain, they should be observers out of the child's view, not participants. Unless specifically allowed by the test manual, parents or others should *not* administer test items.

Preparation of the Student

Scheduling the test at an optimal time, seeing to the student's physical needs, and preparing the student psychologically are critical components in testing. If these factors are neglected by an insensitive tester, the student's attitude may be affected, and it may become impossible to elicit optimal performance.

Schools are busy places. Schedules for classes, lunch, buses, and special events such as assemblies must be considered when setting up a time and place for testing. Usually the tester coordinates scheduling with the classroom teacher. Most teachers, concerned about schoolwork missed during testing, prefer that the student leave the classroom during his or her best subject or during the subjects with which he or she experiences difficulty.

Students' preferences must also be considered. Test performance will likely be affected if students are removed from the classroom during a favorite activity; their attention may be on recess, art, or whatever they are missing, rather than on the testing situation. Many students work more efficiently at certain times of the day, such as the early morning or midafternoon. The classroom teacher should be consulted to determine when the student is most alert, and if possible, the test should be scheduled for that time.

Because tests are usually scheduled well in advance, the tester must check the student's physical and emotional status on the day of the test. If the student is ill, the test should be postponed. A toothache, cold, or other physical ailment can depress performance; pain may distract the student, a cold could impair hearing, and even an over-the-counter medication can interfere with normal functioning. Emotional well-being also affects test performance. If the student is upset (for example, by the death of a pet), testing should be delayed. If the tester learns afterwards that the student was under physical or mental stress, test results should be considered invalid or, at minimum, interpreted with great caution.

Before beginning the test, the tester should attend to the physical needs of the student. Students are best able to focus attention on test tasks if they are not distracted by pressing physiological needs, such as hunger and thirst. Students should visit the drinking fountain and restroom before the test and during breaks. Some students, particularly younger children, will not ask to go to the restroom, even when they are in dire need of a toilet break. In addition, the tester must make sure that students are wearing eyeglasses, hearing aids, or other required prosthetic devices. If the student is receiving medication, the tester should find out if it has been administered that day and, if so, the possible effects upon test performance.

Preparing a student psychologically for testing is called *establishing rapport*. This procedure is explained by Anastasi (1988) as "the examiner's efforts to arouse the test takers' interest in the test, elicit their cooperation, and encourage them to respond in a manner appropriate to the objectives of the test" (p. 35). To establish a good working relationship with the student, the tester should follow these steps.

1. *Introduction of the tester to the student.* The introduction should be friendly and unhurried, and should convey the tester's pleasure at meeting the student. The tester gives his or her name and some indication of profession. For example, the tester might say, "My name is Ms. Geller and I'm a teacher who visits this school twice a week."

2. *Elicitation of general information from the student.* The tester engages the student in conversation by asking for full name, age, grade, and favorite school subjects. This allows the student a chance to relax and provides the tester with some indication of the student's manner of expression and knowledge of personal information.

3. *Explanation of the purpose of testing.* The meeting should be presented as an occasion for work ("We're going to do some work together") rather than play ("Today, we're going to play some games"). If students believe the test is merely a game, they may not put forth their best effort. However, the word *test* should be avoided because students may associate testing with past failures.

4. *Description of test activities.* The tester should explain exactly what will happen during the test situation. This will prepare the student and may relieve some anxiety. Some tests provide instructions describing test activities for the tester to read to the student. If these are not available, Table 4–1 explains important points to cover during pretest preparation.

5. *Encouragement of student questions.* Students should be provided the opportunity to ask questions about the test. The tester determines if the student understands what will occur and also gauges the student's readiness to begin. Discussion continues until the student becomes comfortable, or if the student is obviously upset and ill at ease, testing is postponed.

TABLE 4–1
Pretest information for students

Before test administration begins, each of the following factors should be explained by the tester in language appropriate to the student's age and ability level.

Length of the Test
  Tell the student approximately how long the test will take either in terms of hours and minutes or classroom activities ("You'll be back in Ms. Lloyd's room before lunchtime").

Test Activities
  Briefly describe the types of activities involved: listening, looking at pictures, talking, reading, writing, doing math, and so forth. If several different activities are required, let the student know that test tasks will change.

Test Difficulty
  If appropriate, inform the student that there will be both easy and difficult items. Let the student know that he or she is not expected to answer every question correctly because some were designed for older age groups.

Confirmation of Responses
  Advise the student that he or she will not be told if answers are right or wrong. The tester cannot give information about response accuracy.

Timed Tests
  If parts of the test are timed, tell the student so he or she will know that speed is important. If a stopwatch will be used for timing, show it to the student and demonstrate its use.

TEST ADMINISTRATION

The goal in administration of standardized tests is to obtain the best possible sample of student behavior under standard conditions. Strict adherence to the test manual's guidelines for administration and scoring is an absolute necessity. The manual usually provides instructions and test items to be read to the student. These words often appear in bold print and must be read verbatim. The tester may tell the student that he or she must "read some directions." The tester should *not* attempt to recite information from memory, and test items and directions may not be paraphrased, unless specifically allowed by the manual. However, they should be read in a natural tone of voice. The test manual also specifies the order of administration, if there are several parts or subtests within the test. Generally, the subtests must be given in a set order which the tester may not vary. The manual informs the tester if it is permissible to delete some subtests and, if so, which ones.

Testing requires strict conformance to administration rules, together with the establishment of a dynamic working relationship between student and tester. Achieving this balance is particularly difficult for educators because of the differences between testing and teaching. The teacher automatically praises, prompts, and provides information; the tester can do none of these, yet must maintain an atmosphere of encouragement to promote the student's best efforts. As early as 1905, Binet and Simon observed,

An inexperienced examiner has no idea of the influence of words; he talks too much, he aids his subject, he puts him on the track, unconscious of the help he is thus giving. He plays the part of pedagogue, when he should remain psychologist. (as quoted by Kessen, 1965, p. 199)

Because each test is different, it is always necessary to refer to the manual for specific administration rules. However, standardized measures have many commonalities, making it possible to provide a set of general guidelines, as shown in Table 4–2.

Recording Student Responses

The tester is often responsible for keeping a record of student responses. As the student replies to each question, the tester writes down the answer on the score sheet or record booklet. Once the test record form has been filled in, it is known as the test protocol. The protocol serves as the minutes of the testing situation. Because this record is used to evaluate and score the student's responses, it must be both accurate and complete. Recording student responses takes skill, and several rules should be followed.

Concealment of the test protocol. The test protocol is hidden from student view. Students should not be allowed to look at it unless, of course, it is necessary for test administration. A protocol may contain correct answers to the questions, and should students see them, test results would be invalidated. The protocol also contains the tester's record and evaluation of the student's responses.

TABLE 4–2
General guidelines for test administration

Test administration is a skill, and testers must learn how to react to typical student comments and questions. The following general guidelines apply to the majority of standardized tests.

Student Requests for Repetition of Test Items
Students often ask the tester to repeat a question. This is usually permissible as long as the item is repeated verbatim and in its entirety. However, repetition of memory items measuring the student's ability to recall information is not allowed.

Asking Students to Repeat Responses
Sometimes the tester must ask the student to repeat a response. Perhaps the tester did not hear what the student said, or the student's speech is difficult to understand. However, the tester should make every effort to see or hear the student's first answer. The student may refuse to repeat a response or, thinking that the request for repetition means the first response was unsatisfactory, answer differently.

Student Modification of Responses
When students give one response, then change their minds and give a different one, the tester should accept the last response, even if the modification comes after the tester has moved to another item. However, some tests specify that only the first response may be accepted for scoring.

Confirming and Correcting Student Responses
The tester may not in any way—verbal or nonverbal—inform a student whether a response is correct. Correct responses may not be confirmed; wrong responses may not be corrected. This rule is critical for professionals who both teach and test, because their first inclination is to reinforce correct answers.

Reinforcing Student Work Behavior
Although testers cannot praise students for their performance on specific test items, good work behavior can and should be rewarded. Appropriate comments are, "You're working hard" and, "I like the way you're trying to answer every question." Students should be praised between test items or subtests to ensure that reinforcement is not linked to specific responses.

Encouraging Students to Respond
When students fail to respond to a test item, the tester can encourage them to give an answer. Students sometimes say nothing when presented with a difficult item, or they may comment, "I don't know" or "I can't do that one." The tester should repeat the item and say, "Give it a try" or "You can take a guess." The aim is to encourage the student to attempt all test items.

Questioning Students
Questioning is permitted on many tests. If in the judgment of the tester the response given by the student is neither correct nor incorrect, the tester repeats the student's answer in a questioning tone and says, "Tell me more about that." This prompts the student to explain so that the response can be scored. However, clearly wrong answers should not be questioned.

Coaching
Coaching differs from encouragement and questioning in that it helps a student arrive at an answer. The tester must *never* coach the student. Coaching invalidates the student's response; test norms are based on the assumption that students will respond without examiner assistance. Testers must be very careful to avoid coaching.

Administration of Timed Items
Some tests include timed items; the student must reply within a certain period to receive credit. In general, the time period begins when the tester finishes presentation of the item. A watch or clock should be used to time student performance.

Seeing how answers were scored would provide students information about response accuracy; knowing they made several errors might upset some students and affect test performance.

Hiding the protocol may take some manipulation of test materials, because several objects must be managed by the tester at the same time (manual, protocol, stimulus materials for the student, writing implements, and perhaps a stopwatch). The method used to conceal the protocol depends upon the specific materials involved and the tester's preference. Some testers place the protocol behind a propped-up test manual; others keep it on a clipboard that rests on the edge of the table. Each tester should find his or her most comfortable method.

Verbatim recording of student responses.
The tester keeps an exact record of student responses for scoring purposes and to assist in interpretation of results. It is often of interest to examine not only which test items were missed by the student but also what responses he or she gave to these items. For example, knowing what types of errors a student made on a reading test may be just as valuable as knowing the score, particularly when planning instructional strategies. The specific information noted by the tester in verbatim recording depends upon the nature of the test task. The tester may make a prose record of student comments or simply write the number of the picture selected by the student from four options. The conventional notation for recording an "I don't know" response is *DK* and for indicating the student did not answer is *NR* (no response).

Accurate scoring during administration.
Some tests require that the tester make an on-the-spot decision whether the student's response is correct. Each response must be carefully but quickly evaluated; otherwise, the student will lose interest. The response is scored and then recorded. Recording systems vary across measures. On some tests, correct responses are denoted by a *1* and incorrect responses by a *0*; on others, + indicates a correct answer and − an incorrect answer. Testers must observe the recording conventions of the particular test so other professionals can interpret the protocol. If a different system is used for some reason, the tester should write a key for that system on the protocol.

Use of mechanical recording devices. Unless allowed by the manual, no mechanical recording equipment, such as tape recorders or video cameras, should be introduced into the testing environment. Many novice testers tape record a session and then later review the tape to check their scoring of student responses or even to enter student responses on the protocol. This is a bad practice for several reasons. Mechanical devices are typically not part of the standard conditions for test administration, and recording equipment may distract the student. Even if recording is unobtrusive, tapes should not be trusted as the sole source of results. Breakdowns do occur; and if a tape were to fail, the only recourse would be readministration of the test. Although taping practice sessions can assist in learning a new test, testers should acquire the skills of recording student responses during test administration. Few practicing professionals have the leisure to review tapes of each testing session.

Administering Test Items

Before beginning the test, the tester and student should complete the identification section of the test form. Most forms provide space for the name of the student, the tester's name, the date of testing, and pertinent student data, such as age, gender, grade, and teacher. If appropriate, the student can fill in a portion of the form. Recording this information is a necessary step in testing; a form with only the student's first name is virtually useless. At minimum, a protocol should contain the student's full name, the date of testing, and the tester's name.

Some tests are designed so each item is administered to each student; students begin with the first item and continue until the last is completed. More typically, standardized tests cover a wide range of difficulty, and students attempt only that portion of the test appropriate to their skill level. For example, no student could complete all items in measures for use with grades 1 through 12. Some items would likely be too easy and others too hard, and the time required for test administration would be prohibitive. Test items are arranged in order of difficulty, and whereas one student might receive items 10 to 30, another might attempt items 50 to 95.

Demonstration items may be provided for administration at the start of the test or subtest. Demonstration items are activities similar to but usually easier than test tasks. They acquaint students with the type of items to follow and, if necessary, allow the tester to teach the student how to perform test tasks. The rules of teaching, not testing, apply to the presentation of demonstration items. The tester can and should coach the student, reinforce correct answers, and correct wrong ones. If the tester cannot elicit correct responses to these items, testing should be discontinued. Demonstration items are never included in the student's score.

Most test manuals tell how to locate the appropriate point within the test to begin presentation of items. For some students, the very first item is the suggested starting place; for others, it would be unrealistic to begin at the easiest item. Because guidelines differ across measures, the test manual must always be consulted. The *Peabody Picture Vocabulary Test–Revised* (Dunn & Dunn, 1981), for example, recommends beginning at item 1 for children age $2\frac{1}{2}$ to 3 and at item 30 for children age 5.

After selecting a starting point, the tester presents items to the student in an attempt to locate items of appropriate difficulty. The basal or range of successful performance is determined. Testing then continues to establish the ceiling or the level at which the student is no longer successful.

The basal is the point in the test at which it can be assumed that the student would receive full credit for all easier items. To establish a basal, the tester administers items until the student has correctly completed some specified number of items. The student is then given credit for passing earlier, easier items, even though these were not administered. The basal allows the tester to skip items that would be too easy for the student, thereby saving time. The student, having answered several questions correctly, begins the test with a feeling of success.

Tests vary as to the number of items required to establish a basal. On some, the student must correctly answer three consecutively numbered items; for example, a basal would be established by correct responses for items 9, 10, and 11. On other measures, the student must correctly answer five or even eight consecutively numbered

items for the tester to assume success on all easier items.

Determining the basal is not always easy. The tester begins administration at the suggested starting point and proceeds through the test items. If a 10-year-old is to be tested and the manual recommends beginning with item 20 for students ages 10 to 12, the tester begins with item 20. As shown in the following example, the student answers the question correctly, and the tester writes a + in the space next to the item number. The student also answers items 21 and 22 correctly. Because the basal requirement is three consecutive correct responses, a basal is established. The tester will continue administration with item 23.

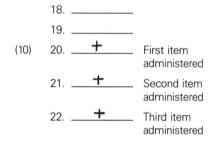

BASAL: 3 consecutive correct responses

	18. _____	
	19. _____	
(10)	20. ___+___	First item administered
	21. ___+___	Second item administered
	22. ___+___	Third item administered

In this example, the starting point designated by the manual was appropriate for the student. Items were not too difficult and the student quickly achieved three consecutive correct responses. This is not always the case. Sometimes the first or second item administered to the student is answered incorrectly. When this happens, the tester has to present items out of order to establish the basal. Generally, when a student makes an error during the search for the basal, the tester immediately begins to proceed backwards through the test. Table 4–3 explains this procedure.

Suggested starting points can also be too low. For example, the student may begin with item 5 and answer the next 15 questions correctly. At the start of a test, if there is indication that items are too easy for the student, the tester may move forward to more difficult items. Testers should take care, however, not to present very difficult items before students have achieved some success. It is far worse to discourage students than to use extra administration time presenting easy items.

TABLE 4–3
Establishing the basal

Sometimes the tester begins a test at exactly the right starting point, and the basal is easily achieved as the student correctly answers the first several questions. It is just as usual, however, for the student to miss one of the first items presented. When this occurs, the tester must present earlier, easier items.

Presume that a sixth grader was given a test in which the basal is four consecutive correct responses. The recommended starting point for sixth grade students is item 11, and the tester began there. The student answered the first item correctly but missed item 12. Here is what the protocol looked like at this point.

BASAL: 4 consecutive correct responses

```
        8. _____
        9. _____
       10. _____
(6)    11. ____+_____   First item administered
       12. ____−_____   Second item administered
       13. _____
       14. _____
```

The basal cannot be established without four consecutive correct responses. The tester proceeds backward until a basal of four consecutively numbered correct items is established. As shown in the following example, after the student missed item 12, the tester administered item 10, then item 9, then item 8. When the student answered these correctly, there was a basal. Testing will continue with item 13.

BASAL: 4 consecutive correct responses

```
        8. ____+_____   Fifth item administered
        9. ____+_____   Fourth item administered
       10. ____+_____   Third item administered
(6)    11. ____+_____   First item administered
       12. ____−_____   Second item administered; when missed, the tester moved to item 10
       13. _____
```

In this example, the tester moved backward item by item until a basal was achieved. However, some tests require that the tester skip back several items or move back to a previous page. The tester should check each manual for specific instructions.

Once the basal is determined, testing continues until a ceiling is reached. The ceiling is defined as the point at which it can be assumed that the student would receive no credit for all more difficult test items. The ceiling is established by a specified number of incorrect responses; the test ends when the ceiling is determined. Like basals, tests differ in the number of items required for the ceiling. Some measures specify 3 consecutive incorrect responses on consecutively numbered items; others require 5, 8, or even 10 consecutive errors. A ceiling can also be defined in terms of a range of items; for example, the ceiling might be 5 errors within 7 consecutive responses.

Ceilings are established the same way as basals, except the tester seeks a series of incorrect responses. In the following example, the ceiling is three consecutive incorrect responses. The suggested starting item for third graders is item 3. The tester therefore began at item 3; a basal was achieved when the third grader answered items 3, 4, and 5 correctly. The student then missed items 6, 7, and 8, establishing a ceiling.

BASAL: 3 consecutive correct responses

CEILING: 3 consecutive incorrect responses

(3)
1. —————
2. —————
3. —— + ——
4. —— + ——
5. —— + ——
6̶. —— − ——
7̶. —— − ——
8̶. —— − ——

Students often achieve a basal and then answer several questions correctly before any missing. When they encounter items difficult for them, they may answer some correctly and others incorrectly before reaching the ceiling. The following example depicts this type of response pattern. The tenth grade student began the test at the recommended starting point, item 15. The student answered several items correctly and did not make an error until item 19. Item 20 was correct, 21 incorrect, and 22 correct; a ceiling was established with errors on items 23, 24, and 25.

BASAL: 3 consecutive correct responses

CEILING: 3 consecutive incorrect responses

(10)
15. —— + ——   2̶1̶. —— − ——
16. —— + ——   22. —— + ——
17. —— + ——   2̶3̶. —— − ——
18. —— + ——   2̶4̶. —— − ——
1̶9̶. —— − ——   2̶5̶. —— − ——
20. —— + ——   26. —————

The test manual is the best source for information about suggested starting points and basal and ceiling rules. Some test forms also provide this information. Although no substitute for studying the manual, these brief notations on the test record serve as reminders during test administration.

Ending the Test and Retesting

The testing session should include periodic breaks to ward off fatigue. The length of the session and the endurance of the participants determine how often these breaks should occur. With elementary students, a short rest break should be given at least every half hour; more frequent breaks may be necessary with preschool children. Secondary grade students and adults can usually work from 45 minutes to an hour before needing a rest period. Breaks should occur at a logical stopping point in administration, such as at the end of a test or subtest. During the break, students should be encouraged to stand up, move about, and visit the restroom and drinking fountain.

Testing ends when all scheduled activities are completed, the time allotted is exhausted, or the student is no longer able to work efficiently due to fatigue or loss of concentration. At the end of the session, the tester should thank the student for his or her cooperation and explain what will happen next. This might be further testing on another day, a meeting of the student and tester to go over results, or testing with another professional. The tester answers any questions the student may have and then accompanies the student back to the classroom. The tester should review the session as soon as possible and attempt to evaluate the quality of his or her relationship with the student and the adequacy of the administration process.

It may be necessary to readminister a test at some later date. Readministration of achievement measures to assess progress is routine; students may be given a reading test at the beginning of the school year and then again at the end to measure their growth. Sometimes, however, retesting must occur after only a brief interval. For example, the tester may need to readminister the test within a period of days or weeks, if the original administration was invalidated due to tester error or a student health problem.

Retesting can take place immediately if the test has multiple forms. For instance, if the results of form A were invalid for some reason, form B could be administered the next day. To determine the equivalency of alternate forms of a test, the tester should check the manual's description of equivalent-form reliability.

For measures with only one form, readministration should be delayed as long as possible, preferably for 2 to 4 weeks. If this is impossible, results of the second administration should be interpreted cautiously because a practice effect is likely. The test manual may provide information on how scores are affected by practice in a test-retest situation.

OBSERVATION OF TEST BEHAVIOR

Skilled testers handle the mechanics of test administration automatically so they can concentrate on observing the student's behavior during testing. How students act in the testing situation—what they do and say, how they approach a task, and what their general work methods are—is important in interpreting results. The student who is eager, attentive, and anxious to perform well during testing is quite different from one who is withdrawn and uncooperative. Such behavioral descriptions assist in interpretation of results and provide a beginning for planning instructional strategies.

Observation is a process of collecting data on student behavior. In the observation of test behavior, the tester records information about the student's words and actions. Observational data are objective, precise descriptions of how students behave, and they easily communicate what occurred during testing. Statements, such as "John left his seat 13 times during the first 10 minutes of testing," provide useful assessment information. Judgments or opinions, such as "Janice was shy and retiring" or "Darren was easily distracted," do not, unless substantiated by observational data. The specific techniques used in observation of student behavior are explained in Chapter 5.

One of the first things the tester should observe is the student's approach to the testing situation. How does the student act when presented with directions and the first few tasks? Is he or she able to adjust quickly to the demands of this new working environment? The tester should be alert for both verbal and nonverbal clues. Students may comment, "I don't wanna stay here," "I like writing with pencils," or "I'm ready to work." They may also express themselves by actions, such as failure to establish eye contact. Also of interest is how students begin the first test task. Some start working immediately, whereas others appear to have difficulty focusing their attention on a new activity.

The tester should also observe the student's style of responding: the response mode selected, the latency between question and answer, the length of the response, and so forth. Table 4–4 describes several important dimensions of response style.

Another major concern is the general work style of the student. The following factors should be considered in observation:

1. *Activity level.* The tester should note obvious signs of activity (standing up, walking around the testing room), as well as more subtle behaviors. Students can be very active without ever leaving their seats. They can squirm around, tap their fingers, and jiggle their legs up and down. High activity levels can distract the student from the test tasks, thereby lowering test performance.

2. *Attention to task.* Some students are able to sustain attention to test tasks for several minutes or for the entire administration period; others appear to become distracted after a very short time. The tester can quantify inattention by counting the number of student remarks unrelated to test activities or the number of times the student looks away from test materials. When the student's attention is away from the task 25% or more of the time, the tester should consider taking a break or ending the session.

3. *Perseverance.* When presented with an activity, is the student able to persevere until the task is finished? Or does the student give up after a brief attempt? The tester can collect data by timing how long the student works on a particular task.

4. *Need for reassurance.* Many students, anxious about their performance, query the tester about the accuracy of their responses. Even though it has been explained at the beginning of the test that the tester cannot tell them if their answers are right or wrong, students often end a response with the question, "Is that right?" The tester should reiterate that it is against the rules to let them know. An attempt should be made to reassure such students with positive comments such as, "You're working hard." The tester should begin to collect observational data if students persist with this concern.

Comments made during testing may provide information about student attitudes and feelings. Students may talk about how they perceive their abilities ("I'm dumb in school" or, "I can do puzzles real good'') or their performance on various test tasks (''I can read pretty well now'' or, ''I'm lousy at spelling''). They may also comment about the test by asking, ''Can I do more of these?'' or ''Are we almost done?'' Testers should listen when students talk, answer when appropriate, and record any statements that may be useful in interpreting results.

Testers should also be alert to any warning signs of handicapping conditions. The student's speech should be considered in terms of its intelligibility, articulation, pitch, and volume. Loud or unclear speech may be an indication of hearing problems, as are frequent requests for repetition of test items. Symptoms of vision problems include bringing reading materials close to the face, having red and watery eyes, and rubbing the eyes. If any aspect of the student's test behavior suggests possible speech, hearing, vision, physical, or emotional problems, the tester should refer the student to the appropriate professional for further assessment. If some severe difficulty is confirmed, test results will probably be invalid.

As observational data are collected during testing, they should be recorded. Testers should not trust their memories, particularly their recall of

---

TABLE 4–4

Observation of response style

Response Mode

Which response mode—verbal or nonverbal—does the student favor? If a question can be answered either by pointing to a response or saying it, which mode does the student select? With questions requiring a yes or no response, does the student speak or gesture? Some students accompany even written responses with talk; others speak only when absolutely necessary.

Latency

Latency is the delay between presentation of the test task and the beginning of a response. Students may begin to answer as soon as or even before the tester finishes introducing the task; others may delay a few seconds. Some students wait for as long as a minute but then respond correctly. Very short or long response latencies are noteworthy, particularly in relation to classroom performance.

Length

The length of an answer is not necessarily an indication of its accuracy; depending upon the content of the response and the scoring standards of the test, a brief response may earn as many points as a lengthy one. Verbal responses of students may be characterized by brevity or length. Such patterns should be noted by the tester.

Organization

Although the organization of the response may not be germane to scoring, it is important. A response may be logical and well organized; an equally correct one may be rambling and poorly ordered. How students organize answers provides information about their ability to structure, order, and clearly present their thoughts.

Method of Expressing Inability to Respond

The tester should watch for the student's method of responding when he or she does not know the answer to a question. Some will simply say, ''I don't know.'' Others will say they don't know but will then attempt to explain their inability to answer (''That's fifth grade stuff and I haven't had it yet'') or will substitute something they do know (''I can't spell *dog* but I can do *cat:* c-a-t''). Students who express ignorance before the tester has finished the question or who routinely respond to certain types of questions with ''I can't do that'' should be encouraged to attempt the item. With students who say nothing when they do not know an answer, the tester should wait a reasonable length of time and then encourage the student to at least take a guess. It is important to consider the student's typical response latency so as not to confuse a long delay before answering with inability to respond.

Idiosyncratic Responses

Occasionally students will give responses that appear to have no relationship to the question. The tester should repeat the question to make sure the student understood what was asked, then ask the student to explain the answer. This is done by repeating the student's answer in a questioning tone and saying, ''Tell me what you mean.''

---

student comments. Some test forms provide space for notations about behaviors; others include checklists for use in rating the student's behavior. However, because space is limited on most forms, experienced testers often bring along extra paper to record observational data and student comments.

SCORING THE TEST

The standard conditions that form the basis of norm-referenced tests also apply to conversion of student responses into test scores. Scoring is a critical step that transforms the student's test responses into comparative data. Accuracy is imperative; every count and calculation must be correct. The amount of time and number of computations required for scoring differ with each test. Some are scored quickly with few calculations, whereas others may take as long or longer to score than administer.

Tests should be scored as soon as possible after administration. At this time, the tester should also review the observational data, because these may aid in the interpretation of numerical scores. Many experienced testers score the test right after it is given and again later to recheck their accuracy.

TABLE 4–5
Calculating chronological age

To determine the student's exact age at the time of testing, subtract the birthdate from the test date. The year, month, and day of testing are written first, then the same information for the student's date of birth.

To subtract, the tester begins with the right-hand column and first subtracts days, then months, and finally years.

Year	Month	Day	
1989	11	29	Date of testing
− 1977	8	11	Date of birth
12	3	18	Chronological age

If borrowing is required, convert 1 year into 12 months and 1 month into 30 days. In the following example, it was necessary to borrow 1 month (from 6 months) to convert 4 days to 34 days.

Year	Month	Day	
	5	34	
1990	8̶	4̶	Date of testing
− 1976	3	31	Date of birth
14	2	3	Chronological age

In the next example, both years and months were converted before subtracting. First, 2 months were reduced to 1, and 8 days were increased to 38; then, 1989 years were reduced to 1988 and 1 month increased to 13.

Year	Month	Day	
	13		
1988	1̶	38	
1̶9̶8̶9̶	2̶	8̶	Date of testing
− 1979	10	28	Date of birth
9	3	10	Chronological age

Chronological age is generally reported in terms of years and months, but not days. However, the number of days is considered. The convention is to add 1 month if the number of days is greater than 15; if days equal 15 or less, the number of months is not changed. Thus,

8 years, 4 months, 9 days = 8–4
10 years, 6 months, 20 days = 10–7

TABLE 4–6
Computing raw scores

Steps in Computing the Raw Score
  Step 1: Rate each response correct or incorrect.
  Step 2: Assign point values to each response.
  Step 3: Calculate number of points earned (4).
  Step 4: Calculate number of points assumed earned (2).
  Step 5: Add the number of points earned and the number of points
            assumed earned (4 + 2 = 6).

Example of Raw Score Computation
  BASAL: 3 consecutive correct responses
  CEILING: 3 consecutive incorrect responses
  Each item is worth 1 point

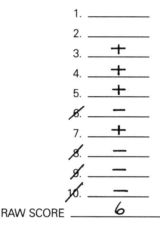

RAW SCORE _____ 6 _____

Sometimes in scoring, it is necessary to know the student's exact chronological age—the number of years and months since birth. Calculation of the student's actual age at the time of testing requires both the student's birthdate and the date of testing. Table 4–5 explains the computational procedure. Chronological age (CA) is generally written as two numbers separated by a hyphen. For instance, CA 6–3 refers to 6 years, 3 months. The hyphen cannot be replaced with a decimal point. CA 10.6 is not the same as CA 10–6. CA 10.6 is 10 years and $\frac{6}{10}$ of a year, an older age than $10\frac{1}{2}$; CA 10–6 is 10 years, 6 months, equal to $10\frac{1}{2}$ years.

Computing Raw Scores

Raw scores, the first to be computed by the tester, describe the number of points earned by a student on a test or subtest. The first step is to determine which test items were answered correctly. This is often done during administration. The tester then assigns point values to each correct response. On many tests, each item is simply worth 1 point; on others, a student can earn 0, 1, 2, or 3 points

depending upon response accuracy. Items within a test can vary in point value. For example, easier items may be worth 1 point; more difficult items, 2 points; and the most difficult, 3 points. The test manual provides scoring guidelines with information on item point values.

The raw score is computed by adding the total number of points earned by the student to the total number of points assumed to be earned. Credit is given for the items below the basal that, although not administered, were assumed to be answered correctly. If items below the basal take on a range of possible points, the student is credited with the highest number; for instance, if correct responses receive either 1, 2, or 3 points, it is assumed the student would have earned a score of 3, had the item actually been administered.

Table 4–6 presents an example of raw score computation. The test began at item 3, and a basal was achieved when the student correctly answered items 3, 4, and 5. Incorrect responses on items 8, 9, and 10 established the ceiling. Because each item is worth 1 point, the student earned a total of 4 points by correctly answering questions 3, 4, 5, and 7. Credit must also be given for items 1 and 2, the items below the basal assumed to be correct. When the number of points earned (4) is added to the number of points assumed to be earned (2), a total raw score of 6 is obtained.

Converting Raw Scores to Derived Scores

Raw scores must be converted to other scores for a student's performance to be contrasted with that of the norm group. Depending on the test, several types of derived scores may be available: age equivalents, grade equivalents, percentile ranks, standard scores, and others.

Test manuals provide tables for converting raw scores into other scores. This student's raw score is computed, the correct norms table is located, and the derived score is read from the table. Table 4–7 presents sample test norms for students age 9–0 to 9–6. The tester finds the student's raw score in the first column, then reads across to determine age equivalent, grade equivalent, percentile rank, and standard score. For example, a raw score of 5 for someone age 9–3 would be equivalent to a percentile rank of 35 and a standard score of 94. When no scores are listed for a

particular raw score, the student's performance is considered either above or below norms. On the sample norms table, a raw score of 1 would be below norms and a raw score of 12 above norms.

Sometimes the tester must consult more than one table to obtain all needed scores. For instance, one table may be used to convert raw scores to percentile ranks, and a second to convert percentile ranks to standard scores. Tests also differ in how tables are arranged; raw scores can be listed across the top of the table, down the left-hand side, or even down the middle. Testers should be careful to select appropriate tables for the age or grade of the student and to read each table accurately. Some testers find it helpful to use a ruler or index card to help keep their place.

Many test protocols include graphs or profiles for plotting the student's derived scores. This visual representation may assist in interpreting and explaining test results to students and parents. Test manuals provide instructions for plotting the profile; as with all aspects of scoring, accuracy should be a prime concern.

INTERPRETING TEST RESULTS

Results of standardized tests are used to make educational decisions. Tests are administered and

TABLE 4–7
Sample norms table

AGE 9–0 TO 9–6				
Raw Score	Age Equivalent	Grade Equivalent	Percentile Rank	Standard Score
1	—	—	—	—
2	6–0	1.0	5	75
3	6–9	1.7	15	84
4	7–5	2.4	20	87
5	8–2	2.9	35	94
6	9–0	3.5	50	100
7	9–5	3.8	55	102
8	9–11	4.4	60	104
9	10–5	4.8	75	110
10	11–0	5.5	85	116
11	12–1	6.2	90	119
12	—	—	—	—

scored and their results interpreted to determine how students perform in relation to age or grade peers. Interpretation of results involves a number of considerations. These include determining the relationship of test behavior to test scores, weighing which test scores provide the most valuable information, allowing for measurement error when reporting results, and evaluating test performance in relation to norm-referenced criteria.

Test Behavior

During test administration, the tester observes the student's behavior. Observational data are then evaluated in relation to the student's scores. Some important questions the tester should consider in interpreting test behavior are

1. Did the student show *consistent* test behavior? Or did behavior change from task to task or from early in the testing session to later?
2. What types of behaviors were exhibited during tests or subtests that assessed the student's *strengths,* that is, the areas where the student earned the highest scores?
3. What types of behaviors were exhibited during tests or subtests that assessed the student's *weaknesses*?
4. Was the student's test behavior *representative* of usual classroom behavior? Of behavior in the home?

These factors influence test performance. For example, a student may attend well to the tasks presented at the start of assessment, whether those tasks represent strengths or weaknesses. However, he or she may soon lose interest in testing and respond quickly and carelessly. Or a student may refuse to attempt all tasks relating to a certain skill, such as reading or mathematics. Test behaviors should be described in detail when reporting results.

Choice of Test Scores

A standardized test may offer several types of scores—age and grade equivalents, percentile ranks, standard scores, and so forth. In interpreting test results, it is necessary to choose the scores that will be most useful for quantifying the student's performance and for reporting results to parents and professionals.

As Chapter 3 explained, age and grade equivalents appear to be the simplest scores to inter-

pret but are in fact quite complicated. Their use is not recommended for this and other reasons. One major limitation is that they do not provide information about whether a student's performance is within average limits. If a 7-year-old earns a score of age 6 on a measure, this does not indicate the student's standing in relation to others of the same age. The performance of the student could be quite average for 7-year-olds or could fall below the average range of functioning for this age group. If a student in grade 4.3 earns an achievement score of grade 3.9, is the difference significant enough to suggest an achievement problem? Age and grade scores are not useful for answering such questions.

Age and grade scores only *appear* to provide precise information about a student's instructional or developmental level. If a student earns a grade score of 7.3, this means only that he or she earned a raw score roughly equivalent to that of the seventh grade students in the norm group, if there were seventh grade students in the norm group and the score is not the result of extrapolation. Grade scores do not describe the student's current instructional level. They are not even indicative of which test questions were answered correctly. Two students can earn the same age or grade score but not answer any of the same questions correctly. Anastasi (1988) sums up this problem in the interpretation of age and grade scores.

If a fourth-grade child obtains a grade equivalent of 6.9 in arithmetic, it does *not* mean that she has mastered the arithmetic processes taught in the sixth grade. She undoubtedly obtained her score largely by superior performance in fourth-grade arithmetic. It certainly could not be assumed that she has the prerequisites for seventh-grade arithmetic. (p. 80)

Unfortunately, sometimes age and grade equivalents are the only available scores from a particular test. In this situation, they should be reported, but findings should be worded carefully to prevent misinterpretation.

Grade Equivalents

John earned a grade equivalent score of 6.3 on Test X. This may mean that John's raw score on this test was equal to the average raw score of grade 6.3 students in the test's norm group. However, because it is likely the decimal grade equivalents on Test X were derived from the scores earned by grade 6 students, it is more accurate to say that John's raw score approximated the average raw score earned by grade 6 students in the test's norm group.

Age equivalent scores are reported in a similar fashion.

Percentile rank scores are preferable to age and grade equivalents because they are comparative scores. They are straightforward indicators of an individual's standing within a group and are easily interpreted. Percentile rank scores are reported by referring to that portion of the norm group against which the student is being compared.

Percentile Ranks

Harvey, aged 10–3, scored at the 32nd percentile on Test X when compared with age peers. This means that Harvey's performance on this test was equal to or better than that of 32% of the 10-year-old students in Test X's norm group.

Standard scores have many advantages. They are comparative, and when based upon a normal or normalized distribution of raw scores, they can be directly translated into percentile ranks. Also, because standard scores have a uniform mean and standard deviation, they can be compared from one subtest to the next and from one test administration to another.

In addition, standard scores provide information about whether a student's performance is within average limits. They describe the relationship of a student's score to the average score of the comparison group within the norming sample. For example, if standard scores on a particular test are distributed with a mean of 100 and a standard deviation of 15, a standard score of 70 indicates performance two standard deviations below the mean performance of the comparison group for students of any grade or age. That comparison group would be the grade 8 students within the norm group if an eighth grader's performance is being evaluated; if a first grader is under study, the comparison group would be the first graders within the norm group.

Standard Scores

Barbara, a seventh grader, received a standard score of 115 on Test X when compared with grade peers. Because the mean standard score on this test is 100 and the standard deviation is 15, Barbara's score indicates performance one standard deviation above the mean of seventh grade students in Test X's norm group.

Percentile ranks can be reported along with the student's standard scores.

Measurement Error

Test scores, like any other measurement, always contain some element of error. Even if a test is administered and scored in strict adherence to standardization conditions, the scores will be observed scores, consisting of the student's hypothetical true score plus an error component. Fortunately with standardized tests, the standard error of measurement can be used to estimate the amount of error likely to occur within scores. As Chapter 3 explained, the standard error of measurement is based upon the test's reliability and standard deviation. Tests with poor reliability and large standard deviations produce large standard errors. The smaller the standard error of measurement, the more accurate the results. In most cases, standard errors are reported in the test manual. If not, they can be calculated by means of the formula provided in Chapter 3.

The standard error of measurement is used to construct confidence intervals around observed scores. With confidence intervals, a student's performance is reported as a range of scores in which it is highly likely that the true score will fall, rather than as a single score known to include both the true score and error. Sattler (1988) recommends reporting scores in this way:

The student obtained a score of 100 ± 4. The chances that the range of scores from 96 to 104 includes the student's true score are about 68 out of 100.

The procedure for constructing confidence intervals is quite straightforward. After an observed score has been obtained and the standard error of measurement for that score is known, a decision is made about the degree of confidence desired.

The tester may be satisfied with 68% confidence that the student's true score will fall within the range of scores to be constructed. Or a higher degree of confidence may be called for, such as 90%, 95%, or even 99%. The standard error of measurement is then multiplied by a factor related to the level of confidence. The factors, the z scores associated with the confidence levels, are

Confidence Level Desired	Factor by which Standard Error is Multiplied
68%	1.00
85%	1.44
90%	1.64
95%	1.96
99%	2.58

The product of the standard error times the factor is added to the student's observed score to determine the upper limit of the range. The product is then subtracted from the student's observed score to determine the lower limit.

For example, a student's observed score is 100 and the standard error of measurement for that score is 5. If the desired confidence level is 68%, the standard error (5) will be multiplied by the factor (1) to equal 5. The upper limit of the confidence interval becomes 105 (100 + 5) and the lower limit 95 (100 − 5). The student's score is reported as 100 ± 5, with a probability of 68% that the student's true score lies within that range.

If a more conservative estimate is needed, the confidence level could be set at 95%. In this case, the standard error (5) would be multiplied by 1.96 to equal 10. The confidence interval would then extend from 90 to 110, increasing the chances that this range would include the student's true score to 95 out of 100.

When the level of confidence is increased, the width of the confidence interval also increases. In the previous example, increasing the confidence level from 68% to 95% changed the range of scores within the confidence interval from 95–105 to 90–110. The magnitude of the standard error of measurement also affects the width of the confidence interval. Consider these examples.

Example 1

Observed score	100
Standard error of measurement	5
Confidence level	68%
Confidence interval	95 to 105

Example 2

Observed score	100
Standard error of measurement	20
Confidence level	68%
Confidence interval	80 to 120

In these examples, the student's observed score and the level of confidence remain the same. When the standard error is 5, the confidence interval is 95 to 105. However, when the standard error increases to 20, the confidence interval becomes much larger. Tests with small standard errors of measurement allow more precision in the estimation of true scores.

Criteria for Evaluating Test Performance

Norm-referenced tests compare one student's performance against the performance of counterparts in the norm group. Standard score ranges should be used for this purpose.

Many standardized measures provide guidelines for test interpretation. These systems often are based upon a set of standard score ranges, each of which is given a descriptive label. For example, the manual for the *Wechsler Intelligence Scale for Children–Revised* (Wechsler, 1974) uses these labels to describe its standard score (IQ) ranges: "average" (the range from IQ 90 to 109), "low average" (80 to 89), "borderline" (70 to 79), "mentally deficient" (69 and below). However, this system is not used consistently from test to test. Some measures use different labels to describe student performance, and on others, the ranges into which standard scores are divided are defined in a different way.

Although there is no universally accepted system for describing ranges of performance, judicious use of standard score ranges can facilitate the interpretation of test results. In this book, we describe ranges of standard scores in terms of their distance from the test mean. Score ranges are defined in standard deviation units—within one standard deviation of the mean, between one and two standard deviations below the mean, and so forth. Ranges of performance are also defined in relation to the percentage of population each includes.

Thus, the *average range of performance* is the standard score range within one standard deviation from the mean. On a test with standard scores distributed with a mean of 100 and a standard deviation of 15, this range extends from standard score 85 to standard score 115. If the test is normally distributed, that range encompasses 68% of the norm group.

The *low average range of performance* is the standard score range between one and two standard deviations below the mean. It extends from standard score 70 to standard score 84 and includes approximately 14% of the population. Similarly, the *high average range of performance* is defined as the standard score range between one and two standard deviations above the mean. It includes standard scores 116 to 130 and represents approximately 14% of the population.

At the extreme ends of the distribution are the *below average range of performance* and the *above average range of performance*. Each represents approximately 2% of the population. The below average range encompasses standard scores 69 and below, and the above average range encompasses standard scores 131 and above. Figure 4–2 shows the ranges of performance in relation to the normal distribution.

Labels such as "average" and "low average" are arbitrary, although in this system they are tied to percentages of the population. Deciding that a score indicates below average performance by a

standard such as "2 years below grade level" is even more arbitrary and is fraught with measurement difficulties. When linked with percentile ranks, standard score ranges fulfill the purpose of norm-referenced testing and compare the student's performance with that of his or her peers.

In reporting the results of standardized tests, keep in mind several factors. First, standard scores are preferred over other types of scores. Second, report scores as confidence intervals rather than single scores, noting the level of confidence associated with the interval. Third, describe scores in relation to their range of performance, such as average, low average, and so on. Following these recommendations, a standard score of 79 on a test with a standard score mean of 100, standard deviation of 15, and a standard error of measurement of 3 would be reported in the following way:

Standard Scores Expressed in Confidence Intervals

Priscilla, a fifth grader, earned a standard score of 79 ± 3 on Test X when compared with grade peers. The chances that the range of scores from 76 to 82 includes Priscilla's true score are about 68 out of 100. A score within this range

FIGURE 4–2
Test interpretation using standard score ranges

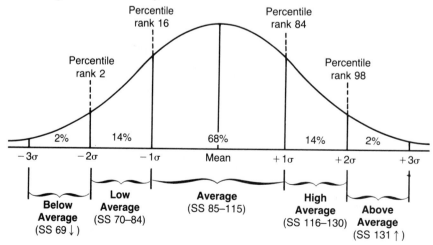

SS = standard score with a mean of 100 and a standard deviation of 15

indicates low average performance in comparison to the fifth grade students in Test X's norm group.

MODIFICATION OF TESTING PROCEDURES

In many cases, test manuals dictate the exact words the tester is to use in presenting tasks to students, how the student may respond, and the ways the tester may respond to the student. If specified procedures are not followed, norm-referenced scores become meaningless because the norms assume administration under standard conditions. However, sometimes professionals believe test results do not adequately reflect the student's capabilities. Certain administration requirements may, in fact, depress a student's performance. For example, a student may be able to complete a test task successfully but not within the required time limits. On most timed tests, students receive no credit for a late, albeit correct, response.

It *is* possible to modify administration procedures for standardized tests, although tests should be given under standard conditions before attempting any modification. In this way, the student's performance under both standard and altered conditions can be studied.

Results of tests administered under altered conditions must be interpreted with great caution. An example is allowing a fourth grade student to use a calculator for a computation test normed with students provided only with paper and pencil. With the aid of the calculator, the student's test score may improve; he or she may achieve a score indicating average performance for a fourth grader. However, it is no longer possible to compare the student's performance to that of students in the norm group. If the norm group had been supplied with calculators, perhaps the performance of the student in question would fall within the low average or below average range. There is simply no way to determine this. However, despite the necessity for caution in interpretation, results from tests given under altered conditions can provide useful information about the student's capabilities to perform test tasks. Results may also suggest ways to alter instructional strategies and requirements to increase chances for classroom success.

Before modifying administration procedures, the professional should consider the possible problems that may arise if the test is to be used sometime again in the future with the same student. If the student somehow learns the questions and responses and is able to recall those responses, the test can no longer be used to compare the student's performance with the performance of others.

Sattler (1988) discusses the modification of administration procedures and calls this practice *testing of limits:*

There may be times when you want to go beyond the standard test procedures in order to gain additional information about the child's abilities. The information from testing-of-limits procedures can occasionally be helpful, especially in clinical or psychoeducational settings. (p. 111)

Administration conditions can be modified in several ways to determine if students are able to improve their performance. Methods include the following:

1. *Instructions* to the student may be paraphrased into simpler language.
2. The tester can provide a *demonstration* of how test tasks are to be performed.
3. *Time limits* for the completion of tasks can be extended or removed.
4. The *presentation mode* for tasks may be changed. For example, the tester could read items aloud to the student rather than requiring the student to read them.
5. The *response mode* required of the student may be changed. For example, instead of writing the answers, the student could respond orally.
6. The student may be allowed to use *aids* such as paper and pencil or a calculator.
7. The tester may provide the student with *prompts.* For example, the first step in the test task could be performed by the tester. Or the tester could question the student about his or her problem-solving method and then suggest an alternate approach.
8. The tester may give *feedback* to the student. This could include confirmation of correct responses or even correction of incorrect responses.

9. *Positive reinforcement* could be offered for correct responses and other appropriate work behaviors.
10. The *physical location* of the test may be changed. The test could be administered on the floor rather than at a table, or in a playroom rather than a testing room.
11. The *tester* may be changed. Someone with whom the student is comfortable, such as a parent or classroom teacher, could administer the test.

When administration procedures are altered, the modification must be described in a report of test results. Results obtained under nonstandard conditions should be reported as *alternate scores*. Although interpretation of these scores is difficult, successful performance with modified tasks may provide clues to ways for improving student functioning. For example, praising a student for each completed test item may increase the number of questions he or she is willing to attempt. Or spelling may improve when the student is allowed to spell orally rather than write the words. Although these results are not determined in accordance with the rules of standardized testing, they may help identify specific problems in learning and suggest remedies for these problems.

AVOIDING BIAS IN TESTING

The potential for bias in assessment does not end with careful selection of assessment instruments. Even if standardized tests are deemed the most appropriate tools, discrimination remains a possibility during test administration and scoring and in the critical step of test interpretation.

Bias can be introduced into test administration in a number of ways. One important consideration is the professional preparation of the tester. Testing skill is absolutely essential for nonbiased assessment. Placing a standardized test in the hands of an untrained examiner is as poor a practice as the selection of a technically inadequate measure.

Professionals should also have knowledge about the types of students they assess, particularly if these include individuals from cultures different from their own. Information about variations in age, gender, cultural group, and handicapping condition and the potential impact of these factors upon test performance is essential.

Tester attitudes are another important factor. If the tester holds strong beliefs about certain groups, he or she may fail to see students as individuals. For example, the belief that girls do not excel in mathematics may influence how diligently the tester attempts to elicit a female student's optimal performance on a math test. Tester attitudes affect expectations, which in turn affect test administration and scoring practices.

The working relationship between the student and tester is critical. Testers may need to take special care in building rapport with students of different races, cultures, or experiential backgrounds. The tester may represent an unfamiliar culture to such students, requiring extra effort to help them feel at ease in the testing situation. Recommendations for the assessment of minority group students include the following:

Make every effort to enlist the child's motivation and interest by helping him or her feel as comfortable as possible in the assessment situation. You should take as much time as needed to ensure the child's cooperation. If at all possible, the clinician should be someone who is familiar to the child. (Sattler, 1988, p. 590).

It has been suggested that minority group students be tested only by examiners from the same group. However, a review of the research on assessment of black and Mexican-American students showed that white testers did not have harmful effects upon the test performance of minority group students. Alley and Foster (1978) consider the matching of tester and student on race a simplistic approach to nonbiased assessment: it overlooks the impact of class differences within minorities, the need for empathy on the examiner's part, and the issue of tester competence.

Selection of the tester becomes an important issue when the student's primary mode of communication is not English. Testers must be chosen carefully for students who speak a language other than English and for students who are deaf and communicate using sign language. In best practice, the tester will be able to communicate directly with the student using the student's communication mode. However, this is not always possible, particularly for students who speak one of the less common languages. When an interpreter must be used to translate the tester's questions to the student and the student's answers to the tester, standardized tests cannot be used for comparative purposes. At best, they provide informal information which must be evaluated with great care.

The potential for bias is also present during the interpretation of test results. Professionals can have a positive influence on this portion of the assessment process by using appropriate procedures for the interpretation of test scores, by understanding the limitations of standardized testing, examining the attitudes they hold toward students from minority cultures, and becoming more familiar with the languages and cultures of the students they assess. To assist professionals in the identification of possible sources of bias during test interpretation, Turnbull, Strickland, and Brantley (1982) have prepared the checklist shown in Figure 4–3.

FIGURE 4–3
Checklist for minimizing bias during interpretation of results

Name _____School _____
Examiner _____Date _____

Examine Child's Score   *A check (✓) indicates potential bias*

_____ Compare them to the adaptive behavior information
_____ Look for characteristics of the child which might bias or influence the results such as:
      _____ native language
      _____ age, health, nutrition
      _____ handicapping conditions
      _____ mode of communication
      _____ sensory and performance modalities
_____ Look for characteristics of the tests and techniques which might bias or influence the results, such as:
      _____ purpose
      _____ communication modalities (a) child-test (b) child-examiner
      _____ norms
      _____ reliability and validity
      _____ type of measure
      _____ relevance of items
      _____ scoring criteria
      _____ type of scores
_____ Look for characteristics of the examiner which might bias or influence the results, such as:
      _____ appropriate training
      _____ communication mode and language
      _____ previous experience
      _____ attitudes
      _____ skills
      _____ knowledge
_____ Look for conditions within the assessment situation which might bias the performance
      _____ time of day
      _____ distractions
      _____ testing materials
      _____ inappropriate use of cues
      _____ length of session
      _____ comfort and accessibility of materials
      _____ order of assessment activities
_____ Look for conditions between the examiner and child which might bias the performance
      _____ rapport
      _____ attending behavior
      _____ initial success or failure
      _____ maintaining responding behavior
      _____ communication
      _____ dress and/or mannerisms
_____ Try to determine if the child's performance is representative and/or approximates his/her potential
_____ Compare the results of multiple measures

Note. From *Developing and Implementing Individualized Education Programs* (2nd ed.) (p. 86) by A. P. Turnbull, B. B. Strickland, and J. C. Brantley (developed in conjunction with G. Harbin), 1982, Columbus, OH: Merrill. Copyright 1982 by Bell & Howell Company. Reprinted by permission.

STUDY GUIDE

Review Questions

1. Check all of the statements describing an adequate testing environment.
   _____ a. One of the student's parents or the student's teacher is present in the testing room.
   _____ b. Chairs and a table are available for the student and the tester.
   _____ c. All the equipment and test materials needed for the session are placed on the test table ready for use.
   _____ d. The temperature and ventilation in the room are comfortable for the student.
   _____ e. The testing room is located near popular school activities such as music and physical education.

2. Which of the following is *not* good practice in introducing the student to the testing situation?
   _____ a. Tests should be scheduled at the same time as the student's favorite classroom activities.
   _____ b. Physical needs of the student should be attended to before testing begins.
   _____ c. The student should be informed about the purpose of testing.
   _____ d. The tester should explain to the student what will happen during the test, including the length of the session, types of test activities, and so forth.

3. Suppose a professional began test administration with item number 10 in an attempt to establish a basal of four consecutively numbered correct responses. If the student failed item 10, what test item should be administered next?

4. Match each term in Column A with the appropriate description from Column B.

Column A	*Column B*
a. Basal	_____ Test questions used to teach students how to do test tasks
b. Coaching	_____ The point in the test when it can be assumed the student would receive full credit for all easier items
c. Demonstration items	_____ The practice of helping a student arrive at the answer to a test question
d. Ceiling	_____ The point when it can be assumed the student would receive no credit for all the more difficult items

5. Give two reasons why it is important to observe the student's behavior during test administration.

6. Calculate the student's chronological age in these examples.

Student's Birthdate	*Date of Testing*	*Chronological Age*
a. 12–2–81	1–3–89	_____
b. 6–28–73	9–15–90	_____
c. 11–20–84	10–6–89	_____

7. Find the raw scores for each of the following tests. Each item is worth 1 point. The basal is three consecutive correct responses, and the ceiling is three consecutive incorrect responses.

Test A		*Test B*	
(1)	_____	(18)	___+___
(2)	_____	(19)	___+___
(3)	___+___	(20)	___+___
(4)	___+___	(21)	___−___
(5)	___+___	(22)	___+___
(6)	___−___	(23)	_____
(7)	___+___	(24)	___+___
(8)	___−___	(25)	___−___
(9)	___−___	(26)	___−___
(10)	___−___	(27)	___−___
Raw score _____		Raw score _____	

8. Choose the statement that best explains the meaning of the score.
   _____ a. When a student earns a percentile rank score of 54, this means that 54% of the test questions were answered correctly.

_____ b. An age equivalent score of 10–3 indicates that the student's raw score is equal to the average raw score of grade 10.3 students in the norm group.

_____ c. If test standard scores are distributed with a mean of 100 and a standard deviation of 15, a standard score of 85 indicates performance one standard deviation below the mean.

_____ d. If test standard scores are distributed with a mean of 50 and a standard deviation of 10, a standard score of 70 indicates performance two standard deviations below the mean.

9. A student received a standard score of 100 on a test in which the mean standard score is 100, the standard deviation is 15, and the scores are normally distributed. This score

_____ a. Falls at the 50th percentile.

_____ b. Is within the 5th stanine.

_____ c. Indicates performance at the mean.

_____ d. All of the above statements are true.

10. Match the standard score with the appropriate score range. The standard scores are normally distributed with a mean of 100 and a standard deviation of 15.

Standard Score	Range of Performance
a. 117	_____ Above average performance
b. 83	_____ High average performance
c. 68	_____ Average performance
d. 135	_____ Low average performance
e. 105	_____ Below average performance

11. A student earned a standard score of 73 on a test with a standard error of measurement of 6. In what range of scores would the student's true score be expected to fall 68% of the time?

12. Testing procedures can be modified if the professional is interested in studying the student's performance under alternate administration conditions. One example is to extend or to remove the time limits for test tasks. Give four other examples.

Activities

1. Select one of the individual achievement tests used in special education and examine its manual. See if these topics are discussed:
   a. Setting up the testing environment
   b. Introducing the student to the testing situation
   c. Observing the student's test behavior
   d. Training requirements for testers

2. Observe a professional administering a standardized test. Follow along in the test manual during administration.

3. Observe a student taking a standardized test. Collect data on the student's test behavior.

4. Practice test administration and scoring with a peer, using a norm-referenced test approved by the course instructor.

5. Interview two or more professionals who administer educational tests. You might talk with a special educator, a school psychologist, and a speech-language pathologist. Ask each to describe the types of test scores he or she prefers and why.

6. Suggest ways to modify test administration procedures for students who
   a. Work very slowly.
   b. Have reading problems.
   c. Have handwriting problems.
   d. Have short attention spans.

Discussion Questions

1. Why is it important that tests only be administered by trained professionals? Identify some errors that untrained persons would make when administering tests and scoring student responses.

2. Explain this statement: "Testing skills should be so well learned that they are automatic, so professionals can devote their attention to observation of the student's behavior."

3. Compare the advantages and disadvantages of percentile ranks and standard scores for reporting test results.

4. When test administration procedures are modified, the results are called *alternate scores*. Discuss the usefulness of these scores and the cautions that must be observed in their interpretation.

5. Describe how bias can intrude into assessment during test administration and scoring. Suggest strategies for preventing bias.

5

Informal Assessment

Teachers use informal assessment techniques every day—when they observe the behavior of a student in the classroom, or examine a student's paper and attempt to find a pattern of errors, or interview a student about the procedures he or she has used to solve a problem or answer a question. The major advantage of informal assessment techniques is their relevance to instruction. In fact, many of the informal assessment strategies used in special education can be viewed as *curriculum-based* measures. Informal techniques provide information about the student's current levels of performance, aid in the selection of instructional goals and objectives, point to the need for instructional modifications, document student progress, and suggest directions for further assessment. Whereas norm-referenced measures focus on the student's ability to function in a structured testing situation, informal measures more closely approximate typical classroom conditions.

Informal assessment is useful not only for the evaluation of student performance but also for the study of instructional settings and curricular tasks. Because it extends beyond the student to the characteristics of the task to be learned and the instructional environment, informal assessment allows a more ecological approach to the study of special needs.

Informal assessment tools help the professional gather information about the current status of the student, the task, or the setting. Tools are designed to describe current conditions, not to predict future performance. There are several other important areas of difference between formal and informal measures.

The first is *standard of reference*. With norm-referenced tests, the student's performance is compared to that of a norm group. With informal measures, the student's performance is compared to specific instructional concerns such as the sequence of learning tasks within the curriculum of the school or the conduct standards of a particular classroom.

The second difference is *technical adequacy*. Most informal tools are not standardized, and few provide information about reliability and validity. If teachers design informal measures for use in their own classrooms, no information about psychometric quality is available unless it is gathered by teachers themselves. It is not that the quality of

informal assessment is poor; rather, it is generally unknown.

Efficiency is the third area. Norm-referenced tests are usually efficient measures. When evaluating the efficiency of an informal assessment tool, the time and personnel requirements for its design, administration, scoring, and interpretation must all be taken into account. Designing, administering, and scoring an informal tool is a time-consuming process. However, administration procedures are often quite straightforward in comparison to those for norm-referenced tests. Paraprofessionals such as instructional aides can be trained to administer some of the easier informal measures. Despite this, the teacher must be involved in the critical steps of designing the measure and interpreting its results. Even in administration, some measures require the expertise of a professional familiar with the school curriculum and the expectations for performance within the classroom learning environment.

The fourth difference between informal and formal measures is *specificity*. Formal measures generally assess larger segments of the curriculum, and their coverage of these segments is selective rather than comprehensive. A norm-referenced test may include a broad range of items chosen to represent a general curriculum area, but each specific skill within that curriculum area is measured by only a few test items or none at all. In contrast, informal measures tend to focus on one or more subskills within a curriculum area in an attempt to assess these thoroughly.

There are many types of informal assessment techniques, and it is useful to have some way of conceptualizing them. One important dimension is whether informal strategies introduce a test task into the assessment situation, that is, how obtrusive they are. With procedures such as observation, no test task is presented to the student; he or she is simply observed within the natural environment of the classroom or whatever setting is of interest. Informal inventories, classroom quizzes, and criterion-referenced tests, on the other hand, exemplify assessment procedures in which something is added to the environment; the tester introduces test tasks to the student in order to observe how these specific tasks are carried out.

A second dimension of importance is whether measures are direct or indirect. Direct measures attempt to answer an assessment question about a particular student or classroom condition by assessing that characteristic or condition. If the question concerns a student's ability to read a fourth grade science text, the student is asked to read the science text. Indirect measures rely upon some less direct source such as an informant. An indirect means of determining a student's ability to read a science text would be to interview the student's teacher.

The dimensions of directness and obtrusiveness can be used to sort informal assessment techniques into three classes: (a) observation, task analysis, and other direct and unobtrusive procedures; (b) curriculum-based measures such as inventories and criterion-referenced tests that are direct but obtrusive; and (c) procedures using informants such as checklists and interviews that are indirect and obtrusive. These and other characteristics of the many different types of informal techniques are summarized in Table 5–1.

OBSERVATION, WORK SAMPLE ANALYSIS, AND TASK ANALYSIS

These are fundamental assessment strategies basic to all types of assessment. Skill in the use of these procedures is critical for any assessment professional. These techniques allow the direct examination of student behaviors, tasks, and settings without the introduction of test tasks. They are important tools for gathering assessment information in the classroom, where they also serve as instructional tools. In addition, they are often used in conjunction with other data-collection strategies. For example, observation of the student's test behavior is a critical part of norm-referenced testing. Observation and other direct unobtrusive procedures can be adapted for use with individuals of any age, in any curriculum area, and in any instructional setting or assessment situation.

Observation

Teachers are continually watching and listening to their students. They may not call this procedure observation, but by taking note of what their students say and do, teachers are conducting simple observations. When a potential problem is discovered during casual observation, then more systematic observational procedures can be begun.

Although observational techniques are often associated with the study of classroom conduct problems, they are just as appropriate for the study of academic, social, self-help, and vocational skills. Because observation involves the examination of student behaviors within the context of the natural environment, it produces information that often cannot be obtained from any other type of assessment procedure.

Systematic observation techniques help the teacher in specifying, recording, and analyzing student behaviors. In the most basic type of observation, the teacher simply observes and records all the behaviors a student exhibits during some set time period. This technique, called continuous recording or narrative recording (Cooper, 1981), provides preliminary information to help the teacher determine if there is a problem that requires further study. For example, Figure 5–1 presents the record of a continuous observation of Minnie's behavior. The teacher decided to conduct this observation because Minnie seemed to be out of her seat "constantly" during times when she was expected to work at her desk. However, in analyzing the results of the observation, Minnie left her seat only five times in the half-hour period, and all of her excursions had reasonable purposes.

Sequence analysis is a second observational technique that is useful for gaining an overall picture of a student's performance (Sulzer-Azaroff & Mayer, 1977). As with continuous recording, the teacher observes and records all the behaviors of the student within a specified time period. In addition, an attempt is made to record the events or actions preceding and following each behavior. Identification of the antecedents and consequences of a student's behaviors provides information about how events in the environment may influence the student's actions. Consider the sequence analysis of John's classroom behavior in Table 5–2. Few conclusions can be drawn if only the student's actions are considered. However, when antecedents and consequences are taken into account, a more complete picture of the instructional interaction emerges. John's hand-raising behavior appears to be influenced by the actions of the teacher.

Continuous recording and sequence analysis are most often used in the initial stages of assessment to determine if a student's behavior

TABLE 5-1
Informal assessment techniques

Assessment Technique	Description	Source of Information	Direct or Indirect Measure	Test Task Introduced?	PURPOSE OF ASSESSMENT TECHNIQUE		
					Direction for Further Assessment	Estimation of Current Performance and/or Progress	Direction for Planning or Modifying Instruction
Observation	Direct measure of student performance	Student setting	Direct	No		*	
Work Sample Analysis	Direct examination of sample of student's work	Student's work sample	Direct	No	*	*	
Task Analysis	Direct examination of tasks within curriculum	Curricular task	Direct	No	*		*
Inventories and Classroom Quizzes	Direct measure of student performance in selected curriculum area	Student	Direct	Yes	*	*	*
Criterion-Referenced Tests	Direct measure of student performance with specific criteria for success	Student	Direct	Yes		*	*
Diagnostic Probes and Diagnostic Teaching	Direct measure of student performance under differing instructional conditions	Student	Direct	Yes	*	*	*
Checklists and Rating Scales	Indirect measure based on informant's assessment of student performance	Student or other informants	Indirect	Yes	*	*	
Questionnaires and Interviews	Indirect measure based on informant's assessment of student performance	Student or other informants	Indirect	Yes	*	*	

merits further study. They provide a global picture of the student's actions in relationship to situational variables and assist the teacher in selecting specific behaviors requiring intervention. However, they are time-consuming procedures and are best considered as screening tools to identify specific student behaviors for further observation.

As soon as a particular behavior or set of behaviors has been selected for study, plans can be made for conducting an observation focusing on these specific behaviors. The teacher follows several steps.

Describe the behavior to be observed. First, the behavior or behaviors of interest are clearly and precisely described. This facilitates communication among persons conducting the observation and allows discussion of results with the student, parents, and concerned professionals.

To conduct an observation, the behaviors must be both observable and measurable. A behavior is considered observable if its performance can be detected by an outside observer; "understanding the reading assignment" is not an observable behavior but "writing answers to comprehension questions" is. Descriptions of observable behaviors usually contain an action verb. Verbs such as *write, point to, name,* and *throw* describe actions that an observer can see or hear; verbs such as *understand, know, appreciate,* and *perceive* do not.

Behaviors that have clearly definable beginnings and endings are discrete behaviors; examples are writing spelling words and reading a paragraph aloud. Discrete behaviors are measured by counting their frequency or timing their duration. Some behaviors are not discrete; for example, it is difficult to detect the precise starting and ending points of behaviors such as staying on-task and swearing in the classroom. Nondiscrete behaviors are also measurable, because during any given time period an observer can determine whether a student is displaying the behavior.

FIGURE 5–1
Continuous observation

Student __Minnie__	Date __April 3, 1989__

Observer __Ms. Brown__

Classroom Activity: __Independent seatwork__

Reason for Observation: Minnie seems to be out of her seat constantly when she should be at her seat working on her worksheet.

Time	Event
11:00–11:02	Minnie comes in from playground, goes directly to her desk, and sits
11:02–11:05	Minnie sits while teacher hands out and explains spelling worksheet
11:05–11:08	Minnie gets pencil from desk, reads worksheet
11:08–11:09	Minnie begins to write, breaks pencil
11:09–11:13	Minnie gets up, walks to pencil sharpener, sharpens pencil, returns to seat
11:14–11:18	Minnie writes on worksheet
11:18–11:20	Minnie drops pencil on floor, gets up, picks up pencil, returns to seat
11:20–11:25	Minnie writes on worksheet
11:25–11:27	Minnie gets up, places worksheet in folder on teacher's desk
11:27–11:28	Minnie returns to seat, puts pencil in desk, looks around room
11:28–11:30	Minnie gets up, walks to teacher's desk, asks teacher if she can get a drink of water, teacher tells Minnie to return to seat
11:30	Minnie begins to return to seat, lunch bell rings

TABLE 5–2
Sequence analysis

Time	Antecedent	Behavior	Consequence
9:05	Teacher asks the class a question.	John raises hand.	Teacher calls on Bill.
9:07	Teacher asks question.	John yells answer.	Teacher reprimands John.
9:11	Teacher asks question and reminds students to raise hands.	John raises hand.	Teacher calls on John and compliments him for raising his hand.

Note. From *Teaching Special Students in the Mainstream* (2nd ed.) (p. 93) by R. B. Lewis and D. H. Doorlag, 1987, Columbus, OH: Merrill. Copyright 1987 by Merrill Publishing Company. Reprinted with permission.

Select a measurement system. If the behavior of interest is a discrete behavior, it is possible to measure its frequency, its duration, or both. Frequency refers to the number of times a behavior occurs; for example, the teacher may be interested in the frequency with which Joe completes math assignments. Duration is a measure of the length of a behavior, that is, how long it lasts in terms of seconds, minutes, or hours. For instance, if punctuality is a concern, information can be collected on the number of minutes late Jaime arrives to class each day. Or, a parent may have identified a young child's tantruming behavior as a target for observation; for this behavior, it may be important to consider both duration and frequency.

The following measurement systems are used to collect data about discrete behaviors (Alberto & Troutman, 1986):

☐ *Event recording.* The frequency of the behavior is noted in event recording. The observer simply makes a notation each time the behavior of interest occurs. The first example in Figure 5–2 shows how the teacher tallied Susie's behavior of throwing paper airplanes in class.
☐ *Duration recording.* Here the observer records the time a behavior begins and the time it ends to determine its length. The second example in Figure 5–2 is the teacher's daily record of the amount of time Philip spent sleeping in class.

Another option is *latency recording.* In this system, the observer determines the amount of time it takes a student to begin doing something. For example, the teacher might be interested in how long it takes Jennifer to begin reading her library book after she returns to the classroom from recess.

For nondiscrete behaviors such as working independently or talking with peers, the use of interval recording and time sampling is recommended (Alberto & Troutman, 1986; Cooper, Heron, & Heward, 1987). With these techniques, the observer determines whether a behavior occurs during a specified time period. The class day, period, or activity is broken down into short intervals of a few minutes or even a few seconds, and a record of the presence or absence of the target behavior is kept for each interval. These techniques can also be used with discrete behaviors if a complete record of every occurrence is not necessary.

Several variations of interval recording and time sampling are available.

☐ *Whole-interval recording.* The student is observed for the entire interval, and the observer notes if the target behavior occurs continuously throughout the interval. Observation intervals are very brief, usually only a few seconds.
☐ *Partial-interval time recording.* The student is observed for the entire interval, but the observer notes only if the behavior occurred at least once during the interval. Again, time intervals are very brief.
☐ *Momentary time sampling.* The student is observed only at the end of each interval; at that time, the observer checks to see if the behavior is occurring. Intervals are usually longer—3, 5, or even 15 minutes—making this a more convenient method for classroom teachers. However, it is less accurate than interval recording techniques because much of the student's behavior goes unobserved.

Figure 5–3 provides an example of momentary time sampling. Note that the *X* indicates occurrence of the target behavior and the *O*, nonoccurrence. Results are expressed as the number or percentage of time intervals in which the behavior of interest was displayed.

Set up the data-collection system. The next step in planning an observation is to determine logistics. Questions to be answered include

□ When and where will the observation take place?
□ How many observation periods will there be, and how frequently will these occur?
□ Who will act as the observer?
□ How will observational data be recorded?

Determining the time and place of the observation must take into account the nature of the behavior. With infrequent behaviors, it may be desirable to collect observational data for each occurrence. However, if the behavior occurs frequently, it is usually impractical to observe every instance. Instead, it makes sense to select those times and settings where the behavior is of greatest concern. For example, if Henry's rough play on the playground during recess is a possible problem, he should be observed on the playground at that time.

One observation is not sufficient. More than one observation should be planned, and these should take place over time. A common practice is to observe daily for a minimum of 5 days. Observation should continue until a complete picture of the behavior has emerged. For example, if a behavior occurs only 3 or 4 times daily from Monday through Thursday but 10 times on Friday, it is advisable to observe for at least another week to determine if frequency will level off or continue to increase.

Data are usually collected by the professional designing the observation system. If the teacher is the observer, there is less disruption in classroom routine and less danger that the presence of an

FIGURE 5–2
Observing discrete behaviors: event and duration recording

Example 1: Event Recording
Student: Susie
Behavior: Throwing paper airplanes in math class
Measurement System: Event recording (the number of times Susie throws paper airplanes in math class)
When Measured: Math period (9:00–9:30 a.m.) on 5 consecutive school days

Day 1	Day 2	Day 3	Day 4	Day 5
‖‖	‖‖‖	‖‖	‖‖	‖‖
Total = 4	Total = 5	Total = 3	Total = 3	Total = 4
Grand total for 5 days = 19 times				

Example 2: Duration Recording

Student: Philip

Behavior: Sleeping during class

Measurement System: Duration recording (the number of minutes Philip sleeps in class)

When Measured: Every occurrence during class time for 5 consecutive school days

Day 1	Day 2	Day 3	Day 4	Day 5
11:15 – 11:30 2:05 – 2:25	—	1:55 – 2:10	2:00 – 2:20	10:35 – 10:40
Total = 35	Total = 0	Total = 15	Total = 20	Total = 5
Grand total for 5 days = 75 minutes				

outsider will cause students to act differently. Although it takes some advance planning, teachers can collect observational data while they are teaching. Several techniques for facilitating teacher observations are presented in Table 5–3. Classroom observations may also be conducted by other professionals, instructional aides, volunteers, or even students, if the behavior is clearly stated, procedures well specified, and observers adequately trained.

Results of observations should be recorded on paper during the observational period or immediately thereafter to insure data are not forgotten. Although tally sheets such as those shown in Figures 5–2 and 5–3 are the most usual way of recording data, there is no set format. However, records forms should be designed to allow easy entry of information and encourage accurate reporting. Some teachers carry observational record forms on clipboards, and others enter data on index cards or in small notebooks. There is no set method; teachers should experiment until they find a comfortable strategy. Another option for recording data is audio- or videotaping. Although an observer is still required to listen to or view tapes to summarize results, taping is permanent.

If a behavior is missed or difficult to interpret, the tape can be replayed for clarification.

Select a data-reporting system. Observational data can be reported in statements such as "Susie threw paper airplanes in math class 19 times in a 5-day period." However, the more usual practice is to present results in a visual format such as a graph or chart. Graphs communicate large amounts of information quickly and facilitate the detection of trends and patterns. The most typical procedure is to plot observation results on a line graph where the x-axis, or abscissa, represents time and the y-axis, or ordinate, represents the behavior.

The simplest way to present frequency data is to plot the observed number of occurrences of the target behavior. The y-axis becomes a scale for the number of times the behavior is exhibited, and the x-axis depicts the different observational sessions. This procedure makes sense, however, only if all observational sessions are of equal duration and if each offers the student the same opportunity to perform the target behavior. If observations vary in duration, then it is more appropriate to report rate data than frequency data. For

FIGURE 5–3
Observing nondiscrete behaviors: interval recording

Momentary Time Sampling

Student: Fred

Behavior: Writing on assigned worksheets

Measurement System: Momentary time sampling (determination if the behavior is occurring at the end of the interval)

Length of Interval: 3 minutes

When Measured: Independent study time (10:30–11:00 a.m.)

Interval Ends		Interval Ends	
10:33	X	10:48	X
10:36	O	10:51	O
10:39	X	10:54	O
10:42	X	10:57	X
10:45	O	11:00	O

X = Fred was writing on a worksheet at the end of the interval.

O = Fred was not writing on a worksheet at the end of the interval.

Results: Fred wrote on assigned worksheets in 5 of the 10 time intervals sampled, or 50%.

TABLE 5–3
Classroom observation techniques for teachers

It is not necessary to stop teaching to observe: in fact, it is almost impossible to teach without observing! Try the following suggestions for integrating observations into your classroom procedures.

1. Carry a small card such as an index card; on it list the names of one or two target students and the problem behaviors you wish to observe (e.g., hitting, out-of-seat, talking to others). Place a tally mark on the card each time the behavior occurs. Start this system with one or two students and gradually expand as your skills improve.

2. Require students to record on their in-class work their starting and finishing time. This permits the calculation of rate as well as frequency and accuracy data. They can also note the times they leave and return to their desks; then the total amount of time in-seat each day or each period can be calculated.

3. Carry a stopwatch to measure the duration of behaviors. For example, start the watch each time Maynard leaves his seat, and stop it when he returns. Continue this (without resetting the watch) and time each occurrence of the behavior. At the end of the observation period, note the total amount of time recorded.

4. Have a seating chart in front of you as you talk to the class. Make a tally mark by a student's name for each target behavior, such as asking a question, talking out, answering a question correctly.

5. Recruit volunteers to observe in the classroom. Older students, parents, senior citizens, college students, or other students in the class can be excellent observers. If the teacher has clearly stated the behavior to be observed, a nonprofessional should be able to conduct the observation.

6. The teacher can use wrist counters (golf counters), supermarket counters, paper clips moved from one pocket to another, navy beans in a cup, and other inexpensive devices to count behaviors without interfering with the operation of the class.

Note. From *Teaching Special Students in the Mainstream* (2nd ed.) (p. 97) by R. B. Lewis and D. H. Doorlag, 1987, Columbus, OH: Merrill. Copyright 1987 by Merrill Publishing Company. Reprinted with permission.

example, if the teacher observed the student 10 minutes on Monday, 15 minutes on Tuesday, and 12 minutes on Wednesday, results could be compared across observational sessions by converting the *number of occurrences* of the behavior into the *number of occurrences per minute* (calculated by dividing the observed number of occurrences by the number of minutes in the observational session). If, on Monday, the behavior occurred 20 times during the 10-minute observation period, its rate of occurrence would be 2 times per minute. That rate could then be directly compared to the rate of occurrence on Tuesday (e.g., 1.3 times per minute), Wednesday, and so forth.

Likewise, if the behavior of interest is the number of times the student correctly answers questions in science class, the student may have the opportunity to respond to 15 questions one day but only 8 the next. In such situations, the *number of occurrences* of the target behavior should be converted into *percentage of occurrences*. This is calculated by dividing the observed number of occurrences by the number of opportunities for occurrence during the observational period; this quotient is then multiplied by 100. If, for example, the student answered 10 out of 15 questions

correctly, the percentage correct would be 67%. That percentage could then be directly compared to percentages achieved at other times when the student was provided with a different number of opportunities.

With duration data, it is possible to plot the actual number of seconds, minutes, or hours that the behavior persisted. However, if observational sessions vary in length, duration data should be converted to percentage data to express the *percentage of time* in which the behavior occurred. This is accomplished by dividing the observed duration of the behavior by the total length of the observation period and then multiplying the quotient by 100. Figure 5–4 presents examples of some of the ways that frequency and duration data for discrete behaviors can be depicted by graphing.

Graphs can also present results of observations of nondiscrete behaviors. Whatever technique is used to record data—whole-interval recording, partial-interval recording, or momentary time sampling—results can be plotted as the number of intervals in which the behavior occurred. If there is variation across observation sessions in the total number of time intervals observed, frequency data

FIGURE 5–4
Reporting observation results for discrete behaviors

Example 1: Event Recording, Graphing Actual Frequency of Occurrence

    Target Behavior: Throwing paper airplanes in math class

    When Measured: Math period (9:00–9:30 a.m.) on 5 consecutive school days

    [Observational sessions are equal in duration and offer equal opportunity for the behavior to occur.]

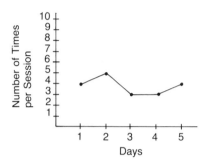

Example 2: Event Recording, Graphing Rate of Occurrence

    Target Behavior: Talking out in class

    When Measured: Independent work time for 5 consecutive school days

    [Observational sessions offer equal opportunity for the behavior to occur but are of unequal duration.]

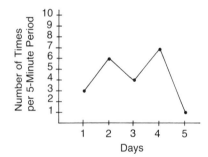

Example 3: Duration Recording, Graphing Percentage of Time

    Target Behavior: Tantruming

    When Measured: Grocery shopping for 5 consecutive shopping trips

    [Observational sessions offer equal opportunity for the behavior to occur but are of unequal duration.]

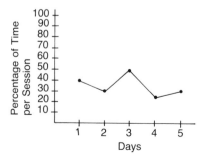

should be converted to percentage data. For example, Sara may stare out of the window in 13 of the 24 time intervals sampled on Monday and in 32 of the 55 time intervals sampled on Tuesday. Comparison becomes possible when these results are stated in terms of percentages: Sara's target behavior occurred in 54% of the time intervals sampled on Monday and in 58% of the time intervals sampled on Tuesday.

Carry out the observations.   The final step is to actually carry out the planned observations. As this occurs, the observer should be alert to potential problem areas. Is the target behavior stated with sufficient precision? Is the measurement system appropriate for this behavior? Do data-collection procedures provide an adequate sampling of the student's typical responses? If two or more observers are involved in the data collection, interobserver reliability becomes an important concern. As Chapter 3 discussed, the percentage of agreement among observers is easily calculated. However, if percentage of agreement falls below 80%, interobserver reliability is in question. It may be necessary to describe the target behavior with more precision or provide observers with additional training.

Work Sample Analysis

Teachers also employ observation to study students' products. The teacher obtains a sample of student work—a test, a written assignment, an essay, an art project, or even a tape recording of oral reading responses or a classroom discussion—and analyzes it to determine areas of successful performance and areas in which the student may require assistance. Work sample analysis is most often used to assess academic skills, but it could be applied to any area in which a product results. This technique is a special type of observation, and it is sometimes referred to as permanent product analysis or outcome recording (Alberto & Troutman, 1986; Cooper, 1981).

Response analysis.   This technique considers both the correct and incorrect responses of the student. Like other types of observation, it involves the steps of describing the behavior, selecting a measurement system, and deciding upon a data-reporting system. In response analysis, the teacher is usually interested in these dimensions

of human behavior: frequency, duration, rate, and percentage.

Figure 5–5 presents a work sample and several examples of the ways in which responses can be analyzed. Most typically, the teacher will select only one or two aspects of the student's behavior for study. The teacher is focusing on Louie's spelling in this response analysis. Although Louie's essay contains several errors, the response analysis shows that 78% of the words were spelled correctly.

Like other types of observation, response analysis should not be limited to a single sample of student behavior. Several work samples should be gathered over a period of time to determine the student's typical manner of responding. Results of response analyses can be graphed to facilitate interpretation.

Error analysis.   A second, more common approach to the study of student work samples is error analysis, which has a long history in special and remedial education. In the 1930s, Monroe suggested a procedure for the study of oral reading in which errors were categorized as additions, omissions, substitutions, repetitions, and so forth. Today error analysis techniques are available for most subject areas.

The goal is identification of error patterns. The work sample is scored, all errors are noted, and then an attempt is made to sort the errors into meaningful categories. For example, on a math worksheet of 15 single-digit multiplication problems, Casey made six errors that fell into the categories:

Error	Error category
$8 \times 6 = 54$	8 fact/6 fact
$9 \times 7 = 64$	9 fact/7 fact
$9 \times 8 = 81$	9 fact/8 fact
$8 \times 7 = 48$	8 fact/7 fact
$8 \times 8 = 62$	8 fact
$9 \times 9 = 72$	9 fact

Results are then summarized to locate patterns of errors.

Error category	Frequency of occurrence
9 fact	3
8 fact	4
7 fact	2
6 fact	1

FIGURE 5–5
Response analysis of a student work sample

Task: Students are asked to write a short description of a favorite animal.

Transcription of Louie's essay:
My favorit animal is giraf. They got a long nek and spots. They eat leafs and trees and are vary tall. They run fast in the jugle.

Time begun: 9:20 a.m.   Time finished: 9:35 a.m.

Response Analysis

Dimension	Analysis Results
Frequency	Number of words written = 27
	Number of words spelled correctly = 21
	Number of words spelled incorrectly = 6
Duration	Number of minutes required to write essay = 15

Rate

Rate of writing words
$$\frac{\text{Number of words written}}{\text{Number of minutes of writing}} = 1.8 \text{ words per minute}$$

Rate of spelling words correctly
$$\frac{\text{Number of words spelled correctly}}{\text{Number of minutes of writing}} = 1.4 \text{ words per minute}$$

Percentage

Percentage of words spelled correctly
$$\frac{\text{Number of words spelled correctly}}{\text{Number of words written}} \times 100 = 78\%$$

Percentage of words spelled incorrectly
$$\frac{\text{Number of words spelled incorrectly}}{\text{Number of words written}} \times 100 = 22\%$$

Casey has difficulty with some but not all multiplication facts. The problems Casey missed required knowledge of the 6, 7, 8, and 9 facts. All errors took place in problems with some number multiplied by either 8 or 9. Because of this error pattern, the teacher's next move would be to assess Casey's knowledge of 8 and 9 multiplication facts with a criterion-referenced test or informal inventory.

The key to a successful error analysis is identification of one or more patterns of errors. However, not all error patterns are as easily detected as the one in the previous example. Sometimes a pattern does not emerge; the student may make several different types of errors or mistakes may seem random. In many ways, error analysis is a subjective technique, relying upon judgments made by the teacher. He or she must decide which responses should be marked as errors, select the category system for classifying errors, and then determine if the student's mistakes fall into some sort of pattern. Also, there are no set criteria for judging the number or proportion of errors that constitute a possible problem. Thus, results of error analyses are best viewed as a guide for further assessment.

Task Analysis

Task analysis is an unobtrusive informal technique that focuses on curricular tasks rather than student performance. It is as much an instructional technique as an assessment strategy, and its purpose is to break down complex tasks into teachable subcomponents. Howell, Kaplan, and O'Connell (1979) define task analysis as "the process of isolating, sequencing, and describing all the essential components of a task" (p. 81).

The major role of task analysis in the instructional process is to assist in curricular design and specification of the instructional sequence. An instructional goal is selected and analyzed to determine the specific subskills that will support its accomplishment. Then the subskills or task subcomponents are arranged for instruction in an order that facilitates their acquisition. This is done in three steps.

1. Identify a specific instructional goal or objective.
2. Analyze the instructional objective into its essential component parts (i.e., the movements, actions, or responses that, when taken cumulatively, constitute the instructional objective).
3. Determine the entry level of the skill and specify the prerequisite skills (in other words, state at what point the particular skill sequence begins). (Berdine & Cegelka, 1980, p. 160)

There are several ways to approach the problem of analyzing a task into its subcomponents: analysis by temporal order, by developmental sequence, by difficulty level, and by structural task analysis. The method selected is determined to some extent by the nature of the task under consideration.

Analysis by temporal order. Some tasks follow a temporal order. In washing one's hands, the tap water must be turned on *before* hands can be rinsed. The teacher may choose to teach such tasks in the order they are performed or, in some cases, may proceed in a backward order by beginning with the last subtask in the sequence. This is called backward chaining; it is most useful when the task is difficult for the learner. By beginning at the end, backward chaining assures successful task completion in the early stages of learning.

Analysis by developmental sequence. Task subcomponents can also be ordered by developmental sequence. Affleck, Lowenbraun, and Archer (1980) explain a developmental sequence as "one in which a gradual progression of steps is built on previously acquired skills" (p. 87). One of the best examples is the standard curriculum for the arithmetic operations of addition, subtrac-

tion, multiplication, and division. There is a definite hierarchy of subskills, and difficulty with a later skill may be due to failure to master an earlier, prerequisite skill.

Analysis by difficulty level. Some tasks have neither a definite temporal order nor a natural developmental sequence; however, they can be analyzed according to the ease with which their subcomponents can be acquired. A good example is the skill of writing letters in manuscript. This skill can be task analyzed by dividing lowercase letters into several clusters, beginning with the least difficult (Affleck et al., 1980, p. 90):

Straight line letters	l t i
Straight line and slant letters	v x w y z
Circle and curve letters	o c s
Circle and line letters	a b e p g d q
Curve and line letters	j h m k n f r u

In assessment, task analysis serves a somewhat different purpose than in instruction. It is used with tasks where a student experiences difficulty. Troublesome tasks are analyzed, and the student's ability to perform each subtask or task subcomponent is assessed to locate the source of the difficulty. For example, if writing sentences with correct capitalization and punctuation appears to be a problem for Frank, the teacher could task analyze this skill and then assess Frank's ability to perform each step in the developmental sequence. A sample skill hierarchy for capitalization and punctuation appears in Table 5–4. To utilize this sequence for assessment, informal measures such as criterion-referenced tests are designed for each step of interest. With Frank, the teacher could begin by assessing the skills listed for third graders, and then work backward through the sequence to identify prerequisite skills not yet mastered. Instruction would then focus on mastery of these skills.

There are several strategies for conducting a task analysis in assessment. If the task in question is part of the standard curriculum, the teacher may have access to curriculum guides, scope and sequence charts, or published materials that describe the task's subcomponents. Otherwise, it is up to the teacher to determine the important task components. This is usually easiest for tasks with a definite temporal sequence. The teacher can perform the task and note each step that is taken.

TABLE 5–4
Hierarchy for capitalization and punctuation skills

Grade 1

Copies sentences correctly.
Capitalizes first word of a sentence.
Capitalizes first letter of a proper name.
Uses period at the end of a sentence.
Uses question mark after a written question.
Uses period after numbers in a list.

Grade 2

Capitalizes titles of compositions.
Capitalizes proper names used in written compositions.
Uses comma after salutation and after closing of a friendly letter.
Uses comma between day of the month and the year.
Uses comma between names of city and state.

Grade 3

Capitalizes the names of months, days, holidays; first word in a line of verse; titles of books, stories, poems; salutation and closing of letters and notes; and names of special places.
Begins to apply correct punctuation for abbreviations, initials, contractions, items in a list, quotations, questions, and exclamations.
Uses proper indention for paragraphs.

Note. From *Teaching Students with Learning Problems* (3rd ed.) (pp. 563–564) by C. D. Mercer and A. R. Mercer, 1989. Columbus, OH: Merrill. Copyright 1989 by Merrill Publishing Company. Reprinted by permission.

According to Berdine and Cegelka (1980), ''To check the adequacy of the breakdown, the teacher should perform the task a second time following the steps outlined, adding or deleting steps as necessary'' (p. 164).

It is also important to determine if the task can be performed in more than one acceptable sequence. For example, tying one's shoe is a task for which there are several successful sequences. Thus, the teacher should observe other adults and, if possible, students as they complete the task.

With tasks that do not follow a temporal order, subcomponents and their sequence must be determined by logic. One method is to list all the subtasks or subcomponents that appear to be involved in the task. These are then arranged in order, ranging from the least difficult to the most difficult, or by utility, ranging from the most necessary for task completion to the least necessary. Obviously, such a task analysis is somewhat subjective, and two teachers generating a subtask sequence for the same skill might disagree. However, flaws in the task analysis usually become apparent in the assessment phase. If the student can perform each subtask but not the task itself, it is likely that an important subtask has been omitted. If the student can perform what are considered to be difficult subcomponents but cannot perform easier ones, then the specified sequence is incorrect, at least for that student.

Structural task analysis. Another approach that may provide instructional information is an analysis of task demands (McLoughlin & Kershman, 1978). Rather than specifying task subcomponents and sequence, the goal is to describe the task in terms of the demands placed upon the learner. This is sometimes called a structural task analysis and it includes consideration of the following task characteristics:

☐ *Task directions.* The directions for completing the task may be presented verbally or in writing. They vary in number and can be either clear and concise or complex and confusing.

☐ *Presentation mode.* This refers to the way in which information necessary for task completion is provided to the learner; for example, the student may be required to listen to, read, or look at one or more sources of information.

☐ *Response mode.* This is the method used by the student in performing the task. The student may need to respond orally or make some sort of written response such as writing numbers, letters, words, sentences, or paragraphs.

☐ *Quantity requirements.* This task dimension is concerned with the number of responses the student must produce: the number of questions to answer, problems to solve, sentences to write, and so on.

☐ *Time requirements.* Some tasks are timed, and their successful completion depends on the speed of the learner.

☐ *Accuracy requirements.* These criteria specify the accuracy standards for successful task performance. For example, a teacher might require a minimum of 80% accuracy on in-class assignments.

Structural analysis of a classroom task helps identify specific instructional expectations. When these expectations are known, one can consider ways to modify the task demands to facilitate successful performance. In assessment, diagnostic probes are used to evaluate the effects of changing task demands systematically, and this strategy is described in the next section.

CURRICULUM-BASED MEASURES

Many types of informal assessments are curriculum-based. These measures and strategies assess school skills directly. Their content is determined by the standard school curriculum or the special course of study designed to meet the needs of a particular exceptional student. They are obtrusive, because they require that a test task or a series of tasks be added to the instructional environment. However, curriculum-based measures are used often in classrooms, and their results relate directly to instructional decision making.

A growing body of research supports the usefulness of curriculum-based measurement for monitoring student progress and modifying instruction based on student performance (Deno, 1985; Deno & Fuchs, 1988; Deno, Marston, & Mirkin, 1982; Deno, Mirkin, & Chiang, 1982; Deno, Mirkin, Lowry, & Kuehnle, 1980; Fuchs, 1986; Fuchs, Deno, & Mirkin 1984). For curriculum-based measurement to be effective, the behaviors of interest should be assessed directly, and measurement should be frequent so that needed instructional changes can be made quickly. Deno and his colleagues recommend the use of brief probes of critical target behaviors such as reading words aloud, writing numbers, and writing words. For example, to assess oral reading proficiency, students can read aloud from a reading or content area textbook for one minute while the teacher tabulates the number of words read correctly. This measure is administered frequently (e.g., twice weekly), data are graphed, and the results are analyzed to determine whether the student's progress is adequate.

Curriculum-based measurement can use any type of informal assessment strategy, even observation. However, the most common techniques are informal inventories, classroom quizzes, and criterion-referenced tests. The next sections describe these measures as well as diagnostic probes and diagnostic teaching. Information about the use of curriculum-based measurement for the identification of students with school performance problems is presented in Chapter 7.

Inventories and Classroom Quizzes

Informal inventories and quizzes assess a student's performance in a school skill area. Their standard of comparison is the curriculum. For example, the teacher may wonder about a new student's knowledge of geography or of punctuation and capitalization rules; another teacher might want to find out if the class has learned the American history material presented over the last few weeks. Inventories and quizzes answer these types of questions about present levels of functioning.

Inventories and quizzes are screening devices that assess selected portions of curricular areas; they are not intended to measure mastery of every fact, concept, and subskill in a particular domain. Because they assess only representative skills, they can sample a greater number of skill areas. For example, an arithmetic inventory might present some, but not all, addition fact problems, some subtraction facts, and some multiplication and division facts. The intent is to identify the general level of student functioning within the curricular area. However, more precise measures such as criterion-referenced tests are needed to find out about student performance in relation to all skills within this domain.

A major difference between informal inventories and classroom quizzes is the purpose for which they are used. Quizzes—or, as they are sometimes called, tests or examinations—typically assess whether students have acquired some body of knowledge or skills taught by the teacher. They are progress measures, and their results are used to evaluate the effects of teaching and learning. Inventories are more of a preteaching assessment tool. They are usually administered before instruction to determine where a need for instruction exists. Also, inventories generally cover a larger segment of the curriculum than quizzes. A spelling inventory might contain selected words from several levels of difficulty (grade 1, grade 2, and so forth), whereas a classroom spelling quiz would include only those words for which instruction had been provided.

Informal inventories.   Inventories may be created by the teacher or purchased from test publishers. Inventories are commercially available for many subject areas, but the most common is the informal reading inventory. Teachers should understand the steps involved in designing an inventory so they can create such a measure if an appropriate one is not readily available. To design an informal inventory, the teacher should

1. Determine the curriculum area in which the student is to be assessed.
2. Isolate a portion of the curriculum appropriate for the student's age, grade, and skill level.
3. Analyze the curriculum into testable and teachable segments. Like in task analysis, the curriculum may be broken down into sequential steps, developmental steps, or difficulty levels.
4. Prepare test items for each segment of the curriculum, emphasizing the most important aspects of each segment.
5. If necessary, reduce the number of test items so the inventory is of manageable length.
6. Sequence the test items from easiest to most difficult or in random order if the student is expected to answer all items.

Figure 5–6 presents an example of such an informal inventory. The content area is handwriting, and it is designed for elementary grade students. The test items are representative of the content domain, but only include selected subskills. In designing this inventory, the teacher analyzed the skill of handwriting into developmental steps: students learn to print their name, then print the lowercase and capital letters, and so forth. Be-

cause students usually acquire these skills in this order, the test items are arranged in the developmental sequence to assure successful performance for students who have not yet mastered more advanced skills. However, test items are sometimes arranged in random order. If students are expected to answer all test items, random order reduces the possibility that clues from one item will help them answer others.

Because informal inventories do not typically include performance standards, students do not pass or fail these measures. Instead, the goal is to estimate the students' current levels of performance and identify areas in the curriculum requiring further assessment. Teachers should be cautious about basing instruction solely on the results of informal inventories. First, the quality of an inventory, like most informal measures, is usually unknown. With no information about reliability and validity, it is difficult to judge a measure's accuracy. However, Turnbull, Strickland, and Brantley (1982) maintain that informal inventories ''can be constructed so that they exhibit content validity—that is, the test items included are specifically designed to measure the objectives of the curriculum'' (p. 68). Second, because inventories do not usually contain standards for acceptable performance, the professional must decide how many errors constitute a potential skill weakness. If a student misses one or two items out of several of a particular type, is this a cause for concern? With informal inventories, the teacher is responsible for making that judgment.

If the teacher determines that inventory results indicate a potential problem area, the next step is to assess the skill area more closely. For example, if a student completes an addition skills inventory and performs successfully until encountering regrouping problems, the teacher should find out more about the student's skills in regrouping. The teacher could construct a criterion-referenced test to assess these skills and, if results indicated they were not yet mastered, begin instruction at this point in the curriculum.

Classroom quizzes.   Classroom quizzes are usually designed by teachers, although sample quiz items may be available in teachers' manuals for textbooks or instructional materials. The first step in the development of a quiz is to identify the content of the instructional unit to be assessed.

FIGURE 5–6
Informal inventory of handwriting skills

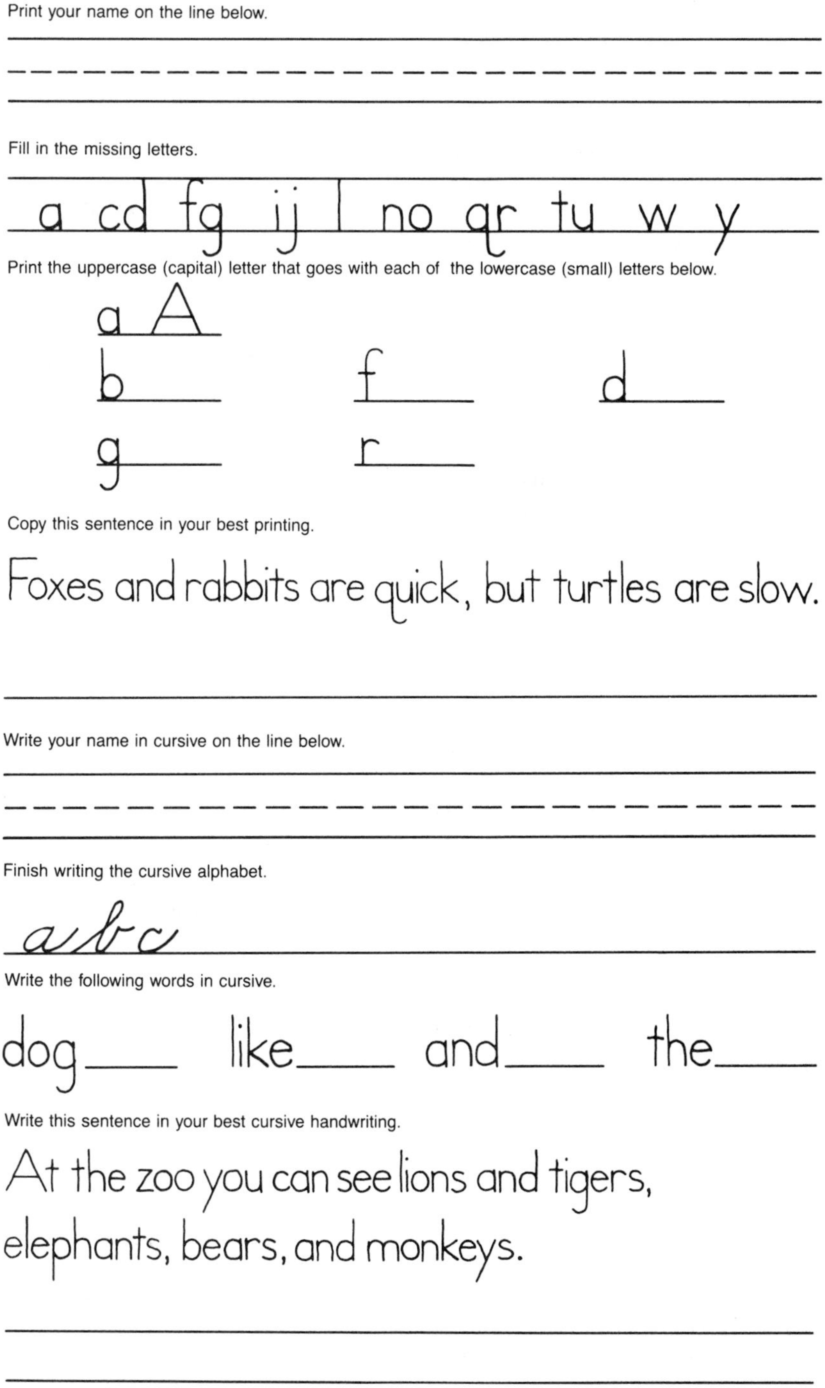

Print your name on the line below.

_____
– –
_____

Fill in the missing letters.

_a_ cd fg ij l no qr tu w y

Print the uppercase (capital) letter that goes with each of the lowercase (small) letters below.

a A

b _____   f _____   d _____

g _____   r _____

Copy this sentence in your best printing.

Foxes and rabbits are quick, but turtles are slow.

_____

Write your name in cursive on the line below.

_____
– –

Finish writing the cursive alphabet.

abc _____

Write the following words in cursive.

dog_____   like_____   and_____   the_____

Write this sentence in your best cursive handwriting.

At the zoo you can see lions and tigers,
elephants, bears, and monkeys.

_____

Note. From *Teaching Special Students in the Mainstream* (2nd ed.) (p. 77) by R. B. Lewis and D. H. Doorlag, 1987, Columbus, OH: Merrill. Copyright 1987 by Merrill Publishing Company. Reprinted with permission.

Because instruction has already taken place, instructional objectives should be available, and these are used to generate quiz items. If time constraints permit, each important objective should be represented by at least one quiz item.

The next step is to determine the type or types of items to be included in the quiz. Objective items are those for which the correct answer is readily identifiable (e.g., true–false and multiple-choice questions). Objective items are easily scored but time-consuming to construct. In contrast, more subjective items such as essay questions require less time to construct but are more difficult to score because the teacher must exercise judgment in evaluating student responses. In selecting the type of items to prepare, the teacher must also consider the nature of the subject matter to be assessed. Some curriculum areas, particularly those with a body of factual information, lend themselves well to measurement by objective questions. Other areas are better assessed with essays and other types of more subjective questions. The most common types of quiz items used by classroom teachers are

- □ *True–false*—In this type of question, the student determines whether a statement is true or false.
- □ *Multiple-choice*—The student selects a word, phrase, or sentence that best completes a partial statement or answers a question.
- □ *Matching*—The student selects from one set of words, phrases, or sentences the one that best fits each of the words, phrases, or sentences in another set.
- □ *Completion*—The student finishes an incomplete sentence by furnishing a word or phrase.
- □ *Short answer*—The student provides a brief response such as a definition, a list of steps or examples, or a short description.
- □ *Problem*—The student solves some sort of mathematical problem.
- □ *Essay*—The student provides a prose response, usually of some length.

In designing quizzes for special learners, it is also important to consider academic skill demands. Students must be able to read quiz questions; a test is not an adequate measure of a curriculum area if a student fails because he or she could not decode the questions. For students with writing skill problems, objective items requiring a response

of only one letter or number would be less difficult than, for example, an essay exam. Another concern is the physical appearance of the quiz. The print should be clear and readable, and pages should be uncluttered.

Classroom quizzes can be power tests or speed tests. With power tests, there are no time limits because the aim is to determine the extent of the student's knowledge in the curriculum area under assessment. In general, classroom quizzes should be power measures unless the instructional goal requires that students perform both accurately and quickly. However, with skills subjects, particularly basic academic skills, speed often is important.

The reliability of classroom quizzes can be determined by means of the Kuder-Richardson 21 formula, an estimate of interitem consistency. The teacher needs to know three things to use this formula: K, the number of items in the test; $\overline{X}$, the mean of the scores; and σ^2, the variance of the scores (computed by squaring the standard deviation). These values are used in the following formula to yield r, the total test reliability.

$$r = \frac{K\sigma^2 - \overline{X}(K - \overline{X})}{\sigma^2(K - 1)}$$

It is also possible to gather information about characteristics of specific quiz items. One concern is the difficulty of the item, and this is determined by calculating the proportion of students who respond to the item correctly. To do this, simply divide the number of students with correct responses by the total number of students attempting the item. Brown (1981) recommends separating the class into two groups of students, those who score in the upper half on the quiz and those who score in the lower half, in order to use the following formula:

$$\text{Item difficulty} = \frac{\substack{\text{Proportion correct} \\ \text{(upper half)}} + \substack{\text{Proportion correct} \\ \text{(lower half)}}}{2}$$

The proportion correct for the upper half of the class is determined by dividing the number of upper-half students who answered the item correctly by the total number of students in the upper half; the proportion for the lower half is determined in the same way. This allows the teacher to compare the difficulty levels for these two segments of the class. Brown (1981) suggests that a difficulty level of .60 to .75 (60% to 75% of students responding correctly) is appropriate for most classroom exam items.

The discrimination index of a quiz item is a measure of how well the item differentiates between students who score well and those who do not. To determine the discrimination index, use this formula (Brown, 1981):

Item discrimination = Proportion correct − Proportion correct
                     (upper half)   (lower half)

According to Gay (1985), when an item's discrimination index is greater than .30, that item is doing an adequate job of distinguishing between upper- and lower-half students. If the discrimination index is less than .30, the item should be reexamined and possibly rewritten. The index can be a negative number. For example, if 50% of the upper-half students and 80% of the lower-half students answer a quiz question correctly, the item's discrimination item would be −.30, a sign that the question is a misleading one. There are some situations in which a teacher would not want an item to discriminate. For example, the instructional goal might be that all students will tell time to the nearest minute with 100% accuracy.

Some objective items offer students a choice of responses. For instance, with multiple-choice questions, the student must select one response from the several possible answers presented. With this type of item, it is important to look at the wrong answers, sometimes called distractors. To conduct this type of analysis, the teacher records the number of students who select each of the possible responses. If a particular distractor is chosen by a large proportion of students, this may signal a poorly written item or an area of misunderstanding that merits further explanation or instruction.

Criterion-Referenced Tests

Like informal inventories and classroom quizzes, criterion-referenced tests (CRTs) compare a student's performance to the goals of the curriculum rather than to the performance of a norm group. However, CRTs typically sample more restricted curricular domains than inventories. An inventory might reveal a possible problem in decoding short

vowels; a criterion-referenced test would identify the short vowels the student could read and those he or she could not. Another important feature of CRTs is their emphasis on mastery. These measures are scored as pass or fail: either the student has mastered the skill under study or the student has not. This has direct implications for instruction; unmastered skills or their prerequisites may become the next curricular goal.

Placement tests are quite similar to criterion-referenced tests. Often furnished as part of an instructional material or textbook series, placement tests identify the point within the material where instruction should begin. Placement tests assess mastery of the content presented by the text or material. When the student achieves with a specified level of accuracy, it is assumed the content has been mastered. When he or she drops below this specified mastery level, the starting point for instruction is identified. Competency tests, too, are much like CRTs. A common school use of competency tests is to determine whether students have met literacy standards for high school graduation. Again, specific skills are assessed and performance is compared to a prespecified level of mastery.

Criterion-referenced tests, placement tests, and competency tests are all commercially available. CRTs are easy to construct, and teachers may wish to design their own to match their instructional goals. Usually, however, teachers use the placement tests that accompany commercial materials, although it is certainly possible to adapt or even construct such measures. Because competency tests are used with large groups of students, perhaps even an entire school population, they are typically developed at the school or district level or purchased from a test publisher.

CRTs can be used to assess any behavior for which an instructional objective can be specified. They are easy to design, but their construction does require an investment of time and energy. The major steps are

1. Decide what specific questions you want answered about a student's behavior. What ability (i.e., skill and knowledge) do you want to test?
2. Write a performance objective which describes how you are going to test the student. It should include (a) what the student must do (i.e., what behavior must be engaged in); (b) under what con-

ditions the student will engage in this behavior; and (c) how well the student must perform in order to pass the test.

3. Use the performance objective to help you construct (i.e., write) your CRT. All of the necessary components of a CRT may be found in your performance objective. These components are (a) the directions for administration and scoring, (b) the criterion for passing the test, and (c) the materials and/or test items necessary. (Howell et al., 1979, pp. 96–97)

Questions about student performance can be generated from many sources. After observing a student in the classroom for a few days, the teacher can easily come up with several! Standardized test results may also suggest areas for further assessment. Other valuable sources are the results of informal measures such as inventories and work sample analyses.

Once an assessment question is specified, an instructional objective is selected. If the question concerns a standard area of the curriculum, it is likely that the appropriate instructional objective will be available in a curriculum guide or a similar source. If necessary, the teacher can construct the objective by specifying three things: the desired student behavior, stated in observable terms; the conditions under which the behavior should occur; and the criterion for acceptable performance of the behavior (Mager, 1975). Just as a target behavior must be pinpointed before it can be observed, the behavior to be assessed with a CRT must be clearly specified. For example, "knowing the alphabet" is too imprecise. It could be interpreted in many ways—reciting the alphabet, writing it in manuscript or cursive, saying the names or sounds of the letters, and so forth. If the teacher is interested in whether the student can recite the alphabet, the objective can begin as

Say the names of the letters of the alphabet in order from memory.

The teacher then specifies the conditions under which the behavior should occur. What directions will the teacher provide? What materials will be available to the student? What constraints will be imposed upon performance? For the alphabet recitation example, the teacher decided to give one simple direction ("Say the alphabet"). No time constraints were imposed and no materials were necessary. The objective is

When told by the teacher to "say the alphabet," the student will say the names of the letters of the alphabet in order from memory.

The last step is to set the criterion for acceptable performance. How well must the student perform to demonstrate mastery of the skill? Are any errors allowed? If so, how many or what percentage? Howell et al. (1979) suggest establishing criteria by means of "expert" populations. They recommend that the teacher identify individuals who possess the skill being assessed by the CRT, then administer the CRT to this group and use their minimum level of performance as the mastery standard. This may not be necessary with some skills if the teacher believes the skill should be performed without errors. If this is the case in alphabet recitation, the objective becomes

When told by the teacher to "say the alphabet," the student will say the names of the letters of the alphabet in order from memory with no errors.

The criterion-referenced test in Figure 5–7 measures this instructional objective. The information at the beginning of the test is derived from the objective. The student behavior becomes the test task; the conditions under which the behavior is to be performed provide information about needed materials and directions, both for the student and the tester; and the objective's criterion for acceptable performance becomes the criterion for passing the CRT. Additional scoring standards may also be necessary. In this case, the teacher decided to allow mispronunciations of letter names if they were intelligible. On the score sheet, the teacher records identifying information about the student and the test and then writes down the student's responses.

If a student passes a CRT, the teacher assumes that the student has mastered the objective and an assessment can progress to the next instructional step. If a student does not pass, the teacher moves backwards through the curricular sequence and assesses a prerequisite skill. Instructional planning can begin once the skills the student has mastered are established.

However, the teacher must exercise some caution in interpreting results. First, CRTs tell only what a student can or cannot do; because they

FIGURE 5–7
Criterion-referenced test and score sheet

Criterion-Referenced Test

Task: Say the alphabet in order from memory.

Materials: Score sheet

Directions (to student): "Say the alphabet."

Directions (to tester): Record student responses verbatim. Do not allow the student to look at the score sheet.

Scoring: Count correct if the student says each of the 26 letters of the alphabet in the correct order. Count correct if letter names are intelligible even if not articulated perfectly. Count as incorrect if a letter name is omitted, added, or said out of order.

Criterion for Acceptable Performance: 100% accuracy

Score Sheet

Skill: Knowledge of the alphabet

Task: Say names of letters of the alphabet in order from memory

Student _____ Date _____

Age _____ Grade _____ Tester _____

Student responses (record verbatim):

_____

_____

_____

_____

---

are not normed, they do not tell what a particular student is expected to do. If a student fails a CRT on shoe tying, the instructional implication appears to be to teach this skill. Although it would likely be appropriate for a young school-aged child, it would not be for a toddler. Other factors to be considered before translating CRT results into instructional action are the age of the student, the age-appropriateness of the skill, and the priority of the skill in relation to other possible instructional goals.

Another caveat common to all informal measures is the lack of information about reliability and validity. Teachers can improve the CRTs they construct by specifying standard procedures for test administration and scoring and by establishing mastery levels empirically rather than arbitrarily; procedures are also available for determining reliability and validity of CRTs (Howell et al., 1979).

Diagnostic Probes and Diagnostic Teaching

Diagnostic probes and diagnostic teaching involve the systematic manipulation of instructional con-

ditions to determine the most appropriate strategy for teaching a particular skill to a student. The difference between these two procedures relates to the thoroughness with which they evaluate instructional alternatives. Diagnostic probes are typically brief, one-time measures of a single instructional option. Diagnostic teaching, on the other hand, takes place over an extended time period to investigate fully the differential effects of various instructional interventions.

Diagnostic probes. Diagnostic probes are used to discover whether changing some aspect of a classroom task will have a positive effect upon student performance. For example, if the history teacher observes that a student is having difficulty with the daily quizzes on reading assignments, the teacher could design one or several diagnostic probes to investigate the relationship between the demands of the task and the student's ability to perform. The daily quiz could be modified in a number of ways, depending upon the type of difficulty the student is experiencing. For instance, if the student answers the first few questions but does not complete the quiz, the amount of time allowed for this task could be increased or the number of questions reduced. Or if the student's writing skills appear to interfere with performance, the student could be permitted to respond orally or to tape record answers.

The general procedures for the design of a diagnostic probe are

1. The student's performance is assessed under the standard instructional condition.
2. Some aspect of the task or of the instructional conditions that relate to the task is modified.
3. The student's performance is assessed under the modified condition and compared with previous performance.

This sequence of steps usually takes place within one instructional session. The teacher observes a possible performance problem and identifies a possible solution. Data are collected before the modification is made to establish the student's current performance level and again after the modification is in place. If necessary, a series of diagnostic probes are devised until the teacher has sufficient information to design a diagnostic teaching sequence.

The teacher can make several types of changes to improve student performance. Two major types of modifications relate to task characteristics and the instructional strategies used to teach the task. Structural task analysis is a useful way to analyze task characteristics. Among the factors to be considered are the difficulty level of the task; the conditions under which the student is expected to perform; the directions provided for task completion; presentation and response modes; and requirements for quantity, speed, and accuracy.

Table 5–5 summarizes several general methods of adapting instruction. Included are strategies for modifying the task itself and for changing the instructional conditions that relate to task performance. These suggestions are by no means exhaustive, but they do provide some direction for the development of diagnostic probes. Dimensions of instruction to consider are the methods used to present new information to students (lecture, discussion, demonstration, and so forth), the number and type of practice opportunities available, how feedback is provided, the consequences for successful performance, the instructional materials, and the pace of instruction.

Another type of instructional change involves modifying the strategies that the student uses to approach the classroom task. It is the student's behavior that is altered, not a condition of instruction. The first step is observation of the student's interaction with the task. The methods the student employs in task performance are analyzed, and ineffective strategies are identified. Then the teacher attempts to modify the student's strategy or substitute another, more effective strategy. For example, if a student's handwriting is poor and he or she grips the pencil awkwardly, the teacher may attempt to change the student's hand position. Or if a student studies new biology terms by staring at a page in the text, the teacher may demonstrate an alternative technique that requires active rehearsal.

Diagnostic probes are most useful for gathering preliminary information about the possible effectiveness of an instructional modification. Only in rare instances do probes yield sufficient information to justify making a change in the instructional environment. Probes provide hypotheses about modifications that may make a difference in student performance. These hypotheses can then be tested through diagnostic teaching.

Diagnostic teaching. Diagnostic teaching systematically evaluates the relative effectiveness of two or more instructional techniques. It assists the teacher in deciding upon an instructional strategy for a particular student or group. The teacher carefully monitors student performance while presenting instruction first in one manner and then in another. Assessment data collected under each instructional condition are then compared to determine the more effective teaching technique.

For example, if Yvonne is having difficulty learning multiplication facts, the teacher might want to try some different types of practice activities for this skill. First, the teacher would identify the current instructional condition and assess the student's performance under this condition. In Yvonne's case, worksheets are the current practice activity; over a one-week period, Yvonne has received scores ranging from 30% correct to 55% correct. Next, the teacher decides upon a new instructional strategy. This decision may be based on the results of a series of diagnostic probes. For multiplication facts, two alternatives to worksheets are flash card drills and computer-based drill and

TABLE 5–5
Designing diagnostic probes

Instructional Dimension	Possible Modifications
Task Characteristics	
The difficulty level of the task	Divide the task into component subtasks for the student to perform separately; or, substitute an easier, prerequisite task
The conditions under which the task is performed	Alter the conditions by allowing the use of aids (e.g., calculators for mathematics tasks) or by providing cues or prompts
Task directions	Simplify and reduce the number of directions; provide oral as well as written directions
Presentation mode	Change the presentation mode to one that takes advantage of the student's strengths (e.g., change to oral presentation for students with reading problems); or, present information in more than one way
Response mode	Change the response mode to one that takes advantage of the student's strengths (e.g., change to oral responses for students with poor writing skills)
Quantity requirement	Reduce the number of required student responses
Speed requirement	Increase the amount of time allowed for task performance; or, remove time limits altogether
Accuracy requirement	Decrease the standards for successful task performance
Instructional Procedures	
Presentation of new information to students	Change the method of instruction to a more direct approach (e.g., use lecture or demonstration rather than discussion or discovery); or, explain new information in several different ways; or, increase the number of times new information is presented
Practice opportunities for students	Increase the number of practice opportunities provided to students; improve the quantity and quality of feedback students receive during practice; alter the types of practice activities to relate more directly to target behaviors
Feedback to students on task performance	Give feedback more often; relate feedback not only to the accuracy of the response but also to the specific aspect of the task that the student performed correctly or incorrectly
Consequences to students for successful performance	Make the consequences for success more attractive
Learning materials	Revise or modify learning materials (e.g., texts, workbooks, worksheets) to a simpler level; or, substitute alternate materials
Pace of instruction	Slow the pace of instruction so less information is presented and practiced at one time
Providing students with alternate strategies for task performance	Change the way in which students approach the task by modifying current strategies; or, introduce new, more effective strategies

Note. From *Teaching Special Students in the Mainstream* (2nd ed.) (pp. 79–83) by R. B. Lewis and D. H. Doorlag, 1987, Columbus, OH: Merrill. Copyright 1987 by Merrill Publishing Company. Adapted by permission.

practice programs. These techniques allow practice of the skill while providing the learner with immediate feedback about the accuracy of her responses. The teacher then implements one of the new instructional approaches for a few days and continues to collect student performance data, usually on a daily basis.

The steps in diagnostic teaching are

1. Identify the current instructional condition, the baseline condition.
2. Select or design an informal assessment tool to monitor student performance.
3. Assess the student's performance under the current instructional condition. Daily data collection for a one-week period usually provides an adequate picture of current performance.
4. Select one or more new instructional strategies to evaluate.
5. Implement the first new instructional strategy for a brief period (e.g., one week). This is the first intervention phase.
6. Continue to regularly assess the student's performance.
7. Implement a second new instructional strategy, if desired.
8. Continue to regularly assess the student's performance.

9. Plot performance data for the baseline condition and the intervention phases on a graph. Compare performance across the conditions.

Only one thing at a time should be changed in diagnostic teaching. The baseline condition and the treatment phase should differ on only one important instructional variable. The instructional factor that produced the change in student behavior can then be identified. For instance, if the teacher changes the practice activity and sees an increase in student accuracy, the change in performance can be linked to the change in the practice activity. However, if several changes occur (a new practice activity is introduced, a peer tutor replaces the teacher, and the amount of instructional time is doubled), the teacher cannot attribute improved student performance to any single modification.

The graph in Figure 5–8 presents the results of the intervention with Yvonne, the girl having difficulty learning multiplication facts. Yvonne's teacher collected daily data on the percentage of questions Yvonne answered correctly. As can be seen from the graph, the new treatment, flash card drill, appears to be a more effective instructional strategy than worksheet activities for Yvonne.

FIGURE 5–8
Diagnostic teaching results

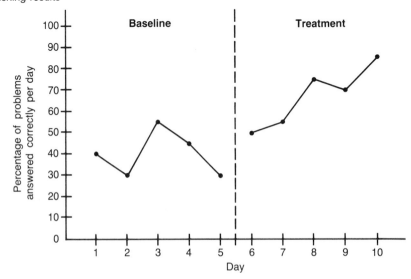

Diagnostic teaching is really classroom research. Because one student is studied, it is single-subject research. Diagnostic teaching can be approached in more than one way. The method just discussed is the simplest design: baseline followed by treatment (or AB). Although the AB design provides important information for classroom decision making, its major limitation is that some factor other than the treatment could be responsible for a change in student behavior. One way to overcome this limitation is by means of a reversal design; baseline followed by treatment, followed by a return to baseline conditions (ABA). Other methods such as multiple baseline designs are beyond the scope of this book. See Cooper et al. (1987) for a description of available methodologies.

PROCEDURES USING INFORMANTS

Checklists, rating scales, questionnaires, and interviews are informal assessment procedures that make use of the expertise of an informant—a teacher, parent, employer, the student, or peers. These measures are obtrusive and indirect; they access information about nonobservables such as values and opinions or past events. Informants are used in assessment for three purposes. First, they can provide a historical perspective. For example, the student's parents are likely the best source of information about acquisition of developmental milestones in the preschool years. Second, informants who have had extensive experience with the student can summarize their observations and offer opinions, judgments, and interpretations. A teacher, for instance, can provide information about the student's current levels of performance in each of the subject areas taught in the classroom. Third, informants can comment upon less observable concerns such as attitudes, values, and perceptions. Students can describe their attitudes toward school, for example.

However, there is always the danger of inaccuracy when information is gathered indirectly. Informants may not recall past events with clarity; their opinions may be based upon incomplete information. They may even report less than the truth. Information gathered from informants is subjective and should be interpreted as such. If this is kept in mind, informants can be a valuable

addition to the assessment process. In fact, for some assessment questions, informants may be the only source of information available to the teacher.

The measures used to gather data from informants are very flexible. They can be designed to assess almost any domain: health and developmental history, educational background, current educational status, social and interpersonal skills, and attitudes toward school subjects. Such measures can be very structured, prompting the informant for every specific response. Or they can be quite open-ended, providing the informant with general questions that he or she can choose how to answer.

Checklists and Rating Scales

Checklists and rating scales are structured assessments. Specific questions are posed, and the informant selects a response rather than generating one. These measures are usually administered in written form to adult informants, although they can be presented orally to young children.

With checklists, the informant is provided with a list of descriptions, and the task is simply to check each description that applies to the student under assessment. The teacher, parent, or other informant reads each description, making a check beside each that is accurate. Checklists can be used for a variety of purposes, and Figure 5–9 presents two examples. The first is a curriculum checklist for teachers. The teacher considers each educational objective, then marks those attained by the student. The skills listed on this measure could be assessed directly if the teacher had insufficient information. In the second example, parents read descriptions of problem behaviors and circle those that apply to their child. Because this measure is written in less behavioral terms, it requires more interpretation. The parent must decide upon the meaning of statements such as "is very distracted" before determining if the description is accurate.

Rating scales require more from informants than a yes–no response. A description or statement is presented, and informants express their agreement with the description by selecting one of a series of ratings. Among the most common rating instruments are Likert-type scales (Likert, 1932), as noted in Chapter 3. The informant

FIGURE 5–9
Examples of checklists

CURRICULUM CHECKLIST: Social Studies—Primary[a]

Understanding One's Heritage
    1. Associates a few well-known persons and stories with holidays.
        _____ a. Tells that Columbus discovered America.
        _____ b. States that Indians and Pilgrims were the first to celebrate Thanksgiving in America.
        _____ c. Associates Santa Claus with Christmas by being able to recognize his picture.
    2. Participates in patriotic customs.
        _____ a. Pledges the flag in the correct manner: puts hand over heart, stands at attention.
        _____ b. Names or sings a patriotic song.
        _____ c. Recognizes the American flag.
_____ 3. Tells the name of his race.
_____ 4. States the name of his religion.

PARENT PROBLEM BEHAVIOR CHECKLIST[b]

Directions: Read through the following list carefully and circle the number in front of each statement that describes a problem related to your child.

1. Lacks self confidence
2. Is hypersensitive—feelings easily hurt
3. Is frequently depressed—sad
4. Is easily flustered and confused
5. Is unsure
6. Is very distracted
7. Has short attention span and poor powers of concentration
8. Behavior not predictable—is sometimes good, sometimes bad
9. Exhibits poor muscular coordination—clumsy and awkward
10. Often has physical complaints: headaches, stomachaches, etc.
11. Is nervous and jittery—easily startled
12. Usually feels tired—drowsy
13. Is shy, bashful
14. Is attention-seeking, engages in "show-off" behavior
15. Quarrels and fights with other children.

Note. a. From *Developing and Implementing Individualized Education Programs* (2nd ed.) (p. 322) by A. P. Turnbull, B. B. Strickland, and J. C. Brantley, 1982, Columbus, OH: Merrill. Copyright 1982 by Bell & Howell Company. Reprinted by permission.
b. From "Parent Problem Behavior Checklist" by S. C. Larsen. Reprinted in *Educational Assessment of Learning Problems: Testing for Teaching* (p. 115) by G. Wallace and S. C. Larsen, 1978, Boston: Allyn & Bacon. Copyright 1978 by Allyn & Bacon. Reprinted by permission of Stephen C. Larsen.

chooses one of the specified responses (see p. 60). The responses to Likert-type scale items are often tied to numerical values (e.g., Strongly Disagree = 1). This allows the informant's responses to be statistically summarized. For example, if a teacher responds to several items about a student's school achievement, the teacher's ratings can be summarized by calculating the mean.

Rating scales are used for many purposes in education. A very common one is grading. The traditional letter grades of A, B, C, D, and F make up a rating scale. Other examples appear in Figure 5–10. The first is a Likert-type scale for rating pupil behavior. The teacher considers each skill (e.g., "Ability to follow directions") and rates the student's acquisition of the skill on a scale of 1 to 5. To facilitate the rating process, each possible choice is further described. A rating of 1 for following directions, for instance, means that the student is "always confused; cannot or is unable to follow directions." The second rating scale is a pupil progress report form. Each grading period, the teacher considers the list of skills and rates the student's progress.

Ranking is another strategy that can be used to question informants. In a ranking task, several alternatives are presented and the person must place them in order. For example, a student might be asked to rank several school activities by writing a number 1 by his or her favorite, a number 2 by the next favorite, and so forth. Ranking measures are sometimes valuable for obtaining information about preferences. However, they are less common than either checklists or rating scales, possibly because their results are somewhat more difficult to interpret.

Questionnaires and Interviews

Questionnaires are written measures designed to elicit information from informants. They may be very structured and contain questions similar to those found on checklists and rating scales. They may also contain other types of structured questions such as multiple-choice and true–false items. Less structured, open-ended questions can also be included. The open-ended questionnaire in Figure 5–11 is designed for use by regular teachers in referring a student for special education services.

Interviews are the oral equivalent of questionnaires. An interview might be more appropriate than a questionnaire in several situations: if there is a literacy barrier, if the informant needs help in feeling at ease before questioning begins, and if the task directions are complex and need explanation. In addition, an interviewer can guide the informant through the questioning, keep him or

FIGURE 5–10
Examples of rating scales

PUPIL BEHAVIOR RATING SCALE[a]				
1	2	3	4	5
Ability to follow directions				
Always confused; cannot or is unable to follow directions	Usually follows simple oral directions but often needs individual help	Follows directions that are familiar and/or not complex	Remembers and follows extended directions	Unusually skillful in remembering and following directions
Comprehension of class discussion				
Always inattentive and/or unable to follow and understand discussions	Listens but rarely comprehends well; mind often wanders from discussion	Listens and follows discussions according to age and grade	Understands well and benefits from discussions	Becomes involved and shows unusual understanding of material discussed
Ability to retain orally given information				
Almost total lack of recall; poor memory	Retains simple ideas and procedures if repeated often	Average retention of materials; adequate memory for age and grade	Remembers procedures and information from various sources; good immediate and delayed recall	Superior memory for both details and content
Comprehension of word meanings				
Extremely immature level of understanding	Fails to grasp simple word meanings; misunderstands words at grade level	Good grasp of grade level vocabulary for age and grade	Understands all grade level vocabulary as well as higher level word meanings	Superior understanding of vocabulary; understands many abstract words

Note. a. From *Learning Disabilities* (p. 21) (2nd ed.) by B. R. Gearheart, 1977, St. Louis: C. V. Mosby. Copyright 1977 The C. V. Mosby Company. Adapted from a project developed under Research Grant, USPHS Contract 108-65-42, Bureau of Neurological and Sensory Diseases. Reprinted by permission.

FIGURE 5–10
continued

PUPIL PROGRESS REPORT[b]

MARKING SYSTEM

1. Improvement shown   *Skill mastered   3. No improvement
2. Improvement needed   0. Not taught

Quarterly grading periods

Reading readiness	1	2	3	4
Sees likenesses and differences in objects				
Sees likenesses and differences in pictures				
Reads pictures from left to right				
Identifies and recognizes colors				
Can work simple puzzles				
Can follow simple directions concerning objects				
Can observe and remember objects in a picture				
Can recite address and telephone number				
Can write address and telephone number				
Knows first and last name				
Knows birthdate				
Writes first and last names using proper letter formation				
Matches color words and colors				
Can use scissors correctly				

b. From Pupil Progress Report by the Cahokia Area Joint Agreement, Cahokia, IL. Reprinted in *Teaching Children with Behavior Disorders* (p. 235) by T. M. Shea, 1978, St. Louis: C. V. Mosby. Copyright 1978 by the C. V. Mosby Company. Reprinted with permission of the Cahokia Area Joint Agreement.

---

her on track, and probe for additional information when necessary.

Interviews are often used to gather information from parents, professionals, and students. With students who have academic difficulties, interviews are usually preferable to questionnaires. Several questions can be used when interviewing students about their school performance.

□ What are your best subjects in school? Why do you think you do your best in these subjects?
□ What are your weakest subjects? What seems to cause the problems in these subjects?
□ If you could change anything about your school day, what would it be? (Turnbull et al., 1982, p. 241)

Interviews, questionnaires, and other assessments that rely upon informants are indirect measures. The value of their results depends upon the informant's accuracy. Poor memory of past events, inadequate interpretation of current observations, faulty judgment, and lack of veracity can result in poor information. The teacher must be aware of these possibilities when interpreting reports of informants.

Clinical Interviews

Clinical interviews are a special type of assessment procedure. They are interviews in which the student acts as informant, and the interview questions are designed to identify the strategies the student uses when attempting to perform a task. For example, the teacher may be interested in learning more about how students go about solving mathematics problems, planning essays, or studying textbook chapters. Clinical interviews focus on the *process* the student follows in completing a task. The product is of secondary interest.

Some strategies are observable. Thus, when conducting a clinical interview, the professional carefully notes the student's behaviors. However, cognitive strategies cannot be observed, and the student's report becomes the basis of information about this aspect of task performance. The teacher takes note of what the student does and then asks the student to describe the thinking process that accompanies those actions.

Clinical interviews usually take place while the student is performing a task. For example, if the task is solving mathematics word problems, the student is supplied with several problems at an appropriate level of difficulty. Then, to find out about her nonobservable strategies, the student is directed to "think out loud as you solve these problems." The professional watches, listens to the student's report, and asks questions to clarify meaning or to probe areas that were not discussed.

In some cases, interviews are conducted immediately after the student has finished the task. In the assessment of writing skills, for instance, it is not wise to interrupt the student in the act of composition. Instead, the interview takes place as soon as the student has finished writing. There should be no delay between the completion of the task and the start of the interview. Otherwise, the student may not be able to recall the exact series of steps taken in responding to the task.

Clinical interviewing is a sophisticated assessment technique. It requires expertise in the use of observation and interviewing techniques, knowledge of the curriculum area under assessment, and the types of cognitive strategies that students are likely to employ in various types of tasks. The resulting data are subjective in that they are an informant's report of nonobservable behaviors. However, clinical interviews are the most direct means of gathering information about students' cognitive strategies and may provide important directions for the structuring of the teaching process.

FIGURE 5–11
Referral questionnaire

DIRECTIONS: Teachers or other individuals referring a student for special education services should complete all sections of this form. The completed form should be sent to the principal's office for processing. Complete and specific information will assist the placement committee in determining the student's need for service. Use behavioral descriptions whenever possible.

Teacher _____ Grade/Class _____ Report Date _____
Student _____ Age _____ Birthdate _____

1. What is the student's problem? How does it affect his or her ability to participate in classroom activities?

2. How frequently does the problem occur? (For example, once a week? six times a day?)

3. What changes have occurred in the behavior during this school year?

4. What changes in classroom activities, assignments, procedures, etc. have you made to try to solve the problem? What were the results of each of these changes?

5. What are the student's major strengths and talents?

6. What special interests, hobbies, or skills does the student have?

Note. From *Teaching Special Students in the Mainstream* (2nd ed.) (p. 29) by R. B. Lewis and D. H. Doorlag, 1987, Columbus, OH: Merrill. Copyright 1987 by Merrill Publishing Company. Reprinted with permission.

INTERPRETING INFORMAL ASSESSMENT RESULTS

One of the hallmarks of informal assessment is its relevance to instruction. When informal procedures are designed by teachers to answer specific assessment questions about their students, results are immediately applicable to the solution of instructional problems. The data assist in the identification of areas for further assessment, in the description of the student's current classroom performance, and in the planning or modification of instructional strategies.

Despite the advantages of informal measures, there are also limitations that become apparent in the interpretation of assessment results. These concerns are summarized here.

Technical Adequacy

The greatest limitation of informal assessment tools is the lack of information about reliability and validity (Bennett, 1982). In many cases, the professional simply does not know whether a particular informal procedure is technically adequate. If technical data are not available for a measure, interpretation of its results must be approached with great caution.

All measurements contain error. With norm-referenced tests, the amount of error can be estimated using the standard error of measurement, and confidence intervals are constructed around observed scores to quantify the error factor. However, when there is insufficient psychometric information, the professional is left with the knowledge that assessment results are inaccurate, but the *degree* of inaccuracy is unknown.

The procedures for gathering information about the technical quality of some types of informal tools have been discussed throughout this chapter. For example, interrater reliability can be determined in observation, and there are techniques to study the reliability and other characteristics of criterion-referenced tests. Professionals should take advantage of any such available procedures.

At minimum, content validity should be evaluated. This type of validity relates to how well the tool fulfills the purpose of assessment by addressing the content of interest. Among the most important considerations are whether the assess-

ment device includes a representative sample of the content domain and whether the assessment tasks are appropriate. If the student's problem is fighting on the playground, an observation conducted during shop class does not assess the domain of interest. If oral reading is the concern, the assessment task should be reading out loud, not matching words and pictures.

Selection of the Appropriate Tools for Assessment

The more direct the measure, the more useful the results. For example, if the student's handwriting skills are a concern, direct measures such as observation and work sample analysis provide instructionally relevant information. Reviewing the student's report card grades in handwriting is a less direct measure.

However, it is necessary to consider the purposes of assessment to determine whether a tool is appropriate. If the purpose is to find out if the student's handwriting skills are adequate for success in a regular classroom, interviewing the regular classroom teacher may be the most direct means of gathering the needed information.

Many informal assessment tools provide professionals with a wealth of information. However, the amount of data can become overwhelming and confuse, rather than facilitate, decision making. Assessment should be a carefully planned, systematic process. Once it has been learned that a student's spelling performance is satisfactory, it is not useful to continue gathering information about spelling. Only areas that represent educational needs should be assessed in depth. The more intensive informal procedures—criterion-referenced testing, diagnostic teaching, and clinical interviews—should be reserved for in-depth assessment.

Quality of the Sample of Behavior

All formal and informal measures rely upon behavior samples. It is impractical to observe all behaviors of a student or test skill in solving all the possible mathematics computation problems. As Bachor (1979) notes, "objective based or not, most formal and informal tests provide only a 'snapshot' of the child's performance" (p. 45). Thus, interpretation of assessment results must take into account the quality of the behavior sample. This holds true for all types of informal assessment tools, from observation and work sample analysis to curriculum-based measures to procedures that rely upon informants.

If the student's behavior is under assessment, that is the behavioral sample that is evaluated for representativeness. When persons other than the student contribute information, the representativeness of their behaviors must also be considered. The performance of teachers and parents, like that of students, can fluctuate over time.

Criteria for Evaluating Performance

One of the major difficulties in interpreting the results of many types of informal procedures is that there are no guidelines for determining whether a problem exists and, if one does, whether it is serious enough to warrant some kind of intervention. In most cases, it is left up to the professional to set the criteria. If an observation shows that the student talks out in English class once every 10 minutes on the average, the teacher must decide if this is a problem. Likewise, there are no set standards for evaluating the adequacy of a writing sample with 20% of the words misspelled.

Criterion-referenced tests do include performance criteria that are often based on professional judgment rather than empirical evidence. If a professional has set 80% accuracy as the standard for mastery on a CRT, other professionals may disagree and choose 70%, 90%, or even 100% as the criterion.

For the most part, informal procedures are designed to describe the behaviors that the student exhibits, the tasks he or she can complete, and the skills that are mastered and those that continue to require instruction. However, such procedures make no attempt to match the student's current performance with the performance appropriate for age, grade, and ability. For example, a CRT will reveal whether or not a student is able to multiply 3-digit by 3-digit numbers. Results will not show that this skill is not expected of first and second graders. Again, the professional must make this decision.

Translating Results into Instruction

If limitations are kept firmly in mind, professionals can draw and then act upon conclusions from informal data. Then assessment continues as information is collected to evaluate the effectiveness of instruction. By building ongoing assessment into the program, the teacher can monitor student progress and determine when instruction is working and when modifications are needed.

Bennett (1982) provides several suggestions for increasing the usefulness of informal data in planning the instructional program. These are

1. Recognize that a variety of reasons may exist for a child's correct or incorrect performance on assessment tasks.
2. Try to determine reasons for correct and incorrect performance.
3. Try to determine the conditions under which the child performs the task best.
4. Use informal procedures as complements to formal procedures. (p. 339)

The third suggestion is important. The assessment process tends to focus on the student's problems. The information gathered describes inappropriate behaviors, unlearned skills, and unmastered tasks. But even more crucial is learning how to help the student succeed. A major purpose of assessment must be identification of the classroom conditions and instructional strategies that are likely to improve student performance.

Bennett's last suggestion also deserves comment. Informal assessment is best viewed as a complement to formal assessment. Neither type of procedure is best; both have their uses. Informal assessment is particularly valuable when it augments the results of standardized testing. For example, if a student's score on a formal reading test falls below the average range of performance for age peers, informal assessment can provide critical information about that student's reading performance. Among the possible informal strategies are observing the student during reading instruction, administering an informal reading inventory, analyzing correct and incorrect oral reading responses, interviewing the student to learn about attitudes toward reading and preferences in reading materials, designing a diagnostic teaching sequence, and conducting a clinical reading interview. Informal procedures can be a rich source of information for instruction. When coupled with formal tests, they complete the assessment picture.

AVOIDING BIAS IN INFORMAL ASSESSMENT

Unlike norm-referenced tests, informal measures have not been criticized as contributors to discriminatory assessment and placement practices. In fact, the opposite has occurred. Informal measures—criterion-referenced tests, in particular—have been suggested as one possible solution to the problem of bias in assessment. Because CRTs compare performance to the goals of the local curriculum rather than to the performance of a norm group, it is assumed that the standard of comparison is fair. In addition, informal measures tend to assess skill areas in more depth than norm-referenced tests, and thus they are more sensitive to small changes in pupil behavior.

However, teacher-constructed tests may also contain discriminatory language and content (Bailey & Harbin, 1980). If teachers are insensitive to and have insufficient information about the languages and cultures of their students, they may prepare biased measures. In constructing or selecting informal assessment tools, teachers should consider the same issues in nondiscriminatory assessment that they attend to when evaluating norm-referenced tests.

☐ Is the standard of comparison appropriate for the student in terms of race, culture, and gender?
☐ Are test items free from cultural bias?
☐ Is the language appropriate for the student?
☐ Does the measure bypass the limitations imposed by the handicapping condition?

Other considerations in the use of informal measures are the time, money, and personnel resources needed to implement a comprehensive criterion-referenced testing system (Duffey et al., 1982), the narrow scope of such measures (Oakland, 1980), and the lack of information about their reliability and validity (Harris & Wolf, 1979).

Although informal measures may not replace norm-referenced tests as the instrument of choice for eligibility assessment, they do offer obvious advantages for classroom use. Teachers can design informal tools to answer specific assessment questions about a particular student. Results assist in making decisions about further assessment, current performance, and modification of instruction. Thus, results are instructionally relevant and directly applicable to classroom practice.

McCormack (1976) maintains that the assessment tools that meet your needs are the ones you construct. Such measures must also be nonbiased to meet the needs of all students. According to Bailey and Harbin (1980), this can be done if

1. The importance of the skills measured by the instrument and taught in the curriculum are agreed upon by culturally diverse groups within the school system.
2. Criterion-referenced items are constructed so as not to measure the skills of children from a particular cultural group unfairly.
3. Alternative instructional strategies are incorporated to meet the learning needs of individual children.(p. 593)

STUDY GUIDE

Review Questions

1. Several of the purposes of assessment are listed below. Check each of the purposes that apply to informal procedures.
   _____ a. Provide direction for further assessment
   _____ b. Compare a student's performance to that of other students
   _____ c. Provide direction for planning or modifying instruction
   _____ d. Describe the student's current performance
2. Decide whether each of these statements about observation is true or false.
   T F a. Continuous observation, in which all the behaviors of the student are observed and recorded, is a preliminary technique used to identify possible problem behaviors.
   T F b. In sequence analysis, the observer records the student's behavior and the events that precede and follow that behavior.
   T F c. The first step in setting up an observation is to determine who will observe.

T F **d.** In duration recording, the observer counts the number of times the student displays the target behavior.

T F **e.** Graphs are used to report observational data.

3. There are two ways in which work samples can be analyzed. In _____ analysis, the student's incorrect answers are studied. In _____ analysis, both correct and incorrect answers are considered.

4. Match the types of task analysis in Column A with the descriptions in Column B.

Column A	*Column B*
a. Temporal	_____ The characteristics of the task—directions; presentation and response modes; quantity, time, and accuracy requirements—are analyzed.
b. Developmental sequence	_____ Task subcomponents are identified, then put in order by ease of learning.
c. Difficulty	_____ The task is analyzed according to which behavior is performed first, which comes next, and so on.
d. Task structure	_____ Subtasks are arranged in a hierarchy according to which are typically learned or taught first, second, and so on.

5. The standard of comparison used to evaluate student performance on informal inventories, classroom quizzes, and criterion-referenced tests is the _____ , not the performance of other students.

6. Suppose a teacher wanted to design a criterion-referenced test to measure mastery of this objective:
   When given a worksheet with 20 2-digit plus 2-digit addition problems requiring regrouping, the student will write the correct answer to at least 15 of the problems within 5 minutes.
   a. What materials would be needed to administer the test?
   b. What instructions would the teacher give to the student?
   c. What would be the criterion for acceptable performance?

7. Find the *false* statement.
   _____ **a.** Diagnostic probes and diagnostic teaching are both indirect, rather than direct, measures of student performance.
   _____ **b.** Diagnostic probes and diagnostic teaching are instructional procedures as much as they are assessment procedures.
   _____ **c.** With diagnostic probes, the teacher changes one element of the instructional situation to determine whether the student's performance will improve.
   _____ **d.** Diagnostic teaching is a type of classroom research. The teacher observes the student's behavior under baseline conditions, then introduces an intervention and analyzes its effect on performance.

8. What are three informal assessment techniques used to gather data from informants?

9. In a clinical interview, the professional observes the student perform a task and also asks the student to describe his or her thinking process. (True or False)

10. Interpretation of informal assessment results is difficult because
   _____ **a.** Results are relevant to classroom instruction.
   _____ **b.** The technical quality of informal assessment tools is usually unknown.
   _____ **c.** Informal assessments generally do not offer standards for evaluating the acceptability of student performance.
   _____ **d.** Answers *b* and *c*.

Activities

1. Obtain a copy of a published informal assessment device such as an informal inventory or a criterion-referenced test. Examine its manual. Does it describe the procedures used to develop the assessment device? Are reliability and validity discussed? Analyze the content validity of the measure.

2. Pick a specific behavior of a friend or classmate. Set up and carry out a plan for observing that behavior. If possible, enlist the aid of another observer and determine interobserver reliability.

3. Task analyze one of the following: writing a letter, making change, reading the want ads, baking a cake, or fixing a flat tire.
4. Write an instructional objective for one of the subtasks identified in Activity 3. Then develop a criterion-referenced test to measure mastery of the objective.
5. Visit a classroom and obtain several samples of student work. Do error analyses and then response analyses.
6. Prepare a questionnaire for use with elementary grade students to find out about their television viewing habits.

Discussion Questions

1. Informal assessment techniques have many advantages, particularly in relation to classroom instruction, but they also have disadvantages. Discuss the pros and cons of informal assessment.
2. Compare and contrast direct and indirect informal procedures. Explain why direct measures of student performance are generally preferred.
3. Several informal techniques rely upon informants for the collection of assessment data. Discuss some of the cautions needed with informants.
4. Choose five informal techniques and describe how each could be used to monitor students' progress in instructional programs.
5. Bias can be found in informal assessments as well as norm-referenced tests. Discuss some of the factors that teachers should keep in mind when attempting to design or select a nonbiased informal assessment tool.

6

The Computer as a Tool for Assessment

From 1986 to 1987, the number of computers in American elementary and secondary schools increased by 18% ("Educational Technology," 1987), and today most teachers have access to computers. There may be a computer in the special education classroom that the teacher and students use for instructional purposes, or handicapped students may visit a centralized computer lab or media center for computer learning activities. Computers may be available in the library, in the teachers' work area, or even in teachers' homes. Wherever computers are located, they can provide valuable assistance in the assessment process.

Much has been written about the instructional advantages of computers for handicapped students (e.g., Behrmann, 1988; Cain & Taber, 1987; Johnson, Maddux, & Candler, 1987; Lindsey, 1987; Male, 1988). The computer can serve as an instructional medium, presenting new information to learners and providing an environment for the practice of skills and information. In addition to acting as a tutor, the computer can also be a tool for accomplishing tasks related to instruction (Taylor, 1981). For example, word processing has become one of the most important tool uses of computers for mildly handicapped students (Hummel, 1988; Lewis & Doorlag, 1987).

In assessment, it is the teacher who uses the computer as a tool. Computers can store, sort, and retrieve large amounts of information quickly, and this capability can expedite many aspects of the assessment process. As this chapter discusses, computers can provide assistance in the selection of tests and other formal measures; the administration of tests, particularly to adults; test scoring and interpretation; report writing and the management of assessment information, including the preparation of IEPs; and the gathering of informal assessment data.

The equipment needed to take full advantage of the computer's assistance in assessment includes a computer, a printer, and a modem. Many types of computers are available, but most applications in assessment (like those in special education instruction) are designed for one or more of the Apple *II* family of computers: the Apple II +, *II*e, *II*c, or the most recent addition to the family, the IIGS (Johnson, 1987). Some application programs are also available for IBM computers (usually

the PC, XT, or AT). What is typically needed is the computer itself, with one disk drive, and a monitor; two disk drives may be required for some programs. A printer is necessary if a printed copy of results is desired; this is certainly the case in most assessment applications. A modem is a device that links one computer with another over telephone lines. Modems are not needed for all assessment applications, but they are essential for communicating with electronic information services and for sending electronic mail.

TEST SELECTION

One of the first steps in assessment is selecting the most appropriate tools to answer the assessment questions that have been posed about a particular student. To do this, the teacher must be acquainted with the assessment instruments currently available and the strengths and weaknesses of these instruments. However, keeping up with the publication of new and revised measures and the research pertinent to the assessment process is not an easy task. Computers can make this task somewhat less difficult by providing ready access to a variety of information sources.

Teachers can use computers to consult several electronic data bases that store information relevant to the assessment process. This process is called telecommunication, which is simply the transfer of information from computer to computer over telephone lines. A modem is needed, as well as a special software program called a terminal or communications program. Also, because most electronic data bases are components of commercial information services, a subscription is necessary. The teacher, school, or district must pay the subscription fees and the hourly charges for use of the system.

One electronic data base familiar to many educators is ERIC (Educational Resources Information Center). ERIC computer searches are a service of most college and university libraries; after connecting via computer and modem with the ERIC system, the user can conduct a literature search by typing in descriptors of the topics of interest. The computer searches the data base for documents having those descriptors and then displays their abstracts on the computer screen.

Schools, other institutions, and even individuals can subscribe to electronic information services. One well-known service is BRS (Bibliographic Retrieval Services) Information Technologies. This system offers on-line access to data bases such as ERIC, PsycINFO, and Exceptional Child Education Resources (ECER). Also available on BRS is *The Mental Measurements Yearbooks* on-line data base, an up-to-date source of current test reviews, and the Educational Testing Service Test Collection. Individuals interested in electronic information systems can subscribe at reduced rates to BRS/After Dark, a system limited to evenings and weekends, or to Knowledge Index, a similar system offered by Dialog Information Services. For further information, contact BRS Information Technologies (1200 Route 7, Latham, NY 12110) and Dialog Information services, Inc. (3460 Hillview Avenue, Palo Alto, CA 94304).

SpecialNet is an electronic information system designed specifically for special educators. This subscription service has three features: electronic mail, bulletin boards, and data bases. The electronic mail system allows users to send messages to and receive messages from all other SpecialNet subscribers. The electronic bulletin boards are organized by topic; users can access the boards of their choice, read the messages posted on the boards, and send messages to others reading the board or to the person or agency responsible for the board. The bulletin boards cover a wide variety of topics including assessment (the ASSESSMENT board), bilingual special education, early childhood special education, litigation and federal legislation, mental retardation, behavior disorders, and parents of exceptional children. SpecialNet also offers data bases that can be searched for information about specific topics; examples are the Apple Special Education Solutions data base, Promising Educational Practices, and Program Evaluation. Further information about SpecialNet is available from National Systems Management, Inc. (2021 K Street, N.W., Suite 315, Washington, DC 20006).

TEST ADMINISTRATION

Just as computers can deliver instruction to students, they can also administer some types of tests. In this application of computer technology to assessment, the student would sit down at a computer, read the on-screen instructions, and type in answers to questions. The computer program would then evaluate the student's responses, calculate test scores, and prepare a written report for the teacher.

At present, computer-assisted testing is rarely used with handicapped children and adolescents. One major reason for this is that test administration by computer may depress the performance of handicapped students. Mildly handicapped students, as a group, have difficulty reading, writing, controlling their behavior, and focusing their attention on task. Using computers for test administration could exacerbate these difficulties. The current generation of school computers rely upon students' ability to read and understand the text that appears on the screen and their ability to answer questions by typing on the computer's keyboard. Reading problems can be circumvented to some extent with taped or synthesized speech, and the technology exists to produce programs that listen to students' oral responses, although this is not yet affordable for most schools. However, the major drawback to computer test administration is the inability of the machine to monitor the student's behavior, provide motivation and encouragement, observe the student's interaction with the task, and direct the student's attention back to the task as necessary. Individual administration of tests by a trained examiner remains the preferred practice for handicapped students, at least at present.

In addition, few measures have been designed for (or converted to) computer administration, and most of those available are adult measures. Most typically, computer-administered procedures are career counseling tools or adult personality measures. One example applicable to some special education populations is the collection of vocational assessment systems produced by Valpar International Corporation, many of which include measures that are administered by computer. Another is the *Piers–Harris Children's Self-Concept Scale* (Piers & Harris, 1984), a self-report measure that can be administered and then scored by computer. Computers also could be used with adult informants such as teachers and parents if computerized versions of measures such as behavior rating scales and checklists were available.

Hasselbring (1984) describes two computer-administered measures specifically designed for students with learning problems. The *Computerized Test of Reading Comprehension* is an adaptation of an existing print test of silent reading comprehension; the student interacts directly with the computer, reading silently and typing responses. The *Computerized Test of Spelling Errors* is a dictation spelling test. In this measure, the words to be spelled are on tape, and the computer drives the tape recorder. When the student has typed a response, the program continues and the next word is read. Hasselbring (1984) reports that computer-based assessments such as these yield results similar to those of paper-and-pencil tests, even with handicapped students. In addition, the computerized tests reduce the amount of time teachers must spend in test administration.

As more computer-administered measures become available for use in special education, professionals will need to learn how to evaluate, select, and interpret the results of these instruments, taking into account the ways in which the introduction of a computer alters the testing situation. The American Psychological Association (1986), in its *Guidelines for Computer-Based Tests and Interpretations,* sets forth several recommendations for professionals who use computers for test administration. These include the following:

□ Influences on test scores due to computer administration that are irrelevant to the purposes of assessment should be eliminated or taken into account in the interpretation of scores.
□ The environment in which the testing terminal is located should be quiet, comfortable, and free from distractions.
□ Test items presented on the display screen should be legible and free from noticeable glare.
□ Test performance should be monitored, and assistance to the test taker should be provided, as is needed and appropriate. If technically feasible, the proctor should be signalled automatically when irregularities occur.
□ Test takers should be trained on proper use of the computer equipment, and procedures should be established to eliminate any possible effect on test scores due to the test taker's lack of familiarity with the equipment.
□ Reasonable accommodations must be made for individuals who may be at an unfair disadvantage in

a computer testing situation. In cases where a disadvantage cannot be fully accommodated, scores obtained must be interpreted with appropriate caution. (pp. 10–12)

The last recommendation is of particular importance with lower performing students. No test, computerized or teacher-administered, should discriminate against the student on the basis of handicap. If a student has poor reading skills, knowledge of general science should not be assessed by forcing that student to read questions from the computer screen or from a printed page.

TEST SCORING AND INTERPRETATION

Computers can also be used in assessment to score tests and, in some cases, to assist in the interpretation of test results. Test scoring by computer is not a new application. Publishers of group-administered measures such as the achievement tests used in regular education have long provided computer scoring services to schools. These services typically require that students respond to test questions on special answer sheets; these sheets are then mailed to the scoring service, and results are returned to the school or district at some later date.

A more recent development is the use of microcomputers by teachers at the school site for test scoring. Within the past few years, several programs have appeared on the market for scoring the individual tests commonly used in special education. These programs, designed for computers like the Apple and the IBM, represent an excellent use of computer technology; they decrease the probability of computation errors in scoring and speed up the scoring process, freeing the professional for other, more meaningful duties.

Most test-scoring programs for individual tests require that the professional administer the test and compute the raw scores for each subtest. Identifying information such as the student's name is entered into the program along with raw scores, and there may be choices to make about the types of scores to be calculated. Usually, it takes only a minute or two to enter the necessary data, and then only a few seconds for the computations. This is a substantial time savings, because for some tests it takes 15 or even 30 minutes to compute derived scores by hand.

Test-scoring programs are available for several of the individual measures used in special education, as Table 6–1 illustrates. Publishers tend to develop scoring programs for tests that are both popular and difficult and/or time-consuming to score. Information about scoring programs can be obtained from publishers' catalogues and from sources such as *Apple Computer Resources in Special Education and Rehabilitation* (1988), *Psychware Sourcebook* (Krug, 1987, 1988), and *Computer Use in Psychology: A Directory of Software* (Stoloff & Couch, 1987). Test-scoring programs are typically developed by the publisher of the test for which the program is designed;

TABLE 6–1

Test-scoring programs

Test	Scoring Program	Source of Program
AAMD Adaptive Behavior Scale, School Edition	ABSOFT	CTB/McGraw-Hill
Adaptive Behavior Inventory	ABI PRO-SCORE System	PRO-ED
Detroit Tests of Learning Aptitude–2	DTLA–2 Software Scoring System	PRO-ED
Detroit Tests of Learning Aptitude–Primary	DTLA–P Software Scoring System	PRO-ED
Diagnostic Achievement Battery	DAB PRO-SCORE System	PRO-ED
Diagnostic Achievement Test for Adolescents	DATA PRO-SCORE System	PRO-ED
Kaufmann Assessment Battery for Children	K-ABC ASSIST™	American Guidance Service
KeyMath Revised	KeyMath–R ASSIST™	American Guidance Service
Peabody Individual Achievement Test–Revised	PIAT–R ASSIST™	American Guidance Service
Quick-Score Achievement Test	Q-SAT PRO-SCORE System	PRO-ED
Scales of Independent Behavior	COMPUSCORE: Scales of Independent Behavior	DLM Teaching Resources
Stanford Diagnostic Mathematics Test	Computer Scoring™ for SDMT	Psychological Corporation
Stanford Diagnostic Reading Test	Computer Scoring™ for SDRT	Psychological Corporation
Test of Adolescent Language–2	TOAL–2 Software Scoring System	PRO-ED
Test for Auditory Comprehension of Language	COMPUSCORE: Auditory Comprehension of Language	DLM Teaching Resources
Test of Language Development–2, Intermediate	TOLD–2 Intermediate PRO-SCORE System	PRO-ED
Test of Language Development–2, Primary	TOLD–2 Primary PRO-SCORE System	PRO-ED
Test of Written Language–2	TOWL–2 PRO-SCORE System	PRO-ED
Vineland Adaptive Behavior Scales	Vineland ASSIST™	American Guidance Service
Woodcock-Johnson Psycho-Educational Battery–Revised	COMPUSCORE: Woodcock-Johnson Psycho-Educational Battery–Revised	DLM Teaching Resources
Woodcock Reading Mastery Tests–Revised	WRMT–R ASSIST™	American Guidance Service

publishers may also certify as accurate programs developed by another agency. Prices for scoring programs vary, but most are in the $100 to $200 range.

Most scoring programs allow the teacher to store student data for later use. In addition, score reports can be displayed on the screen or printed. Reports take different formats, depending on the test, but they include the same types of results that would appear on a hand-scored protocol. A sample computer-generated report is shown in Figure 6–1. This is a report of results from the *Detroit Tests of Learning Aptitude–Primary* (Hammill & Bryant, 1986), prepared with the *DTLA–P Software Scoring System* (Bryant, 1986). The first section presents the identifying information about the student, and derived scores appear in section 2. Section 3 is a score profile. The last two sections report the results of score comparisons. The student's scores on the various domains of the *Detroit Tests of Learning Aptitude–Primary* are com-

pared, and then, to determine whether results indicate a discrepancy between expected and actual achievement, *Detroit* performance is compared to results from a test of academic achievement. To obtain this report, the only information the teacher needed to supply was the demographic data for the student, subtest raw scores, and achievement test results.

Computer-generated reports vary in their length and complexity. All include identifying student information and basic test scores, but some add profiles and other more detailed analyses of student performance. For example, the *WRMT–R ASSIST*™ program (Hauger, 1988) for the *Woodcock Reading Mastery Tests–Revised* (Woodcock, 1987) provides both an instructional level profile and also a standard score and percentile rank profile for subtest and cluster results; confidence intervals are plotted on the profiles, rather than single scores. The computer-generated report for the *KeyMath Revised* (Connolly, 1988) includes

FIGURE 6–1
Sample computer-generated Score Report for the *Detroit Tests of Learning Aptitude–Primary*

Sample Summary Report
DETROIT TESTS OF LEARNING APTITUDE–PRIMARY
SUMMARY REPORT

SECTION I. IDENTIFYING INFORMATION
NAME: ADAM H. BRYANT   DATE OF TESTING: 9/5/85
EXAMINER: MS. DIAGNOSTICIAN   DATE OF BIRTH: 1/30/78
TEACHER: MR. EDUCATOR   AGE: 7 YRS., 7 MOS.
SCHOOL: ANYTOWN ELEMENTARY   CITY, STATE: AUBURN, MAINE

SECTION II. DTLA–P PERFORMANCE

DOMAIN/SUBTEST	RAW SCORE	QUOTIENT	%ILE RANK	RATING
1. LINGUISTIC				
VERBAL (VBQ)	42	91	27	AVERAGE
NONVERBAL (NVQ)	62	112	79	ABOVE AVERAGE
2. COGNITIVE				
CONCEPTUAL (COQ)	48	98	45	AVERAGE
STRUCTURAL (STQ)	56	103	58	AVERAGE
3. ATTENTIONAL				
ATTENTION-ENHANCED (AEQ)	42	95	37	AVERAGE
ATTENTION-REDUCED (ARQ)	62	113	81	ABOVE AVERAGE
4. MOTORIC				
MOTOR-ENHANCED (MEQ)	34	88	21	BELOW AVERAGE
MOTOR-REDUCED (MRQ)	70	126	96	SUPERIOR
5. GENERAL				
GENERAL APTITUDE (GIQ)	104	101	52	AVERAGE

FIGURE 6–1

continued

SECTION III: PROFILE OF DTLA–P SCORES

QUOTIENT	LINGUISTIC		COGNITIVE		ATTENTIONAL		MOTORIC		GENERAL	QUOTIENT
	VBQ	NVQ	COQ	STQ	AEQ	ARQ	MEQ	MRQ	GIQ	
140	—	—	—	—	—	—	—	—	—	140
135	—	—	—	—	—	—	—	—	—	135
130	—	—	—	—	—	—	—	—	—	130
125	—	—	—	—	—	—	—	*	—	125
120	—	—	—	—	—	—	—	—	—	120
115	—	—	—	—	—	*	—	—	—	115
110	—	*	—	—	—	—	—	—	—	110
105	—	—	—	*	—	—	—	—	—	105
100	—	—	*	—	—	—	—	—	*	100
95	—	—	—	—	*	—	—	—	—	95
90	*	—	—	—	—	—	*	—	—	90
85	—	—	—	—	—	—	—	—	—	85
80	—	—	—	—	—	—	—	—	—	80
75	—	—	—	—	—	—	—	—	—	75
70	—	—	—	—	—	—	—	—	—	70
65	—	—	—	—	—	—	—	—	—	65
60	—	—	—	—	—	—	—	—	—	60
55	—	—	—	—	—	—	—	—	—	55

SECTION IV. COMPARISON OF SUBTESTS FOR SIGNIFICANT DIFFERENCES

1. LINGUISTIC DOMAIN

NVQ IS SIGNIFICANTLY GREATER THAN VBQ, HOWEVER, NEITHER SCORE FALLS BELOW AVERAGE.

2. COGNITIVE DOMAIN

NO SIGNIFICANT DIFFERENCE EXISTS BETWEEN COQ AND STQ. THUS THE CHILD APPEARS TO PERFORM EQUALLY WELL ON CONCEPTUAL (ABSTRACT) AND STRUCTURAL (CONCRETE) TASKS, A NORMAL OR TYPICAL PATTERN.

3. ATTENTIONAL DOMAIN

ARQ IS SIGNIFICANTLY GREATER THAN AEQ. HOWEVER, NEITHER SCORE FALLS BELOW AVERAGE.

4. MOTORIC DOMAIN

MRQ IS SIGNIFICANTLY GREATER THAN MEQ, THUS THE POSSIBILITY OF A SERIOUS MOTOR (OR SIGHT) DISABILITY MUST BE CONSIDERED.

SECTION V. COMPARISONS BETWEEN DTLA–P AND ACHIEVEMENT SCORES

DIAGNOSTIC ACHIEVEMENT BATTERY RESULTS

ADMINISTRATION DATE: 1/27/84

LISTENING	82
SPEAKING	86
READING	115
WRITING	114
MATHEMATICS	115
SPOKEN LANGUAGE	84
WRITTEN LANGUAGE	112
TOTAL ACHIEVEMENT	112

DISCREPANCY ANALYSIS

LISTENING PERFORMANCE IS SIGNIFICANTLY BELOW APTITUDE PERFORMANCE.
SPEAKING PERFORMANCE IS SIGNIFICANTLY BELOW APTITUDE PERFORMANCE.
SPOKEN LANGUAGE PERFORMANCE IS SIGNIFICANTLY BELOW APTITUDE PERFORMANCE.

scores and profiles as well as a summary of the student's performance on each of the specific skill domains assessed by the *KeyMath–R.*

As these examples illustrate, many of the newer scoring programs go beyond simple reporting of scores and begin to contribute to the interpretation of test results. In special education software, the most typical type of interpretation offered on computer-generated reports is a comparison of scores

to determine whether there is a statistically significant difference between them. There is also a body of software designed specifically to interpret test results.

Most of the interpretation software has been developed for psychological, rather than educational, tests. For instance, there are several programs to assist psychologists in writing interpretive reports of the results of intelligence tests such as

FIGURE 6–2

Excerpts from sample computer-generated interpretive report for the *Wechsler Intelligence Scale for Children–Revised*

Interpretive Information

Stephen's Full Scale IQ of 120 falls at the 91st percentile in comparison with children of his age, and places Stephen in the Superior classification. This IQ provides an assessment of general intelligence and scholastic aptitude.

Stephen obtained a Verbal IQ of 133, which falls at the 99th percentile. This IQ provides an indication of his verbal comprehension, which includes the ability to reason with words, to learn verbal material, and to process verbal information.

Stephen's Performance IQ of 101 falls at the 53rd percentile. This IQ contributes an understanding of his perceptual organization, which includes nonverbal reasoning, the ability to employ visual images in thinking, and the ability to process visual material efficiently.

As noted earlier, the Verbal IQ is significantly higher than the Performance IQ. Furthermore, the size of the difference is not common in samples of normal children, and efforts should be made to uncover reasons for this difference. Possible interpretations of the difference include the following:

1. Expressive language skills are better developed than nonverbal skills.
2. Auditory processing is better developed than visual processing.
3. Academic opportunities and interests may be a factor.

These possibilities are not necessarily the only ones. None should be accepted as applying to Stephen unless supported by independent evidence such as the results of other tests, behavioral observations, and background information.

Because the Verbal and Performance IQs differ considerably, Stephen's Full Scale IQ appears to summarize diverse abilities.

Only one of the scores contributing to the Verbal IQ differed significantly from Stephen's average verbal score. Therefore the Verbal IQ is probably a good indication of his abilities in this area.

Only one of the scores contributing to the Performance IQ differed significantly from Stephen's average performance score. Therefore the Performance IQ is probably a good indication of his abilities in this area.

The relatively low scores on the Arithmetic, Digit Span, and Coding subtests may be associated with distractibility, short attention or memory span, poor concentration, or lack of facility in handling numbers, in comparison with others of Stephen's ability.

The score on the Comprehension subtest suggests good practical judgment and common-sense reasoning in comparison with the other verbal abilities measured by the WISC–R. Such scores imply the effective use of one's knowledge.

The score on Picture Arrangement may reflect any of several relative strengths—for example, the ability to appraise a total situation that is shown in segments, to anticipate the consequences of social actions, and to distinguish essential from unimportant details.

This report is based only on the subject's WISC–R scores and age. Other information about the individual must be considered when interpreting results.

Note. From the *Wechsler Intelligence Scale for Children–Revised Microcomputer-Assisted Interpretive Report.* Copyright © 1986 by The Psychological Corporation, San Antonio, Texas. Reproduced by permission. All rights reserved.

the *Wechsler Intelligence Scale for Children—Revised* (Wechsler, 1974). Figure 6–2 presents the interpretive information section from a report produced by the *WISC–R Microcomputer-Assisted Interpretive Report* program (1986). Like scoring programs, interpretation programs require only that the tester enter the student's identifying information and raw scores; the program then generates descriptions and analyses of the student's performance.

There are a limited number of interpretation programs for special education purposes, and these programs are typically designed to interpret relationships among several measures of student performance. For example, the *Severe Discrepancy Analyzer* (Reynolds & Stowe, 1985) compares IQ and achievement test data to determine whether a significant discrepancy exists. *Computer Assisted Reading Assessment* (McKenna) is a program that integrates, analyzes, and interprets reading performance data from a variety of sources. The *McDermott Multidimensional Assessment of Children* program (McDermott & Watkins, 1985) analyzes information about children ages 2 to 8 to make both classification decisions and recommendations for the design of instructional programs.

When evaluating a computer program for test interpretation, it is extremely important to understand the decision-making rules the program uses to arrive at its conclusions. For example, the program *CLASS.LD* (Hofmeister, 1984) is an expert system used to analyze psychological and educational data to make decisions about classifying students as learning disabled. This system is based on expert opinion as well as federal regulations and the guidelines of the state of Utah. The rules used to arrive at a classification decision in this program may or may not be acceptable to professionals in other states. Programs that interpret data should be selected with great care to assure that the assumptions underlying the program are sound. They are best used as an aid to decision making, not as a substitute for the deliberations of the multidisciplinary team.

REPORT WRITING AND DATA MANAGEMENT

One aspect of assessment is the preparation of reports summarizing findings and conclusions. In some situations, test-scoring programs or those that assist in interpretation can be used to generate written reports. However, scoring programs are not available for all of the measures used by special educators, and often assessment reports need to describe and interpret the results of several measures, both formal and informal. In cases such as these, word processing programs can be used to facilitate report writing.

Word processors are writing programs. The user enters text, which can be stored and retrieved for later use. One major advantage of word processing is the ease with which text can be edited, altered, and manipulated. Errors are easily corrected, and the sequence and format of the text can be changed. Another advantage is that once something has been written, it can be saved and used again later, either in its original form or in a revised version. This allows professionals to create shells or templates for documents that they must routinely write.

In assessment, reports often follow the same format and organization. Some districts may suggest or even mandate a specific format for assessment reports. Professionals can save time by creating a shell that includes all the necessary components of the report but leaves room for adding the actual content. Figure 6–3 presents an example. The report begins with identifying information with the tester's name filled in. When preparing an actual report, the tester would add the student's name, grade, teacher, school, birthdate, age, the date(s) of testing, and the measure(s) administered. Additional information such as gender could be added as necessary. The body of the report is organized into four major sections: Reason for Referral, Test Behavior, Test Results, and Conclusions and Recommendations. At the end of the report is a space for the tester's signature. In writing the report, the tester would supply the needed information under each heading. For example, in Test Results, the name of the first test to be reported would be inserted, along with the date of administration, subtests, and results stated as standard score ranges. The statement about true score probability would remain the same (unless a different confidence level was selected), and this would be followed by a discussion of the results (e.g., "Jeff scored within the average of range of performance on the Mathematics subtest but showed low average performance in Reading and Written Language").

FIGURE 6–3

Sample word processing shell for an assessment report

Assessment Report

Name: Tester: Marjorie Smith
Grade: Date(s) of Testing:
Teacher: Test(s) Administered:
School:
Birthdate: Age:

Reason for Referral

Test Behavior

Test Results

The XXX was administered on XXX, and the following results were obtained:

Subtest   Standard Score Range

The chances that these ranges of standard scores include the student's true scores are about 68 out of 100.

Conclusions and Recommendations

_____
Marjorie Smith, Special Education Teacher

Another need of special educators is the management of information. For example, a teacher might keep records on several students and their assessment results, including the findings of the initial assessment for special education placement, yearly IEP evaluations, and more frequent classroom performance checks. One way to organize this information is a paper-filing system, but computers offer another alternative—data base management programs. These programs create an electronic filing system, and their major advantage is that once information has been entered and stored, it can be sorted and retrieved quickly and easily. For example, if the teacher has created a record for each student, it would be possible to search for all students who have IEPs more than 6 months old, those with identified needs in oral expression, or those who have successfully completed one of the minimum competencies for high school graduation.

Integrated programs like *AppleWorks* include both a word processor and a data base. The advantage is that information can be transferred from one part of the program to the other. Thus, information is entered once into the data base, then copied into the word processor where it can be edited or formatted, as needed. A system like this could be used to set up a student data base, then import information from that data base for assessment reports and for IEPs.

Computerized IEP programs are specialized data bases. There are several IEP programs available commercially, and they range in price from around $100 to more than $2,000. The simplest programs are IEP shells that the team completes by selecting from a limited collection of annual goals and objectives. More sophisticated programs offer extensive collections of goals and objectives that may be keyed to information about instructional materials; these programs are often capable of generating administrative reports such as class lists, pupil count data, and notices to staff and parents about testing and IEP meeting schedules. One example is the *Talley*™ *Special Education Management System* (Talley, 1986), which includes a referral management system, a student data base, a bank of annual goals and objectives, and a program for writing child count reports. A less expensive system, designed for use by individual teachers, rather than district wide use, is the *Talley*™ *Goals and Objectives Writer* (Talley, 1987). This program is an IEP shell with sets of objectives correlated to the *BRIGANCE*® *Diagnostic Inventories* (Brigance, 1977, 1978, 1981, 1983a, 1983b) and the *ENRIGHT*™ *Diagnostic Inventory of Basic Arithmetic Skills* (Enright, 1983).

According to Jenkins (1987), computerized IEP programs reduce the amount of time teachers spend in preparation for IEP meetings and may improve the quality of the IEPs produced. Also, computer-generated IEPs are easier to read and may contain more objectives than handwritten IEPs (Male, 1988). Certainly, the ability to edit and make corrections without rewriting or retyping is an advantage. Teachers may find, however, that the goals and objectives included in commercial programs are not suitable for all students, which means that existing goals and objectives must be modified and/or new ones typed in. Because of this and the expense involved for the more sophisticated IEP generation systems, it is becoming more common for teachers to devise their own IEP shells using word processing programs or integrated programs such as *AppleWorks* (Mattke & Reinhardt, 1987).

INFORMAL ASSESSMENT

An often neglected application of computers is their use in the more informal aspects of the assessment process. Just as computers can serve as a tool for the teacher in formal testing, they can assist in the collection and analysis of informal assessment data. One major example is the use of computer-assisted instruction programs for assessment purposes. In computer-assisted instruction, the computer serves as a tutor, presenting new information to students, and/or the computer provides students with opportunities to practice and receive immediate feedback on skills and knowledge to which they have previously been introduced.

Many instructional software programs collect data on student performance, and special educators consider this feature important in the selection of quality software (Lewis & Harrison, 1988). Some record-keeping programs simply provide students with information about the number of questions or problems answered correctly. Others store student data for the teacher's use so that the teacher can review the results at some later time. Performance data may be presented on the screen, and/or the program may produce a written report.

The amount of information collected by instructional programs varies from program to program. The examples in Figure 6–4 are reports from two programs published by Hartley Courseware, Inc., a company that offers a record-keeping capability in much of its software. The first example, from the program *Clock,* tells the student's name and the type of task with which he was working (i.e., when shown a drawing of a clock with hands showing the time, the student types the corresponding digital time to the nearest 5 minutes). This student attempted 10 problems, 8 of which were correct on the first try. The report then provides the student's answers to the problems missed, along with the correct answers. The second example, from *Reading for Meaning 2,* begins with the student's name, the name of the lesson, and the percentage correct. The number of questions attempted is followed by a breakdown of the types of questions (e.g., main idea, detail) and the number of each the student answered correctly. These reports, which are quite detailed in comparison to those of many commercial programs, can be viewed on the screen or printed.

Instructional software can be designed to keep even more detailed records. Hasselbring (1984), for example, describes a spelling program that

FIGURE 6–4

Sample student performance reports from instructional software programs: a. report from the *Clock* program; b. report from the *Reading for Meaning 2* program.

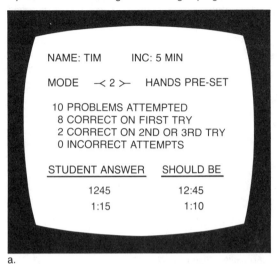

a.   b.

From *Clock Manual* (p. 12), 1983, and *Reading for Meaning 2 Manual* (p. 19), 1984, Dimondale, MN: Hartley Courseware, Inc. Copyright 1983 and 1984 by Hartley Courseware, Inc. Reprinted by permission.

analyzes students' errors. It categorizes each word missed as regular, predictable, or irregular, and analyzes errors according to type (e.g., vowels, consonants, generalizations, and patterns). In addition, the student's error tendencies are noted by a count of the number of errors that were omissions, insertions, substitutions, or errors in order. Although this program was designed to administer spelling tests, its error analysis capability would be a useful addition to instructional programs for spelling.

Another example is *Automath,* an experimental software program described by Semmel, Semmel, Gerber, and Adoradio (1988). Although the major purpose of this program is development of automaticity of math facts, it includes a dynamic assessment component. When a student makes a basic fact error, the program takes the student through a series of similar problems to determine the probable cause of the error. The first step is to present the problem a second time, to insure the student's attention. If another error is made, one component of the problem is changed (e.g., 2 + 6 is changed to 2 + 7). This sequence proceeds developmentally until the original prob-

lem is presented via a concrete representation, then in picture-story form.

Even more sophisticated is "smart" software, based on the work in artificial intelligence, which can analyze the errors made by students and use this information to differentiate the type of instruction and the number and types of practice activities presented. Although not yet available for use in special education classrooms, this type of software illustrates the computer's potential for meeting the diverse needs of handicapped learners and for providing important information to teachers about how individual students approach learning tasks.

However, even the current generation of instructional software provides teachers with excellent opportunities for observing students' interactions with computer-based learning activities in a variety of skills and content areas. As Zinsser (1983) notes, because the computer screen is visible to onlookers, using a computer is somewhat like a spectator sport. Teachers can take advantage of this to observe how students approach learning tasks, how often (or if) they read task directions, what strategies they use when presented with questions and problems, and how they react to error messages and confirmation of correct responses. Writing skills and strategies are particularly easy to observe on the computer. Observation can also be combined with clinical interviewing to gain more information about the student's thinking process as he or she interacts with an instructional program or writing task.

Computers can also become a vehicle for data analysis. One program that helps teachers analyze student performance data is *Aimstar* (Hasselbring & Hamlett, 1983). In effect, *Aimstar* is an electronic graphing program. The teacher selects a specific student behavior (e.g., the number of words read correctly in daily 2-minute reading probes) and sets the instructional goal and the target date for reaching that goal. Student data are then entered and a graph is produced. To aid in decision making, a line is plotted on the graph showing the minimum rate of progress the student must achieve to reach the instructional goal by the target date; a line representing the student's actual progress can also be plotted. In addition, the program will evaluate the student's progress using built-in decision rules and inform the teacher whether the instructional program is successful; if it is not, strategies for increasing student performance will be suggested. According to Thomas (1988), this program is a significant improvement over graphing by hand, because the teacher can easily change the decision rules and review the student's progress under the revised parameters. Others suggest that computers can be used to collect as well as analyze daily performance data, thereby saving teachers' time but possibly increasing the time students must spend in data-collection activities (Fuchs, Hamlett, Fuchs, Stecker, & Ferguson, 1988).

These examples provide some indication of the value of computers in informal assessment. As computers become commonplace fixtures in American classrooms, special educators need to learn how to take advantage of their capability to reduce the amount of time that must be spent in clerical and other noninstructional duties. As this chapter has described, computers can be valuable assessment tools, assisting not only in informal assessment but also in the selection and evaluation of tests and other measures; test administration, scoring, and interpretation; and the preparation of reports and management of student data.

STUDY GUIDE

Review Questions

1. Check all the ways in which computers can assist in assessment:
   - _____ a.   Record keeping
   - _____ b.   Report writing
   - _____ c.   Task analysis
   - _____ d.   Test scoring
   - _____ e.   Drill and practice

2. In assessment, teachers use computers as tutors. (True or False)

3. List the three pieces of equipment needed to use computers in assessment.

4. Which of the following is not an electronic data base?
   a.   *Aimstar*
   b.   PsycINFO
   c.   *Mental Measurements Yearbooks*
   d.   ERIC

5. SpecialNet is an electronic information service that offers electronic mail, _____ , and data bases.

6. At present, computer-assisted testing is rarely used with handicapped students. (True or False)

7. According to the American Psychological Association, when computers are used for test administration
   a.   Students should be taught how to use the computer equipment.
   b.   Test items on the computer screen should be legible and free from glare.
   c.   Accommodations should be made for individuals who might be at a disadvantage in computer testing.
   d.   All of the above.

8. Test-scoring programs are usually more expensive than IEP programs. (True or False)
9. Test-scoring programs
   a. Are not available for measures used in special education.
   b. Require that teachers compute raw scores and derived scores.
   c. May compare scores to see if significant differences exist.
   d. Usually provide fewer results than a hand-scored protocol.
10. Match the program in Column A with the type of application it represents in Column B.

Column A	Column B
a. *K-ABC Assist*	_____ Test administration
b. *Reading for Meaning 2*	_____ Word processing and data management
c. *Talley™ Special Education Management System*	_____ IEP generation
d. *Computer Assisted Reading Assessment*	_____ Instructional record keeping
e. *AppleWorks*	_____ Test scoring

11. Teachers can devise their own shells for assessment reports and IEPs using word processing programs. (True or False)
12. Instructional software can be used in assessment to
    _____ a. Find out what types of questions and problems students typically miss.
    _____ b. Determine how students perform in relation to peers.
    _____ c. Investigate student attitudes toward school.
    _____ d. Prepare pupil count reports.
13. "Smart" software
    _____ a. Is designed for gifted and talented learners.
    _____ b. Bases instruction on student responses.
    _____ c. Is available for most of the curriculum areas taught in special education.
    _____ d. Includes tutorials, but no practice activities.
14. Word processing software
    _____ a. Helps teachers manage and retrieve large amounts of data quickly.
    _____ b. Is best used by students rather than teachers.
    _____ c. Facilitates writing by making revisions easy to make.
    _____ d. Allows teachers to interact with information services like SpecialNet.
15. Give three reasons why mildly handicapped students might experience difficulty taking a test administered by computer.

Activities

1. Interview a special education teacher who uses computers in assessment. Ask the teacher to describe how computers are used and to evaluate whether computers have changed the way in which his or her professional duties are accomplished.
2. Preview one or more of the test-scoring programs discussed in this chapter. Try the program with sample data to determine how long the scoring process takes. Compare this with the time needed for hand scoring. Also, evaluate the report that the program generates to see if it contains all needed information.
3. Using the sample word processing shell in Figure 6–3 as a model, design a shell for reporting results of an informal assessment strategy such as an observation, interview, or diagnostic teaching sequence.
4. Visit a classroom where computers are used for instruction and observe a student interacting with an instructional program. Watch to see how that program informs the student about the accuracy of responses and how the student reacts to these messages. Talk with the teacher and/or consult the manual for the program to find out about its record-keeping capabilities.
5. Contact a district in your area that uses a computerized IEP program. Obtain a sample IEP and talk with IEP team members about the advantages and disadvantages of the system. Does the system contain a data base for storing assessment data?

Discussion Questions

1. Computers can serve as tutors or tools for students. Explain how computers can become a tool for teachers.

2. Computers can administer some types of tests. Discuss the advantages and disadvantages of this application. In your response, be sure to consider the needs of mildly handicapped students.

3. Test interpretation programs analyze data and draw conclusions for professionals. Debate the merits of these programs, and suggest ways to prevent their misuse.

4. Using a computer is a public event; anyone near can see what appears on the screen. Consider how this might affect students with school performance problems.

PART THREE

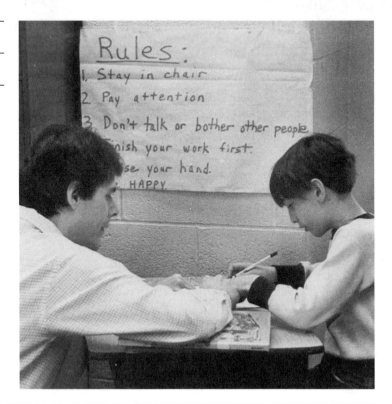

General Considerations

In answering the assessment questions about the eligibility of students for services for the mildly handicapped, the areas that are generally assessed include school achievement, intellectual performance and adaptive behavior, specific learning abilities and strategies, and classroom behavior. In Part III, we suggest the skills to be assessed, describe the major issues and trends involved in such assessments, and provide a perspective of current practices. Of particular interest are descriptions of information sources (for example, school records, the student, teachers, and parents) and strategies for gathering these data.

Several widely used tests are described in each chapter. Parts of the test, the appropriate student population, types of scores obtained, psychometric quality, and methods for interpreting results to answer the assessment questions are all covered. Suggestions from practical experience will prepare you for potential difficulties, and examples will show you how to score and interpret these measures.

In addition to formal tests, each chapter also describes informal techniques for assessing the area under consideration. The chapters conclude with a discussion of how to organize information gathered on a particular topic. Thus, you will learn how to relate data on the basis of the different types of procedures and tasks. Each chapter is geared toward answering the relevant assessment questions. A sample case study helps illustrate the assessment process.

Chapter 7 begins with an overview of the ways school achievement is studied: from school records, student examinations, teacher ratings, and parent perceptions. Then, group achievement tests are reviewed, and three individual tests are described in detail. Attention is focused on ways to confirm test results with informal strategies.

Chapter 8 considers measures of intellectual functioning and adaptive behavior. Although special educators do not give individual intelligence tests, they should be familiar with them. Adaptive behavior scales are included because they help determine whether a student meets eligibility criteria for services for the mentally retarded. The impact of the student's race or culture on this area of assessment must be recognized, so a number of nonbiased assessment systems are described. Other sources of information are identified to avoid overreliance on test scores.

Another common element in the assessment of special students, specific learning abilities and strategies, is discussed in Chapter 9. Screening procedures for vision and hearing problems are described. An overview of traditional specific learning abilities—visual and auditory perception, motor skills, attention, and memory—is presented. The shift from this approach to analysis of learning strategies is discussed, as well as the practice of using discrepancy analysis to determine eligibility for learning disabilities services.

Classroom behavior is the focus of assessment in Chapter 10. Like the other chapters in this section, discussion of formal measures is prefaced with a description of how available data can be gathered. In addition to the rating scales critiqued, this chapter focuses on direct observation and interviews for gathering information about problems in behavior, self-concept, peer acceptance, and school attitudes and interests. Influential elements in the learning environment include teacher and peer expectations and demands, interpersonal interactions, and physical factors.

7

School Performance

School performance is usually equated with academic achievement. Parents and educators alike tend to view adequate performance in reading, language arts, mathematics, and other school subjects as the primary index of successful school performance. Although factors such as classroom behavior, study skills, and interpersonal skills may provide the foundation for successful achievement, school performance is evaluated in terms of classroom functioning, report card grades, and scores on achievement tests.

Special students are characterized by school performance problems. They may have difficulty with one or two of the standard school subjects or be unable to cope with any of the demands of the regular class curriculum. Poor school performance is one of the most common reasons students are referred by teachers, parents, and others for special education assessment.

However, referral for special education assessment should not be the teacher's first response to a student's academic achievement problem. In fact, it should be one of the last steps. When an academic problem is identified, that should signal investigation of the student's current levels of proficiency *and* the instructional factors within the classroom. The teacher can implement one or a series of instructional modifications and gather data to determine if this change improves the student's performance.

In some school systems, teams of educators (sometimes called child study committees) meet on a regular basis to help educators solve instructional problems. Teachers can use this resource as a prereferral strategy. The teacher describes the student's academic difficulties so the team can suggest ways to modify the classroom learning environment to improve the student's performance or to circumvent the academic skill problem. Or the team may recommend other resources such as remedial reading services or evaluation for the bilingual education program as alternatives to special education assessment.

Of course, special education is the appropriate option for some students. When this is the case, the teacher can assist by providing the assessment team with specific information about the student's current classroom performance. Among the types of information that the teacher can contribute are samples of the student's work, records of class-

room activities and the student's success (or lack of success) in these activities, observational data, test scores, and data on the effects of instructional modifications.

When students are first referred for special education assessment, the multidisciplinary team asks, *Is there a school performance problem?* Academic status is also a concern in planning the special education program, evaluating its effectiveness, and determining the continuing eligibility of handicapped students for specialized services. School performance is generally assessed with measures of academic achievement, and the assessment team asks, *What is the student's current level of academic achievement? Are there apparent strengths and weaknesses in the various areas of school learning?*

At this level of questioning, the special education team is concerned with the student's overall academic performance. Once it has been established that a school skill problem exists, the team will do an in-depth examination of the student's performance in each pertinent area. Here, the focus is on assessment strategies that provide a global picture of the student's current achievement status. For example, consider the case of Joyce, a fourth grader who has difficulty coping with the demands of the regular classroom.

Joyce

Joyce is a new student in Mr. Harvey's fourth grade class. Her family recently moved to town from another state, and Joyce is having trouble adjusting to her new classroom. Mr. Harvey is concerned about Joyce. She is unable to read any of the fourth grade textbooks, her spelling and handwriting skills are poor, and she doesn't seem to like coming to school. Mr. Harvey has attempted to modify some aspects of the program for Joyce. She is currently working in a beginning third grade reading book and a second grade spelling book. However, although Joyce is making some progress, she remains far behind her classmates.

For these reasons, Mr. Harvey referred Joyce for special education assessment. The assessment team, including the resource teacher, Ms. Gale, decided that Joyce should be evaluated and secured permission from Joyce's parents.

Individualized Assessment Plan

For: _____ Joyce Dewey _____   _4_   _10–0_   _12/1/89_   _Ms. Gale_

     Student's Name   Grade   Age   Date   Coordinator

Reason for Referral: Difficulty keeping up with fourth grade work in reading, spelling, and handwriting.

Assessment Question	Assessment Procedure	Person Responsible	Date/Time
What is the student's current level of academic achievement?	Interview with Mr. Harvey, Joyce's fourth grade teacher	Ms. Gale, Resource Teacher	12/7/89 3:30 p.m.
	Review of Joyce's school records	Ms. Kellett, School Psychologist	12/5/89 9 a.m.
	Interview with Joyce's parents	Ms. Kellett, School Psychologist	12/8/89 7 p.m.
	Peabody Individual Achievement Test–Revised	Ms. Gale, Resource Teacher	12/11/89 9 a.m.
	Portions of other achievement tests, if necessary	Ms. Gale, Resource Teacher	to be determined

Joyce's mother and father share Mr. Harvey's concerns. They say that Joyce has always had a hard time with schoolwork but that this year seems even more difficult.

The team plans to begin its evaluation of Joyce by reviewing her school records and conducting interviews with her parents and her current classroom teacher. Then an individual achievement test that assesses several school subjects will be administered. The *Peabody Individual Achievement Test–Revised* was selected because it provides information about current skills in reading, mathematics, and spelling. As necessary, other tests or portions of tests may be administered. The results of these assessments will help the team determine the severity of Joyce's school performance problem, a necessary step in deciding whether she is in need of special education services.

CONSIDERATIONS IN ASSESSMENT OF SCHOOL PERFORMANCE

In the assessment process, school performance is generally operationalized as academic achievement. In the elementary grades, the main concerns are the basic subjects of reading, spelling, handwriting, written expression, and mathematics. In

the later elementary and secondary grades the focus of the curriculum shifts to content area subjects such as science, history, and English and to vocational areas. However, basic school subjects such as reading and mathematics remain an important assessment consideration even during the high school years for lower performing students who have not yet mastered these skills.

Purposes

School performance is assessed for several reasons. It is a standard area of concern for classroom teachers, and school systems routinely evaluate the achievement status of their entire population. In special education, poor school performance is a necessary condition for the provision of extraordinary instructional services. Once students begin to receive special education services, their progress in the acquisition of school skills becomes an important evaluation concern.

In seeking information about a student's school performance, the assessment team evaluates current academic achievement in relation to the demands of the least restrictive instructional environment, the regular classroom. Results from achievement measures help the team discover whether the student has benefited from past instruction and has the necessary skills to learn successfully in the mainstream environment. If a school performance problem is identified, it may be determined that there is a mismatch between the needs of the student and the regular learning environment. The team may then decide that the student requires special education services. Before eligibility for special education is determined, the relationship of the school performance problem to a handicapping condition must be documented.

Academic achievement assessment may also contribute information to instructional decisions. Global measures of school learning are useful for identifying the major curriculum areas where students may require special assistance. Such measures also contribute information about the general effectiveness of special education programs by monitoring students' progress toward instructional goals. Of course, general measures of academic achievement can provide only preliminary information for instructional decisions. Their results must be supplemented with results from more specific tests and informal techniques to gain an accurate picture of students' strengths and weaknesses in various school subjects.

Issues and Trends

School performance and its assessment have raised many issues in the last few years. Although most of these pertain to general education, they influence special education because of the mainstreaming of handicapped students. One major area has been the public's concern with the quality of the American educational system. In the late 1970s, the "back-to-basics" movement gained popularity as the public demanded that school curricula emphasize instruction in the basic skills. Americans were concerned about the educational system's ability to produce literate citizens (Gallup, 1978), due in part to a national decline in achievement scores (Copperman, 1979; Munday, 1979).

One outgrowth of the back-to-basics movement was the trend toward minimum competency requirements for high school graduation. By the late 1970s, the majority of states had taken action to require minimum competency tests for grade advancement and/or graduation (Pipho, 1978). In an attempt to guarantee the literacy of those leaving the public school system, these measures were designed to assess basic skills in reading, writing, and mathematical computation (Klein, 1984).

The minimum competency testing movement has raised several issues relating to students receiving special education. According to Pullin (1980), these include

(a) the extent to which handicapped students should participate in or be exempt from the testing program;

(b) whether tests and scoring criteria should be adapted for individual handicapped students or categories of students; and

(c) whether differential diplomas should be awarded to handicapped students on the basis of school performance. (p. 109)

At present, states vary in their policies for minimum competency testing with handicapped students. Many states have some form of testing program for students receiving special education. Some require that some or all handicapped students take competency tests (Wiederholt, Cronin, & Stubbs, 1980). Others have established alternative procedures for this population, such as exemption from testing, special performance standards, and test modifications (Grise, 1980).

The basic skills and minimum competency testing movements did not put an end to public concern about American education. The early 1980s saw increased debate as several major commissions issued reports and recommendations. Among these were *A Nation at Risk: The Imperative for Educational Reform* by the National Commission on Excellence in Education (1983), *Action for Excellence* by the Education Commission of the States (Task Force on Education for Economic Growth, 1983), and *High School: A Report on Secondary Education in America* by Boyer (1983) for the Carnegie Foundation. The opening words from the report of the President's Commission on Excellence in Education convey its stand on the current state of American education:

Our Nation is at risk. Our once unchallenged preeminence in commerce, industry, science, and technological innovation is being overtaken by competitors throughout the world . . . the educational foundations of our society are presently being eroded by a rising tide of mediocrity that threatens our very future as a Nation and a people. (p. 5)

The educational reforms called for in this and other reports marked the beginnings of the excellence in education movement. Rather than stressing basic skills and minimum literacy, these reports recommended increased emphasis on content area curricula in the sciences, social studies, mathematics, English, foreign languages, and computer science. Longer school days and years, firmer discipline requirements, higher expectations and grading criteria, and improved preparation and remuneration of teachers were also stressed. States were quick to take action on these recommendations. For example, since 1975, 36 states have increased the number of academic units required for high school graduation (Bodner, Clark, & Mellard, 1987).

The excellence in education movement continued throughout the 1980s and engendered more than 25 major reports. In 1988, Secretary of Education William Bennett released a 5-year evaluation of the reform effort. Although acknowledging that progress had been made, Bennett concluded that "we are certainly not doing well enough, and we are not doing well enough fast enough."

This movement has important implications for special education. One critical concern is competition for fiscal resources (Moran, 1984). As a result of more rigorous standards, the number of students at risk for school failure increases, while funds are diverted from remedial programs to educational reform efforts. The changing nature of the school-age population, where one child in four lives below the poverty line (Reeves, 1988), suggests the need for more support for low performing students, not less.

Another concern is the way in which educational excellence is defined and assessed. In its "Reply to *A Nation at Risk*," the Council for Exceptional Children (1984) points out that traditional curricula rely on normative standards such as college entrance examination scores and grade point averages for evaluation. These normative criteria make sense for some learners but not for others. Likewise, a traditional content subject curriculum is appropriate for only some of the student population.

Current Practices

Assessment of academic achievement is a routine practice in regular education today. Classroom teachers regularly assess pupil growth with tests or other measures they have devised. When handicapped students are mainstreamed, they typically take part in these assessment activities. They may also participate in schoolwide testing programs, including minimum competency testing to evaluate basic skill development along with the periodic administration of group achievement tests to monitor academic progress.

One problematic feature of regular education assessment for students with learning problems is group test administration. Although group measures can provide some information, handicapped students typically perform poorly on them. Individual tests of academic achievement are preferred for these students. Individual administration allows the tester to direct the student's attention toward the test task, provide encouragement, and explain requirements. The student can be carefully observed to determine whether environmental factors influence performance. In addition, many individual tests attempt to separate out skills so assessment of one does not require mastery of another. Thus, reading skills are not required except on measures of reading. The necessity for writing skills is also minimized, except when these are the subject of evaluation.

One of the first steps in special education assessment is the administration of an individual norm-referenced test of academic achievement. Tests surveying several areas of the curriculum, usually basic skill subjects, are most usual. Because the purpose at this point in the assessment process is to determine whether significant school performance problems exist, norm-referenced measures are appropriate. There is much debate over the relative merits of norm-referenced versus criterion-referenced measures in achievement testing (Ebel, 1978; Perrone, 1977; Popham, 1978; Rudman, 1977), but norm-referenced tests remain the most common strategy for eligibility assessment. Norm-referenced measures provide the comparative information necessary for determining eligibility, and they are much more time-efficient. Criterion-referenced tests and other informal measures are typically used after eligibility has been established to provide more detailed descriptions of student performance in areas of educational need.

At present, the three major individual tests used to assess academic achievement in special education are the *Peabody Individual Achievement Test–Revised,* the *Wide Range Achievement Test–Revised,* and the achievement portion of the

Woodcock-Johnson Psycho-Educational Battery– Revised. These three measures, along with others such as the *Kaufman Test of Educational Achievement* and the *Diagnostic Achievement Battery* are described in later sections of this chapter. In addition, two types of informal strategies are discussed later: criterion-referenced tests and curriculum-based measures. Although curriculum-based assessment relies on informal tools such as classroom quizzes, it has gained popularity as a method for determining whether students show school performance problems in the regular classroom.

SOURCES OF INFORMATION ABOUT SCHOOL PERFORMANCE

The assessment team can gather information about the student's school performance in several ways. In addition to individual tests of academic achievement, four major sources of information are school records, students themselves, teachers, and parents.

School Records

School records provide information about the student's past performance and educational history. Although current performance is the main concern, the team needs a picture of how the student has functioned in previous years and the type of services received. Records may also contain some current data, such as this year's report card grades.

School grades. Both current and past report card grades and teachers' comments should be reviewed. Is the problem new, or does it reflect a continuing pattern of school performance difficulty? Do grades suggest academic achievement deficiencies in all areas or only in selected subjects?

Retentions. School records may show that a student has been retained or considered for retention. If retention was suggested, was poor academic achievement one of the major reasons? If the student was retained, what grade or grades were repeated? What were the effects of the grade repetition?

Special services. Referral to special services may be part of a student's record. Has the student been recommended for remedial tutoring, bilingual evaluation, special education assessment, or other services? If so, what were the reasons for the referral, and what was its disposition? Did special services result in substantial improvement of school performance?

Attendance record. Has the student been absent an excessive number of days in this school year or past years? What were the reasons for the attendance problem? Also consider the student's record in terms of the number of schools attended. Was the student enrolled in several different schools over the past few years? How similar were the academic curricula to the current course of study?

Group achievement test results. With the cautions about group testing in mind, records should be examined to determine the student's scores on current and past group tests of academic achievement, measures of minimum competencies, and any other assessments relating to academic achievement. Are the student's scores indicative of a problem in school performance? Does he or she consistently score within the bottom one third of age or grade peers in one or more academic areas? Are past and present results approximately the same, or is a problem just beginning to become apparent?

The Student

The assessment team can involve students in the evaluation process in several ways.

Individual achievement tests. One of the first steps after referral for special education services is participation in individual achievement tests. These measures provide an overview of the student's current standing in relation to others in the major school subjects. In evaluating the results of these tests, the team considers both the student's behavior during the testing situation and the final scores.

Current classroom performance. School records and teachers provide some information about current classroom performance, but the student is the primary source. The team may want to observe the student in the classroom to see how he or she responds to instruction. Does the student participate by listening and watching, asking questions, and attempting to respond to the teacher's questions? What level of accuracy does the student achieve in classwork? In independent academic activities, is the student able to sustain attention, work without assistance, and achieve an acceptable level of accuracy? Samples of student work can also be analyzed.

Attitudes, viewpoints, and academic goals.
Interviews help determine students' perceptions of their own performance. Information can also be gathered with questionnaires, if the measures do not exceed the student's current reading and writing skills. Among the areas the team may wish to explore are the student's attitude toward school, favorite and most disliked school subjects, and perceptions of the reason for referral. In addition, students can report on their academic goals and perhaps their vocational aspirations. They may perceive a difficult subject as unimportant to their academic or vocational future and therefore expend little energy in attempting to master it.

Teachers

Teachers are an important source of information about current classroom functioning. Often the teacher initiates the referral for special education assessment after careful observation of the student's daily performance. Teachers should be consulted about several different aspects of school performance.

Reason for referral. If the student's regular teacher was the source of the referral for special education assessment, the team should interview this teacher to find out more about the reasons for referral. Is the student able to meet regular classroom expectations for achievement in any subject areas? In what specific areas is the student experiencing difficulty? How does the student's performance compare with that of the rest of the class?

Past classroom performance. The student's former teachers may also be of assistance. They can describe classroom performance in past years, perhaps documenting a history of learning difficulties. Or they may be able to report about instructional strategies that proved successful.

Current classroom performance. Current teachers can provide up-to-date report card grades,

results of classroom quizzes, and samples of assignments and other completed work. They can also report their daily observations of the student in the instructional environment. In addition, teachers can describe the academic level and quality of work the student is able to perform. Is the student using grade level materials? If so, is he or she able to master these? If the student is placed in more elementary materials, what level are they? Are they appropriate for current skills? Is the student attentive during instruction? Does he or she participate by asking and answering questions? Is the student able to work independently?

Instructional modifications. Past and present teachers can provide information about the modification of instruction. If the student is unable to meet the demands of the regular classroom, what changes were made to increase the probability of success? What were the results of these changes? Does the student require more complete explanations of new concepts than most learners? Is it necessary to repeat and explain task instructions? Does the student need more opportunities for practice? Does allowing the student additional time increase accuracy? Or is it necessary to assign less or easier work?

Parents

Whereas teachers have the best opportunity for observing academic performance in the classroom, parents and other family members are best able to report about use of academic skills at home and in the community.

Reason for referral. If the student's parents initiated the referral for special education assessment, the team will want to find out why. Are the student's parents concerned about academic achievement? What led to this concern—poor grades, lack of skills or difficulty with academic tasks, discrepancies between siblings' performance?

Past educational performance. Parents can usually provide information about when their child first began showing signs of academic difficulties. Parents often become concerned about their child's school achievement long before the school takes official notice. Sometimes this is due to unrealistic expectations and aspirations for their child. Many times, however, parents make an accurate assessment because they know their child well and have ample opportunity to observe his or her performance.

Current performance at home and in the community. Parents are the best source of information about how the student uses academic skills in the home and community. For example, parents can talk about how their child handles money, if and what he or she reads for pleasure, and how the child copes with composition tasks such as writing notes to family members. Parents can also report whether their child can tell time and make change, and whether he or she is able to read road signs, television schedules, and restaurant menus. Parents make a valuable contribution to the assessment team's study of school performance.

GROUP TESTS OF ACADEMIC ACHIEVEMENT

Group academic achievement tests are typically administered in regular, not special, education. Their results help evaluate the performance of individuals and classes and determine the effectiveness of school programs. Many special students are mainstreamed and so take group tests along with their peers in the regular classroom.

Group tests of academic achievement usually contain several levels so one test series can be used from the earliest elementary grades through junior high or high school. The subject areas assessed by group measures are the basic skills of reading, mathematics, and language arts. Some tests also evaluate reference or study skills and content area subjects such as science and social studies. Because group administration procedures do not allow oral responses, assessment of reading is limited to silent reading skills. Handwriting, written expression, and written spelling are rarely included because test items tend to be multiple choice to facilitate scoring.

Students are usually furnished with test booklets containing the items and directions. Directions

are also orally presented to the group. Younger students may be allowed to record their answers directly in the test booklets, but older students use separate answer sheets. Some group measures provide practice tests that introduce students to the types of questions used and procedures for marking the answer sheet. Group tests can be scored by hand, and publishers may offer machine scoring services. With sophisticated computer-generated reports, results can be presented by class, grade, school, district, pupil, and test item.

Many types of scores are available for group measures. The most typical are grade equivalents, percentile ranks, and stanines. Many tests also link items to instructional objectives, so individual or class reports include a listing of mastered and unmastered skills.

Table 7–1 describes the major group tests of academic achievement. The range of grade levels for which each is appropriate, the number of available levels, and a listing of assessed subject areas are included. Special features are also noted.

Group administration procedures are not optimal for lower performing students for these reasons:

□ Group tests require reading ability, even when assessing skills other than reading.
□ Group tests are often timed.
□ Students must write their answers, usually on a separate answer sheet.
□ Group administration procedures assume students can work independently, monitor their own behavior, and sustain attention to test tasks.

When interpreting results of group testing, it should be remembered that these measures tend to produce a low estimate of handicapped students' performance. In addition, very low test scores tend to be less reliable than scores within the average range.

However, group tests do have some uses in special education, particularly in the screening process. Results of the achievement tests administered at regular grade intervals should be carefully reviewed to identify students needing further assessment. Such tests can also provide information about the academic progress of mainstreamed students in relation to their nonhandicapped peers.

TABLE 7–1
Group tests of academic achievement

Test	Grades	Number of Levels	SUBJECT AREAS ASSESSED				Features
			Reading, Language, Spelling	Math	Reference Skills	Science, Social Studies	
California Achievement Tests (1985, 1986, 1987)	K–12	11	*	*	*	*	Series also includes criterion-referenced tests in reading and mathematics and the *Test of Cognitive Skills*
Comprehensive Tests of Basic Skills (1981, 1982, 1983, 1984, 1985, 1987)	K–12	10	*	*	*	*	Spanish edition available; series includes citerion-referenced tests in reading and mathematics and the *Test of Cognitive Skills*
Iowa Tests of Basic Skills (Hieronymus, Hoover, & Lindquist, 1986)	K–9	10	*	*	*	*	Series includes *Tests of Achievement and Proficiency* (Gr. 9–12) and the *Cognitive Abilities Test*
Metropolitan Achievement Tests (6th ed.) (Prescott, Balow, Hogan, & Farr, 1985, 1986, 1987)	K–12	8	*	*	*	*	Series includes instructional tests of reading, mathematics, and language, and the *Otis–Lennon School Ability Test*
SRA Achievement Series (Naslund, Thorpe, & Lefever, 1985)	K–12	8	*	*	*	*	Level H (Gr. 9–12) includes *Survey of Applied Skills*; an optional test, the *Educational Ability Series*, is available at all levels
Stanford Achievement Test Series (7th ed.) (Gardner, Rudman, Karlsen, & Merwin, 1982, 1983, 1984, 1986, 1987)	K–13	10	*	*	*	*	Series includes *Stanford Early School Achievement Test* (K–1), *Stanford Test of Academic Skills* (Gr. 8–13), diagnostic tests of reading and mathematics, and the *Otis–Lennon School Ability Test*

INDIVIDUAL TESTS OF ACADEMIC ACHIEVEMENT

Individual achievement tests are preferred for assessment of school performance in special education. Like group measures, they are designed for a wide span of grades, usually kindergarten through grade 12. Instead of having separate versions for different grade levels, individual tests are usually limited to one version that includes a wide range of items arranged in order of difficulty.

As Table 7–2 shows, most individual achievement tests assess the basic skills of reading, mathematics, and spelling. Content subjects such as science and social studies are not included as often. Because these tests are individually administered, student responses can be written, oral, or even gestural. This allows the assessment of oral as well as silent reading, and permits students with poor writing skills to bypass this difficulty when answering questions in other subject matter areas.

The following sections describe and critique several individual academic achievement tests used in special education. In the first section, the *Peabody Individual Achievement Test–Revised* is discussed. Next are the *Wide Range Achievement Test–Revised* and the achievement portion of the *Woodcock-Johnson Psycho-Educational Battery–Revised*.

PEABODY INDIVIDUAL ACHIEVEMENT TEST–REVISED

The *Peabody Individual Achievement Test–Revised (PIAT–R)* is a norm-referenced measure commonly used in special education for identifying academic deficiencies. Originally published in 1970 as the *PIAT* (Dunn & Markwardt), the revised edition of this test offers updated norms and test items, an expanded number of items per subtest, and a new optional subtest to assess composition skills. According to its manual, the *PIAT–R* is "an individually administered achievement test providing wide-range screening in six content areas" (Markwardt, 1989, p. 1).

The *PIAT–R* is made up of six subtests: General Information, Reading Recognition, Reading Comprehension, Mathematics, Spelling, and Written Expression. The most typical response format on the *PIAT–R* is multiple-choice. The student is shown a test plate with four possible answers and asked to select the correct response.

□ *General Information*—On this subtest, questions are read aloud by the tester. There are no visuals, and no choices are presented. The student listens to the question and responds orally. Test items sample several areas of knowledge, including science, social studies, fine arts, humanities, and recreation.

□ *Reading Recognition*—The first 16 test items, in multiple-choice format, begin with simple matching questions where students must select the letter or word identical to the stimulus, then progress to items that require students to locate words that begin with the same sound as that of a pictured object. Beginning with item 17, students are presented with words to read orally. Words are presented in isolation without context cues.

□ *Reading Comprehension*—Students read a sentence silently and then select the picture that best depicts that sentence from a set of four pictures. The sentence may not be read more than once, and the student is not allowed to look at the sentence after the pictures have been exposed.

□ *Mathematics*—On most items, the tester reads a question as the student views four possible responses. Test items begin with exercises requiring matching of numerals and progress to areas such as numeration, basic operations, measurement, geometry, graphs and statistics, estimation, algebra, and advanced mathematics.

□ *Spelling*—This subtest begins with multiple-choice items in which the student must discriminate the one response of four that is different; more difficult items require students to select a letter that makes a particular sound. Beginning with item 16, the format of this subtest changes; the student is shown four ways of spelling a word and asked to identify the correct spelling after hearing the word pronounced and read in a sentence.

□ *Written Expression*—This optional subtest contains two levels. Level I is designed for students in kindergarten and grade 1, and Level II for grades 2 through 12. On Level I, students are asked to write their name, copy letters and words, and write letters, words, and sentences

TABLE 7–2
Individual tests of academic achievement

Name (Author)	Ages or Grades	SUBJECT AREAS ASSESSED				
		Reading	Math	Spelling	Written Language	Content Subjects
Basic Achievement Skills Individual Screener (1983)	Gr. 1–8	*	*	*	*	
Diagnostic Achievement Battery (Newcomer & Curtis, 1984)	Age 6-0 to 14-11	*	*	*	*	
Diagnostic Achievement Test for Adolescents (Newcomer & Bryant, 1986)	Age 12-0 to 18-11	*	*	*	*	*
Kaufman Test of Educational Achievement (Kaufman & Kaufman, 1985)	Age 6-0 to 17-11	*	*	*		
Peabody Individual Achievement Test–Revised (Markwardt, 1989)	Age 5-0 to 18-11, Gr. K-12	*	*	*	*	*
Quick-Score Achievement Test (Hammill, Ammer, Cronin, Mandlebaum, & Quinby, 1987)	Age 7-0 to 17-11	*	*	*	*	*
Wide Range Achievement Test–Revised (Jastak & Wilkinson, 1984)	Age 5-0 to 74-11	*	*	*		
Woodcock-Johnson Psycho-Educational Battery–Revised (Woodcock & Johnson, 1989)	Age 2 to 90+, Gr. K-12 and college	*	*	*	*	*

from dictation. On Level II, students are shown a stimulus picture and directed to write a story about that picture within a 20-minute time period. The tester can choose from two stimulus pictures, Prompt A and Prompt B.

Students must be able to attend to test tasks for several minutes at a time to participate in *PIAT–R* administration. English-language skills are a necessity for comprehension of directions and questions. However, the multiple-choice format used in several subtests reduces response requirements; students can answer either by pointing to the correct response, saying the answer, or saying the number of the answer. The student is required to speak only on General Information and later items of the Reading Recognition subtest. Writing is required only in the Written Expression subtest. Reading skills are not needed for the Mathematics and General Information subtests because the tester reads the questions to the student. Only the Written Expression subtest (Level II) is timed.

Technical Quality

The *PIAT–R* was standardized in 1986 with 1,738 students in kindergarten through grade 12 (ages 5 to 19). Approximately half of the students were males and half were females. Students were drawn primarily from public schools, and students in special education classes were excluded. The sample was selected to resemble the U.S. population as reflected in 1985 U.S. Census data. The final sample appears to resemble the nation as a whole in terms of geographic region, parental education level (an indicator of socioeconomic status), and race or ethnic group.

The *PIAT–R* appears most appropriate for students enrolled in regular classes from kindergarten to grade 12. Although handicapped students receiving services in special education classes were excluded from the sample, the manual does not discuss whether mainstreamed handicapped students or non-English-speaking students were excluded. However, because regular classes are likely to contain students with mild handicapping conditions, it is probable that such students were part of the standardization sample.

Reliability and validity are also of concern in evaluating the technical quality of a norm-referenced test. On the *PIAT–R,* reliability was studied by several methods. For the five required *PIAT–R* subtests and the Total Test score, split-half and Kuder-Richardson reliability coefficients were above the suggested .80 minimum at all grade and age levels. Test-retest reliability was generally adequate for these subtests, although coefficients fell in the .70s for some subtests for grade 6/age 12 students.

Reliability was studied somewhat differently for the optional subtest, Written Expression. Level I of that subtest shows high interrater reliability (.90

PEABODY INDIVIDUAL ACHIEVEMENT TEST–REVISED (PIAT–R)
F. C. Markwardt (1989)

Type: Norm-referenced test
Major Content Areas: General information, reading, mathematics, spelling, and written expression
Type of Administration: Individual
Administration Time: Approximately one hour
Age/Grade Levels: Grades K through 12, ages 5–0 to 18–11
Types of Scores: Grade and age equivalents, standard scores, percentile ranks; for the Written Expression subtest, grade-based stanines and developmental scaled scores
Typical Uses: A broad-based screening measure for the identification of strengths and weaknesses in academic achievement
Cautions: In administration, special rules apply concerning "false" basals and ceilings. Scoring is complicated by the need to use two sets of standard errors of measurement, one for raw scores and age/grade equivalents, another for standard scores. Results of the optional Written Expression subtest should be interpreted cautiously due to concerns about reliability.

for kindergarten and .95 for grade 1); however, internal consistency coefficients ranged from .60 to .69 and test-retest reliability was .56. On Level II of Written Expression, most internal consistency coefficients fell at .80 or above. In contrast, the median correlation coefficient for interrater reliability was .58 for Prompt A and .67 for Prompt B. In addition, the average degree of relationship between student performance on Prompts A and B was .63, indicating less than satisfactory alternate-form reliability.

Also of interest is the relationship between results of the original version of this test, the *PIAT*, and results from the *PIAT–R*. Median correlation coefficients between 1970 and 1989 versions of subtests range from .66 to .83 by grade and from .76 to .88 by age. Total test results, however, show much greater agreement (.88 by grade and .91 by age). It appears that the revision process has resulted in individual subtests that produce somewhat different results than their original versions. One explanation for this is the updating of item content. According to its manual, the *PIAT–R* incorporated only about 35% of the items from the 1970 *PIAT*.

Concurrent validity of the *PIAT–R* was studied by assessing its relationship to the *Peabody Picture Vocabulary Test–Revised (PPVT–R)* (Dunn & Dunn, 1981), which the *PIAT–R* manual describes as a measure of "verbal ability independent of reading ability or expressive language" (p. 66). The median correlation coefficient between *PPVT–R* results and results of individual *PIAT–R* subtests ranged from .50 to .72. Factor analysis was also used to investigate the *PIAT–R*'s validity. Three factors emerged, all of which appear to represent verbal skills. The first, described in the manual as "a general verbal-educational ability factor" (p. 72), includes the General Information, Mathematics, and Reading Comprehension subtests. The second factor includes Spelling and Reading Recognition and appears to relate more to verbal skills associated with symbol systems. The third factor is associated with the Reading Comprehension and Written Expression (Level II) subtests.

There is need to study the relationship of the *PIAT–R* to other tests of academic achievement. The manual does provide summaries of more than 50 validity studies of the original *PIAT*. In general, the 1970 *PIAT* showed moderate correlations with individual measures such as the *Wide Range Achievement Test* (Jastak & Jastak, 1978), the *Woodcock-Johnson Psycho-Educational Battery* (Woodcock & Johnson, 1977), the *Woodcock Reading Mastery Tests* (Woodcock, 1973), and the *KeyMath Diagnostic Arithmetic Test* (Connolly, Nachtman, & Pritchett, 1971, 1976). However, all of these tests have undergone revisions, and new research is needed to examine the ways in which they relate to each other.

Administration Considerations

According to the test manual, "The qualifications for administering the *PIAT–R* are minimal" (p. 3). Before *PIAT–R* results are used for educational decisions, however, the manual advises that testers study the administration and scoring procedures and practice test administration. Interpretation of test results requires additional expertise, particularly in the areas of measurement and curriculum.

The *PIAT–R* is relatively easy to administer and score, and Parts II and III of the manual provide guidelines for these procedures. The testing materials include the manual, four administration booklets (called test easels), the Test Record in which the examiner records the student's responses, and the Written Expression Test Booklet in which the student writes responses. Three of the four administration booklets are in easel format. The tester sits across the corner of the table from the student so that the tester can view both sides of the easel, as needed. On the Reading Comprehension subtest, a book is laid on the table in front of the student. If the tester wishes to continue the easel-type administration, the book can be placed over the easel for one of the other subtests.

Subtests must be administered in a standard order, beginning with General Information, and the Test Record and test easels are arranged in that order. It is possible to omit a subtest, but the standard order must be maintained for the remaining subtests. The Reading Comprehension subtest is not administered to students who receive raw scores of less than 19 on the Reading Recognition subtest; when this occurs, the Reading Recognition raw score is also entered as the raw score for Reading Comprehension.

The *PIAT–R* begins with standard introductory remarks that the tester reads to all students. Training exercises are available for all required subtests and for Level I of Written Expression. For the first subtest, General Information, the Test Record lists suggested starting places by grade level. According to the manual, the tester should adjust this starting place if there is reason to suspect that the student's achievement is either below or above that of typical grade peers. For the remaining required subtests, the suggested starting place is the raw score earned by the student on the previous subtest. Procedures for the Written Expression subtest are somewhat different. Level I is administered to students showing less than grade 2 achievement in written expression skills, and Level II to those with grade 2 achievement or better; it is also possible to administer both levels of this subtest to the same student.

There is no basal or ceiling on the Written Expression subtest; all items are administered on Level I, and Level II consists of only one task. On all other subtests, the basal is five consecutively numbered correct items, and the ceiling is five errors out of seven consecutively numbered items. The manual suggests that, if the student misses the first item administered, the tester move backward five items in an attempt to locate the student's optimal performance range. It is possible on the *PIAT–R* to encounter situations where students appear to attain more than one basal or ceiling. For example, a student might answer items 5 to 9 correctly, miss item 10, then answer 11 to 15 correctly. In this case, the lower-numbered items (5 to 9) are considered a "false basal"; the *higher-numbered* range of items (11 to 15) is considered the true basal, and failures below that basal are disregarded. Likewise, if two ceilings are established, that composed of *lower-numbered* items is considered the true ceiling; successes above that ceiling are disregarded.

Only Level II of the Written Expression subtest is timed. Students are allowed 20 minutes to write a story. However, the manual advises that students be encouraged to respond within 30 seconds to Mathematics items and within 15 seconds on other subtests.

The *PIAT–R* Test Record is well designed. It clearly states the basal and ceiling rules and suggested starting points at the beginning of each subtest. The tester should circle the number of the first item administered and draw a bracket

around the basal items and the ceiling items. As each item is administered, the student's response is recorded on the protocol and scored. On multiple-choice items, the number of the student's response is entered; on open-ended items, the tester records the student's actual response. Incorrect answers are indicated by a diagonal slash through the item number. On the Written Expression subtest, the student writes in a separate booklet. Criteria for evaluating performance are presented in the manual and Test Record. For example, in Level II, the tester uses a 24-item rating scale to evaluate the story the student has written. The scoring guidelines should be carefully followed, and as a check for accuracy, the manual suggests that a second professional be asked to score students' stories.

Results and Interpretation

The *PIAT–R* offers several types of total test and subtest scores. Both age and grade norms are available, and the tester must decide whether to compare the student's performance with that of age or grade peers. Grade norms are generally the most appropriate, and the *PIAT–R* offers grade norms for fall, winter, and spring test administrations. However, if the student is placed in an ungraded or special class, the tester may choose to use age peers for comparison.

A variety of scores are available for the five required subtests: grade or age equivalents, standard scores, and percentile ranks. Standard scores are distributed with a mean of 100 and a standard deviation of 15. Using the interpretation system suggested in Chapter 4, the range of average performance on the *PIAT–R* is standard score 85 to 115. The manual provides guidelines for determining if differences between required subtests are statistically significant.

Confidence intervals can be constructed around each score. The Test Record provides standard error of measurement values for raw scores by grade and age levels and by confidence level (68%, 90%, and 95%). Somewhat different procedures are used for standard scores; the tester must refer to an appendix in the manual for the standard errors of measurement. Values are usually decimals, which are rounded to the nearest whole number. For numbers ending in .5, the number is rounded up if it is odd (e.g., 3.5) and down if it is even (e.g., 4.5). Standard scores are converted to percentile ranks by means of a table.

These types of results are not available for the Written Expression subtest. Raw scores on both Level I and Level II are converted to grade-based stanines. Stanines are a nine-point scale distributed with a mean of 5 and a standard deviation of approximately 2. On Level II, it is also possible to determine developmental scaled scores which allow comparison of a student's performance to that of all individuals within the standardization sample. These scores range from 1 to 15; the mean is 8 and the standard deviation is approximately 3.

In addition to subtest scores, the tester can obtain a Total Reading Composite, Written Language Composite, and Total Test score. Total Reading includes both reading subtests, and the Total Test score is a composite of the five required subtests. The Written Language score combines the Spelling and Written Expression subtests. The Test Record does not provide space for entering the Written Language composite, but directions for its computation are included in an appendix in the manual. All global scores can be expressed as standard scores and percentile ranks.

PIAT–R results can be plotted on two profiles, the Developmental Score Profile for age or grade equivalents, and the Standard Score Profile. General guidelines are provided on the Test Record for evaluating whether differences between scores indicate true differences in achievement; however, the manual should be consulted for specific criteria for determining whether differences are statistically significant.

Figure 7–1 presents sample PIAT–R results for Joyce, the fourth grader with possible school performance problems. Note that grade norms were used to evaluate her performance and that a 68% confidence level was selected. The confidence interval for Joyce's Total Test performance is standard score 79 to 83. The chances that this range of scores includes Joyce's true score are about 68 out of 100. It can be concluded that, in overall academic achievement, Joyce is currently functioning within the low average range of performance when compared to grade peers. Inspection of the Standard Score Profile shows no overlap

between some sets of scores (e.g., Mathematics and Spelling). By consulting the manual, it is possible to determine that a standard score difference of 26 between these two subtests (Mathematics standard score 95 − Spelling standard score 69) is statistically significant at the .01 level for students in grade 4. Likewise, according to the table in the manual, there is a significant difference at the .05 level between Joyce's performance in Mathematics and Reading Recognition but no significant difference between Mathematics and Reading Comprehension.

In evaluating PIAT results, it is sometimes useful to analyze the student's responses to individual test items. For subtests with multiple-choice formats, this may not prove very informative. However, some young or immature children will select their answers by position, perhaps choosing responses in the upper right quadrant of the page. The tester should check the student's response pattern for this. On the General Information, Reading Recognition, and Written Expression subtests, items are open-ended rather than multiple-choice. Response analysis of these subtests may provide clues to the student's storehouse of general knowledge, word attack strategies, and a variety of writing skills.

The PIAT–R appears to be a useful tool for the assessment of school performance across a range of academic subjects. It includes measures of general knowledge and skills such as reading, mathematics, spelling, and composition. Caution is necessary, however, in interpreting results of the Written Expression subtest because its reliability is not well established. If information about writing skills is desired, the tester may choose to use this subtest as an informal measure. Like most broad-based achievement measures that survey several academic subjects, the PIAT–R does not produce results specific enough to provide direction for instructional planning; its main function is the identification of school subjects in which the student shows poor performance in relation to age or grade peers. It is also important to note that the PIAT–R assesses some skills with test tasks dissimilar to typical classroom activities. For instance, classroom spelling tasks usually require students to write spelling words, not select the correct spelling from several choices.

FIGURE 7–1

Sample results from the *Peabody Individual Achievement Test–Revised*

Student's name __Joyce__

Testing date __12 - 11 - 89__

Scores

Grade Placement __4.4__
Chronological Age __9 - 8__

	RAW SCORES	Grade Equivalents ☑ / Age Equivalents ☐ *(Table G.1 or G.3)*	Standard Scores ☑Grade*(G.2)* F ⓦ S *(circle one)* ☐Age*(G.4)*	Percentile Ranks *(Table G.5)*

RAW SCORES — __68__ % confidence
DERIVED SCORES
Grade Equivalents — __68__ % confidence
Standard Scores — __68__ % confidence³
Percentile Ranks — __68__ % confidence

General Information
Raw Score SEM Values by Confidence Level

Grade / Age	68%	90%	95%
K - 7 / 5 - 13	③	5	6
8 - 12 / 14 - 18	2	3	4

−SEM		+SEM	−SEM		+SEM	−SEM		+SEM	−SEM		+SEM
48	51	54	3.7	4.0	4.4	91	95	99	27	37	47

Reading Recognition
Raw Score SEM Values by Confidence Level

Grade / Age	68%	90%	95%
K - 12 / 5 - 18	②	3	4

−SEM		+SEM	−SEM		+SEM	−SEM		+SEM	−SEM		+SEM
47	49	51	2.7	2.9	3.1	80	82	84	9	12	14

Reading Comprehension
Raw Score SEM Values by Confidence Level

Grade / Age	68%	90%	95%
/ 5 - 6	4	7	8
K - 12 / 7 - 18	③	5	6

−SEM		+SEM	−SEM		+SEM	−SEM		+SEM	−SEM		+SEM
44	47	50	2.4	2.7	3.0	76	80	84	5	9	14

TOTAL READING ¹
Raw Score SEM Values by Confidence Level *(Add Reading Rec. and Reading Comp. raw scores)*

Grade / Age	68%	90%	95%
1 - 12 / 5 - 15	④	7	8
K / 16 - 18	3	5	6

−SEM		+SEM	−SEM		+SEM	−SEM		+SEM	−SEM		+SEM
92	96	100	2.6	2.8	3.0	79	81	83	8	10	13

Mathematics
Raw Score SEM Values by Confidence Level

Grade / Age	68%	90%	95%
K - 4 / 5 - 9	②	3	4
5 - 12 / 10 - 18	3	5	6

−SEM		+SEM	−SEM		+SEM	−SEM		+SEM	−SEM		+SEM
45	47	49	3.7	3.9	4.2	91	95	99	27	37	47

Spelling
Raw Score SEM Values by Confidence Level

Grade / Age	68%	90%	95%
K - 6 / 5 - 17	②	3	4
7 - 12 / 18	3	5	6

−SEM		+SEM	−SEM		+SEM	−SEM		+SEM	−SEM		+SEM
40	42	44	2.0	2.1	2.3	65	69	73	1	2	4

TOTAL TEST ²
Raw Score SEM Values by Confidence Level *(See Note 2 below)*

Grade / Age	68%	90%	95%
K - 8 / 5 - 14	⑥	10	12
9 - 12 / 15 - 18	5	8	10

−SEM		+SEM	−SEM		+SEM	−SEM		+SEM	−SEM		+SEM
230	236	242	2.9	3.0	3.1	79	81	83	8	10	13

Written Expression
☐ Level I
☑ Level II
 ☑ Prompt A
 ☐ Prompt B

RAW SCORE __27__

Grade-Based Stanine *(Levels I and II)* *(Table G.6 or G.7)*	Developmental Scaled Score *(Level II only)* *(Table G.8)*
	15
	14
9	13
8	12
7	11
6	10
5	9
④	8
3	7
2	6
1	⑤
	4
	3
	2
	1

¹ The Total Reading composite raw score is the sum of the Reading Recognition and Reading Comprehension subtest raw scores.
² The Total Test composite raw score is the sum of the General Information, Reading Recognition, Reading Comprehension, Mathematics, and Spelling subtest raw scores.
³ Values to be used in the standard score confidence intervals are given in Appendix H of the manual.

STANDARD SCORE PROFILE

☑ Grade (Circle one: Fall ⓦⒾⓃⓉⒺⓇ Spring)
☐ Age

norm group mean

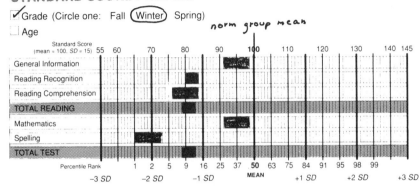

Standard Score (mean = 100, SD = 15) 55 60 70 80 90 100 110 120 130 140 145

General Information
Reading Recognition
Reading Comprehension
TOTAL READING
Mathematics
Spelling
TOTAL TEST

Percentile Rank 1 2 5 9 16 25 37 50 63 75 84 91 95 98 99
−3 SD   −2 SD   −1 SD   MEAN   +1 SD   +2 SD   +3 SD

INTERPRETING DIFFERENCES IN SCORES

Considerable caution should be exercised in interpreting the meaning of observed differences between scores. The following rule of thumb is one approach to evaluating whether a difference between scores indicates a real difference in achievement. Part III in the manual explains this and other approaches to evaluating differences.

For the scores in question, compare the degree to which the shaded confidence intervals on the profile overlap each other. If the intervals —

- overlap by more than half, a real difference is UNLIKELY.
- overlap by half or less, a real difference is POSSIBLE.
- do not overlap at all, a real difference is PROBABLE.

Note. From *Test Record, Peabody Individual Achievement Test–Revised* by F. C. Markwardt, 1989, Circle Pines, MN: American Guidance Service. Copyright 1989 by American Guidance Service, Inc. Reprinted by permission.

WIDE RANGE ACHIEVEMENT TEST–REVISED

Another popular norm-referenced test for assessment of school performance is the *Wide Range Achievement Test–Revised (WRAT–R)*. One of the oldest measures of academic achievement, the *WRAT* first appeared in the 1930s. The fifth revision, the *WRAT–R*, is a new standardization of the previous edition. Test items remain the same except for the addition of a few items to the Arithmetic subtests. According to the *WRAT–R* manual, the purpose of this test is "to measure the codes which are needed to learn the basic skills of reading, spelling, and arithmetic" (Jastak & Wilkinson, 1984, p. 1). Although some portions of the *WRAT–R* can be administered in group fashion, individual administration is preferred.

The *WRAT–R* is divided into Level 1 for students ages 5–0 to 11–11, and Level 2 for those age 12–0 through adulthood. Each level contains three subtests.

□ *Spelling*—Students write spelling words from dictation. The tester reads the word, then a sentence containing the word, and the student must write the word on the test form within a specified time period. Different word lists are used for Levels 1 and 2. A prespelling section is administered to young children (ages 5–0 to 7–11) and to older students who do not meet the specified criterion level on the dictation section of the subtest. In prespelling, students copy geometric shapes and write (or print) their names. Prespelling activities are also timed.

□ *Arithmetic*—Students write answers to arithmetic problems. They are given a page of computation problems and asked to solve as many as possible within 10 minutes. Level 1 contains problems ranging from simple addition and other basic operations to computations involving fractions, decimals, and percentages. On Level 2, items begin with simple arithmetic calculations and extend to problems requiring knowledge of algebra and geometry. A prearithmetic section is administered to young children (ages 5–0 to 7–11) and to older students who fail to meet the specified criterion on the written section. In prearithmetic, students are timed, but responses are oral rather than written. Activities include counting objects, reading numbers, and answering oral addition and subtraction problems.

□ *Reading*—On this subtest, students read lists of words aloud. Words are presented in isolation; each must be pronounced correctly within a specified time limit. Different word lists appear

---

WIDE RANGE ACHIEVEMENT TEST–REVISED (WRAT–R)
S. Jastak & G. S. Wilkinson (1984)

Type: Norm-referenced test
Major Content Areas: Reading recognition, spelling, and arithmetic
Type of Administration: Primarily individual, although portions of the Spelling and Arithmetic subtests may be given to small groups
Administration Time: 15 to 30 minutes
Age/Grade Levels: Ages 5–0 to 74–11
Types of Scores: Grade equivalents, standard scores, percentiles
Typical Uses: A screening measure for the identification of possible strengths and weaknesses in basic school subjects
Cautions: Caution is advised in interpretation of results because of insufficient information on concurrent validity of the 1984 edition. The Arithmetic subtest is a particular concern because its test items appear more difficult for nonwhite persons than white persons. In addition, professionals should keep in mind that the *WRAT–R* is not intended to assess comprehension. Caution is also advised in determining which portions of the test are to be administered to a student.

on Levels 1 and 2. A prereading section is administered to young children (ages 5–0 to 7–11) and to older students who fail to meet the specified criterion on the oral reading section. The prereading section is also timed and includes activities such as matching and naming letters.

To participate in WRAT–R administration, students must be able to attend to test tasks. Knowledge of English is a necessity, except for some portions of the written computation section of the Arithmetic subtest. Response requirements are demanding. Students must write their answers on two of the subtests and respond orally on the third. In addition, all test activities are timed. Reading skills are necessary for the Reading subtest, oral reading of numerals is one of the prearithmetic tasks, and several of the written computation problems contain written directions.

Technical Quality

The WRAT–R was standardized with a stratified national sample of 5,600 persons from 17 states. Twenty-eight age groups were included (ages 5–0 to 74–11). The sample was selected to represent the national population in terms of geographic region, race (white and nonwhite), and type of community (metropolitan and nonmetropolitan). The socioeconomic status characteristics of the sample are not described. In addition, no data are provided regarding the numbers of handicapped persons and those with a primary language other than English.

The WRAT–R appears appropriate for a wide age span of individuals. Norms are based on a large sample representing the total U.S. population on several demographic variables. However, the manual reports a study of item bias: the Arithmetic subtest is more difficult for nonwhite individuals than for white.

The test-retest reliability of the WRAT–R appears adequate. Item difficulty was studied using the Rasch model, and analysis results indicate that the items on each subtest represent a range from very easy to difficult.

According to its manual, "The content validity of the WRAT–R is apparent" (p. 62). The test's purpose is measurement of skill in the rote recall or code aspects of basic skills; the manual states that "the WRAT–R was intentionally designed to

eliminate, as totally as possible, the effects of comprehension" (p. 1). The test authors appear to have attained this goal.

The WRAT–R manual discusses two types of validity studies. One type examined the relationship between the 1984 WRAT–R and earlier editions of the WRAT. Results showed high correlations between the different versions of this test (.91 to .99), a logical outcome because of the number of test items remaining unchanged from edition to edition.

The second type of study investigated the relationship of the WRAT to other tests of academic achievement. No data were reported for the WRAT–R. Instead, the manual refers to the research literature and summarizes results of studies with previous editions of the WRAT. However, some researchers have found significant differences between scores on WRAT Arithmetic and scores on the PIAT Mathematics subtest. In three studies (Harmer & Williams, 1978; Scull & Brand, 1980; Stoneburner & Brown, 1979), students received higher scores on the PIAT measure of arithmetic skills than they did on the WRAT measure.

The first in a series of monographs on the WRAT–R (Wilkinson, 1987) discusses content validity and presents results of one unpublished study of concurrent validity. Correlations between WRAT–R subtests and achievement cluster scores for the Woodcock-Johnson Psycho-Educational Battery ranged from .69 to .84 for percentile ranks, .70 to .85 for standard scores, and .29 to .64 for grade equivalents. Further investigation of the technical quality of the WRAT–R is needed.

Administration Considerations

Although formal training is not required to administer the WRAT–R, the manual must be studied with care because it is a difficult test to correctly administer. Not all sections of the WRAT–R are given to all students. Students between the ages of 5–0 and 11–11 receive Level 1, and those ages 12 and older receive Level 2. In addition, each subtest at each level contains a skill section and a preskill section.

The tester first determines whether to begin each subtest with the skill section or the preskill section. With young Level 1 children (ages 5–0 to

7–11), each subtest is started with the preskill section. With older students in the Level 1 range, testing begins with the skill section. However, if the student does not perform adequately on the skill section, the preskill section must then be administered.

With Level 2 students (ages 12–0 and above), each subtest begins with the skill section. Preskill sections are given only when students fall below specified performance criteria. The Level 2 preskill sections of each subtest differ slightly from the Level 1 versions.

WRAT–R subtests may be administered in any order, and it is not necessary to give all three. *WRAT–R* subtests have no basals as the term is usually used, but the rules for administration of subtest preskill sections can be interpreted as rules for establishing basals. Ceilings of 10 consecutive errors are specified for the Spelling and Reading subtests. Arithmetic has a 10-minute time limit rather than a ceiling. All *WRAT–R* tasks are timed. In Spelling, students are allowed 15 seconds to write a word and, in Reading, 10 seconds to read a word.

The *WRAT–R* manual presents the instructions to be read to the student in boldface type so they are easily located. However, the manual varies in format from subtest to subtest, making it difficult to locate other important information such as time limits, ceiling rules, and rules for preskill administration.

The test form is used to record the student's responses. In some portions of the *WRAT–R,* the tester is the recorder and in others, such as Spelling, the student writes the answers. If handwriting is illegible, the tester should ask the student to read what he or she has written. The *WRAT–R* manual recommends that testers record reading responses by underlining the first letter of words read correctly and marking a slash through the first letter of incorrect words. However, verbatim recording is necessary if the tester later wishes to analyze errors.

Calculation of raw scores on the *WRAT–R* requires an alert tester. If preskill activities are not administered, the student receives full credit for these sections. This is equivalent to giving full credit for all items below the basal. Point values of similar test items also vary from Level 1 to Level 2.

Results and Interpretation

The *WRAT–R* offers several types of scores for each subtest but no total test or summary score. Only age norms are available, extending from age 5 to 75. The derived scores usually obtained from *WRAT–R* raw scores are grade equivalents, standard scores, and percentile ranks. Stanines, scaled scores, and T-scores are also available.

WRAT–R standard scores are distributed with a mean of 100 and a standard deviation of 15. It is expected that approximately 95% of the population will fall between standard score 70 and standard score 130. Thus, the range of average performance on the *WRAT–R* is standard score 85 to 115. The *WRAT–R* manual suggests a somewhat different classification system. Standard score ranges are 10 points, representing two thirds of one standard deviation. For example, standard scores between 90 and 109 are considered Average.

The standard errors of measurement are reported in the *WRAT–R* manual for each subtest in raw score units. Tables are provided so the tester can determine the exact standard error by the age of the person and subtest score received. If this degree of precision is not needed, the test form lists approximate standard errors of measurement for each subtest. On Level 1, these are Reading, 2 raw score points; Spelling, 1.5; and Arithmetic, 1.5. On Level 2, each subtest has an approximate standard error of 2 raw score points.

Sample Level 2 *WRAT–R* results are shown in Figure 7–2 for a junior high school student named David. David is currently in eighth grade and is having trouble in math. Only age norms are available on the *WRAT–R,* so David's performance was compared to that of other students ages 14–0 to 14–11.

David's *WRAT–R* performance is reported in raw scores, standard scores, percentile ranks, and grade equivalents. The grade equivalent scale on the *WRAT–R* is made up of larger units than found on most grade scales. Each grade level only has two possible scores, one indicating performance at the beginning of the grade (e.g., 8B) and the other indicating performance at the end of the grade (e.g., 8E). Grade equivalents are plotted on a profile, as Figure 7–2 shows, and subtest standard errors of measurement are used to construct confidence intervals around each observed score.

FIGURE 7–2
Sample *WRAT–R* results

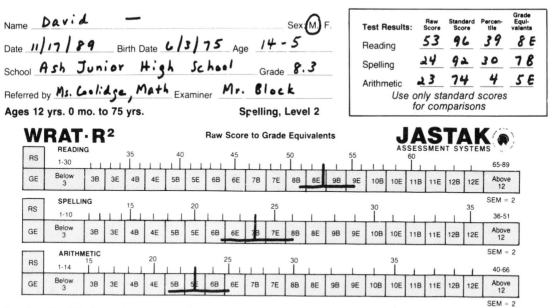

Note. From the *Wide Range Achievement Test–Revised, Level 2* by S. Jastak and G. S. Wilkinson, 1984, Wilmington, DE: Jastak Associates. Copyright 1984 by Jastak Associates, Inc. Reprinted by permission.

Confidence intervals may also be constructed around *WRAT–R* standard scores. However, because standard errors are reported in raw score units, the interval is constructed first in raw scores and then converted into standard scores. On the Arithmetic subtest, David earned a raw score of 23, and the standard error for this subtest is 2 raw score points. If a 68% level of confidence is selected, the interval becomes raw scores 21 to 25. These raw scores correspond to the standard score range of 68 to 80. Thus, the chances that the range of standard scores from 68 to 80 includes David's true score are about 68 out of 100. These results indicate that David's performance on the *WRAT–R* Arithmetic subtest falls between the below average and low average ranges in comparison to age peers.

In evaluating a student's performance on the *WRAT–R,* it may be useful to analyze specific responses. The *WRAT–R* requires students to spell words in writing, write the answers to arithmetic computation problems, and read words orally. Answers may provide some information about how the student approaches these common school tasks. For example, the teacher may be able to compare the student's ability to spell phonetically regular and irregular words or to look at skills in pronouncing certain vowel and consonant sounds. Also, the Spelling and Arithmetic subtests provide samples of the student's handwriting that can be analyzed for legibility and error patterns.

However, in analyzing *WRAT–R* scores and specific student responses, it is necessary to remain aware of the way in which this test assesses basic skills. In all subtests, only a small segment of the curriculum under study is sampled. On the written section of the Level 1 Arithmetic subtest, for example, addition of whole numbers is represented by five problems and subtraction of whole numbers by four. In Reading, only the skill of reading words in isolation is evaluated; the important skill of comprehension is not assessed. In fact, the Reading subtest might better be called "Reading Recognition" because of its failure to include anything but decoding tasks.

The *WRAT–R* should not be used as the sole instrument for determining a student's current levels of academic achievement. It lacks coverage of some basic skill subjects, although the tasks it does contain resemble typical classroom activities. The reliability of the 1984 edition of the *WRAT* is adequate, but its relationship to other measures of academic achievement requires further study. In addition, results are neither specific nor comprehensive enough to assist in planning instructional programs.

WOODCOCK-JOHNSON PSYCHO-EDUCATIONAL BATTERY–REVISED, TESTS OF ACHIEVEMENT

The *Woodcock-Johnson Psycho-Educational Battery–Revised* (*Woodcock-Johnson–R*) is a norm-referenced measure made up of 35 subtests arranged in two main parts, the *Tests of Cognitive Ability* and the *Tests of Achievement*. Of concern here is the portion of the *Woodcock-Johnson–R* that focuses on academic achievement. However, one of the features of the *Woodcock-Johnson–R* is its capacity to assess both learning aptitude and academic performance within one assessment system. This feature is discussed in the next chapter when the *Woodcock-Johnson–R Tests of Cognitive Ability* are described.

The *Woodcock-Johnson* was originally published in 1977. The revised 1989 version features several new subtests and a new organization of subtests into two levels, standard batteries and supplemental batteries. Standard batteries are administered first, then portions of the supplemental batteries are selected if further information is needed. In addition, two alternative forms of the Tests of Achievement are now available.

The *Woodcock-Johnson–R Tests of Achievement* are designed to provide information about four areas of the curriculum: reading, mathematics, written language, and knowledge. In both Form A and Form B, the standard achievement battery contains 9 subtests and the supplemental battery contains 5 subtests. These measures are described in the next paragraphs by curriculum area. In each area, standard battery subtests are discussed first, then supplemental subtests.

Reading

□ *Letter-Word Identification*—On the first test items, the student is shown a colored drawing and two or three small line drawings called rebuses; the student selects the rebus that depicts the colored drawing. Next, when shown a letter, the student must say its name. On more difficult items, the student is asked to pronounce real words.

WOODCOCK-JOHNSON PSYCHO-EDUCATIONAL BATTERY–REVISED (WOODCOCK-JOHNSON–R): TESTS OF ACHIEVEMENT
R. W. Woodcock & M. B. Johnson (1989)

Type: Norm-referenced test
Major Content Areas: Reading, mathematics, written language, and knowledge (science, social studies, and humanities)
Type of Administration: Individual
Administration Time: Approximately one hour for standard battery
Age/Grade Levels: Ages 2 to 90 + ; Grades K–12, college
Types of Scores: Grade and age equivalents, standard scores, percentile ranks, Relative Mastery Index (RMI) scores
Typical Uses: A broad-based screening measure for the identification of strengths and weaknesses in academic achievement
Cautions: Some subtests are not administered if scores on other subtests fall below a specified level. Results are available for more than 30 subtests and skill areas, making scoring time-consuming and interpretation complicated. Test-retest reliability of the Writing Fluency subtest is not well established. Professionals should consult the *Technical Manual* for further information about the *Woodcock-Johnson–R*'s psychometric characteristics.

- *Passage Comprehension*—Early items present several colored drawings and a phrase that describes one of the drawings; the student points to the drawing corresponding to the phrase. Next, the student silently reads a passage of one or more sentences. In each passage is a blank space where one word has been omitted. The student's task is to say a word that correctly completes the sentence.
- *Word Attack* (Supplemental)—The student is presented with nonsense words to read aloud. A pronunciation key is provided for the tester.
- *Reading Vocabulary* (Supplemental)—The subtest is divided into two parts, Synonyms and Antonyms. The student reads a word aloud and then must supply either a word that means the same or one that has an opposite meaning.

Mathematics

- *Calculation*—The student is provided with pages that contain computation problems and writes the answer to each. Beginning items are simple number facts and basic operations. Also included are problems requiring manipulation of fractions and more advanced calculations using algebra, geometry, trigonometry, and calculus.
- *Applied Problems*—The student solves word problems. In the beginning items, the tester reads a question while the student looks at a drawing. On later items, the student is shown the word problem that the tester reads aloud. Answers are given orally on this subtest, but the student may use pencil and paper for computation.
- *Quantitative Concepts* (Supplemental)—The student responds to oral questions concerning mathematics concepts. Items sample skills such as counting, understanding quantitative vocabulary, reading numerals, defining mathematical terms and symbols, and solving computational problems. Visuals accompany most test items.

Written Language

- *Dictation*—Items for young children include making marks, drawing lines, and writing individual letters. With older students, the test takes on a dictation format. Included are spelling items where the tester dictates a word, capitalization items, and punctuation items where the student writes the symbol for a punctuation mark. Usage

items require knowledge of plural forms, comparatives, and superlatives.
- *Writing Samples*—This subtest is made up of a series of brief writing prompts to which the student responds. Early items only require one-word answers. On later items, students must write a complete sentence. Prompts vary in specificity and complexity. For example, in some items, the student must write a sentence describing a drawing; in others, a phrase must be expanded into a sentence or the student must write a sentence to complete a paragraph.
- *Proofing* (Supplemental)—The student is shown a sentence or sentences with one error. After reading the passage silently, the student must locate the error and tell how to correct it. The tester may tell the student an occasional word but not an entire sentence. Like the Dictation subtest, this subtest contains items that assess punctuation and capitalization, spelling, and usage.
- *Writing Fluency* (Supplemental)—Students are given 7 minutes to write sentences. Students write to a series of prompts, each of which contains a drawing and three words. Sentences must describe the picture using the words provided.

Knowledge

- *Science*—The tester reads questions aloud, and the student replies orally. Drawings accompany some of the questions. Items sample general scientific knowledge, including aspects of biology, physics, and chemistry.
- *Social Studies*—Using the same format as the Science subtest, this measure assesses social sciences such as geography, political science, and economics.
- *Humanities*—Again, the same format is used to evaluate knowledge of art, music, and literature.

In addition to these subtests, it is also possible to obtain information about four other areas of Written Expression: Punctuation and Capitalization, Spelling, Usage, and Handwriting. This is accomplished through analysis of specific student responses on subtests such as Dictation and Proofing.

Three of the 14 achievement subtests on the *Woodcock-Johnson–R* are new to the 1989 edition: Writing Samples, Reading Vocabulary, and Writing Fluency. Also, Quantitative Concepts was recategorized as an achievement subtest; on the 1977 version of the *Woodcock-Johnson,* it was included as one of the tests of cognitive ability.

The relationships between *Woodcock-Johnson–R* achievement subtests are shown in Figure 7–3. Of the 9 subtests in the standard battery, 6 are recommended for early childhood assessment. Within each academic area are two or more subskills that make up the broad skill. For example, reading is broken into Broad Reading, Basic Skills, and Comprehension. In selective testing, the two

standard reading measures (Letter-Word Identification and Passage Comprehension) would be administered; then, if Basic Skills appeared to be a problem, the tester could choose to give the supplementary subtest Word Attack. Note that there are no supplementary subtests for the knowledge area.

Students must be able to attend to test tasks for several minutes at a time to participate in *Woodcock-Johnson–R* administration. English-language skills are a necessity, except for the Calculation subtest. However, a Spanish-language version of the original *Woodcock-Johnson* battery

FIGURE 7–3
Selective testing table for the *Woodcock-Johnson–R Tests of Achievement*

TESTS OF ACHIEVEMENT	Early Development	Reading: Broad Reading	Reading: Basic Skills	Reading: Comprehension	Math: Broad Mathematics	Math: Basic Skills	Math: Reasoning	Written Lang: Broad Written Language	Written Lang: Basic Skills	Written Lang: Expression	Written Lang: P.S.U	Written Lang: Handwriting	Broad Knowledge	Intra-Achievement Discrepancies
STANDARD BATTERY														
22. Letter-Word Identification	●	●	●											●
23. Passage Comprehension		●		●										●
24. Calculation					●	●								●
25. Applied Problems	●				●		●							●
26. Dictation	●							●	●		●			●
27. Writing Samples								●		●		●		●
28. Science	●												●	●
29. Social Studies	●												●	●
30. Humanities	●												●	●
SUPPLEMENTAL BATTERY														
31. Word Attack			●											
32. Reading Vocabulary				●										
33. Quantitative Concepts						●								
34. Proofing									●		●			
35. Writing Fluency										●				

Note. From *Woodcock-Johnson–Revised Tests of Achievement* by R. W. Woodcock and M. B. Johnson, 1989, Allen, TX: DLM Teaching Resources. Copyright 1989 by DLM Teaching Resources. Reprinted by permission.

(Woodcock, 1982) is available, and that version contains 7 tests of achievement.

Reading skills are required on the reading and written expression subtests. Students respond orally on 10 of the 14 subtests. Writing is required on Calculation and all written expression subtests except Proofing. The only subtest that is timed is Writing Fluency.

Technical Quality

The *Woodcock-Johnson–R* was standardized from 1986 to 1988 with a total of 6,359 subjects from more than 100 communities throughout the United States. The sample included preschool children ($n = 705$), students in grades K through 12 ($n = 3,245$), college students ($n = 916$), and adults not enrolled in secondary or postsecondary schools ($n = 1,493$). The sample was selected to resemble the national population on a range of variables such as geographic region, community size, sex, race, and Hispanic versus non-Hispanic; weighting procedures were used to assure that the sample distribution conformed to the population distribution on these variables.

Elementary and secondary grade students were randomly selected from the grade lists of regular classes. Severely handicapped students were excluded unless they participated in mainstream classes. Also excluded were students with less than one year of experience in an English-speaking classroom environment.

The manual for the *Woodcock-Johnson–R Tests of Achievement* (Woodcock & Mather, 1989a) reports some information about the technical quality of this measure. Reliability was studied using the split-half procedure, and median results equal or exceed .80 for all subtest and cluster scores. At age 13, however, coefficients fall in the .70s for three subtests. Reliability of the timed Writing Fluency subtest was studied with the test-retest method; the median correlation coefficient across ages is .76, and coefficients fall below .80 for 5 of the 7 age levels sampled. The manual does not discuss test-retest reliability for other subtests, alternate form reliability for the two forms of the *Tests of Achievement,* or interrater reliability for subtests such as Writing Samples and Writing Fluency where professionals must apply scoring criteria.

Results of three studies of the *Woodcock-Johnson–R*'s concurrent validity with other measures of achievement are summarized in the manual. For example, an investigation of age 9 students ($n = 70$) showed moderate correlations between *Woodcock-Johnson–R* achievement clusters and corresponding *PIAT* subtests (.41 to .86) and similar relationships between *Woodcock-Johnson–R* clusters and *WRAT–R* subtests (.63 to .83). Construct validity of the *Tests of Achievement* is supported by data showing systematic patterns of difference between samples of mentally retarded, learning disabled, normal, and gifted students.

Additional information about the technical quality of the *Woodcock-Johnson–R* is presented in a separate publication, the *Technical Manual*. This manual was not yet available when the third edition of *Assessing Special Students* went to press. Professionals wishing to use *Woodstock-Johnson–R* results for educational decisions should consult the *Technical Manual* for a more extensive discussion of the characteristics of the standardization sample and the evidence presented to support reliability and validity. In addition, results of the Writing Fluency subtest should be interpreted with caution due to its less than adequate test-retest reliability.

Administration Considerations

The *Woodcock-Johnson–R* is designed for use by professionals trained in the administration and interpretation of individual tests. In learning this measure, testers should study the procedures for administration and scoring and practice test administration under the supervision of an experienced examiner. Additional expertise is required for the interpretation of test results; professionals should be well grounded in measurement and curriculum and be thoroughly familiar with the range of scores available on the *Woodcock-Johnson–R*.

The achievement portion of the *Woodcock-Johnson–R* is quite easy to administer; instructions in the easel-style test notebook are clear and complete. On the first page of each subtest is information on basal and ceiling rules and suggested starting points. Then each test page provides complete instructions for administration. What the tester should tell the student is highlighted in color. As needed, the tester is provided with a list of student responses that require questioning and the exact wording for queries. Test pages also provide pronunciation guides for difficult words.

The *Tests of Achievement* begin with standard introductory remarks that are read to all students. Then the tester selects the subtests to be administered. As Figure 7–3 illustrates, choices can be made from both the standard and supplemental batteries based on the age of the student and the assessment questions under consideration.

Three of the standard battery subtests provide sample items. On the *Woodcock-Johnson–R*, recommended starting points are given by the student's estimated achievement level, not by actual grade placement. In some cases, starting points are based on performance on another subtest. For example, Writing Samples uses the student's raw score on Dictation to estimate the appropriate starting point; with students who earn raw scores of 7 or less on Dictation, Writing Samples is not administered and a score of 0 is assigned. Some of the supplementary subtests use similar rules, and testers must consider these carefully before selecting additional measures of deficit skill areas.

On most standard *Woodcock-Johnson–R* subtests, basals are established by success on six consecutively numbered items and ceilings by six consecutive failures. On Writing Samples, there are no basals or ceilings as such; the range of items administered is determined by the student's Dictation raw score.

Rules for the supplemental subtests are somewhat more varied. The Word Attack subtest is always administered beginning with item 1. On Reading Vocabulary, the basal is four successes and the ceiling four failures. Writing Fluency is a timed test; students begin with item 1 and continue writing for 7 minutes unless failure is obvious after the first 2 minutes of the test.

Testing on the *Woodcock-Johnson–R* proceeds in complete page units. Thus, if the student misses one of the first six items administered, the tester finishes giving the items on that test page before moving backward to the beginning of an earlier page. Likewise, in establishing the ceiling, the tester completes the test page even if the student has already missed six consecutively numbered items.

During administration, the tester records the student's responses by writing a 1 for a correct answer and a 0 for an incorrect answer or no response. On the subtests where the student writes on a separate answer sheet (Calculation, Dictation, Writing Samples, and Writing Fluency), the tester attempts to observe and score the student's responses as they are written. The test record form provides some space to record verbatim responses and notes about the student's test behavior.

Raw scores are calculated in the usual manner for *Woodcock-Johnson–R* achievement subtests. On the written expression subtests, additional scores can be determined for four additional skill areas. Student responses on the Dictation and Proofing subtests are analyzed to derive scores for Punctuation and Capitalization, Spelling, and Usage. A Handwriting score can be determined by analysis of the student's performance on Writing Samples. The manual provides specific scoring standards for Handwriting and for the Writing Samples and Writing Fluency subtests.

Proceeding from raw scores to final test results on the *Woodcock-Johnson–R* is a time-consuming process because of the number of scores this test produces. However, the test record form provides a shortcut for determining some types of scores. Next to the administration information for each subtest is a norms table that allows the tester to convert the student's raw score to an age and grade equivalent; a W score is also available, and its standard error of measurement is provided. These results can be plotted on an Age/Grade Profile and the student's current age or grade compared with the W score confidence interval. However, the manual must be consulted to derive comparative scores such as percentile ranks and standard scores. A test-scoring program, *COMPUSCORE,* can facilitate this process.

Results and Interpretation

Results of the *Woodcock-Johnson–R* academic tests can be reported by subtest, by academic areas (e.g., Broad Mathematics), and by subskills (e.g., Basic Mathematics and Mathematics Reasoning). More than 30 subtest and area results are produced, and each result can be expressed in a variety of scores: age equivalents, grade equivalents, standard scores, percentile ranks, and Relative Mastery Index (RMI) scores. Confidence intervals can be constructed around standard scores and percentile ranks. Standard scores are distributed with a mean of 100 and a standard deviation of 15.

The *Woodcock-Johnson–R* features extended grade scores for individuals scoring below the average score obtained by kindergarten subjects or above the average score of grade 16.9 students. With extended grade scores, a superscript is added to the grade equivalent to denote percentile rank. Thus, grade K.0[10] would indicate performance at the 10th percentile of kindergarten students. Extended age scores are also available.

The RMI score contrasts the student's performance with that of others of the same grade placement or age. The RMI is stated as a fraction, the denominator of which is 90. The denominator indicates the percentage of mastery (90%) of average students. The numerator denotes the particular student's percentage of mastery. Thus, an RMI of 25/90 indicates that, when average students at the subject's age or grade level achieve 90% mastery, the subject would be expected to perform with 25% mastery.

Results of the *Woodcock-Johnson–R* can be plotted on a series of profiles to assist in interpretation. W scores are plotted in confidence intervals on the Age/Grade Profile to allow comparisons with the student's current age or grade. The Standard Score/Percentile Rank profile, also plotted in confidence intervals, compares student performance to that of age or grade peers in the norm group. Both types of profile are available for individual subtest scores and for broader area scores. In addition, procedures are available for comparing discrepancies in performance across achievement areas.

The *Woodcock-Johnson–R* appears to be a useful measure for the assessment of school performance across a wide range of academic areas and ages. However, like similar broad-based assessment tools, its results are not specific enough to provide direction for instructional planning. Its purpose is the identification of skill areas in which students show poor performance in relation to age or grade peers. One drawback of this test is the time required to score it, if other than age or grade

scores are desired. Also the interpretation process is complicated by the sheer number of scores and profiles produced.

OTHER INDIVIDUAL MEASURES OF ACADEMIC ACHIEVEMENT

Several individual measures of academic achievement are available to the assessment team. One is the *Kaufman Test of Educational Achievement,* which is available in both brief and comprehensive forms. Another, the *Diagnostic Achievement Battery* assesses spoken language as well as the basic school skills. Also of interest are the many criterion-referenced tests of achievement, although these are typically used in later stages of assessment to gather information for instructional planning.

Kaufman Test of Educational Achievement

The *Kaufman Test of Educational Achievement (K-TEA)* by Kaufman and Kaufman (1985) is an individual measure of academic performance for students ages 6–0 to 18–11 and grades 1 through 12. The Brief Form of the *K-TEA* takes 15 to 35 minutes to administer and includes three subtests: Mathematics, Reading, and Spelling. The Mathematics subtest contains written computation problems as well as application questions, the Reading subtest assesses both decoding and comprehension skills, and Spelling is a traditional dictation test. The reading comprehension task on the Brief *K-TEA* is somewhat novel: the student reads a sentence, then follows the directions that the sentence provides (e.g., "Touch your right ear.").

The Comprehensive Form of this test requires about twice as long to administer and offers five subtests:

- Mathematics/Applications
- Reading/Decoding
- Spelling
- Reading/Comprehension
- Mathematics/Computation

These subtests each contain a greater number of items than the Brief Form subtests. Also, the reading skills of decoding and comprehension are assessed in separate subtests, as are the mathematics skills of computation and applications.

The K-TEA provides age and grade norms for Fall (August to January) and Spring (February to July) testing dates. Both forms offer standard scores and percentile ranks for each subtest and for a total test score called the Battery Composite. On the Comprehensive K-TEA, two additional Composite scores are available: Reading Composite and Mathematics Composite.

One feature of the K-TEA's scoring system is a systematic method for comparing results from subtest to subtest to determine whether significant differences exist. For example, on the Brief Form, three subtest comparisons are made: Mathematics versus Reading, Mathematics versus Spelling, and Reading versus Spelling. The tester computes the difference between the standard scores of two subtests, then consults a table to determine whether the observed difference is significant at the .05 level, significant at the .01 level, or not significant. If, for instance, a student's Mathematics score was found to be significantly different from his or her Spelling score at the .05 level, this would mean there was only a 5% chance that the observed difference was due to chance variation rather than being a true difference. The Comprehensive Form allows comparisons of global skills (e.g., Reading Composite versus Mathematics Composite) as well as within-skill comparisons (e.g., Reading Decoding versus Reading Comprehension).

Another important feature of the K-TEA is the error analysis procedure offered on the Comprehensive Form. Every test item is keyed on the protocol to the specific skill category or categories it assesses. For example, the Reading Decoding subtest has nine error categories, including prefixes and word beginnings, suffixes and word endings, and closed syllable (short) vowels. Reading Comprehension, in contrast, contains two types of questions: literal comprehension and inferential comprehension. Errors are noted by category and tabulated so that a student's performance can be compared to the average number of errors made by students in the same grade. These results are used to identify weak, average, and strong skill areas.

Diagnostic Achievement Battery

The Diagnostic Achievement Battery (DAB) by Newcomer and Curtis (1984) is an individual achievement test for students ages 6–0 to 14–11. Unlike most individual tests, it offers measures of listening and speaking skills and a composite index of spoken language. If the assessment team is concerned about a student's spoken language skills as well as performance in basic school subjects, the DAB would be an appropriate instrument to consider. In addition, the DAB was judged as the measure with the highest technical quality in a recent comparison with the PIAT and the WRAT (Brown & Bryant, 1984b).

According to the manual, the DAB "can be used to assess children's abilities in listening, speaking, reading, writing, and mathematics" (p. 1). The test includes 12 subtests, although it is permissable to administer only a portion of these. Each subtest is designed to assess aspects of one area of achievement.

Achievement area	DAB subtest
Listening	Story Comprehension
	Characteristics
Speaking	Synonyms
	Grammatic Completion
Reading	Alphabet/Word Knowledge
	Reading Comprehension
Writing	Capitalization
	Punctuation
	Spelling
	Written Vocabulary
Math	Math Reasoning
	Math Calculation

Listening skills are assessed two ways. In the Story Comprehension subtest, the student listens to brief stories read by the tester and then answers questions about the stories. In the Characteristics subtest, the tester reads a statement ("All trees are oaks"), and the student must determine whether the statement is true or false. Speaking skills are also assessed two ways. The student must supply a synonym for the word presented by the tester in the Synonyms subtest. In Grammatic Completion, the tester reads unfinished sentences, and the student fills in the missing word. Among the grammatic forms assessed are plurals, possessives, and verb tenses.

Standard scores and percentile ranks are available for each DAB subtest. In addition, several composite scores can be determined. These include the Total Achievement Quotient, an index of overall test performance; quotients for each of the basic skill areas (listening, speaking, reading, writing, and mathematics); a Spoken Language Quotient (summarizing listening and speaking skills); and a Written Language Quotient (summarizing reading and writing skills).

Criterion-Referenced Tests

The purpose of criterion-referenced tests is evaluation of student performance in relation to specific instructional objectives. Test items are tied to objectives, so results are immediately applicable to instructional planning. However, because criterion-referenced tests are designed to thoroughly assess mastery of specific skills and subskills, they typically take a long time to administer. The detailed information they provide, although very appropriate for instructional decisions, is not the type of information needed for eligibility decisions. Therefore, criterion-referenced measures are most often used in the later stages of assessment to pinpoint specific skills for instruction. But if criterion-referenced test results are available for a student referred for special education assessment, the team should consider these data in its study of the student's current levels of school performance.

Several of the major criterion-referenced tests are described in Table 7–3. Each assesses a range of basic skill subjects, and some include other areas as well. For example, *System FORE* (Bagai & Bagai, 1979) is a criterion-referenced curriculum that contains progress records and lists of instructional materials keyed to learner objectives. In the area of reading, for instance, more than 5,000 materials are linked to over 300 instructional objectives.

CURRICULUM-BASED ASSESSMENT STRATEGIES

Curriculum-based assessment, or curriculum-based measurement as it is sometimes called, is a method of evaluating student performance using the school curriculum as the standard of comparison. It differs from formal tests because "the stimulus material that provides the occasion for student responses is the actual curriculum of the local school rather than a set of independent items or problems created by commercial test developers" (Deno & Fuchs, 1988, p. 483). According to Tucker (1985), "In curriculum-based assessment

the essential measure of success in education is the student's *progress in the curriculum* of the local school" (p. 199).

In a sense, any informal assessment device designed to investigate students' mastery of what has been taught in the classroom is a curriculum-based strategy. However, the research literature contains a set of simple assessment procedures that have come to be identified with curriculum-based measurement. These procedures assess basic academic skills with brief (e.g., 1-minute) quizzes or probes. For example, reading is evaluated by having students read aloud from basal readers or content area textbooks for 1 minute; the teacher counts the number of words read correctly and the number of errors. Spelling can be assessed by the number of words or letters students write on a 2-minute dictation spelling test, and written expression by the number of words or letters written within 3 minutes in response to a prompt such as a story starter (Deno & Fuchs, 1988). Any curriculum area—even social skills—can be assessed in this way as long as the assessment tool directly measures the skill or behavior of interest and measurement is repeated over time to detect changes in performance (Germann & Tindal, 1985).

Curriculum-based assessment is most useful for gathering information for instructional decisions. According to Blankenship (1985), there are three stages in the teaching process when curriculum-based measures provide important data: (a) at the planning stage before instruction begins, (b) immediately after instruction to determine whether mastery has occurred, and (c) periodically throughout the year to evaluate long-term retention. Curriculum-based measures have been shown to be valid, sensitive to pupil growth, and cost-effective (Marston & Magnusson, 1985).

It has also been suggested that curriculum-based assessment is a useful strategy for gathering information for decisions about pupil eligibility for services such as special education. Deno (1985) describes a simple procedure for peer referencing of curriculum-based measures. To obtain classroom or grade level "norms," the measure is administered to regular class students; their average performance on the curricular task is then used as the standard for evaluating the performance of an individual student. In one example

TABLE 7–3
Criterion-referenced tests of academic achievement

Test	Grade or Age Levels	SUBJECT AREAS ASSESSED						Other Areas
		Readiness	Spoken Language	Reading	Spelling	Writing	Math	
BRIGANCE® Diagnostic Inventories								
Inventory of Basic Skills (1977)	Grades K–6	*		*	*	*	*	Reference Skills
Comprehensive Inventory of Basic Skills (1983a)	Grades K–9	*	*	*	*	*	*	Functional Word Recognition, Reference Skills, Graphs & Maps
Inventory of Essential Skills (1981)	Grades 4–12			*	*	*	*	Functional Word Recognition, Reference Skills, Schedules & Graphs, Vocational, several daily life academic skills
Criterion-Referenced Test of Basic Skills (Lundell, Brown, & Evans, 1976)	Grades 1–5 (functioning level)	*		*		*	*	None
Hudson Education Skills Inventory (Hudson, Colson, Welch, Banikowski, & Mehring, 1989)	Grades K–12	*		*	*	*	*	None
Instructional Based Appraisal System (Meyen, Gault, & Howard, 1976)	Ungraded			*			*	Social Skills (for Mildly Handicapped), Career Education, Pre-Vocational Skills, Physical Education, Science, other areas for severely handicapped
Multilevel Academic Skills Inventory (Howell, Zucker, & Morehead, 1982)	Grades 1–8			*	*	*	*	Content Vocabulary (e.g., math, science, social studies)
System FORE (Bagai & Bagai, 1979)	First 9 years of development, secondary level covers next 5 years	*	*	*			*	Study Skills

provided by Deno (1985), an individual sixth grader was reading from 30 to 55 words per minute, whereas the average rate for regular class grade 6 students was 120 words per minute.

Curriculum-based measures do discriminate between successful members of regular classes and those with achievement problems. Marston and Magnusson (1985) compared regular education, Title I, and special education students on number of words read correctly; regular education students were superior to the other two groups. Peterson, Heistad, Peterson, and Reynolds (1985) used a cutoff score on reading and math curriculum-based measures to discriminate between achievers and nonachievers; 100% of the special education students studied fell below the 20th percentile cutoff on one or both measures, whereas 89% of regular class students fell above the 20th percentile on both reading and math.

Results of curriculum-based measures can add to the data base the assessment team assembles to determine whether a student shows poor school performance. Measures can be peer referenced with norms based on one classroom, a grade level within a school, or an entire district; or the assessment tool can stand by itself, with the curriculum as the standard of comparison. The resulting information is best used in eligibility decisions as an indicator of the magnitude of the school performance problem. In the prereferral stage, for example, curriculum-based measures can help teachers not only identify students who are not responding to instruction but also evaluate the effects of instructional modifications introduced in the regular classroom.

However, curriculum-based assessment is most valuable as one source of information for planning and monitoring instruction. According to Blankenship (1985), data from curriculum-based measures can be used in the IEP process to "(a) summarize a student's present levels of performance, (b) suggest appropriate goals and objectives, and (c) document pupil progress" (p. 238).

ANSWERING THE ASSESSMENT QUESTIONS

The assessment team gathers information about the student's academic achievement to determine current levels of school performance. One major

concern in the assessment of any skill or ability is the technical adequacy of the measurement tool. Measures of academic achievement should be selected for use only after careful consideration of the evidence supporting their reliability and validity. Results should be interpreted with caution, with the measure's limitations kept firmly in mind.

Two other factors important in evaluating assessment results are the types of procedures used in data collection and the nature of the assessment tasks.

Types of Procedures

Many types of procedures are used to gather information about school performance: group and individual measures, norm-referenced and criterion-referenced tests, curriculum-based assessment devices, school record reviews, observations, work sample analyses, questionnaires, and interviews of informants. Each of these methods is likely to produce somewhat different results, because each approaches the question of current school performance from a different perspective.

Group tests of academic achievement generally underestimate school performance abilities of students with academic difficulties. Group tests depend heavily upon reading skills and independent work skills, two areas where lower performing students tend not to excel. Individual measures tend to produce more accurate estimates of current performance and permit the sampling of a broader range of student skills. Therefore, they are preferred in special education.

Norm-referenced measures provide the most appropriate type of results for determining the existence and severity of a school performance problem. Although criterion-referenced measures are superior in describing specific instructional needs, norm-referenced test results tell where the student's performance falls in relation to other students. This type of data is necessary for legal decisions such as eligibility for special education services.

Test results must be confirmed with information about how the student is coping with the demands of the current instructional environment. School records provide historical data and may contain current report card grades. School grades are one index of school performance, although they may be based upon subjective criteria and provide little information about a student's standing in relation to peers. Classroom observations and analyses of student work samples add descriptive data about specific student actions and responses. If considered in relationship to the teacher's expectations and the standards for classroom performance, such data may corroborate school grades and test results. Curriculum-based assessments also serve to document academic difficulties, particularly if their results reflect peer performance standards as well as curricular goals. Judgmental information is available from informants knowledgeable about the student's current school performance. Parents, teachers, and others have observed the student over long periods of time, forming opinions about the student's academic competence. The student can also provide information.

Nature of the Assessment Tasks

Assessment techniques differ in the ways they attempt to measure academic skills. There are obvious differences between group and individual administration, criterion-referenced standards and norm-referenced standards, and direct measures and techniques using informants. What may be less obvious are the variations among the individual norm-referenced tests commonly used to assess achievement.

Comprehensiveness. This concern relates to the number of academic skills assessed and the breadth of coverage within each skill area. For example, a test may say it measures mathematics skills, but it may limit coverage to simple computation. Of the three major achievement tests described in this chapter, the *WRAT–R* is clearly the least comprehensive.

All three measures assess reading recognition skills, math computation, and spelling. Reading comprehension, mathematical problem solving, and written expression are added by the *PIAT–R* and the *Woodcock-Johnson–R,* as is the study of content area knowledge. All three tests require written responses, allowing analysis of the student's handwriting. Areas covered only by the *Woodcock-Johnson–R* are reading nonsense words, knowledge of word meanings, punctuation and capitalization, and English usage.

Test tasks. The ways skill areas are assessed differ from measure to measure. Task characteristics such as timing factors, type of question, presentation mode, and response mode may influence student performance. Also, some test tasks approximate typical classroom activities, whereas others do not.

The methods used by the *PIAT–R, WRAT–R,* and *Woodcock-Johnson–R* to assess reading recognition are very similar. The test task is oral reading of isolated words. However, as Table 7–4 shows, test tasks for reading comprehension are quite different. The *Woodcock-Johnson–R* uses a cloze procedure; the student reads a passage with a word omitted and then attempts to supply the missing word. On the *PIAT–R,* the student reads a passage and then selects the drawing that best illustrates the meaning of the sentence. Neither of these tasks resembles classroom reading comprehension activities. In the typical classroom, students read passages and then answer comprehension questions orally or in writing.

In Spelling, both the *WRAT–R* and the *Woodcock-Johnson–R* Dictation subtest use a written test format. This task should be familiar to most students because it is routinely used in classroom assessment. On the *PIAT–R,* spelling items are multiple choice and do not require writing. The student must differentiate between the correctly spelled word and three misspelled versions. This is a recognition task, whereas written spelling is a recall task. The Proofing subtest of the *Woodcock-Johnson–R* assesses the proofreading skills of error detection and correction, and is much more realistic than the *PIAT–R* task.

Math computation is evaluated by written tests on the *WRAT–R* and the *Woodcock-Johnson–R* Calculation subtest. This format is often used in classroom practice activities and quizzes; most adults also solve computation problems with paper and pencil (or with calculators). The *PIAT–R* again presents multiple choice questions.

Both the *PIAT–R* and the *Woodcock-Johnson–R* assess composition skills. The writing task for older students on the *PIAT–R* is quite open-ended. Students must write a story describing a stimulus picture. The *Woodcock-Johnson–R,* in contrast, provides a variety of prompts designed to elicit brief, one-sentence writing samples. On the Writing Samples subtest, students write sen-

TABLE 7–4
Test tasks used to assess academic skills

Curriculum Area	PIAT–R	WRAT–R	Woodcock-Johnson–R
Reading Comprehension			
Subtest	Reading Comprehension	——	Passage Comprehension
Presentation Mode	Look at a page that contains a sentence, then look at another page with four drawings.	——	Look at a page that contains a reading selection with one word missing.
Response Mode	Read the sentence silently, then point to the drawing that illustrates the sentence.	——	Read the selection silently, then say the word that completes the sentence.
Spelling			
Subtest	Spelling	Spelling	Dictation/Proofing
Presentation Mode	Listen to the tester read a word and a sentence containing the word; look at a page that shows four versions of the word, one of which is spelled correctly.	Listen to the tester read a word and a sentence containing the word.	Dictation: Listen to the tester read a word and a sentence containing the word. Proofing: Look at a sentence containing one spelling error.
Response Mode	Point to the correct spelling.	Write the dictated word within the 15-second time limit.	Dictation: Write the dictated word. Proofing: Identify the misspelled word and orally correct its spelling.
Math Computation			
Subtest	Mathematics	Arithmetic	Calculation
Presentation Mode	Look at a test page with four possible answers, listen to the tester read a problem.	Look at a page of written computation problems.	Look at pages of written computation problems.
Response Mode	Point to the correct answer.	Write the answers to the problems within the 10-minute time limit.	Write the answers to the problems.

tences to describe a drawing, expand a phrase, or complete a paragraph. On the Writing Fluency subtest, students write sentences in response to prompts containing a drawing and three words.

Content area knowledge is also assessed by both the *PIAT–R* and the *Woodcock-Johnson–R*. The *Woodcock-Johnson–R* contains three knowledge subtests whereas the *PIAT–R* combines all content area questions into one subtest, General Information. The test format is the same across the four subtests: the tester asks a question and the student answers orally.

An important difference between the *PIAT–R* and the other tests is the *PIAT–R's* use of multiple choice questions. This is both a strength and a limitation. Because the *PIAT–R* bypasses writing skills on its Spelling and Mathematics subtests, it is a more appropriate measure of these subjects for students with severe writing disabilities or those with physical handicaps that impede writing. However, writing is integral to classroom spelling and mathematics tasks and to the use of these skills in adult life. Also, with multiple-choice questions, students are not asked to recall information, only recognize it. If one of the concerns in assessment is classroom performance in either spelling or mathematics, measures requiring recall of information and written responses should be administered in place of or in addition to the *PIAT–R.*

One of the major differences between the *WRAT–R* and the other two measures is its imposition of time limits. All test tasks on the *WRAT–R* are timed. Speed requirements may penalize students who work accurately but slowly. However, classroom success usually depends on both speed and accuracy, particularly in the upper elementary grades and beyond.

Motivational factors. In addition to comprehensiveness of content and the methods used to assess skills, tests may vary in their appeal to the student. For students with a history of school failure, tests that look like school tasks may seem demanding, difficult, or even forbidding. The *PIAT–R* and the *Woodcock-Johnson–R* appear less threatening than many, because they are in easel format and the test pages include drawings in addition to words and numbers. In contrast, the *WRAT–R* test form gives every appearance of schoolwork. The first page contains three columns of blank lines to write spelling words, the middle pages are covered with math computation problems, and the last page is filled with rows of reading words. In addition, the *WRAT–R* imposes stringent ceiling rules. For example, the student must misspell 10 words in a row before the Spelling subtest is discontinued. Prolonging a failure experience to this extent may affect the student's willingness to attempt other test tasks.

DOCUMENTATION OF SCHOOL PERFORMANCE

The assessment question that guides the team in its study of the student's academic functioning is this: *Is there a school performance problem?* The team determines the student's current levels of achievement in important school subjects and decides whether there are apparent strengths and weaknesses in the various areas of learning. To do this, the team gathers information from many different sources.

Usually the team will examine past records including group test data, interview the student's parents and teachers, observe and possibly interview the student, and administer an individual test of academic achievement. In some cases, a second individual test will be used to add to or help corroborate the results of the first. The team must also gather evidence that the student's academic difficulty is evident in the classroom, not just on standardized tests. Usually this is not an issue, because poor classroom performance is often the reason for the original referral. However, the team must try to explain any discrepancies between teacher reports and test results.

In its review of assessment results, the team attempts to describe the student's current levels of academic performance. At this point in the assessment process, these descriptions focus on the student's standing in relation to others. This type of interpretation was used to evaluate the assessment information gathered about Joyce, the fourth grader introduced at the beginning of the chapter.

Joyce

Joyce has been referred for special education assessment by Mr. Harvey, her fourth grade teacher, because she is having difficulty with reading, spelling, and handwriting tasks. Her parents are also concerned, and they have given their permission for assessment.

The assessment team begins by reviewing Joyce's school records. She had taken a group achievement test in third grade at her previous school, and her reading and spelling scores fell between the 20th and 30th percentiles. Joyce's school grades have been average, and she has never been retained or referred for special services. She began kindergarten at her previous school, making this only the second school she has attended in 5 years.

Ms. Gale, the special education resource teacher, administers the *Peabody Individual Achievement Test–Revised* to Joyce. On the *PIAT–R,* Joyce scores within the average range on General Information and Mathematics, the low average range in Reading Recognition and Reading Comprehension, and the below average to low average range in Spelling. Joyce's performance on Level II of the Written Language subtest falls within the average range, although her printing was difficult to read and she made numerous spelling errors. (See Figure 7–1 for Joyce's *PIAT–R* results).

To confirm these test results, portions of the *Wide Range Achievement Test–Revised* and the *Woodcock-Johnson Psycho-Educational Battery Revised* are administered. Joyce's performance on the written spelling test of the *WRAT–R* also indicates achievement in the below average range. She printed the spelling words, and her letters were large, poorly spaced, and difficult to read. On the *Woodcock-Johnson–R,* Joyce scores within the low average range in Broad Reading.

The reports of Joyce's teacher and parents agree with the team's test results. In the regular classroom, Joyce is placed in a beginning third grade reading book and a second grade spelling program. She is learning cursive writing but continues to print most of her assignments. At home, she likes to look at the pictures in her favorite storybooks but is unable to read most of the words. Last summer, when she was on vacation, she wrote postcards to her friends, but her father helped spell many of the words.

In its review of these results, the assessment team has concluded that Joyce is an average achiever in mathematics with probable school performance problems in reading, spelling, and handwriting. The team will continue assessment to determine whether Joyce's academic deficiencies are related to a handicapping condition.

STUDY GUIDE

Review Questions

1. Read these statements and tell whether they are true or false.
   - T F **a.** The major concern in the assessment of school performance is academic achievement.
   - T F **b.** Students must show a school performance problem to be eligible for special education services.
   - T F **c.** When a regular classroom teacher is concerned about a student's school performance, the teacher's first step is referral for special education assessment.

2. What are two reasons for assessing school performance?

3. Check *each* of the assessment devices and procedures that can be used to document school performance.
   - _____ **a.** Classroom observations
   - _____ **b.** Standardized tests
   - _____ **c.** Personality measures
   - _____ **d.** Group and individual achievement tests
   - _____ **e.** Criterion-referenced measures
   - _____ **f.** IQ tests
   - _____ **g.** Interviews with parents, teachers, and students
   - _____ **h.** Review of school records

4. Which of these statements is true?
   - _____ **a.** Public concern over the state of American education led to the back-to-basics movement emphasizing basic skills such as reading, writing, and mathematics.
   - _____ **b.** As a result of the back-to-basics movement, many states now require that students pass minimum competency tests for grade advancement and high school graduation.
   - _____ **c.** The excellence in education movement stresses achievement in traditional content area subjects, not basic literacy skills.
   - _____ **d.** All of the above statements are true.

5. Find the best description of current practices in special education assessment of school performance.
   - _____ **a.** Only group tests are used.
   - _____ **b.** Only individually administered tests are used.
   - _____ **c.** Both group and individual measures are used, but individual tests are preferred.
   - _____ **d.** Both group and individual measures are used, but group tests are preferred.

6. What are two of the factors in group testing that may affect how well special students perform?

7. Match the assessment device or procedure in Column A with the description in Column B.

Column A		*Column B*
a.	Review of school records	_____ The best source of information about the student's ability to use academic skills at home and in the community
b.	Teacher interviews	_____ An individual achievement test for ages 5 through adult that assesses reading recognition, spelling, and arithmetic skills
c.	Parent interviews	_____ A test system that includes measures of cognitive performance as well as academic achievement tests
d.	*Peabody Individual Achievement Test–Revised*	_____ A standardized measure of reading, spelling, and mathematics with both a brief and comprehensive form
e.	*Wide Range Achievement Test–Revised*	_____ An individual measure that offers tests of reading comprehension, written expression, and general information
f.	*Woodcock-Johnson Psycho-Educational Battery–Revised*	_____ The best source of data about the types of instructional modifications effective in improving classroom performance
g.	*Diagnostic Achievement Battery*	_____ A strategy for finding out about the student's past grades, attendance history, and other historical data
h.	*Kaufman Test of Educational Achievement*	_____ An individual achievement test that includes measures of listening and speaking

8. Which score interpretation is *not* accurate?
    _____ a. A standard score of 109 on the *PIAT–R* indicates performance in the average range.
    _____ b. A standard score of 89 on the *PIAT–R* indicates performance in the low average range.
    _____ c. A standard score of 76 on the *WRAT–R* indicates performance in the low average range.
    _____ d. A standard score of 135 on the *WRAT–R* indicates performance in the above average range.

9. Tests with similar purposes such as the *PIAT–R* and the *WRAT–R* contain similar assessment tasks. (True or False)

10. If the special education assessment team finds that a student's current school achievement falls within the below average range of performance, which of the following conclusions can be drawn?
    _____ a. The student is eligible for special education services.
    _____ b. The student is not eligible for special education services.
    _____ c. The student has school performance problems, and assessment should continue.
    _____ d. The student has school performance problems that should be handled in the regular classroom.

Activities

1. Review several group achievement tests. Compare the school subjects they assess, the time required for administration, and the scores.

2. Work with a peer to develop a parent checklist about children's use of academic skills at home and in the community.

3. Under the supervision of the course instructor, administer one of the individual achievement tests described in this chapter. Calculate all possible scores and analyze the results.

4. Design an interview procedure to determine students' perceptions about their school performance.

Discussion Questions

1. The back-to-basics movement of the 1970s has been replaced by the excellence in education movement. Discuss how this new direction may change the school curriculum and educational assessment. What effects might these changes have upon students with academic achievement problems?

2. Debate the relative merits of group achievement tests and individually administered achievement tests for students with school performance problems.

3. Identify the subject matter areas usually assessed by individual achievement tests. Explain why these tests tend to include basic skills rather than content area subjects.

4. Compare and contrast the *PIAT–R*, the *WRAT–R*, and the *Woodcock-Johnson–R*. For what purposes and with what types of students are each of these measures best used?

5. Explain how informal assessment procedures such as record reviews and teacher and parent interviews help in answering questions about overall school performance.

6. Discuss the purposes of curriculum-based assessment and the best uses of this technique for eligibility and instructional decisions.

8

Learning Aptitude

When students perform poorly in school, educators are interested in finding out why. One explanation for school performance problems is handicaps such as mental retardation, behavior disorders, and learning disabilities. To determine whether a handicapping condition is influencing school learning, the special education assessment team begins to gather information about the student's current functioning in several major domains. One of these is general aptitude for learning.

General aptitude is important to consider in the assessment of students with poor school performance. Some handicapped students show below average general aptitude and, as a consequence, below average school achievement. Others achieve poorly in school despite average potential for learning.

When students are referred for special education assessment, the team may begin by evaluating current school performance. If an achievement problem is documented, the team moves to a study of the student's cognitive and behavioral characteristics. The assessment question being addressed at such a point is this: *Is the school performance problem related to a handicapping condition?*

The team typically starts to investigate the possibility of a handicap by evaluating general learning aptitude. The assessment of learning aptitude is traditionally associated with standardized measures of intellectual performance, known also as intelligence (IQ) tests. However, general aptitude for learning can also be estimated by assessing adaptive behavior—the student's ability to adapt to and comply with environmental demands. Thus, the team is able to pose more specific questions: *What is the student's current level of intellectual performance? What is the student's current functioning level in adaptive behavior?*

At this level of questioning, the major goal is to obtain a global picture of the student's aptitude. In the process of investigation, however, the team may note indications of specific strengths and weaknesses. Consider the case of Joyce.

Joyce

Joyce, a student in Mr. Harvey's fourth grade class, has been referred for special education assessment. The team began by investigating Joyce's current school performance, and results of individual achievement tests suggested low to below average achievement in reading, spelling, and handwriting.

Next the team will assess Joyce's general aptitude for learning. Mental retardation is not suspected, because Joyce appears able to learn some types of material quite easily. For example, her mathematics performance is average for her

---

Individualized Assessment Plan

For: _____ Joyce Dewey _____   4   10–0   12/1/89   Ms. Gale

| Student's Name | Grade | Age | Date | Coordinator |

Reason for Referral: Difficulty keeping up with fourth grade work in reading, spelling, and handwriting

Assessment Question	Assessment Procedures	Person Responsible	Date/Time
What is the student's current level of intellectual performance?	Interview with Mr. Harvey, Joyce's fourth grade teacher	Ms. Gale, Resource Teacher	12/7/89 3:30 p.m.
	Review of Joyce's school records	Ms. Kellett, School Psychologist	12/5/89 9 a.m.
	Wechsler Intelligence Scale for Children–Revised	Ms. Kellett, School Psychologist	12/13/89 9 a.m.
What is the student's current functioning level in adaptive behavior?	*Adaptive Behavior Inventory for Children*	Ms. Gale, Resource Teacher	12/15/89 7 p.m.

age and grade. Other handicaps remain a possibility, so the school psychologist will administer an individual test of intellectual performance, the *Wechsler Intelligence Scale for Children–Revised*. To evaluate Joyce's learning abilities in tasks other than school activities, the team will interview her parents using the *Adaptive Behavior Inventory for Children*. The results of these two measures, along with the data gathered in reviews of school records and interviews with Joyce's classroom teacher, will assist the team in studying the relationship between poor school performance and possible handicapping conditions.

CONSIDERATIONS IN ASSESSMENT OF LEARNING APTITUDE

Learning aptitude refers to an individual's capacity for altering behavior when presented with new information or experiences. Learning aptitude is required in many environments, and the classroom is only one example. Thus, general learning aptitude is assessed to gain a better understanding of the student's ability to cope with the demands of the instructional and other environments requiring changes in behavior.

Purposes

General learning aptitude is a concern in the identification of several different handicapping conditions. The handicap most directly related to learning aptitude is mental retardation. It is defined by the American Association on Mental Retardation as "significantly subaverage general intellectual functioning existing concurrently with deficits in adaptive behavior and manifested during the developmental period" (Grossman, 1983, p. 1). This definition—the one used in federal law—conceptualizes retardation as a developmental phenomenon that becomes apparent during childhood. It identifies two important indicators of mental retardation: below average intellectual performance and impaired adaptive behavior.

Intelligence is a complex construct, and there have been many attempts to define it. According to Wechsler, the author of several measures of intellectual functioning, intelligence is "the overall capacity of an individual to understand and cope

with the world around him" (1974, p. 5). In assessment, intellectual functioning is operationalized as performance on standardized tests of intelligence. Such measures claim to assess reasoning abilities, learning skills, and problem-solving abilities. However, most intelligence tests are essentially measures of verbal abilities and skills in dealing with numbers and other abstract symbols (Anastasi, 1988). Because these skills and abilities are required in school learning, tests of intelligence are best viewed as measures of scholastic, not general, aptitude.

Adaptive behavior refers to "the effectiveness or degree with which individuals meet the standards of personal independence and social responsibility expected for age and cultural group" (Grossman, 1983, p. 1). Expected adaptive behavior varies with the age of the individual. Preschool children are expected to learn to walk, talk, and interact with family members. School-aged children are expected to widen their circle of acquaintances and add academic skills to their repertoire. The clusters of skills identified with the various age levels are

Infancy and Early Childhood
1. Sensorimotor Skills Development
2. Communication Skills (including speech and language)
3. Self-Help Skills
4. Socialization (development of ability to interact with others)

Childhood and Early Adolescence
5. Application of Basic Academic Skills in Daily Life Activities
6. Application of Appropriate Reasoning and Judgment in Mastery of the Environment
7. Social Skills (participation in group activities and interpersonal relationships)

Late Adolescence and Adult Life
8. Vocational and Social Responsibilities and Performance (Grossman, 1983, p. 25)

A student's adaptive behavior can be assessed by direct observation. Because this would be a time-consuming process, it is more usual to rely upon information provided by informants such as parents, teachers, and others who know the student well.

Both intelligence tests and measures of adaptive behavior seek to determine how well the student can adapt to and cope with environmental demands. However, these devices assess different environments. Tests of intellectual performance relate to the academic demands of school, whereas adaptive behavior measures look at performance in nonschool environments that require personal care, communication, social, civic, and vocational skills. By looking at both of these dimensions, it is possible to derive a global picture of the student's current aptitude for learning.

In mental retardation, intellectual performance must be below average *and* there must be one or more deficits in adaptive behavior. Poor scores on tests of intelligence are not sufficient evidence to support the identification of retardation. The individual must also be unable to meet age level expectations in an important area of adaptive behavior.

General learning aptitude is also a concern with other handicapping conditions. In learning disabilities and behavior disorders, the possibility of mental retardation must be ruled out. Thus, intelligence tests are used to gather evidence of average potential for learning. In addition, a major criterion for learning disabilities is a discrepancy between expected and actual achievement. Tests of intellectual performance provide the basis for predicting expected achievement. Assessment of adaptive behavior is less usual with learning disabilities and behavior disorders, even though it can provide important information about the student's ability to cope with nonscholastic environments.

Issues and Trends

Intelligence testing has engendered more controversy than any other area in assessment. The issues raised by the intelligence testing debate concern the nature and definition of intelligence, the relative contributions of heredity and environment to intellectual performance, the usefulness and accuracy of IQ tests, and the appropriateness of these measures for minority group members (Ebel, 1977; Herrnstein, 1971; Jones, 1988; Perrone, 1977; Tyler, 1969).

One factor underlying the controversies is a basic misunderstanding of the purpose of intelligence tests. Measurement of current intellectual performance has become confused with measurement of innate potential. Intelligence tests do not assess potential; they sample behaviors already learned in an attempt to predict future learning.

They are built upon the premise that current performance is an indicator of future performance. Individuals who have learned from their environment and are able to perform certain tasks are assumed able to continue learning and achieving. Robinson and Robinson (1976) commented that intelligence tests "seem to measure with reasonable accuracy about half of what we need to know to predict how well individuals will do in school. This is, of course, what they were designed to do" (p. 22).

The use of intelligence tests in special education drew heated criticism in the 1970s, particularly in relation to the placement of minority group students. The major issue was the finding that special classes for the mentally retarded contained disproportionate numbers of minority students (Jones & Wilderson, 1976; Mercer, 1973). This overrepresentation was attributed to many factors, including reliance on only IQ scores for special education placement and the cultural loadings of intelligence measures.

In addition, the practice of administering English-language tests of intelligence to students whose primary language was not English resulted in lawsuits such as *Diana* v. *The State Board of Education* (1970) and *Guadalupe* v. *Tempe Elementary School District* (1972). Other litigation charged that intelligence tests were culturally biased and therefore discriminated against minority group members (*Larry P.* v. *Riles,* 1972, 1979, 1984; *Parents in Action on Special Education* v. *Joseph P. Hannon,* 1980). The courts clearly supported the use of tests in the child's own language. However, test bias decisions have been contradictory. In the *Larry P.* case, it was ruled that intelligence tests are culturally biased and must not be used to assess black students for possible placement in classes for the mildly mentally retarded; in the *Parents in Action* case, the court held that intelligence tests are not racially or culturally biased.

In the mid-1970s, legislative action was taken in an attempt to address the concerns about intelligence testing held by professionals, parents of students identified as handicapped, and others. The Education for All Handicapped Children Act of 1975 contained two major provisions to safeguard against testing abuses. The first was its adoption of the American Association on Mental Retardation definition of mental retardation. In this definition, mental retardation is identified by concurrent deficits in intellectual performance and adaptive behavior. Social adaptation has long been of interest to professionals in the field of mental retardation (Cegelka & Prehm, 1982). However, the need to consider nonscholastic performance was underscored by the findings of Mercer (1973) and others that some students labeled mentally retarded in school performed quite adequately at home and in their community.

The second major provision of federal law is a set of procedures for special education assessment. These procedures, described in detail in Chapter 3, require that testing be conducted in the language of the student, that measures be non-discriminatory and validated for the purpose for which they are used, and that no single test score be the sole basis for determining special education placement.

Today, school systems and professional educators are aware of clear guidelines for the appropriate use of intelligence tests in special education assessment. That is not to say that procedures mandated by law are followed in all instances or that all questions about intelligence testing have been answered. Debate continues over measures of intellectual performance, their proper use, and social consequences (Bersoff, 1981; Carroll & Horn, 1981; Reschly, 1981; Scarr, 1981).

The study of intelligence also continues. For example, Sternberg (1984) proposed a new theory of intelligence with implications for the development of better, or at least more comprehensive, measures of intellectual performance. In Sternberg's theory, human intelligence is conceptualized in terms of the individual's mental mechanisms for processing information, the tasks or situations that involve the use of intelligence, and the sociocultural context in which the individual lives. Such new theories may revolutionize not only the way educators conceptualize intelligence but also the way they assess it.

Current Practices

Assessment of general learning aptitude takes place in both regular and special education. In regular education, many school districts administer group intelligence tests to elementary grade populations, although this practice is far less common

than group achievement testing. At the secondary level, measures such as the *Scholastic Aptitude Test* (n.d.) of the College Entrance Examination Board are used to predict success in higher education.

Group measures of general learning aptitude share the drawbacks of group achievement tests for lower performing students. In nationwide testing programs such as the *Scholastic Aptitude Test,* special administration procedures are available for students identified as handicapped. In general, however, individual tests are preferred because they provide a more accurate picture of current academic aptitude.

Individual tests of intellectual functioning are part of the assessment battery for most students under serious consideration for specialized services. Information about general learning aptitude is needed for initial decisions for many handicaps as well as for the periodic reevaluation of eligibility. As a rule, individual tests of intelligence are administered in educational settings only by school psychologists, specially trained and licensed professionals who perform this kind of assessment. However, some available individual intelligence tests may be administered by any professional, without any formal training. This may bring about a major change in the way school assessment teams operate. If this occurs, it will be necessary to make sure that the professionals responsible for assessment of intellectual performance are adequately trained in the administration, scoring, and interpretation of these tests.

The first intelligence test was developed in 1905 in France by Alfred Binet and Theodore Simon. This measure, adapted for use in the United States and revised several times, is the *Stanford-Binet Intelligence Scale.* The individual measure most often used in schools today, the *Wechsler Intelligence Scale for Children–Revised,* is one of a family of intelligence tests developed by David Wechsler. The Wechsler scale along with the *Tests of Cognitive Ability* of the *Woodcock-Johnson Psycho-Educational Battery–Revised* are discussed in this chapter. Other measures of intellectual performance, including the *Stanford-Binet* and the *Kaufman Assessment Battery for Children,* are also described.

Adaptive behavior is also of concern in the assessment of general learning aptitude, particularly with students under consideration for services for the mentally retarded. Most states include impaired adaptive behavior as one of the requirements for mental retardation (Bruininks, Thurlow, & Gilman, 1987; Patrick & Reschly, 1982). However, adaptive behavior is not routinely assessed in the identification of learning disabilities and behavior disorders. This is unfortunate because many students with these mild handicaps experience difficulty in meeting expectations in nonscholastic environments as well as the classroom.

Adaptive behavior is typically evaluated by interviewing parents, teachers, or others well acquainted with the student or by having them complete questionnaires. There has been interest in the assessment of adaptive behavior for several decades. In 1935, the first edition of the *Vineland Social Maturity Scale,* a parent interview form, was published by Doll; the latest edition appeared in 1984. This scale and others are discussed later in this chapter. More complete descriptions are also provided for two adaptive behavior measures often used in schools today: the *Adaptive Behavior Inventory for Children,* part of the *System of Multicultural Pluralistic Assessment,* and the School Edition of the *AAMD Adaptive Behavior Scale.*

SOURCES OF INFORMATION ABOUT LEARNING APTITUDE

There are several sources of information about learning aptitude in addition to formal measures. For example, the student's performance in actual learning situations at school or at home may provide clues about ability to acquire new skills and information. However, norm-referenced measures are usually the best source of comparative information about learning aptitude, at least for majority group students whose characteristics match those of the norm group. Informal measures are less useful in this area of assessment and are best used to verify and elaborate the results of formal measures.

School Records

School records contain information about the student's past performance. Unlike achievement, learning aptitude is a relatively stable characteristic,

and past performance data may be worth considering.

Group intelligence test results. Results of any current or past group tests of intellectual performance should be reviewed. Keeping in mind the limitations of group administration procedures for students with school performance problems, the team can evaluate test results to determine the student's standing in relation to age or grade peers.

Individual intelligence test data. The student may have been referred for individual assessment in the past, and individual intelligence test data may be available. If the assessment took place within the recent past, results should be compared with current findings. If an individual intelligence test has been administered very recently (e.g., within the last year), the assessment team may decide that another administration is unnecessary.

Developmental and school histories. School records may contain the student's developmental history furnished by parents, perhaps at the time of entry to school. Histories typically provide information about the student's early development and therefore are most useful in the lower elementary grades. Included may be the ages at which developmental milestones such as talking and walking were achieved, any birth or other medical problems, family history, and data about attendance in early education programs. Developmental histories may suggest delays in early development, a possible indication of depressed learning aptitude. Likewise, school histories may reveal information on retentions, past referrals, chronic problems in school learning, or teachers' comments about the student's general learning aptitude.

The Student

The student assists the study of learning aptitude by participating in test administration and, on occasion, performing nonschool tasks under observation. Students can also talk about how they perceive their own abilities as a learner.

Individual tests of intellectual performance. The most usual way of gathering information about general learning aptitude is the administration of individual intelligence tests. During the hour or more of test administration, the tester observes the speed and accuracy with which the student completes each task. The tester also notes the way the student approaches each problem and plans and implements a strategy for a solution.

Current adaptive behavior. Adaptive behavior may be assessed by direct observation, especially if available informants are not able to provide important information. Students themselves may be used as informants. Older students may be able to report whether they can tell time, make change, or get along with peers. As with all informants, students' responses may not be accurate, particularly if the questions are unclear to them.

Teachers

Teachers observe the student in everyday learning situations and are important sources of information about aptitude.

Observed learning aptitude. Teachers can report about how a student learns new skills, information, and classroom routines and procedures. Does the student learn as quickly as class peers? Is more practice needed or a greater number of explanations? How does the student go about learning, and what instructional strategies have proven successful in facilitating learning?

Current adaptive behavior in nonscholastic school activities. Teachers also observe their students participating in many activities unrelated to academic learning. For instance, they see students at play during recess and observe social interactions throughout the day. They may also see students in community settings on field trips. From this experience base, teachers can provide at least partial information about the student's current adaptive behavior.

Parents

Parents are the best source concerning the student's performance at home, in the neighborhood, and in the community. Their perspective is valuable because of the lifetime experience with their child in a wide range of activities and environments.

Developmental history. If school records do not contain the student's developmental history,

parents can provide it. This information is most useful for younger elementary children; for older students, school histories are of interest.

Observed learning aptitude. Like teachers, parents have numerous opportunities to observe learning aptitude. Within their child's first few years of life, parents watch a great variety of learning experiences: the first step, the first words, the first friends, and the first moves toward independence as children begin to acquire skills in caring for themselves. Parents may be able to compare one child's rate of learning with siblings or age mates. They may also identify tasks the child learns easily and tasks he or she finds difficult.

Current adaptive behavior at home and in the community. Parents are the primary source of information about the student's nonschool adaptive behavior. Two methods used to gather these data are interviews and questionnaires. For example, the assessment team can interview the student's parents about the student's current interaction skills, personal hygiene, responsibility for household chores, handling of money, use of public transportation, and so forth.

GROUP TESTS OF INTELLECTUAL PERFORMANCE

Group intelligence tests are sometimes used in regular education; their results may be available for students referred for special education assessment. Like all group-administered measures, their scores are likely to be low estimates of actual abilities of students with school performance problems. In particular, most group intelligence tests rely heavily upon reading skills. Poor scores on these measures may reflect poor reading ability as opposed to below average intellectual performance. Because of this and the other limitations, results of group intelligence tests should be used only as an indicator of the need for further assessment with individual tests.

Group tests of intellectual performance are typically designed with several levels, so one test series can be used for grades 1 through 12. The content of group tests varies somewhat, but most attempt to assess both verbal and quantitative reasoning skills. Some provide separate measures of verbal and nonverbal abilities, and some contain several subtests, each of which addresses a different cognitive skill. Most, however, produce total test scores similar to IQ scores that indicate overall cognitive functioning. Other summary scores such as percentile ranks and stanines for total test performance are usually also available.

As with group achievement tests, test items are typically in multiple-choice format. Directions are presented orally by the tester, and the student reads each question and responds in writing. Most tests are timed, and older students record their responses on separate answer sheets.

Many of the group tests available today are current editions of long-used measures. The *Otis-Lennon School Ability Test,* for example, is the modern version of *Otis Group Intelligence Scale,* one of the earliest measures of its type developed in the United States. Several current group intelligence tests are described in Table 8–1. Included for each measure is the range of grade levels for which it is appropriate, the number of available levels, and the type of results produced.

Like group achievement measures, group intelligence measures are most useful in screening programs. When group measures are administered to large segments of the school population, results should be reviewed to identify students needing further assessment.

INDIVIDUAL TESTS OF INTELLECTUAL PERFORMANCE

Individual tests may be designed for a special age group, such as preschool children or students between the ages of 6 and 18, or may be appropriate for the entire age range from early childhood through adulthood. Unlike group tests, they usually only have one version divided into sections by either subtests or age levels. Subtests contain items that attempt to assess the same skill or ability, and test items are arranged in order of difficulty. When tests are broken into age levels, each age level usually contains a variety of tasks that assess different skills and abilities.

Most individual tests of intellectual performance assess both verbal and nonverbal reasoning. Verbal skills may be emphasized, but nonverbal abilities are evaluated by means of figural or mathematical problem-solving tasks. Measures of memory are often included, as are visual-motor coordination tasks. Academic skill demands are deemphasized on individual intelligence tests. Reading is not required, and written responses are usually limited to drawing or writing numbers. Information is presented orally or with pictures or objects, and students answer orally or with some type of motoric response.

TABLE 8–1
Group tests of intellectual performance

Name (Author)	Grades	Number of Levels	Results
Cognitive Abilities Tests (Thorndike & Hagen, 1986)	1–12	10	Standard scores, percentile ranks, and stanines for Verbal, Quantitative, and Nonverbal batteries
Henmon-Nelson Tests of Mental Ability (Lamke & Nelson, 1973; Nelson & French, 1974)	K–12	4	Deviation IQ, percentile rank, and stanine
Kuhlmann-Anderson Tests (Kuhlmann & Anderson, 1981)	K–12	7	Cognitive Skills Quotient (CSQ) for verbal, nonverbal, and full batteries; standard scores, percentile ranks, and stanines
Otis-Lennon School Ability Test (Otis & Lennon, 1979, 1982)	1–12	5	School Ability Index (SAI), percentile ranks, stanines
Test of Cognitive Skills (1981) (a revision of the *Short Form Test of Academic Aptitude*)	2–12	5	Cognitive Skills Index (CSI), subtest scores

Several well-known individual tests of intellectual performance are listed in Table 8–2. Each is described in terms of age span and types of results. The next sections of this chapter discuss intelligence measures for school-aged children beginning with the *Wechsler Intelligence Scale for Children–Revised*. Tests designed specifically for preschool children are covered in Chapter 18.

WECHSLER INTELLIGENCE SCALE FOR CHILDREN–REVISED

The *Wechsler Intelligence Scale for Children–Revised (WISC–R)* (Wechsler, 1974) is the individual test most often used to assess general intellectual performance of school-aged individuals. It is one of a family of tests that spans all age levels. The *Wechsler Preschool and Primary Scale of Intelligence (WPPSI)* (Wechsler, 1967) is appropriate for children between the ages of 4–0 and 6–6, and the *Wechsler Adult Intelligence Scale–Revised (WAIS–R)* (Wechsler, 1981) is used for persons between the ages of 16 to 74. There is a version of the *WISC–R* adapted for deaf children (Anderson & Sisco, 1977) and a Spanish-language adaptation, the *Escala de Inteligencia Wechsler para Niños–Revisada* (1982). Spanish versions developed in Puerto Rico are available for the original *WISC* (Roca, 1967) and for the original *WAIS* (Green & Martinez, 1968).

The *WISC–R* assesses general intellectual functioning by sampling performance on many different types of activities. According to Wechsler (1974), intelligence is not a single trait but "a multidetermined and multifaceted entity" (p. 5). In special education assessment, the *WISC–R* is often used to gain an overall estimate of the student's current global intellectual performance. This measure may also provide information about strengths and weaknesses in specific areas of aptitude.

The *WISC–R* contains 12 subtests; 10 are required and 2 are supplementary. Only the required subtests are used to determine IQ scores. Subtests are classified as either Verbal or Performance, and these are alternated in administration.

Verbal scale subtests require students to listen to questions and answer orally. To preserve the confidentiality of the test items, the examples cited are similar, but not identical, to *WISC–R* tasks.

☐ *Information*—The student responds orally to general information questions such as "How many eyes do you have?" and "From what animal do we get hamburger?"

☐ *Similarities*—The student must describe how two things (pony and cow, or car and airplane) are alike.

☐ *Arithmetic*—The tester reads arithmetic problems to the student, and the student responds orally. All computations must be done mentally; paper and pencil are not furnished. Visuals are used with the first four test items. On the last three items, the student is given a word problem and told to read it aloud. The tester may read the problems if the student cannot.

WECHSLER INTELLIGENCE SCALE FOR CHILDREN–REVISED (WISC–R)
D. Wechsler (1974)

Type: Norm-referenced test
Major Content Areas: General verbal aptitude, general performance aptitude
Type of Administration: Individual
Administration Time: 50 to 75 minutes
Age/Grade Levels: Ages 6–0 to 15–11
Types of Scores: Three IQ scores (Verbal, Performance, and Full Scale), scaled scores for each subtest, Test Ages by subtest
Typical Uses: A wide-range measure of general intellectual performance
Cautions: This test is not appropriate for students who do not understand and speak English.

TABLE 8–2

Individual tests of intellectual performance

Name (Author)	Ages	Results
Columbia Mental Maturity Scale (Burgemeister, Blum, & Lorge, 1972)	3½ to 10	Age score, percentile rank, stanine, Maturity Index
Kaufman Assessment Battery for Children (Kaufman & Kaufman, 1983)	2½ to 12½	Global standard scores (Mental Processing Composite, Sequential Processing, Simultaneous Processing, and Nonverbal) and subtest scaled scores and percentile ranks
Learning Potential Assessment Device (Feuerstein et al., 1979)	Children and youth	Clinical description of the student's cognitive modifiability
Leiter International Performance Scale (Leiter, 1948; Arthur, 1952)	2 to 18	Mental Age (MA), IQ
McCarthy Scales of Children's Abilities (McCarthy, 1972)	2½ to 8½	General Cognitive Index, MA, and scaled scores for five scales: Verbal, Perceptual-Performance, Quantitative, Memory, and Motor
Nonverbal Test of Cognitive Skills (Johnson & Boyd, 1981)	Grades K–7	Age score, percentile rank, Cognitive Skills Index
Raven Progressive Matrices (Raven, 1938, 1947, 1962)	5 to adult	Percentile rank
Slosson Intelligence Scale (Slosson, 1983)	2–0 to adult	Mental Age (MA), IQ, percentile rank, stanine
Stanford-Binet Intelligence Scale (Terman & Merrill, 1973; Thorndike, Hagen, & Sattler, 1986)	2–0 to adult	1973 edition: Mental Age (MA), IQ 1986 edition: test scaled scores, composites for Verbal Reasoning, Abstract-Visual Reasoning, Quantitative Reasoning, Short-Term Memory, and total test
System of Multicultural Pluralistic Assessment (Mercer & Lewis, 1977b)	5 to 11	School Functioning Level (*WISC–R* IQ scores) and Estimated Learning Potential (*WISC–R* results rescored using alternate norms)
Test of Nonverbal Intelligence (Brown, Sherbenou, & Johnsen, 1982)	5–0 to 85–11	*TONI* quotient, percentile rank
Wechsler Adult Intelligence Scale–Revised (Wechsler, 1981)	16 to 74	Verbal IQ, Performance IQ, Full Scale IQ, and subtest scaled scores
Wechsler Intelligence Scale for Children–Revised (Wechsler, 1974)	6–0 to 15–11	Verbal IQ, Performance IQ, Full Scale IQ, and subtest scaled scores
Wechsler Preschool and Primary Scale of Intelligence (Wechsler, 1967)	4–0 to 6–6	Verbal IQ, Performance IQ, Full Scale IQ, and subtest scaled scores
Woodcock-Johnson Psycho-Educational Battery–Revised (Woodcock & Johnson, 1989)	2 to 90+	Age and grade equivalents, standard scores, percentile ranks, and Relative Mastery Index (RMI) scores for individual subtests; Broad Ability; cognitive factors (Long-Term Memory, Short-Term Memory, Processing Speed, Auditory Processing, Visual Processing, Comprehension-Knowledge, Fluid Reasoning); and several areas of scholastic aptitude

□ *Vocabulary*—The student must tell the meaning of words. The tester asks, "What is a _____ ?" or "What does _____ mean?"

□ *Comprehension*—The student answers questions requiring social reasoning, such as "What are some reasons why we need firemen?"

□ *Digit Span* (Supplementary)—The tester reads a series of numbers to the student at the rate of one digit per second. On the first portion of the test, the student attempts to repeat the digits in the order the tester read them. On the second portion, digits are repeated backwards.

Performance subtests are visual-motor tasks. The student listens to oral directions, looks at stimulus materials, and responds motorically. Performance subtests are timed.

□ *Picture Completion*—The student is shown a drawing of an object or a scene missing some important part. The student must point to or say what is missing.

□ *Picture Arrangement*—Several cards with pictures are presented, and the student arranges these to tell a story.

□ *Block Design*—The student is given several colored cubes or blocks and a picture of a design. The cubes must be arranged into an identical design.

□ *Object Assembly*—Puzzle pieces must be arranged into the correct shape.

□ *Coding*—In this paper-and-pencil task, the student is shown a code, such as one geometric design for each of the digits. Then rows of digits are presented, and the student must write in the correct geometric design for each digit. The code remains available to the student during the task.

□ *Mazes* (Supplementary)—This subtest is another paper-and-pencil task in which the student attempts to solve mazes.

The *WISC–R* is appropriate for students who can sustain attention for extended periods of time. This test is long and may be administered in more than one session. English-language competence is a necessity. Students must be able to understand test directions and questions and answer questions in English. Both oral and motor responses are required. No reading, handwriting, or spelling skills are needed, but mental arithmetic is assessed.

Technical Quality

The *WISC–R* was standardized on 2,200 individuals ages 6–6 to 16–6. Equal numbers of males and females were included at each age level. The standardization sample was selected to resemble the United States as described in the 1970 Census. Several variables were used in the stratified sampling plan: race (white and nonwhite), geographic region, occupation of head of household, and urban–rural residence. The final sample approximated the total population on these variables. In the case of race, however, 15% of the U.S. population was nonwhite, which resulted in only 330 nonwhite individuals in the standardization sample. Of these, 305 were classified as black, leaving 25 individuals to represent American Indians, Orientals, Puerto Ricans, and Chicanos.

The manual states that "the standardization sample was limited to 'normal' children" (p. 19). Excluded were institutionalized mentally retarded children, those with severe emotional problems, and bilingual children unable to speak and understand English. Mentally retarded individuals were included if they lived at home. Thus, the *WISC–R* comparison group is made up of English speakers who are primarily white and nonhandicapped or mildly handicapped.

The reliability of the *WISC–R* was studied by the split-half method for most subtests. Verbal, Performance, and Full Scale IQs have average reliabilities of .94, .90, and .96 respectively across all ages. Average reliability coefficients range from .77 to .86 for Verbal subtests and from .70 to .85 for Performance subtests.

WISC–R concurrent validity was investigated with other measures of intelligence including the *Stanford-Binet Intelligence Scale,* 1972 norms. Average correlations of the *WISC–R* Verbal, Performance, and Full Scale IQs with the *Stanford-Binet* IQ were .71, .60, and .73 respectively. The *Stanford-Binet* is considered to be highly weighted with verbal items, thus its lower correlation with Performance IQ. Also of interest in relation to the *WISC–R* is its predictive validity; this question is not addressed in the *WISC–R* manual. However, Sattler (1982) concludes from a review of research that the *WISC–R* has "acceptable validity using as criteria (a) achievement tests, with median correlations between .56 and .60, and (b) school grades, with a median correlation of .39" (p. 168).

Administration Considerations

According to the manual, the *WISC–R* "should be administered and scored by a competent, trained examiner" (p. 53). Licensed school psychologists are usually the only professionals permitted to administer individual intelligence tests like the *WISC–R* in school settings. Other professionals, however, should be knowledgeable about such tests, even if they are not responsible for administering and scoring them.

Results and Interpretation

The *WISC–R* provides both global IQ scores and, for each subtest, scaled scores. Derived scores are determined by age norms; grade norms are not available.

The global scores available from the *WISC–R* are: Verbal IQ, based on performance on the 5 required Verbal subtests; Performance IQ, based on performance on the 5 required Performance subtests; and Full Scale IQ, based on performance on all 10 required subtests. These IQ scores are standard scores distributed normally with a mean of 100 and a standard deviation of 15. Standard errors for IQ scores are low (Verbal IQ, 3.6 IQ points; Performance IQ, 4.7 IQ points; Full Scale IQ, 3.2 IQ points).

Standard scores called scaled scores are obtained for each subtest. These are distributed normally with a mean of 10 and a standard deviation of 3. Standard errors vary according to subtest. Average errors on Verbal subtests range from 1.2 to 1.4; those on Performance subtests range from 1.2 to 1.7. Subtest scaled scores are plotted on a profile that appears on the front of the record form.

The *WISC–R* manual provides guidelines for analyzing differences among IQ scores and among scaled scores. When comparing Verbal IQ and Performance IQ, Wechsler (1974) suggests that "a difference of 15 [IQ] points or more is important and calls for further investigation" (p. 34). In comparing scaled scores from one subtest to another, Wechsler recommends a minimum difference of 3 scaled score points.

However, Kaufman (1981) suggests that Wechsler's criteria are not stringent enough. Kaufman points out that "one out of four normal children has a significant V-P difference at the .01 level, i.e., 15+ points" (p. 523). Likewise, professionals can expect normal children to show scatter (i.e.,

differences between the highest and lowest subtest scales scores). On the average, such differences are 7 ± 2 scaled score points (Kaufman, 1981).

IQ and scaled scores can be interpreted using the standard score range system suggested in Chapter 4. However, Wechsler provides a somewhat different system. IQ scores between 90 and 109 are considered Average, and this range incorporates approximately 50% of the population. IQs 80 to 89 are rated as Low Average (Dull), 70 to 79 as Borderline, and 69 and below as Mentally Deficient. Above the mean, IQs 110 to 119 are classified as High Average (Bright), 120 to 129 as Superior, and 130 and above as Very Superior.

Results of individual tests such as the *WISC–R* provide information about one criterion for mental retardation, subaverage intellectual functioning. According to the classification manual of the American Association on Mental Retardation (Grossman, 1983), general intellectual functioning is operationally defined as results of one or more individual, standardized intelligence tests. Mental retardation is indicated when general intellectual functioning is significantly subaverage. The manual explains

Significantly subaverage is defined as IQ of 70 or below on standardized measures of intelligence. This upper limit is intended as a guideline; it could be extended upward through IQ 75 or more, depending on the reliability of the intelligence test used. This particularly applies in schools and similar settings if behavior is impaired and clinically determined to be due to deficits in reasoning and judgment. (Grossman, 1983, p. 11)

These guidelines take the standard error of measurement of IQ scores and the clinical judgment of the assessment team into account. On the *WISC–R*, the standard error for Full Scale IQ is 3 IQ points. Thus, a Full Scale IQ of 70 would fall in the range 67 to 73, and an IQ of 72 would fall in the range 69 to 75. Determination of whether these scores indicate subaverage intellectual performance is left to the assessment team. Of course, the individual's adaptive behavior must also be evaluated.

Figure 8–1 presents *WISC–R* results for Joyce, the fourth grader described at the start of this chapter. Joyce was 10–0 at the time of testing, so her performance was compared to that of other

10-year-olds. Note how subtest scaled scores are plotted on *WISC–R* profile.

In reporting *WISC–R* results, confidence intervals are constructed around each IQ and subtest scaled score, so scores are presented as ranges rather than individual scores. For example, the standard error of the Full Scale IQ is 3 IQ points, so Joyce's observed Full Scale IQ score (101) becomes 98 to 104. In writing the report on Joyce's *WISC–R* performance, the psychologist might say:

On the *Wechsler Intelligence Scale for Children–Revised,* Joyce earned a Verbal IQ in the range 104 to 112, a Performance IQ in the range 87 to 97, and a Full Scale IQ in the range 98 to 104. The chances that these score ranges include the true scores of the student are about 68 out of 100. The IQ results indicate that Joyce is currently functioning within the average

range in verbal abilities, performance abilities, and general intellectual functioning.

WISC–R IQ scores provide information about general intellectual functioning. Individual subtest scores may indicate strengths and weaknesses in specific aspects of general aptitude. In addition, it is possible to look at performance on clusters of subtests. Kaufman (1981) notes that three subtest clusters are typically identified in factor analytic research:

☐ *Verbal Comprehension*—composed of the Verbal Scale subtests of Information, Similarities, Vocabulary, Comprehension, and to some extent Arithmetic

☐ *Perceptual Organization*—composed of the Performance Scale subtests of Picture Completion,

FIGURE 8–1
Sample *WISC–R* results

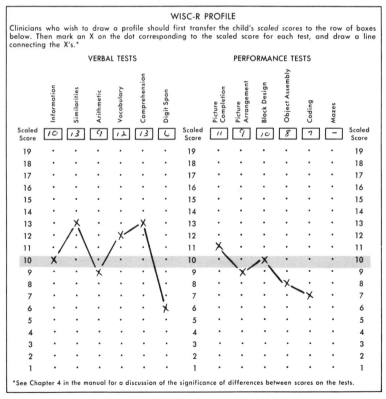

Picture Arrangement, Block Design, Object Assembly, and Mazes

☐ *Freedom from Distractibility*—composed of Arithmetic, Digit Span, and Coding.

The *WISC–R* appears to be an appropriate individual measure of general intellectual functioning. It is well standardized and reliable, and the available validity data are adequate. The results of this measure provide information about general levels of intellectual performance as well as more specific mental abilities. This and other Wechsler tests have a long history, and they are well known and widely accepted in education. The *WISC–R* is likely the individual intelligence test most frequently used in schools today.

WOODCOCK-JOHNSON PSYCHO-EDUCATIONAL BATTERY–REVISED, TESTS OF COGNITIVE ABILITY

The *Woodcock-Johnson Psycho-Educational Battery–Revised (Woodcock-Johnson–R)* was introduced in Chapter 7, where part two of the battery, the *Tests of Achievement,* was discussed as a measure of school performance. The first part, the *Tests of Cognitive Ability,* is presented here. A later section of this chapter describes a measure of adaptive behavior designed to accompany the 1977 *Woodcock-Johnson,* the *Scales of Independent Behavior* (Bruininks, Woodcock, Weatherman, & Hill, 1984).

The *Tests of Cognitive Ability* serve several purposes. First, they provide an estimate of overall intellectual functioning, similar to the Full Scale IQ of the *WISC–R.* Second, subtests are clustered into seven cognitive factors to allow description of more specific abilities. The factors, based on the Horn-Cattell theory of intellectual processing (Woodcock & Mather, 1989b), are Long-Term Retrieval, Short-Term Memory, Processing Speed, Auditory Processing, Visual Processing, Comprehension-Knowledge, and Fluid Processing. Third, subtests are also arranged into aptitude clusters to allow prediction of academic achievement in reading, mathematics, written language, and knowledge. Fourth, the student's performance on the *Tests of Cognitive Ability* can be compared with achievement scores from part one of the battery to contrast expected and actual achievement.

There are 21 cognitive ability tests arranged in two levels, the standard battery (7 subtests) and the supplemental battery (14 subtests). As with the *Woodcock-Johnson–R* achievement tests, the standard battery is administered first, then

---

WOODCOCK-JOHNSON PSYCHO-EDUCATIONAL BATTERY–REVISED (WOODCOCK-JOHNSON–R): TESTS OF COGNITIVE ABILITY
R. W. Woodcock & M. B. Johnson (1989)

Type: Norm-referenced test

Major Content Areas: Broad cognitive ability, seven cognitive factors, four types of scholastic aptitude

Type of Administration: Individual

Administration Time: Less than one hour for standard battery

Age/Grade Levels: Ages 2 to 90 + ; Grades K–12, college

Types of Scores: Grade and age equivalents, standard scores, percentile ranks, Relative Mastery Index (RMI) scores

Typical Uses: A broad-based measure of general cognitive functioning, specific cognitive abilities, and academic aptitudes

Cautions: Administration rules vary from subtest to subtest. Results are available for more than 35 subtests and cognitive areas, making scoring time-consuming and interpretation complicated. Results of some subtests should be interpreted cautiously due to reliability concerns. Professionals should consult the *Technical Manual* for additional information about the *Woodcock-Johnson–R's* psychometric characteristics.

portions of the supplemental battery are selected if further information is needed. Alternate forms are not available for the *Tests of Cognitive Ability*.

The cognitive ability subtests are described in the next paragraphs by cognitive factor. Within each factor, standard battery subtests are discussed first, then supplemental subtests.

Long-Term Retrieval

☐ *Memory for Names*—The tester teaches the student the names of line drawings of space creatures. A page containing several drawings is exposed and, when the tester names a creature, the student must point to it. The tester corrects any errors the student makes.

☐ *Visual-Auditory Learning* (Supplemental)—The tester teaches the student a series of visual symbols that stand for words. Then the student is asked to "read" sentences made up of the symbols. The tester corrects student errors or supplies a word if the student hesitates more than five seconds.

☐ *Delayed Recall—Memory for Names* (Supplemental)—This subtest is administered one to eight days after Memory for Names is given. The task is the same except the tester does not teach the names of the space creatures and errors are not corrected.

☐ *Delayed Recall—Visual-Auditory Learning* (Supplemental)—This subtest is administered one to eight days after Visual-Auditory Learning is given. The task is the same except the tester does not teach the labels for visual symbols and errors are not corrected.

Short-Term Memory

☐ *Memory for Sentences*—The student listens to sentences read by the tester or presented by the Test Tape and attempts to repeat each sentence verbatim. Young children begin by repeating single words and short phrases.

☐ *Memory for Words* (Supplemental)—The tester or Test Tape reads a series of unrelated words and the student repeats the words in order.

☐ *Numbers Reversed* (Supplemental)—The tester or Test Tape reads a series of digits at a rate of one digit per second; the student repeats the digits in backward order.

Processing Speed

☐ *Visual Matching*—On this paper-and-pencil task, the student is shown rows of numbers. The student must circle the two identical numbers in each row. Three minutes are allowed.

☐ *Cross Out* (Supplemental)—This paper-and-pencil task requires the student to look at a row of 20 small drawings and cross out the 5 drawings identical to the first drawing in the row. Three minutes are allowed.

Auditory Processing

☐ *Incomplete Words*—The tester or Test Tape presents words with one or more phonemes missing (e.g., tele-ision for television); the student must pronounce the word.

☐ *Sound Blending* (Supplemental)—The tester or Test Tape presents words broken into parts and the student must say the word. On earlier items, words are broken into two parts; on more difficult items, each phoneme is pronounced.

☐ *Sound Patterns* (Supplemental)—The Test Tape is used for all but the first few sample items. The student listens to pairs of sound sequences to tell if they are the same or different. Sound sequences may differ in an individual phoneme, in the order or speed with which sounds are presented, in tone or intonation, or in length of tones or pauses.

Visual Processing

☐ *Visual Closure*—The student must tell what a drawing or photograph depicts. Drawings are incomplete and/or partially obscured by superimposed lines; photos show objects from unusual perspectives.

☐ *Picture Recognition* (Supplemental)—The student is shown a stimulus page with one or more drawings on it; after five seconds, a new page is revealed which contains some of the stimulus drawings and others that are similar. The student must identify the stimulus drawings.

☐ *Spatial Relations* (Supplemental)—A geometric figure divided into two or more pieces is presented. The student must select from a series of shapes those that, when combined, make the original figure.

Comprehension-Knowledge

- *Picture Vocabulary*—The student is shown a drawing and is asked to say what it is. In early items, the tester presents a set of drawings, names one, and directs the student to point to it.
- *Oral Vocabulary* (Supplemental)—In the first part of this subtest, the tester reads a word and the student must give its synonym. In the second part, the student provides an antonym for the word read by the tester. Test pages show the words that the tester reads.
- *Listening Comprehension* (Supplemental)—The tester or Test Tape reads a sentence or paragraph with one word missing, and the student must supply that word.
- *Verbal Analogies* (Supplemental)—The tester reads verbal analogies (e.g., "Big is to little as up is to . . .") and the student completes them.

Fluid Reasoning

- *Analysis-Synthesis*—The student is shown a key that defines a relationship between colors. For example, red with green may equal black. With the key present, the student solves puzzles where one or more colors have been omitted. Error responses are corrected. There is a one-minute time limit for more difficult items.
- *Concept Formation* (Supplemental)—The student is shown two sets of drawings, one set of which is inside boxes. The student must tell one or more concepts that differentiate the boxed drawings. Examples are color, size, shape, and number.
- *Spatial Relations* (Supplemental)—This subtest assesses both Fluid Reasoning and Visual Processing; see the Visual Processing section for a description.
- *Verbal Analogies* (Supplemental)—This subtest assesses both Fluid Reasoning and Comprehension-Knowledge; see the Comprehension-Knowledge section for a description.

All of the cognitive ability subtests from the 1977 *Woodcock-Johnson* were retained in the 1989 edition, although Quantitative Concepts was recategorized as an achievement test. Ten of the 21 cognitive subtests, almost half, are new: Memory for Names, Incomplete Words, and Visual Clo-

sure on the standard battery; Delayed Recall—Memory for Names, Delayed Recall—Visual-Auditory Learning, Memory for Words, Cross Out, Sound Patterns, Picture Recognition, and Listening Comprehension on the supplementary battery.

Figure 8-2 shows the relationships between *Woodcock-Johnson-R* cognitive ability subtests. Of the seven subtests in the standard battery, five are recommended for early childhood assessment. All subtests in the standard battery are administered to derive a Broad Ability score. Subtests may be combined in a number of ways to obtain information about various cognitive factors and areas of scholastic aptitude. For example, the cluster score for the cognitive factor of Long-Term Retrieval is determined by performance on one standard battery subtest, Memory for Names, and one supplementary subtest, Visual-Auditory Learning. Two other supplementary subtests are available if further information is needed about this factor.

Students must be able to attend to test tasks for several minutes at a time to participate in *Woodcock-Johnson-R* administration. English-language skills are a necessity, except perhaps for Processing Speed subtests and some Visual Processing subtests. However, a Spanish-language version of the original *Woodcock-Johnson* battery (Woodcock, 1982) contains 10 tests of cognitive ability.

No reading is required. On the standard battery, the most typical response mode is oral. However, on Memory for Names, the student points to the answer, and Visual Matching is a paper-and-pencil task. The Processing Speed subtests are timed. The Test Tape is used to present items on all Short-Term Memory and Auditory Processing subtests and on one Comprehension-Knowledge subtest. With immature students and others having difficulty with the Test Tape, the tester may read the items, except on the Sound Patterns subtest. The student must be able to discriminate colors on the Analysis-Synthesis subtest.

Technical Quality

As discussed in Chapter 7, the *Woodcock-Johnson-R* was standardized from 1986 to 1988 with more than 6,300 subjects ranging in age from 2-0 to 90+. Preschool children, K–12 students, college students, and adults were included. The K–

12 group was drawn from regular classes, and students were excluded only if their sole placement was special education or if they had less than one year's experience in an English-language classroom. Weighting procedures were used to assure that that the entire standardized sample resembled the national population on variables such as geographic region, community size, sex, race, and Hispanic versus non-Hispanic.

At the time the third edition of *Assessing Special Students* went to press, the *Technical Manual* for the *Woodcock-Johnson–R* was not yet avail-

FIGURE 8–2

Selective testing table for the *Woodcock-Johnson–R Tests of Cognitive Ability*

TESTS OF COGNITIVE ABILITY	Early Development Scale (G)	Standard Scale (G)	Extended Scale	Long Term Retrieval (Glr)	Short Term Memory (Gsm)	Processing Speed (Gs)	Auditory Processing (Ga)	Visual Processing (Gv)	Comprehension-Knowledge (Gc)	Fluid Reasoning (Gf)	Oral Language	Reading	Mathematics	Written Language	Knowledge	Intra Cognitive Discrepancies	Oral Language
STANDARD BATTERY																	
1. Memory for Names	●	●	●	●												●	
2. Memory for Sentences	●	●	●		●						●	●			●	●	
3. Visual Matching		●	●			●						●	●	●		●	
4. Incomplete Words	●	●	●				●								●	●	
5. Visual Closure	●	●	●					●								●	
6. Picture Vocabulary	●	●	●						●		●					●	
7. Analysis-Synthesis		●	●							●			●			●	
SUPPLEMENTAL BATTERY																	
8. Visual-Auditory Learning	○	●		●										●		●	
9. Memory for Words	○	●			●											●	
10. Cross Out		●				●										●	
11. Sound Blending	○	●					●					●		●	●	●	
12. Picture Recognition	○	●						●								●	●
13. Oral Vocabulary		●							●		●	●	●	●		●	
14. Concept Formation		●								●			●		●	●	●
15. Delayed Recall — Memory for Names				○													
16. Delayed Recall — Visual-Auditory Learning				○													
17. Numbers Reversed					○											●	
18. Sound Patterns							○										●
19. Spatial Relations								○		○							
20. Listening Comprehension									○		●						
21. Verbal Analogies									○	○	●						

● = Tests to administer for a cluster score
○ = Tests which can supply additional information

Note. From *Woodcock-Johnson–Revised Tests of Cognitive Ability* by R. W. Woodcock and M. B. Johnson, 1989, Allen, TX: DLM Teaching Resources. Copyright 1989 by DLM Teaching Resources. Reprinted by permission.

able. However, the examiner's manual for the *Woodcock-Johnson–R Tests of Cognitive Ability* (Woodcock & Mather, 1989b) reports some information about the technical quality of this measure. Reliability was studied with the test-retest method for timed tests (Visual Matching and Cross Out) and with the split-half procedure for other tests and for clusters. Median reliabilities across ages fall at or above .80 for all cluster scores and many subtests. However, four subtests show median reliability coefficients of less than .80: Visual Matching, Visual Closure, Memory for Words, and Cross Out. Also, subtests at some age levels fall below minimum standards. For example, for age 13 subjects, reliabilities on 8 of the 21 Cognitive Ability tests are in the .60s or .70s.

Results of three studies of the *Woodcock-Johnson–R*'s concurrent validity with other measures of intellectual performance are summarized in the manual. Findings indicate relationships in the mid to high .60s between the Broad Cognitive Ability Standard Scale of the *Woodcock-Johnson–R,* the *WISC–R* Full Scale, and the *Stanford-Binet IV* Composite. Construct validity of the *Tests of Cognitive Ability* is supported by results of a factor analysis and by data showing systematic patterns of difference between samples of mentally retarded, learning disabled, normal, and gifted students.

Professionals wishing to use *Woodcock-Johnson–R* results for educational decisions should consult the *Technical Manual* for a more extensive discussion of the characteristics of the standardization sample and the evidence presented to support reliability and validity. Of particular interest is the predictive validity of the scholastic aptitude cluster scores derived from the *Tests of Cognitive Ability.* In addition, results of the Visual Matching, Visual Closure, Memory for Words, and Cross Out subtests should be interpreted with caution due to concerns about reliability.

Administration Considerations

The *Tests of Cognitive Ability* are more difficult to administer than the achievement portion of the *Woodcock-Johnson–R.* Consider the diversity of the seven subtests in the standard battery. Five subtests require that all students begin with item 1; basal rules on the other two subtests are either 4 or 6 consecutively numbered successes. Two

subtests use cutoff scores in lieu of ceilings; on the other subtests, ceiling rules vary from 4 to 8 consecutively numbered failures. One subtest, Visual Matching, is timed. Two use the Test Tape. On the two subtests that are controlled learning tasks (Memory for Names and Analysis-Synthesis), student errors are to be corrected by the tester.

The *Tests of Cognitive Ability* begin with standard introductory remarks that are read to all students. Then the tester selects the subtests to be administered. As Figure 8–2 illustrates, choices can be made from both the standard and supplemental batteries based on the age of the student and the assessment questions under consideration. Suggested starting points are given by the student's estimated ability level, not by actual grade placement.

Raw scores are calculated in the usual manner. As with the achievement tests, the test record booklet provides tables for converting raw scores to age and grade equivalents. The tables for the subtests where cutoff scores are used instead of ceilings (e.g., Memory for Names and Analysis-Synthesis) are a bit more complicated; norms are arranged by the number of items administered. As with the *Tests of Achievement,* the manual must be consulted to derive comparative scores such as percentile ranks and standard scores. This time-consuming process can be shortened with the test-scoring program *COMPUSCORE.*

Results and Interpretation

The *Tests of Cognitive Ability* produce a great number of results. The Broad Ability Standard Scale summarizes performance on the standard battery. A Broad Ability Extended Scale is also available; it takes into account all standard battery subtests as well as seven of the supplementary subtests. Results can also be reported by subtest, by cognitive factor, and by areas of scholastic aptitude. More than 35 subtest and area results are produced, and each result can be expressed as an age and grade equivalent, standard score, percentile rank, and Relative Mastery Index (RMI) score. Extended age and grade scores are provided, and standard scores are distributed with a mean of 100 and a standard deviation of 15.

Results of the *Woodcock-Johnson–R* can be plotted on a series of profiles to assist in interpretation. W scores are plotted in confidence intervals on the Age/Grade Profile to allow comparisons with the student's current age or grade. The Standard Score/Percentile Rank profile, also plotted in confidence intervals, compares student performance to that of age or grade peers in the norm group. Both types of profile are available for individual subtest scores and for broader area scores. In addition, procedures are provided for comparing discrepancies in performance across cognitive ability areas and between scholastic aptitudes and areas of achievement.

The *Tests of Cognitive Ability* are an interesting set of measures that span a wide age range. In contrast to the *WISC–R,* the *Woodcock-Johnson–R* addresses a number of cognitive factors. Several of these factors are of particular interest in the assessment of learning disabilities. The drawbacks of this measure include its length (a total of 21 subtests), the time required for scoring if other than age or grade scores are needed, and the difficulties associated with interpreting the large number of scores and profiles produced.

OTHER INDIVIDUAL MEASURES OF INTELLECTUAL PERFORMANCE

The assessment team can choose from several other individual tests of intellectual performance. The *Kaufman Assessment Battery for Children,* like the *Woodcock-Johnson–R,* contains aptitude measures as well as measures of academic achievement. Also available are age scales such as the 1973 *Stanford-Binet Intelligence Scale* where test items are arranged by age levels rather than by subtest. The *Stanford-Binet Intelligence Scale: Fourth Edition,* the most recent version, represents a major revision of this classic test; it is no longer an age scale. In addition, there are a number of nonverbal tests of intellectual performance.

Kaufman Assessment Battery for Children

The *K-ABC* (Kaufman & Kaufman, 1983) is an individual measure, designed to be administered by professionals such as school psychologists who are trained in individual intelligence testing. The battery is appropriate for children ages $2\frac{1}{2}$ to $12\frac{1}{2}$ and contains mental processing and achievement subtests. Among the global scores derived from the mental processing subtests is the Mental Pro-

cessing Composite, an index of overall intellectual performance. Two other global scores are measures of more specific abilities, Sequential Processing and Simultaneous Processing. All global scores are distributed with a mean of 100 and a standard deviation of 15.

According to the *K-ABC*'s Interpretive Manual, "sequential processing places a premium on the serial or temporal order of stimuli when solving problems; in contrast, simultaneous processing demands a gestalt-like, frequently spatial, integration of stimuli to solve problems with maximum efficiency" (p. 2). *K-ABC* subtests are

Sequential Processing Subtests
Hand Movements (ages 2–6 through 12–5)
Number Recall (ages 2–6 through 12–5)
Word Order (ages 4–0 through 12–5)

Simultaneous Processing Subtests
Magic Window (ages 2–6 through 4–11)
Face Recognition (ages 2–6 through 4–11)
Gestalt Closure (ages 2–6 through 12–5)
Triangles (ages 4–0 through 12–5)
Matrix Analogies (ages 5–0 through 12–5)
Spatial Analogies (ages 5–0 through 12–5)
Photo Series (ages 6–0 through 12–5)

Achievement Subtests
Expressive Vocabulary (ages 2–6 through 4–11)
Faces and Places (ages 2–6 through 12–5)
Arithmetic (ages 5–0 through 12–5)
Riddles (ages 3–0 through 4–11)
Reading/Decoding (ages 5–0 through 12–5)
Reading/Understanding (ages 7–0 through 12–5)

The *K-ABC* manual contains instructional suggestions for teaching academic skills by using students' sequential or simultaneous processing strengths. Although remedial suggestions are based upon research results, further validation of this intervention approach is needed. Anastasi (1988) cautions that the simultaneous and sequential subtests on the *K-ABC* could also be interpreted as measures of verbal and nonverbal reasoning.

On the *K-ABC,* it is possible to make comparisons between processing scale scores, and between each of these and achievement. A supplementary scoring system (Kamphaus & Reynolds, 1987a, 1987b) allows computation of two additional aptitude scores (Verbal Intelligence Composite and General Intelligence Composite) and provides a system for determining whether global scores are significantly different. For example, it is possible to compare General Intelligence and Reading.

Also available on the *K-ABC* is a Nonverbal Scale composed of several mental processing subtests. On these subtests, directions can be given in pantomime, and only motor responses are required. The Nonverbal Scale is recommended for students with hearing impairments, speech and language disorders, and those who do not speak English. For bilingual Hispanic students, the *K-ABC* manual provides information for Spanish-speaking examiners about giving test directions in Spanish and allowing Spanish responses.

The *K-ABC* appears to be a promising measure of intellectual performance with several interesting features, including a nonverbal scale and tests of two types of processing abilities. However, norms are available only up to age 12–6, its use is restricted to trained professionals such as school psychologists, and further validation of its remedial approach is needed. In addition, criticism has been leveled at the *K-ABC* in reference to its theoretical base (Sternberg, 1984), its sequential-simultaneous factor structure (Strommen, 1988), and its relevance to instructional planning (Salvia & Hritcko, 1984).

Age Scales

Two age scales used in educational evaluation are the 1973 edition of the *Stanford-Binet Intelligence Scale* (Terman & Merrill) and the *Slosson Intelligence Test* (Slosson, 1983).

1973 Stanford-Binet Intelligence Scale. This version of the *Stanford-Binet* is composed of many different types of items arranged in order of difficulty by age levels. Items assessing similar skills and abilities are not grouped together into subtests. The *Stanford-Binet* begins at age 2 with tasks such as block building and identification of body parts. It extends through the Superior Adult range and, at that level, includes test items such as reasoning, vocabulary, and opposite analogy questions. This test requires approximately one hour for administration and is typically administered by school psychologists.

On early versions of the *Stanford-Binet,* subjects earned a Mental Age (MA) score that was converted into a ratio Intelligence Quotient (IQ) by the formula $IQ = (MA/CA) \times 100$, where CA denotes chronological age. For example, if a 10-year-old child earned an MA of 8–0, the IQ would be 80. This system, although intuitively appealing, has several faults:

1. The same mental age score may have very different meanings for individuals of different chronological ages.
2. The mental age scale is uneven because growth occurs more rapidly at younger ages.
3. Mental age is not an informative concept with adults.
4. Ratio IQs have different standard deviations at different ages, making interpretation difficult.

For these reasons, ratio IQs on the *Stanford-Binet* were replaced with deviation IQs, standard scores with a mean of 100 and a standard deviation of 16 at all ages.

Slosson Intelligence Test. The *Slosson Intelligence Test* (*SIT*) (Slosson, 1983) is also based on age levels rather than subtests. It is designed for quick and easy administration and for attainment of IQ results equivalent to those of the 1973 *Stanford-Binet.*

The *SIT* contains a series of items, each of which is assigned an age level. Items begin at age 0.5 months and extend to 27 years, 0 months. Test questions are similar to those found on the *Stanford-Binet.* They include vocabulary, verbal reasoning, memory, numerical reasoning, general information, and visual-motor questions. At the higher age levels, verbal items and those assessing numerical reasoning are the most common.

New norms established for the *SIT* in 1981 are provided in a separate manual (Armstrong & Jensen, 1981). The purpose of renorming was to keep pace with the 1972 renorming of the *Stanford-Binet.* The current *SIT* offers deviation IQ scores for the first time. These are distributed with a mean of 100 and a standard deviation of 16. IQ scores can also be converted to percentile ranks and stanines. Norms tables have recently been expanded (Jensen & Armstrong, 1985) to extend the lower score range of the test.

When the *SIT* was renormed, the sample was not selected randomly, and subjects were drawn only from the Northeast. The manual reports a correlation of .95 between *SIT* and 1973 *Stanford-Binet* IQs in the norm sample, and no difference was found between scores. However, a high degree of relationship is expected between these measures. Many *SIT* items are adaptations of items from the *Stanford-Binet,* and the procedures used in renorming the *SIT* were specifically designed to produce equivalent scores. Thus, the *SIT* is best viewed as a quick screening measure rather than a substitute for more comprehensive tests such as the *WISC–R* and the newest edition of the *Stanford-Binet,* at least in special education assessment.

Stanford-Binet Intelligence Scale: Fourth Edition

The 1986 edition of the *Stanford-Binet* (Thorndike, Hagen, & Sattler) is not an age scale. Although it retains many of the same types of items as earlier editions, this test is organized by subtests. This new edition represents several major changes: items are arranged by skill areas rather than age; several scores are available, not just one global IQ score; and abilities other than verbal aptitude are emphasized. These changes make the 1986 *Stanford-Binet* much more similar to measures such as the *WISC–R* and the *Woodcock-Johnson–R.*

Designed for persons age 2 through adult, the 1986 *Stanford-Binet* contains 15 subtests that assess four areas of intellectual performance:

Verbal Reasoning
Vocabulary
Comprehension
Absurdities
Verbal Relations

Abstract/Visual Reasoning
Pattern Analysis
Copying
Matrices
Paper Folding and Cutting

Quantitative Reasoning
Quantitative
Number Series
Equation Building

Short-Term Memory
Bead Memory
Memory for Sentences
Memory for Digits
Memory for Objects

According to the manual, Verbal Reasoning and Quantitative Reasoning subtests measure crystallized abilities, whereas Abstract/Visual Reasoning subtests assess fluid-analytic abilities. Experiences outside of school provide the knowledge base for fluid-analytic abilities, but schooling is the major influence on crystallized abilities. Thorndike and colleagues (1986) say that "the crystallized-abilities factor could also be called a scholastic- or academic-ability factor" (p. 4).

Results on the 1986 *Stanford-Binet* are normalized standard scores called Standard Age Scores (SAS), a term that is somewhat misleading. These are standard scores based on age norms, not age equivalents. Subtest Standard Age Scores are distributed with a mean of 50 and a standard deviation of 8. Subtest results can be combined into four area scores (Verbal Reasoning, Abstract/Visual Reasoning, Quantitative Reasoning, and Short-Term Memory) and an overall composite similar to a global IQ score. Area and total test Standard Age Scores have a mean of 100 and a standard deviation of 16.

Several important changes were made in the *Stanford-Binet* in its fourth revision. These changes may help to overcome some of the criticisms of previous editions, particularly concerns about overemphasis of verbal aptitude. As research begins to accumulate on this measure, it will become possible to make comparisons between it and other tests such as the *WISC–R* and the *Woodcock-Johnson–R* that attempt to assess a variety of intellectual abilities.

Nonverbal Measures

Nonverbal measures of intelligence may be useful for students with hearing, speech, or language disorders, or for those whose language is not English. The Performance scale of the *WISC–R,* for example, deemphasizes verbal skills and is sometimes considered a nonverbal intelligence measure, even though directions are given verbally. Other well-known nonverbal tests include the *Raven Progressive Matrices* (1938, 1947, 1962) and the *Leiter International Performance Scale* (1948).

Raven Progressive Matrices. The *Raven Progressive Matrices* are nonverbal tests in which the subject is shown a design or matrix with a part missing. The subject must then select from several choices the piece that best completes the matrix. This task requires figural reasoning and is the only task used on the three versions of the

Matrices. These are the *Standard Progressive Matrices* (Raven, 1938) for ages 8 to 65, the *Coloured Progressive Matrices* (Raven, 1947) for ages 5 to 11 and mentally retarded adults, and the *Advanced Progressive Matrices* (Raven, 1962) for adolescents and adults. These tests were originally standardized in England, but recent American norms are available for the *Standard* and *Progressive Matrices* (Raven et al., 1986).

Leiter International Performance Scale.
The *Leiter International Performance Scale* (Leiter, 1948) is another nonverbal measure of intellectual performance. Directions are given in pantomime. A stimulus card is shown, and the subject arranges blocks to complete matching, copying, memory, analogies, classification, and other types of figural reasoning tasks. Test items are arranged in age scales from ages 2 to 18, and Mental Age scores are converted to ratio IQs. An adaptation of this measure designed for children ages 3 to 8 was developed by Arthur (1952). However, only ratio IQ scores are available, norms are dated, and there is insufficient evidence of technical adequacy.

Test of Nonverbal Intelligence.
A much newer nonverbal measure is the *Test of Nonverbal Intelligence (TONI)* (Brown, Sherbenou, & Johnsen, 1982). On this test, the examiner pantomimes instructions, and the subject responds by pointing to one of several possible answers. Test items assess problem solving with abstract, figural designs. The subject is shown a set of figures with one or more figures missing. The individual must determine the rule or rules governing the set (e.g., matching, analogies, progressions) and then select the figure that best completes the set from several options.

The *TONI* offers two alternate forms. Results are reported as standard scores with a mean of 100 and standard deviation of 15. The test was standardized on approximately 2,000 persons, ages 5–0 to 85, and the standardization sample resembles the U.S. population in terms of sex, race, ethnicity, geographic location, and urban–rural residence. Internal consistency and alternate forms reliability is adequate, and results of validity studies with limited numbers of subjects indicate *TONI* results are related to results from other nonverbal measures of intelligence. Although further research is needed to substantiate the validity of the

TONI, it appears to be a promising tool for the measurement of nonverbal problem-solving ability.

NONBIASED ASSESSMENT OF LEARNING APTITUDE

Concern about the cultural bias of traditional measures of intellectual performance has led to the development of alternative strategies for the assessment of learning aptitude in students with a heritage other than the dominant American culture. One early effort was the design of the *Culture Fair Intelligence Tests* (Cattell, 1950; Cattell & Cattell, 1960, 1963). These group-administered measures stress figural reasoning and deemphasize verbal skills and school learning. Nonverbal tests, such as those described in the previous section, are used with students whose primary language is not English; some standard measures of learning aptitude are available in languages other than English, most notably Spanish. Such strategies attempt to reduce linguistic bias by replacing English with the student's language or by minimizing the role of language. Cultural bias, although related to the language of testing, is a separate issue. The sections that follow describe two attempts to overcome cultural bias in the assessment of general learning aptitude.

System of Multicultural Pluralistic Assessment

The *System of Multicultural Pluralistic Assessment (SOMPA)* (Mercer & Lewis, 1977b) is a battery of nine measures that provides information about the general learning aptitude of children ages 5 to 11. The *SOMPA* is designed to aid in the evaluation of students from diverse sociocultural backgrounds and white, black, and Hispanic ethnic groups.

To describe current functioning comprehensively, the *SOMPA* assesses performance from three separate perspectives: Medical, Social System, and Pluralistic. Medical measures evaluate the student's current health status to determine whether pathological conditions are interfering with physiological functioning. They include visual and auditory acuity checks; physical dexterity tasks; evaluation of weight by height; the *Bender Visual Motor Gestalt Test* (Bender, 1938; Koppitz, 1963), used to assess "perceptual maturation and neurological impairment'' (Mercer, 1979, p. 68); and a Health History Inventory completed by the child's parent. *SOMPA* information is collected either in parent interviews or by direct student assessments.

Social System measures determine whether the student is meeting performance expectations for school and social roles. In this context, the *WISC–R* is used as a measure of academic role performance. Social role performance is assessed with the *Adaptive Behavior Inventory for Children* (*ABIC*), a parent interview form that elicits information about the student's ability to cope with nonacademic environments.

The third perspective on the *SOMPA* is the Pluralistic perspective. This concerns whether the student is meeting performance expectations for age and sociocultural group. The student's current environment is assessed with the Sociocultural Scales, part of the parent interview. Included are questions about family size and structure, socioeconomic status, and urban acculturation. The second pluralistic measure is the *WISC–R,* rescored to compare the student with his or her sociocultural group rather than standard norms. According to the *SOMPA*, standard *WISC–R* scores may be poor predictors of learning aptitude, particularly for students whose sociocultural background is different from that of dominant culture students. Thus, an appropriate comparison group for the student is identified with the Sociocultural Scales, and *WISC–R* results are ''rescored'' using these alternative norms. The new *WISC–R* scores are considered measures of Estimated Learning Potential.

Results are plotted on profiles to allow comparison of Medical, Social System, and Pluralistic findings. A portion of a sample profile from the *SOMPA* manual appears in Figure 8–3. The scores are for a 9-year-old black girl, Bernice. Her performance was within normal limits on all Medical measures. Adaptive behavior is adequate on the Social System profile, but the School Functioning Level, measured by standard *WISC–R* results, is within the ''At Risk'' range, the lowest 3%. On the Pluralistic profile, however, the rescored *WISC–R* places the student's Estimated Learning Potential clearly within the range of adequate performance. On the Sociocultural Scales, Bernice scores at higher percentiles within her own ethnic

group than when compared to the culture of the school.

The *SOMPA* has been heavily criticized for its lack of national norms (standardization took place in California only), its failure to include school performance tasks, its lack of validity data for the Estimated Learning Potential score, and failure to provide guidelines for use of the battery in educational decisions (Clarizio, 1979; Goodman, 1979; Oakland, 1979). Salvia and Ysseldyke (1988) conclude that the *SOMPA,* at best, should be viewed as an experimental measure. Sattler (1988) makes a stronger statement in his criticism of the Estimated Learning Potential (ELP) score:

> The use of the ELP for placement or clinical decisions is not warranted. Any use of the ELP violates the widely accepted test standards of the American Psychological Association and Public Law 94–142.... *There is no justification for using the ELP for any clinical or psychoeducational purpose.* (p. 354)

Learning Potential Assessment Device

The assessment system proposed by Feuerstein and colleagues (1979) is a nontraditional approach to evaluation of learning aptitude. According to Feuerstein, children learn through interactions with adults in mediated learning experiences. In these interactions, the adult ''mediates'' the world to the child ''by framing, selecting, focusing, and feeding back environmental experiences'' (p. 71). In Feuerstein's view, cultural deprivation results from inadequate mediated learning; culturally deprived children have not assimilated their own culture.

In the *Learning Potential Assessment Device* (*LPAD*), the tester becomes a teacher and attempts to provide the student with mediated learning. To accomplish this, the *LPAD* is administered using a test-teach-test format. This device is actually a collection of measures, some adapted from experimental tasks, others from published instruments such as Raven's *Progressive Matrices.* The student first performs reasoning tasks without assistance from the examiner. The examiner then steps into the instructional role and attempts to provide the student with more sophisticated strategies for task solution. Test tasks are then presented again without coaching.

The aim is to assess the student's cognitive modifiability rather than current intellectual status.

FIGURE 8-3
Sample *SOMPA* profile

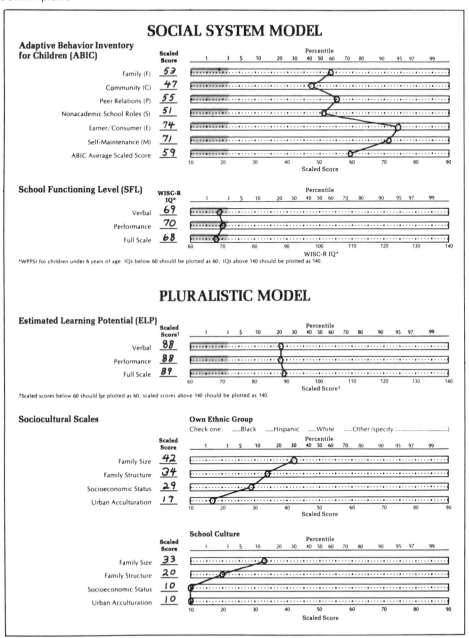

The examiner observes the student's performance and forms a judgment about deficient cognitive functions and the ability to learn. Test tasks are not normed and scores not emphasized. Instead, the *LPAD* is intended for clinical use, and its results are primarily descriptive rather than quantitative.

This measure and the accompanying intervention program, Instrumental Enrichment (Feuerstein, 1980), are still under study (Feuerstein et al., 1981; Feuerstein, Miller, Rand, & Jensen, 1981; Harth, 1982). Although the *LPAD* is an interesting system that attempts to address the central question of ability to learn, it is unlikely to be widely used in schools. It is a clinical measure tied to the expertise of the individual examiner with results that appear less objective than those of traditional tests.

ADAPTIVE BEHAVIOR MEASURES

Adaptive behavior is usually not measured directly. Instead, the student's parents or teachers are used as informants about the student's current nonacademic functioning. Interviews are typically used with parents and written questionnaires with teachers.

There are several norm-referenced measures of adaptive behavior available today, as Table 8–3 illustrates. This table lists the names of the measures, the ages for which each is appropriate, the person or persons who act as informants, and the type of measure (interview or questionnaire). In the next sections, the *Adaptive Behavior Inventory for Children* and the *AAMD Adaptive Behavior Scale, School Edition* are described. Other measures are then discussed briefly.

ADAPTIVE BEHAVIOR INVENTORY FOR CHILDREN

The *Adaptive Behavior Inventory for Children (ABIC)* (Mercer & Lewis, 1977a) is a standardized parent interview form designed to aid in the assessment of children from diverse cultural backgrounds. It is one of the measures of the *SOMPA;* its purpose is assessment of the student's ability to meet expectations for social role performance. A Spanish version of the interview is available for bilingual examiners.

TABLE 8–3
Measures of adaptive behavior

Name (Author)	Ages	Informant	Type of Measure
AAMD Adaptive Behavior Scale, School Edition (Lambert & Windmiller, 1981)	3 to 16	Parent Teacher	Interview Questionnaire
Adaptive Behavior Inventory (Brown & Leigh, 1986)	5 to 18–11	Teacher	Questionnaire
Adaptive Behavior Inventory for Children (Mercer & Lewis, 1977a)	5 to 11	Parent	Interview
Comprehensive Test of Adaptive Behavior (Adams, 1984a)	Birth to 60	Student Parent	Direct measure Questionnaire
Normative Adaptive Behavior Checklist (Adams, 1984b)	Birth to 21	Parent or Teacher	Checklist
Scales of Independent Behavior (Bruininks, Woodcock, Weatherman, & Hill, 1984)	Infants to 40 + years	Parent or Teacher	Interview
Vineland Adaptive Behavior Scales (Sparrow, Balla, & Cicchetti, 1984)			
Interview editions	Birth to 18–11 and low functioning adults	Parent	Interview
Classroom edition	3 to 12–11	Teacher	Questionnaire
Weller-Strawser Scales of Adaptive Behavior for the Learning Disabled (Weller & Strawser, 1981)	Students identified as learning disabled	Teacher	Questionnaire

---

ADAPTIVE BEHAVIOR INVENTORY FOR CHILDREN (ABIC)
J. R. Mercer & J. F. Lewis (1977a)

Type: Norm-referenced interview form

Major Content Areas: Adaptive behavior in the home, community, and nonscholastic aspects of school

Type of Administration: Individual interview

Administration Time: Approximately 30 minutes

Age/Grade Levels: Ages 5 to 11

Types of Scores: Scaled scores for each of six scales, average scaled score, percentile ranks

Typical Uses: An indirect measure of several dimensions of adaptive behavior

Cautions: This measure was standardized with residents of only one state, California, and its use is restricted to similar states. Results must be interpreted with great caution because the manual does not provide validity information.

Seven types of questions appear on the *ABIC*. Veracity questions describe roles not expected to be mastered by students age 5 to 11; these items are used to evaluate the accuracy of the informant's answers. The remaining questions are categorized according to dimensions of adaptive behavior: Family, Community, Peer Relations, Nonacademic School Roles, Earner/Consumer, and Self-Maintenance. Figure 8–4 presents the first few items on the *ABIC* and the introductory information read to parents. Question 1 assesses Self-Maintenance, and questions 2 and 3 Family.

The person being interviewed can choose between five possible responses. The respondent may answer that he or she has no knowledge of the student's ability to perform a particular activity or that the student has no opportunity to take part in this activity. The responses read by the interviewer are coded as 0, 1, or 2. Latent Role, or 0, responses indicate the student does not yet engage in the activity. Emergent Role, or 1, responses mean infrequent participation or participation only with adult supervision. Mastered Role, or 2, responses indicate frequent participation with little or no supervision.

The *ABIC* is administered to a parent or other adult in the household who knows the child best. The informant must be familiar with the child's activities in the home and in other nonschool environments and must be able to communicate in either English or Spanish.

Technical Quality

The *ABIC* was standardized in 1972–73 on 2,085 students enrolled in public schools in California. Three samples of equivalent size were independently selected: black, Hispanic, and white students. During standardization, students' parents were interviewed by persons of the same ethnic group as themselves.

The reliability of the *ABIC,* as reported in the *SOMPA* Technical Manual (Mercer, 1979), appears adequate. Over 300 newly trained interviewers observed an actual interview and independently recorded responses and computed scores. Interobserver reliability was reported as high.

The predictive validity of the *ABIC* was not studied. According to the Technical Manual, the quality of a direct measure of social role performance should be judged by its interrater reliability, not its predictive validity. Mercer says,

The validity of the ABIC is judged by its ability to reflect accurately the extent to which the child is meeting the expectations of the members of the social systems covered in the scales, *not* by its correlation with teacher judgments, school performance, or performance on measures of achievement, such as academic achievement tests, aptitude tests, or "intelligence tests." (1979, p. 109)

Despite Mercer's position, the validity of the *ABIC* is of interest. What is the relationship between *ABIC* results and the results of other measures of

FIGURE 8–4
Sample items from the *ABIC*

"We are now going to talk about children's activities, the kinds of things they do at home and around the neighborhood. I will ask some questions and give you answers to choose from. Choose the answer that best describes what _____ does. Please let me know if you don't allow _____ to do the activity, or if _____ doesn't have an opportunity to do the activity, or if you don't know whether _____ does the activity. If you are ready, let's begin."

If there are any questions, repeat or clarify the instructions. Then begin with question 1 and ask all questions through question 35. Remember that numbers (0, 1, or 2) printed in front of the responses are *not* to be read aloud.

1. Some children are afraid of a lot of things. Is _____ afraid of
    0 many things,   **1** a few things, or   **2** not much of anything?

2. Children get along better with some people than they do with others. How does _____ get along with his/her brother(s)?
    2 very well,   **1** fairly well, or   **0** not so well

3. How does _____ get along with his/her sister(s)?
    0 not so well,   **1** fairly well, or   **2** very well

Note. Reproduced from the *System of Multicultural Pluralistic Assessment* by J. R. Mercer and J. F. Lewis. Copyright 1977, 1979 by The Psychological Corporation. All rights reserved. Reproduced by special permission.

adaptive behavior? Is there agreement between parents' reports of their child's adaptive behavior and direct measures of child performance? Does current adaptive behavior, as measured by the *ABIC*, predict future performance on the same instrument?

Administration Considerations

Either professionals or paraprofessionals may administer the *ABIC*. Interviewers must have good reading and writing skills, be similar to respondents in ethnic and sociocultural background, and receive training in *ABIC* administration and scoring. The interviewers using the Spanish version of the instrument must be able to speak, read, and write both English and Spanish.

The *ABIC* begins with a series of questions asked of all informants. Questions are then divided into age levels. The interviewer determines the appropriate starting place in the age-graded questions from a table in the manual and continues administration until a basal and ceiling are achieved.

Results and Interpretation

The *ABIC* standardization samples were selected to represent three ethnic groups, but norms for this measure are provided only by age. According to the *SOMPA* Technical Manual, "The social roles played by 5- through 11-year-old children of differ-

ent ethnic backgrounds appear to be quite similar" (p. 105).

In scoring the *ABIC,* the interviewer first checks to see if Veracity, No Knowledge (DK), and No Opportunity (N) scores are within acceptable limits. Then, raw scores are computed for each of the six adaptive behavior scales. Raw scores are converted to scaled scores, and a total test score, the Average Scaled Score, is determined by summing the six scaled scores and dividing by 6. The scaled score mean is 50 with a standard deviation of 15. Scaled scores of 10 and 90 are approximately equivalent to the 1st and 99th percentiles. The standard error of measurement varies across ages, scales, and ethnic group, but the technical manual suggests using 5 scaled score points as an approximation.

Scaled scores from the *ABIC* are plotted on the *SOMPA*'s Social System profile (see Figure 8–3). The *ABIC* classifies a student "At Risk" if scaled scores fall at or below the 3rd percentile (scaled score 21 or below), and the At Risk section of the profile is colored red.

The *ABIC* has several strong points, including provision of interview questions in both Spanish and English. However, it fails to provide national norms and information about its validity. Because of these limitations, results should be interpreted cautiously, particularly when the *ABIC* is used in states dissimilar to California.

AAMD ADAPTIVE BEHAVIOR SCALE, SCHOOL EDITION

The *AAMD Adaptive Behavior Scale, School Edition (ABS–SE)* (Lambert & Windmiller, 1981) is the current version of a measure designed originally for institutionalized populations (Nihira, Foster, Shellhaas, & Leland, 1974). It was adapted and standardized for school use (Lambert, Windmiller, Cole, & Figueroa, 1975) and revised to its current form in 1981.

The *ABS–SE* is an indirect measure of adaptive and maladaptive behavior in school children age 3 to 16. According to the *ABS–SE* manuals (Lambert, 1981a; Lambert, Windmiller, Tharinger, & Cole, 1981), its results can be used for screening, instructional planning, diagnosis and placement, evaluation of progress, and IEP evaluation.

The *ABS–SE* may be used either as a print questionnaire or an interview form. In First Person Assessment, a teacher or trained aide answers the questions by reading the form and writing down ratings. In Third Party Assessment, a teacher, psychologist, or other professional reads the questions on the scale to the child's parent or another adult who knows the child well. The administration manual suggests that, whenever possible, ratings be obtained from both teachers and parents.

The *ABS–SE* contains 95 items that assess 21 domains of behavior. Part One domains are concerned with adaptive behavior, and Part Two with maladaptive behavior. Table 8–4 lists the contents of the *ABS–SE.*

Technical Quality

The *ABS–SE* was originally standardized in 1972–73 with students enrolled in California public school programs. Part of this sample was used in the current standardization along with Florida and California samples of preschool children, high school students, and special education students. A total of 6,523 students in three types of educational placements were included: Regular Class, programs for Educable Mentally Retarded (EMR) students, and programs for Trainable Mentally Retarded (TMR) students. The technical manual describes the sample but does not compare it with any larger group, such as the national school-aged population.

During standardization, the *ABS–SE* was used as a questionnaire completed by teachers. Teachers were selected, rather than parents, to involve them in the assessment process, because they are more accessible than parents, and because their reports are probably reliable. To support this procedure, the technical manual cites the results of a study (Cole, 1976) in which no differences were found between teacher and parent ratings of white and Spanish-surnamed children enrolled in EMR classes.

The reliability of the *ABS–SE* was evaluated only for factor scores, composite scores derived

---

AAMD ADAPTIVE BEHAVIOR SCALE, SCHOOL EDITION (ABS–SE)
N. Lambert & M. Windmiller (1981)

Type: Norm-referenced questionnaire or interview

Major Content Areas: Adaptive and maladaptive behavior

Type of Administration: Print questionnaire or individual interview

Administration Time: 15 to 45 minutes

Age/Grade Levels: Ages 3 to 16

Types of Scores: Percentile ranks by age and educational placement for each domain, scaled scores for each factor, and an overall Comparison Score

Typical Uses: An indirect measure of several dimensions of adaptive and maladaptive behavior

Cautions: Norms are based on residents of only two states, and only teachers were used as informants during standardization. Results should be interpreted cautiously and with special attention to standard errors of measurement, because factor scores show low reliabilities at some age levels and for some educational placements.

from the results on individual domains. Internal consistency varies across factors, ages, and educational placements. For example, on Factor 1, Personal Self-Sufficiency, coefficients range from .44 to .89, with the majority in the .70s and .80s; on Factor 5, Personal Adjustment, coefficients range from .27 to .82, with the majority in the .50s and .60s. The technical manual provides no information about test-retest or interrater reliability.

The concurrent validity of ABS–SE domain scores was studied by examining their relationship with IQ results. Factor scores were studied in relation to IQ tests and results of academic achievement measures. ABS–SE scores were not compared to results of other measures of adaptive behavior. The summary score on the ABS–SE,

called the Comparison Score, was used to reclassify a subset of the students in the standardization sample by educational placement. Over all ages, this score correctly reclassified an average of 74% of the students.

The technical quality of this version of the ABS–SE is improved over the earlier one, because the geographic distribution of the standardization sample has been broadened and reliability data are now available. However, the current norm group includes students from only two states, and some factor score reliabilities are low. Information about the relationship between the ABS–SE and other measures of adaptive behavior, including direct measures of child performance, would also be useful.

TABLE 8–4
Contents of the ABS–SE

Part One Domains and Subdomains	Part Two Domains
DOMAIN 1 Independent Functioning	DOMAIN 10 Aggressiveness
Eating Subdomain	DOMAIN 11 Antisocial vs. Social Behavior
Toilet Use Subdomain	DOMAIN 12 Rebelliousness
Cleanliness Subdomain	DOMAIN 13 Trustworthiness
Appearance Subdomain	DOMAIN 14 Withdrawal vs. Involvement
Care of Clothing Subdomain	DOMAIN 15 Mannerisms
Dressing & Undressing Subdomain	DOMAIN 16 Interpersonal Manners
Travel Subdomain	DOMAIN 17 Acceptability of Vocal Habits
Other Independent Functioning Subdomain	DOMAIN 18 Acceptability of Habits
DOMAIN 2 Physical Development	DOMAIN 19 Activity Level
Sensory Development Subdomain	DOMAIN 20 Symptomatic Behavior
Motor Development Subdomain	DOMAIN 21 Use of Medications
DOMAIN 3 Economic Activity	
Money Handling & Budgeting Subdomain	
Shopping Skills Subdomain	
DOMAIN 4 Language Development	
Expression Subdomain	
Comprehension Subdomain	
Social Language Development Subdomain	
DOMAIN 5 Numbers & Time	
DOMAIN 6 Prevocational Activity	
DOMAIN 7 Self-Direction	
Initiative Subdomain	
Perseverance Subdomain	
Leisure Time Subdomain	
DOMAIN 8 Responsibility	
DOMAIN 9 Socialization	

Note. From Administration and Instructional Planning Manual: AAMD Adaptive Behavior Scale, School Edition (p. 5) by N. Lambert, M. Windmiller, D. Tharinger, and L. Cole, 1981, Monterey, CA: Publishers Test Service. Copyright 1981 by the American Association on Mental Deficiency. Reprinted by permission.

Administration Considerations

Either professionals or paraprofessionals may complete the *ABS–SE* as a questionnaire, but trained professionals are needed when the scale is used as an interview form with parents. If the student's parents communicate in a language other than English, the administration manual advises the use of an interpreter.

Results and Interpretation

Depending upon the purpose of the assessment, *ABS–SE* results may be determined in two ways. If the aim is screening, instructional planning, or IEP development, the professional is directed to complete the Instructional Planning Profile. If the aim is diagnosis or placement, the Diagnostic Profile is recommended.

On the Instructional Planning Profile, raw scores for each domain are converted to percentile ranks. Three sets of norms are available: Regular Class, EMR, and TMR. The profile allows the professional to plot the student's performance in relation to two of these comparison groups. Norms extend from age 3–3 to 17–2, except there are no EMR norms for 3- to 6-year-olds and no Regular Class norms for 16-year-olds. According to the technical manual, domain percentile scores below the 10th percentile indicate "serious deficits in adaptive behavior" (p. 10).

The Diagnostic Profile allows the conversion of domain scores to factor scores. There are five factors.

- *Factor 1, Personal Self-Sufficiency,* is composed of items from the domains of Independent Functioning, Physical Development, and Economic Activity.
- *Factor 2, Community Self-Sufficiency,* is composed of items from Independent Functioning, Language Development, Numbers and Time, and Prevocational Activity.
- *Factor 3, Personal-Social Responsibility,* is composed of items from Prevocational Activity, Self-Direction, Responsibility, and Socialization, and Part Two items from Withdrawal.
- *Factor 4, Social Adjustment,* is composed of items from Aggressiveness, Antisocial vs. Social Behavior, Rebelliousness, Trustworthiness, Habits, Activity Level, and Symptomatic Behavior.

- *Factor 5, Personal Adjustment,* is composed of items from Mannerisms, Appropriateness of Interpersonal Manners, and Vocal Habits.

Raw factor scores are computed and converted to scaled scores with a mean of 10 and a standard deviation of 3. Standard errors for raw factor scores vary widely, and the manual should be consulted for each student assessed. According to the technical manual, factor scaled scores one or more standard deviations below the mean (scores of 7 or lower) indicate significant deficits.

A summary score for the *ABS–SE* is computed by a weighted combination of the raw scores for Factors 1, 2, and 3. Called the Comparison Score, it is an index of the student's overall adaptive behavior in relation to Regular Class, EMR, or TMR peers. The Comparison score is a cumulative percentage of reference group students receiving lower scores than the student under study. The technical manual recommends considering Comparison Scores in the bottom 2 to 5% of the Regular Class distribution as possibly signifying mental retardation. Of course, results of measures of intellectual performance must be considered before mental retardation can be confirmed.

Figure 8–5 contains the Diagnostic Profile for Lori, a case study student described in the *ABS–SE* manuals. Lori is age 8–9 and in second grade. She was retained in kindergarten, and her current academic performance ranges from readiness to first grade level. On the *ABS–SE,* her performance was more similar to that of EMR students than to that of Regular students. On the profile, the solid lines indicate Lori's standing in relation to regular class students, and the broken lines in relation to EMR class students. Her adaptive behavior appears to be within the average range when EMR students are the reference group. When compared with regular class students, Lori shows below average performance in the Community Self-Sufficiency Factor.

The *ABS–SE* appears to be useful for the study of various dimensions of adaptive behavior in preschool and school-aged children. This version of the *ABS–SE* has many improvements over the previous version. However, it is still not free from technical limitations. Therefore, results should be interpreted with caution, with special attention to standard errors of measurement.

FIGURE 8–5
Sample *ABS–SE* diagnostic profile

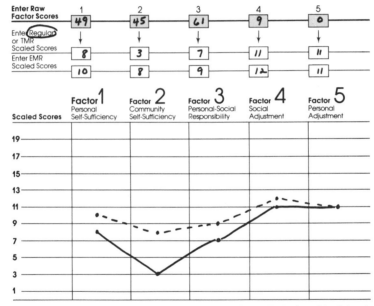

Note. From *Diagnostic and Technical Manual: AAMD Adaptive Behavior Scale, School Edition* (p. 13) by N. Lambert, 1981, Monterey, CA: Publishers Test Service. Copyright 1981 by American Association on Mental Deficiency. Reprinted by permission.

OTHER MEASURES OF ADAPTIVE BEHAVIOR

Until quite recently, few up-to-date measures of adaptive behavior were available to assessment professionals. However, the *Vineland Social Maturity Scale* (Doll, 1935, 1965), one of the earliest measures of adaptive behavior, has been updated. In addition, several new instruments have appeared on the market, including the *Scales of Independent Behavior* (considered part of the *Woodcock-Johnson* battery) and the *Weller-*

Strawser Scales of Adaptive Behavior for the Learning Disabled.

Vineland Adaptive Behavior Scales

The *Vineland Adaptive Behavior Scales* (Sparrow et al., 1984) are updates and revisions of Doll's *Vineland Social Maturity Scale.* Doll's instrument was a parent interview form, but the new *Vineland* contains three separate scales: two interview editions in survey or expanded form, and a classroom edition.

The interview editions are used by trained interviewers with parents or others who know the student well. The survey form includes fewer items than the expanded interview form and consequently requires less administration time. Interviews are conducted in a semistructured format; that is, the interviewer uses his or her own words to probe respondents about the student's current functioning. Interview items are not read. When the interviewer has gathered sufficient information about the student's participation in specific activities, he or she rates the student on the scale's items. Interview editions of the *Vineland* are designed for assessment of children from birth to 18–11 and low functioning adults. A Spanish version of the survey form is available.

The classroom edition is a print questionnaire completed by the student's teacher. It is appropriate for ages 3 to 12–11 and requires approximately 20 minutes. The classroom and interview editions assess four adaptive behavior domains and several subdomains.

□ *Communication* domain—includes the subdomains Receptive, Expressive, and Written.
□ *Daily Living Skills* domain—includes the subdomains Personal, Domestic, and Community.
□ *Socialization* domain—includes the subdomains Interpersonal Relationships, Play and Leisure Time, and Coping Skills.
□ *Motor Skills* domain—includes the subdomains Gross and Fine.

The Motor Skills domain is intended for children up to age 6, but it can be used with older persons with physical or other disabilities. The interview editions also contain Maladaptive Behavior, an optional domain for individuals age 5 and above.

The interview editions were standardized with a national sample of 3,000 persons, ages birth to 19, and a supplementary sample of 1,788 handicapped individuals, including mentally retarded adults and children in residential facilities for the emotionally disturbed, visually handicapped, and hearing impaired. For the classroom edition, the national standardization sample contained 2,925 students, ages 3 to 13. Each of the national samples was selected to represent the U. S. population as described in 1980 Census data. However, the classroom edition sample appears to differ from the national population on several variables. For instance, 7.2% of the sample represents rural communities, whereas 29% of the nation's population is classified as living in rural communities.

Standard scores are available for each of the adaptive behavior domains and for the Composite score, a summary of the four domains. Standard scores are distributed with a mean of 100 and a standard deviation of 15. Only Age Equivalent scores can be computed for subdomains. On the interview editions, students can be compared to both national norms and norms derived from the supplementary sample of handicapped persons. Also, a standard score is available for the optional domain, Maladaptive Behavior.

The revised *Vineland* scales, particularly those designed for use with parents, appear to be useful instruments for the study of several areas of adaptive behavior. One limitation is the amount of training needed to properly administer the semistructured parent interview. The *Vineland* manuals restrict administration of the interview editions and scoring and interpretation of all editions to "a psychologist, social worker, or other professional with a graduate degree and specific training in individual assessment and test interpretation."

Scales of Independent Behavior

The *Scales of Independent Behavior* (*SIB*) (Bruininks et al., 1984) are considered part of the 1977 *Woodcock-Johnson Psycho-Educational Battery*. The *SIB* adds adaptive behavior and problem behavior to the domains of cognitive ability and achievement assessed in this multidimensional battery.

The *SIB* is a structured interview that is appropriate for gathering information about persons ranging in age from infancy through 40+ years. The respondent can be anyone who knows the child or adult well. In some cases—for example, when adults are assessed—the subject can act as respondent. A Spanish version of the interview questions is available.

The *SIB* is made up of four Adaptive Behavior clusters, each of which contains several subscales:

Motor Skills
Gross-Motor Skills
Fine-Motor Skills

Social Interaction and Communication Skills
Social Interaction
Language Comprehension
Language Expression

Personal Independence Skills

Eating and Meal Preparation
Toileting
Dressing
Personal Self-Care
Domestic Skills

Community Independence Skills

Time and Punctuality
Money and Value
Work Skills
Home–Community Orientation

These 14 subscales require 45 to 60 minutes to administer, and results are summarized by a Broad Independence (Full Scale) score. A Short Form Scale is also available, as well as an Early Development Scale for children with developmental ages of less than $2\frac{1}{2}$ years. The optional Problem Behaviors Scale assesses eight areas of maladaptive behavior: hurtful to self, hurtful to others, destructive to property, disruptive behavior, unusual or repetitive habits, socially offensive behavior, withdrawn or inattentive behavior, and uncooperative behavior.

Norms are based on a national sample of more than 1,700 persons. A variety of scores are available, including age scores, percentile ranks, standard scores, instructional ranges, Relative Performance Indexes (RPIs), and Maladaptive Behavior Indexes (MBIs). Because the *SIB* is part of the 1977 *Woodcock-Johnson* system, its results can be directly related to results of that battery's cognitive ability tests.

Weller-Strawser Scales of Adaptive Behavior for the Learning Disabled

Unlike most adaptive behavior measures, the *Weller-Strawser Scales of Adaptive Behavior* (Weller & Strawser, 1981) are designed for use with only one population: students already identified as learning disabled. The *Weller-Strawser* is a checklist completed by professionals after a period of observation of the student under study. Its purpose is not to determine eligibility for special services but rather to identify areas of need for instructional planning.

Weller and Strawser (1981) describe the four areas of adaptive behavior assessed by this instrument:

☐ Social Coping—"assesses the manner in which the learning disabled student deals with environmental situations."

☐ Relationships—"assesses how the learning disabled student relates to others."
☐ Pragmatic Language—"assesses the learning disabled student's use of language in those social situations which are language based."
☐ Production—"assesses *how* the learning disabled produces rather than *what* is produced." (pp. 11–12)

Both an Elementary and a Secondary scale are available, each containing 35 items. On each item, the teacher reads descriptions of appropriate and inappropriate behavior and selects the one that best describes the student.

The two language subtests on the *Weller-Strawser* assess areas not usually included on measures of adaptive behavior. The Pragmatic Language subtest is concerned with areas such as ability to interpret gestures and facial expressions, the use of intuition and reasoning, and sense of humor. The Production subtest attempts to assess concentration, generalization of learning, organizational skills, and need for modification of instruction. Although these areas may be of concern with some learning disabled students, they are not usually considered dimensions of adaptive behavior.

One major limitation of this instrument is that it classifies student performance into only two categories: mild–moderate deficit or moderate–severe deficit. Even if a student's behavior is rated as appropriate on all items, results will indicate mild–moderate deficits in all areas. Another major concern is the lack of information about the standardization sample. Teachers of the learning disabled from urban and rural areas of six states rated the behavior of learning disabled students. The manual reports that "a total of 236 students between the ages of six and eighteen were selected by the teachers for inclusion in the rating. Of these 236 students, 154 were of elementary age and 82 were of secondary age" (p. 66). No other descriptive data about the standardization sample are provided.

ANSWERING THE ASSESSMENT QUESTIONS

The assessment team gathers information about intellectual performance and adaptive behavior to arrive at an estimate of the student's current learning aptitude. In evaluating assessment results, the team compares and contrasts the student's academic aptitude measured by tests of intellectual performance with current levels of functioning in nonacademic activities. The handicap of mental retardation is indicated only when both intellectual performance and adaptive behavior are below average. In learning disabilities and behavior disorders, intellectual performance must be within the average range, and adaptive behavior may be either adequate or below average.

Types of Procedures

Several types of assessment strategies are used to study learning aptitude: group tests of intellectual performance, individual intelligence tests, school records, parent interviews, questionnaires and checklists for teachers, and direct observation of students' adaptive behavior. Each of these methods is likely to produce somewhat different results.

Results from measures of intellectual performance are not expected to be equivalent to those from measures of adaptive behavior. These two strategies assess different skill domains, and although there is some relationship between academic aptitude and adaptive behavior (Harrison, 1987), students may perform poorly in one of these areas but adequately in the other.

Intellectual performance is assessed with group and individual tests, and parents and teachers may provide supplementary information about the student's aptitude for school learning. Individual tests are preferred over group measures. In special education assessment, there is no substitute for individually administered tests of intellectual performance. The information provided by parents and teachers is useful to corroborate test results; if major discrepancies occur, the team should continue its investigation, perhaps by administering a second individual test. Like group test results, the reports of parents and teachers should be considered preliminary data, less accurate than results of individual measures. As Robinson and Robinson (1976) observe, "There is little doubt that a much higher percentage of individuals were inappropriately labeled as mentally retarded, or, conversely, not retarded, when such labels depended completely on the subjective appraisal of teachers and physicians" (p. 23).

Adaptive behavior may be assessed directly through the presentation of test tasks or by ob-

servation, but usually informants are asked about the student's typical performance. Direct measurement is very time-consuming; for a comprehensive assessment, the professional would have to observe and evaluate the student's behavior in a wide range of situations. The primary persons who serve as informants regarding adaptive behavior are parents and teachers. Because of their different perspectives, parents and teachers may provide different estimates of the student's current functioning (Harrison, 1987). Parents see their child in settings that impose quite different demands from those of the classroom. Also, parents and children share experiences over a number of years. Teachers, in contrast, see students in academic situations and nonscholastic school activities. They are usually acquainted with students for only one school year but are able to evaluate the performance of a particular child in relation to the typical performance of agemates. Neither the parent's nor the teacher's perspective is the "right" one. Each is able to provide only part of the picture of adaptive behavior.

Another factor influencing adaptive behavior assessment is the method used to question informants. The typical strategies are face-to-face interviews and print questionnaires. Interviews allow personal contact, and the interviewer can explain the purpose of the assessment, answer any questions, and probe the informant's unclear responses. In addition, interviews do not require reading and writing skills. However, interviews take more time than print methods, and respondents may be more willing to answer personal questions on paper. Interviews typically are used with parents and print methods with teachers, but of course there are exceptions.

Nature of the Assessment Tasks

Assessment instruments differ in the ways they attempt to measure learning aptitude. Among the important differences are the comprehensiveness of measures and tasks that assess the domains of interest. In the evaluation of intellectual performance, most measures attempt to be comprehensive. Individual intelligence tests typically sample several types of reasoning skills, although some of the nonverbal tests restrict assessment to one type (e.g., figural reasoning or problem solving).

However, the comprehensiveness of a measure is influenced by the nature of its assessment tasks.

The *WISC–R,* for example, and the *Woodcock-Johnson–R,* are designed to evaluate several different reasoning skills. In contrast, tests such as the 1973 *Stanford-Binet* and the *SIT* emphasize verbal tasks. At the opposite extreme, nonverbal tests like the *Leiter* and *Raven's Progressive Matrices* deemphasize verbal abilities and rely solely on performance tasks to evaluate intellectual performance.

Tests that differ on the nature of the tasks used to assess performance may produce quite different results. For example, if a student were to score notably higher on *WISC–R* performance subtests than verbal subtests, results of nonverbal tests would probably produce higher estimates of current intellectual performance than results of tests emphasizing verbal abilities. This would not necessarily mean that either type of measure was inappropriate, only that each provided merely part of the picture.

The content across adaptive behavior measures is quite similar (Kamphaus, 1987). Most scales include items that assess self-help or daily living skills, socialization and interpersonal relations, and independent functioning in the home and community. Also common are questions about communication skills, motor development, and sensory capabilities. Some measures include additional areas. Examples are the Nonacademic School Roles subtest on the *ABIC* and the *ABS–SE*'s two factors on maladaptive behavior. Although measures may be similar in content, they vary in the persons used as informants and the ways information is collected. These differences may influence the estimated level of current adaptive behavior.

Documentation of Learning Aptitude

The broad assessment question that guides the team in its study of the student's learning aptitude is this: *Is the school performance problem related to a handicapping condition?* This question is multifaceted, and the team usually begins its investigation by gathering data about one major concern: general learning aptitude. Two specific assessment questions provide the structure for this part of the process: *What is the student's current level of intellectual performance? What is the student's current functioning level in adaptive behavior?*

Information is gathered from many sources. School records are reviewed for results of group tests of intellectual performance and data on the student's developmental and school history. Intellectual performance is assessed with individual norm-referenced tests, usually administered by school psychologists. To obtain information about adaptive behavior, teachers and parents may be interviewed or asked to complete questionnaires.

The team reviews assessment results and attempts to describe the student's current levels of learning aptitude. These descriptions are norm-referenced; they depict the student's standing in relation to peers. If current performance is within the below average range in both intellectual performance and adaptive behavior, the team may decide the student meets eligibility criteria for mental retardation—provided, of course, that a school performance problem has been documented. If intellectual functioning is not below average, the student may still be eligible for special education services. In such a case it would be necessary to satisfy eligibility criteria for either learning disabilities or behavior disorders. For example, consider the results of the learning aptitude assessment for Joyce, the fourth grader with school performance problems.

Joyce

Results of individual achievement tests have confirmed that Joyce is experiencing difficulty in reading, spelling, and handwriting. Continuing the assessment, the team begins an investigation of general learning aptitude. No results of group intelligence tests are found in the school records, and the brief developmental history Joyce's mother completed at the beginning of the school year does not suggest major developmental delays. Mr. Harvey, Joyce's teacher, reports that Joyce learns some skills quite easily, and Joyce's parents confirm this.

The school psychologist, Ms. Kellett, meets with Joyce and administers the *Wechsler Intelligence Scale for Children–Revised.* Joyce scores within the average range in verbal abilities, performance abilities, and general intellectual functioning. However, Joyce's lowest subtest scores are on Digit Span (6 $\pm$ 2 scaled score points) and Coding (7 $\pm$ 1 scaled score points), subtests within the *WISC–R* Freedom from Distractibility factor (see Figure 8–1 for Joyce's *WISC–R* profile).

Although the team does not suspect mental retardation, it decides to assess Joyce's adaptive behavior to determine whether her school learning problems extend to other areas. Ms. Gale, the special education resource teacher, meets with Joyce's parents at their home and administers the *Adaptive Behavior Inventory for Children.* No scores fall within the "At Risk" range. Joyce is rated above the 50th percentile on all areas except Nonacademic School Roles. That

domain of adaptive behavior may be a possible area of weakness.

The assessment team concludes that Joyce shows average intellectual performance with possible weaknesses in specific cognitive abilities. In addition to her academic deficiencies, she may also experience difficulty in nonacademic school roles. The team will continue assessment and explore the possibility of learning disabilities.

STUDY GUIDE

Review Questions

1. What is learning aptitude?
2. Read these statements and tell whether they are true or false.
   - T F **a.** Learning aptitude is assessed by evaluating two dimensions of behavior, intellectual performance and adaptive behavior.
   - T F **b.** Adaptive behavior is operationalized as performance on standardized tests of intelligence.
   - T F **c.** Intelligence tests contain items requiring reasoning, problem solving, and scholastic aptitude.
   - T F **d.** Measures of adaptive behavior assess competence in areas such as self-help, socialization, communication, and motor development.
3. Select the statement that best describes current practices in the assessment of learning aptitude.
   - _____ **a.** Learning aptitude is assessed only when the handicap of mental retardation is suspected.
   - _____ **b.** All students referred for special education assessment are evaluated in terms of adaptive behavior.
   - _____ **c.** When students show below average performance on tests of intellectual performance, adaptive behavior is assessed.
   - _____ **d.** Group tests are preferred for the study of intellectual performance.
4. Many of the controversies related to special education assessment center around misuse of intelligence tests. List two safeguards of PL 94–142 that help prevent the inappropriate use of these measures.
5. Check *each* of the assessment devices and procedures that can be used to document learning aptitude.
   - _____ **a.** Group intelligence tests
   - _____ **b.** Measures of adaptive behavior
   - _____ **c.** Norm-referenced achievement tests
   - _____ **d.** Parent and teacher interviews
   - _____ **e.** Early developmental history
   - _____ **f.** Individual measures of intellectual performance
   - _____ **g.** Criterion-referenced tests of reading and mathematics
   - _____ **h.** Observation of the student's behavior in nonacademic settings
6. Match the test of intellectual performance in Column A with the description in Column B.

Column A	Column B
a. *Wechsler Intelligence Test for Children–Revised*	_____ A measure for school-aged children that provides scores for Sequential Processing and Simultaneous Processing
b. *Woodcock-Johnson Psycho-Educational Battery–Revised, Tests of Cognitive Ability*	_____ Includes both a Verbal Scale and a Performance Scale

c. *Kaufman Assessment Battery for Children* _____ Results include scores for Verbal Reasoning, Abstract/Visual Reasoning, and Quantitative Reasoning

d. *Stanford-Binet Intelligence Scale: Fourth Edition* _____ Provides estimates of Reading Aptitude, Mathematics Aptitude, and Written Language Aptitude

e. *Test of Nonverbal Intelligence* _____ Test items assess one ability area: problem solving with abstract, figural designs

7. Decide whether these statements about measures of adaptive behavior are true or false.
   T F a. The *ABIC* is a teacher interview form.
   T F b. The *ABS–SE* can be used either as a parent interview or a teacher questionnaire.
   T F c. The *SIB* assesses both adaptive and problem behaviors.
   T F d. The *Vineland Social Maturity Scale* assesses four major adaptive behavior domains: Communication, Daily Living Skills, Socialization, and Motor Skills.
   T F e. The *ABIC* contains norms for different ethnic groups, and the *ABS–SE* contains norms for different school placements (e.g., regular class, EMR, TMR).

8. Which statement best describes the assessment system used to evaluate intellectual functioning and other areas related to school performance?
   _____ a. The *Woodcock-Johnson Psycho-Educational Battery–Revised* provides tests of cognitive ability and academic achievement as well as the *Scales of Independent Behavior,* a measure of adaptive behavior.
   _____ b. The *Kaufman Assessment Battery for Children* assesses mental processing, school achievement, and classroom behavior.
   _____ c. The *System for Multicultural Pluralistic Assessment* is a comprehensive battery for the assessment of medical status, academic achievement, sociocultural characteristics, adaptive behavior, and estimated learning potential.

9. Match the range of performance in Column A with the assessment results in Column B.

   Column A
   a. Above average performance
   b. High average performance
   c. Average performance
   d. Low average performance
   e. Below average performance

   Column B
   _____ *WISC–R* Verbal IQ 72
   _____ *WISC–R* subtest scaled score 12
   _____ Scaled score 50 on the *ABIC*
   _____ IQ score 140 on the *Stanford-Binet*

10. Which type of measure is typically used in the assessment of intellectual performance?
    _____ a. Norm-referenced tests
    _____ b. Informal measures such as criterion-referenced tests

11. If the special education assessment team finds that a student performs in the below average range in academic achievement, intellectual performance, and adaptive behavior, which of the following conclusions can be drawn?
    _____ a. The student is eligible for special education services because of learning disabilities.
    _____ b. The student is eligible for special education services because of mental retardation.
    _____ c. The student is eligible for special education services because of behavior disorders.
    _____ d. The student is not eligible for special education services.

Activities

1. Observe a professional administering either the *Wechsler Intelligence Scale for Children–Revised* or the *Stanford-Binet Intelligence Scale: Fourth Edition.* Analyze the results.

2. Under the supervision of the course instructor, practice assessing adaptive behavior either by completing a questionnaire or interviewing a parent.

3. Obtain one of the assessment systems described in this chapter (e.g., *Woodcock-Johnson–R, K-ABC*). Review its contents and the directions for administration.

4. Read one of the reviews of literature on the *WISC–R* performance of mildly handicapped students. For example, see the 1981 article by Kaufman. Summarize the conclusions reached in the review.

5. Review several of the articles in the Spring 1987 special issue of the *Journal of Special Education* on adaptive behavior. Identify the major criticisms of adaptive behavior measures.

Discussion Questions

1. Explain why both intellectual performance and adaptive behavior are considered in the assessment of learning aptitude.

2. Discuss the reasons why learning aptitude is of interest for all special students, not just mentally retarded students.

3. In the assessment of learning aptitude, the special education team gathers data to help determine whether a school performance problem is related to a handicapping condition. Explain why norm-referenced measures are preferred.

4. Review the information presented in this chapter about the technical quality of measures of adaptive behavior. For what purposes and with what types of students are each of these measures best used?

5. There have been several attempts to develop nonbiased measures of intellectual performance. These include the *SOMPA,* the *Learning Potential Assessment Device,* and the tests that emphasize nonverbal abilities. Discuss the rationale behind each approach.

9

Specific Learning Abilities and Strategies

Specific learning abilities and strategies are one of the assessment team's major concerns in considering a student's eligibility for special education services. Students may show school performance problems despite average intellectual performance; one reason for this may be deficits in specific learning abilities. Such students are usually identified as learning disabled. Individuals with other handicaps may also experience difficulty in certain learning abilities and strategies. For example, attentional problems are often associated with students identified as behavior disordered.

In planning a student's assessment, the special education team poses several questions about handicapping conditions. The major concern is this: *Is the school performance problem related to a handicapping condition?* Usually assessment begins with study of the student's current school performance and general aptitude for learning. Then the team continues by investigating other domains, including specific learning abilities.

Vision and hearing are important considerations for all students, including those with possible deficits in specific learning abilities. Screening for vision and hearing problems is routinely conducted in schools. The results of screening procedures should be reviewed when students are referred for special education assessment. Although vision and hearing are not considered specific learning abilities, they are closely related. Thus, the assessment team asks: *What is the status of the student's sensory abilities?*

Assessment of specific learning abilities has traditionally emphasized discrete ability areas such as memory, visual perception, auditory discrimination, and so forth. Professionals are also becoming interested in the ways students use their specific abilities in situations requiring learning, that is, in their learning strategies and study skills. These concerns lead the team to two assessment questions: *What is the student's current level of development in specific learning abilities? What is the student's current functioning level in strategies for learning and study skills?* In the assessment of learning disabilities, it is also necessary to determine whether there is a discrepancy between expected and actual school performance. Therefore, the team asks: *Is there a substantial discrepancy between the student's actual achieve-*

ment and the achievement level expected for that student?

At this stage in assessment, the team attempts to identify specific strengths and weaknesses in the student's repertoire of skills for school learning. Observations made in the evaluation of academic achievement, intellectual performance, and adaptive behavior may prove useful if they indicate potential difficulties in specific learning abilities and strategies. In the case of Joyce, for example, the team was interested in learning more about Joyce's specific abilities after observing her performance on the *WISC–R.*

Joyce

Joyce, a student in Mr. Harvey's fourth grade class, has been referred for special education assessment because of concerns about her current classroom functioning. Thus far in the assessment process, it has been established that Joyce has a school performance problem despite average intellectual performance and adaptive behavior.

The team will next consider Joyce's specific learning abilities and strategies. The first areas of investigation will be vision and hearing; the team will consult school records to determine the results of the most recent screenings. On the *WISC–R,* Joyce's areas of lowest performance were the Digit Span and Coding subtests, measures of freedom from distractibility. The team will investigate these possible problem areas further by observing Joyce's learning strategies in classroom tasks and by interviewing Joyce and her fourth grade teacher. For example, Ms. Gale, the special education resource teacher, will observe Joyce's techniques for learning new spelling words and then interview Joyce about her choice of strategies.

As more is learned about Joyce's specific abilities and the ways she uses them in classroom learning, the team may decide to assess her development in one or more abilities using a norm-referenced test such as the *Detroit Tests of Learning Aptitude* (2nd ed.). As a final step, if learning disabilities are suspected, the team will compare Joyce's current achievement levels

---

Individualized Assessment Plan

For: _____ Joyce Dewey _____   4   10–0   12/1/89   _____ Ms. Gale _____

       Student's Name   Grade   Age   Date   Coordinator

Reason for Referral: Difficulty keeping up with fourth grade work in reading, spelling, and handwriting

Assessment Question	Assessment Procedures	Person Responsible	Date/Time
What is the status of the student's sensory abilities?	Review of Joyce's school records for results of hearing and vision screens	Ms. Kellett, School Psychologist	12/5/89 9 a.m.
What is the student's current level of development in specific learning abilities and strategies?	Classroom observation and interview	Ms. Gale, Resource Teacher	12/15/89 9:30 a.m.
	Detroit Tests of Learning Aptitude (2nd ed.), if necessary	Ms. Gale, Resource Teacher	To be determined
Is there a substantial discrepancy between actual and expected achievement?	Discrepancy analysis	All members of the assessment team	12/18/89 3:30 p.m.

---

with expected achievement to determine whether a substantial discrepancy can be documented.

CONSIDERATIONS IN ASSESSMENT OF SPECIFIC LEARNING ABILITIES

Specific learning abilities refer to an individual's capacity to participate successfully in certain aspects of the learning task or in certain types of learning. Among the specific abilities that interest educators are attention, perception, memory, and the processes of receiving, associating, and expressing information. Specific abilities are more circumscribed than general learning aptitude; they usually do not affect all areas of learning. In young children, the development of specific abilities is often viewed as a precursor to the acquisition of academic skills. In this context, specific abilities may be regarded as readiness skills; this type of assessment is described in Chapter 18 on evaluation in the preschool years. Specific abilities are also a concern for older students who fail to acquire basic academic skills at the expected rate.

Learning strategies are a newer area of interest. Educators are concerned with the ways individuals utilize specific learning abilities in situations that require the acquisition of new skills or information. Alley and Deshler (1979) define learning strategies as "techniques, principles, or rules that will facilitate the acquisition, manipulation, integration, storage, and retrieval of information across situations and settings" (p. 13). Whereas assessment of specific abilities is essentially a static process, learning strategy assessment is dynamic. Its primary focus is the methods employed by the individual to interact with the demands of the learning task.

Purposes

Learning abilities and strategies are assessed to determine the student's strengths and weaknesses in various types and methods of learning. This information may help those who plan instructional interventions for any student, and it is also important in determining whether school performance problems are related to the handicapping condition of learning disabilities.

The handicap of specific learning disabilities is defined by federal law as:

. . . a disorder in one or more of the basic psychological processes involved in understanding or in using language, spoken or written, which may manifest itself in an imperfect ability to listen, think, speak, read, write, spell, or to do mathematical calculations. [PL 94–142, 121a. 5b(9)]

In this definition, the term *basic psychological processes* refers to learning abilities such as attention, perception, and memory. Learning disabilities are viewed as specific ability deficits that contribute to performance problems in basic school skills.

In determining whether students are eligible for special education services for the learning disabled, the assessment team typically evaluates current levels of development in specific abilities. However, federal guidelines specify three criteria for eligibility, none of which is directly concerned with specific learning abilities.

1. A severe discrepancy between achievement and intellectual ability must be documented. The discrepancy must occur between expected and actual achievement in at least one of the following skill areas: oral expression, listening comprehension, written expression, basic reading skill, reading comprehension, mathematics calculation, or mathematics reasoning.
2. The discrepancy must exist despite the provision of appropriate learning experiences. Underachievement cannot be simply due to lack of instruction.
3. The discrepancy cannot be the result of other handicaps or conditions. Excluded from consideration are learning problems due primarily to visual, hearing, or motor handicaps; mental retardation; emotional disturbance; and environmental, cultural, or economic disadvantage.

Thus, assessment of specific learning abilities and strategies is only one part of the process of establishing eligibility for learning disabilities services.

This type of assessment is not limited to students with suspected learning disabilities. With students identified as handicapped in other areas, the assessment team may gather information about specific abilities and strategies in an attempt to better understand individual learning problems. Mildly retarded students and those with behavior disorders may also show strengths in certain areas and weaknesses in others. Knowledge about study skills and learning strategies may provide the team with important data for planning the educational intervention program.

Issues and Trends

Study of specific abilities and strategies in the field of special education has focused on one population, students with learning disabilities. The issues and trends discussed here have resulted from learning disabilities research and practice but clearly have implications for the assessment of students with other types of handicaps.

There has been much debate in the learning disabilities literature about the definition of this handicap, appropriate procedures for its assessment, and effective strategies for educational intervention (Lewis, 1988). Much controversy has centered around the notion of specific learning abilities. In the early years of the field, special educators hypothesized that school achievement problems were related to deficits in specific learning abilities and that achievement could be improved by either remediating (remedying) the weakness or circumventing it by teaching through the student's strengths. For example, a student with poor reading skills might also score poorly on measures of visual perception. In the remediation of deficits approach, educational treatment would focus on improving the student's visual perception, in the hope that he or she would then become able to acquire skills in reading. In the utilization of strengths approach, the educational program in reading would emphasize auditory skills such as phonics and avoid visual skills such as sight word recognition. This second approach is also known as the preferred modality method because students are typically classified according to their strongest learning modality—visual, auditory, or kinesthetic.

Many of the pioneers in the learning disabilities field developed tests and other measures to detect specific deficits. For example, Frostig worked in the area of visual perception (Frostig & Horne, 1964; Frostig, Lefever, & Whittlesey, 1966), Kephart in perceptual-motor skills (Roach & Kephart, 1966), and Kirk in psycholinguistic processing (Kirk & Kirk, 1971; Kirk et al., 1968). Several of these measures were accompanied by instructional programs designed to remediate problem areas. The tests identified deficits; the companion educational programs provided activities to remediate the deficits.

In the 1970s, researchers began to study the effectiveness of these interventions. First to come under scrutiny were perceptual and perceptual-motor treatments (Coles, 1978; Hallahan & Cruickshank 1973; Hammill & Larsen, 1974b; Larsen, Rogers, & Sowell, 1976), particularly tests and instructional programs that focused on visual perceptual deficits (Hammill, Goodman, & Wiederholt, 1974; Hammill & Wiederholt, 1972; Larsen & Hammill, 1975; Wiederholt & Hammill, 1971). In assessing the usefulness of perceptual-motor training programs, Hammill (1982) concluded that "the efficacy of providing such training to children has not been sufficiently demonstrated to warrant the expenditure of the school's funds or the teacher's time" (p. 408). The effectiveness of remediating deficit psycholinguistic abilities has also been studied, with the debate continuing today (Hammill & Larsen, 1974a; Kavale, 1981; Larsen, Parker, & Hammill, 1982; Minskoff, 1975; Newcomer & Hammill, 1975, 1976; Sowell, Parker, Poplin, & Larsen, 1979; Sternberg & Taylor, 1982; Torgesen, 1979). In their critical appraisal of the deficit remediation approach, Arter and Jenkins (1979) reached the following conclusions:

There have been many attempts to train specific abilities. Psycholinguistic, visual perceptual, auditory perceptual, and motor abilities have all been the focus of training. . . . Ability training succeeded about 24% of the time in well designed investigations. It is difficult to escape the conclusion that abilities measured in differential diagnosis are highly resistant to training by existing procedures.

Given this, it would certainly be surprising to find that ability training improved academic performance. Indeed, the research shows that more often than not academic performance is not improved. (p. 547)

Similar conclusions have been reached in evaluations of the preferred modality approach (Larrivee, 1981; Meyers, 1980; Ringler & Smith, 1973; Tarver & Dawson, 1978; Waugh, 1973). Larrivee summarized the findings in her review of research on modality preferences and beginning reading instruction.

1. Regardless of the measure used to classify learners, only a relatively small percentage of children showed a marked preference for either modality;
2. Most current measurement instruments did not demonstrate the necessary reliability to be used in decisions concerning differential assignment of children to instructional programs; and

3. Differentiating instruction according to modality preference apparently does not facilitate learning to read. (p. 180)

In addition to the criticism of the instructional programs derived from specific ability tests, many of the instruments themselves have come under attack. The major charge has been lack of adequate technical quality (Arter & Jenkins, 1979; Coles, 1978; Salvia & Ysseldyke, 1988). Certainly some measures of specific abilities are technically adequate; however, many of the older tests fail to meet minimum reliability and validity requirements.

Despite the controversies surrounding evaluation and training of specific learning abilities, many special educators remain interested in their assessment. Recent studies of school practices indicate that perceptual-motor and information-processing tests remain part of the assessment battery for many students considered for learning disability services (Davis & Shepard, 1983; Mardell-Czudnowski, 1980; Thurlow & Ysseldyke, 1979). The reason for continued interest may be the apparently logical relationship between readiness skills, such as visual perception, and more advanced school skills, such as reading. Also, Lewis (1983) points out the intuitive appeal of some notions underlying the specific ability approach: "It makes sense that instructional procedures should take into account the strengths and weaknesses of the learner" (pp. 232–233).

This concept is known as aptitude-treatment interaction (Cronbach & Snow, 1977). According to Lloyd (1984), an aptitude-treatment interaction occurs "when instruction differentiated on the basis of learner characteristics leads to greater achievement" (p. 8). This concept remains appealing, although its usefulness has not yet been demonstrated in special education (Lloyd, 1984).

Another issue in specific ability assessment is definition of the handicap of learning disabilities. Most of the traditional definitions emphasize perceptual and/or information-processing deficits, and the characteristics they describe are difficult to operationalize into assessment practices. A newer definition, proposed by the National Joint Committee on Learning Disabilities (1981), shifts focus away from specific abilities, instead emphasizing performance problems in basic school skills.

Learning disabilities is a generic term that refers to a heterogeneous group of disorders manifested by significant difficulties in the acquisition and use of listening, speaking, reading, writing, reasoning or mathematical abilities. These disorders are intrinsic to the individual and presumed to be due to central nervous system dysfunction.

This definition, however, does not translate directly into a plan for assessment.

One of the most important trends is the movement toward consideration of learning strategies, in addition to or in place of specific learning abilities. Researchers have begun to identify characteristic strategies of low performing students, and some evidence shows that learning strategies may be susceptible to training (Hallahan, 1980; Schumaker, Deshler, Alley, Warner, & Denton, 1982; Wong, 1980). Although preliminary results are promising, further study is critical. There is a particular need to develop reliable and valid measures of learning strategies and study skills appropriate for classroom use. If practitioners are to begin to assess the learning strategies and study skills of students with school performance problems, they will require a set of technically adequate assessment tools.

Current Practices

Specific learning abilities and strategies are a concern in both regular and special education. In regular education, young children in the early elementary grades often take part in group readiness testing. Readiness tests evaluate development in preacademic skills such as listening, memory, matching, letter recognition, and language. Results of such measures may be available for special students but, like all group test results, should be interpreted with caution. Sensory abilities are also of interest in regular education, and most schools routinely screen students for possible hearing and vision impairments. These results are extremely important for special students because undetected vision or hearing problems can contribute to difficulties in school performance.

In special education, the assessment team often decides to evaluate specific learning abilities, particularly if learning disabilities are suspected. The team can use one or more of the many currently available individual tests. Some of these measures are designed to assess one ability area. Examples are the *Goldman-Fristoe-Woodcock Test of Auditory Discrimination* (Goldman, Fristoe, & Woodcock, 1970) and the *Bruininks-Oseretsky Test of Motor Proficiency* (Bruininks, 1978). Other measures, such as the revised *Detroit Tests of Learning Aptitude* (Rev.) (Hammill, 1985), attempt to evaluate several different abilities.

Another tactic is administration of those portions of individual tests of intellectual performance that include measures of specific abilities. For instance, the team may be interested in the specific learning abilities assessed by the *Wechsler Intelligence Scale for Children–Revised* (Wechsler, 1974) or the *Stanford-Binet Intelligence Scale: Fourth Edition* (Thorndike et al., 1986).

Great caution must be exercised in selecting tests or subtests to assure that reliable and valid measures are chosen. If no adequate formal measure can be found, the team may decide to use informal techniques. This is often the case in the assessment of learning strategies and study skills because few formal measures are available. Caution is needed here too. Validity and reliability are just as important in the selection of informal measures as in the selection of formal measures. If technical data are not available for an informal test or procedure, the team should make every effort to gather such data, or select another measure.

Another type of assessment that may be conducted by the special education team is discrepancy analysis. This occurs when information is needed about eligibility for learning disabilities services. Discrepancy analysis does not usually involve gathering new data. Results of current achievement tests are compared with results of current intellectual performance tests to determine whether important differences between actual and expected achievement exist.

SOURCES OF INFORMATION ABOUT SPECIFIC LEARNING ABILITIES

There are several sources of information about students' specific learning abilities, learning strategies, and study skills. School records, teachers, parents, and the students themselves are all able to make important contributions.

School Records

School records may provide some clues to a student's past or current levels of functioning. Of particular importance are records of results of periodic vision and hearing screenings.

Readiness test results. Results of group tests of school readiness may be available for some students. Readiness measures are usually administered at the end of kindergarten or at the beginning of first grade, so results are most meaningful for first and second graders.

Results of vision and hearing screening. The team should review the student's health record to determine the dates and results of vision and hearing screenings. If possible problems were indicated, the team should check to see if the student was referred for further assessment and what the results were. Were recommended treatments carried out? For example, if corrective lenses were prescribed, were eyeglasses or contact lenses purchased, and does the student wear them as directed? If there is no record of recent vision and hearing checks, the team should arrange for these as soon as possible.

Information about aptitude–achievement discrepancies. There may be some information in the school records that points to discrepancies between the student's aptitude for learning and actual achievement. For example, past teachers may have commented about the student's failure to achieve to capacity. Or the school record may contain results of group achievement and intelligence tests administered earlier in the student's school career. Although these types of data are historical rather than current, they may indicate a continuing pattern of performance.

The Student

The student is an important participant both in the formal assessment of specific abilities and strategies and in informal assessment. Older students in particular can assist the team by describing their strategies for learning.

Individual measures of specific learning abilities. Students may participate in the administration of individual tests of specific abilities when technically adequate measures are available. Specific ability tests are usually designed for elementary grade students. With older students, the team may administer pertinent subtests of individual tests of intellectual performance. During test administration, the student is carefully observed to determine the strategies he or she uses for task completion.

Current learning strategies and study skills. Informal techniques are typically used to evaluate these. Students can be observed in the classroom to determine what methods they use to learn new material. For example, an observer can record a student's behaviors during lectures, class discussions, or independent work periods. Interviewing is another technique. Students can be asked to describe the study methods they use in school and at home. They can also be interviewed while engaged in a learning task. In addition, samples of the student's work may provide clues about poor work habits or inefficient study strategies.

Teachers

Teachers have many opportunities to observe the specific learning abilities, strategies, and study skills of students in their classroom.

Current abilities and strategies for learning. Teachers can describe how students go about learning new skills and information. In particular, teachers should be asked to discuss any learning problems the student exhibits. For example, does the student have difficulty paying attention to relevant aspects of the task at hand? Is he or she unable to remember previously learned material? Teachers can also report about students' current study skills. Does the student listen to directions and ask questions when necessary? Is he or she able to follow directions?

Current aptitude–achievement discrepancies. Teachers may be able to comment about the match between the achievement expected of a particular student and that student's current performance. For instance, a teacher may observe that a student appears to understand the course material in class discussions but performs poorly on written examinations. Such observations are important indicators of aptitude–achievement discrepancies.

Parents

Like teachers, parents have many opportunities to observe their child in learning situations. Parents also have information about their child's current health status and medical history in relation to vision and hearing problems.

History of treatment for vision and hearing problems. If school records do not contain information about the student's vision and hearing, parents may be able to supply this. If routine vision or hearing checks at school or by the family physician indicated possible problems, the student's parents can describe what treatments, if any, were recommended and carried out. If necessary, parents can refer school personnel to the appropriate medical professional for more information.

Home observations of current learning abilities and strategies. Based upon their observations of their child in many learning situations, parents can describe typical strategies for learning and recurrent problems. They may comment, for example, on their child's attention span, perseverance in problem solving, or ways of remembering things. Parents can also describe the study strategies used at home to complete class assignments.

SCREENING FOR SENSORY IMPAIRMENTS

A first priority in the assessment of any student referred for school performance problems is to determine current status in vision and hearing. Undetected and untreated sensory impairments can interfere with school learning. Sensory acuity in hearing and vision is the concern in screening. Acuity refers to the ability of the sense organ to register stimuli. Sensory screening programs identify students in need of in-depth assessment. These persons are then referred to appropriate health professionals for a comprehensive examination.

Vision

Vision can be impaired in many ways. Students may have difficulty seeing objects at a distance. In this condition, known as nearsightedness or myopia, near vision is clearer than far vision. Farsightedness or hyperopia is the opposite; vision is clearer for objects at a distance. A third type of disorder, astigmatism, is a condition in which vision is blurred or distorted. Myopia, hyperopia, and astigmatism are considered refractive disorders. They are very common among school-aged children but are usually correctable with eyeglasses or contact lenses (Caton, 1985). When a vision problem can be corrected, it is not considered a disability.

Other types of vision problems are muscle disorders, restricted peripheral vision, and impairments in color vision. Muscle disorders involve the external muscles that control the eye movement. An example is strabismus or "crossed eyes," in which a muscle imbalance prevents the eyes from focusing simultaneously on the same object. Peripheral or "side" vision refers to the wideness of the visual field. If peripheral vision is severely impaired, the visual field is limited so the individual only sees objects directly in front of him or her; this condition is known as tunnel vision. Tunnel vision, if uncorrected, is considered a severe enough handicap to be included as a type of legal blindness. Disorders can also occur in color vision, reducing the ability to distinguish between colors. Although color blindness is not considered a disability, it can have a deleterious effect upon some aspects of school performance. Teachers must know when they have color-blind students so color-cued materials and other educational uses of color can be minimized.

The most usual method of screening for vision problems is the *Snellen Chart*. The chart used with older children and adults contains several different letters of the alphabet. The letters vary in size, with the largest placed at the top. The individual stands 20 feet away and attempts to read all the letters, first covering one eye and then the other. A modified version of the chart is available for young children and those unable to read. It contains only the letter *E*, but that letter is rotated into four different positions (see Figure 9–1). The person responds by telling or showing which way the letter is pointing.

The Snellen Chart measures far distance vision, and results are expressed as a fraction. For instance, the fraction 20/20 indicates normal vision.

The numerator of the fraction stands for the distance the individual stands from the chart when reading letters, and the denominator stands for the distance at which persons with normal vision are able to read the same letters. Thus, a person with 20/100 vision is able to read at 20 feet what a person with normal vision can read at 100 feet.

FIGURE 9–1
Snellen Chart

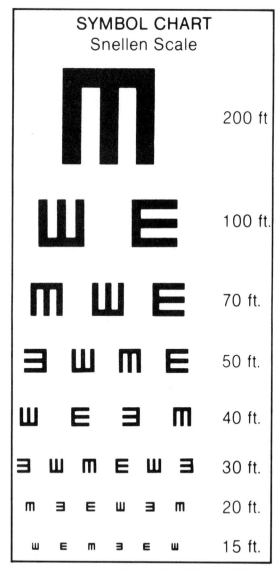

Note. National Society for the Prevention of Blindness. 79 Madison Avenue. New York, NY 10016.

Students are considered legally blind when visual acuity is 20/200 or less in the better eye after the best possible correction (American Foundation for the Blind, 1961).

Far distance vision, although important, is only one of the areas where visual disorders may occur. To detect possible problems in other aspects of visual acuity, different techniques are available. For instance, the Keystone Telebinocular device allows appraisal of far distance vision, near distance vision, depth perception, color discrimination, and other abilities. Other instruments that assess several aspects of visual acuity are the Titmus Vision Tester and the Bausch and Lomb Orthorater. Such devices offer a more comprehensive picture of the student's current vision than the standard chart method.

Teachers, other professionals, and parents can assist in the detection of potential vision problems by being aware of warning signs. These include physical manifestations such as red or watery eyes, a pronounced squint, irritation of the eyelids, irregularities of the pupils, or obvious muscle imbalances such as crossed eyes (National Society for the Prevention of Blindness, 1969; Smolensky, Bonvechio, Whitlock, & Girard, 1968). Among the behavioral symptoms are lack of attention to information presented visually, holding of reading materials very close to or far away from the eyes, and inability to see the chalkboard and other distant objects (Smolensky et al., 1968).

When possible vision problems are identified, the student is referred to an appropriate vision specialist, usually an ophthalmologist or an optometrist. Ophthalmologists are physicians who specialize in eye disorders; not only do they conduct comprehensive vision examinations, they may also prescribe drugs or perform surgery. Optometrists conduct vision examinations and prescribe corrective lenses, but they are not physicians and do not provide medical or surgical treatment. A third professional, the optician, prepares corrective lenses according to the optometrist's or ophthalmologist's prescription.

Many visual impairments can be treated through medical intervention, surgery, and/or the relatively simple prescription of corrective lenses. If vision specialists recommend a treatment regimen, the school should be aware of what is occurring and cooperate as necessary. For example, if eyeglasses are prescribed to correct poor near distance vision, the classroom teacher can assist by making sure the student wears the glasses during reading and writing activities.

Hearing

The two primary types of hearing loss are conductive and sensorineural. With conductive losses, some obstruction or interference in the outer or middle ear blocks the transmission of sound. The inner ear is intact, but sound does not reach it. Among school-aged children, conductive losses are the most common type of hearing impairments (Frank, 1988). They may be caused by excessive buildup of wax in the auditory canal or collection of fluid in the middle ear (serous otitis media). Many conductive losses can be corrected by medical or surgical treatment (Moores & Moores, 1988). For example, fluid in the middle ear can be treated with a surgical procedure called a myringotomy in which small tubes are placed in the eardrum to allow drainage (Frank, 1988). Hearing aids usually benefit individuals with conductive losses.

Sensorineural losses are caused by damage to the inner ear. Sound travels to the inner ear but is not transmitted to the brain. Sensorineural hearing losses are not as responsive to medical and surgical treatment as conductive hearing losses (Heward & Orlansky, 1988), although hearing aids that amplify sounds may prove beneficial. Individuals can also show a mixed hearing loss—both a conductive and a sensorineural hearing loss.

Hearing screening, like vision screening, is routine in most schools today. However, teachers and parents should also be aware of some hearing loss symptoms, so that they can initiate hearing checks for students with possible problems. This is particularly important because some hearing losses are intermittent; a student with impaired hearing may be able to pass a routine screening (Frank, 1988). Some of the signs of hearing loss are physical problems associated with the ears, poor articulation of sounds and confusion of similar sounding words, turning of the head toward the source of sound, extreme watchfulness when people are speaking in an attempt to lip-read, frequent requests to speakers for repetitions, speaking in a monotone, and speaking very quietly (Smolensky et al., 1968; Stephens, Blackhurst, & Magliocca, 1982).

The dimensions of sound important in the assessment of hearing are intensity and frequency. Intensity refers to the loudness of sound and is measured in units called decibels (dB). Zero decibels is the threshold of normal hearing. At a distance of 5 feet, a whisper registers 20 dB, conversational speech 40 to 65 dB, and a loud shout 85 dB (Green, 1981). The frequency of a sound refers to its pitch, whether it is high or low. For example, the keys on a piano are arranged by pitch, from low to high. Frequency is measured in hertz units (Hz), and the range of frequencies considered most important for hearing conversational speech is from 500 to 2000 Hz (Heward & Orlansky, 1988).

In school hearing screening programs, an instrument called a pure tone audiometer is used to produce sounds of different frequencies and intensities. Students are usually individually tested. The student wears earphones, listens for tones generated by the audiometer, then raises a hand or pushes a button when a tone is heard. In pure tone audiometric screening, or sweep testing, tones are generated at several frequencies, first for one ear, then for the other. If the student fails this screening procedure, it is typically repeated at a later date. The next step is a pure tone threshold test, usually administered by a trained professional such as an audiologist. In this procedure, sounds are presented at several frequencies, and the intensity is varied to determine the exact decibel level at which the student can detect the sound.

Figure 9–2 shows the record of a pure tone threshold test for a student with a mild hearing impairment. This graph is called an audiogram. The horizontal axis is marked off in frequency units, and the range of frequencies critical for speech is shaded. The vertical axis represents the hearing threshold level, the lowest intensity at which sound can be detected. For example, at 500 Hz, the student was able to hear sounds at 45 dB with the left ear (marked on the audiogram by an *x*) and sounds at 50 dB with the right ear (marked by an *o*). Persons with normal hearing would be able to detect sounds at intensities somewhere between 0 and 10 dB. If a person's threshold exceeds normal limits, a hearing loss is indicated. For example, if the threshold is 60 dB, a 60-dB loss is reported.

FIGURE 9–2
Sample audiogram

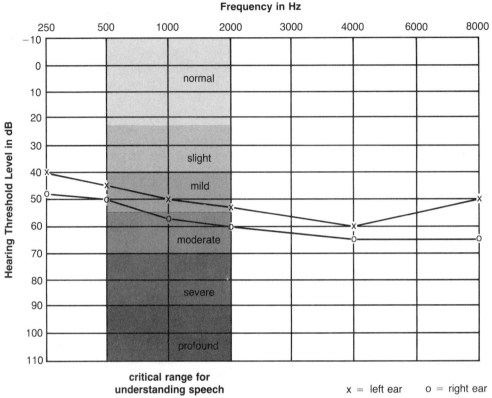

Frequency in Hz

Note. From *Exceptional Children* (3rd ed.) (p. 261) by W. L. Heward and M. D. Orlansky, 1988, Columbus, OH: Merrill. Copyright 1988 by Merrill Publishing Company. Reprinted by permission.

When possible hearing losses are identified, students are referred to hearing specialists. Otologists are physicians who specialize in disorders of the ear; they conduct comprehensive hearing examinations and provide medical and surgical treatments. Audiologists are not physicians, although they often work closely with otologists. The audiologist evaluates hearing and prescribes hearing aids for losses that cannot be corrected. Otologists and audiologists use several techniques to evaluate hearing in addition to pure tone audiometry. These include speech audiometry, where the threshold levels for speech are determined, and special assessment procedures for infants, young children, and other persons difficult to test (Green, 1981; Moores & Moores, 1988).

MEASURES OF PERCEPTUAL-MOTOR SKILLS AND OTHER SPECIFIC LEARNING ABILITIES

Traditional measures of specific learning abilities are concerned with factors such as attention, perception, and memory and with the information-processing abilities of reception, association, and expression. Specific abilities are difficult to delimit and define because they are based on inferences about mental processes. For instance, it is impossible to observe or measure directly how a person perceives incoming sensory information. It is possible only to study the person's overt responses or his or her report of the experience and then make inferences about what may have occurred during perception.

Perception can be defined as the psychological ability to process or use the information received through the senses. According to Lerner (1985), perception is "the term applied to the recognition of sensory information, the intellect's ability to extract meaning from the data received by the senses" (p. 280). Perception depends on the physiological ability of the sense organs to receive information. Visual and auditory acuity are of primary concern to educators, but there is also interest in information received through other senses, particularly tactile and kinesthetic input. Tactile information is received through the sense of touch and kinesthetic information from the feelings of muscles and body movements.

Memory is the ability to recall previously learned information. The memory process can be described in many ways. For example, memory is differentiated according to the period of time that has elapsed since original learning. Educators are usually most concerned with long-term memory ability, but information must pass through short-term memory before it is stored for long-term recall.

Attention is the process whereby an individual's awareness is directed toward some stimulus or set of stimuli. Kirk and Chalfant (1984) define attention as "the process of selectively bringing relevant stimuli into focus" (p. 77). Attention can be considered a prerequisite not only for other specific abilities such as memory and perception but also for any type of learning activity. Although the importance of attention cannot be denied, it is very difficult to separate from other factors.

Information processing refers to the set of abilities that govern the way people receive and respond to incoming information. The three major components of information processing are reception of information, association of incoming information with previously stored information, and expression. Information processes are also referred to as psychological processes. The term *psycholinguistic abilities* describes the psychological processing of linguistic information. Language disorders are often a concern in the assessment of information-processing abilities, as are disorders of thinking and reasoning. In fact, measures of information processing often share many charac-

teristics of language and intellectual performance tests.

Table 9–1 presents a listing of well-known tests of specific learning abilities, although many are no longer widely used in educational assessment, particularly those related to perception. In fact, the Council for Learning Disabilities (1986) recommends a moratorium on perceptual assessment until research support for this approach is available.

The next sections of this chapter briefly describe several measures of specific learning abilities. Discussion is limited because of the technical problems of many of these instruments and because these measures represent a traditional, rather than a contemporary, approach to assessment of learning disabilities.

Tests of Perception

Measures of perceptual abilities usually focus either on auditory or visual perception, rather than the perceptual process as a whole. Among the assessment concerns in visual perception are visual discrimination, figure-ground discrimination, spatial relationships, and form perception (Wallace & McLoughlin, 1979). Discrimination is the ability to detect likenesses and differences among stimuli, and figure-ground discrimination is the ability to differentiate relevant stimuli (the figure) from irrelevant stimuli (the background). Spatial relationships refer to perception of the relative positions of objects in space, and form perception is concerned with the size, shape, and position of visual stimuli. In auditory perception, auditory discrimination and figure-ground are of interest, as is auditory blending (Wallace & McLoughlin, 1979). Auditory blending is the ability to combine separate sounds into a whole.

Visual perception was considered one of the most important specific abilities in early assessment programs because of the hypothesized relationship between visual perception deficits and reading disorders. One of the best-known measures is the *Developmental Test of Visual Perception* (Frostig et al., 1966). This early measure, designed for young children, contains five subtests: Eye-Motor Coordination, Figure-Ground, Constancy of Shape, Position in Space, and Spatial Relationships. The Frostig test has been criticized for its failure to separate motor skills from perceptual skills, the limited representativeness of its standardization sample, the low reliabilities of sub-tests, and the lack of adequate evidence of validity (Hammill & Wiederholt, 1972). This test is not commonly used in schools today.

Another measure of several visual perception skills is the *Motor-Free Visual Perception Test* (*MVPT*) (Colarusso & Hammill, 1972). The *MVPT* manual describes this individual, norm-referenced measure as ''a test of visual perception which avoids motor involvement . . . a quick, highly reli-able, and valid measure of overall visual perceptual processing ability in children'' (p. 7). Like most perceptual measures, it offers norms only for young children. Five different tasks are used to assess visual perception.

☐ *Figure-Ground*—The student is shown a page with a stimulus figure at the top and four pos-sible response drawings at the bottom. The student must select the correct response by

TABLE 9–1
Tests of specific learning abilities

Name (Author)	Ages	SPECIFIC ABILITIES ASSESSED			
		Perception	Motor Skills	Memory and Attention	Information Processing
Auditory Discrimination Test (2nd ed.) (Reynolds, 1987; Wepman, 1975)	4 to 8–11	*			
Bender Gestalt Test for Young Children (Koppitz, 1963, 1975)	5 to 9		*		
Bruininks-Oseretsky Test of Motor Proficiency (Bruininks, 1978)	4–6 to 14–6		*		
Detroit Tests of Learning Aptitude (2nd ed.) (Hammill, 1985)	6–0 to 17–11		*	*	*
Detroit Tests of Learning Aptitude–Primary (Hammill & Bryant, 1986)	3–6 to 9–11	*	*	*	*
Developmental Test of Visual-Motor Integration (3rd. rev.) (Beery, 1989)	4–0 to 17–11		*		
Developmental Test of Visual Perception (Frostig, Lefever, & Whittlesey, 1966)	4–0 to 7–11	*	*		
Goldman-Fristoe-Woodcock Auditory Skills Test Battery (Goldman, Fristoe, & Woodcock, 1976)	3 to adult	*		*	
Goldman-Fristoe-Woodcock Test of Auditory Discrimination (Goldman, Fristoe, & Woodcock, 1970)	5–0 to adult	*			
Illinois Test of Psycholinguistic Abilities (Kirk, McCarthy, & Kirk, 1968)	2–4 to 10–3	*		*	*
Motor-Free Visual Perception Test (Colarusso & Hammill, 1972)	4–0 to 8–11	*			
Purdue Perceptual-Motor Survey (Roach & Kephart, 1966)	6 to 10		*		
Test of Gross Motor Development (Ulrich, 1985)	3 to 10		*		

locating the drawing in which the stimulus figure is imbedded. The tester points to the possible responses and says, "Find it here. Where is it hiding?"

☐ *Spatial Relationships*—The student is shown a page with a stimulus figure at the top and four possible response drawings at the bottom. The student must select the correct response by locating the drawing in which the stimulus figure is reproduced. The tester points to the possible responses and says, "Find one here. It might be smaller, bigger, darker, or turned on its side."

☐ *Visual Memory*—The student is shown a stimulus figure for 5 seconds. Then the stimulus page is removed, and the student is shown another page with four possible responses. The student must select the response identical to the stimulus.

☐ *Visual Closure*—The student is shown a page with a stimulus figure at the top and four possible response drawings at the bottom. The student must select the drawing that, if completed, would be identical to the stimulus.

☐ *Visual Discrimination*—The student is shown a page with four drawings and must select the one different from the other three.

Although the *MVPT* assesses several skills, only total test scores are available. These include a Perceptual Age score and a standard score called a Perceptual Quotient.

The technical quality of the *MVPT* is better than that of many tests of specific abilities. The standardization sample was composed of an unselected group of 881 normal children from 22 states. The lack of data about sample selection methods and subgroup characteristics has been criticized (Compton, 1984). However, test reliabilities appear adequate. In support of the *MVPT's* validity, the test authors note that it "correlated higher with other measures of visual perception (median $r = 0.49$) than it did with tests of intelligence (median $r = 0.31$) and school performance (median $r = 0.38$)" (p. 19).

Auditory perception has also been a concern in special education assessment, particularly in relationship to speech and language problems. Measures evaluating several auditory skills are available. For example, the *Goldman-Fristoe-Woodcock Auditory Skills Test Battery* (Goldman et al., 1976) contains tests assessing aspects of auditory selective attention, discrimination, and memory, along with sound-symbol relationships. However, auditory discrimination has been the main focus in assessing auditory perceptual skills.

The *Goldman-Fristoe-Woodcock Test of Auditory Discrimination* (Goldman et al., 1970) is an individual, norm-referenced test of discrimination under both quiet and noise conditions. It is designed for age 5-0 through adulthood. The individual looks at four line drawings, listens to a tape, and then selects the drawing that depicts the word read on the tape. The four drawings have names similar in sound (for example, *wake, rake, lake,* and *make*). This test was standardized on a limited sample representing only three states, and small samples were used to study test-retest reliability and concurrent validity. More information is needed to substantiate the technical adequacy of this measure.

One of the best-known measures of perceptual ability is the *Auditory Discrimination Test* by J. M. Wepman (1975). This test has recently been standardized on a national sample of more than 1,800 children age 4 through 8 (Reynolds, 1987). According to the manual for the second edition, the Wepman test is "a brief, easy-to-administer procedure for the assessment of children's ability to discriminate between commonly used phonemes in the English language" (p. 1).

About 5 minutes are required for administration. Two alternate forms are provided, and the test task is the same on each: the tester reads a pair of words, the student listens and tells whether the words are the same or different. Of the 40 word pairs read to the student, 30 differ in only one sound (for example, *tub* versus *tug*), and 10 pairs contain identical words.

Standard scores are available on the Wepman test for the first time with the second edition. They are normalized *T*-scores with a mean of 50 and a standard deviation of 10. The student's raw score is converted to a standard score, percentile rank, and a Qualitative Score, which describes current functioning level (i.e., very good development, above average ability, average ability, below average ability, or below the level of adequacy). The test-retest and alternate form reliability of the Wepman test appears satisfactory, and its validity is supported by its moderate correlations with other measures of auditory discrimination.

The Wepman test has typically been used as a screening device to identify students with poor auditory discrimination skills. However, before using this measure, the student's ability to comprehend the concepts of *same* and *different* and sustain attention during test administration must be considered, along with the tester's ability to accurately pronounce the word pairs.

Tests of Motor Skills

Motor skills are required in many school endeavors. In the classroom, for example, handwriting is a very important mode of expression. The development of motor skills may be impaired in students with physical handicaps such as missing limbs, paralysis, and cerebral palsy. Physicians have the major responsibility for treatment of physical impairments, but they are often assisted by physical therapists, occupational therapists, and adaptive physical education teachers.

Problems in motor skill development may also occur in students without obvious physical impairments. The two major areas of concern to educators are gross motor development and fine motor development. Gross motor skills, such as running, jumping, and throwing, involve the large muscles of the body. In contrast, fine motor skills involve the small muscles. Examples of school-related fine motor tasks are cutting with scissors, tracing, copying, and writing. Many of these skills involve both fine motor ability and visual perception; this combination is called eye-hand coordination. Other motor skills of interest are balance, rhythm, laterality, directionality, body image, and body awareness (Wallace & McLoughlin, 1979).

Some measures of motor development are comprehensive in an attempt to assess both gross and fine motor skills. An early example is the *Purdue Perceptual-Motor Survey* (Roach & Kephart, 1966). It evaluates five types of motor skills: Balance and Posture, Body Image and Differentiation, Perceptual-Motor Match, Ocular Control, and Form Perception. This measure is no longer widely used.

A more recent measure is the *Bruininks-Oseretsky Test of Motor Proficiency* (Bruininks, 1978), based on the *Lincoln-Oseretsky Motor Development Scale* (Sloan, 1954). The *Bruininks-Oseretsky* is an individual, norm-referenced test for students aged $4\frac{1}{2}$ to $14\frac{1}{2}$; it contains eight subtests.

Gross Motor Skills

Subtest 1: Running Speed and Agility
Subtest 2: Balance
Subtest 3: Bilateral Coordination
Subtest 4: Strength

Gross and Fine Motor Skills

Subtest 5: Upper-Limb Coordination

Fine Motor Skills

Subtest 6: Response Speed
Subtest 7: Visual-Motor Control
Subtest 8: Upper-Limb Speed and Dexterity

The *Bruininks-Oseretsky* produces two scores for each subtest, a standard score and an age equivalent. Composite scores are available for gross motor performance, fine motor performance, and total performance.

The *Bruininks-Oseretsky* is a well-constructed test that appears to be useful for the assessment of fine and gross motor functioning. It was standardized in 1977 on a sample of 765 students selected to resemble the U.S. population. Test-retest and interrater reliability are adequate, and content validity appears satisfactory. Test validity was also studied by comparing the performance of normal students with that of mentally retarded and learning disabled students; normal students showed superior performance.

The *Test of Gross Motor Development (TGMD)* (Ulrich, 1985) assesses two areas of gross motor development in children ages 3 to 10: locomotor skills and object control skills. On the Locomotion subtest, students are asked to demonstrate skills such as running, hopping, leaping, and skipping. The Object Control subtest includes tasks such as striking a ball with a bat, bouncing a ball, and catching a ball.

The test manual clearly describes the procedures for administration and the criteria for evaluating student performance. Results include subtest standard scores and percentiles and a global standard score, the Gross Motor Development Quotient.

The *TGMD* was standardized on 909 subjects from eight states. This sample resembled the U.S. population in terms of gender, race, and community size; the geographic distribution of the sample was somewhat different from that of the nation as a whole. The manual provides evidence to support the reliability of the *TGMD,* its content validity, and its ability to differentiate between handicapped and nonhandicapped children. Information is also needed on the relationship of the *TGMD* to other measures of motor development.

Many of the instruments developed to assess motor skills are concerned with only one ability, the fine motor skill of eye-hand coordination. This skill is emphasized because it is required in many educational activities, most notably handwriting. Among the measures designed to evaluate eye-hand coordination are the *Bender Visual-Motor Gestalt Test* (Bender, 1938) and its adaptation for young children (Koppitz, 1963, 1975), the *Slosson Drawing Coordination Test* (Slosson, 1967), and the *Developmental Test of Visual-Motor Integration* (Beery, 1989). These tests all require students to copy geometric designs to evaluate the development of eye-hand coordination. On the *Bender Gestalt Test for Young Children* (Koppitz, 1963, 1975), for instance, children ages 5 to 11 copy nine geometric designs. Although the *Bender Gestalt* has been recommended as an indicator of intellectual functioning level, minimal brain dysfunction, and emotional disturbance (Koppitz, 1975), it is best viewed simply as a test of eye-hand coordination.

The *Developmental Test of Visual-Motor Integration (VMI)* (Beery, 1989) is a popular measure of eye-hand coordination. This test was originally published in 1967, and new norms appeared in the 1982 revision, although the test itself was not altered. The 1989 revision added new subjects to the norm group, bringing its total number to 5,824 students. In addition, the test's scoring system was changed so that more difficult items are weighted more heavily than easier items. The *VMI* may be administered individually or to groups; administration requires less than 15 minutes. Norms are provided for ages 4–0 through 17–11 years.

The *VMI* contains 24 geometric forms to be copied by the student (see Figure 9–3). Testing continues until the student fails three consecutive forms. *VMI* administration is fairly easy, but scoring can be quite complicated. Each item is scored pass or fail using the criteria and examples provided in the manual, and a protractor is needed to evaluate some forms. For example, to pass the form called "Vertical-Horizontal Cross" [**+**], the student's drawing must contain two lines that are fully intersecting *and* continuous *and* at least one half of each line must be within 20 degrees of its correct

orientation. The student's performance is summarized in one global score which can be expressed as an age equivalent, percentile rank, or standard score.

Measures of Memory and Attention

Like perception, memory is often separated into two separate abilities on the basis of sensory input channel. Although the auditory-visual distinction may be of interest, memory can be described in several other important ways.

☐ *Type of information to be recalled*—In some memory tasks, the information to be stored for later retrieval is familiar and meaningful to the learner. This type of information is usually easier to recall than unfamiliar or nonmeaningful material.

☐ *Time since original learning*—Another variable is the amount of time intervening between original learning and recall. Short-term memory tasks require recall immediately after learning. Long-term memory tasks impose an interval of at least several seconds or minutes between learning and recall.

☐ *Type of memory*—This dimension distinguishes between the recognition of information learned previously and its recall. In recognition memory, the learner simply says whether or not information has been presented earlier. In recall

FIGURE 9–3

Sample items from the *Developmental Test of Visual-Motor Integration*

Item 10, Open Square and Circle

Item 15, Circle and Tilted Square

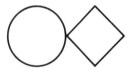

Note. From the *Developmental Test of Visual-Motor Integration* by Keith Beery and Norman Buktenica. Copyright © 1967 by Keith Beery and Norman Buktenica. Used by permission of Modern Curriculum Press, Inc.

TABLE 9–2
Measures of memory

Type of Memory	Auditory or Visual	Type of Information to Be Recalled	Test	Subtest
Short-term recognition	Visual	Meaningful (people's faces)	K-ABC	Face Recognition
Short-term serial recall	Auditory	Meaningful (commands)	DTLA–2	Oral Directions
	Auditory	Meaningful (sentences)	DTLA–2	Sentence Imitation
	Auditory	Meaningful (sentences)	S-B	Memory for Sentences
	Auditory	Meaningful (sentences)	W-J–R	Memory for Sentences
	Auditory	Nonmeaningful (isolated words)	DTLA–2	Word Sequences
	Auditory	Nonmeaningful (isolated words)	K-ABC	Word Order
	Auditory	Nonmeaningful (isolated words)	W-J–R	Memory for Words
	Auditory	Nonmeaningful (digits)	ITPA	Auditory Sequential Memory
	Auditory	Nonmeaningful (digits)	K-ABC	Number Recall
	Auditory	Nonmeaningful (digits)	S-B	Memory for Digits
	Auditory	Nonmeaningful (digits)	WISC–R	Digit Span
	Auditory	Nonmeaningful (digits)	W-J–R	Numbers Reversed
	Visual	Nonmeaningful (geometric forms)	DTLA–2	Design Reproduction
	Visual	Nonmeaningful (letters)	DTLA–2	Letter Sequences
	Visual	Nonmeaningful (unrelated objects)	DTLA–2	Object Sequences
	Visual	Nonmeaningful (geometric shapes)	ITPA	Visual Sequential Memory
	Visual	Nonmeaningful (hand movements)	K-ABC	Hand Movements
	Visual	Nonmeaningful (position of stimuli)	K-ABC	Spatial Memory
	Visual	Nonmeaningful (shapes, colors)	S-B	Bead Memory
	Visual	Nonmeaningful (unrelated objects)	S-B	Memory for Objects

TABLE 9–2
continued

Type of Memory	Auditory or Visual	Type of Information to Be Recalled	Test	Subtest
Long-term paired-associate recall	Visual and Auditory	Nonmeaningful (words associated with shapes)	W–J–R	Visual-Auditory Learning
	Visual and Auditory	Nonmeaningful (words associated with shapes)	W–J–R	Delayed Recall–Visual-Auditory Learning
	Visual and Auditory	Nonmeaningful (words associated with drawings)	W–J–R	Memory for Names
	Visual and Auditory	Nonmeaningful (words associated with drawings)	W–J–R	Delayed Recall–Memory for Names

Key to test names

DTLA–2—Detroit Tests of Learning Aptitude–2 (Hammill, 1985)

ITPA—Illinois Test of Psycholinguistic Abilities (Kirk, McCarthy, & Kirk, 1968)

K-ABC—Kaufman Assessment Battery for Children (Kaufman & Kaufman, 1983)

S-B—Stanford-Binet Intelligence Scale: Fourth Edition (Thorndike, Hagen, & Sattler, 1986)

WISC–R—Wechsler Intelligence Scale for Children–Revised (Wechsler, 1974)

W–J–R—Woodcock-Johnson Psycho-Educational Battery–Revised (Woodcock & Johnson, 1989)

memory, a more difficult task, the learner must reproduce the information.

☐ *Organization of recall*—In memory tasks, information can be retrieved in more than one way. Free recall is the retrieval of information in any order. In contrast, serial recall requires a fixed order. Serial recall is required in school tasks such as counting from 1 to 100 and reciting the alphabet in order. In paired-associate recall, the learner associates a response with a particular stimulus; when the stimulus is produced, the learner must recall the response. A common classroom task requiring paired-associate recall is saying letter names when written letters are presented.

Despite the many types of memory required in classroom learning, the majority of memory tests assess only short-term recall, usually in the serial mode. The most usual type of memory task on norm-referenced measures is short-term serial recall of nonmeaningful information. Auditory memory is often assessed with digit span tasks, where students listen to and attempt to repeat series of numbers. Visual memory tasks are more varied; some use nonmeaningful shapes or isolated letters, and others employ pictures or photographs.

Most of the commonly used measures of auditory and visual memory are subtests from tests of intellectual performance or comprehensive specific ability batteries. Several of these are described in Table 9–2.

Attention is another specific ability of interest in special education assessment. It is a difficult ability to measure because a learner's attention cannot be separated from the task. When persons attend, they attend *to* something, and that task or situation may influence how well attentional resources are deployed. Because of the inability to isolate attention from other factors, attention is assessed informally.

Observation is the major technique used. Before attending behavior can be observed, it must be operationally defined. For instance, paying attention to a workbook assignment might be defined by behaviors such as looking at the workbook page and writing answers to questions on the page. Of course, such observable behaviors are only indicators of the process of attention. Attention is inferred when the student engages in behaviors related to task completion.

Another source of information is the reports of teachers and parents. The following series of questions proposed by Chalfant and King (1976) can be developed into a teacher or parent interview form:

1. Does the child have difficulty narrowing or focusing attention on relevant stimuli?
2. Does the child have unusual difficulty shifting attention from one stimulus within or between the visual, auditory, or haptic channels?
3. Does the child have difficulty shifting attention from one stimulus to another? In spatial order? In temporal order?
4. Does the capability to focus on relevant stimuli diminish at an unusually rapid rate? Is the duration of attending behavior usually brief?
5. Is the inattentive behavior related to specific kinds or classes of tasks and not to others?
6. Does the child have difficulty focusing on specific kinds of stimuli? Is the attending behavior channel specific? Auditory? Visual? Haptic?
7. Does increasing reinforcement contingencies *fail* to make an appreciable change in eliciting, maintaining, or increasing the focus or duration of attending behavior?
8. Does making the task easier by reducing irrelevant cues and increasing relevant cues *fail* to make an appreciable difference in the child's attending behavior?
9. Does altering conditions which precede, occur during or immediately following inattentive behavior *fail* to result in any appreciable change in attending behavior?

    (*Note.* From "An Approach to Operationalizing the Definition of Learning Disabilities" by J. C. Chalfant and F. S. King, 1976, *Journal of Learning Disabilities, 9,* pp. 228–43. Copyright 1976 by The Professional Press, Inc. Reprinted by special permission of The Professional Press.)

Several of these questions suggest ideas for diagnostic teaching sequences. For example, Question 7 is concerned with the influence of reinforcement upon attention. A diagnostic teaching sequence could be designed to determine whether reinforcement increases the frequency or duration of attending behaviors.

Test Batteries for Specific Ability Assessment

Whereas some measures are designed to assess one particular learning ability, others attempt a more comprehensive evaluation. Such measures are made up of several subtests, each focusing on one or more specific abilities. Among the best-known measures of this type are the *Illinois Test of Psycholinguistic Abilities,* an information-processing test battery developed by Kirk, McCarthy, and Kirk (1968), and the *Detroit Tests of Learning Aptitude* (Baker & Leland, 1967), a traditional measure that has recently been revised (Hammill, 1985) and extended to include preschool children (Hammill & Bryant, 1986).

Illinois Test of Psycholinguistic Abilities (ITPA). According to its manual, the *ITPA* is an individual, norm-referenced test that "is used to delineate areas of difficulty in communication more than to determine overall ability. It is a diagnostic test of specific cognitive abilities" (Kirk et al., 1968, p. 5).

The *ITPA* is based upon the communication model of Osgood and is organized around three dimensions of cognition: (a) channels of communication or input-output modes (namely, auditory-vocal and visual-motor); (b) psycholinguistic processes (reception, association, and expression); and (c) levels of organization (representational and automatic). Table 9–3 describes the various levels and processes and lists the subtests designed to measure each. The *ITPA* was constructed so each subtest represents one level, process, and channel. Thus, the Auditory Reception subtest is designed to measure the process of reception at the representational level through the auditory-vocal channel. The Visual Reception subtest is designed to assess the same process and level using the second channel of communication, visual-motor.

The *ITPA* provides norms for students ages 2–4 to 10–3. Each subtest produces an age equivalent score called a Psycholinguistic Age (PLA) and a Scaled Score. Total test scores include Composite Psycholinguistic Age, Mean Scaled Score, and Median Scaled Score. Scaled Scores are distributed with a mean of 36 and a standard deviation of 6.

The *ITPA* has come under heavy criticism due to questions about its technical adequacy (Salvia & Ysseldyke, 1988). According to the technical manual for the *ITPA* (Paraskevopoulos & Kirk, 1969), the sample was drawn from only five communities and represented just two states. Only "average" children were included rather than a sample of children representative of the total population. Reliability of the *ITPA* varies, and test-retest reliabilities are very low for some subtests. For example, correlations for the Visual Sequential Memory subtest are .38 for age 6 and .28 for age 8 when corrected for restricted intelligence range. Limited information is provided about the validity of the *ITPA*. One study cited in the technical manual found moderate correlations between the *ITPA* composite test score and *Stanford-Binet* results. Another study reported a correlation of .96 between chronological age and *ITPA* composite test scores for the standardization sample. Clearly, more information about test validity is needed. The authors of the technical manual appear to agree. Among areas of needed research, they include studies of the relationship between the *ITPA* performance of young children and later school performance.

Detroit Tests of Learning Aptitude. This measure was first developed in the 1930s by Baker and Leland and then revised in 1967. In 1985, a new version of the *Detroit Tests of Learning Aptitude* (Hammill) appeared. The *DTLA–2,* as this edition is called, is a complete revision and restandardization. A new version for young children, the *Detroit Tests of Learning Aptitude–Primary* (Hammill & Bryant, 1986), is also available.

The *DTLA–2* is an individual, norm-referenced test designed to assess a variety of specific cognitive abilities. It is appropriate for students aged 6–0 to 17–11 and contains 11 subtests. These subtests, as described in the *DTLA–2* manual, are

- *Word Opposites*—The examiner says a word aloud; the student responds by saying another word that has precisely the opposite meaning of the examiner's word.
- *Sentence Imitation*—The examinee repeats sentences exactly as the examiner has said them.
- *Oral Directions*—The examiner says a series of commands which a student executes in pencil on a sheet of paper.
- *Word Sequences*—The student repeats in order a series of meaningfully unrelated words spoken by the examiner.
- *Story Construction*—The student is shown a picture . . . and is asked to make up a story about the picture. The story is told to the examiner, who scores its conceptual, insightful, and coherent qualities.

TABLE 9–3
Contents of the *Illinois Test of Psycholinguistic Abilities*

I. **Representational Level**—The use of symbols which carry the meaning of an object.
  A. *The Receptive Process* (*Decoding*)—The ability to comprehend visual and auditory symbols.
    SUBTESTS: Auditory Reception
             Visual Reception
  B. *The Organizing Process* (*Association*)—The ability to relate, organize, and manipulate visual or auditory symbols in a meaningful way.
    SUBTESTS: Auditory Association
             Visual Association
  C. *The Expressive Process* (*Encoding*)—The ability to use verbal or manual symbols to transmit an idea.
    SUBTESTS: Verbal Expression
             Manual Expression

II. **Automatic Level**—Habits of functioning which are less voluntary (than those at the representational level) but highly organized and integrated.
  A. *Closure*—The ability to fill in the missing parts in an incomplete picture or verbal expression.
    SUBTESTS: Grammatic Closure
             Visual Closure
             Auditory Closure (Supplementary)
             Sound Blending (Supplementary)
  B. *Sequential Memory*—The ability to reproduce a sequence of auditory or visual stimuli.
    SUBTESTS: Auditory Sequential Memory
             Visual Sequential Memory

Note. From the *Illinois Test of Psycholinguistic Abilities* (rev. ed.) by S. A. Kirk, J. M. McCarthy, and W. D. Kirk, 1968, Urbana: University of Illinois Press. Copyright 1968 by the Board of Trustees of the University of Illinois. Reprinted by permission.

□ *Design Reproduction*—The examinee is shown a complex design for a short period of time, the design is withdrawn from view, and he or she is asked to draw the design from memory.

□ *Object Sequences*—The examinee is briefly shown a card that has a row of pictures printed on it, the pictures are covered, and another stimulus row containing the same pictures in a different order is presented. Under each picture on this second row there is a number. The student is asked to indicate the original order of the pictures by writing the numbers in sequence.

□ *Conceptual Matching*—The examinee is shown a card with one picture at the top and a series of 10 pictures at the bottom. He or she is to choose by pointing which of the 10 pictures is most closely related to the picture at the top.

□ *Symbolic Relations*—The examinee is shown a card with some designs on it. At the top of the card, the designs are arranged in a pattern that has a missing part. At the bottom of the card is a series of designs, one of which is the missing part needed to complete the pattern pictured above. The student points to the correct answer.

□ *Word Fragments*—The examinee is shown a known printed word which has a significant amount of print missing. He or she says the word aloud if the fragmented form triggers a recognition.

□ *Letter Sequences*—The examinee is briefly shown a card containing a series of letters. The card is removed from view and the examinee is asked to write down the letters in the same order as they appeared on the card.

(*Note.* From *Detroit Tests of Learning Aptitude* (2nd ed.) (pp. 65–71) by D. D. Hammill, 1985, Austin, TX: PRO-ED. Copyright 1985 by Donald D. Hammill. Adapted by Permission.)

Standard scores and percentile ranks are computed for each subtest; subtest results can be combined into several Composite Quotients. The General Intelligence Quotient is a total test score that reflects performance on all subtests. More interesting are the two composite quotients for each of the *DTLA–2*'s domains: Linguistic, Cognitive, Attentional, and Motoric.

On the Linguistic Domain, these are the Verbal Aptitude Quotient and the Nonverbal Aptitude Quotient. Verbal aptitude is measured by the *DTLA–2* subtests that stress word knowledge and use. Nonverbal aptitude is assessed by subtests that deemphasize reading, writing, and verbal abilities. Likewise, there are two Cognitive Domain composite quotients: the Conceptual Aptitude

Quotient, which reflects skill in problem solving and abstract reasoning; and the Structural Aptitude Quotient, a measure of more concrete types of reasoning tasks such as sequencing. On the Attentional Domain, subtests that require attention, concentration, and short-term memory make up the Attention-Enhanced Aptitude Quotient, and subtests that stress long-term memory contribute to the Attention-Reduced Aptitude Quotient. The Motoric Domain combines subtests with high motor skill demands into the Motor-Enhanced Quotient and those that are relatively motor-free into the Motor-Reduced Quotient. One of the purposes of the *DTLA–2* is "to determine strengths and weaknesses among intellectual abilities" (p. 11), and the composite quotients provided by this measure facilitate this task.

The *DTLA–2* was standardized in 1984 with 1,532 persons from 30 states. The sample included ages 6–0 to 17–11, and it appears to approximate the national population in gender, urban-rural residence, race, and geographic region. The internal consistency reliability of composite quotient scores is adequate as is their test-retest reliability, although coefficients for some subtests at some age levels fall below the .80 suggested minimum. Validity was investigated in several ways, including study of the *DTLA–2*'s concurrent validity. In general, *DTLA–2* results appear related to results of group achievement tests and tests of intellectual performance such as the *WISC–R*. However, further study of validity is necessary. The concurrent validity research described in the manual was conducted with small samples of students, and investigation was limited to only a few measures of intellectual performance and academic achievement. There is also need to look at the relationship of the *DTLA–2* to some of the newer measures such as the *Woodcock-Johnson Psycho-Educational Battery–Revised* and the *Kaufman Assessment Battery for Children*.

The *Detroit Tests of Learning Aptitude–Primary* is a downward extension of the *DTLA–2* for children ages 3–6 to 9–11. It employs many of the same kinds of test tasks and produces the same General Intelligence and Domain Composite Quotients as the *DTLA–2*. There are two major differences between the tests. The *Primary* version is not organized by subtests; items of all types are merged into one sequence by difficulty level. Also, the *DTLA–Primary* contains some tasks not found on the version for older students: Articulation, Digit Sequences, Draw-a-Person, Motor Directions, Picture Fragments, Picture Identification, and Visual Discrimination.

The standardization sample for the *DTLA–Primary,* composed of 1,676 children from 33 states, appears representative of the national population. Internal consistency and test-retest reliabilities are adequate. Concurrent validity was studied by reviewing records of children in the standardization sample for other test results. Despite small numbers of children, the correlations obtained support the relationship of the *DTLA–Primary* to the *DTLA–2* and measures of intellectual performance, school readiness, and academic achievement.

Intelligence Tests as Measures of Specific Cognitive Abilities

Subtests from measures of intellectual performance are sometimes used to assess specific cognitive abilities. This practice may occur when a technically adequate specific ability test is not available and/or when available measures do not provide age-appropriate norms. The norms of many specific ability tests do not extend to the junior or senior high ages.

The individual intelligence test most often used as an information source about specific abilities is the *WISC–R,* the *Wechsler Intelligence Scale for Children–Revised* (Wechsler, 1974). *WISC–R* results are available for most students assessed for possible special education placement, and these results are examined to determine strengths and weaknesses in various cognitive abilities.

WISC–R analysis is often recommended as part of the process in the identification of learning disabilities. However, interpretation of *WISC–R* results can take many forms, from identification of the lowest subtest scores to a search for subtest scatter and Verbal-Performance discrepancies. Many of these procedures have been thoroughly studied, and reviews of research (Kaufman, 1981; Kavale & Forness, 1984) are beginning to indicate a consensus on the utility of various approaches.

This body of research suggests that analysis of Verbal-Performance discrepancies, subtest scatter, and recategorized *WISC–R* scores are not fruitful procedures for identification of learning disabilities.

However, examination of scores on individual subtests may provide information about a student's relative strengths and weaknesses. Of particular interest are the subtests where learning disabled students typically show their poorest performance: Arithmetic, Coding, Information, Digit Span, and Mazes.

Use of intelligence tests as measures of specific abilities has resulted in part from the criticism leveled at traditional specific ability measures. Faced with a shortage of technically adequate tests, practitioners turned to well-respected instruments such as the *WISC–R.* In addition, many of the newer tests of intellectual performance are designed to assess both global learning aptitude and specific cognitive abilities. As described in Chapter 8, the *Woodcock-Johnson Psycho-Educational Battery–Revised* (Woodcock & Johnson, 1989) assesses seven cognitive factors, and the *Kaufman Achievement Battery for Children* (Kaufman & Kaufman, 1983) offers measures of two types of processing—simultaneous and sequential. The newest edition of the *Stanford-Binet Intelligence Scale* (Thorndike et al., 1986) provides information on short-term memory as well as verbal, quantitative, and abstract/visual reasoning. As yet, there is not a rich research literature about the utility of these approaches, as there is in relation to the *WISC–R.* Thus, caution is necessary as professionals begin to use newer measures to help in the study of specific learning abilities.

ASSESSMENT OF LEARNING STRATEGIES

Within the last few years, the emphasis in assessment has shifted from the study of isolated specific abilities to consideration of learning strategies. Learning strategies are the methods students employ when faced with a learning task. This change is due in part to the criticism leveled against traditional specific ability assessments and treatment programs. It is also due to current research findings about the nature of learning disabilities.

Research Findings

Results of recent research indicate that many students with learning disabilities are characterized by inefficient and ineffective strategies for learning (Lewis, 1983). This finding has been reported in relation to the specific learning abilities of both attention and memory. Hallahan and Reeve (1980), in their summary of research on selective attention, conclude,

At this time, it appears that the most parsimonious explanation for the learning disabled child's tendency to have problems in attending to relevant cues and ignoring irrelevant cues is his inability to bring to the task a specific learning strategy. (p. 156)

Research on memory supports this (Torgesen, 1980). Learning disabled students tend to recall less information than nonhandicapped students. They approach the learning task differently and are less likely to engage in active rehearsal during the study period. However, when learning disabled students are required to rehearse, their recall improves to the level of nonhandicapped students (Torgesen & Goldman, 1977). These findings have led Torgesen (1977) to hypothesize that learning disabled students are passive learners.

Deshler and other researchers at the University of Kansas have carried out a series of studies on the learning characteristics of adolescents identified as learning disabled (Alley, Deshler, Clark, Schumaker, & Warner, 1983; Deshler, Schumaker, Alley, Warner, & Clark, 1982; Schumaker, Deshler, Alley, & Warner, 1983). Their results indicate that many learning disabled adolescents exhibit immature executive functioning; that is, these students are unable to create and apply an appropriate strategy to a novel problem (Schumaker et al., 1983). In addition, the study skills and strategies of secondary-aged learning disabled students are deficient. Among the areas of difficulty are note taking, attention to teachers' statements, listening comprehension, scanning of textbook passages, monitoring of writing errors, and test-taking skills (Deshler et al., 1982).

Although deficient learning strategies and study skills appear to characterize learning disabled students, these strategies may be susceptible to training (Lewis, 1983). Torgesen's (1980) work in memory illustrates this point. Research at the University of Kansas on the efficacy of learning strategy interventions also supports the feasibility of training (Deshler et al., 1982). The instructional model proposed by Deshler, Alley, Warner, and Schumaker (1981) begins with assessment of the

student's current strategies for learning. New strategies are then taught, first in isolation, then with controlled academic materials, and finally with actual school texts and assignments.

The Learning Strategies Curriculum described by Schumaker and colleagues (1983) includes two major strands: strategies for gaining information from written and oral materials, and strategies for expressing information in permanent products (e.g., written assignments and tests). Among the strategies included in this curriculum are Word Identification, Self-Questioning, Sentence Writing, Test Preparation, and Memorization.

Approaches to Assessment

Although progress has been made in the development of instructional models, the assessment of learning strategies has received little attention. At present, professionals must rely upon informal measures. Specific ability tests do not provide sufficient information, because they measure abilities in isolation rather than in the context of actual learning tasks. More pertinent data are produced by observations, work sample analyses, student questionnaires and interviews, and teacher interviews.

Suggestions for the design of informal tools for the assessment of learning strategies are available in the study skills literature. However, study skills are not the same as learning strategies. The term *learning strategy* is usually reserved for the general cognitive strategies that students apply to tasks where learning is expected: strategies for the deployment of attention, for the rehearsal of skills and information to be learned, for generating and evaluating solutions to problems, and so forth. In contrast, study skills are more closely tied to specific school tasks and often require at least rudimentary proficiency in reading and writing. Despite these differences, both learning strategies and study skills are concerned with the student's *use* of specific abilities. Evaluation of study habits can provide some insight into the ways the student interacts with the learning task.

According to Cohen and de Bettencourt (1983), students are responsible for five aspects of independent learning activities: following directions, approaching tasks, obtaining assistance, gaining feedback, and gaining reinforcement. These five components could form the basis for designing an observation of student study behavior.

Brown (1978) discusses study behaviors and suggests methods for informal assessment. First, the student's work habits should be observed within the context of the classroom. Among the factors to be considered are the frequency and duration of on-task and off-task behaviors; any classroom conditions or events that appear to distract the student; and variations in performance from one time, subject matter area, or teacher to another. A second assessment method is discussion with the student. Students can be asked to describe their usual methods of approaching and completing class assignments. The interview can be informal with open-ended questions or have a more structured approach. Brown provides a set of descriptions for use in student interviews. They are as follows:

A. Finish assigned work
B. Do as well as I can
C. Usually understand assignments
D. Don't understand purpose of most assignments
E. Collect all materials needed
F. Budget time for study
G. Can explain what "studying" means
H. Can't stand studying
I. Check over completed assignments
J. Concentrate well
K. See little real value in studying
L. Use textbooks well
M. Study with tests in mind
N. Learn a lot from assignments
O. Take notes well
P. Begin assigned work
Q. Prefer to study alone
R. Study as well as my friends do
S. Take notes well
T. Keep "study" records
U. Easily distracted from study
V. Ask for help with studying
W. Organize study time well
X. (Your own idea) _____
Y. Can outline study materials
Z. Study only subjects I like
(*Note.* From "Independent Study Behaviors: A Framework for Curriculum" by V. Brown, 1978, *Learning Disability Quarterly, 1* (2), p. 80. Copyright 1978 by the Division for Children with Learning Disabilities. Reprinted by permission.)

These descriptions could be used as a checklist, with students checking each item that applies to their usual study behavior. Or students could rate themselves on each item using a Likert-type scale with descriptions such as usually, often, sometimes, rarely, and never.

Students can be interviewed while they are working on a study task or just after they have completed it. This allows the interviewer to ask specific questions about a particular task. Students simply report their actions, rather than attempting to recall or make judgments about their typical behaviors. Some questions that could be asked in situations where students are learning new information are

☐ Think about the things you just did in studying _____ . What did you do first?
☐ Did you begin by looking over the information to be learned?
☐ Did you try to organize the information in any way? If so, how did you organize it?
☐ Was there anything in the material that you didn't understand? If there was, how did you try to figure it out?
☐ In your studying, did you do anything to help you remember the information? What did you do? Did you look at it? Say it to yourself? Picture it in your mind? Take notes? Outline the information?
☐ Can you recall the information now? Do you think you'll be able to remember it tomorrow?
☐ Will you study this information again? If so, will you use the same study methods?

These questions attempt to elicit student comments about the use of strategies such as previewing, organizing, problem solving, and rehearsing. In light of the research findings about students' lack of active task participation, the questions about rehearsal techniques are of special interest. Some students may report using verbal rehearsal where the material to be learned is said aloud or subvocally. Others may talk about visual imagery, the construction of mental visual images, as a strategy for learning. Both verbal rehearsal and visual imagery have been found useful as mnemonic devices or memory aids for learning disabled students. (Rose, Cundick, & Higbee, 1983). Students who report no rehearsal strategy or say they simply look at the material may be in need of strategy training.

The *Study Skills Counseling Evaluation* (*SSCE*) (Demos, 1976) is a published assessment device designed to "rapidly and objectively identify study weaknesses" (p. 1). It is a printed questionnaire with norms for high school students, 2-year college students, and 4-year college students.

The *SSCE* contains 50 items that assess five study skill areas.

- Study-Time Distribution
- Study Conditions
- Taking Notes
- Preparing and Taking Examinations
- Other Habits and Attitudes

The student reads each statement (e.g., "I study in several short sessions") and then marks the best description of his or her current study habits: very often, often, sometimes, seldom, or very seldom. The *SSCE* total test raw score is converted to a percentile rank. In addition, the manual provides guidelines for rating performance in each of the study skill areas as Very Strong, Strong, Average, Weak, or Very Weak. These ratings can be plotted on a summary profile to provide a graphic representation of strengths and weaknesses.

The *SSCE* is a normed instrument, but very little information is provided in the manual about the standardization sample. Although this is a concern, the *SSCE* could be used as an informal device, or local norms could be developed. In interpreting results of this or other self-report measures, it must be remembered that not every student is able—or willing—to provide totally accurate information.

Most published study skills questionnaires are designed for high school and college students. The *Study Attitudes and Methods Survey* (Michael, Michael, & Zimmerman, 1985) includes the dimensions of academic interest and drive, study habits, and lack of study anxiety. An older measure, the *Study-Habits Inventory* (Wrenn, 1941), assesses reading and note-taking techniques, concentration, time management, and work attitudes and habits. One measure, the *Survey of Study Habits and Attitudes* (Brown & Holtzman, 1953, 1967), extends down to grade 7 and is available both in English and Spanish. It evaluates study methods, motivation for studying, and attitudes toward scholastic activities.

Levine, Clarke, and Ferb (1981) report the results of a study in which learning disabled students, ages 9 and above, rated themselves on several dimensions of learning behavior. The instrument, the *Self-Administered Student Profile,* was made up of quotations gathered from children with learning disabilities. The items represented the categories of Memory, Selective Attention, Visual-Spatial Orientation, Gross Motor Function, Fine Motor Function, Sequential Organization, Language, Academic Performance, Social Interaction, and Overall Working Efficiency.

The most common problems identified by students in this study were in the areas of memory and selective attention. For example, 45% of the sample reported that, "A lot of times I do things too fast without thinking"; 36% said, "It's hard for me to keep my mind on work in school"; and 28% said, "I have trouble remembering things the teacher just said a little while ago." In general, there was good agreement between students' reports and those of their teachers, parents, and clinic staff.

Assessment of learning strategies is a new endeavor in special education. At present, assessment teams must rely on informal techniques if there is interest in evaluating strategies for learning and study skills. The previous paragraphs have provided some suggestions about important factors to consider in designing student observations, interviews, and questionnaires. For other sources of information about study skills assessment, see Cronin and Currie (1984).

DISCREPANCY ANALYSIS

One of the major criteria for the identification of learning disabilities is a discrepancy between expected and actual performance. It is assumed that this handicap will have a negative effect upon school functioning so students will not achieve as well as would be expected from their general intellectual level. According to federal guidelines, for a student to qualify for learning disabilities services, the team must establish a severe discrepancy between ability and achievement in one or more of these subject matter areas: oral expression, listening comprehension, written expression, basic reading skill, reading comprehension, mathematics calculation, and mathematics reasoning.

The discrepancy notion appears clear and straightforward until it must be operationalized; then numerous questions arise. These include choice of measures of ability and achievement, and the setting of standards to determine how large a difference between scores indicates a discrepancy and how large that discrepancy must be to be considered severe. The simplest of these decisions is the choice of measures. In practice, ability is assessed with tests of intellectual performance and achievement with achievement tests. But even this choice is complicated by factors such as the range of scores available on many measures.

Several methods have been suggested for discrepancy analysis, although none has escaped criticism. One common method often used by practitioners is the years-below-grade-level procedure. In this procedure, the student's grade score on some measure of academic achievement is subtracted from current grade placement. A discrepancy is indicated when the student is found to be more than 2 years below grade level. For example, if a midyear fourth grade student (grade placement = 4.5) earns a grade equivalent of 1.3 on a reading test, the student could be said to achieve 3.2 years below grade level, a difference considered indicative of a discrepancy. Although this method is easy to use, it is not an appropriate way to analyze discrepancies. It does not take differences in ability into account. It assumes average ability by making actual grade placement the standard of comparison.

Another major difficulty with this method is its use of grade scores. As Chapter 3 explained, grade equivalents are not equal-interval scores; thus, they may not legitimately be added or subtracted. Berk (1982) discusses some of the deficiencies of grade equivalent scores. These scores

1. Invite seemingly simple but misleading interpretations
2. Assume that the rate of learning is constant throughout the school year . . .
3. Are derived primarily from interpolation and extrapolation rather than from real data
4. Are virtually meaningless in the upper grade-levels for subjects that are not taught at those levels
5. Do not comprise an equal-interval scale
6. Exaggerate the significance of small differences in performance
7. Vary markedly from test to test, from subtest to subtest within the same test battery, from grade to grade and from percentile to percentile. (p. 12)

Because of these deficiencies and its other limitations, the years-below-grade-level method is not recommended for discrepancy analysis.

A second method makes use of expectancy formulas to estimate the student's expected level of achievement. For example, the expectancy formula of Harris (1970) is calculated by subtracting 5.0 years from the student's measured mental age (MA). Thus, a student of MA 9.0 would be expected to achieve at the 4.0 grade level. This expected grade level is then compared to the student's grade score on some test of achievement. The Bond and Tinker (1967) formula is similar, but IQ, rather than MA, is used as the aptitude measure. Several other expectancy formulas have also been proposed (Bureau of Education for the Handicapped, 1976; Monroe, 1932; Myklebust, 1968).

Expectancy formulas share one of the major limitations of the years-below-grade-level approach: current achievement is expressed in grade equivalent scores. In addition, age equivalent scores such as mental ages are subject to the same deficiencies as grade equivalent scores. Another major criticism of expectancy formula methods is that they do not consider reliability. The reliability of each of the compared scores is of interest, as is the reliability of the obtained discrepancy score.

One way of overcoming the limitations of age and grade scores is to replace them with standard scores. Standard scores are interval data and may be manipulated arithmetically by addition or subtraction. Standard scores must be distributed with the same mean and standard deviation to compare them from one measure to another. Norm groups used to derive these standard scores must also be comparable. One way to insure this is to choose measures standardized on the same sample. Some of the newer measures such as the *Woodcock-Johnson–R* (Woodcock & Johnson, 1989) and the *K-ABC* (Kaufman & Kaufman, 1983) provide both ability and achievement scores.

The simplest method of discrepancy analysis using standard scores is to subtract one score from another. For example, if a student receives a standard score of 105 on an IQ test and a standard score of 82 on an achievement test, the difference between the two scores would be 23. This new score, 23, is called a difference score. However, because this approach does not take into account the measurement error present in each of the two scores, Anastasi (1988) suggests an alternative procedure. Instead of comparing scores, confidence intervals are constructed around each obtained score using each test's standard error of measurement. Then these score ranges are compared to determine whether there is an overlap. For example, using a 95% confidence interval, the IQ score range might be 99 to 111 and the achievement score range 72 to 92. If there is no overlap between the score ranges, it is likely there is a difference between the obtained ability and achievement scores.

To gain even more precision, Anastasi (1988) recommends calculation of the standard error of difference between scores. The standard error of difference is used to determine whether an observed difference occurred by chance or whether the difference is likely a true difference. It is computed with the formula

$$SE_{diff} = SD\sqrt{2 - r_1 - r_2}$$

where SE_{diff} is the standard error of the difference, SD is the standard deviation of the two tests, r_1 is the reliability coefficient for test 1, and r_2 is the reliability coefficient for test 2. For example, if the standard deviation of each test is 15, and the tests' reliabilities are .90 and .92, the standard error of the difference would be 6.36.

To find out how large a difference is needed at various levels of confidence, the standard error of the difference is multiplied by

   1.64 to determine the difference likely to occur by chance 10% of the time

   1.96 to determine the difference likely to occur by chance 5% of the time

   2.58 to determine the difference likely to occur by chance 1% of the time

If the 5% (.05) level is selected, the standard error of the difference is multiplied by 1.96: 6.36 × 1.96 = 12.46. Thus, the difference between the two scores must be at least 12 to signify a real difference at the .05 level. That is, there is 95% probability that a difference of 12 signifies a true difference and only 5% probability that this difference is due to chance.

The standard error of difference method is not a perfect solution to the problem of score comparisons. If the tests being compared are related, the reliability of the difference score is affected. The higher the correlation between the tests, the lower the reliability of the difference score. Schulte and Borich (1984) provide procedures for computing the reliabilities of difference scores when the correlation between measures is known. Other factors that influence the accuracy of difference scores are regression effects and the lack of homogeneity among the standard errors of measurement within a particular test.

The following case provides an example of the standard error of difference method using IQ and achievement test data for Joyce, the fourth grader described at the start of this chapter. In this example, Joyce's Full Scale WISC–R IQ score is compared to the standard score she earned on the WRAT–R Spelling subtest. According to Schulte and Borich (1984), the reliabilities of difference scores based on WISC–R Full Scale and WRAT Spelling results range from .86 to .89.

Joyce

Joyce, the fourth grader referred for school performance problems, has been tested with the WISC–R and several measures of academic achievement, including the Spelling subtest from the WRAT–R. To determine whether Joyce's measured achievement is different from her current intellectual performance, the assessment team decides to conduct a discrepancy analysis.

The team chooses to evaluate Joyce's aptitude–achievement discrepancies using the standard error of the difference between two scores. This method will allow them to determine whether the discrepancies are likely due to true differences between aptitude and achievement or to chance.

To compute the standard error of the difference, the team needs to know the reliabilities of the scores to be compared. According to the WISC–R manual, the internal consistency reliability of the Full Scale IQ score is .96 for students ages $10\frac{1}{2}$ to $11\frac{1}{2}$. The WRAT–R manual lists the internal consistency reliability of the Spelling subtest for 10-year-olds as .94.

WISC–R Full Scale IQ reliability = .96

WRAT–R Spelling reliability = .94

The standard error of difference now can be calculated for IQ versus spelling achievement. The computations are

$$SE_{diff} = SD \sqrt{2 - r_1 - r_2}$$
$$SE_{diff} = 15\sqrt{2 - .96 - .94}$$
$$SE_{diff} = 4.74$$

The standard error of the difference, 4.74, is then multiplied by 1.96 to determine the difference likely to occur by chance 5% of the time.

$$SE_{diff} \times 1.96 = 9.29$$

Thus, at a 95% level of confidence, the observed difference between Joyce's *WISC–R* Full Scale IQ and her standard score on the *WRAT–R* Spelling subtest must equal or exceed 9 to indicate a true difference. The observed difference is

101	(*WISC–R* Full Scale IQ)
− 69	(*WRAT–R* Spelling standard score)
32	observed difference

The observed discrepancy is greater than the minimum discrepancy needed to indicate a true difference at the 95% confidence level. Therefore, the team concludes that it is probable that Joyce's current performance in spelling is discrepant from her intellectual performance.

Salvia and Ysseldyke (1988) suggest a more detailed procedure for the evaluation of different scores. The reliability of the difference score, its standard deviation, and its standard error are calculated to determine whether the difference is reliable and, if so, to estimate the true difference score.

Other authors (Algozzine, Forgnone, Mercer, & Trifiletti, 1979; Hanna, Dyck, & Holen, 1979) have suggested additional methods of discrepancy analysis, most notably the regression approach (Cone & Wilson, 1981; Reynolds, 1984). At present, there does not appear to be agreement about the most appropriate method, although criticism of expectancy formulas and the years-below-grade-level

approach is consistent (Berk, 1982, 1984; Cone & Wilson, 1981; Sattler, 1988).

Some research has compared the effects of using various discrepancy analysis procedures. Forness, Sinclair, and Guthrie (1983) applied seven expectancy formulas and a "years-behind" method to the ability and achievement scores of 92 students. The eight methods of discrepancy analysis produced quite different results. The percentage of children identified as learning disabled by the different formulas ranged from a low of 10.9% to a high of 37.0%. Ysseldyke, Algozzine, and Epps (1983) reported similar findings. In addition, it appears that some regular class students would be classified as learning disabled, if ability–achievement discrepancy was the sole criterion.

Many unanswered questions about discrepancy analysis remain. Despite this, assessment teams must evaluate students for placement in learning disability programs. One approach to the problem is use of some of the newer measures of ability and achievement that have built-in procedures for discrepancy analysis. For example, both the *Woodcock-Johnson–R* and the *K-ABC* provide methods for comparing intellectual performance and academic achievement. Also, the *Woodcock Reading Mastery Tests–Revised* (Woodcock, 1987) allows comparison of a student's reading performance with results of aptitude measures such as the *WISC–R, Woodcock-Johnson,* and *K-ABC.* However, not all tests offer systems for discrepancy analysis.

In attempting to determine whether a discrepancy exists between expected and actual achievement, the assessment team should consider the following suggestions. The last two suggestions are pertinent for all discrepancy analyses, even those simplified by newer measures.

1. When comparing ability and achievement scores, use scores from valid and reliable tests with comparable norm groups.
2. Construct confidence intervals around each score and determine whether there is an overlap in score ranges.
3. Compute the standard error of the difference to determine whether the observed difference is likely due to chance.
4. If the degree of relationship between the ability and the achievement tests is known, determine the reliability of the difference score.

5. Even if it is highly probable that the difference score is reliable and that the observed difference is a true one, confirm that the discrepancy exists within the school environment. Substantiate that the student's actual classroom performance is below expectation levels.
6. Keep in mind that a discrepancy between ability and achievement is only one of the criteria for the identification of learning disabilities.

ANSWERING THE ASSESSMENT QUESTIONS

The assessment team gathers several types of information to describe the student's current specific learning abilities and strategies. Visual and auditory acuity are checked to determine whether a sensory impairment is influencing school performance. Specific ability tests may be administered if perceptual-motor skills, memory, or information-processing abilities are of interest. The team may use informal techniques such as observations, questionnaires, and interviews to learn more about learning strategies and study skills. If learning disabilities are suspected, the student's current scores on measures of ability and achievement will be compared to determine if there is a substantial discrepancy between expected and actual achievement.

Types of Procedures

A wide range of assessment techniques are used to study specific learning abilities, learning strategies, and study skills. Because these techniques provide information for several different assessment questions, they are not expected to produce equivalent results. For example, the evaluation of sensory acuity is a separate procedure from the evaluation of specific learning abilities. A student may perform adequately in both of these areas, in neither, or in only one.

Results of specific ability measures are not expected to be equivalent to the findings of informal evaluations of learning strategies and study skills. There are several reasons for this. First, students may perform differently in these two areas of functioning. An individual can show adequate specific abilities when these are assessed in isolation but have difficulty applying them in actual school learning tasks. A student also might compensate for poor specific abilities by developing appropriate learning strategies and study skills.

Second, the types of measures typically used in the evaluation of specific learning abilities are quite different from those used to assess learning strategies and study skills. Most specific ability measures are individual, norm-referenced tests. In contrast, learning strategies and study skills are usually assessed informally. Students are observed while engaged in learning activities or are questioned about study strategies through interviews or questionnaires. Such informal techniques do not produce comparative data. For example, if an observation reveals that a student attends to the teacher's lecture in 60% of the time intervals sampled, this may or may not indicate typical performance for the student's age and grade.

A third consideration is the directness of the measures. Specific ability tests and student observations are more direct methods of assessment than interviews and questionnaires used to elicit students' descriptions of their typical learning strategies and study skills. Indirect measures that rely upon informants may produce less accurate results than direct assessment of behaviors under consideration.

Technical quality is a fourth concern. Most specific ability measures are standardized tests, with information available concerning their standardization, reliability, and validity. Most informal learning strategy measures do not have such information. Yet norm-referenced tests are not always preferable to informal strategy assessments. Many norm-referenced measures of specific learning abilities fail to meet minimum criteria for adequate reliability and validity and thus should not be used as tools in educational decision making. In many cases, informal measures are the only alternative to technically inadequate tests. Regardless, technical quality is still an important concern. The assessment team should attempt to identify informal techniques that are documented as both reliable and valid.

Nature of the Assessment Tasks

Assessment devices that appear to measure the same skill or ability may in fact be measuring quite different factors. This may occur because different test tasks are used for assessment. For example, evaluation of auditory discrimination is the purpose of both the *Goldman-Fristoe-Woodcock Test of Auditory Discrimination* and the Wepman *Auditory Discrimination Test,* but these measures demand different skills. On the Wepman, the student simply listens to the tester read a pair of words. No visual stimuli are presented, and the test is administered in a quiet environment. The student responds by saying whether the words presented were the same or different. In contrast, the *Goldman-Fristoe-Woodcock* uses a taped presentation, and the student hears one word. The student is also shown four pictures and must select the picture that represents the word read on the tape. This test includes two subtests, one where the listening environment is quiet and the other where a noisy environment is simulated.

Likewise, tests of visual perception may use dissimilar assessment tasks. For instance, the *Developmental Test of Visual Perception* requires students to trace and to copy, whereas the *Motor-Free Visual Perception Test* does not. These two tests each assess five areas of visual perception, but only figure-ground perception and spatial relationships are common to both measures.

Several types of assessment tasks evaluate memory. Some emphasize the auditory presentation of information, others visual input. The required response mode may be verbal or motor. Most memory tasks assess short-term recall, but the type of information to be recalled varies widely: numbers, words, sentences, shapes, pictures of common objects, photographs of people's faces, and so on. The student may be required to recall in the exact order of presentation, in reverse order, or in no particular order. Because there are important differences between test tasks, it is certainly possible for a student to perform well on one type of memory task and poorly on another.

Documentation of Specific Learning Abilities and Strategies

Specific learning abilities and strategies are one major concern of the assessment team as they attempt to answer the question: *Is the school performance problem related to a handicapping condition?* The handicapping condition under consideration in this phase of the assessment process is learning disabilities. Four specific assessment questions are pertinent.

1. *What is the status of the student's sensory abilities?*
2. *What is the student's current level of development in specific learning abilities?*
3. *What is the student's current functioning level in strategies for learning and study skills?*
4. *Is there a substantial discrepancy between the student's actual achievement and the expected achievement level?*

The first question, relating to vision and hearing, is asked for all students referred for special education assessment. Although the other questions relate most directly to learning disabilities, they may also be of interest for students with other types of mild handicaps.

The assessment team gathers information from many sources to answer these questions. School records are reviewed for results of group measures of school readiness and vision and hearing screenings. Specific learning abilities are assessed with individual norm-referenced tests, provided technically adequate measures are available. To evaluate learning strategies and study skills, students are observed, or they may complete questionnaires or participate in interviews. Teachers and parents contribute by sharing observations of the student's specific abilities and strategies. When learning disabilities are considered a possibility, IQ and achievement data are compared using discrepancy analysis techniques.

Determination of eligibility for learning disabilities services rests upon discrepancy analysis. The team must demonstrate there is a severe discrepancy between the student's expected achievement, based upon intellectual performance, and actual achievement. In addition, the assessment team is usually interested in identifying some reason for poor achievement, such as low or below average performance in one or more specific abilities or evidence of ineffective learning strategies or study skills. According to federal guidelines, the team must also establish that underachievement is *not* primarily due to another handicapping condition; to lack of instruction; or to environmental, cultural, or economic disadvantages.

Joyce

At this point in Joyce's assessment, the team has substantiated the school performance problems noted by Mr. Harvey, Joyce's fourth grade teacher. It has also been established that Joyce's current intellectual performance is within the average range. The assessment team then moves on to an investigation of specific learning abilities and strategies.

School records are reviewed for the results of Joyce's most recent hearing and vision tests. Both vision and hearing were checked at the beginning of the year when Joyce entered the school district, and no problems were noted. According to Joyce's parents, she has never been treated for a vision or hearing impairment.

When Joyce was given the *WISC–R,* the assessment team noticed two possible areas of difficulty, the Digit Span and Coding subtests, both of which are related to the *WISC–R* Freedom from Distractibility factor. To learn more about Joyce's attention to tasks and memorization strategies, the resource teacher, Ms. Gale, observes Joyce as she studies her new spelling words for the week. No attentional problems are noted. Joyce starts the task immediately and appears to remain on task during the entire study period.

Joyce's assigned task is to study each word and then write it 10 times. Ms. Gale observes that Joyce begins by writing her name on her paper. She then copies five new words from the book to the first line of her paper. Joyce's strategy for writing each word 10 times is this: to write the first word, *home,* she copies the *h* 10 times down her paper, then she copies the *o* 10 times, and so forth until she has finished that word. She repeats this procedure with each of the new spelling words. After the observation, Ms. Gale talks with Joyce about her study tactics. Joyce says she has always written her spelling words that way because it is quicker. When asked what she did to try and remember how to spell the words, Joyce says she looked at their shapes.

Ms. Gale then interviews Joyce's teacher. Mr. Harvey reports that Joyce seems to remember some things, such as math facts, quite well but has difficulty with reading and spelling words. He also mentions that Joyce has problems remembering a series of oral directions. He often has to

repeat instructions for her, especially if they contain several steps. Ms. Gale also questions Joyce's teacher about fine motor skills. According to Mr. Harvey, Joyce prints most of her assignments. Her printing is large, the spacing is poor, and many of the letters are difficult to read.

To gather more information about Joyce's memory and motor skills, Ms. Gale administers the *Detroit Tests of Learning Aptitude* (2nd ed.). Joyce's overall General Intelligence Quotient on this measure is within the average range of performance. However, her quotient scores fall within the low average range in Attention-Enhanced Aptitude and Motor-Enhanced Aptitude. She earned her lowest subtest score on Oral Directions, a measure of short-term memory with a motor component. These test results are in agreement with the results of the informal assessments of specific learning abilities. In addition, because the *DTLA–2* is a norm-referenced measure, these results suggest that Joyce performs memory and motor tasks less well than the majority of her peers.

After reviewing these data, the assessment team decides to continue its investigation of the possibility of learning disabilities by carrying out a discrepancy analysis. The team uses the standard error of the difference method to evaluate the observed difference between Joyce's performance on the *WISC–R* Full Scale, a measure of aptitude, and her performance on the *WRAT–R* Spelling subtest, a measure of achievement. From the analysis results, the team determines that the discrepancy between aptitude and reading achievement is likely a true difference.

The team concludes there is evidence to suggest a discrepancy between ability and achievement. From the information gathered about specific abilities and strategies, it appears that Joyce's underachievement may be related to poor memory, inefficient memorization strategies, and a possible problem in fine motor skills. Although learning disabilities seem highly probable, the team will continue its assessment by studying Joyce's classroom behavior and social-emotional status.

STUDY GUIDE

Review Questions

1. Specific learning abilities and strategies are assessed for which of the following reasons?
   - _____ a. To assist in determining whether school performance problems are related to the handicap of learning disabilities
   - _____ b. To aid in the planning of instructional interventions for any student
   - _____ c. To identify students with behavior disorders
   - _____ d. Answers a and b
   - _____ e. All of the above

2. The specific learning abilities most often studied are memory, _____ , and _____ .

3. In the assessment of learning strategies, educators are concerned with the ways students use specific learning abilities in situations that require the acquisition of new skills or information. (True or False)

4. According to federal law, which of the following are criteria for eligibility for learning disabilities services? Check all that apply.
   - _____ a. A deficit in one or more specific learning abilities or strategies.
   - _____ b. Poor school performance.
   - _____ c. A severe discrepancy between achievement and intellectual ability.
   - _____ d. The discrepancy must exist despite the provision of appropriate learning experiences.
   - _____ e. The discrepancy cannot be the result of other handicaps or conditions.

5. Read these statements and determine whether each is true or false.
   - T F **a.** Most of the research on specific learning abilities comes from study of mentally retarded students.
   - T F **b.** The traditional approach to assessment of specific learning abilities stresses identification of deficits in areas such as visual perception, auditory discrimination, and eye-hand coordination.
   - T F **c.** One of the problems in the assessment of specific learning abilities is that many of the available measures show poor technical quality.
   - T F **d.** Learning strategies and study skills are a new area of interest in the study of learning disabilities, but as yet there are few measures available to assess them.

6. Check each of the assessment devices and procedures that can be used to gather information about specific learning abilities and strategies.
   - _____ a. Individual tests of intellectual performance
   - _____ b. Informal inventories and criterion-referenced tests
   - _____ c. Interviews with parents and teachers
   - _____ d. Measures of adaptive behavior
   - _____ e. Discrepancy analysis
   - _____ f. Behavior problem checklists
   - _____ g. Classroom observations

7. Complete this sentence. Vision and hearing screening . . .
   - _____ a. should be conducted with all students, not only those referred for special education assessment.
   - _____ b. is designed to identify students with possible problems in auditory or visual discrimination.
   - _____ c. uses devices like the audiometer to identify vision problems and measures like the Snellen Chart to identify hearing problems.
   - _____ d. produces results that allow teachers to prescribe remedial treatments.

8. Match the perceptual-motor measure in Column A with the description in Column B.

Column A	Column B
a. *Auditory Discrimination Test*	_____ A battery of tests for young children that assesses reception, association, and expression through both the auditory-vocal and visual-motor channels
b. *Motor-Free Test of Visual Perception*	_____ A measure of eye-hand coordination in which students copy geometric designs

c. *Illinois Test of Psycholinguistic*   _____ A test where students listen to pairs of words and
    Abilities   tell whether the words are the same or different
d. *Developmental Test of Visual*   _____ Assesses visual perception by having students point
    Perception   to the correct answer
e. *Detroit Tests of Learning Aptitude*   _____ Assesses several types of abilities including
                                                            linguistic, conceptual, attentional, and motoric
                                                            aptitudes
f. *Developmental Test of Visual-Motor*   _____ A measure of visual perception containing five
    Integration   subtests including Eye-Motor Coordination, Figure-
                                                            Ground, and Constancy of Shape

9. Find the true statements about learning strategies.
    _____ a. Many learning disabled students show inefficient and ineffective strategies for learning.
    _____ b. Learning disabled students recall less information than nonhandicapped students because they
                actively rehearse the material to be learned.
    _____ c. It is not possible to teach students new strategies for learning.
    _____ d. There are few measures available for the assessment of learning strategies.
    _____ e. Measures of study skills provide some information about the ways students go about learning
                tasks.

10. Complete this sentence. Discrepancy analysis . . .
    _____ a. is used to determine whether there is a significant discrepancy between expected and actual
                achievement.
    _____ b. is used to determine whether there is a significant discrepancy between general intellectual
                performance and performance on one or more measures of specific learning abilities.
    _____ c. is best accomplished with expectancy formulas.
    _____ d. is best accomplished by determining the difference between the student's current grade in
                school and grade scores on an achievement test.

11. If the special education team finds that a student with average intelligence performs in the low average or
    below average range in academic achievement, what conclusion can be drawn?
    _____ a. The student may be eligible for special education services for mentally retarded students.
    _____ b. The student may be eligible for special education services for learning disabled students.
    _____ c. The student is not eligible for special education services.
    _____ d. The student is eligible for special services in reading.

Activities

1. Locate one of the specific ability tests described in this chapter. Examine its manual for information on
    standardization procedures, reliability, and validity.

2. Under the supervision of the course instructor, administer one of the tests described in this chapter. Calculate
    the scores and analyze the results.

3. Select a classroom learning task and analyze its components. Consider the specific learning abilities and
    strategies required by the task.

4. Design an interview procedure to determine the learning strategies that students use in school tasks such as
    answering reading comprehension questions or solving mathematics problems.

5. Read the article by Arter and Jenkins (1979) or another critical review of the research on training perceptual-
    motor or psycholinguistic deficits. For another point of view, read Minskoff (1975). Summarize the conclusions
    of each article and point out the areas of difference.

6. Talk with school personnel in your area to see how they go about assessing students with learning disabilities.
    Do they use tests of specific learning abilities and, if so, which ones? Do they consider learning strategies and
    study skills? How do they assess these? Do they conduct discrepancy analyses? What methods are used?

Discussion Questions

1. Describe how specific learning abilities and strategies can affect students' performance in school subjects
    such as reading, mathematics, handwriting, and composition.

2. Compare the relative merits of the learning strategies approach to the assessment of learning disabilities and the specific learning abilities approach.

3. Discuss the research findings on the *WISC–R* performance of learning disabled students. From these findings, would you conclude there is a typical *WISC–R* profile for this group?

4. Explain the rationale for discrepancy analysis. List and describe three of the ways that discrepancy analysis can be accomplished. Tell why the standard score method is preferred.

10

Classroom Behavior

Some students are referred for special education assessment because their school behavior is judged inappropriate. Such students may be disruptive in class, disturbing instruction. They may be disobedient, unresponsive, or even aggressive. They fail to meet the teacher's expectations for appropriate classroom conduct, and their behavior calls attention to itself. These students may be eligible for special education services, if they meet criteria for the handicap of behavior disorders and if this handicap adversely affects school performance. Of course, students with behavior disorders are not the only ones who exhibit inappropriate classroom behaviors. School conduct problems may also be found in mildly retarded students, individuals with learning disabilities, and even nonhandicapped students.

Problem behaviors are the most obvious concern in assessment of classroom behavior, but there are several other important dimensions. These include the student's self-concept and self-esteem, how well the student is accepted by peers, and the student's interests and attitudes toward school. Also of interest are the characteristics of the classroom learning environment and its effects on the student's ability to behave appropriately. These dimensions of behavior are important considerations for all students referred for special education assessment.

Assessment of classroom behavior starts with a general question: *What is the student's current status in classroom behavior and in social-emotional development?* Answers to this question provide the team with an overall view of the student's current behavioral competence. Other, more specific questions may be asked if preliminary data indicate a need. For example, if the student under study appears to exhibit inappropriate behaviors, the team may ask: *Is there evidence of a severe conduct problem? What are the characteristics of the classroom learning environment?* The first question helps the team describe the student's current performance, and the second focuses attention on classroom factors that may influence behavior. If self-concept or peer interactions are of concern, the assessment question would be: *What is the student's current status in self-concept and acceptance by peers?* To find out more about the student's perceptions of school and ways to motivate him or her, the team could

ask: *What are the student's current interests and attitudes toward school and learning?* For some students, all of these questions are pertinent. With other students, the team may concentrate on one or two areas.

The results of the classroom behavior assessment assist the team in determining eligibility for special education services for individuals with behavior disorders. Results also provide the basis for designing instructional programs to improve classroom behavior. Very specific information is needed for program design, so the assessment tools selected for the study of classroom behavior usually include informal techniques. Formal, norm-referenced measures may also be used, but informal assessment is stressed. In evaluating Joyce's classroom behavior, for example, the team relied heavily upon techniques such as interviews, observations, and inventories.

Joyce

The assessment team has almost finished its initial evaluation of Joyce, the fourth grader referred for academic skill problems. The team has established that Joyce has a school performance problem despite average intellectual performance, and her underachievement is probably due to a learning disability. Next, the team will consider Joyce's classroom behavior.

Although Joyce's teacher reported no classroom conduct problems, Joyce's lowest score on the *Adaptive Behavior Inventory for Children* was in the area of Nonacademic School Roles. To study this further, the team will observe Joyce interacting with her fourth grade classmates. The observer, Ms. Gale, will look at Joyce's peer interactions in the classroom and in at least one nonacademic setting such as the lunchroom or the playground. In the classroom observation, Ms. Gale will also take note of the characteristics of the learning environment and Joyce's interactions with her teacher.

The team is also interested in Joyce's self-concept and attitudes toward school and learning. In a previous interview, Joyce's parents described her as a generally happy child who has many friends in her neighborhood. This year, however, they noticed that Joyce doesn't seem to like school as well as she used to. She's not

Individualized Assessment Plan

For: _____Joyce Dewey_____   ___4___   __10–0__   __12/1/89__   ____Ms. Gale____
            Student's Name   Grade   Age   Date   Coordinator

Reason for Referral: Difficulty keeping up with fourth grade work in reading, spelling, and handwriting

Assessment Question	Assessment Procedures	Person Responsible	Date/Time
What is the student's current status in self-concept and acceptance by peers?	Observation of peer interactions in the classroom and in nonacademic settings	Ms. Gale, Resource Teacher	1/3/90, 1/4/90, 1/5/90— Times vary
	Self concept measure such as the *Coopersmith Self-Esteem Inventory*	Ms. Kellett, School Psychologist	1/8/90 1:30 p.m.
What are the student's current interests and attitudes toward school and learning?	Informal interest inventory	Ms. Gale, Resource Teacher	1/8/90 2 p.m.
What are the characteristics of the classroom learning environment?	Classroom observation	Ms. Gale, Resource Teacher	1/3/90 and 1/5/90

interested in practicing her reading or other academic skills at home, and sometimes talks about how different she feels from the other students in her class.

To assess Joyce's self-concept, the team will administer one of the self-concept measures designed for elementary grade students. At present, the team plans to informally evaluate Joyce's attitudes toward school. An informal interest inventory will be used to find out about Joyce's current preferences in school and leisure activities. If more information is needed, Ms. Gale will interview Joyce.

CONSIDERATIONS IN ASSESSMENT OF CLASSROOM BEHAVIOR

Classroom behavior is a broad term that encompasses a range of nonacademic school behaviors. Included are the student's conduct within the school setting, response to school rules, interpersonal relationships with teachers and other students, and self-concept and attitude toward school. A classroom behavior problem can interfere with academic performance; likewise, poor academic achievement can influence classroom conduct, precipitating inappropriate social behaviors.

Purposes

Classroom behavior and social-emotional development are assessed to gain information about a student's current ability to meet the nonacademic demands of the classroom and other learning environments. The student's classroom behavior is an important consideration when planning instructional programs. It is also of interest in the identification of mild handicapping conditions, particularly behavior disorders.

Students with behavior disorders are characterized by the seriously inappropriate behaviors they exhibit over time. According to federal law, students with this handicap are called seriously emotionally disturbed.

(i) The term means a condition exhibiting one or more of the following characteristics over a long period of time and to a marked degree, which adversely affects educational performance:
   (a) An inability to learn which cannot be explained by intellectual, sensory or health factors;
   (b) An inability to build or maintain satisfactory relationships with peers and teachers;
   (c) Inappropriate types of behaviors or feelings under normal circumstances;
   (d) A general pervasive mood of unhappiness or depression; or

(e) A tendency to develop physical symptoms or fears associated with personal or school problems.

(ii) The term includes children who are schizophrenic. The term does not include children who are socially maladjusted, unless it is determined that they are seriously emotionally disturbed.
(*Federal Register*, 1977, *42*, 42474, as amended in *Federal Register*, 1981, *46*, 3866)

To meet eligibility criteria for the handicap of serious emotional disturbance, students must show a behavior disorder that is both severe and persistent. In addition, the disorder must act as a negative influence upon school performance.

The definition lists several characteristics of behavior disorders; the student must display one or more of these. One possible disorder is an inability to learn. Students whose learning problems can be explained by other handicapping conditions are excluded from consideration here. For example, if a student's difficulties in learning can be attributed to mental retardation, that student is not considered emotionally disturbed under the "inability to learn" criterion. Other characteristics listed as indicators of emotional disturbance are unsatisfactory interpersonal relationships, inappropriate behavior, depression and other mood disorders, and fears and physical symptoms associated with school and personal problems.

In assessment, there are two major approaches to the identification of behavior disorders. In the first approach, teachers, instructional aides, parents, and others well acquainted with the student provide information about the student's current behavioral status. The purpose is to determine whether the student's behavior is perceived as inappropriate by important persons in the environment. Various assessment strategies are used to gather information from informants: rating scales, checklists, interviews, and questionnaires. Some of these provide norms in addition to eliciting informants' judgments. In the second approach, emphasis is on direct observation of the student and the environment where the student is experiencing difficulty.

Direct observation and the questioning of informants are not mutually exclusive. In fact, both are typically used. Teachers and parents point to the existence of a behavior problem, and direct observation allows intensive study of that problem.

Issues and Trends

Many of the issues related to assessment of classroom behavior are tied to issues within the field of behavior disorders. One basic concern is what to call this handicapping condition. *Emotional disturbance* is the more traditional term, and federal law uses a variation of this, *seriously emotionally disturbed*. However, many educators prefer the term *behavior disorders* because it emphasizes behaviors and behaviors can be changed. For example, within the Council for Exceptional Children, the professional organization for educators of students with this handicap is called the Council for Children with Behavioral Disorders (CCBD), and it publishes a journal entitled *Behavioral Disorders*.

Differences in terminology are reflections of theoretical differences. There are several theoretical approaches to the study of behavior disorders; in each, the handicap is viewed in a somewhat different way. As Table 10–1 shows, each theoretical model has its own way of describing disordered behavior, goals for educational intervention, and methods of instruction. Each also approaches assessment differently. For example, the behavioral model holds that behavior disorders are the result of learning; the student has learned inappropriate behaviors or failed to learn appropriate behaviors. Its focus is on the overt behaviors of the student. In contrast, the ecological approach emphasizes the student's interactions with the environment. Behavior disorders are seen as problems in interaction, not as a dysfunction within the student. In assessment, both student and environmental characteristics are studied.

Another major issue is definition of the handicap. As Shea (1978) observed, "There appear to be as many definitions of behavior-disordered children and youth as there are authors to write about them and purposes for writing them" (p. 5). Defining this handicap is difficult for several reasons:

☐ Lack of an adequate definition of mental health and normal behavior
☐ Difficulties in measuring emotions and behavior
☐ Relationships between ED/BD and other handicapping conditions
☐ Differences in the functions of socialization agents who categorize and serve children (Hallahan & Kauffman, 1988, p. 162)

TABLE 10–1
Theories of behavior disorders

	Psychoanalytic Approach	Psycho-educational Approach	Humanistic Approach	Ecological Approach	Behavioral Approach
The problem	A pathological imbalance among the dynamic parts of the mind (id, superego, ego).	Involves both underlying psychiatric disorders and the readily observable misbehavior and underachievement of the child.	The ED/BD child is out of touch with his or her own feelings and can't find fulfillment in traditional educational settings.	The child interacts poorly with the environment; child and environment affect each other reciprocally and negatively.	The child has learned inappropriate responses and failed to learn appropriate ones.
Purpose of educational practices	Use of psychoanalytic principles to help uncover underlying mental pathology.	Concern for unconscious motivation/underlying conflicts *and* academic achievement/positive surface behavior.	Emphasis on enhancing child's self-direction, self-evaluation, and emotional involvement in learning.	Attempt to alter entire social system so that it will support desirable behavior in child when intervention is withdrawn.	Manipulation of child's immediate environment and the consequences of behavior.
Characteristics of teaching methods	Reliance on individual psychotherapy for child and parents; little emphasis on academic achievement; highly permissive atmosphere.	Emphasis on meeting individual needs of the child; reliance on projects and creative arts.	Use of nontraditional educational settings in which teacher serves as resource and catalyst rather than as director of activities; nonauthoritarian, open, affective, personal atmosphere.	Involves all aspects of a child's life, including classroom, family, neighborhood, and community, in teaching the child useful life and educational skills.	Involves measurement of responses and subsequent analyses of behaviors in order to change them; emphasis on reward for appropriate behavior.

Note. From David P. Hallahan & James M. Kauffman, *EXCEPTIONAL CHILDREN: Introduction to Special Education* (4th ed.), © 1988, p. 188. Reprinted with permission of Prentice-Hall, Inc., Englewood Cliffs, NJ.

Deciding if behaviors are inappropriate is a somewhat subjective process. The same behavior may be judged appropriate at one age but not at another. For example, ceaseless activity and exploration are expected of 2-year-olds, but not of sixth graders. Culture and gender influence behavioral expectations. What is viewed as normal play among boys may be labeled aggressive in girls. Because it is not possible to set up one standard for normal behavior, it is also difficult to state criteria for disordered behavior, except in very severe cases. Obviously, there would be little debate over the inappropriateness of behaviors such as assault or arson.

At present, school practices in the assessment and treatment of behavior disorders appear to be most influenced by the behavioral model. In this approach, applied behavioral analysis techniques are used to identify behaviors of interest, observe and measure those behaviors, and then change them through manipulation of environmental events (Alberto & Troutman, 1986; Cooper et al., 1987). The ecological perspective has also gained support, at least in assessment. Thus, there is interest in the characteristics of the environment where the student must function (Swap, 1974; Thurman, 1977).

Current Practices

Classroom behavior is a concern of all teachers, and assessment of student behavior is a regular occurrence in both regular and special education. At the classroom level, teachers typically rely on informal techniques such as observation to gather information about student behavior. When assessment is conducted to determine a student's eligibility for special programs, more formal instruments may be used.

In general, special education assessment begins with the questioning of informants. Most typically, informants are interviewed or asked to complete one of the many available behavioral rating scales or checklists. Many of the commonly used rating scales are formal, normed instruments. This chapter describes several of these rating scales, including the *Behavior Rating Profile* (Brown & Hammill, 1983a) and the *Walker Problem Behavior Identification Checklist* (Walker, 1983).

Both formal and informal measures are available to study other aspects of student behavior such as self-concept, acceptance by peers, interests, and attitudes toward school. These too are described in this chapter. Formal measures are typically selected if the goal of assessment is to determine whether a problem exists. If the goal is to gather information for program planning, informal tools are preferred. Informal techniques are also used to investigate the classroom learning environment and its effects upon student behavior.

As Table 10–2 shows, current practices in the educational assessment of behavior problems incorporate many types of formal measures. However, tests of personality are seldom included. Personality tests are indirect measures, not direct measures of behavior or even attitude or opinion surveys. For example, on projective tests, the student is presented with ambiguous stimuli, and then personality traits are inferred from the student's descriptions of these stimuli. One problem with such measures is their lack of technical adequacy (Salvia & Ysseldyke, 1988). Another is their lack of educational relevance. Because of these limitations, personality measures are rarely used in schools today.

SOURCES OF INFORMATION ABOUT CLASSROOM BEHAVIOR

Several sources can contribute information about the student's current and past classroom behavior: school records, parents, teachers, and the student himself or herself. In addition, the student's peers may be questioned about their perceptions to determine how well the student is accepted by classmates.

School Records

School records may help the team gain a historical perspective of the student's classroom behavior problem. If the problem is long-standing, particular attention should be paid to the results of past interventions.

Discipline and attendance records. Educational records usually contain information about school disciplinary actions. For example, if the student has been sent to the principal or vice-principal for breaking classroom or school rules, there will likely be a record of the incident and the disciplinary action that resulted. The team should

TABLE 10–2
Formal measures of classroom behavior and related concerns

Name (Authors)	Ages or Grades
CLASSROOM BEHAVIOR AND SOCIAL-EMOTIONAL DEVELOPMENT	
Behavior Evaluation Scale (McCarney, Leigh, & Cornbleet, 1983)	Gr. K–12
Behavior Rating Profile (Brown & Hammill, 1983a)	Gr. 1–12, Ages 6–6 to 18–6
Burks' Behavior Rating Scales (Burks, 1977)	Gr. 1–9
Child Behavior Rating Scale (Cassell, 1962)	Gr. K–3
Devereux Behavior Rating Scales (Spivack, Haimes, & Spotts, 1967; Spivack & Spotts, 1966; Swift, 1982)	Gr. 1–6 and Ages 8 to 18
Hahnemann High School Behavior Rating Scale (Spivack & Swift, 1972)	Gr. 7–12
Mooney Problem Check Lists (Mooney & Gordon, 1950)	Gr. 7–12, college
Pupil Behavior Rating Scale (Lambert, Bower, & Hartsough, 1979)	Gr. K–7
Pupil Rating Scale Revised (Myklebust, 1981)	Gr. K–6
Revised Behavior Problem Checklist (Quay & Peterson, 1987)	Gr. K–8 regular class, Gr. K–12 special class
School Behavior Checklist (Miller, 1977)	Ages 4 to 13
School Social Skills Rating Scale (Brown, Black, & Downs, 1984)	School ages
Social-Emotional Dimension Scale (Hutton & Roberts, 1986)	Ages 5–6 to 18–5
Test of Early Socioemotional Development (Hresko & Brown, 1984)	Ages 3–0 to 7–11
Walker Problem Behavior Identification Checklist (Walker, 1983)	Ages 2 to 5, Gr. K–6
Walker-McConnell Scale of Social Competence and School Adjustment (Walker & McConnell, 1988)	Gr. K–6
SELF-CONCEPT	
Coopersmith Self-Esteem Inventories (Coopersmith, 1981)	Ages 8 to adult
Piers-Harris Children's Self Concept Scale (Piers & Harris, 1984)	Gr. 4–12
Dimensions of Self-Concept (Michael, Smith, & Michael, 1984)	Gr. 4–12 and college
Tennessee Self-Concept Scale (Fitts & Roid, 1988)	Age 12 and above
PEER ACCEPTANCE	
Behavior Rating Profile (Brown & Hammill, 1983a)	Gr. 1–12, Ages 6–6 to 18–6
Peer Attitudes Toward the Handicapped Scale (Bagley & Greene, 1981)	Gr. 4–8
Test of Early Socioemotional Development (Hresko & Brown, 1984)	Ages 3–0 to 7–11
Pupil Behavior Rating Scale (Lambert, Bower, & Hartsough, 1979)	Gr. K–7
SCHOOL INTERESTS AND ATTITUDES	
Estes Attitude Scales (Estes, Estes, Richards, & Roettger, 1981)	Gr. 2–12
School Interest Inventory (Cottle, 1966)	Gr. 7–12
Survey of School Attitudes (Hogan, 1973, 1975)	Gr. 1–8
Woodcock-Johnson Psycho-Educational Battery, Part Three, Tests of Interest (Woodcock & Johnson, 1977)	Ages 3 to 80 +

examine these records to determine whether the student has a history of conduct problems. Also, attendance records should be reviewed for information about truancy, chronic tardiness, and excessive school absences. If the student has come into conflict with the law, school records may contain information about the charges and their disposition (probation, referrals for counseling or other services, jail sentences, and so forth). In addition, the team should take special note of any information about reported incidents of child abuse, alcohol or substance abuse, or attempted suicide.

Observations of former teachers. The student's former teachers may have left some written records of their observations of the student's classroom behavior. The team should consider report cards from previous years, copies of letters from teachers to parents, and any past referrals for special education assessment.

Past services. Also of interest are any services that the student received in relation to behavior problems. For example, the student may have received school counseling services, or the school may have suggested counseling services to the student's family. If records are available, the team should attempt to determine the types of services provided and the effects of those services on the student's behavior.

The Student

The student assists in the assessment of classroom behavior by participating in observations and by answering questions about current behavior, attitudes, and perceptions.

Current classroom behavior. Direct observation of student behavior is one of the most valuable techniques for gathering data about classroom conduct. The student's role in this assessment technique is simply to behave as usual. This is facilitated if the observer takes care not to call attention to the observation process or to the particular student under study.

Current attitudes and perceptions. The student can also participate by acting as an informant about his or her own behavior and attitudes. For instance, some behavior rating scales are designed to be completed by students, allowing them to

rate their own behaviors. In the assessment of self-concept, interests, and attitudes toward school, students are the primary source of information. They may complete interest inventories, talk about their attitudes about school and learning, or reply to questions on measures of self-concept.

Teachers

Teachers have the best opportunity of all professionals to observe and evaluate the student's day-to-day behavior in the classroom. Teachers are also an excellent source of information about the characteristics of the classroom learning environment.

Observations of current behavior. Behavioral rating scales and checklists are often used to gather information from teachers about student behavior. These measures allow teachers to share their observations of the student's typical behavior patterns and their judgments about the appropriateness of the student's classroom conduct. Interviews are also useful for eliciting teachers' opinions.

Characteristics of the learning environment. Teachers can provide firsthand information about the characteristics of their classroom. Among the major considerations are the teacher's rules for classroom conduct, strategies for rewarding appropriate behavior, and standard disciplinary techniques. Because there may be wide variations among the behavioral demands of different classrooms, it is important to consider the teacher's standards when interpreting his or her reports of problem behaviors.

Peers

Peers are usually not participants in special education assessment, but in the area of classroom behavior, they can contribute information about the student's social acceptance and interpersonal relationships.

Peer acceptance and interactions. Peers can be involved in the assessment process in two major ways. The first area of interest is the general attitudes of regular class peers toward students with learning and behavior problems. These attitudes can be surveyed through interviews or with a questionnaire designed for this purpose. This provides information about peer attitudes toward handicapped students in general. To find out about acceptance of a particular student, it is necessary to use sociometric techniques, another assessment strategy. These techniques sample students' opinions about the peers with whom they would like to work and play. The results provide a picture of the social interactions within a classroom, identifying students who are and are not accepted by their classmates.

Parents

Parents may be unfamiliar with classroom behavior, but they can discuss their child's behavior in the home and other nonschool settings.

Observations of current behavior. A student with classroom behavior problems may or may not act inappropriately at home. The same types of inappropriate behavior could occur both at school and at home, the student could show a different set of problem behaviors at home, or home behavior could be acceptable. Parents can discuss their observations of their child's typical conduct and any concerns they might have. They can describe what approaches they have used in trying to improve problem behaviors and the results of these efforts. If the problem is long-standing, parents may be able to share information about intervention programs in which the child and perhaps the family have participated.

Characteristics of the home environment. Because the rules for behavior at home may be quite different from school demands, parents should be asked to describe the behavioral expectations they hold for their child. Also of interest are their strategies for encouraging appropriate behavior and discouraging inappropriate behavior. What type of discipline system is used in the home? What consequences does the child face for breaking the rules? The child's parents can also provide information about family makeup. Are both parents present in the home? Does the child have brothers and sisters? Are there other individuals or family members living in the home as part of the family? In addition, the assessment team should be alert to any major changes or stresses within the family such as divorce, unemployment, or the protracted illness or death of a family member. Such changes affect family dynamics and may have an influence on the student's ability to behave appropriately in school.

BEHAVIOR RATING SCALES AND CHECKLISTS

A wide variety of rating scales and checklists are available for assessing classroom behavior. These measures vary in several ways: the age of the student to be rated, the person or persons used as informants, the types of behaviors included on the scale, and the scores produced. The next sections describe two of the scales that focus on in-school behaviors.

Behavior Rating Profile

The *Behavior Rating Profile (BRP)* is an interesting norm-referenced measure because it attempts to provide a comprehensive picture of the student's current behavioral status. Information may be gathered from four types of informants—students themselves, teachers, parents, and peers—to assess the student's performance in the home, at school, and in interpersonal relationships.

The *BRP* is made up of four measures that correspond to the different types of informants. The self-rating scale, called the *Student Rating Scale*, is composed of 60 items. One third of the items are concerned with school behaviors, one third with home behaviors, and one third with peer interactions. For instance, "I often break rules set by my parents" is a home item, whereas "I can't seem to concentrate in class" is a school item. The student reads each item and checks whether it is true or false. If necessary, the tester may read the questions aloud to the student and explain the meaning of unknown words.

The *Teacher Rating Scale* is made up of 30 descriptions of school behaviors. The teacher reads each item and determines whether the description is "very much like the student," "like the student," "not much like the student," or "not at all like the student." An example of an item on the teacher scale is "The student doesn't follow class rules." The manual recommends that the student be in the classroom at least a month before teacher or peer ratings are taken.

The *Parent Rating Scale* is quite similar to the teacher scale, except that it contains descriptions of home behaviors (for example, "My child is shy and clings to me"). Each description is rated as "very much like my child," "like my child," "not much like my child," or "not at all like my child." The *Parent Rating Scale* can be completed by the

---

BEHAVIOR RATING PROFILE (BRP)
L. L. Brown & D. D. Hammill (1983a)

Type: Norm-referenced teacher rating scale, parent rating scale, student checklist, and sociogram

Major Content Areas: School behavior, home behavior, interpersonal relationships

Type of Administration: Individual for teachers, parents, and students; group for peers

Administration Time: 10–15 minutes for teachers, 15–20 minutes for parents, 15–30 minutes for students, 5–10 minutes for peers

Age/Grade Levels: Ages 6–6 to 18–6, grades 1–12

Types of Scores: Standard scores, percentile ranks

Typical Uses: Identification of students with possible behavior disorders who may be in need of further assessment

Cautions: On the *Student Rating Scale,* some students may require assistance in reading the checklist items.

---

child's mother or father, or both parents can rate their child independently.

The peer portion of the *BRP* is not a rating scale. Instead, a sociometric technique is used, and the student's classmates are asked questions such as "Which of the students in your class would you most (least) like to . . . " Several sets of questions are available, each tapping a different aspect of interpersonal relationships. For example, students can name the peers with whom they'd most like to be friends. According to the *BRP* manual, a minimum of 20 peers must participate for scoring to be accurate.

As Figure 10–1 illustrates, results from the *BRP* can be plotted on a profile. Standard scores are produced by each of the rating scales and the sociograms, and percentile ranks are also available. Standard scores are distributed with a mean of 10 and a standard deviation of 3; the range of average performance is standard score 7 through 13. Several scores are available from the *BRP* depending upon which of the scales were administered. If the student under study completed the *Student Rating Scale,* three separate scores are reported: Home, School, and Peer. There is one score for each teacher who rated the student and one for each parent. Also, each sociometric question answered by the student's peers produces a score. Data can be gathered from all of these sources, or depending upon the purposes of assessment, only one portion of the *BRP* can be selected for administration.

The *BRP* was standardized on approximately 2,000 regular class students, 1,000 teachers, and 1,200 parents from 15 states. The internal consistency of the scales appears adequate, as does the test-retest reliability. The standard error of measurement is low. On the parent, teacher, and student scales, standard error ranges from 0.4 to 1.6 standard score points over all grade levels.

Concurrent validity was studied by examining the relationships between *BRP* scores and results from other rating scales. In general, *BRP* results were found to be consistent with those from other measures. The diagnostic validity of the *BRP* was investigated by comparing the ratings of four groups of students, and different group profiles emerged. Normal students were rated as showing fewer problem behaviors than handicapped students. Among handicapped students, institutionalized emotionally disturbed students were rated as showing more problem behaviors than either public school emotionally disturbed or learning disabled students.

The *BRP* appears to be a reliable and valid tool for gathering information from a range of informants about perceptions of a student's behavior in several different ecologies. It is one of the few instruments that allows students to rate themselves and that involves peers in the assessment process. Also of note is the availability of a Spanish-language version of the *BRP*, the *Perfil de Evaluacion del Comportamiento* (Brown & Hammill, 1983b) and a version for preschool children, the

FIGURE 10–1

Sample *Behavior Rating Profile* results

B R P

BEHAVIOR RATING PROFILE SHEET

LINDA L. BROWN & DONALD D. HAMMILL

Name *Joey Stewart*

Parent's Name *David & Ellen Stewart*

Address *110 Allen St.*

School *David Brewer*

Teacher (Grade) *Ms. Brooks* (*3*)

Examiner *Dr. J. Brothers—School Psch.*

Referred by *Ms. Brooks*

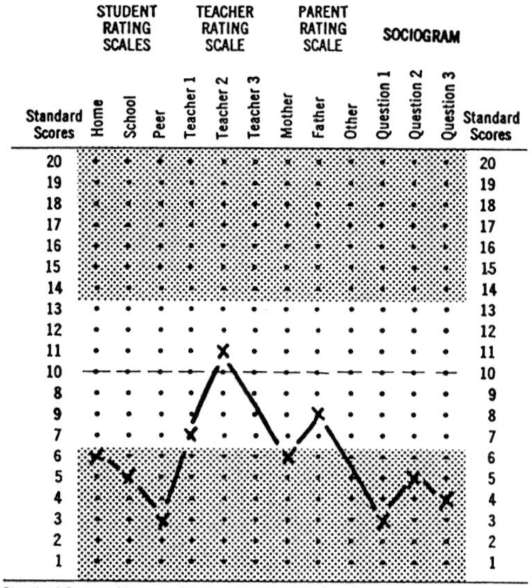

Date Tested *82* YEAR *10* MONTH

Date of Birth *74* YEAR *1* MONTH

Age *8* YEARS *9* MONTHS

Profile graph — STUDENT RATING SCALES (Home, School, Peer), TEACHER RATING SCALE (Teacher 1, Teacher 2, Teacher 3), PARENT RATING SCALE (Mother, Father, Other), SOCIOGRAM (Question 1, Question 2, Question 3); Standard Scores 1–20.

Standard Scores: Mean = 10, Standard Deviation = 3

COMMENTS:

BRP Scales	Raw Scores	Standard Scores	Percentile Ranks
Student Rating Scales			
Home Scale	8	6	10
School Scale	6	5	5
Peer Scale	2	3	1
Teacher Rating Scale			
Teacher # 1	47	7	16
Teacher # 2	79	11	64
Teacher # 3	—	—	—
Parent Rating Scale			
Mother	54	6	10
Father	66	9	36
Other	—	—	—
Sociogram			
Question # 1	27/27	3	1
Question # 2	25/27	5	5
Question # 3	26/26	4	2

Test of Early Socioemotional Development (Hresko & Brown, 1984).

Walker Problem Behavior Identification Checklist

The *Walker* is a norm-referenced behavior checklist designed as a screening instrument for use by teachers of preschool and elementary grade children. According to the manual, the *Walker* is a tool for "identifying children with behavior problems and disorders who should be referred for further psychological evaluation, referral, and treatment" (p. 1).

The *Walker* contains 50 statements that describe inappropriate classroom behaviors. The teacher's task is to read each statement and identify those that describe the student under study. Parents can also be asked to complete the checklist. Although norms are based upon teacher ratings, Walker (1983) cites evidence of a strong relationship between teachers' and parents' responses to this checklist. However, parents and teachers may rate a student's behavior differently because they view the student from different perspectives.

Five scales, representing five types of behavior problems, are included on the *Walker:* Acting Out, Withdrawal, Distractibility, Disturbed Peer Relations, and Immaturity. For example, "Reacts with defiance to instructions or commands" is an item from the Acting Out scale and "Does not engage in group activities" is an example from the Withdrawal scale. Each scale is scored separately, and a total score is available.

The *Walker* provides norms for three ranges of grade levels: preschool through kindergarten, grades 1–3, and grades 4–6. High raw scores and corresponding T-scores indicate maladaptive behavior. According to the *Walker* manual, T-scores of 60 or above (that is, one or more standard deviations above the mean) signal a need for further evaluation.

The *Walker* was normed with samples of approximately 500 preschool/kindergarten children, 900 primary grade children, and 500 intermediate grade children. However, only 85 teachers participated in the norming study. Another concern is that subjects were selected from only two locations, a city in Oregon and a school district in the state of Washington. This may limit the usefulness of this instrument for students different from those in the standardization sample.

Split-half reliability of the *Walker* is adequate. Test-retest reliability is higher for the total test score than for the scores from the individual scales. For example, in a study by Walker and Bull (1970), the test-retest coefficients for individual scales ranged from .43 to .88. Interrater reliability was studied by having regular and special education teachers rate the same group of handicapped students. On four of the five *Walker* scales, regular teachers rated the students' behavior as more

---

WALKER PROBLEM BEHAVIOR IDENTIFICATION CHECKLIST
H. M. Walker (1983)

Type: Norm-referenced teacher checklist
Major Content Areas: School behavior
Type of Administration: Individual
Administration Time: Approximately 15 minutes
Age/Grade Levels: Preschool (ages 2 to 5), kindergarten, grades 1 through 6
Types of Scores: T-scores
Typical Uses: Identification of students with possible school behavior problems who may be in need of further assessment
Cautions: Results should be interpreted with caution because of the lack of representativeness of the standardization sample, low test-retest reliabilities for some scales, poor interrater reliability between regular and special education teachers, and the need for further information about the *Walker*'s relationship to other behavior rating scales and checklists.

inappropriate than special teachers. Walker (1983) suggests several explanations for this finding: regular teachers may hold higher expectations for student behavior than special teachers, handicapped students may behave more inappropriately in regular classes than in special classes, or regular teachers may believe that handicapped students are less competent than nonhandicapped students.

Validity of the *Walker* checklist was investigated by comparing the teacher ratings of normal students and students identified as behaviorally disturbed. Teachers rated the behavior of handicapped students as more maladaptive than that of normal students. Several other validity studies are described in the manual, including intervention studies and factor analyses. However, there is need for further investigation of the relationship between the 1983 *Walker* and other behavioral rating scales and checklists.

The *Walker* is often used in schools for the identification of students with possible behavior disorders. It is a quick measure that can be completed by classroom teachers. However, limitations include the lack of representativeness of its norm group and the lack of information about its relationship to other rating scales and checklists. On the positive side, instructional programs have been developed for improving three of the types of maladaptive behaviors assessed by the *Walker:* acting out (Hops et al., 1978; Walker & Hops, 1979), social withdrawal (Hops, Walker, & Greenwood, 1979), and distractibility (Greenwood et al., 1979).

Other Measures

The *BRP* and the *Walker* are but two of the many behavior rating scales and checklists available, as Table 10–3 shows. Most of these measures are designed for school-aged populations, particularly elementary grade students. However, the *Walker* applies to the preschool years, the *Test of Early Socioemotional Development* is intended primarily for preschool children, and the *Child Behavior Rating Scale* concentrates on the early school years, kindergarten through grade 3. Measures have also been developed specifically for adolescents, most notably the *Devereux Adolescent Behavior Rating Scale* and the *Hahnemann High School Behavior Rating Scale.*

Most behavior rating scales and checklists use teachers, or teachers and parents, as informants. Rarely are the student and peers involved. Exceptions to general practice are the *Behavior Rating Profile,* which includes teachers, parents, students, and peers, and the *Pupil Behavior Rating Scale,* which includes teachers, students, and peers.

Measures also vary on the types of behaviors they ask informants to consider and the theoretical frameworks used to interpret behavioral ratings. For example, on the *Walker,* results are interpreted according to the five theoretical classes of behavior problems mentioned earlier. Likewise, the research instrument developed by Quay and Peterson, the *Revised Behavior Problem Checklist,* classifies student behaviors according to six domains: Conduct Disorder, Socialized Aggression, Attention Problems-Immaturity, Anxiety-Withdrawal, Psychotic Behavior, and Motor Excess. According to Gresham (1982), the *BPC* is the teacher rating scale with the strongest base of empirical support.

In contrast, measures such as the *Burks' Behavior Rating Scales* emphasize personality traits rather than behavior disorders. According to its manual, the *Burks* is "specifically designed to identify patterns of pathological behavior shown by children" (p. 5). This measure clusters items into 19 categories, such as Excessive Self-Blame, Excessive Anxiety, Poor Ego Strength, and Poor Reality Contact.

At the other extreme are measures such as the *Behavior Rating Profile* that focus on observable school and home behaviors. The *Behavior Evaluation Scale* provides the teacher with descriptions of common school behaviors, and the teacher rates the frequency with which those behaviors occur. Items are grouped according to the types of behavior disorders described in the federal definition of emotional disturbance: Learning Problems, Interpersonal Difficulties, Inappropriate Behavior, Unhappiness/Depression, and Physical Symptoms/Fears. In addition, a supplemental Data Collection Form is provided for professionals who wish to conduct direct observations.

A great many behavior rating scales and checklists are available to screen students with possible behavior disorders, so it is necessary to select the most appropriate measure for the assessment task at hand. Psychometric quality, theoretical characteristics, the type of informants consulted, and the

TABLE 10–3
Behavior rating scales and checklists

Name	Rating Scale (R) or Checklist (C)	Ages or Grades	INFORMANTS			
			Teachers	Parents	Student	Peers
Behavior Evaluation Scale	R	Gr. K–12	*			
Behavior Rating Profile	R, C	Gr. 1–12, Ages 6–6 to 18–6	*	*	*	*
Burks' Behavior Rating Scales	R	Gr. 1–9	*	*		
Child Behavior Rating Scale	R	Gr. K–3	*	*		
Devereux Adolescent Behavior Rating Scale	R	Ages 13–18		*		
Devereux Child Behavior Rating Scale	R	Ages 8–12		*		
Devereux Elementary School Behavior Rating Scale II	R	Gr. 1–6	*			
Hahnemann High School Behavior Rating Scale	R	Gr. 7–12	*			
Mooney Problem Check Lists	C	Gr. 7–12, college			*	
Pupil Behavior Rating Scale	R	Gr. K–7	*		*	*
Pupil Rating Scale Revised	R	Gr. K–6	*			
Revised Behavior Problem Checklist	R	Gr. K–8 regular class, Gr. K–12 special class	*	*		
School Behavior Checklist	C, R	Ages 4 to 13	*			
School Social Skills Rating Scale	R	School ages	*			
Social-Emotional Dimension Scale	R	Ages 5–6 to 18–5	*			
Test of Early Socioemotional Development	R, C	Ages 3–0 to 7–11	*	*	*	*
Walker Problem Behavior Identification Checklist	C	Ages 2 to 5, Gr. K–6	*			
Walker-McConnell Scale of Social Competence and School Adjustment	R	Gr. K–6	*			

age and grade of the student must be considered. In addition, there may be considerable overlap among the factors measured by similar teacher scales (Harris, Drummond, Schultz, & King, 1978); one teacher rating scale or checklist is usually sufficient. If adaptive behavior has been assessed, results should be reviewed, because adaptive behavior measures often include questions about student behavior, interpersonal relationships, and social-emotional development.

DIRECT OBSERVATION AND OTHER INFORMAL TECHNIQUES

Behavior rating scales and checklists provide preliminary information about student conduct problems. Like teacher and parent interviews, they are screening techniques. Further study is needed for two reasons. First, rating scales, checklists, and interviews rely upon informants rather than direct evaluation of student behavior. Direct measures are needed to substantiate the existence of a behavioral problem. Second, the results of many screening measures are too general to assist in program planning.

Direct observation of student behavior is the recommended procedure for in-depth study of the possible problem behaviors identified by rating scales, checklists, and interviews. Another way to explore potential behavior problems is through measures that focus on one specific behavioral domain such as hyperactivity, impulsivity, or self-control.

Direct Observation

Observation is a versatile assessment technique that can be used to study any type of student behavior—appropriate or inappropriate, academic or social, at home or at school. In the assessment of school behavior problems, data are gathered about the frequency and/or duration of specific student behaviors within the classroom learning environment.

The first step in planning an observation is to decide which behavior will be studied. It is possible to observe and record all the behaviors that a student displays within a certain time period, but usually observations focus upon one or more specific behaviors. Results of rating scales, checklists, and teacher and parent interviews may suggest

possible behaviors of concern. These sources are most useful for identifying possible inappropriate behaviors because they tend to focus on classroom conduct problems. In classroom observations, it is also important to consider the student's academic behaviors. Wallace and Kauffman (1986) have identified four significant classes of academic behavior: (a) accepting tasks provided by the teacher, (b) completing tasks within a reasonable amount of time, (c) working neatly and accurately, and (d) participating in group activities.

The procedures for conducting behavioral observations were described in detail in Chapter 5, the chapter on informal assessment. The major steps are briefly reviewed.

Describe the behavior to be observed. Before a behavior can be observed, it must be clearly and precisely described. "The student is disruptive" is too general a statement; it must be translated into one or more precise descriptions. For example, a disruptive student might be described as one who talks or yells out during class without permission. Talking and yelling are behaviors that can be observed and counted, and as such they are suitable targets for observation.

Select a measurement system. There are several systems available for the measurement of behaviors. Discrete behaviors can be measured by counting their frequency and/or by timing their duration. With nondiscrete behaviors such as talking with peers, interval recording or time sampling is used. The observation period is broken into several short time intervals, and the observer notes whether the behavior is or is not occurring at some point in each interval.

Set up the data-collection system. There are several considerations in setting up the data-collection system: who will collect the data, when and where the observations will occur, how many observations will take place, and how data will be recorded. In general, observations should be scheduled at the time and location where the target behavior is most likely to occur. The student's teacher may collect observational data or another member of the assessment team may act as observer. Several observations should be conducted; one observation is not sufficient to provide a picture of the student's typical pattern of behavior. If classroom conduct is the concern, the student should be observed daily for a minimum of 5 school days.

Select a data-reporting system. The results of observations are usually graphed. Graphs communicate large amounts of information quickly and allow identification of trends and patterns in behaviors. Graphs can be used to report any type of observational data: frequency, rate, and percentage of occurrence; duration; percentage of time; and so forth. Examples of several types of graphs were provided in Chapter 5. A graph that reports the results of a series of observations of several behaviors is depicted in Figure 10–2.

FIGURE 10–2
Sample graph of observation results

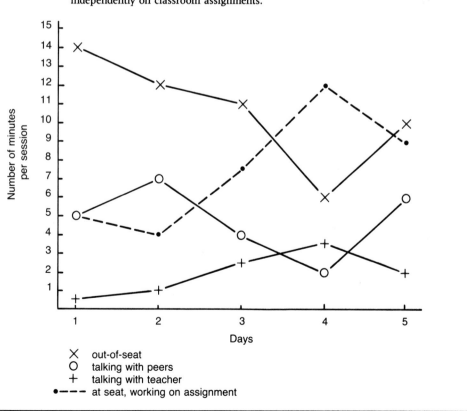

Student: Michael   Grade: 4
Observer: Ms. Garcia, Resource Teacher
Target Behaviors: Out-of-seat
                  Talking with peers
                  Talking with teacher
                  At seat, working on assignments
Measurement System: Duration recording
Data-Collection System: Observations were conducted in Michael's fourth grade classroom during the daily
                        independent work period (10:00 to 10:20 a.m.) for 5 consecutive school days. During
                        this period, students are expected to remain in their seats and work quietly and
                        independently on classroom assignments.

Number of minutes per session (vertical axis)
Days (horizontal axis)

X   out-of-seat
O   talking with peers
+   talking with teacher
●——— at seat, working on assignment

In this example, Michael was observed during the daily classroom work period to determine how long each day he sat at his seat and worked quietly on his assignment without talking with others. Also of interest were three behaviors incompatible with quiet, independent, in-seat work: out-of-seat, talking with peers, and talking with the teacher.

Carry out the observations. Observations are carried out, and then the final step—interpretation of results—takes place. Data are evaluated to determine whether or not a behavior problem exists, that is, whether or not intervention is needed. The process of making this decision is complex. Observations are informal techniques without norms or other guidelines to assist in evaluating whether a particular student's behavior is acceptable. There are no criteria that indicate how frequent or of what duration a behavior must be to warrant special attention. Thus, professionals must rely on their own best judgments when interpreting observation results.

Eaves (1982) has proposed a possible alternative. In Eaves's model, information is collected about student behavior in two ways: rating scales are completed by important persons in the student's environment, and student behavior is directly observed. A major feature of this model is that local or regional norms are developed for specific student behaviors. Observation becomes a norm-referenced technique, and it is possible to determine how one student's behavior compares to that of age or grade peers. In an example provided by Eaves, a student showing disruptive behavior 24% of the time scores at the 98th percentile in disruptiveness. One who is noncompliant 1.8% of the time scores at the 99th percentile in noncompliance. Such a system would greatly facilitate the interpretation of observational data. However, as Eaves points out, this proposal is not yet a reality. Before such a system could be used, standardized observation schedules would have to be developed and normative data collected for different regions, age levels, and types of classrooms.

Measures of Specific Problem Behaviors

Some problem behaviors are of such concern to educators and other professionals that specific measures have been developed for their assessment. For example, there is much interest in the set of behaviors related to self-control, particularly the problem behaviors of hyperactivity and impulsivity.

Hyperactivity means excessive activity. The term refers to a level of activity perceived as excessive for the age of the student and the situation where it is displayed. Obviously, judgments about hyperactivity must be somewhat subjective. There are no established criteria for normal activity levels. Thus, it is difficult to differentiate between active and hyperactive student behavior.

Several measures are available to assist in evaluating activity level. Poggio and Salkind (1979) have evaluated many of the procedures used to study hyperactivity, reaching these conclusions:

1. A variety of behavioral assessment scales and techniques to assess activity level have been devised.
2. The majority of instruments have documented interrater reliability that, while not always high, tends to be acceptable.
3. Evidence regarding other types of reliability such as test-retest, internal consistency, and standard error of measurement is typically lacking.
4. Authors often make no attempt to improve the reliability of their measures.
5. Independent validity studies are seriously lacking.
6. The source of the items on the scales often has no theoretical rationale.
7. Few authors have established norms. (p. 21)

These findings suggest the need for caution in selecting measures of hyperactivity.

The *Conners' Teacher Rating Scale* (Conners, 1969) is one of the more popular tools for assessing activity level. An abbreviated version of this scale appears in Figure 10–3. It is a teacher rating instrument, and Sprague and Sleator (1973) recommend that the student be observed in the classroom for 1 to 4 weeks before behavior is rated. The teacher completes the form by rating the student's activity level on a 4-point scale, from "not at all" (0) to "very much" (3), for behaviors such as restlessness, excitability, and inattentiveness.

Impulsivity is a second problem behavior related to self-control. Impulsivity refers to a tendency to act quickly without careful thought. Impulsivity may have a negative effect upon school learning, if students' hasty responses are inaccurate. At the other end of the continuum is reflective behavior. The *Matching Familiar Figures Test (MFFT)* by Kagan (1965) is the assessment tool most often

FIGURE 10–3
Conners' Abbreviated Teacher Rating Scale

Child's Name _____

TEACHER'S OBSERVATIONS

Information obtained _____ By _____
　　　　　　　　　　Month　　　Day　　　Year

Observation	Degree of Activity			
	Not at all 0	Just a little 1	Pretty much 2	Very much 3
1. Restless or overactive				
2. Excitable, impulsive				
3. Disturbs other children				
4. Fails to finish things he starts, short attention span				
5. Constantly fidgeting				
6. Inattentive, easily distracted				
7. Demands must be met immediately—easily frustrated				
8. Cries often and easily				
9. Mood changes quickly and drastically				
10. Temper outbursts, explosive and unpredictable behavior				

OTHER OBSERVATIONS OF TEACHER (Use reverse side if more space is required.)

_____

_____

Note. From "Effects of Psychopharmacologic Agents on Learning Disorders" by R. Sprague and E. Sleator, 1973. *Pediatric Clinics of North America, 20,* p. 726. Copyright 1973 by W. B. Saunders Co. Reprinted by permission.

used in research studies to investigate impulsivity and reflectivity. On this test, the student is shown a familiar figure such as a house or a tree. He or she then attempts to select an identical figure from six choices. Two factors are considered in evaluating student performance: the number of incorrect responses, and response latency (the time required for the student to respond). Two scores are obtained and are used to determine whether a student's response style is slow and inaccurate, slow and accurate (reflective), fast and accurate, or fast and inaccurate (impulsive).

The *MFFT* is primarily a research tool, rather than an assessment device for school use, and its psychometric quality has been criticized. Becker, Bender, and Morrison (1978) and others are concerned about the *MFFT*'s low test-retest reliability and lack of normative data.

Fagen and Long (1979) have developed a curriculum for teaching students skills in self-control. The curriculum is based upon eight skill clusters: Selection, Storage, Sequence and Order, Anticipate Consequences, Appreciate Feelings, Manage Frustration, Inhibit and Delay, and Relaxation. Included in the system are two assessment tools. The first is a self-rating form for students. Eight descriptions, each corresponding to a skill area, are presented; and students select from "I can do it very well," "OK," and "I need to improve." The statements are

1. I can pay attention to the teacher.
2. I can remember what I am supposed to do.
3. I can finish my work after I understand what to do.
4. I can guess what will happen if I start trouble.
5. I can talk about different feelings that I have.
6. When I get upset and can't do what I want, I can think of ways to make things better.
7. I can stop myself from doing things that I know are wrong.
8. I can relax when things are going wrong.
   Note. From "A Psychoeducational Curriculum Approach to Teaching Self-Control" by S. A. Fagen and N. J. Long, 1979, *Behavioral Disorders, 4,* p. 74. Copyright 1979 by The Council for Children with Behavioral Disorders. Reprinted by permission.

The second measure is a self-rating form for teachers. Teachers are asked to describe the extent to which they assist students in the development of self-control skills.

Measures that assess specific behaviors such as hyperactivity, impulsivity, and self-control play the same role in assessment as the more general behavior rating scales and checklists. They help identify possible areas of need that may warrant further evaluation. If further assessment is needed, direct observation is the recommended procedure.

SELF-CONCEPT AND PEER ACCEPTANCE

Students with school performance problems may have poor self-concepts, perceiving themselves as failures in academic pursuits. Students may also experience difficulty in their interactions with classmates. Their peers may fail to accept them as friends or as regular members of the classroom social group. The next sections describe several of the measures available for exploring these areas.

Self-Concept

Both formal, norm-referenced measures and informal assessment devices are available for the study of self-concept and self-esteem. One popular norm-referenced measure is the *Piers-Harris Children's Self-Concept Scale*. It is a self-report form, and norms are available for grades 4 through 12. According to its manual, the *Piers-Harris* was designed primarily as a research instrument. However, it is often used in schools as a screening device to identify students who have possible self-concept problems.

The *Piers-Harris* is made up of 80 declarative statements such as "My classmates make fun of me," "I am smart," and "I give up easily." In the elementary grades, the tester reads the statements aloud to students. In junior high and high school, students are expected to read the statements themselves. Items are written at a third grade reading level, and both positive and negative statements are included. Students respond by circling "yes" if they feel the statement describes them or "no" if they feel the statement does not.

Raw scores on the *Piers-Harris* range from 0 to 80, with higher scores indicating more positive

---

"THE WAY I FEEL ABOUT MYSELF," THE *PIERS-HARRIS CHILDREN'S SELF-CONCEPT SCALE*
E. V. Piers & D. B. Harris (1984)

Type: Norm-referenced student checklist
Major Content Area: Self-concept
Type of Administration: Group
Administration Time: 15 to 20 minutes
Age/Grade Levels: Grades 4 through 12
Types of Scores: Percentile ranks, stanines
Typical Uses: Designed as a research tool; also used in the identification of students with possible needs in the area of self-concept development
Cautions: Best used as an informal measure unless local norms are developed.

self-concepts. For students in grades 4 through 12, raw scores can be converted to percentile ranks and stanines. Six cluster scores can also be obtained, although these are raw scores. The clusters correspond to six dimensions of self-concept: Behavior, Intellectual and School Status, Physical Appearance and Attributes, Anxiety, Popularity, and Happiness and Satisfaction.

Although its manual was revised in 1984, the *Piers-Harris* was standardized in the 1960s. Piers and Harris (1969) recommend caution in the use of these norms because "they are based on data from one Pennsylvania school district and are therefore generalizable only to similar populations" (p. 13). Users of the test are encouraged to develop local norms, rather than rely upon the norms provided in the manual. The reliability of the *Piers-Harris* appears adequate, with 11 of the 16 reliability coefficients reported by Piers (1977) at the .80 level or above. With respect to validity, correlations between the *Piers-Harris* and other measures of self-concept range from .40 to .85.

The *Coopersmith Self-Esteem Inventories* are another set of measures available for the assessment of self-concept. Three measures make up the set: the School Form, the Adult Form, and a teacher rating scale entitled *Behavioral Academic Self-Esteem* (Coopersmith & Gilberts, 1981). Of interest here is the School Form, the only one of the three measures that is normed.

The School Form of the *Coopersmith* contains 58 statements such as "I have a low opinion of myself" and, "I'm proud of my schoolwork." Both positive and negative statements are included. Students read each statement and then check whether the statement is "like me" or "unlike me." The tester is allowed to read the statements aloud if students have difficulty reading. If a short form of the measure is desired, only the first 25 items are administered. However, norms are not available for the short form.

Items on the *Coopersmith* school inventory are divided into four subscales: General Self, Social Self-Peers, Home-Parents, and School-Academics. Raw scores from each of the subscales are added together; the sum is then multiplied by 2 to produce the Total Self raw score. In addition, there is a Lie Scale used to evaluate the veracity of students' responses. Total Self scores can be converted to percentile ranks, but norms are not available for subscale scores or the Lie Scale.

Norms for the *Coopersmith* School Form were developed by Kimball (1973) with a sample of approximately 7,600 public school students in grades 4 through 8. According to Coopersmith (1981), the standardization sample included "all socioeconomic ranges and Black and Spanish-surname students" (p. 17). No further description is offered. Coopersmith advises caution in the use of these norms and strongly recommends the development of local norms. The *Coopersmith*'s reliability appears adequate, and there is some support for its validity. The manual states that significant correlations have been found between the *Coopersmith* and other measures of self-esteem.

COOPERSMITH SELF-ESTEEM INVENTORIES
S. Coopersmith (1981)

Type: Norm-referenced student checklist (a teacher rating scale without norms and an adult form without norms are also available)

Major Content Area: Self-esteem

Type of Administration: Group or individual

Administration Time: Approximately 10 minutes

Age/Grade Levels: School Form for students ages 8 to 15, Adult Form for ages 16 and up

Types of Scores: Percentile ranks for students in grades 4 through 8 (School Form); no norms available for the Adult Form or teacher rating scale

Typical Uses: Identification of students with possible needs in the area of self-esteem

Cautions: Best used as informal devices unless local norms are developed.

Like the *Piers-Harris*, the *Coopersmith* is best used as an informal device. If norms are desired, local norms should be developed. In addition, Coopersmith (1981) recommends supplementing the results of the student checklist with teacher ratings and observations.

Several informal student checklists are also available for the study of self-concept. Two examples, provided by Smith (1969), appear in Figure 10–4. Students can also be interviewed about their perceptions of self-worth, or some types of observational data can be collected. For example, it is possible to count the number of negative statements a student makes about himself or herself and compare that with the number of positive statements. Some students make frequent comments such as, "I'm dumb" or, "I can't do that," whereas others are much more positive in their self-appraisal.

Peer Acceptance

Attitude scales are used to evaluate regular students' perceptions of individuals with school performance problems. These scales provide information about peer attitudes toward handicapped students in general. They do not assess how well peers accept a particular student. One example of a general attitude scale is the *Peers*

Attitudes Toward the Handicapped Scale (*PATHS*) (Bagley & Greene, 1981).

The *PATHS* contains 30 statements, each of which describes a handicapped student and a problem experienced by that student. For example, one description is

Stephen cannot follow directions, and his teacher must tell him at least three times what to do; even then, Stephen might still not know what to do. He is unable to do the classwork and is failing every subject.

Students are directed to read each description and then select the place where the handicapped student should work: "Work with me in *My Group*," "Work in *Another Group* (with someone else)," "Work in *No Group* (with no other students)," "Work *Outside of Class* (in another class or room)," or "Stay at *Home* (and not come to school)."

The *PATHS* includes descriptions of students with physical, learning, and behavioral handicaps. These correspond to the Physical, Learning, and Behavioral subscales of the *PATHS*. Raw scores can be converted to percentile ranks for each of the subscales and for the total test score. The manual provides guidelines for classifying student scores as showing a Very Positive Attitude, Above Average Attitude, Average Attitude, Below Average Attitude, or Very Negative Attitude.

FIGURE 10–4
Sample self-concept checklists for students

Adjective Check List

Directions: Put an X by each word that describes you.

_____ 1. smart	_____ 7. quarrelsome	_____ 13. bothersome
_____ 2. funny	_____ 8. fidgety	_____ 14. cranky
_____ 3. tired	_____ 9. energetic	_____ 15. eager
_____ 4. happy	_____ 10. friendly	_____ 16. honest
_____ 5. blue	_____ 11. shy	_____ 17. lazy
_____ 6. busy	_____ 12. sad	_____ 18. selfish

Behavioral Check List

Directions: Put an X by each description that fits you.

_____ 1. makes friends easily	_____ 6. seems to lack confidence
_____ 2. not as smart as most kids	_____ 7. is a good leader
_____ 3. likes to be alone	_____ 8. enjoys school
_____ 4. is fun to be with	_____ 9. feelings are easily hurt
_____ 5. laughs a lot	_____ 10. daydreams a lot

Note. From *Teacher Diagnosis of Educational Difficulties* (p. 192) by R. M. Smith, 1969. Columbus, OH: Merrill. Copyright 1969 by Bell & Howell Company. Reprinted by permission.

To find out about how a particular student is perceived by his or her classmates, sociometric techniques are used (Asher & Taylor, 1981). The most common technique is the nomination method. Students nominate the peers they would most or least like to associate with in some activity. Several activities appropriate for the students' age are presented: playing a game, working on a class art project, attending a school assembly, and so forth. For example, students can be asked to respond to questions such as

1. Name the students in this class you would most (least) like to play with during recess.
2. Name the students you would most (least) like to sit next to in class.
3. Name the students you would most (least) like to work with on a class assignment.

A measure of this kind is included in the *Behavior Rating Profile* (Brown & Hammill, 1983a), described earlier in this chapter, and norms are provided for students in grades 1 through 12. Or sociometric data can be collected informally. Class results are then analyzed to determine how many positive and negative nominations each student received.

Rating scales can also be used to collect sociometric data. For instance, on the *Peer Acceptance Scale* (Bruininks, Rynders, & Gross, 1974), each student in the class rates every other student using the picture rating scale shown in Figure 10–5. The possible ratings are "Friend" (illustrated by two persons playing together), "All Right," and

FIGURE 10–5
A picture rating scale

A STUDENT'S NAME

A

All right
Friend
Wouldn't like

Note. From the "Peer Acceptance Scale" by R. H. Bruininks, J. E. Rynders, and J. C. Gross, 1974, *American Journal of Mental Deficiency, 78,* pp. 377–83. Copyright 1974 by the American Association on Mental Deficiency. Reprinted by permission.

"Wouldn't Like." An advantage of this procedure is that results are available for all members of the group, not just those students nominated by their peers.

Sociometric instruments such as the ones just described can be used to determine how well individual students are accepted by their peers. However, student ratings of other students must remain confidential. Students should be encouraged not to share their responses with others (Lewis & Doorlag, 1987), and teachers should not report results to students. Informing students that they are poorly accepted by their peers is likely to have a negative effect upon self-concept.

SCHOOL ATTITUDES AND INTERESTS

A student's interests and attitudes may be related to how well that student performs in school. Poor academic achievement, frustration in complying with classroom rules, and difficulty relating to teachers and peers do not lead to positive attitudes toward the school experience. Likewise, disinterest and negative attitudes can contribute to school performance problems. The relationships between interests, attitudes, and school behaviors are complex, usually making it impossible to determine which factors were causes and which were effects.

Attitudes Toward School

Several measures are available for gathering information from students about their perceptions of the school experience. These measures assess students' attitudes toward various school subjects or their attitude towards specific classroom practices. In both of these important areas, the majority of assessment tools are informal and include interviews, questionnaires, and checklists. A few formal measures have been developed to assess school attitudes. One example is the *Estes Attitude Scales (EAS)* (Estes, Estes, Richards, & Roettger, 1981), with one level for the elementary grades and another for secondary grades. The elementary *EAS* is made up of three attitude scales: Mathematics, Reading, and Science. Reading skills are not required. The tester reads statements such as "It is easy to get tired of math" and "Reading is fun for me" aloud to the students. Students respond by checking "I agree," "I don't know," or "I disagree."

The secondary *EAS* assesses attitudes toward English and social studies in addition to math, reading, and science. Reading is required, but test items are written at a grade 6 reading level. Examples of secondary level items are, "Work in English class helps students do better work in other classes" and "Much of what is taught in social studies is not important." Students respond to each statement by checking "I strongly agree," "I agree," "I cannot decide," "I disagree," or "I strongly disagree."

The *Survey of School Attitudes* (Hogan, 1973, 1975) is another formal measure designed for group administration. Its target audience is students in elementary and junior high school. Attitudes toward four school subjects are assessed: reading and language arts, mathematics, social studies, and science.

If the purpose in assessment is to compare one student's attitudes to those of others, then measures like the *EAS* and the *Survey of School Attitudes* are appropriate. If comparative information is not needed, informal measures may suffice. Interviews or questionnaires could be used to elicit students' views about the school subjects they like most and least and those they perceive as most and least valuable.

Several informal devices are available for assessing students' perceptions of classroom practices. For example, Figure 10–6 presents an attitude survey appropriate for use with secondary students (Hawisher, 1975). This questionnaire contains items pertaining to school attitudes, self-concept, interactions with teachers, and peer relationships. Students are asked to decide whether things at school are better this year than last year. The student reads each item (e.g., "I get along better with the other students") and then selects a response: "much more," "more," "the same," "less," or "much less."

Another technique for gathering information about attitudes involves the use of incomplete sentences. For example, students could be asked to complete sentences such as the following:

□ For me, school is _____ .
□ Learning new things in school makes me feel _____ .

□ When the teacher asks me to read out loud in class, I _____ .
□ When I have some math problems to solve, I _____ .
□ In my opinion, writing a story or a composition is _____ .

Interests

Interests are assessed to learn more about students' likes and dislikes. Information about students' preferences among subjects may prove useful in academic counseling. Knowledge of preferred leisure activities may help teachers select rewards for classroom behavior management programs or choose high interest instructional materials.

The simplest way to find out about interests is to ask students to describe their favorite activities, the things that they most enjoy doing. Kroth (1975) has developed an informal survey that is a series of open-ended questions about student preferences:

□ The things I like to do after school are:
□ If I had ten dollars I'd:
□ My favorite TV programs are:
□ My favorite game at school is:
□ My best friends are:
□ My favorite time of day is:
□ My favorite toys are:
□ My favorite record is:
□ My favorite subject at school is:
□ I like to read books about:
   (p. 18)

These questions could be used as the basis for an informal interest interview or questionnaire.

Student interests are usually assessed informally, but norm-referenced measures can be used if comparative data are needed. For example, the first edition of the *Woodcock-Johnson Psycho-Educational Battery* (Woodcock & Johnson, 1977) includes tests of interest level that assess five areas of interest. The Academic Interest Cluster has three subtests: reading interest, mathematics interest, and written language interest. The physical interest and social interest subtests make up the Nonscholastic Interest Cluster. Physical interest refers to preferences for individual or group physical activities, and social interest is concerned with preferences for activities involving other persons. On the *Woodcock-Johnson*, the interest

FIGURE 10–6
Attitude survey for secondary students

Student Questionnaire

I'd like to know if things are different for you at school this year. I will read you a statement. Think about the sentence and then check one of the blanks on your paper (*much more, more, the same, less,* or *much less*).

1. I get along better with the other students.
2. Other children in the class tease me about my school work.
3. My teachers are more patient with me when I have problems in my work.
4. I like school more this year.
5. My school work seems easier.
6. My principal knows me better this year.
7. Other people understand my learning problems in school.
8. My guidance counselor has helped me understand my learning problems.
9. I have really improved my school work in the resource room.
10. My mother helps me more with my homework.
11. My father helps me more with my homework.
12. My parents are more patient with me with my school work.
13. My parents yell at me when I get poor grades.
14. My parents see my teacher more this year.
15. My parents are pleased with my homework.
16. The resource room has helped me do my school work better in all my classes.
17. I feel better about myself.
18. Learning is more fun.
19. I know that I'll continue to improve my school work even though I'll be slow in some subjects.
20. I have talked with my principal more this year.
21. Many of my classroom assignments are too hard for me to do.
22. I have problems learning things that other kids learn very easily.
23. If other children tease me about school, I can control myself because I understand myself better.
24. I know why it's important to do well in school.
25. I don't think I'm stupid.
26. I take pride in my accomplishments.
27. I learn more in the resource room than in my other classes.
28. I feel that I'll be successful some day.
29. When I do poorly in school, it depresses me.
30. I think my teachers understand me better.

Note. From *The Resource Room: An Access to Excellence* (pp. 181–182) by M. F. Hawisher, 1975, Lancaster: South Carolina Region V Educational Services Center. Copyright 1975 by South Carolina Region V Educational Services Center. Reprinted by permission.

---

subtests are administered together, as if they are one test. Students read descriptions of two activities and then choose the one they prefer. Results take the form of percentile rank scores by age or grade for the two interest clusters, Scholastic Interest and Nonscholastic Interest.

THE LEARNING ENVIRONMENT

The assessment techniques described so far have focused on the student: problem behaviors, self-concept, acceptance by peers, interests, and attitudes toward school. Although this is a necessary part of the assessment process, it is also important to consider the characteristics of the classroom and the other environments where the student must function (Feagans, 1972; Rhodes, 1967). In the ecological approach to assessment, both student and environmental characteristics are of interest.

Ecological assessment studies the match (or mismatch) between the behaviors of the student and the constraints imposed by the environment. Thurman (1977) has identified three factors to consider: (a) the student's deviant or nondeviant behavior, (b) the student's functional competence, and (c) the tolerance of the microecology (that is, the classroom) for deviant and/or incompetent student behaviors. Environments with a high tolerance for differences accept greater ranges of student behaviors.

Smith, Neisworth, and Greer (1978) also recommend comprehensive assessment of the learning environment. In addition to evaluation of student performance, they identify four major environments for assessment: instructional (curriculum, methods, and materials), social, services within the school and classroom, and physical.

The next sections describe strategies for assessing school learning environments. Included are techniques for gathering information about the expectations teachers hold for behavior, the instructional demands placed upon the student in the classroom learning environment, interactions between students and teachers, and physical characteristics of the environment.

Observations, interviews, and other informal procedures are typically used to assess the classroom learning environment. One published system for this purpose is *The Instructional Environment Scale* (*TIES*) (Ysseldyke & Christenson, 1987b). This system is made up of three components: a classroom observation, structured student interview, and structured teacher interview. When these data have been collected, the Instructional Rating Profile is completed. The Profile describes the learning environment in terms of 12 factors identified as critical for student learning. The factors are Instructional Presentation, Classroom Environment, Teacher Expectations, Cognitive Emphasis, Motivational Strategies, Relevant Practice, Academic Engaged Time, Informal Feedback, Adaptive Instruction, Progress Evaluation, Instructional Planning, and Student Understanding. *TIES* is not a normed measure, but each of the factors is described in detail, and examples are provided of appropriate practices.

Behavioral Expectations

Teachers differ in the behavioral expectations they hold for students. The same student behavior may be considered appropriate by one teacher but inappropriate by another. Thus, consideration of the teacher's standards for classroom conduct is necessary in the investigation of student behavior problems. The most straightforward way of gathering this information is to interview the teacher. Classroom observations are another useful source of data.

One area of interest is classroom rules. In many classrooms, the rules for behavior are stated explicitly so students understand which behaviors are acceptable and which are not. Rules may even be posted on a bulletin board as a reminder to students. Affleck, Lowenbraun, and Archer (1980) recommend that classroom rules

1. Be very few in number.
2. State what behavior is desired from the children (e.g., Complete your work. Stay at your desks. Work quietly.) rather than stating all of the behaviors you do not wish children to exhibit (e.g., Don't walk around the room. Don't hit others.).
3. Be simple and clearly stated.
4. Be guidelines that you, the teacher, can directly enforce. (pp. 35–36)

In some classrooms, the rules for conduct are not clearly spelled out. If students are confused about the rules for behavior, they may be unable to comply with those rules. To help students understand class rules, Clarizio and McCoy (1983) suggest "listing the rules on the board, having the student explain in his own words what the rules mean, minimizing distractions while giving directions, and keeping rules short" (p. 547).

Closely related to the rules for conduct is the classroom behavior management system. This system may be a formal, explicit contingency management program or a less formal approach. Among the questions to consider in studying the classroom behavior management system are

☐ Do students have a clear understanding of the expectations for classroom conduct? Are they aware of which behaviors are considered acceptable and which are considered unacceptable?

☐ Are students aware of the consequences of appropriate and inappropriate behavior?

☐ What happens in the classroom when students behave appropriately? Is appropriate behavior rewarded in some way?

☐ What types of rewards or reinforcers are provided? Are students rewarded with social reinforcers like teacher praise? Can they earn activity reinforcers such as free time in the media center or the opportunity to do a special art project? Are tangible rewards like stars, notes home to parents, or school supplies used for reinforcement? Are edible rewards provided?

☐ Is there a formal system for rewarding appropriate behavior? For example, do students earn points for good behavior and later trade their points for reinforcers? If a formal system is in place, does it include provisions for inappropriate behavior?

☐ What happens in the classroom when students behave inappropriately? Is inappropriate behavior ignored or are there consequences?

☐ What are the consequences of inappropriate behavior? Does the teacher verbally rebuke the student? Does the student lose privileges or previously earned rewards? Is the student sent to the principal or kept in at recess or after school?

☐ Are consequences delivered consistently to all students at all times?

☐ How does the classroom behavior management system relate to the rules of the school and the school's behavior management system?

Instructional Demands

The instructional demands in the classroom learning environment can have an influence upon student behavior. If students are faced with academic expectations that they are unable to fulfill, they may react by displaying inappropriate classroom behaviors. In assessing problem classroom behaviors, it is important to consider not only the behavior itself but also the instructional events and conditions that precede it. Clarizio and McCoy (1983) suggest several questions to ask about the antecedents of problem behaviors.

☐ At what time of the class, day, week, or year does the problem occur?

☐ In what subject matter does the problem occur?

☐ What degree of accuracy is demanded for a given assignment?

☐ Who is present? What are they doing?

☐ Where is the child?

☐ By whom does the child sit when the student misbehaves?

☐ What is the size of the group when the student misbehaves?

☐ Is the student academically capable of completing assignments? (p. 549)

These questions relate to instructional antecedents, but the consequences of a problem behavior in terms of instruction are also important. What happens when a student behaves inappropriately? Do the academic demands change in some way?

The school curriculum has major impact upon the instructional conditions of the classroom be-cause curriculum dictates what students are taught. The curriculum specifies not only the particular skills and information students should learn but also the scope of these skills and the sequence of instruction.

Instructional materials, methods, and activities are used to implement the curriculum. Whereas curriculum is concerned with *what* is taught, instruction is concerned with *how* new skills and information are taught. Included under instructional considerations are learning materials such as texts and workbooks, specific learning activities such as classroom and homework assignments, and the instructional methods used by the teacher to present new information. In evaluating instructional materials, some major characteristics to consider are content, instructional procedures, opportunities for practice, initial and ongoing assessment, review activities, and motivational value.

Many of the factors considered in the evaluation of instructional materials are also pertinent to the evaluation of classroom learning activities. In addition, these questions may prove useful:

1. Do the learning activities match the instructional goals and objectives for the student?

2. Has the student mastered the prerequisite skills necessary for the learning activity?

3. Are the directions for the activity clear and comprehensible?

4. Does the activity present information in a way appropriate for the student? For example, if the task requires the student to read, is the level of the reading material appropriate for the student?

5. Are the types of responses required by the activity appropriate for the student?

6. Does the activity provide adequate opportunity for practice of newly learned skills and information?

7. Is there adequate feedback to students about the accuracy of their responses?

8. Is the activity motivating? Is some type of reinforcement provided for successfully completing the activity?

9. Is the classroom environment conducive to participation in and completion of the learning activity?

Popham and Baker (1970) provide additional questions that focus on the student's involvement with the learning task: Does the student know the point of the activity? Precisely what is expected? The value of the activity? Does the student have adequate practice to do the task well?

Also of interest are teachers' instructional strategies and the ways they attempt to modify instruction for students with learning problems. Lewis and Doorlag (1987) discuss four kinds of instructional adaptations teachers can make when students encounter problems with classroom learning tasks. The most drastic modification involves removing the task students are experiencing difficulty with and substituting an alternative task. This adaptation should be considered a last resort. Table 10–4 shows several other changes that can be tried first, including modifying the learning materials and activities, changing the procedures used to teach new skills and information, and altering the requirements for successful task completion. The teacher can be observed or interviewed to determine what types of instructional modifications have been tried and the results. In addition,

TABLE 10–4
Ways of adapting instructional activities

IF students experience difficulty in task performance,
TRY these adaptations of . . .

Materials and Activities:
1. clarify task directions
2. add prompts
3. teach to specific student errors

Teaching Procedures:
4. give additional presentation of skills and information
5. provide additional guided practice
6. make consequences for successful performance more attractive
7. slow the pace of instruction

Task Requirements:
8. change the criteria for successful performance
9. change task characteristics
10. break tasks into smaller subtasks

BEFORE selecting an alternate task.
IF NECESSARY, substitute a similar but easier task or a prerequisite task.

Note. From *Teaching Special Students in the Mainstream* (2nd ed.) (p. 80) by R. B. Lewis and D. H. Doorlag, 1987, Columbus, OH: Merrill. Copyright 1987 by Merrill Publishing Company. Reprinted by permission.

when the student, rather than the learning environment, is under assessment, this hierarchy for altering instructional procedures can form the basis of a series of diagnostic probes or diagnostic teaching sequences.

Student–Teacher Interactions

Interactions between teacher and student are one of the key factors in the classroom learning environment. Teachers can influence student conduct and academic performance by how they react to students' appropriate and inappropriate behaviors. For example, if a student volunteers to answer questions in class but is repeatedly ignored by the teacher, the student may stop attempting to participate or may resort to inappropriate behavior to gain the teacher's attention.

Assessment of student–teacher interactions is best accomplished by observation. The assessment team can design its own observation system or adopt one of the many available systems and modify it, if necessary. For example, the *Brophy-Good Teacher-Child Dyadic Interaction System* (Brophy & Good, 1969) is designed to assess the verbal interactions between the teacher and each individual student in the classroom. For each interaction, information is gathered about the classroom activity, the initiator of the interaction, the nature of the interaction, the appropriateness of student's response, and the type of feedback provided by the teacher. Chapman, Larsen, and Parker (1979) describe the five types of student–teacher interactions of interest in the *Brophy-Good* system.

A *response opportunity* occurs when the child publicly attempts to answer a question or problem posed by the teacher. *Recitation* occurs when the child reads aloud, describes some experience, goes through the arithmetic tables, or makes some other extended oral presentation. A *procedural contact* refers to an interaction between the teacher and the child concerning supplies and equipment or to matters concerning the child's individual needs. A *work-related contact* is any interaction involving homework, seat work, or other written work assigned to the child. A *behavioral contact* occurs when the teacher disciplines the child or makes comments regarding his classroom behavior. (pp. 227–228) [italics added]

In this system, data are recorded on each interaction as it occurs, so that the sequence of events in classroom interactions can be analyzed.

The *Flanders' Interaction Analysis Categories* (Flanders, 1970) are another system for observing teacher–student interactions. This system targets three types of behavior for observation: teacher talk, pupil talk, and silence. These behaviors are further broken down into 10 categories used for coding. The observer uses the codes to record the type of interaction that occurs every 4 seconds for a short period of time each day over several days. For example, an observer might note the following events:

Event	Flanders code
A student expresses an opinion on a topic	9. Pupil-talk—initiation
The teacher agrees with the student	3. Accepts or uses ideas of pupils
The teacher continues with the lecture	5. Lecturing
The teacher asks a question	4. Asks questions
A student responds	8. Pupil-talk—response
The teacher praises the student for answering correctly	2. Praises or encourages

If these events occurred within a 1-minute period, the coding for the 4-second intervals might be

9 9 9 3 3 3 5 5 5 5 5 5 4 8 2

The *Brophy-Good* and *Flanders* systems may be modified as needed. Depending upon the purpose of the observation, it may become necessary to add or delete behavioral categories. The behaviors of interest in observation depend upon the particular situation: the grade level of the classroom, the specific classroom activities, the characteristics of the student and teacher, and the assessment questions under study. However, an unfavorable learning environment is indicated when observations show few interactions between students and teacher and few positive teacher responses to student behaviors.

Students may be able to contribute information about student–teacher interactions or at least their perceptions of those interactions. For example, the rating scales in Figure 10–7 are designed to probe students' opinions of the teacher's performance. Each contains several descriptions of teacher behavior in language tailored to the level of elementary or secondary students. Included on the scales are items relating to the teacher's attention to individual differences and strategies for providing praise and encouragement.

The Physical Environment

Physical conditions can influence the effectiveness of the classroom learning environment. A noisy room, poorly arranged surroundings, and uncomfortable temperatures can impair both students' and teachers' ability to perform at their best. Reynolds and Birch (1977) have developed a system for evaluating the physical conditions of classrooms, including factors such as space and facility accommodations, teaching–learning settings, and instructional materials. Provided as guidelines are contrasting descriptions of poor and adequate physical environments. For example, the following characteristics indicate a learning environment with inadequate space and facility accommodations:

(a) The classroom is essentially untreated for sound.
(b) Access to the class involves difficult elevation and entry problems for students in wheelchairs.
(c) There are no amplification devices.
(d) There are no partitioned areas for small group work.
(e) Movement to washrooms, lunchrooms, and other essential areas is difficult for the orthopedically or visually impaired students.
(f) Space is very limited—thus inflexible.
(g) Storage space is almost totally lacking in the classroom. (p. 134)

A more ideal classroom in terms of space and facilities has these features:

The classroom is carpeted and/or otherwise treated effectively for sound control; access and entry present no problems for any student; storage, flexible partitioning possibilities, sound amplification, varied furniture, and like matters are provided adequately. (p. 134)

These and other descriptions can be used to rate the suitability of the physical conditions in classroom learning environments.

Whatever classroom space is available should be carefully arranged to facilitate instruction. Lewis and Doorlag (1987) suggest several factors to consider:

1. *Sound.* Separate quiet areas from noisy areas.
2. *Convenience.* Store equipment, supplies, and materials near where they are used; locate instructional groups near the blackboard.

FIGURE 10–7
Student rating scales for evaluating the teacher's performance

Interaction Checklist (Elementary)

	Always 3	Seldom 2	Never 1
1. I can get extra help from the teacher when I need it.	☐	☐	☐
2. The teacher praises me when I do well.	☐	☐	☐
3. The teacher smiles when I do something well.	☐	☐	☐
4. The teacher listens attentively.	☐	☐	☐
5. The teacher accepts me as an individual.	☐	☐	☐
6. The teacher encourages me to try something new.	☐	☐	☐
7. The teacher respects the feelings of others.	☐	☐	☐
8. My work is usually good enough.	☐	☐	☐
9. I am called on when I raise my hand.	☐	☐	☐
10. The same students always get praised by the teacher.	☐	☐	☐
11. The teacher grades fairly.	☐	☐	☐
12. The teacher smiles and enjoys teaching.	☐	☐	☐
13. I have learned to do things from this teacher.	☐	☐	☐
14. When something is too hard, my teacher makes it easier for me.	☐	☐	☐
15. My teacher is polite and courteous.	☐	☐	☐
16. I like my teacher.	☐	☐	☐

Interaction Checklist (Secondary)

The teacher

	Always 5	Sometimes 4	Often 3	Seldom 2	Never 1
1. is genuinely interested in me	☐	☐	☐	☐	☐
2. respects the feelings of others	☐	☐	☐	☐	☐
3. grades fairly	☐	☐	☐	☐	☐
4. identifies what he or she considers important	☐	☐	☐	☐	☐
5. is enthusiastic about teaching	☐	☐	☐	☐	☐
6. smiles often and enjoys teaching	☐	☐	☐	☐	☐
7. helps me develop skills in understanding myself	☐	☐	☐	☐	☐
8. is honest and fair	☐	☐	☐	☐	☐
9. helps me develop skills in communicating	☐	☐	☐	☐	☐
10. encourages and provides time for individual help	☐	☐	☐	☐	☐
11. is pleasant and has a sense of humor	☐	☐	☐	☐	☐
12. has "pets" and spends most time with them	☐	☐	☐	☐	☐
13. encourages and provides time for questions and discussion	☐	☐	☐	☐	☐
14. respects my ideas and concerns	☐	☐	☐	☐	☐
15. helps me develop skills in making decisions	☐	☐	☐	☐	☐
16. helps me develop skills in using time wisely	☐	☐	☐	☐	☐

Note. From *The Exceptional Student in the Regular Classroom* (4th ed.) (p. 107) by B. R. Gearheart, M. W. Weishahn, and C. J. Gearheart, 1988, Columbus, OH: Merrill. Copyright 1988 by Merrill Publishing Company. Reprinted by permission.

3. *Movement Efficiency.* Make traffic patterns direct; discourage routes that lead to disruptions (e.g., students distracting others when turning in assignments or moving to activities).
4. *Flexibility.* Ensure that all classroom activities can be accomplished; make areas multipurpose, or use different arrangements for different tasks.
5. *Density.* Arrange student seating so that personal space is preserved; avoid crowding. (p. 143)

In arranging the classroom, there are a great many alternatives to the traditional configuration of straight rows of desks. Turnbull and Schulz (1979) recommend that classroom learning environments include such features as individual and group work areas, manipulative and listening centers, and rest and recreation areas. There are a number of options for arranging seating for classroom instruction: students can be seated at a table, on a rug, or on the floor; in chairs; or in more permanent arrangements such as groupings of desks and chairs.

Comprehensive checklists for evaluating the physical environment of the classroom and of the school have been developed by Smith, Neisworth, and Greer (1978). Among the areas of concern are the safety of the learning environment, its accessibility to students with physical handicaps and other disabilities, and physical factors such as lighting, temperature, noise, and color. Some of the questions that relate to physical conditions in instructional settings include the following:

☐ Are related compatible activities arranged together and unrelated, incompatible activities separated within the classroom?
☐ Have an appropriate time and place been designated and assigned for all activities?
☐ Is there a variety of places where different sized groups can meet and work?
☐ Are there special places that individual children can go (a) for isolation, (b) for rest and quiet, (c) to let off steam, (d) to reward themselves, (e) for private instruction, (f) to work independently, (g) to be disciplined privately?
☐ Are the furnishings (desks, displays, etc.) moveable to provide a variety of groupings and areas within the room for different learning tasks?
☐ Can the teacher control visual distractions between groups of children (by separating groups, raising room dividers, etc.)?
☐ Are storage facilities accessible to the students for getting out and putting away materials which they are allowed access to? (pp. 151–52)

ANSWERING THE ASSESSMENT QUESTIONS

The assessment team can choose to gather several types of information in its study of the student's current classroom behavior. Behavior rating scales and checklists serve as screening measures to identify possible problem behaviors. If problems are indicated, assessment continues with in-depth study of the behaviors of interest by direct observation. The characteristics of the learning environment are also investigated to determine whether classroom factors are contributing to the student's behavioral difficulties. With some students, other dimensions of behavior may be assessment concerns—the student's self-concept, acceptance by peers, attitudes toward school, and current interests.

Types of Procedures

The assessment techniques used to study classroom behavior supply information for several different assessment questions; thus, they are not expected to produce equivalent results. Dimensions such as classroom behavior and self-concept are viewed as separate concerns, and results in one area are not expected to duplicate results in the other.

Assessment of classroom behavior relies heavily upon the information provided by informants. Teachers, parents, peers, and students themselves share their views through rating scales, checklists, interviews, and questionnaires. In interpreting these data, it is important to recognize that measures depending upon informants are indirect. Whenever possible, results of indirect measures should be confirmed with more direct techniques.

Another characteristic of the strategies used in the study of classroom behavior is that many are informal techniques. Some dimensions of classroom behavior do not lend themselves to norm-referenced assessment; an example is the study of environmental influences. Available norm-referenced tools tend to be either screening devices like behavior rating scales and checklists or measures of student characteristics such as self-concept. However, some of these normed instruments have been criticized because of poor or unsubstantiated technical quality.

Informal measures have both advantages and disadvantages. In general, informal tools are designed to provide instructional information, and their results are more detailed and specific than those from formal measures. If the purpose in assessment is to learn more about the student and the learning environment to devise an instructional program, informal techniques are preferred. However, a major disadvantage of informal measures is that their technical quality is typically unknown. They may be valid and reliable or technically inadequate. Therefore, results of informal measures must be interpreted with caution, particularly when used for decisions about program eligibility.

Nature of the Assessment Tasks

Assessment devices that appear to measure the same behavioral domains may in fact be evaluating quite different dimensions. In selecting measures for the study of classroom behavior and interpreting their results, it is important to take into account how each measure goes about assessment.

Behavioral rating scales and checklists provide an excellent example of the range of variations that can occur among measures with similar purposes. For example, rating scales and checklists differ in the person or persons they select to act as informants; the identity of the informant is an important consideration in the selection of an assessment tool. Teachers and parents view students from different perspectives, and if classroom behavior is the major concern, teachers are likely the better source of information. The observations of parents may be different from those of teachers, and peers may disagree with both teachers and parents. If students are given the opportunity to rate themselves, their self-perceptions may provide another perspective different from the perceptions of others. One way to account for divergent views from various informants is to include them all in the assessment process.

Rating scales and checklists can also vary on several other dimensions. These include types of student behaviors that informants are asked to consider, the underlying theoretical frameworks that influence the selection of behaviors and the methods used to derive results, and the ways in which informants are required to respond. Because of these areas of possible difference, rating scales and checklists that appear similar may in fact measure quite different aspects of student behavior.

Other types of procedures also bear scrutiny. Observations of student behaviors are influenced by the way the behavior is defined, the measurement system selected, the times and places that observations occur, the number of times the student is observed, and so forth. Likewise, observations of student–teacher interactions are affected by the coding system used to categorize behaviors. On sociograms, the specific questions that students are asked may determine their willingness to accept or reject a particular peer. Important differences are also likely to be found among measures of self-concept, attitude scales, and informal interest inventories.

Documentation of Classroom Behavior

Classroom behavior is one of the primary concerns of professionals on the assessment team as they attempt to answer the question, *Is the school performance problem related to a handicapping condition?* However, classroom behavior is an important consideration for all students referred for special education assessment, not only those who qualify for services for behavior disorders. The general question under study is, *What is the student's current status in classroom behavior and social-emotional development?* This question is pertinent for any student with a school performance problem because of the possible relationship between poor achievement and inappropriate school behavior.

More specific questions about classroom behavior include

- □ *Is there evidence of a severe conduct problem?*
- □ *What are the characteristics of the classroom learning environment?*
- □ *What is the student's current status in self-concept and acceptance by peers?*
- □ *What are the student's current interests and attitudes toward school and learning?*

These specific questions may be germane for some students but not for others.

The assessment team gathers data from many sources to answer the questions about classroom behavior. School records are reviewed for information about disciplinary history and attendance.

Current classroom behavior is studied by administering norm-referenced rating scales and checklists to informants such as teachers and parents. If the results of these screening measures point to possible conduct problems, classroom observations are conducted and information is gathered about the environment in which the student is expected to perform. With some students, other dimensions of classroom behavior are of interest, and the assessment team may investigate the student's self-concept, level of acceptance by peers, or current interests and attitudes toward school. In the study of classroom behavior, teachers, parents, the student, and even peers share their observations and perceptions of the student's ability to conform to the behavioral expectations of the classroom learning environment.

In analyzing the assessment results, the team's task is to describe the student's current behavioral status. This description is based to some extent on the norm-referenced data provided by behavior rating scales and checklists. However, many of the techniques used to study specific aspects of the student's behavior are informal strategies. Informal techniques are an excellent source of instructional information but do not provide comparative data. Thus, the team must proceed cautiously in interpreting their results and drawing conclusions about performance deficiencies.

Determination of eligibility for programs for students with behavior disorders rests upon documentation of a severe and persistent behavioral disability. The assessment team must demonstrate that a behavior disorder exists, that it is neither a mild nor a transitory problem, and that the disorder exerts an adverse effect upon school performance. According to federal law, several types of disorders are possible: an inability to learn not explainable by other factors, unsatisfactory relationships with peers and teachers, inappropriate behaviors and feelings, a general mood of unhappiness or depression, and physical symptoms or fears developed in association with school or personal problems.

Classroom behavior is also an important concern for students who do not exhibit behavior disorders. Any student, handicapped or not, can require educational intervention at some time during his or her school career because of a behavioral difficulty. Consider, for instance, the case of Joyce, the fourth grader with school performance problems.

Joyce

The assessment team continues its study of Joyce by investigating several aspects of classroom behavior. Conduct problems are not a concern, because Joyce's teacher had reported earlier that Joyce was a well-behaved student. However, Joyce's lowest score on the *Adaptive Behavior Inventory for Children* was in the area of Nonacademic School Roles, so the team has decided to begin assessment by observing Joyce's interactions in the classroom and in nonacademic activities such as recess.

Ms. Gale, the resource teacher, conducts a series of observations over several days. One purpose of these observations is to determine how Joyce relates to her peers in the fourth grade classroom, and no problems are noted in this area. Joyce appears to have many friends among the boys and girls in her class. She interacts socially with the other students in the classroom, and at recess she is always included in one of the play groups.

The second purpose for observation is study of the classroom learning environment and Joyce's interactions with her teacher, Mr. Harvey. Although Joyce does not exhibit inappropriate classroom behavior, some areas of difficulty are identified. First, Joyce frequently asks the teacher to repeat or further explain the directions for academic tasks. This occurs at an average of three times per hour, a much higher rate than that of other students in the class. In addition, Joyce often requests help from the teacher when attempting to complete her classroom assignments. Again, her request rate is high in comparison to other students. Because of Joyce's requests for attention, Mr. Harvey interacts with her more frequently than with most other students. Despite this, Joyce often fails to complete her work on time. Seventy percent of her assignments are turned in either late or unfinished.

The School Form of the *Coopersmith Self-Esteem Inventories* is administered to Joyce to learn more about her self-concept and self-perceptions. Items are read to Joyce because of her difficulties in reading. Test norms are not used, but Joyce's responses are tallied for the four types of questions included on the *Coopersmith*: General Self, Social Self-Peers, Home-Parents, and School-Academics. In only one area, specifically School-Academics, do the majority of Joyce's responses indicate a negative self-concept.

Ms. Gale then interviews Joyce about her attitudes toward school. Joyce reports that she likes some parts of school, such as art and recess and sometimes math, but that she is "dumb" in reading and spelling. She says she might like to read stories and books if she knew how, but that reading is "very hard to do." Joyce completes an informal interest inventory with Ms. Gale's assistance. Joyce's least favorite school activities are reading, doing workbooks, and writing her spelling words. For leisure activities, she prefers playing with her friends and her new puppy. She says she does not read for pleasure, but she sometimes looks at magazines and books with pictures.

In reviewing these results, the assessment team concludes that Joyce's peer interactions are satisfactory and her classroom behavior is acceptable. However, the team notes that Joyce appears to have difficulty remembering and understanding the directions for classroom assignments. Joyce's difficulties may be due in part to problems in memory and in part to the difficulty level of her classroom work. Thus, the team suggests that Joyce's classroom teacher provide her with less difficult assignments in an attempt to decrease her need for assistance and increase her rate of completion. The team also determines that Joyce shows needs in the areas of self-concept and attitude toward school. These needs probably are related to her poor academic performance.

The team has now gathered sufficient information to make a decision about Joyce's eligibility for special education services. School performance problems in reading, spelling, and handwriting have been documented, and the handicap of learning disabilities has been substantiated through discrepancy analysis and the identification of deficits in memory, memorization strategies, and fine motor coordination. Mental retardation, sensory impairments, and behavior disorders have been ruled out as causes of Joyce's difficulties in academic achievement. Given these data, the team concludes that Joyce meets eligibility criteria for programs for students with learning disabilities. The next steps in assessment will focus on gathering data about Joyce's specific instructional needs to plan her individualized program.

STUDY GUIDE

Review Questions

1. Assessment information about classroom behavior is used to make eligibility decisions and to plan classroom intervention programs. (True or False)

2. What are three areas of classroom behavior that may be assessed?

3. Which of the following statements is false?
   _____ a. One of the handicaps included under PL 94–142 is serious emotional disturbance.
   _____ b. In the field of emotional disturbance, there is a lack of consensus about both terminology and definition.
   _____ c. There are several theoretical models of behavior disorders.
   _____ d. School practices in the assessment and treatment of students with behavior problems are most influenced by the psychoanalytic model.

4. Check each of the assessment devices and procedures that can be used to gather information about classroom behavior.
   _____ a. Behavior rating scales and checklists
   _____ b. Individual tests of intellectual performance

_____ c. Self-concept measures and sociograms
_____ d. Observations of student behavior and student–teacher interactions
_____ e. Measures of reading, mathematics, and study skills
_____ f. Environmental checklists
_____ g. Tests of memory, perception, and attention

5. Rating scales and checklists are used to obtain information about the student's behavior from informants such as _____ , _____ , and _____ .

6. Most of the behavior rating scales and checklists designed to identify students with conduct disorders are based upon the same set of problem behaviors. (True or False)

7. Match the assessment device or procedure in Column A with the description in Column B.

Column A	Column B
a. Behavioral observation	_____ Teachers, parents, students themselves, and students' peers act as informants
b. *Woodcock-Johnson Psycho-Educational Battery*	_____ A measure of self-concept
c. *Walker Problem Behavior Identification Checklist*	_____ Used by teachers to report on students' activity levels
d. *Conners' Teacher Rating Scale*	_____ One portion of this collection of tests assesses students' interests
e. *Coopersmith Self-Esteem Inventories*	_____ This device is designed for teachers to report on classroom conduct problems
f. *Behavior Rating Profile*	_____ A very flexible technique used to study a wide range of student and teacher behaviors

8. Conducting a classroom observation requires several steps. The first is: *Describe the behavior to be observed.* What are the other four steps?

9. To find out about how a particular student is perceived by his or her classmates, _____ techniques can be used. For example, the teacher can ask each student to nominate the peers they would most like to play with during recess.

10. Find the true statements.
_____ a. Measures of personality are often used in the assessment of classroom behavior because they provide educationally relevant information.
_____ b. In ecological assessment, the student is considered to be the source of the learning problem.
_____ c. Among the concerns in the study of the student's learning environment are behavioral expectations, instructional demands, student–teacher interactions, and the physical environment of the classroom.
_____ d. When assessing the instructional environment, consider the classroom curriculum and the instructional methods, materials, and learning activities used to teach that curriculum.

11. If the special education team finds that a student with average intelligence performs in the low average or below average range in academic achievement *and* in one or more areas of classroom behavior, what conclusion can be drawn?
_____ a. The student may be eligible for special education services.
_____ b. The student should receive counseling or psychotherapy services.
_____ c. The student is not eligible for special education services.
_____ d. The student should be returned to the regular classroom.

Activities

1. Locate one of the measures of student behavior described in this chapter. Examine its manual for information on standardization procedures, reliability, and validity. Check the *Mental Measurements Yearbook* series for a review of the measure.

2. Administer a measure such as the *Behavior Rating Profile*. Calculate the scores produced and analyze the results.

3. Construct a checklist for use by students to assess one of the following:
   a. Self-concept
   b. Attitude toward school
   c. Interactions with teachers
   d. Peer relationships
4. Design a questionnaire or an interview procedure for use with teachers to find out about the major instructional characteristics of the classroom learning environment.
5. Talk with school personnel in your area to see how they go about assessing students with behavior disorders. Do they use behavior rating scales or checklists? If so, which ones? Is the student's classroom behavior observed as part of the assessment process? How does the assessment team go about gathering information from teachers and parents? Is the classroom learning environment considered as a possible contributor to the student's behavioral difficulties? How is the impact of the learning environment assessed?

Discussion Questions

1. Describe how classroom behavior can affect students' performance in subjects such as reading, mathematics, handwriting, and composition.
2. One of the areas of debate in behavior disorders is definition of the condition. Identify the essential components of a definition of behavior disorders, and for each component, prepare a list of relevant assessment procedures.
3. Two major approaches to the identification of behavior disorders are direct observation of student behavior and reliance on the information provided by informants such as teachers and parents. Discuss the pros and cons of each approach, and tell why both are necessary for a balanced picture of the student's current behavioral status.
4. Explain the rationale for assessing the student's environment as a possible contributor to behavioral problems. Consider classroom instructional demands and the behavioral expectations that teachers hold for students.

PART FOUR

Academic Areas

The academic skill areas of reading, mathematics, written language, and oral language are considered in Chapters 11 through 14. Assessment questions in these areas are central to eligibility and programming decisions. Each chapter begins with an explanation of the reasons for assessment, the skills to be studied, and the way professionals currently go about assessment in this area. Major formal tests are then fully described, including techniques for the interpretation of results. Equal attention is given to informal strategies.

A special feature of Part IV is each chapter's discussion of academic assessment in relation to the student's current instructional program, interpersonal relations, and the physical aspects of the learning environment. To further aid in interpretation of results, a comparison of assessment tools in each skill area is provided. Associations among disabilities are clarified, and assessment questions are readdressed. A case profile of Joyce, the student introduced in Part III, is continued throughout this section.

Chapter 11 critiques three popular formal reading tests, covering decoding, comprehension, and the use of reading for learning. Informal reading inventories are also highlighted. Examples of informal techniques in reading—error analysis, the cloze procedure, interviews, and so forth—then follow.

Chapter 12 covers mathematics, with a comprehensive listing of available tests. Descriptions (from selection through interpretation) of four major tests provide a broad scope of skill assessment, including computation and problem solving. Work sample analysis, criterion-referenced tests, and clinical math interviews are informal ways to assess mathematical abilities. A sample student profile summarizes assessment in this area.

Chapter 13 discusses assessment in written language. Joyce, the student in the sample profile, has problems in this area, and her IAP calls for formal tests and other strategies covered in this chapter. Formal tests and informal techniques are applied in assessing spelling, handwriting, and composition. Joyce's disabilities in these areas can be linked to problems with other skills such as reading.

Oral language is a complex assessment area with potential for relationships to other skill deficits. In addition to the comprehensive oral language measures described in Chapter 14, formal and informal measures of articulation, morphology and syntax, semantics, and pragmatics are discussed. The special educator cooperates with speech-language clinicians in the use of these screening and formal procedures. Many handicapped students, although they are not language disordered, may have language-related problems. Additionally, Chapter 14 provides information on consideration of the language background of students speaking either nonstandard English or languages other than English.

11

Reading

Teachers, parents, and the American citizenry place great value on literacy, and reading is considered to be the most important of the basic literacy skills. In the elementary grades, much of the curriculum focuses on skill acquisition in reading, and in the secondary grades, reading is a major vehicle for the presentation of information in content area subjects. In our society, people are expected to be proficient readers; illiteracy is a definite handicap.

Reading is often an area of difficulty for handicapped students. Young students may not learn the basic skills of reading at the expected rate; they may fall far behind their classmates in their ability to decode and understand the written word. Older students, even farther behind in reading, may lack the skills needed to use reading as a tool for learning other skills and subjects.

Once students are found eligible for special education services, the focus in assessment shifts to instructional planning. The question that guides this phase of assessment is, *What are the student's educational needs?* Because reading is often an area of need for mildly handicapped students, the assessment team may ask, *What is the student's current level of reading achievement? What are the student's strengths and weaknesses in the various skill areas of reading?*

At this level of questioning, the team is concerned more about the student's ability to perform important reading tasks than about how performance compares with that of other students. Although norm-referenced information can be useful in determining which reading skills are areas of need, criterion-referenced information and other types of informal data provide specific descriptions of the student's current status in skill development. Consider, for example, the assessment team's plans for evaluating the reading skills of Joyce. Joyce is the fourth grader described in the last few chapters who was recently found eligible for special education services for students with learning disabilities.

Joyce

Joyce's problem in reading is one of the reasons she was referred for special education assessment by Mr. Harvey, her fourth grade teacher. Joyce is unable to read any of the fourth grade texts in her classroom, and she is now working in a beginning third grade reading book. Results of individual achievement tests such as the *PIAT–R* have confirmed that Joyce's reading performance is below that expected for her age and grade. Joyce considers reading one of her least favorite of school subjects; she feels that she is "dumb" in reading.

Individualized Assessment Plan

For:	Joyce Dewey	4	10–0	12/1/89	Ms. Gale
	Student's Name	Grade	Age	Date	Coordinator

Reason for Referral: Difficulty keeping up with fourth grade work in reading, spelling, and handwriting

Assessment Question	Assessment Procedures	Person Responsible	Date/Time
What is the student's current level of reading achievement?	*Woodcock Reading Mastery Tests–Revised*	Ms. Gale, Resource Teacher	1/9/90 10 a.m.
	Informal reading inventory such as the *New Sucher-Allred Reading Placement Inventory*	Ms. Gale, Resource Teacher	1/10/90 9 a.m.
What are the student's strengths and weaknesses in the various skills areas of reading?	Error analysis of oral reading responses on formal tests	Ms. Gale, Resource Teacher	1/10/90 2 p.m.
	Additional informal strategies, selected on the basis of the results of formal testing	Ms. Gale, Resource Teacher	to be determined

The assessment team believes that instruction in reading will be an important part of Joyce's individual education program. Evaluation of Joyce's current reading skills will begin with administration of the *Woodcock Reading Mastery Tests–Revised,* a norm-referenced measure that evaluates several components of the reading process including sight word vocabulary, word attack skills, and passage comprehension. In addition, an informal reading inventory will be administered to gather information about Joyce's oral reading skills and her ability to derive meaning from the material she reads.

Then, informal assessment strategies will be selected to further explore the particular reading skills that appear to be areas of weakness for Joyce. For example, if sight word vocabulary seems to be a need, the team could devise a criterion-referenced test to assess Joyce's mastery of standard lists of sight words for first, second, and third grade students. Or, if comprehension skills are a concern, the team could analyze the types of errors Joyce makes in her attempts to answer comprehension questions.

The results obtained from these assessments will be used to develop part of the individualized special education program for Joyce.

CONSIDERATIONS IN ASSESSMENT OF READING

Of all academic skills, reading is most often the subject of special education assessment. For many educators, reading is one of the most critical of all school subjects, particularly in the elementary curriculum that focuses on the acquisition of basic skills. In the secondary grades, students are expected to use their reading skills to gain information in subject areas such as English, history, and the sciences. Because many special students do not meet these expectations, reading is a major concern in special education assessment.

Purposes

Students' reading skills are assessed for several reasons. In determining eligibility for special education programs, overall school performance is investigated, and reading is an important compo-

nent of school achievement. In addition, regular teachers monitor their students' progress in reading, group achievement tests include subtests to evaluate reading skills, and reading proficiency is one of the minimum competencies assessed by many schools and districts for grade advancement and high school graduation.

In special education, reading skills are assessed not only for determining program eligibility but also for planning instruction, and that is the focus of this chapter. Information from general achievement tests such as the *PIAT–R* is insufficient. It is necessary to gather additional data about the student's specific strengths and weaknesses to describe current levels of reading performance. It then becomes possible to project annual goals for the student and specify instructional objectives.

Reading assessment does not stop when the student's individualized educational program has been planned. Special educators begin to monitor the student's progress in acquiring targeted skills, and in ongoing assessment, data are gathered on a weekly or even a daily basis. Reading assessment continues throughout the student's special education program, if reading is a focus of specialized instruction. At least once a year, the educational plan is reviewed, and evaluation data are gathered to determine the student's current levels of reading achievement.

Skill Areas

Reading is a complex process involving many skills. There is continuing debate over the nature of the reading process, but most experts acknowledge that reading involves the recognition and decoding of printed text and the comprehension of that text as meaningful information. According to Schreiner (1983), "The act of reading consists of two separate but interrelated stages: (a) decoding or pronouncing the printed elements and (b) assigning some meaning to these same elements" (p. 71).

Currently, there are three divergent models of proficient reading (Chall & Stahl, 1982). These models differ in the amount of importance they attach to text and meaning, two aspects of the reading process. In the *bottom-up* model, it is hypothesized that proficient readers proceed from text to meaning; first, individual letters and words are perceived and decoded, and then comprehension of the text's meaning takes place. Reading is considered a text-driven or stimulus-driven activity;

it depends on the reader's skill in lower-level processes such as word recognition. In contrast, the *top-down* model emphasizes what are considered the higher-level processes of comprehension. The skilled reader relies on prior knowledge and previous experience, questioning and hypothesis testing, and comprehension of the meaning of textual material rather than decoding of individual text elements. The third model is the *interactive* model, and it emphasizes both text and meaning. In this model, reading is viewed as "an interactive process where the reader strategically shifts between the text and what he already knows to construct his response" (Walker, 1988, p. 6).

The debate over the relative importance of text versus meaning or decoding versus comprehension carries over into the classroom and the strategies selected for reading instruction (Lapp & Flood, 1983). In the bottom-up sequential approach, decoding skills are taught first, followed by instruction in comprehension. Examples are phonics-based reading programs, linguistic methods, and programmed instruction. The top-down model is the basis for the spontaneous approach to reading instruction. Reading for meaning is emphasized from the first stages of instruction, as in the language experience approach to teaching reading and the individualized reading instruction method.

In assessment, traditional measures focus on the student's ability to decode text and respond to questions about the meaning of the text he or she has read. As Garner (1983) observed, these measures are product-oriented, and they are based on a bottom-up view of the reading act. Reading tests and inventories do not stress the interaction between the reader and the text. Thus, informal assessment strategies are needed to gather information about the student's background knowledge, language facility, knowledge of text structure, and the metacognitive strategies he or she chooses to use when interacting with text (Samuels, 1983).

Formal reading tests and inventories typically include measures of students' decoding and comprehension skills. Decoding skills are word recognition skills; decoding occurs when a student looks at a word, or the letters that make up the word, and then pronounces the word. Decoding can be accomplished in several ways. Words that are familiar to the student may be recognized by sight; such words are called sight words or sight vocabulary. When words are unfamiliar, the student may attempt to use phonic analysis. The student looks at each letter, or grapheme; recalls the sound, or phoneme, associated with the letter; and blends the sequence of sounds into a word. Another method of decoding unfamiliar words is structural analysis. In this method, words are broken into syllables to analyze prefixes, suffixes, root words, and endings. In the third approach to decoding, the context of the sentence or paragraph where the unfamiliar word appears is the subject of analysis. The student uses the meaning of the passage and the grammatical structure of the text as aids in word recognition. Phonic, structural, and contextual analysis are not necessarily independent strategies; students can use one, two, or all three of these methods to decode an unfamiliar word.

Decoding skills are assessed in several ways by reading tests and inventories. One typical method is to present students with a list of words to read aloud. The task may be untimed to allow students the opportunity to use phonic and structural analysis skills. However, tasks are timed if the purpose is to assess sight vocabulary or if the speed of decoding is a concern. Lists of phonetically regular words or nonsense words may be used to evaluate the student's ability to apply phonic analysis skills. Nonsense words force students to analyze each word rather than relying upon sight recognition. Another common method of assessing decoding involves the reading of connected text rather than isolated words. Students are presented with sentences or paragraphs to read aloud. Passage reading provides students with the opportunity to use contextual analysis skills as well as other methods of decoding. Also, it becomes possible to observe the student's oral reading fluency and phrasing and his or her rate of reading connected text.

On traditional reading tests and inventories, comprehension skills are assessed by asking students questions about material they have just read. Students may read the text silently or orally, depending upon whether decoding skills are also under study. The text may be a sentence, a paragraph, or a series of paragraphs making up a story or essay. Comprehension questions may be multiple choice or completion items, but most typically, the student provides oral responses to open-ended questions. Comprehension questions may probe the student's understanding of the literal meaning of the passage or require inferential thinking and critical analysis (Bartel, 1986b). For example, students may be asked to recall the details of the passage, remember a sequence of events, state the main ideas, explain the meaning of vocabulary words, make judgments, draw conclusions, or evaluate ideas or actions.

The ability to use reading skills in everyday situations is an area rarely included on measures of reading performance; informal techniques are needed to evaluate students' ability to apply their skills in decoding and comprehension to real reading tasks. Reading is a useful skill only when the student is able to read quickly and accurately enough to use it as a tool to gain new information. For example, in everyday life, readers apply their skills when they read signs, posters, letters, magazines and newspapers, television schedules, and the like. These important applications of reading should not be neglected in assessment.

Current Practices

In schools today, the assessment of reading achievement is common practice both in regular and special education. Because of the high interest in reading and the complexity of this skill area, a great number and variety of measures and techniques are available to assess reading performance.

Academic achievement tests typically include one or more subtests designed to evaluate students' mastery of reading skills. This is true both for the group-administered achievement measures used in regular education and for the individual tests preferred in special education. The school performance measures described in Chapter 7 each contain at least one reading achievement measure.

More directly related to instructional planning are norm-referenced reading tests. Sometimes called diagnostic reading tests, these measures survey several subskills within the broad area of reading to identify specific strengths and weaknesses. Because these tests are norm-referenced, the information they provide is comparative.

There are a number of reading tests available, and these vary somewhat in the range of skills they assess. Some tests are designed for comprehensive assessment of the reading process and include measures of several of the important reading skills. One example is the *Woodcock Reading Mastery Tests–Revised* (Woodcock, 1987). Other measures concentrate on a particular component of reading. There are tests that assess only comprehension skills and others that assess only word recognition skills. On some measures, oral reading is the concern, whereas on others it is silent reading. The majority of reading tests are administered individually to allow testers the opportunity to observe students' performance.

Another type of measure often used in reading assessment is the informal reading inventory. Reading inventories are made up of graded word lists and graded reading selections. For instance, an inventory might contain a series of word lists and passages ranging from a primer reading level up to grade 8 reading level. Students begin by reading material at the lower grade levels; they continue reading until the material becomes too difficult to decode and/or to comprehend. These measures are grade-referenced, not norm-referenced. The standard of comparison is the grade level of the material the student is reading, not the performance of other students. There are several informal reading inventories available.

Inventories are only one type of informal strategy used in reading assessment. There are a great many informal assessment tools for reading, and these represent all of the standard types of measures and techniques. Among the most commonly used are criterion-referenced tests of specific reading objectives, error analysis of students' oral reading performance, teacher checklists, diagnostic teaching, and clinical reading interviews. Informal techniques are also used to investigate the classroom learning environment and its relationship to students' reading performance.

Table 11–1 provides a listing of several of the reading measures used in special education. Each is categorized by type—formal test, informal reading inventory, or criterion-referenced test—and information is included about the grades or ages for which each measure is intended and whether administration is group or individual. In addition, the table notes if the measure is designed to assess decoding skills, comprehension skills, or both.

TABLE 11-1
Measures of reading

Name (Authors)	Type of Measure[1]	Ages or Grades	Group or Individual	Decoding	Comprehension
Analytical Reading Inventory (4th ed.) (Woods & Moe, 1989)	I	Primer to Gr. 9 Functioning Level	Individual	*	*
BRIGANCE® Diagnostic Comprehensive Inventory of Basic Skills (Brigance, 1983b)	C	Gr. K–9	Individual	*	*
BRIGANCE® Diagnostic Inventory of Basic Skills (Brigance, 1977)	C	Gr. K–6	Individual	*	*
BRIGANCE® Diagnostic Inventory of Essential Skills (Brigance, 1981)	C	Gr. 4–12	Individual	*	*
Classroom Reading Inventory (5th ed.) (Silvaroli, 1986)	I	Preprimer to Gr. 8 Functioning Level	Individual	*	*
Diagnostic Reading Scales (Spache, 1981)	T	Gr. 1–8 Functioning Level	Individual	*	*
Doren Diagnostic Reading Test of Word Recognition Skills (Doren, 1973)	T	Elementary grades	Group	*	
Durrell Analysis of Reading Difficulty (3rd ed.) (Durrell & Catterson, 1980)	T	Gr. 1–6	Individual	*	*
Ekwall Reading Inventory (2nd ed.) (Ekwall, 1986)	I	Preprimer to Gr. 9 Functioning Level	Individual	*	*
Formal Reading Inventory (Wiederholt, 1986)	T	Ages 7–18	Individual	*	*
Gates-McKillop-Horowitz Reading Diagnostic Test (Gates, McKillop, & Horowitz, 1981)	T	Gr. 1–6	Individual	*	
Gilmore Oral Reading Test (Gilmore & Gilmore, 1968)	T	Gr. 1–8	Individual	*	*

Test	Type[1]	Grade/Age	Administration		
Gray Oral Reading Tests—Revised (Wiederholt & Bryant, 1986)	T	Ages 7–18	Individual	*	*
Hudson Education Skills Inventory (Hudson, Colson, Welch, Banikowski, & Mehring, 1989)	C	Gr. K–12	Individual	*	*
Iowa Silent Reading Tests (Farr, 1973)	T	Gr. 6 to college	Group	*	*
Multilevel Academic Skills Inventory (Howell, Zucker, & Morehead, 1982)	C	Gr. 1–8	Individual	*	*
New Sucher-Allred Reading Placement Inventory (Sucher & Allred, 1981)	I	Primer to Gr. 9 Functioning Level	Individual	*	*
Reading Miscue Inventory (Goodman, Watson, & Burke, 1987)	I	Gr. 1–8+ Functioning Level	Individual	*	*
Slosson Oral Reading Test (Slosson, 1963)	T	Gr. 1 to high school	Individual		*
Standardized Reading Inventory (Newcomer, 1986)	I	Preprimer to Gr. 8 Functioning Level	Individual	*	*
Stanford Diagnostic Reading Test (3rd ed.) (Karlsen, Madden, & Gardner, 1984)	T	Gr. 1–12, college	Group	*	*
System FORE (Bagai & Bagai, 1979)	C	Gr. K–12	Individual	*	*
Test of Early Reading Ability (Reid, Hresko, & Hammill, 1981)	T	Ages 4–8	Individual	*	*
Test of Reading Comprehension (rev. ed.) (Brown, Hammill, & Wiederholt, 1986)	T	Ages 7–18	Individual, small group		*
Wisconsin Tests of Reading Skill Development (1972, 1977)	C	Gr. K–6	Individual	*	*
Woodcock Reading Mastery Tests—Revised (Woodcock, 1987)	T	Gr. K to college senior, Ages 5–75+	Individual	*	*

[1] T stands for standardized test, I for informal inventory, and C for criterion-referenced test.

This chapter describes each of the major strategies used in schools today for the assessment of reading. Discussed first are formal reading tests, and the next sections introduce three of these. Included is a comprehensive measure of reading, the *Woodcock Reading Mastery Tests–Revised* and two measures that each concentrate on one major reading skill, the *Gray Oral Reading Tests–Revised* and the revised edition of the *Test of Reading Comprehension.*

WOODCOCK READING MASTERY TESTS–REVISED

The *Woodcock Reading Mastery Tests–Revised* (*WRMT–R*) is a norm-referenced measure used to pinpoint students' strengths and weaknesses. The original version of this test was published in 1973 and the revision in 1987. According to its manual, the *WRMT–R* is "suitable for a variety of applications in both educational and noneducational settings" (p. 10); its uses include clinical assessment and diagnosis, individual program planning, selection and placement, and research.

Two forms of the *WRMT–R* are available, Form G and Form H. The forms are not identical. Form G, the complete battery, is made up of four tests of reading achievement and a readiness section; Form H contains only alternate forms of the reading achievement tests. The four subtests common to both forms are:

- *Word Identification*—Students are shown rows of individual words (e.g., *is, listen*), and they must pronounce each word within about 5 seconds.
- *Word Attack*—Nonsense words and syllables (e.g., *ift, lundy*) are presented instead of real words. The student reads each aloud.
- *Word Comprehension*—This subtest includes three parts. On Antonyms, the student reads a word aloud and supplies its opposite. On Synonyms, the student reads a word and supplies a word that means the same. On Analogies, the student reads a row of three words representing an incomplete analogy (e.g., *mother—big, baby—_____*) and supplies the missing word.
- *Passage Comprehension*—This subtest uses a cloze procedure to assess comprehension skills. The student is presented with a brief passage with one word omitted. The student reads the passage silently and then attempts to supply the missing word. Easier passages are accompanied by drawings.

Form G also contains three measures of reading readiness:

WOODCOCK READING MASTERY TESTS–REVISED (WRMT–R)
R. W. Woodcock (1987)

Type: Norm-referenced test
Major Content Areas: Reading readiness, basic reading skills (word identification and word attack), word and passage comprehension
Type of Administration: Individual
Administration Time: 30 to 45 minutes
Age/Grade Levels: Grades K through 16.9 (college senior), ages 5–0 through 75+
Types of Scores: Grade and age equivalents, percentile ranks, standard scores, and Relative Performance Index scores for subtests and clusters
Typical Uses: A broad-based reading test for the identification of strengths and weaknesses in reading skill development
Cautions: Care should be taken in the interpretation of results because of the unusual assessment tasks used to evaluate comprehension. More information is needed about the concurrent validity of the *WRMT–R*. Scoring the test is time-consuming if results such as standard score ranges are desired.

- *Visual-Auditory Learning*—This subtest, borrowed from the *Woodcock-Johnson Psycho-Educational Battery,* is a "miniature 'learning-to-read' task" (p. 4). The student is shown visual symbols which the tester labels. The student repeats the word associated with each symbol, then attempts to read sentences composed of the symbols.
- *Letter Identification*—Individual letters are arranged in rows, and the student must say the name (or sound) of each. Letters appear in upper and lowercase, in manuscript and cursive, and in a variety of type styles.
- *Supplementary Letter Checklist*—This two-part checklist (Capital Letters and Lowercase Letters) is a supplementary informal measure that can be used to determine a student's ability to give either the names or sounds of the letters. The only results are raw scores.

The *WRMT–R* is designed for students from kindergarten through college, but young children and nonreaders may experience success only on the readiness subtests. English-language skills are particularly important for the Word Comprehension and Passage Comprehension subtests where students must supply missing words. Students respond orally on all *WRMT–R* subtests; no writing is required.

Technical Quality

The *WRMT–R* was standardized from 1983 to 1985 with more than 6,000 persons from 60 communities. The school-age sample contained 4,201 students in grades K to 12, the college/university sample included 1,023 students, and the adult sample was made up of 865 persons ages 20 to 80 and older. Samples were weighted so that the final samples corresponded to 1980 U.S. census data for geographic region, community size, sex, and race. The college sample was weighted for type of college (e.g., public vs. private) and the adult sample for education, occupational status, and occupation type. The *WRMT–R* manual does not discuss whether handicapped or non-English-speaking persons were included in the standardization samples.

Split-half reliability of the *WRMT–R* is generally adequate. For subtest and cluster scores on Forms G and H, most reliability coefficients fell above .80. Low coefficients were found for grade 5 students

on Letter Identification (.34) and the Readiness Cluster (.54); Passage Comprehension was somewhat low for both grade 5 (.73) and grade 11 (.68) students. Information is also needed on test-retest and alternate form reliability.

Concurrent validity of the *WRMT–R* was studied by examining its relationship to the reading tests of the *Woodcock–Johnson.* Correlations ranging from .85 to .91 were found between total reading scores on these two measures. The manual also presents data to support the relationship of the 1973 *WRMT* with measures such as the reading subtests on the *PIAT* and *WRAT.* However, further information is needed about the 1987 *WRMT* and its relationship to newer measures such as the *PIAT–R* and *WRAT–R.*

Administration Considerations

Although formal training is not required to administer the *WRMT–R,* inexperienced testers should study the test manual, administer at least two practice tests, and be observed and evaluated by an experienced examiner. Practice activities for administration, scoring, and interpretation are provided in the *WRMT–R* manual. The *WRMT–R* is a relatively easy test to administer, although its scoring is somewhat complicated.

Test books are in easel format. Each subtest begins with a tabbed page that contains any special administration information, scoring directions, basal and ceiling rules, and suggested starting points. Starting points are based on the student's estimated reading grade level, not the current grade in school. However, all individuals begin the Visual-Auditory Learning and Word Attack subtests with item one. Sample items are provided for Word Attack, Word Comprehension, and Passage Comprehension.

The *WRMT–R* is set up for administration by page units. The tester always begins with the first item on a test page and continues until the last item is administered. This procedure influences how basals and ceilings are established. On all subtests except Visual-Auditory Learning, the basal is six consecutive items passed, and the ceiling is six consecutive items failed. If it is necessary to move to easier items to establish a basal, the tester first finishes the page where testing was begun, then moves backwards one page and begins with its first item. Likewise, in locating the ceiling, testing continues to the end of the page, even if the student has already made six consecutive errors. As stated on the Test Record, the basal is "the first 6 consecutive correct responses that begin with the first item on an easel page" and the ceiling is "the last 6 consecutive failed responses that end with the last item on an easel page."

Test items are scored as they are administered, and on most subtests, correct responses are marked "1" and incorrect responses "0." The Test Record is well designed, and there is ample room to record students' error responses on all subtests. The procedures for the Visual-Auditory Learning subtest are somewhat different from those for the rest of the test. Students' errors are circled, and the numbers of errors are counted. Also, there is no basal or ceiling. Instead, at certain points in the subtest, the tester compares the cumulative number of errors to a cutoff criterion to determine whether to continue testing. For example, after Test Story 4, testing is stopped if the student has made 25 or more errors.

It is not necessary to administer all subtests of the *WRMT–R;* the tester can select any portion of the battery that is of interest. The Word Attack subtest can be omitted (and a score of 0 recorded) if the students earns 0 or 1 on Word Identification. However, the tester may choose to administer Word Attack if there is reason to believe that the student will achieve success. Subtests may be administered in any order.

Results and Interpretation

The *WRMT–R* offers a variety of scores. For each subtest it is possible to obtain a grade equivalent, age equivalent, percentile rank, Relative Performance Index (RPI), and standard score. *WRMT–R* grade and age scores are extended scales. At the upper and lower ends, percentile rank superscripts are added to make scores more precise. For example, a grade equivalent of K.0^{35} indicates performance at the 35th percentile for beginning kindergarten students. The Relative Performance Index (RPI) score is a ratio; for example, an RPI of 85/90 indicates that the student is expected to perform tasks at 85% mastery that average students of his or her age or grade would perform at 90% mastery. Several types of standard scores are available, including *T* scores, stanines, normal curve equivalents, and standard scores with a

mean of 100 and standard deviation of 15. It is also possible to construct confidence intervals around scores so that RPI, percentile rank, and standard scores are expressed as ranges.

Subtest scores can be combined into cluster scores. The Readiness Cluster is made up of the two readiness subtests, the Basic Skills Cluster consists of the Word Identification and Word Attack subtests, and the Reading Comprehension Cluster of the two comprehension subtests. The Full Scale Total Reading Cluster is a global score for the four reading achievement tests; the Short Scale Total Reading Cluster includes only Word Identification and Passage Comprehension. The same types of scores available for subtests can be computed for clusters.

Figure 11–1 shows a sample Summary of Scores from the *WRMT–R* Test Record. Form G was administered, although the readiness portion was omitted. The gray area in each block of scores contains what the manual calls optional scores. It would be possible to compute only those in the unshaded area: the RPI and percentile rank. If standard score ranges are desired, however, computation is a lengthier process. The *ASSIST*™ computer scoring program for the *WRMT–R* can be used to minimize scoring time.

The *WRMT–R* offers several profiles that can be plotted to help with interpretation of test results. An Instructional Level Profile appears in Figure 11–2; the results shown are those of the sample case presented in the previous figure. Across the top of the profile is the grade equivalent scale, and the shaded portion of the graph for each subtest indicates the student's instructional range. The lower end corresponds to the student's easy reading level (the grade level at which the student's RPI would be 96/90). The upper end is the difficult reading level corresponding to an RPI of 75/90. The heavy vertical line marks the instructional reading level (RPI 90/90).

The tester can also plot the Percentile Rank Profile and three Diagnostic Profiles: readiness, basic skills, and comprehension. The Diagnostic Profiles show *WRMT–R* results as well as results from the *Woodcock–Johnson Psycho–Educational Battery* (Woodcock & Johnson, 1977) and the *Goldman–Fristoe–Woodcock Auditory Skills Test Battery* (Goldman, Fristoe, & Woodcock, 1976). For example, on the comprehension profile, oral comprehension can be compared with reading comprehension.

FIGURE 11–1

Sample Summary of Scores from the *Woodcock Reading Mastery Tests–Revised*

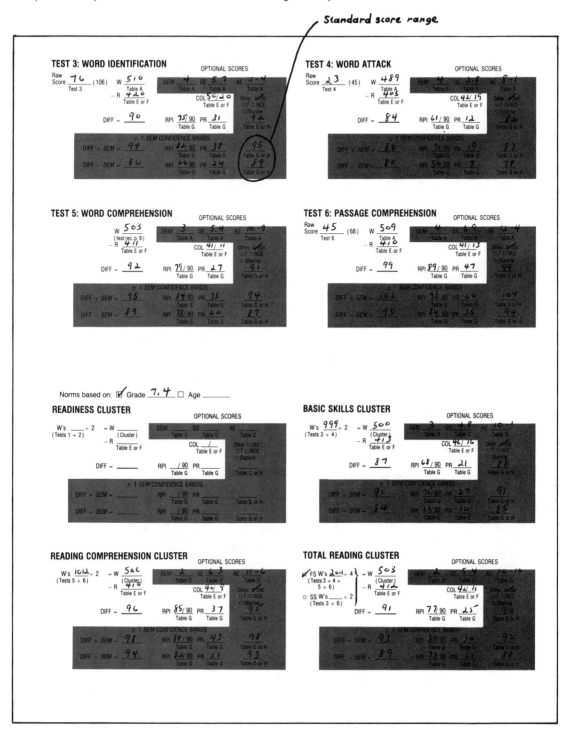

Note. From *Woodcock Reading Mastery Tests–Revised, Forms G and H, Examiner's Manual* (p. 47) by R. W. Woodcock, 1987, Circle Pines, MN: American Guidance Service. Copyright 1987 by American Guidance Service, Inc. Reprinted by permission.

FIGURE 11–2

Sample Instructional Level Profile from the *Woodcock Reading Mastery Tests–Revised*

INSTRUCTIONAL LEVEL PROFILE

(Instructional Range   Easy ◄———— Grade Equivalent ————► Difficult)

Word Identification
Grade Equivalent

Raw 76
RPI 23/90

Word Attack
Grade Equivalent

Raw 23
RPI 61/90

Word Comprehension
Grade Equivalent

W 503
RPI 79/90

Passage Comprehension
Grade Equivalent

Raw 45
RPI 89/90

TOTAL – FULL SCALE
Grade Equivalent

W 503
RPI 77/90

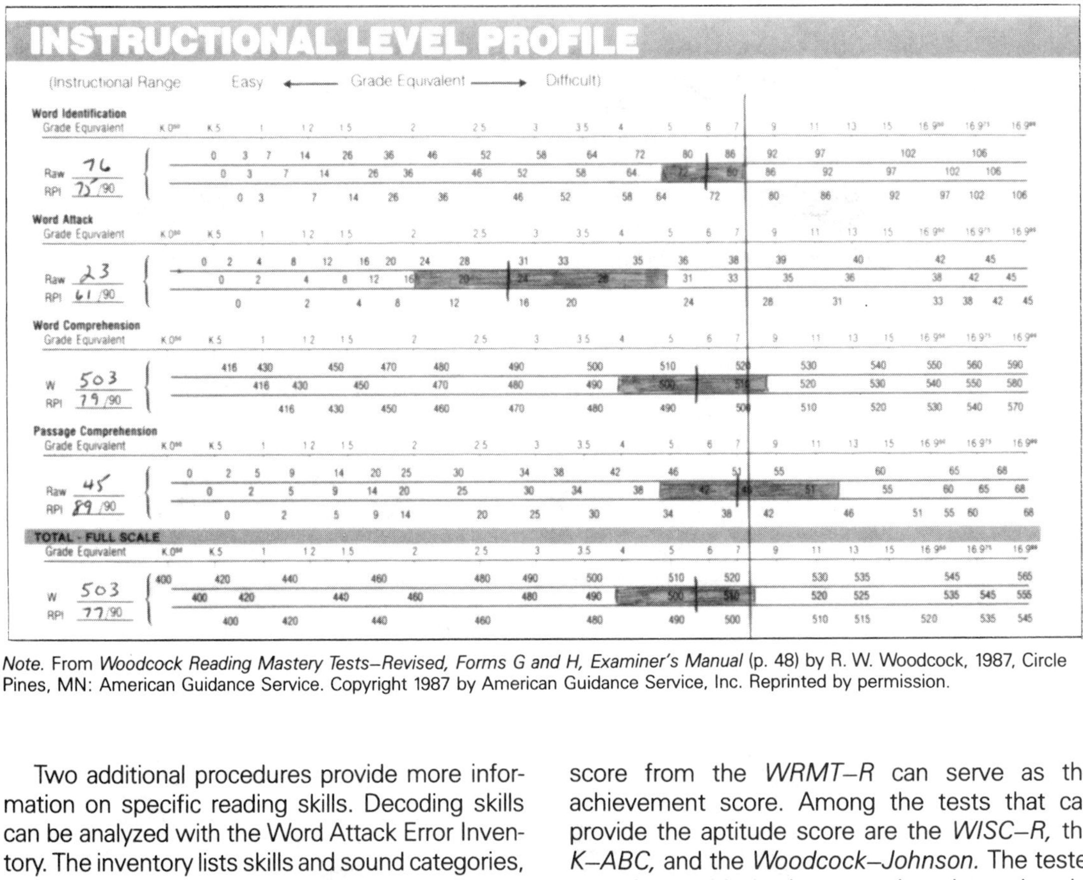

Note. From *Woodcock Reading Mastery Tests–Revised, Forms G and H, Examiner's Manual* (p. 48) by R. W. Woodcock, 1987, Circle Pines, MN: American Guidance Service. Copyright 1987 by American Guidance Service, Inc. Reprinted by permission.

Two additional procedures provide more information on specific reading skills. Decoding skills can be analyzed with the Word Attack Error Inventory. The inventory lists skills and sound categories, and items from the Word Attack subtest are linked to appropriate categories. The skill areas included are single consonants and digraphs, consonant blends, vowels, and multisyllabic words. If a student read *wab* as *wid* on the Word Attack subtest, two errors would be marked on the inventory: the short sound of the vowel *a,* and the consonant *b.* It is also possible to look at vocabulary skills as measured by the Word Comprehension subtest. Each item on that test is categorized by the type of vocabulary it assesses: general reading, science-mathematics, social studies, or humanities. The number correct in each category is counted, and the results are plotted on the Content Area portion of the Diagnostic Comprehension Profile.

A useful feature of the *WRMT–R* is the procedure it offers for aptitude–achievement discrepancy analysis. Any subtest or cluster standard score from the *WRMT–R* can serve as the achievement score. Among the tests that can provide the aptitude score are the *WISC–R,* the *K–ABC,* and the *Woodcock–Johnson.* The tester consults a table in the manual to determine the expected correlation between the two tests, then finds the expected achievement score in another table. If actual achievement is less than expected, the difference is computed, and another table is used to determine the percentage of the population showing the same or greater discrepancy.

The *WRMT–R* produces many scores, and interpretation should focus on the results most pertinent to the assessment questions under investigation. Standard score ranges help the examiner determine the reading skills in which the student shows low or below average performance in comparison to peers. The Relative Performance Index provides information about the student's expected mastery relative to grade peers; this score may be of interest when the assessment team is considering the advisability of mainstreaming handicapped students into regular classes for reading instruction. The instructional range may prove helpful in estimating the student's current instructional level on various reading tasks.

It is also possible to compare performance in different reading skill areas. In the area of decoding, results of the Word Identification subtest, a measure of sight vocabulary, can be compared with results of the Word Attack subtest, a measure of phonic and structural analysis. Results of the two comprehension subtests can also be contrasted. However, these subtests are not traditional measures of comprehension skills. Word Comprehension, in addition to being a measure of vocabulary, also assesses reasoning ability in its analogies portion. Passage Comprehension employs a cloze procedure to evaluate students' understanding of the material they have read; this procedure is quite different from the comprehension tasks used in classroom reading instruction.

Further information about strengths and weaknesses can be gathered by analyzing students' responses to specific test items. The WRMT–R provides systems for analysis of word attack errors, vocabulary knowledge, and skill in identification of upper- and lowercase letters. The tester might also want to consider the student's responses to items of the Word Identification subtest.

Results of the WRMT–R help the professional determine the student's current levels of achievement in reading readiness, basic reading skills, and comprehension. These results are most useful for identifying areas of strengths and educational needs. They also provide valuable direction for further assessment. Informal strategies are used to further investigate weaknesses suggested by WRMT–R results and to probe skills not assessed (e.g., oral reading of connected text).

GRAY ORAL READING TESTS–REVISED

The Gray Oral Reading Tests–Revised (GORT–R) assess students' ability to read passages aloud quickly and accurately with adequate comprehension. The current version of this test is an update of a popular measure developed by William S. Gray (1967). According to the manual, the GORT–R is designed to identify students with problems in reading, determine students' strengths and weaknesses, and document progress in reading.

Two alternate forms of the GORT–R are available, Forms A and B. Each contains 13 reading passages that increase in difficulty, and each passage is followed by five comprehension questions. The task remains the same throughout the test. The student reads the passage aloud, as the tester records errors and times the student. Then, the tester reads comprehension questions and four possible answers as the student follows along; the student selects the correct response (A, B, C, or D). Several types of questions are asked, including those that assess literal, inferential, critical, and affective comprehension.

The GORT–R is designed for students ages 6–6 to 17–11, but beginning readers may experi-

---

GRAY ORAL READING TESTS–REVISED (GORT–R)
J. L. Wiederholt & B. R. Bryant (1986)

Type: Norm-referenced test
Major Content Areas: Oral reading speed, accuracy, and comprehension
Type of Administration: Individual
Administration Time: 15 to 30 minutes
Age/Grade Levels: Ages 6–6 to 17–11
Types of Scores: Percentile ranks, standard scores, Oral Reading Quotient (ORQ)
Typical Uses: Identification of strengths and weaknesses in oral reading skills
Cautions: The GORT–R is a measure of oral reading skills; some students may show better comprehension when reading silently. Results should be interpreted with caution because of the need for further evidence of the validity of this test.

ence difficulty because the first passages are written at a grade 1 (rather than a preprimer) readability level. English-language skills are a necessity for success on the *GORT–R*. Writing is not required; all student responses are oral.

Technical Quality

The *GORT–R* was standardized with 1,401 students from 15 states. The sample appears to approximate the national population in terms of sex, urban–rural residence, race, ethnicity, and geographic region. No information is provided on whether handicapped or non-English-speaking students were included as part of the norm group.

Internal consistency reliability is adequate for all scores on the *GORT–R*. Alternate form reliability is also acceptable. Concurrent validity was studied by examining the relationship between *GORT–R* results and those from other measures of reading. In general, modest correlations were found with reading results from tests such as the *Iowa Tests of Educational Development, Formal Reading Inventory,* and *Comprehensive Test of Basic Skills;* coefficients ranged from .38 to .54. Higher correlations were found between *GORT–R* results and teachers' ratings of students' reading skills (.63 to .74). Also, the *GORT–R* appears to be related to results of intellectual performance measures (.51 to .80). More information is needed about the validity of this test, particularly its relationship to individual tests of reading commonly used in special education assessment.

Administration Considerations

Because there is only one type of task on the *GORT–R,* administration is straightforward. Suggested starting points are provided by grade level. For example, students in grades 3 and 4 should begin with Story 3. Testing begins with the suggested story and continues until the ceiling is reached. A ceiling is defined as at least three errors on the five comprehension questions following any story. After the ceiling is reached, the tester may need to administer easier passages to obtain a basal. The basal is the point at which all comprehension questions for a story are answered correctly.

For each passage administered, the tester reads a sentence or two about the story as motivation, then tells the student to begin reading orally from the appropriate page in the Student Book. When the student has completed the passage, the tester turns to the page with comprehension questions and reads these aloud as the student looks on. The tester records the student's responses.

When the student is reading orally, the tester must do two things: (a) record any errors the student makes and (b) time how many seconds it takes the student to read each passage. Two systems are available for recording errors. In the first system, a slash mark (/) is used to denote deviations from the printed page. A slash is made on each word that is not read correctly and in the space between words when errors such as additions, repetitions, or self-corrections occur. Each word and space can account for only one error. Thus, if the student read "The big cat" as "The great really big cat," only one error would be marked in the space between "The" and "big." If the student hesitates, the word is supplied by the tester and counted as an error. Students are allowed 10 seconds to sound out a word but only 5 seconds if there is no audible attempt to read the word.

The second recording system is used if the tester wants to analyze student errors. It combines slashes with verbatim recording. The manual contains guidelines for marking the Examiner Record Form. Tape recording the student's oral reading for later analysis is allowed, although print deviations should be marked with a slash during test administration.

Results and Interpretation

Each passage on the *GORT–R* produces two raw scores. The Comprehension raw score is simply the number of comprehension questions answered correctly. The Passage raw score reflects both the student's accuracy and his or her speed. Tables in the manual are used to derive the Passage Score from the student's Rate and Deviations from Print scores.

Total test Comprehension and Passage scores are then converted to percentile ranks and standard scores. Standard scores are distributed with a mean of 10 and a standard deviation of 3. Two summary scores are available that reflect overall test performance: a percentile rank score and the Oral Reading Quotient (ORQ), a standard score distributed with a mean of 100 and standard deviation of 15. Standard errors of measurement for Comprehension and Passage scores are 1 standard score point or less; those for the ORQ fall between 3 and 4 standard score points.

An important feature of the *GORT–R* is the procedure it provides for analysis of student errors or miscues. The Examiner's Worksheet is used to record each substitution error and categorize the way in which it was similar to the text word. This system is based on the work of the Goodmans (K. S. Goodman, 1969, 1976; Y. M. Goodman & Burke, 1972). Types of miscues include errors similar in meaning to the text word, errors similar in grammatical function, and errors with graphic/phoneme similarity. The *GORT–R* system also provides for other types of miscues such as self-corrections, omissions, additions, reversals, and dialectical interference.

The *GORT–R* is a useful measure for analyzing students' skills in oral reading. It is not as complete a measure as the *WRMT–R,* but it assesses areas that the *WRMT–R* does not, specifically oral reading of connected text and reading rate. However, the *GORT–R* may underestimate the comprehension skills of those students for whom silent reading improves understanding. Results of the *GORT–R* provide information about strengths and weaknesses related to oral reading, and they are best used to identify areas needing further assessment.

TEST OF READING COMPREHENSION (REVISED EDITION)

The *Test of Reading Comprehension* (rev. ed) (*TORC*) does not attempt to measure all aspects of the reading process. Instead, it emphasizes comprehension skills, silent reading, and knowledge of word meanings.

The *TORC* contains eight subtests. Instructions for each subtest are read to the student, and most subtests include one or two demonstration items. The student reads the test questions silently and then records responses on a separate answer sheet. No time limits are imposed.

It is not necessary to administer the entire battery. However, four subtests are used to determine the Reading Comprehension Quotient, an index of general reading comprehension ability. If this information is desired, the entire General Comprehension Core should be administered.

General Comprehension Core

☐ *General Vocabulary.* The student is presented with three stimulus words related in some way. He or she then considers four possible responses and chooses two that relate to the stimulus words. For example, if the stimulus words are *white, red,* and *green,* the possible responses might be

    A. *blue*

    B. *sky*

TEST OF READING COMPREHENSION (REV. ED.) (TORC)
V. L. Brown, D. D. Hammill, & J. L. Wiederholt (1986)

Type: Norm-referenced test

Major Content Areas: Silent reading comprehension and vocabulary

Type of Administration: Individual or small group

Administration Time: 10 to 30 minutes per subtest, between $1\frac{1}{2}$ and 3 hours for the entire battery

Age/Grade Levels: Ages 7–0 to 17–11

Types of Scores: Percentile ranks, standard scores, Reading Comprehension Quotient (RCQ)

Typical Uses: Identification of strengths and weaknesses in the development of comprehension skills and knowledge of word meanings

Cautions: The *TORC* is a measure of silent reading comprehension. To participate in *TORC* administration, students must be able to work independently. Testers should take care in scoring this measure; items on several subtests require two responses, and on the Sentence Sequencing subtest, responses can earn 0, 2, 3, 4, or 5 points.

C. *yellow*

D. *no*

The student should select answers A and C.

☐ *Syntactic Similarities.* In this subtest, the student reads five sentences and chooses the two that are most similar in meaning. In the following example from the *TORC* manual, sentences A and D are most similar.

A. Sam plays.

B. Sam will not play.

C. Sam played.

D. Sam is playing.

E. Sam is going to play.

☐ *Paragraph Reading.* Students read six one- or two-paragraph selections and answer five multiple choice questions about each. The questions require students to select the best title for the passage, recall details, and make inferences and negative inferences. On the negative inference questions, students identify the sentence that does not go with the selection.

☐ *Sentence Sequencing.* Five sentences that make up a paragraph are listed in random order. The student's task is to determine the sequence in which the sentences should appear. The student responds by writing the letters that correspond to the sentences.

Diagnostic Supplements

☐ *Mathematics Vocabulary.* As in the first subtest, General Vocabulary, the student is shown three stimulus words related in some way. Four possible responses are presented, and the student selects the two that are related to the stimulus words. The vocabulary assessed on this subtest includes numerals, mathematical symbols, number words, and mathematical terms.

☐ *Social Studies Vocabulary.* The format for this subtest is the same as for Mathematics Vocabulary, but the words are drawn from social studies.

☐ *Science Vocabulary.* The format remains the same, but the vocabulary words are drawn from science.

☐ *Reading the Directions of Schoolwork.* On this subtest, the student reads directions and then attempts to follow them. According to the *TORC* manual, "Directions range in difficulty from 'Write your name' to 'Arrange these sentences in order by numbering them correctly' " (p. 14).

The *TORC* is designed for students ages 7–0 to 17–11. The supplementary subtest, Reading the Directions of Schoolwork, is recommended for beginning and remedial readers; norms extend only through age 14–11. The manual points out that, because the *TORC* requires only silent reading, it is appropriate for students who speak a dialect, those with articulation problems, and deaf students.

On the *TORC,* students must be able to work independently. Students answer all questions by writing. Proficiency in taking tests is expected, because students write their answers on a separate answer sheet. Six of the eight subtests are multiple choice, and students respond by making an *X* on the letter of the correct answer or answers. On Sentence Sequencing, students write letters in blank spaces on the answer sheet. It is possible to allow students to write directly in their test booklets if the separate answer sheet causes difficulties. If students are unable to write, they can respond orally or point to the correct response. The answer sheet is not used for the Reading Directions subtest. A separate page is provided so that students can draw lines and circles; make check marks; and write words, numbers, and sentences as directed after each question.

Technical Quality

The standardization sample for the revised edition of the *TORC* contains 2,492 students from 13 states. Included were most of the children from the original version of the *TORC;* however, 6-year-olds were excluded because the test tasks were judged unsuitable for beginning readers. The original sample was "augmented in the spring of 1985" (p. 38), and the final sample appears to approximate the national population in terms of sex, urban–rural residence, and geographic region. No information is provided about race or ethnicity or whether the sample included handicapped and non-English-speaking students. Ages 7 to 17 are represented, but the number of students in the 15-, 16-, and 17-year-old age groups is quite small compared to those for elementary grade age groups.

Internal consistency reliability of the *TORC* is adequate. Test-retest reliability was studied with 59 low socioeconomic students from one parochial school; coefficients ranged from .64 to .91.

Five studies of concurrent validity are described in the manual. Results indicate a moderate relationship between *TORC* results and those of other measures of reading. For example, correlations between *TORC* subtest scores and results of the *PIAT* Reading Comprehension subtest range from .48 to .87. Evidence is also presented to support the *TORC*'s ability to differentiate between normal readers and students with reading difficulties. However, additional information is needed about the *TORC*'s relationship to reading tests commonly used in special education assessment, particularly newer measures such as the *WRMT–R*.

Administration Considerations

Administration of the *TORC* requires no special training. In learning to administer this test, professionals should "give the test to at least three different students, preferably while being observed by someone who knows the test well" (p. 16).

The *TORC* is quite easy to administer. The tester reads the instructions for the subtest to the student, administers available demonstration items, and then allows the student to work independently. Students begin each subtest with item 1 and continue until a ceiling is reached. For most subtests, the ceiling is three errors out of any five consecutive items. There is no ceiling on the Reading Directions subtest; students attempt all items. Testers should consult the manual for specific ceiling rules for the Paragraph Reading and Sentence Sequencing subtests.

Scoring the *TORC* is somewhat more difficult. For example, on the five subtests that require students to mark two responses, credit is given only if both responses are correct. Raw scores should be calculated carefully, particularly on Sentence Sequencing. On this subtest, students can earn 0, 2, 3, 4, or 5 points for each question, depending on the order in which they arrange the sentences to form a paragraph.

Results and Interpretation

The *TORC* provides standard scores and percentile ranks for each subtest. Subtest standard scores have a mean of 10 and a standard deviation of 3. The Reading Comprehension Quotient (RCQ) is a global score indicative of the student's overall skill level in reading comprehension. This score is based on the results of the General Comprehension Core

subtests. The RCQ is a standard score distributed with a mean of 100 and a standard deviation of 15. Standard errors of measurement range from 3 to 7 standard score points for the Reading Comprehension Quotient; those for subtest scores are either 1 or 2 standard score points, depending on the particular subtest and the student's age.

The RCQ and subtest scores are plotted on the *TORC* profile, as Figure 11–3 illustrates. These results are for an 8-year-old student who shows low average performance on two *TORC* subtests: Mathematics Vocabulary and Science Vocabulary.

More important than classifying students' scores in *TORC* interpretation is the identification of strengths and weaknesses in reading comprehension. The general comprehension subtests provide information about the student's ability to comprehend silently read material. The diagnostic subtests assess performance of classroom-related comprehension tasks. Of particular interest with younger elementary students is skill in reading and following written directions. With older elementary students and those in junior high and high school, content areas become important, particularly when students are mainstreamed into regular classes for these subjects.

TORC results are helpful in determining the student's current levels of performance in several different comprehension skills. Informal techniques are then used to gather information about the specific skills that may require educational intervention. However, comprehension is related to the student's ability to recognize and pronounce words, and the *TORC* does not assess decoding skills or oral reading speed, as does the *GORT–R*. Also, it is not as complete a measure as the *WRMT–R*. However, it addresses other important aspects of the reading process. Among the *TORC*'s features are the use of a standard classroom task to assess silent reading comprehension, the inclusion of a reading directions task for younger students, and the provision of standard score results for content area vocabulary subtests.

INFORMAL READING INVENTORIES

Standardized tests are but one of the many types of assessment tools available for the study of students' reading skills. Another popular kind of

FIGURE 11–3
Sample *Test of Reading Comprehension* (rev. ed.) profile

SECTION II. TORC SUBTEST RESULTS

GENERAL READING COMPREHENSION CORE

	Raw Scores	%iles*	Std. Scores
General Vocabulary	11	75	12
Syntactic Similarities	2	37	9
Paragraph Reading	5	50	10
Sentence Sequencing	6	37	9
Total of Standard Scores			40
Reading Comprehension Quotient (RCQ)			100

*Percentiles are available only for the 1986 edition.

DIAGNOSTIC SUPPLEMENTS

	Raw Scores	%iles*	Std. Scores
Mathematics Vocabulary	1	9	6
Social Studies Vocabulary	1	16	7
Science Vocabulary	0	9	6
Reading Directions	21	75	12

SECTION III. TORC PROFILE

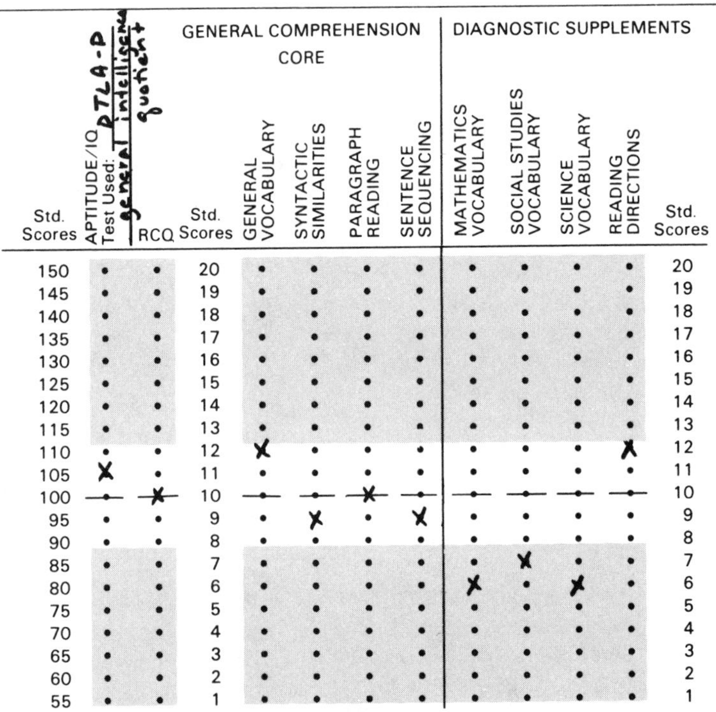

Note. From *Test of Reading Comprehension* (rev. ed.) (p. 26) by V. L. Brown, D. D. Hammill, & J. L. Wiederholt, 1986, Austin, TX: PRO-ED. Copyright 1986 by V. L. Brown, D. D. Hammill, & J. L. Wiederholt. Reprinted by permission.

measure, particularly for classroom use, is the informal reading inventory (IRI). IRIs assess both decoding and comprehension skills. They are made up of graded word lists and reading selections that the student reads orally. The tester notes any decoding errors and records the student's answers to the comprehension questions accompanying each reading selection.

IRIs are grade-referenced measures; the word lists and passages are arranged in order of difficulty according to school grade levels. They are informal measures, and their purpose is to provide information about the student's reading skills in relation to the grade level system of the regular school curriculum.

The results obtained from IRIs are grade level scores. Typically, informal inventories provide three reading levels: the Independent Level, the Instructional Level, and the Frustration Level. A student's Independent Level is the level of graded reading materials that can be read easily with a high degree of comprehension and few errors in decoding. At this level, the student reads independently, without instruction or assistance from the teacher. Reading materials at the student's Instructional Level are somewhat more difficult; this is the level appropriate for reading instruction. Materials at the Frustration Level are too difficult for the student; decoding errors are too frequent and comprehension too poor for instruction to occur. According to Kirk, Kliebhan, and Lerner (1978), the usual criteria for determining these three reading levels are

□ 98% to 100% word recognition accuracy and 90% to 100% accuracy in comprehension for the Independent Level,
□ 95% word recognition accuracy and 75% accuracy in comprehension for the Instructional Level, and
□ 90% or less word recognition accuracy and 50% or less accuracy in comprehension for the Frustration Level.

These standards have been criticized by some experts as too stringent. For instance, Spache (1972) warned that "if the teacher employs an Informal Reading Inventory (IRI) for his estimate of instructional level, he may be expecting children to read with a very unrealistic degree of oral accuracy" (p. 25).

Figure 11–4 presents a sample grade 1 reading passage from the *New Sucher-Allred Reading Placement Inventory* (Sucher & Allred, 1981). The tester introduces the task by reading a sentence that provides a purpose for reading. The student reads the selection orally and then responds to five comprehension questions read by the tester. The number of word recognition and comprehension errors made by the student is recorded to determine whether the selection falls at the student's Independent, Instructional, or Frustration reading level.

Several published informal reading inventories are available for classroom use, or professionals can construct their own IRIs by selecting reading passages of various difficulty levels from a series of reading textbooks (Gillespie-Silver, 1979). Designing an IRI requires time and effort, but the advantage is that locally prepared inventories can reflect the reading series used in a particular school or district.

Selecting an Informal Reading Inventory

All informal reading inventories share several general characteristics. Their major emphasis is oral reading, they use lists of words and reading passages to assess reading skill, and they take both decoding and comprehension into account when determining the student's Instructional Reading Level. As Table 11–2 illustrates, however, there are some differences that should be evaluated when selecting an IRI for use in assessment. Among the factors to consider are the number of forms provided, whether measures of listening skill and silent reading are included, the number and grade levels of word lists and passages, the types of comprehension questions asked, and the availability of optional tests and other features.

The *Analytical Reading Inventory (ARI)* (4th ed.) by Woods and Moe (1989) is worthy of note for several reasons. First, it is one of the few inventories that provides a complete description of the procedures used in development and validation. Readability results are presented for each of the passages on the *ARI* along with vocabulary diversity scores and information about average sentence lengths.

Second, the reading passages are original writings carefully prepared to be "motivational for both boys and girls and also nonsexist in nature" (p. 9). In addition, the content of the graded selections is consistent across the three forms of the *ARI*. At the Grade 6 level, for example, all passages describe famous inventors or scientists who developed a device or technique for saving lives. Because the content of a passage affects its appeal to readers, consistency helps to insure the equivalence of alternate forms.

Third, the *ARI* offers a wide range of types of comprehension questions. The eight questions that accompany each reading selection measure six aspects of comprehension: main ideas, facts, terminology, cause and effect, inference, and conclusions.

A fourth feature of the *ARI* is that it encourages both quantitative and qualitative analysis of decoding errors. Drawing from the work of the Goodmans and others (K. Goodman, 1973a; Goodman & Burke, 1972), the authors of the *ARI* use the term *miscue* instead of *error*. Miscues are defined as deviations from the printed text. All readers make miscues, and miscues are not necessarily evidence of a problem in reading.

FIGURE 11-4

Sample scoring page from the Oral Reading Test of the *New Sucher–Allred Reading Placement Inventory*

SELECTION B, GRADE 1—DIRECTIONS: READ THIS STORY TO FIND OUT WHAT HAPPENED TO MARY.

Mary wanted a black and white puppy at the pet store. Grandfather gave her a dollar for her birthday to buy the puppy.

"Thank you, Grandfather!" said Mary. She put the dollar in her pocket. On the way to the store Mary and her friend Jack played a jumping game.

At the store, Mr. Bond gave Mary the puppy. But when Mary started to get the dollar for Mr. Bond, it was not in her pocket.

"I have lost it!" said Mary sadly.

Mary and Jack went back and looked for the dollar. Finally they found it by the fence.

They ran back to the store and Mary bought the puppy.

"Yap! Yap!" said the puppy.

"He is glad to see me," said Mary.

M ——— N ——— O ——— L ——— S ——— R ———

Comprehension Questions and Possible Answers

——— 1. What would be a good name for this story?
——— 2. What did Mary's grandfather give her for her birthday?
——— 3. What did they do after they couldn't find the dollar?
——— 4. How did Mary lose her dollar?
——— 5. Do you think $1.00 is very much to pay for a puppy? Why?

Possible Answers

1. Mary and the Puppy
2. A dollar
3. Ran back to look in the place where they had been jumping
4. Playing a jumping game
5. Any reasonable answer

W.R. Errors	Comp. Errors		
This is the student's (check one)	**W.R. Errors**		**Comp. Errors**
☐ Ind. level If	0-4	and	0-1
☐ Inst. level If	5-10	and	1¼-2
☐ Frust. level If either	11 or more	or	2¼ or more
☐ Listening Capacity (optional)			1 or fewer

Note. From *New Sucher–Allred Reading Placement Inventory* by R. Sucher and R. A. Allred, 1981, Oklahoma City, OK: The Economy Company. Copyright 1981 by The Economy Company. Reprinted by permission.

TABLE 11–2
A comparison of informal reading inventories

| | MEASURES | | | |
FEATURES	Analytical Reading Inventory	Classroom Reading Inventory	Ekwall Reading Inventory	New Sucher-Allred Reading Placement Inventory
Number of forms	3	4	4	2
Includes measure of silent reading	Yes	Yes	Yes	No
Includes measure of listening skills	Yes	Yes	Yes	Yes
Number of graded word lists (per form)	7	8	11 (same list for all forms)	12
Grade levels of word lists	Primer, first reader, grades 2–6	Preprimer, primer, grades 1–6	Preprimer, primer, grades 1–9	Primer, first reader, 2^1, 2^2, 3^1, 3^2, grades 4–9
Number of graded passages (per form)	10	10 (8 for Forms C and D)	10	12
Grade levels of passages	Primer, first reader, grades 2–9	Preprimer, primer, grades 1–8	Preprimer, grades 1–9	Primer, first reader, 2^1, 2^2, 3^1, 3^2, grades 4–9
Types of comprehension questions	Main idea, factual, terminology, cause and effect, inferential, conclusion	Facts, inference, vocabulary	Factual, inference, vocabulary	Main idea, facts, sequence, inference, critical thinking
Optional tests	Two sets of graded expository passages (social studies and science)	Graded Spelling Survey	Ekwall Basic Words, Letter Knowledge, Syllables and Vowels, Contractions, Quick Survey Word List, El Paso Phonics Survey	None
Other features	□ Manual describes development, field testing, and readability studies □ Content of passages is consistent across forms □ Decoding errors can be analyzed qualitatively	Forms C and D are designed to appeal to the interests of secondary grade students and adults	Manual describes development of the IRI and its reliability	Well-designed manual

For example, miscues such as the substitution of *the* for *a* do not change the meaning of the text and thus do not affect comprehension. On the *ARI,* miscues can be analyzed quantitatively by following the traditional procedure of counting the different types of errors made by the student. Or the Qualitative Analysis Summary Sheet can be used to analyze the nature of each deviation from the text. Figure 11–5 provides a sample qualitative analysis of the miscues made by John, a fourth grade student.

Most informal reading inventories are designed for elementary grade students. One exception is the *Classroom Reading Inventory* (5th ed.) (Sil-

varoli, 1986). The content of one form of this IRI addresses the interest levels of junior high students, and the content of another is geared to interests of high school students and adults.

Some IRIs include supplementary measures. For example, the *Ekwall Reading Inventory* (2nd ed.) (Ekwall, 1986) provides several strategies for the evaluation of reading and readiness skills. Among these are the Ekwall Basic Sight Words test and the El Paso Phonics Survey. In addition, the graded word list on the Ekwall inventory is the San Diego Quick Assessment (LaPray & Ross, 1969), an informal measure often used to estimate word recognition skill level.

FIGURE 11–5

Sample qualitative analysis of miscues from the *Analytical Reading Inventory*

FORM _____ C _____

Level	# of Miscues	STUDENT: *John Stone* — MISCUE IN CONTEXT	Meaning Change	DATE: 1/18/88 — NATURE OF MISCUE
2	②	"Look out, ~~you'll~~ (*you're*) get hit!"	yes	final substitution – used wrong sight word – no self-correction
		"Thud!" was the noise I heard, then I saw my pup ~~lying~~ (*down*) in the street.	no	whole word substitution meaning based
		"Mom! Dad!" I yelled as I ran ~~straight~~ (*street*)(SC) home.	sc	reader is self-correcting to insure meaning
		But they started rolling down my face anyway as I blasted ~~through~~ (*thought*)(SC) the door.	sc	reader is self-correcting to insure meaning
3	⑦	These are the signs which Jack ~~read~~ (*reed*) ...	yes	medial vowel – possible tense change no self-correction
		Jack was the new boy and he really wanted to ~~belong~~ (*become*) to the club.	yes	medial/final substitution no self-correction
		~~Suddenly~~ (*Sunday*) he dashed home and returned with a bucket....	yes	medial/final substitution no self-correction
		He began ~~pounding~~ (*banging*) on the clubhouse door.	no	whole word substitution no self-correction
		"I don't know the secret word," he ~~remarked~~ (*said*), "but ...	no	whole word substitution no self-correction
		~~All~~ (*and*) the kids thought ~~this~~ was a great idea and quickly ~~invited~~ (*invented*) Jack to belong!	? yes	whole word sub. – no SC medial vowel – no SC

Note. From *Analytical Reading Inventory* (4th ed.) (p. 31) by M. L. Woods and A. J. Moe, 1989, Columbus, OH: Merrill. Copyright 1989 by Merrill Publishing Company. Reprinted by permission.

Two recently published measures are attempts to make reading inventories less informal. The *Standardized Reading Inventory (SRI)* (Newcomer, 1986) has set procedures for administration and scoring, and information is available about its reliability and validity. Reading passages on the *SRI* are composed of words drawn from five popular basal reading series; criteria for classifying a passage as within the student's independent, instructional, or frustration reading level were determined from the performance of individuals whose reading levels ranged from preprimer to grade 8. Although the *SRI* is standardized, it is not norm-referenced. The *Formal Reading Inventory (FRI)* (Wiederholt, 1986) does offer norms. The *FRI* is composed of a series of passages that students read silently and orally; standard score results are available for silent reading, and oral reading miscues can be analyzed informally.

OTHER INFORMAL STRATEGIES

Assessment for instructional planning in reading relies upon informal strategies, including the informal reading inventories described in the previous section. Here the focus is on other types of informal techniques: teacher checklists, error analysis, cloze procedures, diagnostic teaching and clinical reading interviews, criterion-referenced tests, and questionnaires and interviews.

Teacher Checklists

Checklists are a quick and efficient means of gathering information from teachers and other professionals about their observations and perceptions of students' reading skills. The reading behaviors described on checklists can be of any kind: decoding, comprehension, oral reading, silent reading, or a combination. Most typically, checklists are designed to identify difficulties in reading or are curriculum checklists used to record and monitor reading skills development. An example of a reading difficulty checklist appears in Figure 11–6.

Error Analysis

One of the most frequently used techniques in the informal assessment of reading is error analysis. It is a traditional technique that dates back to the 1930s when Marion Monroe (1932) described common types of oral reading errors. Error analysis is a study of the mistakes students make. Unlike the more general procedure, response analysis, it does not take into consideration both correct and incorrect responses. In reading assessment, incorrect responses provide information about how the student is processing the text and suggest directions for instructional interventions.

Error analysis is generally used to investigate decoding mistakes in oral reading. The first step in conducting an error analysis is to select material for the student to read. That material may be a word list or some sort of connected text. If the teacher is interested in the student's ability to read common words—words that appear with high frequency in reading books and other text materials—the teacher could select a list like that in Table 11–3. This high-frequency word list is Johnson's (1971) updated version of the *Dolch Basic Sight Word List* (Dolch, 1953). It includes 220 words commonly found in reading texts for the primary grades.

Also available are lists of "survival" reading words. These contain words believed necessary for minimal literacy in today's society. Included are words found on warning signs and notices (e.g., "Danger," "Keep Out," "Poison") and words used to provide information (e.g., "Rest Rooms," "This Way Out," "Restaurant") (Kaluger & Kolson, 1978).

If connected text is the concern, the teacher can choose from the passages provided on informal inventories and some standardized tests, a series of graded textbooks for reading instruction, or other materials such as content area textbooks or library books on topics of interest. The school's reading series is a good source of reading selections, particularly if the teacher is also interested in determining the student's instructional reading level. The teacher should gather several levels of graded readers so the student can begin reading at a level where he or she can experience success.

The next step is to decide what types of responses will be considered errors and how these errors will be classified. In the reading of word lists, mispronunciations and nonpronunciations are typically viewed as errors. Mispronunciations occur when the student decodes a word incorrectly; for example, he or she may read *who* when the text says *how*. Mispronunciation errors are often classified by the types of letter sounds in which the

FIGURE 11-6
Reading difficulty checklist

		1st Check	2nd Check	3rd Check		
1					Word-by-word reading	
2					Incorrect phrasing	
3					Poor pronunciation	
4					Omissions	
5					Repetitions	
6					Inversions or reversals	
7					Insertions	
8					Substitutions	Oral Reading
9					Basic sight words not known	
10					Sight vocabulary not up to grade level	
11					Guesses at words	
12					Consonant sounds not known	
13					Vowel sounds not known	
14					Vowel pairs and/or consonant clusters not known (digraphs, diphthongs, blends)	
15					Lacks desirable structural analysis (Morphology)	
16					Unable to use context clues	
17					Contractions not known	
18					Comprehension inadequate	Oral Silent
19					Vocabulary inadequate	
20					Unaided recall scanty	
21					Response poorly organized	
22					Unable to locate information	
23					Inability to skim	Study Skills
24					Inability to adjust rate to difficulty of material	
25					Low rate of speed	
26					High rate at expense of accuracy	
27					Voicing-lip movement	
28					Lacks knowledge of the alphabet	Other Abilities
29					Written recall limited by spelling ability	
30					Undeveloped dictionary skills	

NAME _____
GRADE _____

TEACHER _____
SCHOOL _____

D—Difficulty recognized
P—Pupil progressing
N—No longer has difficulty

The items listed above represent the most common difficulties encountered by pupils in the reading program. Following each numbered item are spaces for notation of that specific difficulty. This may be done at intervals of several months. One might use a check to indicate difficulty recognized or the following letters to represent an even more accurate appraisal:

Note. From *Locating and Correcting Reading Difficulties* (5th ed.) (p. 6) by E. E. Ekwall, 1989, Columbus, OH: Merrill. Copyright 1989 by Merrill Publishing Company. Reprinted by permission.

mistakes occur: consonant sounds, vowel sounds, blends (e.g., the first two letters in *tree* and *glass*), digraphs (e.g., the first two letters in *ship* and *chalk*), and diphthongs (e.g., the last two letters in *cow* and *toy*). Nonpronunciation occurs when the student fails to say a word. If word recognition speed is a major concern, the teacher can set a time limit for responding. For example, if 2 seconds are established as the time limit, correct responses produced after the 2-second time period would be scored as nonpronunciations.

Several types of errors can occur when students read connected text. Most systems of error analysis include at least four classes of errors.

- *Additions*—The reader adds words or parts of words to the printed text. For example, if the text is "the brown dog," the reader says "the *big* brown dog."
- *Substitutions*—The reader mispronounces a word or parts of words; this type of error is also called a mispronunciation. For example, if the text is "the small house," the reader says "the small *horse*."
- *Omissions*—The reader fails to pronounce words or parts of words. This error occurs when readers skip words, when they hesitate in responding, or when they say they do not know a word and the teacher supplies it. For example, if the text is "the gnarled old tree," the reader might omit the word "gnarled" and read "the old tree."
- *Reversals*—The reader changes the order of the words in a phrase or sentence or the order of sounds within a word. For example, if the text is "There were many seagulls," the reader says, "*Were there* many seagulls."

Repetitions are another type of reading behavior considered an error by some professionals. A repetition occurs when the reader repeats a word or a series of words. For example, if the text is "The man walked to the levee," the reader says, "The man walked to the *walked to the* levee." Other behaviors sometimes viewed as errors are disregard of punctuation and poor phrasing in oral reading. However, most educators agree that if a student makes and then corrects an error, the error is not counted.

When collecting a reading sample for error analysis, two copies of the reading material are needed: one for the student to read and another for the teacher's use in recording the student's responses. A standard set of symbols is used for noting errors:

- The symbol ∧ indicates an *addition;* the ∧ is placed in the text where the word or word part has been added, and the addition is written above the text. For example,

  big
  "The∧brown dog."

- A *substitution* is marked by crossing out the mispronounced word and writing the substituted word above it. For example,

  horse
  "The small ~~house~~."

- *Omissions* are shown by drawing a circle around the word, word part, or series of words the student left out. For example,

  "The (gnarled) old tree."

- The symbol ∽ indicates a *reversal* of words or parts of a word. For example,

  "There were many seagulls."

- *Repetitions* are marked by drawing an arrow under the word or words repeated. For example,

  "The man walked to the levee."

The next step is analysis of the student's errors. In the traditional approach to analysis, the professional simply counts the number of errors that occurred in each class. However, it is also necessary to decide which errors are instructionally important for the student under study. Most educators would agree that substitutions and omissions have instructional relevance, but other types of errors may be of less concern. Errors such as the addition of an *-s* ending or an occasional repetition usually do not alter the sense of the passage.

An alternate method of error analysis takes into account the quality of the errors readers make.

TABLE 11–3
High-frequency word list

Preprimer	Primer	First	Second	Third
1. the	45. when	89. many	133. know	177. don't
2. of	46. who	90. before	134. while	178. does
3. and	47. will	91. must	135. last	179. got
4. to	48. more	92. through	136. might	180. united
5. a	49. no	93. back	137. us	181. left
6. in	50. if	94. years	138. great	182. number
7. that	51. out	95. where	139. old	183. course
8. is	52. so	96. much	140. year	184. war
9. was	53. said	97. your	141. off	185. until
10. he	54. what	98. may	142. come	186. always
11. for	55. up	99. well	143. since	187. away
12. it	56. its	100. down	144. against	188. something
13. with	57. about	101. should	145. go	189. fact
14. as	58. into	102. because	146. came	190. through
15. his	59. than	103. each	147. right	191. water
16. on	60. them	104. just	148. used	192. less
17. be	61. can	105. those	149. take	193. public
18. at	62. only	106. people	150. three	194. put
19. by	63. other	107. Mr.	151. states	195. thing
20. I	64. new	108. how	152. himself	196. almost
21. this	65. some	109. too	153. few	197. hand
22. had	66. could	110. little	154. house	198. enough
23. not	67. time	111. state	155. use	199. far
24. are	68. these	112. good	156. during	200. took
25. but	69. two	113. very	157. without	201. head
26. from	70. may	114. make	158. again	202. yet
27. or	71. then	115. would	159. place	203. government
28. have	72. do	116. still	160. American	204. system
29. an	73. first	117. own	161. around	205. better
30. they	74. any	118. see	162. however	206. set
31. which	75. my	119. men	163. home	207. told
32. one	76. now	120. work	164. small	208. nothing
33. you	77. such	121. long	165. found	209. night
34. were	78. like	122. get	166. Mrs.	210. end
35. her	79. our	123. here	167. thought	211. why
36. all	80. over	124. between	168. went	212. called
37. she	81. man	125. both	169. say	213. didn't
38. there	82. me	126. life	170. part	214. eyes
39. would	83. even	127. being	171. once	215. find
40. their	84. most	128. under	172. general	216. going
41. we	85. made	129. never	173. high	217. look
42. him	86. after	130. day	174. upon	218. asked
43. been	87. also	131. same	175. school	219. later
44. has	88. did	132. another	176. every	220. knew

Note. From "The Dolch List Reexamined" by D. D. Johnson, 1971, *The Reading Teacher, 24,* pp. 455–56. Copyright 1971 by the International Reading Association. Reprinted with permission of Dale D. Johnson and the International Reading Association.

Woods and Moe (1989) call this approach qualitative analysis. In this system, errors are called miscues (K. Goodman, 1973a, 1973b; Goodman & Burke, 1972). According to Burke (1973), "Even proficient adult readers make miscues with some regularity" (p. 21). As noted earlier in this chapter, miscues are not necessarily cause for alarm. Efficient readers are still able to comprehend the meaning of text, because the types of errors they make tend to preserve meaning. Inefficient readers, in contrast, make errors that change the meaning of the text (Goodman, 1973b).

Figure 11–5 (p. 314) provides an example of qualitative analysis. Miscues are analyzed to determine whether they represent a change in meaning from the original text. For example, the substitution of *said* for *remarked* is semantically correct and does not alter meaning, but the substitution of *invented* for *invited* does change the sense of the passage.

The miscues that produce changes in meaning can be further analyzed. Burke (1973) suggests that the student's miscue and the original text be compared in three ways:

1. Graphic Similarity: How much do the two words *look* alike?
2. Sound Similarity: How much do the two words *sound* alike?
3. Grammatical Function: Is the grammatical function of the reader's word the same as the grammatical function of the text word? (p. 23)

These questions are drawn from the short form of the *Reading Miscue Inventory* (Goodman & Burke, 1972). The most acceptable miscue is semantically correct. Less acceptable are errors that are grammatically correct but semantically incorrect and errors that fit the graphic or phonic characteristics of the text but are semantically and grammatically incorrect.

Error analysis techniques can be used to study comprehension as well as decoding skills. One way to do this is to ask students comprehension questions after they have finished reading a passage. Or students can be asked to retell the story they have read or summarize the major points of an expository passage. In selecting reading materials for the assessment of comprehension, the type of material is an important consideration. Expository, narrative, and other types of texts such as poetry and plays are organized differently, and

the reader's experience with the type of text may affect comprehension. According to Lapp and Flood (1983), comprehension is influenced "not only by linguistic cues and semantic content but also by the knowledge that we bring to a passage" (p. 167).

Several kinds of questions can be used to assess students' understanding of the meaning of a passage. To evaluate literal comprehension, the student can be asked to state the main idea of the passage, propose a title for the selection, recall details from the passage, remember a series of events or ideas, and explain the meaning of vocabulary words introduced in the reading selection. Inferential thinking is assessed by asking questions that force students to go beyond the information provided in the passage; students can be asked to draw conclusions, make predictions, evaluate ideas or actions, suggest alternative endings for a narrative, and so forth. In preparing comprehension questions to accompany a reading selection, professionals should ensure that the questions are text-dependent. Questions should be answerable only by students who have read the text.

Analysis of comprehension errors is conducted in the same way as analysis of decoding errors. A sample of the student's responses is gathered, and errors are noted and classified. Most typically, the classification system is based on the various types of comprehension questions: main idea, fact, sequence, vocabulary, inference, conclusion, and so forth. The number of errors in each category is totaled to help the professional identify the comprehension skills in which the student requires additional instruction.

The Cloze Procedure

The cloze procedure (Bormuth, 1968; Jongsma, 1971) is an informal technique for determining whether a particular textbook or other reading material is within a student's instructional reading level. To use the cloze procedure, the teacher selects a passage of approximately 250 words. The first and last sentences of the passage are left intact. In the rest of the passage, every fifth word is deleted and replaced with a blank. For example, the sentence "The little dog sat down beside the boy" would become "The little dog sat _____ beside the boy." The student reads the passage and attempts to fill in each of the blanks.

If the student correctly supplies between 44% and 57% of the missing words, the passage is considered to be at the student's instructional level (Bormuth, 1968; Burron & Claybaugh, 1977).

This technique is also useful for assessing comprehension skills. By omitting every fifth (or seventh or *n*th word), the teacher forces the student to rely on the context clues within the passage to derive meaning. Figure 11–7 provides an example.

Diagnostic Teaching and Clinical Reading Interviews

In reading assessment, diagnostic teaching procedures are often based on the results of a clinical reading interview. Clinical reading interviews combine the techniques of observation, interviewing, and diagnostic probes. The professional observes the student engaged in some type of reading task,

but assessment does not stop with observation. Students are questioned about their reading strategies, comprehension of the material, and background knowledge about passage content. In addition, the teacher can alter the nature of the reading task to determine how instructional adaptations will affect the student's reading performance. Consider the following example:

Theresa was referred to Mr. Considine, a Chapter I teacher, for help with her reading. Theresa was in the lowest group in a third-grade classroom and seemed to have great difficulty reading with comprehension.

Remembering a recent workshop for Chapter I teachers that he had attended, Mr. Considine reached for the easiest book in a set of graded readers instead of the diagnostic reading test he typically used. He asked Theresa to read for him from successively more difficult readers until she could proceed no further without his assistance. Then he began to prompt her,

FIGURE 11–7
The cloze procedure as a measure of comprehension skills

Teacher reads these directions: Here is a story with some words left out. Each time a word is left out, it has been replaced with a line. When you come to a line, try to figure out what word should be in that blank. Ready—begin.

Jan has a cat.

The cat's <u>name</u> is Tab.

Tab does not <u>like</u> dogs.

One day <u>a</u> dog ran after Tab.

<u>Tab</u> ran up a tree.

The dog could not go <u>up</u> the tree.

Then <u>the</u> dog went away.

Grade one reading level

- -

Jan has a cat.

The cat's _____ is Tab.

Tab does not _____ dogs.

One day _____ dog ran after Tab.

_____ ran up a tree.

The dog could not go _____ the tree.

Then _____ dog went away.

Note. From *Locating and Correcting Reading Difficulties* (5th ed.) (p. 251) by E. E. Ekwall, 1989, Columbus, OH: Merrill. Copyright 1989 by Merrill Publishing Company. Reprinted by permission.

to read in unison with her, to read sentences before she read them, to read all of the words that surrounded an unfamiliar one to cue it, and to employ other techniques for helping Theresa read orally with good expression. He also asked her to dictate a story from her personal experience; then he printed the story and helped her to read it with good expression.

From all of the techniques Mr. Considine used he got a good diagnostic picture of Theresa's strengths and weaknesses in reading. In addition, and perhaps more important, he was able to identify some promising strategies for helping Theresa read with understanding. (Otto & Smith, 1983, pp. 24–25)

As this example illustrates, clinical reading interviews are dynamic procedures. The professional observes, questions, changes the reading task, and then observes and questions again. The goal of the process is to provide information about promising strategies for reading instruction.

Clinical interviews focus on the interaction between the reader and the text; they allow the professional to go beyond the product of the reading act to evaluate the process. There are many important factors to consider when exploring the reading process, including the student's background knowledge, familiarity with the structure of the text (e.g., narrative or expository), understanding of anaphoric terms, facility with language, and use of metacognitive strategies (Samuels, 1983).

For example, students may or may not have background knowledge about the content and structure of the passage. These factors are critical for comprehension; if the student is totally unfamiliar with the content being presented, comprehension will suffer despite adequate decoding skills.

Anaphoric terms are words used as substitutes for words or phrases that have already appeared in a text. In the text "The dog and cat ate their supper. They liked it," there are three anaphoric terms: *their* and *they,* referring to the dog and cat, and *it,* referring to the supper. Students unable to identify the referents of anaphoric terms will lose the meaning of the passage.

Metacognitive strategies are the methods readers use to think about their interactions with the text. Effective readers think about both the content of the material and the reading process. According to Samuels (1983), the active reader asks such questions as

□ Why am I reading this?
□ Do I want to read this for superficial overview or for detail?
□ Do I know when there is a breakdown in comprehension?
□ When there is a breakdown in understanding, what can I do to get back on the track again?
□ What are the major and minor points of this text?
□ Can I summarize or synthesize the major points made in this text? (pp. 6–7)

The professional can adapt these questions and use them to investigate the way the student interacts with text during a clinical reading interview.

In addition to asking questions during the clinical interview, the professional can introduce diagnostic probes. For example, if decoding skills are a concern, the teacher can change the task by reading aloud with the student, pronouncing the difficult words for the student, or providing clues for the difficult words. Sometimes the teacher may wish to have the student read the entire passage alone without assistance and then intervene. If the teacher discovers that the student has difficulty with a particular set of decoding skills such as medial vowel sounds or word endings, those skills can be taught, and then the student can attempt the passage again with the teacher providing help as needed. Having the student do repeated readings of a passage is an excellent technique for evaluating his or her ability to learn and apply new skills.

What is learned about the student's skill levels and responsiveness to various types of instruction during the clinical reading interview is then used to design a diagnostic teaching sequence. Diagnostic teaching is a more structured process. Data are collected to describe the student's entry level skills; then an instructional intervention is begun and consistently continued over several days. The student's performance is monitored daily to determine whether the intervention is effective and should be included as part of the instructional program.

Criterion-Referenced Tests

Criterion-referenced tests assess the student's mastery of specific skills within the reading curriculum. They are based upon instructional objectives and, as Chapter 5 described, are quite easy to construct. For example, if mastery of high-frequency reading words is a goal of the instructional program, the teacher could use the word list presented in Table 11–3 as the basis of a criterion-referenced test. The objective for this test might be *The student will read the high-frequency list aloud and pronounce at least 200 of the 220 words correctly.* The teacher would present each of the words to the student, keep track of errors, and then evaluate the student's performance to determine whether the objective had been achieved.

Several criterion-referenced tests of reading are commercially available, and professionals may select from these rather than constructing measures themselves. It is less time-consuming to use a criterion-referenced test that has already been prepared, but the time saved is wasted unless the measure adequately reflects the classroom curriculum. In evaluating criterion-referenced tests, professionals should carefully study the objectives upon which these measures are based to insure that the skills included are important ones. Results of criterion-referenced tests should be relevant to the student's curriculum and immediately applicable to instruction.

The series of criterion-referenced tests by Brigance is one of the more popular sets of measures. This series includes the *BRIGANCE® Diagnostic Inventory of Early Development* (1978) for children from birth through age 7, the *BRIGANCE® Diagnostic Inventory of Basic Skills* (1977) for kindergarten through grade 6, the *BRIGANCE® Diagnostic Comprehensive Inventory of Basic Skills* (1983a) for kindergarten through grade 9, and the *BRIGANCE® Diagnostic Inventory of Essential Skills* (1981) for grades 4 through 12. A Spanish edition of the *Basic Skills* inventory (Brigance, 1983b) is also available. Each of these measures contains several tests of reading; even the inventory for preschool children offers tests of readiness and basic reading skills.

The *Basic Skills* measure, designed for the elementary grades, provides criterion-referenced tests of readiness, word recognition, oral reading and comprehension, word analysis, and vocabulary. The *Comprehensive Inventory* for elementary and junior high students assesses several types of reading skills: word recognition grade placement, oral reading, reading comprehension, word analysis, and functional word recognition. Table 11–4 lists the names of the tests assessing these

skill areas. In all, 48 tests of reading skill are included on the *Comprehensive Inventory.*

The *Essential Skills* measure is intended for older elementary and secondary grade students. It contains the same types of tests as the *Comprehensive Inventory,* but skills are assessed at somewhat higher grade levels. For example, the reading comprehension portion of *Essential Skills* extends through the grade 11 level. Other features of both these measures are the tests that assess functional skills such as reading direction words, warning and safety signs, and informational signs.

Many other criterion-referenced tests attempt to provide comprehensive coverage of the reading skill area. Among the available measures are

- *Multilevel Academic Skills Inventory* (Howell et al., 1982)—A collection of general survey tests, placement tests, and specific skill tests of decoding and comprehension for grades 1 to 8; testing begins at the general level to identify skills and subskills that require further evaluation with the specific skill tests.
- *System FORE* (Bagai & Bagai, 1979)—A criterion-referenced curriculum that offers objectives, assessment devices, and suggestions for selecting instructional materials; *FORE Reading* contains over 300 objectives in decoding, study skills, and comprehension, and *FORE Secondary* continues the skill sequence into the high school grades.
- *Wisconsin Tests of Reading Skills Development* (1972, 1977)—A series of field-tested measures of word attack, comprehension, and study skills for kindergarten through grade 6; the system includes a set of skills and objectives, criterion-referenced tests, the Teacher's Resource Files for instruction, and a management system.

In using criterion-referenced tests such as these, the professional selects and administers only those tests that address the skills of interest for the particular student.

Questionnaires and Interviews

Questionnaires and interviews are used in reading assessment to gather information about students' views and opinions: their attitudes toward reading, perceptions of the reading process, opinions of their own reading abilities, likes and dislikes in

TABLE 11–4

Reading tests on the *BRIGANCE®*
Diagnostic Comprehensive
Inventory of Basic Skills

WORD RECOGNITION GRADE PLACEMENT
    Word Recognition Grade Placement, Forms A and B

ORAL READING
    Reads Orally at Preprimer or Primer Level
    Reads Orally at Lower or Upper First-Grade Level
    Reads Orally at Lower or Upper Second-Grade Level
    Reads Orally at Lower or Upper Third-Grade Level
    Reads Orally at Fourth or Fifth-Grade Level
    Reads Orally at Sixth or Seventh-Grade Level
    Reads Orally at Eighth or Ninth-Grade Level

READING COMPREHENSION
    Reading Vocabulary Comprehension Grade Placement, Form A
    Reading Vocabulary Comprehension Grade Placement, Form B
    Comprehends at Primer Level
    Comprehends at Lower First-Grade Level
    Comprehends at Upper First-Grade Level
    Comprehends at Lower Second-Grade Level
    Comprehends at Upper Second-Grade Level
    Comprehends at Lower Third-Grade Level
    Comprehends at Upper Third-Grade Level
    Comprehends at Fourth-Grade Level
    Comprehends at Fifth-Grade Level
    Comprehends at Sixth-Grade Level
    Comprehends at Seventh-Grade Level
    Comprehends at Eighth-Grade Level
    Comprehends at Ninth-Grade Level

WORD ANALYSIS
    Auditory Discrimination
    Identifies Initial Consonants in Spoken Words
    Pronounces Written Initial Consonants
    Substitutes Initial Consonant Sounds
    Substitutes Short Vowel Sounds
    Substitutes Long Vowel Sounds
    Identifies Final Consonants in Spoken Words
    Substitutes Final Consonant Sounds
    Pronounces Written Initial Blends and Digraphs
    Substitutes Initial Blend and Digraph Sounds
    Reads Words with Common Endings
    Reads Words with Vowel Digraphs and Diphthongs
    Reads Words with Phonetic Irregularities
    Reads Suffixes
    Reads Prefixes
    Identifies Number of Syllables in Spoken Words
    Divides Words into Syllables

FUNCTIONAL WORD RECOGNITION
    Basic Sight Vocabulary
    Direction Words
    Contractions
    Abbreviations
    Warning and Safety Signs
    Informational Signs
    Warning Labels
    Food Labels
    Number Words

Note. From *BRIGANCE® Diagnostic Comprehensive Inventory of Basic Skills* by A. H. Brigance, 1983, N. Billerica, MA: Curriculum Associates, Inc. Copyright 1983 by Curriculum Associates, Inc. Adapted by permission.

reading materials, and so on. Interviews are preferred for younger students and those with poor reading skills; print questionnaires are reserved for more mature students who are able to read with comprehension and answer in writing.

Students can be interviewed to find out their attitudes toward reading and preferences in reading materials. The teacher could ask questions such as

☐ Is reading one of your better subjects in school?
☐ What types of reading activities are the easiest for you? Which are the hardest?
☐ If you could read a story about anything in the world, what would the story be about?
☐ What magazines do you read or look at?
☐ Do you ever read the newspaper? If so, what parts of the paper do you read?
☐ Would you rather read true stories or stories that the author makes up?
☐ What are your hobbies? Have you ever read a book, a story, or a magazine article about one of your favorite activities?
☐ What was the last thing you read for fun? When did you read it? What did you enjoy about it?

The questionnaire in Figure 11–8 is designed for secondary grade students, but some of the questions could be adapted for interviews with younger readers. The purpose of this measure is to elicit information from students about their attitudes toward reading, their study skills and work habits, and reading interests. In addition, students are asked to describe the strategies they use when reading and to evaluate their own reading performance.

WITHIN THE CONTEXT OF THE CLASSROOM

The assessment procedures described so far have been student-centered measures designed to evaluate the student's current levels of performance in important reading skills. In this section, the emphasis shifts to assessment tools and techniques for studying the classroom learning environment and its influence on the student's reading abilities.

The Instructional Environment

In the elementary grades, assessment of the instructional environment must take into account the reading curriculum and the instructional methods and materials used to implement that curriculum. The most common elementary reading program centers around a basal reading series. A basal series is a set of graded reading textbooks that span a number of grade levels, usually from the beginning reading levels (preprimer and primer) through the end of grade 6 or grade 8.

Assessment of the instructional factors that influence younger students begins with a study of the classroom reading program.

1. Does the basal reading series used in the classroom stress text, meaning, or the interaction between text and meaning? If the reading program is not based on a basal series, what is the major component?
2. Do the reading selections provided in the basal series build on the students' language and background experiences, or do they present unfamiliar content?
3. How many levels of the reading series are in use? Is there a range of reading textbooks available to accommodate the range of student skills? Or if a third grade classroom is under study, are only grade 3 reading books available?
4. What instructional materials supplement reading textbooks? Workbooks? Worksheets? Computer-based instructional programs? Reading games? Leisure reading books?
5. What types of reading skills are stressed in classroom instruction? Decoding? Comprehension? Oral reading? Silent reading?
6. What decoding skills are emphasized? Sight vocabulary? Phonic analysis? Structural analysis? Contextual analysis? A combination?
7. Is the reading curriculum organized so the sequence of instruction is logical and the instructional steps are of appropriate size?
8. Is reading instruction based on ongoing assessment? How often are performance data collected for monitoring students' progress? What strategies are used to determine the starting points for students entering the program?
9. How are students grouped for reading instruction? Does the entire class receive instruction at one time? Is the class divided into large groups of 10 to 15 students each? Smaller groups of 5 to 8 students? How much individualization takes place in each group?

10. What instructional techniques does the teacher use to present new skills and information? Lecture? Discussion? Demonstration and modeling?

11. In what types of learning activities do students participate? Oral reading? Silent reading? Completing workbook pages or worksheets? Writing book reports?

FIGURE 11–8
Reading questionnaire for older students

A. Strategies of effective reading

1. Which one of the following statements best describes what you do when you can't seem to understand what you're reading?
   (a) I re-read.
   (b) I stop reading and do something else for awhile.
   (c) I keep reading to the end.
   (d) I ask someone else to read it and explain it to me.
   (e) I try to find something easier to read.
2. Which one of the following is most descriptive of your rate of reading?
   (a) I read everything at about the same speed.
   (b) I adjust my rate according to the difficulty of the reading materials.
   (c) I adjust my rate according to my interest in the reading materials.
   (d) I adjust my reading rate according to my purpose for reading.
3. When I want to get an idea of what a book is about, I
   (a) read the book from beginning to end
   (b) look for the author's name
   (c) consult the book's index
   (d) consult the book's table of contents
   (e) ask the librarian or my teacher

B. General attitude toward reading

1. Choose one of the following that best describes your attitude toward reading:
   (a) I like to read almost anything.
   (b) I like to read, but only what interests me.
   (c) I do some reading, but I don't really like it.
   (d) I don't like to read at all.
2. If I had to learn about the writing of the Declaration of Independence, I would rather
   (a) have my teacher tell us about it
   (b) see a movie or TV program about it
   (c) read about it
3. How many books have you read during the past month that weren't assigned in school?
   (a) None
   (b) One
   (c) Two
   (d) Three or more

C. Self-evaluation

1. With which one of the following do you have the most trouble in reading?
   (a) Understanding the meaning of difficult words

   (b) Remembering what I read
   (c) Understanding the main ideas
   (d) Reading fast enough
2. In which of the following school subjects do you find the reading most difficult?
   (a) Science
   (b) Social Studies
   (c) Mathematics
   (d) English
3. Do you think you need extra help in reading?
   (a) Yes
   (b) No

D. Work-study skills and library habits

1. Did you go to the library to find reading materials during the past month?
   (a) Not at all
   (b) Once or twice
   (c) Three or more times
2. Which of the following have you used most often to find a book in the library?
   (a) The card catalog
   (b) Browsing
   (c) Asking someone
3. Choose one of the following to describe why you usually go to a library (school or community library):
   (a) To study or read on my own
   (b) To look up information for homework assignments
   (c) To take books out to read for fun
   (d) I hardly ever go to a library

E. Reading interests

This is best tested by a format that allows the student to rate his interests from high to low:

Directions: For each of the types of reading matter listed below, choose the rating that best describes your interest in it.

Ratings: (a) high interest
         (b) medium interest
         (c) low interest — read only if assigned
         (d) no interest at all — dislike

1. A short story or novel
2. An article that tells how to make or repair something
3. Newspapers and magazines
4. An article or book about something I have a special interest in (such as sports, clothes, music)
5. An article, story, or book about a person I admire

12. How is supervised practice incorporated into the reading program? On the average, how many minutes per day do students spend practicing their reading skills?
13. What changes, if any, have been made in the standard reading program to accommodate the needs of special learners such as the student under assessment?

The nature of the materials that students are required to read is an important factor both for beginning readers and for secondary students expected to use reading as a tool for learning in other subject areas. Among the critical characteristics of reading materials are the topic of the text, the style in which the text is written, format, and readability (Samuels, 1983).

The topic of the text has a direct effect on the reader's ability to read with comprehension; more familiar topics are more easily understood. The clarity of the author's writing style also affects text comprehensibility. Passages containing too many anaphoric terms, those with poor transitions from event to event or idea to idea, and those containing long sentences with too much information are difficult to comprehend. In addition, if there is a mismatch between the information presented in the text and the background knowledge of the reader, the author may fail to communicate with the intended audience. Format also plays a role in text comprehensibility. Reading materials should be clearly printed, and the text should be organized to facilitate reading and review. In evaluating the format of textbooks, professionals should check to see if chapters are structured with design features such as headings, subheadings, abstracts, summaries, and review questions.

The readability of a passage is influenced by its content, vocabulary, and organization, and by the structure of its sentences. However, most of the readability formulas available for measuring reading levels take only one or perhaps two of these factors into account. For example, Fry's (1968) readability graph, presented in Figure 11–9, uses sentence length and the number of syllables per word to estimate readability. The professional selects three 100-word passages from a book or article, counts the number of sentences and syllables in each passage, and then uses the graph to determine readability; readability estimates are stated in terms of grade level.

Readability formulas and graphs can help the professional evaluate reading materials and match the difficulty levels of materials to students' skill levels. This is particularly important with content area textbooks. Science, social studies, and other content subject texts are graded, but their grade levels refer to the difficulty of the subject matter, not to reading difficulty. Thus, a grade 9 science book is likely to contain grade 9 science material, but it may or may not be written at a grade 9 reading level. Readability graphs and formulas can also be used to determine the approximate reading levels of other types of materials, such as library books, short stories, passages in reference books, and magazine or newspaper articles. The Fry (1968) graph is a relatively quick and easy method for estimating readability. It can be used for materials that range from grade 1 to college level, and extensions are available for preprimer and primer materials (Maginnis, 1969) and for materials at college and graduate school levels (Fry, 1977).

The Interpersonal Environment

The major factors that relate to reading within the interpersonal environment of the classroom are the interactions between students and teachers and the social relationships among students. The most effective way of assessing these interpersonal dimensions is observation. Classroom observations scheduled when students are engaged in reading activities can provide answers to the following questions:

☐ What occurs when a student makes an error in oral reading? Does the teacher correct the student? Ignore the error? Ask another student to assist?
☐ How does the student react to the teacher's corrections?
☐ What do other students do when a peer makes oral reading errors? Do they laugh, tease, or ridicule the student?
☐ Are poor readers accepted by others in the classroom? Do they participate with their peers in social and free time activities?
☐ What happens when a student reads correctly? Does the teacher confirm the correct responses? Praise the student? Provide a tangible reward or token?
☐ Are students able to work independently on silent reading assignments and workbook activ-

FIGURE 11–9

Fry readability graph

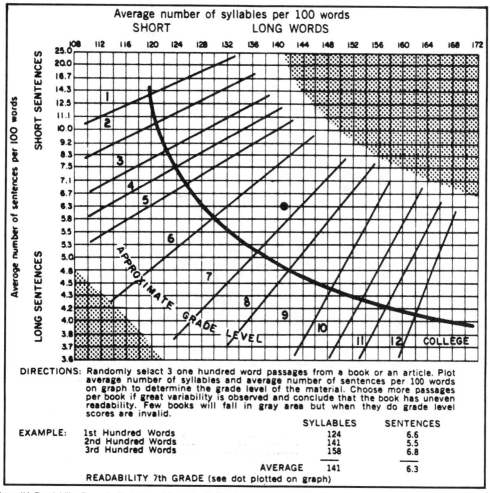

Average number of syllables per 100 words

DIRECTIONS: Randomly select 3 one hundred word passages from a book or an article. Plot average number of syllables and average number of sentences per 100 words on graph to determine the grade level of the material. Choose more passages per book if great variability is observed and conclude that the book has uneven readability. Few books will fall in gray area but when they do grade level scores are invalid.

	SYLLABLES	SENTENCES
EXAMPLE: 1st Hundred Words	124	6.6
2nd Hundred Words	141	5.5
3rd Hundred Words	158	6.8
AVERAGE	141	6.3

READABILITY 7th GRADE (see dot plotted on graph)

Note. From "A Readability Formula That Saves Time" by E. Fry, April 1968. *Journal of Reading, 11,* pp. 513–16.

ities? Or do certain students require frequent assistance from the teacher?

Another factor to consider when evaluating student–teacher interactions is the amount of time teachers spend teaching reading and students spend practicing reading skills. Studies of programs for mildly handicapped students indicate that students are actively engaged in reading for only a few minutes each day (Leinhardt, Zigmond, & Cooley, 1981; Thurlow, Graden, Greener, & Ysseldyke, 1983; Zigmond, Vallecorsa, & Leinhardt, 1980). The amount of time students and teachers spend in instructional interactions is likely to have a direct effect on the amount of progress students make in their attempts to develop reading skills.

The Physical Environment

The physical environment of the classroom can also affect students' reading performance. Environmental factors such as lighting, temperature, and ventilation influence the students' and the teacher's comfort levels and can either facilitate or hinder the teaching–learning process. In addition, the physical arrangement of the classroom is an important consideration, particularly in relation to seating configurations and allocation of classroom space.

Some of the questions that can be asked about the classroom's physical environment and its impact on reading instruction are

1. What seating arrangements are used for reading instruction? Are students seated so they can easily see and hear the teacher?
2. Is the lighting in the classroom adequate for reading?
3. Is classroom space structured so areas for noisier activities are separated from the areas for quieter activities like reading?
4. How are students' seats arranged for independent work? Are students' desks or tables positioned so students do not distract one another?
5. Are there any quiet work areas or "offices" within the classroom where students can go to escape from distractions?
6. Is there a variety of reading materials in the classroom for student use? Do the materials cover a wide range of topics, interest levels, and reading levels? Are the materials accessible to students?
7. Is a computer available in the classroom for students to practice reading skills? Are students trained in the operation of computer equipment? Do students have access to a variety of educationally sound software programs in reading?
8. What types of reading materials are available in the school library or media center? Are these materials accessible to students?

ANSWERING THE ASSESSMENT QUESTIONS

The major purpose of reading assessment is description of students' current levels of educational performance. There are many assessment tools designed for this purpose. They represent numerous types of techniques: diagnostic reading tests, informal reading inventories, error analysis procedures, clinical reading interviews, diagnostic teaching, cloze procedures, criterion-referenced tests, teacher checklists, interviews, observation, and

other informal strategies. Because of the great number and diversity of assessment tools for reading, it is particularly important that the assessment process be carefully planned. Assessment begins with comprehensive measures that sample several reading skills. When potential problem areas are identified, these areas are assessed further, usually with informal measures and techniques.

Nature of the Assessment Tools

Tools for reading assessment vary in the range of reading skills they assess. Comprehensive measures such as the *Woodcock Reading Mastery Tests–Revised* attempt to evaluate a wide range of reading skills, whereas an instrument such as the *Test of Reading Comprehension* focuses on a narrower set of skills. However, most measures today are comprehensive, and they assess both decoding and comprehension skills. Table 11–1 illustrated this point. Of the 26 reading measures described, only 4 assess either decoding or comprehension but not both.

Assessment tools can also vary in depth of skill coverage. Standardized tests typically sample several skills and levels but provide only a few representative test items in each area. For example, a subtest on phonic analysis may devote only two or three test items to the skill of decoding consonant-vowel-consonant words. Informal measures, particularly criterion-referenced tests, allow study of specific skills in much greater depth.

Measures of reading may also differ by the types of reading tasks students are required to perform. Table 11–5 describes several of the more common measures of decoding and comprehension and the ways these measures go about assessment. In the area of decoding, all of the measures except the *GORT–R* require students to read lists of words aloud. However, measures differ on the number of words on each list, the actual words included, and whether time limits are imposed.

In the area of comprehension, assessment tasks are much more varied. The *GORT–R* and the *Sucher-Allred* use the standard tasks of reading graded passages and answering comprehension questions based on the content of the passages. However, questions are open-ended on the *Sucher-Allred* but multiple-choice on the *GORT–R*. The task on the *TORC* is somewhat

TABLE 11–5
Assessment tasks used to evaluate reading skills

Reading Skill	Measure	Subtest	Presentation Mode	Response Mode
Decoding	*Gray Oral Reading Tests–Revised*	(entire test)	Look at a series of graded passages.	Read each passage aloud as quickly and accurately as possible.
	New Sucher-Allred Reading Placement Inventory	Word Recognition Test	Look at lists of isolated words.	Read each word aloud within a 2-second time limit.
	Woodcock Reading Mastery Tests–Revised	Word Attack	Look at lists of nonsense words and syllables.	Read each word or syllable aloud.
	Woodcock Reading Mastery Tests–Revised	Word Identification	Look at lists of isolated words.	Read each word aloud within 5 seconds.
Comprehension	*Gray Oral Reading Tests–Revised*	(entire test)	Look at a series of graded passages; listen to multiple-choice comprehension questions read aloud by the tester.	Read the passages orally; answer the comprehension questions by saying the letter of the correct answer.
	New Sucher-Allred Reading Placement Inventory	Oral Reading Test	Look at a series of graded passages; listen to comprehension questions read aloud by the tester.	Read the passages orally; answer the comprehension questions orally.
	Test of Reading Comprehension	Paragraph Reading	Look at paragraphs, then read multiple-choice comprehension questions.	Silently read each paragraph and the comprehension questions that accompany it; mark answers on the separate answer sheet.
	Woodcock Reading Mastery Tests–Revised	Passage Comprehension	Look at a passage with one word missing.	Read the passage silently and say the missing word.

different; students read standard types of passages, then read the multiple-choice comprehension questions themselves, rather than listening to the tester read them. The *WRMT–R* uses a cloze procedure to assess comprehension; no questions are asked. The student reads passages silently and then attempts to supply the word missing in each.

Oral reading is required on the comprehension tasks on the *GORT–R* and the *Sucher-Allred;* the *WRMT–R* and the *TORC* employ silent reading tasks. Students respond orally on each of the measures except the *TORC.* The *TORC* and the *GORT–R* use multiple-choice comprehension questions; the *WRMT–R,* a completion task; and the *Sucher-Allred,* open-ended questions.

Clearly, there are important differences among measures of reading in the ways they assess decoding and comprehension skills. These differences must be considered in selecting the tools for reading assessment and in interpreting the results of the assessment.

The Relationship of Reading to Other Areas of Performance

When the assessment team begins to evaluate and interpret its results, one of the major tasks is study of the relationships among areas of performance. Academic skills such as reading may influence or be influenced by several other areas.

A student's general aptitude for learning can have an effect on the ease and speed with which reading skills are acquired. In general, students with lower than average general intelligence are expected to progress at a somewhat slower rate than students of average intellectual ability. There have been several attempts to quantify the relationship between IQ and reading, and reading expectancy formulas have resulted (Bond & Tinker, 1967; Harris, 1970; Myklebust, 1968). These formulas use the student's current intellectual performance and sometimes other factors such as age or years in school to predict an expected reading level.

Expectancy formulas have several limitations, most notably their reliance on age and grade scores, and their use is not recommended. Instead, the standard score procedures described in Chapter 9 are preferred for comparing and contrasting IQ test results and results from measures

of reading. Also, the *WRMT–R* provides a procedure for the analysis of aptitude–achievement discrepancies.

Like general learning aptitude, specific learning abilities and strategies can influence the student's success in the acquisition and application of reading skills. Problems in attention, memory, or other areas such as auditory discrimination can hinder skill development, particularly the acquisition of basic decoding skills. Inefficient learning strategies can interfere when students attempt to read with comprehension. In the secondary grades, poor learning strategies may combine with poor reading skills to prevent students from successfully using reading as a study technique.

Classroom behavior may be related to reading performance. Inappropriate classroom conduct can impede classroom learning, including acquisition and application of reading skills. Poor achievement can also affect a student's behavior. Difficulty in reading can result in lowered self-concept and negative attitudes toward school and learning. Achievement problems can even influence peer relationships and the student's conduct in social and instructional situations.

Reading pervades the school curriculum. It has a direct impact on several other areas of school performance, particularly language arts subjects. Writing skills such as spelling and composition are directly affected by delayed development in reading. In written language, the expressive skill of writing is built upon the receptive skill of reading. Likewise, the development of beginning reading skills is influenced by the student's oral language proficiency.

Reading can also affect the student's ability to perform successfully in mathematics and other subjects. Although arithmetic computation usually does not require reading skills, other mathematics tasks do. Students are often asked to read explanations in mathematics textbooks, to read the directions for mathematics worksheets or workbook pages, and to read word problems.

Reading is almost a necessity for content area subjects such as science, history, English, and social studies. Even in the elementary grades, students may be expected to use reading to acquire content area information. At the secondary level, reading assignments are routine. Students are expected to learn by reading textbooks and other materials. Students can bypass their poor reading skills by using aids such as taped versions of textbooks, but mainstreamed students will still be expected to achieve at least a minimal level of reading proficiency.

In addition, there are very real reading demands in the adult world. Reading is a necessity for most occupations, and the average adult is constantly faced with text to read: street and traffic signs, signs on buildings and restroom doors, commercial ads, want ads, newspapers, magazines, television schedules, job application forms, postcards and letters, grocery labels, labels on cosmetics and medications, menus, and the like. The ability to read and comprehend everyday reading materials such as these is an important concern for all students, particularly older students with special instructional needs.

Documentation of Reading Performance

The general question that guides the assessment team in its study of reading skills is, *What are the student's educational needs?* The purpose of this phase of assessment is to describe precisely the student's current skill levels; these data then serve as the basis for planning the student's educational program. The first question that the team attempts to answer is *What is the student's current level of reading achievement?* Then additional information is gathered about areas where the student appears to be experiencing difficulty. The result is a description of the student's current performance in reading that is specific enough to answer the question *What are the student's strengths and weaknesses in the various skill areas of reading?*

Data are gathered from many sources using many types of assessment tools. The team usually begins by reviewing school records, results of individual achievement tests, interviews with parents and teachers, and classroom observations to plan the reading assessment. Next, a diagnostic reading test may be administered to survey the student's skills in several areas of reading. Test results are used to identify potential problem areas, and these skills and subskills are further assessed with informal measures and techniques.

There are many alternatives for reading assessment—tests, inventories, error analysis procedures, and clinical reading interviews, among others—and the assessment team must choose

its tools carefully to avoid duplication and ensure that assessment is as efficient as possible. As a general rule, the more specific measures and techniques such as criterion-referenced tests and clinical reading interviews are reserved for in-depth analysis of potential weaknesses.

Answering the assessment questions about reading is one step toward planning the student's Individualized Education Program. For example, Joyce, the fourth grader, was referred for problems in reading.

Joyce

Joyce is unable to read any of the grade 4 textbooks in her classroom. She is now working in a beginning third grade reading book with some success. Previous assessment with the *PIAT–R* and interviews with Mr. Harvey, Joyce's teacher, confirm that Joyce's current reading performance is below that expected for her age and grade.

The assessment team begins its study of Joyce's reading skills by administering Form H of the *Woodcock Reading Mastery Tests–Revised*. Joyce earns these scores:

Subtest	Standard Score Range
Word Identification	71–76
Word Attack	79–88
Word Comprehension	84–91
Passage Comprehension	79–87
Cluster	
Basic Skills	74–79
Reading Comprehension	79–86
Full Scale Total Reading	77–81

Joyce's overall performance on the *WRMT–R* falls within the low average range. Her comprehension skills appear stronger than her decoding skills. Joyce shows low average performance on the Word Identification subtest, a measure of sight vocabulary, and low average to average performance on the Word Attack subtest, a measure of skill in phonic analysis of unknown words.

Next, the *New Sucher-Allred Reading Placement Inventory* is administered to gain more information about Joyce's oral reading abilities. According to this inventory, Joyce's Independent Reading Level is grade 2^1, her Instructional Level is grade 2², and her Frustrational Level is grade 3¹. On the reading passages, Joyce makes very few comprehension errors until she reaches frustration level.

Joyce's oral reading responses on the *WRMT–R* and the *Sucher-Allred* are analyzed to identify patterns of errors. Joyce can recognize only a few words by sight. When she does not recognize a word, she attempts to decode it by sounding it out and by using available context clues. However, Joyce shows weak phonic analysis skills, and the majority of her decoding errors are substitutions that involve mispronunciation of vowel sounds. In reading connected text, Joyce appears to look at the initial consonant of the word and then guess from context. Most of her substitutions make sense in context and begin with the correct initial consonant sound.

A series of criterion-referenced tests are used for further analysis of Joyce's decoding skills. On the *BRIGANCE® Diagnostic Inventory of Basic Skills,* Joyce shows strengths in knowledge of consonant sounds, short vowel sounds, and consonant blends. However, results indicate that Joyce has not yet mastered long vowel sounds, consonant digraphs, and diphthongs. The up-

dated version of the Dolch high-frequency word list (Table 11–3) is used to assess Joyce's sight word vocabulary. Of the 220 words, Joyce is able to recognize 97; most of her errors occur in the second and third grade lists.

After careful analysis of these results, the assessment team is ready to describe Joyce's current levels of reading performance. Their conclusions are as follows:

□ Joyce's current instructional reading level is grade 2², as measured by the *New Sucher-Allred Reading Placement Inventory.* At this level, Joyce comprehends well but requires assistance in decoding.
□ In general, Joyce's comprehension skills are more advanced than her decoding skills. She uses context to help her decode unknown words.
□ Joyce can recognize most preprimer and primer sight words. She has not yet mastered grade 1, 2, and 3 sight words.
□ Joyce knows the sounds of consonants and consonant blends and the short sounds of vowels. She has not yet mastered long vowel sounds, consonant digraphs, and diphthongs.

STUDY GUIDE

Review Questions

1. Which of the following is the major reason for assessing reading skills?
   _____ a. To determine whether the student has a handicapping condition
   _____ b. To gather information about specific learning abilities
   _____ c. To aid in planning the instructional program
   _____ d. To evaluate the effectiveness of instructional practices in the regular classroom
2. The two skill areas of primary concern in the assessment of reading are decoding and _____ . In addition, there is growing interest in the _____ between the reader and the text he or she is reading.
3. Decoding can be accomplished in many ways. Check each of the strategies available to readers for decoding *unfamiliar* words:
   _____ a. Sight recognition
   _____ b. Structural analysis
   _____ c. Phonic analysis
   _____ d. Readability analysis
   _____ e. Contextual analysis
4. In schools today, reading is assessed by
   _____ a. Group and individual measures
   _____ b. Norm-referenced and criterion-referenced tests
   _____ c. Informal inventories and clinical interviews

        _____ **d.** Answers *a* and *c*

        _____ **e.** Answers *b* and *d*

5. Diagnostic reading tests usually assess a wide range of reading skills rather than one single skill area. (True or False)

6. Match the assessment device or procedure in Column A with the description in Column B.

Column A	Column B
a. *Woodcock Reading Mastery Tests–Revised*	_____ Assesses content area vocabulary skills and the ability to follow written directions
b. *Test of Reading Comprehension*	_____ A test that considers both speed and accuracy in decoding
c. *Classroom Reading Inventory*	_____ An informal reading inventory for persons reading between the primer and grade 9 levels
d. *Gray Oral Reading Tests–Revised*	_____ An informal inventory that contains a spelling test
e. *New Sucher-Allred Reading Placement Inventory*	_____ Includes readiness measures such as Visual-Auditory Learning and Letter Identification

7. Which of these statements about reading measures are true and which are false?

    T F **a.** Decoding skills are assessed on the *Woodcock Reading Mastery Tests–Revised* and the *Gray Oral Reading Tests–Revised.*

    T F **b.** Most reading measures include a test of structural analysis skills.

    T F **c.** Informal inventories evaluate both decoding and comprehension skills.

    T F **d.** The *Test of Reading Comprehension* uses oral reading to assess comprehension skills.

8. Match the description with the assessment results.

a. An area of strength	_____ Reading Comprehension Quotient 110 on the *Test of Reading Comprehension*
b. A possible area of educational need	_____ Grade 1.6 Instructional Level on an informal reading inventory for a grade 4 student
	_____ RPI score of 50/90 on one of the *WRMT–R* subtests
	_____ Scaled score 4 on the Paragraph Reading subtest of the *TORC*

9. The results of informal reading inventories are estimates of three reading levels: the _____ level, the _____ level, and the _____ level.

10. Find the true statements about informal assessment of reading.

    _____ **a.** Two types of reading checklists are most common: those that list typical reading difficulties, and curriculum checklists to record and monitor reading skill development.

    _____ **b.** In reading assessment, response analysis is used to identify the errors students make in decoding and comprehension.

    _____ **c.** Having students read high-frequency word lists is one way of assessing comprehension of connected text.

    _____ **d.** With the cloze procedure, the student reads a selection from which words have been omitted and attempts to fill in the missing words.

    _____ **e.** Clinical reading interviews are one way of studying how the student interacts with the text.

    _____ **f.** An example of a criterion-referenced test that includes reading skills is the *BRIGANCE® Diagnostic Inventory of Basic Skills.*

11. Check each type of response that is commonly considered to be a decoding error on informal reading inventories and oral reading tests.

    _____ **a.** Omissions

    _____ **b.** Substitutions

    _____ **c.** Disregard of punctuation

    _____ **d.** Listening comprehension

    _____ **e.** Inference and main idea

    _____ **f.** Additions

12. What three aspects of classroom environments should be evaluated when students experience difficulty in reading?

13. Poor reading skills would likely have the most effect on which school subject?
    _____ a. Mathematics
    _____ b. Spelling
    _____ c. Speaking and listening skills
    _____ d. Physical education

14. If the special education team finds that a student shows poor performance in reading comprehension, what conclusion can be drawn?
    _____ a. The student is eligible for special education services for mentally retarded students.
    _____ b. The special education program should focus on improving decoding skills.
    _____ c. The student does not qualify for special education services.
    _____ d. A possible IEP goal would be improving reading comprehension.

Activities

1. Interview elementary and secondary teachers about their perceptions of the importance of reading skills. Ask them to identify activities in their classrooms where students with poor reading skills would have difficulty. Are there major differences between the viewpoints of elementary and secondary educators?

2. Locate several group achievement tests and examine how each assesses reading. Are all the major skills covered?

3. Under the supervision of the course instructor, administer one of the reading measures discussed in this chapter. Calculate all possible scores and analyze the results to determine strengths and weaknesses.

4. Under the supervision of the course instructor, administer relevant portions of one of the criterion-referenced tests of reading discussed in this chapter. Prepare a report that includes recommendations for instructional objectives.

5. Do a work sample analysis of a student's oral reading performance. Identify and analyze all errors according to a system presented in this chapter.

6. Observe in a classroom and note the important features of the instructional, interpersonal, and physical environments that may influence reading performance.

Discussion Questions

1. Reading is the primary literacy skill, and literacy is highly valued in today's society. Discuss some barriers to adult success that face persons who read poorly.

2. Describe how reading skills can affect how well a student is able to perform in school subjects such as mathematics, composition, and content areas.

3. One of the current areas of debate in the field of reading concerns the relative importance of two aspects of the reading process, text and meaning. Describe the three major models of proficient reading—bottom-up, top-down, and interactive—and tell which one you favor and why.

4. Explain the rationale for assessing the instructional environment of the classroom as a possible contributor to reading problems. Then describe some of the ways classroom demands can be altered so students with difficulty in reading can successfully participate in learning activities.

12

Mathematics

Mathematics, like reading, is one of the basic school subjects. Young students are expected to acquire the vocabulary of mathematics; learn to count, recognize, and write numerals and mathematical symbols; and understand quantitative terminology. Arithmetic operations are also a part of the elementary curriculum; students learn to manipulate quantities with the computational processes of addition, subtraction, multiplication, and division. Mathematics learning continues in the secondary grades; at this level, students are required to apply their knowledge of mathematics in solving quantitative problems. Some students also expand their repertoire of skills by studying algebra, geometry, trigonometry, and perhaps even calculus.

Many special students encounter difficulty in their attempts to learn the basic skills of mathematics and in their efforts to apply these skills in mathematical problem solving. Although mathematics does not pervade the school curriculum in the same way that reading does, quantitative thinking is a necessity in the adult world. Mathematics-based tasks such as handling money, telling time, and measuring are a common part of daily life, as are problem-solving situations such as comparative shopping. Poor skill development in mathematics is a cause for concern, particularly when planning the educational program for students with special needs.

Math skills are assessed in order to gather information for instructional planning. The general question that the assessment team seeks to answer is, *What are the student's educational needs?* Two specific questions are asked: *What is the student's current level of mathematics achievement? What are the student's strengths and weaknesses in the various skill areas of mathematics?*

The major concern is description of the student's current levels of performance. Informal measures and techniques are preferred because they provide specific information about the student's status in skill development. Results of norm-referenced tests may help professionals differentiate educational needs from skills where the student shows adequate progress.

Assessment for program planning is a selective process that concentrates on the skills and subskills that have been identified as possible problems. If a student's progress in an academic subject such as reading or mathematics is satisfactory, that subject will not be part of the student's special educational program and thus in-depth assessment is not necessary. For example, Joyce, the fourth grader whose assessment was described in previous chapters, is successful in mathematics. Therefore, the assessment team will not gather additional data about Joyce's mathematics abilities. In place of Joyce, consider the needs of another student, David. David is an eighth grader whose primary area of difficulty is mathematics.

David

David has been referred for special education assessment by his eighth grade math teacher, Ms. Coolidge. David's math grades were poor in seventh grade, and this year he is failing. In the classroom, he is not able to cope with eighth grade math tasks and instead is reviewing basic number facts and operations. The results of individual achievement tests such as the *WRAT–R* and the *Woodcock-Johnson–R* confirm that David's math performance is below that expected for his age and grade.

The assessment team has determined that David is eligible for special education services, and it is anticipated that specialized instruction in mathematics will be an important part of David's individualized program. To begin the study of David's math performance, the *KeyMath Revised* will be administered. This measure assesses a wide variety of skills, and results will help the team determine the directions for further assessment.

As appropriate, informal measures and techniques will be used to explore the particular skills that appear to be areas of weakness for David. For example, if problem solving seems to need strengthening, the team may conduct a clinical math interview, observing and talking with David as he verbalizes his steps in solving a quantitative problem. Or if David's knowledge of number facts is a concern, the team may devise or select an informal inventory or criterion-referenced test to evaluate his command of specific addition, subtraction, multiplication, or division facts. David's individualized program in mathematics will be based upon the results of these assessments.

Individualized Assessment Plan

For: _____ David Burke _____ | 8 | 13–7 | 11/6/89 | Mr. Block
Student's Name | Grade | Age | Date | Coordinator

Reason for Referral: David is failing grade 8 math; he is working on basic number facts and operations rather than grade level material.

Assessment Question	Assessment Procedures	Person Responsible	Date/Time
What is the student's current level of mathematics achievement?	*KeyMath Revised*	Mr. Block, Resource Teacher	11/17/89 9:40 a.m.
	Error analysis of current math homework assignments and quizzes	Mr. Block, Resource Teacher, and Ms. Coolidge, Grade 8 Math Teacher	11/13/89 3 p.m.
What are the student's strengths and weaknesses in the various skill areas of mathematics?	Error analysis of David's responses on the *KeyMath Revised*	Mr. Block, Resource Teacher	11/17/89 2 p.m.
	Additional tests and/or informal assessments, as indicated by the results of formal testing	Mr. Block, Resource Teacher	To be determined

CONSIDERATIONS IN ASSESSMENT OF MATHEMATICS

Students' mathematics and arithmetic skills are often the subject of special education assessment. One of the primary aims of the elementary school curriculum is the development of proficiency in mathematical thinking and computation, and elementary mathematics skills become the foundation for the secondary grade mathematics. When students fail to meet the expectations of the regular curriculum in the acquisition and application of mathematics skills, mathematics becomes a major assessment concern.

Purposes

In regular education, teachers routinely monitor their students' progress in mathematics, and it is one of the school skills evaluated by the group achievement tests administered at regular intervals throughout the grades. In addition, mathematics proficiency is a competency area assessed by many schools and districts for grade advancement and high school graduation.

In special education, mathematics skills are investigated at the start of assessment to determine the student's eligibility for special education ser-

vices. When mathematics is identified as an area of need for a particular student, assessment continues in order to gather the detailed information necessary for program planning. Precise information about the student's current status in mathematics is the basis for establishing the instructional goals of the Individualized Education Program.

Assessment continues throughout the student's special education program. The cycle of gathering data about current skills, planning instructional interventions, and monitoring the success of those interventions is repeated for as long as the student needs specially designed mathematics instruction.

Skill Areas

Mathematics is a complex body of knowledge, but its skill hierarchy is developmental. Mathematical thinking begins in the preschool years when children acquire the rudiments of a quantitative vocabulary and start to learn counting and other fundamental skills. The written language of mathematics, made up of numerals and symbols, is built upon this conceptual framework. Young students learn to read and write numerals and mathematical symbols and to manipulate quantities through computation. Mathematical problem solving is also introduced to young students once they have some facility with computational operations.

The developmental nature of mathematics is apparent in the school curriculum. Skills are built one on the other, and there is a set order for the acquisition of new learning. For example, the general mathematics skills taught in the elementary grades are prerequisite to the higher mathematics of the secondary grades and college.

It is important to distinguish between *mathematics,* the general field of study, and one of its components, *arithmetic.* Reid and Hresko (1981) provide these definitions:

Mathematics refers to the study or development of relationships, regularities, structures, or organizational schemata dealing with space, time, weight, mass, volume, geometry, and number.

Arithmetic refers to the computational methods used when working with numbers. (p. 292)

Arithmetic is a computational skill. It is concerned with the operations of addition, subtraction, multiplication, and division, and the algorithms involved in these operations. Algorithms are step-by-step procedures for solving computational problems (Ashlock, 1986).

Mathematics is much broader in scope than arithmetic. Although it includes computation, it also encompasses mathematical readiness, number systems and numeration, quantitative problem solving, geometry, measurement, the applications of time and money, and higher mathematics such as algebra and calculus. Although skill in computation is often equated with mathematics proficiency, there are other fundamental areas of mathematics. The basic mathematics skills identified by the National Council of Supervisors of Mathematics (1978) include

☐ Arithmetic computation
☐ Problem solving
☐ Applying mathematics in everyday situations
☐ Alertness to the reasonableness of results
☐ Estimation and approximation
☐ Geometry
☐ Measurement
☐ Reading, interpreting, and constructing tables, charts, and graphs
☐ Using mathematics to predict
☐ Computer literacy (Fey, 1982, p. 1168)

In the 1960s, the new math curriculum dominated mathematics instruction with its emphasis on exploration, discovery, and conceptual understanding. The back-to-basics movement of the 1970s changed the instructional focus to the development of basic skills. In the 1980s, groups such as the National Council of Teachers of Mathematics (1980) called for educators to give problem-solving skills the highest priority in mathematics instruction. However, results of the recent National Assessment of Educational Progress study of the mathematics performance of American youth indicate that serious gaps remain in students' mathematics knowledge and skills (National Council of Teachers of Mathematics, 1988).

In assessment, traditional measures tend to focus on computational skills, problem solving, and the more common applications such as geometry and measurement. Computational skills are typically evaluated with paper-and-pencil tasks. The student is presented with written problems that require addition, subtraction, multiplication, or division of whole numbers, fractions, or decimals.

$$\begin{array}{ccc} 5 & 26 & 639 \\ +\,4 & -\,19 & \times\,748 \\ \hline \end{array}$$

$$4.2)\overline{509.3} \qquad \frac{3}{16} + \frac{5}{32} =$$

The student then attempts to solve the problems, often within a specified time limit. On most tests, students are allowed to use pencil and paper for calculation; however, some measures require mental computation. To solve computational problems, the student must read and understand numerals and symbols. Math facts must be recalled from memory or calculated. Then the student must select and correctly apply the appropriate algorithm when solving the problem.

Mathematical problem solving is often assessed by means of story problems that present a quantitative problem in a prose format. Within the story is the problem situation, the numerical data the student must manipulate, and information about the type of manipulation necessary. For example, the problem might state

George had five apples. He gave two apples to Susan. How many apples did George have left?

The student must read or listen to the story, identify the problem and the pertinent data for its solution, select the appropriate operation and algorithm, and correctly perform the computation. On some tests, students are required to read the story problems themselves; this is not the best method of assessment for students with poor reading skills. As with computational tests, some measures of problem solving allow the use of paper and pencil, whereas others require mental computation.

In some ways, the distinction between computation and problem solving in mathematics is analogous to that between decoding and comprehension in reading. Just as comprehension relies on decoding, mathematical problem solving relies on arithmetic computation.

As in reading, traditional measures of mathematics performance are product-oriented, not process-oriented. To investigate the interactions between the student and the mathematical "text," it is necessary to use informal strategies. Error analysis procedures provide some information about the student's strategies; clinical math interviews are useful when investigating the student's methods of interacting with story problems.

Mathematics measures often attempt to assess application skills as well as computation and problem solving. Most typically, the applications involve the everyday uses of geometry, time, money, and measurement. Application skills are based on mathematics fundamentals, but because they incorporate new subject matter, they extend beyond simple calculation. For example, to apply mathematics skills to money, the student must learn new symbols such as $ and ¢, new terms such as *penny* and *nickel,* and new facts and equivalencies such as *1 nickel = 5 pennies.* Application skills are an important part of mathematics competency because they represent the most typical ways the average adult uses mathematics in daily life and the world of work.

Current Practices

Assessment of mathematics achievement is common practice today in both regular and special education. Next to reading, mathematics is probably the most frequently assessed school skill. Mathematics assessment is a standard part of the elementary school curriculum, and both group and individual tests of academic achievement include measures of mathematics proficiency.

More directly related to instructional planning in special education are the assessment tools listed in Table 12–1. Included are standardized tests of mathematics performance, informal inventories, and criterion-referenced tests. Fewer measures are available for the assessment of mathematics than for assessment of reading.

Most standardized tests of mathematics are survey instruments. They assess a wide range of skills within the broad area of mathematics in an attempt to identify the student's strengths and weaknesses. An example is the *KeyMath Revised* (Connolly, 1988). Its predecessor, the *KeyMath Diagnostic Arithmetic Test* (Connolly, Nachtman, & Pritchett, 1971, 1976) was consistently identified as one of the most often used tests in special education assessment (Mardell-Czudnowski, 1980; Thurlow & Ysseldyke, 1979), perhaps because there were few alternatives for the assessment of mathematics skills. At present, however, there are several standardized instruments available, including the *Stanford Diagnostic Mathematics Test* (Beatty, Madsen, Gardner, & Karlsen, 1984) and the *Test of Mathematical Abilities* (Brown & McEntire, 1984).

In addition, there is a rich array of informal assessment strategies for the study of mathematics performance. These include all the standard types of informal techniques, but among the most common are informal inventories, criterion-referenced tests of specific skills, error analysis procedures, and clinical math interviews. As Table 12–1 shows, many of the criterion-referenced tests described as informal measures of reading assess mathematics skills as well.

This chapter describes each of the major strategies used in schools today for mathematics assessment. First to be discussed is the *KeyMath Revised.* Then other formal measures of mathematics performance are described. Later sections of the chapter present information about informal measures and techniques.

KEYMATH REVISED: A DIAGNOSTIC INVENTORY OF ESSENTIAL MATHEMATICS

The *KeyMath Revised* (*KeyMath–R*) is an individually administered test designed to "provide a

TABLE 12–1
Measures of mathematics performance

Name (Authors)	Type of Measure[1]	Ages or Grades	Group or Individual
BRIGANCE® Diagnostic Comprehensive Inventory of Basic Skills (Brigance, 1983a)	C	Gr. K–9	Individual
BRIGANCE® Diagnostic Inventory of Basic Skills (Brigance, 1977)	C	Gr. K–6	Individual
BRIGANCE® Diagnostic Inventory of Essential Skills (Brigance, 1981)	C	Gr. 4–12	Individual
Diagnostic Test of Arithmetic Strategies (Ginsburg & Mathews, 1984)	I	Gr. 1–6	Individual
ENRIGHT™ Diagnostic Inventory of Basic Arithmetic Skills (Enright, 1983)	I, C	Less than Gr. 7 functioning level	Group or Individual
Hudson Education Skills Inventory (Hudson, Colson, Welch, Banikowski, & Mehring, 1989)	C	Gr. K–12	Individual
KeyMath Revised (Connolly, 1988)	T	Gr. K–9, Ages 5–0 to 16–0	Individual
Multilevel Academic Skills Inventory (Howell, Zucker, & Morehead, 1982)	C	Gr. 1–8	Individual
Sequential Assessment of Mathematics Inventories–Standardized Inventory (Reisman, 1985)	T	Gr. K–8	Individual
Stanford Diagnostic Mathematics Test (3rd ed.) (Beatty, Madden, Gardner, & Karlsen, 1984)	T	Gr. 1–12	Group
System FORE (Bagai & Bagai, 1979)	C	Gr. K–12	Individual
Test of Early Mathematics Ability (Ginsburg & Baroody, 1983)	T	Ages 4–0 to 8–11	Individual
Test of Mathematical Abilities (Brown & McEntire, 1984)	T	Gr. 3–12, Ages 8–6 to 18–11	Group or Individual

[1]*T* stands for standardized test, *I* for informal inventory, and *C* for criterion-referenced test.

comprehensive assessment of a student's understanding and application of important mathematics concepts and skills" (Connolly, 1988, p. 1). It is a norm-referenced test that also offers some of the features of criterion-referenced assessment. Test items are linked to skill domains and instructional objectives.

There are two forms of the *KeyMath–R*. Each contains 13 subtests organized into three major areas of mathematics. According to the manual, "Basic Concepts represent foundation knowledge; Operations represent computational skills; and Applications represent the use of knowledge and computational skills" (p. 8).

Basic Concepts Subtests

□ *Numeration*—Items on this subtest are designed to evaluate the student's understanding of the number system. Among the skills assessed are counting, reading numbers, sequencing numbers, place value, and rounding.

□ *Rational Numbers*—This subtest is concerned with the student's ability to identify, order, and compare fractions, decimal numbers, and percentages.

□ *Geometry*—Included here are questions about spatial relations, likenesses and differences, pattern development, two- and three-dimensional shapes, and coordinate geometry.

Operations Subtests

□ *Addition*—On the first few problems of this subtest, the student looks at a drawing, listens to problems read by the tester, and responds orally. On later items, the format changes to a paper-and-pencil task; the student is given a page of problems and asked to write the answers. Included are problems requiring addition of multidigit numbers (with and without regrouping), fractions, decimals, and mixed numbers.

□ *Subtraction*—The tasks on this subtest are the same as on Addition, but the computations involve subtraction of multidigit numbers (with and without regrouping), fractions, decimals, and mixed numbers.

□ *Multiplication*—Again, the same test tasks are used, but the problems require multiplication of whole numbers, fractions, decimals, and mixed numbers.

□ *Division*—The test tasks remain the same, but the student must solve problems involving division of whole numbers, fractions, decimals, and mixed numbers.

□ *Mental Computation*—Paper and pencil are not allowed on this subtest. The tester reads a computation problem or a series of problems at the rate of one computation per second; problems cannot be repeated, and the student must respond orally within approximately 15 seconds. On other questions, the student looks at a problem as the tester reads it aloud; again, the student must answer within 15 seconds.

Applications Subtests

□ *Measurement*—In this subtest, the student answers questions relating to common units of measurement (both standard and metric) and the use of measurement tools such as rulers and thermometers.

□ *Time and Money*—Items evaluate the student's ability to complete tasks such as telling time, reading calendars, sequencing chronological events, identifying and counting coins and currency, and making change.

□ *Estimation*—Here, the student solves problems by estimating the answer. Most items have a range of acceptable responses. Included are problems involving whole numbers, fractions, and units of measurement.

□ *Interpreting Data*—This subtest assesses the student's ability to read and interpret graphs, charts, and tables. Simple problems involving probability and statistics are also included.

□ *Problem Solving*—Both routine and nonroutine problems appear on this subtest. Routine problems provide direct cues to the correct operational procedures; nonroutine problems require the student to identify pertinent information, disregard extraneous information, and determine whether all needed information is available. The student must solve both types of problems and describe strategies for attacking nonroutine problems.

The *KeyMath–R* is designed for students from kindergarten through grade 9. Reading skills are

---

KEYMATH REVISED: A DIAGNOSTIC INVENTORY OF ESSENTIAL MATHEMATICS (KEYMATH–R)

A. J. Connolly (1988)

Type: Norm-referenced and domain-referenced test
Major Content Areas: Basic concepts, operations, and applications in mathematics
Type of Administration: Individual
Administration Time: 30 to 50 minutes
Age/Grade Levels: Grades K through 9, ages 5–0 through 16–0
Types of Scores: Standard scores and percentile ranks for subtests, area scores, and total test; optional age and grade equivalents for area scores and total test
Typical Uses: A broad-based mathematics test for the identification of strengths and weaknesses in mathematics skill development
Cautions: Reliability of the *KeyMath–R* is best for total test and area scores; further information is needed about concurrent validity. In administration, the Numeration Basal Item determines starting points for later subtests. Scoring is straightforward but can be time-consuming if all types of results are desired.

not needed, because the tester reads all questions and problems to the student. However, English-language skills are a necessity, particularly for sub-tests such as Problem Solving. On most *Key-Math–R* subtests, students respond orally, but writing is required on four of the Operations sub-tests. All subtests except Mental Computation are untimed.

Technical Quality

To provide both fall and spring norms, the *Key-Math–R* was standardized in fall 1985 with 873 students and in spring 1986 with 925 students. The goal was to select 100 students per grade level (K to 8), half girls and half boys, both in spring and fall; ninth graders were included only in the spring, and the goal was a total of 50 students. Some grades fell short of these goals because of student absences or transfers. However, the total sample appears to resemble the national school-age population in geographic region, sex, race or ethnic group, and parental education level. No information is provided about whether handi-capped or non-English-speaking students were in-cluded in the sample.

Total test and area scores on the *KeyMath–R* show adequate split-half and alternate form relia-bility. However, several individual subtests do not meet minimum criteria. Alternate form reliability coefficients for grade-based scores fall below .80 for all 13 subtests; reliabilities are in the .70s for six subtests and in the .60s or .50s for the rest. Split-half reliability is lowest for grade-based scores earned by students in kindergarten and grades 1 and 2; in these grades, more than half the reliability coefficients fall below .70.

Concurrent validity of the *KeyMath–R* was stud-ied by examining its relationship to the original *KeyMath* and to mathematics subtests on the *Comprehensive Tests of Basic Skills* and the *Iowa Tests of Basic Skills*. Total test scores of the two versions of the *KeyMath* are strongly related (.90); total mathematics subtest results from the group achievement tests show moderate correlations (.66 to .76) with *KeyMath–R* results. Further in-formation is needed about the relationship of the *KeyMath–R* to other individual tests of mathe-matics performance and to the individual measures of general achievement (e.g., *PIAT–R*) commonly used in special education.

Administration Considerations

No special training is required to administer the *KeyMath–R*. According to the manual, this test can be administered by "regular and special edu-cation teachers, classroom aides and other para-professionals, as well as counselors, school psychologists, and others with special psycho-metric training" (p. 11). Test interpretation, how-ever, is best accomplished by professionals with training in psychometrics and experience in teach-ing mathematics.

There are consistent basal and ceiling rules for all *KeyMath–R* subtests. Basals are established by three consecutive correct responses and ceil-ings by three consecutive errors. *KeyMath–R* sub-tests must be administered in order. The test record provides a starting point for the first subtest, Numeration; students in kindergarten and grade 1 begin with item 1, those in grades 2 and 3 begin with item 6, and so forth. Starting points for the rest of the test are determined by the student's performance on Numeration. The basal is estab-lished and the "Numeration Basal Item" identified; this is the *first* item in the string of three consec-utive responses needed for the basal. For example, if the basal was established with successes on items 12, 13, and 14, the Numeration Basal Item would be item 12. This number is then used to locate the appropriate starting item for later sub-tests. The test record form indicates, for instance, that students earning a Numeration Basal of 0 to 17 should begin the Rational Numbers subtest with item 1.

Test books are in easel format. On the exam-iner's side are the directions and questions to be read to the student, the correct answers, and any special scoring instructions. On some items, the tester must point to information on the student's side of the easel. On most *KeyMath–R* subtests, there are no time limits and testers can repeat items for students as needed. However, on the Mental Computation subtest, items can be read only once and students have approximately 15 seconds to respond. Written computation is re-quired on the four basic operation subtests; the test record form contains the problems with ample space for computation.

On the *KeyMath–R,* test items are scored as they are administered. Correct responses are marked "1" and incorrect responses "0." As Figure

12–1 shows, each item is keyed to a domain. On the Numeration subtest, the first domain is "Numbers 0–9" and it is evaluated in items 1 through 6. The tester records the student's performance (0 or 1) in the space provided for each item so that domain scores can be obtained. A line is drawn above the easiest item passed and below the most difficult item administered. All domains contain six items. Raw scores for domains are determined by counting the number of successes and the items assumed correct below the basal. The subtest's ceiling item is noted, and the total raw score for the subtest is computed by adding the domain scores.

Results and Interpretation

Unlike its predecessor, the *KeyMath–R* offers a variety of scores. Norms are available by age and

FIGURE 12–1
Sample subtest scoring on the *KeyMath Revised*

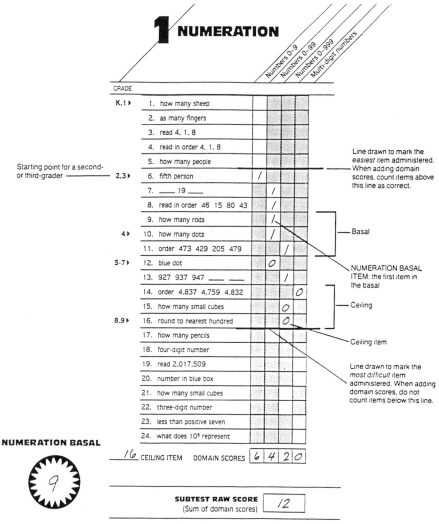

Note. From *KeyMath Revised Manual, Forms A and B* (p. 14) by A. J. Connolly, 1988, Circle Pines, MN: American Guidance Service. Copyright 1988 by American Guidance Service, Inc. Reprinted by permission.

grade and for fall and spring testing dates. Subtest results are expressed as percentile ranks and scaled scores (standard scores with a mean of 10 and a standard deviation of 3). Additional scores are available for the three areas (Basic Concepts, Operations, and Applications) and for the Total Test: percentile ranks, standard scores with a mean of 100 and standard deviation of 15, and optional scores such as age and grade equivalents, normal curve equivalents, and stanines.

Results can be plotted on a Score Profile. The tester chooses a confidence level (68% or 90%) and consults a table to determine the values needed to construct intervals around observed scores. Standard scores are plotted for Total Test and area results and scaled scores for subtests. It is also possible to compare the student's performance on the three areas assessed by the *KeyMath–R*. The tester computes the observed difference between area standard scores and consults a table to determine whether these differences are significant at the .01 level, significant at the .05 level, or not significant.

Figure 12–2 presents the Score Profile and Area Comparisons for David, the eighth grader introduced at the start of this chapter. Form A was administered, and fall grade norms were used. The *KeyMath–R* manual recommends selecting a 90% confidence level for profiling Total Test and area standard scores and a 68% confidence level for subtest scaled scores. David's overall mathematics performance fell within the low average range. The Basic Concepts area score was indicative of low average to average performance, and it was significantly higher than both Operations and Applications area scores. David had particular difficulty with the skills assessed on the Multiplication, Division, and Problem Solving subtests.

The *KeyMath–R* provides procedures for analysis of students' performance by domain and by individual test item. As Figure 12–1 shows, each item is keyed to a specific domain. For example, there are three domains within the Division subtest: models and basic facts, algorithms to divide whole numbers, and dividing rational numbers. The Summary of Domain Performance, a table that appears on the test record, is used to evaluate the student's status in each domain. The student's domain scores are listed, and a table in the manual is checked to determine average domain scores

for the student's grade. Then, the student's performance in each domain is rated as Weak, Average, or Strong. On the Division subtest, David showed Average skill in models and basic facts but Weak performance in the other two domains.

Test items on the *KeyMath–R* are also linked to specific objectives. For example, the objective for one of the Division items that David missed is, "The student can divide a three-digit number when regouping is required." This feature can be very helpful in preliminary planning of instruction if the objectives are ones that are addressed in the student's school mathematics program. Further assessment would be necessary, however, because *KeyMath–R* objectives are evaluated by only one or two test items. Professionals can devise measures themselves or select a published material such as *KeyMath Teach and Practice* (Connolly, 1985).

KeyMath–R results help evaluators determine the student's current achievement in basic mathematics concepts, computational operations, and applications such as problem solving, estimation, time, money, and measurement. The *KeyMath–R* is most useful as a screening device to identify possible strengths and weaknesses. Although further information must be gathered about each potential area of educational need, the *Key-Math–R's* organization of mathematics skills into domains and objectives facilitates this process. Results can be linked to specific skills and subskills, thereby proving helpful in the selection or design of appropriate informal tools for in-depth assessment.

OTHER FORMAL MEASURES

There are several other formal measures of mathematics skills in addition to the *KeyMath–R,* and three of these are described in the next sections. Included are the *Stanford Diagnostic Mathematics Test* (3rd ed.), a set of group-administered survey tests designed for grades 1 through high school; the *Test of Mathematical Abilities,* an instrument that assesses mathematical aptitudes and students' attitudes toward math; and the *Diagnostic Test of Arithmetic Strategies,* a formal measure of the strategies students use to solve computation problems.

FIGURE 12–2

Sample Score Profile and Area Comparisons from the *KeyMath–R*

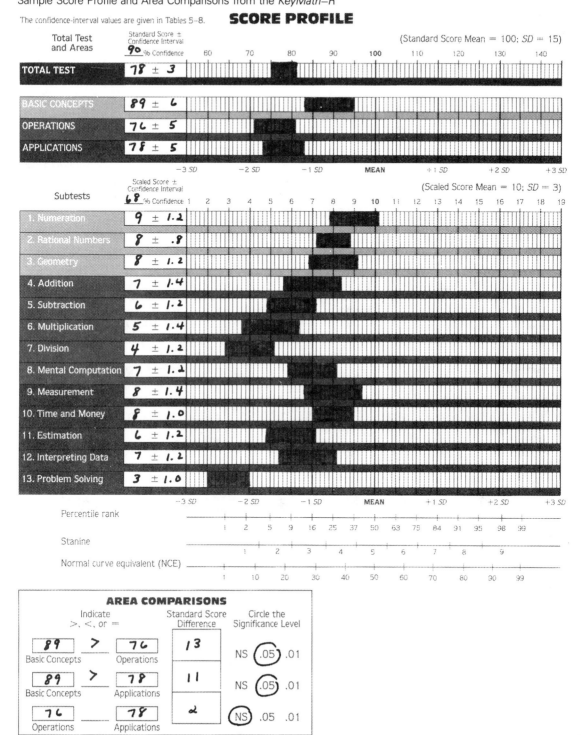

Stanford Diagnostic Mathematics Test (SDMT)

The *SDMT* is a norm-referenced test of several types of mathematics skills. Designed for group use, its major purpose is identification of areas of educational need.

Four levels of the *SDMT* are available to meet the needs of students in grades 1 through high school, and there is some overlap between levels to accommodate students with problems in mathematics. For example, both the Red and Green Levels provide norms for fourth graders, but the Red Level is more appropriate for low achievers because its content is based on the skills taught in the early elementary grades. To facilitate retesting, parallel forms are available for each level.

Each level contains the following three tests of mathematics skills, although content varies somewhat from level to level:

□ *Test 1: Number System and Numeration* assesses the Concept/Skill domains of Whole Numbers and Decimal Place Value, Rational Numbers and Numeration, and Operations and Properties.
□ *Test 2: Computation* assesses the Concept/Skill domains of Addition with Whole Numbers, Subtraction with Whole Numbers, Multiplication with Whole Numbers, Division with Whole Numbers, Fractions, Decimals, Percent, and Number Sentences.
□ *Test 3: Applications* assesses the Concept/Skill domains of Problem Solving, Tables and Graphs, and Geometry and Measurement.

It is possible to administer all three tests or select only one or two. If all tests are given, they may be administered on different days to avoid tiring the students.

The *SDMT* is designed for group administration. To participate, students must be able to listen and attend to test directions and to work independently. All questions are multiple-choice. On the upper levels, students mark their responses on separate answer sheets. Students are provided with scratch paper for their calculations. Several of the tests are timed. On the lower levels, reading skills are not required because the tester reads the word problems aloud. On the upper levels, students may request assistance in reading the questions.

The *SDMT* was standardized in 1983 and 1984, and stratified random sampling was used to select a sample resembling the national school population. The reliability and validity of this instrument appear adequate. However, it would be useful to have information about the relationship between the *SDMT* and individual mathematics tests such as the *KeyMath–R*.

STANFORD DIAGNOSTIC MATHEMATICS TEST (3rd ed.) *(SDMT)*
L. S. Beatty, R. Madden, E. F. Gardner, & B. Karlsen (1984)

Type: Norm-referenced test
Major Content Areas: Number system and numeration, computation, and applications
Type of Administration: Group
Administration Time: From 85 to 100 minutes, depending on the level of the test
Age/Grade Levels: Red Level, Grades 1.5 to 4.9; Green Level, Grades 4.1 to 6.9; Brown Level, Grades 6.1 to 8.9; Blue Level, Grades 8.1 to 12.9
Types of Scores: Percentile ranks, stanines, scaled scores, grade equivalents, Progress Indicators
Typical Uses: A broad-based test for the identification of strengths and weaknesses in mathematics skill development
Cautions: The *SDMT* is designed for group administration. Questions are multiple-choice, some portions of the test are timed, and older students record their responses on a separate answer sheet. If students experience difficulty with group administration, the *SDMT* can be administered individually as long as the tester adheres to standard administration procedures.

The *SDMT* is quite easy to administer. There are no basals or ceilings, and all responses are recorded by the student. The tester simply reads the specified directions to the student and times some of the tests. The *SDMT* can be hand scored by the tester or sent to a commercial service for machine scoring. Sets of stencil keys are provided to assist in hand scoring.

Several types of scores are available on the *SDMT,* including percentile ranks, scaled scores, stanines, and grade equivalents. A total test score may be calculated as well as scores for each of the three subtests. For comparison of student performance across subtests, the *SDMT* manual recommends either percentile ranks or stanines; use of grade scores is not advised.

One feature of the *SDMT* is that each test is described in terms of the Concept/Skill domains it assesses. In addition, each domain is linked to a set of instructional objectives. For example, the Whole Number domain in Test 1 can be broken down into a series of objectives for Comparing Sets of Objects and for Naming Numbers and Counting.

Another feature is the Progress Indicator score. This score provides information about how well the student is progressing in each Concept/Skill domain. The student's raw score on each domain is compared to a cutoff score that indicates mastery of skills in that domain. If the student's score equals or exceeds the criterion, the Progress Indicator (PI) is +, meaning adequate progress. If the student's score falls below the criterion, the PI is −. The *SDMT* calls the Progress Indicator a content-referenced score because its reference point is the test's content, not test norms.

Although the *SDMT* is a group test, it has several advantages for the assessment of students with special needs in mathematics. Its norms extend through grade 12, so it can be used with older high school students, unlike the *KeyMath–R*. It offers precise descriptions of the skills it assesses and provides information about skill mastery through the Progress Indicators. Skill and content domains are linked to instructional objectives that assist in planning further assessment efforts. The *SDMT* is best used as a broad-based survey of several areas of mathematics proficiency. If students have difficulty with the group administration, the *SDMT* can be administered individually as long as standard testing procedures are followed.

Test of Mathematical Abilities (TOMA)

The *TOMA* is an interesting test because it attempts to extend mathematics assessment beyond the traditional skills of computation and problem solving. According to the *TOMA* manual, other important factors are the "attitudes a student might have toward mathematics, the understand-

---

TEST OF MATHEMATICAL ABILITIES (TOMA)
V. L. Brown & E. McEntire (1984)

Type: Norm-referenced test
Major Content Areas: Attitude toward math, vocabulary, computation, general information, story problems
Type of Administration: All subtests may be group administered except General Information
Administration Time: 45 to 105 minutes
Age/Grade Levels: Grades 3 to 12, ages 8–6 to 18–11
Types of Scores: Scaled scores, percentiles, Math Quotient
Typical Uses: Evaluation of attitudes toward mathematics and identification of strengths and weaknesses in mathematics skill development
Cautions: Students need both reading and writing skills to complete test tasks on the *TOMA*. Professionals should take extra care when grading student's responses to the open-ended questions on the Vocabulary and General Information subtests. *TOMA* results must be interpreted cautiously because of the need for further information about validity.

ing of vocabulary used in a mathematical sense, and the understanding of how information about mathematics is used in our general culture" (p. 1).

The *TOMA* contains five subtests:

□ *Attitude toward Math*—The tester reads aloud statements such as "Math is easy for me." Students listen and then check whether they agree with the statement, disagree, or don't know. This subtest is an adaptation of the mathematics portion of the *Estes Attitude Scales* (Estes, Estes, Richards, & Roettger, 1981) described in Chapter 10.

□ *Vocabulary*—Students are presented with 20 mathematical terms. They read the words and then write a brief definition of the term as it is used in a mathematical sense. This test is to be administered only to students at least 11 years old.

□ *Computation*—Twenty-five computational problems appear on a page in the student booklet. These problems sample the basic operations as well as manipulation of fractions, decimals, money, percentages, and other types of mathematical expressions. Students write their responses directly in the test booklet.

□ *General Information*—This subtest must be individually administered. The tester reads questions to the student, who replies orally. For example, the tester might ask, "How many pennies are there in a dime?"

□ *Story Problems*—The student reads brief story problems that contain extraneous information. Work space is provided for calculation, and the student writes the solution in this space and circles it.

The tester may choose to administer all the subtests on the *TOMA* so the total test score, the Math Quotient, may be calculated. The Vocabulary subtest is not administered to students younger than age 11, but Math Quotients can be computed if scores from the other four subtests are available.

Both reading and writing are required on the *TOMA,* and students with skill problems in these areas may have difficulty with some subtests. However, test tasks are not timed. The manual advises that the Story Problems subtest not be administered to nonreaders. On the Vocabulary subtest, students must read terms and write definitions, although spelling and capitalization errors are not penalized. Clearly, English-language facility

is a prerequisite for participation in the *TOMA*. If group administration procedures are used, then students must also be able to attend to test directions and work independently in a group.

The *TOMA* was standardized on approximately 1,500 students from five states, and this sample resembled the national population in terms of sex, residence, race, and geographic region. Students were selected from regular classes, and the manual states that handicapped students were included "to the extent that they were mainstreamed into the classes chosen for testing" (p. 17). The internal consistency of the *TOMA* appears adequate. Test-retest reliability was studied with two small samples ($n = 23$ and $n = 38$); all coefficients were at or above .70 and the majority fell above .80. To investigate validity, a small sample of learning disabled students ($n = 38$) was administered the *TOMA,* the *KeyMath,* and the mathematics subtests from the *PIAT* and *WRAT.* Moderate correlations (.34 to .45) were found. Additional studies using larger and more diverse samples are needed to substantiate the *TOMA's* concurrent validity.

No special training is required to administer the *TOMA,* but testers should study the manual and administer at least three practice tests. In administration, the Attitude toward Math subtest is presented first and Computation last. Other subtests may be presented in any order. Students answer all items on the Attitude subtest. On the other subtests, the basal is defined as three consecutive correct responses and the ceiling as three consecutive incorrect responses. When subtests are administered to groups, students are directed to complete as many items as they can; the tester then applies the ceiling rules when scoring the test.

Care must be taken in grading students' responses. In particular, the Vocabulary and General Information subtests require the tester to exercise judgment in determining whether responses are correct or incorrect. The manual provides scoring standards to assist in evaluating students' responses on these two subtests.

Scaled scores and percentile ranks are available for each *TOMA* subtest. The scaled scores are distributed with a mean of 10 and a standard deviation of 3. A total test score, the Math Quotient (MQ), is derived by combining subtest results; it is distributed with a mean of 100 and a standard deviation of 15. The standard error of measurement for the *TOMA* subtests is either 1 or 2 scaled score points, depending on the subtest and the age of the student. For all ages, the standard error of the MQ score is 6.

Results of the *TOMA* are plotted on a profile, as Figure 12–3 illustrates. These are the scores of a 12-year-old girl who shows average performance in mathematics skill areas. However, her score on the Attitude toward Math subtest is below average, indicating a possible problem in this area.

The student booklet for the *TOMA* is designed so testers can analyze the student's responses and make comments about their findings. For example, on the Computation subtest, testers are encouraged to record the number of problems the student attempted, the number of problems answered correctly, which problems showed care-

FIGURE 12–3
Sample results of the *Test of Mathematical Abilities*

SECTION I. TOMA SUBTEST SCORES

	Raw Scores	Standard Scores	Percentiles
1. Attitude toward Math	23	4	2
2. Vocabulary	5	11	63
3. Computation	17	13	84
4. General Information	25	10	50
5. Story Problems	6	8	25
Sum of Standard Scores	46	= 94 TMQ	

Note. For students under the age of 11, the Vocabulary subtest is not given. For children this age, only four subtests are combined to obtain the sum of the standard scores.

SECTION II. TOMA SUBTEST PROFILE

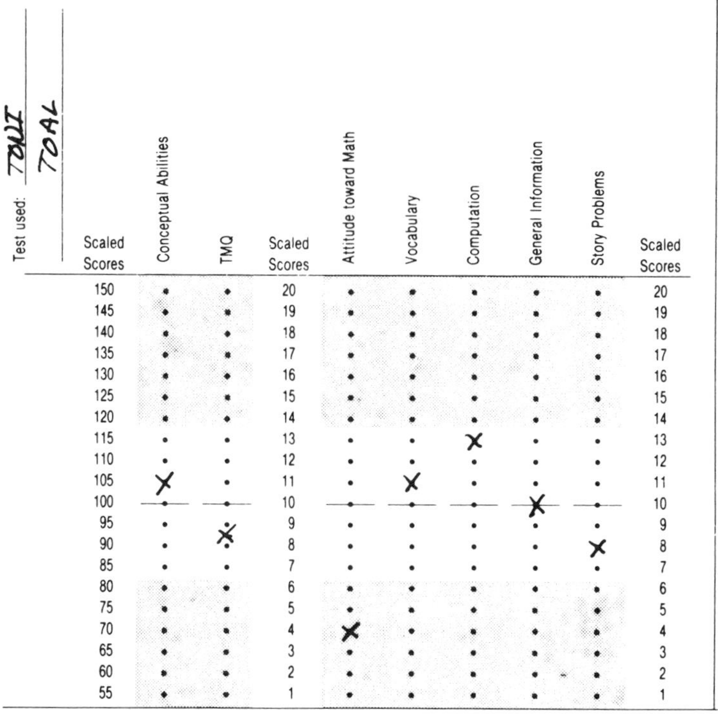

RECOMMENDATIONS

Attitude related to class-room situation. Miss W. will be working with teacher to increase assignments that require "thinking." More hands-on work within the classroom. Partner learning with story problems. Cornale will assist with management techniques.
Implement Tobin's Study Skills ideas.

Note. From *Test of Mathematical Abilities* (p. 30) by V. L. Brown and E. McEntire, 1984, Austin, TX: PRO-ED. Copyright 1984 by PRO-ED. Reprinted by permission.

less errors, and the types of systematic errors made by the student.

The *TOMA* is a norm-referenced mathematics test that surveys several areas of performance. It assesses traditional mathematics skills and also offers measures of attitudes toward mathematics, mathematics vocabulary, and general mathematics information. As with other survey tests, the results of the *TOMA* are used to direct further assessment.

Diagnostic Test of Arithmetic Strategies (DTAS)

The *DTAS* is a measure of the strategies students use in solving arithmetic computation problems. Although not norm-referenced, it is a formal assessment device with standard procedures for administration and scoring. Its scope is quite limited in comparison to tests like the *KeyMath–R, SDMT,* and *TOMA.* Its purpose is the in-depth assessment of one important component of mathematical ability, arithmetic computation.

The *DTAS* contains four subtests: Addition, Subtraction, Multiplication, and Division. Their focus is not the answers students give to computation problems. Instead, they are designed to elicit information about the ways students go about solving computation problems. To accomplish this, each subtest is divided into four sections.

Section 1: Setting Up the Problem.   The tester reads problems to the student, who writes down each problem; the student is not required to solve the problems. For example, the tester might say, "Write down twenty-four plus eighteen." The student's responses are checked for several types of errors. Errors in writing numerals occur when the student writes 7 as Γ. Errors in writing numbers occur when numbers are written as they sound (e.g., 204 for twenty-four) or when numbers are reversed. In addition, subtraction, and multiplication, alignment is incorrect if the student aligns numbers to the left rather than to the right. Sloppy alignment is also considered an error.

Section 2: Number Facts.   Students are shown a simple facts problem and told to say the answer that comes into their head. The tester records how long it takes the student to respond and whether or not the response is correct. The skill under assessment is the student's ability to recall number facts quickly, accurately, and automatically. The tester observes the student and notes whether the student attempts to solve the problems by counting fingers, using whispered counting, or counting aloud.

Section 3: Written Calculation.   The student is presented with 12 computation problems of increasing difficulty. He or she is directed to read each problem out loud, show all work on the answer sheet, and "Tell me out loud what you are doing." The tester then analyzes several aspects of the student's work. To illustrate this, Figure 12–4 presents the scoring sheet for the Written

---

DIAGNOSTIC TEST OF ARITHMETIC STRATEGIES (DTAS)

H. P. Ginsburg & S. C. Mathews (1984)

Type: Diagnostic inventory with standard administration and scoring procedures

Major Content Areas: Setting up problems, number facts, written calculation, and informal skills

Type of Administration: Individual

Administration Time: 20 minutes per subtest

Age/Grade Levels: Students in the elementary grades

Types of Scores: Norm-referenced scores are not available; results are the number and types of errors made by the student

Typical Uses: Identification of successful and unsuccessful strategies for addition, subtraction, multiplication, and division

Cautions: The *DTAS* provides descriptive results rather than norm-referenced scores.

Calculation section of the Addition subtest. The results are those of a 6-year-old second grader described in the *DTAS* manual.

First the professional determines whether the student's answer is correct or incorrect. Then the student's method of solving the problem is considered to see if the student used the standard school method or an informal one. The standard school method for addition involves beginning with the ones column and carrying when necessary. Informal methods are nonstandard procedures. For example, the student may begin with the larger number and count upwards; or a problem such as 42 + 54 might be simplified into two problems, 40 + 50 and 2 + 4.

Second, the tester looks for any number fact errors that may have occurred. "Bugs" are another concern. Also called defective algorithms (Ashlock,

FIGURE 12–4

Sample results of the *Diagnostic Test of Arithmetic Strategies*

SECTION IIB: WRITTEN CALCULATION

					Problems							
	5	6	7	8	9	10	11	12	13	14	15	16
1. Answer												
Correct (circle)	㊴	㉗	㊻	㉘	126	135	42	64	643	730	36	36
Incorrect (write in)	—	—	—	—	*136*	*145*	*312*	*514*	*533*	*620*	*30*	*38*
2. Standard school method	✓	✓	✓	✓	✓	✓	—	—	—	—	—	—
3. Informal method	—	—	—	—	—	—	—	—	—	—	—	—
4. Number fact error	—	—	—	—	✓	✓	—	—	—	—	—	—
5. Bugs												
A. Addition like multiplication	—	—										
B. Zero makes zero			—	—								
C. Add from left to right					—	—						
D. No carry: All digits on bottom								—	—	—	—	
E. No carry: Vanishing digit							✓	✓	—	—		
F. Carries wrong digit							—	—	✓	✓		
G. Wrong operation	—	—	—	—	—	—	—	—	—	—	—	—
H. Add individual digits	—	—	—	—	—	—	—	—	—	—	—	—
I. Other	—	—	—	—	—	—	—	—	—	—	—	—
6. Slips												
A. Skips numbers	—	—	—	—	—	—	—	—	—	—	✓	—
B. Adds twice	—	—	—	—	—	—	—	—	—	—	—	✓
C. Other	—	—	—	—	—	—	—	—	—	—	—	—

Notes: *Debbie started out by doing the standard school method on problems 5–8 which do not involve carrying. When carrying was introduced, she obviously did not know how to deal with it and either put all digits on the bottom or ignored the numbers to be carried. On the last two problems, she was sloppy, making two slips.*

Note. From *Diagnostic Test of Arithmetic Strategies* (p. 34) by H. P. Ginsburg and S. C. Mathews, 1984, Austin, TX: PRO-ED. Copyright 1984 by PRO-ED. Reprinted by permission.

1986), bugs are systematic but inappropriate procedures for problem solving. The *DTAS* scoring sheet lists several possible types of bugs. For instance, the student might approach an addition problem as if it were a multiplication problem. Or the student might follow the rule that "0 makes 0." With this bug, the sum of 15 + 20 would be calculated as 30, because 0 plus any number is 0.

"Slips" are another error category in Written Calculation. According to the *DTAS* manual, slips are "relatively minor execution errors, and do not seem to result from basic faults in understanding or serious defects in the calculational procedure" (p. 4). Examples of slips in addition are skipping numbers and adding the same number twice.

Section 4: Informal Skills. Here the tester reads computation problems and the student must solve them mentally. For example, the tester might ask, "How much is twenty-seven and fourteen?" The purpose of this activity is to require the student to go beyond the standard school methods of problem solving. The student is presented with nontraditional problems (nontraditional because they require mental computation), and informal problem-solving procedures are observed. The tester then records which strategy the student employs. For example, on the Addition subtest, the tester notes whether the student used counting, simplification, imaginary column addition, or some other informal strategy. If the student fails to use an informal procedure, the tester prompts the student by suggesting a strategy.

According to the manual, the *DTAS* is appropriate for students "who are experiencing difficulty with addition, subtraction, multiplication, or division (roughly in grades 1–6)" (p. 9). Students must possess sufficient English-language skills to understand test directions and respond to questions. No reading skills are required, and students do not need to write letters or words. However, they are expected to write computation problems and solutions. None of the subtests are timed, but students are urged to work quickly on the Number Facts task. At first, students may be somewhat reluctant to explain how they are solving the problems on Written Calculation, but most will cooperate when encouraged by the tester.

Special training is not needed to administer the *DTAS*, but professionals should study the manual carefully and administer several practice tests. Subtests can be administered in any order, and it is not necessary to administer all subtests to any one student. The manual advises that a student be given only one of the four subtests during any one testing session. There are no basals and ceilings because students are encouraged to attempt all of the test items.

Scoring the *DTAS* requires more expertise than many measures. The tester must evaluate the accuracy of the student's responses and also describe the methods the student used to arrive at these responses. The manual provides guidelines for scoring each subtest, standards for scoring, and examples. Testers should take advantage of these resources.

The *DTAS* does not produce norm-referenced results. Instead, the results are descriptive. For each basic operation, it is possible to identify the strategies the student uses and the types of errors that consistently occur. For example, the results that appeared in Figure 12–4 indicate that the student experiences difficulty with carrying. When faced with addition problems requiring carrying (or regrouping), the student relies upon two types of bugs. She fails to carry and writes all digits:

$$\begin{array}{r} 15 \\ + \ 29 \\ \hline 314 \end{array}$$

or she fails to carry but writes only the ones digit:

$$\begin{array}{r} 345 \\ + \ 296 \\ \hline 531 \end{array}$$

Descriptive results have direct implications for instruction, if the skill in question is an area of educational need for the student. Because the *DTAS* is not normed, it is impossible to compare the student's performance with age or grade peers. For example, the student may be progressing satisfactorily but simply not have reached the point in the mathematics curriculum where regrouping skills are taught. However, if the skill deficiency is perceived as a problem, *DTAS* results may be used to plan a course of instructional action. The manual provides suggestions for remedial activities.

INFORMAL ASSESSMENT PROCEDURES

Assessment for instructional planning relies upon informal measures and techniques and, in mathematics, there are a variety of informal strategies. Among the most common are teacher checklists, informal inventories, error analysis, diagnostic teaching and clinical math interviews, criterion-referenced tests, questionnaires, and interviews.

Teacher Checklists

Checklists are a quick and efficient method for gathering information from teachers and other professionals about their observations of students' performance in mathematics. Some checklists are designed so they are general in nature, surveying a wide range of mathematics content. Others are quite specific, focusing on a particular set of skills.

One major use of checklists is to document and monitor students' acquisition of mathematics skills. Curriculum checklists, such as the one shown in Figure 12–5, serve this purpose. It addresses application skills such as telling time, using a calendar, reading a thermometer, and applying consumer economics. This checklist could be completed during assessment and then updated as the student learns new skills.

FIGURE 12–5
Curriculum checklist for mathematics application skills

Early Childhood Education

N. Applied Mathematics
  1. Measurement (9.14.0)—Time/Calendar
    _____ a. Can show time to the hour.
    _____ b. Can read time to the hour.
    _____ c. Can *show* time to the minute.
    _____ d. Can *identify* time to the minute, by stating "so many minutes after the hour."
    _____ e. Can tell time by fractions:____half hour,____quarter hour.
    _____ f. Can count by 5-minute intervals.
    _____ g. States there are 60 minutes in an hour,____30 minutes in half-hour,____12 hours in half-day,____distinguishes A.M. and P.M.
    _____ h. Can read so many minutes before the next hour.
    _____ i. States the number of days in a week,____months in a year.
    _____ j. Tells names of days in a week.
    _____ k. Can read names of days,____months.
    _____ l. Uses the calendar to interpret date.
    _____ m. Tells his or her birthday by____month,____day,____year.

Middle School Education

    _____ n. Interprets written notation of time, e.g. 3:00, 3:01, 3:30, 3:45, etc.
    _____ o. Writes time shown on a clock face.
    _____ p. States number of seconds in a minute.
    _____ q. Sets an alarm clock.
    _____ r. Constructs time schedules, such as for homework or TV.
    _____ s. Uses time schedules—bus, train, plane, subway.
    _____ t. Reads public transportation schedules.
    _____ u. Explains Daylight Saving Time.

High School Education

    _____ v. Can use a time clock.
    _____ w. Can explain meaning of *time and a half, double time.*

    _____ x. Is on time for school, work.
    _____ y. Explains and identifies different time zones in the world and can compute equivalent time across zone.
    _____ z. Uses time in relationship to____speed,____distance,____cooking.
  2. Measurement—clothing size
    _____ a. Can interpret sizes of____clothes,____shoes,____underwear.
  3. Measurement—temperature
    _____ a. Can read and interpret temperature on a thermometer.
    _____ b. Can use temperature in cooking.
  4. Metric Measure
    _____ a. Can relate metric measures to decimal notation.
    _____ b. Can use metric measures in cooking; weights.
    _____ c. Can convert values from one measure to another—metric to nonmetric, metric to metric, nonmetric to nonmetric (inches to feet, gallon to quarts).
    _____ d. Tells approximate distance between two locations in either kilometers or miles.
    _____ e. Uses measure in basic shop work.
    _____ f. Uses legend on map to estimate kilometers or miles.
    _____ g. Tells how to use an odometer; a speedometer.
  5. Economics (9.15.0)
    _____ a. States the approximate money value of objects, such as soda pop, crayons, movie ticket, postage stamps.
    _____ b. Recognizes paper money to $20.00.
    _____ c. Makes change up to $25.00.
    _____ d. Writes all money amounts in decimal form.
    _____ e. Uses ads in newspapers, on radio, TV, and on store front windows to compare prices of food, clothing, etc.
    _____ f. Keeps daily record of expenditures.
    _____ g. Can check sales tax on purchases computing percent.
    _____ h. Computes hourly wage.
    _____ i. Displays understanding of state and federal taxes.
    _____ j. Displays understanding of social security tax and purpose of tax.
    _____ k. Can estimate living expenses, such as rent, utilities.
    _____ l. Can estimate cost of various licenses—auto, driver's, business.
    _____ m. States basic bank interactions and their purpose: checking account, savings account, loan, interest on savings accounts, interest on loans.
    _____ n. Can interpret bank statement.
    _____ o. Can keep checking account balanced.
    _____ p. States pros and cons of installment buying.

Note. From *Teaching Mathematics to Children with Special Needs* (pp. 252–53) by F. K. Reisman and S. H. Kauffman, 1980. Columbus, OH: Merrill. Copyright 1980 by Bell & Howell Company. Reprinted by permission.

Informal Inventories

Informal inventories survey a variety of skills to determine where the student's strengths and weaknesses lie. For example, an informal inventory that assesses arithmetic computation skills appears in Figure 12–6. It contains problems that require the basic operations of addition, subtraction, multiplication, and division. However, the inventory provides only one or two items at most to evaluate a particular skill such as addition of 2-digit numbers with regrouping. If results point to a possible skill deficiency, it is necessary to collect further data with more precise measures such as criterion-referenced tests.

Inventories are quite easy to construct, and professionals can design their own to assess whatever skill areas are of interest. For instance, if the teacher is curious about a student's understanding of place value concepts, he or she could devise a set of questions to probe this area of mathematics. The teacher might include activities such as the following:

> The number 48 is the same as 4 tens and 8 ones. Tell how many tens and ones make up these numbers.
> 15 = _____ tens + _____ ones
> 36 = _____ tens + _____ ones
> 72 = _____ tens + _____ ones

Or if the teacher is interested in the student's ability to tell time, the teacher could prepare a set of drawings of clock faces, each showing a different time. One set might assess telling time to the hour (e.g., 4:00), another telling time to the half hour (e.g., 7:30), and so forth. The teacher should also consider including clocks with digital displays (e.g., 8:42 or 4:23:15).

Mathematics skills are usually assessed with paper-and-pencil tasks, but there are many other alternatives. If the teacher wants to learn more about the student's knowledge of basic math facts, problems could be presented orally, on paper, on the chalkboard, with flashcards, in horizontal notation (2 + 3 = _____) or vertical notation, and so forth. Students could respond orally instead of writing their answers. If speed is a concern, the inventory can be timed. A popular technique is to present students with a set of problems to complete in 1 minute. The students' answers are scored for accuracy, and the number of problems attempted can be compared with the number of problems answered correctly.

Error Analysis

Mathematics is one of the school subjects best suited for error analysis because students respond in writing on most tasks, thereby producing a permanent record of their work. Also, there is usually only one correct answer to mathematical problems and questions, and scoring is unambiguous. Error analysis is a traditional technique in mathematics assessment; it dates back to the 1920s when professionals began to study the types of errors that characterize written computation (Brueckner, 1930; Buswell & John, 1925; Osborn, 1925).

Today the most common use of error analysis in mathematics is assessment of computation skills. Cox (1975) differentiates between systematic computation errors and errors that are random or careless mistakes. With systematic errors, students are consistent in their use of an incorrect number fact, operation, or algorithm. Roberts (1968) studied the written computation of elementary grade students and identified four error types:

1. *Incorrect operation*—The student selects the incorrect operation. For example, if the problem requires subtraction, the student adds.
2. *Incorrect number fact*—The number fact recalled by the student is inaccurate. For example, the student recalls the product of 6 × 9 as 52.
3. *Incorrect algorithm*—The procedures used by the student to solve the problem are inappropriate. The student may skip a step, apply the correct steps in the wrong sequence, or use an inaccurate method. For example, in the subtraction problem 24 − 18, the student may begin by subtracting 4 from 8, using the algorithm "subtract the smaller number from the larger."
4. *Random error*—The student's response is incorrect and apparently random. For example, the student writes 100 as the answer to 42 × 6.

According to Roberts, the most frequent type of error among students with achievement problems is the random error. For other students, incorrect algorithms are most common.

FIGURE 12–6
Informal inventory of computation skills

Addition

6	3	4	10	8	11
+ 2	+ 5	+ 0	+ 5	+ 3	+ 4

17	33	67	11 12	42	523
+ 5	+ 15	+ 71	+ 9	+ 9	+ 162

692
+ 349

Subtraction

6	3	4	17	98	47
− 4	− 3	− 0	− 3	− 4	− 32

10	14	27	7 − 5 = _____
− 3	− 6	− 24	

17 − 12 = _____   18 − 9 = _____   462
− 321

176	253
− 36	− 89

Multiplication

3	2	2	6	33	22	3
× 2	× 2	× 8	× 0	× 1	× 4	× 22

232	204	8 × 6 = _____	7 × 7 = _____
× 3	× 2		

1403	105	2675	1760	22	17
× 2	× 3	× 3	× 5	× 33	× 12

46	60	328	6023
× 32	× 16	× 21	× 34

Division

$3\overline{)3}$ $2\overline{)4}$ $3\overline{)963}$ $6\overline{)18}$ $5\overline{)155}$ $2\overline{)1864}$

$3\overline{)10}$ $4\overline{)1208}$ $7\overline{)56714}$ $7\overline{)1500}$ $22\overline{)484}$

$36\overline{)864}$ $15\overline{)3666}$

Note. From *Clinical Teaching* (2nd ed.) (pp. 249–50) by R. M. Smith, 1974. New York: McGraw-Hill. Copyright 1974 by McGraw-Hill Book Company. Reprinted by permission.

The first step in conducting an error analysis is to gather a sample of the student's work. The professional could administer an informal mathematics inventory or a computation subtest from a formal test. Or samples of recent classroom work could be obtained from the student's teacher; these might be homework assignments, worksheets, workbook pages, or classroom tests or quizzes.

The math sample is then graded to identify the errors that the student has made. In most cases, scoring is a straightforward process. However, difficulties may arise when a student's handwriting is hard to read. If an answer is illegible, the professional should ask the student for help in deciphering it. By using this procedure, the teacher can evaluate the student's math skills separately from writing skills.

Next, the student's errors are categorized by type. Random errors, incorrect operations, inaccurate number facts, and defective algorithms are the usual categories. The professional may also want to consider two other types of errors assessed by the *Diagnostic Test of Arithmetic Strategies:* slips (careless, nonsystematic errors) and mistakes in setting up the problem.

Sometimes the answer to a computational problem is wrong for more than one reason. For instance, the student may recall a number fact inaccurately *and* employ an inappropriate operation or algorithm. In the following problem, the student used addition rather than subtraction and also recalled one addition fact incorrectly:

$$
\begin{array}{r}
\overset{1}{36} \\
-\ 18 \\
\hline
\mathbf{55}
\end{array}
$$

Another concern is whether errors are systematic. If the student correctly adds $8 + 4$ in four problems but not in the fifth, the error is probably a slip rather than a number facts problem. A response analysis of the student's work, where both correct and incorrect answers are analyzed, can provide this kind of information. One error on one problem does not constitute an error pattern. The errors most relevant to instructional planning occur consistently over several problems and frequently over time.

Error analysis can also be used with mathematical problem-solving tasks such as story problems. Goodstein (1981) suggests that students'

word problem errors be analyzed by following these steps:

1. Check to determine the magnitude of the discrepancy between the incorrect and correct response. Small discrepancies for large numbers will often indicate carelessness in the computational aspect of the task.
2. Check to determine if the magnitude of the response indicates selection of the proper operation. . . .
3. Check to determine if the response could have been the combination of other numerical data in the problem. (Obviously, this step is only used when extraneous information is present). (pp. 42–43)

Cawley, Miller, and School (1987) report that secondary grade learning disabled students find indirect problems and those with extraneous information particularly difficult. Indirect problems, like the nonroutine problems on the *KeyMath–R,* do not provide direct cues to the correct operation. If it appears that the student has chosen the incorrect operation or the wrong numerical data for computation, the next step would be to conduct a clinical interview to determine how the student goes about solving story problems.

Clinical Math Interviews and Diagnostic Probes

Whereas error analysis techniques focus on students' written products, clinical interviews elicit information about the procedures students use to arrive at those products. Clinical interviews are the most appropriate technique for process analysis.

In conducting a clinical interview, the professional combines several informal techniques. The student is observed going about the mathematics task, and the professional takes note of any behaviors of interest. For example, on a computation task the student may attempt to solve problems by counting fingers or by making hatchmarks on the paper. The student is interviewed to find out about the cognitive strategies used to accomplish the task. Diagnostic probes are introduced to determine whether alternative strategies will improve the student's performance.

According to Cawley (1978), clinical math interviews are conducted *after* students have completed some mathematics task. The student's paper is scored, and then "the student is asked to verbalize the procedure that he or she used to do both the correct and incorrect problems" (p. 224). However, Bartel (1986a) recommends that the interview take place *while* students are engaged in the mathematics activity. Bartel suggests these guidelines for math interviews:

1. One problem area should be considered at a time.
2. The easiest problem should be presented first.
3. A written record or tape should be made of the interview.
4. The student should simultaneously solve the problem in written form and "explain" what he or she is doing orally.
5. The student must be left free to solve the problem in his or her own way without a hint that he or she is doing something wrong.
6. The student should not be hurried. (p. 200)

Neither approach is the perfect solution (Ashlock, 1986). When interviews are conducted during the activity, the process of thinking out loud may influence the way the student approaches the problem. When interviews take place after the work has been completed, the student may be unable to recall all the steps that were followed or the reasoning that prompted those steps. To compensate for the shortcomings of these methods, Ashlock advises using both. Thus, the professional could interview the student after he or she has completed one set of tasks and then conduct a second interview as the student attempts another set of tasks.

One use of clinical interviews is the study of computational processes. For example, the *Diagnostic Test of Arithmetic Strategies* incorporates an interview procedure into its evaluation of students' written computation skills. In the classroom, teachers can present the student with arithmetic problems and then listen to the student's explanation of the strategies selected for problem solving. Mercer and Mercer (1989) provide an example:

The teacher gave Mary three multiplication problems and said, "Please do these problems and tell me how you figure out the answer." Mary solved the problems in this way:

$$\begin{array}{ccc} \overset{2}{27} & \overset{4}{36} & \overset{3}{44} \\ \times\ 4 & \times\ 7 & \times\ 8 \\ \hline 168 & 492 & 562 \end{array}$$

For the first problem, Mary explained, "7 times 4 equals 28. So I put my 8 here and carry the 2. 2 plus 2 equals 4 and 4 times 4 equals 16. So I put 16 here."

Her explanations for the other two problems followed the same logic.

By listening to Mary and watching her solve the problems, the teacher quickly determined Mary's error pattern: She adds the number associated with the crutch (the number carried to the tens column) *before* multiplying the tens digit. (p. 204)

Clinical interviews can also provide information about how students solve story problems. The solution involves several steps, and interviews are the best means for studying the student's skill in selecting and carrying out the appropriate procedures. According to Goodstein (1981), students must follow a four-step process in solving story problems:

1. Identification of the required arithmetic operation
2. Identification of the relevant set(s) of information
3. Appropriate and accurate display of the computation (this step is often unnecessary for simple computations and would be replaced by "accurate entry of the computational factors" if a calculator were to be used)
4. Accurate performance of the indicated computation (this step would automatically follow successful completion of steps 1–3, if a calculator were used) (p. 34)

To accomplish these steps, students must first read and comprehend the story problem. For many students with special needs, poor reading skills interfere with their ability to take this important first step. Next, the student must be familiar with the meanings of the quantitative terms that appear in the problem and the relationship between these terms and arithmetic operations. For example, when the problem asks, "How many are there *altogether?*" the addition operation is usually implied. When the student has identified the appropriate operation, the problem must be carefully studied to locate the values to add, subtract, multiply, or divide. To do this, relevant information must be recognized and irrelevant data discarded. For instance, if the problem says, "John has 3 kittens, Mary has 2 cats, and Hortense has 5 puppies," Hortense's pets are irrelevant if the student must determine "How many cats and kittens are there altogether?"

The professional can learn a great deal about the student's problem-solving skills by incorporating diagnostic probes into the clinical math interview. To do this, the student is given several story problems to solve and instructed to "think out loud" throughout the entire process. When a problem area becomes apparent, the professional intervenes and provides a cue or an alternate strategy for accomplishing the task. Table 12–2 presents several diagnostic probes for use with story problems. For example, if the teacher suspects that poor reading skills are affecting the student's performance, the teacher can read the problem aloud to the student. If the student is then able to solve the problem successfully, reading becomes the instructional concern rather than mathematical problem-solving skills.

Criterion-Referenced Tests

Criterion-referenced tests are used to assess mastery of specific mathematics skills. For example, if the results of an informal math inventory or

standardized test point to possible weaknesses in a particular set of skills, the professional can select or design a criterion-referenced test to evaluate the student's ability to perform those skills.

Professionals can prepare their own criterion-referenced measures based on the goals and objectives of the local curriculum or can select from commercially available tests. The *Multilevel Academic Skills Inventory* (Howell et al., 1982) and *System FORE* (Bagai & Bagai, 1979) contain a large number of mathematics assessments, as do the measures prepared by Brigance (1977, 1981, 1983).

For example, the *BRIGANCE® Diagnostic Inventory of Basic Skills* (1977), which is designed for elementary students, includes tests of several

TABLE 12–2
Diagnostic probes for the study of problem-solving skills

Suspected Area of Difficulty	Suggested Intervention
Decoding the words in the story problem	Read the story problem aloud to the student, and see if he or she can then solve the problem correctly.
Understanding the meaning of the situation described in the story problem	Ask the student to draw a picture that illustrates the problem.
	Provide the student with a picture illustrating the problem.
Selecting the appropriate operation (addition, subtraction, multiplication, or division)	Ask the student to explain the meaning of key quantitative terms that appear in the problem (e.g., "How many apples are there *altogether?*" or "How many children were *left?*").
	Tell the student which operation to use, and see if he or she can then solve the problem correctly.
Identifying the relevant and irrelevant information in the problem	If the problem requires knowledge of conceptual categories (e.g., dogs and cats are animals, but a doll is a toy), assess the student's understanding of the categories.
	Tell the student that the problem contains extra information, and ask him or her to try and find it.
Writing down the computational problem	Have the student dictate the problem while the professional writes it down.
Remembering number facts	Provide the student with manipulatives such as sticks or beans to use in figuring out the number facts that are needed.
	Provide the student with a calculator, and see if he or she can then solve the problem correctly.
Selecting the appropriate computational algorithm	If the student's algorithm is inaccurate, teach the student the appropriate procedure.
	Provide the student with a calculator, and see if he or she can then solve the problem correctly.

types of mathematics skills. For younger students, readiness tests assess skills such as counting, recognition of numerals, and number comprehension. For older students, 64 additional tests are organized into four major sections: Numbers, Operations, Measurement, and Geometry. A Math Grade Level Test is also provided. On this written test, the student completes a page of computation problems, and the raw score earned is converted to a grade equivalent. However, these grade equivalents should be interpreted with caution because the *BRIGANCE®* manual does not explain how the scores were established.

The measure for grades 4 through 12, the *BRIGANCE® Diagnostic Inventory of Essential Skills* (1981), stresses vocational as well as school skills and offers several tests of vocationally related mathematics abilities. For instance, there are 11 tests of Money and Finance, each of which is directed toward a real-world application of mathematics such as reading price signs and making change.

Another criterion-referenced test worthy of note is the *ENRIGHT™ Diagnostic Inventory of Basic Mathematics Skills* (Enright, 1983). The purpose of this measure is the evaluation of computational skills. It includes basic number facts as well as the addition, subtraction, multiplication, and division of whole numbers, fractions, and decimals. There are three levels of assessment on the *ENRIGHT™* inventory: (a) a broad-based placement test that assesses several skills, (b) a set of skill placement tests and number fact tests that assess one skill area each, and (c) a series of criterion-referenced tests that assess one specific subskill. The professional would begin by administering the Wide-Range Placement Test. If results point to a possible problem in addition, the next step would be to administer the Skill Placement Test for Addition of Whole Numbers and the Basic Facts Addition Test. The results of these measures would then be used to select the appropriate criterion-referenced tests. For example, the professional might choose these two Skill Tests from the Addition of Whole Numbers strand: Two 2-Digit Numbers with No Regrouping, and Two 2-Digit Numbers, Regrouping Ones.

An interesting feature of the *ENRIGHT™* measure is that error analysis is incorporated into the scoring procedures for the criterion-referenced Skill Tests. The administration page for each Skill Test lists the correct responses for the problems and examples of incorrect responses. The incorrect responses were derived by employing an inappropriate computational algorithm. The professional can then match the student's wrong answers with the examples provided to determine whether the student is making a systematic algorithmic error. For instance, Figure 12–7 shows the administration page for one of the multiplication Skill Tests. Five different types of systematic algorithm errors are described. If the student answers the first problem incorrectly and writes 812, the error analysis chart indicates that the inappropriate algorithm is, "writes entire product of each column without regrouping."

Questionnaires and Interviews

In mathematics assessment, questionnaires and interviews are used to gather information about students' viewpoints: their attitudes toward mathematics, perceptions of computation and the problem-solving process, opinions of their own abilities in the skill area of mathematics, and so forth. Interviews are preferred for younger students and those with poor reading skills. Questionnaires are used only with students who can cope with reading and writing requirements.

Mercer and Mercer (1989) recommend sentence completion tasks for assessing students' attitudes toward arithmetic. In this procedure, the teacher reads an incomplete sentence to the student, who fills in the missing part. Examples of possible sentences are

1. Math is very _____ .
2. My best subject is _____ .
3. During math sessions I feel _____ .
(p. 205)

Interviews can also be used to find out about students' attitudes toward mathematics and perceptions of its usefulness in everyday life. For example, young students could be asked these open-ended questions:

☐ Is math (or arithmetic) one of your better subjects in school?
☐ What types of math activities are the easiest for you? Which are the hardest?

FIGURE 12–7
Sample administration page from the ENRIGHT™ Diagnostic Inventory of Basic Arithmetic Skills

C. Multiplication of Whole Numbers

SKILL: Multiplies a 2-digit number by a 1-digit number, regrouping ones.

GRADE LEVEL TAUGHT: 3.6

ARITHMETIC RECORD BOOK: Page 4

MATERIALS: Copy of S-94 and a pencil.

ASSESSMENT METHODS: Individual or group written response.

DISCONTINUE: When student has completed the five test items at the top of S-94.

ACCURACY: At least 4/5 (80%) on the test items is required. When the review items are used for post testing, 4/5 (80%) is also required.

NEXT: If the student's accuracy is 4/5 (80%) on this skill test, proceed to the next higher test. If the student has responded incorrectly to two or more test items, do not proceed to the next higher skill test. Instead, begin remediation based on the error analysis shown here.

NOTES:
* Check to see if student works left to right instead of right to left. Working left to right also results in answers shown here.

REVIEW ITEMS:

a. 45 ×2 = 90 b. 18 ×5 = 90 c. 26 ×3 = 78

d. 15 ×4 = 60 e. 37 ×2 = 74

DIRECTIONS: Give each student a copy of S-94 and a pencil. Tell the students to do the five items at the top of S-94. Tell the students to work carefully and take as much time as needed.

2-Digit Number by a 1-Digit Number, Regrouping Ones

	a. 46 ×2 = 92	b. 24 ×3 = 72	c. 18 ×4 = 72	d. 39 ×2 = 78	e. 16 ×4 = 64	ERROR ANALYSIS
	812	612	432	618	424	**Regrouping 13:** Writes entire product of each column without regrouping.* (example: 46 ×2 = 812)
	101	81	63	141	82	**Regrouping 14:** Writes tens value of each subproduct, and regroups ones value into next column. (example: 46 ×2 = 101)
	82	62	42	68	44	**Regrouping 15:** Writes ones value of each subproduct, but doesn't regroup tens value into next column. (example: 46 ×2 = 82)
	20	18	36	24	28	**Process Substitution 31:** Adds digits of multiplicand, and multiplies. (example: 4+6=10 ×2 = 20)
	44	21	14	37	12	**Attention to Sign 193:** Subtracts. (example: 46 −2 = 44)

Examiner's Notes:

(C-4)
OBJECTIVE: By _____ (date), when given five test items for multiplying a 2-digit number by a 1-digit number, regrouping ones, __(student's name)__ will correctly compute at least four of the five test items (80%).

C-4 MULTIPLICATION OF WHOLE NUMBERS:
2-Digit Number by a 1-Digit Number, Regrouping Ones

Note. From ENRIGHT™ Diagnostic Inventory of Basic Arithmetic Skills by B. E. Enright, 1983, North Billerica, MA: Curriculum Associates, Inc. Copyright 1983 by Curriculum Associates, Inc. Reprinted by permission.

- ☐ Do you like to work addition problems? Subtraction problems? Multiplication? Division? Why or why not?
- ☐ Do you like to try to solve story problems? Why or why not?
- ☐ Most people use math skills every day. Can you name three things that people do with numbers?
- ☐ When was the last time you went to the store to buy something? How did you find out how much it cost? Did you pay for it? If you did, how did you figure out whether the salesperson gave you back the right change?
- ☐ Can you tell time? How do you do it?
- ☐ Suppose you wanted to find out how much you weighed. How would you do it? How could you find out how tall you are?
- ☐ Have you ever used a calculator to add or subtract numbers, or to multiply and divide? Is using a calculator easier than doing it in your head? Why or why not?

Several of these questions could be adapted into a questionnaire for older students by changing some of the terminology and substituting age-appropriate examples of everyday math activities.

WITHIN THE CONTEXT OF THE CLASSROOM

Up to this point, discussion has focused on assessment tools for gathering information about the student's performance. Here the emphasis shifts to procedures and techniques for studying the classroom learning environment and its influence on the student's mathematics abilities.

The Instructional Environment

Assessment of the instructional environment must take into account the mathematics curriculum and the instructional methods and materials used to implement that curriculum. In the elementary grades, basal textbook series are the foundation of most mathematics programs. Basal series vary in their approach to the teaching of mathematics, but most emphasize both computation and problem-solving skills.

The questions that follow provide a framework for studying the classroom mathematics program:

1. Which basal mathematics series is used in the classroom?
2. Is more than one level of the mathematics series in use in the classroom?
3. What instructional materials supplement the mathematics textbooks in the basal series? Are manipulatives provided as computational aids? Are calculators available?
4. What types of mathematics skills are stressed in classroom instruction? Computation? Problem solving? Mathematics applications such as time, money, and measurement?
5. Is the mathematics curriculum organized so development of new skills is based on the mastery of prerequisite skills? Are the instructional steps of appropriate size?
6. Is instruction based upon ongoing assessment? How often are performance data collected for monitoring students' progress? What procedures are used to determine the starting points for students entering the mathematics program?
7. How are students grouped for mathematics instruction? How much individualization takes place in each group?
8. What instructional techniques does the teacher use to present new skills and information? Lecture? Demonstration? Discussion? Exploration?
9. In what types of learning activities do students participate? Do all mathematics activities involve paper-and-pencil tasks, or do students sometimes have the opportunity to respond orally?
10. How is supervised practice incorporated into the mathematics program? On the average, how many minutes per day do students spend practicing their mathematics skills?
11. What changes, if any, have been made in the standard mathematics program to accommodate the needs of special learners such as the student under assessment?

Wiederholt, Hammill, and Brown (1978) suggest it is also important to consider the teacher's attitudes, capabilities, and expectations in relation to mathematics instruction.

One major concern is the focus of the mathematics curriculum. The back-to-basics movement is still a powerful force in shaping instructional programs in mathematics, despite the recent emphasis on the teaching of problem solving. Basic skills programs tend to emphasize drill and practice as a means to achieving computational proficiency. The basic skills approach to mathematics is, to some extent, a reaction against the new math curriculum of the 1960s that stressed exploration and discovery learning (Glennon, 1976).

Also of importance are the academic skill demands placed on the student in mathematics activities. Reading is a part of many mathematics tasks, particularly in the upper elementary and secondary grades. Poor reading skills can interfere with the student's ability to read mathematics textbooks, the directions on math worksheets, story problems, and so forth. If reading is a concern, the reading level of the mathematics textbook or other material should be determined using the procedures described in Chapter 11. If the material is too difficult for the student's current skills, the text could be rewritten at an easier reading level or a more suitable text substituted.

Many mathematics activities also require writing skills. Students are expected to write the answers to computational problems, and students must sometimes copy questions or problems onto their papers from the chalkboard or their textbooks. Such tasks may interfere with the mathematics performance of students with handwriting difficulties. Students who write slowly may be unable to finish their work. If the student's writing is difficult to read, both the student and the teacher may be unable to decipher it.

It is also useful to look at other characteristics of mathematics tasks: the number of questions or problems students are expected to complete, the requirements for speed, and the expectations for accuracy. Sometimes students have the necessary skills to succeed with mathematics assignments, but they fail because they cannot meet performance criteria. They may work the first few problems correctly and then become discouraged by the number of problems left to complete. Or they may work too slowly to finish within the required time period. It may be that classroom standards are unduly stringent and some adjustment can be made. For example, the teacher might be willing to allow more time for each assignment or reduce the number of problems students are expected to complete.

The Interpersonal Environment

Social relationships among students are an important component of the classroom's interpersonal environment. Students with achievement problems are often not well accepted by their peers, but difficulties in mathematics seem to be better tolerated than difficulties in reading. Perhaps this is because, in mathematics, students make most of their responses privately, and peers are less aware of each others' performances. Another possible explanation relates to students' experiences with mathematics. All students make computational errors at one time or another, and this experience with failure may make achieving students more tolerant of those with persistent problems with mathematics. It is also possible that students value reading more highly than mathematics or that they perceive mathematics as the more difficult subject. Whatever the reason, mathematics skill deficiencies appear to be less socially debilitating than reading problems.

Interactions between students and teachers are also part of the interpersonal environment. In mathematics instruction, one of the primary ways the teacher communicates with students is by grading their math papers. There are several methods of grading, and some are more likely than others to encourage students in their efforts to learn mathematics skills. For example, for students with achievement problems, it is probably better to mark the correct responses rather than the errors. Such a paper is much less threatening than one covered with red checkmarks and a message such as "F—Try harder."

These questions should be considered when evaluating student-teacher interactions:

□ In grading students' math papers, how does the teacher respond to errors? Does the teacher identify an incorrect response as an error? Correct it? Ignore the error?

□ If the situation is a public one (for example, students are solving problems at the board), what occurs when a student makes an error? Does the teacher use the same correction procedures as in private interactions?

□ How does the student react to the teacher's corrections? Is there a difference when the student is corrected in front of peers?

□ What do other students do when a peer makes an error?

□ What occurs when the student makes a correct response? Does the teacher confirm the response? Praise the student? Provide a tangible reward or token?

□ Are students able to work independently on mathematics activities? Do certain students require frequent assistance from the teacher?

The Physical Environment

The physical environment of the classroom can also affect students' mathematics performance. The environment should be physically comfortable with lighting, temperature, and ventilation at appropriate levels, and classroom space should be arranged to facilitate mathematics instruction. In assessing the classroom's physical characteristics, some of the questions that can be asked are the following:

1. Are all students seated so they can easily see and hear the teacher? Can they see the chalkboard, if necessary?
2. Is the lighting in the classroom adequate?
3. Is the classroom space structured so areas for noisier activities are separated from areas for quieter activities?
4. How are the students' seats arranged for independent work? Are students' desks or tables positioned so students do not distract each other?
5. Are there any quiet work areas or "offices" within the classroom where students can go to escape from distractions?
6. Does the classroom offer a variety of mathematics learning materials, or are textbooks the only resource? If other materials are available, do they cover a wide range of skill levels? Are they accessible to students?
7. In elementary classrooms, is there a learning center for mathematics? If so, what materials and activities does it contain? Are manipulative materials such as computational aids available for student use?
8. Are calculators available to students? Are they accessible at all times, or are they reserved for special activities?
9. Is a computer available in the classroom for students to practice mathematics skills? Do students have access to a variety of education-

ally sound software programs in the area of mathematics?

ANSWERING THE ASSESSMENT QUESTIONS

Mathematics skills are assessed in order to describe the student's current levels of educational performance. A wide variety of assessment tools are available for this purpose, including both formal and informal measures and techniques.

Nature of the Assessment Tools

Measures of mathematics performance vary in the range of skills they assess. Some are quite comprehensive, whereas others are more limited. Three of the formal tests described in this chapter—the *KeyMath Revised,* the *Stanford Diagnostic Mathematics Test,* and the *Test of Mathematical Abilities*—are considered wide-range measures because they assess a variety of skills. However, each covers a somewhat different set of skill areas. For example, the *KeyMath–R* and the *SDMT* include computation, problem solving, and mathematics applications. The *TOMA* does not assess mathematics applications but evaluates areas that the *KeyMath–R* and *SDMT* do not.

The criterion-referenced tests by Brigance are somewhat more restricted in range because they assess only application and computational skills. Even narrower in scope are the *Diagnostic Test of Arithmetic Strategies* and the *ENRIGHT™ Diagnostic Inventory of Basic Arithmetic Skills.* These measures assess only computational skills. However, they also provide error analysis procedures for studying students' mistakes in computation.

Another area of difference is the thoroughness with which skills are assessed. Comprehensive tests such as the *KeyMath–R* and the *SDMT* sample several skills and skill levels but provide only a few representative test items in each area. For example, on the *KeyMath–R,* three test items are used to evaluate the student's skill in addition of fractions. Informal measures evaluate skills in much greater depth. On the *ENRIGHT™ Diagnostic Inventory,* for example, addition of fractions is assessed with 10 separate criterion-referenced tests.

Measures can also differ in the types of assessment tasks used to evaluate skill development. For instance, there are many differences between the *KeyMath–R* and the *SDMT*, even though they both assess the same general skill areas. The *SDMT* requires written responses, whereas students usually answer orally on the *KeyMath–R*. *SDMT* questions are multiple choice, and many of the subtests are timed. The *KeyMath–R* imposes time limits on only one subtest, and most test questions are open-ended. On the *SDMT*, students are provided with scratch paper for written computations. On the *KeyMath–R*, students calculate mentally, except on portions of some of the Operations subtests.

Mathematics measures are most similar in the assessment tasks they use to evaluate students' computational skills. Typically, paper-and-pencil tasks are used; students read the problem and then write the answer. There are fewer similarities in the ways problem-solving skills are assessed, as Table 12–3 illustrates. Although story problems are the basic tasks for evaluating problem solving on the *KeyMath–R*, the *SDMT*, and the *TOMA*, task characteristics differ from measure to measure. Such differences can affect the student's ability to respond to test tasks. They are important considerations in selecting the tools for assessment and in interpreting assessment results.

The Relationship of Mathematics to Other Areas of Performance

When assessment is complete, the special education team begins to interpret the results and study the relationships between areas of performance. Academic skills such as mathematics may influence or be influenced by several other areas.

General learning aptitude is a consideration in the acquisition of any skill, and the student's progress in mathematics should be evaluated in relation to estimated intellectual potential. In general, students with lower than average general intelligence are expected to progress at a somewhat slower rate than students of average intellectual ability.

TABLE 12–3
Assessment tasks used to evaluate mathematical problem solving

Measure	Subtest	Presentation Mode	Response Mode
KeyMath Revised	Problem Solving	Listen to word problems read aloud by the tester; look at a test page with drawings and/or statements related to the problem.	Compute mentally and say the answer.
		Listen to nonroutine word problems read aloud by the tester; look at a test page with drawings and/or statements related to the problem.	Tell how to solve the problem or identify extraneous or missing information.
Stanford Diagnostic Mathematics Test	Applications	Read brief story problems and a series of possible responses (students with reading problems may request the tester's assistance.)	Write computations on scratch paper, as needed; select a response; mark the letter of the response on the appropriate space on the separate answer sheet; or, on the Red Level, mark the response in the test booklet.
Test of Mathematical Abilities	Story Problems	Read brief story problems.	Write computations in the workspace on the test page; write and circle the answer on the test page.

However, IQ may be a better predictor of mathematical problem-solving ability than rote computational skills. As with reading, expectancy formulas are not the best means of estimating the student's expected level of achievement. Standard score procedures are preferred. For example, if the student's current scores on a measure of intellectual performance fall within the average range, that student would be expected to show average achievement in mathematics.

Specific learning abilities and strategies also play a role in the student's ability to acquire and apply mathematics skills. Difficulties in attention, memory, or other areas such as visual and auditory perception can hinder skill development, particularly the acquisition of mathematics readiness skills and computational proficiency. Inefficient learning strategies may interfere with the student's practice of mathematics skills, resulting in further underachievement. In the secondary grades, poor learning strategies may combine with poor mathematics skills to prevent students from applying mathematics in other subject areas.

Classroom behavior may be related to mathematics performance. Inappropriate conduct in the classroom can impede academic learning. Likewise, poor achievement can affect a student's behavior. For example, a student who is unable to cope with a classroom mathematics assignment may react by causing a disturbance. Poor achievement can also influence the student's self-concept, relationships with peers, and the attitudes the student holds toward both school and mathematics.

The student's skills in mathematics may have an impact on other areas of school performance. Basic mathematics competencies are needed in any classroom. To locate page 42 in a spelling book, the student must be able to count and read numerals. Teachers' directions often include quantitative terminology such as *first, last, next,* and *greater than.* In art class, the student may need to measure the dimensions of a canvas; in physical education, students may be asked to "count off by 2s."

In the secondary grades, students are expected to use mathematics in several school subjects. Proficiency in mathematics is often a requirement in the sciences, and even in social studies, students must be able to read and interpret graphs and tables. Mathematics is necessary in almost all vocational subjects, and measurement skills are particularly important. Measurement is needed for cooking, sewing, carpentry, mechanics, agriculture, and many other vocational areas. Skills in handling money and telling time are also important, not only in vocational preparation classes but also in daily life. Students who have not learned to tell time or deal with simple money exchanges will face real barriers in their attempts to deal with the demands of adult life.

Achievement problems in other curriculum areas can interfere with the acquisition of mathematics skills. Oral language is the foundation for all school learning, and students with language problems may have difficulty acquiring and using the quantitative vocabulary of mathematics. Reading is needed for many mathematics tasks and is a critical component of the process of solving story problems. Difficulties with handwriting can be a real liability. In beginning math instruction, students must learn how to read and write numerals and mathematical symbols, and writing continues to be a necessary part of math activities throughout the school years.

Documentation of Mathematics Performance

The general assessment question that guides the special education team in its investigation of mathematics is, *What are the student's educational needs?* In this phase of assessment, the goal is to obtain sufficient data to describe the student's current levels of educational performance. The team begins by asking, *What is the student's current level of mathematics achievement?* A wide range of mathematics skills is surveyed, and then additional information is gathered about the areas where the student appears to experience difficulty. This results in a specific description of the student's current skills, and the assessment team is able to answer the question: *What are the student's strengths and weaknesses in the various skill areas of mathematics?*

In mathematics assessment, data are gathered from many sources using many types of assessment tools. Usually, the team begins by reviewing school records, the results of individual achievement tests, and the data collected in interviews with parents and teachers and in classroom observations. Next, a test that evaluates a range of mathematics skills is administered to identify possible problem areas. Informal measures and techniques are then used to learn more about potential weaknesses. For example, the team may administer a series of criterion-referenced tests to assess specific computational skills. Or a clinical math interview may be conducted to learn more about the student's problem-solving strategies.

There are many types of tools available for mathematics assessment. The assessment team should select its tools with care so duplication is avoided and the assessment process is as efficient as possible. In general, the more specific procedures such as clinical interviews and criterion-referenced tests should be reserved for in-depth assessment of potential problem areas.

By answering the assessment questions about mathematics, the team moves closer to planning the student's Individualized Education Program. Current levels of educational performance in mathematics are documented and the areas of educational need in mathematics identified. For instance, David was referred for assessment because of his difficulties with mathematics.

David

David is failing eighth grade mathematics. In math class, he is working on basic number facts and operations because he lacks the skills to participate in any of the regular eighth grade activities. Special education assessment has begun, and results of the *WRAT–R* and *Woodcock-Johnson–R* have confirmed that David's current performance in mathematics is far below that expected for his age and grade.

To gather more information about David's skills across several areas of mathematics, Mr. Block, the special education resource teacher, administers the *KeyMath Revised* (Figure 12–2). David's total test performance is within standard score range 75 to 81, which indicates overall low average performance. His Operations and Applications skills are significantly lower than Basic Concepts. David shows relative strengths in Numeration, Rational Numbers, Geometry, Measurement, and Time and Money. The areas where David earns his lowest scores are Problem Solving, Division, and Multiplication. Based

on these results, the team decides to concentrate its efforts on assessing David's problem-solving and computation skills.

Next, the *ENRIGHT™ Diagnostic Inventory of Basic Arithmetic Skills* is administered to pinpoint David's computational difficulties. David shows mastery of addition and subtraction number facts but is less successful with multiplication and division facts. The majority of David's errors occur on problems involving multiples of 6, 7, 8, and 9. On the Skill Tests of basic operations with whole numbers, David consistently has difficulty with problems requiring regrouping. In addition and multiplication, he often fails to carry and instead writes the entire number as part of the answer. When multiplying two multidigit numbers, David uses the same strategy, and he does not cross-multiply. For example:

$$\begin{array}{r} 25 \\ \times\ 34 \\ \hline \mathbf{6\,20} \end{array}$$

In this problem, David multiplies 4×5 and writes the answer as 20. He then moves to the tens column and multiplies 3×2. In subtraction, he sometimes subtracts the smaller number from the larger, disregarding which is the minuend and which is the subtrahend. In division, he refuses to attempt problems requiring regrouping, saying, "I can't do ones like this."

To assess David's skills in solving story problems, the team asks Ms. Coolidge, David's math teacher, to provide several samples of David's work. All of the papers provided to the assessment team had been graded F. However, most of David's errors were due to his failure to attempt all problems. On one assignment, for example, David had solved the first two problems correctly and made a minor computational error on the third; he did not attempt the remaining seven problems, so his score on this paper was 20%.

The team uses clinical interviewing techniques to explore David's problem-solving skills. He is given 10 story problems and instructed to "think out loud" when solving them. He reads the problems accurately and is able to explain what operations are required. With simpler problems, David can identify the numbers to be used in computation and write the computational problem correctly. However, David's strategy is to include all the numbers that the problem provides. With more difficult problems that contain extraneous information, this strategy is not successful. David also has difficulty carrying out the calculations. He works slowly, sometimes, making hatchmarks on his paper to help him figure out number facts, and 7 of his 10 solutions are incorrect. David says that he likes "the thinking part of these problems, but not the math part."

After a careful analysis of these results, the assessment team is ready to describe David's current levels of mathematics performance. Their conclusions are as follows:

□ At present, David's overall level of achievement in mathematics is within the low average range of performance, as measured by the *KeyMath Revised*. His greatest areas of weakness are mathematics operations and applications.

□ David shows adequate knowledge of addition and subtraction facts. He has not yet mastered multiplication and division facts and has particular difficulty with multiples of 6, 7, 8, and 9.

□ David has some knowledge of regrouping procedures but fails to use them consistently. In addition and multiplication, David does not always carry, and in subtraction, he sometimes subtracts the smaller number from the larger. David does not appear to know how to solve division problems requiring regrouping or how to cross-multiply in multidigit multiplication.

□ David receives failing grades on story problem assignments because he completes only a few problems.

□ David is able to determine how to solve simple story problems, but many of his answers are incorrect because of computational errors.

STUDY GUIDE

Review Questions

1. Mathematics performance is assessed to gain information about the student's educational needs and strengths and weaknesses in specific mathematics skills. (True or False)
2. Three major skill areas are considered in the assessment of mathematics: computation, _____ , and the _____ of mathematics skills to daily life situations.
3. In current school practices, mathematics is assessed by
   _____ a. Both formal and informal measures
   _____ b. Individual and group tests
   _____ c. Error analyses, informal inventories, and clinical math interviews
   _____ d. Standardized tests
   _____ e. All of the above
4. Which is the most frequently used comprehensive measure of mathematics skills for students in grades kindergarten to 9?
   _____ a. *KeyMath Revised*
   _____ b. *Stanford Diagnostic Mathematics Test*
   _____ c. *Test of Mathematical Abilities*
   _____ d. *Diagnostic Test of Arithmetic Strategies*
   _____ e. None of the above
5. The *Stanford Diagnostic Mathematics Test* is both norm-referenced and criterion-referenced. (True or False)
6. Match the assessment device or procedure in Column A with the description in Column B. (The answers in Column A may be used more than once.)

Column A	*Column B*
a. *KeyMath Revised*	_____ A group test for students in grades 1 through 12
b. *Test of Mathematical Abilities*	_____ Used to identify the strategies students use for addition, subtraction, multiplication, and division
c. *Diagnostic Test of Arithmetic Strategies*	_____ Assesses Basic Concepts, Operations, and Applications with 13 subtests

     d. *Stanford Diagnostic Mathematics Test*   _____ Assesses Number System and Numeration, Computation, and Applications
    _____ An individual test with items referenced to skill domains and objectives
    _____ Includes a measure of attitude toward mathematics and a test of mathematics vocabulary

7. Write the letter *S* before each test result that indicates an area of strength; write the letter *N* if results point to a possible area of educational need.
    _____ a. Stanine 1 Total score on the *Stanford Diagnostic Mathematics Test*
    _____ b. *KeyMath–R* Geometry subtest scaled score of 11
    _____ c. *SDMT* Progress Indicator of + on the Addition Facts subtest
    _____ d. Math Quotient 75 on the *Test of Mathematical Abilities*
    _____ e. Scaled score 13 on a *TOMA* subtest

8. Students may arrive at incorrect answers to mathematics computation problems if they use correct facts but inappropriate _____ .

9. One feature of the academic achievement tests by Brigance is that they include instructional objectives. (True or False)

10. Find the true statements.
    _____ a. Many mathematics tests assess both computation and problem-solving skills.
    _____ b. Mathematics measures may evaluate application skills such as time, money, and measurement.
    _____ c. The difference between informal mathematics inventories and criterion-referenced tests is that inventories tend to measure skill domains thoroughly, rather than assessing only a few representative skills.
    _____ d. The four most common types of computation errors are incorrect operations, number facts, algorithms, and random errors.
    _____ e. Clinical math interviews are used to determine how well students perform when they are provided with computational aids such as calculators.

11. In assessing mathematics performance within the context of the classroom, it should be determined whether the curriculum stresses _____ or _____ skills.

12. Motor skills are necessary for what mathematics task?

13. If a student shows average intellectual performance, in what standard score range would you expect mathematics scores to fall?
    _____ a. Less than standard score 70
    _____ b. Standard score 70 to 84
    _____ c. Standard score 85 to 115
    _____ d. Standard score 116 to 130
    _____ e. Greater than standard score 130

14. If the special education team finds that a student shows poor performance in mathematics computation, what conclusion can be drawn?
    _____ a. The special education program should focus on improving problem-solving skills.
    _____ b. The special education program should emphasize the use of computational skills in problems concerning time, money, and measurement.
    _____ c. A possible educational goal would be to increase accuracy in addition, subtraction, multiplication, and division.
    _____ d. The student should remain in the regular classroom and be provided with a calculator.

Activities

1. Interview two special educators, one who serves elementary grade students and the other who serves students in junior high or high school. Ask each to describe the mathematics skills they consider most important and to explain how they assess mathematics performance. Are there any differences in the skill areas they assess? For example, are application skills more of a concern to the secondary teacher?

2. Locate several group achievement tests and examine how each assesses mathematics. Are all the major skills covered?

3. Under the supervision of the course instructor, administer one of the mathematics measures discussed in this chapter. Calculate all possible scores and analyze the results to determine strengths and weaknesses.

4. Obtain a set of word problems appropriate for adult learners. Use these to conduct a clinical math interview with one of your peers. Then reverse roles so your peer becomes the interviewer and you act as the student. Compare the findings from the two interviews. Did you approach the problems in different ways and use different strategies for the solution?

5. Do a work sample analysis of a student's mathematics paper. Identify and analyze all errors according to one of the systems presented in this chapter.

6. Devise a set of diagnostic probes to investigate the reasons for failure on computational problems. Use the problem-solving probes in Table 12–2 as a guide.

Discussion Questions

1. Mathematics plays an important role in daily activities. Discuss some of the ways adults use mathematics at home and in the workplace.

2. Explain why mathematics is considered one of the basic school skills.

3. Discuss this statement: In some ways, the distinction between computation and problem solving in mathematics is analogous to the distinction between decoding and comprehension in reading.

4. Compare and contrast the three individual tests of mathematics performance described in detail in this chapter—the *KeyMath Revised,* the *Test of Mathematical Abilities,* and the *Diagnostic Test of Arithmetic Strategies.* Include in your discussion a comparison of the content assessed by each measure and a description of the population for which each is appropriate. Conclude by presenting your recommendations regarding the best use of each test.

13

Written Language

Written language is a basic method of communication in today's society. Adults are expected to be literate, and literacy includes not only the ability to read but also the ability to write. As part of the routine of daily life, adults write shopping lists, business letters, and notes to friends. They complete job applications, fill out tax forms, and write checks. Writing skills are a requirement for most occupations, and some jobs demand a high degree of proficiency in written language.

Writing is also an important skill during the school years, and its acquisition is stressed in the elementary grades. In the upper elementary grades and in junior high and high school, students are expected to be able to express their thoughts in writing. This poses grave difficulties for individuals with poor written expression skills, and many special students fall within this group.

In special education assessment, students' written language skills are studied to gather information for instructional planning. The broad question that guides this portion of the assessment process is, *What are the student's educational needs?* When written language is the concern, this general question is refined into two specific questions: *What is the student's current level of achievement in written language? What are the student's strengths and weaknesses in the various skill areas of written language?*

At this point in assessment, the major goal is description of the student's current status in important areas of the written language curriculum: spelling, handwriting, and composition. Consider how both formal and informal assessment strategies are part of the plan for learning more about the written expression skills of Joyce, the fourth grader whose assessment we've been following in the past few chapters.

Joyce

The team is now gathering data to assist in planning Joyce's Individualized Education Program. From the reports of Joyce's fourth grade teacher and from the results of individual achievement tests, the team is quite certain that Joyce could benefit from specially designed instruction in at least two areas of written language, spelling and handwriting.

In spelling, Joyce showed below average performance on both the *PIAT–R* and the *WRAT–R*, and she is working in a grade 2 spelling book in her fourth grade classroom. To learn more about Joyce's spelling skills, the team will administer the *Test of Written Spelling–2*, a measure that assesses the student's ability to spell phonetically regular and irregular words. Then informal techniques will be used to explore the particular spelling skills that appear to be areas of weakness for Joyce. For example, if regular words appear to be a problem, the team may administer an informal inventory or criterion-referenced test that probes the student's ability to write the letters that correspond to various letter sounds.

Handwriting may also be an area of need for Joyce. In the school that Joyce attended last year, cursive writing was not introduced in the third grade, so Joyce entered fourth grade at a disadvantage. Mr. Harvey, her fourth grade teacher, has begun to teach Joyce cursive writing, but she continues to print the majority of her assignments. Despite 3 years of instruction, Joyce's printing is not good. To gather more information about handwriting, the assessment team will observe Joyce as she writes and collect several samples of her printing and cursive writing. The observational data and writing samples will be carefully analyzed to detect any pattern of errors.

As yet, the assessment team has no information about Joyce's composition skills. Joyce's ability to write sentences, themes, essays, stories, and the like was not mentioned by Mr. Harvey when he referred Joyce for assessment, so the team will begin by interviewing Mr. Harvey. Then a broad range measure such as the *Test of Written Language–2* will be administered to help the team pinpoint Joyce's strengths and weaknesses in various composition skills. As necessary, informal procedures will be used to gather further information about specific areas of educational need.

Joyce's individualized program in written language will be based on the results of these assessments.

Individualized Assessment Plan

For: _____Joyce Dewey_____ ___4___ __10–0__ __12/1/89__ _____Ms. Gale_____

Student's Name   Grade   Age   Date   Coordinator

Reason for Referral: Difficulty keeping up with fourth grade work in reading, spelling, and handwriting

Assessment Question	Assessment Procedures	Person Responsible	Date/Time
What is the student's current level of achievement in written language?	*Test of Written Language–2*	Ms. Gale, Resource Teacher	1/12/90 9 a.m.
What are the student's strengths and weaknesses in the various skill areas in written language?	*Test of Written Spelling–2*	Ms. Gale, Resource Teacher	1/12/90 1 p.m.
	Observation and work sample analysis of handwriting	Ms. Gale, Resource Teacher	1/8/90 morning
	Additional informal strategies, as needed	Ms. Gale, Resource Teacher, and other team members, as needed	To be determined

CONSIDERATIONS IN ASSESSMENT OF WRITTEN LANGUAGE

Written language skills are critical for successful school performance. Students with poor written language are at a decided disadvantage in attempting to meet the academic demands of the regular curriculum. Because many students with mild handicaps experience difficulty in this area, written language is often one of the areas of focus in special education assessment.

Purposes

Written language skills are assessed for many different reasons. Writing is considered an important part of the regular education curriculum; teachers routinely monitor their students' progress in the acquisition of spelling, handwriting, and composition skills. Spelling and some aspects of composition are often included among the skills assessed by group achievement tests, and proficiency in written language is frequently one of the competency areas evaluated for grade advancement and high school graduation.

In special education, written language skills may be investigated at the start of assessment to determine the student's eligibility for special education services. In many cases, however, assessment is limited to only one aspect of written language, spelling, because that is the language skill emphasized on the traditional individual tests of achievement used in special education. Further investigation is needed if there is reason to believe that other aspects of written language may be areas of educational need.

Several measures of written language are currently available to assist the assessment team in identifying academic skill deficiencies. Norm-referenced tests help pinpoint specific areas of difficulty, and informal techniques and procedures are then used to gather the detailed information needed for planning the educational program. The student's current levels of performance are described and specific strengths and weaknesses noted in preparation for the establishment of the instructional goals and objectives of the individualized program plan.

Assessment continues when special education services begin, but it changes somewhat in character. The purpose becomes continuous monitoring of the student's educational progress. On an ongoing basis, special educators monitor the student's acquisition of targeted skills, and at least once each year, the educational plan is reviewed and modified as necessary.

Skill Areas

When considering the complex of skills and processes that contribute to proficiency in written language, it is important to understand the relationship between writing and other dimensions of language. Language is a communication system characterized by the use of symbols for the transmission of information. Language can either be spoken or written, and in both oral and written language there is an expressive and a receptive mode. In the expressive mode, the speaker or writer attempts to communicate ideas; in the receptive mode, the listener or reader attempts to comprehend the ideas expressed by the speaker or writer.

In the developmental sequence, oral language generally precedes written language. Most children begin to understand and use speech for communication within the first 3 years of life. Reading and writing skills come later, usually after children have completed some formal schooling. It also appears that receptive language skills emerge first: young children learn to listen, then to speak; school-aged children learn to read, then to write.

In this developmental perspective, writing is the last skill to be acquired, and to some extent, it is dependent on the other language skills that underlie it. Poor oral language can inhibit the development of written language, just as lack of proficiency in reading can interfere with the acquisition of writing skills. However, students need not wait until they are proficient readers to begin writing; these skills can be developed simultaneously (Wells, 1981).

Writing is quite different from speech. Speech is essentially a social act (Litowitz, 1981). Both the sender and receiver of the communication are present and are able to interact if a breakdown in communication occurs. Writing is a solitary act, and the writer is unable to exchange messages with the reader. In oral communication, information is transmitted in many ways, not only through spoken words. The facial expressions, gestures, posture, and body language of the participants all contribute to communication, as do the speaker's tone of voice and the loudness and speed with which the message is delivered. These methods of transmitting information are not available to the writer; the written symbols must stand alone.

In writing, the sender of the message must first conceptualize its content and then record the message so it is available and comprehensible to the receiver. To do this, the writer must have some skill in handwriting (or typing) and in spelling. In recording the message, the writer uses a pencil or pen (or a typewriter or computer keyboard) to form the smallest elements of written language, the individual letters, or graphemes. Letters are then combined into words, and the conventions of spelling determine how these letters are sequenced. As words are arranged into sentences, other conventions must be observed including the rules for sentence formation, written syntax, and English usage. In addition, the writer must attend to the mechanical aspects of writing, factors that are not concerns in oral language: capitalization, punctuation, paragraphing, page format, and so forth.

In Smith's (1982) view, the act of writing imposes two distinct roles on the writer—author and secretary. The author's task is to generate ideas and compose the content of the writing. The secretary transcribes what the author composes. The secretary is concerned with the form of the writing and so attends to spelling, handwriting, capitalization, punctuation, and the like. Smith's analogy of the thinker and the scribe is a useful way of conceptualizing the writing process. It points up the range of skills required in writing (Nodine, 1983) and provides a framework for thinking about those skills.

Writing is a process that involves (or should involve) several steps, and each step places different demands on the writer. Polloway, Payne, Patton, and Payne (1985) identify three stages of writing: prewriting, writing, and postwriting. In the prewriting stage, the author is the dominant participant. Influenced by past input, motivation, and the purpose for writing, the author plans the content. The writing stage requires both author and secretary. As the author composes, the secretary performs the physical act of writing with attention to legibility, spelling accuracy, and other print conventions. The postwriting stage is the evaluation stage. While the secretary checks the accuracy of the mechanical aspects of the product, the author reviews the content: organization and sequence, logic and clarity, and the style in which it is written.

Teaching students how to write clearly and cogently appears to be a major goal of American education. Together with reading and mathematics, writing is considered one of the basic school skills. However, although writing may be perceived as a valued skill, this perception has not been translated into actual classroom practice (Graves, 1978; Isaacson, 1987). According to Freedman (1982), writing is "the neglected basic skill" (p. 34). Another concern is that, when writing instruction does occur, it is directed more toward improving the performance of the writer-as-secretary than that of the writer-as-author. Writing instruction tends to emphasize mechanical aspects such as handwriting, spelling, and usage (Alexander, 1983).

However, changes are beginning to occur in the ways that the teaching of writing is conceptualized (Moran, 1988; Nodine, 1983). One new direction is increased emphasis on writing as a thinking process and the stages that make up that process. Another is the "writing across the curriculum" movement in which writing instruction takes place in all subject matter areas.

Assessment practices are also undergoing changes, but there is still heavy emphasis on the more mechanical aspects of writing (Freedman, 1982; Moran, 1988). Poplin (1983) says, "Today most of our assessment devices tap very little of what is considered meaningful writing behavior" (p. 69). Instead, most measures concentrate on the secretarial dimensions of writing, perhaps because these dimensions are less difficult to assess.

Traditional measures of writing skills tend to focus on the skills of spelling, handwriting, and composition. Spelling is usually assessed with a paper-and-pencil task. The tester reads a word to the student, the word is read again in the context of a phrase or sentence, and the student responds by writing the word. Students can also be asked to spell orally, or spelling tasks can be designed in multiple-choice format. Multiple-choice tests usually present the student with several words, and the student selects the one that is correctly or incorrectly spelled.

Handwriting is generally informally assessed by comparing a sample of the student's writing with a set of performance criteria. An existing sample of the student's handwriting can be evaluated, or a new sample can be elicited. Depending upon the age and skill level of the student, the sample may be written in manuscript (printing) or cursive handwriting.

Composition can be defined as the process by which a writer creates a written product. On measures of composition skills, students are typically presented with a writing task; the sample that the student produces is then subjected to analysis. Several aspects of the sample can be evaluated: content, vocabulary, organization, logic, writing style, productivity, creativity, and the more mechanical dimensions such as handwriting and spelling.

Traditional measures of composition are concerned with the product of writing, not the process. Their purpose is the evaluation of the student's responses, not the interaction between the student and the task throughout the series of stages involved in writing. To gather information about the process of writing and how the student approaches and completes the task of composition, informal assessment strategies are a necessity.

Another area that traditional measures often neglect is the ability to apply composition skills in daily life tasks. Writing is a common part of daily living. Students should be competent in performing tasks such as writing notes, friendly letters, memoranda, and shopping lists; completing job applications and tax forms; and the like.

Current Practices

Writing assessment receives much less attention than either reading or mathematics assessment. There are fewer measures of writing skills available, and those that exist tend to emphasize the more mechanical aspects of the process. Although most survey tests of academic achievement contain some measure of written language, the skills most often assessed are spelling, usage, and grammar. However, newer tests such as the *Peabody Individual Achievement Test–Revised* (Markwardt, 1989) and the *Woodcock-Johnson Psycho-Educational Battery–Revised* (Woodcock & Johnson, 1989) do include measures of composition, as Chapter 7 described.

More directly related to instructional planning for handicapped students are the assessment tools listed in Table 13–1. These include not only standardized tests but also criterion-referenced tests and other types of informal measures. The number of written language measures has increased dramatically in the past few years.

TABLE 13–1
Measures of written language

Name (Authors)	Type of Measure[1]	Ages or Grades	Group or Individual	Spelling	Handwriting	Composition
BRIGANCE® Diagnostic Comprehensive Inventory of Basic Skills (Brigance, 1983a)	CR	Gr. K–9	Varies	*	*	*
BRIGANCE® Diagnostic Inventory of Basic Skills (Brigance, 1977)	CR	Gr. K–6	Varies	*	*	
BRIGANCE® Diagnostic Inventory of Early Development (Brigance, 1978)	CR	Birth to age 6	Individual		*	
BRIGANCE® Diagnostic Inventory of Essential Skills (Brigance, 1981)	CR	Gr. 4–12	Varies	*	*	*
Checklist of Written Expression (Poteet, 1980)	C	All	Individual	*	*	*
Denver Handwriting Analysis (Anderson, 1983)	I	Gr. 3–8	Group or Individual		*	
Diagnostic Achievement Test in Spelling (Wittenberg, 1980)	T	Gr. 2–10	Group	*		
Diagnostic Evaluation of Writing Skills (Weiner, 1980)	E	All	Individual	*	*	*
Diagnostic Spelling Test (Kottmeyer, 1970)	I	Gr. 2–6	Group	*		
Hudson Education Skills Inventory (Hudson, Colson, Welch, Banikowski, & Mehring, 1989)	CR	Gr. K–12	Individual	*	*	*
Picture Story Language Test (Myklebust, 1965)	T	Ages 7 to 17	Group or Individual			*
Spellmaster Assessment and Teaching System (Greenbaum, 1987)	I	Gr. K–10	Group	*		
Test of Adolescent Language–2 (Hammill, Brown, Larsen, & Weiderholt, 1987)	T	Ages 12–0 to 18–5	Group			*
Test of Early Written Language (Hresko, 1988)	T	Ages 3–0 to 7–11	Individual	*	*	*
Test of Written Language–2 (Hammill & Larsen, 1988)	T	Ages 7–6 to 17–11	Group or Individual	*		*
Test of Written Spelling–2 (Larsen & Hammill, 1986)	T	Ages 6–6 to 18–5	Group or Individual	*		
Woodcock Language Proficiency Battery (Woodcock, 1980)	T	Ages 3 to 80 +	Individual	*		
Zaner-Bloser Evaluation Scales (1984)	R	Gr. 1–8	Group		*	

[1]Key to Type: C—Checklist
CR—Criterion-referenced test
E—Error analysis procedure
I—Inventory
R—Rating scale
T—Test

Some of the measures that are currently available are survey instruments. They are designed to assess a range of skills in order to identify the student's strengths and weaknesses. For instance, the *Test of Written Language–2* (Hammill & Larsen, 1988) assesses not only spelling and grammar but also composition. Other measures concentrate on one specific skill area. The *Test of Written Spelling–2* (Larsen & Hammill, 1986), for example, is limited to the investigation of spelling ability.

Informal strategies are a necessity in the assessment of writing skills because of the limited number of formal tools and the narrowness of their scope. Among the informal techniques most often used in writing assessment are observation, informal inventories, criterion-referenced tests, clinical interviews, and work sample analysis procedures. Informal strategies provide information not only about the student but also about the characteristics of the classroom learning environment.

This chapter is organized around three major skill areas in written language assessment: spelling, handwriting, and composition. Spelling is the first topic of discussion, and the section that follows describes the major formal and informal assessment strategies available for the study of special students' spelling skills. Techniques for assessing handwriting are described next, followed by procedures for evaluating proficiency in composition.

STRATEGIES FOR ASSESSING SPELLING

Spelling is an academic skill usually included on the individual achievement tests used in special education assessment to establish the presence of a school performance problem. However, it is important to recognize that broad range achievement tests assess spelling skills in different ways. Many, like the *Wide Range Achievement Test–Revised* (Jastak & Wilkinson, 1984), use recall tasks where the student is required to remember and then write the correct spelling of words. Others, like the *Peabody Individual Achievement Test–Revised* (Markwardt, 1989), employ recognition tasks where the student must identify the correctly spelled word. Recognition tasks are essentially proofreading and are related to the post-

writing stage of the writing process; recall tasks are more related to the writing stage. The *Woodcock-Johnson Psycho-Educational Battery–Revised* (Woodcock & Johnson, 1989) offers measures of both types of spelling skills in its Dictation and Proofing subtests.

Broad range achievement tests do not provide sufficient information for planning instructional programs in spelling. Thus, when a problem in spelling is indicated, further assessment must take place. The assessment team can select a norm-referenced test of spelling such as the *Test of Written Spelling–2*. In addition, a variety of informal techniques and procedures can be used to learn more about students' current spelling skills.

Test of Written Spelling–2 (TWS–2)

The *Test of Written Spelling–2 (TWS–2)* is a norm-referenced measure designed for students ages 6–6 to 18–5. It contains two subtests: Predictable Words, a test of skill in spelling words that conform to the rules of phonics (e.g., *bed, him*), and Unpredictable Words, a measure of skill in spelling irregular words (e.g., *people, knew*). The *TWS–2* manual states that both types of spelling skills are important. Results of this test allow professionals "to ascertain whether a pupil will require training on the commonly used rules of English orthography that underlie the spelling of 'predictable' words as well as the words that do not conform to rules (frequently referred to as 'spelling demons')" (p. 4).

Both *TWS–2* subtests are standard dictation tests. The tester reads a word to the student, reads the word in a sentence, and then reads the word again. The student responds by writing the word on the test answer sheet; no time limits are imposed. The two subtests each contain 50 words, and the manual provides suggested starting points by grade level. Testing begins at the starting point and continues until a ceiling of five consecutive errors is reached; at that point, it may be necessary to administer items below the starting point to establish a basal of five consecutive correct responses. Also available in the manual are guidelines for group administration of the *TWS–2*.

The *TWS–2* was standardized with 3,805 students from 15 states. The sample appears to approximate the national population in terms of

---

TEST OF WRITTEN SPELLING–2 (TWS–2)

S. C. Larsen and D. D. Hammill (1986)

Type: Norm-referenced test

Major Content Areas: Spelling predictable words (i.e., words that adhere to phonics rules) and unpredictable words

Type of Administration: Individual or group

Administration Time: 15 to 25 minutes

Age/Grade Levels: Ages 6–6 to 18–5

Types of Scores: Percentile ranks and standard scores for subtests and total test

Typical Uses: Evaluation of students' skills in spelling two types of words, predictable and unpredictable

Cautions: Information is needed about the *TWS–2*'s concurrent validity.

---

sex, urban–rural residence, geographic region, race, and ethnicity. No information is provided about how the sample was selected or whether handicapped or non-English-speaking students were included.

The reliability of the *TWS–2* is satisfactory. Coefficients for both test-retest reliability and internal consistency exceed .80 for all scores at all age levels. The manual presents evidence of the relationship of the *TWS–2* to its predecessor, the *TWS,* and reports research supporting the concurrent validity of the *TWS.* However, information is needed about the relationship of the *TWS–2* to other group and individual measures of spelling achievement.

Percentile rank and standard scores are available for each *TWS–2* subtest and for the total test. Standard scores are distributed with a mean of 100 and a standard deviation of 15. The standard errors of measurement for *TWS–2* standard scores appear in the manual. For the total test score, the standard error is 3 standard score points for all ages except age 6, where it is 4 standard score points.

TWS–2 results are plotted on the Profile of Scores on the test form. The student's performance on the two subtests can be compared to identify patterns of strengths and weaknesses. Three different patterns are possible: adequate performance on both *TWS–2* subtests, poor performance on both subtests, or adequate performance on one subtest but poor performance on the other.

Informal Techniques

Among the informal strategies that can provide information about spelling are work sample analysis, informal inventories, criterion-referenced tests, observation, and clinical interviews.

Work sample analysis. Spelling, like all written language skills, is well suited to work sample analysis because a permanent product is produced. Within every classroom, there are many types of spelling samples available for analysis: students' essays, book reports, test papers (including spelling tests), daily homework assignments, workbooks, and so forth. Error analysis procedures can be used to evaluate the spelling samples of older students who have achieved some proficiency. However, with younger students and others only beginning to acquire spelling skills, response analysis is the preferred technique.

Poplin (1983) points out that learning to spell is a developmental process, and young children go through a number of stages as they begin to acquire written language skills. Writing begins in the preschool years as young children observe and begin to imitate the act of writing. They practice with paper and pencil by drawing and scribbling and ask adults to write words for them so they can attempt to copy them. Soon children begin to write words and phrases on their own, using invented spellings. According to Poplin, spelling skills emerge in the following sequence:

a. Only 1–2 consonants represent words or phrases.

b. Most consonant sounds in words or phrases are represented, few or no vowels.

c. Tense (long) vowels emerge without their silent counterparts; lax (short) vowels are missing.

d. Lax vowels are represented by phonologically nearest tense vowel.

e. Most consonants are present and correct—except possibly double consonants, consonant blends, consonant diagraphs, final consonant blends, those associated with morphological endings (e.g., *ing, ed, er, tion* and *sion*).

f. Rules are overapplied to regular words (e.g., *goed*).

g. Correct forms appear in a majority of instances. (p. 71—italics added)

These stages provide a framework for the work sample analysis of the spelling of beginning writers.

When students' skills mature to the extent that many of their written words are spelled correctly, error analysis becomes an appropriate procedure. Several systems for categorizing spelling errors have been devised. Edgington (1968), for example, includes additions, omissions, reversals, and phonetic spelling of nonphonetic words as errors.

The *Spellmaster Assessment and Teaching System* (Greenbaum, 1987) contains a series of inventories to assess students' skill in spelling regular words, irregular words, and homophones. There are eight levels of the Regular Word Test, corresponding roughly to grades kindergarten to 10, and the score sheet for each level is designed for analysis of the student's responses. A portion of a sample score sheet is shown in Figure 13–1. Across the top are the spelling skills assessed on this level: beginning consonants, beginning blends, short vowels, and so on. The first spelling word, *lap,* is divided into three parts, and each letter appears under the appropriate heading. The tester circles the letter or letters where substitution errors occur; additions and omissions can also be noted on the score sheet. When all of the student's responses have been analyzed, a count is made of the number of errors in each category.

Others have suggested a simpler way to conceptualize errors in spelling: phonetic and nonphonetic misspellings (Howell & Kaplan, 1980; Mann, Suiter, & McClung, 1979). Phonetic misspellings take place when the student attempts, unsuccessfully, to use the rules of phonics to spell a word. Either the student applies the rules incorrectly or the word does not adhere to those rules. For instance, a student might write *kat* instead of *cat.*

Nonphonetic spellings, in contrast, do not appear to be based upon the application of phonics rules. Some nonphonetic spellings are close approximations of the correct sequence of letters. For example, the student may recall most of the appropriate letters correctly but forget one or two, add an extraneous letter, or jumble the sequence somewhat (e.g., *lenght* for *length*). In some cases, nonphonetic spellings bear little or no resemblance to the word in question (e.g., *ob* for *house*). Such attempts are usually considered random spellings.

Informal inventories. Teachers may find it useful to design an informal inventory to learn more about students' current levels of performance. One strategy involves selecting representative words from the basal spelling series used in the school or classroom. A short list of words from the first grade spelling textbook is assembled, a list from the second grade text, and so on, depending upon the skill level of the student. Then the teacher dictates the lists to the student and asks him or her to write each word. Results provide a rough estimate of the student's status in relation to the skill demands of the classroom spelling program.

Another strategy is to design an inventory around specific spelling skills. Mercer and Mercer provide an example designed to assess grade 2 and 3 spelling skills; it appears in Table 13–2. This is a diagnostic test, because each item is intended to measure one particular aspect of spelling. Thus, skill in writing the letters that correspond to the short vowel sounds is assessed by the first five items. By evaluating the student's performance in terms of the specific spelling skills assessed, the teacher can determine which areas may be in need of further assessment with criterion-referenced tests and other procedures.

Criterion-referenced tests. These measures can help professionals identify which spelling skills have been mastered and which remain in need of instruction. Teachers can prepare their own criterion-referenced tests to measure progress toward curriculum objectives. For example, if spelling common words is an educational goal, the teacher could use the word list that appears in Figure 13–2 to construct a CRT. This list contains 250 words arranged in order of difficulty; each of the words included on the list is commonly found in children's writings. Criterion-referenced tests could also be designed to assess students' mastery of words that are often misspelled (spelling demons) or evaluate progress in the classroom spelling program.

There are also several published CRTs that offer tests of spelling. One example is the collection of tests by Brigance (1977, 1981, 1983a). The test for elementary students, the *BRIGANCE® Diagnostic Inventory of Basic Skills* (Brigance, 1977), features a Spelling Dictation Grade Placement Test and measures of skill in spelling initial consonants, initial clusters, suffixes, and prefixes. These measures are also available on the secondary level test, the *BRIGANCE® Diagnostic Inventory of Essential Skills* (Brigance, 1981), along with tests entitled Number Words, Days of the Week, and Months of the Year.

FIGURE 13–1
Spellmaster error analysis score sheet

SPELLMASTER — **REGULAR WORD TEST 1**

Name:

Grade: Date:

Number Right:

	Beginning Consonants	Beginning Blends	Short vowels a	e	i	o	u	Ending Consonants	Ending Blends	Additions	Omissions
1	l		a					p			
2	r						u	g			
3	h				i			d			
4		fl				o		p			
5	v			e				t			
6	y		a					m			
7	g				i				ft		
8		dr					u	m			
9	v		a					n			
10	f					o			nd		

Note. From *Spellmaster Assessment and Teaching System* by C. R. Greenbaum, 1987, Austin, TX: PRO-ED. Copyright 1987 by C. R. Greenbaum. Reprinted by permission.

TABLE 13–2
Diagnostic spelling test

Spelling Words	Spelling Objectives	Spelling Words Used in Sentences
1. man 2. pit 3. dug 4. web 5. dot	short vowels and selected consonants	The *man* is big. The *pit* in the fruit was hard. We *dug* a hole. She saw the spider's *web*. Don't forget to *dot* the i.
6. mask 7. drum	words beginning and/or ending with consonant blends	On Halloween the child wore a *mask*. He beat the *drum* in the parade.
8. line 9. cake	consonant-vowel-consonant-silent *e*	Get in *line* for lunch. We had a birthday *cake*.
10. coat 11. rain	two vowels together	Put on your winter *coat*. Take an umbrella in the *rain*.
12. ice 13. large	variant consonant sounds for *c* and *g*	*Ice* is frozen water. This is a *large* room.
14. mouth 15. town 16. boy	words containing vowel diphthongs	Open your *mouth* to brush your teeth. We went to *town* to shop. The *boy* and girl went to school.
17. bikes 18. glasses	plurals	The children got new *bikes* for their birthdays. Get some *glasses* for the drinks.
19. happy 20. monkey	short *i* sounds of *y*	John is very *happy* now. We saw a *monkey* at the zoo.
21. war 22. dirt	words with *r*-controlled vowels	Bombs were used in the *war*. The pigs were in the *dirt*.
23. foot 24. moon	two sounds of *oo*	Put the shoe on your *foot*. Three men walked on the *moon*.
25. light 26. knife	words with silent letters	Turn on the *light* so we can see. Get a fork and *knife*.
27. pill	final consonant doubled	The doctor gave me a *pill*.
28. bat 29. batter	consonant-vowel-consonant pattern in which final consonant is doubled before adding ending.	The baseball player got a new *bat*. The *batter* hit a home run.
30. didn't 31. isn't	contractions	They *didn't* want to come. It *isn't* raining today.
32. take 33. taking	final *e* is dropped before adding suffix	Please *take* off your coat. He is *taking* me to the show.
34. any 35. could	nonphonetic spellings	I did not have *any* lunch. Maybe you *could* go on a trip.
36. ate 37. eight 38. blue 39. blew	homonyms	Mary *ate* breakfast at home. There are *eight* children in the family. The sky is *blue*. The wind *blew* away the hat.
40. baseball	compound words	They played *baseball* outside.

Note. From *Teaching Students with Learning Problems* (3rd ed.) (pp. 416–417) by C. D. Mercer and A. R. Mercer, 1989, Columbus, OH: Merrill. Copyright 1989 by Merrill Publishing Company. Reprinted by permission.

FIGURE 13-2
High-frequency spelling words

title: SPELLING: 250 MOST OFTEN USED WORDS   #7509

THE **STEP** SYSTEM
Sequential **T**asks for **E**ducational **P**lanning

CAJON VALLEY UNION SCHOOL DISTRICT
Special Education Department

Most appropriate for CA	0-3	4-6	7-9	10-12	13+
Reg. Class		X	X	X	X
Lrng Hdcp			X	X	X
Comm Hdcp			X	X	X
Phys Hdcp		X	X	X	X
Sev Hdcp		X			

#7509

title: SPELLING: 250 MOST OFTEN USED WORDS

type: Curriculum Milestones

Instructions

Student _____

1.0 Spells a, an, am, as, at, be, by, do, go, he.

2.0 Spells I, if, in, is, it, me, my, no, of, on.

3.0 Spells or, so, to, up, us, we, all, and, any, are.

4.0 Spells bed, big, boy, but, can, car, day, did, dog, eat.

5.0 Spells few, for, fun, get, got, had, has, her, him, his.

6.0 Spells how, let, man, may, men, new, not, now, off, old.

7.0 Spells one, our, out, put, ran, saw, say, see, she, tell.

8.0 Spells the, too, two, use, was, way, who, you, also, cold.

9.0 Spells away, back, best, book, boys, been, came, city, come, days.

10.0 Spells dear, don't, door, down, each, ever, find, fire, five, four.

11.0 Spells from, gave, girl, give, good, have, hard, help, here, home.

12.0 Spells hope, into, just, keep, kind, know, last, left, like, live.

13.0 Spells long, look, made, make, many, more, most, much, must, name.

14.0 Spells next, nice, once, only, over, play, read, room, said, side.

15.0 Spells snow, some, soon, stay, still, sure, take, than, that, them.

16.0 Spells then, they, this, time, told, took, town, tree, used, very.

17.0 Spells want, week, well, went, were, what, when, will, with, work.

18.0 Spells year, your, about, after, again, along, asked, comes, could, every.

19.0 Spells found, girls, going, great, happy, heard, house, large, lived, money.

20.0 Spells never, night, other, place, ready, right, small, their, there, these.

21.0 Spells thing, think, three, today, until, water, where, which, while, white.

22.0 Spells would, write, years, always, around, before, better, called, coming, didn't.

23.0 Spells enough, father, first, friend, letter, little, looked, mother, people, pretty.

24.0 Spells school, should, summer, things, wanted, winter, another, because, brother, country.

25.0 Spells getting, morning, started, teacher, thought, through, beautiful, children, Christmas, something.

DEVELOPED BY: Marie J. Griffith

DATE DEVELOPED: 1/2/79
Suggested Criterion: 80% Mastery

Note. Reprinted with permission of the Special Education Department of the Cajon Valley Union School District, El Cajon, California. STEP #7509 was developed by Marie J. Griffith.

381

Observation.   Observations can help determine how the student approaches the task of spelling. The observation should be scheduled during a time when the student will be writing an essay or engaging in any other type of activity that requires spelling. The observer must be quite near the student to see exactly how the student proceeds. Of special interest are any strategies the student employs when unsure of the spelling of a word.

In the elementary grades where spelling is taught directly, students can also be observed as they attempt to learn new spelling words. The observer should watch for the ways the student attacks or fails to attack the memorization task. Does the student open the spelling book and simply stare at the words? Or is there some indication that the student is actively rehearsing the new words? For example, does he or she write the words? Say the letters of each word aloud or subvocally? Look at a word, cover it, and then attempt to write it?

Clinical interviews.   Clinical interviews can take place while students are writing, but there is danger of interrupting the students' thought processes and distracting them from the task at hand. Because of this, it is probably best to simply observe until students have finished writing. Then they can be questioned about the ways they coped with the spelling demands of the writing task. Some of the questions that can be asked are

☐ When you're writing a sentence or a paragraph and you write down a word, how do you tell if you've spelled the word correctly?
☐ When you're not sure how to spell a word, what do you do?
    Do you guess at the spelling?
    Try to sound the word out?
    Write two or three possible spellings and then pick the one you think is right?
    Ask the teacher or a friend how to spell the word?
    Look the word up in a dictionary?
    Choose another word, one that you can spell?
☐ After you've finished writing, do you read and check what you've written?
☐ In checking your writing, what do you do if you find a word that you think may be spelled incorrectly?

Students can then be asked to look over the writing they've just completed and mark any words that they think might be incorrectly spelled. This provides some information about proofreading skills and the student's ability to spot errors in spelling.

STRATEGIES FOR ASSESSING HANDWRITING

Handwriting skills are evaluated with informal assessment tools rather than norm-referenced measures. Informal strategies such as rating scales, observation, error analysis, inventories, and criterion-referenced tests are used to assess the student's current proficiency in handwriting. With younger children, manuscript handwriting (i.e., printing) is the concern. With older students, cursive handwriting is analyzed.

Rating Scales

Rating scales provide a method for judging whether a student's handwriting is poor enough to be considered an area of educational need. However, rating scales rely on the judgment of the professional who evaluates the student's handwriting sample, and thus their results can be somewhat subjective. Ratings can be made more objective if professionals are furnished with standards for judging students' handwriting, such as those with the *Zaner-Bloser Evaluation Scales*.

The *Zaner-Bloser Evaluation Scales* (1984) provide teachers with a standard method of collecting and rating handwriting samples. A separate scale is available for each grade from 1 through 8; manuscript writing is evaluated on the scales for grades 1 and 2, and cursive writing on the scales for grades 3 through 8. A cursive scale for grade 2 is also available. Each scale contains a handwriting selection for the students to copy.

The administration procedures are quite simple. The teacher writes the selection on the chalkboard, and students copy it twice: once for practice, and the second time in their best handwriting. Their second attempt is evaluated.

Five factors are considered in judging handwriting skill:

1. Letter formation
2. Vertical quality in manuscript; slant in cursive
3. Spacing
4. Alignment and proportion
5. Line quality

To help the teacher evaluate these factors, the *Zaner-Bloser* provides examples of Excellent, Good, Average, Fair, and Poor handwriting at each of the grade levels. Figure 13–3 shows two examples from the Grade 3 Scale, Average and Poor.

The teacher rates the student's handwriting in relation to the five factors listed in the figure. Each is judged either as Satisfactory or Needs Improvement. If four of the five factors are judged satisfactory, the student's handwriting is considered Excellent. If three of the five factors are judged satisfactory, the sample is considered Good. Two satisfactory areas result in a rating of Average, one satisfactory area in a rating of Fair, and no satisfactory areas in a rating of Poor.

The *Zaner-Bloser Evaluation Scales* are most useful for providing an estimate of the overall quality of the student's handwriting. However, in interpreting results, it is necessary to remember that these scales are not designed to assess a typical sample of the student's handwriting. Instead, the student copies a selection, first practicing it and then attempting to write it in his or her best handwriting. Having the opportunity to practice may result in an improvement from the student's usual performance. On the other hand, fatigue may interfere with the second attempt. It is also important to note that the *Zaner-Bloser* is untimed. The quality of the student's handwriting may change dramatically when speed becomes a necessity.

Observation and Error Analysis

Both observations and error analyses can provide information about how students approach handwriting. A student can be observed during an activity that requires writing, and then error analysis procedures can be applied to the writing sample the student produces. In implementing these informal assessment techniques, it is important to consider not only the legibility of the student's writing but also speed. A student must be able to write quickly if handwriting is to become a useful tool for communication.

Speed can be studied in several ways. For example, the teacher can ask the student to copy a passage of 100 words (or some other known length) and time how long it takes the student to complete this task. Or the teacher can time the student during a writing activity and then count

the number of letters or words the student produced. These data can then be transformed into a rate measure such as the average number of letters the student writes per minute.

In classroom observations of handwriting performance, the professional should take note of several student behaviors:

- □ How is the student seated? Are the desk and chair of appropriate size? Is the student sitting upright with both feet on the floor under the desk?
- □ In what position is the student's paper? Is he or she holding it so it will not slip?
- □ How does the student hold the writing implement? Does the student grip the pen or pencil too tightly?
- □ Is the student writing with a pen or a pencil? Is it an appropriate size?
- □ On what type of paper is the student writing? What size is it? Is it lined? Are there guidelines between the lines? Are there margins?
- □ Does the student write with the right or left hand?
- □ When the student writes, does he or she move the entire hand smoothly across the page or move just the fingers in an attempt to draw each letter?
- □ Does the student press down when writing? Does he or she exert a great deal of pressure on the paper? If writing with a pencil, does the student break pencil points frequently?
- □ How often does the student erase or cross out mistakes?

When students are copying from the board or from a text or worksheet on the desk, they may make errors because they are unable to see the model clearly. If this occurs, it is important to determine if vision problems are a factor.

Any writing sample produced by the student can be used for error analysis, and daily classroom assignments are likely to provide the most typical sample of a student's handwriting. However, if written assignments require spelling and other language skills, poor handwriting may be the result of an attempt to compensate for poor skills in other areas. For instance, if a student is unsure whether to write *receive* or *recieve*, he or she may write the letters indistinctly, placing the dot for the *i* in the center between the two letters.

FIGURE 13–3
Handwriting samples from the *Zaner-Bloser Evaluation Scales,* Grade 3

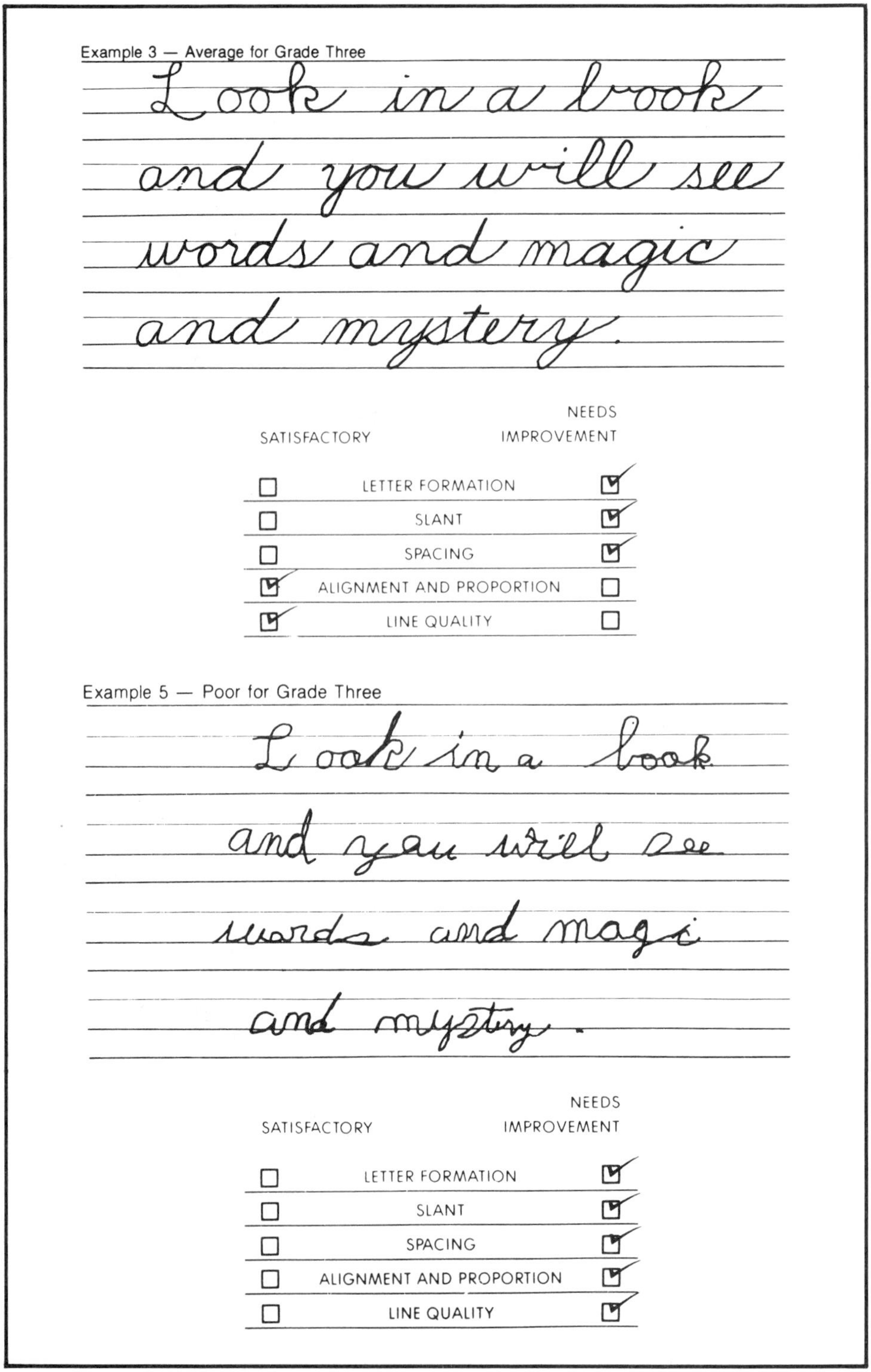
Example 3 — Average for Grade Three

Look in a book
and you will see
words and magic
and mystery.

SATISFACTORY		NEEDS IMPROVEMENT
☐	LETTER FORMATION	☑
☐	SLANT	☑
☐	SPACING	☑
☑	ALIGNMENT AND PROPORTION	☐
☑	LINE QUALITY	☐

Example 5 — Poor for Grade Three

Look in a book
and you will see
words and magi
and mystery.

SATISFACTORY		NEEDS IMPROVEMENT
☐	LETTER FORMATION	☑
☐	SLANT	☑
☐	SPACING	☑
☐	ALIGNMENT AND PROPORTION	☑
☐	LINE QUALITY	☑

Note. From *Zaner-Bloser Evaluation Scales,* 1984. Used with permission of the publisher Zaner-Bloser, Inc., Columbus, OH. Copyright 1984.

Because such tactics interfere with the evaluation of handwriting, the teacher may wish to consider obtaining at least one writing sample in which the student copies the material.

Several systems of categorizing handwriting errors have been proposed. For example, Wiederholt, Hammill, and Brown (1978) suggest that the teacher examine the following features of students' manuscript writing:

1. Position of hand, arm, body, and/or paper
2. Size of letters: too small, large, etc.
3. Proportion of one letter or word to another
4. Quality of the pencil line: too heavy, light, variable, etc.
5. Slant: too much or irregular
6. Letter formation: poor circles or straight lines, lines disconnected, etc.
7. Letter alignment: off the line, etc.
8. Spacing: letters or words crowded or too scattered
9. Speed: too fast or too slow (p. 183)

Howell and Kaplan (1980) add that, in analyzing cursive handwriting, the teacher should take note of alignment, letter size, spacing, letter form, and spatial orientation.

Inventories and Criterion-Referenced Tests

Teachers can design informal inventories to gain general information about students' handwriting abilities. An inventory assessing both manuscript and cursive writing skills appeared in Chapter 5 on informal assessment. That chapter also presented a task analysis of the lowercase manuscript alphabet (Affleck, Lowenbraun, & Archer, 1980) in which letters were divided into several clusters based on difficulty (e.g., straight line letters, straight line and slant letters, and so forth). That analysis and one of cursive letters by Graham and Miller (1980) provide a framework for developing informal inventories of basic handwriting skills. According to Graham and Miller, the cursive alphabet can be divided into the following clusters based on how the letters are formed:

Lowercase Letters	Uppercase Letters
i, u, w, t, r, s	C, A, E
n, m, v, x	N, M, P, R, B, D, U, V, W,
e, l, b, h, k, f	K, H, X
c, a, g, d, q	T, F, Q, Z, L
o, p, j	S, G
y, z	O, I, J, Y

The *Denver Handwriting Analysis* (Anderson, 1983) is a published inventory that assesses several cursive writing skills. It is designed for students in grades 3 to 8, but it can be used with other ages if cursive handwriting is a concern. The skills sampled include near-point and far-point copying, writing the cursive alphabet from memory, and writing the cursive equivalent of manuscript letters.

Criterion-referenced tests can also provide information about students' current handwriting skills. For example, the measures by Brigance (1977, 1978, 1981, 1983a) offer several tests of handwriting. Manuscript writing is assessed on the *BRIGANCE® Diagnostic Inventory of Early Development* and the *BRIGANCE® Diagnostic Inventory of Basic Skills*, and cursive writing is assessed on the basic skills measure as well as the *BRIGANCE® Diagnostic Comprehensive Inventory of Basic Skills* and the *BRIGANCE® Diagnostic Inventory of Essential Skills*. In addition, the essential skills battery includes measures of daily life handwriting tasks such as Addresses Envelope, Letter Writing, and Simple Application for Employment.

STRATEGIES FOR ASSESSING COMPOSITION

A student's ability to plan, write, and revise a piece of original writing can be assessed formally with the aid of standardized tests or informally with techniques such as rating scales, work sample analysis, criterion-referenced tests, observation, and clinical interviews. Most of these assessment strategies focus on the written product the student creates. Only the informal procedures of observation and clinical interviewing allow the professional to assess the process the student engages in to produce a sample of writing.

The primary concern in the assessment of composition skills is the content of the student's writing, not its form. Areas of interest include the organization of the writing, the vocabulary used to express ideas, the style in which the composition is written, and the originality of the ideas expressed. However, the mechanical aspects of writing also play a role, albeit a secondary one, because a composition's intelligibility can be impaired by mechanical errors. Thus, some measures of composition take into account areas such as syntax, usage, capitalization, punctuation, and even spelling and handwriting.

The sections that follow introduce a wide range of strategies for the assessment of composition skills. First to be discussed is the *Test of Written Language–2*, a formal measure that evaluates several of the important skills in writing. Next, other formal tests are introduced, and finally, a variety of informal techniques are described. Because few formal tests are available, informal strategies play a major role in the assessment of composition skills.

Test of Written Language–2

According to its manual, the *Test of Written Language–2* (*TOWL–2*) is designed to accomplish several purposes:

(a) To identify students who perform significantly more poorly than their peers in written expression and who as a result need special help;

(b) To determine a student's particular strengths and weaknesses in various writing abilities;

(c) To document a student's progress in a special writing program; and

(d) To conduct research in writing. (Hammill & Larsen, 1988, p. 6)

The 1988 edition of this test offers two forms. Each form assesses three components of language: (a) conventions or the rules for punctuation, capitalization, and spelling; (b) the linguistic component, which is concerned with written grammar and vocabulary; and (c) the conceptual component, which relates to the ability to produce written products that are logical, coherent, and sequenced. Writing is elicited through both contrived and spontaneous formats. Spontaneous writing is assessed by means of a writing sample that the student produces. The student is shown a picture (see Figure 13–4 for the stimulus picture from Form A) and directed to write an original story about it. Contrived formats are artificial ways of eliciting written language responses, and they typically focus on one discrete element of language such as written grammar or spelling. Contrived methods include such devices as dictation spelling tests, proofreading tasks, and multiple-choice items.

There are 10 subtests on the *TOWL–2*. The student begins the test with the spontaneous writing task: writing a story in fifteen minutes. The five contrived format subtests are then administered. After the test is completed, the tester scores the student's story to obtain results for the five spontaneous writing subtests.

Contrived Format Subtests

□ *Vocabulary*—In the Student Response Booklet is a list of words. The student reads each word, then writes a meaningful sentence that includes the word.

□ *Spelling*—The tester dictates sentences, and the student writes them with attention to spelling (and to capitalization and punctuation). In

---

TEST OF WRITTEN LANGUAGE–2 (TOWL–2)
D. D. Hammill & S. C. Larsen (1988)

Type: Norm-referenced test
Major Content Areas: Conventional, linguistic, and conceptual components of written language
Type of Administration: Individual or group
Administration Time: $1\frac{1}{2}$ to 2 hours
Age/Grade Levels: Ages 7–6 to 17–11
Types of Scores: Standard scores and percentile ranks for subtests; composite standard scores called quotients for Contrived Writing, Spontaneous Writing, and Overall Written Language
Typical Uses: Identification of strengths and weaknesses in several of the written language skills involved in composition
Cautions: Both reading and writing skills are required; students cannot be given reading assistance. Scoring the *TOWL–2* is time-consuming. The tester must be thoroughly familiar with the scoring standards for evaluating both the writing sample and subtest responses.

FIGURE 13–4
Stimulus picture from the *Test of Written Language–2, Form A*

Note. From *Test of Written Language–2, Form A, Student Response Booklet* by D. D. Hammill and S. C. Larsen, 1988, Austin, TX: PRO-ED. Copyright 1988 by PRO-ED. Reprinted by permission.

scoring this subtest, only spelling errors are noted.

☐ *Style*—The sentences written on the Spelling subtest are evaluated for capitalization and punctuation errors.

☐ *Logical Sentences*—The student reads sentences with errors in logic (e.g., "Sally is as sweet as salt") and must rewrite each sentence so that it makes sense.

☐ *Sentence Combining*—The student reads two sentences and must write one new sentence that combines the original sentences. For example, the sentences "Tom is big" and "Tom is a man" could be combined into "Tom is a big man."

Spontaneous Format Subtests

☐ *Thematic Maturity*—The content of the student's writing sample is evaluated on 30 criteria.

Among the criteria are writing in paragraphs, naming objects shown in the picture, developing the personalities of one or more characters, and writing a story with a definite ending.

☐ *Contextual Vocabulary*—The writing sample is examined to determine the number of unique words with seven or more letters included in the student's story.

☐ *Syntactic Maturity*—Clauses in the writing sample that contain errors in syntax are crossed out; the student's score for this subtest is the number of words remaining in the story.

☐ *Contextual Spelling*—The score on this subtest is the number of words spelled correctly in the student's story.

☐ *Contextual Style*—The student earns points for each punctuation or capitalization rule used correctly in the story. Credit is given only once for each rule, and more sophisticated rules (e.g., a comma after an introductory clause or phrase) receive more credit than elementary rules (e.g., a period at the end of a statement).

The *TOWL–2* requires that students have both reading and writing skills. On several subtests, the student must read the words or sentences that prompt the writing task. If group administration procedures are used, students must listen and attend to test instructions as the tester reads them, then work independently. All tasks are untimed, except the 15-minute writing sample.

The *TOWL–2* was standardized in 1987 with 2,216 students from 16 states. The sample was identified through professionals who used the original *TOWL;* this sample was augmented by testing conducted in four major census districts. The final sample approximates the national population in sex, race, and geographic region, although there is a slight overrepresentation of rural areas and American Indian and Hispanic students. The manual does not tell whether handicapped and non-English-speaking students were included.

The reliability of *TOWL–2* global scores is well established. Interscorer reliability, internal consistency, and test-retest reliability coefficients all exceed .80 for total test and composite score results. However, coefficients fall below .80 for some types of reliability for some subtests. Internal consistency coefficients for Thematic Maturity, Contextual Vocabulary, and Contextual Style are in the .70s; and test-retest reliability is .75 for Sentence Combining, .77 for Syntactic Maturity, and .59 for Contextual Spelling.

The concurrent validity of the *TOWL–2* was studied by examining its relationship to the Language Arts composite of the *SRA Achievement Series;* moderate correlations were found between results of the *TOWL–2's* contrived format subtests and results of the group achievement test. In another study, stories of 51 students were holistically scored, and results were examined to determine relationships to the students' *TOWL–2* performance; low to moderate correlations resulted. Results of a factor analysis support the construct validity of the two formats used to elicit writing on the *TOWL–2,* contrived and spontaneous.

According to the manual, formal training in assessment is needed to administer and interpret results of the *TOWL–2.* Administration rules are straightforward. All students begin with the writing sample. Contrived subtests are then administered, and entry points are suggested by students' grade levels. Testing continues until a ceiling of five consecutive errors is reached; if a basal of five consecutive correct responses has not yet been established, items below the entry point are administered. The manual also provides guidelines for group administration of *TOWL–2* subtests.

All the student's answers are written in the Student Response Booklet. During administration, the tester must observe what the student is writing in order to determine basals and ceilings on the contrived subtests. The manual explains the rules for scoring and lists acceptable answers; the tester should study the scoring standards carefully. Each item is either correct (marked as "1") or incorrect ("0").

After testing, the writing sample is scored, and the manual estimates that this will take around 30 minutes. Again, it is necessary to study the scoring standards, and the manual provides sample stories for practice. On the Syntactic Maturity subtest, the tester identifies instances of unacceptable grammar and draws a line through the clauses that contain errors; the subtest score is the number of words left in the story. On Contextual Style, the story is evaluated to discover what rules of punctuation and capitalization the student has demonstrated. Only the first instance of each rule is credited, and rules receive varying numbers of points based on their sophistication. For example, placing a period after a statement receives one point, but placing a period after an abbreviation receives two points. However, if the student wrote five declarative sentences and ended each with a period, only the first period would receive one point.

TOWL–2 results include percentile ranks and standard scores (mean = 10, standard deviation = 3) for each of the subtests and three global scores: the Contrived Writing Quotient, Spontaneous Writing Quotient, and Overall Written Language Quotient. Quotients are standard scores with a mean of 100 and standard deviation of 15. Standard errors of measurement are 2 standard score points for Thematic Maturity and Contextual Style, 1 standard score point for all other subtests, 4 for the Contrived and Spontaneous Writing Quotients, and 4 for the total test score.

Results can be plotted on a profile form, and Figure 13–5 shows the profile for a 14-year-old student described in the *TOWL–2* manual. This student's overall test performance is within the below average range (standard score 69). However, he shows strengths in Thematic Maturity, Contextual Vocabulary, and Syntactic Maturity, all of which fall within the average range of performance.

The *TOWL–2* is a useful test because it includes methods for evaluating several important components of written language. To do this, the *TOWL–2* departs from the typical format of standardized tests. While remaining within a norm-referenced framework, it incorporates one of the most valuable informal strategies for studying composition, the writing sample. Results are best used to identify strengths and weaknesses and to provide direction for further assessment.

Other Formal Measures

The *Test of Written Language–2* is only one of the formal measures that address composition skills. Among the others are the *Picture Story Language Test* (Myklebust, 1965), an early standardized measure of writing ability, and two measures that assess a wide range of oral and written language skills: the *Woodcock Language Proficiency Battery* (Woodcock, 1980) and the *Test of Adolescent Language–2* (Hammill, Brown, Larsen, & Wiederholt, 1987).

Picture Story Language Test (PSLT). The *PSLT* was published in the 1960s. The manual for the test appears in book form as Volume I of *Development and Disorders of Written Language* (Myklebust, 1965). Volume II of this work (Myklebust, 1973) contains case studies of normal and handicapped children.

FIGURE 13–5
Sample results of the *Test of Written Language–2*

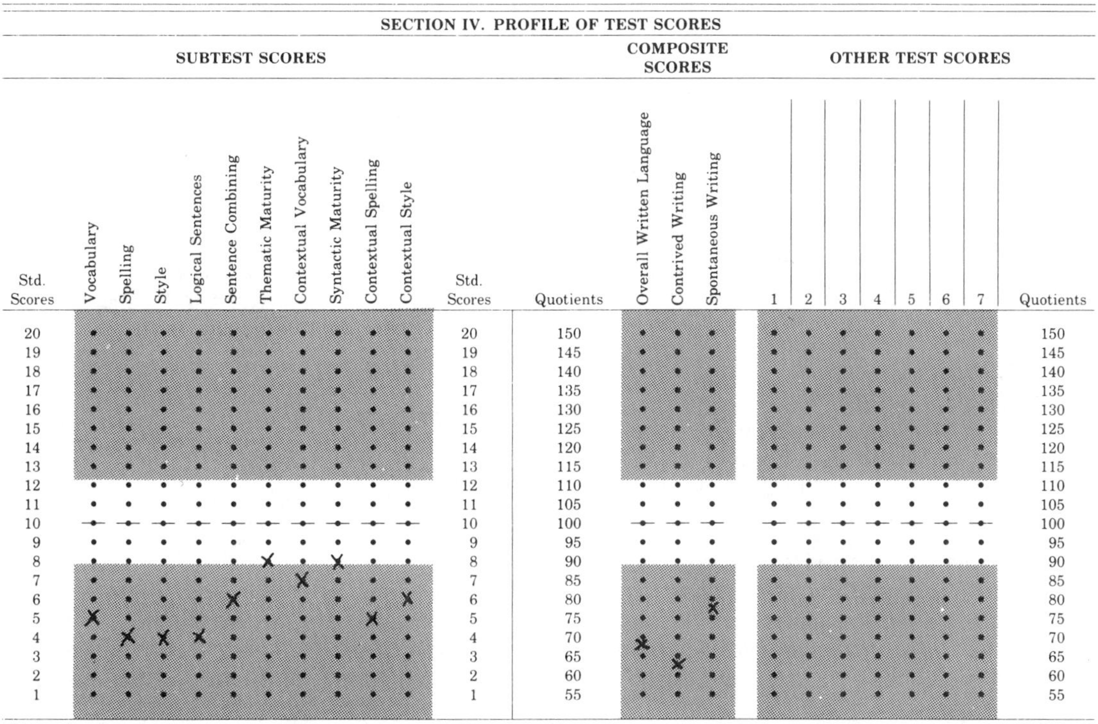

Note. From *Test of Written Language–2, Profile/Story Scoring Form* by D. D. Hammill and S. C. Larsen, 1988, Austin, TX: PRO-ED. Copyright 1988 by PRO-ED. Adapted by permission.

The *PSLT* is a norm-referenced measure in which students write a story about a standard stimulus picture. It may be administered either individually or to groups, and norms are provided for ages 7 to 17. Administration is quite simple. The stimulus picture, which shows a young boy playing, is presented to the student, who is asked to write a story about the picture. No time limits are imposed, and most students finish within 20 minutes.

The writing sample is then scored in terms of three aspects of written language: productivity, correctness, and meaning. The three scales of the *PSLT* correspond to these dimensions:

- *Productivity Scale*—The length of the writing sample is used to evaluate the student's productivity. The words in the sample are counted, as are the sentences. The average number of words per sentence is then determined.
- *Syntax Scale*—The purpose of this scale is evaluation of the student's accuracy in the mechanical aspects of writing. The writing sample is analyzed to identify errors in word usage, word endings, and punctuation; incorrect spellings are not counted as errors. A Syntax Quotient is determined by comparing the number of correct words to the total number of words produced by the student.
- *Abstract–Concrete Scale*—This scale attempts to assess the content of the student's writing. The sample is rated in terms of the abstractness of the ideas expressed. First, the sample is assigned to one of five possible levels:
    - I. Meaningless Language
    - II. Concrete—Descriptive
    - III. Concrete—Imaginative
    - IV. Abstract—Descriptive
    - V. Abstract—Imaginative

A score is then determined by the sample's placement within the level. For example, Level III samples receive from 7 to 12 points, depending on their content.

PSLT results are reported as age equivalents; percentile ranks and stanines are available by age and by sex. However, age norms are presented in 2-year intervals; thus, norms are provided for only six age groups: ages 7, 9, 11, 13, 15, and 17. Standard scores are not available, and the *PSLT* manual does not discuss the standard errors of measurement for test scores.

The *PSLT* represents one of the first attempts to quantify the written language of students with learning problems. However, this test is no longer widely used. Its norms are dated, and serious questions have been raised about its technical adequacy, particularly in relation to validity and the representativeness of the standardization sample (McLoughlin & Lewis, 1981). In addition, scoring the writing sample on the *PSLT* is a lengthy and somewhat subjective process. For these reasons, professionals today are much more likely to choose a measure such as the *Test of Written Language–2* in place of the *PSLT*.

Woodcock Language Proficiency Battery.

The *Woodcock Language Proficiency Battery* (Woodcock, 1980) is a shortened version of the first edition of the *Woodcock-Johnson Psycho-Educational Battery* (Woodcock & Johnson, 1977). The *Language Battery* is composed of eight subtests that assess oral language, reading, and written language. Two written language tests are included: Dictation and Proofing.

These subtests evaluate the student's knowledge of the rules of punctuation, capitalization, spelling, and usage. On the Dictation subtest, the student writes the letter, word, or punctuation mark the tester dictates. On the Proofing subtest, the student reads a passage with an error and must identify and tell how to correct the error.

These measures provide some information about the student's skill in dealing with the more mechanical aspects of written language. If the student's test performance indicates possible special needs in these areas, assessment should continue with criterion-referenced tests or other informal procedures.

Test of Adolescent Language–2.

The *TOAL–2* (Hammill et al., 1987) is a norm-referenced measure developed for use with students ages 12–0 to 18–5. Like the *Language Battery*, it assesses a wide range of language skills: listening, speaking, reading, and writing. In addition, the test is designed so professionals can view the student's current language skills in several different ways. For example, spoken language performance can be compared to written language performance, receptive language can be contrasted with expressive language, and vocabulary skills can be compared to grammar skills.

The *TOAL–2* contains two subtests that assess written language:

☐ *Writing/Vocabulary*—The student is given a word and asked to write a meaningful sentence that includes the word.

☐ *Writing/Grammar*—Two sentences are presented. The student must write a new sentence that combines the meaning of the original sentences.

These test tasks are the same as those used for two of the *TOWL–2's* contrived writing subtests, Vocabulary and Sentence Combining.

Subtest results are expressed as percentile ranks and standard scores. The student's performance on Writing/Vocabulary and Writing/Grammar is summarized by the Writing Quotient, a standard score with a mean of 100 and standard deviation of 15. The *TOAL–2* manual provides guidelines for determining whether composite scores are significantly different. For example, there must be at least an 11-point discrepancy between the *TOAL–2* Writing and Reading Quotients to consider these results different at the .05 confidence level.

The *TOAL–2* is one of the few tests of language designed specifically for older students. It is a survey of several important language skills, and its format encourages the comparison of performance across different dimensions of language. Results of the *TOAL–2* are most useful for identification of broad areas of educational need. As with most norm-referenced measures, further assessment is necessary before instructional planning can begin.

Informal Techniques

Writing skills are usually evaluated with informal techniques rather than formal, norm-referenced tests. Results of informal measures and techniques are used to describe current skill levels, particularly in areas for which no test results are available. They are invaluable for providing direction for instructional planning.

Rating scales and checklists. There are several ways to analyze students' writing samples, and one common approach is the use of a rating scale or checklist. For example, Figure 13–6 contains an expressive writing rating scale prepared by Affleck, Lowenbraun, and Archer (1980). The teacher selects one or, preferably, several samples of the

student's writing and then analyzes content, vocabulary, sentences, paragraphs, mechanics, handwriting, and spelling. To direct the teacher's examination of these skill areas, the scale provides specific questions such as, "Do the sentences in the paragraph relate to one topic?"

Poteet's (1980) *Checklist of Written Expression* covers four major concerns in writing: penmanship, spelling, grammar, and ideation. Composition skills are included in the section on ideation, which appears in Figure 13–7. When using this checklist, the teacher considers several aspects of the student's writing sample: type of writing, level of abstraction (or substance), productivity, comprehensibility, and relationship to the reality of the writing task. The last section in the checklist, Style, is divided into three subsections: sentence sense, tone, and word choice.

Checklists and rating scales typically assess skill development by breaking the broad skill of composition down into more specific subskill areas. Another approach to the assessment of writing is holistic evaluation. This method, as its name implies, considers the writing sample as a whole, not in relation to individual elements (Moran, 1988). Errors or particular features of the writing are not counted. According to Graham (1982), "The examiner reads the student's essay to obtain a general impression of its quality. . . . With this approach, the paper is to be read rapidly, and a score assigned on the basis of the examiner's instantaneous judgment" (p. 11). Dagenais and Beadle (1984) suggest that training is needed before professionals can conduct holistic evaluations.

Writing sample analysis. In addition to checklists and rating scales, work sample analysis techniques can be used to study students' writing samples. Error analysis is most valuable for identifying possible areas of need in the mechanics of writing: spelling, handwriting, punctuation, capitalization, and so on. Response analysis, which takes into account both errors and correct responses, is the more useful technique for the evaluation of composition skills.

The *Diagnostic Evaluation of Writing Skills* (*DEWS*) (Weiner, 1980) is an error analysis procedure that focuses attention on six aspects of written language:

☐ Graphic (visual features)
☐ Orthographic (spelling)

FIGURE 13–6
Expressive writing rating scale

```
Child_____ Type of writing analyzed_____

Rating scale:              1          2          3
                          poor     adequate   excellent

CONTENT
    1  2  3      A.  Does the writing clearly communicate an idea or ideas to the
                     reader?
    1  2  3      B.  Is the content adequately developed?
    1  2  3      C.  Is the content interesting to the potential reader?

VOCABULARY
    1  2  3      A.  Does the writer select appropriate words to communicate
                     his/her ideas?
    1  2  3      B.  Does the writer use precise/vivid vocabulary?
    1  2  3      C.  Does the writer effectively use verbs, nouns, adjectives and
                     adverbs?
    1  3  3      D.  Does the vocabulary meet acceptable standards for written
                     English (e.g., "isn't" vs. "ain't")?

SENTENCES
    1  2  3      A.  Are the sentences complete (subject and predicate)?
    1  2  3      B.  Are run-on sentences avoided?
    1  2  3      C.  Are exceptionally complex sentences avoided?
    1  2  3      D.  Are the sentences grammatically correct (e.g., word order,
                     subject-verb agreement)?

PARAGRAPHS
    1  2  3      A.  Do the sentences in the paragraph relate to one topic?
    1  2  3      B.  Are the sentences organized to reflect the relationships between
                     ideas within the paragraph?
    1  2  3      C.  Does the paragraph include a topical, introductory or transition
                     sentence?

MECHANICS
    1  2  3      A.  Are the paragraphs indented?
    1  2  3      B.  Are correct margins used?
    1  2  3      C.  Are capitals used at the beginning of sentences?
    1  2  3      D.  Are additional capitals used as necessary in the written sample?
    1  2  3      E.  Is correct end of sentence punctuation used?
    1  2  3      F.  Is additional punctuation used as necessary in the written
                     sample?

HANDWRITING
    1  2  3      A.  Is the handwriting legible?
    1  2  3      B.  Is the handwriting neat?

SPELLING
    1  2  3      A.  Does the writer correctly spell high frequency, irregular words?
    1  2  3      B.  Does the writer correctly spell phonetic words?
```

NOTES. Using these guidelines, the teacher can carefully examine a child's written work and pinpoint instructional needs. For example, it might be determined that the child needs instruction on writing complete sentences, using correct punctuation or proofing for spelling errors. Evaluation of more than one sample would increase the accuracy of these conclusions.

Note. From *Teaching the Mildly Handicapped in the Regular Classroom* (2nd ed.) (pp. 72–73) by J. Q. Affleck, S. Lowenbraun, and A. Archer, 1980, Columbus, OH: Merrill. Copyright 1980 by Bell & Howell Company. Reprinted by permission.

FIGURE 13–7

Checklist of composition skills

IV. IDEATION
  A. Type of Writing
    1. Story _____ 2. Poem _____ 3. Letter _____ 4. Report _____ 5. Review _____
  B. Substance
    1. Naming _____ 2. Description _____ 3. Plot _____ 4. Issue _____
  C. Productivity
    1. Number of words written _____ 2. Acceptable number _____ 3. Too few _____
  D. Comprehensibility
    Easy to understand _____ Difficult to understand _____ Cannot understand _____
                    _____ perseveration of words _____ illogical
                    _____ perseveration of ideas _____ disorganized
  E. Reality
    _____ Accurate perception of stimulus or task
    _____ Inaccurate perception of stimulus or task
  F. Style
    1. Sentence Sense
      a. Completeness   Tallies:
        (1) complete sentences _____
        (2) run-on sentences _____
        (3) sentence fragments _____
      b. Structure
        (1) simple _____
        (2) compound _____
        (3) complex _____
        (4) compound/complex _____
      c. Types
        (1) declarative _____
        (2) interrogative _____
        (3) imperative _____
        (4) exclamatory _____
    2. Tone
      a. intimate _____ b. friendly _____ c. impersonal _____
    3. Word Choice (N = none, F = few, S = some, M = many)
      a. Formality
          formal _____ informal _____ colloquial _____
      b. Complexity
          simple _____ multisyllable _____ contractions _____
      c. Descriptiveness
          vague _____ vivid _____ figures of speech _____
      d. Appropriateness
          inexact words _____ superfluous/repetitions _____ omissions _____

Note. From "Informal Assessment of Written Expression" by J. A. Poteet, 1980. *Learning Disability Quarterly, 3* (4), p. 92. Copyright 1980 by Council for Learning Disabilities. Reprinted by permission.

☐ Phonologic (sound components)
☐ Syntactic (grammatical)
☐ Semantic (meaning)
☐ Self-Monitoring Skills

In the use of this procedure, students are asked to write an autobiography; approximately 30 minutes are allowed for writing and 15 minutes for revision. The writing sample is then studied to identify errors that may indicate a need for instruction. In the meaningful language category, the professional looks for errors in flexible vocabulary, coherence, logical sequencing, transitions, distinction between major and minor points, inferential thinking, and idiomatic and figurative language.

According to Wallace and Larsen (1978), content, organization, word choice, and usage are among the critical factors that should be taken into account in the evaluation of composition skills. As an example, consider the writing sample that appears in Figure 13–8. This essay was written by a 17-year-old student in grade 11 in response to an assignment in history class to describe the pilgrims' journey to the New World. The first few sentences of the essay are presented in the student's own handwriting, followed by a verbatim transcription of the entire essay. Last is a record of the essay as read aloud by the student; note that, in reading the essay, the student filled in missing words and corrected many punctuation errors. An error analysis of this writing sample would document the extent of the student's difficulties with handwriting, spelling, capitalization, punctuation, and usage. However, a response anal-

ysis would reveal that the essay is meaningful, its content is expressed in an organized manner, and the student's word choice is accurate, if immature.

A number of other factors may be taken into account when analyzing students' writing (Polloway & Smith, 1982; Polloway, Patton, & Cohen, 1983). These include

☐ *Productivity*, sometimes called fluency, refers to the quantity of writing produced by the student. The simplest way to evaluate productivity is to count the number of words and sentences in the writing sample and then determine the number of words per sentence. Another method involves T-units (Hunt, 1965), or thought units. Hammill and Larsen (1983) define a T-unit

FIGURE 13–8
Student writing sample

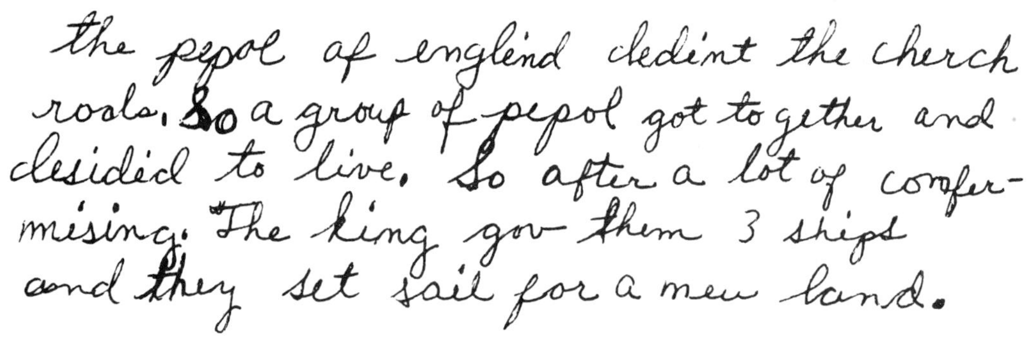

TRANSCRIPTION OF THE ENTIRE ESSAY
the pepol of englind didint the cherch roals. So a group of pepol got to gether and desidid to live. So after a lot of comfermising. The king gov them 3 ships and they set sail for a mew land. they sailed a long ways for a to long tine. then they saw it land it was North amareca. they landid on plymouth rock. ther they started to beld the ferst coliny. the firs winter wase the hardes a lot of pepol dide from being sick. After the winter was over the ingin's becom frinds with them and to them how to hunt and grow food.

ENTIRE ESSAY AS READ BY THE STUDENT
The people of England didn't like the church rules. So a group of people got together and decided to leave. So after a lot of compromising the King gave them three ships and they set sail for a new land. They sailed a long ways for a long time. Then they saw it. Land! It was North America. They landed on Plymouth Rock. Then they started to build the first colony. The first winter was the hardest and a lot of people died from being sick. After the winter was over the Indians became friendly with them and taught them how to hunt and grow food.

as "a segment of meaningful expression that contains an identifiable verb and its subject and that can stand alone" (p. 44). The number of T-units in the sample is counted and the average number of words per T-unit determined. In general, longer T-units, like longer sentences, indicate a more mature writing style.

□ *Sentences* can be analyzed according to their structure (simple, compound, complex, or fragment) and their type (declarative, interrogative, imperative, and exclamatory) (Polloway & Smith, 1982). Complete sentences are preferred to sentence fragments, and compound and complex sentences are considered more advanced forms of expression than simple sentences. In relation to sentence type, diversity is desirable when appropriate to content.

□ *Vocabulary*, or the words selected by the student for inclusion in the writing sample, is another important consideration. The type–token ratio is a measure of the diversity of the vocabulary used by the writer. This ratio is determined by dividing the number of unique words in the writing sample by the total number of words in the sample. Polloway and Smith (1982) say that "a ratio of 1.0 would therefore indicate no redundancy while a ratio of .5 would suggest frequent repetition" (p. 344). In general, diversity of vocabulary is viewed as an indicator of mature writing.

Criterion-referenced tests. Criterion-referenced tests are a very flexible type of assessment tool that can be used to measure a variety of different composition skills. For example, the teacher could develop CRTs to assess a student's ability to write complete sentences, an organized paragraph containing both a topic sentence and several supporting sentences, or a brief story describing interactions between characters.

Published criterion-referenced tests such as the measures by Brigance (1977, 1981, 1983a) also offer assistance in the study of composition skills. A Sentence-Writing Level Placement test is provided on both the *BRIGANCE® Diagnostic Inventory of Basic Skills* (1977) and the *BRIGANCE® Diagnostic Comprehensive Inventory of Basic Skills* (1983a). This test assesses the student's ability to write complete and correct sentences that incorporate several stimulus words. For example, the student

might be asked to compose a sentence that includes these words: *circus, escaped, after,* and *elephant.*

Criterion-referenced tests of practical writing skills appear on some of the Brigance measures. For example, the *BRIGANCE® Diagnostic Inventory of Essential Skills* (1981) provides measures of daily life writing skills. Included are tests that assess skill in completing several common types of applications—employment, Social Security number, credit card, and driver's permit—as well as common forms such as income tax returns and forms for unemployment compensation.

A new measure, the *Hudson Education Skills Inventory* (Hudson et al., 1989) contains an array of composition measures that may be useful in classroom planning. Among the skills assessed are capitalization, punctuation, grammar, vocabulary, sentences, and paragraphs.

Observation and clinical interviews. Even though writing is essentially a private act, aspects of the writing process can be studied by observation. With classroom writing tasks, for example, it is possible to observe some of the actions the student takes in the three major steps of writing: preparing to write, writing, and reviewing what has been written.

When a writing task is assigned, some students appear to engage in a planning process, whereas others begin to write immediately. Such observable behaviors are open to the scrutiny of the professional. For instance, the teacher could observe how much time is spent in the prewriting and postwriting stages as well as in the actual act of writing.

Table 13–3 lists the three stages of writing and the typical behaviors expected of skilled and unskilled writers at each stage. For example, in the planning stage, skilled writers may discuss the assigned topic, spend time thinking about what to write, and make notes or draw diagrams. The descriptions in this table could be converted into an observation checklist or a set of questions for a student interview.

However, it is important to recognize that the writing process is not always made up of three separate and distinct stages. As Graham (1982) observes, people approach writing in different ways. One person might write down thoughts as fast as they occur and then revise them later.

TABLE 13–3
The stages of writing for skilled and unskilled writers

Stage	Unskilled Writer	Skilled Writer
Planning	Does not participate in prewriting discussions.	Explores and discusses topic.
	Spends little time thinking about topic before beginning composition.	Spends time considering what will be written and how it will be expressed.
	Makes no plans or notes.	Jots notes; draws diagrams or pictures.
Transcribing	Writes informally in imitation of speech.	Writes in style learned from models of composition.
	Is preoccupied with technical matters of spelling and punctuation.	Keeps audience in mind while writing.
	Stops only briefly and infrequently.	Stops frequently to reread. Takes long thought pauses.
Revising	Does not review or rewrite.	Reviews frequently.
	Looks only for surface errors (spelling, punctuation.)	Makes content revisions, as well as spelling and punctuation corrections.
	Rewrites only to make a neat copy in ink.	Keeps audience in mind while rewriting.

Note. From "Effective Instruction in Written Language" (p. 291) by S. L. Isaacson, 1988, in *Effective Instructional Strategies for Exceptional Children* by E. L. Meyen, G. A. Vergason, and R. J. Whelan (Eds.), Denver: Love. Copyright 1988 by Love Publishing Company. Reprinted by permission.

Another might write and rewrite the first sentence until it is satisfactory and then proceed to the second sentence. Still another might carefully outline the story or essay and then write and edit it. A writer can also combine these strategies or switch from one to another during the act of writing.

Clinical interviews provide a method for gathering information about the nonobservable aspects of writing and the ways that the student interacts with the writing task. Interviews can be conducted before the student begins to write or after writing is completed (or both). However, while the student is writing, the professional should simply observe and not interrupt the student's thoughts with questions.

Among the dimensions of writing that can be explored in clinical interviews are the student's perceptions of the purposes for writing and the audience for which the writing is intended. Martin (1983) summarizes these dimensions with the questions, "What is the writing for?" and "Who is it for?" According to Martin, the function (or purpose) of expressive writing can be viewed as a continuum, with transactional writing at one end and poetic writing at the other.

Transactional writing, often called "expository," is concerned with some direct result or transaction like giving information, presenting an argument or a literary judgment, or writing reports, essays, or notes. It is the language of science, commerce, and technology and it is taken for granted that the writer can be challenged for truthfulness. . . .

Poetic writing on the other hand is without any such *direct* practical purpose, and includes stories, poems, and plays. It is taken for granted that true or false is not a relevant question at the literal level . . . (p. 3)

Phelps-Gunn and Phelps-Terasaki (1982) suggest that these purposes are related to the different modes of discourse—narration, description, exposition, and argument—that writers select to communicate their ideas to readers.

In school writing tasks, there are several different audiences: peers; the teacher, viewed as a trusted adult; the teacher, in the role of critic and dispenser of grades; the student himself or herself (as in writing a journal, class notes, and memoranda); or the general public (Martin, 1983). How students perceive the audience and the function of writing can influence how they approach the writing task. To find out about these and other dimensions of writing, the professional can ask these questions before the student begins to write:

☐ You're going to be writing something in a few minutes. Tell me about the assignment. What are you expected to do?

☐ Who will you be writing to? With whom will you try to communicate? Your teacher? A friend? Yourself? If you'll be writing to your teacher, do you expect the teacher to give you a grade—or to read what you have written and then help you make it better?

☐ What purpose will you try to accomplish in writing? Will you try to tell an exciting story? Give the reader information? Present an argument?

☐ What will you do before you begin writing? Will you think about what you're going to write? Make notes? Prepare an outline?

The interview can be continued after the student has completed the writing task.

☐ You've finished your essay (or paragraph, story, book report, etc.) Tell me about what you've written.

☐ When you finished, did you read over what you had written? Did you make any changes? What did you change?

☐ While you were writing, what did you think about? Did you consider . . .

The ideas you were writing about?

What should come first, second, and so on?

Choosing the exact words to express your meaning?

Spelling the words correctly, using correct punctuation, and following all the other rules for correct English?

☐ Do you think that you've accomplished your purpose in writing? Why or why not? If not, what do you need to change?

☐ You said that you would be writing to your teacher (or friend, self, etc.). Is your writing appropriate for that person? For example, is the vocabulary suitable? The tone? If not, what do you need to change?

WITHIN THE CONTEXT OF THE CLASSROOM

Students and their written products have been the focus of discussion up to this point in the chapter.

Now the emphasis shifts to study of the classroom learning environment and its influence upon students' spelling, handwriting, and composition skills.

The Instructional Environment

Assessment of the influence of the instructional environment on students' written language must take into account the classroom curriculum and instructional methods and materials used to implement that curriculum. However, investigating the written language program may be a bit more difficult than studying classroom practices in reading and mathematics. In the elementary grades, written language is typically divided into several subjects, each of which is taught directly but separately from the others: spelling, handwriting, and English (or language). There are usually separate basal textbook series for each of these subjects, with composition subsumed under the subject of language or English. In the secondary grades, writing skills become part of the English curriculum, although students are expected to communicate in writing in all classes.

Two fundamental concerns in the evaluation of any instructional environment are the amount of time devoted to instruction and the types of skills emphasized. These concerns are particularly important in written language instruction. There is evidence from the research literature (e.g., Alexander, 1983; Freedman, 1982; Leinhardt, Zigmond, & Cooley, 1981) that suggests teachers do not allocate a great deal of instructional time to teaching writing skills. When classroom time *is* spent on written language, it may be on the more mechanical aspects of writing such as spelling and handwriting rather than composition. Thus, one of the first steps in assessing the learning environment should be a study of the classroom schedule and how that schedule is implemented.

The following questions provide a framework for evaluating the classroom program for teaching written language skills:

1. Are spelling skills included within the written language curriculum? If so, what does the curriculum stress—regular words, irregular words, spelling rules, or a combination?

2. Are handwriting skills included? If so, is manuscript or cursive writing taught? Does the

curriculum emphasize accuracy in letter formation? Speed? Legibility?

3. Are composition skills included? Are they taught as part of the language or English program? Or is there a separate program for teaching composition? If so, what are its major components?

4. Where do skills such as capitalization and punctuation fit? Are they taught in conjunction with composition or as a separate skill area?

5. What basal textbook series are used in the classroom to teach written language skills? Is there a text for spelling? Handwriting? Language? English?

6. Are multiple levels of each of the written language textbooks in use in the classroom?

7. What instructional materials supplement the textbooks in the basal series? Are there word processing programs for the computer?

8. What types of writing skills are stressed in classroom instruction? Writing mechanics? Composition and the use of writing as a means of communication?

9. Is any attempt made to integrate the teaching of composition with instruction in spelling, handwriting, and usage? If so, how is this accomplished?

10. Is the written language curriculum organized so the sequence of instruction is logical?

11. Is instruction based on ongoing assessment?

12. How are students grouped for instruction? How much individualization takes place in each group?

13. What instructional techniques does the teacher use to present new skills and information? Lecture? Demonstration? Discussion? Exploration and discovery?

14. In what types of learning activities do students participate? In spelling and handwriting, do they complete workbook pages or worksheets? Do they copy each spelling word several times as a strategy for learning? In handwriting, do students practice writing letters, words, and symbols by copying from a model? What types of composition activities are available? Do students keep a journal? Write paragraphs? Stories? Letters? Poems? Book reports? Is expository or creative writing emphasized?

15. How is supervised practice incorporated into the written language program? On the average, how many minutes per day do students spend practicing their spelling skills? Handwriting skills? Composition skills?

16. What changes, if any, have been made in the standard program to accommodate the needs of special students such as the one under assessment?

Graham (1982) and Graham and Miller (1979, 1980) have summarized the research on effective methods for the teaching of spelling, handwriting, and composition in order to offer specific recommendations for classroom practice. These recommendations could serve as a set of standards for the evaluation of classroom practices.

According to Graham and Miller (1979), "The single most important factor in learning to spell is the student correcting his or her own spelling test under the teacher's direction" (p. 10). Some of the other research-based practices these authors advocate are

□ The presentation of spelling words in lists or columns to focus the student's attention on each word

□ Use of the test-study-test method in which students study only the words that they are unable to spell (in preference to the study-test method in which all words are studied)

□ The allocation of 60 to 75 minutes per week for spelling instruction

Graham and Miller (1979) also describe instructional procedures not supported by research. These include the assumption that "writing words several times ensures spelling retention" (p. 10).

Some of the recommendations that Graham and Miller (1980) offer for an effective program in handwriting instruction are

□ Handwriting instruction is direct and not incidental.

□ Handwriting is taught in short daily learning periods during which desirable habits are established.

□ Skills in handwriting are overlearned in isolation and then applied in meaningful context assignments.

□ Teachers stress the importance of handwriting and do not accept, condone, or encourage slovenly work.

□ Although students do develop personal idiosyncrasies, the teacher helps them maintain a consistent, legible handwriting style throughout the grades. (pp. 5–6)

In relation to the teaching of composition skills, Graham (1982) suggests

1. Students should be exposed to a broad range of writing tasks.
2. Strategies for reducing the number of cognitive demands inherent in the act of writing should be an integral part of a remedial composition program.
3. Writing error should not be overemphasized.
4. The composition program should be both pleasant and encouraging.
5. The composition program should be planned, monitored, and evaluated on the basis of assessment information. (pp. 6–9)

It is also important to consider the performance demands imposed on students in writing tasks. These include expectations for quantity (that is, the number of words, sentences, or paragraphs expected), the requirements for speed, and the expectations for accuracy. Performance demands become a concern whenever writing activities are a part of instruction: writing a composition in English class, copying mathematics problems from the board, writing answers to questions on a history test, writing entries in a science lab notebook, and so on.

Classroom standards should be considered in relation to the student under assessment. Standards may be unrealistically high for this student, and some adjustment can be made to better the student's chances for success. For example, the teacher may be willing to allow the student more time for composition activities or reduce the amount of writing required. Or if handwriting is an area of difficulty, the teacher may permit the student to type, tape record, or dictate assignments to a peer.

The Interpersonal Environment

The major factors within the interpersonal environment that are of concern in assessment are social relationships among students and student–teacher interactions. Often, students with achievement problems are not well accepted by their peers. This can occur when students experience difficulty with written language, particularly when their attempts to communicate in writing are open to view by their peers. In most classrooms, students have many opportunities to see and read what other students write. For instance, it is routine practice to ask students to write on the board and collect their themes, stories, essays, and the like, placing them on public display on classroom bulletin boards.

In written language instruction, most teacher–student interactions center around the student's written product. The student writes in an attempt to communicate, and the teacher reads and then grades the communication. There are several methods of grading, and some are more likely than others to encourage students in their efforts to learn writing skills. Covering a student's paper with red ink by marking every error may only discourage the student from further attempts. For students with an achievement problem in some aspect of written expression, it is better to emphasize what they have done correctly by drawing attention to their correct responses rather than errors. Graham (1982) says, "Only the most frequent and flagrant errors that appear in a child's writing should be treated" (p. 9). It is also possible to assign more than one grade to a paper. For example, the teacher might give one grade for spelling, handwriting, and other form considerations and another for the content.

These questions are of interest when evaluating interactions between students and teachers in written language instruction:

☐ In private student–teacher interactions (for example, when the teacher communicates with students by grading their papers), how does the teacher respond to an error? Does the teacher identify the response as an error? Correct it? Ignore the error?
☐ If the writing situation is a public one (for example, students are writing on the board), what occurs when a student makes an error? Does the teacher use the same correction procedures as in private interactions?
☐ How does the student react to the teacher's corrections? Is there a difference when the student is corrected in front of peers?
☐ What do other students do when a peer makes errors in writing?
☐ What happens when a student makes a correct writing response? Does the teacher confirm the

response? Praise the student? Provide a tangible reward or token?

☐ Are students able to work independently on writing activities? Do certain students require frequent assistance from the teacher?

The Physical Environment

The physical environment of the classroom is an important consideration in written language instruction. General environmental factors such as lighting, temperature, and ventilation can affect the physical comfort of teachers and students, thereby influencing the teaching–learning process. In addition, the seating arrangements for students and the writing tools provided can have an impact on their ability to perform, particularly in relation to handwriting. In assessing the classroom's physical environment, some of the major questions to consider are

1. Are appropriate chairs provided for students? Can each student sit comfortably with hips touching the back of the chair and both feet resting on the floor (Graham & Miller, 1980)?
2. Are student desks (or other types of writing surfaces such as tables) an appropriate height for writing?
3. What types of writing implements are available in the classroom? Is there a selection of different types?
4. Are writing implements selected to meet the needs of individual students? For example, some students find primary-sized pencils easier to grip.
5. What types of paper are available in the classroom? Is there a selection of different types? For example, for younger students and those with severe handwriting problems, is there a supply of primary paper with guidelines between each pair of widely spaced lines?
6. Is the lighting in the classroom adequate for writing?
7. What seating arrangements are used for instruction in written language?
8. How are students seated for independent work?
9. Is the classroom space organized so areas for noisier activities are separated from areas for quieter activities such as writing?
10. Are there any quiet areas within the classroom where students can escape from distractions?

11. Does the classroom offer a variety of learning materials, or are textbooks the only resource? For example, is there a typewriter available in the classroom? A computer with a word processing program and a printer?

ANSWERING THE ASSESSMENT QUESTIONS

The major purpose of assessing written language is to describe the student's current levels of educational performance in this important school skill, and a number of different types of assessment tools are available for this purpose.

Nature of the Assessment Tools

The tools available for the study of written language vary in several ways. One important dimension is the range of skills they are designed to assess. Some measures are comprehensive and evaluate a number of the major skill areas of written language. Others are more limited in scope. For example, handwriting is the sole concern of the *Zaner-Bloser Evaluation Scales,* and the *Test of Written Spelling–2* concentrates on spelling.

Of the 18 assessment tools listed in Table 13–1, 6 could be considered comprehensive measures. Of these, all are informal measures, except the *Test of Early Written Language.* If norm-referenced information is needed for decisions about the severity of students' skill deficits, relatively few formal tests are available. The most comprehensive is the *Test of Written Language–2,* although it does not assess handwriting performance.

Assessment tools can also vary in the depth with which skills are assessed. In general, informal measures are likely to provide the most thorough coverage of individual skills. For example, the *BRIGANCE® Diagnostic Inventory of Basic Skills* offers several tests of spelling, and each considers a specific skill in depth: spelling initial consonants, spelling initial clusters, spelling prefixes, and so forth.

Another way that assessment tools may differ are the types of tasks used to evaluate skill development. For example, as Table 13–4 shows, there are three basic strategies for the study of spelling: dictation tests, analysis of students' writing samples, and error detection tasks. Error detection, the least frequently used assessment

TABLE 13–4
Assessment tasks used to evaluate written language skills

Written Language Skill	Assessment Task	Presentation Mode	Response Mode	Examples of Measures Using This Type of Task
Spelling	Dictation test	Listen to a word (or a word and a sentence containing the word) read by the tester.	Write the word.	*Test of Written Spelling–2,* Kottmeyer's *Diagnostic Spelling Test, Spellmaster Assessment and Teaching System*
		Listen to a sentence read by the tester.	Write the sentence.	Spelling subtest of the *Test of Written Language–2*
	Analysis of a classroom writing sample	An existing sample of the student's writing is analyzed.	—	*Checklist of Written Expression, Diagnostic Evaluation of Writing Skills*
	Error detection	Read a sentence that contains an error.	Identify the error and correct it.	Proofing subtest of the *Woodcock Language Proficiency Battery*
Handwriting	Copying test	Look at a sentence or paragraph written in legible handwriting.	Copy the model.	*Zaner-Bloser Evaluation Scales, Denver Handwriting Analysis*
	Analysis of a classroom writing sample	An existing sample of the student's writing is analyzed.	—	*Checklist of Written Expression, Diagnostic Evaluation of Writing Skills*
Composition	Elicitation of a writing sample	Look at a picture.	Write a story about the picture.	*Test of Written Language–2, Picture Story Language Test*
	Sentence writing	Read a word.	Write a sentence containing the word.	Vocabulary subtest of *Test of Written Language–2,* Writing/Vocabulary subtest of *Test of Adolescent Language–2*
		Read a sentence with a logical error in it.	Rewrite the sentence and correct the error.	Logical Sentences subtest of *Test of Written Language–2*
	Sentence combining	Read two sentences.	Write a new sentence that combines the meanings of the original sentences.	Sentence Combining subtest of *Test of Written Language–2,* Writing/Grammar subtest of *Test of Adolescent Language–2*

strategy, is essentially a proofreading task. It is important to remember that detecting spelling errors is not the same skill as recalling correct spellings from memory. If both skills are of interest, both should be assessed.

A variety of assessment tasks are used to evaluate handwriting skills. Two major strategies are based on analysis of a sample of the student's handwriting, but they differ in the way the writing sample is obtained. On copying tests, students are provided with a model and directed to copy that model in their best handwriting. In contrast, classroom writing samples tend to represent the student's typical handwriting. A comparison of the handwriting samples that the student produces under these divergent conditions can provide useful assessment information.

Composition skills are assessed in many ways, but writing samples are the most common assessment task. The student is directed to write a story about a standard stimulus such as one or a series of pictures. This technique is somewhat different from the collection of classroom writing samples. Because the task is standard for all students, norms can be developed for evaluating various aspects of written language performance. On the *Test of Written Language–2*, for example, the content of the writing sample is evaluated; vocabulary level is assessed; and spelling, syntax, capitalization, and punctuation errors are noted.

The Relationship of Written Language to Other Areas of Performance

A student's general aptitude for learning can affect the ease and speed with which academic skills are acquired. Hence, the student's current status in written language should be evaluated in relation to estimated intellectual performance. In general, students with lower than average general intelligence are expected to progress at a somewhat slower rate than students of average intellectual ability. The Verbal IQ is likely the best measure for estimating a student's potential for learning spelling and composition skills. In contrast, the Performance IQ may provide a better estimate of handwriting ability because of the motor components of this skill.

Specific learning abilities and strategies can influence the student's success in the acquisition

and use of written language skills. Difficulties in attention, memory, or other areas such as visual perception and auditory discrimination can impede skill development, particularly the acquisition of basic spelling and handwriting skills. Fine motor skills and eye-hand coordination are important considerations in relation to handwriting, the motor component of written language. Also, inefficient learning strategies can interfere with the student's attempts to learn new skills and apply already learned skills to the process of planning, writing, and revising a written product.

Classroom behavior may be related to written language performance. Inappropriate classroom conduct can impede any type of learning, including the acquisition of spelling, handwriting, and composition skills. Likewise, poor achievement can affect a student's behavior. Classroom writing activities often require that students work independently, and when written language is an area of difficulty, students may be unable to comply. The result may be disruptive behavior, frequent bids for the teacher's attention, and/or withdrawal from the academic situation.

In addition, achievement problems in other school skill areas can interfere with the acquisition of written language skills. In this regard, oral language and reading skills are the major concerns. Difficulties in the comprehension or expression of oral language can have a major impact on the student's ability to express thoughts in writing. Likewise, a lack of reading proficiency may inhibit the development of writing skills. Generally, students first learn to read words, then learn to write and spell them. Also, reading exposes students to the formal conventions of written language—sentences, paragraphs, capitalization, punctuation, and the like—and to the structural, syntactical, and vocabulary differences between written and oral language.

Just as other school skills can affect written language, writing skills influence the student's chances for success in other academic areas. Beginning in the early elementary grades, writing is a primary way that students demonstrate what they have learned. As the student proceeds through the various levels of education—from the primary grades to the intermediate grades to junior high school and so on—an increasing proportion of school tasks require writing.

Writing, like reading, is a skill that pervades the entire curriculum. Students with poor spelling, handwriting, and composition skills will have difficulty not only when these skills are taught directly but also when writing proficiency is a requirement in other curriculum areas. Almost all school subjects involve some degree of writing. Students who write very slowly will have difficulty completing their assignments on time. Those who write illegibly may fail an exam or assignment even though their responses are correct. Poor spelling and syntax may lower students' grades, even in subjects like history or biology.

Writing skills are also necessary for adult life. Adults use writing as a memory aid when they make note of a telephone number, write down an address, or make out a shopping list. People also write to communicate with others; they write postcards and notes to friends, fill out mail order forms, and compose business letters. Job applications are another feature of adult life, as are the forms that must be completed for a Social Security number, a driver's license, income taxes, and so on. In addition, some degree of writing proficiency is required in most occupations. In the assessment of written language, it is important to consider the student's ability to cope with adult writing tasks as well as the degree of success in meeting classroom writing requirements.

Documentation of Written Language Performance

What are the student's educational needs? is the general assessment question that guides the special education team in its study of written language. The goal in this phase of assessment is to gather sufficient information for a precise description of the student's current levels of educational performance. The first question the team attempts to respond to is, *What is the student's current level of achievement in written language?* Additional data are then gathered about the writing skills that are possible areas of educational need. The result, a description of the student's current status in relation to written language, allows the team to answer this question: *What are the student's strengths and weaknesses in the various skill areas of written language?*

Answers to the assessment questions about written language make up one part of the data base used to plan the student's Individualized Education Program. Results of formal tests and informal procedures document the student's current levels of performance in written language. From this information the team identifies the areas of educational need that may become the priorities for special instruction. For example, consider the case of Joyce, the fourth grader with problems in spelling and handwriting.

Joyce

At this point in assessment, the team has some information about Joyce's current skills in spelling and handwriting. In both areas, Joyce's performance appears to be below average, and in her fourth grade classroom, she is working in a second grade spelling book and just beginning to learn cursive writing. However, little information is available about Joyce's composition skills. Mr. Harvey, Joyce's teacher, did not discuss composition when he made the referral, so the team decides to begin its in-depth study of written language by talking with him. In this interview, Mr. Harvey reports that Joyce writes quite slowly, her handwriting is difficult to read, and her spelling is poor. Despite this, Joyce seems to have good ideas. Although her compositions are short and hard to read because of her difficulties with handwriting and spelling, she is able to express her thoughts in writing.

The team administers the *Test of Written Language–2* to learn more about Joyce's composition skills, and these results are obtained:

Contrived Subtests	Standard Score
Vocabulary	7
Spelling	5
Style	5
Logical Sentences	6
Sentence Combining	6
Spontaneous Subtests	
Thematic Maturity	10
Contextual Vocabulary	8
Syntactic Maturity	9
Contextual Spelling	6
Contextual Style	5
Composites	
Contrived Writing Quotient	71
Spontaneous Writing Quotient	83
Overall Written Language Quotient	76

Joyce's overall performance on the *TOWL–2* indicates low average achievement in written language skills. However, on the writing sample, she shows strengths in Thematic Maturity, Contextual Vocabulary, and Syntactic Maturity. Spelling and Style (capitalization and punctuation) are areas of weakness, on both the contrived and spontaneous subtests. On the contrived subtests, Joyce asked for assistance in reading several of the words and sentences.

To investigate Joyce's difficulties with spelling, the *Test of Written Spelling–2* is given. Joyce's performance on this measure is consistent with her scores on the spelling subtests of the *PIAT–R* and *WRAT–R*. The results are as follows: Predictable Words Quotient, 74; Unpredictable Words Quotient, 68; and Written Spelling Quotient, 70. These scores indicate below average performance in spelling irregular words and low average performance in spelling regular words.

Ms. Gale, the special education resource teacher, administers an informal spelling inventory (see Table 13–2) to determine Joyce's pattern of errors with regular words. On this measure, Joyce is able to spell the short sounds of vowels and words that follow the vowel-consonant-e pattern (e.g., *line* and *cake*). In the 15 words that she attempts, she makes no errors with consonants. However, she is unable to spell words with two vowels together (e.g., *coat*), with *ow-ou* spellings of the *ou* sound, long and short *oo*, and final *y* as short *i*. Joyce is then asked to write the spellings of a portion of words in a high-frequency word list (Figure 13–2). She spells the first two groups of 10 words correctly but then begins to experience difficulty. For example, she spells *any* as *ene* and *eat* as *et*.

Handwriting is the next area of study. Samples of Joyce's manuscript and cursive writing are obtained from Mr. Harvey and analyzed for possible error patterns. In manuscript, Joyce's letters are large, poorly spaced, and often difficult to read. As the following sample shows, she seems to have special difficulty writing circular letters like *a, o,* and *e.*

My name is Joyce.

Joyce has just begun to learn cursive writing. She is able to write all of the lowercase letters and has started to learn capitals. Her cursive writing is also large, but the spacing between letters and words is adequate. Letter formation is satisfactory, but she has not yet learned how to join some letters together with others.

my name is jayce.

A classroom observation is conducted when Joyce is participating in a writing activity. Joyce writes in manuscript to copy a paragraph from the board. Her chair and desk are of appropriate size, her posture is adequate, and she holds her paper and pencil correctly. However, she writes with a standard pencil on lined paper with narrow spaces and no guidelines. In forming letters, she makes one line, lifts her pencil from the paper, repositions the pencil, then writes a second line. For example, in writing an uppercase *M,* she makes four separate lines, lifting her pencil each time. This strategy, along with her frequent erasures, affects her writing speed.

After a thorough analysis of these results, the assessment team is prepared to describe Joyce's current levels of written language performance. They have reached these conclusions:

□ At present, Joyce is functioning within the low average range in composition skills, as measured by the *Test of Written Language–2.*

□ Joyce's spelling skills are quite deficient. On the *Test of Written Spelling–2,* she showed below average performance in spelling unpredictable words and low average skill in spelling predictable words.

□ Joyce's knowledge of regular spellings is limited to consonant and short vowel sounds and words that follow the vowel-consonant-e pattern. She is able to spell only a very few irregular words.

□ On most classroom assignments, Joyce writes in manuscript. Her manuscript writing is large, poorly spaced, and difficult to read because of poor formation of some letters (e.g., *a, e,* and *o*). A larger pencil and paper with guidelines between widely spaced lines might help improve her legibility.

□ Joyce's manuscript writing is slow because she lifts her pencil after each stroke and erases frequently.

□ In cursive, Joyce's spacing and letter formation are adequate, and her writing is legible.

She needs to learn the uppercase cursive alphabet and procedures for joining letters together.

STUDY GUIDE

Review Questions

1. The major purpose for the assessment of written language skills is _____ .

2. What three skill areas are most often considered in the assessment of written language?

3. Find the true and false statements.

   T F **a.** In the developmental sequence, oral language generally precedes written language.
   T F **b.** Reading is an expressive language skill, whereas writing is a receptive language skill.
   T F **c.** Writing is often assessed by multiple choice exams.
   T F **d.** One strategy frequently used to assess written expression is to obtain a writing sample.
   T F **e.** The most commonly assessed skill area in written language is composition.

4. Are traditional measures of written language more concerned with the process of writing, or with the product?

5. Match the assessment device or procedure in Column A with the description in Column B.

Column A	*Column B*
a. *Test of Written Language–2*	_____ A standardized test that assesses the student's ability to spell both regular and irregular words
b. *Picture Story Language Test*	_____ Assesses two aspects of written language, Dictation and Proofing
c. *Zaner-Bloser Evaluation Scales*	_____ A rating scale for the evaluation of handwriting skills
d. *Test of Adolescent Language–2*	_____ Includes these subtests: Thematic Maturity; Syntactic Maturity; and Contextual Vocabulary, Spelling, and Style
e. *Test of Written Spelling–2*	_____ Includes tests of written vocabulary and grammar as well as tests of listening, speaking, and reading
f. *Woodcock Language Proficiency Battery*	_____ A writing sample is obtained and scored for productivity, correctness, and meaning

6. Find the test results that indicate possible areas of educational need.
   _____ **a.** Percentile rank 65 on a scale from the *Picture Story Language Test*
   _____ **b.** Overall Written Language Quotient 80 on the *Test of Written Language–2*
   _____ **c.** Standard score 92 on one of the composite scores from the *Test of Adolescent Language–2*
   _____ **d.** Predictable Words Quotient of 117 for a grade 4 student on the *Test of Written Spelling–2*

7. There are several systems for the analysis of spelling errors, but the simplest recognizes only two types of errors. Name the two types of misspellings.

8. Check each of the areas that should be considered in the evaluation of handwriting skills.
   _____ **a.** Letter formation
   _____ **b.** Spelling
   _____ **c.** Alignment and proportion
   _____ **d.** Size of letters and spacing
   _____ **e.** Punctuation and capitalization
   _____ **f.** Speed

9. On both the *Test of Written Language–2* and the *Picture Story Language Test,* a writing sample is elicited by asking students to _____ .

10. Writing samples can be analyzed for spelling, handwriting, grammar, punctuation and capitalization, and content and organization. (True or False)

11. Two fundamental concerns in the evaluation of the instructional environment of the classroom are the amount of _____ devoted to instruction and the types of _____ that are emphasized.

12. If a student shows high average intellectual performance, in what standard score range would you expect the student to perform in written language?

_____ a. Less than standard score 70

_____ b. Standard score 70 to 84

_____ c. Standard score 85 to 115

_____ d. Standard score 116 to 130

_____ e. Greater than standard score 130

13. If the special education team finds that a student shows poor performance in one aspect of written language, what conclusion can be drawn?

_____ a. If the problem is in spelling, it is likely that the student's handwriting is also poor.

_____ b. A problem in one area usually means that the student will show poor performance in all dimensions of written language.

_____ c. The student can perform poorly in one aspect of written language while showing adequate performance in other aspects.

_____ d. Written language skill is related to reading competence; if a student writes poorly, he or she also reads poorly.

Activities

1. Write an Individualized Assessment Plan for an elementary grade student who has been referred because of problems in written language. Then tell how you would modify that plan for a secondary grade student with the same referral information.

2. Analyze the content of the group and individual achievement tests described in Chapter 7. Do these measures include tests of written language? If so, what writing skills are emphasized?

3. Under the supervision of the course instructor, administer one of the measures discussed in this chapter. Calculate all possible scores and analyze the results to determine strengths and weaknesses.

4. Obtain a writing sample from a student receiving special education services. Analyze that sample in terms of spelling, handwriting, form (written syntax, capitalization and punctuation, and so on), and content and organization. When you have completed your analysis, rate the adequacy of the sample using a scale such as Figure 13–6. Compare your ratings with those of another professional.

5. Devise a criterion-referenced test to assess some aspect of written expression. Be sure to base your CRT on an instructional objective that clearly specifies the student behavior of interest, the conditions under which that behavior should occur, and the criteria for acceptable performance.

Discussion Questions

1. Writing, like reading and mathematics, is considered a basic school skill. Discuss the importance of written expression in the school curriculum and in adult life.

2. Freedman (1982) calls writing "the neglected basic skill." Explain some reasons for this and offer suggestions for change.

3. In most classrooms, writing is a way students can demonstrate what they have learned. Discuss how writing requirements can affect student performance in other school subjects. Consider teachers' expectations for quantity, speed, and accuracy in your answer.

4. Compare the ways that writing samples are analyzed on the *Test of Written Language–2*, the *Picture Story Language Test*, and the *Checklist of Written Expression* (Table 13–4). Do these measures consider the same skill dimensions? Include in your discussion a comparison of the skills assessed by each measure and a description of the population for which each is appropriate. Conclude by presenting your recommendations regarding the best use of each measure.

14

Oral Language and Bilingual Assessment

Oral language is the most basic communication skill. One person talks, another listens, and information is transmitted. This communication process begins in infancy when babies first learn to attend to the sound of their parents' voices. By the time most children enter school, they are experienced oral communicators, able to understand the messages spoken by others and to express their own thoughts in speech. Oral language is the foundation for school learning. In the first few years of school, most new information is presented orally; students learn by listening and demonstrate what they have learned by talking. As students progress through the grades, reading and writing skills take on increased importance, but oral language remains a basic means of communication between teacher and student. It is also the fundamental communication process for daily life. In most communication situations at home, at work, and at play, people exchange information by talking.

For many students with special needs, oral language is an area of concern. Handicapped students may have difficulty understanding the language of others, expressing themselves in speech, or in both comprehension and production of oral language. Language is also a concern with students who speak nonstandard English or languages other than English. If standard English is the only language of communication in the classroom, language minority students may face real barriers in their attempts to understand and participate in instructional activities.

The purpose of oral language assessment is to gather information for instructional planning. The general question that guides this phase of assessment is, *What are the student's educational needs?* When oral language is the skill area under study, two specific questions are asked: *What is the student's current level of development in oral language?* and *What are the student's strengths and weaknesses in the various skill areas of oral language?* These questions apply to both language minority students and those whose only language is standard English. The goal in this phase of the assessment process is description of the student's current levels of educational performance.

Assessment for instructional planning is a selective process. If the student is making satisfac-

tory progress in oral language or another skill area, the student's special education program will probably not address this skill, and thus extensive assessment is unnecessary. However, it is often the case that the assessment team has little information about a student's current status in oral language. Before this or any other skill can be ruled out as an area of educational need, it is necessary to gather data to document the student's current performance. For example, consider Joyce, the fourth grader with achievement problems in the written language skills of reading, spelling, and handwriting.

Joyce

The assessment team has almost completed its evaluation of Joyce. Results suggest a discrepancy between Joyce's expected school performance and her actual achievement, and three major areas of educational need have been identified: reading, spelling, and handwriting.

To date, oral language has not been a concern in assessment. The original referral from Mr. Harvey, Joyce's classroom teacher, did not mention oral language, and Joyce's parents did not include listening and speaking skills among the areas that they perceived as possible problems. In its study of Joyce's performance in other areas, the team has not noticed any severe problems in oral communication, although classroom observation results indicate that Joyce has difficulty following oral directions. This difficulty probably is related to Joyce's poor performance on memory tasks, but it could also be influenced by problems in the comprehension of oral language.

To find out more about Joyce's proficiency in oral language, the team will administer the intermediate level of the *Test of Language Development–2*, a comprehensive measure of several areas of language functioning. If results of this test suggest that one or more components of oral language are possible areas of educational need, the assessment team will continue its investigation. Depending on the language skill to be assessed, the team may decide to administer another norm-referenced test, collect a language sample, conduct an observation, or use some other type of informal assessment strategy.

Individualized Assessment Plan				
For: _____Joyce Dewey_____	_____4_____	_10–0_	_12/1/89_	_____Ms. Gale_____
Student's Name	Grade	Age	Date	Coordinator

Reason for Referral: Difficulty keeping up with fourth grade work in reading, spelling, and handwriting

Assessment Question	Assessment Procedures	Person Responsible	Date/Time
What is the student's current level of development in oral language?	*Test of Language Development–2, Intermediate*	Mr. Bell, Speech-Language Pathologist	1/15/90 10 a.m.
What are the student's strengths and weaknesses in the various skill areas of oral language?	Additional tests and/or informal assessments, as necessary	Mr. Bell, Speech-Language Pathologist, and other team members as needed	To be determined

CONSIDERATIONS IN ASSESSMENT OF ORAL LANGUAGE

Students' oral language skills are the subject of study in regular, special, and bilingual education. This skill area, more than many others, illustrates the multidisciplinary nature of the assessment process. Regular, special, and bilingual teachers are interested in promoting the language development of their students. They gather assessment data to measure students' progress. Speech-language pathologists serve students with severe oral communication disorders; their role in assessment is the administration of specialized measures to identify and describe disorders of speech and language. Bilingual educators are concerned with the communication skills of students who speak languages other than English. They contribute by providing information about the student's competency in the first language and by reporting on progress in the acquisition of English-language skills.

Purposes

In regular education, teachers monitor oral language skills to determine pupil progress and evaluate the effectiveness of the instructional program. However, after the early elementary grades, oral language is not usually taught as a separate school subject. Also, oral communication is not assessed by the group achievement tests used to measure students' school performance (although listening skills may be). This lack of attention to oral language reflects the assumption that students learn to listen and speak during the preschool years. Once in school, students are expected to be oral communicators, so the curriculum focuses on the acquisition of higher-level academic skills such as reading, writing, and mathematics.

When students have difficulty with oral communication in the regular classroom, they may be referred for special education assessment and/or bilingual assessment. The purpose of bilingual assessment, like special education assessment, is to determine whether the student is eligible for special services and, if so, what services are needed. If the student is identified as limited in English proficiency (LEP), special services may be offered. Among the services available in some school districts are bilingual education programs where instruction takes place both in English and in the students' language and ESL programs where English is taught as a second language.

In special education assessment, oral language is usually a concern of the assessment team as it begins to gather data for planning the student's Individualized Education Program. Many students identified as mildly handicapped have special instructional needs in oral language. In particular, mildly retarded students may show an overall delay in the acquisition of listening and speaking skills, and students with learning disabilities in written language may have equivalent needs in oral language. In addition, there is a large group of handicapped students for whom oral language is the primary disability area. This handicap is called a communication disorder.

When oral language is identified as an area of educational need for a particular student, assessment is continued to gather the detailed information necessary for program planning. This occurs for all students with language needs, whatever the handicap of the student or the language the student speaks. The goal at this point in assessment is description of the student's current performance so an appropriate educational program can be designed. Once that program is implemented, the cycle of gathering data about current skills, planning instructional interventions, and evaluating the success of those interventions is repeated for as long as the student remains in need of specially designed instruction.

Skill Areas

Language is a symbol system used for communication, and speech is one medium used to express language. Like written language, oral language can be receptive or expressive, depending on the person's role in the communication process. In oral language, speech is the expressive component and listening the receptive component. Polloway and Smith (1982) suggest that, just as language is a vehicle for communication, it is a vehicle for thought. In this view, thinking is conceptualized as a type of communication process in which inner language plays a major role.

There are many ways that language can be described, and the reception-expression dimension is only one. Another useful system is that proposed by Bloom and Lahey (1978). They suggest that language is composed of three interacting dimensions: form, content, and use. Language competence is the integration of these three dimensions of language.

Wiig and Semel's (1984) model of language includes similar components, as Figure 14–1 illustrates. In this model, four dimensions of language are described: language as sound sequences, language as a structured rule system (form), language as a meaning system (content), and language in communicative context (use).

The form of language is determined by the rules used to combine speech sounds into meaning units and meaning units into communications. Three aspects of language are involved: phonology, morphology, and syntax. Phonology is concerned with the smallest units of oral language, the speech sounds (phonemes). Expressive phonology is called articulation. Receptive phonology, the ability to recognize and comprehend phonemes, is auditory discrimination. The next level of language is morphology. A morpheme is the smallest meaningful unit of language. A morpheme may be a word such as *flower* or a meaningful part of a word such as the *-ing* in *growing*. Syntax refers to the grammatical rules for combining morphemes into comprehensible utterances. Like phonology, morphology and syntax have receptive and expressive components. For example, expressive syntax refers to the ability to produce grammatically acceptable speech.

For communication to occur, language must have meaning as well as form, and language meaning is called semantics. Semantics is concerned with the meaning of individual words and with the meaning that is produced by combinations of words. Receptive semantics is language comprehension, and expressive semantics is the production of meaningful discourse.

Pragmatics, or language use, is concerned with the speaker's purposes for communication and the ways language is used to carry out those intents. Adults are able to analyze the social contexts in which communications occur and alter their language accordingly. They are influenced by the setting of the communication, the characteristics of the participants, the topic of conversation, and the goals and objectives of each participant (Wiig & Semel, 1984). For example, if the communicative intent is to announce that dinner is ready, the language used to convey that message to one's family is likely to be different from that used with dinner guests.

Thus, oral language involves both reception and expression of communications, and those communications can be analyzed according to the dimensions of phonology, morphology, syntax, semantics, and pragmatics. In addition, oral communication is influenced by other aspects of the speech act (e.g., intonation, pitch, loudness, and stress) and by the nonverbal communications that

FIGURE 14–1

Dimensions of oral language

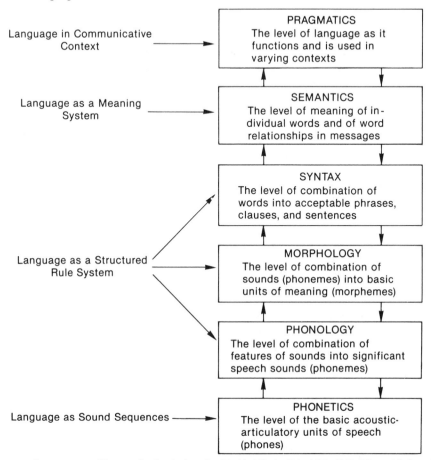

Language in Communicative Context →
PRAGMATICS
The level of language as it functions and is used in varying contexts

Language as a Meaning System →
SEMANTICS
The level of meaning of individual words and of word relationships in messages

SYNTAX
The level of combination of words into acceptable phrases, clauses, and sentences

Language as a Structured Rule System
MORPHOLOGY
The level of combination of sounds (phonemes) into basic units of meaning (morphemes)

PHONOLOGY
The level of combination of features of sounds into significant speech sounds (phonemes)

Language as Sound Sequences →
PHONETICS
The level of the basic acoustic-articulatory units of speech (phones)

Note. From *Language Assessment and Intervention for the Learning Disabled* (2nd ed.) (p. 23) by E. H. Wiig and E. Semel, 1984, Columbus, OH: Merrill. Copyright 1984 by Bell & Howell Company. Reprinted by permission.

accompany speech (e.g., facial expressions, body language, gestures). Children and adolescents can experience difficulty with any one or several of these dimensions.

In assessment, measures of oral language focus on the comprehension and production of language form and content. Pragmatics is a new area of study, and as yet few measures have been developed for its assessment. In addition, traditional language measures are designed to evaluate students' products, not the process by which those products are created. When information is needed

about a student's ability to use language in a variety of communicative contexts or about the cognitive processes that interact with language comprehension and production, informal measures are often the only type of assessment strategy available.

Many measures of oral language are designed for young children (preschoolers and children in the first few grades of school) because of the rapid rate at which language skills develop during this age period. Most measures are individually administered, a necessity when oral responses are required. Because language competence is such a complex skill area, many types of assessment tasks are used to evaluate students' oral language abilities.

Expressive phonology—the articulation of speech sounds—is assessed by eliciting samples of the student's speech. Auditory discrimination (receptive phonology) is measured by listening tasks. Tests of auditory discrimination were discussed in Chapter 9, the chapter on specific learning abilities and strategies, and thus will not be covered here.

Like articulation, expressive morphology and syntax are assessed by eliciting samples of the student's speech. With these skills, however, the concern is the structural adequacy of the utterance, not its phonological characteristics. Receptive skills are measured in a variety of ways, but one common technique involves having the student select a picture that illustrates a sentence read by the tester. For example, if the sentence is, "The girl is talking to her mother," one picture might show a girl talking to her mother, another the mother talking while her daughter listens, and so forth.

The meaning component of language, semantics, is the subject of assessment not only on measures of oral language but also on many tests of intellectual performance. Most often, expressive skills are the concern, and a typical test task is word definition. Recognition tasks are used to assess receptive skills. With this type of task, the student listens to a word and selects from several drawings or photos the one that best represents the word's meaning.

Similar techniques are used to assess student's proficiency in languages other than English, and the same language dimensions are of interest. In bilingual assessment, the language that the child speaks upon entry to school is called the first language (L1), or the home or native language. The second language the child learns is usually English and is called L2. The purpose of language assessment for bilingual learners is to determine the extent of their language proficiency in both languages so learning needs can be identified. The language in which the student is most proficient is called the dominant, or primary, language. Also of interest, particularly with older students, is language preference. The language in which a speaker is most proficient may not be the language in which he or she prefers to converse.

Whatever languages the student speaks, the ability to use oral language in everyday communication situations should not be neglected in assessment. Pragmatics is one facet of the application of language skills and is a necessary assessment concern. It is also important to evaluate the student's ability to deal with the form and meaning of language in everyday interactions. Tests measure language competence, but language performance is another matter. Although a student may define a word correctly on a test, he or she does not necessarily use the word correctly in discourse or, indeed, ever use the word in communication situations.

Current Practices

Assessment of oral language skills is not as common a practice as assessment of academic skills such as reading and mathematics. The group achievement and competency tests used in regular education focus on written, not oral, language, and even individual tests of academic achievement rarely include listening and speaking skills. One notable exception is the *Diagnostic Achievement Battery* (Newcomer & Curtis, 1984), an individual test for students ages 6–0 to 14–11.

Although oral language is not typically assessed by tests of academic achievement, it is often included on other types of measures. Tests of intellectual performance (unless they are designed as nonverbal measures) usually assess language skills in some way. For example, half of the subtests on the *Wechsler Intelligence Scale for Children–Revised* (Wechsler, 1974) are considered verbal subtests, and a Verbal Reasoning composite score is one of the results of the *Stanford-Binet Intelligence Scale–Fourth Edition* (Thorndike, Hagen, & Sattler, 1986). In addition, oral language skills are frequently one of the performance domains assessed by measures of adaptive behavior. Some of the instruments used to assess specific learning abilities also evaluate oral language.

More directly related to instructional planning are measures designed specifically for the study of oral language skills. Several of these assessment tools are listed in Table 14-1. These measures are divided into five categories according to the skills they assess. First are survey measures (instruments that assess more than one aspect of oral language), and these are followed by measures of phonology, measures of morphology and syntax, measures of semantics, and measures of pragmatics.

As Table 14–1 illustrates, there are a great many tools for the assessment of oral language, and these tools vary in the skill areas they address. Some measures are comprehensive, whereas others are limited to one domain. With the exception of pragmatics, each dimension of language is represented by a number of measures. For the most part, oral language assessments are designed for children in the elementary grades. However, some currently available measures extend oral language assessment into the secondary grades and even adulthood.

Informal techniques also play a role in oral language assessment. All of the standard types of informal devices and procedures are available, but the most common are criterion-referenced testing, informal inventories, language sample analysis, and checklists and rating scales.

This chapter describes many of the major strategies used in schools today for oral language assessment. First to be discussed are comprehensive measures of oral language. These are followed by sections on measures of phonology, morphology and syntax, and semantics and pragmatics. In each section, formal and informal strategies are described briefly because of the number of devices and techniques available. Techniques for the assessment of language minority students are discussed later in the chapter.

COMPREHENSIVE MEASURES OF ORAL LANGUAGE

Of the oral language measures available today, several are designed to assess a wide range of language skills. Described here are two versions of the *Test of Language Development–2*, the primary level for young children and the intermediate level for students in the later elementary grades. Also discussed are the *Clinical Evaluation of Language Fundamentals–Revised*, the *Woodcock Language Proficiency Battery*, and the *Test of Adolescent Language–2*.

Test of Language Development–2, Primary

The *TOLD–2 Primary* is an individual test of oral language for preschool and early elementary grade children. There are seven subtests on the *TOLD–2 Primary*, and these assess both reception and expression in three of the major dimensions of oral language: phonology, syntax, and semantics.

TEST OF LANGUAGE DEVELOPMENT–2 (TOLD–2),
PRIMARY AND INTERMEDIATE

P. L. Newcomer and D. D. Hammill (1988), D. D. Hammill and P. L. Newcomer (1988)

Type: Norm-referenced test
Major Content Areas: Primary: receptive and expressive phonology, syntax, and semantics; Intermediate: receptive and expressive syntax and semantics
Type of Administration: Individual
Administration Time: 30 to 60 minutes each
Age/Grade Levels: Primary: ages 4–0 to 8–11; Intermediate: ages 8–6 to 12–11
Types of Scores: Percentile ranks and standard scores for subtests, composite standard scores (quotients)
Typical Uses: A broad-based test for the identification of strengths and weaknesses in oral language development
Cautions: The phonology subtests on the *TOLD–2, Primary* are most useful for children under age 6.

TABLE 14–1
Measures of oral language

Name (Authors)	Ages or Grades	Group or Individual	SKILL AREA(S) ASSESSED	
			Reception	Expression
SURVEY MEASURES				
BRIGANCE® Diagnostic Inventory of Early Development (Brigance, 1978)	Ages birth to 7 years	Individual	*	*
Clinical Evaluation of Language Fundamentals–Revised (Semel, Wiig, & Secord, 1987)	Ages 5–0 to 16–11	Individual	*	*
Houston Test for Language Development (Crabtree, 1963)	Ages 6 months to 6 years	Individual	*	*
Illinois Test of Psycholinguistic Abilities (Kirk, McCarthy, & Kirk, 1968)	Ages 2–4 to 10–3	Individual	*	*
Test of Adolescent Language–2 (Hammill, Brown, Larsen, & Wiederholt, 1987)	Ages 12–0 to 18–5	Varies by subtest	*	*
Test of Early Language Development (Hresko, Reid, & Hammill, 1981)	Ages 3–0 to 7–11	Individual	*	*
Test of Language Development–2, Intermediate (Hammill & Newcomer, 1988)	Ages 8–6 to 12–11	Individual	*	*
Test of Language Development–2, Primary (Newcomer & Hammill, 1988)	Ages 4–0 to 8–11	Individual	*	*
Woodcock Language Proficiency Battery (Woodcock, 1980)	Ages 3–0 to 80+	Individual		*
PHONOLOGY				
Arizona Articulation Proficiency Scale (2nd ed.) (Fudala & Reynolds, 1986)	Ages 1–6 to 13–11	Individual		*
Auditory Discrimination Test (Reynolds, 1987; Wepman, 1975)	Ages 4 to 8–11	Individual	*	
Goldman-Fristoe Test of Articulation (Goldman & Fristoe, 1986)	Ages 2 to 16+	Individual		*

Test	Ages	Administration		
Goldman-Fristoe-Woodcock Test of Auditory Discrimination (Goldman, Fristoe, & Woodcock, 1970)	Ages 4 to 70 +	Individual	*	
Photo Articulation Test (Pendergast, Dickey, Selmar, & Soder, 1984)	Ages 3 to 12	Individual		*
Templin-Darley Tests of Articulation (2nd ed.) (Templin & Darley, 1969)	Ages 3 to adult	Individual		*
Test of Articulation Performance (Bryant & Bryant, 1983a, 1983b)	Ages 3-0 to 8-11	Individual		*

MORPHOLOGY AND SYNTAX

Test	Ages	Administration		
Carrow Elicited Language Inventory (Carrow-Woolfolk, 1974)	Ages 3-0 to 7-11	Individual		*
Developmental Sentence Analysis (Lee, 1974)	Ages 2-0 to 7-11	Individual		*
Language Sampling, Analysis, and Training (rev. ed.) (Tyack & Gottsleben, 1977)	Young children	Individual		*
Northwestern Syntax Screening Test (Lee, 1971)	Agess 3-11 to 7-1	Individual	*	*
Test for Auditory Comprehension of Language–Revised (Carrow-Woolfolk, 1985)	Ages 3 to 10	Individual	*	

SEMANTICS

Test	Ages	Administration		
Assessment of Children's Language Comprehension (Foster, Giddan, & Stark, 1972)	Ages 3 to 7	Individual	*	
Boehm Test of Basic Concepts–Preschool Version (Boehm, 1986)	Ages 3 to 5	Individual	*	
Boehm Test of Basic Concepts–Revised (Boehm, 1986)	Grades K-2	Group	*	
Environmental Language Inventory (MacDonald, 1978)	Ages 2 to adult	Individual		*
Peabody Picture Vocabulary Test–Revised (Dunn & Dunn, 1981)	Ages 2½ to 40	Individual	*	

PRAGMATICS

Test	Ages	Administration		
Let's Talk Inventory for Adolescents (Wiig, 1982c)	Ages 9 to adult	Individual	*	*
Let's Talk Inventory for Children (Bray & Wiig, 1987)	Ages 4 to 8	Individual	*	*
Test of Pragmatic Skills (rev. ed.) (Shulman, 1986)	Ages 3-0 to 8-11	Individual	*	*

- *Picture Vocabulary* (Receptive Semantics)—The tester reads a word, and the child points to the picture that best represents the word. The child chooses from four pictures.
- *Oral Vocabulary* (Expressive Semantics)—The tester reads a word and asks the child to define it orally.
- *Grammatic Understanding* (Receptive Syntax)—The tester reads a sentence, and the child must choose the picture that best illustrates the meaning of the sentence. The three pictures presented to the child represent syntactically similar sentences. As the *TOLD–2 Primary* manual explains, "In response to the stimulus sentence 'He had ridden,' the child must select the picture that most closely depicts the sentence from among pictures of a boy mounting a horse, a boy riding a horse, and a boy walking away from a horse." (p. 5).
- *Sentence Imitation* (Expressive Syntax)—On this subtest, the tester reads a sentence, and the child must repeat it verbatim. This test task is based on the assumption stated in the manual that "it is easier for children to repeat or imitate grammatic forms that are part of their linguistic repertoires than it is to repeat those that are unfamiliar" (p. 5).
- *Grammatic Completion* (Expressive Syntax)— The tester reads an unfinished sentence, and the child must supply the missing word. For example, the child might be asked to finish this sentence, "Cats are small, but birds are even _____." Included are items that assess plurals, possessives, verb tenses, and comparative and superlative adjectives.
- *Word Discrimination* (Receptive Phonology)— The tester reads two words, and the child must say whether the words are the same or different. Different word pairs differ in only one phoneme.
- *Word Articulation* (Expressive Phonology)— Here the tester shows the child a picture and reads a sentence that describes it. The child is asked to name the picture. If he or she fails to respond correctly, the tester says the word and asks the child to repeat it (e.g., "That's a dog. Say *dog*."). The purpose is to assess articulation, not vocabulary.

According to the *TOLD–2 Primary* manual, the two phonology subtests are most useful for children under the age of 6. However, norms are available for older children.

To participate in *TOLD–2 Primary* administration, children must understand and speak English and be able to respond to oral questions. The subtests are not timed, and reading and writing skills are not required. This test is quite easy to administer and score. All subtests begin with item 1, and the ceiling for all subtests is five consecutive incorrect responses. It is not necessary to administer all subtests. The manual says that a quick estimate of overall oral language can be obtained from two subtests (Picture Vocabulary and Grammatic Completion), or the tester can select only those subtests that assess a specific language ability such as phonology or syntax.

The original version of *TOLD–2 Primary* was standardized between 1976 and 1981 with 1,836 children. For this edition, 600 additional children were tested, bringing the total sample to 2,436 children from 29 states. This sample appears to approximate the national population in sex, urban–rural residence, and geographic region; ethnic minority children, particularly Hispanics, are somewhat overrepresented. No information is provided about inclusion of students identified as handicapped or about the home language of students in the sample. The manual states that although the *TOLD–2 Primary* should not be given to students who do not speak English, "the norms are designed to be applicable to children with diverse language skills" (p. 7).

The internal consistency of the *TOLD–2 Primary* is adequate; all coefficients exceed .80 except for the Grammatic Understanding subtest at age 8 (.75). Test-retest reliability is generally satisfactory, although one study with a small sample of normal children found coefficients in the .70s for three of the seven subtests. The manual reports several investigations that support the concurrent validity of the *TOLD–2 Primary* with other tests of oral language and with vocabulary measures from tests of intellectual performance.

Percentile rank and standard scores are available for each subtest. These standard scores are distributed with a mean of 10 and a standard deviation of 3. Six composite scores called quotients are also available: Spoken Language Quotient (a summary of performance on all subtests), Listening Quotient, Speaking Quotient, and quotients for

Semantics, Syntax, and Phonology. The quotients are standard scores (mean = 100, standard deviation = 15). Standard errors of measurement are 1 standard score point for *TOLD–2 Primary* subtests and either 3 or 4 standard score points for composite quotients.

TOLD–2 Primary results are plotted on profiles, as Figure 14–2 illustrates. The profile on the left shows the child's quotient scores, and subtest scores are plotted on the other profile. In this example, the child's performance falls within the low average range in two major areas, listening skills and semantics.

The *TOLD–2 Primary* is a useful measure for investigating the oral language skills of young children because it assesses several dimensions of

FIGURE 14–2

Sample results for the *Test of Language Development–2, Primary*

SECTION I   RECORD OF SCORES

SUBTESTS	Raw Scores	% iles	Standard Scores	COMPOSITES	PV	OV	GU	SI	GC	WD	WA		Sums of Std. Scores	Quotients
I Picture Vocabulary	3	2	4	Spoken Language (SLQ)	4	6	6	9	9	9	8	=	51	(81)
II Oral Vocabulary	1	9	6	Listening (LiQ)	4		6			9		=	19	(76)
III Gram. Understanding	11	9	6	Speaking (SpQ)		6		9	9		8	=	32	(87)
IV Sentence Imitation	9	37	9	Semantics (SeQ)	4	6						=	10	(70)
V Gram. Completion	13	37	9	Syntax (SyQ)			6	9	9			=	24	(87)
VI Word Discrimination	14	37	9	Phonology (PhQ)						9	7	=	16	(88)
VII Word Articulation	15	25	8											

SECTION II   PROFILE OF SCORES

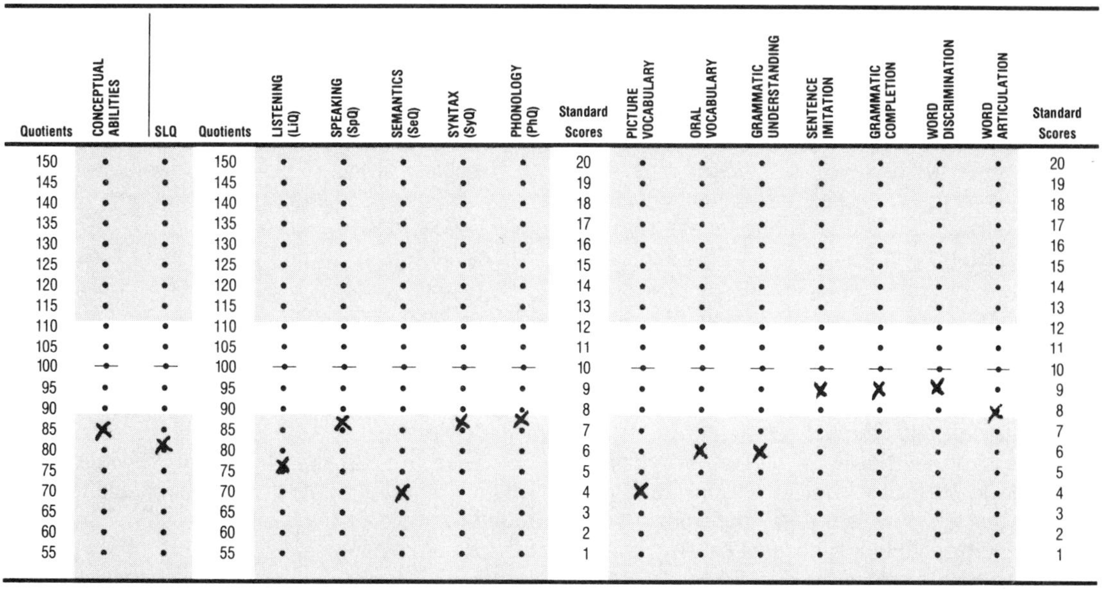

Note. From *Test of Language Development–2, Primary* (p. 24) by P. L. Newcomer and D. D. Hammill, 1988, Austin, TX: PRO-ED. Copyright 1988 by P. L. Newcomer and D. D. Hammill. Reprinted by permission.

language ability. It is best used at the start of language assessment to identify areas where the child is proficient and areas that require further evaluation.

Test of Language Development–2, Intermediate

The intermediate level of the *TOLD–2* is designed for older elementary grade students. Like the primary version, it offers measures of receptive and expressive syntax and semantics. However, phonology measures are not included.

Six subtests make up the *TOLD–2 Intermediate:*

□ *Sentence Combining* (Expressive Syntax)—The tester reads two or more simple sentences, and the student must combine these into one new sentence. As the *TOLD–2 Intermediate* manual explains, "The sentences 'John fell down. He hurt his knee,' may be combined into 'John hurt his knee when he fell down' " (p. 5).

□ *Vocabulary* (Receptive Semantics)—The tester reads pairs of words to the student, who must tell whether the words mean the same, have opposite meanings, or are unrelated.

□ *Word Ordering* (Expressive Syntax)—The tester reads several (four to seven) words in random order, and the student must put the words in order to form a sentence. For example, the words *dog, the, big, is* would be reordered to construct the sentence, "The dog is big."

□ *Generals* (Expressive Semantics)—The tester reads three words, and the student must tell how the words are alike. The manual provides this example: "If the examiner were to say, 'Venus, Mars, and Pluto,' the child might say, 'They are all gods,' 'They are all mythical characters,' or 'They are all planets' " (p. 5).

□ *Grammatic Comprehension* (Receptive Syntax)—The student listens to the tester read sentences, some of which contain syntax errors. The student tells whether the sentence is correct or incorrect, but he or she is not required to provide corrections for errors. Included are items that contain errors in noun-verb agreement, plurals, pronouns, negatives, comparative and superlative adjectives, and adverbs.

□ *Malapropisms* (Receptive Semantics)—Malapropisms are words used in place of similar-sounding words, thereby altering the meaning of the sentence. In this subtest, the tester reads sentences containing malapropisms, and the student must say the word needed to replace the malapropism. The manual says, "For example, upon hearing, 'John took a phonograph of his family,' the child must provide the word *photograph*" (p. 6).

The *TOLD–2 Intermediate* is somewhat more difficult to administer than the primary version of the test. Suggested starting points for each subtest are listed on the test form, based on the age of the student. On each subtest, the basal is five consecutive correct responses. On most subtests, the ceiling is five consecutive incorrect responses. However, on Grammatic Comprehension, a ceiling is reached when the student makes three errors in any five consecutive items. It is not necessary to administer all subtests. The short form, composed of the Generals and Sentence Combining subtests, provides a quick estimate of overall language performance.

The *TOLD–2 Intermediate* was standardized with 1,214 students from 21 states; this sample included the original norm group for the 1982 edition of the *TOLD* plus 471 students added in 1987. The final sample appears to approximate the national population in terms of sex, urban–rural residence, and geographic region; Hispanic students are somewhat overrepresented and black students somewhat underrepresented. No information is provided about handicapping conditions or home languages of students in the sample.

Reliability of the *TOLD–2 Intermediate* is generally adequate. Coefficients for internal consistency were above .80, except for the Generals subtest at age 12; and those for test-retest reliability exceeded .80, except for the Vocabulary subtest (.77). Concurrent validity was studied by examining the relationship of *TOLD–2 Intermediate* results to results from the *Test of Adolescent Language*. Significant correlations were found between the speaking and listening subtests of the *TOAL* and most *TOLD–2* subtests (median correlation .59); *TOAL* reading and writing results were found to relate to many of the *TOLD–2* subtests (median correlation = .47). It would also be useful to have information about the relationship of the *TOLD–2 Intermediate* to other tests of oral language performance.

Subtest scores on the *TOLD–2 Intermediate* are percentile ranks and standard scores. Five composite quotients are derived from subtest results: Spoken Language Quotient (an overall test score), Listening Quotient, Speaking Quotient, Semantics Quotient, and Syntax Quotient. The standard errors of measurement are 1 standard score point for subtest scores and 3 to 4 standard score points for composites.

The *TOLD–2 Intermediate* is a promising measure of oral language for older elementary grade students. Like the primary *TOLD–2,* it is best used at the start of assessment to identify the student's strengths and weaknesses in listening and speaking skills. Its results are not sufficiently specific to direct instructional planning.

Other Comprehensive Measures

Several other comprehensive measures are worthy of note. One is a clinical measure composed of a variety of oral language tests, and two are batteries that assess both oral and written language skills.

Clinical Evaluation of Language Fundamentals–Revised (CELF–R).

The *CELF–R* (Semel, Wiig, & Secord, 1987) is a diagnostic battery containing 11 subtests that assess syntax, semantics, and memory. This test is designed for students ages 5–0 to 16–11. Different sets of subtests are required for children ages 5 to 7 and those ages 8 and above, although all subtests can be used as supplementary measures at all ages.

The three subtests required for all students are

- *Oral Directions* (Receptive Language)—The student looks at a picture that shows several shapes. The tester reads directions that tell the student to point to certain shapes in a set order.
- *Formulated Sentences* (Expressive Language)—The tester shows the student a picture and reads one or two words. The student must compose a sentence about the picture that includes the stimulus word or words.
- *Recalling Sentences* (Expressive Language)—The tester reads a sentence, and the student must repeat it verbatim with no errors.

Other subtests on the *CELF–R* are Linguistic Concepts, Sentence Structure, Word Classes, Semantic Relationships, Word Structure, Sentence Assembly, Listening to Paragraphs, and Word Associations.

Results include subtest standard scores and three global standard scores: Receptive Language (representing performance on three required receptive subtests), Expressive Language (representing performance on three required expressive subtests), and Total Language (summarizing the six required subtests). An age equivalent score is available for Total Language.

The *CELF–R* battery provides several measures of receptive and expressive syntax and semantics, although phonology is not assessed. However, it may be better to begin assessment with a test other than the *CELF–R* in order to pinpoint the student's probable difficulties. Then, the tester can select the specific *CELF–R* subtests that will provide the most pertinent information.

Woodcock Language Proficiency Battery.

This measure by Woodcock (1980) is a shortened version of the *Woodcock-Johnson Psycho-Educational Battery* (Woodcock & Johnson, 1977). It contains three oral language subtests.

- *Picture Vocabulary*—The student looks at a drawing and says what it is.
- *Antonyms–Synonyms*—In Part A of this subtest, the tester reads a word, and the student says its antonym. In Part B, the student provides a synonym for a word read by the tester.
- *Analogies*—The tester reads verbal analogies (e.g., "Big is to little as up is to . . ."), and the student completes them.

These subtests do not represent a range of oral language skills; each is a measure of expressive semantics. If the student's test performance indicates some difficulty in this area, assessment would continue with additional formal tests or informal procedures.

Test of Adolescent Language–2 (TOAL–2).

The *TOAL–2* (Hammill, Brown, Larsen, & Wiederholt, 1987) is a norm-referenced measure designed for students ages 12–0 to 18–5. It requires 1 to 3 hours to administer, but most subtests can be administered to groups. Two subtests assess listening skills and two evaluate speaking.

- *Listening/Vocabulary*—The student looks at four pictures in the booklet while the tester reads a word. The student chooses the two pictures that relate to the word.

□ *Listening/Grammar*—The tester reads three sentences. The student selects the two sentences most similar in meaning.

□ *Speaking/Vocabulary*—The tester reads a word. The student is asked to produce a meaningful oral sentence that incorporates the word. (This subtest must be administered individually.)

□ *Speaking/Grammar*—The student listens to a sentence read by the tester and attempts to repeat the sentence verbatim. (This subtest must be administered individually.)

These subtests assess two dimensions of receptive and expressive language, semantics and syntax.

The *TOAL-2* is constructed so professionals can compare a student's language skills in several ways. Subtest results are expressed as standard scores, and combinations of subtests produce a variety of language quotients. An overall test score, the Adolescent Language Quotient, is available along with quotients for these areas: Listening, Speaking, Reading, Writing, Spoken Language, Written Language, Vocabulary, Grammar, Receptive Language, and Expressive Language. Thus, listening skills can be contrasted with speaking skills, and spoken language performance can be compared with written language performance. Subtest and composite results are plotted on profiles to facilitate comparisons, and the manual provides guidelines for determining whether differences are statistically significant.

STRATEGIES FOR ASSESSING ARTICULATION

Articulation refers to the production of speech sounds or phonemes. There are 44 speech sounds in the English language (Polloway & Smith, 1982). Twenty-five are consonantal sounds such as the initial phonemes in *mother* and *baby*. Consonantal sounds are produced by movements of the articulators (tongue, lips, teeth, palate and so forth). There are also 19 vocalic sounds (e.g., the initial phonemes in *at* and *open*); when these are produced, the air passes through the mouth without obstruction. Table 14–2 presents the phonemes in the English language and examples of words containing these sounds.

TABLE 14–2
Phonemes of the English language

I. Consonantal (25)		II. Vocalic (19)	
/b/	ball	/ă/	cat
/ch/	chip	/ā/	cake
/d/	dog	/â/	air
/f/	farm	/ä/	art
/g/	goat	/ĕ/	leg
/h/	home	/ē/	meal
/j/	jump	/ĭ/	pin
/k/	kite	/ī/	ice
/l/	lamp	/ŏ/	log
/m/	moon	/ō/	road
/n/	nut	/ô/	stork, ball
/ng/	song	/oi/	boy
/p/	pig	/oo/	book
/r/	rug	/o͞o/	moon
/s/	sun	/ou/	cow
/sh/	ship	/ū/	cube
/t/	top	/ŭ/	duck
/th/	thumb	/û/	fur, fern
/th/	that	/ə/	sofa, circus
/v/	vine		
/w/	witch		
/wh/	white		
/y/	yo-yo		
/z/	zipper		
/zh/	pleasure		

Note. From *Teaching Language Skills to Exceptional Learners* by E. A. Polloway and J. E. Smith, 1982, Denver: Love. Copyright 1982 by Love Publishing Company. Reprinted by permission.

Some experts separate vocalic sounds into two categories: vowels and diphthongs. Diphthongs are made up of a combination of two vowel sounds. Examples are the medial phonemes in each of these words: *paid, time, couch,* and *boil* (Culatta & Culatta, 1985).

In the assessment of articulation, a sample of the child's speech is gathered, and the speech sounds produced are evaluated in terms of accuracy and intelligibility. One way to gather a speech sample is simply to record the spontaneous utterances of the child. However, this is not efficient, because it may take the child some time to produce all of the speech sounds. Standardized measures of articulation use other strategies, and one of the most common is to present pictures or other stimuli to elicit the production of specific phonemes. For example, the *Photo Articulation*

Test (Pendergast, Dickey, Selmar, & Soder, 1984) contains 72 color photographs of objects. In naming these objects, the child produces all of the consonant, vowel, and diphthong sounds.

The *Goldman-Fristoe Test of Articulation* (Goldman & Fristoe, 1986) employs three strategies for eliciting speech sounds. The Sounds-in-Words subtest is a picture-naming task; the student is shown pictures of familiar objects and is asked to name or answer questions about them. The Sounds-in-Sentences subtest is more unusual. It contains two stories accompanied by action pictures. The stories include words that have the speech sounds with which children most often have difficulty. The tester reads a story and then asks the student to retell it. The third subtest, Stimulability, is administered last. On this measure, the tester attempts to stimulate the student to produce phonemes misarticulated earlier in the test. The student is directed to watch and listen as the tester pronounces the target sound in a syllable, within a word, and in the context of a sentence.

The *Test of Articulation Performance* (Bryant & Bryant, 1983a, 1983b) also uses a variety of procedures to elicit speech production. There are two versions of this measure—a screening test (1983b) and a diagnostic test (1983a)—and both offer a picture-naming task. The diagnostic test also includes five other measures. The first, Distinctive Features, is an error analysis system used to study the articulation errors made by the student on the first subtest. Phonemes are classified in three ways: place, or the location in the mouth where they are produced; manner, or the way they are produced (stop, nasal, fricative, etc.); and voicing, whether they are voiced or unvoiced sounds. Also available is the Selective Deep Test, which examines the influence of adjacent sounds on the production of target phonemes. On the Continuous Speech subtest, a sample of connected speech is elicited by asking the student to read or repeat sentences. The last subtest, Stimulability, looks at the student's ability to learn to articulate target phonemes when production is modeled.

Norm-referenced tests of articulation are usually administered by specially trained professionals such as speech-language pathologists. However, other professionals can collect preliminary data on students' articulation skills with informal procedures. The most common method is observation

and analysis of the student's spontaneous speech. Also, any of the strategies used by formal measures can be adapted for informal assessment. For example, the student can be asked to name pictures or objects selected to represent the speech sounds.

Figure 14–3 provides a checklist in which speech sounds are listed in the order that they are typically acquired. The teacher can use this checklist to record observation results or the findings from other informal assessments.

STRATEGIES FOR ASSESSING MORPHOLOGY AND SYNTAX

Morphology and syntax, like phonology, are dimensions of language that relate to form. Morphology is concerned with the smallest meaningful units of language, morphemes, and how these are combined into words. Syntax is the relationship of words in phrases and sentences. Several formal measures of morphology and syntax are available for young children; in normal development, most of the formal features of language are learned during the preschool and early school years. The paragraphs that follow discuss formal measures of morphology and syntax as well as techniques for the analysis of language samples.

Formal Measures

Northwestern Syntax Screening Test (NSST). The *NSST* (Lee, 1971) is designed to identify problems in either receptive or expressive syntax. Syntax, as defined by this test, includes morphology. It is an individual test appropriate for young children ages 3–0 to 7–4.

Two subtests are included, Receptive and Expressive. On the Receptive subtest, the student is shown a page containing four line drawings. The tester reads a sentence, and the student must select the drawing that represents its meaning. Two sentences are read for each page of four drawings, and the sentences vary in only one grammatical element. For example, the first sentence might be "The dog is *in front of* the couch" and the second "The dog is *on top of* the couch."

On the Expressive subtest, the student looks at two drawings while the tester reads a sentence describing each. Then, for each drawing, the tester asks, "Now, what's this picture?" The student is expected to recall the sentences read by the tester. Again, the sentence pairs differ in only one grammatical element (verb tense, preposition, singular or plural verb, etc.).

Percentile rank scores are available for each subtest. According to the manual, scores at the second to third percentile are considered below average, and children earning such scores "are almost certain to be in need of interventional language teaching" (p. 9).

The *NSST* is a screening test, and thus its purpose is to identify children in need of further assessment. However, it is best used as an informal measure because of lack of information about technical quality. The manual does not discuss reliability and validity. In addition, the sample used to standardize this measure is inadequate. Only 344 children were included, half of whom were between the ages of 5–0 and 5–11. The children represented only seven schools from "middle-

FIGURE 14–3
Speech checklist

Student _____ Age _____ Grade _____

Teacher _____ Date of evaluation _____

1. Voice Quality (check all that are appropriate)

    The student's *usual* voice quality is

    _____ pleasant to listen to   _____ like a whisper   _____ low-pitched

    _____ unpleasant to listen to   _____ nasal   _____ very loud

    _____ hoarse or husky   _____ high-pitched   _____ very soft

2. Speech Fluency (check one)

    The student's *usual* speech is

    _____ very fluent

    _____ generally fluent with occasional hesitations, repetitions, and/or prolongations of sounds and syllables

    _____ frequently dysfluent and characterized by hesitations, repetitions, and/or prolongations of sounds and syllables

3. Sound Production (check each sound that the student *usually* produces clearly and correctly)*

    *Sounds expected by age 5***

    _____ /p/ as in *pal*   _____ /g/ as in *goat*   _____ /n/ as in *not*   _____ /t/ as in *tap*

    _____ /m/ as in *map*   _____ /d/ as in *dog*   _____ /b/ as in *ball*   _____ /ng/ as in *ring*

    _____ /f/ as in *fat*   _____ /h/ as in *hit*   _____ /k/ as in *kill*   _____ /y/ as in *year*

    _____ /w/ as in *water*

    *Sounds expected by age 6***

    _____ /r/ as in *rag*   *Sounds expected by age 8***

    _____ /l/ as in *lad*   _____ /s/ as in *son*

    *Sounds expected by age 7***   _____ /z/ as in *zoo*

    _____ /ch/ as in *church*   _____ /v/ as in *very*

    _____ /sh/ as in *ship*   _____ /th/ (voiced) as in *this*

    _____ /j/ as in *junk*   *Sounds expected after age 8***

    _____ /th/ (voiceless) as in *thank* _____ /zh/ as in *azure* or *pleasure*

*Only consonant sounds are listed because most children are able to produce vowel and diphthong sounds upon entry to school
**Age norms derived from Sander (1972)

Note. From *Teaching Special Students in the Mainstream* (2nd ed.) (p. 254) by R. B. Lewis and D. H. Doorlag, 1987, Columbus, OH: Merrill. Copyright 1987 by Merrill Publishing Company. Reprinted by permission.

income and upper-middle-income communities" (p. 7).

Test for Auditory Comprehension of Language–Revised (TACL–R).

The purpose of the *TACL–R* (Carrow-Woolfolk, 1985) is assessment of receptive syntax. It is an individual test for ages 3 through 10, and three subtests are included: Word Classes and Relations, Grammatical Morphemes, and Elaborated Sentence Constructions. The test format is similar to other measures of receptive language. A page with three line drawings is shown to the student, and the student must select the drawing that best represents the meaning of the word or sentence read by the tester.

The *TACL–R* was standardized with a national sample of over 1,000 students selected to represent the U.S. population in terms of sex, race, and geographic region. Several types of scores are available, including percentile ranks and standard scores.

Carrow Elicited Language Inventory (CELI).

The *CELI*, also by Carrow-Woolfolk (1974), is a measure of expressive morphology and syntax for children ages 3–0 to 7–11. It is an individual test with one type of task: the tester reads and the child repeats a sentence. The imitation task was selected because research findings indicate a relationship between the form of children's spontaneous speech and the form of sentences they can imitate.

The 52 sentences on the *CELI* were constructed to assess several different grammatical categories and features: articles, adjectives, nouns, noun plurals, pronouns, verbs, negatives, contractions, adverbs, prepositions, demonstratives, and conjunctions. Percentile ranks are provided for the total test score as well as for each grammatical class. In addition, the student's errors are analyzed by type (substitution, omission, addition, transposition, reversal) and a percentile rank score determined for each type. A Verb Protocol is available for in-depth analysis of the child's mastery of verb forms. Scoring the *CELI* is time-consuming.

A small, restricted sample from only one city was used to standardize the *CELI*. Standardization took place in 1973 in Houston, Texas, and the sample contained 475 white children "from middle socioeconomic level homes" (p. 8). Reliability and validity were investigated, but the study samples included only 20 to 25 children. For these reasons, the *CELI* is best used as an informal measure of expressive syntax and morphology.

Analysis of Language Samples

Language samples are another method for the assessment of expressive syntax and morphology. A sample of the child's language is elicited, tape-recorded, and transcribed. The transcription is then analyzed using one of the methods described in the following paragraphs.

Mean length of utterance. The simplest way of analyzing a child's language sample is to compute the mean length of utterance (MLU). A sample of 50 consecutive utterances, at minimum, is needed for this procedure. The professional counts the number of morphemes that the child produced and divides this total by the number of utterances. MLU, according to Wiig and Semel (1984), "correlates positively (.80) with psychological scale values of degree of language development" (p. 370).

Brown (1973) developed a set of procedures for calculating MLU that has been adopted by most language development researchers (Bartel & Bryen, 1982). In Brown's system, analysis begins with the second page of the transcription of the child's language sample. The first 100 utterances are counted, although 50 are sufficient for a preliminary estimate. Counted as separate morphemes are inflections such as the possessive *s* and the regular past tense *d*. Repetitions are not counted nor are fillers such as "um" and "oh." Compound words are counted as one morpheme, as are diminutives (e.g., "kitty") and catenatives (e.g., "gonna," "wanna").

According to Brown, these procedures are reasonable only for language samples with mean lengths of utterance up to approximately 4.0. Thus, this technique is most useful for young children and children with serious language disorders.

Developmental Sentence Analysis.

Another technique is *Developmental Sentence Analysis* (Lee, 1974). This is a norm-referenced procedure, designed for children ages 2–0 to 6–11. In an interview situation, a clinician elicits a sample of the child's language using stimulus materials such as toys or pictures. The sample is transcribed and analyzed to determine what proportion of the child's utterances are complete sentences. In this system, a complete sentence is defined as a noun and verb in subject–predicate relationship. Thus, "doggie bark" is considered a complete sentence.

Fifty complete, consecutive sentences are needed to use the Developmental Sentence Scoring system. First, each word is categorized by its grammatical type. Lee states that the categories of grammatical forms included are those "showing the most significant developmental progression in children's language" (p. 136). These are

1. Indefinite pronoun or noun modifier
2. Personal pronoun
3. Main verb
4. Secondary verb
5. Negative
6. Conjunction
7. Interrogative reversal in questions
8. *Wh-* question

A chart is then consulted to assign a point value to each word. Words representing higher developmental status receive higher point values. For example, among personal pronouns, first and second person pronouns such as *I* and *you* receive 1 point, third person pronouns such as *he* and *she* receive 2 points, and plurals such as *we* receive 3 points. Point values range from 1 to 8.

The total number of points assigned to words in the sample of sentences is determined and then divided by the number of sentences (50) to produce the Developmental Sentence Score (DSS). This score can be expressed as a percentile rank. A chart is provided for determining where the score falls in relation to the 10th, 25th, 50th, 75th, and 90th percentiles for each 6-month age group between ages 2–0 and 6–6.

The norms for this procedure were derived using a sample of 200 children. Thus, there were only 20 boys and 20 girls at each age level. The children were from middle-class, monolingual homes in four states. Split-half reliability was reported as .73 over all ages, but coefficients fell in the .50s for children aged 2, 3, and 4. No information is provided about concurrent validity.

Because norms are based on a limited sample, reliability is low for very young children, and validity is not established, this technique is best viewed as an informal assessment strategy.

STRATEGIES FOR ASSESSING SEMANTICS AND PRAGMATICS

Semantics is concerned with the meaning of language. A variety of tests and other procedures are available to assess students' comprehension of language content and production of meaningful discourse. In contrast, pragmatics is concerned with language use or, in the words of Wiig and Semel (1984), language in a communicative context. Meaning is one aspect of pragmatics, but the major focus is the speaker's intent and the way language is used to fulfill that intent. To date, most of the strategies for assessing pragmatics are informal rather than formal.

Assessment of Language Meaning

Most formal measures of semantics deal with receptive skills, and the most typical test format is a picture-identification task. The tester reads a word or a sentence, and the student selects from several pictures the one that best illustrates the meaning of the word or sentence. Two well-known tests that use this format are the *Peabody Picture Vocabulary Test–Revised* and the *Boehm Test of Basic Concepts–Revised.*

Peabody Picture Vocabulary Test–Revised (PPVT–R). The *PPVT–R* (Dunn & Dunn, 1981) is an individual test of receptive vocabulary designed for ages 2½ through 40. Two forms of the test are available, and administration requires only 10 to 20 minutes. The test task remains the same throughout the *PPVT–R.* The student is shown a page containing four line drawings. The tester reads a word, and the student points to or says the number of the drawing that represents that word.

There are five training items for children under 8, and Figure 14–4 shows the stimulus pictures for the first. In presenting this item, the tester says, "Put your finger on *doll.*" The *PPVT–R* also includes 175 test items arranged in order of difficulty. In presenting these items, the tester can change the directions to "Point to _____" or "What number is _____?"

The *PPVT–R* is not divided into subtests, and only one result is obtained, an index of total test performance. Several types of scores are used to report that result: a standard score, percentile rank, stanine, and age equivalent. The manual provides norms by age, and grade norms are available from

FIGURE 14–4
Sample training item from the *Peabody Picture Vocabulary Test–Revised*

1

2

3

4

A

Note. From *Peabody Picture Vocabulary Test–Revised* by L. M. Dunn and L. M. Dunn, 1981, Circle Pines, MN: American Guidance Service. Copyright 1981 by American Guidance Service. Reprinted by permission.

the publisher. The student's score is plotted on a profile in the record form, and a confidence interval is constructed around the score.

The *PPVT–R* manual describes this test as both an achievement and a scholastic aptitude test. It is considered a test of achievement because it measures acquisition of English vocabulary, and an aptitude test because it assesses verbal skills, one of the components of many tests of intelligence. But as Dunn and Dunn observe, "It is *not,* however, a comprehensive test of general intelligence" (p. 2). The *PPVT–R* is best viewed as a measure of

one of the many dimensions of oral language development, receptive vocabulary.

The 1981 edition of the *Peabody Picture Vocabulary Test* was standardized with 4,200 individuals between the ages of 2–6 and 18–11 and 828 adults. The child sample was selected to represent the U.S. population as described in the 1970 census, and this aim was achieved. The adult sample resembled the national population only in terms of occupation.

The *PPVT–R* is a quick, easy-to-administer measure of receptive vocabulary. Its child standardization sample is adequate, although test reliability is a concern with young children, and the manual does not report validity data for the 1981 edition. The *PPVT–R* is best used as a screening tool.

Boehm Test of Basic Concepts–Revised. The *Boehm–R* (Boehm, 1986a) evaluates receptive vocabulary in young school-aged children. According to the manual, it is "designed to assess children's mastery of basic concepts that are both fundamental to understanding verbal instruction and essential for early school achievement" (p. 1). There are two forms of the test, and it is administered in group fashion to kindergarten children and students in grades 1 and 2. Administration requires approximately 30 to 40 minutes.

The test task for the *Boehm–R* is picture identification. The student looks at a row of three drawings in the test booklet. The tester reads directions that include a target concept, and the student marks an *X* on the appropriate drawing. For example, if the student is asked to "mark the paper with the star at the *top*," the test booklet might show a drawing of a paper with the star at the top, another with the star at the bottom, and the third with the star in the middle.

Students respond to a total of 50 test items. The concepts assessed are basic vocabulary words that often appear in instructional materials for young school-aged children and in teachers' directions. Included are four types of relational concepts: space (e.g., *top, between*), quantity (e.g., *some, few*), time (e.g., *after, beginning*), and miscellaneous (e.g., *different, matches*).

A supplementary Applications test is also available. This test assesses students' ability to understand basic concepts when they are used in combination and to follow multistep directions, make comparisons, and place objects in order. For example, when shown a drawing of black and white cats of different sizes, the student might be told to mark all the cats that are both white *and* small. The Applications test is most appropriate for first and second graders.

Results of the *Boehm–R* are expressed as percentile ranks. Raw scores on the basic concept task and on Applications can be converted to percentile ranks by grade, socioeconomic level, and time of year (beginning of year or midyear). In addition, the performance of an entire class can be analyzed to identify the basic concepts with which several children are unfamiliar.

The *Boehm–R* is a group test of receptive vocabulary for young school-aged children. Its standardization sample is impressive in terms of numbers, but reliability is not well established. Both alternate form and test-retest reliability coefficients are less than .80 for grades 1 and 2, although those for kindergarten are adequate. Split-half reliability varies by test form and students' grade and socioeconomic level; half of the coefficients reported for kindergarten and grade 1 students and all of those for grade 2 students fell below .80. Predictive validity was studied, and results indicate moderate relationships (.24 to .64) between *Boehm–R* scores and results of academic achievement measures given one year later.

The *Boehm–R* can be administered to an individual, rather than a group, as long as standard procedures are followed. Results are used to identify students with possible weaknesses in receptive vocabulary and to identify basic concepts that students have not yet mastered.

Measures of expressive semantics. Few tests are designed specifically for the assessment of expressive semantics. However, subtests that evaluate the ability to produce meaningful language are included on many tests of language, intellectual performance, and specific learning abilities. Table 14–3 lists several examples. A wide variety of test tasks are used. Tasks such as labeling pictures, giving synonyms and antonyms, and completing analogies require only one-word responses. Longer responses are expected on tasks such as defining words, using a word in a sentence, describing objects, describing similarities, and telling a story.

One measure that does concentrate on expressive semantics is the *Environmental Language Inventory (ELI)* (MacDonald, 1978). The *ELI* is a formal procedure for gathering information about a child's ability to produce meaningful language. Part of the procedure is the collection of a spontaneous sample of the child's language. In addition, the tester attempts to elicit eight specific types of utterances (for example, Agent + Action, Action + Object). If the goal is to elicit "Throw ball" (Action + Object), the tester pretends to throw a

TABLE 14–3
Measures of expressive semantics

Task	Subtest	Test
Complete analogy	Analogies	*Woodcock Language Proficiency Battery*
	Verbal Analogies	*Woodcock-Johnson Psycho-Educational Battery–Revised*
Define words	Oral Vocabulary	*Test of Language Development–2, Primary*
	Vocabulary	*Wechsler Intelligence Scale for Children–Revised*
	Vocabulary	*Stanford-Binet Intelligence Scale: Fourth Edition*
Describe object	Verbal Expression	*Illinois Test of Psycholinguistic Abilities*
Give antonym	Antonyms/Synonyms	*Woodcock Language Proficiency Battery*
	Oral Vocabulary	*Woodcock-Johnson Psycho-Educational Battery–Revised*
	Word Opposites	*Detroit Tests of Learning Aptitude–2*
Give synonym	Antonyms/Synonyms	*Woodcock Language Proficiency Battery*
	Oral Vocabulary	*Woodcock-Johnson Psycho-Educational Battery–Revised*
Label picture	Expressive Vocabulary	*Kaufman Assessment Battery for Children*
	Picture Vocabulary	*Woodcock Language Proficiency Battery*
	Picture Vocabulary	*Woodcock-Johnson Psycho-Educational Battery–Revised*
Tell how words are alike	Generals	*Test of Language Development–2, Intermediate*
	Similarities	*Wechsler Intelligence Scale for Children–Revised*
Tell a story about a picture	Story Construction	*Detroit Tests of Learning Aptitude–2*
Use word in a sentence	Formulated Sentences	*Clinical Evaluation of Language Fundamentals–Revised*
	Speaking/Vocabulary	*Test of Adolescent Language–2*

ball to the child and says, "What do you want me to do?" If the child does not respond, the tester says, "Say 'Throw ball'."

Informal assessment strategies. It is also possible to use informal procedures to evaluate a student's ability to comprehend and produce meaningful language. Any of the tasks used on formal tests could be adapted for this purpose. For example, if receptive vocabulary is the area of interest, the teacher can present a set of pictures or objects, name one, and direct the child to point to it. Or the child can be asked to demonstrate the meaning of action words ("Show me *jump*") or prepositions ("Put the apple in *front* of the doll"). If expressive semantics is the concern, the student can be asked to label pictures or objects, define words, use words in sentences, provide synonyms or antonyms, describe objects or events, or tell a story.

Figure 14–5 presents a checklist for recording information about vocabulary development. It lists 38 types of vocabulary—body parts, clothing, classroom objects, and so forth—and two of the major language dimensions, identification (reception) and production. In using this form, it would be helpful to generate lists of words for each vocabulary type. These lists would vary from child to child due to differences in age, gender, interests, and environments. Once this checklist was expanded, it could form the basis for a series of observations of the student's language behavior. It could also provide the professional with a structure for designing a set of informal inventories to learn more about the student's receptive and expressive vocabulary.

FIGURE 14–5
Vocabulary checklist

Basic Vocabulary/Semantics	Identifies				Produces		
	Identifies persons, things or events labeled	Comprehends words in sentences in familiar contexts	Comprehends words in sentences in unfamiliar contexts	Labels persons, things or events	Uses words in sentences in familiar contexts	Uses words in sentences in unfamiliar contexts
1. Body Parts							
2. Clothing							
3. Classroom Objects							
4. Action Verbs							
5. Verb Tasks							
6. Animals and Insects							
7. Outdoor Words							
8. Family Members							
9. Home Objects							
10. Meals							
11. Food and Drink							
12. Colors							
13. Adverbs							
14. Occupations							
15. Community							
16. Grooming Objects							
17. Vehicles							
18. Money							
19. Gender							
20. School							
21. Playthings							
22. Containers							
23. Days of the Week							
24. Months							
25. Emotions							
26. Numbers							
27. Celebrations and Holidays							
28. Spatial Concepts							
29. Quantitative Concepts							
30. Temporal Concepts							
31. Shapes							
32. Greetings and Polite Terms							
33. Opposites							
34. Materials							
35. Music							
36. Tools							
37. Categories							
38. Verbs of the Senses							

Note. From ''Language'' (p. 24) by T. Serpiglia in *Diagnosing Basic Skills* by K. W. Howell and J. S. Kaplan, 1980. Columbus, OH: Merrill. Copyright 1980 by Bell & Howell Company. Reprinted by permission.

Assessment of Language Use

Pragmatics refers to the way language is used for communication in different situations. As language skills develop, children learn to modify their choice of words and grammatical structures according to the message they intend to convey and the situation in which the communication takes place. The context of the speech act is an important variable determined by several factors:

1. The social setting and occasion of the interaction
2. The location of the interaction
3. The characteristics of the participants (gender, race, ethnicity, etc.) in the interaction
4. The topic and purpose of the interaction
5. The spatial deployment of the participants (face-to-face, at a distance, nonvisible) in the interaction
6. The role or intent of the speaker (Wiig & Semel, 1984, p. 57)

The speaker's intent influences the content and form of language and the way the message is delivered. There are several different purposes of communication, and one system for categorizing these has been proposed by Wells (1973). According to Wiig and Semel (1984), this system includes five distinct language uses.

☐ *Ritualizing*—the ritualized use of language in social situations, as in greetings, farewells, introductions, turn taking, responses to requests, and so forth.

☐ *Informing*—the use of language to give or request information.

☐ *Controlling*—the use of language to control or influence the actions of the listener.

☐ *Feeling*—the use of language to express feelings or to respond to feelings or attitudes expressed by others.

☐ *Imagining*—the use of language to create an imaginary situation, as in storytelling, role playing, speculation, or the creation of fantasies.

By the end of the elementary grades, students are expected to comprehend the different functions of language and use language appropriately to accomplish each of these purposes (Wiig & Semel, 1984). Like other dimensions of language, competence in pragmatics develops over time. Findings from research by Wiig (1982b) and others suggest that children around the age of 6 communicate from a self-oriented perspective. However, by age 12, students adapt to the listener's

needs. They are able to alter expectations, negotiate, state reasons and justifications, and communicate bad news so its impact is softened.

Let's Talk Inventories.   The *Let's Talk Inventory for Adolescents* (Wiig, 1982c) and its companion, the *Let's Talk Inventory for Children* (Bray & Wiig, 1987), are two of the few formal tools available for the assessment of pragmatic competence. They are individual measures that span the age ranges from 4 to 8 years and from 9 years to adulthood.

The assessment task is interesting. The student is shown a picture that illustrates a communication situation. Some pictures show peer interactions, others interactions between a child and adult. A short narrative is read to the student describing the situation and the intent of the speaker. The student's task is to formulate a speech act appropriate to the context, the audience, and the stated communicative intent.

Items are available to assess four of the major functions of language: ritualizing, informing, controlling, and feeling. The imagining function is not assessed, but the format of the test is role playing, a communication strategy that requires use of the imagining function. Items are also provided to assess receptive pragmatics, if the student experiences difficulty with the expressive tasks.

Test of Pragmatic Skills (rev. ed.).   Shulman's (1986) *Test of Pragmatic Skills (rev. ed.)* is designed for students ages 3 to 8. The test tasks are four guided play interactions in which the tester follows a script to elicit responses from the child. For example, in the first interaction, the student and tester use puppets to converse about favorite television shows. The test probes 10 types of communicative intents: requesting information, requesting action, rejection/denial, naming/labeling, answering/responding, informing, reasoning, summoning/calling, greeting, and closing conversation.

Informal assessment strategies.   Informal strategies can also be used to investigate pragmatic performance. Mercer and Mercer (1989) suggest that a spontaneous sample of the student's speech can be analyzed to determine the types of language functions the student uses. Videotaping is the best way to record the language sample, because it allows the professional to study the situation in which the communication occurred. If this is not possible, the student can be audiotaped while an observer records the events that occur before and after each speech act. The professional evaluates each utterance in relation to the events that preceded and followed it and then assigns the utterance to a function category.

There are several other strategies for informal assessment of pragmatic competence. Students can be observed as they engage in conversational interactions with peers and adults, or the teacher can set up a role playing situation to evaluate specific types of communications. For example, if observations reveal that a student rarely uses language for the ritualizing function, the student could be asked to participate in role plays such as meeting a friend on the way to school, leaving a party, and so on. Receptive skills can be probed with videotapes or pictures that present conversational interactions. For example, if the controlling function of language is of interest, the teacher could show a picture of two children, one of whom is playing with a toy truck. The student would then be asked to select the more appropriate request: "Give me that truck!" or "May I please play with the truck a little while?"

Figure 14–6 presents a checklist (Wiig, 1982b) designed to record the pragmatics performance of preadolescents and adolescents. It covers four language functions, and several language behaviors are listed for each of the functions. For example, behaviors such as "Introduces him/herself appropriately" are included under the ritualizing function. The student is rated according to how often he or she engages in each language behavior. In addition, the professional can record the quality of the speech acts observed: informal, formal, direct, or indirect. This checklist is used to record results of observations and can also serve as a guide for planning further assessment of expressive pragmatics.

ASSESSING STUDENTS WHO SPEAK NONSTANDARD ENGLISH

Not all persons who speak English pronounce the speech sounds in the same way, nor do they use the same syntax, morphology, and vocabulary. The variations that occur within languages are called dialects, and there are many dialects of English.

For example, the English spoken in Great Britain is not the same as that spoken in America or in Australia. Within the United States, there are regional variations. Words are pronounced differently in Maine, New York, and Louisiana, and variations occur in grammatical structure and word meaning. In addition, some American English dialects are related to population characteristics rather than geographic region. Examples are Black English and the English spoken by some persons whose first language was Spanish.

Many variations of English are spoken in the United States, and Standard English is only one. Other dialects should be considered different from, but not inferior to, Standard English. This is the issue of language difference versus language deficit (Polloway & Smith, 1982). The deficit position holds that the language of persons from lower socioeconomic levels is a restricted code and therefore represents a deficit; it is substandard, rather than nonstandard, English. The difference position, based primarily on studies of Black English, maintains that nonstandard English is a complete linguistic system, different from, but not inferior to, the standard dialect. Most educators today support the difference position.

The language that a child or adult uses for communication is influenced by several factors. Wiig and Semel (1984) suggest that the major influences include

□ First language community and culture
□ Race and ethnicity
□ Geographic region
□ Social class, education, and occupation
□ Age
□ Gender
□ Peer group association and identification
□ Situation-context (pp. 54–57)

The last factor, situation-context, refers to the setting in which a particular communication takes place. Speakers alter their language to fit the communicative context. This is called style switching, and bidialectical speakers are able to change from one dialect to another depending upon the situation, setting, and audience of the communication. For example, a person who speaks nonstandard English in one context (e.g., a conversation with a close friend) may speak Standard English in another (e.g., a job interview) (Cohen & Plaskon, 1980).

FIGURE 14–6
Communication skills checklist

Name _____ Birth Date _____ Sex _____

Address _____

Classroom _____ Teacher _____ Date _____

Other Information _____

COMMUNICATION ACTS			RATINGS			QUALITY
	Never	Seldom	Sometimes	Often	Always	

Ritualizing

	Never	Seldom	Sometimes	Often	Always
1. Greets others appropriately	1	2	3	4	5
2. Introduces him/herself appropriately	1	2	3	4	5
3. Introduces people to each other appropriately	1	2	3	4	5
4. Greets others appropriately when telephoning	1	2	3	4	5
5. Introduces him/herself appropriately when telephoning	1	2	3	4	5
6. Asks for persons appropriately when telephoning	1	2	3	4	5
7. Says farewell appropriately	1	2	3	4	5
8. Asks others to repeat appropriately	1	2	3	4	5
9. Gives name (first and last) on request	1	2	3	4	5
10. Gives address (number, street, town, etc.) on request	1	2	3	4	5
11. Gives telephone number on request	1	2	3	4	5

Informing

	Never	Seldom	Sometimes	Often	Always
1. Asks others appropriately for name	1	2	3	4	5
2. Asks others appropriately for address	1	2	3	4	5
3. Asks others appropriately for telephone number	1	2	3	4	5
4. Asks others appropriately for the location of belongings and necessities	1	2	3	4	5
5. Asks others appropriately for the location of events	1	2	3	4	5
6. Responds appropriately to requests for the location of events	1	2	3	4	5
7. Asks others appropriately for the time of events	1	2	3	4	5
8. Responds appropriately to requests for the time of events	1	2	3	4	5
9. Asks others appropriately for preferences or wants	1	2	3	4	5
10. Responds appropriately to requests for preferences or wants	1	2	3	4	5
11. Tells others realistically about abilities	1	2	3	4	5
12. Tells realistically about the levels of various abilities	1	2	3	4	5
13. Asks appropriately for information by telephone	1	2	3	4	5
14. Asks appropriately for permission to leave messages	1	2	3	4	5
15. Tells appropriately who a message is for	1	2	3	4	5
16. Leaves appropriately expressed messages	1	2	3	4	5

continued

FIGURE 14–6 *continued*

COMMUNICATION ACTS	Never	Seldom	Sometimes	Often	Always	QUALITY
Controlling						
1. Suggests places for meetings appropriately	1	2	3	4	5	
2. Suggests names for meetings appropriately	1	2	3	4	5	
3. Asks appropriately for permission	1	2	3	4	5	
4. Asks appropriately for reasons	1	2	3	4	5	
5. Tells reasons appropriately	1	2	3	4	5	
6. Asks appropriately for favors:	1	2	3	4	5	
7. Responds appropriately to requests for favors:						
a. Accepts and carries out	1	2	3	4	5	
b. Evades or delays	1	2	3	4	5	
c. Rejects	1	2	3	4	5	
8. Offers assistance appropriately	1	2	3	4	5	
9. Makes complaints appropriately:	1	2	3	4	5	
10. Responds to complaints appropriately:	1	2	3	4	5	
a. Accepts blame and suggests action						
b. Evades or refers	1	2	3	4	5	
c. Rejects blame	1	2	3	4	5	
11. Asks for intentions appropriately	1	2	3	4	5	
12. Responds appropriately to requests for intentions	1	2	3	4	5	
13. Asks to discontinue actions appropriately	1	2	3	4	5	
14. Asks appropriately for terms of contract:						
a. Pay	1	2	3	4	5	
b. Work hours	1	2	3	4	5	
c. Vacations, etc.	1	2	3	4	5	
d. Other	1	2	3	4	5	
15. Asks appropriately for changes in contractual terms:						
a. Pay	1	2	3	4	5	
b. Work hours	1	2	3	4	5	
c. Vacations, etc.	1	2	3	4	5	
d. Other	1	2	3	4	5	
Feelings						
1. Expresses appreciation appropriately	1	2	3	4	5	
2. Apologizes appropriately	1	2	3	4	5	
3. Expresses agreement appropriately	1	2	3	4	5	
4. Expresses disagreement appropriately	1	2	3	4	5	
5. Expresses support appropriately	1	2	3	4	5	
6. Compliments appropriately	1	2	3	4	5	
7. Expresses affection appropriately	1	2	3	4	5	
8. Expresses positive feelings and attitudes appropriately	1	2	3	4	5	
9. Expresses negative feelings and attitudes appropriately	1	2	3	4	5	

Note. From *Let's Talk: Developing Prosocial Communication Skills* (pp. 23–25) by E. H. Wiig, 1982. Copyright © 1982 by The Psychological Corporation, San Antonio, Texas. All rights reserved. Reproduced by permission.

In discussing the possible goals of language instruction for nonstandard English speakers, Cohen and Plaskon review three alternatives: eradication of the nonstandard dialect, complete acceptance of the nonstandard dialect, and bidialectalism. Of these options, the last is most commonly accepted. Teaching students to speak Standard English while maintaining their competence in the original dialect allows them to meet linguistic demands in a variety of communication settings.

Dialectical Differences

Dialects differ along the major dimensions of language: phonology, morphology, syntax, semantics, and pragmatics. However, the areas of dialectical difference that have been studied most extensively are phonological differences and variations in morphology and syntax.

Black English is a dialect spoken by Blacks in large urban centers (Polloway & Smith, 1982). There are two recognized variations of Black English: standard Black English, used by educated Blacks for interpersonal communications; and Black English vernacular, spoken primarily by working-class people (Wiig & Semel, 1984). Although there are systematic differences between Black English and Standard English, Wiig and Semel point out that "the overwhelming majority of utterances in Black English conform with the linguistic rules of Standard English" (p. 55).

Pronunciation of speech sounds is one area of difference. Engquist (1974) describes the most common phonological variations in Black English:

1. Softening of the r sound (e.g., sister/sistah, poor/po', Carter/Cahtuh).
2. Lessening of the l sound (e.g., help/hep, all/awe, tool/too).
3. Weakening of final consonants in clusters (e.g., past/pass, hold/hol, bent/ben).
4. Specific sound substitutions (e.g., f for th, as in mouth/mouf; d for th, as in this/dis; i for e, as in pen/pin; ah for i, as in I/ah).
   (as cited in Polloway & Smith, 1982, pp. 72–73)

Some phonological characteristics of Black English have morphological consequences. According to Bartel, Grill, and Bryen (1973), the most common morphological variations involve omissions of the final sounds of words. Final sounds are omitted in verbs (present, past, and future tense), possessives, and plurals. For instance, when final /t/ and /d/ sounds are omitted, past tense verbs sound like present tense verbs ("pass" for "passed") (Cohen & Plaskon, 1980). When the final /l/ sound is omitted, future tense sounds like present ("she" for "she'll"). When the final /s/ or /z/ sound is omitted, singular verbs sound like plural verbs ("hit" for "hits"), and plural nouns sound like singular nouns ("cent" for "cents").

In Black English, variations occur in all parts of speech, but most often in verbs. Use of the verb to be in Black English is quite different from standard English. For example, the copula may be omitted (e.g., "He tired") or be used in place of other verb forms (e.g., "They always be messing around") (Ruddell, 1974).

Dialectical differences also occur in English speakers whose first language was Spanish. English is influenced by the first language, and several phonological, morphological, and syntactical variations result. The speech sounds in Spanish are not the same as those in English. For example, Spanish does not have the vowel sounds in pig, fat, or sun (Wiig, 1982a). Several English consonant sounds are either not present or pronounced differently in Spanish. Thus, when Spanish-speakers learn English, they substitute phonemes they can pronounce for those not in their speech sound repertoire. For example, "bit" is pronounced "beat" and "bat" is pronounced "bet" (Cohen & Plaskon, 1980).

Similarly, the morphology, syntax, and semantics of the Spanish language may interfere with English expression. A word or phrase in one language may convey an entirely different meaning when translated into another. Condon, Peters, and Sueiro-Ross (1979) cite these examples from Lado (1968):

☐ The Spanish compliment "Que grueso estas," which is translated literally as "how fat you are," becomes an insult in English.
☐ The use of the name "Jesus" for a boy is quite common in Hispanic society, but not in the Anglo-Saxon community, where it is regarded as inappropriate, if not sacrilegious.
☐ To be "informal" in Spanish is "to be neglectful," but to be so in English simply conveys the notion of "casual" behavior. (Condon, Peters, & Sueiro-Ross, 1979, p. 82)

Descriptions of some of the morphological and syntactical variations of Spanish-influenced English are provided in Table 14–4.

Information is available about the characteristics of other, less common dialectical variations of English. Interested readers should refer to Wiig and Semel (1984) for descriptions of Appalachian English and the Southern White dialect, to Adler and Birdsong (1983) for the phonological characteristics of Mountain English, and to Cheng (1987) for a discussion of the influences of the Asian languages on English.

TABLE 14–4
Morphological and syntactical characteristics of Spanish-influenced English

Spanish uses equivalents of *more* and *most* to form all comparatives and superlatives of adjectives. Thus, interference may produce sentences such as

> Elephants are *more* big than cows.
>
> Dotty is the *most* nice of all.
>
> Likewise, since Spanish does not form noun plurals and noun possessives with suffixes as English does, the speaker whose dominant language is Spanish may make the following kinds of mistakes:
>
> The *car are* new.
>
> That is the car *of my mother.*

Similarly, suffixes used to form verbs in English have no Spanish equivalents, so the Spanish influence may lead to sentences like these:

> Baby is sleep＿＿＿ . (-ing)
>
> John walk＿＿＿ to school. (-s)
>
> Betty walk＿＿＿ to school yesterday. (-ed)

In addition, differences in word order and vocabulary interfere in learning grammar, as indicated in these sentences:

> *No* go now. (Don't)
>
> Iris is *no* here. (not)
>
> *Jorge can* come? (Can Jorge?)
>
> *You* like ice cream? (Do you)
>
> I *have thirst.* (am thirsty)
>
> Dinner is *in* the table. (on)
>
> The *car red* is mine. (red car)
>
> Mrs. Jones is *teacher.* (the teacher)

Note. From "Communication Disorders" (p. 92) by E. H. Wiig, in *Exceptional Children and Youth* (3rd ed.) by N. G. Haring (Ed.), 1982, Columbus, OH: Merrill. Copyright 1982 by Bell & Howell Company. Reprinted by permission.

Assessment Strategies

Dialect must be considered in the assessment of oral language. A dialect is not a language disorder, but it can be mistaken for one if the professional conducting the assessment does not recognize its influence on receptive and expressive language. Terrell and Terrell (1983) discuss three types of errors that can occur if the role of dialect is not well understood. First, professionals can assume that all minority group students are normal dialect speakers and thus fail to assess their language competence. Second, if students are assessed, professionals can overcompensate for dialect and assume that true disorders are dialectical characteristics. Third, professionals can undercompensate for dialect and mistake dialectical differences for language disorders.

Dialect is a concern in the assessment of skills other than oral language. Adler and Birdsong (1983), in their discussion of bias in standardized testing, point out the effects of dialect on students' performance on measures of auditory discrimina-

tion. For example, on the *Auditory Discrimination Test* by Wepman (1975), Adler and Birdsong identify six pairs of words that may sound alike to children who speak dialects (e.g., "tub/tug" and "pen/pin"). This is a serious problem. On the second edition of the *Auditory Discrimination Test* (Reynolds, 1987), a 7-year-old making six errors scores at the 16th percentile.

Dialectical differences also affect performance of academic skills. Variations in the pronunciation of phonemes may result in what appear to be decoding errors in reading. Written language may be affected, too. If students spell words as they pronounce them, their spelling will not conform to Standard English expectations. Likewise, dialectical variations in morphology, syntax, and semantics can result in compositions that contain nonstandard English sentences and paragraphs.

Unfortunately, there are no widely accepted standardized techniques for the assessment of language competence in students who speak dialects. Terrell and Terrell (1983) observe that "the development of dialect-sensitive or culture-fair language tests has not kept pace with the development of testing materials designed to assess the speech and language of standard-English speakers'' (p. 3). This presents a major obstacle to the responsible professional. Whether a student speaks a dialect must be established in assessment. It cannot be assumed because of some ethnic, cultural, or social characteristic.

One strategy for the assessment of speakers of dialects is to rely on informal procedures. Leonard and Weiss (1983) recommend the collection of spontaneous speech samples in naturalistic settings; these samples are analyzed for instances of dialectical usage. However, in some cases, dialectical variations are similar to the speech produced by young, normally developing children and older children with language disorders. For example, both these children and persons who speak Black English may omit -s endings on possessives and plurals. Thus, it is most productive to concentrate on dialectical variations that are different from the variations that occur in normal development.

Sentence repetition is another useful informal technique (Adler & Birdsong, 1983). Sentence repetition tasks are based on the assumption that when children are asked to repeat a sentence, they will reconstruct the sentence and say it in their own dialect. Adler and Birdsong (1983) also suggest strategies for determining whether a particular utterance is nonstandard (dialectical) or substandard (an error). One approach is to interview other children who speak the dialect. If a significant number of children (e.g., 50%) use the linguistic pattern, it can be assumed to be part of the dialect.

Once the characteristics of the student's dialectical language have been established, it is possible to begin selecting tools for assessment. This process must take into account the possibility of bias. Taylor and Payne (1983) suggest that the language characteristics of individual test items be analyzed. Such an analysis would take into account the language characteristics of each test item, in relation to Standard English and the dialect of the student. In many cases, items will be answered in one way if the rules of Standard English are followed and in another way (that would be scored as incorrect) if the rules of the nonstandard dialect are followed.

When tests contain such items, professionals face a limited number of options. The best solution is to eliminate the test from the battery and substitute another, more appropriate test. If a better measure is not available, the test can still be eliminated and informal procedures used in its place. Sometimes, however, comparative data are needed and informal procedures will not suffice. In such cases, there are two legitimate courses of action. First, the test can be renormed with members of the student's language group (Adler & Birdsong, 1983; Taylor & Payne, 1983). This is an expensive and impractical option unless a large number of students need revised norms. The second approach is to administer the test in the standard fashion and report two types of results: the student's score in relation to test norms and the expectations for Standard English, and an alternate score where dialectical responses (if correct according to the rules of the dialect) are scored as correct. Like all alternate scores, these must be interpreted with caution. However, by using this technique, the characteristics of the student's language are considered rather than ignored, and the student is not penalized for language differences. In addition, some information is produced about the student's relative proficiency in Standard English and the dialect.

ASSESSING STUDENTS WHO SPEAK LANGUAGES OTHER THAN ENGLISH

According to a report by the National Advisory Council for Bilingual Education (1980–81), the number of persons of non-English-language background in the United States will reach almost 40 million by the year 2000, and by 1990 there will be approximately 3 million school-aged children with limited proficiency in the English language. The great majority will speak Spanish as their first language. Among the other languages to be represented are Chinese, Filipino, French, German, Greek, Italian, Navajo, Polish, Portuguese, and Vietnamese.

Assessment of students who speak languages other than English has two purposes. The first is determination of the student's language proficiency, both in the first language (L1) and in English, the language of the school. With most students, English is the second language (L2), although English can be the third or even fourth language of the child. Assessment of language proficiency provides professionals with information about the student's relative competence in each language, so that the language or languages of assessment can be determined. Once this decision is made, assessment continues to explore the need for educational intervention.

With this population, intervention can take several forms, and one of the most common is bilingual education. Bilingual education programs are designed primarily for students with limited English proficiency (LEP). Bergin (1980) describes the major components of bilingual instructional programs:

☐ Native language instruction
☐ English as a second language (ESL)
☐ Cultural heritage
☐ Content area instruction (p. 21)

Several different models are used in the United States to deliver bilingual education (Baca & Cervantes, 1984). In the transitional model, first language instruction is provided only as a transition to English; when English skills have been developed, English becomes the language of instruction. The full bilingual model, in contrast, attempts to develop competency in both languages. Instruction takes place in the first language and in English for all school subjects throughout the program.

The development and maintenance of both languages has several advantages. Bilingualism itself is an advantage. The ability to communicate in more than one language is a strength that the regular curriculum of secondary schools attempts to impart to monolingual students via foreign language instruction. In addition, Cummins (1981, 1983) suggests that first and second language academic skills are interdependent. This is the theory of common underlying proficiency. Although the surface features of the first and second languages may differ, the cognitive and academic skills learned in one language will transfer to another language. Cummins (1983) explains this concept in relation to a Spanish-English bilingual program:

Spanish instruction which develops first-language reading skills for Spanish-speaking students is not just developing *Spanish* skills, but also a deeper conceptual and linguistic proficiency which is strongly related to the development of *English* literacy and general academic skills. (p. 376)

When students are identified as both limited in English proficiency *and* handicapped, decisions

about appropriate services become more complex. In some cases, the student will receive both bilingual and special education services. In other cases, a bilingual special education program may be available. There are a number of ways that special and bilingual services can be combined: bilingual education with support from special education, special education with bilingual support services, special education with a bilingual teacher, and special education with a bilingual aide, volunteer, or peer tutor (Plata, 1982).

Language Proficiency

Payan (1989) defines language proficiency as

the degree to which the student exhibits control over the use of language, including the measurement of *expressive* and *receptive* language skills in the areas of phonology, syntax, vocabulary, and semantics and including the area of pragmatics or language use within various domains or social circumstances. (p. 127)

Proficiency in one language is judged independently from proficiency in other languages. It is possible for students to show proficiency in both the first language (L1) and English (L2), in L1 but not in L2, or in L2 but not in L1.

Language proficiency is not a simple, unitary skill. According to Cummins (1981), there are two major dimensions of language proficiency. Basic interpersonal communication skills (BICS) are the spoken skills of the language community and are acquired by almost all community members. Cognitive/academic language proficiency (CALP), in contrast, is the set of language skills needed to function in the academic environment of school.

In second language learning, proficiency in basic interpersonal communication is acquired much more quickly than cognitive/academic proficiency (Cummins, 1982). In face-to-face interpersonal communications, a variety of extralingual supports are available to assist communication: intonation, facial expression, loudness of voice, gestures, body language, and so forth. The communication is context-embedded. In the classroom, there are fewer extralingual cues, making the communication situation more context-reduced.

These differences have important implications for assessment. Evidence of competence in basic communication skills does not guarantee that the student will also speak and understand the language necessary for classroom communications.

Mercer (1983) contends that "a thorough linguistic assessment of the bilingual student requires assessment of basic interpersonal communication skills in *both* languages and cognitive/academic skills in *both* languages" (p. 49).

Current practices in the assessment of language proficiency include two major steps. The home language is determined through a language background questionnaire or interview, and the student's skills are assessed with one of the available language proficiency measures. The language background questionnaire or interview is used to gather information from the child's parents about which language or languages are spoken in the home. If a language other than English is spoken, this alerts the school that the student *may* also speak this language. As Payan (1989) comments, "The types of questions commonly presented in language background questionnaires will not directly identify the language the child commands readily but will describe the child's linguistic environment, the amount of language input received, and impressions of the child's communicative abilities" (p. 132).

To determine the child's language proficiency, it is necessary to assess the child. There are several measures available for this purpose, as Table 14–5 illustrates. However, except for the *Basic Inventory of Natural Language,* a formal procedure for the collection of language samples, and the *Ber-Sil* tests, most measures are designed for students whose first language is Spanish. Although Spanish-speakers are the largest language minority group in the United States, many professionals are also interested in assessing the language proficiency of students who speak languages other than Spanish. According to Lynch and Lewis (1987), a major problem in assessment is "the lack of appropriate measures in many of the languages spoken by students in schools today; particular difficulties arise with the Pan-Asian group" (p. 404).

Cheng (1987) presents several informal tools for assessing the oral language skills of Asian students. She also lists a number of language proficiency tests appropriate for this population that are available from school districts and other noncommercial sources.

Most of the instruments for assessing language proficiency in Spanish and English are designed to determine the student's dominant language. The dominant language (also called primary language)

is the language in which the student is most proficient. A more complex method of categorizing language proficiency was recommended in the *Lau Remedies* (Office for Civil Rights, 1975). The *Lau Remedies* were proposed by a federal task force established in response to the landmark *Lau v. Nichols* case (1974). The issue in this class-action suit was denial of equal educational opportunity to non-English-speaking students by providing instruction only in English. The *Lau Remedies* recognize five categories of language proficiency, and Cegelka (1988) describes these as

1. Monolingual speaker of a language other than English; speaks this language exclusively.
2. Predominantly speaks the language other than English, although some English is spoken.
3. Bilingual, speaks both English and primary language with equal ease.
4. Predominantly speaks English, although not exclusively.
5. Monolingual speaker of English; speaks this language exclusively (p. 555).

One issue in the use of tests that assess languages other than English is who will administer them. According to Juárez (1983), native-English speakers should administer English versions of tests, and native-minority-language speakers should administer minority-language versions. Bilingual professionals are able to fill both roles, provided, of course, they have adequate training in test administration. Some measures attempt to minimize the need for minority-language proficiency by the tester by using audiotapes to present test items. This practice may help standardize administration procedures, but it does not eliminate the need for a tester who can speak the student's own language, understand the student's communications, and record responses to test items.

Another issue relates to the equivalency of language proficiency measures. Wald (1982) reports the results of a study that compared three of these measures, the *Basic Inventory of Natural Language (BINL),* the *Bilingual Syntax Measure (BSM),* and the *Language Assessment Scales (LAS).* Minimal correlations were found between the measures, and each identified a different portion of the population as limited in English proficiency (LEP). With the *BINL,* 73% of the students participating in the study were identified as LEP.

TABLE 14–5
Measures of language proficiency

Name (Authors)	Ages or Grades	Language(s)	Oral Language Skills Assessed
Basic Inventory of Natural Language (Herbert, 1977, 1979, 1983)	Gr. K to 12	Spanish and 31 other languages	A language sample is scored for fluency, complexity, and average sentence length
Ber-Sil Elementary and Secondary Spanish Tests (Beringer, 1987, 1984)	Ages 5 to 12 and 13 to 17	Spanish, Tagalog, Ilokano; Elementary also available in Cantonese, Mandarin, Korean, Persian	Receptive vocabulary
Bilingual Syntax Measure I and II (Burt, Dulay, & Chávez, 1978)	Gr. pre-K to 12	Spanish, English	Expressive syntax
Dos Amigos Verbal Language Scales (Critchlow, 1973)	Ages 5 to 13	Spanish, English	Expressive vocabulary
Language Assessment Scales–Oral (DeAvila & Duncan, 1975–1985)	Gr. K to 12	Spanish, English	Phonemic, lexical, syntactical, and pragmatic aspects of language
Prueba de Desarrollo Inicial de Leguaje (Hresko, Reid, & Hammill, 1982)	Ages 3 to 7	Spanish	Receptive and expressive syntax and semantics
Woodcock Language Proficiency Battery, English Form and Spanish Form (Woodcock, 1980, 1981)	Ages 3 to 80 +	Spanish, English	Receptive and expressive semantics

Fewer were identified by the *LAS* (30%) and the smallest percentage by the *BSM* (19%).

Juárez (1983) contends that "informal measures tend to be more accurate predictors of communicative competence than formal tests" (p. 60). Generally, informal techniques are the only alternative if pragmatics is the concern. In addition, for many languages, informal assessment may be the only approach available if there is interest in evaluating both basic interpersonal communication skills and cognitive/academic language proficiency. Among the available informal strategies are observation of the student in communication situations, collection and analysis of samples of the student's natural language, and administration of informal inventories and criterion-referenced tests to evaluate specific receptive and expressive language skills.

Special Education Assessment for Bilingual Students

When students who speak languages other than English are referred for special education assessment, a first step is the study of language proficiency. If one language is clearly dominant, then special education assessment will take place in that language. For example, if the student speaks only Spanish, Spanish-language assessment tools should be selected.

When students show some proficiency in both English and their first language, then the decision about the language of assessment is not as straightforward. In general, the best course of action in this situation is to assess in both languages. Baca and Cervantes (1989) explain,

Overall, it would be in the student's best interest to have as much data as possible regarding functioning in both languages in order to determine strengths and weaknesses, as well as to aid in the development of prescriptive measures for remediation. (p. 171)

The language of assessment is not the only consideration. The recent history of special education has been marked by controversy over the assessment of minority group students and the disproportionate placement of such students in special education classes for the mentally retarded. Although concerns about testing abuses and inappropriate placement abated somewhat in the late 1970s with the passage of PL 94–142 with its guarantees of due process and requirements for nondiscriminatory assessment, the issues continue to command attention today. As Messick (1984) reports, "For the past 12 years, national surveys by the Office for Civil Rights (OCR) of the U.S. Department of Education have revealed an overrepresentation of minority children and males in special education programs for mentally retarded students" (p. 3).

In response to these data, the National Academy of Sciences Panel on Selection and Placement of Students in Programs for the Mentally Retarded was formed. The report of that panel, *Placing Children in Special Education: A Strategy for Equity* (Heller, Holtzman, & Messick, 1982), addresses both assessment and instruction, and a two-phase comprehensive assessment process is recommended for eligibility decisions.

The first phase in assessment should be study of the student's learning environment and investigation of the nature and quality of regular classroom instruction. In Messick's (1984) words,

Only after deficiencies in the learning environment have been ruled out, by documenting that the child fails to learn under reasonable alternative instructional approaches, should the child be exposed to the risks of stigma and misclassification inherent in referral and individual assessment. (p. 5)

Four types of information are gathered during the first phase of the comprehensive assessment process:

1. Evidence that the school is using programs and curricula shown to be effective not just for students in general but for the various ethnic, linguistic, and socioeconomic groups actually served by the school in question.
2. Evidence that the students in question have been adequately exposed to the curriculum by virtue of not having missed many lessons due to absence or disciplinary exclusions from class, and that the teacher has implemented the curriculum effectively (e.g., evidence that the teacher makes effective use of the flexibility afforded by the curriculum in choosing instructional strategies and materials, that the child receives appropriate direction, feedback, and reinforcement, that other children in the class are performing acceptably, etc.).
3. Evidence that the child has not learned what was taught.
4. Evidence that systematic efforts were, or are being, made to identify the learning difficulty and to take corrective instructional action, such as intro-

ducing remedial approaches, changing the curriculum materials, or trying a new teacher. (Messick, 1984, p. 5)

The second phase of assessment is undertaken only if it is established that an achievement problem exists despite the provision of appropriate instruction in the regular classroom.

With students who speak languages other than English, special education assessment is conducted in the language or languages in which students are most proficient. Several measures are available in a variety of skill areas for Spanish-speaking students, as Table 14–6 shows. As with language proficiency tests, Spanish is the language most often represented on minority-language versions of special education assessment devices. Most of the measures listed in Table 14–6 have English-language counterparts that have been discussed earlier.

Obviously, the methods used to develop Spanish-language tests affect both technical adequacy and educational usefulness. According to Payan (1989), minority-language tests should not be direct translations of English-language tests. Literal translation may not take into account the subtle differences between languages and cultures, so items on the minority-language version of the test become either more difficult or easier than their English-language counterparts.

The characteristics of the standardization sample are a critical concern in selection of minority-language tests. Tests based on English-language measures may not have been renormed with minority-language speakers. If that is the case, professionals are forced to develop local norms or use the test as an informal measure; norms developed with English-speakers are inappropriate for non-English-speaking students. If norms are available, the characteristics of the standardization sample must be carefully evaluated. As with English, there are many dialects of Spanish and of other languages. Lynch and Lewis (1987) caution that "Spanish-language tests prepared for use in Mexico may not be appropriate for Cuban refugees in urban areas of Florida or for Mexican-American students in the rural southwest" (p. 404).

The selection of appropriate tools for assessment becomes even more difficult when students speak languages other than Spanish. Often, no technically adequate measures are available in the student's language. When this occurs, professionals could choose not to assess the student or assess with English-language measures. However, neither of these tactics is acceptable. Failure to assess may result in inappropriate placement of the student in special education or retention in regular education. Testing non-English-speakers with English-language tests is clearly discriminatory.

More acceptable options are the use of interpreters to assist in administration of English-language measures and the development of informal measures in the student's language. Interpreters are not a perfect solution, although in many cases they may be the only alternative if the language of the student is not a common one. Plata (1982) describes several pitfalls in the use of interpreters for test administration:

(a) On-the-spot translation is very difficult, especially when the interpreter does not know the technical language found in test items.
(b) Many words lose their meaning in the translation process.
(c) The interpreter may not know all the possible terms or dialects applied to a word or concept, especially if the child being tested is from a different geographic region than that of the interpreter.
(d) There may be hostile feelings toward the examiner on the part of an interpreter who feels that he or she is "being used" to "cover up" inadequacies of the examiner or if the interpreter perceives the remuneration to be minimal for doing the work of a highly paid professional. (p. 4)

However, Plata concedes that "using interpreters to try to compromise the effect of the examinee's language on test results is better than no attempt at all" (p. 4). When English-language tests are administered via an interpreter, test norms no longer apply. Results should be viewed as alternate scores, or more realistically, the test should be treated as an informal measure.

The other strategy available to professionals is development of informal measures in the language of the student. As with norm-referenced tests, these should not be direct translations of English-language measures. The design of informal inventories, criterion-referenced tests, and other informal instruments requires proficiency in the child's language. If this is not available among the professional staff of the school or district, translators become necessary for the development of the assessments and interpreters for their administration. Again, this is not a perfect solution to the problem, but it is sometimes a workable alternative for students who speak uncommon minority languages.

WITHIN THE CONTEXT OF THE CLASSROOM

The classroom learning environment is an important concern in the assessment of oral language skills, both for special students with educational needs in the area of oral language and for those who speak nonstandard English dialects or languages other than English. So far discussion has focused on assessment strategies for gathering information about the student's performance. The emphasis now shifts to procedures and techniques for studying the classroom learning environment and its influence on the student's oral language skills.

The Instructional Environment

Oral language is usually not taught as a separate subject in regular classrooms, except in the early elementary grades. However, oral language demands pervade the entire curriculum. Students are expected to listen to and understand the teacher and others in the classroom. They are also expected to be fluent in the language of the classroom and to be able oral communicators.

One aspect of the learning environment is the communication skill of the teacher. This is important both in the early elementary grades, where most of the instructional content is delivered orally, and in the secondary grades, where teachers rely heavily on lecture as a method for the presentation of new information. Factors to consider are as follows:

☐ When oral directions are given, does the teacher prepare the students for what is to come?
☐ Does the teacher make sure that the purposes for listening are clear to each student?
☐ Is the teacher usually talking, or does the teacher listen to students as speakers? (Russell & Russell, 1959)

Other dimensions of teacher behavior that may influence students' ability to listen effectively are described by Alley and Deshler (1979):

1. *Nonlinguistic communication.* Does the teacher make effective use of gestures, eye contact, pauses?

2. *Preorganizers.* Does the teacher present an overview that stresses the major points of the material to be covered?
3. *Organization.* Does the teacher present information in a logical, organized fashion?
4. *Pace.* Does the teacher present the information at varied paces—slowing down for important points and repeating them for emphasis?
5. *Examples.* Does the teacher use examples to illustrate points and give concrete examples of abstract information? (p. 289)

Another area of interest is the number and types of oral responses required of students in the classroom learning environment. In the early years of elementary school, speaking is a primary way that students respond to classroom activities. They read aloud, answer questions orally, and participate in group discussions. In junior high and high school, teachers continue to expect students to communicate orally. In a study by Knowlton and Schlick, reported in Schumaker and Deshler (1984), secondary teachers considered communication skills important and identified specific skills such as "speaking clearly, making oral reports, participating in discussions, and explaining reasons for one's actions" (p. 25).

The teacher's instructional response to students with language differences or disorders should also be considered in assessment. In correcting student errors, does the teacher stress language form (i.e., articulation and grammar) or meaning and usage? What changes, if any, have been made in the standard instructional program to accommodate the needs of learners such as the student under assessment? Are listening tasks restructured for students with difficulty in receptive language? Are speaking tasks modified in any way for students with problems in language production?

Polloway and Smith (1982) provide specific suggestions for the instruction of students with special language needs, particularly those who speak nonstandard English or languages other than English. These include the following:

☐ Avoid negative statements about the child's language, exercising particular caution in front of large groups. Rather than saying, "I don't understand you" or "You are not saying that right" several times, the teacher should use a statement such as, "Could you say that in a different way to help me understand?"

TABLE 14–6
Assessment devices for Spanish-speaking students

Assessment Area	Name (Authors)	English-Language Counterpart
Academic Achievement	*Batería Woodcock Psico-Educativa en Español* (Woodcock, 1982)	*Woodcock-Johnson Psycho-Educational Battery* (Woodcock & Johnson, 1977)
	BRIGANCE® Diagnostic Inventory of Basic Skills, Spanish Edition (Brigance, 1983b)	*BRIGANCE® Diagnostic Comprehensive Inventory of Basic Skills* (Brigance, 1983a)
	Prueba de Lectura y Lenguaje Escrito (Test of Reading and Writing) (Hammill, Larsen, Wiederholt, & Fountain-Chambers, 1982)	none
	Spanish Assessment of Basic Education (1987)	Linked to *Comprehensive Tests of Basic Skills* and *California Achievement Tests*
	Woodcock Language Proficiency Battery, Spanish Form (Woodcock, 1981)	*Woodcock Language Proficiency Battery, English Form* (Woodcock, 1980)
Intellectual Performance	*Batería Woodcock Psico-Educativa en Español* (Woodcock, 1982)	*Woodcock-Johnson Psycho-Educational Battery* (Woodcock & Johnson, 1977)
	Escala de Inteligencia Wechsler para Niños–Revisada (1982)	*Wechsler Intelligence Scale for Children–Revised* (Wechsler, 1974)
Adaptive Behavior	*Adaptive Behavior Inventory for Children* (Mercer & Lewis, 1977a)	Both English-language and Spanish-language versions are included.
	Scales of Independent Behavior (Bruininks, Woodcock, Weatherman, & Hill, 1984)	A Spanish version offers a Spanish-language test book and English-language manual and response booklets.
	Vineland Adaptive Behavior Scales (Sparrow, Balla, & Cicchetti, 1984)	A Spanish-language version of the Survey Form for the Interview Edition is available.

Specific Learning Abilities	*Language Assessment Scales—Oral* (DeAvila & Duncan, 1975–1985)—Minimal Pairs subtest (auditory discrimination)	Both English-language and Spanish-language versions are included.
	Prueba Illinois de Habilidades Psicolingüísticas (von Isser & Kirk, 1980)	*Illinois Test of Psycholinguistic Abilities* (Kirk, McCarthy, & Kirk, 1968)
	Survey of Study Habits and Attitudes, Spanish Edition (Brown & Holtzman, 1967b)	*Survey of Study Habits and Attitudes* (Brown & Holtzman, 1967a)
Classroom Behavior	*Perfil de Evaluación del Comportamiento* (Brown & Hammill, 1983)	*Behavior Rating Profile* (Brown & Hammill, 1983)
Oral Language[1]	*Boehm Test of Basic Concepts—Revised* (Boehm, 1986)	A manual with Spanish directions is available.
	Prueba de Desarrollo Inicial de Lenguaje (Hresko, Reid, & Hammill, 1982)	*Test of Early Language Development* (Hresko, Reid, & Hammill, 1981)
	Screening Test of Spanish Grammar (Toronto, 1973)	*Northwestern Syntax Screening Test* (Lee, 1971)
	Test de Vocabulario en Imágenes Peabody (Dunn, Lugo, Padilla, & Dunn, 1986)	*Peabody Picture Vocabulary Test–Revised* (Dunn & Dunn, 1981)
	Woodcock Language Proficiency Battery, Spanish Form (Woodcock, 1981)	*Woodcock Language Proficiency Battery, English Form* (Woodcock, 1980)

[1]See also the measures of language proficiency described in Table 14–5.

□ Reinforce oral and written language production. A first goal in working with language-different students is to maintain and subsequently increase the language output. Reinforcing desired production will insure that this goal is reached.

□ Set aside at least a short period during the day to stress language development.

□ Involve persons from the linguistically different community in the total school program as much as possible so that these persons, as well as "native" speakers, can share language experiences.

□ As the teacher, you should model standard English usage. For example, when a student says, "Dese car look good," you could say, "Yes, these cars do look good." (pp. 83–84)

The Interpersonal Environment

The interpersonal environment of the classroom is an important area of concern in the study of oral language performance because communication is a social event. At least two persons must participate, a speaker who transmits information and a listener who acts as the recipient.

In assessing the interpersonal dimension, it is necessary to determine whether students have opportunities to practice oral language skills as part of classroom activities. Some of the questions that can be asked are

□ Is the teacher the primary speaker in the classroom? That is, are students expected to act as listeners rather than speakers? How many opportunities per day, on the average, do students have to respond orally in class? What types of responses are most typical—yes and no answers, short responses of a few words, several sentences?

□ Are there opportunities for students and the teacher to communicate in large group settings?

□ Do students speak with the teacher individually or in small group settings?

□ Are students allowed or encouraged to communicate with each other?

□ Are there opportunities for students to communicate in structured situations such as small group discussions, role playing activities, class meetings, debates, panel discussions, and the like?

It is also important to evaluate the instructional interactions when classroom activities require oral communication. For example, when students make errors in speaking, how does the teacher respond? Is the error identified? Does the teacher correct it?

The Physical Environment

The way the physical environment of the classroom is arranged influences students' opportunities for interaction and the practice of oral communication skills. Cohen and Plaskon (1980) describe two classroom seating arrangements, one that inhibits student interaction and another that encourages communication among students. In the traditional classroom environment, students are seated at desks arranged in rows, so each student is isolated from all but a few peers.

As Figure 14–7 shows, the modified classroom environment represents a more ideal arrangement.

There will be multiple opportunities for children to engage in conversation, discussion, and problem solving with each other, and therefore, with the mildly handicapped child.

The teacher will be able to group, organize for instruction, and modify materials or presentations for the mildly handicapped child as a natural course of action. Such "changes" would not single out the mildly handicapped child and would be more a part of the daily class routine.

Implied in the room arrangement is the freedom to move about as assignment, topics, and activities warrant. Mildly handicapped children can readily select working partners or those individuals with whom they easily relate and do so in an unobtrusive manner. (Cohen & Plaskon, 1980, p. 202)

The physical environment can also affect listening skills. Soundproofing or carpeting decreases the overall noise level of the room. The areas of the classroom used for listening and independent study should be separated from the areas where less quiet activities take place. Some classrooms have listening centers where one or several students can listen to tapes or records through earphones. These centers can be used to provide instruction in listening skills and for free time activities such as listening to music or stories.

ANSWERING THE ASSESSMENT QUESTIONS

The purpose of the study of oral language is to describe the student's current levels of performance in this important area of functioning. There are a great many assessment strategies available

FIGURE 14-7
Classroom seating arrangements

Traditional Classroom Environment

▲ = Mildly handicapped child

Modified Classroom Environment

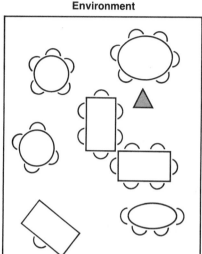

▲ = Mildly handicapped child

Note. From *Language Arts for the Mildly Handicapped* (pp. 201, 203) by S. B. Cohen and S. P. Plaskon, 1980, Columbus, OH: Merrill. Copyright 1980 by Bell & Howell Company. Reprinted by permission.

for this purpose. Many are norm-referenced tests, whereas others are informal measures such as language samples and informal inventories. These tools aid the assessment team in gathering information about the student's current status in oral language development.

Nature of the Assessment Tools

Measures of oral language vary along several dimensions, one of the most obvious being the language they assess. The most common language is, of course, English. However, several tests evaluate students' skills in Spanish, and some assess both English- and Spanish-language proficiency. Formal tests of proficiency in other languages are less common, although informal measures may be available.

Language measures also vary in the range of skills they assess. Some measures attempt to be comprehensive, whereas others concentrate on one or perhaps two of the major dimensions of language. Several current test batteries include measures of phonology, morphology, syntax, and

semantics. However, these measures are not truly comprehensive because they fail to include the newest area of language study, pragmatics.

Oral language is a complex skill made up of many subskills. Because of this, some measures attend to only one specific area of functioning. Examples are measures of articulation, those that assess morphology and syntax, and vocabulary tests. Some tests are so specific they address an area as restricted as expressive syntax or receptive semantics.

Measures also differ in depth of skill coverage. Thus, norm-referenced tests tend to sample several skills and/or several skill levels, but only a few representative test items are provided in each area. Most informal measures are designed to evaluate skills in much greater depth. An example is language sample analysis where every utterance is recorded, transcribed, and analyzed. A wealth of information concerning the student's productivity, the semantic aspects of the communication, and the specific morphological and syntactical characteristics of the student's language is the result.

Measures use different assessment tasks to evaluate similar oral language skills. For example, the student's command of morphology and syntax is assessed by tasks such as sentence repetition, sentence combination, and identification of pictures that best represent the meaning of sentences. Table 14–3 provided examples of the many tasks used to evaluate expressive semantics. Clearly, differences among test tasks must be considered in the selection of the tools for assessment and in the interpretation of results.

The Relationship of Oral Language to Other Areas of Performance

When assessment is complete, the special education team begins to interpret the results and study the relationships between areas of performance. General learning aptitude is one area of interest. Because general aptitude can influence the rate and success with which skills are acquired, the student's progress in oral language should be evaluated in relation to the estimated level of intellectual functioning. Verbal IQ scores are most appropriate for this purpose. However, the relationship between language and intelligence is reciprocal. Just as intelligence can affect language development, students' language skills can affect performance on measures of intellectual performance. This is a particular concern with students whose language is dissimilar from the formal Standard English used on IQ tests.

Specific learning abilities also play a role in the student's ability to acquire and use oral language skills. Difficulties in attention and memory can hinder language development, as can poor auditory discrimination. Again, the relationship is reciprocal. Language is an integral part of learning strategies such as verbal rehearsal, and students use language to regulate their own learning behavior and focus attention.

Classroom behavior may be influenced by language development. Students with poor receptive language skills may appear inattentive, fail to follow directions, or seem to ignore the teacher. Students with poor expressive skills may be reluctant to speak in class, especially in situations where peers can take notice of their errors or the differences between their language and Standard English. Such students may refuse to answer questions and participate in class discussions; they may engage in disruptive behavior to draw attention away from their difficulties with language. Also, self-concept and attitude toward school are likely to be affected.

Oral language skills have an impact on other areas of school performance. All school subjects require listening and speaking skills, at least to some extent. In classrooms at all grade levels, from preschool through college, students are expected to learn by listening. The demands for speaking skills are almost as great. No matter what subject or what grade level, the teacher will ask questions and expect students to respond orally. Students who enter school with delays in receptive or expressive language development are likely to experience difficulty in the acquisition of reading, mathematics, and written language skills as well as content area subjects.

Oral language also pervades daily life. At home and at work, people communicate with each other through speech. They talk face-to-face and on the telephone to family members, friends, neighbors, and acquaintances; they talk to facilitate vocational pursuits and to accomplish routine tasks such as shopping. Students with severe language disorders may require training to succeed at the oral communication tasks that make up much of the fabric of daily life.

Documentation of Oral Language Performance

The general question that guides the assessment team in its study of student performance is, *What are the student's educational needs?* Two specific questions are asked in relation to the student's oral communication skills: *What is the student's current level of development in oral language? What are the student's strengths and weaknesses in the various skill areas of oral language?*

Many types of data are gathered to answer these questions. The team may begin by reviewing school records and the information collected in classroom observations and interviews with teachers and parents. Formal tests may then be administered to evaluate the student's oral language performance in relation to that of age or grade peers. Informal assessment strategies such as language sampling, informal inventories, and criterion-referenced tests may also play a role by describing the specific skill areas in which the student shows educational needs.

As with other areas of assessment, the team should select its tools with care so duplication is avoided and the assessment process is as efficient as possible. This is an important concern in the study of oral language skills because of the great number of available formal measures. In addition, the more specific procedures such as language sampling should be reserved for in-depth assessment of potential problem areas.

By answering the assessment questions about oral language, the team moves closer to planning the student's individualized education program. In the case of Joyce, assessment results indicated that oral language was not a skill area requiring special instruction.

Joyce

The assessment team has identified Joyce as learning disabled, and to date three areas of academic underachievement have been documented. Although Joyce's oral language skills appear adequate, she has difficulty following oral directions in the classroom, a problem that may relate to receptive language. Thus, the team decides to investigate language development by

administering the intermediate level of the *Test of Language Development–2*.

Joyce's scores on all subtests of the *TOLD–2* fall within the average range of performance. To corroborate these results and gather further information about Joyce's difficulty with oral directions, the assessment team develops an informal inventory to assess comprehension of typical classroom directions. For example, the first direction is, "Write your name on the upper left-hand corner of the paper." Joyce follows single directions without difficulty. However, when directions are combined into a series (e.g., "Next to number 3 on your paper, write your last name and draw a circle around it"), Joyce is unable to comply. These results substantiate the team's belief that Joyce's failure to follow classroom directions is related to memory, not receptive language.

The special education team has completed its evaluation of Joyce and the learning environment of her fourth grade classroom. Results indicate that Joyce is in need of specialized instruction in reading, spelling, and handwriting. Next, Joyce's parents will meet with members of the school staff to plan the individualized educational program.

STUDY GUIDE

Review Questions

1. Oral language skills are assessed to
   - _____ a. Determine whether students are eligible for special education services from a speech-language pathologist
   - _____ b. Identify educational needs in the area of speech and language
   - _____ c. Find out if students are in need of bilingual education services
   - _____ d. All of the above
   - _____ e. Answers *a* and *b*
2. What five dimensions of oral language are of interest in special education assessment?
3. Which of the following statements are true and which are false?
   - T F **a.** In the developmental sequence, receptive language generally precedes expressive language.
   - T F **b.** Listening is an expressive language skill, whereas speaking is a receptive language skill.
   - T F **c.** Another term for receptive phonology is auditory discrimination.
   - T F **d.** Articulation is the production of morphemes, the smallest meaningful units of language.
   - T F **e.** Pragmatics refers to the use of language in communicative contexts.
4. Most measures of oral language assess language form, content, and use. (True or False)
5. Students who speak a nonstandard version of English are said to speak a _____ of English.
6. Match the assessment device or procedure in Column A with the description in Column B.

	Column A		Column B
a.	*Test of Language Development–2, Primary*	_____	Assesses expressive phonology
b.	*Clinical Evaluation of Language Fundamentals–Revised*	_____	Used to evaluate receptive and expressive phonology, syntax, and semantics in preschool and early elementary grade children
c.	*Test of Adolescent Language–2*	_____	Available in both an English and Spanish form to assess Picture Vocabulary, Antonyms–Synonyms, and Analogies
d.	*Goldman-Fristoe Test of Articulation*	_____	A collection of 11 subtests that assess syntax, semantics, and memory
e.	*Woodcock Language Proficiency Battery*	_____	Contains four oral language subtests: Listening Vocabulary and Grammar, and Speaking Vocabulary and Grammar

7. Which measure would you select if you wished to assess both receptive and expressive syntax?
   _____ a. *Northwestern Syntax Screening Test*
   _____ b. *Test for Auditory Comprehension of Language–Revised*
   _____ c. *Carrow Elicited Language Inventory*
   _____ d. Language sampling

8. Which measure would you choose to assess pragmatics?
   _____ a. *Peabody Picture Vocabulary Test–Revised*
   _____ b. *Boehm Test of Basic Concepts–Revised*
   _____ c. *Let's Talk Inventory for Adolescents*
   _____ d. *Test of Language Development–2, Intermediate*

9. There are many ways to analyze samples of students' oral language. In most systems, the words uttered by the student are analyzed according to their morphological and syntactical characteristics. However, the simplest method is calculation of the mean _____ of _____ , an indicator of overall language development.

10. Nonstandard forms of English such as Black English and Spanish-influenced English are considered language deficits, not language differences. (True or False)

11. With students who speak languages other than English
    _____ a. The first step in assessment is determination of the student's language proficiency in the first language and in English
    _____ b. Special education assessment takes place in the student's primary language, whenever feasible
    _____ c. Bilingual education services may be provided as well as special education services
    _____ d. All of the above

12. Oral language development is most related to _____ aptitude.

13. If a student shows low average intellectual performance, in what standard score range would you expect that student to perform in oral language?
    _____ a. Less than standard score 70
    _____ b. Standard score 70 to 84
    _____ c. Standard score 85 to 115
    _____ d. Standard score 116 to 130
    _____ e. Greater than standard score 130

14. Poor oral language skill development may affect
    _____ a. Reading
    _____ b. Composition
    _____ c. Mathematics
    _____ d. Classroom behavior
    _____ e. Interactions with peers and teachers
    _____ f. All of the above

15. If the special education team finds that an English-speaking student shows poor performance in oral language, what conclusion can be drawn?

     _____ a. The student may be eligible for bilingual education services.

     _____ b. The student requires individualized instruction in reading, writing, listening, and speaking.

     _____ c. Special education services should be provided in the area of oral language, if the student meets eligibility criteria for one of the handicapping conditions.

     _____ d. The student will require an interpreter for all assessments.

Activities

1. Write an Individualized Assessment Plan for an elementary grade student who has been referred because of problems in oral language. In writing the plan, attempt to include measures of all major dimensions of language: phonology, morphology, syntax, semantics, and pragmatics.

2. Under the supervision of the course instructor, administer one of the oral language survey measures discussed in this chapter. Calculate all possible scores and analyze the results to determine strengths and weaknesses.

3. Obtain a language sample from a student receiving special education services. Analyze that sample using a method described in this chapter.

4. Devise an interview form for use with parents of young school-aged children to find out about the language environment of the home.

5. Observe in a classroom and note the important features of the instructional, interpersonal, and physical environments that may influence oral language performance.

Discussion Questions

1. Oral language is the communication mode most often used in everyday discourse among adults. Why then is oral language not included among the basic school skills?

2. Pragmatics is the newest area of language study. Explain what is meant by pragmatics and tell how this dimension of language can be assessed.

3. Explain why it is necessary to consider the oral language of students who speak nonstandard English when assessing intellectual performance, reading, written language, and other school subjects.

4. The primary language of the student should be the language in which the special education assessment is conducted. However, technically adequate assessment tools are not always available in the student's language. Discuss the alternatives open to the assessment team when this occurs. Include in your discussion the advantages and disadvantages of each alternative.

PART FIVE

Application of Assessment Results

After considering the many different ways there are to evaluate major assessment topics, we now turn to a final question—how to interpret and use the information gathered. At this point in the assessment process, we apply and report the data. Using the structure of an IAP, Chapter 15 considers the interpretation and reporting of results. Principles of analyzing, interpreting and organizing information into a report are illustrated with examples and a sample case study. Guidelines for conducting a conference and sharing the results are also provided.

To stress the importance of continuing the assessment once a student's program is implemented, Chapter 16 illustrates how assessment procedures (especially informal ones) are put to that purpose. The informal inventories, criterion-referenced tests, interviews and other informal strategies described throughout this text are now used for monitoring instruction. An IAP for the student profiled in Chapter 15 is used to structure this phase. You will see how monitoring student performance lends itself to answering questions about the student's IEP.

Special attention will be given in Chapter 17 to parents, vital team members in the assessment process. The roles of parents of exceptional students in assessment are described. Professionals need to know ways to involve parents, both as mandated by PL 94–142 and PL 99–457 and on the basis of good practice. Reporting data to and conferencing with parents (and special students themselves, when appropriate) are treated in detail, along with strategies for successfully communicating assessment results.

15

Interpreting, Reporting, and Using Assessment Data

Analyzing and reporting the results of the total assessment are the natural extensions of the assessment itself. These steps follow the identification of a student with learning problems, the completion of the referral process, the design of an Individual Assessment Plan (IAP), and the administration, scoring, and interpretation of individual procedures. Now all the assessment data must be combined in an intelligible form based on the main assessment questions.

As discussed in Chapter 1 (Figure 1–1, p. 18), the assessment process is directed by a set of assessment questions. Before special education services can be made available to a student, the following questions must be answered:

□ Is there a school performance problem?
□ Is it related to a handicapping condition?
□ What are the educational needs?

Throughout the process, parts of these questions have been addressed. However, because no single procedure or piece of information can provide sufficient data to answer all questions, one must arrange the available data so solutions are apparent. The assessment questions that must ultimately be answered and to which the interpretation and report of the results must lead are

□ What are the educational needs, annual goals, and objectives?
□ What kinds of special education and related services are necessary?
□ What is the least restrictive and most appropriate educational environment?

GENERAL GUIDELINES FOR REPORTING ASSESSMENT RESULTS

The interpretation and reporting of assessment results are guided by a set of general principles.

Follow a structured format. When analyzing and reporting assessment results, remember the reasons for referral and work toward answering the main assessment questions. Whether the interpretation and report are verbal or written, you must proceed in an orderly fashion to present a cohesive picture of the student's learning problems. If the assessment was conducted and structured by the series of assessment questions recommended in this text, the interpretation and reporting of the data are straightforward.

The major components of an assessment report are

1. *Identification data*—All essential demographic information about the student: full name, address, birth date, and so forth
2. *Reason for referral*—The basis for and source of the referral
3. *Relevant background*—Significant information about the student's medical, developmental, educational, and sociocultural background
4. *Behavioral observations*—Descriptions of the student's behavior during assessment
5. *Assessment results and discussion*—Scores and other results in pertinent areas, such as reading, mathematics, and so forth
6. *Summary and conclusions*—A brief statement of the level of performance and strengths and weaknesses in the areas assessed
7. *Suggested goals and services*—Major foci for the instructional program and possible ways to provide the services
8. *Data sheet*—All the formal and informal results for independent analysis and reference

Report only relevant data. Choose the most pertinent data to answer the assessment questions and disregard the rest.

Report information once and then mention it only as needed. Avoid making the same point again and again. For example, distractible behavior has bearing upon all the results. Discuss it once in the appropriate place and then clarify its significance at a crucial point.

Avoid making recommendations or giving ideas for solutions throughout the report. Recommendations should be saved for the appropriate place, generally at the end of the report.

Report facts and data accurately and simply. Avoid making unfounded statements or inferences.

Insert sensitive information tactfully. When information may be offensive or unpleasant to someone (for example, information about child abuse, a recent death in the family, or teacher–parent disagreements) and is significant for interpreting the data, choose diplomatic language to make the point.

Note the source of any information and report the data accurately. When appropriate, attribute statements to the parents, teachers, and other people who made them. Useful phrases are, "As his mother reported . . . " or "From an interview with her teacher. . . . " Use similar references in the case of tests and informal procedures, including observations and task analysis: "As measured by the *WISC–R . . .* " or "From observations in the classroom. . . . "

When reporting data from previous assessments, do so briefly and with full reference to the source. For example, a useful phrase may be, "The results of a recent psychological examination at Children's Clinic. . . . " If appropriate, similarities or differences with the data to be reported can be noted in the discussion of results.

Mention the absence of critical data, such as recent vision and hearing assessments. Such data may be necessary for a full interpretation. When unavailable, it may be one of the recommended areas for further assessment.

Report any test administration errors or problems and reservations about the findings. This should also be done only once and at the most significant point. Of course, if there were major problems in the administration of tests and the results are highly questionable, you should discard and not report them.

Consider information about instructional factors in the classroom and noninstructional correlates (medical, social, and cultural). Test results must be interpreted in relationship to many factors. Among instructional variables are past educational experience and current conditions in the classroom. For example, a teacher may be using a particular procedure that enhances or limits good achievement. In addition, the student's medical, social, and cultural background may have bearing on school performance. For example, a vision problem may be compounding reading difficulties.

Address discrepancies between data and present possible explanations. For example, there may be disagreement among test results or between test results and a teacher's opinion. It may be possible to explain these discrepancies by referring to test construction, student behavior, classroom procedures, and so forth.

When interpreting test results, remember that there are two levels of analysis: statistical and clinical. Interpret tests and other procedures individually and statistically first. Statistical analysis is

computing the scores, identifying the important scores for interpretation, and perhaps arranging them on a profile. Clinical analysis establishes whether the performance is average, what the strengths and weaknesses are, and how the performance on the tests relates to other factors. Placing values on and making judgments about test performances fall into the clinical analysis category.

Selectively use theoretical constructs. Their use in interpreting and reporting results may be considered part of a description of the pattern of learning problems or an attempt to unify the results of assessment. However, these efforts may lead to unwarranted statements of cause and effect. Concepts originally generated as descriptors can become explanations or causes. For example, a number of a student's behaviors may be called "immature"; before long, the child's difficulties in learning become related to or caused by "immaturity."

Keep a variety of stylistic points in mind. Interpreting and reporting the results require both an excellent understanding of the data and a good grasp of communication skills. Sattler (1988), Reed (1980), and others urge diagnosticians to be clear, simple, and neat; use simple sentence structure, perhaps 8 to 20 words in length; be consistent in use of tenses; distinguish between making conclusions and simply reporting facts (e.g., "It appeared/seemed . . . " or, "The mother said . . . "); if necessary, refer to oneself in the third person (e.g., "The examiner gave . . . "); and use the student's name or the personal pronoun. They should not use extra verbiage; go off on tangents; make unwarranted conclusions; use technical jargon; explain away the student's performance; express surprise, sadness, or happiness at the results; use conjecture (e.g., "probably," "perhaps"); make overstatements or use superlatives (e.g., "The most fantastic performance . . . ").

REPORTING BACKGROUND INFORMATION

A comprehensive report of assessment results includes certain essential components. As Table 15–1 shows, each component contains different and critical information for understanding the student's current status. The sources of information are the many formal and informal assessment procedures discussed throughout this book. By referring to the assessment questions used to organize the assessment process, you can arrange the gathered information appropriately.

Although ideal, this comprehensive and detailed assessment format is often abbreviated by school districts. To portray a variety of reporting styles, we provide both a fuller, clinical report example in Appendix B and a more common type of case report in this chapter. See Figure 15–1.

Phillip

Phillip is a 15-year-old high school student in a resource room for the mildly retarded. The assessment that follows was performed for the 3-year reevaluation required to justify special services. (See Figure 15–1 on pp. 458–459.)

Identification

Identifying information is essential and must be accurate and complete. The following data are frequently provided.

Student
Name, address, and phone number. If the student's last name is different from the parents', provide both names, addresses, and so forth.
Age
Birthday
Sex

School
Grade placement
School, school address, phone number, and principal's name
Teacher's name

Testing
Testing date(s)
Reporting date
Names of assessment personnel

Reason for Referral

Students are referred for educational assessment for many reasons. Reasons frequently involve problems in learning to read, write, or speak. Teachers, parents, and others may also express concerns about disruptive behavior, immaturity,

and other problems. As discussed in Chapter 2, considerable care must be taken to specify the reasons for referral so the assessment can be well organized. In addition to stating the reason(s) for assessment, this section of the report should indicate the referral agents.

The information for this section comes from developmental case histories and referral forms filled out by parents, teachers, and others. Prior interviews with parents and teachers will help direct the assessment. Their statements can also be used to explain its purpose and expected outcome. For example, the referral statement for Phillip recounts his past placement in special education and the areas to be reevaluated for the 3-year review mandated by PL 94–142.

Relevant Background

This section summarizes relevant information about the student's medical, educational, and sociocultural background. It is used to briefly report data with specific significance in answering the referral questions. Medical history generally includes the status of general health, vision, and hearing ability, medical treatments (for example, diet or drugs), accidents or surgery, handicapping conditions, and so forth. Unusual events in the student's growth and development, such as delays in motor or language maturation, should be mentioned. This information is available from case histories; interviews with parents, physicians, and others; school records; and medical reports. To avoid duplication or misdirection, these reports should be procured before the assessment begins.

Educational data to be reported include past grades, types of educational placement (for example, special or bilingual education), retention or advancement, performance on group or individual assessments, attendance at school, teacher reactions and comments, number of schools attended, and so forth. Efforts to remediate learning problems in the regular classroom should be briefly described. This information is highly significant in specifying general problems to be initially assessed as well as in interpreting the results. It can be drawn from reports of individual assessments, group achievement testing, report cards, and teacher and student interviews.

TABLE 15–1
Key components of an assessment interpretation and report

Sections	Contents	Sources
I. Identification information	1. Demographic data 2. Particulars about assessment	School records Referral form Parent/teacher interviews
II. Reason for referral	1. Source and reason for referral	Referral form Parent/teacher interviews
III. Relevant background	1. Medical 2. Educational 3. Sociocultural	Referral form Developmental history Parent/teacher interviews Medical records School records Psychological testing Home visits
IV. Behavioral observations	1. Behavior during the assessment	Comments on the test protocols Informal observations

V. Assessment results and discussion	1. List of the names of procedures
	2. Overall academic performance and strengths and weaknesses
	3. Comparison of overall academic performance to referents
	
	4. Level of reading performance and strengths and weaknesses
	  a. Overall achievement
	  b. Skills in oral reading, comprehension, and application
	  c. Comparison among reading skills
	  d. Comparison to instructional and noninstructional factors
	5. Level of mathematical performance, strengths, and weaknesses
	  a. Overall achievement
	  b. Skills in computation, problem solving, and application
	  c. Comparison among math skills and to reading skills
	  d. Comparison to instructional and noninstructional factors
		Test protocols and other forms
		Individual achievement batteries (See Chapter 7)
		Other sources (See Chapter 7)
		Chronological age
		Grade placement
		Intellectual functioning and adaptive behavior measures (see Chapter 8)
		Individual reading batteries (see Chapter 11)
		Formal and informal procedures (see Chapter 11)
		See guidelines
		See guidelines
		Individual math batteries (see Chapter 12)
		Formal and informal procedures (see Chapter 12)
		See guidelines
		See guidelines

6. Level of oral language performance, strengths, and weaknesses

   a. Overall oral language development — Individual oral language batteries (see Chapter 14)

   b. Oral skills in receptive and expressive semantics, syntax, morphology, phonology, and pragmatics — Formal and informal procedures (see Chapter 14)

   c. Comparison among oral language skills and to reading and math skills — See guidelines

   d. Comparison to instructional and noninstructional factors — See guidelines

7. Level of written language performance, strengths, and weaknesses

   a. Overall written language development — Individual written language batteries (see Chapter 13)

   b. Written skills in spelling, handwriting, and composition — Formal and informal procedures (see Chapter 13)

   c. Comparison among written language skills and to reading, math, and oral language skills — See guidelines

   d. Comparison to instructional and noninstructional factors — See guidelines

8. Level of development of specific learning abilities and strategies

   a. Skill development in attention, perception, and memory areas — Formal and informal procedures (see Chapter 9)

   b. Use of learning strategies — See Chapter 9

   c. Comparison to reading, math, and language skills — See guidelines

   d. Comparison to instructional and noninstructional factors — See guidelines

9. Status of classroom behavior and social-emotional development

   a. Overall status of problem behaviors — Broad survey procedures (see Chapter 10)

   b. Specific status of problem behavior, student behavior, and environmental influences — Formal and informal procedures (see Chapter 10)

   c. Comparison among behavioral areas and to academic skills — See guidelines

   d. Comparison to instructional and noninstructional factors — See guidelines

VI. Summary and conclusions

   1. Overall level of performance in academic areas, and strengths and weaknesses — "Results and Discussion" section

   2. Mastered and unmastered skills in each skill area —

   3. Significant relationships among skill areas and to other factors — "Results and Discussion" section

VII. Suggested goals and services

   1. Suggested goals for instruction — "Results and Discussion" and "Summary and Conclusions" sections

   2. Possible needed special education and related services —

VIII. Appendix Data Sheets

   1. Test scores — Protocols

   2. Informal data —

FIGURE 15–1
Sample assessment report

Name: Phillip Hughes
Date of Birth: April 2, 1974
Age: 15 / Sex: Male
Date(s) tested: April 4, 6, and 9, 1989

School: Glenover J.H. School
Teacher: Mr. Thompson
Grade: 8.8
Date of report: May 2, 1989

Reason for Referral: Phillip has been receiving services for the mildly retarded since grade 2, and is now in a resource room for 4 of 6 daily school hours. This assessment was performed as the mandated 3-year evaluation. Phillip's eligibility for special education and related services must be reexamined and the effectiveness and appropriateness of his IEP established. The goals of his current program encompass reading, mathematics, and written language with special therapy for eye-hand coordination problems.

Relevant Background

Phillip lives at home with his mother, stepfather, three stepbrothers and two sisters. His mother's divorce occurred when Phillip was 5 years old. She remarried 3 years ago.

Phillip was assessed at the end of grade 2 and placed in a full-time special class for the educable mentally retarded. His program consisted of the basic skills of reading, mathematics, and language, along with physical therapy for gross and fine motor deficits. At that time he also was hyperactive and disruptive in the classroom; his parents and teachers found him overly dependent.

By the end of grade 5, Phillip's behavior and reading, mathematics, and language skills had improved to warrant a change in program. Now he is in a resource room for part of the school day and only receives fine-motor assistance once a week. However, his immaturity and overreliance on others have continued to be a problem.

Phillip's mother reports that he gets along well with other people, although he has only a few friends and they tend to be younger. He basically watches television or rides his bicycle. He likes to go to school to see his friends but does not like to do schoolwork. Phillip has no major medical problems.

Testing Observations

Phillip behaved well during the testing situation, speaking freely with the examiner. He was cooperative and generally followed directions well. A number of times he requested to have material repeated. When required to write, he said that he did not do well but would try.

Tests and Procedures Used

The following tests and informal procedures were used: *Wechsler Intelligence Scale for Children–Revised (WISC–R), AAMD Adaptive Behavior Scale–School Edition (ABS–SE); Woodcock-Johnson Psycho-Educational Battery–Revised (Woodcock-Johnson–R), Test of Written Language-2 (TOWL–2), BRIGANCE® Diagnostic Inventory of Essential Skills, Detroit Tests of Learning Aptitude (DTLA–2), Reading-Free Vocational Interest Inventory–Revised (R–FVII), the Purdue Pegboard, and Behavior Rating Profile (BRP).* Phillip's special education teacher and other teachers were interviewed. He was observed a number of times in his classroom, and a written work sample analysis was done.

Assessment Results

Phillip's overall performance on the *WISC–R* was significantly below average, over 2 standard deviations. His verbal skills were somewhat better than his performance skills. Stronger performances were in similarities, arithmetic, and picture completion; weaker performances were evident in vocabulary, general information, block design, and coding. When questioned with the *ABS–SE,* Phillip's parents perceived his adaptive skills as being more similar to mildly retarded students than regular classroom peers. His relative strengths were in personal and community self-sufficiency (e.g., physical development, numbers, and time), and social adjustment (e.g., trustworthiness). Particular weaknesses were in personal-social responsibility (e.g., self-direction) and personal adjustment (e.g., mannerisms).

On the *Woodcock-Johnson–R,* Phillip's performance in major academic areas is in the below average range for his grade placement. Additionally, Phillip was retained and should be in grade 9. Reading and mathematics skills are 1 standard deviation below average performance, and written language and knowledge areas (science, social studies, and humanities) are 2 standard deviations below.

Based on the *Woodcock-Johnson–R, BRIGANCE®,* and other informal measures, Phillip's oral reading skills are approximately 2 years behind his current grade placement and 4 years behind in comprehension skills of read material; his comprehension is better when Phillip reads silently. Error analysis of oral miscues indicates a tendency to guess at the ends of words, incorrectly blend sounds, and substitute words that do not fit the meaning of the passage but are visually similar to the printed word. Phillip's teachers indicate that he understands and uses read material when the material and vocabulary are discussed beforehand and when the tasks to be completed are examined first.

Corrective Reading materials have been successful with Phillip. Skill deficits continue to be recognizing critical sight words, performing word analysis, recognizing and remembering critical details, and identifying the main idea of read material.

Math tends to be a favorite subject for Phillip. He performs about 2 years behind in computation and 4 years in problem solving according to the *BRIGANCE®* and other measures. His use of multiplication and division procedures is inconsistent; he has not yet mastered computing averages and using fractions. Although Phillip can make change and tell time, he is still learning conversion of measurement units and application of formulas. Consistent use of basic mathematical terms is a noticeable skill deficit. Phillip enjoys using a calculator and practicing skills on the classroom computer. His teachers indicate that he has learned to detect and correct his own errors.

A readministration of the *TOWL–2* after $1\frac{1}{2}$ years of instruction indicates some areas of growth, although overall written language performance is below average. His spelling, punctuation, and capitalization skills are in the low average range. His major deficits are in use of vocabulary, grammar, creativity and handwriting. Fine motor deficits continue to interfere with written work and copying. Phillip's teachers indicate that an integrated language experience program has encouraged growth in this area, but memory and language problems interfere with concept generation for writing. Deficit areas are letter formation, letter writing, completion of forms (e.g., job applications), and arrangement of information on charts.

Phillip's overall performance on the *DTLA–2* was below average and consistent with his scores on the *WISC–R* and academic measures. Verbal and nonverbal skills are evenly matched, but Phillip was better on fine detail, structural aptitude tasks than on abstract, symbolic tasks. Short-term memory subtest performances were somewhat superior to long-term ones. Also, tests requiring fine eye-hand coordination responses were more troublesome than those requiring speech or pointing.

On the *R–FVII* Phillip indicated higher interests in animal care, food service, and horticulture than in clerical, automotive and building trades. Responses to items on the *BRIGANCE®* in this area indicate need to improve work attitudes and related skills, knowledge of employment signs and vocabulary, and ability to read want ads and complete job applications. The tasks on the *Purdue Pegboard* were difficult for him.

Phillip's behavioral needs at home and school are evident from parent, teacher, and self-reports on the *BRP* and classroom observations. Although Phillip's disruptive and hyperactive behavior has improved in response to behavioral management programs, his peer relationships are a concern. He also tends to be naive and overly dependent on others for direction.

Summary and Conclusions

Phillip is a mildly retarded 15-year-old whose academic and social development approximates his intellectual and adaptive abilities in some areas but not others. In recent years he has overcome hyperactive and disruptive behavior and has developed basic oral reading, spelling, and computational skills; his gross motor abilities have also improved. However, deficits continue to exist in oral word analysis and in comprehension of read material (i.e., memory for detail and main ideas). Improving weak mathematical skills (consistent use of computations, fractions, measurement, and problem solving) is also a priority. Written language deficits include handwriting and use of vocabulary, concepts and grammar. Fine motor deficits hamper writing; language and long-term memory problems interfere with all academic areas.

Phillip's current vocational interests are in the nonmanual areas. He has special needs in the fine-motor area. Improved peer relationships and independent living skills are also required.

Suggested Goals and Services

A variety of curricular needs must be addressed when an IEP is composed. In reading, Phillip has deficits in completing structural analyses, self-correcting substitutions, remembering details of material read silently, and completing tasks based on read material. Appropriate instructional goals in mathematics are performing multiplication and division and solving problems using averaging, fractions, and necessary formulas. Identified written language problems are ability to verbalize material to write about, grammar, and legibility and speed in handwriting. Phillip's vocational interests, work attitude and skills, and knowledge of jobs and application procedures require attention. He also needs to learn how to function independently and relate to his peers better.

Certain special education and related services are suggested by these results. Most of Phillip's needs could be met through assignment to a special education basic skills class and a regular ninth grade homeroom. A vocational counselor can perform assessments in vocational interests and aptitudes, and Phillip can attend the vocational awareness/preparation program. The school counselor can assist Phillip with interpersonal skills and independence. Fine motor therapy may be provided by an occupational therapist.

The sociocultural aspects of a student's background may also affect the problems being considered. Factors that merit attention include size of the family, living and studying conditions, educational values, family status and crises, and the student's relations with parents and other family members. Information about favorite recreational activities and types of friendships may also contribute to a better understanding of the issues. These data may be obtained from a developmental history form, a home visit, interviews with students and parents, and reports from social workers.

An essential rule here is to avoid making value judgments or interpreting information. Be selective in the choice of data to report; the data should be relevant and significant in answering the assessment questions. For example, information about Phillip's preschool experience may not be useful in understanding his current learning problems in high school. But information about recent academic and behavioral improvement and continuing social maturity problems is relevant.

Observations

The student's behavior during formal and informal assessment may be highly relevant. A student may be inattentive, hesitant, impulsive, self-correcting, or questioning. These behaviors may indicate learning strategies as well as responses to the testing situation. Anxiety, fatigue, emotional upset, and other factors may explain some test performances. These data should be recorded on test protocols and other record forms and reported in this section. For example, Phillip's need for repetition of information or hesitancy to write responses may help explain his test performances or illustrate a point.

These essential components of the report provide background and contextual information that can be used to interpret assessment data. Test scores and informal data must be considered in relation to such information so they can be truly meaningful and relevant to the individual.

REPORTING CURRENT ASSESSMENT RESULTS

The discussion of the results of testing and other forms of assessment follows the assessment questioning format (Figure 1–1, p. 18). Before be-

ginning, report the full names of all tests and other assessment procedures to avoid any confusion about their identity; commonly used test abbreviations can be placed in parentheses and used throughout to refer to the source of data. Furthermore, actual test scores and other data can be appended to the report for easy reference. The body of the discussion does not generally require all the specific test scores, but they can be inserted in parentheses, if desired. As indicated in Phillip's sample case report, he received the *WISC–R* and *Test of Written Language–2*, among other measures. Informal procedures used were observations and work sample analyses.

Each assessed academic and behavioral performance area of concern should be discussed. The findings concerning levels of performance and strengths and weaknesses in reading, mathematics, and so forth must be related to the general considerations (intellectual functioning, adaptive behavior, specific learning abilities and strategies, classroom behavior, and socioemotional development); to environmental demands in the classroom; and to medical, social, and cultural correlates. Making the appropriate relationships is a critical aspect of interpreting and reporting results.

This discussion can be organized around the assessment questions that guided the choice of procedures. However, some rearrangement of the information may be necessary, especially with data that must be related to a variety of findings. For example, difficulty in discriminating certain sounds might be affecting low performance in both reading and spelling.

However, all possible disability areas do not have to be discussed, although a comprehensive study of the student's learning problems is desirable. The goal at this point is to present a clear and full description of the student's learning problem areas and a clarification of the connection of the learning problems with other factors. The criterion for the organization and choice of data discussed is their significance in making eligibility and planning decisions.

Organizing the Report

Discussion of the test data and other information is governed by specific guidelines that will facilitate the integration of data on different skills from various sources.

Use referents or guidepoints when reporting data. When a level of performance is presented, it is difficult to appreciate the degree of under-achievement without a criterion. The referents generally used are the student's age, current grade level, or level of intellectual functioning. As discussed earlier, a standardized test provides ways to judge whether the student's performance is average or not, in comparison to peers of similar age and/or grade level.

Note early in the report whether the student has been retained so the full degree of under-achievement can be understood. State whether the grade placement is the one that the student is actually in or the one he or she should be in, and use it throughout.

Group data by major skill areas. Discuss the results of the assessment in each academic and behavioral area separately. Describe all aspects of performance in an area such as reading before introducing information about a second area such as handwriting. As indicated in Table 15–1, a useful order of presentation is reading, mathematics, oral language, written language (including spelling and handwriting), specific learning abilities and strategies (including motor development), classroom behavior, and social-emotional development. If the suggested assessment questions have been used, data organization is straightforward.

Begin a discussion of each area with a statement of the student's current level of performance. This statement can take different forms, depending on the measurement unit used to describe performance: age levels, grade levels, percentiles, and so forth. Choose one comprehensive test battery upon which to base this statement and the subsequent discussion of strengths and weaknesses. For example, a standardized measure such as the *Test of Written Language–2* (Hammill & Larsen, 1988) offers both the needed data and an overview of the area of written language. Also compare the stated level of performance to a criterion, such as current grade placement or age.

Divide the discussion in each area into appropriate subdivisions. Typically assessed academic and behavioral areas have a number of subdivisions.

□ *Reading*—Oral reading, comprehension, and application to subject matter
□ *Mathematics*—Computational skills, problem solving, and their application
□ *Oral Language*—Receptive and expressive vocabulary, syntax, morphology, phonology, and pragmatics
□ *Written Language*—Spelling, handwriting, and composition (including written language, creativity, and mechanics)
□ *Learning Strategies and Specific Learning Abilities*—Attention, perception, and memory
□ *Classroom Behavior and Social-Emotional Development*—Problem behavior; student classroom skills, attitudes, and interactions with teachers and peers; and curricular and physical environmental influences

When appropriate, identify strengths and weaknesses within an area. For example, a student like Phillip may be considerably more skilled in the creation and use of vocabulary in written passages than in spelling and punctuation. These data can be used in developing a set of prioritized goals.

Specify the mastered and unmastered skills in each academic and behavioral area. These data are typically generated by criterion-referenced procedures and other informal methods. They support the development of necessary goals and objectives required for instruction.

Analyze the data on an intraindividual, as well an interindividual, basis. Normative comparisons include statements about a student's current level of performance and about the degree of disparity with expectations on the basis of age, grade placement, IQ, and so forth. They are the result of comparisons with other students; that is, they are interindividual. However, exceptional students may be underachieving in many areas. Interindividual data merely indicate how far behind they are.

Comparison of one student's various performances against each other gives a better picture of intraindividual strengths and weaknesses. Some skills may be higher or lower than others. Although all of the scores may be low or below average compared to scores of other students, a student may have some relative strengths and weaknesses. For example, an eighth grader like Phillip whose overall reading performance is on the third grade level may have relative strengths in reading real and nonsense words in isolation (sixth grade level) and relative weaknesses in understanding the meaning of words and passages (fourth grade level).

Indicate the nature of tasks by rewording the names of subtests or by giving examples of the task whenever necessary. As indicated earlier, note the test or other procedures used to gather the data being reported. However, explain the nature of the subtest, because its name does not necessarily explain its content. Therefore, reword the name of the subtest; for example, in reference to spelling performances on the *Test of Written Spelling–2 (TWS–2)* (Larsen & Hammill, 1986) and *Peabody Individual Achievement Test–Revised (PIAT–R)* (Markwardt, 1989), an appropriate statement might be, "Phillip did better in written spelling of dictated words *(TWS–2)* than in detection of spelling errors *(PIAT–R),* that is, choosing the correct spelling visually from four choices."

Report the same kind of scores as often as possible. A consistent pattern in reporting scores avoids potential confusion. Choose one type of score and use it as much as possible. However, when another type of score must be used, the change should be clearly noted. For example, a report may generally contain standard scores but use percentile ranks in reference to language tests. For convenience, the scores can be placed in parentheses when the source and performance are reported.

Use standard scores or percentiles when comparing test performance. You may need to compare scores from different measures or scores from different subtests within the same battery, such as the *Wechsler Intelligence Scale for Children–Revised* (Wechsler, 1974) or *Woodcock-Johnson Psycho-Educational Battery–Revised* (Woodcock & Johnson, 1989). Standard scores or percentiles are statistically more appropriate for use than grade or age equivalents. In fact, these types of scores are generally more useful in interpreting standardized test performances. Consider the standard error of measurement (SEM) and standard error of measurement of differences (SEM$_{diff}$) when comparing test

scores. As discussed in Chapter 9, these two statistics supply a basis for deciding the significance of differences between scores.

Report a student's performances in ranges indicating the meaning of the numerical scores. Establish a common criterion or yardstick to judge performances on formal and informal measures. The five-level system recommended earlier is

☐ *Above average*—Performance more than 2 standard deviations above the mean
☐ *High average*—Performance from 1 to 2 standard deviations above the mean
☐ *Average*—Performance within 1 standard deviation above or below the mean
☐ *Low average*—Performance from 1 to 2 standard deviations below the mean
☐ *Below average*—Performance more than 2 standard deviations below the mean

This system can be used to report levels of performance, with standard scores inserted in parentheses. The system is based upon the use of standard scores and a consideration of SEM and SEM$_{diff}$. However, grade or age equivalents could be reported in parentheses to make the results more intelligible. This solves the problem of using the different interpretation systems of various tests, such as the *Woodcock Reading Mastery Tests–Revised* (Woodcock, 1987) and the *Test of Language Development–2, Primary* (Newcomer & Hammill, 1988).

Indicate other test scores and data to corroborate findings. One measure should be initially chosen that is a base for a statement about performance. However, other available test scores and data can be used to substantiate this statement. Any discrepancy in the findings should be addressed and reconciled.

Use correct and incorrect student responses and other examples to illustrate a learning problem. Informal analysis of correct and incorrect responses often yields rich illustrations of patterns of learning behavior. They can be integrated into the report to make the findings clearer.

Whenever learning performance in one area seems to be affecting performance in another area, indicate the relationship. Sometimes a student's strengths or weaknesses in one skill affect performance in other areas. For example, poor handwriting skills may partially explain difficulty on written spelling tests and math worksheets. Draw relationships among these associated areas of learning in an orderly and logical way. As indicated before, the results of the assessment in each area should initially be presented separately and sequentially; that is, reading, mathematics, and so forth. Then you can make statements about appropriate relationships. Furthermore, these relationships should be stated only for data that have been reported previously. For example, discussion of the relationship between mathematical and reading performances occurs after the data in mathematics itself have been discussed; the association of the language data with the reading and math performance must be delayed until after the language data are reported. This procedure considerably simplifies the interpretation and reporting of results. Relationships are mentioned only once, in the most appropriate place, and random and repetitious discussions are avoided.

Table 15–2 will help you consider possible relationships of assessed areas based on the content of the assessment tasks. As explained earlier, each area has subdivisions that can be compared on the basis of content and current research. For example, performance in reading word attack skills can be compared to reading comprehension skills. Furthermore, comparisons can be made across areas. As shown in Table 15–2, problem-solving skills in mathematics may be related to a variety of other areas: reading comprehension, mathematical computation, oral language (vocabulary, syntax, and morphology), and written language (handwriting). Strengths or weaknesses in these areas can affect math problem-solving ability.

Another basis for comparison is the structural composition of the assessment tasks themselves: directions, presentation and response modes, and time and accuracy requirements. Within the same general areas (such as reading) and across areas (such as reading and oral language), there may be a similarity in the tasks that the student performs well or poorly. For example, a student may do well in all areas when an oral response is appropriate, but poorly when a written response is expected.

These comparisons should be made both formally and informally. Formally, available test scores are used and statistically compared. Informally, the logical connection of content and structural components suggests possible relationships. Informal analysis must suffice for data not in the form of test scores. Formal and informal interpretations help the assessment team see patterns in the student's learning performance profile. Information about strengths and weaknesses contributes to the data base for making decisions concerning goals, objectives, and so forth.

Integrate information about educational and noneducational correlates at the appropriate point. This information can be useful in interpreting assessment results. Data about classroom tasks, materials, methods, and the physical environment can be used to explain different performances on the tests and on classroom tasks, if necessary. Information can be integrated into the report wherever appropriate. The noninstructional correlates (medical, social, and cultural) should also be included if the student's academic and behavioral performance seems connected to any of these factors. For example, the student's linguistic and cultural background may be affecting school performance. Report this information early under "Relevant Background," but mention it again if and when it is germane to the discussion.

Reserve specific statements about instructional plans and appropriate services for the team designing the IEP. The assessment data will naturally indicate the student's instructional deficits and suggest areas for emphasis in the educational plan. However, because a team of professionals and the student's parents must develop the IEP, it would be inappropriate to specify the necessary program in the assessment report. The major deficits should be stated under the final section of the report called "Suggested Goals and Services," along with some general statements about possible appropriate services.

These specific guidelines structure the analysis and discussion of the assessment data. They represent practical suggestions for developing a comprehensive, integrated profile of a student's learning performance. As applied in the following section, they address key assessment questions in an orderly manner.

TABLE 15-2
Relating areas of assessment

	Reading			Mathematics			Oral Language					Written Language			Specific Learning Abilities & Strategies				Classroom Behavior/ Social-Emotional Development	Correlates	
	1	2	3	1	2	3	1	2	3	4	5	1	2	3	1a	1b	1c	2	1	1	2
Reading																					
1. Oral Reading		*	*	*			*		*	*		*			*	*	*	*	*	*	*
2. Comprehension	*		*		*	*	*	*	*						*	*	*	*		*	*
3. Application	*	*				*	*	*	*	*	*	*	*		*	*	*	*	*	*	*
Mathematics																					
1. Computation	*				*	*	*	*	*	*		*			*	*	*	*	*	*	*
2. Problem Solving		*	*	*		*	*	*	*			*	*		*	*	*	*	*	*	*
3. Application	*		*	*	*		*	*	*	*	*	*	*	*	*	*	*	*	*	*	*
Oral Language																					
1. Semantics	*	*	*	*	*	*		*	*	*	*	*			*	*	*	*	*	*	*
2. Syntax	*	*	*	*	*	*	*		*	*	*	*	*		*	*	*	*	*	*	*
3. Morphology	*	*		*		*	*	*		*	*	*	*		*	*	*	*	*	*	*
4. Phonology	*				*		*	*	*		*				*	*	*	*	*	*	*
5. Pragmatics	*		*			*	*	*	*	*				*	*	*	*	*	*	*	*
Written Language																					
1. Spelling	*						*		*				*	*	*	*	*	*	*	*	*
2. Handwriting									*			*	*		*	*	*	*	*	*	*
3. Composition	*	*				*	*	*	*	*	*	*	*		*	*	*	*	*	*	*
Specific Learning Abilities & Strategies																					
1. Abilities																					
a. Attention	*	*	*	*	*	*	*	*	*	*	*	*	*	*	*	*	*	*	*	*	*
b. Perception	*	*	*	*	*	*	*	*	*	*	*	*	*	*	*	*	*	*	*	*	*
c. Memory	*	*	*	*	*	*	*	*	*	*	*	*	*	*	*	*	*	*	*	*	*
2. Strategies	*	*	*	*	*	*	*	*	*	*	*	*	*	*	*	*	*	*	*	*	*
Classroom Behavior and Social-Emotional Development	*	*	*	*	*	*	*	*	*	*	*	*	*	*	*	*	*	*	*	*	*
Correlates																					
1. Instructional	*	*	*	*	*	*	*	*	*	*	*	*	*	*	*	*	*	*	*	*	*
2. Noninstructional	*	*	*	*	*	*	*	*	*	*	*	*	*	*	*	*	*	*	*	*	*

464

Answering the Assessment Questions

For the purposes of a report, consider assessment questions in the fashion outlined here. Although this organization constitutes a modification of the assessment question model in Figure 1–1 (p. 18), there is a clearer flow of the information needed to address questions of eligibility for special services and program needs.

What is the level of intellectual functioning and adaptive behavior? Indicate the range (e.g., below average) where the total test score falls. If you used the *WISC-R* (Wechsler, 1974), report the three major IQ scores and indicate any difference. Traditional psychological reports may also include a student's performance on other developmental measures such as visual-motor ones. The results of relevant observations, interviews, and other informal procedures should also be reported here.

Eligibility for special education services often requires additional information about adaptive skills, as compared to performance on measures of intellectual performance. For example, the *AAMD Adaptive Behavior Scale, School Edition* (Lambert & Windmiller, 1981) can indicate comparison with students in similar age groups and ability levels. The results of relevant observations and other informal procedures should also be reported here. For example, the results of Phillip's psychological and adaptive behavior assessments showed that he is below average in these areas.

What is the level of academic achievement; what are strengths and weaknesses in school learning? Begin by stating a student's current level of overall academic performance. One of the individual achievement batteries, such as the *Woodcock-Johnson Psycho-Educational Battery–Revised* (Woodcock & Johnson, 1989), will supply a global level of performance and an indication of strengths and weaknesses. The results from the achievement battery can be compared to the student's age, grade placement, intellectual performance and adaptive behavior, and so forth.

Thus, this early section of the discussion of results establishes the level of general academic achievement and indicates whether it is appropriate for the student's ability—whether there is a match between expected and actual achievement. This point must be established to determine eli-gibility for special education services. But criteria vary across handicaps; for example, learning disabilities occur when a student with average or above average intelligence and adaptive behavior is achieving below that level of development. However, as in Phillip's case, his aptitude–achievement profile is similar to that of mentally handicapped students where both ability and achievement levels are significantly below average.

What is the level of reading achievement; what are strengths and weaknesses? Begin the discussion by stating the student's overall reading performance, strengths, and weaknesses. As discussed in Chapter 11, a standardized reading battery such as the *Woodcock Reading Mastery Tests–Revised* (Woodcock, 1987) offers this kind of preliminary data. Comparisons among subtests indicate strengths and weaknesses. Further confirmation of the student's general reading ability can be gained from other available test data.

Next, oral reading skills, reading comprehension, and use of reading skills may be discussed separately. Draw information from the standardized tests available in each area, as described in Chapter 11. That data can be supplemented with lists of specific mastered and unmastered skills in each area. Data are available from criterion-referenced tests, such as the *BRIGANCE® Diagnostic Inventory of Essential Skills* (Brigance, 1981), and other informal procedures. A comprehensive treatment of the main subdivisions of reading would include a discussion of at least the following:

☐ *Decoding*—Real and nonsense words in isolation; words in phrases, sentences, and paragraphs; typical kinds of errors (such as substitutions, omissions, reversals)

☐ *Comprehension*—Words in isolation and in passages, comprehension after reading orally and silently, different kinds of comprehension (such as factual recall, sequence, main idea, inferences)

☐ *Application*—Application of the skills to different subject matter areas such as science and history and to daily life

This discussion should include comparisons of these different types of reading skills and an indication of their distinctive strengths and weaknesses. Refer to the specific guidelines for directions to accomplish this type of discussion regarding reading achievement. As an example, Phillip's reading skills are described as being more advanced in oral reading than comprehension areas. However, there are deficit skills in both areas.

One must establish the necessary comparisons and relationships in reading achievement to other areas such as oral language and to instructional correlates. Table 15–2 contains many suggestions for possible relationships, such as to mathematical problem solving or spelling. However, as previously noted, delay such discussions until the other area is discussed.

What is the level of mathematical achievement; what are strengths and weaknesses?

The answer to this question can best be stated initially in terms of the student's overall performance, strengths, and weaknesses in mathematics. As discussed in Chapter 12, a standardized mathematics battery, such as the *KeyMath Revised* (Connolly, 1988), offers such preliminary data. Strengths and weaknesses among subtests can be indicated in the fashion described earlier. Other similar data can be used to substantiate or qualify the results.

Next, computational and problem-solving skills, and their application in real life, may be discussed individually. These data are available from the many standardized and informal procedures also described in Chapter 12. Definitely include a list of specific mastery objectives. These data are available from a variety of sources, including criterion-referenced tests such as the *BRIGANCE® Diagnostic Inventory of Basic Skills* (Brigance, 1977). Other informal techniques such as task analysis and error analysis can also be used.

A comprehensive presentation of mathematics skill performance would include a treatment of at least the following:

- □ *Computational Skills*—Verbal and written addition, subtraction, multiplication, and division
- □ *Problem-Solving Skills*—Verbal and written use of computational skills to solve word problems
- □ *Application Skills*—Verbal and written use of computational and problem-solving skills in real-life situations

This discussion should also include comparisons of different kinds of mathematical skills and an indication of distinctive strengths and weaknesses.

Finally, establish the relationship of mathematical performance with any other areas affecting it. Because the data concerning reading achievement have been presented, comment upon the association of reading and mathematics performance. As indicated in Table 15–2, there seems to be a logical connection between computational skills and word recognition; between problem solving and reading comprehension; and between both problem-solving skills and use of reading skills in learning other material. In addition, this information about mathematics performance can be related to both instructional demands, such as classroom procedures, and noninstructional correlates, such as visual or hearing problems. Specific guidelines previously described outline procedures for making these associations. For Phillip, such a discussion notes inconsistent use of computational skills and inadequate grasp of mathematical terms.

What is the level of oral language development; what are strengths and weaknesses?

The student's overall level of oral language development, strengths, and weaknesses can be established early by reporting the results from one of the standardized batteries described in Chapter 14, such as the *Test of Language Development–2, Intermediate* (Hammill & Newcomer, 1988). Use a procedure that samples as many components of oral language as possible. Strengths and weaknesses may be identified from formal analysis of subtest scores and/or informal procedures. Other formal and informal data, such as classroom observations, can be used to support this initial effort to establish the level of the student's performance in oral language.

The second level of discussion involves a separate treatment of the comprehension and use of syntax, morphology, phonology, vocabulary, and pragmatics. As described in Chapter 14, many formal and informal procedures yield data specific to each of these areas of oral language. Although procedures comparable to the criterion-referenced tests in reading and mathematics are not as readily available, an effort must be made through other informal techniques to identify mastered and unmastered skills in each area. The expertise of a speech-language specialist may be required to supply this information.

A discussion of oral language skills may be considered adequate if the following topics are discussed:

□ *Receptive Language*—Phonology, syntax, morphology, semantics, and pragmatics
□ *Expressive Language*—Phonology (articulation), syntax, morphology, semantics, and pragmatics

Performance in these subdivisions of oral language can be compared, and strengths and weaknesses noted. This information will be used in prioritizing needed goals and objectives.

After this within-area discussion, establish any of the relationships of oral language performance with the previously reported reading and mathematics data. For example, poor understanding of the meaning of words (receptive vocabulary) may be related to poor memory of sight vocabulary. In addition, difficulty in understanding syntax and grammar may be part of the problem in reading comprehension and/or math problem solving.

Classroom factors such as the physical environment, and medical, social, and cultural correlates may also shed light on the nature of a student's language performance. In the area of language, note any factors such as hearing disabilities or linguistic background that may partially explain poor language performance.

What is the level of written language development; what are strengths and weaknesses? As described in Chapter 13, there are a number of procedures from which a preliminary statement about a student's overall level of performance in written language can be drawn. For example, the *Test of Written Language–2* (Hammill & Larsen, 1988) yields an overall indication of the development of written language skills and the basis for identifying strengths and weaknesses across a variety of skills. Information concerning performance of written assignments at school, use of written language skills in everyday life, and error analysis of written products can also be used to compose this statement.

The main subdivisions of spelling, handwriting, and composition may then be discussed individually, if necessary. The measures of these specific areas from which the necessary data can be drawn were presented in Chapter 13. For example, the *Test of Written Spelling–2* (Larsen & Hammill,

1986) can be used to distinguish the types of spelling words with which the student may have more difficulty.

However, as is the case in oral language, you will need to rely heavily on informal techniques to specify mastered and unmastered written language skills. Task and error analyses and teacher and student interviews are the main sources for this important level of interpretation and reporting. For example, specify the letters the student can and cannot make, whether the use of commas or periods is creating problems, and so forth. Without this information, it would be extremely difficult to develop instructional goals and objectives.

A full treatment of the student's written language skills, which can serve as a basis for identifying strengths and weaknesses, should at least contain the following:

□ *Spelling Skills*—Oral and written spelling, predictable and unpredictable words, error detection and dictated spelling
□ *Handwriting Skills*—Readiness skills such as copying, upper- and lowercase writing, manuscript and cursive writing
□ *Composition Skills*—Language factors (semantics, syntax), creativity and productivity, and mechanics (punctuation and capitalization)

There are many possible relationships among skills (see Table 15–2). If a student's written language skills seem to be influencing other skills or vice versa, that association should be stated. For example, poor handwriting skills may be keeping the student from completing classroom mathematics assignments, or poor written composition may be the result of inadequate oral vocabulary and comprehension of syntax and grammar. Conversely, well-conceptualized written products may reflect high achievement in reading comprehension and verbal expression.

The student's written language skills should be considered in relationship to instructional conditions in the classroom and noninstructional variables. Written language performance can be influenced by the type of pencils and paper used, the presence of handwriting models, the opportunity for practice, and other classroom variables. In addition, poor eyesight or medication may influence written language production. In Phillip's case, the written language assessment indicates deficits in vocabulary, grammar, creativity, and handwriting.

What is the level of development of specific learning abilities and strategies?

After interpreting and reporting the results of learning performance in reading, mathematics, and oral and written language, it may be necessary to discuss specific learning abilities and strategies that may be involved in the development of these academic skills. As discussed in Chapter 9, the specific learning abilities, such as visual memory or auditory perception, represent readiness factors; the specific learning strategies, such as verbal mediation, represent techniques or approaches to learning.

This area of assessment does not lend itself to the same type of organization previously discussed. Rather, expand upon the following skills that seem to be involved in the learning performance of the student:

□ *Specific Learning Abilities*—Perception, motor skills, memory and attention, and information processing
□ *Learning Strategies*

The data gathered through the formal and informal measures of these skills can be compared to the results of academic performance. Problems in reading or mathematics may be partially connected to deficits in attention or memory. Poor use of specific learning strategies, such as organization, may adversely affect achievement in mathematical problem solving and written composition.

Another set of data are the results of analyzing the instructional demands placed on the student in the classroom. Information about the structural components of tasks (e.g., presentation and response modes) may be compared to the results of visual, auditory, and motor skill assessments. For example, a student with poor fine motor skills may have problems on most tasks that require a written response.

In addition, medical problems may affect the development of specific learning abilities such as attention. For example, hyperactivity or the use of medication may affect the student's ability to pay attention. Social and cultural practices can also influence specific learning abilities and strategies in many ways. Some cultural groups use different cognitive strategies than others and employ auditory, visual, and motor skills differently. These cultural practices may influence the development of required specific learning abilities and strategies.

This treatment of specific learning abilities and strategies can be drawn upon when considering questions about eligibility for special education services and about instructional programming. Although this area is of particular interest for learning disabled students, it is also a relevant assessment question to ask about all mildly handicapped students. In Phillip's case, the report indicates problems with abstract, symbolic material as well as with long-term memory demands. However, his positive responses to certain instructional strategies in reading, mathematics, and written language indicate intact learning strategies.

What is the status of classroom behavior and social-emotional development?

It may be initially useful to present the results of a broad survey of possible behavior problems; a number of procedures offering this type of assessment such as the *Behavior Rating Profile* (Brown & Hammill, 1983a) were discussed in Chapter 10. They also include a consideration of strengths and weaknesses.

A more specific description of problems in this area may then be given. The results of classroom observations, interviews with parents and teachers, and sociograms are useful for discussing specific behavior problems, strengths, and weaknesses. The major factors to be considered in such a discussion are

□ *Problem Behavior*
□ *Self-concept and Peer Acceptance*
□ *School Attitudes and Interests*
□ *Learning Environment*

This treatment of the results of behavioral assessment should be reserved until the end of the discussion, because it can be related to all the other areas assessed. Underachievement and specific learning problems in reading, mathematics, and oral and written language may be more understandable when related to behavioral data. For example, students with disruptive behavior or poor study habits may have difficulty doing well in all basic subjects.

Furthermore, there may also be a behavioral basis for poor development and use of general aptitude (intelligence), of specific learning abilities such as attention, and of specific learning strategies such as organization. For example, hyperactive students may also have problems maintaining attention or recalling information. Poor performance on measures of intellectual functioning and adaptive behavior may be partially due to behavioral problems.

Instructional factors like strategies the teacher uses to present information and reward accomplishments are critical influences on how a student behaves in the classroom. As discussed in Chapter 10, the classroom represents a broad arena of social and emotional interactions that affect what and how a student learns. There may also be a physical basis for behavioral problems. Or, as in the case of poor behavioral management skills, a student's disruptive behavior may be partially related to inappropriate techniques used by parents and others. The results of the assessment of adaptive behavior and the ability to cope with the demands of the home and other settings may also be appropriate to consider at this point.

This discussion of behavioral problems is useful for answering questions about eligibility for special education as well as instructional planning. Although germane to any of the mildly handicapped conditions, severe behavior problems and emotional difficulties are critical in decisions about services for the emotionally disturbed. They may also be the basis for instructional goals and objectives, as well as useful in designing general classroom conditions. For Phillip, the answer to this assessment question is that he lags behind his peers in interactional skills and independent living skills. However, he has reacted well to behavior management strategies.

Summary and Conclusions

After analyzing and discussing the particulars of a student's learning problem, summarize the main points and present an integrated view of the student's disabilities. This section is not a repetition of all the points made already. However, the major aspects of the student's abilities and disabilities must be included to give clear direction in composing recommendations.

First, indicate the overall level of functioning in all areas measured, specifying relative strengths and weaknesses. Second, report the current level of performance for each area separately (reading, mathematics, etc.), including strengths and weaknesses. Third, mention specific mastered and un-

mastered skills. Fourth, indicate prominent relationships among the various problems and the possible impact of correlates such as sensory problems. For Phillip, such a summary profiles the slow but gradual progress achieved in recent years and indicates new goals, including one in the vocational area.

Suggested Goals and Services

The student's major academic and behavioral deficits are transformed into suggested instructional needs. For infants and preschoolers they will be developmental in nature, and for adolescents and young adults, vocational and transitional in nature. This information can facilitate the discussion of the IEP team that must develop a full program based on the assessment data. Although the ultimate IEP plan will have greater specificity, these suggestions pinpoint major learning deficits and provide suggestions about possible services. In Phillip's case, needs are indicated in academic, behavioral, and vocational areas, and some ways to provide assistance in these areas are noted.

This assessment report should provide the team of professionals and the student's parents a data base from which to develop the kind of individual program required by PL 94–142. The IEP team must discuss and determine the following key elements of the plan:

1. A statement of current levels of performance, with strengths and weaknesses
2. Annual goals and short-term instructional objectives
3. The special education and related services needed
4. The extent of participation in the regular education program
5. Projected beginning and ending dates of the special program
6. The criteria, procedures, and schedule for the review process

PREPARING THE IEP

The IEP may be designed at the same conference as the assessment results are explained or at another one. As described in Chapter 2, the team designing the IEP should include someone familiar with the assessment results. The information that is the basis of the IEP should also be readily available in assessment reports. Some components of the IEP may be drawn directly from the assessment report (depending upon how thorough it was), whereas other aspects of the plan are decided from a combination of the assessment data and other key factors. The team designing the IEP will have to deliberate on many of its specific items, because the assessment data is only one source of direction. The following sections indicate how to compose the main elements of an IEP from assessment data and other sources. The components of these IEP factors are mandated by PL 94–142 (as clarified in the 1981 *Federal Register*) and by good practice.

Current Levels of Educational Performance

The statements used to indicate a student's current levels of performance should demonstrate the effect of the disability on academic and nonacademic skill development. Diagnostic labels cannot be substituted (*Federal Register*, 1981). Statements should be presented in objective, measurable terms, including test scores when and if they are easily understandable and meaningful. There must also be a clear relationship between the stated levels of performance and the other IEP components to follow.

There are a variety of strategies to use in stating this information. Always review the assessment data gathered. The student's performance can be stated in quantitative terms and compared to others of the same age, grade placement, and so forth based on formal and informal data.

Levels of performance should also refer to the subject and skill area assessed and for which the IEP is being developed (Turnbull et al., 1982). Levels can be based on a student's strengths and weaknesses, the curriculum currently available in the mainstream, and relevance to the student's needs, age, and interests. It may be necessary to gather additional data to compose this component of the IEP. Take particular care to base it on current data and use measurable and specific terms, for example, "cannot follow a three-part oral command" or "can name all primary colors."

As indicated in the sample IEP (see Figure 15–2), Phillip is described as having an overall delayed level of development and poor achievement. However, he has some definite strengths and areas where he has benefited from instruction and therapy.

Annual Goals

The stated goals in the IEP should be directly related to the current levels of performance and should be connected with other components of the IEP (*Federal Register*, 1981). Goals should serve as a basis for the specifics to follow and should focus the general direction of the IEP. They represent the achievement anticipated for the student over a period of time, generally a year, and are an educated guess.

When composing these annual goals (Turnbull et al., 1982) the IEP team must

- Examine a student's past achievement and rate of progress
- Refer to the stated levels of performance and especially the student's weaknesses
- Consider the practicality and relevance of the goals for a student
- Prioritize the student's needs from the simple to complex and on the basis of immediate need
- Consider the amount of time to be devoted to the instruction of a goal
- Use specific, measurable terms, e.g., "Phillip will use appropriate punctuation marks when writing."

As illustrated in Phillip's IEP, annual goals encompass academic, social-emotional, and vocational areas. They are to be pursued in a coordinated fashion.

Short-term Objectives

The IEP's short-term objectives are measurable, intermediate steps in accomplishing the goals (*Federal Register*, 1981). They should describe what a child is expected to accomplish in a particular area over a specified period of time. Further, they are a means to determine the extent to which the student is progressing toward the program goals.

By their nature they are more specific than annual goals, referring to weekly or monthly, rather than yearly, activities and yet are not as detailed as daily lesson plans (*Federal Register*, 1981). They must be specific, observable, and measurable statements (e.g., "will use 10 commonly used oral vocabulary words in written material with 100% accuracy") and yet stop short of indicating instructional materials and procedures of daily lesson plans.

The IEP team should sequence and arrange their short-term objectives in a logical and systematic fashion (Turnbull et al., 1982). Task analysis can be used to arrange the objectives in a variety of ways in relationship to the annual goals. Refer to the discussion of task analysis in Chapter 5.

Another important feature of short-term objectives is instructional value; that is, they need to specify

1. What the student is expected to do
2. The particular skill area for which the objective is written
3. Within what specific time period the objective should be accomplished or another means for determining the extent to which the objective is met (such as number of correct responses, percent of correct responses, etc.)
(*Federal Register,* 1981, p. 5470)

An example objective might be: "Given his own written paragraph, Phillip will circle all the misspelled words in 5 minutes." It is no coincidence that these requirements seem similar to those of an instructional objective. Such short-term objectives are meant to structure and focus instruction.

The IEP team must apply the same rules of appropriateness, relevance, and manageability in drafting short-term objectives as in composing annual goals. They can rely on the same types of information just outlined, especially data generated by criterion-referenced testing, task analysis, and behavioral observations. A number of resources are also available to assist the IEP team in framing IEP objectives: (a) curriculum guides and curriculum checklists available in many school systems, (b) commercially developed resource banks of goals and objectives such as the *Instructional Based Appraisal System* (Meyen, Gautt, & Howard, 1976), and (c) commercial materials with skill scope and sequence charts. The topic of developing and evaluating objectives is discussed in Chapter 16. As illustrated in Phillip's IEP, the short-term objectives specify intermediate steps toward goals in the various areas. They are more applied and resemble what happens regularly in the classroom.

Specific Special Education and Related Services

The IEP also indicates the kind of special educational and related needs that handicapped students have and the type of services they require. According to PL 94–142, special education means "specially designed instruction, at no cost to the parents, to meet the unique needs of a handicapped child, including classroom instruction, instruction in physical education, home instruction, and instruction in hospitals and institutions" (§121a.14). It includes speech pathology, vocational education, or any related service—transportation and support such as psychological services, physical and occupational therapy, recreation, early identification and assessment of disabilities in children, counseling, and medical diagnosis. The service must be specially designed to meet the unique needs of the student. The student may also receive school health services, social work services, and family counseling, if needed.

The IEP team must decide which of these services are required, based on the stated goals and objectives. Related services (e.g., transportation) must be substantiated by evaluation results and supported by the recommendations of a qualified service provider regarding the nature, frequency, and amount of service to be provided the student (*Federal Register,* 1981). All the needed services must be indicated on the IEP.

Special education services for mildly handicapped students are available for mild mental retardation, emotional disturbance, and specific learning disabilities. State departments usually supply definitions of these exceptionalities. The assessment team can use these definitions to decide if the student is eligible for services. In the IEP, the types of services for which the student is eligible can be indicated in several ways. The student may be labeled as "learning disabled," "behavior disordered," and so forth. Another approach is to designate the teachers and their titles, such as "Mr. Thompson, the teacher of the mildly retarded class" or "the EMR teacher." In states using cross-categorical services, the program may be called "educationally handicapped." Sometimes only the type of service or professional needed will be indicated, such as "speech-language services" or "speech-language clinician." The parents or students themselves may be designated as responsible for accomplishing certain goals.

In the sample IEP in Figure 15–2, Phillip will not only receive special education but also counseling and occupational therapy. He will have contact with his normal peers and also benefit from the vocational program.

FIGURE 15–2
Sample IEP

Child's Name: Phillip Hughes   Birthdate: 4/20/74   Grade: 8.8

School: Glenover H.S.   Date Referred: 3-year reevaluation   Date Tested: 4/4/89–4/9/89

Current Levels of Performance (Strengths and Weaknesses)

Phillip's intellectual development is significantly below average for his age; his adaptive behavioral skills are similar to those of mildly retarded students, especially in personal-social responsibility and adjustment. All academic skills are below average; however, reading and mathematics are relative strengths, and written language and knowledge areas are relative weaknesses.

Phillip's oral reading skills are better than his comprehension in remembering details and central ideas. Phillip is somewhat better in mathematical computations than in problem solving, but consistency and correct use of fractions, measurement, and other concepts to solve problems are weaknesses. Phillip's handwriting, language, and grammar restrict his written work.

Phillip's current vocational interests are in nonmanual areas like animal care, food service, and horticulture; his attitudes and preparatory skills for the world of work need instruction. His social-emotional priority needs are in the area of peer relationships and developing greater independence.

Performance Data

RANGE OF PERFORMANCE

	Below Average	Low Average	Average	High Average	Above Average
WISC–R	*				
DTLA–2	*				
ABS–SE	*				
Woodcock-Johnson–R					
Reading		*			
Math		*			
Written Language	*				
TOWL–2	*				
BRP	*				
Purdue	*				

LONG-TERM GOALS

Area: Reading
1. Phillip will apply structural analysis in orally decoding words.

2. Phillip will remember requested details of material he reads silently.

3. Other goals will follow.

Area: Mathematics
1. Phillip will use averaging to solve daily problems.

2. Phillip will use fractions to solve daily problems.

3. Other goals will follow.

SHORT-TERM OBJECTIVES

Area: Reading
1. Given 25 three-syllable words, Phillip will identify the prefix, root, and suffix of words with 100% accuracy.
2. Given 25 three-syllable words, Phillip will read them orally with 90% accuracy.
1. Having been told five facts to identify in a passage beforehand, Phillip will underline these items with 100% accuracy.
2. Given five factual questions after reading a passage, Phillip will answer with 100% accuracy.

Area: Mathematics
1. Given the shooting average of five University of Louisville basketball players, Phillip will compute the overall team average accurately.
2. Given a pizza, Phillip will compute what part each of his eight classmates will receive. He will cut the pieces accurately.

Area: Written Language
1. Phillip will use appropriate grammatical rules in writing.

2. Phillip will verbalize familiar terms for a written passage.
3. Other goals will follow.

Area: Vocational
1. Phillip will clarify his vocational interests.

2. Other goals will follow.

Area: Social-Emotional
1. Phillip will learn to relate appropriately to peers.

2. Other goals will follow.

Area: Written Language
1. Given a passage with 10 grammatical errors in use of tenses and plurals, Phillip will circle all the errors in 5 minutes.
2. After a field trip, Phillip will write 10 terms to be used in a written passage.

Area: Vocational
1. Given a series of work samples, Phillip will indicate his entry skills, interests, and work habits. Phillip will answer all questions correctly.

Area: Social-Emotional
1. Given the picture of his classmates, Phillip will verbalize their appealing and unappealing qualities.

Responsible Personnel
Academic and Vocational Goals: Mr. Thompson (special education teacher), Ms. Smith (vocational education teacher), and Mr. Wright (ninth grade homeroom)
Motor and Social-Emotional Goals: Ms. Tribble (occupational therapist) and Ms. Swift (counselor)

Placement Recommendation
Phillip will remain in the special education program. He will be assigned to a regular homeroom for an hour a day, with 3 hours in the special education resource room and 2 hours in the vocational laboratory. Phillip will see the counselor twice a week for 1 hour; he will receive occupational therapy for 1 hour a week.

Timeline
The program starts 8/25/89 and continues until review on 6/3/90.

Evaluation
BRIGANCE® subtests will be used to monitor skills development and the *Woodcock-Johnson Psycho-Educational Battery–Revised* will be readministered. Interviews with Phillip, his parents, the counselor, and the teachers will be used for behavioral goals. Results of vocational work sample analyses will be studied.

Committee Members	Member Name	Signature
Parent	Ed Hughes	*Ed Hughes*
Special education teacher	Tom Thompson	*Tom Thompson*
Vocational education teacher	Barbara Smith	*Barbara Smith*
Counselor	Jane Swift	*Jane Swift*
Occupational therapist	Terry Tribble	*Terry Tribble*

For Parent Use
I agree with this plan and grant permission for continued placement in special education.

Ed Hughes
Signature

_6/6/89_
Date

Extent of Time in the Regular Classroom

When the type of program and appropriate goals and objectives are identified, choose an appropriate method of delivering the services to the student. It must be decided where, how, and by whom the services will be supplied. This decision about the student's placement is governed by the following regulation:

1. That to the maximum extent appropriate, handicapped children, including children in public or private institutions or other care facilities, are educated with children who are not handicapped, and
2. That special classes, separate schooling or other removal of handicapped children from the regular educational environment occurs only when the nature or severity of the handicap is such that education in regular classes with the use of supplementary aids and services cannot be achieved satisfactorily. (PL 94–142, §121a.550)

This principle of the least restrictive environment guides the educational placement of the student. The handicapped student must be educated in the regular classroom with normal peers as much as feasible, considering the needs of both handicapped and nonhandicapped students.

Specifically, the placement of exceptional students must be based on the needs stated in the IEP; must be as close to the student's home as possible, preferably in the school where the student would normally go if not handicapped; and must indicate attention to any potentially harmful effects on the student or the quality of the program. Therefore, choice of a service delivery method is based on both individual needs and the principle of the least restrictive environment.

The major service delivery models are the following:

1. *Regular classroom model*—The handicapped student is in the regular classroom all day and receives any needed assistance from the teacher. This arrangement constitutes no special education service in itself.
2. *Consultant teacher model*—The handicapped student is in the regular classroom all day, and the classroom teacher receives needed support from a consultant teacher. The special service is for the teacher and indirectly for the student.
3. *Itinerant teacher model*—The handicapped student is in the regular classroom most of the day and is taken out periodically (perhaps once or twice a week) for special help, such as speech therapy.
4. *Resource room model*—The handicapped student is in the regular classroom for part of the day and in the special education resource room for the rest of the day to receive special help, such as reading instruction. Generally, the exceptional student is considered a member of the regular classroom group and the responsibility of that teacher.
5. *Special class model*—The handicapped student is in the special class with other handicapped students for most of the day, although he or she may participate in some regular class activities. The special educator has primary responsibility for the student.
6. *Special day school model*—The handicapped student attends a special school with other exceptional students each day and returns home at night.
7. *Residential model*—The handicapped student lives at a special school, institution, or hospital, and receives all special services there.

There should be a choice of these alternative service arrangements. These models can be arranged on a continuum to indicate the degree to which students participate with their normal peers. The regular classroom model allows the maximum contact between handicapped and nonhandicapped students and may partially serve large numbers of exceptional students. Two additional models that facilitate integration are the consultant teacher, who offers the classroom teacher necessary support, and the itinerant specialist, who trains the student in certain skills. The resource room model permits partial integration, while supplying specialized assistance within the school building.

The special class, although more restrictive than the other models, is used for the student with more complex, severe, and global learning problems. The same is true of the day school and residential models. Although the student's educational needs are the primary basis for placement, a special day school may also be chosen because of the need to house all specialists and materials in one place, because of cooperative planning among school districts, or because of parental preference. When the handicapped student has multiple needs and local services are unavailable, the residential model is used. In such cases, the school district must pay all costs.

These choices of how to serve the student are not mutually exclusive. For example, an exceptional student in a special class may also require speech therapy from an itinerant speech teacher. The goal is to offer all the necessary services and still keep handicapped students with their peers. When and if a more restrictive model is needed, the goal is to return the student to full-time education in the regular classroom as soon as possible. Furthermore, handicapped students in special classes and day schools can be integrated with normal peers on a limited basis in, for example, art and physical education.

The placement decision is based on the nature, number, and severity of the student's needs, as indicated in the IEP. It is also necessary to be aware of the pros and cons of different kinds of placements (Wallace & McLoughlin, 1988). Emphasis in placement decisions should be on *how* to get services to handicapped students, not necessarily *where*. Services should be provided on the basis of educational needs of students, not teacher or program labels.

Most mildly handicapped students are or have been in the regular classroom. Many are served in the regular classroom part of the day and in the resource room during the rest, or through itinerant and consultant services in the regular classroom. Special classes, special schools, and residential facilities are used far less frequently. Sometimes the regular classroom placement is not the best model, because the student's needs cannot be met in that environment. In that case, the regular classroom placement is not truly the least restrictive.

The placement decisions are reported in the IEP in many ways. The type of model may be designated, such as "special class." It may also be labeled for a particular exceptionality, for example, "the resource room for learning disabilities." Another technique used is to name the teachers and their titles, such as "Mrs. Jones, the LD resource teacher."

However, the IEP must always indicate the extent to which the handicapped student will participate in regular educational programs. The amount of time (30 minutes per day), a percentage

of the school day (75% of the day), and the type of activity (fourth grade PE) are examples. As shown in the sample IEP, Phillip will be mainstreamed part of his school day and receive specialized assistance during other parts. He will be with normal peers during homeroom, vocational education, and nonacademic activities.

Projected Dates

The dates of starting the program and projected dates of goal completion must be documented in the IEP. This timeline requirement guarantees that the IEP is implemented and that a reasonable amount of time is allowed for the completion of the goals. It is an effort to make the placement in special education temporary; in the past, some handicapped students were placed in special programs and remained there past the time they needed special services—some until they finished their schooling. This information is usually indicated on the IEP by dates. As shown in the sample IEP, Phillip's program will continue through the next school year and be reviewed in June 1990.

Evaluation and Annual Review

The IEP must be evaluated annually, or more often if necessary. It must contain appropriate objective criteria and evaluation procedures to measure the effectiveness of the program, and a schedule for assessing the achievement of short-term instructional objectives.

The purpose of yearly evaluations is to determine student progress and plan the next year's instructional program. In the annual evaluation, the IEP team reviews the student's progress of the last year in a summative fashion and decides whether broad program modifications are necessary.

Many alternative decisions are available. For example, the IEP team may decide that the student no longer needs special education services. Or they may find that progress was not sufficient and thus increase the amount of special education services.

Additionally, formative evaluation or ongoing assessment takes place in the classroom throughout the school year. It provides information about the student's achievement of objectives. It also helps the educator make the following instructional decisions.

1. Is progress sufficient to justify continuation of the present instructional procedures?
2. Do progress data indicate whether the instructional objective is appropriate or inappropriate for the student?
3. Is the criterion level appropriate for the instructional objective?
4. If the objective is reached, what is the appropriate next step? (Lilly, 1977, pp. 28–29)

Affleck, Lowenbraun, and Archer (1980) recommend program modification when student progress appears unsatisfactory. Inadequate progress is indicated when the student's rate of learning decreases significantly, when no change is seen over a period of time, or when the student or parent expresses dissatisfaction with the progress. Strategies to accomplish these evaluations and reviews are discussed in Chapter 16.

In the IEP, the specific procedures and schedule for the annual review are indicated several ways. Specific tests or other assessment procedures are mentioned. Sometimes the general assessment strategy, such as criterion-referenced testing, is indicated; the person to gather the data can also be mentioned. The IEP may have a place to record completion of goals and objectives or any current academic achievements. The schedule for the review is composed of the appropriate dates. The annual review often occurs in June, after a school year of instruction. The accomplishment of goals and objectives will be evaluated by the team using an assortment of criterion-referenced and standardized tests as well as informal procedures and continuous monitoring.

The development of such Individual Education Programs and the assessment process preceding them are the work of a team. Although much of the work is done prior to the meeting, major decisions are made at team conferences. Professionals and parents may study the assessment data beforehand and outline the possible elements of a program to facilitate the team discussion. For efficiency, such meetings need to be guided by certain principles. Whereas Chapter 17 is devoted to a detailed treatment of parental participation in such conferences, the next section summarizes general points about team conferencing.

THE TEAM CONFERENCE

The session or sessions where the results of the assessment are reported and used for planning the initial IEP or other instructional changes are a critical event. Assessment results must be shared and discussed with other educators, related professionals, parents, and perhaps the student. Then, if the student is considered eligible for special education, the elements of a program are discussed and agreed upon. The style of explanation of the assessment results must be shaped to the audience, and in this situation there may be many audiences. The priorities and interests of the various parties may also complicate the conference. There may be hidden agendas or differences of opinion among the people at the session. However, this meeting must be effective, because this group is likely to be the core of individuals involved in the student's program.

There are a number of procedural guidelines to keep in mind when participating in an assessment and/or IEP conference. First, the written assessment reports should be available to everyone involved, preferably before the conference. Second, the conference should begin and end at a specific time and be of reasonable duration. Third, the chairperson of the conference should arrange for introductions, establish the purpose and method of proceeding, and otherwise facilitate and direct the discussion. Fourth, each participant should personally report the results of his or her own assessment. After the individual reporting is completed, participants can comment on the findings and relate the results to already reported information. For example, after the reports from the psychologist and classroom teacher, the special educator may be able to confirm a common finding or contribute a particular insight about the student's behavior. It is essential to allow each report to be completed, to reserve comment until all information has been presented, and to avoid repetitions and irrelevant comments.

Fifth, parents, the student (if present), and others should be actively encouraged to participate in the conference. Students should participate if they and their parents agree it would be helpful and contribute to the discussion. In Chapter 17 we discuss strategies for encouraging participation.

Sixth, every participant in the conference should follow the flow of the discussion and attempt to identify a pattern within the assessment results or appropriate solutions to deliberations about IEP components.

Seventh, professionals should not read their reports or attempt to cover all information in detail. In fact, the written report should be abbreviated and reorganized for the verbal presentation. The main points to cover are the reason for referral, the student's behavior during the assessment, a brief summary of the results, and the curricular recommendations. Delay the discussion of the needed special education and related services, as well as the service delivery models to be used, until after all the participants have contributed their input.

Eighth, when sharing the results of the assessment or describing programmatic options, attempt to avoid technical language as much as possible. This practice may facilitate sharing among the professionals as well as with the parents and student, because different disciplines often use different terminology and constructs. Confusion and misunderstanding can be avoided if everyone attempts to communicate in everyday language.

Ninth, the assessment results should be reported as graphically and clearly as possible. Examples of test items and other tasks can be given. It helps to supply samples of the student's work or behavior, perhaps with audio or visual records. Some types of assessment procedures are particularly intelligible and easy to report; for example, charts of observed behaviors or lists of mastered and unmastered skills do not pose any translation problems.

Tenth, it is helpful to everyone, particularly lay participants, to reduce the many results to a common scale or form. Some of the tests and other procedures described in Chapters 7 through 14 supply profiles to facilitate reporting. However, an informal presentation of the current level of performance across all assessed areas, indicating strengths and weaknesses, is also very useful in conceptualizing the student's abilities and disabilities. For example, Drew, Freston, and Logan (1972) suggest a procedure for profiling data. The results of teacher referral and formal assessment data are reduced to a 5-point scale, with 1 meaning very low and 5 meaning very high. Similar profiles can be constructed with more specific breakdowns in each major area, such as reading.

It is also possible to reduce all of the assessment data into the interpretative system of ranges described throughout this text. As noted in Figure 15–3, Phillip's performances in all the areas assessed have been recorded as being average or not. That decision is made on the basis of one or more formal or informal measures in each area. This kind of display may help the team appreciate relative strengths and weaknesses. Further, the articulation of IEP components, such as levels of performance and annual goals, may occur more easily. Such a reporting device is particularly helpful with parents.

Another possibility is to follow the model of the profiles used by measures such as the *Test of Language Development–2, Primary* (Newcomer & Hammill, 1988). Standard scores are arranged in the margins, parallel to columns for areas assessed. A mark is made in each column, and lines are drawn between marks to establish a pattern. Lines can be drawn across the profile to signify levels of expectation or criterion, or shaded or colored areas can be used to designate high and low performances. However, such procedures, although helpful in sharing information, may result in the loss and sometimes distortion of data.

Eleventh, all conference participants should contribute to the discussion of recommendations concerning special education services, the most appropriate service delivery model, and so on. After all the assessment results have been reported and discussed, those questions can be answered. They should be team decisions, as the assessment itself has been.

Twelfth, the student's IEP may be designed as part of the postassessment conference or can be done in a later meeting. Whenever it is being composed, the data can be easily abstracted from the assessment report. Given the described structure for a report, the information for the IEP can be drawn mainly from the "Summary and Conclusions" and "Suggested Goals and Services" sections.

The completion of an assessment and the development of an appropriate IEP set in motion a program that must be monitored regularly and

FIGURE 15–3

Profile of Phillip's performance

	Below Average	Low Average	Average	High Average	Above Average
School Performance	X				
Intellectual Performance	X				
Adaptive Behavior	X				
Attention		X			
Perception		X			
Memory		X			
Student Behavior		X			
Self-Concept		X			
Reading: Oral Reading	X				
Reading: Comprehension		X			
Reading: Application		X			
Math: Computation		X			
Math: Problem Solving	X				
Math: Application	X				
Listening		X			
Speaking		X			
Handwriting	X				
Spelling		X			
Composition	X				
Career/Vocation		X			
Fine-Motor	X				

reviewed at least annually. This continuation of the assessment process is integrated into instruction and serves to create a consistent flow of information about the students and their programs. As discussed in the next chapter, the monitoring and evaluation process uses the same procedures described throughout this text but coordinated with an intervention program.

STUDY GUIDE

Review Questions

1. What are the three major assessment questions to be answered after interpreting and reporting results?
2. What are the main components of an assessment report?
3. Indicate whether the following statements are true or false in regard to interpreting and reporting assessment results.
   - T F **a.** Report all the data gathered.
   - T F **b.** Only the sources of test scores should be referenced.
   - T F **c.** Consider only educational matters.
   - T F **d.** Make recommendations freely at any time.
   - T F **e.** Ignore results from other assessments.
   - T F **f.** Use only the present tense.
   - T F **g.** Refer to the examiner in the first person.
   - T F **h.** Avoid making inferences.
4. Information in "Relevant Background" includes _____ , _____ , and _____ areas.

5. It (is) (is not) important to indicate the student's behavior during the assessment.

6. The major referents to judge levels of underachievement are _____ , _____ , and _____ .

7. What is a useful order for reporting data about skills?

8. The discussion of assessment results in oral language can be divided into _____ , _____ , _____ , _____ , and _____ .

9. Indicate whether the following statements are true or false in regard to interpreting and reporting results.
   - T   F   **a.** A list of mastered and unmastered skills is useful in designing instructional objectives.
   - T   F   **b.** An intraindividual interpretation compares students to a normative group.
   - T   F   **c.** A "relative" strength in a skill may not be a true strength.
   - T   F   **d.** A test name may not clearly indicate the nature of a test.
   - T   F   **e.** Report one kind of score as often as possible.

10. Two statistics that assist in interpreting test scores for significant differences are _____ and _____ .

11. Match the ranges in Column A to the appropriate descriptors in Column B.

Column A	Column B
a. Above Average	_____ Within 1 standard deviation above or below the mean
b. High Average	_____ More than 2 standard deviations above the mean
c. Average	_____ More than 2 standard deviation below the mean
d. Low Average	_____ From 1 to 2 standard deviations below the mean
e. Below Average	_____ From 1 to 2 standard deviations above the mean

12. Skill areas may be compared on the basis of _____ and _____ .

13. Oral reading skills may be related to which of the following skills?
    - _____ **a.** Reading comprehension
    - _____ **b.** Computation skills
    - _____ **c.** Phonology
    - _____ **d.** Spelling
    - _____ **e.** Auditory and visual skills

14. Indicate whether the following statements about the assessment conference are true or false.
    - T   F   **a.** Written assessment reports should be available to conference participants before the conference.
    - T   F   **b.** One professional view should dominate the conference.
    - T   F   **c.** Parents should maintain a low profile at the conference.
    - T   F   **d.** The most appropriate procedure for professionals is to read their reports aloud.
    - T   F   **e.** It is difficult to report assessment information graphically.

15. It is useful to delay discussion of suggested goals and services until all the assessment results and educational needs have been discussed. (True or False)

Activities

1. Read a report of an assessment. Can you find any problems with it? How would you improve it?

2. Interview professionals who perform assessments. Ask them how they analyze and report the data.

3. Compare assessment reports written by a neurologist, psychologist, and special educator. How do they differ?

4. Given data from a student's assessment, write or verbally discuss the results. Did you observe the practices mentioned in this chapter?

5. Given a discussion of the results of an assessment, write the summary and suggested goals and services. What kind of assessment data was most helpful in developing recommendations?

6. Read an assessment report and then verbally present the results briefly in everyday terms.

Discussion Questions

1. Discuss the statement, "The real point of educational assessment is drawing appropriate relationships among the data."

2. An overworked colleague says, "How comprehensive do they think these assessments should be?" What points would you make in the discussion?

3. Many professionals in noneducational fields do not have a high regard for informal educational assessment. Discuss ways to make a positive case for such strategies and data at assessment conferences.

16

Monitoring and Evaluating the Instructional Program

The IEP described in Chapter 15 is a general plan, lacking many specifics left to teachers and other implementors to develop. Further assessments provide such particulars and suggest ways to modify an inappropriate objective or strategy. Valid instruction of exceptional students must include regular evaluation. Further, the nature of educating exceptional students dictates a level of monitoring and accountability not legally mandated for others. The implementation of the Individualized Education Plan must be monitored to determine whether its goals are accomplished, the student has been mainstreamed as planned, and the special education service is still necessary.

RATIONALE

Reasons for Ongoing Assessment

There are a variety of purposes for assessment during this program phase. One is to monitor the instructional progress of the student and the appropriateness of the program. Another is to guide any needed program modifications. Also, the special education placement may need to be re-adjusted, and these data will permit such a consideration.

Such evaluation information also indicates when teachers should stop instruction and insures they do not continue working on an objective too long nor stop too soon. The information is a record of the effort by students and teachers to accomplish objectives, a necessary feature of accountability. If shared with students, such data can also be motivating. The information can also facilitate communication between professionals and parents.

Additionally, the completion, efficiency, and broader impact of the program must be measured. It is not sufficient to evaluate only student progress; the cost, program coordination, and quality of services must also be assessed. Program continuation and improvement depend on that level of evaluation (Borich & Nance, 1987).

Targets of Evaluation

The targets for this monitoring process are the same considered throughout this text—the student and the teachers, the instructional task demands, and environmental conditions. Student progress as revealed by observed behaviors, test scores, attitudes, and so forth are subjects for data gathering. Teacher interactions with students, attitudes, and teaching style will also be considered. The physical, curricular, and cultural environments impinging on the student's program are other factors to be taken into account.

Monitoring and evaluation of IEP implementation takes a form similar to the previously outlined assessment process. Formal and informal assessment strategies are used. However, the nature of the task dictates that most are informal and include task analysis, behavior observation, and error analysis. The few formal tests are used to provide comparative data to reconsider eligibility status for special education placement and perhaps achievement of IEP goals.

These evaluation activities are best regarded as an extension of the initial assessment effort. Educators readily admit that experience in teaching the student clarifies preliminary impressions from an assessment. In many cases, teachers must perform additional diagnostics to specify general information. The instructional process may be used to explore appropriate approaches, materials, and reinforcements. Sometimes assessments are done to confirm an impression arising from a particular student response or events that occur during a lesson. Evaluation is a tool educators can use to structure readily available data about a student or answer a more refined, specific question generated by the instructional experience.

Thus, teachers turn to formal and informal assessment strategies as part of implementing and evaluating the IEP. In order to design the specifics suggested by the IEP, educators perform evaluations that direct the design of daily lesson plans, the selection of curriculum and materials, the choice of reinforcement schedules, and so forth. The initial assessment offers structure, guides preliminary efforts, and guarantees an appropriate start to the program. However, almost from the start teachers are using their assessment skills on a daily basis.

The number of indicators of program efficacy continually grows. Recent research on the role of instructional environment, effective schooling, and mainstreaming has suggested new targets for monitoring and evaluation beyond measurement of basic skill achievement on tests (Wang, 1987). The quality of students' functioning inside and outside the school learning environment, students' ability to learn on their own and from others, and students' perceptions of self-competence need to be considered. Borich and Nance (1987) urge that attention be given to such issues as compliance to rules and standards, coordination of services, and measures of change. PL 99–457 encourages greater focus on the family and home environment when measuring program impact. Such an expanded view of evaluation is imperative in the case of minority and linguistically different students and their families.

Types of Evaluation

Evaluation of instruction may be either formative or summative (Heron & Harris, 1987). Formative evaluation is conducted during the implementation of the IEP to find out whether the plan is working and being completed. Direct and frequent measures of student performance and other instructional variables are necessary and usually are informal, including quizzes, anecdotal records, observations, and criterion-referenced tests. The information gained can be used to guide necessary instructional modifications.

Summative evaluation is performed after the IEP is implemented and can represent the annual review called for by PL 94–142. The purpose is to document the completion of the IEP, including its goals and objectives. Thus, the data gathered during formative evaluation can be very useful. At this point, standardized tests may be used as well as informal measures. Behavioral evaluation plans can also provide useful data (Smith, 1981).

Formative and summative evaluation differ in purpose, time, and level of generalization. Performed during instruction, formative evaluation is directed at improvement of the specific content of the lesson. Summative evaluation occurs at the end of an instructional plan or unit and is a more general assessment of broader outcomes. For example, the former may be a series of quizzes, and the latter a final exam (Sherman, 1980).

A particular challenge in evaluation is to avoid discounting educational outcomes that are not easily quantifiable (Heron & Harris, 1987). Standardized tests often do not detect student gains on more specific objectives. Furthermore, some goals of a program affect the process of teaching and should be directly evaluated. There are also many ethical and methodological concerns in eval-

uation: influence of personal bias in deciding the value of a program, matching of an evaluator to a program, and the effect of evaluation on individuals and groups.

As with assessments for initial placement in special education, an assessment plan is very useful in conceptualizing an appropriate set of strategies. The IEP specifies the criteria, techniques, and timeline for this evaluation. The IAP in Figure 16–1 is based on Phillip's IEP from Chapter 15 (Figure 15–2, p. 472) and specifies in detail how the evaluation process will be conducted.

There are two additional types of evaluation (Borich & Nance, 1987). One of these, value evaluation, attempts to provide evidence of the linkage between outcomes occurring at the end of a program and longer-term outcomes valued in some context larger than the program itself. Program outcomes (e.g., improved writing skills) are viewed as means toward a more valued end (e.g., getting and holding a job or going to college). Another approach is systems evaluation through which attainment of program goals is related to some larger instructional program of which those goals are a part; for example, improved reading skills contribute to ability to learn American history.

AREAS FOR EVALUATION

The IEP provides a set of goals and objectives around which a curriculum or course of instruction must be designed. These preliminary directives are a major source of attention in the monitoring effort. Also, the provisions for mainstreaming and related services must be examined.

Instructional Objectives

Developing objectives. Teachers may find themselves generating more specific instructional objectives for IEP goals on the first day of class. IEPs serve as roadmaps, whereas instructional objectives mark the routes. Criterion-referenced assessment is a major tool in focusing instruction. Also, teachers can rely on task analysis to break down general directions to more specific instructional objectives with specific outcome behavior, instructional condition, and criteria for mastery.

FIGURE 16–1
Individualized Assessment Plan for evaluation

For:	Phillip Hughes	8.8	15	5/3/89	Jane Swift
	Student's Name	Grade	Age	Date	Coordinator

Reason for Assessment: The following procedure will be followed to monitor Phillip's program and gather data for the IEP annual review.

Assessment Questions	Instrument	Personnel	Timeline
What progress has been made in reading, mathematics, and written language skills?	*Woodcock-Johnson Psycho-Educational Battery Revised,* appropriate *BRIGANCE®* subtests	Mr. Thompson, Special education teacher	5/4/90– 5/10/90
What progress has been made in social-emotional areas?	Behavioral observations and interviews	Ms. Swift, Counselor	5/4/90– 5/11/90
What are his vocational entry skills, attitudes, and work habits?	Work sample analyses Motor tests	Ms. Smith, Vocational education teacher & Mrs. Tribble, Occupational therapist	5/4/90– 5/10/90

Team members can also draw on their own experience with the student to suggest more specific objectives to obtain a goal. Parents are often aware of opportunities at home and in the community where a student can get additional practice. Classroom teachers, vocational teachers, and other specialists may pinpoint necessary objectives.

Another type of information available to educators is skill hierarchies. These lists may be the stated objectives around which a curriculum is constructed, such as a reading series. School systems frequently have published skill lists representing competencies for students at different levels. These hierarchies can offer an excellent basis for a set of instructional skill surveys (Zigmond, Vallecorsa, & Silverman, 1983).

Assessing objectives. A major way to assess student progress is to use the instructional objectives stated in the student's IEP and the teacher's lesson plans. They contain the specific outcome ("Johnny will say the answers to 12 factual questions after silently reading a chapter in his history text"), instructional conditions ("When given a review of key vocabulary words and major topics to look for, . . . "), and criteria ("with 85% accuracy"),

greatly increasing the possibilities for evaluation. A teacher can record whether the objective is being pursued, has been accomplished, has been modified, or has not been achieved at all.

A teacher can generate questions or tasks to measure whether the objective is accomplished. A criterion-referenced test with a more complete coverage of the skill area may also be appropriate. Sometimes the testimony of another teacher, parents, or someone else may be enough. Such is often the case when documenting progress in generalizing skills to the regular classroom, home, playground, and so forth.

Changing objectives. A teacher may have to change an instructional objective because of a student's response. If the student responds incorrectly or not at all in spite of the instruction and practice opportunities, a modification is called for. Any of the features of an objective can be changed, such as the condition, outcome, or criteria. The educator manipulates each systematically, observing the student's response. Additional information can be gathered from questioning the student, peers, and others involved in the lesson.

Some objectives prove inappropriate because they are too difficult for the student. Student reluctance to respond, annoyance with the task, and erratic responses may be telltale signs. Task analyzing the objectives for component and prerequisite skills then becomes a sensible assessment activity. As described in Chapter 5, a hierarchical list of finer skills provides an excellent assessment framework. When the missing skill or skills are identified, more appropriate instructional objectives can be chosen. Ultimately, the original one can be addressed after the necessary prerequisite skills are established.

Here too, additional assessment, even formal tests, may be called for. The realization that the exceptional student may have problems listening, may suffer from an interfering allergy, and so forth would spur the teacher to work with other professionals and the parents to make the necessary referral. Problems in accomplishing an objective in oral reading that requires writing skill may encourage an educator to perform a survey of cursive writing and other language functions.

Instructional Process

Educators tend to structure the monitoring and evaluation process around the stages of learning. Although there are a number of ways to conceptualize these phases, Idol-Maestas (1983) suggests acquisition, reversion, proficiency, maintenance, generalization, and adaptation. The focus and intensity of evaluation vary according to the student's phase of learning.

Acquisition. At this stage, a student does not respond or errs consistently. For example, a child simply does not know any multiplication facts. A teacher at this point is noting the first few correct responses on perhaps one type of multiplication, (e.g., the 5's table).

Reversion. A student knows some information but does not consistently respond correctly. For example, a student may know the 6's table in multiplication but confuses 6×7 and 6×9. In this case, the teacher is alert to the particular items needing instruction and does not waste time on the others.

Proficiency. This stage is a matter of fluency and speed. A student consistently completes multiplication drills correctly, but is slow. A teacher will not need to evaluate each and every multiplication fact. A work sample arranged into timed drills is a typical monitoring format at this point.

Maintenance. Teachers expect students to remember information and retain skills outside of the actual lesson or reinforcement plan. As the need for knowledge of multiplication facts arises during the school day, teachers listen for lapses in student performance. Regularly scheduled games are used by some teachers to refresh student memories and informally monitor retention over time. An informal checklist organized by student names and multiplication table can be used to direct a more intense probe of a particular set of facts.

Generalization. Because the ultimate goal of instruction is the use of a skill or knowledge in a variety of situations, this stage of learning merits particular evaluation. Here we are looking for consistent accuracy in novel situations that were not present during an actual lesson. Because each teacher and lesson varies, this ability to generalize skills is imperative. In mainstreamed programs, students must often respond in a variety of settings to similar demands for knowledge and skills.

For example, a student may use multiplication facts to respond to flash cards in the resource room and to written problems in the regular classroom. Monitoring this level of proficiency must be cooperative. A regular, informal, easy-to-use system must be established to find out whether a student is using a skill. Teachers, parents, and others provide observations from their respective settings. The students themselves should also be asked.

Questions teachers can use to analyze whether their instructional conditions encourage generalization (Idol-Maestas, 1983) include the following:

- ☐ Are cues and prompts being gradually removed?
- ☐ Are tangible reinforcers being replaced by attention and social praise?
- ☐ Are the curriculum and materials similar to other ones used in other school settings?
- ☐ Are other teachers and the parents informed of useful and reasonable strategies to use?
- ☐ Have students been taught and encouraged to monitor their own performance?

Adaptation. We expect students to apply learned skills and knowledge in solving problems. This phase in learning is the most demanding because they must often use their newly acquired knowledge without direct teacher guidance. For example, a student who applies computational facts to divide candy among friends is working at this level. Evaluation in this context is more complex, because a variety of component skills are usually demanded. Thus, teachers in this case would maintain a record of percentage of correct division problems and, in the event of difficulties, perform an error analysis to ascertain the deficit subskill.

Monitoring and evaluation vary in intensity and form across these stages of learning. Initially, there must be many specific measures taken of performance. Later, monitors of retention and application are less frequent, but nonetheless necessary. The evaluation may also be more global and indirect. For example, daily probes of multiplication fact knowledge with flash cards are necessary during acquisition and proficiency development. However, checks for retention and the use of math skills in the regular classroom or at home are apt to involve examining written worksheets or asking teachers and parents.

Instructional Conditions

Teachers should check their own instructional repertoire throughout these stages of learning; sound instructional procedures are imperative. Lewis and Doorlag (1987) discuss some appropriate conditions for learning that teachers should arrange.

☐ Are lessons meaningful and motivating?
☐ Has the student been shown what to do and how to do it?
☐ Is the student free to ask questions and seek feedback?
☐ Is there an element of novelty and variety across lessons?
☐ Are there opportunities for students to practice appropriate skills?
☐ Are prompts and other supports gradually withdrawn?
☐ Are the conditions for and consequences of learning pleasant?

Curriculum and Materials

The selection, development, modification, and evaluation of curriculum and materials also require assessment by educators. Brown (1975) suggests asking the following questions:

1. What is the stated rationale for developing the program?
2. What is the scope and sequencing of skills, items, or units?
3. How is the curriculum paced?
4. How independently can the material be used?
5. How is reinforcement used in the program?
6. What is the interest level of the material? (pp. 412–15).

Entry. The entry into a curriculum or material is sometimes complex. Unless the teacher starts at the beginning lesson or activity, a placement decision is necessary. Placement tests provided by the publishers are available to a teacher. Guidelines may also be provided based on the student's age, grade level, skill development, and so forth.

Some published materials contain scope-and-sequence charts of the skills they purport to develop. This feature is particularly useful in matching instructional objectives and activities in materials. A teacher or therapist can examine a list of skills and identify sections of the material devoted to that skill. The *DISTAR* reading series (Englemann & Bruner, 1983) contains a scope-and-sequence chart to guide the teacher.

Regular classroom teachers, special educators, and other specialists must communicate about the materials and programs they intend to use. When both regular classroom teachers and special educators are responsible for working together toward common academic and behavioral goals, materials and programs must not conflict. Students must have consistency in their educational programs. Furthermore, there must not be undue overlap, lest the student become bored. This need for cooperation also applies to parents and other professionals.

In addition, the instructional team may specify teaching and management strategies or behaviors to use with the students. Typically, these are indications of the way teachers, therapists, and others can best communicate with the students. Examples of such directions are to give tangible reinforcers, repeat directions twice, face the child when speaking, model expected responses, and so forth.

Team input is also essential. Everyone who has worked with the student has amassed useful information through trial-and-error experiences; by sharing, they can save one another and the student much time and effort. Specialists in hearing, vision, and so forth may point out strategies to accommodate students' needs; for example, students with listening and/or hearing problems may need to see the teacher's face and be close to the source of sound. These strategies frequently pertain to managing social behavior at school and elsewhere. Team members interacting with handicapped students must use similar, if not identical, behavior management strategies.

In addition, environmental arrangements must be determined. Meyen, Gautt, and Howard (1976) list the following possible environmental entries: study carrels, cubicles, teaching machines, and audiovisual equipment. These special arrangements are often needed to accomplish the specified goals and objectives. Team input is needed to determine the special features in the classroom and anywhere else the child is to be taught, as well as to find out if these resources are available. Assessment data and past experience with the student indicate whether a student needs a nondistracting environment, can use a computer independently, and so forth.

Changes. Modifications must sometimes be made in both the curriculum and the use of materials based on the student's progress, reaction to the plan, and the teacher's and others' satisfaction. Some materials provide unit tests or intermediate checks of progress. One may even find available published criterion-referenced tests. If not, teachers must devise their own quizzes.

Student, teacher, and parent satisfaction with the curricular emphasis, particular materials, and types of activities can be established with interviews and questionnaires. Observations may also yield important data to guide modifications. For example, if materials meant to allow independent work and encourage generalization require teacher supervision, the student and material are inappropriate for one another.

Exit. When and where to stop instruction are other questions teachers must face. The obvious answer is when the instructional objective is completed. Some curricula and materials provide exit measures to demonstrate achievement. Often the tests are more general or curriculum-specific and do not measure IEP objectives. A teacher may turn to criterion-referenced tests to demonstrate mastery. Or if comparative data are needed, a suitable norm-referenced test may be useful. Additional ideas for monitoring the suitability and effectiveness of these factors are contained in Chapter 10.

Instructional Environment

Comprehensive evaluation of a student's program must take into account the environment. Current research indicates that student achievement is linked to school district conditions (e.g., teacher–student ratio, amount of homework, attendance), within-school conditions (e.g., school climate, principal leadership, high expectations), and general family characteristics (e.g., educational and income levels, peer group) (Ysseldyke & Christenson, 1987a). One way to gather data about these environmental factors in a systematic way is *The Instructional Environment Scale* (*TIES*) (Ysseldyke & Christenson, 1987b). Based on observations and interviews with the student and teachers, *TIES* is used (a) to describe the extent to which a student's academic and behavior problems are a function of factors in the instructional environment; (b) to identify starting points in designing appropriate instructional interventions; and (c) to facilitate other aspects of program implementation, including progress monitoring.

The main components of *TIES* are the instructional presentation, teacher expectations, cognitive emphasis, motivational strategies, relevant practice, academic engaged time, informed feedback, adaptive instruction, progress evaluation, instructional planning, and student understanding.

Placement and Mainstreaming

A key feature of evaluation of all IEPs is the student's maintenance and success in the least restrictive environment. The main evaluation question is, *Was the student physically, socially, and academically integrated into a setting with typical peers?* These elements in mainstreaming are the main dimensions by which to judge success.

Physical. Criteria to evaluate physical mainstreaming include the ratio of mildly handicapped to typical students, the frequency and duration of such integration, and the nature of the activity. Put negatively and in an exaggerated fashion, one would judge that mainstreaming was *not* accomplished if the LD child was placed in a room with children 3 years younger; the mildly retarded student was with normal peers only once a week; behavior disordered students were integrated only during a 10-minute recess each day.

Social. Although there may be indications that the IEP was abided by and students were physically integrated with typical students, social integration may not necessarily follow. The main criteria for successful student integration are the frequency and quality of social interactions. How often students make contact with peers and teachers is important to monitor, because each contact provides opportunity for practice. An occasional verbal exchange or wave of the hand does not constitute valid mainstreaming. Also, we must be cognizant of interactions in nonschool settings and with others, such as relatives, doctors, and store clerks.

The quality of interactions must be evaluated in a variety of ways. Some dimensions that monitor meaningful integration are verbal and nonverbal exchange with typical peers and special and regular classroom teachers; mildly handicapped students' perceptions of other students and teachers and of themselves; attitudes of students, professionals, and parents toward mainstreaming; and the quality of teacher and peer modeling. The strategies described in the discussion of classroom behavior (Chapter 10) can be used for these analyses. Observations, interviews, rating scales, and questionnaires offer direct and indirect measures of social integration.

The need to focus on the nature and quality of social integration is underscored by recent research (Heron & Harris, 1987). Mildly handicapped students not only may be rejected and ignored by typical peers but also may receive few and largely negative or task-related comments from teachers. They may also have unrealistic estimates of their own social status in the classroom. Although there are many dimensions to conceptualize evaluation in this area, here are some possibilities:

1. Acceptance v. rejection
2. Inclusion v. exclusion
3. Liked v. disliked
4. High social/self-ranking v. low social/self-ranking

Sociometric measures are popular in gathering data in this social integration area (Lewis & Doorlag, 1987). Three possibilities are nomination ("Name three students you like (dislike) having near you"); rating scale ("Given a scale of 1 to 5 (High), indicate how much you like to do things with Billy, Jim, etc."); and paired comparison ("Given pairs of students in the class, choose the one you like more") (Asher & Taylor, 1981). Nomination tends to measure friendship, whereas rating scales address level of acceptance. The same cautions apply in their use as discussed in Chapter 10.

Teacher attitudes, knowledge, and skills also must be examined in connection with effective mainstreaming (Schulz & Turnbull, 1983). Research indicates that teacher competence can be improved in this area and that student social integration is directly affected (Leyser & Gottlieb, 1980). Some questions that teachers can ask themselves (or can be asked about them) are

☐ Do I project a positive and constructive attitude about having exceptional students in my class?

☐ Are my typical students sensitized to the goal of the mainstreaming program, and do they know what is expected of them?

☐ Am I modeling and encouraging friendship skills, such as sharing, cooperation, verbal complimenting, and so on between handicapped and typical students?

☐ Am I providing exceptional students ways to gain social status in the classroom, such as allowing for errors, praising work, and offering extra support?

Academic. Integration of mildly handicapped students into the regular curriculum may be the most difficult goal of the IEP. The challenge is clear to teachers: provide individualized instruction to the mildly handicapped along with teaching other students. Teachers are to offer a program in the least restrictive environment; that is, an educational setting that maximizes the handicapped student's opportunity to respond and achieve, permits the regular education teacher to interact proportionally with all the students in the classroom, and fosters acceptable social relationships between nonhandicapped and handicapped students (Heron & Skinner, 1981).

What are indications that a student is being successfully taught in the mainstream? First, students should be afforded opportunities to respond: Do they ask and answer questions? Join in discussion? Complete assignments? Participate in classroom activities?

Second, there must be evidence of student achievement and success: Are students passing subjects? Reaching skill mastery? Retaining and applying skills? Graduating from school? Realistically, mildly handicapped students may not be competing on par with typical peers. They may be working at a lower level, completing tasks differently, and taking exams under special conditions. But given the instructional conditions prescribed by their disabilities, can one document accomplishment of objectives to the criteria stated?

Third, a valid evaluation of academic and social mainstreaming requires examination of what Heron and Skinner (1981) refer to as *proportional interaction*. Do *all* of the students receive the teacher's attention for appropriate behavior on a consistent enough basis to maintain performance? If a regular classroom teacher can approximate the amount of attention given in a resource room, then integration is being accomplished. However, the bottom line is need—each student should have his or her fair share.

Fourth, there are myriad ways to individualize instruction. Evaluation must focus on the presence or absence of teacher strategies to maintain a student in a mainstreamed setting. Some ways to individualize instruction are selecting learning tasks based on assessment data and teaching experience; providing demonstrations, necessary cues and prompts, and both guided and independent practice; giving clear directions; providing consequences for successful task performance; and selectively and minimally modifying methods (Lewis & Doorlag, 1987).

Fifth, the curriculum activities and materials should be as similar to those of typical students as possible. Direct observation will indicate what degree of variation exists and whether student needs dictate the differences. Sometimes the continued use of a particular approach is dictated more by teacher or institutional habit than student need. In some school systems, every classroom has a particular material because of a salesperson's initiative, rather than documented student needs. Full integration has been accomplished when the special conditions for academic learning resemble regularly used ones without requiring undue time or drawing attention to exceptional students.

Factors to be examined are the following:

☐ Are aides available to facilitate individualized instruction?

☐ Are the academic curricula and materials for special students similar enough in visual and management characteristics to those in the regular program?

☐ Do learning activities permit performing tasks on different levels and in different ways?

☐ Are students' special and regular classroom programs coordinated and reinforcing?

This approach ensures that mildly handicapped students are not coloring pictures while typical students calculate math problems. Another travesty of ineffective academic mainstreaming results when no relationship exists between activities in the resource room and the regular classroom.

Eligibility

Generally, during the course of a school year, students change their level of performance and learning needs. Special education and related services may need to be revised or discontinued. Gaps between ability and reading achievement may be narrowed, disruptive behaviors decreased, and organizational and retention skills improved. Perhaps a student's behavioral problems are solved, but academic and language needs remain severe. Another possibility is that the IEP team realizes after a period of instruction and continuous evaluation that the child has a hearing or vision deficit or speech problems and needs related services.

As discussed earlier, the eligibility criteria for special education services for mildly retarded, learning disabled, and behavior disordered children are set forth by federal, state, and local guidelines and involve gathering formative data and adding necessary formal assessments for comparison.

Although an assessment as extensive as the initial one may not be done on an annual basis, there is a federal requirement for a complete assessment every 3 years.

Annual IEP Review

All the previous evaluation considerations culminate in a summative annual review of the IEP document. Formal and informal data are examined in regard to these questions:

1. Is the child progressing as specified in the goal statements in the IEP?
2. Is the child approaching a point where he/she will/can exit to another program?
3. If the plan does not seem to be appropriate, what adjustments appear to be necessary in
   a. Goal statements?
   b. Timelines?
   c. Strategies?
   d. Materials?
   e. Methods?
   f. Resources?
   g. Implementors?
   h. Monitoring systems?
      (National Association of State Directors of Special Education [NASDSE], 1976, p. 42)

COLLECTING DATA

Both formal and informal information must be gathered and interpreted to monitor and evaluate students' IEPs. Educators use a variety of techniques to gather information about successful implementation. The rule of thumb is to use strategies that fit into the instructional format and minimize additional work for the teacher, students, and others.

Anecdotal Records

Many teachers take daily notes on student performance, including what the teacher did and how the student responded. Written comments might include questions the teacher needs to answer and reminders for follow-up activities. Some examples are the words misread by one or more students in an oral reading lesson, or a concern about the appropriateness of a learning center for a student. This type of system provides a day-to-day account of things to act on through testing, modified instruction, or consultation. However, due to fatigue and distractions, teachers may not remember details accurately or may be subjective (Smith, 1981). The solution is to record events as

they occur. For most teachers, these anecdotal records are their main recording system and represent critical information for classroom instruction and behavioral management.

Observation

Teachers are continually watching and listening to students and making mental or written notes of their observations. As discussed in Chapter 5, teachers use observation as a direct but unobtrusive monitoring technique of both student behavior and the impact of instructional tasks and setting. Observation is frequently used to evaluate social skill development, but it also can be applied to particularly troublesome academic behaviors.

One such structured format for taking daily observations concerning academic and social behavior is antecedent-behavior-consequence (ABC) analysis (Smith, 1981). For example, using this approach, notes are organized as

☐ *Antecedent*—description of the preceding and precipitating event ("When we begin the math lesson . . .")
☐ *Behavior*—the actual problem behavior (". . . Tim gets hyperactive and starts looking around . . .")
☐ *Consequence*—the events immediately following the problem behavior (". . . and then the teacher goes to Tim's desk and turns him so he faces the front of the room.")

This format permits the recording of more details and encourages precise descriptions. Environmental factors that influence the student may be pinpointed and the role of the teacher and classmates clarified.

Teachers use a variety of time-saving devices to keep tallies of academic and social behaviors in the classroom (Lewis & Doorlag, 1987). Some possibilities described in Chapter 5 are using wrist counters and tape-recorders.

Checklists

With experience and knowledge of curriculum, teachers devise checklists to monitor individual and small group sessions. They design sheets with student names along one side and the predictable areas of concern along the top, for example, vowel sounds in reading, main aspects of a composition, and so forth. The checklist illustrated in Figure 16–2 can be used to analyze the written compositions of students with frequent problems. Then teachers can follow up by administering tests, conducting drills, or modifying the activity.

Another possibility is very detailed checklists of skills. For example, a list of basic phonics could be used to record deficit skills during an oral reading session. This level of evaluation, however, may be unwieldy. Such procedures are more appropriate on an individual basis in an assessment. Refer to the discussion in Chapter 5 of the use of checklists for such purposes.

Coding Systems

Teachers employ a variety of coding systems to categorize or organize incorrect oral or written responses. These systems allow teachers to record and analyze observations as the lessons progress or as they examine a permanent product like a worksheet. These codes are more elaborate than correct–incorrect or pass–fail. Examples are codes used in many informal oral reading inventories, as described in Chapter 11. The use of such codes fit in with error analysis, another handy approach for monitoring and evaluating instruction.

Work Folders

Work folders can be incorporated into the evaluation process and are an excellent way to provide daily assignments. Students pick them up at the beginning of a session, placing completed work there for later teacher examination. The students can be given answer keys and asked to mark their own papers. Grades are kept in the folders themselves.

There are advantages and disadvantages to using individual work folders to monitor student

progress (Stowitschek, Gable, & Hendrickson, 1980). Folders permit storage of papers, easy checks of past ratings, and a place to examine current work. More entries can be made for one subskill, and remedial ideas can be noted for the individual. However, there is much duplication when many students are involved. Summaries have to be made separately to provide an overview of the class and facilitate grouping decisions. Also, when records of student progress are kept only in individual folders, a graph of student performance is unavailable to motivate student effort.

Charts

Charts indicating a whole class's performance are useful in monitoring progress, and they overcome the limitations of folders. They can supply an overview, whereas student folders are used to collect daily work (Stowitschek et al., 1980). Charts offer a quick reference, give an overview of past and future instructional goals, relate tests and materials to skills, and provide a visual display.

As illustrated in Figure 16–3, Stowitschek et al. (1980) have built into a chart recordings of the starting point, progress check points, mastery points, and retention for each skill learned and for each student. These are defined as follows:

□ *Entry Point*—A plus or minus, date, or test score is recorded on the first, second, third, and so on point until Mastery (M) is attained.
□ *Mastery*—A check or date is used when competence is attained.
□ *Retention of Mastery*—A check or date is noted when students demonstrate retention of the information.

FIGURE 16–2
Written composition checklist

Student Names	LANGUAGE			MECHANICS		
	Vocabulary	Grammar	Spelling	Punctuation	Capitalization	Handwriting
Sam	✓	✓				✓
Mary Lou			✓		✓	
Jenny		✓				✓
Phil	✓		✓	✓		

FIGURE 16–3
Reading Skill Profile Chart

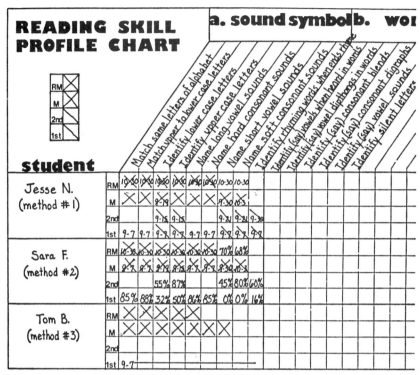

Note. From *Instructional Materials for Exceptional Children* (p. 139) by J. J. Stowitschek, R. Gable, and J. M. Hendrickson, 1980, Austin, TX: PRO-ED. Copyright 1980 by PRO-ED. Reprinted with permission of PRO-ED.

As noted in Figure 16–3, Sara had 85% mastery on her first attempt at matching the same letters of the alphabet. On September 7, she mastered all the material and could still do the activity at the end of October when the material was reviewed. Chapter 5 explains the design and use of charts to report observational data. See Howell and Morehead's (1987) treatment of charting, including the use of six-cycle charting procedures.

Self-checking Materials

Self-checking sheets and self-correcting materials allow students to check their own work and gain immediate feedback (Mercer & Mercer, 1989). However, lest students change their answers, they should use a colored pen for correcting papers and/or correct work in a special supervised area. The teacher should randomly check student use

of the correcting system regularly, encouraging accuracy.

Self-evaluation procedures have also proven effective in reducing inappropriate behavior and in changing other behavior. Students who maintain self-ratings of their behavior and match them to those maintained by their teachers significantly modify their disruptive and inattentive behavior (Smith, Young, West, Morgan, & Rhode, 1988). The self-evaluation activities serve as a behavior management program in the classroom.

Integrating Materials

Many activities and materials used daily or at least regularly lend themselves to a continuous monitoring system (Stowitschek et al., 1980). Teachers often use a variety of permanent products across skill areas where responses can be tallied and analyzed. Examples include drill sheets for mathematic facts; flash cards for computation, sight vocabulary, or spelling; and quizzes and workbook pages. These materials yield data that can be recorded on graphs as percentages and as rates of performance.

Daily Probes

Daily measurement of a specific academic response is usually the most desirable way to assess the impact of an instructional technique (Stowitschek et al., 1980). Daily probes are based on specific objectives, usually last from 1 to 5 minutes, and are administered before or after instruction. The key element is that the instructional approach is consistent and materials used do not vary. For example, a teacher may have students spend 1 minute a day completing a sheet of 25 or more 2-digit addition problems requiring regrouping. As the instruction has its impact, the students should do more problems correctly. Or the time allowed could be varied, and percentages of correct responses calculated.

Daily probes allow much flexibility in application to different content areas, including the response mode, location of administration, and administration and scoring procedures (Haring & Gentry, 1976). These probes are measures of rate of performance as well as accuracy. The format should stay the same each day, but the number of items may need to be adjusted so students cannot complete all the problems in the allotted time. Otherwise, the probes are not monitoring growth. Teachers should examine the activities and materials they usually use to structure daily probes and other evaluation methods.

Diagnostic Teaching

Teachers may observe that their students are having difficulty in performing a task and wish to make the necessary modifications for greater success. The assessment questions they are asking themselves are, *What would be a more effective strategy?* and *Which element of the instructional activity do I change?* As described in Chapter 5, diagnostic teaching is called for because it is a curriculum-based procedure and will provide direction for needed changes. An alternate activity or instructional condition must be designed or chosen, and its differential impact compared to the previous strategy. New and previous strategies may be referred to as diagnostic probes.

Probe design. When designing or choosing instructional alternatives, task analysis can be helpful, particularly structural task analysis. As described in Chapter 5, the task demands are analyzed by examining the task directions, presentation mode, response mode, time requirements, and accuracy requirements. This form of analysis focuses on key elements of any instructional objective.

Level of difficulty is another dimension along which instructional alternatives may be designed. The diagnostic probe may be somewhat easier or more difficult than the original instructional activity or condition. There are a variety of ways to conceptualize these levels of difficulty. Zigmond et al.'s hierarchy (1983) includes matching (e.g., copying), recognition (e.g., multiple-choice), aided recall (e.g., provided context cues or fill-ins), and recall or unaided production from memory. Gagné (1970) also describes a hierarchy of difficulty in terms of task design.

Many other possible considerations can modify instruction, including reinforcement for appropriate behavior, and task completion and accuracy. The discussion in Chapter 10 concerning the assessment of instructional demands is relevant here, especially suggestions for ways to adapt instructional activities.

Sources. Informal techniques are the basis for probes to be used in diagnostic teaching. Task analysis, observation, work sample analysis, and classroom quizzes may provide the needed insights. Clinical interviews with the students before, during, and after task completion may be particularly helpful.

Probe use. The key to instructional probes besides their design is how they are used. The teacher must know what aspects of the task to watch as the student responds. Then one knows what to change in the instructional task for the desired effect.

Probes are called for at various times. Student errors, impulsive or erratic answers, slow pace of responding, or lack of motivation dictate probing during a lesson. A word of caution, though, lest a lesson plan be prematurely altered: One or two student errors may not indicate anything more than a student having a bad day. The number of items in a probe should be sufficient for a teacher to feel justified in restructuring tasks and objectives based on the data.

As recommended in Chapter 5, the diagnostic teaching process should be extended over a number of days. You should gather data on the impact of the original teaching strategy for a week and then monitor the student's response to the modified approach for another week. With that comparative information you can then judge which is the more successful one. There is no sense in using a modified activity or different learning condition unless it proves better than the one currently in use.

Surveys and Interviews

Surveys can be used to gather important evaluative data from students, teachers, other professionals, parents, employers, and others. Written or verbal feedback can be obtained about the mastery of skills, their transfer to nonclassroom settings, satisfaction with the program, new skills needed by students, and so forth. For example, students in prevocational and vocational classes can evaluate their own job performance by completing ratings of their attitude at work, work completion, interaction with co-workers and employers, and work behaviors such as being on time (Lund, Montague, & Reinholtz, 1987). They can also describe both their strengths and weaknesses and their successes and difficulties on the job. Job support discussion groups, during which students can discuss reasons for their problems and discuss ways to improve, provide an ideal evaluation companion to the surveys. Simulations and role playing can be used.

Teachers too can evaluate their own performance in critical areas. Englert (1984) suggests they can ask themselves whether they make optimal use of class time, that is, keeping transition time between lessons short, maintaining a high level of student attention and interaction, circulating among students as they do seatwork, and so forth. Classroom management questions that teachers could put to themselves would include some about physical organization of the classroom to minimize disruptive traffic flow, clear statements and examples of appropriate student behavior and

student rehearsal of the same, and maintenance of rules and procedures through such strategies as regular visual scanning and eye contact with students and use of nonverbal signals to direct student attention. Ysseldyke, Samuels, and Christenson (1988) have designed *Teacher Evaluation Rating Scales* for supervisors and teachers themselves. Teachers can also use self-charting procedures to evaluate their own performance.

ANALYZING AND REPORTING DATA

The data used for monitoring and evaluation of instruction are generally gathered through informal procedures and analyzed by teachers through self-made procedures. Although standardized tests may also be used, evaluation data often need to be organized to facilitate interpretation and use.

Quantifying Data

In the case of formal tests, the same scores as discussed in Chapter 3—raw scores, age and grade scores, percentile ranks, and standard scores—can be expected. The type of data typically gathered through informal means can be translated into quantitative terms, thus facilitating analysis and interpretation of information. The four main forms used are frequency, duration, rate, and percentage. Daily worksheets, quizzes, and so forth are analyzed for right and wrong items or for the length of time taken.

One can also quantify other important information such as number of objectives accomplished, skills mastered, and pages read accurately. See Figure 16–4 for an illustration of how the correct completion of homework assignments was monitored over a week. Chapter 3 explains the possible uses of these scores to evaluate growth. Percentages can be compared from day to day, as well as rates for speed and fluency. Rates may be more sensitive to small changes in academic skills (Stowitschek et al., 1980) and incorporate both accuracy and speed in one measure.

Graphs

A handy way to portray formal and informal data is on graphs. Possible dimensions are number of correct and incorrect responses, number of such responses per specified time period, or amount of time during which a behavior occurred (Affleck,

FIGURE 16–4
Record of homework accuracy

Day	Number of Questions	Number of Responses	Number of Correct Responses	Percentage of Correct Responses
Student: Juan				
Subject: Science 9				
Task: Homework Assignments				
Monday	7	7	3	43%
Tuesday	9	9	4	44%
Wednesday	6	6	3	50%
Thursday	10	10	5	50%
Friday	8	8	3	38%

Note. From *Teaching Special Students in the Mainstream* (2nd ed.) (p. 78) by R. B. Lewis and D. H. Doorlag, 1987, Columbus, OH: Merrill. Copyright 1987 by Merrill Publishing Company. Reprinted by permission.

Lowenbraun, & Archer, 1980). Figure 16–5 contains a completed graph of Susan's performance on 1-minute probes of multiplication facts. Each day the teacher corrected the drill sheet with Susan, who recorded the number correct and incorrect. The goal was 30 correct in a minute. See Chapter 5 for an explanation of how to design graphs and examples. Also, see Wesson (1987) for some suggestions on developing and maintaining graphs efficiently.

Evaluation Design

How do you decide whether progress was made, enough work was done, or appropriate services were provided? We need to document learning, certify completion of tasks, and appraise the quality of services. Positive change, growth, and achievement indicate goal completion. Thus, much depends on the criteria initially established for progress and the level of performance recorded at that time. The standardized and informal data gathered through formative and summative evaluation are compared.

In the case of documenting services, we need to indicate that timelines were met and that the types of specialists prescribed in the IEP actually worked with the student. The amount of instructional time and quality of social and academic interactions must be established. Thus, the evaluation design used is a combination of data comparison, job completion, and measures of satisfaction.

There are many ways to organize an evaluation; they vary in ease, technical superiority, and usefulness. One may choose to use pretest-posttest, only posttest, or continuous measurement designs.

In the pre- and posttest approach, educators administer similar, sometimes identical, measures of performance at the beginning and end of instruction. A behavioral observation taken in September and another in December would reveal whether a desired outcome is accomplished. In educating exceptional students, school year beginning and ending designs are usually modified to include more frequent periodic checks (Gay, 1985).

FIGURE 16–5

Correct and incorrect responses in one-minute probes on multiplication facts

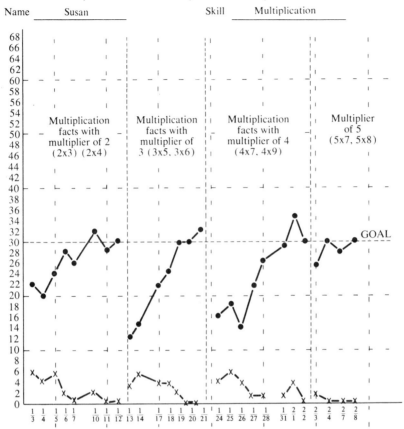

Number of correct responses (●) and incorrect responses (*x*) on one-minute probe.

NOTE: Though the teacher provided Susan with many interventions on multiplication facts, he used a one-minute probe for the consistent measurement event. Each day Susan was given a one-minute probe on multiplication facts. The teacher corrected the page with Susan. Susan then plotted the number of correct responses and the number of incorrect responses on this graph. (The criterion of movement was ● 30 correct responses in a minute, and no errors.)

Note. From *Teaching the Mildly Handicapped in the Regular Classroom* (2nd ed.) (p. 140) by J. O. Affleck, S. Lowenbraun, and A. Archer, 1980, Columbus, OH: Charles E. Merrill. Copyright 1980 by Bell & Howell Company. Reprinted by permission.

The posttest-only design uses measures independent of those previously used and the course of instruction. This approach documents evaluation criteria unavailable at the beginning or during the program, for example, parent satisfaction or student integration into the regular classroom. No direct comparison is involved.

Continuous measurement incorporates many of the previously described formative monitoring procedures. Before, during, and after instruction, a student is assessed on a specific skill, and a graph or record is kept. Additionally, this approach documents progress during learning and regularly checks skill retention and application. Reversal, multiple baseline, and criterion changing behavioral designs use continuous measurement (Smith, 1981). The latter two designs do not require withdrawal of a helpful procedure. Variations of the three designs are also available.

Ultimately, monitoring and evaluation of programs involve addressing questions of attribution, significance, and relevance (Simeonsson, 1986). It is important to ascertain whether noted changes and improvements are related to the program or some other factors. The full significance of the amount and kind of change should be considered, because some change may not be adequate to satisfy even statistical levels of significance. Also, you must determine whether the change makes any real difference in the student's instructional or broader life.

Feedback to Students and Others

An essential component of the evaluation process is to provide students with timely and meaningful feedback on performance. Unfortunately, teachers delay in grading oral and written work and in reporting to students. Mere grades or marks are not sufficiently directive in correcting student errors and improving performance.

Students value clear, considerate feedback. Teachers who describe or write the correct procedures and answers and show students where they erred are particularly helpful. Interview students concerning their strategies to help them identify their errors. Have them describe their step-by-step approach aloud. Although lengthy, this eventually saves teachers and students time.

Providing students with records of the feedback allows them to review the information at their own pace and in more comfortable surroundings than the classroom. Well-marked papers are a valuable resource to students and ultimately a time-saver to everyone concerned. For example, teachers who use different color pens to model correct handwriting permit students to clearly see their errors. Another effective technique is demonstrating progress on charts.

Teachers must also be considerate in how they provide feedback. One key is to interact with students. Relying totally on corrected papers may be efficient, but not generally effective. Additional verbal comments personalize the message and permit students to ask questions. Also emphasize positive aspects of student performance, not just errors. Monitoring instruction is an excellent opportunity to praise related behaviors and attitudes. When teachers provide regular feedback, students can clarify what they find reinforcing and helpful.

Teachers soon realize that student feedback needs to be a component at each level of learning. As students move through various stages in developing skills, teachers must provide the correct kind and amount of feedback needed. At the early stages, feedback is quite intense, descriptive, and structured. Later, when encouraging generalization, teachers provide less direct comments on the skill itself and more ideas for using the skill.

Regular reports of a student's progress should also be provided to cooperating professionals and the student's family. Because most mildly handicapped students are served in mainstream education, a variety of teachers and auxiliary personnel can use regular feedback to judge the specific impact of their contributions and the overall efficacy of the effort. Such reports also promote cooperative activity among professionals and parents, along with the student. The major behaviors of concern can be incorporated in a simple form or chart, giving common direction to everyone involved. Such reports can be the basis for reinforcement programs and contribute to the grading system used with students.

Evaluation and Grading

"I love to teach but I hate to test and grade my students," is an unfortunate indication of the gap between evaluation and instruction and the common misconception of this process. If instruction is based on individual need and if IEP goals are directed by valid and reliable information, then evaluation should be straightforward. The basis for grading should be more than testing alone.

Student evaluation may take any of the forms described in this text, including classroom quizzes and teacher-made tests. Because many of the mildly handicapped students are mainstreamed, they will be assessed as part of a group as well as individually. Special education teachers may then prepare students for such test formats and conditions by gradually using more traditional group techniques, such as multiple-choice, true–false, fill-ins, matching columns, definitions, short answers, and essay.

Because exceptional students may be tested differently, work at less difficult levels of instruction, and follow different curricula, standard grading practices may not be relevant or practical. Regular classroom teachers, special education teachers, and administrators can modify the major elements of the grading process: measurement devices, performance criteria, grading decision-making process, grading symbols, and the reporting system (Butler, Magliocca, & Torres, 1984). Some alternative test conditions for exceptional students are to read the information for the student, rephrase the question, permit many modes of response (such as speaking or pointing), test more frequently, increase the time, and/or provide incentives (Vasa, 1981). Furthermore, common classroom practices in evaluation should be supplemented with student and teacher interviews, observation, and so forth. The outcome will be a fairer, clearer, and more accurate assessment of student progress and the program impact.

Grading the exceptional student is a related aspect of assessment. The special educator may cooperate with the regular classroom teacher who actually awards the grade, compose a grade for specific areas, or do all the grading if the student is totally in a special class.

The key to grading is the criteria used. The most obvious way is to grade the exceptional student like everyone else. However, because it is likely that the student's grades will always be lower in relationship to nonhandicapped students, alternative forms of grading are needed. Otherwise, true progress and effort are never reflected and rewarded. Thus, use the student's own level of performance, age, entry skills, and so forth for reference.

Differential grading can be accomplished in a variety of ways (Lewis & Doorlag, 1987). One possibility is to state the student's current grade level in the academic subject and grade the performance at that level. Another is to grade the student's work habits rather than skill performance. A third variation is to state the student's IEP goals and objectives in the academic subject and indicate which have been accomplished and which still require work.

Another way is to base grades on accomplishment of IEP objectives (Schulz & Turnbull, 1983).

For example, a letter grade can be based on the overall accomplishment of the criteria stated for IEP objectives—a grade of B for 80% mastery. Or a letter grade can indicate the extent of a student's progress: satisfactory, unsatisfactory, or needing improvement. Schulz and Turnbull (1983) argue that such a system allows mildly handicapped students to receive reports that look similar to other students'. A problem is that the grade may be inflated compared to typical students. One solution is to implement a weighted scale point system to accompany grades. An A for a gifted student is 5 points; for a typical child, 4 points; and for the handicapped student, 3 points. However, such a system may become confusing for students who perform like their peers only in some areas, and not in others.

For older students, Vasa (1981) suggests the use of contracts between teachers and students upon which to base grades. Students participate in agreeing to objectives for the project, activities, and ways to be evaluated. Pass–fail grades are another possibility, as is a checklist of competencies. This alternative or addition to letter or percentage grades indicates skill mastery. A list of skills based on objectives are checked as mastered, in progress, unmastered, or irrelevant. As described in relationship to instructional objectives, mastery can be reported by percentages (70% accuracy), time (30 minutes), or simply as accomplished or not. Criterion-referenced assessment readily supplies this type of data. For example, a teacher can use the *BRIGANCE® Diagnostic Inventory of Basic Skills* (Brigance, 1977) when those tests measure program objectives.

Cohen (1983) encourages the incorporation of corrective feedback on daily assignments as a grading system. Rather than marking an answer right or wrong and adding up the score, teachers provide ideas for improvement and award an intermediate mark. An error analysis may allow the teacher to describe the inappropriate strategy. Ultimately, the collection of performances can be translated to other codes, such as satisfactory/unsatisfactory or letter grades. Checklists and rating scales can be used to translate these subjective, descriptive grades into more quantitative ones.

Grading practices must reflect the minimum competency guidelines in states and school systems that have adopted such standards for promotion and graduation (Bender, 1984). In the cases of mildly handicapped students, there may be options in how or whether they are tested. However, IEP teams should specify an appropriate grading procedure and the basis for promotion and graduation on the IEP, as well as contributors to this process. Ideally, the IEP requirements should be integrated into the grading and minimum competency testing process. The criterion-referenced tests discussed in Chapter 5 are well suited to accomplish this kind of merger between IEPs, minimum competency testing, and grading systems.

EVALUATION MODELS

The preceding procedures need to be conceptualized into a monitoring and evaluation model for decision-making purposes. Curriculum-based measurement is one such approach that can result in greater student growth, enhance teacher decision making, and improve students' awareness of their performance (Deno, 1987). It uses direct observation and recording of student performance in the local school curriculum and provides a closer connection between testing and teaching. The major components are identifying a long-range goal statement based on performance in the curriculum, creating a pool of test items, and measuring student performance at least weekly (Fuchs, 1987).

Two strategies can be used to evaluate the data and make a decision about the need for instructional changes (Fuchs, 1987). The goal-oriented strategy is to compare how quickly the student must progress to a goal in the available time to an estimate of how quickly the student is actually progressing. The experimental approach involves regular, systematic experimentation with alternative interventions.

Different kinds of data can be charted for monitoring and reporting purposes (Tindal, 1987). Performance-monitoring charts contain performance data on a single and constant task over many days or weeks, such as the number of correctly and incorrectly solved multiplication problems (see Figure 16–5). Mastery-monitoring charts contain information about mastery of whole units of a curriculum. The effects of the program can be summarized in various ways: the average rate of

progress over time (number of units of improvement per unit of time), variability, impact of program changes, and overlap of program components.

These data should be reviewed regularly, at least every 2 weeks (Howell & McCollum-Gahley, 1986). You need to have a reference for deciding whether the student is progressing satisfactorily. That goal or aim is based on what a student who is achieving well can accomplish. As illustrated in Figure 16–6, you can portray on a graph the actual performance level (such as reads 80 words per minute correctly) and also the performance goal or aim for the student after a particular period of time (such as reads 160 words correctly in 8 weeks). The line drawn between those two points is the line of expected progress or progress aim around which you array the results of daily measures. If a student's performance falls below the line of expected progress more than 3 days, an instructional change is necessary. Howell and Morehead (1987) provide a full rationale and description of possible ones that can be made and the indicators for them. Bursuck and Lessen (1987) have incorporated elements of curriculum-based evaluation into a Curriculum-Based Assessment and Instructional Design system, which consists of academic skill probes, a Work Habits Perception Check, and an Environmental Inventory.

Another effort to quantify evaluation data into a meaningful whole is the use of formulas into which standardized test results are put. For example, some childhood specialists use formulas to demonstrate the impact of programs, particularly when no control group is available. The formulas are measures of absolute developmental progress during a program or gain scores, measures of the rate of child developmental progress (the months of developmental age gained per month of time between measurements), and measures of change in the rate of developmental progress (comparison of the rate at which a child had developed prior to intervention with his or her rate of progress during intervention) (Rosenberg, Robinson, Finkler, & Rose, 1987). All of these approaches have some error associated with them and are based on the assumption that children develop at a fairly steady, unchanging rate before initiation of services. This approach should be supplemental to other decision-making strategies. Similar efforts to use statistical formulas for evaluating placement of learning disabled students are

FIGURE 16–6
Performance and progress aim

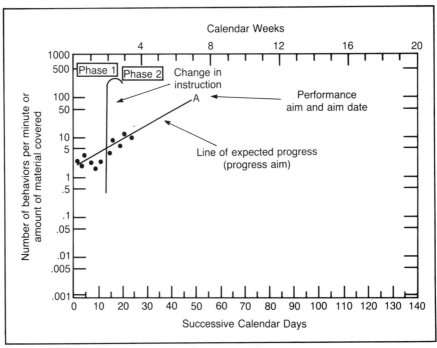

Note. From "Monitoring Instruction" by K. W. Howell and J. McCollum-Gahley, 1986, *Teaching Exceptional Children, 19,* p. 47. Copyright 1986 by The Council for Exceptional Children. Reprinted with permission.

discussed by Wallace and McLoughlin (1988) and in Chapter 9.

Borich and Nance (1987) recommend the development of an evaluation model for special education programs that is suitably comprehensive. The model should focus on compliance (adherence to regulations related to legal and funding constraints), coordination (the degree of overlap in programs), and change (measurement of student progress, parental attitudes, etc.). This approach recognizes the unique demands of special education services and generates information useful in evaluating the full impact of programs rather than student progress alone. See Field and Hill (1988) for a description of the application of a related contextual appraisal system to a school district.

STUDY GUIDE

Review Questions

1. What are two reasons for ongoing assessment?
2. The targets for evaluation are _____ , _____ , _____ , and _____ .
3. _____ evaluation is conducted during the IEP implementation and _____ evaluation occurs at its end.
4. In what three aspects do formative and summative evaluation differ?
5. An IAP can be used to structure program evaluation and annual reviews. (True or False)

6. _____ is the phase of learning during which a student responds or errs inconsistently.
7. The phases of learning often neglected in evaluation are _____ and _____ .
8. Published quizzes are better than teacher-made ones. (True or False)
9. Three dimensions of mainstreaming to evaluate are _____ , _____ , and _____ .
10. Proportional interaction is a concept to measure mainstreaming both _____ and _____ .
11. In a truly mainstreamed environment, curriculum, activities and materials should be similar for exceptional and normal students. (True or False)
12. Most teachers keep _____ as a way of monitoring instruction.
13. What are two devices for gathering data regularly?
14. Match the changeable aspects of diagnostic probes in Column A to examples in Column B.

Column A	*Column B*
a. Number of items	_____ Written
b. Response mode	_____ Five minutes
c. Location of administration	_____ Peer tutor
d. Time	_____ At child's desk
e. Materials	_____ Flash cards
f. Administrator and scorer	_____ Twenty-five items

15. _____ is helpful in designing diagnostic probes.
16. Arrange the following levels of instructional difficulty from easiest to most demanding by numbering the easiest 1, the next one 2, and so forth.
    _____ Aided recall
    _____ Matching
    _____ Recognition
    _____ Unaided recall
17. The four main forms of quantifying data are _____ , _____ , _____ , and _____ .
18. The key to grading is _____ .
19. Grades can be based on the completion of IEP objectives. (True or False)

Activities
1. Attend an annual review meeting and describe the formative and summative evaluation data reported.
2. Take an IEP of a student and develop an IAP for the annual review.
3. Design a self-checking material or identify materials that include an evaluation component.
4. Explain diagnostic teaching to another person and ask whether he or she would use it.
5. Compare the grading systems used for exceptional students in your own and a neighboring school system.

Discussion Questions
1. Discuss whether to discount educational outcomes that are not easily quantifiable.
2. Can evaluation be unethical? How?
3. Discuss this statement: "Students are usually punished, not reinforced, by evaluation and grading systems."
4. What other factors besides instructional ones need to be evaluated? Why?

17

Parental Involvement

Parents of children and adolescents with learning problems must be actively involved in the special education process. They can play vital roles in assessment, in educational decision making, and in all aspects of the educational program. PL 94–142, PL 99–457, and good practice mandate parental participation, despite the possible hesitation and resistance of some professionals. Furthermore, these laws are merely the beginning; they suggest only a few of the many possible ways parents can be full partners with professionals in the education of their children. The nature and extent of current parental involvement are being clarified from both parental and professional perspectives.

ROLES FOR PARENTS

In becoming involved with the student's program, parents can participate in many activities (Wallace & McLoughlin, 1988). These are

1. *Identification/Referral*—The informed parent can be aware of early signs of a disability, know what special educational services are available, and know how to seek services.
2. *Assessment*—Parents can provide valuable assessment information often otherwise inaccessible to the professional. Parental cooperation in the procedural aspects of assessment can immeasurably facilitate the process.
3. *Programming*—The initial conference to discuss the assessment results and, if necessary, to develop the IEP requires full parental participation. Parents help choose IEP goals and objectives as well as the most appropriate educational placement for their child.
4. *Teaching*—Parents may serve as classroom aides and tutors to improve learning or help implement the IEP in the home. As a function of these instructional activities, parents can gather useful information about the student's learning strategies and work habits.
5. *Evaluation*—By supplying feedback to professionals, parents assist in improving programs. They can provide evidence of student growth in situations and places outside the classroom.

Reasons for Involving Parents

There are many reasons for encouraging the parents' involvement in assessment. Parents are aware of many aspects of the student's background and current conditions about which professionals know little. They also can assist by gathering data about the student's performance both before and during the special education program. If parents are alerted to the critical areas being assessed, they can be more supportive of the instructional program. Another key consideration is that all parents, especially culturally different or minority parents, will be less anxious and suspicious of the assessment if they are included throughout the total process.

PL 94–142 requires parental involvement. As indicated in Chapter 2, there are many specific areas of assessment where parental participation is mandated. The major areas are (a) notice of referral, (b) permission to test, (c) information concerning assessment results, (d) participation in IEP development, (e) permission for placement in special education programs, (f) review of the IEP at least annually, and (g) rights to an appeal process regarding the decisions made. Parents must be informed of their legal rights and responsibilities and should be able to respond to basic questions about PL 94–142.

Parent and Professional Expectations

However, the willingness and eagerness of parents to exercise their rights and become fully involved are influenced by a variety of factors. Parents may be realizing for the first time that their child has a problem and may be reluctant to initiate or follow through with the process. For others, assessments have become routine, and their experience shapes their reaction.

Professionals must also adjust their expectations of parental participation because tangential family matters may be drawing parents' attention away from the process. The minority or culturally different family may be suspicious of the true intent of the testing and avoid any involvement. Some parents have had poor experiences with schools and agencies and are leery of any contact. What is becoming increasingly clear is that the language, procedures, and interactions required by full parental participation demand considerable education, interest, and motivation.

Professionals must develop a realistic perspective of what parents can actually be expected to do (Kroth, 1980b). Whether by readiness, inclination, or training, parents may participate in a variety of ways. Professionals must not have universal expectations for parents, even as they work to guarantee parental rights and encourage involvement. The minimal participation of some parents should not be taken as an indication of lack of interest in their child. Nor is zealous involvement by others a sign of self-interest.

It is necessary to individualize parental involvement to suit the needs and preferences of each parent (Allen & Hudd, 1987). Allowances must be made for the social, economic, physical, recreational, and other needs of families. Current research on parent preferences for involvement indicates they generally prefer informal and frequent communication and activities such as giving and receiving information over activities that require active decision making (Turnbull & Turnbull, 1986). Parental preferences for information to be shared between the home and school, forms of communication, and frequency of contacts should be assessed regularly.

FORMS OF INVOLVEMENT

Parents may be involved in the special educational assessment process in many ways, including those required by federal and state laws and good practice. Professionals can encourage parents to contribute their expertise and knowledge in assessment.

Identification and Referral

Parents can provide valuable information in the identification stage of assessment. They are aware of the developmental status of their children and, if provided with information about early signs of handicapping conditions, may be able to identify possible problems during preschool years. Even with school-aged students, parents given information about the characteristics of various handicaps can be of immeasurable assistance in identifying disabled learners. Also, parents should be made aware of the availability of special school services and the procedures for making a referral. In many cases, particularly with preschool children, the parents make the initial referral of their child for special educational assessment.

Since the passage of PL 94–142, better-quality information has become increasingly available. State departments of education develop and dis-

seminate print and media material to make parents and others aware of handicapping descriptors and available services (McLoughlin et al., 1981). Parent groups, such as the Association for Children and Adults with Learning Disabilities, are also active in this effort (McLoughlin, Edge, Petrosko, Strenecky, & Davis, 1983).

Notification and Permission

Parents are informed in writing that their child has been referred for testing. Also, they are informed of their rights to participate in the process and to question any decisions made along the way. However, although prior notices concerning assessments are generally provided, they may not always mention critical rights, as they should (Yoshida, 1982).

Parents also give their permission for testing and are provided with the reason for and details of the planned assessment. Sometimes parents are hard to contact, and phone calls and home visits are necessary to obtain their consent. When parents cannot be reached by mail or phone, the school system or other agency documents its efforts. The critical factor is that parents are encouraged to give their informed consent. Vocabulary control, forms translated into different languages, and accommodations for an individual's disability are frequently necessary to ensure this early level of involvement.

Interviews and Case Histories

Once a student has been referred, parents can provide needed information about the student's past history and current functioning by being interviewed and completing case histories. Often this type of information is available only from them, because professionals have no knowledge of the student's past and may be unable to observe the student in situations outside the school.

As illustrated by the case history in Appendix A, special educators may discuss the student's health and physical history, educational status, personal traits, home and family, work experience, and more (Kroth, 1985). In addition to gathering information about the student, interviews may also be used to obtain information concerning parent–child relationships, including questions such as, "Are there any activities that you particularly enjoy doing with your child?" and "Do you feel that he or she needs a lot of praise and encouragement?"

FIGURE 17–1
Questions about learning problems to ask parents

You see your child in many situations: at home, at family gatherings, playing with friends in the neighborhood, and in other community situations. Help professionals to know your child better by sharing your years of observation and experience.

1. In your opinion, what are things your child does best?
2. What areas are you as a parent most concerned about?
3. Think of one or two things that your child does at home that you would like to change. Describe each and tell how often each occurs.

    a. My child_____
       This happens_____

    b. My child_____
       This happens_____

4. One concern of most teachers is how well children read, write, and do math. Read the statements below, think about your child, and tell if he or she

    a. never does this
    b. sometimes does this
    c. usually does this

    _____ writes letters to family members
    _____ reads the newspaper or magazines
    _____ reads the menu in a restaurant
    _____ tells time with a clock or watch
    _____ reads for fun
    _____ reads the t.v. guide to select programs to watch
    _____ writes down a phone message
    _____ reads signs in the community such as traffic signs, street signs, store names, and so forth
    _____ makes purchases in stores and can tell if correct change is received

    Add any other examples or reading, writing, and math skills that you can think of:

_____

5. What is the major thing you would like your child to accomplish in school this year?

Note. From "Assessing Special Students: Strategies for Increasing Parent and Professional Collaboration in the Assessment Process" by J. A. McLoughlin & R. B. Lewis, 1982. Keynote address given at University of San Diego Symposium on Behavior and Learning Disorders, San Diego, CA. Reprinted by permission.

Pose questions in a way and in a context familiar to parents. Find out what concerns parents have and what they want to see changed in their child. As illustrated in Figure 17–1, questions about language arts and communication skills can be asked in terms of parents' experience with their children.

The interview, whether factual or personal in nature, must be both sensitive and efficient. The interviewer's goal is to encourage the parents to talk, and thus the interviewer should attempt to limit his or her own participation to a minimum. Questions with "yes" and "no" answers should be avoided. Questions should not be posed so the answers are implied—"You didn't like that, did you?" Losen and Diament (1978) suggest that (a) both parents should be involved in the interview, if possible; (b) the purpose of the interview should be made clear to the participants; (c) if necessary, the reasons for the questions in the interview should be explained; and (d) parents should be informed of the use of interview results and the provisions for privacy. PL 93–380, the Family Educational and Privacy Rights Act, guarantees parents the right to inspect and challenge the accuracy of educational records, including information concerning family background and other sociological information. Kroth and Simpson (1977) encourage interviewers to be factual in recording parental statements, to avoid unfounded conclusions about parents and children, and to report the conclusions and the perceptions of the parents rather than of the interviewer. Judgments about parents and their skills should not be allowed to taint the interview report. Chapter 5 contains more ideas about the use of interviews and questionnaires that can be applied to parents.

Formal Assessment

A number of formal assessment procedures depend on parental participation, such as ratings of children's behavior and completion of developmental schedules, as described in Chapter 18. For example, in the *Behavior Rating Profile* (Brown & Hammill, 1983a), the student's behavior is rated by parents, teachers, and by students themselves. Parents are asked to respond to a list of questions, as illustrated in Figure 17–2. The perceptions of the parent are then compared with those of the teacher and the student.

Such systematic comparisons are important. Parents, teachers, and students may disagree le-

gitimately because of the difference in the home and school contexts, or a child's exaggerated perception of the situation. When another dual-questionnaire system (Rosenberg, Harris, & Reifler, 1988) was used with parents and teachers of learning disabled students, the parents and teachers agreed about overt, aggressive behaviors affecting others and differed in their appraisal of more inner-directed problem behaviors.

Kroth's *Target Behavior* (1973) is another procedure that involves parents in assessment. Its aim is to measure and compare parent and teacher concerns. Parents are given 25 cards, each containing a description of a behavior a child might exhibit at home or at school; they must arrange these cards on a grid. The position of the behavioral description on the grid indicates the degree the parent considers that behavior a problem.

Parents of students from culturally different and minority families can be of great assistance in making nondiscriminatory assessments. As part of the *System of Multicultural Pluralistic Assessment* (Mercer & Lewis, 1977b), parents are interviewed with the *Adaptive Behavior Inventory for Children* (Mercer & Lewis, 1977a) to establish the level of their child's coping skills in nonschool settings. Also, questions about and observations on language, communication style, and so forth may yield information about students that clarify the meaning of their behavior.

There are many informal assessment procedures that parents can learn to administer. Parent aides and tutors can be trained to use criterion-referenced tests and informal inventories. The use of developmental scales and criterion-referenced tests by parent volunteers is frequent practice in early childhood programs.

Observation and Charting

Parents of disabled learners can participate in the data-gathering process by observing their child in the classroom, at home, and elsewhere. Cooper and Edge (1981) and Heward, Dardig, and Rossett (1979) describe strategies for parents in systematic observation of their exceptional child's behavior. In these procedures, which are part of the applied behavioral analysis approach, parents first select a behavior to observe. They collect data on the frequency of occurrence or duration, and then plan and implement a behavior change program. For example, parents concerned about their child's

FIGURE 17–2

Parent *Behavior Rating Profile*

My child	Very Much Like My Child	Like My Child	Not Much Like My Child	Not At All Like My Child
1. Is verbally aggressive to parents	☐	☐	☐	☐
2. Doesn't follow rules set by parents	☐	☐	☐	☐
3. Overeats, is obese, fat	☐	☐	☐	☐
4. Complains about doing assigned chores . . .	☐	☐	☐	☐
5. Doesn't follow directions	☐	☐	☐	☐
6. Lies to avoid punishment or responsibility . .	☐	☐	☐	☐
7. Has associates of which parents don't approve	☐	☐	☐	☐
8. Is not a leader among his/her peers	☐	☐	☐	☐
9. Is self-centered, egocentric	☐	☐	☐	☐
10. Is shy; clings to parents	☐	☐	☐	☐
11. Is lazy	☐	☐	☐	☐
12. Has no regular, special activities with parents, e.g., shopping trips, ball games, etc. . .	☐	☐	☐	☐
13. Is self-destructive; pulls out his/her own hair, scratches self to point of drawing blood, etc.	☐	☐	☐	☐
14. Seeks parental praise too eagerly	☐	☐	☐	☐
15. Is unconcerned about personal hygiene; brushing teeth, bathing, combing hair	☐	☐	☐	☐
16. Sleeps poorly; has nightmares, insomnia . . .	☐	☐	☐	☐
17. Has too rich a fantasy life	☐	☐	☐	☐
18. Takes orders from parents unwilling	☐	☐	☐	☐
19. Is overly sensitive to teasing	☐	☐	☐	☐
20. Demands immediate gratification, e.g., must have the bicycle now, can't wait	☐	☐	☐	☐
21. Talks too little; is nonverbal	☐	☐	☐	☐
22. Is unreliable about money; buys compulsively; is not trusted with money	☐	☐	☐	☐
23. Tattles on others	☐	☐	☐	☐
24. Violates curfew	☐	☐	☐	☐
25. Doesn't seem to enjoy participating in family recreational activities	☐	☐	☐	☐
26. Makes "put-down" remarks about him/ herself; self-effacing	☐	☐	☐	☐
27. Won't share belongings willingly	☐	☐	☐	☐
28. Doesn't listen when parents talk	☐	☐	☐	☐
29. Demands excessive parental attention	☐	☐	☐	☐
30. Cries excessively	☐	☐	☐	☐

					Total
Sum of Marks in Each Column =	_____	_____	_____	_____	Points
Multiply Sum by	X 0	X 1	X 2	X 3	Scored
Add Products	0 +	_____ +	_____ +	_____ =	_____

Note. From *Behavior Rating Profile* by L. L. Brown & D. D. Hammill, 1983, Austin, TX: PRO-ED. Copyright 1983 by Linda L. Brown & Donald D. Hammill. Reprinted by permission.

poor use of after-dinner study time first counted the number of minutes actually spent in studying (the baseline). Then they increased the student's study time by introducing a system of rewards.

Parents may also gain a better understanding of their child's learning problems and of the instructional program if they observe in the classroom and other school settings. Teachers should secure the necessary permission and cooperation from school administrators and staff; policies and procedures should be developed cooperatively; and parents should be advised of confidentiality regulations. In addition, the teacher should discuss the possible goals, rules, and procedures for observations (e.g., where parents might sit and how to deal with a student's attention-seeking behavior), as well as appropriate days and times for observations.

Involving the Student in Assessment

Parents can contribute to the success of the assessment process by helping their child understand what will happen so that he or she will feel more comfortable about the testing situation. Because the disabled learner may feel anxious and confused about the assessment and the reasons for it, parents should explain some of the procedures and mechanics of test taking. Parents should be aware of their own attitudes toward assessment so they do not transfer their own anxiety or fear to the child.

Parents should also talk with their child *after* the assessment. Students may have doubts, fears, and questions about the testing, and parents should be prepared to address these feelings. Exceptional students may have found the experience unpleasant, and parents will help to insure their child's cooperation in future assessments if they listen to and immediately discuss any concerns.

Furthermore, parents should explain the results of the assessment to their child, when appropriate. This communication may increase the student's cooperation in the instructional program. Parents may decide that older exceptional students should be present at the postassessment conference.

CONFERENCING WITH PARENTS

Parents attend at least one conference to have the assessment results explained, whether their child is found to be handicapped or not. If the student proves to be eligible for special education, parents and professionals work together at this meeting to decide on a suitable course of action. For them, this conference is an important beginning for a working relationship.

Preparation for the Conference

Parents should be prepared for the postassessment conference by being told the purpose of the meeting, when and where it will occur, and who will participate. Also, parents should be ready to answer questions about the student's interests and about their goals for the student.

It is helpful for the parents to know the major topics to be discussed at the meeting, especially those concerning the development of the key components of the IEP. It may encourage fuller participation if parents know that they may ask questions, volunteer information, and challenge data presented by others.

The Physical Environment

Parental involvement may also be influenced by the conference's physical environment. Kroth and Simpson (1977) suggest that professionals can increase parent participation by scheduling conferences in private rooms; making arrangements so conferences will not be interrupted by phone calls or knocks on the door; gathering all necessary conference materials beforehand; and insuring that parents feel they have the professionals' undivided attention. The parents should be seated among the professionals at a table. The professionals should make every effort to include parents not only physically but also in the actual team deliberations.

Communication Style

The communication style used during conferences can also affect the degree to which parents feel included. Professionals must indicate both verbally and nonverbally that they have a sincere desire to work with the parents (McLoughlin, McLaughlin, & Stewart, 1979). Professionals who are advocates make every effort to insure parents are involved. Advocates do not perceive themselves as adversaries of parents; they are prepared to work with parents, regardless of how uncooperative parents may appear. On the other hand, professionals who display nonadvocate behaviors are not dedicated to increasing parental involvement. Professional advocates can demonstrate their interest and are easily distinguishable from nonadvocates.

However, communications between professionals and parents are also influenced by the parents' behaviors. Most parents fall between two extremes: resistant—they have a predetermined position or opinion and are unwilling to discuss the issues—and compliant—they are reluctant to get involved and concede all decision-making powers to the professionals. With extremely resistant parents, advocates attempt to understand their concerns and examine alternative solutions. With excessively compliant parents, the special educator may need to lead the discussion, ask questions about the student, and solicit the parents' opinions. In both cases, it is essential to use positive nonverbal communication; that is, maintain eye contact, avoid visual distractions, and so forth.

Professionals do not routinely encounter total resistance or compliance, because most parents fall somewhere between the two extremes. Regardless of parent behavior, Litcher (1976) counsels against admonishing, exhorting, blaming, and criticizing them; those strategies only block communication. Instead, the principles of active listening are much more appropriate. Active listening involves

1. Listening for the message of the speaker
2. Restating the basic content and/or feeling of the speaker's message
3. Determining whether the speaker's message was accurately received by observing cues or asking for a response
4. If necessary, allowing the speaker to correct the listener's impression of what was said

Losen and Diament (1978) also caution against falling into such pitfalls as responding angrily to parental outbursts and passively acquiescing to parental opinions. Professionals must fulfill the responsibility to behave assertively but calmly when disagreements occur. Furthermore, teachers should avoid making excuses and denying mistakes.

Reporting Results

Professionals can do much to include parents in the assessment process by reporting all results clearly and graphically. The type of assessment data influences the degree of immediate intelligi-

bility to parents. Standardized tests, with their variety of scores and interpretations, pose a difficult communication problem. Results of informal assessments, such as graphs of observations, criterion-referenced tests, and informal inventories, are much easier to report.

Single scores of standardized tests should not be reported; a range of scores should be given so the significance of an individual score is not misconstrued. Percentile ranks are useful to indicate how well a student performed compared to other students. Grade and age equivalent scores are extremely subjective in meaning; other types of scores, such as standard scores, may be too technical. As illustrated in Chapter 15, parents can be shown where the child scored within a broad range. Charts can be made for other areas tested, such as academic achievement or motor skills.

Other forms of assessment data lend themselves readily to presentation to parents. Results of behavioral observations are truly graphic. The specific description of the behavior in question and the nature of the data are easily understandable. Similarly, data from other informal techniques such as criterion-referenced tests and task analyses may be easily interpreted to parents. Samples of classroom work and test data should be shown when it is necessary to illustrate a point; audio- or videotapes of the student's responses in the testing situation or in the classroom could also be used.

Parents can be helped to view their child's performance on an intraindividual basis. Comparison with other students is only one way to analyze learning behavior; for instructional purposes, consider a student's skills in relationship to his or her general abilities. Professionals also need to inform parents about the nature of test items so parents do not misinterpret the meaning of scores. Special testing conditions, such as tasks that must be performed within strict time limits, should also be pointed out. From the parents' point of view, it is also important to report positive as well as negative results. The child's strengths should be highlighted as well as the weaknesses.

Professionals must be mindful of the interdisciplinary nature of the assessment team and its possible effect on parents. Different disciplines use different terminology and stress different aspects of the student's performance; so much divergent input may be confusing. Special educators can provide a valuable service to parents by summarizing the information received from various sources. You need to streamline the different terms and procedures used by the various disciplines. In order to help parents make sense out of a variety of assessment information, a profile can be used to summarize the results (see Chapter 15).

Also, it is important to take into account family dynamics when deciding what information to share and how to present it. Parents' attitude toward the student assessed, level of cooperation, receptivity to new information about their child, role in family decision making, and other factors must be considered (Fulmer, Cohen, & Monaco, 1985).

Send a letter to parents before or after the conference to summarize the assessment results. Although comprehensive, the summary must also avoid technical jargon as much as possible. As Turnbull, Strickland, and Brantley (1982) explain, the educational level of the parents may reduce the usefulness of this strategy.

Student Involvement

Older students can be included in conferences at which assessment data are explained and other meetings at which IEPs are designed. The advantage is that parents and students will hear the same information, have an opportunity to ask questions, and have a mutual sense of responsibility. Professionals and parents should discuss the inclusion of students beforehand and take into account students' level of understanding and maturity. Also, you need to consider the parents' ability to discuss the information with their child present and whether the parents can act appropriately. Data should be presented in understandable terms and with tact, particularly information about intelligence. In some cases it is a good idea to see the parents first and then include their child. Students can be taught how to participate productively in educational planning conferences using a learning strategy approach (Van Reusen, Bos, Schumaker, & Deshler, 1987).

Parent Advocates

Some parents feel more comfortable having someone accompany them to school conferences. This friend or advocate may offer anything from moral support to technical expertise if they know the regulations governing assessments and programs. Some parent groups offer trained parent advocates for this purpose.

Sometimes a professional attending the conference functions as an advocate for the parents, at least as far as encouraging their involvement. As discussed earlier, the ideal is for everyone to behave with the parents' best interest at heart. Someone who works in the school, such as a counselor, can increase parental comments by introducing them, directing questions to them, reinforcing their contributions, clarifying jargon, and summarizing decisions at the end of the meetings (Goldstein & Turnbull, 1982).

Designing Program Goals

Parents of special students can be better drawn into the assessment process and subsequent deliberations if they are encouraged to describe their own goals and concerns for the child. This information will point out possible areas of conflict between parents and professionals, and steps may be taken to resolve differences. Parents should also be encouraged to help implement IEP goals and objectives, particularly those that apply to the student's behavior in the home and community, including study and self-help skills. These activities increase parents' feelings of involvement in the special education program and can be coordinated with the school instructional program.

Approving Placement

When it comes time to discuss placement at an IEP conference, the parents should be encouraged to participate in this decision, not merely to acquiesce and approve the recommendations of the professionals on the team.

Each service delivery model has both advantages and disadvantages. Parents should be made aware of the pros and cons of placement in the resource room, special class, and so forth, and should be encouraged to visit and observe several different types of services. The placement decision should be presented as a matter of alternatives. Although the mandates of PL 94–142 regarding least restrictive environment must be followed, the team must consider several placement options to determine the most appropriate one for the individual student.

Evaluating the Assessment

Parents can be helpful in evaluating the assessment process. They can monitor the quality of assessment by noting the following:

1. Was the assessment discriminatory in any way?
2. Were the diagnosticians qualified?
3. Were different points of view represented on the team?
4. Was the student's native language or major mode of communication used?
5. Was more than one test used?

Parents can answer many questions about the procedures, personnel, and level of their own involvement in the IEP conference (Hudson & Graham, 1978).

Current Research on Parental Participation

A number of studies over the past few years have profiled the status of parental involvement. Turnbull et al. (1982) conclude that parental attendance at conferences has been at a fairly high level. However, even when parents are involved, they report that they usually only listen, rather than contribute to the decision-making process (Goldstein, Strickland, Turnbull, & Curry, 1980). Parental noninvolvement is evidenced by the significant number of IEPs that lack parent signatures (Say, McCollum, & Brightman, 1980). Parents often cannot seem to remember what happens at IEP conferences (Hoff, Fenton, Yoshida, & Kaufman, 1978) and confuse this type of meeting with others (McKinney & Hocutt, 1982). This may be the result of lack of preparedness for the conferences, the technical jargon typically used, and confusion about their role (Kotin & Eager, 1977). Their confusion may also stem from poor attendance by professionals (Scanlon, Arick & Phelps, 1981) and professionals' own uncertainty about their roles in assessment and IEP conferences (Fenton, Yoshida, Maxwell, & Kaufman, 1979).

Parents are not influential at these meetings. When asked before a conference, all participants rank parents much higher in importance and contribution than after the meeting (Gilliam, 1979). The main contributors are professionals with hard data such as test scores (Gilliam & Coleman, 1981).

Parents may be deferring their decision-making power to other team members (Knoff, 1983).

Actual observations of team meetings have indicated that parents generally ask few questions and respond little, yet these same parents generally report satisfaction with the outcome of the meetings and have few questions about the decisions made (Vaughn, Bos, Harrell, & Lasky, 1988). One reason for this low level of participation may be that the major decisions have been made and the meeting is held to confirm them (Ysseldyke, 1983). Special education teachers have indicated when interviewed that one of their roles is to prepare objectives for the IEP *before* the meetings (White & Calhoun, 1987). Another reason for the low participation is parents' lack of training in the process. Parents who have had training are more likely to participate and contribute.

MINORITY PARENTAL INVOLVEMENT AND PROFESSIONAL CULTURAL COMPETENCE

Low participation of minority parents is a significant problem in conducting assessments and designing IEPs. In one survey of Hispanic parents (Lynch & Stein, 1987), about 75% of the respondents said they were contacted prior to assessment; understood the assessment, their rights, and the goals and objectives on their child's IEP; and signed and received a copy of the IEP. However, only 45% considered themselves part of the assessment process, and 50% felt that they were not an active participant in the development of the IEP.

Professionals must be more culturally competent to work with minority families (Research and Training Center, 1988). The following points are particularly important. First, they need an awareness and acceptance of cultural differences, particularly in regard to communication style, view of life, and definition of disabilities. Second, they must realize how their own culture influences how they think and act.

Third, professionals must appreciate the dynamics of difference that occur when they work with minority parents. Both professionals and minority parents bring culturally prescribed patterns of communication, etiquette, and problem solving; and they may bring stereotypes and feelings about working with someone who is different. Fourth, it is necessary to learn what symbols are meaningful, how disabilities are defined, and how the family support system is organized.

Fifth, professionals must adapt their practices to minority parents' culture. Culture will shape how professionals conduct family interviews, whom they will include in family intervention plans, and what goals will be established for the child and family.

HOME ASSESSMENT

An important consideration in assessment relevant to the family is assessment of the home. One approach to home assessment is to ask the family directly about their habits, customs, support systems, and short- and long-term needs. Observations and more formalized techniques, some focused on the child and others on the family, are also used (Bailey & Simeonsson, 1988). Among those that document how the environment stimulates child development is the *Home Observation and Measurement of the Environment* (Caldwell & Bradley, 1978). *HOME* has two levels (for 0–3 years and 3–6 years) and includes true–false items about the physical, social, and cognitive surroundings provided in the home such as verbal responsivity of the mother, provision of play material, language stimulation, and modeling and encouragement of social maturity. Those that are more family oriented tend to focus on psychological aspects such as child aspiration level, child-rearing practices, and moral or religious emphasis. Bailey and Simeonsson (1988) provide descriptions of these procedures. Other aspects of family assessment are discussed in the context of early childhood assessment in Chapter 18.

DUE PROCESS HEARINGS

As described in Chapter 2, if parents disagree with any aspect of the special education process, including the placement decision, they can ask for an impartial due process hearing. A more informal effort, called mediation, may be made by an intermediary to help the parents and agency reach a mutually acceptable solution. Currently, mediations have proven to be as adversarial, formal, and costly as due process hearings (Yoshida & Bryne, 1979),

but they are improving with experience (Turnbull & Strickland, 1981; Yoshida, 1982).

According to Strickland (1982), due process hearings are also difficult for parents. Parents are using them as a last desperate effort, usually after repeated negative and unsuccessful experiences with the schools. Decisions of the impartial hearing officers often do not get implemented, and parent–school relationships get worse. Turnbull and Strickland (1981) advise considerable thought before seeking such hearings, as do parents who have used them. However, when faced with the alternatives (i.e., live with an unsatisfactory educational program or go to court), due process hearings continue to offer a viable legitimate recourse for dissatisfied parents.

MONITORING THE PROGRAM

Parents are routinely sent report cards and invited to conferences with teachers. However, typical grading systems, whether letters or numbers, do not reveal much about the nature and extent of student progress. At best, a letter or number is a general indicator of performance in comparison to normal peers or other students with disabilities. When true progress is not revealed, the nature and extent of failure may not become apparent until it is too late to make suitable modifications.

Turnbull et al. (1982) and others stress the need to build specific continuous monitoring devices into the IEP. If objectives are stated clearly, then their complete or partial accomplishment can be noted by everyone. Some published IEP systems, such as the *Instructional Based Appraisal System* (Meyen, Gautt & Howard, 1976), assist in monitoring completion of objectives, as well as offering reasons for and the nature of modifications. Copies are available to parents and other involved parties.

The criterion-referenced report card is another alternative technique used to involve parents in the evaluation process. This system supplies parents with information for evaluating the effectiveness of the instructional program without requiring the teacher to grade student performance. These report cards commonly include IEP short-term objectives and a record of the student's progress toward these objectives.

Once special education services have begun, parents have many opportunities to participate in the ongoing evaluation of the student's instructional program. Regular communication between parents and teachers should be encouraged. As discussed in Chapter 16, it is possible to design a system of brief daily or weekly report cards to keep parents abreast of their child's progress. Teachers may require parents to sign and return these reports to insure their review. Parents may also use daily reports as part of a system of rewards in the home.

Communication between parents and teachers can also be fostered by regular phone calls. In one project, parents were called to encourage their tutoring and to report student progress; there was an increase in achievement and an improvement in parental attitude (Heron & Axelrod, 1976). A recorded telephone answering system to transmit instructions for parents, requests, and progress notes has also been used with similar positive results (Chapman & Heward, 1982).

Interviews with the students themselves can be very revealing. The key is to pose the questions appropriately. Parents can help by noting their children's spontaneous and solicited comments about school. Parents can also report their observations of their children's use of skills in different settings. Such data, when shared regularly, may suggest the validity of an instructional approach or the need for change.

Thus, when the time comes for scheduled program reviews, more than hastily gathered test scores or grades are available. The accomplishment of IEP objectives, the attainment of time-lines, the reasons for changes, and so forth are documented. Because parents have been regularly involved, no one is surprised by the accomplishments or lack of them. Also, parents are in a better position to decide if the program is still needed and in what form.

The point here is to establish and maintain regular and meaningful communications about student programs. This exchange of information should occur among special educators, regular classroom teachers, other specialists, and the parents. Parents should not have to rely on piecemeal information to assess the appropriateness of their child's program. Often miscommunication leads to misunderstanding and causes everyone involved a great deal of trouble.

PARENTAL COOPERATION

Professionals may be frustrated by the lack of cooperation from some parents of handicapped students. However, parents go through stages of adjusting to the reality of their child's disability, including shock, denial, fear, anger, and other feelings (McLoughlin, 1985a). Reluctance to share information, absence from meetings, and seeming indifference to decision-making activities may be signs of their struggle to cope.

Culturally different or minority parents may be highly concerned by the whole assessment process (Jones, 1988; Marion, 1980). They may perceive these practices as a reinforcement of their inferiority in the schools and discriminatory in principle and practice. The result may be a total lack of involvement or angry confrontation. You should incorporate these parents informally in the process and use appropriate language and communication styles (Rodriguez, 1981). Ignoring official-looking communications or phone calls and refusing to attend meetings at schools may indicate a coping strategy in dealing with bureaucracies rather than indifference to their child.

Parents also have cultural perceptions and values concerning teachers and schools that may influence how they respond to the assessment process. They may reject teachers as authority figures and resent their intrusion into non-school-related areas. Parents can also blame the schools for their child's failure and hold unrealistic expectations for what the schools can accomplish.

Teachers and other professionals must beware of perceiving parents as the cause of the child's problem or transferring any of their negative feelings for the student to the parents. Teachers may also perceive the child differently than the parents. These different perspectives may contribute to communication blocks and misunderstandings. Thus, parents may respond to professionals' requests for involvement along a continuum from indifference to overzealous participation. Extremes in either case are usually the result of the previously mentioned variables and the lack of an appropriate and functional communication system.

PARENT EDUCATION

Parent education in the area of special education assessment is greatly needed. There are several aspects of the assessment process that may require training parents, such as communication skills, team decision making, special education procedures and practices, and advocacy (McLoughlin, 1985a). Parent education is one of the roles of the special educator, and professionals should give parents many opportunities to gain information about and skills in assessment.

One method of parent education is to acquaint them with various organizations, agencies, and resources that can provide information about assessment. Parents may get information from state departments of education or from national agencies such as the National Information Center for Handicapped Children and Youth (formerly *Closer Look*). The content and appropriateness of this material have improved markedly since passage of PL 94–142, although readability level and some content need improvement (McLoughlin et al., 1981). The state departments of education place a high priority on providing information on parents' rights in regard to assessment and available services (McLoughlin et al., 1983). Periodicals such as *The Exceptional Parent* are recommended.

National, state, and local organizations, such as the Association for Children and Adults with Learning Disabilities (ACLD) and the National Association for Retarded Citizens (NARC), are designed to assist parents of exceptional students. These groups offer conferences to acquaint parents with current issues. A regular feature of recent conferences is advocacy training workshops to foster more active involvement by parents in assessment and programming areas. Advocacy training may include using professional terminology well, asking the right questions, being persistent but diplomatic when answers are less than satisfactory, and evaluating the quality of services (Muir, Milan, Branston-McLean, & Berger, 1982).

The various parent groups frequently have their own newsletters, such as *Newsbriefs* from ACLD, and offer periodicals on relevant topics. Although they often have useful information available or at least the expertise to develop it, these parent groups are limited in resources for dissemination (McLoughlin et al., 1983). However, they and other agencies, like state departments of education, seem interested in devising more cooperative development and dissemination activities.

Parent organizations and similar groups also offer emotional support and counseling when parents first become aware of their child's problems. During the process of gaining appropriate services for their children, parents find such a group helpful and understanding. Another method of training is to provide parents with written information about assessment. Many school districts prepare information packets for their parents, or professionals may obtain materials.

Agencies that can provide copies of suitable information include the following:

- The Council for Exceptional Children, 1920 Association Drive, Reston, VA 22091
- Children's Defense Fund, 1520 New Hampshire Avenue, N.W., Washington, DC 20036
- Educational Testing Service, Princeton, NJ 08540
- The National Information Center for Handicapped Children and Youth, Box 1492, Washington DC 20013
- CTB/McGraw-Hill, Del Monte Research Park, Monterey, CA 93940
- *Exceptional Parent,* P. O. Box 964, Manchester, NH 03105
- National Center for Law and the Handicapped, 211 W. Washington St., Suite 1900, South Bend, IN 46601
- Impact Publishers, P.O. Box 1094, San Luis Obispo, CA 93406

Parents use workshops, speeches, and the like to educate themselves. Some pertinent topics in the area of assessment include decoding professional jargon, understanding assessment procedures used in the local school district, using observation techniques in the home, and analyzing test items. Training sessions may be conducted by professionals, parents, or the two working together as a team. Kroth (1980a) has developed lecture outlines, handouts, tapes, overlays, and modules related to assessment matters. A frequent goal of special projects, such as early childhood education of the handicapped programs, is to train parents in assessment skills. The main emphasis is generally formal and informal observation and interviewing.

Probably the most common type of parent training occurs informally in parent–teacher conferences and conversations. Parents may indicate the need for information by asking questions such as, "Why can't my child do math?" or "How can my child be failing reading when he's so smart?"

Professionals, by being prepared to answer the parents' questions, can help them understand the assessment. Professionals can also directly affect the frequency and quality of parental contributions at conferences (Goldstein & Turnbull, 1982). Classroom teachers who have received in-service training about their role at conferences speak much more than unprepared teachers, direct more comments to the parents, and make more focused points (Trailor, 1982).

Therefore, do not overlook more indirect forms of parental training. Even without formal training sessions, parent behavior can be influenced by how professionals communicate during various phases of the assessment process. Professional training is very important in this area.

STUDY GUIDE

Review Questions

1. In what five areas can parents become involved in assessment?
2. Provide two reasons for encouraging parental participation in assessment.
3. Interviewers should avoid questions with _____ and _____ answers.
4. PL 93–380 is the Family Educational and Privacy Rights Act. (True or False)
5. Parents' perceptions of their child's behavior are useful in educational assessment. (True or False)
6. Some types of assessment data are harder to report and interpret to parents than others. (True or False)
7. Parents can systematically take observational data. (True or False)
8. Parents and staff should be prepared for classroom observations. (True or False)
9. Parents should know what to expect at IEP conferences. (True or False)
10. Professionals cannot afford to be advocates of parents of exceptional children. (True or False)
11. _____ are the most appropriate types of scores to report to parents.
12. Parents should be encouraged to perceive their child's performance on an _____ basis.
13. A journal for parents of exceptional children is _____ .
14. Parents should not be taught particulars about educational assessment because that is the sole concern of professionals. (True or False)
15. Professionals and parents should work together to develop and offer useful parent education experiences. (True or False)

Activities

1. Interview a special education teacher and other professionals concerning their views on the involvement of parents in the assessment process.
2. Select a standardized test and consider whether parents could participate in its administration. Name the assessment devices and procedures that best lend themselves to parental use.
3. Attend an IEP conference and note whether parents are included.
4. Role play a conference where a teacher reports assessment results to a parent.
5. Observe minority and nonminority parents in a postassessment conference, and describe the similarities and differences in the behavior of the parents and professionals attending the conference.

Discussion Questions

1. Discuss whether parental participation in assessment should be restricted to informal procedures or whether parents should be trained to use formal tests.
2. Discuss why parent participation in assessment and IEP conferences has been relatively poor in spite of PL 94–142 mandates.
3. Teachers complain that the parents who most need to attend conferences never show up. Discuss ways to change this situation.

PART SIX

Special Considerations

The special needs of infants and young children and the career and vocational concerns for adolescents and young adults are discussed in this final section. Chapter 18 considers assessment issues related to developmentally delayed children and preschoolers preparing for formal schooling. Assessment questions related to development and readiness for school are answered with various formal and informal strategies in accordance with PL 99–457. An IAP and IEP for a kindergartner with disabilities illustrate the considerations peculiar to assessment at this age level. Additionally, strategies for assessing family needs are described, as is the Individualized Family Services Plan (IFSP).

We have referred to the needs of older students as they prepare for the transition to college or the world of work and careers. In Chapter 19, ways to identify vocational knowledge, aptitudes, interests, and skills of students are considered. This discussion will be placed in the broader context of assessing adolescents' needs in interpersonal and recreational areas. The limitations of current assessment procedures and their failure to meet the needs of more able handicapped adolescents and young adults are clarified. In addition, the status of college assessment strategies is discussed.

Finally, Chapter 20 readdresses the critical issues in assessment outlined in Chapter 1. Hopefully, you will have a greater understanding of these issues, and you will have learned ways to solve or circumvent these concerns. We summarize the current research behind these issues and remind you of ways to grapple with them. Advances in assessment may make some issues obsolete. Others may continue to plague us in the years to come.

18

Early Childhood and Family Assessment

Questions sometimes arise about the developmental status of infants and preschool children. Parents, teachers, physicians, and others notice a lag or disturbing quality about growth in speech, motor skills, socialization, and so on. As children enter nursery school and kindergarten, readiness for traditional schooling becomes the real issue. Parents and others may indicate their concerns about their children's development and school readiness by such comments as, "Billy was premature; he's now 2 and sleeps poorly and responds slowly," or "Tiffany's nursery school teacher claims that she does not listen well and tends to withdraw."

At this level of development, the assessment question is not whether children are learning disabled, mildly retarded, or emotionally disturbed. Most professionals shy away from these types of diagnostic queries with really young children. The main question asked in order to provide suitable developmental interventions is, *What is the developmental status or school readiness level?* Assessment concerning overall development and school readiness is used in parent-child intervention programs, nurseries, and preschools. It is the first step in providing suitable support or assistance in preparing a child for school.

Timmy

Timmy is 5 years old and having problems in kindergarten. His speech is intelligible, but his language usage is odd. Ms. Mahoney, his teacher, indicates that he uses short phrases, often confusing parts of speech and grammatical forms. Timmy's copying skills are poor—whether working with material from the blackboard or at his desk. His teacher questions his readiness for the first grade.

Ms. Mahoney also mentions his withdrawn, quiet moods. She finds him crying sometimes and has to encourage him to participate more than other children. His parents are also aware of this behavior; he often resists going to school. Timmy will be referred to the school's child study team for a thorough assessment. He may need special support at school.

CONSIDERATIONS

The importance of early screening for growth and developmental problems is well accepted. Prevention of inadequate and uneven development of certain skills can remove the need for enormous personal and social effort later on. The domains of language, motor, and so forth do not develop in isolation, and problems in one affect the others. For example, imagine what is involved in a child riding a tricycle and saying hello to someone. Delays in motor or language development would make such a simple act very demanding, if not impossible.

Unprepared children entering preschool and later grades generally have a history of learning problems. School readiness is an important concept in avoiding the failure some young children face without suitable training in obvious preparatory skills. For children with disabilities, early screening and assessment programs can be a vital step toward providing needed support during schooling.

Purposes

The reasons for early childhood assessment are the same as mentioned in Chapter 1. First, there is a need to screen and identify young children with possible disabilities. Then, a more in-depth assessment is performed to determine whether a handicapping condition is involved. This decision-making process is difficult with young children because most criteria—especially for the mildly handicapping conditions—are stated in terms of school.

If there is evidence of such a handicap, data are gathered to design a suitable program to meet the needs of children and their families. Because early childhood interventions include parental involvement components, the family environment is also subject to assessment. Family members are frequently active participants in the whole assessment and programming process.

The final two reasons for assessment—program monitoring and evaluation—are related at this level. As the program is delivered, it is regularly evaluated and changed as needed. Also, at regular intervals and at least annually, the effectiveness of the service is established and recommendations for change and/or continuation are made. As the young child with disabilities nears school age, this transitional phase is critical to guarantee the continuation of vital support services. Throughout the various phases of assessment, the main question remains, *What is the development status or school readiness level, and what are specific strengths and weaknesses?*

Areas Assessed

Assessment of young children encompasses all the main areas of development. Physical factors (hearing, vision, neurological status, etc.) figure prominently in an examination of contributing elements. Concept formation and other cognitive functions like memory and problem solving also must be studied, especially in the context of intelligence. There are also many elements to be assessed in general aptitude and specific learning abilities areas.

Another broad area assessed is language and communication skills, including both receptive and expressive use of vocabulary and grammar. Because of the key role of language in thinking and establishing social relations, language disorders figure prominently in early childhood assessment. Speech, a related factor, is also a regular focus of assessment teams.

Gross and fine motor skills need to be examined because of their crucial role in exploration and play; as noted in Chapter 9, there are many specific elements in these broad categories. Social-emotional development is assessed both in the context of the home and school setting. Another frequently studied area is self-help and adaptive skills.

As the child grows, these areas of development take on different forms for assessment. In preschool and kindergarten, school readiness becomes the focus of evaluation—especially early reading, mathematics, and writing skills. Oral language and motor development continue to be major elements in assessment at this level. The importance of social behavior is studied in the context of classroom demands and expectations of teachers; school attitude and work habits are particularly important. There is a special demand on assessment teams to examine adaptive and self-help skills too.

Legislation

In 1975, PL 94–142 mandated preschool programs for special needs children from the age of 3, but only in states that required preschool education for all children. PL 99–457 of 1986 changed that by requiring all states to provide services for all 3- to 5-year-old handicapped children by 1990–1991. All the requirements of PL 94–142 are applicable, including those for a comprehensive assessment. However, a state department does not need to require school systems and other agencies to attach diagnostic labels to children in order to qualify them for funding. Children only need to be identified as developmentally delayed (that is, as measured by appropriate measures in cognitive development, physical development, language and speech development, psychosocial development, or self-help skills) or as having a diagnosed physical or mental condition that has a high probability of resulting in developmental delay (that is, at risk if early intervention services are not provided). Besides providing assessments and appropriate services for special needs children, PL 99–457 supports parent training and allows local educational agencies to provide services through other public and private agencies and at home or at centers.

The Handicapped Infants and Toddlers Program, another feature of PL 99–457, is aimed at the needs of at-risk children from birth to 3 years and their families. The target populations are children with developmental delays, physical and mental conditions with high probability of resulting in delays, or at-risk circumstances, medically or environmentally. Besides providing handicapped infants and children with services, the family's needs are to be assessed and addressed in an Individualized Family Service Plan (IFSP). PL 99–457 does not mandate participation by states in this program but indicates that states which decide to offer it have up to 4 years to organize an interagency coordinating council and develop other aspects of the program. Funding is based on state census data.

Issues

One issue facing early childhood educators is that they do not want to label young children as handicapped to correct milder forms of cognitive, language, adaptive, and emotional problems. One reason is fear of establishing negative or restrictive expectations for the child. However, PL 99–457 has removed the need to give children a diagnostic label so that state departments can qualify for federal funds, previously one of the major reasons for this practice. Another issue is the firm conviction that services for young children should be provided in a mainstreamed environment with age-appropriate peers.

Conceptualizations of assessment and services for infants and preschoolers with disabilities are also characterized by a fundamental difference of opinion. Some professionals consider the developmental approach the most appropriate way to establish lags or problems in one or more areas of growth. Others stress the need to examine immediately functional skills; they question the usefulness or efficiency of examining skills that seem age-specific and prerequisite and may not be important in performing current relevant tasks. This functional approach to assessment stresses analysis of specific, observable behaviors that form the fabric of the current and future existence of the child.

This need not be an either/or decision for early childhood educators; rather, it is a question of emphasis. A child's age and severity of handicap are crucial factors to consider (Bailey & Wolery, 1984). Additionally, this functional perspective in assessment and programming is essential when mildly handicapped children are getting ready to change from one placement to another and are having particular difficulty in a given learning environment. Then the issue clearly concerns the most immediate and crucial skills for successful, independent functioning.

The availability of valid and reliable measures to locate and program for the young disabled learner represents another pressing issue. Many of the norm-referenced and age-referenced measures are based on a variety of developmental milestones and vary in what they measure in similarly named areas (Bailey & Wolery, 1984). The informal techniques are subject to similar problems inherent with more formal techniques. Also, children in this age range are highly individualistic in their progression through the developmental stages because of a variety of factors, such as home environment.

Thus, there is considerable demand for ecological assessment and not merely testing of the child. The child's development must be considered in light of the family context, as well as other environmental factors. The demands of the current home and preschool environment must be taken into account when interpreting data and designing a program. Observations in the setting and interviews to establish parent and teacher expectations are particularly important, not to mention the behavior and attitudes of peers.

An ethical issue arises when children go through a thorough assessment process only to be incorrectly identified as having disabilities or not (Paget, 1984–85). This situation places undue strain on both the child and family in many ways, including financially. Everything must be done to make procedures as efficient, reliable, and useful as possible. Additionally, because assessments at this developmental level rely so heavily on the input of parents and involve different kinds of procedures, professionals must be prepared to interpret the data in an integrated fashion for parents and reconcile different findings and points of view about the child's behavior. Although parents and others may be expected realistically to hold different perspectives of the child, assessment results should be presented as a cohesive whole and not as fragments and unrelated facts.

To account for all the crucial facets in a child's development, a team of interdisciplinary professionals and the child's parents is needed. The core team usually consists of educators, parents, pediatricians, psychologists, speech-language specialists, and physical and/or occupational therapists. Additional supportive personnel are involved as needed: otologists and audiologists, ophthalmologists and optometrists, neurologists, and so on. Coordinating a group so varied in backgrounds, procedures, and terminology naturally leads to criticism. Awareness of one another's perspective and intercommunication among specialties is sometimes poor. Thus, parents may find the team model difficult to deal with because of the overwhelming number of professionals.

There are recurring complaints that assessment data are not useful for teaching children. Although such data are sometimes helpful in locating children with learning problems and establishing the scope of need, there is often no link between assessment and treatment. Similar arguments about standardized testing with school-aged children also apply at this level. Even curriculum-based assessments are criticized for their lack of practicality to the immediate learning environments.

Current Practices

Current practices in early childhood assessment for learning problems have progressed considerably. A variety of assessment procedures are in use. Brief, broad-based screening devices are available, generally permitting comparison of children to age-appropriate peers.

Highly desirable multidimensional screening instruments have well-defined target behaviors; have demonstrated reliability, predictive validity, and representative standardization; are completed easily, quickly, and economically; provide information about children incorrectly screened; and are acceptable to the professional and lay communities (Scott & Hogan, 1982). Robinson, Rose, and Jackson (1986) have reviewed a number of such instruments using these criteria. More specific, norm-referenced diagnostic tests are employed to examine psychological, emotional, language, preacademic, and other skills.

Particularly popular for program planning and evaluation are criterion-referenced systems and curriculum-based assessments that measure children's competency in a set of developmental or readiness skills. Often, additional task analysis is needed to identify component skills toward which instruction must be directed. Several model programs for handicapped children, such as the Portage Project, have developed both these assessment systems and accompanying instructional programs (Bluma, Shearer, Froham, & Hillard, 1976).

Informal assessment procedures are as relevant for young children as for other age levels. Structured and nonstructured observations are routinely used. Many times, the age of the child dictates against more structured assessment techniques. Parent and teacher interviews are also relied on heavily for convenience as well as effectiveness. Their testimonies concerning certain behaviors are used in lieu of testing every skill. By virtue of their close contacts with the child, parents and teachers have greater access to certain kinds of information than an examiner would.

Assessment practices in early childhood special education are traditionally directed toward identifying and serving children with sensory, physical, and severe handicaps. However, professionals avoid diagnostic labels and conceptualize problems as developmental delays with the mildly handicapped at an early age. This less severely handicapped group is essentially served in mainstream settings.

Although the child's family had an important role to play in the assessment process in the past, PL 99–457 has made analysis of family needs and other aspects of family life an essential feature of a comprehensive assessment (Hanson & Lynch, 1989). The main domains for family assessment are the child's needs and characteristics likely to affect family functioning, parent–child interactions, family needs, critical events, and family strengths (Bailey & Simeonsson, 1988). These data are the basis for the family component of the Individualized Family Service Plan, which is the major distinguishing characteristic from the IEP.

A variety of clear criteria underlie current assessment practices. First, you must directly measure a child's specific observable behavior. Assessments and programming for handicapped infants and preschoolers tend to be highly structured and objective. The outcomes are specific areas needing instruction and directions for related services.

Second, these assessments should be done over time to gather a number of behavioral samples. The danger inherent in any assessment is to conclude from one test or observation that a disability does or does not exist. A number of instances of a recurring behavior problem or speech dysfluency provide a more reliable basis for judgment.

A third guideline is to incorporate the viewpoint of a number of different people in the assessment. Parents, relatives, teachers, aides, neighbors, and playmates can offer valuable input or contribute to a fuller profile of a child's abilities and disabilities. Further, such assessments are team affairs involving a core group such as that just described. Others are consulted as the need arises.

A fourth, related criterion is to perform the assessment in the child's natural environments—the school, home, and so on. The child functions under the regular setting demands, and a truer picture of abilities is seen. Complete reliance on formally administered tests or parent and teacher interviews may provide a partial or biased perspective of abilities and disabilities. On-site observations can be very revealing about the role and interaction of environmental factors and events.

Fifth, focus on critical skills for functioning in current and future settings. With young handicapped children there is a tendency to assess and teach developmental skills that are prerequisite for more formal academic and life skills. Depending on children's memory, motivation, and other learning repertoire, they may stay at the same level of skill development unless a more practical and functional approach is used in assessment and instruction.

The sixth criterion is to identify useful data in planning an instructional or therapeutic program. Although there is a need for standardized, comparative data, preschool programming relies heavily on developmental and curriculum-based assessment systems that lead directly to instructional goals.

These assessments are directed by three main assessment questions:

☐ Is there a developmental problem?
☐ What is the nature of the developmental problem?
☐ What are the educational needs?

DEVELOPMENTAL ASSESSMENT

The tests, survey forms, interviews, and other techniques used for screening developmental disorders generally include some items or questions about physical factors (e.g., vision, hearing), cognitive and concept development, language and communication (including speech development), gross and fine motor skills, social-emotional development, and adaptive self-help skills. More indepth and comprehensive assessment is used as needed. As Table 18–1 indicates, a number of procedures would be appropriate for use with this age group.

Is There a Developmental Problem?

Among the many developmental measures that are available to answer this question are the *Denver Developmental Screening Test* (*DDST*) (Frankenburg, Dodds, Fandal, Kazuk, & Cohrs, 1975) and the *Developmental Profile II* (Alpern, Boll, & Shearer, 1980). They incorporate a combination of assessment techniques (observation, interview, etc.) to develop the needed profile.

Denver Developmental Screening Test (DDST).

The *DDST* is designed "to aid in the early discovery of children with developmental problems" (Frankenburg et al., p. 12). It consists of 105 items arranged in four sectors: Personal-Social (ability to get along with people and to take care of self), Fine Motor-Adaptive (ability to see and use hands to pick up objects and draw), Language (ability to hear, carry out commands, and speak), and Gross Motor (ability to sit, walk, and jump). Because many items may be scored on the basis of observation by the tester or parent, the child need not be administered each item. Children must actively cooperate, but they may be tested while sitting on their parent's lap.

The *DDST* was standardized on 1,036 normal children in Denver, Colorado, ages 2 weeks to 6–4 years. When 20 children were retested by the same examiner after one week, there was 95.8% agreement for all the cases. Interrater reliability indicated an average agreement of 90%. According to the manual, a high level of agreement was found between the *DDST* ratings and quotients on the *Stanford-Binet* and *Bayley*.

The *DDST* is easy to administer and score. Directions are available in the manual and repeated on the back of the record form. As indicated in Figure 18–1, the items are arranged in the Record Form by sectors. An *R* on an item indicates that an item can be passed on the basis of a parent's report; a number is a guide to directions on the back of the form. Age lines are arranged along the top and bottom of the form. The tester draws an age line from top to bottom based on the child's age.

The sectors should be administered in the order presented on the Record Form. The child is allowed three trials per item. Each item is scored as pass (P), fail (F), refusal (R), or no opportunity (NO). The appropriate score is marked directly on the item. Criteria for passing each item vary; they are stated in the manual and repeated briefly for some items on the back of the Record Form.

TABLE 18-1
Early childhood and preschool assessment procedures

NAME	AGE/GRADE RANGE	AREAS						SCOPE		ASSESSMENT QUESTIONS		
		Cognitive	Speech/ Language	Pre-academics	Fine/Gross Motor	Self-Help	Social Emo-tional	Develop-mental	Readiness	A Problem?	Nature of Problem?	Needs?
Basic School Skills Inventory–Diagnostic (Hammill & Leigh, 1983a)	4-6–11		*	*	*	*	*		*		*	*
Battelle Developmental Inventory Screening Test (Newborg, Stock, Wnek, Guidubaldi, & Suinicki, 1984)	0–8	*	*		*	*	*	*		*		
Bayley Scales of Infant Development (Bayley, 1969)	0–2½	*			*		*	*		*		
Behavioral Characteristics Progression (Santa Cruz County, 1973)	0–Adult	*	*	*	*	*	*	*	*		*	*
Boehm Test of Basic Concepts–Preschool Version (Boehm, 1986a)	3–5	*	*	*						*		
Boehm Test of Basic Concepts–Revised (Boehm, 1986b)	K-Gr. 2	*	*	*					*		*	*
BRIGANCE® Diagnostic Inventory of Basic Skills (Brigance, 1977)	K-Gr. 6	*	*	*	*	*	*	*	*		*	*
BRIGANCE® Diagnostic Inventory of Early Development (Brigance, 1978)	0–7	*	*	*	*	*	*	*	*		*	*

Instrument	Age									
BRIGANCE® K & 1 Screen (Brigance, 1982, 1987)	K–Gr. 1			*	*				*	*
BRIGANCE® Preschool Screen for 3- and 4-Year-Olds (Brigance, 1983c)	3–4			*	*				*	*
Carolina Developmental Profile (Lillie, 1975)	2–5	*	*	*		*			*	*
Comprehensive Identification Process (Zehrbach, 1975, 1985)	2½–5½			*		*	*		*	*
Developmental Indicators for the Assessment of Learning–Revised (Mardell-Czudnowski & Goldenberg, 1983)	2–6			*		*	*		*	*
Denver Developmental Screening Test (Frankenburg, Dodds, Fandal, Kazuk, & Cohrs, 1975)	0–6			*		*	*	*	*	*
Developmental Profile II (Alpern, Boll, & Shearer, 1980)	0–9			*		*	*	*	*	*
Developmental Program for Infants and Young Children (Schafer & Moersch, 1981)	0–3	*	*			*	*	*	*	*
Early Learning Accomplishment Profile (Glover, Preminger, & Sanford, 1978)	0–3	*	*			*	*	*	*	*
Gesell Developmental Schedules (Gesell, 1940)	0–6			*		*	*	*	*	*

TABLE 18–1
continued

NAME	AGE/GRADE RANGE	AREAS						SCOPE		ASSESSMENT QUESTIONS		
		Cognitive	Speech/ Language	Pre-academics	Fine/Gross Motor	Self-Help	Social Emotional	Develop-mental	Readiness	A Problem?	Nature of Problem?	Needs?
Hawaii Early Learning Profile (Furuno et al., 1979)	0–3	*	*		*	*	*	*			*	*
Learning Accomplishment Profile–Revised (Sanford & Zelman, 1981)	3–6	*	*	*	*	*	*	*	*		*	*
Learning Accomplishment Profile–Diagnostic Edition (LeMay, Griffin, & Sanford, 1977)	3–6	*	*		*	*		*			*	*
McCarthy Scales of Children's Abilities (McCarthy, 1972)	2½–8½	*	*		*			*	*		*	
McCarthy Screening Test (McCarthy, 1978)	4–6½	*	*		*			*	*	*		
Metropolitan Readiness Tests (Nurss & McGauvran, 1986)	K–Gr. 1			*					*	*		
Minnesota Child Development Inventory (Ireton and Thwing, 1972)	1–6	*	*		*	*	*	*		*		
Portage Project Checklist (Bluma et al., 1976)	0–6	*	*		*	*	*	*			*	*
Preschool Screening System (Hainsworth & Hainsworth, 1980)	2½–6	*	*	*	*	*	*	*	*	*		

Test	Age											
Rockford Infant Developmental Evaluation Scale, Form L–M (Project RHISE, 1979)	0–4	*		*	*	*	*	*	*			*
Stanford-Binet Intelligence Scale (Terman & Merrill, 1973; Thorndike, Hagan, & Sattler, 1986)	2–Adult	*			*				*	*	*	*
System Fore (Bagai & Bagai, 1979)	K up								*			*
Test of Early Language Development (Hresko, Reid, & Hammill, 1981)	3–8	*			*	*					*	
Test of Early Mathematics Ability (Ginsburg & Baroody, 1983)	4–9	*			*				*	*		
Test of Early Learning Skills Development (Somwaru, 1979)	K–Gr. 1	*			*	*			*			
Test of Early Reading Ability (Reid, Hresko, & Hammill, 1981)	4–8	*			*	*	*		*			
Test of Early Socioemotional Development (Hresko & Brown, 1984)	3–8				*	*	*	*				*
Vineland Adaptive Behavior Scales (Sparrow, Balla, & Cicchetti, 1984)	0–Adult	*		*	*	*	*	*	*	*		*
Wechsler Preschool & Primary Scale of Intelligence (Wechsler, 1967)	4–6½	*			*	*			*			*

FIGURE 18–1 *Denver Developmental Screening Test*

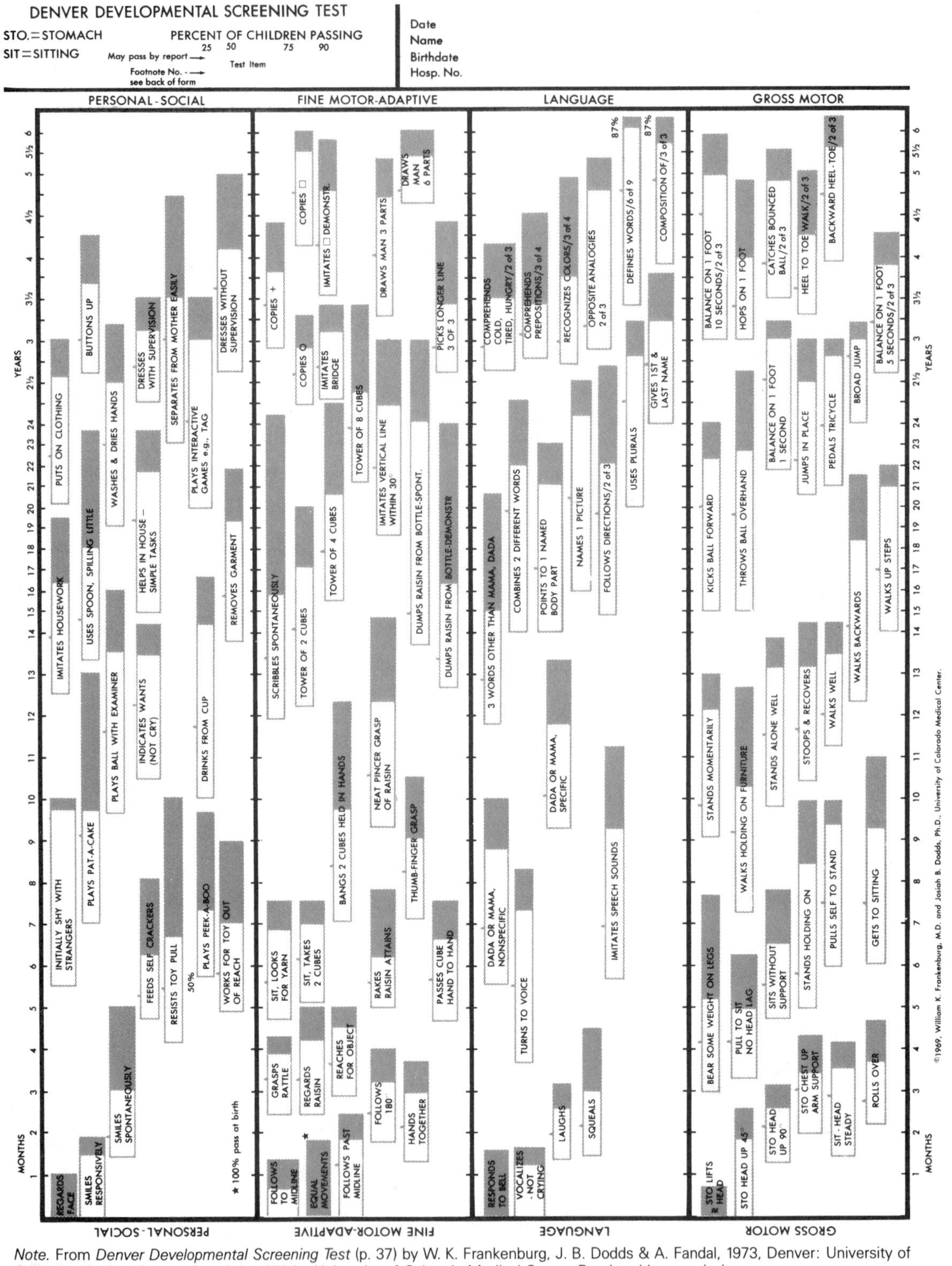

Note. From *Denver Developmental Screening Test* (p. 37) by W. K. Frankenburg, J. B. Dodds & A. Fandal, 1973, Denver: University of Colorado Medical Center. Copyright 1973 by University of Colorado Medical Center. Reprinted by permission.

The tester must decide whether a failed item represents a delay. Each test item is represented on the form by a bar placed between age scales when 25%, 50%, 75% and 90% of normal children can do that item. Additional marks at the right end of the bar indicate other percentages, a star (for 100% passage), or the number noted for directions. A delay is any failed item completely to the left of the age line; that is, the child failed an item that 90% of children normally can pass at a younger age. NOs are not used in the interpretation.

Results from the *DDST*, along with other data, are used to answer the key question, *Is there a developmental delay?* The *DDST* provides an overview of these areas. A child's performance is judged

1. *Abnormal* if [a] two sectors each for 2 or more delays or [b] one sector has 2 or more delays and one other sector has one delay and in the same sector no passes intersect the age line
2. *Questionable* if [a] two or more delays occur in one sector or [b] one or more sectors have one delay and in the same sector the age line does not go through a passed item
3. *Untestable*—When refusals occur frequently enough that if scored as failures the test results would be questionable or abnormal
4. *Normal*—any condition not listed above (p. 26)

According to the manual, the following interpretation would be appropriate for the profile in Figure 18–1.

The performance of J. T. is normal because no sector has two or more delays. Although the Gross Motor sector has one delay (Kicks Ball Forward), the age line

passes through several items which the child passed. In the Personal-Social sector, J. T. did not pass any item the age line goes through but he had no delays in that sector. (p. 14)

The manual suggests retesting children whose performance is judged questionable or abnormal. Parents should be asked whether the child's performance is typical. If the results are the same upon rechecking, the child should be referred for further assessment. Note that there is a revised *DDST* record form (Frankenburg, 1978) that contains the same items as Figure 18–1 and is used in the same way. Items are arranged in stepwise fashion resembling a growth chart. Either form can be used. Also available is the abbreviated version consisting of 39 key *DDST* items, which can be used for prescreening (Frankenburg, Ker, Engelke, Schaefer, & Thorton, 1988).

Developmental Profile II.

The *Profile* is an inventory of skills, classified by age norms in five key areas of development: physical, self-help, social, academic, and communication. The test provides an individual profile of a child's functional developmental age level. The *Profile* was developed to provide a multidimensional description of children's development in the five key areas that is relatively quick, inexpensive, and accurate.

There are 186 items divided into five scales. The items are at 6-month intervals from birth to $3\frac{1}{2}$ years, and at year intervals thereafter. Most age levels contain three items in each area. The administration involves whether the child does or

---

DENVER DEVELOPMENTAL SCREENING TEST (DDST)
W. K. Frankenburg, J. B. Dodds, A. Fandal, E. Kazuk, & M. Cohrs (1975)

Type: Norm-referenced and standarized test
Major Content Areas: Personal-social and fine motor–adaptive, language, and gross motor
Type of Administration: Individual
Administration Time: 10–20 minutes
Age/Grade Levels: Birth to 6 years
Types of Scores: Pass (P), fail (F), refusal (R), or no opportunity (NO); age scores
Typical Uses: Screen for developmental delays
Cautions: Only Denver children in samples; best used with younger children having severe delays

does not have specific skills resulting in a comparison of abilities to the norm. Anyone well acquainted with the child can provide the information.

The standardization study involved 3,008 subjects; the population was restricted to normal children—84% were white, 14% black, and 2% Oriental or other. Interviewed parents were from Indiana and Washington; 89% were from large cities. Studies of interrater and test-retest reliability reported very high agreement; when 8,709 actual observations of items on the *Profile* were compared to parent reports, there was 84% agreement. Comparisons of the *Profile's* IQ Equivalency scores (IQE) to *Stanford-Binet* IQs of retarded and normal children indicated the tendency of the IQE to be lower for normal children and higher for the retarded group.

Parents, older siblings, day care teachers, and anyone else knowledgeable about the child may be interviewed. Items may be rephrased by the tester as long as content is not changed. If the interviewee is uncertain, the child may be tested directly. Scoring is done by circling a zero or the number corresponding to the item number on the scoring sheet. The child is judged on a pass–fail basis. When there is a difference between the child's actual or observed performance and the interviewee's response, primary consideration is given to the child's performance. The age score is the sum of the age at the highest level for which all items were passed plus the month value of any individual items passed beyond that point.

Results can be transferred to a Profile Sheet, giving a graphic display of five developmental ages compared to the child's chronological age. An IQ Equivalency score can be computed from the age score for the Academic Scale; however, the authors of the *Profile* stress cautious use of this figure. Results of the *Profile* show whether the child is advanced or delayed in each developmental area compared with his or her chronological age. Tables are available in the manual to assist in deciding whether individual scale performances are below average for a child's age; however, the tables are based on clinical judgment, not empirical data. Item analysis can locate failures and aid in program planning. If a 7-year-old child with a communication age of 5–3 is delayed in the skill area, passed and failed items in that domain suggest strengths and weaknesses. How significant a few months' lag is depends on the child's age, the other deficit domains, and the interrelationship. Computerized administration, scoring, and reporting are available.

Others. Other assessment formats are frequently referred to in the context of early childhood screening. The *Vineland Adaptive Behavior Scales* (Sparrow et al., 1984) are normed from birth to age 19 and were described in Chapter 8. Another standardized interview discussed in the same chapter that accounts for sociocultural variables and is normed from age 5 is the *Adaptive Behavior Inventory for Children* (Mercer & Lewis, 1977a).

The practice of incorporating a parent questionnaire is evident in several preschool screening systems. The *Revised Denver Prescreening Developmental Questionnaire (R–PDQ)* (Frank-

---

DEVELOPMENTAL PROFILE II

G. D. Alpern, T. J. Boll, & M. S. Shearer (1980)

Type: Developmental, norm-referenced profile
Major Content Areas: Physical, self-help, social, academic, and communication
Type of Administration: Individual (parent interview)
Administration Time: 20 to 40 minutes
Age/Grade Levels: Birth through 9 years
Types of Scores: Developmental ages, IQ Equivalency (IQE)
Typical Uses: Screening for developmental problems
Cautions: Restrict to screening; use IQE cautiously; rural children and most states
    underrepresented in sample

enburg, Fandal, & Thorton, 1987) is an adaptation of the *DDST*. The *DDST* items were modified into yes or no questions for parents and grouped into four age-appropriate questionnaires from age 0 to 6. The results are examined for correspondence with *DDST* results.

Other multidimensional screening systems, such as the *Comprehensive Identification Process* (Zehrbach, 1975, 1985) and the *Preschool Screening System* (Hainsworth & Hainsworth, 1980) include such data. However, these questionnaires do not provide norms or even guidelines for the interpretation of results (Lichtenstein & Ireton, 1984). Also, recall the various cautions voiced in Chapter 5 about the use of questionnaires and interviews. The most reliable parent information is reports of current observable behavior rather than recall of past events (Graham & Rutter, 1968; Yarrow, 1963).

What Is the Nature of the Developmental Problem?

There are a number of extensive batteries among the many measures available for this level of assessment. When supplemented with other data, they serve as a good basis for specifically profiling certain problems. They are particularly useful if administrative decisions about eligibility need to be made. The two included here are the *Bayley Scales of Infant Development* (Bayley, 1969) and the *McCarthy Scales of Children's Abilities* (McCarthy, 1972).

Bayley Scales of Infant Development (BSID).

The *BSID* provides a comprehensive measure of current developmental status and a means to compare children with age peers. It is a three-part evaluation of a child's developmental status, consisting of a Mental Scale (sensory-perceptual abilities; memory, learning, and problem-solving; verbalization and communication; generalization and classification), a Motor Scale (fine and gross motor), and Infant Behavior Record (attitudes, interests, emotions, etc.).

Infants are observed while doing tasks, or parents provide testimony to performance. The *BSID* was standardized on 1,262 children located through hospitals, clinics, and other settings; only normal children were included. The median split-half reliability coefficient for the Mental Scale was .88 and for the Motor Scale was .84; the standard error of measurement (SEM) range for the Mental Scale was 4.2 to 6.9 standard score points and for the Motor Scale, 4.6 to 9.0. When two observers' ratings were compared, there was 89% agreement on the Mental Scale and 93% on the Motor Scale. The relationship of the Mental Development Index (MDI) to the *Stanford-Binet* IQ was .57 in a study reported in the manual.

The record forms for the two scales are color coded to coordinate with the respective pages of directions and tables in the manual. The tester marks the appropriate column with a check: pass, fail, or other (omitted, refused, or reported by mother). The raw scores for the two scales are converted to the Mental Development Index and Psycho-Motor Development Index (PDI), respectively. The mean is 100, with a standard deviation of 16. Indices below 84 are considered below average, and the child should be assessed further. Age equivalent scores are also available.

BAYLEY SCALES OF INFANT DEVELOPMENT (BSID)
N. Bayley (1969)

Type: Norm-referenced test
Major Content Areas: Mental (memory, communication, etc.) and motor (fine and gross)
Type of Administration: Individual
Administration Time: 90 minutes
Age/Grade Levels: 0–2½ years
Types of Scores: Mental Development Index, Motor Development Index, age equivalents, and standard scores
Typical Uses: Screen infants
Cautions: 1960 standardization; needs more validity studies

McCarthy Scales of Children's Abilities (MSCA).

The *MSCA* is a measure of general aptitude ability of young children, as well as specific strengths and weaknesses. The test consists of 18 subtests grouped into 6 scales: Verbal (assessing the child's ability for verbal expression), Perceptual-Performance (assessing reasoning ability through the manipulation of materials), Quantitative (assessing facility with numbers and understanding of quantitative words), Memory (assessing short-term memory), Motor (assessing gross and fine motor skills), and General Cognitive (composed of the first 3 scales and providing a measure of overall cognitive functioning).

The *MSCA* was standardized on 1,000 children in a mix resembling the 1970 U.S. Census Bureau figures. Only normal children were eligible for standardization testing; bilingual children were included only if they could speak and understand English. The reliability of the *MSCA* seems good; the average split-half reliability coefficient for the General Cognitive Scales was .93, and the averages for the other scales ranged from .79 to .88. The average standard errors of measurement for the six scales across all ages ranged from 3.4 to 4.7 points. For 35 children (ages 6–0 to 6–7 years), the *MSCA*'s General Cognitive Index (GCI) correlated .81 with the *Stanford-Binet* IQ and .62 to .71 with the three *Wechsler Preschool and Primary Scale of Intelligence* IQs. Coefficients with the 1970 *Metropolitan Achievement Test* Total Score ranged from .02 to .51; General Cognitive, Perceptual-Performance, and Quantitative Scale Indexes approximated the .50 relationship.

Pass/fail or actual responses are recorded as a score; criteria for scoring each item vary and are in the manual. In addition to numerical scores, some subtests require other information, such as which hand was used, the time taken, and so on. As noted on the Sample Profile in Figure 18–2, the *MSCA* yields six Scale Indexes; the raw scores for the Verbal, Performance, and Quantitative Scales are totaled to compose the General Cognitive Scale. Using the child's age, the raw scores are converted into Scale Index Equivalents; Mental Age equivalents are available for the GCI only. The GCI has a mean of 100 and a standard deviation of 15; other scales have a mean of 50 and standard deviation of 10. SEMs are 3 to 5 points, and SEM_{diffs} are 10 to 13 index points.

MSCA results may be plotted on a profile provided on the front of the protocol. The Scale Indexes of the five subtests and GCI are arranged on the protocol. The GCI can be interpreted using the criteria suggested by the manual.

GCI	Descriptive Classification
130 and above	Very Superior
120–129	Superior
110–119	Bright Normal
90–109	Average
80–89	Dull Normal
70–79	Borderline
69 and below	Mentally Retarded

Thus, the sample protocol indicates an overall cognitive level in the bright normal range. Verbal and memory skills are above average, and perceptual and quantitative ones are average; but motor skills are a relative weakness.

McCARTHY SCALES OF CHILDREN'S ABILITIES (MSCA)
D. McCarthy (1972)

Type: Norm-referenced test
Major Content Areas: Verbal, perceptual, quantitative, memory, motor, and general cognitive
Type of Administration: Individual
Administration Time: 45 to 60 minutes
Age/Grade Levels: Ages 2½ to 8½
Types of Scores: Percentiles and standard scores, mental age and General Cognitive Index (GCI)
Typical Uses: Intelligence measure
Cautions: For English-speaking children without severe disabilities. Standardization was done in 1970, and validity is based on studies of small numbers of children.

FIGURE 18–2
McCarthy Scales of Children's Abilities

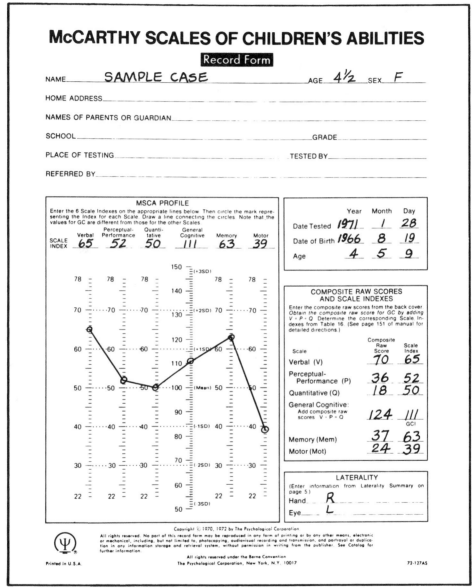

There is also an adapted version of the *MSCA* called the *McCarthy Screening Test* (McCarthy, 1978). According to the manual, it can be used to help schools identify children between 4 and 6½

who are likely to need special education assistance. It consists of 6 of the 18 separate tests that comprise the *MSCA:* Right-Left Orientation, Verbal Memory (Part I), Draw-a-Design, Numerical Memory (Parts I & II), Conceptual Grouping, and Leg Coordination. If the child's performance fits the at-risk classification, then further assessment, possibly with the *MSCA,* is warranted.

Others. Another popular measure used to answer diagnostic questions is the *Wechsler Preschool and Primary Scale of Intelligence (WPPSI)* (Wechsler, 1967). Designed for children ages 4 to 6½ years, it is similar to the *WISC–R* form and content described in Chapter 8. The *WPPSI* has three unique tests (Animal House, Sentences, and Geometric Design) and includes *WISC–R* subtests except for Digit Span, Picture Arrangement, Object Assembly, and Coding, yielding the same three scores as the *WISC–R.* Although *WPPSI* difficulties include long administration time and scoring of certain subtests, it is a well-standardized and carefully developed instrument that should be a valuable tool (Sattler, 1982).

Behavioral observations, parent interviews, and questionnaires can be very useful. Informal observations are essential complements to more formal types of measures. Some areas particularly subject to observation are the child's alertness, responsiveness, interactions, communications, self-concept, confidence, adaptability, and coordination of verbal and motor skills.

The parent questionnaire contained in Appendix A is a good example of the type of material typically covered in a verbal interview or gathered through written form. With parents of younger children you would naturally dwell more on developmental information. The value of parental input is to compare other data with parental concerns and perspectives to achieve a balanced and valid profile of the child. Also, parents can provide excellent insight into cultural expectations and demands.

What Are the Educational Needs?

Given serious concerns about a child's development in one or more of the major areas, you must develop an appropriate plan. The required information to be gathered is similar to data mentioned earlier but should cover developmental areas. Although not mandated by PL 94–142, the elements of the IEP are major factors to consider for inclusion. There are a variety of techniques to use in gathering the data to design a plan. The ones to be discussed in detail are the *Early Learning Accomplishment Profile* (Glover et al., 1978), the

Learning Accomplishment Profile–Revised (Sanford & Zelman, 1981), the *Learning Accomplishment Profile–Diagnostic Edition* (LeMay, Griffin, & Sanford, 1977), and the *BRIGANCE® Diagnostic Inventory of Early Development* (Brigance, 1978).

Early Learning Accomplishment Profile (E–LAP). The *E–LAP* is one of a series of assessment and programming instruments by the Chapel Hill Project in North Carolina. Constructed for children ages 0 to 3 years, the *E–LAP* is designed to generate developmentally appropriate instructional objectives and task analytic programming for young handicapped children in gross and fine motor, cognitive, language, self-help, and social-emotional areas. Technical data about the *E–LAP* are not available in the manual. However, sources are noted for each test item.

Passage of an item is based on actual testing, observation, or testimony of parents, caretakers, teachers, and others familiar with the child. The items are also coded so passage of one item may automatically mean passage of another. A passed item is marked with a plus and a failed one with a minus; if a performance is questionable, a combination plus/minus is used. The child's performance can be arranged on a profile that indicates the items passed and failed and the approximate age level of the highest passed items. The results of the child's pretest are recorded to be compared to the posttest performance after instruction. A planning guide for curriculum design is available to program from the results of the *E–LAP* and other related measures (Sanford, Williams, James, & Overton, 1983).

Learning Accomplishment Profile–Revised (LAP). The *LAP* is identical to the *E–LAP* except it is designed for children 3 to 6 years old and has 400 samples of behavior spread over six areas: gross and fine motor, prewriting, cognitive, language, self-help, and personal-social. The administration, scoring, interpretation, and programming characteristics are the same as for the *E–LAP.*

Figure 18–3 shows that results are easily translatable into instruction. This child has not mastered four skills, such as "Strings four beads," that will become instructional objectives. The planning guide by Sanford et al. also accompanies the *LAP.* Also the *Learning Accomplishment Profile–Diagnostic Edition (LAP–D)* (LeMay, Griffin, & Sanford, 1977) to be described next is an entry into the *LAP.*

Learning Accomplishment Profile–Diagnostic Edition (LAP–D).

The *LAP–D* determines a child's mastery level in five skill areas: fine motor (manipulation and writing), cognitive (matching and counting), language/cognitive (naming and comprehension), gross motor (body movement and object movement), and self-help (eating, dressing, grooming, toileting, and self-direction). The *LAP–D* evaluates a child's entry skills into a program and his or her exit skills at the end, validating the effects of the program. It complements the *LAP* Prescriptive Edition, which is meant for ongoing assessment.

Items included on the *LAP–D* are based on a variety of sources, including major figures from

FIGURE 18–3

Learning Accomplishment Profile

Bibliog. Source	Behavior	Age (Dev.)	Assessment Date	Date of Achievement	Comments (Criteria, materials, problems, etc.)
3	Manipulates egg beater	27 mos.	+ 9/18/73		WHIPPED SOAP SUDS. TEACHER HELD HANDLE.
9	Enjoys finger painting	30-35 mos.	+ 9/20/73		FINGER PAINTED ON FORMICA TABLE. — 10 MIN.
9	Makes mud and sand pies	30-35 mos.	+ 9/24/73		MADE SAND PIES USING TEASET
13	Paints strokes, dots, and circular shapes on easel	30-35 mos.	+ 9/27/73		IMITATED TEACHER w/ ½" BRUSH
6	Cuts with scissors	35 mos.	+ 10/2/73		CUT ½" PARTIALLY CUT STRIPS (2 WHACKS)
13	Picks up pins, thread, etc. with each eye separately covered	36-48 mos.	− 10/3/73		
7	Drives nails and pegs	36-48 mos.	− 10/4/73		THESE WILL
13	Builds tower of 9 cubes	36-48 mos.	− 10/5/73		BECOME
7	Holds crayon with fingers	36-48 mos.	+ 10/8/73		OBJECTIVES
3	Strings 4 beads	36-48 mos.	− 10/8/73		FOR THIS CHILD
13	Can close fist and wiggle thumb in imitation, R & L	36-48 mos.			
11	Puts 6 round pegs in round holes in pegboard	36-48 mos.			

NOTE: ← — — — THE CHILD HAS DEMONSTRATED A DEV. AGE OF 35 MOS. IN FINE MOTOR SKILLS. FAILURE ON 4 OF 5 ITEMS REPRESENTS CEILING.

* Mark + for positive demonstration of skill

  Mark − for negative demonstration of skill

early childhood development. The sample of 35 children was well balanced in terms of sex and race; early editions used larger samples. Test-retest correlations were in the .90s, according to the manual.

The tester begins the *LAP–D* with items designated for the child's chronological age; if the child has a disability, the manual suggests beginning 50% lower than the child's age. A plus is recorded for a pass and a minus for a failure. If children refuse to respond or otherwise do not cooperate, they receive a minus. The number of minuses is subtracted from the number of the next to the last item administered to get the score for each subtest. Raw scores are then converted to percentages and can be displayed on the Assessment Profile. Developmental ages for each item are also available in the manual. The *LAP–D* manual encourages development of local norms and comparison of percentage performances among children. A brief 17-item *LAP–D Screening Edition* (Bright, Martinson, & Covert, 1982) is also available to establish the need to use the *LAP–D*. A standardized edition of the *LAP–D* will be available in Fall 1989.

BRIGANCE® Diagnostic Inventory of Early Development.

Designed for children from birth to 7 years, this *BRIGANCE®* inventory probes the following areas:

1. Preambulatory Motor Skills and Behaviors (e.g., standing)
2. Gross Motor Skills and Behaviors (e.g., hopping)
3. Fine Motor Skills and Behaviors (e.g., cutting with scissors)
4. Self-Help Skills (e.g., dressing)
5. Prespeech (e.g., gestures)
6. Speech and Language (e.g., following verbal directions)
7. General Knowledge and Comprehension (e.g., time concepts)
8. Readiness (e.g., reading common signs)
9. Manuscript Writing (e.g., printing lowercase letters dictated)
10. Math (e.g., recognizing money)

As illustrated in Figure 18–4, this inventory indicates whether a child has mastered a skill such as appropriate language production. For one item the educator uses informal procedures to elicit 10 typical sentences and computes an average sentence length for the sample and compares it to norms suggested by language specialists. If necessary, an instructional objective can be developed for this area.

There is considerable controversy about whether norm-referenced or criterion-referenced procedures are better for early childhood assessment. According to Boehm (1973), criterion-referenced procedures must be closely examined in regard to

1. Who determines the objectives
2. Who sets the behavioral criterion levels
3. Whether the test items accurately reflect the behavioral criteria
4. What constitutes a sufficient sample of test items

LEARNING ACCOMPLISHMENT PROFILE–DIAGNOSTIC EDITION (LAP–D)
D. W. LeMay, P. M. Griffin, & A. R. Sanford (1977)

Type: Criterion-referenced test
Major Content Areas: Fine and gross motor, cognitive, language, and self-help
Type of Administration: Individual
Administration Time: Varies
Age/Grade Levels: 36 to 72 months
Types of Scores: Age scores and percentages
Typical Uses: Program planning and evaluation
Cautions: Needs studies of reliability and validity; content based on work of developmental experts; standardization available in Fall 1989.

FIGURE 18–4

BRIGANCE® Diagnostic Inventory of Early Development

LENGTH OF SENTENCE

SKILLS: Speaks using sentences of a certain length. Average number of words used in sentences:
2-02, 2-63, 3-04, 4-54.5, 5-05, 6-06, 77-0

DEVELOPMENTAL RECORD BOOK: Page 14.

ASSESSMENT METHOD: Observation of the child in assigned or relaxed performances.

DISCONTINUE: After a minimum of ten typical sentences, try to determine the average number of words per sentence.

TIME: Your discretion.

MATERIALS: Situations, topics or items of interest which will encourage talking in sentences.

DIRECTIONS: Make the assessment by counting the number of words in a sample of at least ten sentences typically used by the child. Then compute an average.

Formula:

$$\frac{\text{Number of words used in sample sentences}}{\text{Number of sentences}} = \text{Average sentence length}$$

Example:

$$\frac{54 \text{ words}}{12 \text{ sentences}} = 4.5 \text{ word sentence}$$

Record a sampling of ten or more sentences typically spoken by the child. Use one or more of the following methods.

a. Observe the child's speech in a natural speaking situation.
b. Engage the child in conversation about interests, family trips, etc. Do not ask questions which will encourage a simple "yes" or "no" response.

REFERENCES: The author's research did not yield enough norming data to fully validate the developmental ages indicated for making sentences of specific lengths. The developmental ages listed in this assessment are based on:

Berry (7: 210-11, 225-7)

(F-2)
OBJECTIVE: By ___(date)___, when presented with the appropriate situation or setting, ___(child's name)___ will use sentences with an average length of ___(quantity)___ words.

Note. From *BRIGANCE® Diagnostic Inventory of Early Development* (p. 119) by A. Brigance, 1978, N. Billerica, MA: Curriculum Associates, Inc. Copyright 1978 by Curriculum Associates, Inc. Reprinted by permission.

---

5. Whether test scores obtained actually describe an individual's response pattern

Major concerns with criterion-referenced measures are validity and the sequence of test items.

MacTurk and Neisworth (1978) compared a standardized procedure, the *Gesell Developmental Schedules* (Knoblock & Pasamanick, 1974) with a criterion measure from the HICOMP Curriculum (Neisworth, Willoughby-Herb, Bagnato, Cartwright, & Laub, 1980) and found a high correlation in the evaluation of progress among preschoolers. They conclude that the use of both norm-referenced and criterion-referenced measures for program evaluation during and after implementation is a decided advantage.

Others. Educational needs can be assessed by the *Ordinal Scales of Psychological Development* (Uzgiris & Hunt, 1975). The scales use Piaget's six stages of development to profile the effects of experience on the rate of development of children ages 0 to 2 years. Another useful informal technique (see Chapter 5) at this age is task analysis (McLoughlin & Kershman, 1978).

A number of early childhood projects for handicapped children have developed and field-tested assessment and programming systems. The assessment procedure is usually an age-referenced list of developmental skills in each major area of growth and development—language, motor, and so on. Suitable activities and appropriate materials are referenced to the skill list; the systems are also sometimes accompanied by ideas for parent education. Some examples from Bailey and Wolery (1984) include

☐ *Carolina Developmental Profile* (Lillie, 1975)
☐ *Developmental Program for Infants and Young Children* (Schafer & Moersch, 1981)
☐ *Hawaii Early Learning Profile* (Furuno et al., 1979)

□ *Comprehensive Developmental Scale* (Quick, Little, & Campbell, 1974)
□ *Portage Project Checklist* (Bluma et al., 1976)

Because some of these projects were designed for severely handicapped children, the scope and sequence of skills may need to be modified for the mildly handicapped.

Whereas various questions surround the developmental problems of infants and young children, readiness for school becomes an issue when they get older. In many ways this is an extension of the previous discussion, with the major difference being the entrance of unique setting demands and teacher expectations. The IAP in Figure 18–5 includes some of the readiness measures used to assess Timmy's learning problems. Three main assessment questions are the following: *Is*

there a readiness problem? What is the nature of the readiness problem? What are the educational needs?

SCHOOL READINESS ASSESSMENT

Readiness tests, surveys, interview and rating forms, and observations usually include items in gross and fine motor development, speech and language, prereading, premathematics, prehandwriting, and classroom behavior and study habits. There are also specific tests and informal techniques for in-depth assessment of each. As indicated in Table 18–1, a number of procedures already mentioned in this text would be appropriate here, as well as several others.

FIGURE 18–5
Sample preschool IAP

Timmy Ryan	8/1/83	5/1/89
Child	Birthdate	Referral Date
Elwood	Ms. Mahoney	Kindergarten
School	Teacher	Grade

Reason for Referral: Ms. Mahoney is concerned about Timmy's oral language and fine motor skills. Timmy is withdrawn, frequently cries, and seems immature in his dealing with others.

Assessment Questions	Assessment Tool	Person Responsible	Date/Time
What are his vision and hearing abilities?	Vision and hearing screening	School Nurse	5/9/89 9:00 a.m.
What are his intellectual development and adaptive skills?	*WPPSI Developmental Profile II*	Mr. Swift, Psychologist	5/10/89 9:00 a.m.
What are his readiness skills for academic schoolwork?	*BSSI–D*	Ms. Jones, Resource Teacher	5/11/89 9:00 a.m.
What are his oral language skills?	*TOLD–2, Primary*	Ms. Jones, Resource Teacher	5/13/89 9:00 a.m.
What are his copying skills?	*VMI BRIGANCE*®	Ms. Jones, Resource Teacher	5/13/89 10:30 a.m.
What are his social-emotional skills?	*TOESD* Classroom observations	Ms. Jones, Resource Teacher	5/13/89 11:00 a.m.

For Parental Use: I am aware of the need for testing Timmy and the procedures used. I give my approval.

Sandra Ryan
Parent's Signature

5/3/89
Date

Is There a Readiness Problem?

Among the many readiness measures available to answer this question are the *Metropolitan Readiness Tests* (5th ed.) (Nurss & McGauvran, 1986) and the *BRIGANCE® K and 1 Screen for Kindergarten and First Grade* (Brigance, 1982, 1987). Other formal and informal procedures will be mentioned.

Metropolitan Readiness Tests (MRT). The *MRT* measures preacademic skills in beginning and middle kindergarten (Level I) and more advanced reading and mathematic skills at the end of kindergarten and in grade 1 (Level II). Level I consists of auditory memory, beginning consonants, letter recognition, visual matching, school language and listening, and quantitative language. Level II consists of beginning consonants, sound–letter correspondence, visual matching, finding patterns, school language, listening, quantitative concepts and quantitative operations. Children must listen and view symbols and then mark the appropriate circle from among a number of choices; a practice booklet and activity are provided a day or more before actual testing. There is an optional test of copying a sentence on Level II.

The *MRT* was standardized on over 30,000 children chosen by a stratified random sampling plan based on data from the 1980 Census. Two types of reliability coefficients for the composite score were almost all in the .90s for both Levels I and II. For validity, the *MRT*'s content selection process was described by the manual as an analysis of the prereading and mathematics process,

literature review, task analysis of prerequisite skills, and professional judgment. Predictive comparisons to the *Metropolitan Achievement Tests* (6th ed.) composite score yielded a coefficient of .65 and to the *Stanford Achievement Test* (7th ed.) a coefficient of .83.

The raw score consists of the number of correct items. It is placed in the appropriate box on the back cover of the Test Booklet (see Figure 18–6). Raw scores are combined into skill area scores and a Pre-Reading Skills Composite Percentile and Stanine. Conversions to percentiles, stanines, and scaled scores are available according to the grade and level of *MRT* form. Performance ratings are verbal descriptions based on the raw score ranges: + (skill learned), √ (skill being learned), and − (skill undeveloped). The *MRT* may be scored by hand or computer.

Results for all scores are transferred to the Class Record and are analyzed to establish competency trends in the class. "As a general rule, the SEM for the *MRT* is about one stanine" (p. 20). The child's profile in Figure 18–6 indicates overall average readiness, with particular strengths in language skills.

BRIGANCE® K & 1 Screen for Kindergarten and First Grade (K & 1). The *K & 1* is a brief survey of language and number skills, motor ability, body awareness, and auditory and visual discrimination. Although some items are used for both levels, there are some separate tasks for kindergarten or grade 1, as well as separate Pupil Data Sheets. The *K & 1* can be used to rank order class

---

METROPOLITAN READINESS TESTS (5th ed.) (MRT)
J. R. Nurss and M. E. McGauvran (1986)

Type: Norm-referenced test
Major Content Areas: Preacademic skills
Type of Administration: Group
Administration Time: 80–90 minutes
Age/Grade Levels: Level I (early and middle K) and Level II (late K and early Grade 1)
Types of Scores: Stanines, performance ratings, percentiles, scaled scores
Typical Uses: Readiness screening
Cautions: Children may lose place in booklet; combine results with other data for decision making

FIGURE 18–6
Metropolitan Readiness Tests

Metropolitan Readiness Tests

LEVEL 2

Pupil's Name **Terry Smith**

Teacher **Ziegler**   Age **6**   ☒ Boy ☐ Girl

School **Arkport Elementary**   Grade **1**   Date of Test **Oct. 6-10**

AREAS AND TESTS	PERFORMANCE RATING			NUMBER POSSIBLE	RAW SCORE	PERCENTILE RANK	STANINE
	−	√	+				
AUDITORY SKILL AREA	−	√	+	29	25	56	5
Beginning Consonants			✳	13	12		
Sound-Letter Correspondence		✳		16	13		
VISUAL SKILL AREA	−	√	+	26	22	55	5
Visual Matching		✳		10	7		
Finding Patterns			✳	16	15		
LANGUAGE SKILL AREA	−	√	+	18	16	82	7
School Language			✳	9	8		
Listening			✳	9	8		
QUANTITATIVE SKILL AREA	−	√	+	24	16	41	5
Quantitative Concepts		✳		9	5		
Quantitative Operations		✳		15	11		

	Number Possible	Raw Score	National Percentile Rank–Stanine
Pre-Reading Composite Scores	73	63	68 – 6

members and choose a group of lower achievers for further assessment. The *K & 1* also contains a supplementary Teacher Rating Form and Parent Rating Form with items similar to the *K & 1* screening ones.

Students must do a variety of tasks requiring verbal and written responses on the *K & 1*, including reading and math. Items were chosen from the *BRIGANCE® Diagnostic Inventory of Basic Skills* (K to 6th grade) (Brigance, 1977) and the *BRIGANCE® Diagnostic Inventory of Early Development* (birth to 7 years) (Brigance, 1978). The *K & 1* is not standardized and was field tested by having users around the country rate the appropriateness of items for screening. As a result, all items were kept; some supplementary material was developed, and editorial changes were made.

Paraprofessionals can be taught to administer the *K & 1*, because it requires no special training. Directions, including ceilings and additional assessment questions, are provided for each item. As illustrated in the sample Profile in Figure 18–7, the tester circles each item as it is passed. The total number of passed items for each skill is recorded on the Pupil Data Sheet and multiplied by the point value to obtain the student's score. A total score of 100 is possible, and scores of all children in the class are rank ordered. The manual suggests arranging the students in Higher, Average, and Lower groups based on local criteria for cutoff points. The author recommends further assessment for any student scoring below 60, probably with the *BRIGANCE® Diagnostic Inventory of Early Development*.

These results and those from the Teacher and Parent Ratings (if used) are summarized on the Pupil Data Sheet, and recommendations are made. Figure 18–7 is a completed *K & 1* for a five-year-old. The child is considered average and will enter kindergarten. However, his hearing needs to be tested because of his reactions to directions. The 1987 edition contains additions of picture vocabulary and advanced assessments and some other minor changes.

Others. Two comprehensive but brief screening systems—the *Comprehensive Identification Process (CIP)* (Zehrback, 1975, 1985) and the *Preschool Screening System (PSS)* (Hainsworth & Hainsworth, 1980)—include tests and parent interviews concerning the cognitive, language, speech, fine and gross motor, and social-emotional needs of children $2\frac{1}{2}$ to 6 years old (Lichtenstein & Ireton, 1984). The *CIP* indicates possible referrals for sensory, medical, or comprehensive evaluations. The *PSS*'s screening test has items divided into three areas (body awareness and control, visual-perceptual-motor, and language) and comes in various versions to accommodate nonverbal, bilingual, and other needs. Group administration of the *PSS* is possible.

The *Developmental Indicators for the Assessment of Learning–Revised (DIAL–R)* (Mardell-Czudnowski & Goldenberg, 1983) is a 25- to 30-minute mass screening procedure for children $2\frac{1}{2}$ to $5\frac{1}{2}$ years. Children move through various stations for testing and observation. *DIAL* consists of 150 items spread over four areas (gross and fine motor,

---

BRIGANCE® K & 1 SCREEN (K & 1)
A. H. Brigance (1982, 1987)

Type: Criterion-referenced test
Major Content Areas: Readiness skills
Type of Administration: Ideally individual; some group
Administration Time: 10–12 minutes
Age/Grade Levels: Kindergarten and Grade 1
Types of Scores: Raw scores
Typical Uses: Identify children in kindergarten or first grade needing further assessment
Cautions: Not standardized; needs further study, especially its cutoff points

FIGURE 18-7
BRIGANCE® K & 1 Screen

KINDERGARTEN Pupil Data Sheet for the *BRIGANCE® K & 1 SCREEN*

A. Student's Name Colin Killoran

Parents/Guardian Kristin and Edmund Killoran

Address 310 Locke Street

	Year	Month	Day
Date of Screening	81	6	15
Birthdate	76	1	10
Age	5	5	5

School/Program Vinal School

Teacher Leslie Feingold

Assessor Dennis Dowd

B. BASIC SCREENING ASSESSMENTS

C. SCORING

Page	Assessment Number	Skill (Circle the skill for each correct response and make notes as appropriate.)	Number of Correct Responses	Point Value	Student's Score
2	1	**Personal Data Response:** Verbally gives: ① first name ② full name ③ age 4. address (street or mail) 5. birthdate (month and day)	3 ×	2 points each	6/10
3	2	**Color Recognition:** Identifies and names the colors: ① red ② blue ③ green ④ yellow ⑤ orange 6. purple ⑦ brown ⑧ black ⑨ pink 10. gray	8 ×	1 point each	8/10
5	3	**Picture Vocabulary:** Recognizes and names picture of: ① dog ② cat ③ key ④ girl ⑤ boy ⑥ airplane ⑦ apple 8. leaf ⑨ cup 10. car	8 ×	1 point each	8/10
6	4A	**Visual Discrimination:** Visually discriminates which one of four symbols is different: ① ○ ② ○ ③ ○ ④ ○ ⑤ ○ ⑥ ○ 7. I ⑧ P 9. V 10. X	7 ×	1 point each	7/10
8	5	**Visual-Motor Skills:** Copies: ① ○ ② − ③ + ④ □	4 ×	2 pts. ea.	8/10
9	6	**Gross Motor Skills:** ① Hops 2 hops on one foot. ② Hops 2 hops on either foot. ③ Stands on one foot momentarily. ④ Stands on either foot momentarily. ⑤ Stands on one foot for 5 seconds. ⑥ Stands on either foot for 5 secs. ⑦ Walks forward heel toe and heel 8. Walks backward toe and heel 4 steps. 9. Stands on one foot momentarily with eyes closed. 10. Stands on one foot momentarily with eyes closed.	8 ×	1 point each	8/10
12	8	**Rote Counting:** Counts by rote to: *(Circle all numerals prior to the first error.)* ① ② ③ ④ ⑤ ⑥ 7 8 9 10	6 ×	.5 point each	3/5
13	9	**Identification of Body Parts:** Identifies by pointing or touching: ① chin ② fingernails ③ heel ④ elbow ⑤ ankle ⑥ shoulder ⑦ jaw 8. hips ⑨ wrist 10. waist	8 ×	.5 point each	4/5
15	11	**Follows Verbal Directions:** Listens to, remembers, and follows: ① one verbal direction 2. two verbal directions	1 ×	2.5 points each	2.5/5
17	12	**Numeral Comprehension:** Matches quantity with numerals: ② ① ④ ③ 5	4 ×	2 pts. ea.	8/10
21	15	**Prints Personal Data:** ① Prints first name Reversals: Yes: No: ✓	1 ×	5 points each	5/5
22	16	**Syntax and Fluency:** ① Speech is understandable. ② Speaks in complete sentences.	2 ×	5 pts. ea.	10/10

Total Score 77.5/100

D. OBSERVATIONS:
1. Handedness: Right ✓ Left Uncertain
2. Pencil grasp: Correct ✓ Incorrect
3. Maintained paper in the proper position when writing: Yes No ✓
4. Record other observations below or on the back.

Cooperative. Had difficulty attending to verbal directions and relied on visual clues.

E. SUMMARY: *(Compared to other students included in this screening)*
1. this student scored: .... Lower ____ Average ✓ Higher ____
2. this student's age is: .... Younger ____ Average ✓ Older ____
3. the teacher rates this student: .... Lower ____ Average ____ Higher ✓
4. the assessor rates this student: .... Lower ____ Average ✓ Higher ____

F. RECOMMENDATIONS:
Place in: Preschool ____ Low Kindergarten ____ Average Kindergarten ✓ High Kindergarten ____

Other *(Indicate.)* _____

Refer for: *(Indicate if needed)* Ask mural to check hearing concepts, and communications) that reflect actual expected classroom behaviors. Behavioral observations are made on a checklist after each testing for such behaviors as clumsiness and hyperactivity. A parent information form is completed too. The results indicate the need for retesting on the *DIAL* or referral for further assessment.

Behavioral observations are among the many appropriate informal techniques for screening. Forness and Esveldt (1975) used direct observations of kindergarteners' verbal responses (recitation), attending (watching the teacher), not attending (staring out the window), and disruptions (hitting classmates). Taken early and later in the year, these observations compared very well with teacher ratings of reading readiness and language development, relationships with other children, and attitudes toward classroom rules. Magliocca, Rinaldi, Crew, and Kunzelmann (1977) also obtained highly predictive results of readiness for grade 1 by taking continuous measurements of basic skills. The skills proving more predictive were reproducing letters and naming numbers.

What Is the Nature of the Readiness Problem?

Once there is evidence of possible problems in readiness for school achievement, you should probe the deficit skill areas in more detail. Among the variety of readiness diagnostics mentioned in Table 18–1, the *Basic School Skills Inventory– Diagnostic (BSSI–D)* (Hammill & Leigh, 1983a), the *Test of Early Reading Ability (TERA)* (Reid, Hresko, & Hammill, 1981), the *Test of Early Mathematics Ability (TEMA)* (Ginsburg & Baroody,

1983), and the *Boehm Test of Basic Concepts– Preschool Version (Boehm–Preschool)* (Boehm, 1986) will be described.

Basic School Skills Inventory–Diagnostic (BSSI–D). This is a norm-referenced standardized measure that assesses several aspects of readiness in order to identify children below their peers in readiness, specify strengths and weaknesses for instructional planning, and document instructional progress. The *BSSI–D* contains 110 items and assesses daily living skills, spoken language, reading, writing, mathematics, and classroom behavior.

The *BSSI–D* was standardized on 376 children (ages 4–0 to 6–11) from 15 states resembling the 1980 census population. Test reliability coefficients mostly approximated .90. Comparisons of *BSSI–D* results with teacher ratings yielded significant correlations in the .20s and .30s, a minimally acceptable level according to Anastasi (1988). Comparisons with tests of readiness and school achievement are needed. Construct validity is described in the manual with studies of age comparisons, the interrelationship of items, and distinctions between learning disabled and normal children.

Based on observing and testing the children, or confirming their competency by asking others, a 1 is recorded for items passed and a 0 for those failed. The total passes on a subtest constitute the raw score; when converted to scaled scores, those in the range of 7 to 13 are considered average. In addition to the subtest scores, the *BSSI–D* provides a total test score called the Skill Quotient.

BASIC SCHOOL SKILLS INVENTORY–DIAGNOSTIC (BSSI–D)
D. D. Hammill & J. Leigh (1983)

Type: Norm-referenced test
Major Content Areas: Daily living, spoken language, reading, writing, math, and behavior
Type of Administration: Individual
Administration Time: 30 minutes
Age/Grade Levels: 4–0 to 6–11 years
Types of Scores: Percentiles, standard scores, and total quotient
Typical Uses: Screening and programming
Cautions: Needs further reliability and validity studies

The SQ is distributed with a mean of 100 and a standard deviation of 15. The *BSSI–D* manual rates the SQ range of 85–115 as average; the SQ's SEM is 3 to 4 raw score points.

As illustrated by the sample Profile in Figure 18–8, the child age 5–3 earned a total test Skill Quotient of 86 that indicates average overall readiness skills. The child scored in the average range on all subtests, except Writing, where the student scored in the low average range. Possible strengths include readiness in daily living skills, spoken language, reading, mathematics, and classroom behavior. The results indicate a possible need in writing readiness.

According to the *BSSI–D* manual, further assessment and additional information are necessary before diagnostic decisions or instructional plans are made. There is also a *BSSI Screen* (Hammill & Leigh, 1983b) that consists of 20 of the 110 *BSSI–D* items chosen across the six areas. It takes 5 to 10 minutes to administer and indicates whether a child is at risk and needs further assessment.

Test of Early Reading Ability (TERA).

The *TERA* is a brief reading readiness test. It consists of items clustered around construction of meaning (print in the environment, relations among vocabulary, and print in connected discourse), alphabet and its functions (letter naming, oral reading, and proofreading), and conventions of written language (book handling and other practices). According to the manual, the *TERA* can screen children deficient in reading and document their progress. Students are expected to listen, read orally, express themselves, and point. They examine print, pictures, and numerals.

The *TERA* was standardized on over 1,000 children in 11 states and Canada, a sample similar to statistics in the 1979 *Statistical Abstract of the U.S.* The internal consistency reliability coefficients were all rounded to .90, with SEMs across age ranges of about 2 raw score points. The test-retest reliability coefficient for all groups was .97. For validity, *TERA* performances related significantly to the Reading subtest score of the *Metropolitan Achievement Tests* (.66) and the Composite Score of the *Test of Reading Comprehension* (.52). The manual reports data to support age differentiation on the *TERA* ($r = .85$); significant relationships to a variety of intelligence, language, and readiness tests (median $r = .57$); and identification of poor readers.

An acceptable answer is scored on the Record Form as a 1; a failure is scored as 0. The total raw score can be converted to a Reading Quotient (RQ), a percentile, and an age equivalent. The RQ's mean is 100, with a 15-point standard deviation; the SEM is 2 raw score points. Thus, the average range is 85 to 115. Missed items are profiled on the back of the Record Form under the three clusters described earlier. Possible strengths and weaknesses may be evident. The manual cautions against making diagnostic decisions other than the possible existence of reading problems and the need for further assessment.

TEST OF EARLY READING ABILITY (TERA)
D. K. Reid, W. Hresko, and D. D. Hammill (1981)

Type: Norm-referenced test
Major Content Areas: Prereading and reading skills
Type of Administration: Individual
Administration Time: 15–20 minutes
Age/Grade Levels: 4–0 to 7–11 years
Types of Scores: Reading quotient, percentile, and reading age
Typical Uses: Screening
Cautions: Only for screening

FIGURE 18–8
Basic School Skills Inventory–Diagnostic profile

PART III: CONVERSION OF RAW SCORES INTO STANDARD SCORES AND PERCENTILES

Subtests:	Raw Scores	% iles	Standard Scores	Category Of Performance:
I Daily Living Skills	14	37	9	average
I Spoken Language	17	50	10	average
III Reading	4	16	7	average
IV Writing	2	9	6	Below Average
V Mathematics	6	16	7	average
VI Classroom Behavior	16	25	8	average
OVERALL SKILL LEVEL	59	19	86	average

PART IV   BSSI-D PROFILE

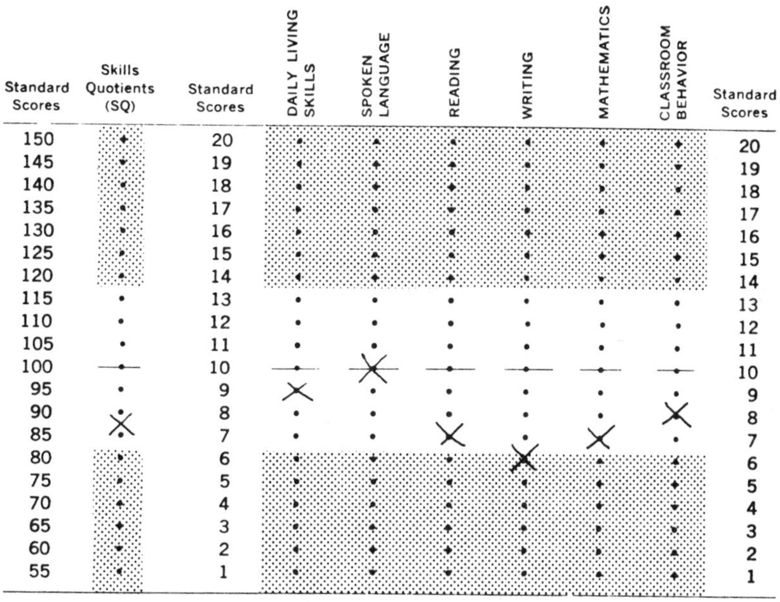

Standard Scores	Skills Quotients (SQ)	Standard Scores	DAILY LIVING SKILLS	SPOKEN LANGUAGE	READING	WRITING	MATHEMATICS	CLASSROOM BEHAVIOR	Standard Scores
150		20							20
145		19							19
140		18							18
135		17							17
130		16							16
125		15							15
120		14							14
115		13							13
110		12							12
105		11							11
100		10		X					10
95		9	X						9
90	X	8						X	8
85		7			X		X		7
80		6				X			6
75		5							5
70		4							4
65		3							3
60		2							2
55		1							1

PART V: COMMENTS

Remedial teaching should emphasize writing activities. Help should also be provided in reading and math areas. This is Bob's first school experience. Has had little exposure to 3 R's

Test of Early Mathematics Ability (TEMA).

This is a measure of both formal and informal knowledge. It can be used to screen children behind in math development and identify strengths and weaknesses. The four kinds of items are knowledge of conventions, number facts, calculation, and base-10 concepts. *TEMA* contains 23 informal and 27 formal problems. Children must listen, respond verbally, read calculations, and write numerical answers.

TEMA was standardized on 617 children in 12 states, similar in most traits to the 1981 U.S. population. Internal consistency reliability was .90, and SEMs were 2 raw score points; the test-retest reliability coefficient was .94. A comparison to the *Diagnostic Achievement Battery* yielded significant coefficients of .40 for 6-year-olds and .59 for 8-year-olds. The *TEMA* differentiates ages (.94), compares well with the *Slosson Intelligence Test* (.66) and the *Test of Early Language Development* (.39), and distinguishes between normal and at-risk children, according to the manual.

A correct answer is scored as 1 and an error as 0. The Total Raw Score, the sum of the correct answers, is placed on front of the Record Booklet and is converted to other scores (Math Quotient, Percentile, and Math Age). An Item Profile is completed by putting a slash mark through each passed item; the profile indicates the age and types of tasks involved.

The Math Quotient (mean = 100, SD = 15, SEM = 2 raw score points) indicates a child's overall grasp of the material tested and should be interpreted as average if in the range of 85 to 115. The Item Profile may provide a pattern of strengths and weaknesses relating to types of math tasks.

Boehm Test of Basic Concepts–Preschool Version (Boehm–Preschool).

The *Boehm–Preschool* (Boehm, 1986a) is designed to measure a child's knowledge of 26 basic relational concepts considered necessary for achievement in the beginning years of school. It is a downward extension of the *Boehm Test of Basic Concepts–Revised* (Boehm, 1986b) described in Chapter 14. It consists of 52 pictorial items, two for each concept being measured, and five practice items. Two administration changes from the *Boehm–R* are that the *Boehm–Preschool* is individually administered, and that the child points to the picture indicated by the examiner's verbal statement, e.g., "Point to the car *nearest* the house." The relational concepts measured include characteristics of persons and objects such as size (*tallest*), direction (*up*), position in space (*under*), quantity (*many*), and time (*after*).

The basic concepts were selected from an examination of educational and psychological research literature, analyses of tape recordings made of preschool teachers' verbal interactions with children, and surveys of widely used curriculum materials. The standardization sample included 433 children drawn from 35 sites in 17 states spread across four regions of the country and attending public and private preschools, nurseries, and day-care facilities. The sample was stratified with respect to race, region, and socioeconomic status according to 1980 Census data; there were almost

---

TEST OF EARLY MATHEMATICS ABILITY (TEMA)
H. P. Ginsburg and A. J. Baroody (1983)

Type: Norm-referenced test
Major Content Areas: Mathematics readiness
Type of Administration: Individual
Administration Time: 20 minutes
Age/Grade Levels: 4 to 8–11
Types of Scores: Math quotient, percentile, math age
Typical Uses: Screening for mathematics deficits
Cautions: Writing may be a problem with some children

BOEHM TEST OF BASIC CONCEPTS–PRESCHOOL VERSION (BOEHM–PRESCHOOL)

A. E. Boehm (1986)

Type: Norm-referenced test
Major Content Areas: Receptive vocabulary and grammar
Type of Administration: Individual
Administration Time: 15 minutes
Age/Grade Levels: 3 to 5 years
Types of Scores: Raw score, percentile rank, and T-score
Typical Uses: Screening of comprehension of basic verbal relational concepts
Cautions: Limited to comprehension and certain directions; should not be the sole measure of school readiness

---

equal numbers of males and females at all age levels. Alpha reliability coefficients across the five age levels ranged from .85 to .91, with the average coefficient being .88. Split-half coefficients ranged from .80 to .87, with the average coefficient being .85. Test-retest stability was at the .94 level for 3½-year-olds and .87 for 4½-year-olds. Content validity was established by the fact that items were represented in curriculum materials and used frequently by preschool teachers. The relationship of the *Boehm–Preschool* and the *PPVT–R* was .63 for 29 typical children and .57 for 19 language-delayed children.

The five practice items should be given to each child, and the test should be discontinued if the child responds incorrectly to two of the last four practice items. Mark a "1" for a correct response on the record form and a "0" for an incorrect one or no answer. After all 52 items are administered, the professional should add the scores for the pair of items that measures each concept and then total all scores. Basic concepts on which a child receives less than "2" may require special instruction. The child's Total Score can be converted to a percentile and to a T-score with a mean score of 50 and standard deviation of 10. These results are indicators of school readiness when included in a comprehensive evaluation battery. Remedial ideas can be found in the *Boehm Resource Guide for Basic Concept Teaching* (Boehm, 1976).

Others. Many age-appropriate oral language procedures are described in Chapter 14. Among them is the *Test of Early Language Development*

(Hresko et al., 1981) which screens for language problems at an early age and indicates possible further assessment. The receptive and expressive aspects of the form (e.g., syntax) and meaning of language are assessed. Children with possible language delays are identified with a Language Quotient (85 to 115 being average) and comparison of the child's language age to chronological age. Additional supportive data are needed to justify further assessment or diagnosis.

The *Test of Early Socioemotional Development (TOESD)* (Hresko & Brown, 1984) is a downward extension (3 to 7–11 years) of the *Behavior Rating Profile* (Brown & Hammill, 1983a) described in Chapter 10. Although retaining the same components, the *TOESD*'s items include age-appropriate ones; the student form is read to the child; and the sociogram asks, "Who would you invite to a party?", "Who are your friends?" and so on. Ratings by the child, teacher, and parents are converted into standard scores (mean = 10, SD = 3) and arrayed on the Profile. A sample interpretation might read that Chris's behavior is below average according to himself, one of his teachers, and both parents. Examination of items of concern indicates problems with immaturity and overdependence.

Among other informal procedures, child interviews and work sample analysis may be helpful. As a result of examining types of errors and questioning children, Spector (1979) identified several possible reasons for failure on the *Boehm Test of Basic Concepts (BTBC)* (Boehm, 1971). This test consists of 50 verbal concepts needed for understanding instructions and verbal directions. A child's performance may be affected by such factors as inability to focus on key words in directions ("Mark the *third* child from the teacher"); complexity of directions ("Look at the . . . ", "Mark the . . . "); deficits in spatial relationships (nearest, farthest); lack of knowledge of concept labels (zero and forward); confusion in terminology (corner instead of edge); level of abstraction (always and never); difficulty with negative concepts; poor auditory memory for sentences; and social considerations.

Once the nature of a child's readiness problem is described in detail, specify the actual needs in terms of objectives for remediation. The kind of information sought at this point would direct the development of an appropriate IEP.

Timmy

Timmy's performance on the assessment indicates average intellectual ability but a significant problem with verbal items on the *WPPSI*. His visual skills seem adequate, but he may have a high-frequency hearing loss. The two major concerns of Timmy's parents are his communication and self-help skills.

According to his *BSSI–D* performance, Timmy is not ready for the first grade. He is below average in all preacademic areas, as well as spoken language and daily living skills. His oral language development is significantly below average, particularly in receptive skills of vocabulary and grammar; these deficits may be related to his problems in hearing. Additionally, Timmy's copying on the *VMI* was below average for his age; he lacks the ability to outline and copy symbols and letters from one paper to another. Timmy's parents and teachers share similar concerns about his social-emotional development. On the *TOESD* they indicated he lacked friends, was withdrawn, and did not respond in social situations.

The goals and objectives in Timmy's program need to be specified. The following section describes the available procedures for this aspect of preschool assessment.

What Are the Educational Needs?

Many of the previously mentioned procedures can be used to specify needs, goals, objectives for instruction, and other planning features dictated by PL 94–142 and PL 99–457. The *LAP* (Sanford & Zelman, 1981) has upper-level items appropriate for school readiness. For example, in the prewriting section the child prints his or her first and last name and writes the numerals 1 to 19; in the cognitive one, names coins, counts, and tells time; and for upper-level language items, follows directions, rhymes words, names animals, and so forth.

Another previously mentioned criterion-referenced measure, the *BRIGANCE® Diagnostic Inventory of Early Development* (Brigance, 1978), encompasses school readiness areas at its upper limits and can be administered at this point. Also, the *BSSI–D* (Hammill & Leigh, 1983a) can be used to identify major problem areas and indicate specific skills for instruction. In both cases more detailed task analysis may be necessary.

The *BRIGANCE® Diagnostic Inventory of Basic Skills* (Brigance, 1977) is a good example of a criterion-referenced test of educational readiness needs. As indicated in Table 18–1, various school preparatory skills are included in the battery. For example, in reading readiness, there are tests of alphabet knowledge and recognition of upper- and lowercase letters.

An ideal approach to this level of assessment is to identify skill competency hierarchies designed by the child's school district. Many school systems have prepared such scope-and-sequence skill charts, especially in response to current demands for minimum competency testing for student promotion. The *System Fore* (Bagai & Bagai, 1979) has been referred to at different points in this text; it encompasses readiness skills and can be used for this type of assessment.

The *Behavioral Characteristics Progression (BCP)* (1973), developed by special educators in Santa Cruz County in California, is another assessment, instructional, and communication tool. A nonstandardized, criterion-referenced chart, the *BCP* contains 2,400 observable behaviors arranged across 59 strands, including early development and readiness. Also, there are identifying behaviors for each strand to help specify exceptional children's needs. For example, some of the identifying behaviors mentioned for the articulation strand are, "omits sounds in words, substitutes one sound for another in words." Each strand is numbered 1 to 59 and describes behaviors from the most primary to the most complex. So in the practical mathematics strand, Item 1 is "Looks at/for clock when asked, 'Is it recess, lunch, or bedtime?' " Item 7 is "names penny," and so forth. The results are composed into a plan, and the dates of estimated and actual accomplishment of objectives are recorded for reporting purposes.

Task analysis, diagnostic teaching, and any of the other informal procedures can be applied here. As discussed in Chapter 16, many potential goals and objectives for preschool programming do not appear in tests, surveys, and other data-gathering forms. For example, the mainstreaming component for preschool handicapped children is particularly important and needs to be included in their plans. Teachers may have to develop the children's awareness of appropriate behaviors being modeled by peers, the ability to indicate reinforcement preferences, and so on. Additionally, the frequency and quality of their interactions with peers and adults may constitute important goals different from any academic concerns.

When a child like Timmy is identified and his needs are outlined, an appropriate IEP is developed (see Figure 18–9). In Timmy's case, retention in kindergarten and placement in special education are needed. His program will include special assistance in readiness skills and language therapy. Depending on the results of the hearing diagnosis, Timmy may require a hearing aid.

As is the case in most preschool programs, Timmy's parents will be involved in a variety of ways. Note the behavior management plan they will participate in. The language clinician will also need their follow-up at home for language development. Timmy will be mainstreamed as much as possible throughout the program.

FAMILY ASSESSMENT

Family assessments need to be performed to meet legal mandates of PL 99–457, understand the child as part of the family system, identify families' needs for services, identify families' strengths that promote family adaptation, and expand the base for evaluating services (Bailey & Simeonsson, 1988a). An effective family assessment should "cover important family domains, incorporate multiple sources and measures, recognize the importance of family values and traditions, determine family priorities for goals and services, vary according to program type and demands, and evaluate family outcomes on a regular basis (Bailey & Simeonsson, 1988a, p. 9). Five important areas to assess are children's needs and characteristics likely to affect family functioning, parent–child interactions, family needs, critical events, and family strengths.

Critical Areas

First, assessment of the child should go beyond assessment of cognition, language, self-help, and so forth. It should include variables that directly affect parent–child interactions such as the child's temperament, responsiveness to others, predictability of behavior, demands for attention and care giving, and so forth (Bailey & Simeonsson, 1988a).

A second important area is interactions between parents and their special needs children. Careful attention must be given to the activity to be observed, the setting for observations, the format (free or structured, live or taped), the materials to be involved, the length of time, and the participants (Bailey & Simeonsson, 1988a). Three types of assessment scales used are (a) a behavioral count of specified parent and/or child behaviors during certain times; (b) a qualitative judgment about observed generic behaviors; and (c) reports of occurrence of specified behaviors during the observed session. Table 18–2 contains the names of some parent–child interaction assessment instruments. Bailey and Simeonsson (1988a) note that information about reliability and validity of these measures is limited, and they advise contacting the authors of the scales for current information.

It is important to watch for strengths and weaknesses in parent-child interactions and for patterns in behavior (Bailey & Simeonsson, 1988a). Parental perspective of the interactions should be taken into account, and the data must be evaluated within the family and environmental contexts. Other observations should be made of the child's interactions with other caregivers.

FIGURE 18–9
Sample preschool IEP

Timmy Ryan	8/1/83	5/1/89	
Child	Birthdate	Referral Date	
Elwood	Ms. Mahoney	Kindergarten	5/10/89–5/14/89
School	Teacher	Grade	Dates Tested

Current Level of Performance, Strengths, and Weaknesses: Timmy is of average intelligence but has communication and self-help deficits and a possible hearing loss. He lacks readiness skills in preacademic and behavioral areas. His oral language is below average, especially in comprehension of words and phrases. He can grasp writing utensils and trace but cannot outline and copy from a paper. He is not a disruptive child but tends to be immature and withdrawn, and lacks friends.

Performance Data:

	Below Average	Low Average	Average	High Average	Above Average
Vision			*		
Hearing		*			
Preacademics	*				
Oral Language	*				
Copying	*				
Socialization	*				

GOALS	OBJECTIVES
Area: Sensory 1. Refer Timmy to an otologist for further assessment.	Area: Sensory
Area: Language 1. Timmy will comprehend vocabulary words. 2. Timmy will comprehend grammatical phrases.	Area: Language 1. Given animals' pictures, Timmy will point to the correct one when it is named. 2. Given three pictures, Timmy will point to the one matching a grammatical phrase.
Area: Copying 1. Timmy will outline shapes of familiar objects. 2. Timmy will copy letters from the board.	Area: Copying 1. Given a sheet of partially outlined objects, Timmy will complete the lines correctly. 2. Given magnetic letters, Timmy will produce the pattern of letters on the blackboard.
Area: Socialization 1. Timmy will play with his classmates. 2. Timmy will approach other children spontaneously.	Area: Socialization 1. Given a common task, Timmy will complete the task at the same table as his classmates. 2. Given three photos, Timmy will pass them out to the appropriate children.

Responsible Personnel:
Academic Goals: Ms. Mahoney (kindergarten teacher), Ms. Jones (special education teacher), and Ms. Miller (language clinician)
Other Goals: Dr. Willis (otologist)

Placement Recommendation: Timmy will be retained in kindergarten. He will work with the special education teacher for 2 hours daily on copying and other readiness skills. Ms. Mahoney, Timmy's kindergarten teacher, and his parents will use a cooperative behavioral management program to encourage socialization and independence. Also, Ms. Miller will provide language therapy an hour a day.

Timeline: The program starts 9/2/89 and continues until review on 6/5/90.

Evaluation: *BRIGANCE®* subtests will be used to monitor Timmy's preacademic progress; the *Woodcock-Johnson Psycho-Educational Battery–Revised* will be given next June. The *Test of Language Development–2, Primary* will be used to reassess language performance. Classroom observation and interviews with teachers and peers are appropriate evaluations in the socialization area.

Committee Members:		Signatures
Sandra Ryan	Parent	*Sandra Ryan*
Patricia Mahoney	Kindergarten teacher	*Patricia Mahoney*
Helen Jones	Special education teacher	*Helen Jones*
Jean Miller	Language teacher	*Jean Miller*

For Parental Use: I agree with this plan and grant permission for placement in special education.

Sandra Ryan   6/3/89
Signature   Date

TABLE 18–2
Parent–child interaction assessment instruments

Name	Purpose	Examples of Behaviors Assessed
Dyadic Parent-Child Interaction Coding System (Robinson & Eyberg, 1981; Eyberg & Robinson, 1982)	To assess degree to which parent's or child's behavior during play is deviant and to evaluate effectiveness of treatment	Parent's direct and indirect commands, labeled and unlabeled praise, positive and physical contact, descriptive statement or question; child's compliance, noncompliance, whining, yelling
Social Interaction Assessment/Intervention (McCollum, 1984; McCollum & Stayton, 1985)	Evaluation of parent–handicapped child interaction pre-/postintervention to increase parent's ability to make independent adjustments to child's behavior during play	Communicative social interaction; individualized target behaviors for parent and child, e.g., imitation, vocalization, turn taking
Parent Behavior Progression (Bromwich, 1976, 1981)	Assess infant-related maternal behaviors to develop short-term goals aimed at changing maternal attitudes and behavior to enhance maternal–infant interaction	Six levels ranging from maternal enjoyment of infant to mother independently providing developmentally appropriate activities; behaviors such as parent's pleasure in watching infant, physical proximity, awareness of signs of distress or comfort, provides stable caregiver, provides variety of stimulation
Nursing Child Assessment Teaching and Feeding Scales (Barnard & Bee, 1984; Bee et al., 1982)	Assessment of parent and child behaviors during teaching and feeding as screening device and pre-/postintervention	Parent's verbalizations, positioning, handling; child's gaze, verbal cues; factor analyzed into six subscales: parent's sensitivity to cues, response to distress, cognitive and socioemotional growth fostering; child's clarity of cues, responsiveness
Interaction Rating Scales (Clark & Siefer, 1985)	Assess parental sensitivity to child behavior and reciprocity of interactions during free play	Parent's imitating, affect; child's gaze aversion, social referencing; dyadic reciprocity; behaviors grouped as interaction style, social referencing, assessment of context
Teaching Skills Inventory (Rosenberg, Robinson, & Beckman, 1984; Rosenberg & Robinson, 1985)	Assessment of parent's teaching skills with handicapped child pre-/postintervention	Parent's clarity of verbal instruction, task modification effectiveness of prompts; child's interest
Maternal Behavior Rating Scale (Mahoney, Finger, & Powell, 1985)	Assess quality of maternal interactive behavior during play with young mentally retarded children for use in program evaluation	Parent's expressiveness, warmth, sensitivity to child state, achievement orientation, social stimulation, effectiveness, directiveness; child's activity level, attention span, enjoyment, expressiveness
Parent/Caregiver Involvement Scale (Farran, Kasari, Comfort, & Jay, 1986; Farran et al., 1987)	Description of parent's involvement in play interaction with handicapped, high-risk, or normally developing children	Adult's amount, quality, appropriateness of involvement via 11 behaviors—e.g., physical, verbal, responsiveness, control; overall impression of affective climate and learning environment

Note: Adapted from *Family Assessment in Early Intervention* by D. B. Bailey & R. J. Simeonsson, 1988, Columbus, OH: Merrill. Copyright 1988 by Merrill Publishing Company. Reprinted by permission.

A third type of assessment is a family needs assessment. There are a variety of procedures available for this purpose, including the following (Bailey & Simeonsson, 1988a):

□ The *Family Information Preference Inventory* (Turnbull & Turnbull, 1986), which has 37 items arranged across five areas: teaching the child at home, advocacy and working with professionals, planning for the future, helping the whole family relax and enjoy life more, and finding and using more support.
□ *Family Needs Survey* (Bailey & Simeonsson, 1988b), which assesses a family's need for information, for support from others, for help in explaining their child to others, for community services, and for financial assistance.

Fourth, it is important to consider critical events, because families of special needs infants and children may experience added stress from both normal life events and events that by their nature are stressful. The diagnosis of a child's disability, developmental milestones, efforts in obtaining services, transitions such as preschool to elementary school programs, medical crises, and the normal life events are likely to pose particular challenges for these families (Bailey & Simeonsson, 1988a). Because most available questionnaires about family events do not contain relevant information for families of special needs children, Bailey and Simeonsson (1988a) recommend the use of informal procedures including the following questions:

□ Has the family learned of diagnosis within the last six months?
□ Does the handicapped child have a younger sibling who is at the point where he/she is matching or beginning to exceed the handicapped child's abilities?
□ Is the family anticipating a program transition (e.g., child will enter a developmental center) within the next six months?
□ Is the child expecting a medical operation within the next six months?
□ Has the child just reached or is s/he about to reach the age at which most children walk and is not walking?
□ Has the child just reached or is about to reach the age at which most children begin to feed themselves independently, and is not self-feeding?

□ Has the child just reached or is about to reach the age at which most children talk and is not talking?
□ Has the child just reached or is about to reach the age at which most children are toilet-trained (bladder control) and is not toilet-trained? (Bailey et al., 1986)

The fifth area that requires attention in a family assessment are the strengths and weaknesses of the family. A key element is to study the roles of family members, support systems that are available to them, and the family environment (Bailey & Simeonsson, 1988a). The major methodologies are questionnaires, clinical interviews, and observations. It is particularly important to consider the family as a unit and not as an aggregate of individuals. Analysis of support systems include those internal to the family such as values, beliefs, and attitudes and those that are external such as extended family, friends, and institutions. Bailey and Simeonsson (1988a) describe a variety of assessments in this area.

Family Interview

Although family assessment utilizes many methods, the family interview is particularly useful for gathering data about family characteristics, family strengths, and family perceptions of situations, events, goals, and services (Bailey & Simeonsson, 1988a). A structured interview is better than paper-and-pencil tests because the interviewer can monitor whether he or she is being intrusive, language and questions can be changed to meet a family's values and culture, a family can more easily screen its responses, and there is more flexibility (Hanson & Lynch, 1989).

There are a number of skills necessary to conduct an effective family assessment (Hanson & Lynch, 1989). Good listening skills are very important, as is the ability to maintain neutrality and not take sides in disputes. Because you are likely to encounter cultures, religions, values, and priorities different from yours, you must be nonjudgmental. Parents and other family members must be regarded as equals, that is, their perceptions must be regarded as having equal value. Finally, competence, openness, and a genuine desire to help the family are essential. Table 18–3 contains a description of five phases in a family-focused interview.

TABLE 18–3
Family-focused interview

Interview Phase	Purpose
1. Preliminary	Prepare for interview by summarizing assessment data
Identify high-priority needs	
Identify difficulties in parent-child interaction	
Specify child characteristics that have potential family impact	
Note upcoming critical events	
2. Introduction	Reduce parents' anxiety and create appropriate listening environment
Explain purpose of the interview	
Confirm time allotted and format	
Discuss confidentiality	
Structure physical environment (if possible)	
3. Inventory	Validate and elaborate information from assessment
Make opening statement	Identify additional areas of family needs, strengths, and resources
Allow parents to do most of the talking	
4. Summary, priority, and goal setting	Clarify consensus and disagreement between parents
Make summarizing statements	Agree on definition of family needs
Explore family's priorities	Establish priorities and set goals
Set goals collaboratively	
5. Closure	Recognize parents' efforts
Express recognition and appreciation of parents' contribution	Allow concerns about interview to emerge
Ask if family members have additional concerns or thoughts about interview	

Note: From *Family Assessment in Early Intervention* (p. 194) by D. B. Bailey and R. J. Simeonsson, 1988, Columbus, OH: Merrill. Copyright 1988 by Merrill Publishing Company. Reprinted by permission.

Individualized Family Services Plan

According to Bailey and Simeonsson (1988a), there are seven components of the Individualized Family Services Plan (IFSP):

1. A statement of the infant's or toddler's current levels of physical development, language and speech development, psychosocial development, and self-help skills, based on acceptable objective criteria
2. A statement of the family's strengths and needs related to enhancing the development of the family's handicapped infant or toddler
3. A statement of major goals for the infant or toddler and the family, and the criteria, procedures, and timelines used to measure progress toward these goals and determine whether modifications of goals or services are necessary
4. A statement of specific early intervention services necessary to meet the unique needs of the infant or toddler and the family, including frequency, intensity, and method of delivering services
5. The projected dates for initiation of services and the anticipated duration of such services
6. The name of the case manager from the profession most immediately relevant to the infant's or toddler's and the family's needs, who will be responsible for implementing the plan and coordinating with other agencies and persons
7. The steps to be taken supporting the transition of the handicapped toddler to services provided for preschoolers to the extent such services are considered appropriate

Figure 18–10 contains a sample of family needs as they might be listed on the family portion of the IFSP.

FIGURE 18–10
Family portion of IFSP

Family Priorities

Need	Resources	Strategies	Person Responsible	Review Date
1. Additional information about developing motor skills	• O.T. + SPL team members	Consultation	Jan Wu, O.T. Dave Bell, SPL	9/89
and language skills	• Books	Provide list of books from program library	Jan Wu, O.T. Dave Bell, SPL	9/89
2. Information about parent support groups	• Parent-to-Parent • UCP Parent Groups • Exceptional Parent magazine	Provide referral & information	Luella Smith, MSW Fam. Coor.	9/89
3. Suggestions for helping Amy eat regular foods	• O.T. • Mrs. J. (Cynthia's mother) who has just done this successfully	Consultation Provide name and telephone	Jan Wu, O.T. Brenda Johns, Tch.	9/89 9/89

Signatures & Dates of Plan:

Mary Whiteson
Parent/Guardian

Richard Whiteson
Parent/Guardian

Jan Wu, O.T.
Case Coordinator/Manager

Mark Ranside
Program Administrator

Note. From *Early Intervention: Implementing Child and Family Services for Infants and Toddlers Who Are At-Risk or Disabled* (pp. 454–455) by M. J. Hanson and E. W. Lynch, 1989, Austin, TX: PRO-ED. Copyright 1989 by PRO-ED. Reprinted by permission.

STUDY GUIDE

Review Questions

1. What are five reasons for early childhood assessment?
2. Screening instruments supply in-depth diagnostic data for programming. (True or False)
3. A developmental and functional perspective in early childhood assessment are mutually exclusive. (True or False)
4. What are two problems with early childhood assessment?
5. Pediatricians are among the (core or supportive) team members of an interdisciplinary assessment team. (Circle one)
6. There seems to be a place for both standardized and criterion-referenced tests in early childhood assessment. (True or False)
7. What are two criteria for early childhood assessment?
8. The *Denver Developmental Screening Test* is a criterion-referenced measure for program planning. (True or False)
9. The *Developmental Profile II* relies on _____ .
10. A General Cognitive Scale score of 125 on the *McCarthy Scales of Children's Abilities* is in the _____ range.
11. Formal standardized testing of young children must be supplemented by data from observations and parent interviews. (True or False)
12. The (*LAP–E, LAP,* or *LAP–D*) is meant for children ages 0 to 3. (Circle one)
13. The average stanine range on the *Metropolitan Readiness Test* is from 4 to 6. (True or False)
14. The *Basic School Skills Inventory–Diagnostic* has a briefer screening version. (True or False)
15. The *Test of* _____ is a downward extension of the *Behavior Rating Profile* for young children.

Activities

1. Find out what agencies in your community assess infants and young children. What procedures do they use?
2. Examine the school readiness testing procedures in your school district. What kinds of data are gathered?
3. Visit a local preschool and interview the director about their assessment activities. How do they know whether their program is beneficial to the children?
4. Examine one of the tests described in this chapter. What additional data should be combined with the results? How would you get it?
5. Observe a person testing a young child. What are the noticeable differences from testing older children?
6. Observe a family interview for a needs assessment. How did the interviewer structure the questions and modify them as needed? What were the family members' reactions to the interview?

Discussion Questions

1. What is the basis of the developmental vs. functional controversy in early childhood assessment? Discuss its implications.
2. One preschool teacher might consider a child's behavior as normal and another teacher might call him hyperactive. Discuss the reasons why.
3. The published measures described in this chapter may not be specific enough to develop a program plan for a child. Why is this so? What can be done about it?

19

Career, Vocational, and College Assessment

When assessing adolescents and young adults with mild handicaps, questions about career and vocational needs and future education invariably arise. Often these individuals' other learning problems preclude them from obtaining the preparation they need to obtain gainful employment or make other career choices. The assessment question to be answered in such cases is, *What are the student's career and vocational awareness, aptitude, interests, and skills?* Although their learning needs must be clarified for instructional purposes, career and vocational needs must also be directly addressed in a systematic fashion. Such was the case with Phillip, whose intellectual and adaptive skills and academic achievement are significantly below average (see Chapter 15). His main needs are in reading, mathematics, and written language; he also has poor fine motor coordination. Phillip has difficulty with remembering, sequencing, and organizing his thoughts, as well as in making decisions. His parents and teachers agree that his program should stress functional skills for post–high school community adjustment, including vocational guidance and training. As part of this year's annual review assessment, Phillip will be administered a number of surveys and tests to measure his awareness and knowledge of occupations and his aptitudes for certain jobs. He will also complete a vocational interest inventory and perform some work samples.

CONSIDERATIONS

Appropriate career and vocational assessment and services are essential to meet the needs of mildly handicapped students. Studies of learning disabled adolescents indicate little evidence of such provisions being available. The actual jobs obtained by learning disabled adults (Association for Children and Adults with Learning Disabilities, 1982a, 1982b; White, Deshler, Schumaker, Warner, Alley, & Clark, 1983) are of low status. The students and their parents tend to hold low expectations of career and vocational prospects.

Only half of the former mildly handicapped high school students surveyed in Vermont indicated that they were employed; and of those, one third had only part-time work (Hasazi, Gordon, & Roe, 1985). The students who had taken vocational education

and had part-time or summer jobs tended to be employed more than those who had not. They found employment through a self-family-friend network, and job changes were frequent.

Another group of former students in Colorado reported that they did not necessarily receive vocational education, and half of them did not report postsecondary training of a vocational or technical nature (Mithaug, Horiuchi, & Fanning, 1985). About 70% had jobs, as many had part-time ones as had full-time ones, hourly wages were less than $4 for most of them, and more than one third had never received a raise. They too had relied on parents and teachers in obtaining employment. Thus, there is a significant need for improved assessment and instructional opportunities in this area to improve the transition from secondary schools to career and other schooling opportunities.

Three major components of vocational preparation are general and continuing education, career education, and specific vocational programming (Brolin, 1982). The first component consists of general knowledge, basic academic skills, aesthetic preparation, physical education, and so forth.

The second, career education, is "the process of systematically coordinating all school, family, and community components together to facilitate each individual's potential for economic, social, and personal fulfillment and participation in productive work activities that benefit the individual or others" (Kokaska & Brolin, 1985, p. 43). It provides the opportunity for students to learn in the least restrictive environment academic, daily living, personal-social, and occupational knowledge and skills to attain economic, personal, and social fulfillment (Brolin, Cegelka, Jackson, & Wrobel, 1978). The objectives of career education offer the exceptional student a broad array of experiences from the awareness level to the evaluation level. In this chapter, career education is considered as an indispensable companion of vocational education, a broad context and preparation for occupational training.

Obtaining specific occupational skills, the third element in preparing for a vocation, is an important aspect of the schooling of mildly handicapped students (Kokaska & Brolin, 1985). Such training cannot be left to chance after they leave school. There is much to be said for demonstrating early that students can learn to have saleable skills.

Such a vocational emphasis in the curriculum often makes schooling more meaningful. Handicapped students with vocational skills are in a more competitive position relative to untrained peers, have had a chance to demonstrate their potential, and can eliminate unrealistic occupational goals.

Purposes

PL 94–142 (1975) and the corresponding vocational education legislation, PL 94–482 (1976), mandate a variety of changes in vocational education of handicapped persons (Sitlington, 1979). First, handicapped students are to be included in the regular vocational program. Second, regular educators must be involved with these students. Third, an IEP in this area of vocational and career development is to be prepared. PL 94–482 also builds on the provisions of the Vocational Education Act of 1963 and the Vocational Education Amendments of 1968 (PL 90–576), which require states to spend at least 10% of the federal/state grant-in-aid funds for vocational programs to meet the needs of handicapped persons. This provision allows that the 10% set-aside monies can be matched with 50% from state and local funds, thus preventing substitution of federal monies for state funds in this area. Other pieces of legislation that particularly safeguard the civil rights of handicapped persons are sections 503 and 504 of the Rehabilitation Act Amendments of 1973, PL 93–112. Section 503 regulates the hiring, training, advancement, and retention of qualified handicapped workers by employers under contract with the federal government for more than $2,500. Section 504 guarantees accessibility to programs; a public education; and the elimination of discriminatory admission procedures, testing, and interviews.

The Carl D. Perkins Vocational Education Act (PL 98–524) of 1984 (*Federal Register,* October 15, 1985) provides federal assistance to local education agencies for vocational education programs, with special mention of including special needs students. Students with disabilities are to have equal access to information about the program at least one year before they enter the grade level when vocational education is available but no later than the beginning of the ninth grade. They also are to have equal access in recruitment, enrollment, and placement and to the full range of vocational programs. Vocational education programs and activities are to be provided in the least restrictive environment and will, when appropriate, be included in their IEP. Of particular significance here is that an assessment of the student's interests, abilities, and special needs with respect to successfully completing the vocational education program is to be prepared.

The assessments and evaluations necessary to provide appropriate career and vocational programs require a cooperative team effort. Regular and special educators and the other core assessment team members call upon vocational educators and rehabilitation counselors for assistance. Together they gather the necessary data. Whereas some assessment measures described in this chapter may be given by any team member, others require specialists. Their expertise is especially important for interpretation.

Assessment Areas and Levels

In order to establish the entry skills of mildly handicapped students for vocational programs and to design such IEPs, a complete and appropriate assessment is necessary. The types of information generally required in a vocational or career assessment are degree of awareness and knowledge of careers and the world of work, general aptitude and work/study habits, interests, and skills for specific occupations. The assessment team must also gather data concerning the student's medical, academic, personal-social, and learning strategy needs required for special education placement; the age-appropriate formal tests and informal procedures described in earlier chapters are used for this purpose. All the information is combined to provide a clear profile of strengths and weaknesses and a base for developing a comprehensive and coordinated program.

Vocational assessment is an ongoing process of identifying individual student characteristics, strengths and weaknesses, and interests, as well as education, training, and placement needs (Illinois State Board of Education, 1987). Because not all students require a full vocational assessment, Illinois and many other states conceptualize the process in levels. As Figure 19–1 indicates, more seriously disabled students require more extensive and intensive assessments to meet their needs.

FIGURE 19–1

The Illinois Model: The three levels of vocational assessment

```
                          LEVEL I

                        Cumulative
                       Data Review
                         Career
                     Interest Testing
                      Aptitude Testing
                       Ability Testing
                      Student Interview
                      Parent Interview
                     Teacher Interview
                 Informal Teacher Assessments
                     Student Observation


                         LEVEL II

          Cumulative Data Review      Aptitude Testing
          Career Interest Testing      Ability Testing
            Student Interview      Parent Interview
      Teacher Interview      Informal Teacher Assessments
                    Student Observation
        Career Maturity Ratings      Job Readiness
        Work Samples      Work-Related Behaviors
              Learning Style Inventories


                         LEVEL III

     Cumulative Data Review      Career Interest Testing      Aptitude Testing
    Ability Testing      Student Interview      Parent Interview      Teacher Interview
          Informal Teacher Assessments      Student Observation
        Career Maturity Ratings      Job Readiness      Work Samples
            Work-Related Behaviors      Learning Style Inventories
     Simulated Job Station      Functional Living Skills      Production Work
            Situational Assessment      Contracted Work
```

MOST STUDENTS

MOST SEVERE DISABILITIES

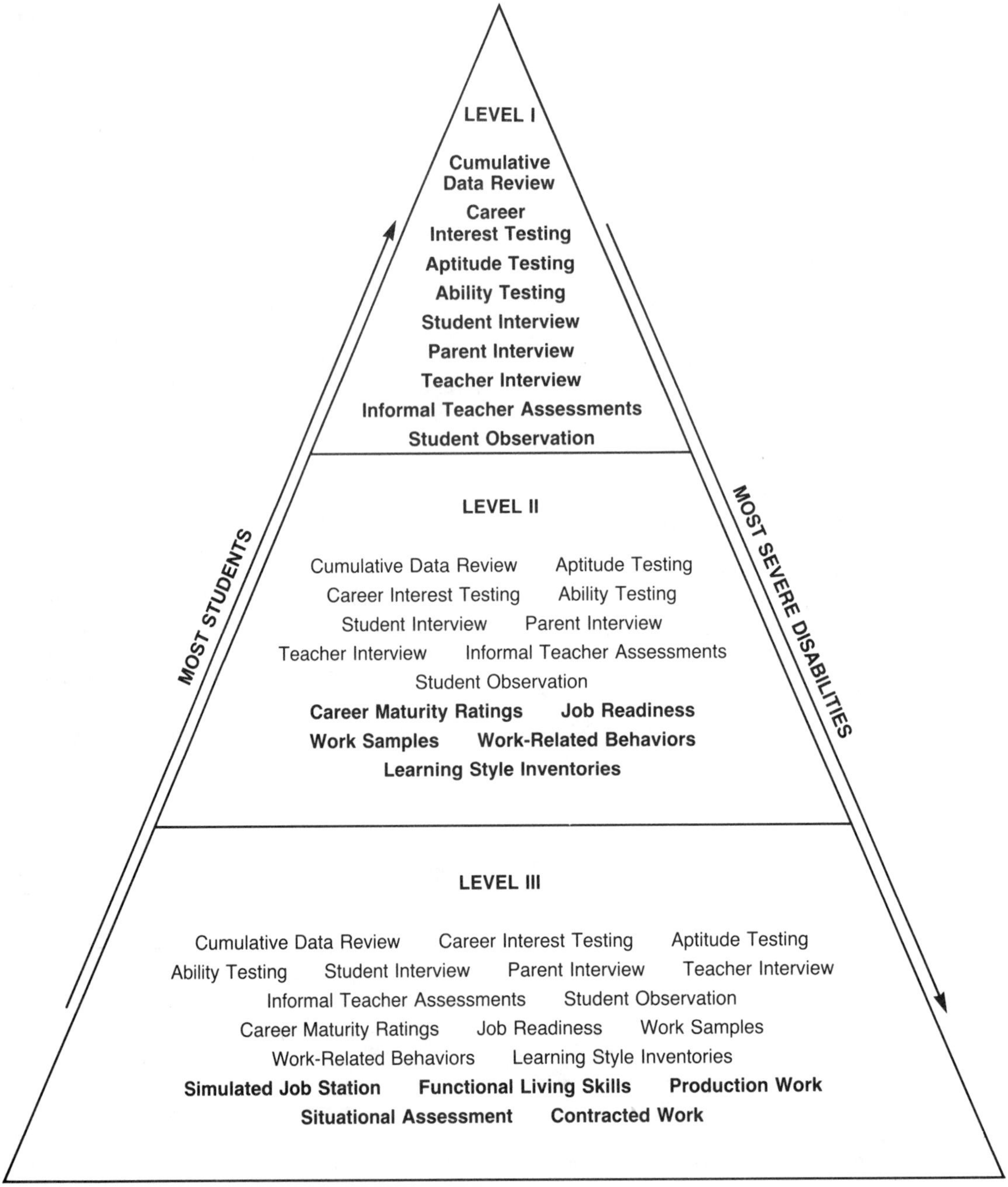

Note. Adapted from *Vocational Assessment of Secondary Special Needs Students* by Illinois State Board of Education, 1987. Springfield, IL: Illinois State Board of Education. Reprinted by permission.

Level 1 assessment is performed with all special needs students and involves reviewing and compiling all preexisting student information into a student profile. Because special students must be thoroughly assessed for academic programming, these data are readily available. Also, student interests are identified, and the perceptions of teachers, parents, and the students themselves are gathered. Of particular interest is assessment of motor and perceptual skills and work-related behaviors, motivation, and attitudes. For most students, this level of assessment should be adequate for assignment to appropriate vocational programs. Existing school personnel should be able to perform this level of assessment.

At Level 2 more information is obtained about learning styles, values, career maturity, and job readiness. Specific formal and informal tests may be used, as well as work sample and work evaluation systems. The latter compensate for difficulties students have with the paper and pencil tests and general ability/aptitude screening instruments frequently used in Level 1 assessment. Personnel trained in the instruments used are necessary, and vocational assessment specialists are needed for administering work samples and other work evaluation systems.

Level 3 assessment in Illinois is reserved for students with limited mental, physical, and social-emotional abilities who do not respond well to the procedures used at other levels and is used to determine appropriate placements such as sheltered employment. Actual placement in a job or training program may be less threatening than other procedures and necessary to gather the kind of information needed. Functional living skills are a particular focus. The assessment may be conducted outside the school by trained specialists utilizing simulated or actual contract work.

Kentucky is using a similar phase approach. Basic related information and vocational knowledge and interests are established in Phase 1 (usually in grades 8–9). In Phase 2 (grades 9–10) assessment information on vocational aptitudes for certain kinds of work and vocational skill performance is analyzed. Finally, in Phase 3 (grades 11–12), individuals requiring more in-depth assessment receive work samples, on-the-job evaluations, and additional interest and aptitude assessment.

More specifically, Fayette County Public Schools in Lexington, Kentucky, organize vocational assessment of mildly handicapped students in the following fashion (Nelson & Hammer, 1985):

☐ Phase 1—Information needed for the initial development of an assessment plan is gathered including data on medical, psychological, academic areas; learning style preferences, problem-solving ability; work and attitude observations; work and social history; work interests and academic reports.

☐ Phase 2—Students who are college bound are given only an appropriate interest inventory. All other students receive appropriate interest and attitude screenings.

☐ Phase 3—All students completing the interest and attitude screenings in Phase 2 undergo approximately 2 hours of hands-on evaluation at the local school and approximately 5 hours of work sample evaluation at an assessment center.

Another approach to conceptualizing vocational assessment is represented by the *McCarron-Dial Evaluation System* (McCarron & Dial, 1986), which measures five factors using the following procedures:

1. Verbal-cognitive: *Wechsler Adult Intelligence Scale–Revised* (Wechsler, 1981) or the *Stanford-Binet Intelligence Scale* (Terman & Merrill, 1973; Thorndike, Hagen, & Sattler, 1986) and the *Peabody Picture Vocabulary Test–Revised* (Dunn & Dunn, 1981)
2. Sensory: *Bender Visual Motor Gestalt Test* (Bender, 1938) and the *Haptic Visual Discrimination Test* (McCarron & Dial, 1976)
3. Motor: *McCarron Assessment of Neuromuscular Development* (McCarron, 1976, 1982)
4. Emotional: *Observational Emotional Inventory* (McCarron & Dial, 1976, 1986)
5. Integration-coping: *Dial Behavior Rating Scale* (McCarron & Dial, 1973)

An individual's strengths and weaknesses in these areas are organized in a standardized individual evaluation profile. The data are used to develop the vocational training and transitional components of an individual plan.

As with the academic areas discussed earlier, the types of information gathered depend on the assessment questions being asked. The first, *What is the student's level of awareness and knowledge about occupations?* identifies the student's general background, experience, use of terminology, and so on, in choosing a career or a job. Second, *What are the general aptitudes and work or study habits?* addresses a broad range of vocational, cognitive and behavioral prerequisites. Third, the student's responses to an array of career and vocational options address this question: *What are the student's career or vocational interests?* Finally, we ask *What are the skills for specific work?* to determine entry level for jobs. These assessment questions occur throughout the process and lead to the development of an appropriate career or vocational education program; they also dictate the types of assessment strategies to be used.

Issues

Although there is general acceptance of career or vocational education for handicapped persons, exceptional students still are not receiving the amount and type of services they need for successful community adjustment (Brolin, 1982). Some reasons for this situation are the lack of flexibility created by the departmental organization of secondary schools, an emphasis on younger handicapped children, segregated vocational programming directed by special educators, unsupportive professional attitudes, and inappropriateness of typical career or vocational programs.

School systems encounter a variety of problems in providing career and vocational assessments (Nelson & Hammer, 1985). Assessment systems are available for students with extremely high abilities or with severe deficits, but these are not very useful with the vast majority of students in-between. They also require too much time to administer. Teachers are resistant to the demands placed on them to gather information about the students and to add instructional objectives generated by the vocational assessment. Vocational assessments are not modified appropriately for individual student needs. Assessment results may not be interpreted meaningfully in light of local programs and jobs nor integrated into the student's IEP. Most of all, the data may not be used properly to counsel and motivate students.

The technical quality of the assessment procedures is also an issue. In addition to the reliability of the tests and observations, the content and use of vocational tests may be sexually discriminatory (Cegelka, 1976). The validity of the work representations can be questioned partly because of the enormous technological advances in the workplace. Persons with mildly handicapping conditions may not be as limited due to some advances and may not need to be prepared as they currently are (Cegelka & Lewis, 1983). In other cases, new challenges may occur; for example, additional reading requirements if shopping by computer.

There is a territorial controversy between special education, vocational education, and rehabilitation counseling that affects mildly handicapped students' access to appropriate assessment and programs. Vocational educators may not be anxious to have many special education students in their classes because they feel the quality of their programs may suffer. In this era of normalization, there are fewer and fewer special vocational schools and programs specifically for disabled students. Further, students with learning disabilities have only recently been considered severely handicapped enough to merit rehabilitative counseling services.

This question of territoriality is also related to who is to do the needed assessments. In schools there are clear divisions between academic and vocational programs. Special educators may administer a vocational aptitude or interest survey, but their expertise often ends there. Arranging for the additional assessment is sometimes a challenge.

Another issue for mildly handicapped students wanting career or vocational guidance and preparation is created by their cognitive, academic, or behavioral problems. These characteristics often prevent entry into programs because they lack prerequisite grades, fail exams, or are judged unfit. Additionally, a student from middle or high socioeconomic status may find the typical vocational program offerings unappealing; to take a job in such areas would be socially stigmatizing. These mildly handicapped students may also want to continue their education after high school but may find their aspirations basically limited by the vocational preparatory perspective. This either/or mentality governs much career counseling of these students and fails to reflect possible accommodations in testing and college entrance requirements.

Many of the issues center around the need to meet the transitional needs of students. Their preparation for postschooling is not only to get a job. They may want to go to school, get married, and engage in leisure and recreational activities. As we discuss later, the evaluation and preparation for these aspects of their lives are necessary and should be conceptualized as a unit.

Current Practices

The answers to the assessment questions require considerable information about not only careers and occupations but also the students. The assessment techniques currently employed are therefore often multidimensional. There are a variety of assessment techniques available, some applicable for gathering many kinds of data and others only useful in specific cases (Illinois State Board of Education, 1987; Sitlington, 1979; Wimmer, 1982).

Cumulative data review. Examination of attendance records, grades, test scores, and available special education assessment of intellectual, academic, and behavioral areas is a vital aspect of a career/vocational assessment. The information provides a context in which vocational needs can be understood and appropriate services chosen. Also, knowledge of a student's task-approach preferences, motivation, and academic abilities shapes how vocational instruction will be delivered.

Medical examination. Students should have a physical as a preliminary measure. Such data may be available in school records, or a physical examination may need to be arranged. Factors that might complicate training and job placement can be avoided or compensated for. Corrective measures, as in the case of vision, or rehabilitation may be necessary.

Student, parent, and teacher interviews.
Students should be asked about interests and leisure-time activities, the types of work they have done at home, and the part-time and summer jobs they have held. Also, their knowledge about and aspirations for jobs and professions could be tapped informally.

It is important to establish parents' aspirations for their children's future employment and schooling, because these shape students' perceptions. Parents also can provide their view of their children's strengths and weaknesses and describe their perceptions of appropriate vocations and professions for their children.

Teachers have a good deal of information about the cognitive and affective skills of students. Their experience with the work-related behaviors of students, like attention and task completion, is a valuable resource. Also, teachers can describe how students like to approach and complete tasks and how they have learned to plan the best instruction for particular students.

Students, teachers, and parents can also provide data about social skill development that is essential to vocational placement and job maintenance. It is important to know how students adapt to school, home, and other settings and how well they interact with peers and authority figures. A comparison of perspectives may reveal the need for socialization training in certain settings or with certain target groups.

Follow-up studies of school leavers can yield useful information about the relevance and quality of secondary school preparation in this area (Peterson, 1988). Responses to written surveys, phone interviews, and face-to-face contacts can confirm or dispute the usefulness of the program. Employers and co-workers, parents and other family members, and the individuals themselves can be called on to profile their job ability and satisfaction, as well as to evaluate the preparation program and current support system.

Interest inventories. Students are asked about occupational and professional preferences through informal and formal ways. Some students can clearly state their likes and dislikes in terms of future work. In other cases, observation of hobbies and leisure-time activities provides useful information. In inventories and surveys students choose among different types of activities and indicate the one they like the most.

Vocational aptitude/ability testing. General aptitude and ability tests are available to assess broad and multiple competencies for certain types of work. Also, there are specific aptitude tests for particular job skills such as fine and gross motor dexterity, use of tools, and speed and accuracy of motor and perceptual-motor performance. Although the results of these types of tests may suggest some aptitude or readiness for certain types of training or work, actual success or failure may be affected by many other factors (Wimmer, 1982). These tests may also present the opportunity to observe students' communication skills, physical endurance, work habits and attitudes, ability to follow directions, and tolerance for stress.

Career maturity ratings.   It is important to note attitudes, values, temperaments, and other personality factors that affect choice of and performance in jobs and professions. These types of measures also assess knowledge of occupational information and establish whether students know the basic requirements of certain occupations and fields.

Job readiness.   This assessment concerns job-seeking skills such as interviewing skills. Job-keeping skills such as punctuality and response to supervision are also important to assess. This analysis can be conducted through a variety of means, including observation, testing, and interviews with teachers and parents.

Job analysis.   This procedure is a task analysis of the specific skills required by a job and is often a prerequisite for other assessments. There are some overview skill descriptions of jobs that enable you to begin a job analysis, such as the *Dictionary of Occupational Titles (DOT)* (U.S. Department of Labor, 1977, 1982, 1986). However, on-site analysis is imperative. For that purpose, use observation and interviews to gather information concerning the following job requirements and characteristics (Sitlington & Wimmer, 1978):

1. Physical (e.g., standing for long periods)
2. Motor dexterity (e.g., use of fingers)
3. Perceptual (e.g., color discrimination)
4. Academic (e.g., computational skills)
5. Familiarity with tools and equipment
6. Affective (e.g., social skills)
7. Worker traits (e.g., handling time pressure)
8. Training
9. Supervision
10. Working conditions (e.g., fumes, noise)
11. Salary and benefits

12. Entry procedures (e.g., testing)
13. Appearance (e.g., clothing)

School systems are analyzing local jobs and using that information as an essential element in designing an appropriate vocational preparation program. Fayette County Public Schools in Lexington, Kentucky, computerize the data and match the information to student characteristics in their decision-making process (Nelson & Hammer, 1985).

Commercial work sample systems.   There are a number of commercially available work sample systems. They vary in the types of tasks required of the students and their resemblance to actual jobs or components of jobs (Sitlington, 1979). Some systems assess student performance on actual features of a job, such as sorting mail. Others assess skills on generic tasks common to a number of jobs, such as independent problem solving. The results indicate specific skill development in those tasks as well as allow for generalizations to similar jobs. Although expensive, these assessment systems do provide comprehensive efforts to establish a clear profile of student entry skills.

Self-developed work samples and simulations.   To reflect job placements in a particular locale, work samples can also be locally developed and standardized. They are simulated representations of work tasks or activities that may or may not represent an actual job or part of a job (Sitlington & Wimmer, 1978). Such procedures not only reveal student competence on specific work tasks but also provide information about work habits, stamina, and social skills. Students have the opportunity to acquire hands-on exposure to job requirements before actually entering the market. Work samples may be a full-scale replica of a local job or a representation of one common job component in a variety of local jobs (e.g., using a cash register).

Behavioral analysis.   This approach permits a systematic and functional analysis of the students' actual job performance and is similar to diagnostic teaching, described in Chapter 5. It involves specifying the work behavior being observed, describing the environmental work conditions, establishing the student's initial level of performance, initiating the job training program or actual job, and continuing observations during the program to establish improved skill competence. A variety of elements can be changed, and the student performance can be observed: environmental conditions (noise level, number of people in the work area, etc.), instructional methods (verbal directions, computer, etc.), types of reinforcement (e.g., praise, tangibles, etc.), and schedule of reinforcement (immediate, daily, etc.). Such information can be used in improving both training and on-the-job performance.

Situational assessment.　Students are also observed regularly by supervisory staff in performing training or actual work activities. This on-site assessment is quantified, or at least structured, on rating forms that cover areas of supervisor interest. Unforeseen strengths and weaknesses that go unnoticed in more artificial training activities often occur in such situations. Although this form of assessment is intentionally flexible and broad-based to permit inclusion of a variety of topics, ratings and other comments are to be as objective as possible.

The typical programs for which these assessments qualify students are usually school- or employer-based (Cegelka, 1985). The school-based approach has the greatest impact on education and is directed toward adult occupational adjustment. This model has three stages: (a) career awareness, during which young students are introduced to the values and types of work; (b) career orientation and exploration, during which they learn about job options and jobs of interest; and (c) career preparation, during which they acquire the technical prerequisites for occupations or college.

Another popular model provides for career or vocational experiences outside the school. Experience-based career education programs draw on academic, general, and vocational curricula. They make use of banks, factories, and other settings by arranging for a series of supervised placements of 2 or more weeks for students.

In the case of mildly handicapped students, an infused approach in a school situation is highly likely; that is, the career education and other curricula are integrated. Therefore, the scope of an assessment must encompass both academic and vocational concerns, as in Phillip's case. As illustrated in the sample IAP (see Figure 19–2), an interest inventory, student interview, and work sample analysis will be used to answer the main career or vocational assessment questions. In the following sections a number of formal and informal procedures representative of some of the types of assessment are discussed.

FIGURE 19–2
Sample career and vocational IAP

Phillip Hughes	9.8	16	4/2/89
Student's Name	Grade	Age	Date
Reason for Assessment: To clarify vocational/career awareness and aptitudes, interests, and skills.			
Assessment Questions	Procedures	Personnel	Date and Time
1. What are the student's general knowledge and awareness of occupations?	Student interview, *BRIGANCE*® subtests	Ms. Smith and Mrs. Tribble (OT)	5/1/89, 9 a.m.
2. What are the student's occupational interests?	*Wide Range Interest-Opinion Test*	Ms. Smith	5/2/89, 9 a.m.
3. What are the student's specific occupational skills?	*Wide Range Employability Sample Test* and Singer Work Samples	Ms. Smith and Mrs. Tribble	5/3/89 and 5/4/89, 9 a.m.

ASSESSMENT PROCEDURES

The four main assessment questions asked in regard to career or vocational needs of mildly handicapped students are, *What is the awareness and knowledge of occupations? What are the general aptitudes and work or study habits? What are the career or vocational interests? What are the skills for specific work?* A variety of standardized procedures are available to assess different aspects of career and vocational preparation. The following sections critique examples of some, including career or vocational knowledge, aptitudes and tests of manual dexterity, interests and opinions, and commercial work samples. The roles of a number of informal techniques are also considered.

What Is the Student's Level of Awareness and Knowledge of Occupations?

An essential aspect of career and vocational assessment is establishing the level of awareness and knowledge students have about careers and jobs. Among the many procedures available are the *Social and Prevocational Information Battery—Revised* (Halpern & Irvin, 1986) and the *Test of Practical Knowledge* (Wiederholt & Larsen, 1983). Additionally, competency and criterion-referenced testing and job analysis are useful, as well as a consideration of the relationship among student performances.

Social and Prevocational Information Battery—Revised (SPIB–R).   The *SPIB–R* is a set of nine

tests directly related to long-range goals of work study or experience programs in secondary schools. They are as follows:

SPIB–R Tests	Long-Range Goals
Job Search Skills	Employability
Job-Related Behavior	
Banking	Economics
Budgeting	Self-Sufficiency
Purchasing	
Home Management	Family Living
Physical Health Care	
Hygiene and Grooming	Personal Habits
Functional Signs	Communication

The tests vary in length from 26 to 36 items and are presented orally—reading is not required. In the revised version, 34 of the 277 items were replaced based on feedback from users about clarity, vocabulary, accuracy, content appropriateness, and difficulty. Students mark a true or false response or select a picture.

The *SPIB* was standardized on over 900 junior and senior high school students with mental retardation in Oregon who were mostly Caucasian. In terms of test construction, 26 secondary teachers of students with mental retardation helped choose long- and short-range objectives in community adjustment. The total battery median internal consistency and test-retest reliability coefficients for both junior and senior high students were above .90. Performance on the *SPIB*, current counselor ratings, and vocational rehabilitation counselors' ratings of postschool adjustment were related at a moderate level. Normative data for the

---

SOCIAL AND PREVOCATIONAL INFORMATION BATTERY–REVISED (SPIB–R)
A. Halpern and L. K. Irvin (1986)

Type: Norm-referenced test
Content Areas: Job search skills, budgeting, purchasing, hygiene and grooming, and others
Type of Administration: Group
Administration Time: 15–25 minutes for each test; spread over three sessions but within a week
Age/Grade Levels: Junior and senior high school; mildly retarded students
Types of Scores: Raw scores, percentage correct, and reference group percentile rank
Typical Uses: Measures knowledge and skills considered important to community adjustment
Cautions: Standardized only on retarded students in Oregon

SPIB–R are being collected during the first several years of use.

The *SPIB–R* can be scored by computer or hand. An answer key can be used to speed manual scoring. Each correct answer is a point, and subtest scores and total scores are converted to percentage correct scores. Conversion tables for each test and the total are available for comparing a student's performance to the percentage correct and percentiles of the reference group, either junior or senior high level. A typical interpretation is

A junior high school student who achieved a raw score of 26 on the Banking Test correctly answered 84% of the items and scored better than approximately 93% of the students in the reference group.

Test of Practical Knowledge (TPK). The *TPK* is a test of knowledge about facts believed to be important for daily functioning. The 100 items are grouped into three factors: Personal Knowledge, Social Knowledge, and Occupational Knowledge (including definitions of terms such as *job reference, strike, interest income;* computation of salary and benefits; and job application procedures). It can be used to identify students with deficits in practical knowledge, establish areas of strengths and weaknesses, and monitor learning. *TPK* is a silent reading test with a multiple-choice format; answers are marked on a separate sheet. Its readability level varies; 12 of 17 measures are written below the eighth grade reading level.

The *TPK* was standardized on 1,398 students in 11 states, with almost equal numbers of males and females. Items were drawn from studies of functional competency and a summary of competencies and were factor analyzed into the three areas in the current test. Internal consistency reliability and test-retest reliability coefficients for the *TPK* Total Score were in the .80s and .90s. The *TPK* compared well to the *Iowa Tests of Educational Development* and the *SRA Achievement Series* (median coefficients being .64 to .57, respectively); it correlated with the *WISC* in a range from .23 to .60 and differentiated normal and disabled students.

For scoring, a template with correct answers can be laid on top of the Student Answer Sheet. The raw score for each subject is recorded on the Student Profile Sheet and converted to stanines and percentiles. The total percentile score can be converted to the Practical Knowledge Quotient (PKQ), with a mean of 100 and SD of 15 points. Stanine scores can be plotted on a profile, the average range being 4 to 6. In the case of the sample Profile in Figure 19–3, the PKQ of 93 is considered average. Practical knowledge in personal and social areas is average, but below average in the occupational area.

Others. Kokaska and Brolin (1985) use a competency-based assessment approach in conjunction with a total career education curriculum. The competencies are divided into three areas: Daily Living Skills, Personal-Social Skills, and Occupational Guidance and Preparation. A student is assessed in the competency areas and, if deficits are found, is given the necessary instruction.

TEST OF PRACTICAL KNOWLEDGE (TPK)
J. L. Wiederholt and S. C. Larsen (1983)

Type: Norm-referenced test
Major Content Areas: Functional competency
Type of Administration: Group
Administration Time: 30–45 minutes
Age/Grade Levels: Grades 8–12 (ages 12–11 to 18–8)
Types of Scores: Raw scores, stanines, percentiles, and Practical Knowledge Quotient
Typical Uses: Measures adaptive behavior and prevocational knowledge
Cautions: Demands for silent reading skills and group administration conditions may adversely affect mildly handicapped students

Therefore, these competencies are the basis of both assessment and programming.

This assessment system generates data that can be directly applied in instructional planning. The student's deficit competencies in daily living and occupational skills are placed in an IEP format and become the basis for goals and objectives. The career education activities are integrated into the student's entire program. The attainment of goals will be measured by the same competency checklist. This assessment approach and curriculum in career education for the handicapped are

FIGURE 19–3
Test of Practical Knowledge profile

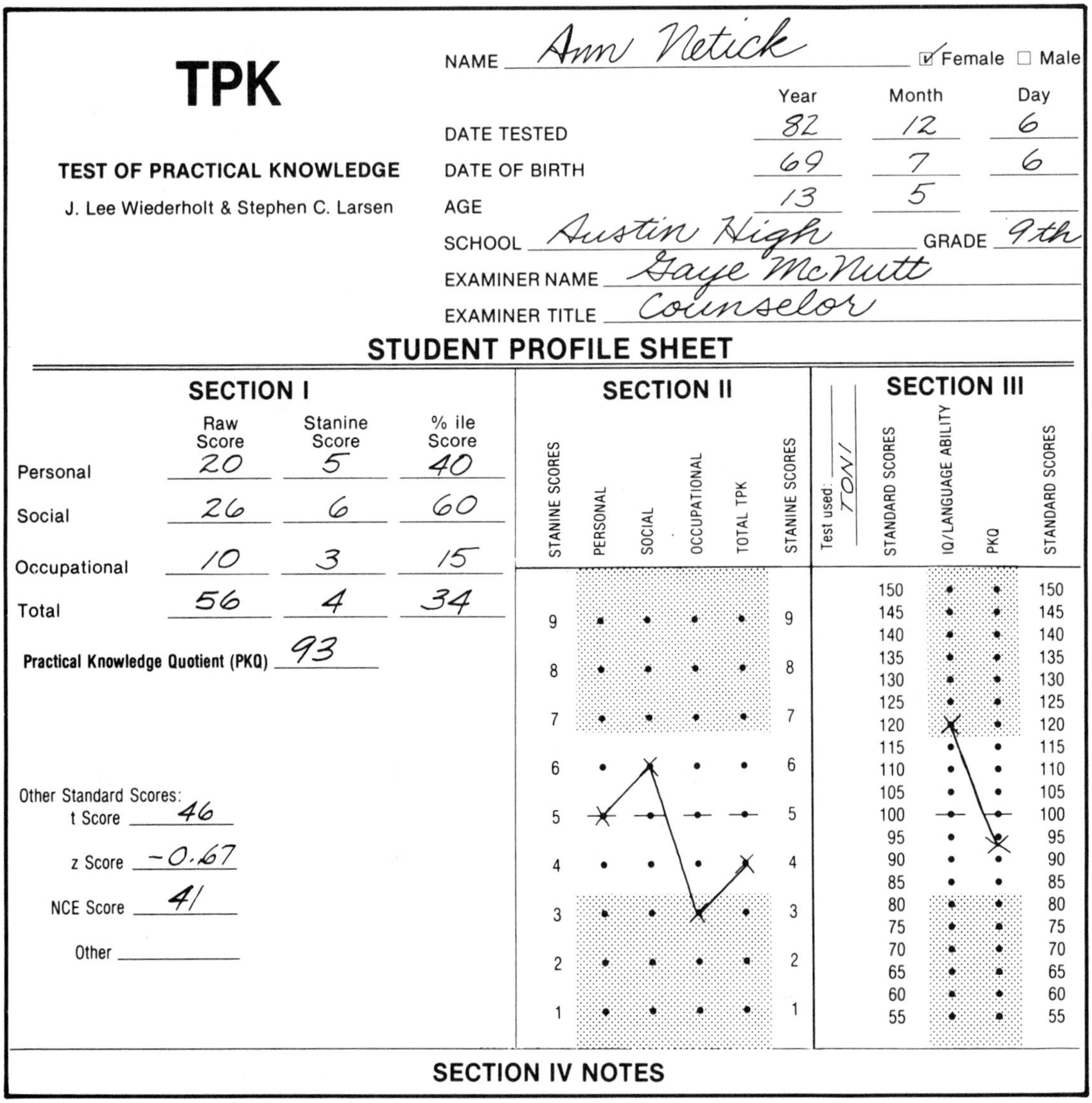

TPK

TEST OF PRACTICAL KNOWLEDGE

J. Lee Wiederholt & Stephen C. Larsen

NAME Ann Netick ☑ Female ☐ Male

	Year	Month	Day
DATE TESTED	82	12	6
DATE OF BIRTH	69	7	6
AGE	13	5	

SCHOOL Austin High GRADE 9th

EXAMINER NAME Gaye McNutt

EXAMINER TITLE Counselor

STUDENT PROFILE SHEET

SECTION I

	Raw Score	Stanine Score	% ile Score
Personal	20	5	40
Social	26	6	60
Occupational	10	3	15
Total	56	4	34

Practical Knowledge Quotient (PKQ) 93

Other Standard Scores:
t Score 46
z Score −0.67
NCE Score 41
Other

SECTION II

SECTION III

SECTION IV NOTES

Note. From *Test of Practical Knowledge* (p. 18) by J. L. Wiederholt and S. C. Larsen, 1983, Austin, TX: PRO-ED. Copyright 1983 by J. L. Wiederholt and S. C. Larsen. Reprinted by permission.

described in *Life-Centered Career Education: A Competency-Based Approach* (Brolin, 1978, 1983).

The *BRIGANCE® Diagnostic Inventory of Essential Skills* (Brigance, 1981) contains aspects of career and vocational assessment to determine a person's level of awareness and knowledge about occupations, as well as to answer other assessment questions concerning reading and understanding employment vocabulary, abbreviations, and ads. The subtests can be used to gather baseline data and later evaluation information and can also be related to other assessment systems or school district competency lists. Kokaska and Brolin (1985, Appendix, pp. 403–409) provide a chart connecting vocational and other skills in this *BRIGANCE® Inventory* with the career education competencies just described.

Another form of assessment is job analysis, a systematic way of observing jobs to determine what the individual does, how and why he or she does it, and the skill involved in performance. During field trips, students can be encouraged to complete a form containing such considerations as a brief description of the work, the skills required for the job (academics, physical demands, etc.), work conditions (noise, heating, lighting, ventilation, etc.), training required, salary and hours, and good and poor features of the job. The information can be reviewed and discussed later with the student in probing realistic knowledge and interests. If students are suitably interested, the jobs can be broken down by task analysis.

Additionally, the assessment team must consider the results of examination of work awareness and knowledge in connection with the students' opportunities for experience, sociocultural background, and so on. Their cognitive, academic, or behavior disabilities may restrict their ability to notice and examine vocational options. Some may be slower than their peers in acquiring interest and knowledge in this area.

What Are the Aptitudes and Work or Study Habits?

The assessment of prerequisite aptitudes can be a complex task. Generally included in this area are intellectual, academic, and linguistic requirements. Aptitudes covered in most vocational aptitude surveys are numerical, spatial, form perception, clerical perception (e.g., proofreading words and

numbers), motor coordination, finger dexterity, manual dexterity, eye-hand-foot coordination, and color discrimination. Many questions are raised about not only the definition and measurement of aptitudes but also the relevance of tasks used in tests and their relationship to actual jobs.

These factors are measured in a variety of ways. For example, the *General Aptitude Test Battery (GATB)* (U.S. Department of Labor, 1970a), written at sixth grade reading level, has 12 subtests covering these areas. The *Nonreading Aptitude Test Battery (NATB)* (U.S. Department of Labor, 1970b) is a nonreading version of the *GATB* that measures the same factors but has no arithmetic problems and presents vocabulary items orally. The work samples listed and described later also probe such aptitudes. Following are descriptions of the *APTICOM® Occupational Aptitude Test Battery* (Jewish Employment & Vocational Services, 1985), *Occupational Aptitude Survey and Interest Schedule (OASIS–AS)* (Parker, 1983), a variety of measures of manual dexterity, and some informal procedures.

APTICOM® Occupational Aptitude Test Battery.

The *Aptitude Test Battery* is a portion of the *APTICOM®* system, which also assesses interests and academically related skills. It is a norm-referenced survey of general learning, verbal, numerical, spatial, form perception, clerical perception, motor coordination, and finger and manual dexterity aptitudes. A group or individually administered test requiring 60 to 90 minutes along with the other portions, the *Aptitude Test Battery* is appropriate for junior and senior high school students and adults. Eleven tests measure aptitudes derived by the Department of Labor and related to occupational success.

APTICOM® is a portable desktop microcomputer. Students electronically mark their responses with a pin. The test is self-scoring, and students can pace themselves.

APTICOM® Occupational Aptitude Test Battery was standardized on over 300 students in different parts of the country whose characteristics are described in the technical manual (p. 12). The validity coefficients with the U.S. Department of Labor's *General Aptitude Test Battery* (GATB) ranged from .37 for motor coordination to .87 for general learning, with the median being .66. Reliability coefficients ranged from .65 to .89, the median being .82.

An individual report is generated with standard scores (mean = 100, SD = 20) and percentiles for each aptitude, as well as a profile of those that are average and below or above average. The percentile ratings allow comparison with the 1–5 rating system used in the *Dictionary of Occupational Titles (DOT)*. These data are also integrated with the results from interest and skill assessment.

Occupational Aptitude Survey and Interest Schedule (OASIS–AS).

The *Aptitude Survey* portion of the *OASIS–AS* is a norm-referenced survey of aptitudes for the world of work. A group or individually administered test requiring about 35 minutes, with norms available for students in grades 8 through 12, the *OASIS–AS* is appropriate for junior and senior high students. There are five subtests: Vocabulary, Computation, Spatial Relations, Word Comparison, and Making Marks. The five subtests represent six different vocational aptitudes:

Subtest	Aptitude Areas
Vocabulary and Computation	General Ability
Vocabulary	Verbal
Computation	Numerical
Spatial Relations	Spatial
Word Comparison	Perceptual
Making Marks	Manual Dexterity

Students read the student booklet and mark the answer sheet; the tester must time each subtest carefully. A stencil with the correct multiple-choice answers for the first four subtests is provided, and criteria are given in the manual for scoring the subtest Making Marks.

The *OASIS–AS* was standardized on 1,398 different 8th through 12th grade students from 11 states; they were mainly whites from urban areas. The median reliability coefficient across five grade levels was approximately .86; the SEM for raw scores ranged from 1.5 to 4.4 points. The majority of comparisons with achievement tests and the *General Aptitude Test Battery (GATB)* fell in the .80s.

Several scores are available on the *OASIS–AS*: raw scores, 5-point score, percentile, and stanine. The 5-point score is used in a variety of vocational guidance materials as an indicator of potential for certain occupations: 1 = the upper 10% of the scores and 5 = the lower 10%. For the stanine scale, the average score is 5 (SD = 1.96).

As shown in the sample profile (Figure 19–4), the 12th grade student's stanines are both above and below the average of 5. Using the aptitude factors measured by the subtests, relative strengths are General Ability, Verbal, Numerical, and Spatial. Perceptual and Manual Dexterity are relative weaknesses. By matching the 5-point score to those needed for a list of occupations provided in the manual (pp. 30–34), this student's aptitudes appear to fit the demands for both electrical engineering and law.

APTICOM® OCCUPATIONAL APTITUDE TEST BATTERY
Jewish Employment and Vocational Services (1985)

Type: Norm-referenced survey
Major Content Areas: General learning, verbal, numerical, spatial, form perception, clerical perception, motor coordination, finger dexterity, manual dexterity
Type of Administration: Group or individual
Administration Time: 90 minutes (including interest and skill batteries)
Age/Grade Levels: Junior and senior high school students and adults
Types of Scores: Standard scores and percentiles
Typical Uses: Screen aptitudes to guide counseling and plan preparation
Cautions: Validation studies with actual field performance are needed; also, complete survey should be administered to a suitable standardization sample

FIGURE 19-4
OASIS Aptitude Survey

OASIS APTITUDE SURVEY
STUDENT PROFILE AND ANSWER SHEET
RANDALL M. PARKER

NAME: _Johnson   John   A._
(PRINT)   Last   First   Middle

DATE OF BIRTH: Mo:_6_ Day:_1_ Yr:_70_   TODAY'S DATE: Mo:_8_ Day:_14_ Yr:_87_

SEX: M_✓_; F____   GRADE:_12_   SCHOOL:_Mary Wanda High_

DO NOT WRITE BELOW THIS LINE

SECTION I — RECORD OF SCORES

SUBTEST	RAW SCORE	APTITUDE FACTOR	FIVE POINT SCORE	PERCENTILE	STANINE
Vocabulary + Computation	54	G	1	90	8
Vocabulary	33	V	1	90	8
Computation	20	N	2	75	6
Spatial Relations	13	S	2	75	7
Word Comparison	33	P	3	50	4
Making Marks	66	M	3	50	5

SECTION II — PROFILE OF SCORES
OASIS APTITUDE FACTORS

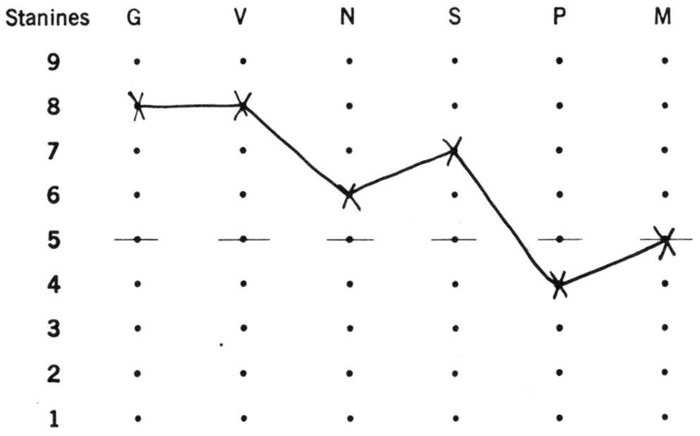

Stanines	G	V	N	S	P	M
9	·	·	·	·	·	·
8	X	X	·	·	·	·
7	·	·	·	X	·	·
6	·	·	X	·	·	·
5	—	—	—	—	·	X
4	·	·	·	·	X	·
3	·	·	·	·	·	·
2	·	·	·	·	·	·
1	·	·	·	·	·	·

Note. From *OASIS Aptitude Survey* by R. M. Parker, 1983, Austin, TX: PRO-ED. Copyright 1983 by R. M. Parker. Reprinted by permission.

*OCCUPATIONAL APTITUDE SURVEY AND INTEREST SURVEY–THE APTITUDE SURVEY
(OASIS–AS)*

R. Parker (1983)

Type: Norm-referenced survey
Major Content Areas: Vocabulary, computation, spatial relations, word comparison, and making marks
Type of Administration: Group or individual
Administration Time: 35 minutes
Age/Grade Levels: Grades 8–12
Types of Scores: 5-point scale, percentile, and stanine
Typical Uses: Screen aptitudes for various types of work
Cautions: Note the time factor and demands for reading and marking the answer sheet with multiple columns; also standardized on mainly white, urban students

Manual dexterity tests. Many occupations require fine motor dexterity and eye-hand coordination. The following tests generally require the placement and/or joining of small screws, bolts and nuts, and similar objects. Tool usage may also be needed. They may serve to establish entry level dexterity skills, help students identify realistic jobs, and provide motivation to acquire needed skills (Kokaska & Brolin, 1985).

☐ *Bennett Hand Tool Dexterity Test* (Bennett, 1969). Students use ordinary mechanic's tools to disassemble and assemble a series of bolts (5–20 minutes).

☐ *Crawford Small Parts Dexterity Test* (Crawford & Crawford, 1956). Students use tweezers to pick up a pin, place it in a hole on a board, and put a collar over it. After all 36 pins and collars are in place, 30 screws are placed through a plate with a screwdriver (15 minutes).

☐ *Purdue Pegboard* (Purdue Research Foundation, 1968). Students place pins in holes with the right, left, and both hands. They also assemble pins, collars, and washers on a board in a minute's time (10 minutes).

☐ *Pennsylvania BiManual Work Sample* (Roberts, 1945). Students assemble and disassemble 105 nuts and bolts and place them in holes on a board (10–15 minutes).

☐ *Talent Assessment Program* (Talent Assessment Inc., 1972, 1980, 1985, 1988). Students perform 10 work samples of gross and fine

finger and manual dexterity, visual and tactile discrimination, and retention of details ($2\frac{1}{2}$ hours).

☐ *McCarron Assessment of Neuromuscular Development–Revised* (McCarron, 1976, 1982). Students perform various fine and gross motor tasks, including bimanual dexterity, persistent control, balance, and muscle power (15 minutes).

☐ *Haptic Visual Discrimination Test* (McCarron & Dial, 1976). Using touch only, students recognize objects by their shape, texture, size and configuration, as well as recognize objects from photographs (15 minutes).

These measures can be very frustrating for mildly handicapped students with fine motor coordination problems and a desire to do these or related kinds of jobs. In such cases, the assessment team may use results to direct remediation in these areas and also explore alternative ways for students to perform similar tasks with automated or other forms of assistance. They must avoid using performance on such measures as a general predictor of vocational ability.

Others. Examination of other available information can also be used to answer the question about aptitudes and work or study skills. Assessment data concerning intelligence, adaptive behavior, academics, communication skills, and so forth can supplement any information gathered by these procedures. Interviews of the students, parents, and teachers can document work experience, current demonstration of required aptitudes, and motivation to work.

Appropriate work or study habits are very important. In addition to broad technical entry skills for work, a set of work and study habits are critical for success on the job, in college, and so forth. Direct questioning of students, parents, and teachers or observations will reveal their presence. Some interview concepts taken from the Attitude Rating Scale of the *BRIGANCE® Diagnostic Inventory of Essential Skills* (Brigance, 1981) are

☐ Applies himself or herself when given a task
☐ Is receptive to direction and suggestions
☐ Accepts criticism without pouting or getting angry (p. 256)

This *BRIGANCE® Inventory* also contains other rating scales in the areas of responsibility, self-discipline, and personality. See Chapter 10 for more information on assessing behavior and social skills.

What Are the Career or Vocational Interests?

Student interests and preferences must be accounted for in developing suitable career and vocational preparation plans. However, assessing interests is not easy. Many well-known and commonly used interest inventories have proven to be unsatisfactory with handicapped persons because of the requirements for verbal abilities and broad work experience (Brolin, 1982). Some persons have inappropriate perceptions about jobs and low expectations for themselves. As Table 19–1 indicates, a number of measures available for special

populations have reduced requirements in reading. The *Reading-Free Vocational Interest Inventory–Revised* (Becker, 1981, 1988) and the *Wide Range Interest-Opinion Test (WRIOT)* (Jastak & Jastak, 1979) are representative of pictorial surveys. In addition, there is a potential assessment role for needs assessment, interviews, criterion-referenced tests, and other informal approaches.

Reading-Free Vocational Interest Inventory–Revised (R-FVII–R). The *R-FVII–R* is a picture interest inventory to measure vocational interests of mentally retarded and learning disabled students. It consists of 55 sets of 3 pictures; in each set, the student chooses the most appealing picture in terms of the work represented. As indicated in Figure 19–5, the student circles a person raking leaves as the job he or she would most like to do. There is no reading or writing involved. Directions are read, and testers check that students are marking the form correctly when working in a group. The results can be used for vocational planning and placement. The 1988 manual provides additional norms for disadvantaged adults and school-aged students with moderate mental retardation.

The *R-FVII–R* was normed on over 8,000 learning disabled and mentally retarded public school students (grades 7 through 12) and over 2,000 mentally retarded persons from community sheltered workshops and vocational training centers in a variety of states. Test-retest reliability coefficients are mainly in the .70s and .80s, with SEMs of 1

READING-FREE VOCATIONAL INTEREST INVENTORY (REVISED) (R-FVII–R)
R. C. Becker (1981, 1988)

Type: Norm-referenced inventory
Content Areas: Vocational areas
Type of Administration: Group
Administration Time: 20 minutes
Age/Grade Levels: Public school (Grades 7 to 12 and ages 13–22); sheltered workshop (ages 17–59)
Types of Scores: T-scores, percentiles, and stanines
Typical Uses: Identify vocational interests
Cautions: Combine results with other data; more studies of validity are needed

TABLE 19–1
Interest inventories

Instrument	Age/Grade Level	Group Admin.	Indiv. Admin.	Approx. Admin. Time	OCCUPATIONS TARGETED			Reading Required (Grade level, if reported)	No Reading Required
					General (Includes both Voc-Tech and professional occupations)	Voc-Tech (Up to 2 yrs. of training)	Professional (Minimum of 4 yr. college degree)		
APTICOM® Occupational Interest Inventory (JEVS, 1985)	9th grade–Adult	up to 4 X	X	20 min.	X			4th grade	
Career Assessment Inventory–Enhanced (Johansson, 1986)	8th grade–Adult	X	X	40 min.	X			8th grade	
Career Assessment Inventory–Vocational (Johansson, 1982)	8th grade–Adult	X	X	20–25 min.		X		6th grade +	
Geist Picture Interest Inventory–Revised (Geist, 1964)	8th grade–Adult	X	X	30–50 min.	X				X
Gordon Occupational Checklist II (Gordon, 1980)	8th grade–Adult	X	X	20–25 min.		X		X	
Kuder General Interest Survey–Form E (Kuder, 1988)	6–8th grade & 9–12th grade	X	X	40–50 min.	X			6th grade	
Kuder Occupational Interest Survey Form–DD (Kuder, 1985)	10th grade–Adult	X	X	30–40 min.			X	6th grade	
Kuder Preference Record–Vocational (Kuder C–Kuder E) (Kuder, 1978)	9th–12th grade	X	X	30–60 min.	X			9th grade	
Minnesota Vocational Interest Inventory (Clark & Campbell, 1966)	9th grade–Adult	X	X	45 min.		X		Approx. 6th grade	
Occupational Aptitude Survey and Interest Schedule (OASIS) (Parker, 1983)	8th–12th grade	X	X	30 min.	X			X	
Reading-Free Vocational Interest Inventory–Revised (Becker, 1981, 1988)	9th grade–Adult	X	X	20 min.		X			X
Strong-Campbell Interest Inventory (Campbell & Hansen, 1981, 1985)	8th grade–Adult	X	X	30–60 min.			X	8th grade	
USES Interest Inventory II (U.S. Department of Labor, 1982)	10th grade–Adult	X	X	25–30 min.	X			X	
Wide Range Interest-Opinion Test (WRIOT) (Jastak & Jastak, 1979)	7th grade–Adult	X	X	40–60 min.	X				X

Note. Adapted from *Vocational Assessment of Secondary Special Needs Students* by Illinois State Board of Education, 1987. Springfield, IL: Illinois State Board of Education. Reprinted by permission.

FIGURE 19-5
Sample item from the *Reading-Free Vocational Interest Inventory*

  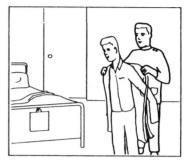

Note. From *Reading-Free Vocational Interest Inventory–Revised* (p. 1) by R. L. Becker, 1981, Columbus, OH: Elbern Publications. Copyright 1981 by Elbern Publications. Reprinted by permission.

or 2 points. The median internal consistency co-efficient was .82. Picture items were chosen from jobs thought appropriate by study teams for the mentally retarded and learning disabled. Comparisons to performances on the *Geist Picture Interest Inventory (GPII)* (Geist, 1964) were almost all significant at the .05 or .01 level; a study of mentally retarded students reported in the manual indicated a high relationship of job occupation and job interest on the *R-FVII–R.*

The raw scores are converted to T-scores, percentiles, and stanines. Percentile scores are plotted on a profile according to the 11 areas. Interests above the 75th percentile are considered high and those below the 25th as low. The student's profile in Figure 19–6 indicates high interests in clerical, patient care, and personal service areas. Low interests are in automotive, building trades, animal care, food service, and horticulture. These results should be combined with other data. The *Occupational Title Lists* (Becker, 1984) can be used to match interests to relevant occupations.

Wide Range Interest-Opinion Test (WRIOT).

The *WRIOT* surveys interests in vocational areas. It consists of 450 pictures arranged in 150 combinations of 3. Males and females are given the same 400 pictures. The activities portrayed are representative of those listed in the *Dictionary of Occupational Titles (DOT).* They cluster into 26 groups: 18 areas of interest (such as sales, social

service, and mechanics) and 8 areas of attitudes (such as sedentariness, risk, and ambition).

Students examine three pictures and mark the letter on an answer sheet corresponding with the most attractive and least appealing ones. Directions are read to students, and they do not need to read or write.

The *WRIOT* was standardized on 9,184 individuals distributed unevenly by sex and across seven age groups. No attempt was made to obtain representative national sampling, and according to the manual, "males and females were selected separately according to mental ability criteria in such a way as to represent appropriate proportions of average, superior, and inferior persons" (p. 32). Split-half reliability coefficients reported in the manual for 150 males ranged from .84 to .95 and for 150 females from .82 to .95. The manual reports comparisons to responses on the *Geist Picture Interest Inventory: Men and Women* (Geist, 1964); some relationships were significant.

The *WRIOT* can be scored by computer through the publisher or with a set of stencils. A T-score (from 21 to 80) is obtained from the appropriate age/sex table for each Raw Score. The T-score is plotted on the Profile by putting a 0 below T-scores of 50, a line of plus signs to the point above 50 where the T-score occurs on the graph, and a line of minus signs to the point below 50 where the T-score occurs. The T-scores are divided into ranges on the Profile with semantic descriptions; for example, 44–56 is average.

FIGURE 19–6
Reading-Free Vocational Interest Inventory

INDIVIDUAL PROFILE SHEET

Last Name __Wilson__ First __Tom__ Date __8-29-81__

Grade __9__ Age: __15__ yrs. __2__ mos. Date of Birth __6-29-66__

School __C.C.S.__ City __Columbus__ State __Ohio__

Male Norm Used __EMR, 13-15__ Female Norm Used _____

Key Letter	Raw Score	T Score	Percentile	Stanine	Interest Area	Symbol	Interest High	Interest Low
A	1	31	3	1	Automotive	Auto		✓
B	4	31	3	1	Building Trades	B Tr		✓
C	11	66	95	8	Clerical	Cl	✓	
D	1	34	5	2	Animal Care	An Cr		✓
E	2	40	15	3	Food Service	F S		✓
F	10	66	95	8	Patient Care	P Cr	✓	
G	3	40	15	3	Horticulture	Hort		✓
H	7	43	25	4	Housekeeping	Hsk		
I	16	71	98	9	Personal Service	P Sv	✓	
J	5	55	70	6	Laundry Service	Ly		
K	5	49	45	5	Materials Handling	M Hg		

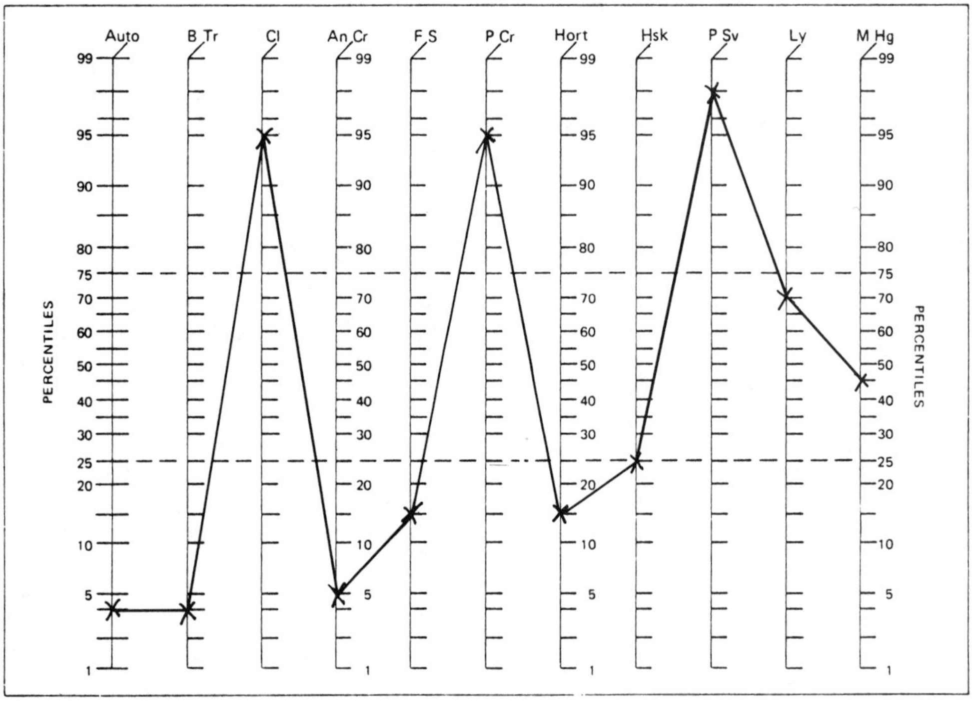

The two parts of the *WRIOT* Profile, vocational areas (A–R) and personal attitudes (S–Z), are interpreted separately. The largest positive interest areas, the largest negative interest areas, and those falling in the median or average range are analyzed. For example, a sample interpretation is

Mike has particularly strong interests in physical science, mathematics, mechanics, machine operation, protective services, and social science. He seems very positive in his attitudes and is highly motivated to do well.

Others. In addition to examining students' interests, it may be necessary to perform needs assessments among faculty, parents, and the community. Also, during the implementation of the plan and afterwards, assessment of the needs and priorities of involved groups can suggest much-needed improvements. Questions such as *Is mainstreaming an effective way to provide career education to these students?* and *Is career education intended for students not able to succeed in an academic program?* can be posed to school personnel to measure their orientation to career education for handicapped students (Brolin et al., 1978). Depending on the audience, questionnaires or interviews can be used to measure priorities and reactions.

Also, the work community needs to be surveyed to establish current perceptions of handicapped students, availability of jobs, and accommodations that need to be and can be made for students. For students interested in occupations requiring advanced training or with aspirations for higher education, technical schools and colleges need to be surveyed. These data should be combined with student interests to aid in realistic planning.

All too often students are simply not asked about their career and vocational aspirations, impressions, and interests. The tests and complex measurement systems structure the assessment process so that they may not get an opportunity to express themselves comfortably. Therefore, interviewing students is a very handy tool and provides an opportunity to observe their physical appearance, communication skills, and so forth. Interviews are also useful vehicles for contacting the families of clients, who influence their career and vocational aims. Parents and other family members shape a person's interests and aspirations by their own type of employment and experience, opinions about careers and work, and so forth. Such information helps explain student entry behavior and alerts educators to environmental factors that might influence student performance and motivation.

Criterion-referenced tests such as the *BRIGANCE® Diagnostic Inventory of Essential Skills* (Brigance, 1981) can also be used to assess student occupational interests, especially Job Interest and Aptitudes. Among the items are, "Do you prefer to work alone or with others? Would you prefer to work with people or to work with objects? and Would you prefer a job which requires a lot of training to develop skills or one that requires little training?" (p. 259).

WIDE RANGE INTEREST-OPINION TEST (WRIOT)
J. Jastak and S. Jastak (1979)

Type: Norm-referenced test
Major Content Areas: 18 areas, including sales, office work, mechanics, machine operation, art, literature, drama, and music
Type of Administration: Group or individual
Administration Time: 40 minutes
Age/Grade Levels: Age 5 through adulthood
Types of Scores: T-scores, percentiles, standard scores, stanines, and scaled scores
Typical Uses: Measures vocational interest and attitude
Cautions: Student may lose place on answer sheet; validity needs further study

What Are the Skills for Specific Work?

Work samples are meant to assess students' skills and attitudes on tasks similar to ones they are apt to perform. Samples offer an opportunity to observe work habits and assess levels of interest. A variety of published work sample analyses are designed for special populations, as indicated in Table 19–2.

The commercially designed analyses are related to the specific jobs or job families noted in the *Dictionary of Occupational Titles (DOT)* (U.S. Department of Labor, 1977, 1982, 1986). In selecting a work sample, consider whether the system takes into account expectancy to fail and academic, verbal, and experiential limitations; allows for more than one trial, repetition of instructions, and checks

for comprehension; and has appropriate content and predictive validity and norms for handicapped persons (Brolin, 1982). The *Wide Range Employability Sample Test* (WREST) (Jastak & Jastak, 1980) and the *Singer Vocational Evaluation System (VES)* (Singer, 1982) will be discussed. Additional assessment possibilities are the design of one's own work samples, the use of simulations, and other informal techniques. It is particularly important to draw on the experience of employers, work supervisors, and co-workers to validate job descriptors as well as to use job clubs.

Wide Range Employability Sample Test (WREST). The *WREST* evaluates productivity and technical work skills through 10 concrete tasks,

TABLE 19–2
Work samples/work evaluation systems

Instrument	Age/Grade Level	Group Admin.	Indiv. Admin.	Approx. Admin. Time
Jewish Employment Vocational Service Work Sample System (JEVS, 1976)	14 yrs.– adult	small group	X	28 work samples, 6–7 days
McCarron-Dial Work Evaluation System (McCarron & Dial, 1976)	14 yrs.– adult		X	1 day of test, 2 weeks observation
Microcomputer Evaluation of Career Areas (MECA) (Schmitz, 1985, 1986)	Grades 6–10	multiple computers	X	15 components, 20 min. each
Micro-Tower (Bachman, 1976)	14 yrs.– adult	small group	X	3–5 days
PREP Work Samples (Prep, 1976)	9th grade– adult	small group	X	26 work samples 2 hrs. each
Valpar Component Work Sample System (Brandon, Balton, Rup & Raslter, 1974)	14 yrs. +	small group	X	varies; timed to completion
Valpar #17–Prevocational Readiness Battery (Valpar Corp., 1978)	14 yrs. +		X	5½ hrs.
Vocational Information and Evaluation Work Samples (VIEWS) (Mandelbaum, Rosen & Miller, 1977)	14 yrs. +	small group	X	30 hours
Vocational Interest, Temperament and Aptitude System (VITAS) (JEVS, 1980)	9th grade and up	small group	X	15 hrs.
Wide Range Employability Sample Test (WREST) (Jastak & Jastak, 1980)	14 yrs. +	up to 6 people	X	1½ –2 hours

Note: Adapted from *Vocational Assessment of Secondary Special Needs Students* by Illinois State Board of Education, 1987. Springfield, IL: Illinois State Board of Education. Reprinted by permission.

WIDE RANGE EMPLOYABILITY SAMPLE TEST (WREST)
J. Jastak and S. Jastak (1980)

Type: Norm-referenced test
Major Content Areas: Folding, stapling, packaging, color matching, and others
Type of Administration: Group and individual
Administration Time: 1½–2 hours
Age/Grade Levels: Ages 16–54
Types of Scores: Standard scores
Typical Uses: Measuring efficiency and attitude
Cautions: Tests are timed; standardized only in one state

---

as indicated in Figure 19–7. Students must perform a series of eye-hand coordination tasks after demonstrations and practice trials. One- and two-step instructions are involved. The test requires minimal math skills and no reading. The practice trials are not timed, but the tests are. However, the worker can complete the task even if the designated time is up. Suggestions for modifications for specific handicapping conditions are given in the manual.

The *WREST* was standardized on about 5,000 persons in Delaware, who were distributed in representative groups of ability on intelligence tests. Test-retest correlations of two administrations of the *WREST* to 428 workers yielded coefficients all above .90 on both time taken and number of errors. For validity, ratings of foperepersons and supervisors of 428 workers were correlated with the quantity standard scores (.86) and quality standard scores (.92). The average variability or spread of scaled scores was 5 to 7 points.

The tester records the amount of time and number of errors after each test on the Summary Profile. Criteria for judging errors are stated clearly in the manual, but in case of doubt the manual encourages leniency. Scaled scores (upper right-hand corner of Profile) for the time scores are recorded from the appropriate tables for three normative groups: general population, sheltered workshop, and industrial sample. Three total scores can be tallied and standard scores recorded on the Profile: production quality (error total), production quantity (time total), and technical productivity rating (average of the two). As noted on the Profile, scaled scores of 8 to 12 are considered

average for worker productivity. Also, workers are observed and rated for behavior and attitudes on the Standard Score Scale (lower right-hand box on Profile) at or near the end of the tests. An Average rating is from 90 to 109, Good is 110 to 119, and so forth.

When Phillip was administered the *WREST,* he appeared slightly below average in production quantity and close to high average in production quality. He had some problems with finger dexterity and spatial abilities but demonstrated better coordination, color discrimination, manual dexterity, and ability to follow oral instructions and demonstrations.

The Singer Vocational Evaluation System (VES). The *VES* is a set of 27 work samples that provide information for vocational training and placement. Some skill areas covered are drafting, electric wiring, plumbing and pipe fitting, refrigeration and air conditioning, sales processing, masonry, sheet metal, cooking and baking, engine service, medical services, cosmetology, data calculation and recording, filing, shipping and receiving, packaging and materials handling, electronics assembly, office services, and basic laboratory analysis. The *VES* was designed to provide simulated hands-on experience in selected occupations from the *Dictionary of Occupational Titles (DOT)* specifically for special needs populations, that is, socially and educationally disadvantaged, mildly retarded, and physically handicapped. The presentation is audiovisual, removing many demands for reading.

FIGURE 19–7 *Wide Range Employability Sample Test*

WREST

WIDE RANGE EMPLOYABILITY SAMPLE TEST

JOSEPH F. JASTAK, Ph.D.
SARAH JASTAK, Ph. D.

SUMMARY PROFILE

NAME: _Bill_ AGE: 19 SEX: Ⓜ F DATE: _____

WORK GOALS: _None_

DISABILITIES: _Below average intellectual level and academic achievement_ EVALUATOR: _____

X General Population
– Sheltered Workshop
o Industrial

EMPLOYABILITY SAMPLE		RAW SCORES			NORMS			PROFILE						
		QUANTITY	QUALITY	TOTAL POPUL.	SHELT. WKSP.	INDUST. SAMPLE	VERY POOR	POOR		AVERAGE		GOOD	VERY GOOD	
		MIN./SEC.	ERRORS	MIN./SEC.	ERRORS	QUANTITY SCALED SCORES		2	4	6	8 10 12	14 16	18	
1. FOLDING	A	0'58"	0	8'11"	0	10	16	11						
	B	7'19"	0											
2. STAPLING	A	2'15"	1	5'10"	1	8	14	8						
	B	2'55"	0											
3. PACKAGING				3'42"	0	10	13	9						
4. MEASURING				2'24"	0	9	15	7						
5. STRINGING				4'39"	1	6	9	0						
6. GLUING				2'54"	0	8	13	5						
7. COLLATING				1'06"	0	8	13	10						
8. COLOR MATCHING				1'46"	0	10	14	13						
9. PATTERN MATCHING				4'00"	2	7	11	6						
10. ASSEMBLING				4'09"	0	7	12	5						
TOTALS FOR ALL SAMPLES			4			83	130	74		60 70 80	90 100 110 120 130 140			
PRODUCTION QUALITY (ERRORS) STANDARD SCORE						110	118	114						
PRODUCTION QUANTITY (TIME) STANDARD SCORE						88	122	82						
TECHNICAL PRODUCTIVITY RATING						99	120	98						

O B S E R V A T I O N S			EVALUATOR RATINGS X—
	APPEARANCE	_Dress appropriate, pleasant but slow manner_ NOTES	
	ATTENDANCE	_One absence_	
	PUNCTUALITY	_Late twice_	
	PERSERVERANCE	_Easily distracted_	
	ORGANIZATION OF WORK	_Not remarkable_	
	RELATIONS, CO-WORKERS	_Little opportunity to observe_	
	RELATIONS, SUPERVISOR	_Reserved, superficially cooperative_	
	FLEXIBILITY	_Slow to switch gears, cautious_	
	SAFETY PRACTICES	_Aware of dangers, cautious_	
	CONFORMITY TO RULES	_Not too aware_	

Note. From *Wide Range Employability Sample Test* (p. 69) by J. F. Jastak and S. Jastak, 1980, Wilmington, DE: Jastak Associates, Inc. Copyright 1980 by Jastak Associates, Inc. Reprinted by permission.

VES accommodates persons with limited reading ability who are poor in testing and lack work experience. The Technical Manual does not recommend use of the *VES* with persons having severe visual and hearing problems, although adaptations are available for the deaf, the blind, and Spanish-speaking persons. Each work sample indicates the instructional reading comprehension level required to decode written material of the program script and the actual activity.

The test-retest reliability of the *VES* was demonstrated by significant coefficients for error (.71) and time (.61) scores as well as interest scores (.61). Content validity is based on the job analysis done from the *DOT* and other sources; it has relatively high predictive power for later employment in specifically related jobs and in more generally related jobs. Normative data are provided in the Technical Manual for each work sample in three ways: (a) a sample of nationwide participants (Participant Norms), (b) a sample of actual workers using the skill called for (Industrial Norms), and (c) ratings according to Methods-Time-Measurement (MTM) Standards. The Singer Career Systems will compute local norms if at least 31 administrations per work sample are sent in.

There is no prescribed sequence to follow in administering the work samples. Each one does not need to be given unless there is student interest, the job is available, and time permits. The work samples are set up at stations, including the filmstrip and cassette programs. Students are given a brief orientation to *VES*. Students record their interests on the Work Activity Ratings Form, using a 4-point scale. Instructions and stop–go points are noted on the tape. There are prescribed check points where evaluators determine the accuracy of student work and reinstruct or repeat the instructions if necessary. Evaluators observe students while they do the tasks and record observations on the Task Observation Record. At the end of the activity the students rate their interest in the job a second time, as well as their performance. The evaluator also rates the performance and discusses the ratings with the student. Work samples may be used again with the same students to measure learning.

Evaluators award 1 point for each student error; typical errors are described in each work sample manual insert. The beginning and ending times are also noted on the Work Activity Form. A student's number of errors and time are translated into ratings on a scale of 1 to 5 based on participant norms provided for each work sample or on other rating systems. These ratings are combined with student interest rating data and evaluator observation. For training placement, this information provides baseline data and possible factors affecting performance that need attention. When administered during or at the end of training, *VES* provides evidence of learning. *VES* may also aid in job placement, particularly for work very similar to the sample used.

Phillip was able to complete all the *VES* cooking and baking, small engine, and bench assembly samples, as long as the evaluator was nearby to

---

THE SINGER VOCATIONAL EVALUATION SYSTEM (VES)
The Singer Company Career Systems (1982)

Type: Norm-referenced and standardized test
Major Content Areas: Drafting, plumbing, cooking, filing, shipping, and others
Type of Administration: Individual or small group
Administration Time: 2–2½ hours
Age/Grade Levels: Adolescents and adults
Types of Scores: Time score, error score, and rating
Typical Uses: To establish interest, aptitude and ability in certain job components
Cautions: Not for severely vision- and hearing-impaired students; students may need assistance with A-V component; some work samples more predictive than others for later employment; an expensive system

intervene in difficult situations and provide encouragement. He recognized some tools at each of the work stations. Difficulties with finger dexterity and spatial abilities persisted on the bench assembly and small engine tasks. He expressed preference for the Cooking Sample above all others, stating that he did not mind the clean-up because he does that at home. Phillip does not seem very ambitious or self-disciplined.

Others. Sometimes it is more appropriate to develop a work or job sample for assessment purposes than to use a commercially prepared one. You may want to capture the key aspects of local work conditions, fill a gap in available work samples, or follow up on a job interest expressed by one or more students. According to Brolin (1982), the major types of work samples are

1. Indigenous work sample, representing the major elements of a local job
2. Job sample, replicating an actual industrial job
3. Cluster trait work sample, developed for a group of worker traits related to a series of jobs
4. Simulated work sample, replicating one segment of related work factors and tools of an industrial job
5. Single-trait work sample, evaluating one isolated characteristic that may be related to one specific job

The use of such samples in assessment accommodates typical problems of handicapped persons (test anxiety, language problems, attention deficits, and so forth), provides a chance to see a person demonstrate potential and interest, and thus develops a realistic basis for planning.

To develop a work sample, a series of activities are necessary (Brolin, 1982). First, local jobs should be catalogued by types of business, perhaps using the *DOT* guidelines. Also, more specific job reviews can be performed to identify particular information such as salaries and benefits, equipment and machines used, physical demands, and so forth. Second, decide what work samples should be developed, based on current availability, time expenditure and expense in development, training for the job possibilities in that area, and long-range usefulness of samples.

Third, the job is carefully analyzed in terms of needed preparation, required licenses, and available supervision, in addition to *DOT* standardized

concerns. A methods analysis about real and potential problem areas leads to improved work samples.

Fourth, construction of a mock-up work sample follows, with special attention given to the needs of the handicapped persons using it. Fifth, the sample should be normed on a large enough representative group, because use of industrial norms is usually inappropriate.

Sixth, work samples should be described in appropriate detail to permit standardized administration and easy understanding. Brolin (1982) considers the following elements essential: *DOT* Code, related jobs, prerequisites, workplace diagram and materials list, instructions for the evaluator, instructions for the evaluees, scoring procedures, interpretation, and special considerations. Seventh, work samples should be validated in a variety of ways, particularly by following up former users. Giving students the opportunity to do the job in actual industry is an important step in work sample design.

Another useful procedure to assess student aptitudes, skills, and interests in certain careers/ jobs is to provide simulated settings. Some schools have set up student-run minibusinesses, such as a store to sell school supplies or food. Even having students perform a project in an industrial fashion (for example, using an assembly line) can prove useful in acquainting them with work basics and in providing a basis for discussion. Schloss, Smith, Hoover, and Wolford (1987) provide a description of an assessment model that integrates many of these informal assessment approaches to assess not only competencies for specific work but also the individual's flexibility and coping skills.

There are a variety of formal measures available to accommodate the psychological, academic, and behavioral limitations of mildly handicapped persons. It is also important to note the many informal assessment techniques, such as student interviews and/or questionnaires, built into published or teacher-made work samples and simulations. Behaviorial observations are a critical aspect of this kind of assessment to measure student work habits, interpersonal skills, and so forth. Of particular interest is how diagnostic teaching techniques are employed at regular intervals to help students analyze their performance, ask questions, and get necessary assistance. These permit necessary task modifications to enhance performance. Appropriate individual plans can then be devised based on defined interests, demonstrated work competency, and observed job performance variables.

Replicating Jobs in Business and Industry for Persons with Disabilities (Tindall & Guserty, 1986, 1987, 1988) provides descriptions of jobs performed by persons with a variety of disabilities. This information can be used to develop more realistic and relevant preparation programs, job simulations, and actual jobs.

PROVIDING SERVICES

An appropriate secondary and postsecondary transitional program should be designed based on the completion of the necessary levels of assessment and the answers to the main assessment questions about career and vocational needs. The information about career and vocational knowledge, aptitude, study and social skills, interests, and technical skills is combined and needs are identified. Also, students' limitations in cognitive, academic, and behavioral areas must be taken into account when designing an IEP and a transitional program for integration into the community. Many of the procedures just described facilitate this program development by providing profiles of strengths and weaknesses and organizing the information into a comprehensive overview. For example, the *McCarron-Dial Evaluation System* (McCarron & Dial, 1986) organizes data from the instruments used to assess its various dimensions into an individual plan that integrates vocational considerations with content areas.

IEP Design

In the case of Phillip (see Chapter 15), vocational education is integrated with instruction in basic skills and content areas, such as social studies and science. Phillip lacks suitable knowledge of the world of work and must familiarize himself with occupational possibilities. Past experience, observations of his behavior on the *WREST* and *VES*, and his responses to items on the *BRIGANCE® Diagnostic Inventory of Essential Skills* (Brigance, 1981) indicate the need for developing appropriate work habits, such as timeliness and self-direction.

Like many mildly handicapped students, his secondary-level instruction of reading, mathematics, and spelling deficits must be done in the context of his total needs. Phillip's IEP indicates goals geared to making such remediation highly functional in terms of survival skills and vocational needs so he can read directions and use technical vocabulary. Language arts instruction is partially related to reading and using job application forms and bus schedules, composing a resume, and communicating on the telephone. Quantitative skills are practiced in reference to money use and management. Compensatory skill development is stressed, such as in the case of using a calculator for computation.

Phillip's IEP includes goals to develop his fine motor skills now for manual dexterity in future employment in food preparation or serving, gardening, and similar occupations. Also, a frequent difficulty in developing and expressing appropriate occupational interests is evident. Phillip needs assistance in analyzing work options and deciding on the more suitable ones.

He must continue to develop appropriate social skills and work habits (such as asking for assistance) useful in a work situation. Like so many students, he needs to mature socially and emotionally to be better prepared to work under supervision, with co-workers, and alone. He must develop a better style of communication, learn how to take feedback and criticism, and prepare to engage in the daily give-and-take of the workplace.

With suitable progress, Phillip should be in a better position to benefit from specific vocational preparation. The next school year will be devoted to establishing prerequisite academic skills, work habits and attitudes, and manual dexterity, as well as providing laboratory and on-site training for interesting work. His current program will place him with his normal peers most of the school day—good preparation for future employment in the mainstream.

Home and Community

Career or vocational assessment and programming must take into account the school, home, and community of the students. Cognitive, academic, and/or behavior deficits of mildly handicapped students dictate special considerations in preparing for careers or vocations. In terms of assessment, special considerations must be made for limited reading, writing, motor, attention, and other skills. Accurate information can often only be gathered by individualized procedures or other special assessment conditions.

Programs must also be coordinated with services for disability areas. Integration of services and mainstreaming are the keynotes of an appropriate program for mildly handicapped students. The collaboration of regular and special education teachers, vocational educators, and others is essential.

Yet recent studies of career and vocational programming in secondary schools suggest that many of these elements still remain future goals (Halpern, 1985). Vocational instruction and mainstreaming opportunities are not being implemented as well as they should be. Role confusion interferes with cooperative planning. Inappropriate curricula and materials and poorly trained teachers are also blamed for problems in implementing career and vocational education.

The home and family of mildly handicapped students also are a factor in providing appropriate services. The parents and other family members serve as models for career and vocational aspirations. From them come awareness and knowledge about work, as well as encouragement for developing appropriate occupational attitudes and habits. The mildly disabled student may be reflecting parental work attitudes and interests on an inventory. Families may or may not have the resources to help their children seek work; finding paid employment for mildly handicapped persons is often the result of assistance from families and friends (Hasazi, Gordon, & Roe, 1985). The sociocultural values of the family need to be considered when directing a student toward certain occupations if family support is needed.

The community is another important consideration in evaluating career or vocational needs and conceptualizing student programs. Assessment personnel must have an excellent grasp of the local job market and conditions of other environments in which students wish to function. A receptive and flexible employment environment is essential for successful preparatory programs because it guarantees not only opportunities for prac-

ticing saleable skills but also holds the promise of continued employment.

Knowing what the community needs now and in the future is important information to combine with the current performance and potential profiles of secondary students. Job analyses are therefore a critical tool for special educators and vocational teachers. They must also monitor available positions and work to maintain good communication between the schools and the community. Of particular usefulness is the analysis of the occupational site's capability and willingness to make accommodations for exceptional students like Phillip.

Appropriate services in this area of preparation must not focus only on career and vocational education. That must be combined with support for students' transition along two other dimensions of community adjustment—the home and neighborhood environment, and the social and interpersonal network (Halpern, 1985). Students like Phillip require a broader preparation for their movement into the adult community. They must learn how to live fully in their homes and neighborhoods and to benefit from available services and recreational opportunities. Also, they need to have and be able to engage in the daily communications, family life, friendships, and other social-emotional mainstays. Success in one area such as employment or social relationships does not mean success in the others (Halpern, 1985). Problems like an inability to maintain a happy home life may have a detrimental effect on a person's overall adjustment, even if he or she is gainfully employed.

It is also important to avoid restrictive projections by limiting occupational and environmental preparations of mildly handicapped students. They may wish to go to trade school or college and accept such challenges in spite of past and current difficulties. They must be taught skills appropriate for those situations and given strategies to get the assistance they need.

COLLEGE ASSESSMENT

It is reasonable to expect that more and more students who have mild handicapping conditions will aspire to technical training and 2- and 4-year college studies. Technical colleges and institutions of higher learning are finding these students already enrolled or seeking admission. The number of university freshman claiming to have learning disabilities is increasing, as are the requests for special testing arrangements (Vogel, 1985). However, one follow-up study of secondary students with behavior disorders indicated that only one in five was in a postsecondary program, as compared to nearly 50% involvement among their nonhandicapped peers (Neel, Meadows, Levine, & Edgar, 1988).

The main legal imperative requiring colleges to offer services is Section 504 of the Rehabilitation Act of 1973 as it applies to postsecondary educational programs that receive federal monies (Vogel, 1982). Accurate identification and assessment procedures pose a particular challenge because the definitions of these handicapping conditions are vague, do not apply to adults, and are not consistently used by colleges and universities.

For mildly handicapped students seeking technical and advanced education there are a few possible admission scenarios (Vogel, 1987). Some schools have open admissions, and special needs students are automatically accepted. Others meet the minimal entrance requirements as other students do, that is, acceptable high school grades, performance on college admission tests like the SATs or ACTs, and so forth. Still others request modifications of test administration procedures because of their learning disabilities, such as taking the tests untimed or having a reader or scribe. Vogel and Sattler (1981) also suggest providing essay exams instead of objective exams or vice versa, allowing an exam to be taken in a separate room with a proctor, allowing alternate methods of demonstrating mastery of course objectives, and permitting the use of references and calculators.

There is no consistently used battery of tests for mildly handicapped students on campuses and universities. Some of the ones frequently mentioned are the *Wechsler Adult Intelligence Scale–Revised* (Wechsler, 1981) and the *Woodcock-Johnson Psycho-Educational Battery–Revised* (Woodcock & Johnson, 1989). Other standardized tests normed ages 19 and above are the *Wide Range Achievement Test–Revised* (Jastak & Wil-

kinson, 1984), *Stanford-Binet Intelligence Scale* (Terman & Merrill, 1973; Thorndike, Hagen, & Sattler, 1986), *Goldman-Fristoe-Woodcock Test of Auditory Discrimination* (Goldman, Fristoe, & Woodcock, 1970), *Goldman-Fristoe-Woodcock Auditory Skills Test Battery* (Goldman, Fristoe, & Woodcock, 1976), and *Mooney Problem Check Lists* (Mooney & Gordon, 1950).

Informal assessment also figures prominently in postsecondary assessment, including observation and interviews. Vogel (1987) suggests asking

- Students about the nature of their learning disability, things that were easy and hard to learn, their best subjects and worst ones, reasons for seeking more education and in what areas, their occupational plans
- Institutions about the number of special needs students on campus, the services available, preparation of advisors and instructors for accommodating students, the willingness of faculty to provide support
- Faculty about their willingness to work with special needs students, instructional style and individualization, and nature and flexibility of evaluation strategies

Areas that should frequently be the object for assessment are study habits (note taking, organization, time management, test taking); listening and comprehension skills for following class lectures and oral expression for participating in class activities; vocabulary, grammar, and production necessary for written expression; and the social and interpersonal skills needed for interaction with teachers and peers (Vogel, 1987).

Much can be accomplished with students like Joyce, whose learning disabilities were described in Chapters 7 through 14, long before they apply to or appear on a college campus. An appropriate career/vocational assessment would establish Joyce's knowledge of and interest in possible fields of study. Many of the academic skills and learning strategies that are the subject of junior and high school assessment are applicable to the college setting and when taught provide an important foundation. Transitional plans for Joyce must prepare for the college environment so that she can explain her needs well to instructors, seek

out available services, independently use strategies to compensate for her disabilities, and cope
with the increased demands for organizational,
interpersonal, and other skills.

Of no less significance is a student's ability to
engage in recreational and leisure-time activities.
Current research indicates that learning disabled
students as well as others need to be well prepared to use their free time (White et al., 1983).
Also, the personal-social goals in the IEP should

be extended to anticipate the transition to adult
relationships, marriage, and childrearing.

Full community adjustment is based on adequate preparation in all of these areas (Halpern,
1985). This perspective is very similar to the one
used for Brolin's career education competency
curriculum described earlier. Students such as Phillip and Joyce require a career or vocational program
conceptualized as part of their total transition to
the adult world.

STUDY GUIDE

Review Questions

1. Define career education.
2. Career education and vocational education are synonymous. (True or False)
3. Other than PL 94–142, no other federal laws regulate vocational and career assessments of a handicapped person. (True or False)
4. What are the four areas generally assessed in career or vocational assessments?
5. Technological advances may make some vocational assessments unrepresentative of the work situation. (True or False)
6. The *DOT* is the _____ .
7. A simulation of an activity in the work world is a _____ .
8. Two academic deficits that affect the design of vocational tests are _____ and _____ .
9. Reading (is/isn't) required on the *Social and Prevocational Information Battery–Revised.* (Circle the correct answer)
10. The response mode on the *Reading-Free Vocational Interest Inventory–Revised* is _____ .
11. A T-score of 65 in the area of sales on the *Wide Range Interest-Opinion Test* indicates (low, average, or high) interest. (Circle the correct answer.)
12. Two commercial work sample analysis systems are _____ and _____ .
13. Reading is required on the *WREST.* (True or False)
14. The two typical measures on work samples are _____ for quantity and _____ for quality.
15. There is a standardized test battery for special students entering college. (True or False)

Activities

1. Visit your local school district's vocational program. Describe and critique their assessment system.
2. Administer a vocational interest inventory to a student. What did you learn? What more do you need to know in order to give suitable guidance?
3. Using the directions in this chapter and the *Dictionary of Occupational Titles,* analyze a job in your community.
4. Interview a special educator, vocational education teacher, and rehabilitation counselor about their mutual roles in career and vocational assessment.
5. Interview a mildly handicapped student in high school about his or her career plans. Are they reflected in current assessment instruments and training programs?

Discussion Questions

1. Read the article by Cegelka and Lewis (1983) mentioned in this chapter. Discuss the implications for career and vocational assessment.

2. Discuss ways to assess a college environment for meeting the needs of a learning disabled student wanting higher education.

3. Halpern (1985) and others in the field of career and vocational education worry that an emphasis on only the work skills of students is short-sighted. Discuss a more comprehensive assessment for making the transition after formal schooling.

20

Current Issues and Future Trends

As mentioned at the beginning of this text, the field is grappling with a set of critical issues. Some are highly specific, such as how to apply current technology in conducting an assessment. Others affect many aspects of the assessment process, for example, the technical quality of the instruments used. It should be helpful to readdress these issues now after considering possible ways to approach them. This summary highlights both the key questions and possible answers.

PURPOSE OF ASSESSMENT

Given recent studies, there are strong concerns about the current purpose of assessing exceptional children. As the arguments go, our assessment practices are not cost-effective, and results obtained are irrelevant to programming and merely confirm initial impressions. In fact, there is evidence that the outcomes of most special education assessments are determined by the referral. Ysseldyke, Thurlow, Graden, Wesson, Algozzine, and Deno (1983) summarize this perspective.

The special education decision-making process is one in which a student is referred, often for vague and subjective reasons; automatically tested, often with technically inadequate devices; usually placed by a team meeting; and is the object of decisions made less on data than on subjective teacher or student variables and on inconsistent and indefensible criteria. (p. 87)

The average exceptional child's assessment may consume 13 to 15 hours; by the time the decision-making process is completed, the cost could be as much as $1,800 (Ysseldyke & Algozzine, 1982). Although PL 94–142 funds may partially defray this expense, one wonders how long school districts can sustain this degree of assessment.

That is particularly true if the results are not even used to make the necessary decisions. In studies of team decision making, very little relationship has been found between the decisions made and the extent that data supported the decision (Ysseldyke, Algozzine, Richey, & Graden, 1982). Analysis of 20 videotaped placement team meetings indicated (a) placements in special education depended on the amount of data provided, (b) 83% of the oral comments made during meetings were irrelevant to the criteria for placement set forth in federal and state guidelines, and (c)

when such relevant statements were made, eligibility for special services did not necessarily follow. If the agreed-upon criteria are not being used to dictate the assessment data sought, then the whole process is suspect. Additionally, this situation raises the concern that less relevant student characteristics, such as sex, race, and physical appearance, are being used to decide placement.

Another concern is that the assessment process seems vague. Surveys of special education directors and Child Service Demonstration Centers indicate that a vast number and variety of assessment devices are used, the common ones being devoted to achievement and ability assessment (Ysseldyke et al., 1982). In a computer-simulated study of the decision-making process, a group of 159 varied professionals chose nearly 50 different devices to make the same outcome decision. There were only a few similarities, such as the *WISC–R* and the *Bender Visual-Motor Gestalt Test* (Ysseldyke et al., 1980). What may be even more alarming is the finding from various studies that tests intended for one purpose are used for others (Ysseldyke & Algozzine, 1982).

What test professionals use for assessment is a function of many factors, including previous training and experience. Sometimes a school district requires only certain tests or does not provide the resources to buy new tests or the time for training. Changes in assessment procedures mean a major expense for a school system.

Therefore, future solutions to these types of concerns require improvements in many areas. Professionals must be dedicated to the study of new procedures. School systems must examine their assessment strategies for cost-effectiveness and usefulness. Most of all, professionals must develop structure and purpose to their assessments. That is why we have emphasized the use of a set of assessment questions to guide the design of an Individualized Assessment Plan. Reasons for selection of tests are clearer, as are the uses of data.

An appropriate prereferral process should be implemented to help students about whom teachers are concerned before decisions are made regarding extensive assessments. There is some evidence that such efforts reduce assessments, further referrals, and placements in special education (Graden, Casey, & Bonstrom, 1985). However, although initial teacher appraisals of such preassessment team efforts are favorable, it is unclear whether recommended classroom interventions are truly new or varied and whether teachers will continue to use this process (Harrington & Gibson, 1986). Greater administrative support, preparation of teachers in referral development, parental assistance, and communication will improve this effort.

Recent trends in removing the need for diagnostic classification promise to change the form of future assessments. PL 99–457 does not require state departments to declare a type of handicapping condition to justify requests for funding of special education services for infants and preschoolers. Wider use of curriculum-based assessment systems is also promising in this regard. Proponents of the regular education initiative or merger of special education and regular education to provide services for mildly handicapped students advocate such a reconceptualization of assessment procedures.

INFORMAL VERSUS FORMAL ASSESSMENT

The problem with much assessment is the overemphasis on standardized procedures and the ambivalent application of informal techniques. In fact, most surveys of assessment practices indicate the predominant use of standardized tests and not very good ones at that (Davis & Shepard, 1983). This trend is prevalent in all phases of assessment, from identification through program design. Some professionals' use of tests has proven improper given the tests' stated purposes (Ysseldyke & Algozzine, 1982).

The imbalance between formal and informal procedures in exceptional student assessment is a concern for a variety of reasons. First, professionals seem to automatically mention formal tests when asked to select a procedure to screen students, gather information for special education program planning, and so forth. Second, this tendency may reflect the low esteem with which informal techniques are held by professionals, especially psychologists. Third, and even worse, it may indicate that educators' information and the ways it is gathered are devalued in the assessment

process. Fourth, there is little awareness of how to establish the reliability and validity of the informal techniques of gathering assessment information.

Some assessment professionals have totally disavowed formal testing for more informal modes. This extreme position overlooks the fact that there are many useful, well-designed standardized tests, as have been described throughout this text. They are technically sound, can identify and clarify the nature of learning problems, and are more efficient than informal procedures. Furthermore, such norm-referenced tests permit comparisons.

The real dilemma of this dichotomy is represented by the concept of clinical judgment. Many professionals have a great deal of confidence in their intuitive abilities to identify and diagnose student disabilities. In fact, for some diagnosticians, clinical judgment is regarded as a cornerstone of their profession—an inviolate right to go beyond the test data to make necessary judgments. To the statement "Test results should clearly be secondary to clinical judgments in arriving at an LD diagnosis," a group of LD teachers, school psychologists, and speech-language specialists voiced strong agreement (Davis & Shepard, 1983).

Unfortunately, professionals in this study and in others vary in their idea of clinical judgment. Some define it as a process to test hypotheses about a student's skills by trying to see a pattern in the student's behavior and matching it to a mental construct about a particular disability. Others equate clinical judgment with informal assessment or some form of guessing. Frequently, they cannot articulate a system (the steps or criteria used) for this process.

Thus, critics of current assessment practices get particularly incensed when clinical judgment is thrown in the face of their findings as an alternative to questionable practices and inadequate tests. The situation also contributes to the devaluing of informal assessment as merely a set of procedures to fall back on when the standardized ones cannot do the job. That is why in this text we have stressed the *accompanying* role of informal techniques in gathering data to answer certain assessment questions. Also remember the ways to establish technical reliability and validity for observations, interviews, work sample analyses, and so forth. There is definitely a trend toward more sophisticated and confident use of informal techniques for a variety of purposes.

Curriculum-based assessment has gained new respect for informal techniques as it becomes more incorporated into the formal decision-making system. Also, the need to attend to environmental and instructional variables has resulted in the greater development of observational and interview assessment materials.

TECHNICAL ADEQUACY

The major concerns just discussed are frequently related to the technical soundness of current standardized tests. The recency of standardization and the nature of norms are criticized as well as the degree and nature of reliability and validity. Given weaknesses in these areas, the most serious charges are often made about the uses to which the questionable data are put.

Surveys of state departments, agencies, and school districts yield a bothersome profile of tests used for exceptional student assessment (Ysseldyke et al., 1982). When one looks at the listed tests and examines the technical features of the more popular ones, surprise soon changes to alarm. Particularly frustrating is the unavailability and/or ambiguity of information provided in test manuals.

When examining the area of standardization, study the recency of norms and their representativeness to the population you are working with. The joint American Psychological Association and American Educational Research Association recommendations explained in Chapter 3 stress the need for regular renorming as well as other features. No doubt you were surprised by the lack of stratification and other features in some tests, particularly ones that are frequently used. Brown and Bryant (1984c) describe the rationale and procedures for norming tests for special populations.

Inadequate reliability (or inconsistency of measurement) is a problem because diagnosticians cannot confidently use tests for various purposes. As discussed earlier, significant correlations are not necessarily indicators of quality. A high degree of relationship (at least .80 and preferably .90) is necessary for individual screening and placement decisions.

The question of valid tests relates to PL 94–142's requirement that assessment procedures be validated for the specific diagnostic task for which they are used. The ways test developers establish this characteristic vary, as do the levels of validity in popularly used tests. Professionals in the fields of mental retardation, emotional disturbance, and learning disabilities should be concerned. Many of the current tests used to determine mildly handicapping conditions, especially learning disabilities, are wanting in validity (Davis & Shepard, 1983; Thurlow & Ysseldyke, 1979). This weakness is particularly evident in tests of perception and information-processing skills.

Such deficiencies are particularly apparent in infant and early childhood assessments and in those required for adolescents and young adults needing transitional services. Efforts to quantify decision making about the nature and scope of student disabilities are plagued by inadequate instrumentation because they play a key role in formulas being developed for the purpose. If the tests themselves have poor reliability, then the formulas that use their data are questionable.

Hammill, Brown, and Bryant (1989) have developed a comprehensive system to summarize and evaluate these key technical aspects, including a description of basic characteristics and an analysis of technical features. A good, acceptable, or unacceptable rating for a test is generated from the mean ratings of reviewers for the technical areas of standardization, reliability, and validity (Brown & Bryant, 1984a). An acceptable rating is possible only if composite ratings are acceptable or good. All three technical aspects of a test must be judged good to have the test so considered, because of the interrelatedness of these factors. Analyses of tests based on this system are a regular feature in the journal *Remedial and Special Education*.

The assessment tool analysis described in Chapter 3 (see p. 67) is conceptualized in a broader way than the system and is the basis for our test reviews. By identifying the requested information about a test, you will be in a good position to decide whether the assessment device can be used to answer your assessment questions.

LITIGATION

A number of highly significant legal actions have influenced assessment practices. *Jose P. v. Ambach* (1979, 1982, 1983) required major administrative changes in how the New York City public schools processed requests for assessment and services in a timely fashion and fulfilled other aspects of the process (Fafard, Hanlon, & Bryson, 1986). Assessment and placement decisions about the least restrictive environment were to occur at the school building level rather than the district level, assessments were to be conducted in a student's native language, placements were to occur within 30 days of recommendations, appropriate parent information and involvement in school-level teams were to be improved, facilities were to be more accessible to the special needs student, periodic reports were to be provided, and an appropriate monitoring system of the areas to be improved was to be put in place.

Lora v. Board of Education of the City of New York (1977, 1980, 1984) arose because of the disproportionate number of black and Hispanic students being placed in special classes for students with emotional disturbance (Wood, Johnson, & Jenkins, 1986). The court mandated that the chief administrative officer of the New York City Public Schools would monitor the implementation of nondiscriminatory practices, information about the procedures would be published widely, multicultural education would be provided all instructional staff, assessment personnel would be trained to implement procedures with sensitivity to a student's ethnicity and native language, comparative referral and placement data would be gathered for majority and minority students, and identified inequities were to be reported to the court and rectified.

The *Larry P. v. Riles* (1972, 1979, 1984) case focused on the inappropriate use of intelligence tests to place a disproportionate number of black students in classes for educable mentally retarded students (Prasse & Reschly, 1986). The State of California was prohibited from using any standardized intelligence tests to identify black educable mentally retarded students or place them in classes for educable mentally retarded students unless it proved the tests were not racially or culturally discriminatory. Also, all tests were to be administered in a nondiscriminatory fashion, and

they were to be validated for use with minority students in such diagnostic and placement situations. The state was to maintain comparative black and white data about referrals and placement decisions, hold public hearings about such practices, and monitor and eliminate disportionate placement, which was defined as occurring when the rate of black pupil enrollment exceeded one standard deviation above the district rate of white pupil enrollment in such classes. All black students had to receive a comprehensive reevaluation without the use of standardized intelligence/ability tests, and misplacements were to be corrected. Although other decisions have been contrary to this one concerning test bias and disproportionate placement, *Larry P. v. Riles* has encouraged a redefinition of the problem of disproportionate placement, stimulated a noncategorical placement movement, questioned the usefulness of the concept of mild mental retardation, and encouraged improvements in the assessment of adaptive behaviors (Prasse & Reschly, 1986).

A review of 1986 through 1988 court cases reported in *Special Education and the Handicapped* (Data Research, Inc., P.O. Box 490, Rosemount, MN 55068) reveals a continuation of such debates, although the majority of the court cases concern programmatic issues rather than only assessment and placement decisions. The Pennsylvania Commonwealth Court found that a former special education student had not been misdiagnosed as educable mentally retarded instead of learning disabled and was not entitled to monetary damages because the school district was to provide an appropriate education, not necessarily develop each student to his or her highest potential (*Agostine v. School District of Philadelphia,* 1988).

In another case related to diagnosis, the court ruled that the State Department of New York could not reclassify a student after an impartial hearing had resulted in a diagnosis (*Hiller v. Board of Education,* 1988). In *Gregory K. v. Longview School District* (1987) the court refused to accept the subjective opinion of a neurologist that a student had a learning disability in favor of the school district's data based on the state department's required objective criteria.

Legal actions such as these court cases continue to shape the implementation of the requirements of PL 94–142 and correct problems arising from deficiencies in the process, instruments, or decisions made. Sage and Burrello (1988) provide a detailed discussion of these and other important legal cases in relationship to constitutions, statutes, and administrative regulations.

NONDISCRIMINATORY ASSESSMENT

The assessment process can be biased against individuals of a certain sex, race, linguistic background, culture, religion, or disability if it includes or excludes them from a service or opportunity because of their nondominant status in society. It may be a matter of underestimating their potential, deciding that they are ineligible or eligible for special education, or perhaps screening them out of a job opportunity.

Discrimination can occur in many ways in the assessment process for special education. Inappropriate referrals may be made because of a student's race, age, and/or sex. The hyperactive child with low socioeconomic status may never get referred for an enriching experience. Or minority students may be overrepresented in referrals for special education.

Test administrators or interviewers also may mistreat, rush, intimidate, or otherwise abuse a student. If they have preconceived notions about how a student looks, talks, and so on, they may not make an effort to establish the kind of rapport discussed in Chapter 4. Incompetence as testers qualifies as a form of bias.

Many of the concerns about discrimination in testing revolve around the technical inadequacies of the instruments and how the data are used. The standardization issue is a key factor because the characteristics of students we test should be represented in the normative group. Otherwise, it is possible to misinterpret performance. That is why we clarified in our test critiques the presence or absence of certain groups in the norming.

Reliability and validity are also to be considered. A test may be a better measure for certain sex, age, or racial groups, and some items may unduly penalize students from different backgrounds. An overemphasis on or absence of content may invalidate the usefulness of a test with certain students.

Major bias is also possible when professionals interpret and apply test results. Various studies have noted that professionals tend to base special education placement decisions more on the student's sex, socioeconomic status (SES), or physical appearance than on the test data (Ysseldyke et al., 1981). Although videotapes of assessment teams at work did not reveal blatant use of such incidental data, the professionals involved did not use the assessment data according to legal and procedural criteria. Their final decisions seemed more related to these extraneous factors.

And discrimination can work both ways. When Frame, Clarizio, & Porter (1984) varied the SES, race, and other traits in a learning disabled child's case profile, professionals recommended special education least often when the child was described as a low SES, black student. The furor raised over the last 10 years about overrepresentation of minorities in special education may be creating an overreaction to the problem.

Discrimination on the Basis of Sex

Although recent efforts have been made to remediate sexist practices in educational material and tests, professionals must be aware how they occur. Concerns about sexism in psychoeducational assessment involve the frequency and nature of portrayals of both sexes in material, language, norming procedures, and interpretation practices. Much of the research on reading material has focused on the facts that boys outnumber girls as major characters in more than 70% of the stories and in 50% of the illustrations, men are more repeatedly shown in more interesting and atypical kinds of occupations, and boys generally have more active, interesting roles in stories (Graebner, 1972). In spite of improvements, females are still underrepresented when compared to males and female activities continue to be passive and inactive (Marten & Matlin, 1976). Such bias may distort the views of both male and female readers; it may carry over in their responses to testing situations and influence them to answer incorrectly. Biased material may be included in assessment instruments in the same manner that passages on reading tests are identical to or designed after basal reading series.

Sex stereotyping is evident in achievement tests, as well as basal readers and curricular requirements, in terms of linguistic factors and test items (Saario, Jacklin & Tittle, 1973). Language bias can result from an inordinate use of male nouns and pronouns. Females may only appear in traditional jobs (like homemakers) and in inactive, passive, and dependent roles. Such test items perpetuate biased views, and the "correct" answers may conflict with the less biased views of the better informed student. Similar problems have been noted in individual speech and language tests (Rabe & Matlin, 1978).

Inventories of vocational interests and aptitudes have been criticized because they categorize occupations by sex and thus limit an exceptional student's choices and because the occupations designated for females are of lower status and yield less money (Gillespie & Fink, 1974). Therefore, boys outnumber girls in secondary work-study programs for the retarded and are provided with higher level vocational training (Cegelka, 1976). The revised version of the *Reading-Free Vocational Interest Inventory* (Becker, 1988), described in Chapter 19, has corrected some of these concerns. The record form is common to both genders and has equal portrayals of males and females doing tasks in all vocational areas. Separate norm tables are used for males and females, and the tester indicates the one used on the Profile.

These modifications are consistent with the National Institute for Education's *Guidelines for Assessment of Sex Bias and Sex Fairness in Career Interest Inventories*. These guidelines urge that items appearing to have sexual bias be eliminated, that references to gender be deleted (e.g., changing policeman to police officer), and that scores be reported on a single profile form used for both sexes (Campbell & Hansen, 1981, 1985). However, Campbell and Hansen also argue that the way to equal treatment is not necessarily through identical treatment, because identical treatment of dissimilar groups will not have identical impact. They conclude from a series of studies with the *Strong-Campbell Interest Inventory* that men and women respond differently to almost half of the inventory items and that the size of the differences is considerable. Further, the differences have not lessened appreciably since 1930, and attempts to develop combined-sex scales appear to be premature, because validity of these scales varies from occupation to occupation. Campbell and Hansen believe separate scales and norms are necessary. However, they stress that these tools should be a means of expanding, not limiting, options. Needed changes are more apt to come as a result of the combined effort of social change (opening more careers to women), revised interventions (establishing guidelines for authors and publishers of tests), and research rather than merely revisions in the assessment procedures themselves.

Discrimination on the Basis of Race and Culture

A nondiscriminatory measure results in similar performance distributions across cultural groups that may differ from one another in language and dialect, value systems, information, and learning strategies (Alley & Foster, 1978). Minority children with suspected handicaps are discriminated against by an assessment procedure when their performance, while more a reflection of their minority status and culture than a handicap, is evaluated as poor.

There are many problems associated with using standardized tests, particularly intelligence tests, with minority children. Classification procedures based on standardized intelligence tests should deem the lowest 3% in intelligence (IQ below 70) and in adaptive behavior as the cutoff level for retardation. This way, individuals who as adults lead fully independent lives will not be labeled as retarded (Mercer, 1974). Furthermore, both IQ and adaptive behavior should be measured, because the ability to function socially distinguishes the clinically retarded and those so labeled merely by performance on an intelligence test. Sociocultural variables must also be considered in the interpretation of clinical scores.

Standardized tests are biased and unfair to persons from cultural and socioeconomic minorities because most tests reflect largely white, middle-class values and attitudes (Oakland & Laosa, 1977). They are used to form homogeneous classroom groups that severely limit educational, vocational, economic, and other societal opportunities. Persons who do not understand the culture and language of minority group children may be unable to elicit a level of performance that accurately reflects the child's underlying competence. Such testing practices foster expectations that may be damaging by contributing to a self-fulfilling prophecy and may rigidly shape school curricula and restrict educational change.

Many minority students may seem to be deficient in motivation, test practice, and reading skills; therefore, they are particularly penalized by standardized tests. They may perform poorly on such tests for reasons extraneous to ability; they lack experience with testing materials, adapt inadequately in the situation, and react emotionally with suspicion or aggression.

The main result of all these concerns is that minority status is misrepresented in special education services, as noted in the cases discussed before. The complaint in the *Parents in Action on Special Education v. Hannon* (1980) case was based on this same issue in Chicago, where black students represented 82% of the enrollment in classes for educable mentally handicapped; only 62% percent of the student body was black. In the California case of *Larry P. v. Riles* (1972, 1979, 1984), the court ultimately ordered the monitoring or elimination of such disproportionate enrollment and banned standardized intelligence tests for that purpose (Lambert, 1981b).

A related concern was the underrepresentation of minority children in learning disabilities classes (Lynch & Lewis, 1987). LD services seemed to be used by primarily white middle- and upper-SES students (Kavale, 1980). This situation may be an indication of the perception that LD placement is more socially acceptable and positive than EMR classes.

The impact of various legal actions, legislation, and pressure from advocacy groups has been a reduction in the number of minority students in some areas of special education. An analysis of California placement practices indicates that, whereas the proportion of black and Hispanic students in EMR classes remains the same, the total number of minority students in special education is less (Lambert, 1981b). In fact, many of the minority students formerly placed in EMR classes seem to be placed now in LD classes. Although the proportion of black students in EMR classes in one urban school system has decreased, the ratio in LD classes has become disproportional (Tucker, 1980).

Particular attention is being focused on the assessments of limited-English-proficient (LEP) students. However, some school districts are having difficulty providing the necessary conditions to account for language differences. A national survey of 21 local school districts indicates that they rely primarily on nonverbal measures and translated tests (Nuttal, 1987). In many cases, translations were done while testing was in progress. An average of 12 psychological, language, and educational tests were used with each LEP child. Only a third of the districts used multicultural pluralistic approaches. Most of the districts reported serious shortages in bilingual assessment personnel. Similar results were found in a statewide study of educational services provided to limited-English-proficient, handicapped students in California (Cegelka, Lewis, & Rodriguez, 1987).

These problems with minority assessment have stimulated a number of solutions, as described in Chapter 14 and elsewhere. Certain groups such as the American Psychological Association have made significant efforts to counter discriminatory practices in existing assessment procedures. The APA's *Standards for Educational and Psychological Testing* (1985) stress the cultural aspects of test administration and interpretation. However, steps to counter the discriminatory aspects of assessment must be taken judiciously. Alteration of test items and other features of the assessment is part of a broader cultural transformation. For some, modifications of educational materials and tests seem like a form of tampering and reversed censorship (Taxel, 1978). However, the constitutional right to express one's views and ideas freely does not supersede the birthright of all children to encounter unbiased and unstereotyped images of themselves. Psychological and educational tests must strive to equitably represent sexual, minority, and other cultural variables. Otherwise, tests will perpetuate the powerless, stereotypical, and so-called inferior status of minorities and women.

As indicated in the preceding discussion of litigation related to assessment and placement decisions, the effort to implement truly nondiscriminatory practices continues. The debate has broadened from questions about the appropriateness of instruments and procedures to concern about the need to test at all to deliver services to needy minority students. To some judges and others, disproportionate placement among minority students is more a sign of lower socioeconomic status than of discrimination (Prasse & Reschly, 1986). Jones (1988) provides a more complete description of current efforts to provide nondiscriminatory assessments.

TEAM PROCESS

Great hopes for fair and appropriate evaluations rest on the principle that more than one person, using more than one source of information, will determine a student's eligibility for special education (Yoshida, 1984). PL 94–142 has based much of its thrust on the ability of the team process to make equitable decisions for exceptional students. The wisdom of this emphasis has been questioned. Particular concerns are (a) who actually participates on these teams, (b) who tends to dominate them, (c) how teams operate, and (d) what the bases for their decisions are.

Many kinds of participants serve on these multidisciplinary teams. When mental retardation is suspected, special education directors from local school districts indicate that special education teachers, psychologists, administrators, classroom teachers, speech pathologists, and parents are most often included on multidisciplinary teams (Frankenberger & Harper, 1986). The average team size is six or seven persons, with some districts reporting three or fewer members.

Team members participate to varying degrees, depending on the phase of the assessment process. In a national survey, 100 directors of special education named 18 different possible participants, including parents and the student (Poland, Thurlow, Ysseldyke, & Mirkin, 1982). Over 60% of the respondents said screening decisions were often made by regular classroom teachers, school administrators, speech-language-audiology specialists, school psychologists, and parents. For actual placement decisions, most of these same professionals were mentioned again by over 80% of the directors, except for the addition of special education teachers and deletion of speech-language-audiology specialists. The most frequently mentioned contributors to instructional planning decisions were special education teachers, parents, and regular education teachers.

Two of the critical variables in evaluating the validity of the team process are the nature and quality of participation. It is possible, at least from studying the signatures affixed to placement decisions and IEPs, to question whether everyone who should be present is always there (Pyecha et al., 1980; Say, McCollum, & Brightman, 1980).

When participants ranked the expected contribution of team members before and after meetings, results indicated that parents were ranked third initially and ninth afterwards (Gilliam, 1979). The most influential team members were (a) psychologists in diagnosis, (b) special educators in planning and implementation, (c) special education directors in placement, and (d) supervisors in due process matters (Gilliam & Coleman, 1981).

That participants with data were the most influential is very consistent with the results of analyses of actual videotaped placement team meetings. The participants have generally tested the student, and the decision-making process is very test oriented (Ysseldyke, Algozzine, & Epps, 1983). Regular education teachers participate very little (present data, ask or answer questions, etc.) and are generally dissatisfied with the team process (Ysseldyke, Algozzine, & Allen, 1981).

Parental participation is also qualitatively limited. Surveys of professional team members indicate that they view the most appropriate roles of parents as providers and receivers of information (Yoshida, Fenton, Kaufman, & Maxwell, 1978). When observed interacting at actual conferences, parents do exactly that—answer questions and listen to the professionals (Goldstein, Strickland, Turnbull, & Curry, 1980). When asked, parents also seem accepting of these roles (Polifka, 1981).

What do all of these people actually do? Poland et al.'s (1982) sample of special education directors could not agree on the number of activities that constituted the team process. They most often identified child referral (97%), assessment (98%), IEP development (77%), and IEP implementation (63%). However, less than 50% said their district's team obtained parental permission for testing or placement, formally assigned team members, and so forth. These obvious gaps in the process are alarming!

Part of the problem is that team members may not know the purpose of their roles. Less than half of a sample of administrators, support personnel, and teachers could describe their roles in these teams (Fenton, Yoshida, Maxwell, & Kaufman, 1979). Can they then be held accountable for how the teams function? How can their performance be evaluated? Furthermore, these professionals come from different fields and possibly from different perspectives; there may be feelings of competition and "turfdom" that contribute to how the team operates (Yoshida, 1984).

Given these conditions, the meetings tend to be unstructured and nongoal oriented, as well as limited in individual contribution (Ysseldyke, Thurlow, et al., 1983). Members basically take turns in reporting test results without any referents. Established criteria from state guidelines and popular definitions are not necessarily mentioned. Observers are often hard pressed to see a relationship between the decisions made and the multitude of data discussed.

That is why we feel strongly about the need for initial structure to assessment through the IAP. This format establishes a rationale for team membership, a direction by which to select assessment tools, and ultimately a framework within which data can be directed for interpretation and use. The team assessment conference can then be devoted to answering questions from a variety of perspectives.

Much progress is also possible in training team participants. Regular classroom teachers have increased their contributions about student performance, behavior, and curriculum after brief training sessions (Trailor, 1982). Parents can also be encouraged to participate more if team members introduce them, direct questions to them, verbally reinforce their comments, and so forth (Goldstein & Turnbull, 1982). The guidelines for conducting conferences described in Chapters 15 and 17 should be helpful in this area.

DECISION-MAKING MODELS

What is very evident from observations of current multidisciplinary assessment and placement teams is the absence of and need for a clear decision-making model or process. Team members do tend to emphasize some variables more than others. In the case of learning disabilities, teachers tend to stress intraindividuality, the difference between actual achievement and potential, academic underachievement, and absence of other disabilities (Valus, 1986). Intelligence test scores may bear more weight in a decision than other data (Knoff, 1984).

Some of the difficulty may be related to the variety and multiplicity of types of tests used in these assessments. When clinicians are provided a great deal of data, such as was done in the study by Epps, McGue, and Ysseldyke (1982), they have a problem arriving at a consensus. Another factor to consider is that it may be more reliable for teams to make decisions than individuals. Professionals arrived at less variable conclusions about placement when they considered the data as a team than when they functioned individually (Pfeiffer & Naglieri, 1983).

To meet the challenge of developing appropriate decision-making models, professionals must select the most relevant information, give it appropriate consideration or weight in arriving at a conclusion, and account for the limitations set by instrument inadequacies and the natural subjectivity involved in clinical judgments. Recent efforts to use quantitative formulas provide a good lesson (Mellard, 1986). A pilot study of the use of the regression true-score formula, standard scores, and clinical judgment to provide some of the data for deciding on learning disabilities services indicated that 62% of the eligibility decisions were based on the formula. Also, the clinicians indicated a level of confidence in the validity of their decisions that far exceeded what was dictated by the reliability of the formula. In spite of stated warnings to the contrary, the temptation to focus on certain data—particularly numbers—is often too great to resist. The National Council for Learning Disabilities voices many of the major reservations about the use of formulas to identify students with disabilities (Board of Trustees of the Council for Learning Disabilities, 1987).

Part of the problem of deciding what data to stress in arriving at a decision is related to professional perception of the adequacy and value of the available information. For example, one group of school psychologists and elementary school teachers judged the data about behavior that had been used to make judgments about behavior disorders as inadequate (Smith, Frank, & Snider, 1984). They considered the traditional academic and intellectual data of higher quality. Because they still valued data about actual behavior, social functioning, and home/family variables, it is clear that professionals may be driven to focus on certain information when their preferred support data are inadequate.

Various models are being experimented with in making decisions about the nature and extent of student disabilities. Potter (1982) and Kavale and Andreassen (1981) have used the Brunswikian Lens Model in studying dimensions of decision making. Wissink, Kass, and Ferrell (1975) and Alley, Deshler, and Warner (1979) have employed Bayes' theorem of subjective probability. Current formulas of regression analysis are based on linear decision-making models.

CATEGORICAL ASSESSMENT

The practice of assessing students with specific diagnostic labels and determining eligibility for special education on the basis of specific categories of disabilities is being strongly questioned. Concerns revolve around issues of ability to do so, the usefulness of such practices, and the broader social implications. Specifically, we must ask ourselves, *Do we have the instrumentation to distinguish learning disabled, behavior disordered, and mildly retarded students from their normal peers?* Related concerns are, *Do we do something distinctive based on those decisions? What are the consequences for students to be so labeled?*

The criteria for making such decisions are not as clear as they could be. When Ysseldyke, Algozzine, and Epps (1983) applied popular definitions of learning disabilities to different categories of students, more than 80% of normal students and 75% of low achievers could be classified as learning disabled. Only 75% of learning disabled students met at least one set of criteria for being considered learning disabled. Further, a national survey of experts' opinions about learning disabled students indicated little consensus (Tucker, Stevens, & Ysseldyke, 1983).

Thus, experts in the field may have problems making these types of decisions. When provided with sample cases of essentially normal students, over 50% of the professionals considered the students eligible for special education, generally learning disabilities services (Algozzine & Ysseldyke, 1981). Getting professionals to agree also may be difficult, depending on the type of classification system used and diagnostic questions asked (Frame, Clarizio, Porter, & Visonhaler, 1982). Various studies of inpatient and outpatient cases with childhood behavioral and emotional problems indicate that professionals may avoid having to make diagnostic decisions and/or chose fairly common ones, like conduct disorders (Clarizio & McCoy, 1983). As discussed earlier, there seems a particular reluctance to label minority students as handicapped, especially mentally retarded.

There is also a fundamental question of whether learning disabled, emotionally disturbed, and mildly retarded students are really different. When 16 learning disabled and 16 emotionally disturbed students were given three standardized tests, there were significant differences in 10 of 12 comparisons (Epstein & Cullinan, 1983). Emotionally disturbed students have been distinguished from learning disabled and mentally retarded students by teachers on behavior rating scales, too (Cullinan, Epstein, & Dembinski, 1979). Gajar's (1980) comparison of 10 achievement tests and behavior ratings of the three mildly handicapping conditions also suggest differences; in addition, though, similarities were noted in IQ of learning disabled and emotionally disturbed students, level of reading ability in mentally retarded and emotionally disturbed children, and behavior ratings for mentally retarded and learning disabled students. Forness, Guthrie, and MacMillan (1982) could not find differences when considering on-task behavior of 900 children in classes for trainable mentally retarded, educable mentally retarded, and educationally handicapped students.

Although the similar versus dissimilar debate continues, there is evidence of separatist policies and attitudes, but combined practices. A survey of practitioner attitudes indicated that special educators, especially learning disabilities teachers, favored separate learning disabilities and mental retardation services (Gaar & Plue, 1983). Assessment personnel strongly concurred, but administrators less so. However, whereas state department policies still are based on separate eligibility requirements (Garrett & Brazil, 1979), many school systems are blending the categories in resource rooms and experimental models (Sparks & Richardson, 1981).

The categorical diagnostic practice is also questionable because the outcome does not seem to be distinctive. It is the common impression that special education methods and placement arrangements are similar across these mildly handicapping problems (Hallahan, Kauffman, & Lloyd, 1985; Miller & Davis, 1982). If we are going to go to all the trouble of establishing categorical eligibility, it should have some basis in practice. Otherwise, we are merely satisfying legal requirements.

Another persuasive force behind cross-categorical approaches is the concern about the labels themselves (Ysseldyke & Algozzine, 1982). There are significant data to support the stigmatizing effects of labels such as "retarded," particularly when coupled with student incompetence. The students dislike being labeled, and peers are adversely influenced. Also, teacher opinion can be negatively affected: teachers tend to establish lower expectations, work less with, and even avoid labeled children.

However, alternatives to categorical diagnosis are not very satisfactory. Developing new definitions and trying out new formulas are not necessarily the answer (Epps, Ysseldyke, & Algozzine, 1983). A behavioral model of specific assessment is one promising direction, as is a full ecological framework by which to organize assessments.

Working from the behavioral model, Deno and his colleagues have developed a system of brief, direct measures that may be helpful with both eligibility and evaluation questions (Marston, Tindal, & Deno, 1984). When 1-minute probes in reading, spelling, and written expression were administered to over 500 randomly chosen students in grades 1 through 6, they provided data by which to determine a percentage of students similar to national incidence figures of mildly handicapped children. Looking for students significantly below criterion performance level yielded percentages of 1% to 9% low functioning students. Such a technique would be considerably less expensive and biased than current ones. Whether or not this system can totally answer eligibility concerns remains to be seen. As discussed in Chapter 5, these informal techniques can short-circuit a complex assessment to begin instruction and serve as a companion to standardized techniques.

The ecological approach is also a viable alternative to categorical diagnosis because it focuses on many factors essential to remedial programs such as physiological factors (hearing, vision, allergy, etc.), physical aspects of the environment (amount of space available, seating arrangement, classroom lighting, and noise), student-to-student interaction, teacher-to-student interaction, home environment, and reinforcement history (Heron & Heward, 1982). We have stressed the ecological

perspective in Chapter 10 and at the end of subsequent chapters by asking assessment questions from this perspective.

Throughout this text we have avoided posing the assessment question, *Is the child learning disabled, emotionally disturbed, or mildly retarded?* We have posed concerns of intelligence, adaptive behavior, behavioral competence, and so forth as common assessment issues. If these categories are distinguishable, it is in the degree of emphasis or concern about social-emotional behavior, adaptive behavior, or specific learning abilities and strategies. We choose to pose the ultimate question of categorical diagnosis as one of eligibility, based on state and local service requirements.

MINIMUM COMPETENCY TESTING

The minimum competency testing (MCT) movement is an effort to make sure all high school graduates possess minimum academic skills and basic knowledge to function in society. Many of the problems anticipated at the initial stages (Madaus & Airasian, 1977; McClung, 1978) have occurred:

1. Teacher emphasis on only the test competencies
2. Measurement of only recall and not real competencies
3. Inadequate phase-in periods
4. Poor matching of test and instructional content
5. Discrimination against disadvantaged minority and handicapped students
6. Inadequate remediation for students who fail

Handicapped students are not generally faring well with this system. A comparative study of their participation in the MCT program of North Carolina (Serow & O'Brien, 1983) indicated that (a) a majority of the handicapped students failed the exam on their first attempt, (b) students who failed the worst received less remediation, and (c) remediated students did not necessarily pass the exam the next time. Mildly retarded students typically continued to fail the exam or dropped out of school. After subsequent attempts, most orthopedically handicapped and learning disabled students were eligible for a high school diploma. During the period of this study, over 60% of attendance certificates awarded (rather than of diplomas) went to mildly retarded students. In Florida only 13 of 38 skill areas were mastered by at least 50% of the LD students who took the test (Linn, Algozzine, Schwartz, & Grise, 1984).

States have implemented various accommodations for disabled students (Gillespie, 1983; Grise, 1980). Test modifications include flexibility in scheduling and setting; various recording modes, including dictation to a proctor; use of mechanical aids like magnifying glasses and pointers; and revisions of the test format with large print, braille, sign language, or audiotape. Special standards are also set, depending on the nature of disabilities; for example, there may be a particular emphasis on career and social-personal skills for retarded students.

Exemption from the tests is another possibility. In Florida, most disabled students are technically exempt from the MCT, but they generally must demonstrate competency either under regular testing conditions or under special standards. If exceptional students meet the minimum regular standards, they get a regular diploma for graduation; if they meet the special standards, they get a special diploma. Otherwise, no diploma or certificate of completion is available.

In Louisiana (Gillespie, 1983), the IEP committee decides whether students will take the MCT. It bases its decision on the match between IEP goals and the state's minimum skills in reading. When there is a match, the students take the regular MCT and work toward a regular diploma. Otherwise, special standards are used, and a certificate of achievement is available. The modifications are then used. Local school districts report scores of special education students separately.

This latter point demonstrates the highly political nature of the MCT movement. What it is truly meant to do and what it will actually accomplish remain to be seen. For the handicapped student, MCT can be highly disruptive and adverse, particularly for mentally retarded individuals (Serow & O'Brien, 1983). Whether it can be suitably modified for exceptional education is still an open question. Olsen (1980) and others point out the disparity in origin and competencies between the MCT and the special education program. However, common ground does seem to lie in integration of the IEP requirements with the MCT process.

ASSESSMENT ETHICS

Ethics must regulate human affairs, including the performance of educational assessment. Respect for individual rights and regard for the principles of a civilized society should be reflected in the technical soundness of assessment techniques; their administration, scoring, and interpretation; and in data use. Many professional organizations, such as the Council for Exceptional Children (CEC), the Council for Learning Disabilities (CLD), and the American Psychological Association (APA) have indicated this level of awareness in formal codes of ethics or statements of standards and competencies.

It is becoming increasingly clear that assessment and instructional personnel face different, but related, challenges. Whether they are one and the same person or not may matter. The "tester" develops a valid data base upon which to make appropriate recommendations—this involves placement and programming decisions for the handicapped student. The "teacher" must use the data gathered, design a suitable program, and instruct the student. However, if the "tester" is not the "teacher," the tester may not feel the same sense of responsibility, urgency, or involvement in making the assessment educationally relevant. Perhaps even the Individualized Assessment Plan (IAP) may be less comprehensive than expected. Or the "teacher" may not base much of the instructional program on the gathered and ongoing assessment data. In either case, both tester and teacher must develop a sense of responsibility for each other's work.

Others who need to reflect these ethical values are professionals who design assessment devices and publishers who provide them to the public. Designers of tests and other procedures are governed by clearly stated, established technical and conceptual rules. However, as discussed in the cases of several formal and informal techniques, there is already a fair amount of latitude in the way rules are followed. Consumers should purchase only tests that follow these standards.

Publishers, for their part, have the responsibility to present the nature of the test or other assessment measure clearly and thoroughly. They need to work closely with professional test designers in supplying all the information necessary to use the device appropriately, including data on reliability, validity, and norms. Professionals and publishers must work together closely to guarantee that assessment devices are of the highest quality and are free of discriminatory features.

The paramount ethical issue related to educational assessment of the handicapped is labeling. The social and psychological implications of using assessment data to designate a student as handicapped, particularly retarded, continue to plague special educators and others. *How can special education services be provided without the stigmatizing aspects of the assessment and placement process?* is a question asked by everyone engaged in serving handicapped students.

It seems there are many types of fallout from the educational assessment. For the student, there seems to be a personal awareness of a learning difficulty. For both student and peers, there is the social impact of being singled out. The challenge for everyone concerned is to find assessment and programming procedures with fewer negative and more positive side effects.

Professionalism

Professionals engaged in educational assessment must learn to monitor their own activities. Many specialty areas involved in serving the handicapped student have developed an assessment role, function, and procedures. Medicine and psychology have well-established positions in assessment; educational psychologists and counselors, reading specialists, speech-hearing-language specialists, and special educators are more recent team members. The professional organizations for these groups attempt to maintain quality practices through policies and professional publications (see Table 20–1). The professional publications of these groups, as well as other periodicals, supply updated descriptions, research, and reviews of assessment procedures, as well as discussions of current issues.

Professionals must recognize the serious threats to the credibility of their efforts. Massive amounts of paperwork, lack of supervision of assessment personnel, uncontrolled accessibility to assessment devices, and use of untrained or partially trained personnel to perform educational evaluations are a few evident abuses. For example, when 95 LD specialists serving on student evalu-

ation teams took a 64-item test of basic measurement concepts, they answered only half the questions correctly (Bennett & Shepherd, 1982). Test coverage included knowledge and application questions on reliability, validity, norms, measures of central tendency and variability, criterion-referenced interpretation, and interpretive aids. Graduate students completing a basic measurement course did significantly better.

The questionable practices of assessment team members described earlier are further documentation of the seriousness of the problem. The repercussions for the students are clear. Unless stringent measures are taken quickly, the validity of the assessment process as a basis for educational planning can be challenged at every level (McLoughlin, 1985).

The task of offering guidance to assessment personnel is not easy. There are many questions that require careful consideration.

1. Why should I use standardized tests when I can use informal ones?
2. If there are no technically adequate measures available right now, what can I do?
3. Can't I learn how to administer the test from the manual?
4. If I'm a teacher, why should I have to learn how to do assessments?
5. If tests are discriminatory, why do we use them at all?
6. In assessment, as in teaching, does every decade have a new fad?
7. Why do they teach one way to do assessments, then change it every few years?
8. Why do we have to know how other professionals do their assessments?
9. Isn't there room in assessment for professional judgment?
10. Must everything be observable and countable to be a valid target for assessment?

Professionals do not totally agree on the best responses. However, these questions represent issues for future research and discussion. Although rigid guidelines for performing assessments of special students do not seem called for, there is an obvious challenge to all professionals to establish acceptable parameters for behavior before the public (consumers, parents, courts, etc.) does.

TABLE 20–1
Selected professional groups and publications

Organizations	Publications
American Association on Mental Retardation 1719 Kalorama Road, N.W. Washington, DC 20009	*Mental Retardation* *American Journal on Mental Retardation*
American Psychological Association 1200 Seventeenth Street, N.W. Washington, DC 20036	*American Psychologist* and many other publications
American Speech, Hearing and Language Association 9030 Old Georgetown Road Washington, DC 20014	*Journal of Speech and Hearing Disorders* *Journal of Speech and Hearing Research* *Language, Speech and Hearing Services in the Schools* *ASHA*
Council for Exceptional Children 1920 Association Drive Reston, VA 22091	*Exceptional Children* *Teaching Exceptional Children*
Council for Children with Behavior Disorders	*Behavioral Disorders*
Division for Early Childhood Education	*Journal for the Division of Early Childhood*
Division on Mental Retardation	*Education and Training of the Mentally Retarded*
Division for Children with Communication Disorders	*Journal of Childhood Communication Disorders*
Council for Educational Diagnostic Services	*Diagnostique*
Division on Career Development	*Career Development for Exceptional Individuals*
Division for Learning Disabilities	*Learning Disabilities Focus* *Learning Disabilities Research*
Technology and Media Division	*Journal of Special Education Technology*
Council for Learning Disabilities P.O. Box 40303 Overland Park, KS 66204	*Learning Disability Quarterly*
International Reading Association 800 Barksdale Road Newark, DE 19711	*Reading Teacher* *Journal of Reading* *Reading Research Quarterly*

Interdisciplinary Assessment

Interdisciplinary assessments are difficult. Educational evaluations of exceptional students require a team approach. Professionals with a variety of orientations, techniques, languages, and priorities must work closely together to develop a clear picture of the student's abilities and needs. Overlaps in function and communication are the two main obstacles to effective cooperation.

PL 94–142 requires that a team perform the assessment and indicates in general terms the makeup of the team, including a professional with knowledge in the area of the suspected disabilities.

The lack of explicitness in the law may have created some confusion about the assessment team. For example, Larsen and Deshler (1978) and Poplin and Larsen (1979) describe the concern of learning disabilities teachers about the lack of explicit mention of themselves as team members.

As the various specialty areas continue to develop their expertise, competition for roles will develop. Exceptional students require the attention of many kinds of professionals, such as school psychologists, counselors, speech and language specialists, and reading teachers, at one time or another. As services for handicapped students expand, the various professions compete for primacy.

The reasons seem to be both altruistic and pragmatic; that is, the good of the handicapped student is everyone's concern, but so are economics and professional pride.

Many professional groups recognize the need for dialogue. For example, the Council for Learning Disabilities, the professional organization of learning disability teachers, has joined in dialogue with the following professional organizations on the Joint Committee on Learning Disabilities: the Orton Society, the Association for Children and Adults with Learning Disabilities, the International Reading Association, the Division for Children with Communication Disorders, and the Division for Children with Learning Disabilities. Regular meetings are devoted to providing discussions of common issues, credentials to professionals, and ways to develop mutual support. A joint definition and various position statements have resulted. These efforts hold a great deal of promise.

Affective Dimensions

One rarely mentioned aspect of educational assessment is the feelings of assessment personnel as they gather, interpret, and use their findings. Testing is different from teaching. Teaching permits a variety of activities to assist and facilitate the student's development; there are opportunities to help students over hurdles. In testing, the standards are set forth in the test manuals; even informal procedures have their administration guidelines. Students are generally on their own and are expected to respond to a standard question under a certain set of conditions. This is the particular challenge for assessment professionals who are also teachers or therapists. The assessment and teaching acts are quite different.

It also seems difficult for some educators to maintain the precision required for assessment: The habit of giving cues and prompts is not a good assessment administration technique. Nor can a teacher who supplies answers to students easily slip into the role of tester.

Furthermore, there is a "mourning" aspect to assessment that complicates it for some professionals. It is hard to test students without wanting them to do well. But in reality, the prospect for underachievers is not good. Consequently, the examiner must strive to get students to produce their best, whatever the quality. At the same time,

the assessment team member is rooting for students and may not want to be too hard on them.

There is also the obviously unpleasant task of explaining the nature of the exceptional condition to the student's parents and others, including perhaps the student. Professionals must use considerable expertise, including affective skills, to do so clearly, positively, and kindly. In working with handicapped children, professionals must be aware of and prepared to deal with their own feelings. Appreciation for the affective dimension of assessment may prove to be as beneficial as technical advancement in tests.

FUTURE GOALS

Assessment continues to be a significant element in education of exceptional students, and procedures and materials are becoming more readily available. Assessment is at a crucial juncture in its development and will need considerable guidance by qualified professionals. The regular education initiative—the movement to provide services to mildly handicapped students through a more integrated system of special and regular education—has many implications for referral, assessment, and placement practices (Hallahan, Kauffman, Lloyd, & McKinney, 1988). Current practices are predicated upon certain assumptions about the educational significance of the characteristics of special needs students, the power of assessment procedures, and the kinds of legal and educational reasons for assessing students. If special education services undergo a major reconceptualization, as is now under study, then many of the current procedures will become inappropriate and useless. However, there should be an even greater call for curriculum-based and other forms of informal assessment related to regular education curriculum and practices. Professional training will be necessary in all these areas (McLoughlin, 1985).

Specific goals to work toward in the near future include the following:

☐ Develop better, simpler, and quicker testing technology.
☐ Enhance the respectability of educational assessment through greater quality control.
☐ Improve the level of meaningful parental participation in the process.

□ Better assess the very young, adolescent, and adult handicapped individual (also account for distinctive needs of the rural and urban, minority, and other groups).

□ Provide for transitional assessment.

□ Try to describe both how and what the students learn.

□ Make a special study of learning environments.

□ Maintain educational assessment as an ongoing process of monitoring and evaluating students' programs.

□ Make team assessment and team decision making smoother.

□ Develop the role of special educators as synthesizers of team results, while continuing their dual role as teachers.

□ Place greater stress on the programming goal for assessment, while clarifying the legal application of data.

□ Maintain a balance between primary direct skill assessment and secondary assessment of correlates and possible etiology.

□ Establish a greater link between regular and special education assessment practices.

□ Encourage school administrators to give educators the time, devices, and conditions needed to conduct thorough educational assessments.

These goals and others will continue to occupy the attention of professionals. Each goal is attainable, but only with considerable application and cooperation among everyone concerned with the needs of special students.

A

Case History Form

To be completed by parent or guardian.

Child's Name _____ Age ____ School Grade ____ Sex ____

Birthdate _____ Birthplace _____

Home Address _____ City _____ State ____ Zip ____

School _____ School Address _____

Name of Present Teacher(s) _____

- -

A. FAMILY HISTORY

   1. Parents: <u>Mother</u>   <u>Father</u>

       Name _____   _____

       Address _____   _____

       Phone _____   _____

       Occupation _____   _____

       Birthplace _____   _____

       Marital Status __ Married __ Divorced   __ Married __ Divorced

                    __ Widowed __ Remarried   __ Widowed __ Remarried

       General Health _____

       Physical Disabilities _____   _____

       Left/Right Handed _____   _____

       Schooling Completed _____   _____

       Educational Difficulties _____   _____

       _____   _____

   2. Brothers and Sisters:

       Age _____ _____ _____

       Sex _____ _____ _____

       School Grade Completed _____ _____ _____

       Educational Difficulties _____ _____ _____

       Physical Difficulties _____ _____ _____

       Left/Right Handed _____ _____ _____

       Living at Home? _____ _____ _____

3. Are there any other persons living in the home? _____ If yes, explain:

_____

4. What languages are spoken in the home? _____

   If other than English, describe extent: _____

B. PHYSICAL HISTORY OF THE CHILD

   1. Name of child's physician _____

      a. Date of last physical examination _____

      b. Major results of this examination _____

      _____

      c. General physical condition _____

   2. Prenatal History

      a. Length of term _____

      b. Any illnesses during pregnancy _____

      c. Any medications during pregnancy _____

      d. Order of the pregnancy (including miscarriages)
         ___ 1st ___ 2nd ___ 3rd (___ Other)

      e. Were the parents Rh incompatible? _____

         Did they change blood? _____ With _____ Before _____ After birth

      f. Other information _____

      _____

   3. Natal

      a. Length of labor _____

      b. Type of delivery: Caesarean _____ Normal _____

         If delivery was normal, were forceps used? _____

      c. Difficulty of labor period _____

      d. Any unusual characteristics of delivery?

         _____ Breech _____ Induced _____ Other (Please specify:

         _____)

4. Postnatal

    a. Condition after birth (color, etc.) _____

    b. Any delay in beginning to breathe or stopping after breathing had

       begun? _____

    c. Incubation period, if any _____

    d. Any delay in establishing successful feeding formula; if so, how long

       was the delay and how drastic were the results? _____

       _____

    e. Was there considerable weight loss? _____

    f. Excessive crying _____

    g. Diarrhea _____ Colic _____ Anemia _____

    h. Was baby normally happy ____; cross ____; nervous ____; other ___

    i. How old was baby when he sat alone? _____

       Were you worried about his being late in sitting alone? _____

    j. How old was the baby when he crawled? _____

       Did he have a good two-sided crawl? ___ Scoot? ___ Other? _____

    k. At what age did the child begin to walk? _____

    l. How early did the baby talk in sentences of three words or more? ___

       Did the baby babble? _____ Coo? _____ Initiate? _____

    m. Check those diseases which your child has had:

Disease	Age	Approximate Length of Absence from School
Measles	—	_____
Whooping Cough	—	_____
Mumps	—	_____
Chicken Pox	—	_____
Pneumonia	—	_____
Diphtheria	—	_____
Scarlet Fever	—	_____
Rheumatic Fever	—	_____
Polio	—	_____
Influenza (severe)	—	_____
Others	—	_____

    n. Was there an <u>extremely high</u> fever accompanying any of the diseases?
       _____ If so, what was the approximate duration? _____ Was there
       any observable change in behavior after or other unusual reaction to
       any of the child's illnesses? _____

o.   Has oxygen ever had to be administered to the child? _____ Under what circumstances? _____

p.   Has child ever lost consciousness? _____ For approximately how long? ___

q.   Has the child had surgery? _____ Type? _____

r.   Has the child at any age had convulsions? _____ Seizures? _____
(Describe conditions--turned red, lost consciousness, etc.) _____
_____

s.   Is there any history of seizures in the family? _____

t.   Any accidents which caused head injuries? _____
Describe briefly _____
Did child lose consciousness? _____

u.   Any orthopedic conditions which interferred with the child's crawling,
walking, or any other kind of movement? _____ Check the type of disorder:

(1) Foot disorders _____   (3) Arm disorders _____
(2) Leg disorders _____   (4) Other _____
                                        _____

What was done to help correct the problem or problems indicated?
_____

v.   Does the child have diabetes? _____ Frequent kidney infections? _____
Frequent respiratory infections? _____ Frequent ear infections? _____
Allergic reactions? _____ Glandular abnormalities? _____ Epilepsy? _____
Cerebral Palsy? _____ Others not previously listed: _____
Is the child currently on medication: _____ If so, what? _____

w.   Does the child have any visual problems? _____ If so, what? _____
Have the eyes always been straight? _____ Has the child ever worn glasses?
_____ If so, when? _____ Is the child wearing glasses now? _____ Has the
child ever had eye surgery? _____ Has the child ever had a professional
visual examination? _____

x.   Does the child have any speech problems? _____ If so, is he having speech
therapy? _____

y. Does the child have hearing problems? _____ If so, how severe are his hearing problems? _____

z. Is your child right handed? _____ Left handed? _____ Mixed? _____ If "mixed," explain: _____

C. PSYCHOLOGICAL AND SOCIAL HISTORY OF THE CHILD

1. Has the child had previous testing or psychological examination? _____

   If yes, give date, agency, reason for examination and a summary of the major results: _____

   _____

2. Describe the child's relationship with father, indicating the nature of the disciplinary procedures used: _____

   _____

3. Describe the child's relationship with the mother, indicating the nature of the disciplinary procedures used: _____

   _____

4. Describe the child's relationships with brothers and sisters: _____

   _____

   _____

5. Describe the child's relationships with playmates, indicating number, ages, and sex of the most frequent playmates: _____

   _____

6. Give a brief description of the neighborhood in which the child lives, indicating facilities and opportunities for play or recreation: _____

   _____

7. Has the child ever been subjected to any unusual family, neighborhood or community influences? _____ If so, please describe: _____

   _____

   _____

8. Is the child as self-reliant or independent as most youngsters of his age?

   _____

   _____

9. Is there any evidence of emotional tension, fear, irritation, or lack of confidence? _____ If yes, please describe: _____

a. Any extreme behavioral symptoms

Tantrums _____

Body rocking _____

Breath holding _____

Excessive bed-wetting _____

      Age of bladder control: _____ night _____ day
      Age of bowel control: _____ night _____ day

Other _____

_____

_____

b. Any unusual behavior patterns

Withdrawal _____

Anger _____

Hostility _____

Overly affectionate _____

Overly sensitive _____

10. Can you recall any time in pre-school or school life when there was a sudden change in child's behavior? If so, was there any particular thing in child's behavior? If so, was there any particular thing (illness, etc.) that preceded this? _____

11. In comparison with other children of this age, would you describe the child's total development as below average, above average, or average? _____

D. EDUCATIONAL HISTORY OF THE CHILD

1. Did the child attend nursery school? _____ Number of years: _____ Age _____

2. Age of entering first grade: _____ Total years of school attended: _____

3. Has the child repeated any grades? _____ If yes, indicate the grades and give reasons for retention: _____

_____

4. Has the child skipped any grades? _____ If yes, indicate the grades and give reasons for acceleration: _____

_____

5. Schools attended by the child:

    Name and Location   Grades   Dates   Reasons for Withdrawal

_____ _____ _____ _____

_____ _____ _____ _____

_____ _____ _____ _____

_____ _____ _____ _____

6. Is the child now receiving any special school services such as special education, speech therapy, reading services, tutoring, etc.? _____

If yes, please detail: _____

_____

_____

7. What is your judgment concerning the adequacy of the general educational program which has been provided for your child? _____

_____

8. What is your opinion concerning the nature of the child's problem or problems? _____

_____

9. What do you think may have contributed to the development of this problem?

_____

_____

_____

10. Is there any additional information which you feel might have significant bearing on this assessment? _____ If yes, please detail: _____

_____

_____

_____

_____

Note. From the Learning Improvement Center, University of Louisville, Louisville, KY. Reprinted by permission.

B

Sample Case Report

Name: John Jones	Parents' Names: Mr. and Mrs. H. W. Nelson
Date of Testing: 3/2/90	Address: 1620 Parkers Mill Road, Boston, MA 02100
Date of Birth: 1/2/80	Phone: 761-2340
Age: 10−2	School Currently Attending: Pines Elementary
Sex: male	School Address: 69 Rhodes Road, Boston, MA 02100
Grade level: 5.7	Phone: 761-3519
Examiner: Jean Thompson	Teacher: Ms. Joan Thomas
Date of Report: 3/15/90	Principal: Mrs. Linda Smith-Lewis

REASON FOR REFERRAL

John was referred by his classroom teacher, Ms. Thomas, because of low achievement in academic areas, particularly reading, math, and writing. She reports that John seems discouraged. John's parents also are concerned by his level of achievement, in spite of extra help in reading.

RELEVANT BACKGROUND

John lives at home with his mother, stepfather, three stepbrothers, and two stepsisters. His mother's divorce occurred when John was 2 years old. She remarried 2 years ago.

John did attend nursery school, but did not attend kindergarten, before entering the first grade at 5-11. In the second grade, John was referred for an intellectual evaluation by the Lee County Schools. Results indicated an IQ in the normal range. He was also given a battery of psychological tests, but no significant problems were found. His vision and hearing have been tested twice; no problems are evident. During the third grade, John was tutored in reading for the entire year. He was also tutored the summer after grade 3, again for reading.

John is currently in a remedial reading class. His academic records show below average performance. Mrs. Nelson, his mother, reports that his mind wanders after a short time period. She also states that John's fifth grade teacher feels John should be retained in the fifth grade due to immaturity.

Mrs. Nelson reports that John gets along well with children in the neighborhood. She also reports that John feels positive toward school and his teachers. However, it is difficult for John to complete his work. Mrs. Nelson said John can be manipulative, if allowed. John has had no unusual medical problems.

OBSERVATIONS

John adjusted well to the testing situation. When he arrived with his mother, he talked freely to the examiner. After his mother left, John remained calm. During the testing session, John was cooperative and generally followed directions well. A number of times he requested to have material repeated. Only one or two times was it necessary to call John's attention back to the test tasks.

TESTS AND PROCEDURES USED

The following tests and informal procedures were administered to John: *Peabody Individual Achievement Test–Revised (PIAT–R)*, *Woodcock Reading Mastery Tests–Revised (WRMT–R)*, *Gray Oral Reading Test–Revised (GORT–R)*, *Test of Reading Comprehension (TORC)*, *KeyMath Revised (KeyMath–R)*, *BRIGANCE® Diagnostic Inventory of Basic Skills (BRIGANCE®)*, *Test of Language Development–2, Intermediate (TOLD–2)*, *Test of Written Language–2 (TOWL–2)*, *Visual-Motor Integration Test (VMI)*, *Behavior Rating Profile (BRP)*, as well as language sampling, error analysis, and interviews with teachers, parents, and the student. The psychological report referred to in this report was completed by the staff of Children's Clinic on March 10, 1990, and the specific results are available through that agency; they administered the *Wechsler Intelligence Scale for Children–Revised (WISC–R)* and *AAMD Adaptive Behavior Scale–Public School Version (ABS)*.

GENERAL APTITUDE

According to the results of a recent psychological report from Children's Clinic, John's overall intellectual functioning on the *WISC–R* is in the low average range (Full Scale IQ 82, Verbal 80, Performance 81). Low average to below average performances are seen in Comprehension (scale score, 6), Similarities (scale score, 5), Arithmetic (scale score, 6), Picture Arrangement (scale score, 6), and Coding (scale score, 5). Performances in other areas are within the average range. In addition, John's adaptive behavior, as indicated on the *ABS*, is average for his age when compared to regular class peers. His teachers and parents confirm his general aptitude in school and home activities, as well as his general ability to cope with environmental demands.

LEVEL OF ACHIEVEMENT

According to the *PIAT–R*, John's overall academic functioning is in the below average range (grade score, 3.0), 2 years below his grade placement. His relative strengths are in reading words in isolation (grade score, 4.1), spelling (grade score, 3.9), and general information (grade score, 4.2), although all are in the low average range. John's rote memory seems particularly good in these areas. However, his relative weaknesses are in reading comprehension (grade score, 1.9) and mathematics (grade score, 2.6), both below average performances. John's teacher reports a similar pattern in the classroom, that is, adequate rote skills but poor comprehension and application ability. There appears to be a significant difference between John's ability level and his academic achievement level.

READING PERFORMANCE

According to John's performance on the *WRMT–R*, his overall reading ability is in the low average range (grade score, 3.0), 2 years below his grade placement. His relative strengths are oral reading of real words (grade score, 4.0) and of nonsense words (grade score, 3.8); these reading recognition skills are in the average to low average range. Reading and providing antonyms, synonyms, and word analogies (grade score, 3.5) was also low average. He seems to use both visual memory skills and phonics in decoding words; his performance in reading real or nonsense words seems similar. However, his relative weakness is in reading comprehension (2.0), that is, substituting a missing word in a passage; the performance is in the below average range and represents a significant problem in understanding and relating read material. A similar pattern was noted on the *PIAT–R*, that is, better word recognition than comprehension skills.

When given the *BRIGANCE®*, John achieved mastery on three-letter consonant blends and syllabication. He was weak in silent letters, unaccented schwa, accents, and possessives. John had severe problems when asked to read passages on the *GORT–R*, obtaining unrecordable scores. His weaknesses were in mispronunciation (for example, *another* for *other*), omissions of words, insertions, and repetitions. Such problems in reading passages, rather than words in isolation, may be related to John's various difficulties in comprehension. He was not able to recall basic facts about the reading passages when asked.

On the *TORC*, John's difficulties in reading comprehension emerged. Although his overall performance was below average (grade score, 3.0), there was a marked difference between knowledge of the meaning of words and the application of language and comprehension skills to passage reading. General vocabulary and vocabulary skills in specific content areas (for example, mathematics) were relative strengths, although in the low average range of performance (grade score, 3.2 to 4.4). However, John's relative weaknesses were in recognizing similar syntactical structures (grade score, 2.5) and comprehending the meaning of passages (grade score, 3.0). In these areas, as well as in sequencing sentences into a story (grade score, 3.2), John's performance was in the below average range.

MATH PERFORMANCE

According to John's performance on the *KeyMath–R*, his overall math ability is in the low average range (grade score, 3.6). His relative strengths are in content areas (numeration, rational numbers, and geometry) and written computation (addition, subtraction, multiplication, and division) and mental computation; these skills are in the average to low average range (grade scores 3.5 to 4.5). However, his relative weaknesses are in most of the problem-solving and other application skills, in which the performances are in the below average range: measurement (grade score 2.0), time and money (grade score 1.9), estimation (grade score 2.0), interpreting data (grade score 2.2), and problem solving (grade score 2.5). There is a major difference in the development of computational skills (written and mental) compared to more conceptual and applied skills. John's teacher and parents also noted these problems in mathematics at school and at home.

An error analysis of John's written products at school indicates problems in adding or subtracting more than 2-digit numbers, especially when regrouping is required. John also has a tendency to reverse the numbers of an answer that is otherwise correct. In an effort to complete assignments, he also seems to write down any answer after a particular point. In an informal interview concerning the area of reading and solving math word problems, John was not able to explain how to analyze the math problem. In particular, he does not know how to identify the key quantitative terms in the problem, choose the appropriate operations or formula needed, and assign meaning and value to the computed answers. Also, on the *BRIGANCE®*, John demonstrates mastery of the following applied skills: money (recognition of and value of money); time (telling time to the hour and half hour); calendar (days, months, and seasons); and linear measurement (measurement with a ruler). However, he lacks mastery of the following and subsequent skills on the *BRIGANCE®*: money (relating coins and making change); time (telling time to finer units, relating and converting time units, etc.); calendar (relating calendar units, using the calendar, etc.); and linear measurement (relating and converting units).

ORAL LANGUAGE PERFORMANCE

When given the *TOLD–2*, John's oral language development is in the average range (Language Quotient 90). His relative strengths are in understanding and using vocabulary. His performance is average in these areas. However, his relative weaknesses are in understanding syntax and grammar and using syntax and grammar.

WRITTEN LANGUAGE PERFORMANCE

In written language, John's performance on the *TOWL–2* also seems in the low average range (Written Language Quotient, 82). His performances in vocabulary, spelling, punctuation and capitalization are in the average or low average range. However, his relative weaknesses are in the level of creative maturity of written material, the use of grammar, and handwriting. An informal analysis of the written grammar performance and other products indicates particular deficits in past and future tense, plurals, and pronouns. Many of these written language problems may be complicating John's effort to compose and develop a passage and are similar to the deficits noted in oral language. Furthermore, the problems may also be related to the conceptual deficits involved in reading and math learning difficulties.

An analysis of the classroom curriculum and materials indicates a particular emphasis on rote academic skills, particularly using written seatwork for practice. These instructional procedures may be associated with John's poor development in comprehension and application skills.

SPECIFIC LEARNING ABILITIES AND STRATEGIES

John seems to have a deficit in motor skills needed for handwriting and copying tasks in the classroom. On the *VMI*, John's efforts to copy various shapes are in the below average range (age score, 6–2). He has similar problems in copying from the board and writing letters, as reported by his teacher. The particular letters he cannot reproduce correctly are cursive *o*, *a*, *d*, *e*, *y*, *h*, *i*, *m*, *r*, and *t*. As noted earlier, he also reverses numbers. This problem may be compounded by the instructional emphasis on written seatwork.

CLASSROOM BEHAVIOR

John's classroom behavior and emotional development seem average. However, on the *BRP*, John indicates a below average perception of himself at school and with peers. Parents and teachers indicate that his behavior is average at home and school respectively. During an informal interview, John's teacher did indicate some concern about John's poor self-concept and lack of interaction with his peers. His parents also report some recent expressions of self-deprecation by John (for example, "I'm stupid" and "I can't seem to get it"). John may be developing a lower sense of self-esteem because of continued academic frustration. From a brief observation in the classroom and school, it appears that John is attentive, keeps to himself, and is one of the last students in the class to complete tasks.

SUMMARY AND CONCLUSIONS

John's overall academic performance is 2 years below his grade placement. Although none of his academic skills are appropriate for his grade level, he is stronger in reading recognition, spelling, and knowledge of general facts than in reading comprehension and mathematics. The developmental level of his general ability and adaptive skills is higher than his academic and language development.

In reading, John's overall performance is 2 years below his grade placement. His abilities to name letters and orally read words in isolation are somewhat better than his understanding and use of read material.

In oral reading, John has particular problems when reading a passage and lacks such specific skills as reading words with silent letters, unaccented schwa, accents, and possessives. In comprehension, John seems to know the meaning of individual words but cannot comprehend the more subtle aspects of passage reading, particularly the syntactical structures involved. Specific deficits in comprehension are remembering details of a passage, sequencing details, having a sense of time, and predicting outcomes of passages.

In mathematics, John's overall performance is nearly 2 years below his grade level. While having relative strengths in content and basic operations, he has particular weaknesses in estimating, solving problems, interpreting data, using money, telling time, and measuring. Specific skills deficits in computation are regrouping in 2-digit problems and reversing numerals. Specific skill deficits in problem solving are processing the steps of a math problem and relating the units of money, time, and measurement.

Although John's oral language is average in many ways, he has specific problems in understanding and expressing grammar correctly, particularly tenses, plurals, pronouns, possessives, and prepositions. They are influencing his ability to follow directions and communicate.

In written language, John's skills are low average for his age. He does have better developed skills in vocabulary, spelling, punctuation, and capitalization, and use of sentence structure than in creativity, use of grammar, and handwriting. Similar language structures seem involved in his oral and written language problems. They may be a common factor across the reading comprehension, math problem solving, and language difficulties. An instructional emphasis on rote skills and written products may be compounding these skill deficits.

Although John's social behavior at home and school is generally acceptable, he does seem to have a poor self-concept, relates poorly to peers, and does not complete his work quickly. These problems may be related to academic failures and a specific motor disability in copying and producing letters and numbers.

SUGGESTED GOALS AND SERVICES

A variety of curricular needs must be addressed when an IEP is composed. In oral reading John must learn to avoid mispronunciations, omissions, additions, and repetitions; particularly troublesome words are those with silent letters, unaccented schwa, accents, and possessives. Appropriate goals in reading comprehension are to remember details in material and to achieve a better understanding of sequence of events, time concepts, and outcomes.

In mathematics, priority should be given instruction in problem solving, measurement, time and money, estimation, and interpretation of data. However, written and verbal computational skills also need reinforcement, especially 2-digit addition and subtraction.

Identified oral language deficits are the understanding and use of tenses, pronouns, possessives, plurals, and prepositions, as well as the ability to follow oral directions. Increased length and creativity in writing, grammatically correct passages (i.e., tenses, plurals, and pronouns), and legible cursive writing (especially, *o, a, d, e, y, h, i, m, r, t*) are needing attention.

Finally, John needs a better self-concept, relationships with peers, and task completion skills.

Certain special education and related services are suggested by these results. The regular fifth grade teacher and a resource teacher should be able to meet the academic and behavioral needs of the student. A language specialist might be helpful in conducting additional assessments and providing any necessary therapy, as well as in helping teachers integrate language training in the curriculum. The school counselor could assist the student in the behavioral areas.

C

Answers to Review Questions

CHAPTER 1

1. It is the systematic process of gathering education- ally relevant information in order to make legal and instructional decisions about the special services to exceptional students.
2. false
3. screening, eligibility, program planning, monitoring student progress, and program evaluation
4. i, h, c, f, a, g, b, d, e
5. false
6. true
7. true
8. true
9. true
10. false
11. c, e, f, b, h, d, g, a
12. true
13. e, a, c, d, f, b
14. false
15. false
16. true
17. Is there a school performance problem? Is it re- lated to a handicapping condition? What are the educational needs?

CHAPTER 2

1. Due process is a procedure that seeks to insure the fairness of educational decisions and the ac- countability of both the professionals and parents making these decisions.
2. true
3. true
4. true
5. true
6. false

7. true
8. true
9. true
10. true
11. true
12. true
13. true
14. Any three of the following: An assessment must
   a. Be in the student's native language
   b. Be administered by trained professionals
   c. Be appropriate for the use for which it is employed
   d. Go beyond intelligence testing
   e. Be tailored to the handicap
   f. Use a variety of procedures
   g. Be as multidisciplinary as necessary
15. a. current level of functioning
   b. annual goals
   c. short-term instructional objectives
   d. type of special education and related services
   e. amount of time in the regular classroom
   f. beginning and ending dates
   g. evaluation schedule and procedures
16. false
17. true
18. Any three of the following: regular classroom, consultant teacher, itinerant teacher, resource room, special class, special day school, residential model
19. false
20. true
21. false
22. g, d, c, f, e, a, b

CHAPTER 3

1. F, T, T, F
2. educational

3. c
4. b
5. Any three of the following: age, grade, and gender of norm group members; method of selection; representativeness of norm group; size of group; recency of test norms
6. e
7. d, b, a, c, e
8. standard error of measurement
9. T, F, T, T
10. Any four of the following: culture-free and culture-fair tests, culture-specific measures, separate norms for minority group students, pluralistic assessment, modification of administration procedures, replacement of standardized tests with informal procedures, moratorium on standardized testing

CHAPTER 4

1. b, d
2. a
3. item 9
4. c, a, b, d
5. Any two of the following: to determine whether the student is comfortable during test administration, to gather information about how the student approaches a work situation, to determine the student's response style and work style, to collect data on the student's attitudes and perceptions, to look for warning signs of handicaps
6. a. 7–1
   b. 17–3
   c. 4–11
7. a. 6
   b. 22
8. c
9. d
10. d, a, e, b, c
11. 67 to 79
12. Any four of the following: paraphrase test instructions; provide a demonstration; change the presentation mode; change the response mode; allow the student to use aids; provide prompts; give feedback; offer positive reinforcement; change the physical location of the test; change the tester

CHAPTER 5

1. a, c, d
2. T, T, F, F, T

3. error, response
4. d, c, a, b
5. curriculum
6. a. a worksheet with twenty 2-digit plus 2-digit addition problems requiring regrouping
   b. "Write the answers to these problems. Do as many as you can in 5 minutes."
   c. fifteen problems correct within a 5-minute time period
7. a
8. Any three of the following: checklists, rating scales, questionnaires, interviews
9. true
10. d

CHAPTER 6

1. a, b, d
2. false
3. computer, printer, modem
4. a
5. bulletin boards
6. true
7. d
8. false
9. c
10. d, e, c, b, a
11. true
12. a
13. b
14. c
15. Any three of the following: poor reading skills, poor writing/typing skills, inability to control behavior, poor attention to task

CHAPTER 7

1. T, T, F
2. Any two of the following: to determine if there is a problem in academic achievement, to identify areas of educational need, to assess academic progress
3. a, b, d, e, g, h
4. d
5. c
6. Any two of the following: time limits, reading skills are required, students respond in writing, instructions are presented orally, independent work skills are assumed

7. c, e, f, h, d, b, a, g

8. b

9. false

10. c

CHAPTER 8

1. Learning aptitude, or the ability to learn, refers to an individual's capacity for altering his or her behavior when presented with new information or experiences.

2. T, F, T, T

3. c

4. Any two of the following: tests must be nondiscriminatory; tests must be administered in the language of the student; tests must be validated for the purpose for which they are used; tests must be administered by trained professionals; no one test score may be the sole basis for determining educational placement

5. a, b, d, e, f, h

6. c, a, d, b, e

7. F, T, T, T, F

8. a

9. d, c, c, a

10. a

11. b

CHAPTER 9

1. d

2. perception, attention

3. T

4. b, c, d, e

5. F, T, T, T

6. a, b, c, e, g

7. a

8. c, f, a, b, e, d

9. a, d, e

10. a

11. b

CHAPTER 10

1. T

2. Any three of the following: conduct problems, self-concept, acceptance by peers, interests and attitudes toward school and learning, influence of the classroom learning environment

3. d

4. a, c, d, f

5. teachers, parents, peers

6. F

7. f, e, d, b, c, a

8. (2) Select a measurement system.
   (3) Set up the data-collection system.
   (4) Select a data-reporting system.
   (5) Carry out the observations.

9. sociometric

10. c, d

11. a

CHAPTER 11

1. c

2. comprehension, interaction

3. b, c, e

4. e

5. T

6. b, d, e, c, a

7. T, F, T, F

8. a, b, b, b

9. independent, instructional, frustration

10. a, d, e, f

11. a, b, f

12. instructional, interpersonal, physical

13. b

14. d

CHAPTER 12

1. T

2. problem solving, application

3. e

4. a

5. T

6. d, c, a, d, a, b

7. N, S, S, N, S

8. algorithms

9. T

10. a, b, d

11. computation, problem solving

12. writing numerals

13. c

14. c

CHAPTER 13

1. to gather information for planning the instructional program
2. spelling, handwriting, composition
3. T, F, F, T, F
4. the product
5. e, f, c, a, d, b
6. b
7. phonetic, nonphonetic
8. a, c, d, f
9. write a story about a picture
10. T
11. time, skills
12. d
13. c

CHAPTER 14

1. d
2. phonology, morphology, syntax, semantics, pragmatics
3. T, F, T, F, T
4. F
5. dialect
6. d, a, e, b, c
7. a
8. c
9. length, utterance
10. F
11. d
12. verbal
13. b
14. f
15. c

CHAPTER 15

1. a. What are the educational needs, annual goals, and objectives?
   b. What kinds of special education and related services are necessary?
   c. What is the least restrictive and most appropriate educational environment?
2. a. Identification
   b. Reason for referral
   c. Relevant background
   d. Behavioral observations
   e. Assessment results and discussion

f. Summary and conclusion
   g. Suggested goals and services
3. a. false
   b. false
   c. false
   d. false
   e. false
   f. false
   g. false
   h. true
4. medical, educational, and sociocultural
5. is
6. age, grade level, and mental age
7. reading, math, oral language, written language, specific learning abilities and strategies, and classroom behavior and social and emotional development
8. receptive and expressive vocabulary, syntax, morphology, phonology, and pragmatics
9. a. true
   b. false
   c. true
   d. true
   e. true
10. SEM and SEM_{diff}
11. c, a, e, d, b
12. content and structural composition of assessment tasks
13. a, b, c, d, e
14. T, F, F, F, F
15. true

CHAPTER 16

1. Any two of the following:
   a. Monitor the appropriateness of the program.
   b. Guide needed modification.
   c. Provide basis for reexamining placement.
   d. Indicate attainment of instructional objectives.
2. the students, their teachers, the instructional tasks, and environmental conditions
3. formative, summative
4. purpose, time, and level of generalization
5. true
6. acquisition
7. generalization and adaptation
8. false
9. physical, social, and academic
10. academically and socially
11. true

12. anecdotal records
13. Any two of the following:
    a. Anecdotal records
    b. Observations
    c. Checklists
    d. Coding systems
    e. Work folders
    f. Charts
    g. Self-checking materials
    h. Integrating materials
    i. Daily probes
    j. Diagnostic teaching
14. b, d, f, c, e, a
15. task analysis
16. 3, 1, 2, 4
17. frequency, duration, rate, and percentage
18. the criteria used
19. true

CHAPTER 17

1. Five areas:
   a. Identification/referral
   b. Assessment
   c. Programming
   d. Implementation
   e. Evaluation
2. Any two of the following:
   a. Access to certain types of information
   b. May aid in gathering data
   c. PL 94–142 and PL 99–457 mandates
   d. Basis of greater cooperation
3. "yes" and "no"
4. true
5. true
6. true
7. true
8. true
9. true
10. false
11. percentiles
12. intraindividual
13. *Exceptional Parent*
14. false
15. true

CHAPTER 18

1. screening, in-depth assessment, program design, program monitoring, and program evaluation
2. false

3. false
4. Any two of the following:
   a. Children may be falsely labeled.
   b. Children may be stigmatized.
   c. Lack of programs and teachers.
   d. Questionable validity and reliability.
5. core
6. true
7. Any two of the following:
   a. Directly measure a child's specific observable behavior
   b. Should be done over a period of time
   c. Incorporate the viewpoint of a variety of people involved with the child
   d. Perform it in the natural environment
   e. Focus on critical skills for current functioning
   f. Gather data useful for instructional planning
8. false
9. parent informants or others very knowledgeable about the child
10. superior
11. true
12. *LAP-E*
13. true
14. true
15. *Early Socioemotional Development*

CHAPTER 19

1. It is the process of systematically coordinating all school, family, and community components together to facilitate each individual's potential for economic, social, and personal fulfillment.
2. false
3. false
4. awareness and knowledge, general aptitude and work/study habits, interests, and specific skills
5. true
6. *Dictionary of Occupational Titles*
7. work sample
8. reading, writing
9. isn't
10. marking an appropriate picture
11. high
12. Any two of the following: *Wide Range Employability Sample Test,* the *Singer Vocational Evaluation System,* or others mentioned on page 000.
13. false
14. time, number of errors
15. false

D

Addresses of Test Publishers

Academic Therapy Publications, 20 Commercial Blvd., Novato, CA 94949

Allyn and Bacon, Inc., 7 Wells Ave., Newton, MA 02159

American Association on Mental Retardation, 1719 Kalorama Rd., N. W., Washington, DC 20009

American Guidance Service, Publishers' Building, P.O. Box 99, Circle Pines, MN 55014

Aspen Systems Corporation, 1600 Research Blvd., Rockville, MD 20850

Behavior Science Systems, Inc., P.O. Box 1108, Minneapolis, MN 55440

The Ber-Sil Company, 3412 Seaglen Drive, Rancho Palos Verdes, CA 90274

Bobbs-Merrill Company, Inc., 4300 West 62nd Street, Indianapolis, IN 46268

Childcraft Education Corporation, 20 Kilmer Road, Edison, NJ 08818

Communication Skill Builders, P.O. Box 42050-D, Dept. 70, Tucson, AZ 85733

Conover Company, P.O. Box 155, Omro, WI 54963

Consulting Psychologists Press, Inc., 577 College Ave., Palo Alto, CA 94306

Nigel Cox, 69 Fawn Dr., Cheshire, CT 06410

CTB/McGraw-Hill, 2500 Garden Road, Monterey, CA 93940

Curriculum Associates, Inc., 5 Esquire Road, North Billerica, MA 01862

Devereux Foundation, 19 South Waterloo Rd., Box 400, Devon, PA 19333

DLM Teaching Resources, One DLM Park, Allen, TX 75002

Early Recognition Intervention Systems, P.O. Box 1635, Pawtucket, RI 02862

Economy Company, Box 25308, 1901 North Walnut, Oklahoma City, OK 73125

EdITS, P.O. Box 7234, San Diego, CA 92107

Edmark Corporation, P.O. Box 3903, Bellevue, WA 98009

Educational Services, P.O. Box 1835, Columbia, MO 65205

Educational Technologies, Inc., 1007 Whitehead Road-Exit, Trenton, NJ 08638

Educational Testing Service, Princeton, NJ 08541

Foreworks Publications, Box 9747, North Hollywood, CA 91609

Grune & Stratton, Inc., Orlando, FL 32887

Hahnemann University, Department of Mental Health Services, Broad & Vine, Philadelphia, PA 19102

Harcourt Brace Jovanovich, Inc.—See Psychological Corporation

Houghton Mifflin Company, One Beacon Street, Boston, MA 02108

Institute for Personality and Ability Testing, P.O. Box 188, Champaign, IL 61820

Jastak Associates, Inc., P.O. Box 4460, Wilmington, DE 19807

LADOCA Project and Publishing Foundation, Inc., East 51st Ave. & Lincoln St., Denver, CO 80216

Learning Multi-Systems, Inc., 340 Coyier Lane, Madison, WI 53713

Modern Curriculum Press, 13900 Prospect Rd., Cleveland, OH 44136

NCE Interpretive Scoring Systems, 4401 West 7th St., Minneapolis, MN 55435

Northwestern University Press, 625 Colfax St., Evanston, IL 60201

PRO-ED, 8700 Shoal Creek Blvd., Austin, TX 78758

Psychological Corporation, 555 Academic Court, San Antonio, TX 78204

Publishers Test Service, 2500 Garden Road, Monterey, CA 93940

Richard C. Owen Publishers, Inc., 135 Katonah Ave., Katonah, NY 10536

Riverside Publishing Company, 8420 Bryn Mawr Ave., Chicago, IL 60631

Scholastic Testing Services, Inc., 480 Meyer Road, Bensenville, IL 60106

Science Research Associates, Inc., 155 North Wacker Dr., Chicago, IL 60606

Slosson Educational Publications, Inc., P.O. Box 280, East Aurora, NY 14052

Stanford University Press, Stanford, CA 94305

Stoelting Company, 1350 South Kostner Ave., Chicago, IL 60623

Talent Assessment, Inc., P.O. Box 5987, Jacksonville, FL 33247

Teachers College Press, Teachers College, Columbia University, New York, NY 10027

United Educational Services, Inc., P.O. Box 605, East Aurora, NY 14052

University of Arizona, Division of Special Education and Rehabilitation, Tucson, AZ 85721

University of Illinois Press, 54 East Gregory Drive, P.O. Box 5081, Station A, Champaign, IL 61820

University of Iowa, Publications Order Dept., Iowa City, IA 52242

University of Miami, c/o Dr. Herbert C. Quay, P.O. Box 248074, Coral Gables, FL 33124

University of Michigan Press, P.O. Box 1104, Ann Arbor, MI 48106

University of Wisconsin-Madison, Vocational Studies Center, 964 Educational Sciences Bldg., 1025 West Johnson St., Madison, WI 53706

Valpar International Corporation, 2450 Ruthrauff Rd., No. 180, Tucson, AZ 85705

Vocational Research Institute, 2100 Arch St. Suite 6104, Philadelphia, PA 19103

VORT, P.O. Box 60132, Palo Alto, CA 94306

Western Psychological Services, 12031 Wilshire Boulevard, Los Angeles, CA 90025

William C. Brown Publishers, 2460 Kerper Blvd., Dubuque, IA 52001

Zaner-Bloser, 2300 West 5th Ave., P.O. Box 16764, Columbus, OH 43216

Glossary

Acuity The physiological ability to receive sensory information.

Adaptive behavior The ability to cope with the demands of the environment; includes self-help, communication, and social skills.

Advocacy Clear expression of support for the rights of exceptional persons and their parents.

Age score Also called *age equivalent;* a score that translates test performance into an estimated age; reported in years and months.

Alternate score A score resulting from the administration of standardized tests under altered conditions.

Anecdotal records Written notes kept by teachers on a daily basis about student performance and needed modifications of instructional programs.

Application skills The ability to use reading, mathematics, and other academic skills in real-life situations.

Articulation The production of the speech sounds or phonemes.

Assessment The systematic process of gathering educationally relevant information in order to make legal and instructional decisions about the provision of special services to exceptional students.

Attention The selective narrowing or focusing on the relevant stimuli in a situation; a prerequisite for perception, memory, and all types of learning activities.

Basal In test administration, the point at which it can be assumed that the student would receive full credit for all easier test items.

Bilingual education The provision of special services to students whose primary language is not English; may include instruction in the primary language, training in English language skills, and development of multicultural awareness.

Ceiling In test administration, the point at which it can be assumed that the student would receive no credit for all more difficult test items.

Checklist An informal assessment device that allows an informant to quickly scan a list of descriptions and check those that apply to the student in question.

Chronological age The number of years and months since birth.

Classroom quiz An informal assessment tool, usually designed by teachers, to assess students' classroom learning.

Clinical analysis A method of interpretation of assessment results that considers student strengths and weaknesses and the interrelationships among the factors assessed.

Clinical interview Asking a student questions about the strategies used to perform a task as it is performed or immediately afterwards.

Cloze procedure A technique for assessing reading skills in which words are omitted from a text and the student is asked to fill in the missing words.

Coaching In test administration, the practice of helping the student arrive at answers.

Composition Also called *written expression;* the subskill of written language in which writers produce connected text.

Comprehension skills In reading, the ability to understand what is read; may be assessed via oral or silent reading.

Computation skills In mathematics, the arithmetic operations of addition, subtraction, multiplication, and division as applied to whole numbers, fractions, and decimals.

Conferences Formal meetings at which professionals and parents of exceptional students discuss assessment results, eligibility, placement, program design, and other matters.

Confidence interval A range of scores in which it is likely that the student's true score will fall; constructed by means of the standard error of measurement.

Continuous recording An observational technique in which all of the student's behaviors are studied.

Correlation A descriptive statistic that expresses the degree of relationship between two sets of scores.

Criterion-referenced test An informal assessment device that assesses skill mastery; compares the student's performance to curricular standards.

Curriculum-based assessment Also called *curriculum-based measurement*; direct and frequent assessment of critical school behaviors to monitor students' progress in the curriculum.

Data base management programs Software programs used on computers for the management of information; allow the user to enter, store, edit, sort, and retrieve data.

Decoding The process by which readers analyze a word in order to pronounce it; includes sight recognition, phonic analysis, structural analysis, and contextual analysis.

Demonstration In test administration, tasks similar to test items that are used to teach test procedures to the student.

Developmental approach An approach to assessment that focuses on stages of development and expectations based on age.

Diagnosis The process of establishing the cause or causes of an illness or condition and prescribing appropriate treatment.

Diagnostic probe An informal technique in which a test task or instructional condition is altered in order to observe if a change in the student's performance results.

Diagnostic teaching An informal assessment strategy in which two or more instructional conditions are compared to determine which is most effective.

Dialect An alternate form of a language that differs in some way from the standard language.

Discrepancy analysis The procedure in which scores are compared to determine whether they are significantly different; most often used to compare expected and actual achievement in the identification of learning disabilities.

Due process Procedural safeguards established to insure the rights of exceptional students and their parents.

Duration recording An observational technique in which the length (or duration) of the target behavior is noted.

Ecological approach An approach to assessment that focuses on the student's interaction with the environment rather than on the deficits of the student.

Error analysis A type of work sample analysis in which the incorrect responses of the student are described and categorized.

Event recording An observational technique in which the frequency of the target behavior is noted.

Expressive language The production of language for communication; for example, speaking and writing.

Family assessment Assessment of child needs and characteristics likely to affect family functioning, parent–child interactions, family needs, critical events, and family strengths.

Fine motor skills In motor development, the use of the small muscles of the body, especially in eye-hand coordination tasks.

First language The language learned first by an individual; also called *home language* or *native language*.

Formal assessment Assessment procedures that contain specific rules for administration, scoring, and interpretation; generally norm-referenced and/or standardized.

Formative evaluation On-going evaluation; results are used for program modification.

Functional approach An approach to assessment that focuses on skills needed for current tasks.

Grade score Also called *grade equivalent;* a score that translates test performance into an estimated grade; expressed in grades and tenths of grades.

Gross motor skills In motor development, the use of the large muscles of the body.

Group test A test administered to more than one student at the same time.

Individual test A test administered to one student at a time.

Individualized Assessment Plan (IAP) A plan in which the steps and procedures of the assessment are organized according to the reasons for the assessment.

Individualized Education Program (IEP) A written educational plan developed for each school-aged student eligible for special education.

Individualized Family Services Plan (IFSP) A written service plan mandated by PL 99–457 that describes the needs of infants and preschoolers and their families and specifies the goals to be achieved and services they will receive to achieve those goals.

Informal assessment Assessment procedures without rigid administration, scoring, and interpretation rules; includes criterion-referenced tests, task analysis, inventories, etc.

Informal Reading Inventory (IRI) An informal assessment device that measures both word recognition and comprehension skills; scores include

Instructional, Independent, and Frustration reading levels.

Intelligence The ability of an individual to understand and cope with the environment; generally assessed with intelligence or "IQ" tests that are measures of academic aptitude.

Interindividual assessment Assessment that compares the performance of the student to the performance of others.

Interval The scale of measurement characterized by equal intervals between points in the scale.

Interview An informal assessment procedure in which the tester questions an informant.

Intraindividual assessment Assessment that compares a student's performance on various measures to one another; results in a statement of "relative" strengths and weaknesses.

Inventory An informal assessment device that samples the student's ability to perform selected skills within a curricular sequence.

IQ Intelligence quotient; a standard score yielded by measures of intellectual performance.

Job analysis A task analysis of the specific skills required by a job.

Language proficiency The degree to which an individual is skilled in a language; when students speak languages other than English, proficiency is assessed to determine the primary language.

Language sample A sample of oral language used for analysis.

Latency In test administration, the amount of time between presentation of the test question and the student's response.

Learning aptitude The capacity for altering one's behavior when presented with new information; the ability to learn; generally measured by tests of intellectual performance and adaptive behavior.

Learning environment The instructional, interpersonal, and physical characteristics of the classroom which may influence student performance.

Learning strategies Methods used by individuals in their interactions with learning tasks.

Least restrictive environment According to PL 94–142, the educational placement for handicapped students that is as close to the regular classroom as feasible.

MA Mental age; a score yielded by some measures of intellectual performance.

Mainstreaming Integration of exceptional students physically, academically and socially with nonhandicapped peers.

Mean The arithmetic average; a measure of central tendency.

Median The middle score in a distribution of scores; a measure of central tendency.

Memory The ability to retrieve previously learned information.

Mildly handicapped Students eligible for services for mild mental retardation, learning disabilities, and mild emotional disturbance (behavior disorders).

Miscue A decoding error in reading.

Mode The most common score; a measure of central tendency.

Modem A device used to link computers with one another over telephone lines; needed to access electronic information services.

Morphology The study of morphemes, or the smallest meaningful units of language.

Motor skills Skills using the small and large muscles of the body; includes fine and gross motor skills.

Nominal The scale of measurement in which data are sorted into categories.

Nondiscriminatory assessment Assessment that does not penalize students for their sex, native language, race, culture, or handicap.

Norm-referenced test A test that compares a student's performance to that of the students in the norm group.

Observation An informal assessment technique that involves specifying, counting, and recording student behaviors.

Oral language The reception and expression of the pragmatic, semantic, syntactical, morphological, and phonological aspects of language; involves listening and speaking.

Ordinal The scale of measurement in which data are arranged in rank order.

Percentile rank A score that translates student test performance into the percentage of the norm group that performed as well as or poorer than the student on the same test.

Perception The psychological ability to process or use information received through the sense organs.

Phonology Study of phonemes or speech sounds, the smallest units of oral language.

Pragmatics Study of the use of language for communication.

Primary language The language in which an individual is most proficient; also called *dominant language*.

Problem-solving skills In mathematics, the use of computational skills to solve a problem; usually assessed via word problems.

Profile A graph upon which scores are plotted.

Proportional interaction Exceptional and typical students receiving the teacher's attention for appropriate behavior on a consistent enough basis to maintain performance.

Protocol The test form or student answer booklet.

Public Law 94–142 The *Education for All Handicapped Children Act of 1975;* mandates free, appropriate, public education for all handicapped students.

Questionnaire An informal assessment device in which the informant reads questions and writes the answers.

Range A descriptive statistic that expresses the spread of a distribution.

Rating scale An informal assessment device in which the informant judges or rates the performance of the student.

Ratio The scale of measurement characterized by equal intervals between points in the scale and a true zero.

Raw score The first test score calculated; usually indicates the number of correct responses plus the number of items assumed correct.

Readability A measure of the ease with which a text can be read; usually expressed as a grade level.

Receptive language The processing of language, as in listening and reading.

Related services Special services that exceptional students may need to benefit from special education; includes transportation, speech pathology and audiology, and counseling.

Reliability Refers to a test's consistency; types of reliability include test-retest, alternate form, split-half, and interrater.

Response analysis A type of work sample analysis in which both errors and correct responses are considered.

Semantics The aspect of language that deals with meaning, concepts, and vocabulary.

Sequence analysis An observational technique in which the antecedents and consequences of the student's behaviors are studied.

Service delivery models A continuum of special education arrangements through which exceptional students receive services.

Sociometric technique An assessment procedure used to determine how students perceive their peers.

Special education Specially designed instruction to meet the unique needs of handicapped students.

Specific learning abilities Readiness skills such as attention, perception, and memory.

Standard deviation A descriptive statistic that expresses the amount of variability within a set of scores.

Standard error of difference between scores A statistic used to estimate whether an observed difference between scores is a true difference.

Standard error of measurement A statistic that estimates the amount of measurement error in a score.

Standard score A derived score with a set mean and standard deviation; examples are IQ scores, scaled scores, and T-scores.

Standardization sample The group used to establish scores on norm-referenced tests.

Standardized test A test in which the administration, scoring, and interpretation procedures are standard or set; usually norm-referenced.

Stanine A derived score equivalent to a range of standard scores; stanines divide the distribution into nine ranges.

Statistical analysis Involves computing test scores, identifying the important scores for interpretation, and arranging scores on a profile.

Structural task analysis A type of task analysis in which the performance demands of the task (e.g., speed and accuracy requirements) are studied.

Summative evaluation Evaluation done at the end of a program to determine its effectiveness.

Surrogate parent A person assigned by the state to represent an exceptional person if the parents cannot be identified, if the parents are unknown, or if the exceptional person is a ward of the state.

Syntax The grammatical structure of language.

Task analysis An informal assessment technique in which a task is broken into its essential components or subtasks.

Team approach An approach to assessment that requires the active involvement of professionals from many fields, parents, perhaps the exceptional person, and other interested parties.

Test A sample of student behavior collected under standard conditions.

Tester One who administers and scores tests.

Test-scoring programs Software programs used on computers to assist in scoring tests.

Time-sample recording An observational technique in which it is noted whether the target behavior occurs at some time within a specified time interval; used with nondiscrete behaviors.

Validity The degree to which a test measures what it purports to measure; types of validity include content, criterion-referenced (predictive and concurrent), and construct.

Word processors Software programs used on computers for writing; allow the writer to enter, store, edit, and retrieve text.

Work sample A permanent product produced by the student (e.g., a homework assignment, test paper, or composition).

Work sample analysis An informal assessment technique in which samples of student work are studied.

Writing Expressive written language; includes spelling, handwriting, usage, and composition.

Writing sample A sample of the written language produced by the student that is used for analysis.

Written language Includes the receptive skill, reading, and the expressive skill, writing.

References

Adams, G. L. (1984a). *Comprehensive test of adaptive behavior.* San Antonio, TX: Psychological Corporation.

Adams, G. L. (1984b). *Normative adaptive behavior checklist.* San Antonio, TX: Psychological Corporation.

Adler, S., & Birdsong, S. (1983). Reliability and validity of standardized testing tools used with poor children. *Topics in Language Disorders, 3*(3), 76–87.

Affleck, J. Q., Lowenbraun, S., & Archer, A. (1980). *Teaching the mildly handicapped in the regular classroom* (2nd ed.). Columbus, OH: Merrill.

Agostine v. School District of Philadelphia. (1988). *Special Education and the Handicapped, 3*(6), 3.

Alberto, P. A., & Troutman, A. C. (1986). *Applied behavior analysis for teachers (2nd ed.).* Columbus, OH: Merrill.

Alexander, N. (1983). A primer for developing a writing curriculum. *Topics in Learning & Learning Disabilities, 3*(3), 55–62.

Algozzine, B., Forgnone, C., Mercer, C., & Trifiletti, J. (1979). Toward defining discrepancies for specific learning disabilities: An analysis and alternatives. *Learning Disability Quarterly, 2*(4), 25–31.

Algozzine, B., & Ysseldyke, J. E. (1981). Special education services for normal children: Better safe than sorry. *Exceptional Children, 48,* 238–243.

Allen, D. A., & Hudd, S. (1987). Are we professionalizing parents? Weighing the benefits and pitfalls. *Mental Retardation, 25,* 133–139.

Alley, G., & Deshler, D. (1979). *Teaching the learning disabled adolescent.* Denver: Love.

Alley, G. R., Deshler, D. D., Clark, F. L., Schumaker, J. B., & Warner, M. M. (1983). Learning disabilities in adolescent and adult populations: Research implications (part II). *Focus on Exceptional Children, 15*(9), 1–14.

Alley, G. R., Deshler, D. D., & Warner, M. (1979). Identification of learning disabled adolescents: A Bayesian approach. *Learning Disability Quarterly, 2,* 76–83.

Alley, G., & Foster, C. (1978). Nondiscriminatory testing of minority and exceptional children. *Focus on Exceptional Children, 9,* 1–14.

Alpern, G. D., Boll, T. J., & Shearer, M. (1980). *Developmental profile II.* Aspen, CO: Psychological Development Publications.

American Educational Research Association, American Psychological Association, & National Council on Measurement in Education. (1985). *Standards for educational and psychological testing.* Washington, DC: American Psychological Association.

American Foundation for the Blind. (1961). *A teacher education program for those who serve blind children and youth.* New York: Author.

American Psychological Association. (1986). *Guidelines for computer-based tests and interpretations.* Washington, DC: Author.

Anastasi, A. (1988). *Psychological testing* (6th ed.). New York: Macmillan.

Anderson, P. L. (1983). *Denver handwriting analysis.* Novato, CA: Academic Therapy Publications.

Anderson, R. J., & Sisco, F. H. (1977). *Standardization of the WISC–R performance scale for deaf children.* Washington, DC: Gallaudet College, Office of Demographic Studies.

Apple computer resources in special education and rehabilitation. (1988). Allen, TX: DLM Teaching Resources.

AppleWorks [Computer program]. Cupertino, CA: Apple Computer, Inc.

Armstrong, R. J., & Jensen, J. A. (1981). *Slosson intelligence test (SIT), 1981 norms tables, application and development.* East Aurora, NY: Slosson Educational Publications.

Arter, J. A., & Jenkins, J. R. (1979). Differential diagnostic-prescriptive teaching: A critical appraisal. *Review of Educational Research, 49,* 517–555.

Arthur, G. (1952). *Arthur adaptation of the Leiter International Performance Scale.* Chicago: Stoelting.

Ary, D., Jacobs, L. C., & Razavieh, A. (1985). *Introduction to research in education* (3rd ed.). New York: Holt, Rinehart & Winston.

Asher, S. R., & Taylor, A. R. (1981). Social outcomes of mainstreaming: Sociometric assessment and beyond. *Exceptional Education Quarterly, 1,* 13–30.

Ashlock, R. B. (1986). *Error patterns in computation: A semi-programmed approach* (4th ed.). Columbus, OH: Merrill.

Association for Children and Adults with Learning Disabilities. (1982a). ACLD vocational committee survey of LD adults, *ACLD Newsbriefs, 145,* 20–23.

Association for Children and Adults with Learning Disabilities. (1982b). ACLD vocational committee survey of LD adults, *ACLD Newsbriefs, 146,* 10–13.

Baca, L. M., & Cervantes, H. T. (1989). Assessment procedures for the exceptional child. In L. M. Baca & H. T. Cervantes (Eds.), *The bilingual special education interface* (2nd ed.) (pp. 153–181). Columbus, OH: Merrill.

Bachman, R. (1976). *MICRO-TOWER.* New York: ICD Rehabilitation & Research Center.

Bachor, D. G. (1979). Using work samples as diagnostic information. *Learning Disability Quarterly, 2*(2), 45–52.

Bagai, E., & Bagai, J. (1979). *System FORE handbook.* North Hollywood, CA: Foreworks Publications.

Bagley, M. T., & Greene, J. F. (1981). *Peer attitudes toward the handicapped scale.* Austin, TX: PRO-ED.

Bailey, D. B., & Harbin, G. L. (1980). Nondiscriminatory evaluation. *Exceptional Children, 46,* 590–596.

Bailey, D. B., & Simeonsson, R. J. (1988a). *Family assessment in early intervention.* Columbus, OH: Merrill.

Bailey, D. B., & Simeonsson, R. J. (1988b). Home-based early intervention. In S. L. Odom & M. B. Karnes (Eds.), *Early intervention for infants and children with handicaps: An empirical base.* Baltimore: Brookes.

Bailey, D. B., Simeonsson, R. J., Winton, P. J., Huntington, G. S., Comfort, M., Isbell, P., O'Donnell, K. J., & Helm, J. M. (1986). Family-focused intervention: A functional model for planning, implementing, and evaluating individualized family services in early intervention. *Journal of the Division of Early Childhood, 10,* 156–171.

Bailey, D. B., & Wolery, M. (1984). *Teaching infants and preschoolers with handicaps.* Columbus, OH: Merrill.

Baker, H. J., & Leland, B. (1967). *Detroit tests of learning aptitude* (rev. ed.). Indianapolis: Bobbs-Merrill.

Barnard, K. E., & Bee, H. L. (1984). The assessment of parent–infant interaction by observation of feeding and teaching. In T. B. Brazelton & B. Lester (Eds.), *New approaches to developmental screening in infants.* New York: Elsevier North Holland.

Bartel, N. R. (1986a). Problems in mathematics achievement. In D. D. Hammill & N. R. Bartel (Eds.), *Teaching students with learning and behavior problems* (4th ed.) (pp. 178–223). Austin, TX: PRO-ED.

Bartel, N. R. (1986b). Teaching students who have reading problems. In D. D. Hammill & N. R. Bartel (Eds.), *Teaching students with learning and behavior problems* (4th ed.) (pp. 23–89). Austin, TX: PRO-ED.

Bartel, N. R., & Bryen, D. N. (1982). Problems in language development. In D. D. Hammill & N. R. Bartel (Eds.), *Teaching children with learning and behavior problems* (3rd ed.) (pp. 283–376). Boston: Allyn & Bacon.

Bartel, N. R., Grill, J. J., & Bryen, D. N. (1973). Language characteristics of black children: Implications for assessment. *Journal of School Psychology, 11,* 351–364.

Basic achievement skills screener. (1983). San Antonio, TX: Psychological Corporation.

Bayley, N. (1969). *Bayley scales of infant development.* San Antonio, TX: Psychological Corporation.

Beatty, L. S., Madden, R., Gardner, E. F., & Karlsen, B. (1984). *Stanford diagnostic mathematics test* (3rd ed.). San Antonio, TX: Psychological Corporation.

Becker, L. D., Bender, N. N., & Morrison, G. (1978). Measuring impulsivity-reflection: A critical review. *Journal of Learning Disabilities, 11,* 626–632.

Becker, R. L. (1981, 1988). *Reading-free vocational interest inventory–Revised.* Columbus, OH: Elbern.

Becker, R. L. (1984). *Occupational title lists.* Columbus, OH: Elbern.

Bee, H. L., Barnard, K. E., Eyres, S. J., Gray, C. A., Hammond, M. A., Spietz, A. L., Snyder, C., & Clark, B. (1982). Prediction of IQ and language skill from perinatal status, child performance, family characteristics, and mother–infant interaction. *Child Development, 53,* 1134–1156.

Beery, K. E. (1989). *Administration, scoring, and teaching manual for the developmental test of visual-motor integration* (3rd rev.). Cleveland: Modern Curriculum Press.

Behrmann, M. M. (Ed.) (1988). *Integrating computers into the curriculum: A handbook for special educators.* San Diego: College-Hill.

Bender, L. (1938). A visual motor gestalt test and its clinical use. *The American Orthopsychiatric Association Research Monographs, 3.*

Bender, W. N. (1984). Daily grading in mainstream classes. *The Directive Teacher, 6,* 4–5.

Bennett, G. K. (1969). *Bennett hand tool dexterity test.* San Antonio, TX: Psychological Corporation.

Bennett, R. E., & Shepherd, M. J. (1982). Basic measurement proficiency of learning disability specialists. *Learning Disability Quarterly, 5,* 177–184.

Bennett, R. L. (1982). Cautions for the use of informal measures in the assessment of exceptional children. *Journal of Learning Disabilities, 15,* 337–339.

Bennett, W. J. (1988). *American education: Making it work.* Washington, DC: U.S. Government Printing Office.

Berdine, W. H., & Cegelka, P. T. (1980). *Teaching the trainable retarded.* Columbus, OH: Merrill.

Bergin, V. (1980). *Special education needs in bilingual programs.* Rosslyn, VA: National Clearinghouse for Bilingual Education.

Beringer, M. L. (1984). *Ber-Sil secondary Spanish test.* Rancho Palos Verdes, CA: Ber-Sil.

Beringer, M. L. (1987). *Ber-Sil elementary Spanish test.* Rancho Palos Verdes, CA: Ber-Sil.

Berk, R. A. (1982). Effectiveness of discrepancy score methods for screening children with learning disabilities. *Learning Disabilities, 1*(2), 11–24.

Berk, R. A. (1984). An evaluation of procedures for computing an ability-achievement discrepancy score. *Journal of Learning Disabilities, 17,* 262–266.

Bersoff, D. N. (1981). Testing and the law. *American Psychologist, 36,* 1047–1056.

Binet, A., & Simon, Th. (1905). Méthodes nouvelles pour le diagnostic du niveau intellectuel des anormaux. *L'Année Psychologique, 11,* 191–255.

Blankenship, C. S. (1985). Using curriculum-based assessment data to make instructional decisions. *Exceptional Children, 52,* 233–238.

Bleil, G. B. (1975). Evaluating instructional materials. *Journal of Learning Disabilities, 8,* 12–24.

Bloom, L., & Lahey, M. (1978). *Language development and language disorders.* New York: Wiley.

Bluma, S. M., Shearer, M. S., Froham, A. H., & Hillard, J. M. (1976). *Portage guide to early education* (No. 12). Portage, WI: Cooperative Educational Agency.

Board of Trustees of the Council for Learning Disabilities. (1987). The CLD position statements. *Journal of Learning Disabilities, 20,* 349–350.

Bodner, J. R., Clark, G. M., & Mellard, D. F. (1987). *State graduation policies and program practices related to high school special education programs: A national study.* Lawrence, KS: University of Kansas.

Boehm, A. E. (1971). *Boehm test of basic concepts.* San Antonio, TX: Psychological Corporation.

Boehm, A. E. (1973). Criteria-referenced assessment for teachers. *Teachers College Record, 75,* 117–126.

Boehm, A. E. (1976). *Boehm resource guide for basic concept teaching.* San Antonio, TX: Psychological Corporation.

Boehm, A. E. (1986a). *Boehm test of basic concepts–Preschool edition.* San Antonio, TX: Psychological Corporation.

Boehm, A. E. (1986b). *Boehm test of basic concepts–Revised.* San Antonio, TX: Psychological Corporation.

Bond, G. L., & Tinker, M. A. (1967). *Reading difficulties: Their diagnosis and correction* (2nd ed.). New York: Appleton-Century-Crofts.

Borich, G. D., & Nance, D. D. (1987). Evaluating special education programs: Shifting the professional mandate from process to outcome. *Remedial and Special Education, 8,* 7–16.

Bormuth, J. R. (1968). The cloze readability procedure. *Elementary English, 45,* 429–436.

Boyer, E. R., for the Carnegie Foundation for the Advancement of Teaching. (1983). *High school: A report on secondary education in America.* New York: Harper & Row.

Brandon, T., Balton, D., Rup, D., & Raslter, C. (1974). *Valpar component.* Tucson, AZ: Valpar Corporation.

Bray, C. M., & Wiig, E. H. (1987). *Let's talk inventory for children.* San Antonio, TX: Psychological Corporation.

Brigance, A. H. (1977). *BRIGANCE® diagnostic inventory of basic skills.* N. Billerica, MA: Curriculum Associates.

Brigance, A. H. (1978). *BRIGANCE® diagnostic inventory of early development.* N. Billerica, MA: Curriculum Associates.

Brigance, A. H. (1981). *BRIGANCE® diagnostic inventory of essential skills.* N. Billerica, MA: Curriculum Associates.

Brigance, A. H. (1982, 1987). *BRIGANCE® K & 1 screen for kindergarten and first grade.* N. Billerica, MA: Curriculum Associates.

Brigance, A. H. (1983a). *BRIGANCE® diagnostic comprehensive inventory of basic skills.* N. Billerica, MA: Curriculum Associates.

Brigance, A. H. (1983b). *BRIGANCE® diagnostic inventory of basic skills. Spanish edition.* N. Billerica, MA: Curriculum Associates.

Brigance, A. H. (1983c). *BRIGANCE® preschool screen for three- and four-year-olds.* N. Billerica, MA: Curriculum Associates.

Bright, B., Martinson, M., & Covert, D. (1982). *LAP–D screening edition.* Winston-Salem, NC: Kaplan.

Brolin, D. E. (1978, 1983). *Life-centered career education: A competency-based approach.* Reston, VA: Council for Exceptional Children.

Brolin, D. E. (1982). *Vocational preparation of persons with handicaps* (2nd ed.). Columbus, OH: Merrill.

Brolin, D. E., Cegelka, P., Jackson, S., and Wrobel, C. (1978). *Official policy of The Council for Exceptional Children as legislated by the 1978 CEC Delegate Assembly.* Reston, VA: Council for Exceptional Children.

Bromwich, R. (1976). Focus on maternal behavior in infant intervention. *American Journal of Orthopsychiatry, 46,* 439–446.

Bromwich, R. (1981). *Working with parents and infants: An interactional approach.* Baltimore: University Park Press.

Brophy, J., & Good, T. (1969). *Teacher-child dyadic interaction: A manual for coding classroom behavior* (Report Series No. 127). Austin, TX: Research & Development Center for Teacher Education, University of Texas.

Brown, F. G. (1981). *Measuring classroom achievement.* New York: Holt, Rinehart & Winston.

Brown, L. J., Black, D. D., & Downs, J. C. (1984). *School social skills rating scale.* East Aurora, NY: Slosson Educational Publications.

Brown, L., & Bryant, B. R. (1984a). A consumer's guide to tests in print: The rating system. *Remedial and Special Education, 5*(1), 55–61.

Brown, L., & Bryant, B. R. (1984b). Critical reviews of three individually administered achievement tests: Peabody Individual Achievement Test, Wide Range Achievement Test, and Diagnostic Achievement Battery. *Remedial and Special Education, 5*(5), 53–60.

Brown, L., & Bryant, B. R. (1984c). The why and how of special norms. *Remedial and Special Education, 5*(4), 52–61.

Brown, L. L., & Hammill, D. D. (1983a). *Behavior rating profile.* Austin, TX: PRO-ED.

Brown, L. L., & Hammill, D. D. (1983b). *Perfil de evaluacíon del comportamiento.* Austin, TX: PRO-ED.

Brown, L., & Leigh, J. E. (1986). *Adaptive behavior inventory.* Austin, TX: PRO-ED.

Brown, L., Sherbenou, R. J., & Johnsen, S. K. (1982). *Test of nonverbal intelligence.* Austin, TX: PRO-ED.

Brown, R. (1973). *A first language: The early stages.* Cambridge, MA: Harvard University Press.

Brown, V. L. (1975). A basic Q-sheet for analyzing and comparing curriculum materials and proposals. *Journal of Learning Disabilities, 8,* 409–416.

Brown, V. L. (1978). Independent study behaviors: A framework for curriculum development. *Learning Disability Quarterly, 1*(2), 78–84.

Brown, V. L., Hammill, D. D., & Wiederholt, J. L. (1986). *Test of reading comprehension* (rev. ed.). Austin, TX: PRO-ED.

Brown, V. L., & McEntire, E. (1984). *Test of mathematical abilities.* Austin, TX: PRO-ED.

Brown, W. F., & Holtzman, W. H. (1953, 1967). *Survey of study habits and attitudes.* San Antonio, TX: Psychological Corporation.

Brown, W. F., & Holtzman, W. H. (1967b). *Survey of study habits and attitudes. Spanish edition.* San Antonio, TX: Psychological Corporation.

Brueckner, L. J. (1930). *Diagnostic and remedial teaching in arithmetic.* Philadelphia: Winston.

Bruininks, R. H. (1978). *Bruininks-Oseretsky test of motor proficiency.* Circle Pines, MN: American Guidance Service.

Bruininks, R. H., Rynders, J. E., & Gross, J. C. (1974). Social acceptance of mildly retarded pupils in resource rooms and regular classes. *American Journal of Mental Deficiency, 78,* 377–383.

Bruininks, R. H., Thurlow, M., & Gilman, C. J. (1987). Adaptive behavior and mental retardation. *Journal of Special Education, 21,* 69–88.

Bruininks, R. H., Woodcock, R. W., Weatherman, R. F., & Hill, B. K. (1984). *Scales of independent behavior.* Allen, TX: DLM Teaching Resources.

Bryant, B. R. (1986). *DTLA–P software scoring system* [Computer program]. Austin, TX: PRO-ED.

Bryant, B. R., & Bryant, D. L. (1983a). *Test of articulation performance–Diagnostic.* Austin, TX: PRO-ED.

Bryant, B. R., & Bryant, D. L. (1983b). *Test of articulation performance–Screen.* Austin, TX: PRO-ED.

Bureau of Education for the Handicapped. (1976, November 29). *Federal Register, 41*(230), 54207.

Burgemeister, B. B., Blum, L. H., & Lorge, I. (1972). *Columbia mental maturity scale* (3rd ed.). San Antonio, TX: Psychological Corporation.

Burke, C. (1973). Preparing elementary teachers to teach reading. In K. S. Goodman (Ed.), *Miscue analysis: Application to reading instruction* (pp. 15–29). Urbana, IL: ERIC Clearinghouse on Reading & Communication Skills.

Burks, H. F. (1977). *Burks' behavior rating scales.* Los Angeles: Western Psychological Services.

Buros, O. K. (Ed.) (1975a). *Intelligence tests and reviews.* Lincoln, NE: University of Nebraska Press.

Buros, O. K. (Ed.) (1975b). *Mathematics tests and reviews.* Lincoln, NE: University of Nebraska Press.

Buros, O. K. (Ed.) (1975c). *Reading tests and reviews.* Lincoln, NE: University of Nebraska Press.

Burron, A., & Claybaugh, A. L. (1977). *Basic concepts in reading instruction* (2nd ed.). Columbus, OH: Merrill.

Bursuck, W. D., & Lessen, E. (1987). A classroom-based model for assessing students with learning disabilities. *Learning Disabilities Focus, 3,* 17–29.

Burt, M. K., Dulay, H. C., & Chávez, E. H. (1978). *Bilingual syntax measure I and II.* San Antonio, TX: Psychological Corporation.

Buswell, G. T., & John, L. (1925). *Fundamental processes in arithmetic.* Indianapolis: Bobbs-Merrill.

Butler, S. E., Magliocca, L. A., & Torres, L. A. (1984). Grading the mainstreamed student: A decision-making model for modification. *The Directive Teacher, 6,* 6–9.

Cain, E. J., Jr., & Taber, F. M. (1987). *Educating disabled people for the 21st century.* San Diego: College-Hill.

Caldwell, B. M., & Bradley, R. H. (1978). *Home observation and measurement of the environment.* Little Rock: University of Arkansas.

California achievement tests. (1985, 1986, 1987). Monterey, CA: CTB/McGraw-Hill.

Campbell, D. P., & Hansen, J. (1981, 1985). *Manual for the SVIB-Strong-Campbell interest inventory.* Stanford, CA: Stanford University Press.

Carroll, J. B., & Horn, J. L. (1981). On the scientific basis of ability testing. *American Psychologist, 36,* 1012–1020.

Carrow-Woolfolk, E. (1974). *Carrow elicited language inventory.* Allen, TX: DLM Teaching Resources.

Carrow-Woolfolk, E. (1985). *Test for auditory comprehension of language–Revised.* Allen, TX: DLM Teaching Resources.

Cassell, R. H. (1962). *The child behavior rating scale.* Los Angeles: Western Psychological Services.

Caton, H. R. (1985). Visual impairments. In W. H. Berdine & A. E. Blackhurst (Eds.), *An introduction to special education* (2nd ed.) (pp. 235–280). Boston: Little, Brown.

Cattell, R. B. (1950). *Culture fair intelligence test: Scale 1.* Champaign, IL: Institute for Personality and Ability Testing.

Cattell, R. B., & Cattell, A. K. S. (1960). *Culture fair intelligence test: Scale 2.* Champaign, IL: Institute for Personality and Ability Testing.

Cattell, R. B., & Cattell, A. K. S. (1963). *Culture fair intelligence test: Scale 3.* Champaign, IL: Institute for Personality and Ability Testing.

Cattell, R. B., & Cattell, A. K. S. (1977). *The culture fair intelligence tests* (rev.). Champaign, IL: Institute for Personality and Ability Testing.

Cawley, J. F. (1978). An instructional design in mathematics. In L. Mann, L. Goodman, & L. L. Wiederholt (Eds.), *Teaching the learning-disabled adolescent* (pp. 201–234). Boston: Houghton Mifflin.

Cawley, J. F., Miller, J. H., & School, B. A. (1987). A brief inquiry of arithmetic word-problem-solving among learning disabled secondary students. *Learning Disabilities Focus, 2*(2), 87–93.

Cegelka, P. T. (1976). Sex role stereotyping in special education: A look at secondary work study programs. *Exceptional Children, 42,* 323–328.

Cegelka, P. T. (1985). Career and vocational education. In W. Berdine & A. E. Blackhurst (Eds.), *An introduction to special education* (2nd ed.) (pp. 573–617). Boston: Little, Brown.

Cegelka, P. T. (1988). Multicultural considerations. In E. L. Lynch & R. B. Lewis (Eds.), *Exceptional children and adults* (pp. 545–587). Glenview, IL: Scott, Foresman.

Cegelka, P. T., & Lewis, R. B. (1983). The once and future world: Portents for the handicapped. *The Journal of Special Educators, 19,* 61–73.

Cegelka, P. T., Lewis, R. B., & Rodriguez, A. M. (1987). Status of educational services to handicapped students with limited English proficiency: Report of a statewide study in California. *Exceptional Children, 54,* 220–227.

Cegelka, P. T., & Prehm, H. J. (1982). The concept of mental retardation. In P. T. Cegelka & H. J. Prehm (Eds.), *Mental retardation* (pp. 3–20). Columbus, OH: Merrill.

Chalfant, J. C., & King, F. S. (1976). An approach to operationalizing the definition of learning disabilities. *Journal of Learning Disabilities, 9,* 228–243.

Chall, J. S., & Stahl, S. A. (1982). Reading. In H. E. Mitzel (Ed.), *Encyclopedia of educational research* (5th ed.) (pp. 1535–1559). New York: Free Press.

Chapman, J. E., and Heward, W. L. (1982). Improving parent-teacher communication through recorded telephone messages. *Exceptional Children, 49,* 79–81.

Chapman, R. N., Larsen, S. C., & Parker, R. M. (1979). Interactions for first-grade teachers with learning disordered children. *Journal of Learning Disabilities, 12,* 225–230.

Cheng, L. L. (1987). *Assessing Asian language performance: Guidelines for evaluating limited-English-proficient students.* Rockville, MD: Aspen.

Clarizio, H. F. (1979). In defense of the IQ test. *School Psychology Digest, 8,* 79–88.

Clarizio, H. F., & McCoy, G. F. (1983). *Behavior disorders in children* (3rd ed.). New York: Harper & Row.

Clark, G. N., & Siefer, R. (1985). Assessment of parents' interactions with their developmentally delayed infants. *Infant Mental Health Journal, 6,* 214–225.

Clark, K. E., & Campbell, D. P. (1966). *Minnesota vocational interest inventory.* San Antonio, TX: Psychological Corporation.

Clock [Computer program]. (1983). Dimondale, MN: Hartley Courseware.

Cohen, S. (1983). Assigning report card grades to the mainstreamed child. *Teaching Exceptional Children, 15,* 86–89.

Cohen, S. B., & de Bettencourt, L. (1983). Teaching children to be independent learners: A step-by-step strategy. *Focus on Exceptional Children, 16*(3), 1–12.

Cohen, S. D., & Plaskon, S. P. (1980). *Language arts for the mildly handicapped.* Columbus, OH: Merrill.

Colarusso, R. P., & Hammill, D. D. (1972). *Motor-free test of visual perception.* San Rafael, CA: Academic Therapy Publications.

Cole, L. J. (1976). *Adaptive behavior of the educable mentally retarded child in the home and school environment.* Unpublished doctoral dissertation, University of California, Berkeley.

Coles, G. S. (1978). The learning disabilities test battery: Empirical and social issues. *Harvard Educational Review, 18,* 313–340.

Comprehensive tests of basic skills. (1981, 1982, 1983, 1984, 1985, 1987). Monterey, CA: CTB/McGraw-Hill.

Compton, C. (1984). *A guide to 75 tests for special education.* Belmont, CA: Fearon Education.

Condon, E. C., Peters, J. Y., & Sueiro-Ross, C. (1979). *Special education and the Hispanic child: Cultural perspectives.* Philadelphia: Teacher Corps Mid-Atlantic Network, Temple University.

Cone, T. E., & Wilson, L. R. (1981). Quantifying a severe discrepancy: A critical analysis. *Learning Disability Quarterly, 4,* 359–371.

Conners, C. K. (1969). A teacher rating scale for use in drug studies with children. *American Journal of Psychiatry, 126,* 884–888.

Connolly, A. J. (1985). *KeyMath teach and practice.* Circle Pines, MN: American Guidance Service.

Connolly, A. J. (1988). *KeyMath revised: A diagnostic inventory of essential mathematics.* Circle Pines, MN: American Guidance Service.

Connolly, A. J., Nachtman, W., & Pritchett, E. M. (1971, 1976). *KeyMath diagnostic arithmetic test.* Circle Pines, MN: American Guidance Service.

Conoley, J. C., Kramer, J. J., & Mitchell, J. V., Jr. (Eds.) (1988). *Supplement to the ninth mental measurements yearbook.* Lincoln, NE: University of Nebraska Press.

Cooper, J. O. (1981). *Measuring behavior* (2nd ed.). Columbus, OH: Merrill.

Cooper, J. O., & Edge, D. (1982). *Parenting: Strategies and educational methods.* Louisville, KY: Eston.

Cooper, J. O., Heron, T. E., & Heward, W. L. (1987). *Applied behavior analysis.* Columbus, OH: Merrill.

Coopersmith, S. (1981). *Coopersmith self-esteem inventories.* Palo Alto, CA: Consulting Psychologists Press.

Coopersmith, S., & Gilberts, R. (1981). *Behavioral academic self-esteem, A rating scale.* Palo Alto, CA: Consulting Psychologists Press.

Copperman, P. (1979). The achievement decline of the 1970s. *Phi Delta Kappan, 60,* 736–739.

Cottle, W. C. (1966). *School interest inventory.* Chicago: Riverside.

Council for Exceptional Children. (1984). Reply to "A Nation at Risk." *Exceptional Children, 50,* 484–494.

Council for Learning Disabilities. (1986). *Board of trustees' statement on perceptual assessment and remediation.* Overland Park, KS: Author.

Cox, L. S. (1975). Diagnosing and remediating systematic errors in addition and subtraction computations. *The Arithmetic Teacher, 22,* 151–157.

Crabtree, M. (1963). *Houston test for language development.* Chicago: Stoelting.

Crawford, J. E., & Crawford, D. M. (1956). *Crawford small parts dexterity test.* San Antonio, TX: Psychological Corporation.

Critchlow, D. C. (1973). *Dos amigos verbal language scales.* East Aurora, NY: United Educational Services.

Cronbach, L. J., & Snow, R. E. (1977). *Aptitudes and instructional methods.* New York: Irvington.

Cronin, M. E., & Currie, P. S. (1984). Study skills: A resource guide for practitioners. *Remedial and Special Education, 5*(2), 61–69.

Culatta, R., & Culatta, B. K. (1985). Communication disorders. In W. H. Berdine and A. E. Blackhurst (Eds.), *An introduction to special education* (2nd ed.) (pp. 145–181). Boston: Little, Brown.

Cullinan, D., Epstein, M. H., & Dembinski, R. J. (1979). Behavior problems of educationally handicapped and normal pupils. *Journal of Abnormal Child Psychology, 7,* 495–502.

Cummins, J. (1981). The role of primary language development in promoting educational success for language minority students. In California State Department of Education, *Schooling and language minority students: A theoretical framework* (pp. 3–49). Los Angeles: Evaluation, Dissemination & Assessment Center.

Cummins, J. (1982, February). Tests, achievement, and bilingual students. *Focus* (National Clearinghouse for Bilingual Education), *9,* 1–8.

Cummins, J. (1983). Bilingualism and special education: Program and pedagogical issues. *Learning Disability Quarterly, 6,* 373–386.

Dagenais, D. J., & Beadle, K. R. (1984). Written language: When and where to begin. *Topics in Language Disorders, 4*(2), 59–85.

Davis, W. A., & Shepard, L. A. (1983). Specialists' use of tests and clinical judgment in the diagnosis of learning disabilities. *Learning Disability Quarterly, 6,* 128–138.

DeAvila, E. A., & Duncan, S. E. (1975–85). *Language assessment scales–oral.* Monterey, CA: CTB/McGraw-Hill.

Demos, G. (1976). *The study skills counseling examination.* Los Angeles: Western Psychological Services.

Deno, S. L. (1985). Curriculum-based measurement: The emerging alternative. *Exceptional Children, 52,* 219–232.

Deno, S. L. (1987). Curriculum-based measurement. *Teaching Exceptional Children, 20,* 41–42.

Deno, S. L., & Fuchs, L. S. (1988). Developing curriculum-based measurement systems for data-based special education problem solving. In E. L. Meyen, G. A. Vergason, & R. J. Whelan (Eds.), *Effective instructional strategies for exceptional children* (pp. 481–504). Denver: Love.

Deno, S. L., Marston, D., & Mirkin, P. K. (1982) Valid measurement procedures for continuous evaluation of written expression. *Exceptional Children, 48,* 368–371.

Deno, S. L., Mirkin, P. K., & Chiang, B. (1982). Identifying valid measures of reading. *Exceptional Children, 49,* 36–45.

Deno, S. L., Mirkin, P. K., Lowry, L., & Kuehnle, K. (1980). *Relationships among simple measures of written expression and performance on standardized achievement tests* (Research Report No. 22). Minneapolis: University of Minnesota Institute for Learning Disabilities. (ERIC Document Reproduction Service No. ED 197 508).

Deshler, D. D., Alley, G. R., Warner, M. M., & Schumaker, J. B. (1981). Instructional practices for promoting skill acquisition and generalization in severely learning disabled adolescents. *Learning Disability Quarterly, 4,* 415–422.

Deshler, D. D., Schumaker, J. B., Alley, G. R., Warner, M. M., & Clark, F. L. (1982). Learning disabilities in adolescent and young adult populations: Research implications. *Focus on Exceptional Children, 15*(1), 1–12.

Diana v. State Board of Education. Civ. No. C-70 37 RFP (N.D. Cal. 1970, 1973).

Dolch, E. W. (1953). *The Dolch basic sight word list.* Champaign, IL: Garrard.

Doll, E. A. (1935). A genetic scale of social maturity. *The American Journal of Orthopsychiatry, 5,* 180–188.

Doll, E. A. (1965). *Vineland social maturity scale* (rev. ed.). Circle Pines, MN: American Guidance Service.

Doren, M. (1973). *Doren diagnostic reading test of word recognition skills.* Circle Pines, MN: American Guidance Service.

Drew, C., Freston, C., & Logan, D. (1972). Criteria and reference in evaluation. *Focus on Exceptional Children, 4,* 1–10.

Duffey, J. B., Salvia, J., Tucker, J., & Ysseldyke, J. (1982). Nonbiased assessment: A need for operationalism. *Exceptional Children, 47,* 427–434.

Dunn, L. M. (1968). Special education for the mildly retarded—Is much of it justifiable? *Exceptional Children, 35,* 5–22.

Dunn, L. M., & Dunn, L. M. (1981). *Peabody picture vocabulary test–Revised.* Circle Pines, MN: American Guidance Service.

Dunn, L. M., Lugo, D. E., Padilla, E. R., & Dunn, L. M. (1986). *Test de vocabulario en imágenes Peabody.* Circle Pines, MN: American Guidance Service.

Dunn, L. M., & Markwardt, F. C. (1970). *Peabody individual achievement test.* Circle Pines, MN: American Guidance Service.

Durrell, D. D., & Catterson, J. H. (1980). *Durrell analysis of reading difficulty* (3rd ed.). San Antonio, TX: Psychological Corporation.

Eaves, R. C. (1982). A proposal for the diagnosis of emotional disturbance. *Journal of Special Education, 16,* 463–476.

Ebel, R. L. (1977). *The uses of standardized testing.* Bloomington, IN: Phi Delta Kappa Educational Foundation.

Ebel, R. L. (1978). The case for norm-referenced measurement. *Educational Researcher, 7,* 3–5.

Edgington, R. (1968). But he spelled it right this morning. In J. I. Arena (Ed.), *Building spelling skills in dyslexic children* (pp. 23–26). San Rafael, CA: Academic Therapy Publications.

Educational technology 1987: A report on *EL's* seventh annual survey of the states. *Electronic Learning, 7*(2), 39–44, 83.

Ekwall, E. E. (1986). *Ekwall reading inventory* (2nd ed.). Boston: Allyn & Bacon.

Englemann, S., & Bruner, E. C. (1983). *DISTAR reading 1: An instructional system, Teacher's guide.* Chicago: Science Research Associates.

Englert, C. S. (1984). Measuring teacher effectiveness from the teacher's point of view. *Focus on Exceptional Children, 17,* 1–14.

Engquist, G. (1974). *Black dialect: Deficient or different?* Unpublished manuscript, University of Virginia.

Enright, B. E. (1983). *ENRIGHT™ diagnostic inventory of basic arithmetic skills.* North Billerica, MA: Curriculum Associates.

Epps, S., McGue, M., & Ysseldyke, J. (1982). Interjudge agreement in classifying students as learning disabled. *Psychology in the Schools, 19,* 209–220.

Epps, S., Ysseldyke, J. E., & Algozzine, B. (1983). Impact of different definitions of learning disabilities on the number of students identified. *Journal of Psychoeducational Assessment, 1,* 341–352.

Epstein, M. H., & Cullinan, D. (1983). Academic performance of behaviorally disordered and learning-disabled pupils. *Journal of Special Education, 17,* 303–308.

Escala de inteligencia Wechsler para niños–revisada (1982). San Antonio, TX: Psychological Corporation.

Estes, T. H., Estes, J. J., Richards, H. C., & Roettger, D. (1981). *Estes attitude scales.* Austin, TX: PRO-ED.

Eyberg, S. M., & Robinson, E. A. (1982). Parent-child interaction training: Effects on family functioning. *Journal of Clinical Child Psychology, 11,* 130–137.

Fafard, M., Hanlon, R., & Bryson, E. (1986). *Jose P. v. Ambach:* Progress toward compliance. *Exceptional Children, 52,* 313–322.

Fagen, S. A., & Long, N. J. (1979). A psychoeducational curriculum approach to teaching self-control. *Behavioral Disorders, 4,* 68–82.

Farr, R. (Ed.). (1973). *Iowa silent reading tests.* San Antonio, TX: Psychological Corporation.

Farran, D. C., Kasari, C., Comfort, M., & Jay, S. (1986). *Parent/caregiver involvement scale.* Unpublished rating scale. Available from Dale Farran, Department of Child Development and Family Relations, University of North Carolina, Greensboro, NC 27412-5001.

Farran, D. C., Kasari, C., Yoder, P., Harber, L., Huntington, G. S., & Comfort, M. (1987). Rating mother-child interactions in handicapped and at-risk infants. In T. Tamir (Ed.), *Stimulation and intervention in infant development.* London: Freund.

Feagans, L. (1972). Ecological theory as a model for constructing a theory of emotional disturbance. In W. C. Rhodes & M. L. Tracy (Eds.), *A study of child variance* (pp. 323–389). Ann Arbor: Institute for the Study of Mental Retardation & Related Disabilities, University of Michigan.

Federal Register. (1977, Aug. 23). Washington, DC: U.S. Government Printing Office.

Federal Register. (1981, Jan. 19). Washington, DC: U.S. Government Printing Office.

Federal Register. (1985, Oct. 15). Washington, DC: U.S. Government Printing Office.

Fenton, K. S., Yoshida, R. K., Maxwell, S. P., & Kaufman, M. J. (1979). Recognition of team goals: An essential step toward rational decision-making. *Exceptional Children, 45,* 638–644.

Feuerstein, R., in collaboration with Rand, Y., & Hoffman, M. D. (1979). *The dynamic assessment of retarded performers.* Baltimore: University Park Press.

Feuerstein, R., in collaboration with Rand, Y., Hoffman, M. D., and Miller, R. (1980). *Instrumental enrichment.* Baltimore: University Park Press.

Feuerstein, R., Miller, R., Hoffman, M. D., Rand, Y., Mintzker, Y., & Jensen, M. R. (1981). Cognitive modifiability in adolescence: Cognitive structure and the effects of intervention. *Journal of Special Education, 15,* 269–287.

Feuerstein, R., Miller, R., Rand, Y., & Jensen, M. R. (1981). Can evolving techniques better measure cognitive change? *Journal of Special Education, 15,* 201–219.

Fey, J. T. (1982). Mathematics education. In H. E. Mitzel (Ed.), *Encyclopedia of educational research* (5th ed.) (pp. 1166–1182). New York: Free Press.

Field, S. L., & Hill, D. S. (1988). Contextual appraisal: A framework for meaningful evaluation of special education programs. *Remedial and Special Education, 9,* 22–30.

Fitts, W. H., & Roid, G. H. (1988). *Tennessee self-concept scale.* Los Angeles, CA: Western Psychological Services.

Flanders, N. (1970). *Analyzing teacher behavior.* Menlo Park, CA: Addison-Wesley.

Forness, S. R., & Esveldt, K. C. (1975). Prediction of high-risk kindergarten children through classroom observation. *Journal of Special Education, 9,* 375–388.

Forness, S. R., Guthrie, D., & MacMillan, D. (1982). Classroom environments as they relate to retarded children's observable behavior. *American Journal of Mental Deficiency, 87,* 259–265.

Forness, S. R., Sinclair, E., & Guthrie, D. (1983). Learning disability discrepancy formulas: Their use in actual practice. *Learning Disability Quarterly, 6,* 107–114.

Foster, C. R., Giddan, J. J., & Stark, J. (1972). *Assessment of children's language comprehension.* Palo Alto, CA: Consulting Psychologists Press.

Frame, R. E., Clarizio, H. F., & Porter, A. (1984). Diagnostic and prescriptive bias in school psychologists' reports of a learning disabled child. *Journal of Learning Disabilities, 17,* 12–15.

Frame, R., Clarizio, H., Porter, A., & Visonhalen, J. (1982). Interclinician agreement and bias in school psychologists' diagnostic and treatment recommendations for a learning disabled child. *Psychology in the Schools, 19,* 319–327.

Frank, T. (1988). Assessment of hearing difficulties. In J. Salvia & J. E. Ysseldyke, *Assessment in special and remedial education* (4th ed.) (pp. 227–236). Boston: Houghton Mifflin.

Frankenberger, W., & Harper, J. (1986). Variations in multidisciplinary team composition for identifying children with mental retardation. *Mental Retardation, 24,* 203–207.

Frankenburg, W. K. (1978). *Denver developmental screening test form–Revised.* Denver: LADOCA.

Frankenburg, W. K., Dodds, J. B., Fandal, A., Kazuk, E., & Cohrs, M. (1975). *Denver developmental screening test.* Denver: LADOCA.

Frankenburg, W. K., Fandal, A., & Thorton, S. (1987). The revised *Denver prescreening developmental questionnaire. Pediatrics, 110,* 653–657.

Frankenburg, W. K., Ker, C. Y., Engelke, S., Schaefer, E. S., & Thorton, S. M. (1988). Validation of the key Denver Developmental Screening Test items: A preliminary study. *Journal of Pediatrics, 112,* 560–566.

Freedman, S. W. (1982). Language assessment and writing disorders. *Topics in Language Disorders, 2*(4), 34–44.

Frostig, M., & Horne, D. (1964). *The Frostig program for the development of visual perception.* Chicago: Follett.

Frostig, M., Lefever, W., & Whittlesey, J. R. B. (1966). *Developmental test of visual perception* (rev.). Palo Alto, CA: Consulting Psychologists Press.

Fry, E. (1968). A readability formula that saves time. *Journal of Reading, 11,* 513–516, 575–577.

Fry, E. (1977). Fry's readability graph: Clarifications, validity, and extension to level 17. *Journal of Reading, 21,* 242–252.

Fuchs, D., Fuchs, L. S., Benowitz, S., & Barringer, K. (1987). Norm-referenced tests: Are they valid for use with handicapped students? *Exceptional Children, 54,* 263–271.

Fuchs, L. S. (1986). Monitoring progress among mildly handicapped pupils: Review of current practice and research. *Remedial and Special Education, 7*(5), 5–12.

Fuchs, L. S. (1987). Program development. *Teaching Exceptional Children, 20,* 42–44.

Fuchs, L. S., Deno, S. L., & Merkin, P. K. (1984). The effects of frequent curriculum-based measurement and evaluation on pedagogy, student achievement, and student awareness of learning. *American Educational Research Journal, 21,* 449–460.

Fuchs, L. S., Hamlett, C. L., Fuchs, D., Stecker, P. M., & Ferguson, C. (1988). Conducting curriculum-based measurement with computerized data collection: Effects on efficiency and teacher satisfaction. *Journal of Special Education Technology, 9*(2), 73–86.

Fudala, J. B., & Reynolds, W. M. (1986). *Arizona articulation proficiency scale* (2nd ed.). Los Angeles: Western Psychological Services.

Fulmer, R. H., Cohen, S., & Monaco, G. (1985). Using psychological assessment in structural family therapy. *Journal of Learning Disabilities, 18,* 145–150.

Furono, S., O'Reilly, K. A., Mosaka, C. M., Inatsuka, T. T., Allman, T. L., & Zeisloft, B. (1979). *Hawaii early learning profile.* Palo Alto, CA: VORT.

Gaar, B. L., & Plue, W. V. (1983). Separate versus combined categories for mental retardation and specific learning disabilities? *Learning Disability Quarterly, 6,* 77–79.

Gagné, R. M. (1970). *The conditions of learning* (2nd ed.). New York: Holt, Rinehart & Winston.

Gajar, A. H. (1980). Characteristics across exceptional children: EMR, LD, & ED. *Journal of Special Education, 14,* 166–173.

Gallup, G. H. (1978). The 10th annual Gallup poll of the public's attitudes toward public schools. *Phi Delta Kappan, 60,* 33–45.

Gardner, E. F., Rudman, H. D., Karlsen, B., & Merwin, J. C. (1982, 1983, 1984, 1986, 1987). *Stanford achievement test series* (7th ed.). San Antonio, TX: Psychological Corporation.

Garner, R. (1983). Correct the imbalance: Diagnosis of strategic behaviors in reading. *Topics in Learning & Learning Disabilities, 2*(4), 12–19.

Garrett, J. E., & Brazil, N. (1979). Categories used for identification and education of exceptional children. *Exceptional Children, 45,* 291–292.

Gates, A. I., McKillop, A. S., & Horowitz, E. C. (1981). *Gates-McKillop-Horowitz reading diagnostic tests* (2nd ed.). New York: Teachers College Press.

Gay, L. R. (1985). *Educational evaluation and measurement* (2nd ed.). Columbus, OH: Merrill.

Geist, H. (1964). *Geist picture interest inventory–Revised.* Beverly Hills, CA: Western Psychological Services.

Germann, G., & Tindal, G. (1985). An application of curriculum-based assessment: The use of direct and repeated measurement. *Exceptional Children, 52,* 244–265.

Gesell, A. (1940). *Gesell developmental schedules.* Cheshire, CT: Nigel Cox.

Gillespie, E. B. (1983). Individualizing minimum competency testing. *Journal of Learning Disabilities, 16,* 565–566.

Gillespie, P. H., & Fink, A. H. (1974). The influence of sexism on the education of handicapped children. *Exceptional Children, 41,* 155–162.

Gillespie-Silver, P. (1979). *Teaching reading to children with special needs.* Columbus, OH: Merrill.

Gilliam, J. E. (1979). Contributions and status rankings of educational planning committee participants. *Exceptional Children, 45,* 466–467.

Gilliam, J. E., & Coleman, M. C. (1981). Who influences IEP committee decisions. *Exceptional Children, 47,* 642–644.

Gilmore, J. V., & Gilmore, E. C. (1968). *Gilmore oral reading test.* San Antonio, TX: Psychological Corporation.

Ginsburg, H. P., & Baroody, A. J. (1983). *The test of early mathematics ability.* Austin, TX: PRO-ED.

Ginsburg, H. P., & Mathews, S. C. (1984). *Diagnostic test of arithmetic strategies.* Austin, TX: PRO-ED.

Glennon, V. J. (1976). Mathematics: How firm the foundations? *Phi Delta Kappan, 57,* 302–305.

Glover, M. E., Preminger, J. L., & Sanford, A. R. (1978). *Early learning accomplishment profile.* Winston-Salem, NC: Kaplan.

Goldman, R. M., & Fristoe, M. (1986). *Goldman-Fristoe test of articulation.* Circle Pines, MN: American Guidance Service.

Goldman, R. M., Fristoe, M., & Woodcock, R. W. (1970). *Goldman-Fristoe-Woodcock test of auditory discrimination.* Circle Pines, MN: American Guidance Service.

Goldman, R. M., Fristoe, M., & Woodcock, R. W. (1976). *Goldman-Fristoe-Woodcock auditory skills test battery.* Circle Pines, MN: American Guidance Service.

Goldstein, S., Strickland, B., Turnbull, A. P., & Curry, L. (1980). An observational analysis of IEP conferences. *Exceptional Children, 46,* 278–286.

Goldstein, S., & Turnbull, A. P. (1982). Strategies to increase parent participation in IEP conferences. *Exceptional Children, 48,* 360–361.

Gonzales, E. (1982). Issues in assessment of minorities. In H. L. Swanson & B. L. Watson (Eds.), *Educational and psychological assessment of exceptional children* (pp. 375–389). St. Louis: Mosby.

Goodman, J. F. (1979). Is tissue the issue? A critique of SOMPA's models and tests. *School Psychology Digest, 8,* 47–62.

Goodman, K. S. (1969). Analysis of oral reading miscues: Applied psycholinguistics. *Reading Research Quarterly, 5,* 9–30.

Goodman, K. S. (Ed.). (1973a). *Miscue analysis: Application to reading instruction.* Urbana, IL: ERIC Clearinghouse on Reading and Communication Skills.

Goodman, K. S. (1973b). Miscues: Windows on the reading process. In K. S. Goodman (Ed.), *Miscue analysis: Application to reading instruction* (pp. 1–14). Urbana, IL: ERIC Clearinghouse on Reading & Communication Skills.

Goodman, K. S. (1976). Behind the eye: What happens in reading. In H. Singer & R. B. Ruddell (Eds.), *Theoretical models and processes in reading.* Newark, DE: International Reading Association.

Goodman, Y., & Burke, C. (1972). *Reading miscue inventory.* New York: Macmillan.

Goodman, Y., Watson, D. J., & Burke, C. L. (1987). *Reading miscue inventory: Alternative procedures.* Katonah, NY: Richard C. Owen.

Goodstein, H. A. (1981). Are the errors we see true errors? Error analysis in verbal problem solving. *Topics in Learning and Learning Disabilities, 1*(3), 31–45.

Gordon, L. V. (1980). *Gordon occupational check list II.* San Antonio, TX: Psychological Corporation.

Graden, J. L., Casey, A., & Bonstrom, O. (1985). Implementing a prereferral intervention system: Part II. The data. *Exceptional Children, 51,* 487–496.

Graebner, D. A. (1972). A decade of sexism in readers. *The Reading Teacher, 26,* 52–58.

Graham, P., & Rutter, M. (1968). The reliability and validity of the psychiatric assessment of the child: Interview with the parent. *British Journal of Psychiatry, 114,* 581–593.

Graham, S. (1982). Composition research and practice: A unified approach. *Focus on Exceptional Children, 14*(8), 1–16.

Graham, S., & Miller, L. (1979). Spelling research and practice: A unified approach. *Focus on Exceptional Children, 12*(2), 1–16.

Graham, S., & Miller, L. (1980). Handwriting research and practice: A unified approach. *Focus on Exceptional Children, 13*(2), 1–16.

Graves, D. (1978). *Balancing the basics: Let them write.* New York: Ford Foundation.

Gray, W. S. (1967). *Gray oral reading tests.* Austin, TX: PRO-ED.

Green, R. F., & Martinez, J. N. (Trans.). (1968). *Escala de inteligencia Wechsler para adultos.* San Antonio, TX: Psychological Corporation.

Green, W. W. (1981). Hearing disorders. In A. E. Blackhurst & W. H. Berdine (Eds.), *Introduction to special education* (pp. 154–205). Boston: Little, Brown.

Greenbaum, C. R. (1987). *Spellmaster assessment and teaching system.* Austin, TX: PRO-ED.

Greenwood, C. R., Hops, H., Walker, H. M., Guild, J., Stokes, J., Young, K. R., Keleman, K. S., & Willardson, M. (1979). A standardized intervention program for academic related behavior during instruction (PASS): Field test evaluations in Utah and Oregon. *Journal of Applied Behavior Analysis, 12,* 235–253.

Gregory K. v. Longview School District. (1987). *Special Education and the Handicapped, 2*(24), 2.

Gresham, F. M. (1982). A model for the behavioral assessment of behavior disorders in children: Measurement considerations and practical application. *Journal of School Psychology, 20,* 131–144.

Grise, P. J. (1980). Florida's minimum competency testing program for handicapped students. *Exceptional Children, 47,* 186–193.

Grossman, H. J. (Ed.). (1983). *Classification in mental retardation* (1983 rev.). Washington, DC: American Association on Mental Deficiency.

Guadalupe v. Tempe Elementary School District. Civ. Act. No. 71-435 (D. Ariz. 1972).

Hainsworth, P. K., & Hainsworth, M. L. (1980). *Preschool screening system.* Pawtucket, RI: Early Recognition Intervention Systems.

Hallahan, D. P. (Ed.). (1980). Teaching exceptional children to use cognitive strategies [Entire issue]. *Exceptional Education Quarterly, 1*(1).

Hallahan, D. P., & Cruickshank, W. M. (1973). *Psychoeducational foundations of learning disabilities.* Englewood Cliffs, NJ: Prentice-Hall.

Hallahan, D. P., & Kauffman, J. M. (1988). *Exceptional children* (4th ed.). Englewood Cliffs, NJ: Prentice-Hall.

Hallahan, D. P., Kauffman, J. M., & Lloyd, J. W. (1985). *Introduction to learning disabilities* (2nd ed.). Englewood Cliffs, NJ: Prentice-Hall.

Hallahan, D. P., Kauffman, J. M., Lloyd, J. W., & McKinney, J. D. (1988). Introduction to the series: Questions about the regular education initiative. *Journal of Learning Disabilities, 21,* 3–5.

Hallahan, D. P., & Reeve, R. E. (1980). Selective attention and distractibility. In B. K. Keogh (Ed.), *Advances in special education* (Vol. 1, pp. 141–181). Greenwich, CT: J.A.I.

Halpern, A. S. (1985). Transition: A look at the foundations. *Exceptional Children, 51,* 479–486.

Halpern, A. S., & Irvin, L. K. (1986). *Social and prevocational information battery–Revised.* Monterey, CA: CTB/McGraw-Hill.

Hammill, D. D. (1982). Assessing and training perceptual-motor skills. In D. D. Hammill & N. R. Bartel (Eds.), *Teaching children with learning and behavior problems* (3rd ed.) (pp. 379–408). Boston: Allyn and Bacon.

Hammill, D. D. (1985). *Detroit tests of learning aptitude* (2nd ed.). Austin, TX: PRO-ED.

Hammill, D. D., Ammer, J. J., Cronin, M. E., Mandlebaum, L. H., & Quinby, S. S. (1987). *Quick-score achievement test.* Austin, TX: PRO-ED.

Hammill, D. D., Brown, L., & Bryant, B. R. (1989). *A consumer's guide to tests in print.* Austin, TX: PRO-ED.

Hammill, D. D., Brown, V. L., Larsen, S. C., & Wiederholt, J. L. (1987). *Test of adolescent language–2.* Austin, TX: PRO-ED.

Hammill, D. D., & Bryant, B. R. (1986). *Detroit tests of learning aptitude–Primary.* Austin, TX: PRO-ED.

Hammill, D. D., Goodman, L., & Wiederholt, J. L. (1974). Visual-motor processes: What successes have we had in training them? *The Reading Teacher, 27,* 469–478.

Hammill, D. D., & Larsen, S. C. (1974a). The effectiveness of psycholinguistic training. *Exceptional Children, 41,* 5–15.

Hammill, D. D., & Larsen, S. C. (1974b). The relationship of selected auditory perceptual skills and reading ability. *Journal of Learning Disabilities, 7,* 429–435.

Hammill, D. D., & Larsen, S. C. (1983). *Test of written language.* Austin, TX: PRO-ED.

Hammill, D. D., & Larsen, S. C. (1988). *Test of written language–2.* Austin, TX: PRO-ED.

Hammill, D. D., Larsen, S. C., Wiederholt, J. L., & Fountain-Chambers, J. (1982). *Prueba de lectura y lenguaje escrito.* Austin, TX: PRO-ED.

Hammill, D. D., & Leigh, J. (1983a). *Basic school skills inventory–Diagnostic.* Austin, TX: PRO-ED.

Hammill, D. D., & Leigh, J. (1983b). *Basic school skills inventory–Screen.* Austin, TX: PRO-ED.

Hammill, D. D., & Newcomer, P. L. (1988). *Test of language development–2, Intermediate.* Austin, TX: PRO-ED.

Hammill, D. D., & Wiederholt, J. L. (1972). Review of the *Frostig Visual Perception Test* and the related training program. In L. Mann & D. Sabatino, (Eds.), *The first review of special education, Volume I* (pp. 33–48). Philadelphia: Journal of Special Education Press.

Hanna, G. S., Dyck, N. J., & Holen, M. C. (1979). Objective analysis of achievement-aptitude discrepancies in LD classification. *Learning Disability Quarterly, 2*(4), 32–38.

Hanson, M. J., & Lynch, E. W. (1989). *Early intervention: Implementing child and family services for infants and toddlers who are at-risk or disabled.* Austin, TX: PRO-ED.

Hargis, C. H. (1987). *Curriculum based assessment.* Springfield, IL: Thomas.

Haring, N., & Gentry, N. D. (1976). Direct and individualized instructional procedures. In N. Haring & R. L. Schiefelbusch (Eds.), *Teaching special children* (pp. 72–111). New York: McGraw-Hill.

Harmer, W. R., & Williams, F. (1978). The *Wide Range Achievement Test* and the *Peabody Individual Achievement Test:* A comparative study. *Journal of Learning Disabilities, 11,* 667–670.

Harrington, R. G., & Gibson, E. (1986). Preassessment procedures for learning disabled children: Are they effective? *Journal of Learning Disabilities, 19,* 538–541.

Harris, A. (1970). *How to increase reading ability* (5th ed.). New York: McKay.

Harris, L. P., & Wolf, S. R. (1979). Validity and reliability of criterion-referenced measures: Issues and procedures for special educators. *Learning Disability Quarterly, 2*(2), 84–88.

Harris, W. J., Drummond, R. J., Schultz, E. W., & King, D. R. (1978). The factor structure of three teacher rating scales and a self-report inventory of children's source traits. *Journal of Learning Disabilities, 11,* 583–585.

Harrison, P. L. (1987). Research with adaptive behavior scales. *Journal of Special Education, 21,* 37–68.

Harth, R. (1982). The Feuerstein perspective on the modification of cognitive performance. *Focus on Exceptional Children, 15*(3), 1–12.

Hasazi, S. B., Gordon, L. R., & Roe, C. A. (1985). Factors associated with the employment status of handicapped youth exiting high school from 1979 to 1983. *Exceptional Children, 51,* 455–469.

Hasselbring, T. S. (1984). Computer-based assessment of special-needs students. In R. E. Bennett & C. A. Maher (Eds.), *Microcomputers and exceptional children* (pp. 7–19). New York: Haworth.

Hasselbring, T. S., & Hamlett, C. L. (1983). *Aimstar* [Computer program]. Portland, OR: ASIEP Education Company.

Hauger, J. (1988). *WRMT–R ASSIST*™ [Computer program]. Circle Pines, MN: American Guidance Service.

Hawisher, M. F. (1975). *The resource room: An access to excellence.* Lancaster: South Carolina Region V Educational Services Center.

Heller, K. A., Holtzman, W. H., & Messick, S. (Eds.). (1982). *Placing children in special education: A strategy for equity.* Washington, DC: National Academy Press.

Herbert, C. H. (1977, 1979, 1983). *Basic inventory of natural language.* Monterey, CA: Publishers Test Service.

Heron, T. E., & Axelrod, S. (1976). Effectiveness of feedback to mothers concerning their children's word recognition performance. *Reading Improvement, 13,* 74–81.

Heron, T. E., & Harris, K. C. (1987). *The educational consultant* (2nd ed.). Austin, TX: PRO-ED.

Heron, T. E., & Heward, W. L. (1982). Ecological assessment: Implications for teaching of learning disabled students. *Learning Disability Quarterly, 5,* 117–125.

Heron, T. E., & Skinner, M. E. (1981). Criteria for defining the regular classroom as the least restrictive environment for LD students. *Learning Disability Quarterly, 4,* 115–121.

Herrnstein, R. (1971). I.Q. *Atlantic Monthly, 228,* 43–64.

Heward, W. L., Dardig, J., & Rossett, A. (1979). *Working with parents of handicapped children.* Columbus, OH: Merrill.

Heward, W. L., & Orlansky, M. D. (1988). *Exceptional children* (3rd ed.). Columbus, OH: Merrill.

Hieronymus, A. N., Hoover, H. D., & Lindquist, E. F. (1986). *Iowa tests of basic skills.* Chicago: Riverside.

Hiller v. Board of Education. (1988). *Special Education and the Handicapped, 3*(9), 1.

Hoff, M. K., Fenton, K. S., Yoshida, R. K., & Kaufman, M. J. (1978). Notice and consent: The school's responsibility to inform parents. *Journal of School Psychology, 16,* 265–273.

Hofmeister, A. M. (1984). *CLASS.LD* [Computer program]. Logan, UT: Utah State University.

Hogan, T. P. (1973, 1975). *Survey of school attitudes.* San Antonio, TX: Psychological Corporation.

Hops, H., Walker, H. M., Fleischman, D., Nagoshi, J., Omura, R., Skinrud, K., & Taylor, J. (1978). A standardized in-class program for acting-out children. II. Field test evaluations. *Journal of Educational Psychology, 70,* 636–644.

Hops, H., Walker, H. M., & Greenwood, C. R. (1979). PEERS: A program for remediating social withdrawal in school. In L. A. Hamerlynck (Ed.), *Behavioral systems for the developmentally disabled: I. School and family environments* (pp. 48–86). New York: Brunner/Mazel.

Howell, K. W., & Kaplan, J. S. (1980). *Diagnosing basic skills.* Columbus, OH: Merrill.

Howell, K. W., Kaplan, J. S., & O'Connell, C. Y. (1979). *Evaluating exceptional children.* Columbus, OH: Merrill.

Howell, K. W., & McCollum-Gahley, J. (1986). Monitoring instruction. *Teaching Exceptional Children, 19,* 47–49.

Howell, K. W., & Morehead, M. K. (1987). *Curriculum-based evaluation for special and remedial education.* Columbus, OH: Merrill.

Howell, K. W., Zucker, S. H., & Morehead, M. K. (1982). *Multilevel academic skills inventory.* San Antonio, TX: Psychological Corporation.

Hresko, W. P. (1988). *Test of early written language.* Austin, TX: PRO-ED.

Hresko, W. P., & Brown, L. (1984). *Test of early socioemotional development.* Austin, TX: PRO-ED.

Hresko, W. P., Reid, D. K., & Hammill, D. D. (1981). *Test of early language development.* Austin, TX: PRO-ED.

Hresko, W. P., Reid, D. K., & Hammill, D. D. (1982). *Prueba de desarrollo inicial de lenguaje.* Austin, TX: PRO-ED.

Hudson, F. G., Colson, S. E., Welch, D. L. H., Banikowski, A. K., & Mehring, T. A. (1989). *Hudson education skills inventory.* Austin, TX: PRO-ED.

Hudson, F. G., & Graham, S. (1978). An approach to operationalizing the IEP. *Learning Disability Quarterly, 1,* 13–32.

Hummel, J. W. (1988). Word processing and related tool applications. In M. M. Behrmann (Ed.), *Integrating computers into the curriculum: A handbook for special educators* (pp. 179–203). San Diego: College-Hill.

Hunt, K. W. (1965). *Grammatical structures written at three levels.* (NCTE Research Report No. 3). Urbana, IL: National Council of Teachers of English.

Hutton, J. B., & Roberts, T. G. (1986). *Social-emotional dimension scale.* Austin, TX: PRO-ED.

Idol-Maestas, L. (1983). *Special educator's consultation handbook.* Rockville, MD: Aspen.

Illinois State Board of Education. (1987). *Vocational assessment of secondary special needs students.* Springfield, IL: Illinois State Board of Education.

International Reading Association. (1981). *Resolution on misuse of grade equivalents.* Newark, DE: Author.

Ireton, H., & Thwing, E. (1972). *The Minnesota child development inventory.* Minneapolis: Behavior Science Systems.

Isaacson, S. L. (1988). Effective instruction in written language. In E. L. Meyen, G. A. Vergason, & R. J. Whelan (Eds.), *Effective instructional strategies for exceptional children* (pp. 288–306). Denver: Love.

Jastak, J. F., & Jastak, S. R. (1978). *Wide range achievement test* (1978 rev. ed.). Wilmington, DE: Jastak Associates.

Jastak, J. F., & Jastak, S. R. (1979). *Wide range interest-opinion test.* Wilmington, DE: Jastak Associates.

Jastak, J. F., & Jastak, S. R. (1980). *Wide range employability sample test.* Wilmington, DE: Jastak Associates.

Jastak, S., & Wilkinson, G. S. (1984). *Wide range achievement test–Revised.* Wilmington, DE: Jastak Associates.

Jenkins, M. W. (1987). Effect of a computerized individual education program (IEP) writer on time savings and quality. *Journal of Special Education Technology, 8*(3), 55–66.

Jensen, J. A., & Armstrong, R. J. (1985). *Slosson intelligence test (SIT), expanded norms tables, application and development.* East Aurora, NY: Slosson Educational Publications.

Jewish Employment and Vocational Service. (1976). *Jewish employment and vocational service work sample system.* Philadelphia: Vocational Research Associates.

Jewish Employment and Vocational Service. (1980). *Vocational interest temperament aptitude system.* Philadelphia: Vocational Research Associates.

Jewish Employment and Vocational Service. (1985). *APTI-COM® occupational aptitude test battery.* Philadelphia: Vocational Research Institute.

Johansson, C. B. (1982). *Career assessment inventory–Vocational.* Minneapolis: NCE Interpretive Scoring Systems.

Johansson, C. B. (1986). *Career assessment inventory–Enhanced.* Minneapolis: NCE Interpretive Scoring Systems.

Johnson, D. D. (1971). The Dolch list reexamined. *The Reading Teacher, 24,* 455–456.

Johnson, D. L. (1987). Selecting a computer for your special education classroom. In D. L. Johnson, C. D. Maddux, & A. C. Candler (Eds.), *Computers in the special education classroom* (pp. 21–28). New York: Haworth.

Johnson, D. L., Maddux, C. D., & Candler, A. C. (Eds.) (1987). *Computers in the special education classroom.* New York: Haworth.

Johnson, G. O., & Boyd, H. F. (1981). *Nonverbal test of cognitive skills.* San Antonio, TX: Psychological Corporation.

Jones, R. L. (1988a). Psychoeducational assessment of minority group children: Issues and perspectives. In R. L. Jones (Ed.), *Psychoeducational assessment of minority group children, A casebook* (pp. 13–35). Berkeley, CA: Cobb & Henry.

Jones, R. L. (Ed.). (1988b). *Psychoeducational assessment of minority group children, A casebook.* Berkeley, CA: Cobb & Henry.

Jones, R. L., & Wilderson, R. B. (1976). Mainstreaming and the minority child: An overview of issues and a perspective. In R. L. Jones (Ed.), *Mainstreaming and the minority child* (pp. 1–13). Reston, VA: Council for Exceptional Children.

Jongsma, E. (1971). *The cloze procedure as teaching technique.* Newark, DE: International Reading Association.

Jose P. v. Ambach. 3EHLR 551:245,27 (E.D.N.Y. 1979); 669 F.2d 865 (2d. Cir. 1982); 557 F.Supp. 1230 (E.D.N.Y. 1983).

Juárez, M. (1983). Assessment and treatment of minority-language-handicapped children: The role of the monolingual speech-language pathologist. *Topics in Language Disorders, 3*(3), 57–66.

Kagan, J. (1965). Impulsive and reflective children: Significance of conceptual tempo. In J. Krumboltz (Ed.), *Learning and the educational process* (pp. 133–161). Chicago: Rand-McNally.

Kaluger, G., & Kolson, C. J. (1978). *Reading and learning disabilities* (2nd ed.). Columbus, OH: Merrill.

Kamphaus, R. W. (1987). Conceptual and psychometric issues in the assessment of adaptive behavior. *Journal of Special Education, 21,* 27–35.

Kamphaus, R. W., & Reynolds, C. R. (1987a). *Clinical and research applications of the K–ABC.* Circle Pines, MN: American Guidance Service.

Kamphaus, R. W., & Reynolds, C. R. (1987b). *Kamphaus/Reynolds K–ABC analysis form.* Circle Pines, MN: American Guidance Service.

Karlsen, B., Madden, R., & Gardner, E. F. (1984). *Stanford diagnostic reading test* (3rd ed.). San Antonio, TX: Psychological Corporation.

Kaufman, A. S. (1981). The WISC–R and learning disabilities assessment: State of the art. *Journal of Learning Disabilities, 14,* 520–526.

Kaufman, A. S., & Kaufman, N. L. (1983). *Kaufman assessment battery for children.* Circle Pines, MN: American Guidance Service.

Kaufman, A. S., & Kaufman, N. L. (1985). *Kaufman test of educational achievement.* Circle Pines, MN: American Guidance Service.

Kavale, K. (1980). Learning disability and cultural-economic disadvantage: The case for a relationship. *Learning Disability Quarterly, 3,* 97–112.

Kavale, K. (1981). Functions of the *Illinois Test of Psycholinguistic Abilities (ITPA):* Are they trainable? *Exceptional Children, 47,* 496–510.

Kavale, K., & Andreassen, E. (1981). Disabled: Analysis of judgmental policies. *Journal of Learning Disabilities, 14,* 273–278.

Kavale, K. A., & Forness, S. R. (1984). A meta-analysis of the validity of Wechsler scale profiles and recategorizations: Patterns or parodies? *Learning Disability Quarterly, 7,* 136–156.

Kessen, W. (1965). *The child.* New York: Wiley.

Kimball, O. M. (1973). Development of norms for the *Coopersmith Self-Esteem Inventory*: Grades four through eight. (Doctoral dissertation, Northern Illinois University, 1972). *Dissertation Abstracts International, 34,* 1131–1132.

Kirk, S. A., & Chalfant, J. C. (1984). *Academic and developmental learning disabilities.* Denver: Love.

Kirk, S. A., & Kirk, W. D. (1971). *Psycholinguistic learning disabilities: Diagnosis and remediation.* Urbana: University of Illinois Press.

Kirk, S. A., Kliebhan, J. M., & Lerner, J. W. (1978). *Teaching reading to slow and disabled readers.* Boston: Houghton Mifflin.

Kirk, S. A., McCarthy, J. J., & Kirk, W. D. (1968). *Illinois test of psycholinguistic abilities* (rev. ed.). Urbana: University of Illinois Press.

Klein, K. (1984). Minimum competency testing: Shaping and reflecting curricula. *Phi Delta Kappan, 65,* 565–567.

Knoblock, H., & Pasamanick, B. (Eds.). (1974). *Gesell and Amartruda's developmental diagnosis: The evaluation and management of normal and abnormal neuropsychologic development in infancy and early childhood* (3rd ed.). New York: Harper and Row.

Knoff, H. (1984). Placement decisions revisited: IQ doesn't always tip the scale. *Exceptional Children, 51,* 122–128.

Knoff, H. M. (1983). Investigating disproportionate influence and status in multidisciplinary child study teams. *Exceptional Children, 49,* 367–369.

Knowlton, H. E., & Schlick, L. (in preparation). *Secondary regular classroom teachers' expectations of learning disabled students: The critical incident technique.* Lawrence, KS: University of Kansas Institute for Research in Learning Disabilities.

Kokaska, C. J., & Brolin, D. E. (1985). *Career education for handicapped individuals* (2nd ed.). Columbus, OH: Merrill.

Koppitz, E. M. (1963). *The Bender gestalt test for young children.* New York: Grune & Stratton.

Koppitz, E. M. (1975). *The Bender gestalt test for young children, Volume II: Research and application, 1963–1973.* New York: Grune & Stratton.

Kotin, L., & Eager, N. (1977). *Due process in special education: A legal analysis.* Cambridge, MA: Research Institute for Educational Problems.

Kottmeyer, W. (1970). *Teacher's guide for remedial reading.* New York: McGraw-Hill.

Kroth, R. L. (1973). *Target behavior.* Bellevue, WA: Edmark.

Kroth, R. L. (1975). *Communicating with parents of exceptional children.* Denver: Love.

Kroth, R. L. (1980a). *Strategies for effective parent-teacher interaction.* Albuquerque: University of New Mexico Institute for Parental Involvement.

Kroth, R. L. (1980b). The mirror model of parental involvement. *Pointer, 25,* 18–22.

Kroth, R. L. (1985). *Communicating with parents of exceptional children* (2nd ed.). Denver: Love.

Kroth, R. L., & Simpson, R. (1977). *Parent conferences as a teaching strategy.* Denver: Love.

Krug, S. E. (Ed.). (1987). *Psychware sourcebook* (2nd ed.). Kansas City, MO: Test Corporation of America.

Krug, S. E. (Ed.). (1988). *Psychware sourcebook 1988–89.* Kansas City, MO: Test Corporation of America.

Kuder, G. F. (1978). *Kuder preference record–Vocational.* Chicago: Science Research Associates.

Kuder, G. F. (1985). *Kuder occupational interest survey–Form DD.* Chicago: Science Research Associates.

Kuder, G. F. (1988). *Kuder general interest inventory–Form E.* Chicago: Science Research Associates.

Kuhlmann, F., & Anderson, R. G. (1981). *Kuhlmann-Anderson tests* (8th ed.). Bensenville, IL: Scholastic Testing Services.

Lambert, N. M. (1981a). *Diagnostic and technical manual: AAMD adaptive behavior scale, School edition.* Monterey, CA: Publishers Test Service.

Lambert, N. M. (1981b). Psychological evidence in *Larry P. v. Wilson Riles*: An evaluation by a witness for the defense. *American Psychologist, 36,* 937–952.

Lambert, N. M., Bower, E. M., & Hartsough, C. J. (1979). *Pupil behavior rating scale.* Monterey, CA: Publishers Test Service.

Lambert, N. M., & Windmiller, M. (1981). *AAMD adaptive*

behavior scale, School edition. Monterey, CA: Publishers Test Service.

Lambert, N., Windmiller, M., Cole, L., & Figueroa, R. (1975). *Manual: AAMD adaptive behavior scale, Public school version* (1974 rev.). Washington, DC: American Association on Mental Deficiency.

Lambert, N., Windmiller, M., Tharinger, D., & Cole, L. (1981). *Administration and instructional planning manual: AAMD adaptive behavior scale, School edition.* Monterey, CA: Publishers Test Service.

Lamke, T. A., & Nelson, M. J. (Rev. by J. L. French). (1973). *Henmon-Nelson tests of mental ability.* Boston: Houghton Mifflin.

Laosa, L. M. (1977). Nonbiased assessment of children's abilities: Historical antecedents and current issues. In T. Oakland (Ed.), *Psychological and educational assessment of minority children* (pp. 1–20). New York: Brunner/Mazel.

Lapp, D., & Flood, J. (1983). *Teaching reading to every child* (2nd ed.). New York: Macmillan.

LaPray, M., & Ross, R. (1969). The graded word list: Quick gauge of reading ability. *Journal of Reading, 12,* 305–307.

Larrivee, B. (1981). Modality preference as a model for differentiating beginning reading instruction: A review of the issues. *Learning Disability Quarterly, 4,* 180–188.

Larry P. v. Riles. C-71-2270-RFP (N. D. Cal. 1972), 495 F. Supp. 96 (N. D. Cal. 1979) Aff'r (9th Cir. 1984), 1983–84 EHLR DEC. 555:304.

Larsen, S. C., & Deshler, D. D. (1978). Limited role for learning disability specialists. *Learning Disability Quarterly, 1,* 2–5.

Larsen, S. C., & Hammill, D. D. (1975). Relationship of selected visual perceptual abilities to school learning. *Journal of Special Education, 9,* 282–291.

Larsen, S. C., & Hammill, D. D. (1986). *Test of written spelling—2.* Austin, TX: PRO-ED.

Larsen, S. C., Parker, R. R., & Hammill, D. D. (1982). Effectiveness of psycholinguistic training: A response to Kavale. *Exceptional Children, 49,* 60–66.

Larsen, S. C., Rogers, D., & Sowell, V. (1976). The use of selected perceptual tests in differentiating between normal and learning disabled children. *Journal of Learning Disabilities, 9,* 85–90.

Lau v. Nichols. (1974). 414 U. S. 562–572.

Lee, L. L. (1971). *Northwestern syntax screening text.* Evanston, IL: Northwestern University Press.

Lee, L. L. (1974). *Developmental sentence analysis.* Evanston, IL: Northwestern University Press.

Leinhardt, G., Zigmond, N., & Cooley, W. (1981). Reading instruction and its effects. *American Educational Research Journal, 18,* 343–361.

Leiter, R. G. (1948). *Leiter international performance scale.* Chicago: Stoelting.

LeMay, D. W., Griffin, P. M., & Sandford, A. R. (1977). *Learning accomplishment profile–Diagnostic edition.* Winston-Salem, NC: Kaplan.

Leonard, L. B., & Weiss, A. L. (1983). Application of nonstandardized assessment procedures to diverse linguistic populations. *Topics in Language Disorders, 3*(3), 35–45.

Lerner, J. W. (1985). *Learning disabilities* (4th ed.). Boston: Houghton Mifflin.

Levine, M. D., Clarke, S., & Ferb, T. (1981). The child as a diagnostic participant: Helping students describe their learning disorders. *Journal of Learning Disabilities, 14,* 527–530.

Lewis, R. (1983). Learning disabilities and reading: Instructional recommendations from current research. *Exceptional Children, 50,* 230–240.

Lewis, R. B. (1988). Learning disabilities. In E. W. Lynch & R. B. Lewis (Eds.), *Exceptional children and adults* (pp. 352–406). Glenview, IL: Scott, Foresman.

Lewis, R. B., & Doorlag, D. H. (1987). *Teaching special students in the mainstream* (2nd ed.). Columbus, OH: Merrill.

Lewis, R. B., & Harrison, P. J. (1988, April). *Effective applications of technology in special education: Results of a statewide study.* Paper presented at Council for Exceptional Children's 66th Annual Convention, Washington, DC.

Leyser, Y., & Gottlieb, J. (1980). Improving the social status of rejected pupils. *Exceptional Children, 46,* 459–461.

Lichtenstein, R., & Ireton, H. (1984). *Preschool screening.* Orlando, FL: Grune & Stratton.

Likert, R. (1932). A technique for the measurement of attitudes. *Archives of Psychology,* No. 140.

Lillie, D. L. (1975). *Carolina developmental profile.* Chicago: Science Research Associates.

Lilly, M. S. (1977). Evaluating IEP's. In S. Torres (Ed.), *A primer on IEP's for handicapped children* (pp. 26–30). Reston, VA: Council for Exceptional Children.

Lindsey, J. D. (Ed.). (1987). *Computers and exceptional individuals.* Columbus, OH: Merrill.

Linn, R. J., Algozzine, B., Schwartz, S. E., & Grise, P. (1984). Minimum competency testing and the learning disabled adolescent. *Diagnostique, 9,* 63–75.

Litcher, P. (1976). Communication with parents: It begins with listening. *Teaching Exceptional Children, 8,* 67–71.

Litowitz, B. E. (1981). Developmental issues in written language. *Topics in Language Disorders, 1*(2), 73–89.

Lloyd, J. W. (1984). How shall we individualize instruction—Or should we? *Remedial and Special Education, 5*(1), 7–15.

Lora v. Board of Education of the City of New York. 74 F.R.D. 565 (E.D.N.Y. 1977); 456 F.Supp. 1211 (E.D.N.Y. 1978), remanded, 623 F.2d 248 (2d. Cir. 1980); 587 F.Supp. 1572 (E.D.N.Y. 1984).

Losen, S. M., & Diament, B. (1978). *Parent conferences in the schools.* Boston: Allyn & Bacon.

Lund, K., Montague, M., & Reinholtz, M. (1987). Monitoring students on the job. *Teaching Exceptional Children, 19,* 58–60.

Lundell, K., Brown, W., & Evans, J. (1976). *Criterion-referenced test of basic skills.* Novato, CA: Academic Therapy Publications.

Lynch, E. W., & Lewis, R. B. (1987). Multicultural considerations. In K. A. Kavale, S. R. Forness, & M. Bender (Eds.), *Handbook of learning disabilities, Volume I, Dimensions and diagnosis* (pp. 399–416). Boston: College-Hill.

Lynch, E. W., & Stein, R. C. (1987). Parent participation by ethnicity: A comparison of Hispanic, Black, and Anglo families. *Exceptional Children, 54,* 105–111.

MacDonald, J. D. (1978). *Environmental language inventory.* Columbus, OH: Merrill.

MacTurk, R., & Neisworth, J. (1978). Norm-referenced and criterion-referenced measures for preschoolers. *Exceptional Children, 45,* 34–41.

Madaus, G. F., & Airasian, P. W. (1977). Issues in evaluating student outcomes in competency-based graduation programs. *Journal of Research and Development in Education, 10,* 79–91.

Mager, R. F. (1975). *Preparing instructional objectives* (2nd ed.). Belmont, CA: Fearon.

Maginnis, G. (1969). The readability graph and informal reading inventories. *The Reading Teacher, 22,* 534–538.

Magliocca, L., Rinaldi, R., Crew, J., & Kunzelmann, H. (1977). Early identification of handicapped children through a frequency sampling technique. *Exceptional Children, 44,* 414–423.

Mahoney, G., Finger, I., & Powell, A. (1985). Relationship of maternal behavior style to the development of organically impaired mentally retarded infants. *American Journal of Mental Deficiency, 90,* 296–302.

Male, M. (1988). *Special magic: Computers, classroom strategies, and exceptional students.* Mountain View, CA: Mayfield.

Mandelbaum, B. L., Rosen, G., & Miller, M. (1977). *Vocational information and evaluation work samples.* Philadelphia: Vocational Research Institute.

Mann, P. H., Suiter, P. A., & McClung, R. M. (1979). *Handbook in diagnostic–prescriptive teaching* (2nd ed.). Boston: Allyn & Bacon.

Mardell-Czudnowski, C. D. (1980). The four Ws of current testing practices: Who; what; why; and to whom—An exploratory survey. *Learning Disability Quarterly, 3*(1), 73–83.

Mardell-Czudnowski, C., & Goldenberg, D. (1983). *Developmental indicators for the assessment of learning–Revised.* Edison, NJ: Childcraft.

Marion, R. C. (1980). Communicating with parents of culturally diverse exceptional children. *Exceptional Children, 46,* 616–625.

Markwardt, F. C. (1989). *Peabody individual achievement test–Revised.* Circle Pines, MN: American Guidance Service.

Marston, D., & Magnusson, D. (1985). Implementing curriculum-based measurement in special and regular education settings. *Exceptional Children, 52,* 266–276.

Marston, D., Tindal, G., & Deno, S. L. (1984). Eligibility for learning disability services: A direct and repeated measure approach. *Exceptional Children, 50,* 554–555.

Marten, L. A., & Matlin, M. W. (1976). Does sexism in elementary readers still exist? *The Reading Teacher, 29,* 764–767.

Martin, N. (1983). Genuine communications. *Topics in Learning & Learning Disabilities, 3*(3), 1–11.

Mattke, R., & Reinhardt, A. (1987, October). *AppleWorks and IEPs: An ideal combination.* Paper presented at Closing the Gap's 5th Annual Microcomputer Technology for Special Education and Rehabilitation Conference, Minneapolis, MN.

McCarney, S. B., Leigh, J. E., & Cornbleet, J. (1983). *Behavior evaluation scale.* Columbia, MO: Educational Services.

McCarron, L. (1976, 1982). *McCarron assessment of neuromuscular development.* Dallas: McCarron-Dial Systems.

McCarron, L., & Dial, J. (1973). *Dial behavior rating scale.* Dallas: McCarron-Dial Systems.

McCarron, L., & Dial, J. (1976). *Haptic visual discrimination test.* Dallas: McCarron-Dial Systems.

McCarron, L., & Dial, J. (1976, 1986). *Observational emotional inventory.* Dallas: McCarron-Dial Systems.

McCarron, L., & Dial, J. (1986). *McCarron-Dial evaluation system manual.* Dallas: McCarron-Dial Systems.

McCarthy, D. (1972). *McCarthy scales of children's abilities.* San Antonio, TX: Psychological Corporation.

McCarthy, D. (1978). *McCarthy screening test.* San Antonio, TX: Psychological Corporation.

McClung, M. S. (1978). Are competency testing programs fair? Legal? *Phi Delta Kappan, 59,* 397–400.

McCollum, J. (1984). Social interaction between parents and babies: Validation of an intervention procedure. *Child: Care, Health and Development, 10,* 301–315.

McCollum, J. A., & Stayton, V. D. (1985). Infant/parent interaction: Studies and intervention guidelines based on the SIAI model. *Journal of the Division for Early Childhood, 9*(2), 125–135.

McCormack, J. E., Jr. (1976). The assessment tool that meets your needs: The one you construct. *Teaching Exceptional Children, 8,* 106–109.

McDermott, P. A., & Watkins, M. W. (1985). *McDermott multidimensional assessment of children* [Computer program]. San Antonio, TX: Psychological Corporation.

McGue, M., Shinn, M., & Ysseldyke, J. (1982). Use of cluster scores on the *Woodcock-Johnson Psycho-Educational Battery* with learning disabled students. *Learning Disability Quarterly, 5,* 274–287.

McKenna, M. (n.d.) *Computer assisted reading assessment* [Computer program]. East Aurora, NY: United Educational Services.

McKinney, J. D., and Hocutt, A. M. (1982). Public school involvement of parents of learning-disabled and average achievers. *Exceptional Education Quarterly, 3,* 64–73.

McLoughlin, J. A. (1985a). The families of children with disabilities. In W. H. Berdine & A. E. Blackhurst (Eds.), *An introduction to special education* (2nd ed.) (pp. 617–660). Boston: Little, Brown.

McLoughlin, J. A. (1985b). Training educational diagnosticians. *Diagnostique, 10*(1–4), 176–196.

McLoughlin, J. A., Edge, D., Petrosko, J., Strenecky, B., & Davis, C. (1983). Interagency cooperation to disseminate materials concerning exceptional people's needs. *Journal of Special Education Technology, 6,* 40–47.

McLoughlin, J. A., Edge, D., Strenecky, B., & Petrosko, J. (1981). PL 94–142 and information dissemination: A step forward. *Journal of Special Education Technology, 4,* 50–58.

McLoughlin, J. A., & Kershman, S. (1978). Including the handicap. *Behavioral Disorders, 4,* 31–35.

McLoughlin, J. A., & Lewis, R. B. (1981). *Assessing special students.* Columbus, OH: Merrill.

McLoughlin, J. A., McLaughlin, R., & Stewart, W. (1979). Advocacy for parents of the handicapped: A professional responsibility and challenge. *Learning Disability Quarterly, 2,* 51–57.

Mellard, D. (1986). *Report of the learning disabilities evaluation study, 1985–1986.* Frankfort, KY: Kentucky Department of Education, Office for Education of Exceptional Children.

Mercer, C. D., & Mercer, A. R. (1989). *Teaching students with learning problems* (3rd ed.). Columbus, OH: Merrill.

Mercer, J. R. (1973). *Labeling the mentally retarded.* Berkeley: University of California Press.

Mercer, J. R. (1974). A policy statement on assessment procedures and rights of children. *Harvard Educational Review, 44,* 125–141.

Mercer, J. R. (1979). *Technical manual, System of multicultural pluralistic assessment.* San Antonio, TX: Psychological Corporation.

Mercer, J. R. (1983). Issues in the diagnosis of language disorders in students whose primary language is not English. *Topics in Language Disorders, 3*(3), 46–56.

Mercer, J. R., & Lewis, J. F. (1977a). *Adaptive behavior inventory for children.* San Antonio, TX: Psychological Corporation.

Mercer, J. R., & Lewis, J. F. (1977b). *System of multicultural pluralistic assessment.* San Antonio, TX: Psychological Corporation.

Messick, S. (1984). Assessment in context: Appraising student performance in relation to instruction quality. *Educational Researcher, 13*(3), 3–8.

Meyen, E. L., Gautt, S., & Howard, C. (1976). *Instructional based appraisal system.* Bellevue, WA: Edmark.

Meyers, M. J. (1980). The significance of learning modalities, modes of instruction, and verbal feedback for learning to recognize written words. *Learning Disability Quarterly, 3*(3), 62–69.

Michael, W. B., Michael, J. J., & Zimmerman, W. S. (1985). *Study attitudes and methods survey.* San Diego, CA: EdITS.

Michael, W. B., Smith, R. A., & Michael, J. J. (1984). *Dimensions of self-concept.* San Diego, CA: EdITS.

Miller, L. C. (1977). *School behavior checklist.* Los Angeles: Western Psychological Services.

Miller, T. C., & Davis, E. E. (1982). *The mildly handicapped student.* New York: Grune & Stratton.

Minskoff, E. H. (1975). Research on psycholinguistic training: Critique and guidelines. *Exceptional Children, 42,* 136–144.

Mitchell, J. V., Jr. (Ed.) (1983). *Tests in print III.* Lincoln, NE: University of Nebraska Press.

Mitchell, J. V., Jr. (Ed.) (1985). *Ninth mental measurements yearbook.* Lincoln, NE: University of Nebraska Press.

Mithaug, D. E., Horiuchi, C. N., & Fanning, P. N. (1985). A Colorado statewide follow-up survey of special education students. *Exceptional Children, 51,* 397–404.

Monroe, M. (1932). *Children who cannot read.* Chicago: University of Chicago Press.

Mooney, R. L., & Gordon, L. V. (1950). *The Mooney problem check lists* (rev. ed.). San Antonio, TX: Psychological Corporation.

Moores, D. F., & Moores, J. M. (1988). Hearing disorders. In E. W. Lynch & R. B. Lewis (Eds.), *Exceptional children and adults* (pp. 276–317). Glenview, IL: Scott, Foresman.

Moran, M. R. (1984). Excellence at the cost of instructional equity? The potential impact of recommended reforms upon low achieving children. *Focus on Exceptional Children, 16*(7), 1–12.

Moran, M. R. (1988). Options for written language assessment. In E. L. Meyen, G. A. Vergason, & R. J. Whelan (Eds.), *Effective instructional strategies for exceptional children* (pp. 465–480). Denver: Love.

Muir, K., Milan, M., Branston-McLean, M., & Berger, M. (1982). Advocacy training for parents of handicapped children. *Young Children, 37,* 41–46.

Munday, L. A. (1979). Changing test scores, especially since 1970. *Phi Delta Kappan, 60,* 496–499.

Myklebust, H. R. (1965). *Development and disorders of written language. Volume one: Picture story language test.* New York: Grune & Stratton.

Myklebust, H. R. (1968). Learning disabilities: Definition and overview. In H. R. Myklebust (Ed.), *Progress in learning disabilities* (Vol. I) (pp. 1–15). New York: Grune & Stratton.

Myklebust, H. R. (1973). *Development and disorders of written language. Volume two: Studies of normal and exceptional children.* New York: Grune & Stratton.

Myklebust, H. R. (1981). *The pupil rating scale revised.* New York: Grune & Stratton.

Naslund, R. A., Thorpe, L. P., & Lefever, D. W. (1985). *SRA achievement series.* Chicago: Science Research Associates.

National Advisory Council for Bilingual Education. (1980–81). *The prospects for bilingual education in the nation. Fifth annual report of the National Advisory Council for Bilingual Education.* Author.

National Association of State Directors of Special Education. (1976). *Functions of the placement committee in special education.* Washington, DC: Author.

National Commission on Excellence in Education. (1983). *A nation at risk: The imperative for educational reform.* Washington, DC: U. S. Government Printing Office.

National Council of Supervisors of Mathematics. (1978). Position statement on basic skills. *The Mathematics Teacher, 71,* 147–152.

National Council of Teachers of Mathematics. (1980). *An agenda for action: Recommendations for school mathematics in the 1980's.* Reston, VA: Author.

National Council of Teachers of Mathematics. (1988, June 15). NAEP: Results of the fourth mathematics assessment. *Education Week,* pp. 28–29.

National Joint Committee on Learning Disabilities. (1981, January 30). *Learning disabilities: Issues on definition.* A position paper of the National Joint Committee on Learning Disabilities.

National Society for the Prevention of Blindness. (1969). *Vision screening in schools.* New York: Author.

Neel, R. S., Meadows, N., Levine, P., & Edgar, E. B. (1988). What happens after special education: A statewide follow-up study of secondary students who have behavioral disorders. *Behavioral Disorders, 13,* 209–216.

Neisworth, J. T., Willoughby-Herb, S. J., Bagnato, S. J., Cartwright, C. A., & Laub, K. W. (1980). *Individualized education for preschool exceptional children.* Rockville, MD: Aspen Systems.

Nelson, D., & Hammer, D. G. (1985). *The Fayette County vocational assessment guide: A practical, secondary-school vocational assessment system.* Lexington, KY: Board of Education of Fayette County.

Nelson, M. J., & French, J. L. (1974). *Henmon-Nelson tests of mental ability, Primary form.* Boston: Houghton Mifflin.

Newborg, J., Stock, J., Wnek, L., Guidubaldi, J., & Suinicki, J. (1984). *Battelle developmental inventory.* Allen, TX: DLM Teaching Resources.

Newcomer, P. L. (1986). *Standardized reading inventory.* Austin, TX: PRO-ED.

Newcomer, P. L., & Bryant, B. R. (1986). *Diagnostic achievement test for adolescents.* Austin, TX: PRO-ED.

Newcomer, P. L., & Curtis, D. (1984). *Diagnostic achievement battery.* Austin, TX: PRO-ED.

Newcomer, P. L., & Hammill, D. D. (1975). ITPA and academic achievement: A survey. *The Reading Teacher, 28,* 731–741.

Newcomer, P. L., & Hammill, D. D. (1976). *Psycholinguistics in the schools.* Columbus, OH: Merrill.

Newcomer, P. L., & Hammill, D. D. (1988). *Test of language development–2, Primary.* Austin, TX: PRO-ED.

Nihira, K., Foster, R., Shellhaas, M., & Leland, H. (1974). *AAMD adaptive behavior scale: Manual* (rev. ed.). Washington, DC: American Association on Mental Deficiency.

Nodine, B. F. (1983). Foreword: Process not product. *Topics in Learning & Learning Disabilities, 3*(3), ix–xii.

Nurss, J. R., & McGauvran, M. E. (1986). *Metropolitan readiness tests, 5th edition.* San Antonio, TX: Psychological Corporation.

Nuttal, E. V. (1987). Survey of current practices in the psychological assessment of limited-English-proficiency handicapped children. *Journal of School Psychology, 25,* 53–61.

Oakland, T. (1979). Nonbiased assessment of minority group children. *Exceptional Education Quarterly, 1*(3), 31–46.

Oakland, T. (1979). Research on the *Adaptive Behavior Inventory for Children* and the Estimated Learning Potential. *School Psychology Digest, 8,* 63–70.

Oakland, T. (1980). Nonbiased assessment of minority group children. *Exceptional Education Quarterly, 1*(3), 31–46.

Oakland, T., & Laosa, L. M. (1977). Professional, legislative, and judicial influences on psychoeducational assessment practices in schools. In T. Oakland (Ed.), *Psychological and educational assessment of minority children* (pp. 21–51). New York: Brunner/Mazel.

Office for Civil Rights. (1975). *Task force findings specifying remedies for eliminating past education practices ruled unlawful under Lau vs. Nichols.* Washington, DC: Author.

Olsen, K. R. (1980). Minimum competency testing and the IEP process. *Exceptional Children, 47,* 176–185.

Osborn, W. J. (1925). Ten reasons why pupils fail in mathematics. *The Mathematics Teacher, 18,* 234–238.

Otis, A. S., & Lennon, R. T. (1979, 1982). *Otis-Lennon school ability test.* San Antonio, TX: Psychological Corporation.

Otto, W., & Smith, R. J. (1983). Skill-centered and meaning-centered conceptions of remedial reading instruction: Striking a balance. *Topics in Learning and Learning Disabilities, 2*(4), 20–26.

Paget, K. (1984–85). Assessment in early childhood education. *Diagnostique, 10,* 76–87.

Paraskevopoulos, J. N., & Kirk, S. A. (1969). *The development and psychometric characteristics of the revised Illinois Test of Psycholinguistic Abilities.* Urbana: University of Illinois Press.

Parents in Action on Special Education v. Joseph P. Hannon. No. 74 C 3586 (N.D. Ill. 1980).

Parker, R. (1983). *Occupational aptitude survey and interest survey–The aptitude survey.* Austin, TX: PRO-ED.

Patrick, J. L., & Reschly, D. J. (1982). Relationship of state educational criteria and demographic variables to school-system prevalence of mental retardation. *American Journal of Mental Deficiency, 86,* 351–360.

Payan, R. M. (1989). Language assessment for the bilingual exceptional child. In L. M. Baca & H. T. Cervantes (Eds.), *The bilingual special education interface* (2nd ed.) (pp. 125–152). Columbus, OH: Merrill.

Pendergast, K., Dickey, S. E., Selmar, J. W., & Soder, A. L. (1984). *Photo articulation test.* Monterey, CA: Publishers Test Service.

Perrone, V. (1977). *The abuses of standardized testing.* Bloomington, IN: Phi Delta Kappa Educational Foundation.

Peterson, M. (1988). *Vocational assessment of special students for vocational education: A state-of-the-art review.* Columbus, OH: National Center for Research in Vocational Education, Ohio State University.

Peterson, J., Heistad, D., Peterson, D., & Reynolds, M. (1985). Montevideo individualized prescriptive instructional management system. *Exceptional Children, 52,* 239–243.

Pfeiffer, S., & Naglieri, J. (1983). An investigation of multidisciplinary team decision making. *Journal of Learning Disabilities, 16,* 578–580.

Phelps-Gunn, T., & Phelps-Terasaki, D. (1982). *Written language instruction.* Rockville, MD: Aspen Systems.

Piers, E. V. (1977). *The Piers-Harris children's self-concept scale* (Research monograph no. 1). Los Angeles: Western Psychological Services.

Piers, E. V., & Harris, D. B. (1969). *The Piers-Harris children's self-concept scale.* Los Angeles: Western Psychological Services.

Piers, E. V., & Harris, D. B. (1984). *The Piers-Harris children's self-concept scale: Revised manual.* Los Angeles: Western Psychological Services.

Pipho, C. (1978). Minimum competency testing in 1978: A look at state standards. *Phi Delta Kappan, 59,* 585–588.

Plata, M. (1982). *Assessment, placement, and programming of bilingual exceptional pupils: A practical approach.* Reston, VA: ERIC Clearinghouse on Handicapped & Gifted Children, Council for Exceptional Children.

Poggio, J. P., & Salkind, N. J. (1979). A review and appraisal of instruments assessing hyperactivity in children. *Learning Disability Quarterly, 2,* 9–22.

Poland, S. F., Thurlow, M. L., Ysseldyke, J. E., & Mirkin, P. K. (1982). Current psychoeducational assessment and decision-making practices as reported by directors of special education. *Journal of School Psychology, 20,* 171–179.

Polifka, J. C. (1981). Compliance with PL 94–142 and consumer satisfaction. *Exceptional Children, 48,* 250–253.

Polloway, E. A., Patton, J. R., & Cohen, S. B. (1983). Written language for mildly handicapped children. In E. L. Meyen, G. A. Vergason, & R. L. Whelan (Eds.), *Promising practices for exceptional children: Curriculum implications* (pp. 285–320). Denver: Love.

Polloway, E. A., Payne, J. S., Patton, J. R., & Payne, R. A. (1985). *Strategies for teaching retarded and special needs learners* (3rd ed.). Columbus, OH: Merrill.

Polloway, E. A., & Smith, J. E. (1982). *Teaching language skills to exceptional learners.* Denver: Love.

Popham, W. J. (1978). The case for criterion-referenced measurements. *Educational Researcher, 7,* 6–10.

Popham, W. J., & Baker, E. L. (1970). *Systematic instruction.* Englewood Cliffs, NJ: Prentice-Hall.

Poplin, M. S. (1983). Assessing developmental writing abilities. *Topics in Learning and Learning Disabilities, 3*(3), 63–75.

Poplin, M. S., & Larsen, S. C. (1979). Current status of learning disability specialists. *Learning Disability Quarterly, 1,* 2–5.

Poteet, J. A. (1980). Informal assessment of written expression. *Learning Disability Quarterly, 3*(4), 88–98.

Potter, M. (1982). *Application of a decision theory model to eligibility and classification decisions in special education* (Research report no. 85). Minneapolis: University of Minnesota, Institute for Research on Learning Disabilities.

Prasse, D. P., & Reschly, D. J. (1986). Larry P.; a case of segregation, testing or program efficacy? *Exceptional Children, 52,* 333–346.

Prep work samples. (1976). Trenton, NJ: Educational Technologies.

Prescott, G. A., Balow, I. H., Hogan, T. P., & Farr, R. C. (1985, 1986, 1987). *Metropolitan achievement tests* (6th ed.). San Antonio, TX: Psychological Corporation.

Project RHISE. (1979). *Rockford infant developmental evaluation scale.* Bensenville, IL: Scholastic Testing Service.

Public Law 94–142, Education of the Handicapped Act of 1975. (1977, August 23). *Federal Register, 42,* 163.

Pullin, D. (1980). Mandated minimum competency testing: Its impact on handicapped adolescents. *Exceptional Education Quarterly, 1*(2), 107–115.

Purdue Research Foundation. (1968). *Purdue pegboard.* Chicago: Science Research Associates.

Pyecha, J., et al. (1980). *A national survey of individualized education programs (IEP's) for handicapped children. Final report.* Research Triangle Park, NC: Research Triangle Institution.

Quay, H. C., & Peterson, D. R. (1983, 1987). *Revised behavior problem checklist.* Coral Gables, FL: University of Miami.

Quick, A. D., Little, T. L., & Campbell, A. A. (1974). *Project MEMPHIS: Enhancing developmental progress in preschool exceptional children.* Belmont, CA: Fearon.

Rabe, M. B., & Matlin, M. W. (1978). Sex-role stereotypes in speech and language tests. *Language, Speech, and Hearing Services in the Schools, 9,* 70–76.

Raven, J., and others. (1986). *Research supplement no. 3: A compendium of North American normative and validity studies.* San Antonio, TX: Psychological Corporation.

Raven, J. C. (1938). *Standard progressive matrices.* London: H. K. Lewis. [American distributor: Psychological Corporation]

Raven, J. C. (1947). *Coloured progressive matrices.* London: H. K. Lewis. [American distributor: Psychological Corporation]

Raven, J. C. (1962). *Advanced progressive matrices.* London: H. K. Lewis. [American distributor: Psychological Corporation]

Reading for meaning 2 [Computer program]. (1984). Dimondale, MN: Hartley Courseware.

Reed, V. (1980). Writing pupil assessment reports. In W. Gearheart & E. Willenberg (Eds.), *Application of pupil assessment information* (pp. 187–201). Denver: Love.

Reeves, M. S. (1988, April 27). "Self-interest and the common weal": Focusing on the bottom half. *Education Week,* pp. 14–21.

Reeve, R. E., Hall, R. J., & Zakreski, R. S. (1979). The *Woodcock-Johnson Tests of Cognitive Ability:* Concurrent validity with the *WISC–R. Learning Disability Quarterly, 2* (2), 63–69.

Reid, D. K., & Hresko, W. P. (1981). *A cognitive approach to learning disabilities.* New York: McGraw-Hill.

Reid, D. K., Hresko, W., & Hammill, D. D. (1981). *Test of early reading ability.* Austin, TX: PRO-ED.

Reisman, F. K. (1985). *Sequential assessment of mathematics inventories—Standardized inventory.* San Antonio, TX: Psychological Corporation.

Reschly, D. J. (1981). Psychological testing in educational classification and placement. *American Psychologist, 36,* 1094–1102.

Research and Training Center, Portland State University. (1988, Summer). Services to minority populations: What does it mean to be a culturally competent professional? *Focal Point, 2*(4), 1–2.

Reynolds, C. R. (1984). Critical measurement issues in learning disabilities. *Journal of Special Education, 18,* 451–476.

Reynolds, C. R., & Stowe, M. L. (1985). *Severe discrepancy analyzer* [Computer program]. Bensalem, PA: TRAIN.

Reynolds, M. C., & Birch, J. W. (1977). *Teaching exceptional children in all America's schools.* Reston, VA: Council for Exceptional Children.

Reynolds, W. M. (1987). *Wepman's auditory discrimination test manual* (2nd ed.). Los Angeles: Western Psychological Services.

Rhodes, W. C. (1967). The disturbing child: A problem of ecological management. *Exceptional Children, 33,* 637–642.

Ringler, L. H., & Smith, I. (1973). Learning modality and word recognition of first grade children. *Journal of Learning Disabilities, 6,* 307–312.

Roach, E. G., & Kephart, N. D. (1966). *The Purdue perceptual-motor survey.* Columbus, OH: Merrill.

Roberts, G. H. (1968). The failure strategies of third grade arithmetic pupils. *The Arithmetic Teacher, 15,* 442–446.

Roberts, J. R. (1945). *Pennsylvania bimanual work sample.* Circle Pines, MN: American Guidance Service.

Robinson, C., Rose, J., & Jackson, B. (1986). Multidomain assessment instruments. *Diagnostique, 11,* 135–153.

Robinson, E. A., & Eyberg, S. M. (1981). The dyadic parent-child interaction coding system: Standardization and validation. *Journal of Consulting and Clinical Psychology, 49,* 245–250.

Robinson, N. M., & Robinson, H. B. (1976). *The mentally retarded child* (2nd ed.). New York: McGraw-Hill.

Roca, P. (Trans.). (1967). *Escala de inteligencia Wechsler para niños.* San Antonio, TX: Psychological Corporation.

Rodriguez, R. F. (1981). The involvement of minority group parents in school. *Teacher Education and Special Education, 4,* 40–44.

Roos, P. (1985). Parents of mentally retarded children—misunderstood and mistreated. In A. P. Turnbull & H. R. Turnbull (Eds.), *Parents speak out: Then and now* (2nd ed.) (pp. 245–260). Columbus, OH: Merrill.

Rose, M. D., Cundick, B. P., & Higbee, K. L. (1983). Verbal rehearsal and visual imagery: Mnemonic aids for learning disabled children. *Journal of Learning Disabilities, 16,* 352–354.

Rosenberg, L. A., Harris, J. C., & Reifler, J. P. (1988). Similarities and differences between parents' and teachers' observations of the behavior of children with learning problems. *Journal of Learning Disabilities, 21,* 189–190.

Rosenberg, S., & Robinson, C. C. (1985). Enhancement of mothers' interactional skills in an infant education program. *Education and Training of the Mentally Retarded, 20,* 163–169.

Rosenberg, S., Robinson, C., & Beckman, P. (1984). Teaching skills inventory: A measure of parent performance. *Journal for the Division for Early Childhood, 8,* 107–113.

Rosenberg, S., Robinson, C., Finkler, D., & Rose, J. (1987). An empirical comparison of formulas evaluating early intervention program impact on development. *Exceptional Children, 54,* 213–219.

Ruddell, R. B. (1974). *Reading language instruction: Innovative practices.* Englewood Cliffs, NJ: Prentice-Hall.

Rudman, H. C. (1977). The standardized test flap. *Phi Delta Kappan, 59,* 178–185.

Russell, D. H., & Russell, E. F. (1959). *Listening aids through the grades.* New York: Bureau of Publications, Teachers College, Columbia University.

Saario, T. N., Jacklin, C. N., & Tittle, C. K. (1973). Sex role stereotyping in the public schools. *Harvard Educational Review, 43,* 386–416.

Sage, D. D., & Burrello, L. C. (1988). *Policy and management in special education.* Englewood Cliffs, NJ: Prentice-Hall.

Salvia, J., & Hritcko, T. (1984). The K–ABC and ability training. *Journal of Special Education, 18,* 345–356.

Salvia, J., & Ysseldyke, J. E. (1988). *Assessment in special and remedial education* (4th ed.). Boston: Houghton Mifflin.

Samuda, R. (1975). *Psychological testing of American minorities.* New York: Dodd, Mead.

Samuels, S. J. (1983). Diagnosing reading problems. *Topics in Learning and Learning Disabilities, 2*(4), 1–11.

Sander, E. K. (1972). When are speech sounds learned? *Journal of Speech and Hearing Disorders, 23*(1) 55–63.

Sanford, A. (1975). *The learning accomplishment profile.* Winston-Salem, NC: Kaplan.

Sanford, A., Williams, J., James, J., & Overton, A. (1983). *A planning guide to the preschool curriculum.* Winston-Salem, NC: Kaplan.

Sanford, A., & Zelman, J. (1981). *Learning accomplishment profile–Revised.* Winston-Salem, NC: Kaplan.

Santa Cruz County. (1973). *Behavioral characteristics progression.* Palo Alto, CA: VORT.

Sattler, J. M. (1982). *Assessment of children's intelligence and special abilities* (2nd ed.). Boston: Allyn & Bacon.

Sattler, J. M. (1988). *Assessment of children* (3rd ed.). San Diego, CA: Author.

Say, E., McCollum, J., & Brightman, M. (1980, April). *A study of the IEP: Parent and school perspectives.* Paper presented at the annual meeting of the American Educational Research Association, Boston.

Scanlon, C., Arick, J., and Phelps, N. (1981). Participation in the development of the IEP: Parents' perspective. *Exceptional Children, 47,* 373–376.

Scarr, S. (1981). Testing *for* children: Assessment and the many determinants of intellectual competence. *American Psychologist, 36,* 1159–1166.

Schafer, D. S., & Moersch, M. S. (Eds.). (1981). *Developmental programming for infants and young children.* Ann Arbor: University of Michigan Press.

Schloss, P. J., Smith, M., Hoover, T., & Wolford, J. (1987). Dynamic criterion-referenced vocational assessment: An alternative strategy for handicapped youth. *Diagnostique, 12,* 74–86.

Schmitz, T. (1985, 1986). *Microcomputer evaluation of career areas.* Omro, WI: Conover.

Scholastic aptitude test. (n.d.). Princeton, NJ: Educational Testing Services. (new edition each year)

Schreiner, R. (1983). Principles of diagnosis of reading difficulties. *Topics in Learning and Learning Disabilities, 2*(4), 70–85.

Schulte, A., & Borich, G. D. (1984). Considerations in the use of difference scores to identify learning-disabled children. *Journal of School Psychology, 22,* 381–390.

Schulz, J. B., & Turnbull, A. P. (1983). *Mainstreaming handicapped students* (2nd ed.). Boston: Allyn & Bacon.

Schumaker, J. B., & Deshler, D. D. (1984). Setting demand variables: A major factor in program planning for the LD adolescent. *Topics in Language Disorders, 4*(2), 22–40.

Schumaker, J. B., Deshler, D. D., Alley, G. R., & Warner, M. M. (1983). Toward the development of an intervention model for learning disabled adolescents: The University of Kansas Institute. *Exceptional Education Quarterly, 4*(1), 45–74.

Schumaker, J. B., Deshler, D. D., Alley, G. R., Warner, M. M., & Denton, P. H. (1982). Multipass: A learning strategy for improving reading comprehension. *Learning Disability Quarterly, 5,* 295–304.

Scott, K., & Hogan, A. (1982). Methods for the identification of high-risk and handicapped infants. In C. Ramey & P. Trohanis (Eds.), *Finding and educating high-risk and handicapped infants.* Baltimore: University Park Press.

Scull, J. W., & Brand, L. H. (1980). The *WRAT* and the *PIAT* with learning disabled children. *Journal of Learning Disabilities, 13,* 350–352.

Semel, E., Wiig, E. H., & Secord, W. (1987). *Clinical evaluation of language fundamentals–Revised.* San Antonio, TX: Psychological Corporation.

Semmel, D. S., Semmel, M. I., Gerber, M., & Adoradio, C. (1988, December). *Dynamic assessment and automatic placement in math drill and practice.* Paper presented at the CEC/TAM Conference on Special Education & Technology, Reno, NV.

Serow, R. C., & O'Brien, K. (1983). Performance of handicapped students in a competency testing program. *Journal of Special Education, 17,* 149–156.

Shea, T. M. (1978). *Teaching children and youth with behavior disorders.* St. Louis: Mosby.

Sherman, T. M. (1980). *Instructional decision-making.* Englewood Cliffs, NJ: Educational Technology.

Shulman, B. B. (1986). *Test of pragmatic skills* (rev. ed.). Tucson, AZ: Communication Skill Builders.

Silvaroli, N. J. (1986). *Classroom reading inventory* (5th ed.). Dubuque, IA: Brown.

Simeonsson, R. J. (1986). *Psychological and developmental assessment of special children.* Boston: Allyn & Bacon.

Singer Company Career Systems. (1982). *Singer vocational evaluation system.* Rochester, NY: Singer.

Sitlington, P. L. (1979). Vocational assessment and training of the handicapped. *Focus on Exceptional Children, 12*(4), 1–11.

Sitlington, P. L., & Wimmer, D. (1978). Vocational assessment techniques for the handicapped adolescent. *Career Development for Exceptional Individuals, 1,* 74–87.

Sloan, W. (1954). *Lincoln-Oseretsky motor development scale.* Chicago: Stoelting.

Slosson, R. L. (1963). *Slosson oral reading test.* East Aurora, NY: Slosson Educational Publications.

Slosson, R. L. (1967). *Slosson drawing coordination test.* East Aurora, NY: Slosson Educational Publications.

Slosson, R. L. (1983). *Slosson intelligence test.* East Aurora, NY: Slosson Educational Publications.

Smith, C. R., Frank, A. R., & Snider, B. C. (1984). School psychologists' and teachers' perceptions of data used in the identification of behaviorally disordered students. *Behavior Disorders, 10,* 27–32.

Smith, D. (1981). *Teaching the learning disabled.* Englewood Cliffs, NJ: Prentice-Hall.

Smith, D., Young, K., West, R., Morgan, D., & Rhode, G. (1988). Reducing the disruptive behavior of junior high students: A classroom self-management procedure. *Behavioral Disorders, 13,* 231–239.

Smith, F. (1982). *Writing and the writer.* New York: Holt, Rinehart, & Winston.

Smith, R. M. (1969). *Teacher diagnosis of educational difficulties.* Columbus, OH: Merrill.

Smith, R. M., Neisworth, J. T., & Greer, J. B. (1978). *Evaluating educational environments.* Columbus, OH: Merrill.

Smolensky, J., Bonvechio, L. R., Whitlock, R. E., & Girard, M. A. (1968). *School health problems.* Palo Alto, CA: Fearon.

Somwaru, J. P. (1979). *Test of early learning skills.* Bensenville, IL: Scholastic Testing Service.

Sowell, V., Parker, R., Poplin, M., & Larsen, J. (1979). The effects of psycholinguistic training on improving psycholinguistic skills. *Learning Disability Quarterly, 2*(3), 69–77.

Spache, G. D. (1972). *Diagnostic reading scales.* Monterey, CA: CTB/McGraw-Hill.

Spache, G. D. (1981). *Diagnostic reading scales* (rev. ed.). Monterey, CA: CTB/McGraw-Hill.

Spanish assessment of basic education. (1987). Monterey, CA: CTB/McGraw-Hill.

Sparks, R., & Richardson, S. O. (1981). Multicategorical/cross categorical classrooms for learning disabled students. *Journal of Learning Disabilities, 14,* 60–61.

Sparrow, S. S., Balla, D. A., & Cicchetti, D. V. (1984). *Vineland adaptive behavior scales.* Circle Pines, MN: American Guidance Service.

Spector, C. (1979). The *Boehm Test of Basic Concepts:* Exploring the test results for cognitive deficits. *Journal of Learning Disabilities, 12,* 564–567.

Spivack, G., Haimes, P. E., & Spotts, J. (1967). *Devereux adolescent behavior rating scale.* Devon, PA: Devereux Foundation.

Spivack, G., & Spotts, J. (1966). *Devereux child behavior rating scale manual.* Devon, PA: Devereux Foundation.

Spivack, G., & Swift, M. (1972). *Hahnemann high school behavior rating scale manual.* Philadelphia: Department of Mental Health Services, Hahnemann Medical College & Hospital.

Sprague, R., & Sleator, E. (1973). Effects of psychopharmacologic agents on learning disorders. *Pediatric Clinics of North America, 20,* 710–736.

Statistical abstract of the United States. (1979). Washington, DC: U.S. Bureau of the Census.

Stephens, T. M., Blackhurst, A., & Magliocca, L. (1982). *Teaching mainstreamed students.* New York: Wiley.

Sternberg, L., & Taylor, R. L. (1982). The insignificance of psycholinguistic training: A reply to Kavale. *Exceptional Children, 49,* 254–256.

Sternberg, R. J. (1984a). The *Kaufman Assessment Battery for Children:* An information-processing analysis and critique. *Journal of Special Education, 18,* 269–279.

Sternberg, R. J. (1984b). What should intelligence tests test? Implications of a triarchic theory of intelligence for intelligence testing. *Educational Researcher, 13*(1), 5–15.

Stoloff, M. L., & Couch, J. V. (Eds.) (1987). *Computer use in psychology: A directory of software.* Washington, DC: American Psychological Association.

Stoneburner, R. L., & Brown, B. A. (1979). A comparison of PIAT and WRAT performances of learning disabled adolescents. *Journal of Learning Disabilities, 12,* 631–634.

Stowitscheck, J. J., Gable, R., & Hendrickson, J. M. (1980). *Instructional materials for exceptional children.* Germantown, MD: Aspen Park.

Strickland, B. (1982). Parental participation, school accountability, and due process. *Exceptional Education Quarterly, 3,* 41–49.

Strommen, E. (1988). Confirmatory factor analysis of the *Kaufman Assessment Battery for Children*: A reevaluation. *Journal of School Psychology, 26,* 13–23.

Sucher, F., & Allred, R. A. (1981). *New Sucher-Allred reading placement inventory.* Oklahoma City: Economy.

Sulzer-Azaroff, B., & Mayer, G. R. (1977). *Applying behavior-analysis procedures with children and youth.* New York: Holt, Rinehart & Winston.

Swap, S. M. (1974). Disturbing classroom behaviors: A developmental and ecological view. *Exceptional Children, 41,* 163–172.

Swift, M. (1982). *Devereux elementary school behavior rating scale II manual* (2nd ed.). Devon, PA: Devereux Foundation.

Talent Assessment Inc. (1972, 1980, 1985, 1988). *Talent assessment program.* Jacksonville, FL: Author.

Talley, M. (1986). *Talley™ special education management system* [Computer program]. North Billerica, MA: Curriculum Associates.

Talley, M. (1987). *Talley™ goals and objectives writer* [Computer program]. North Billerica, MA: Curriculum Associates.

Tarver, S. G., & Dawson, M. M. (1978). Modality preference and the teaching of reading: A review. *Journal of Learning Disabilities, 11,* 5–17.

Task Force on Education for Economic Growth. (1983). *Action for excellence.* Denver: Education Commission of the States.

Taxel, J. (1978). Justice and cultural conflict: Racism, sexism, and instructional materials. *Interchange, 9,* 56–84.

Taylor, O. L., & Payne, K. T. (1983). Culturally valid testing: A proactive approach. *Topics in Language Disorders, 3*(3), 8–20.

Taylor, R. P. (Ed.) (1981). *The computer in the school: Tutor, tool, tutee.* New York: Teachers College Press.

Templin, M. C., & Darley, F. L. (1969). *Templin-Darley tests of articulation* (2nd ed.). Iowa City: University of Iowa.

Terman, L. M., & Merrill, M. A. (1937). *Measuring intelligence.* Boston: Houghton Mifflin.

Terman, L. M., & Merrill, M. A. (1973). *Stanford-Binet intelligence scale, Form L-M, 1972 edition.* Chicago: Riverside.

Terrell, S. L., & Terrell, F. (1983). Distinguishing linguistic differences from disorders: The past, present, and future of nonbiased assessment. *Topics in Language Disorders, 3*(3), 1–7.

Test of cognitive skills. (1981). Monterey, CA: CTB/McGraw-Hill.

Thomas, W. P. (1988). The computer in school and classroom testing. In M. M. Behrmann, *Integrating computers into the curriculum: A handbook for special educators* (pp. 59–78). San Diego: College-Hill.

Thorndike, R. L., & Hagen, E. P. (1986). *Cognitive abilities test.* Chicago: Riverside.

Thorndike, R. L., Hagan, E., & Sattler, J. (1986). *Stanford-Binet intelligence scale: Fourth edition.* Chicago: Riverside.

Thurlow, M. L., Graden, J., Greener, J., & Ysseldyke, J. E. (1983). LD and non-LD students' opportunities to learn. *Learning Disability Quarterly, 6,* 172–183.

Thurlow, M. L., & Ysseldyke, J. E. (1979). Current assessment and decision-making practices in model programs for the learning disabled. *Learning Disability Quarterly, 2,* 15–24.

Thurman, S. K. (1977). Congruence of behavioral ecologies: A model for special education programming. *Journal of Special Education, 11,* 329–334.

Tindal, G. (1987). Graphing performance. *Teaching Exceptional Children, 20,* 44–46.

Tindall, L., & Guserty, J. (1986, 1987, 1988). *Replicating jobs in business and industry for persons with disabilities.* Madison, WI: Vocational Studies Center, University of Wisconsin–Madison.

Torgesen, J. K. (1977). The role of nonspecific factors in the task performance of learning disabled children: A theoretical assessment. *Journal of Learning Disabilities, 10,* 5–17.

Torgesen, J. K. (1979). What shall we do with psychological processes? *Journal of Learning Disabilities, 12,* 514–521.

Torgesen, J. K. (1980). Conceptual and educational implications of the use of efficient task strategies by learning disabled children. *Journal of Learning Disabilities, 13,* 364–371.

Torgesen, J. K., & Goldman, T. (1977). Rehearsal and short-term memory in reading disabled children. *Child Development, 48,* 56–61.

Toronto, A. S. (1973). *Screening test of Spanish grammar.* Evanston, IL: Northwestern University Press.

Trailor, C. B. (1982). Role clarification and participation in child study teams. *Exceptional Children, 48,* 529–530.

Tucker, J. A. (1980). Ethnic proportions in classes for the learning disabled: Issues in nonbiased assessment. *Journal of Special Education, 14,* 93–106.

Tucker, J. A. (1985). Curriculum-based assessment: An introduction. *Exceptional Children, 52,* 199–204.

Tucker, J. A., Stevens, L., & Ysseldyke, J. E. (1983). Learning disabilities: The experts speak out. *Journal of Learning Disabilities, 16,* 6–14.

Turnbull, A. P., & Schulz, J. B. (1979). *Mainstreaming handicapped students.* Boston: Allyn & Bacon.

Turnbull, A. P., & Strickland, B. (1981). Parents and the educational system. In J. L. Paul (Ed.), *Understanding and working with parents of children with special needs* (pp. 231–263). New York: Holt, Rinehart, & Winston.

Turnbull, A. P., Strickland, B. B., & Brantley, J. C. (1982). *Developing and implementing individualized education programs* (2nd ed.). Columbus, OH: Merrill.

Turnbull, A. P., & Turnbull, H. R. (1986). *Families, professionals, and exceptionality.* Columbus, OH: Merrill.

Tyack, D., & Gottsleben, R. (1977). *Language sampling, analysis, and training* (rev. ed.). Palo Alto, CA: Consulting Psychologists Press.

Tyler, L. E. (Ed.). (1969). *Intelligence: Some recurring issues.* New York: Van Nostrand-Reinhold.

U. S. Department of Labor. (1970a). *General aptitude test battery.* Washington, DC: U. S. Government Printing Office.

U. S. Department of Labor. (1970b). *Nonreading aptitude test battery.* Washington, DC: U. S. Government Printing Office.

U. S. Department of Labor. (1977, 1982, 1986). *Dictionary of occupational titles* (4th ed.). Washington, DC: U. S. Government Printing Office.

U. S. Department of Labor. (1982). *USES interest inventory II.* Washington, DC: U. S. Government Printing Office.

Ulrich, D. A. (1985). *Test of gross motor development.* Austin, TX: PRO-ED.

Uzgiris, I. C., & Hunt, J. M. (1975). *Assessment in infancy: Ordinal scales of psychological development.* Urbana: University of Illinois Press.

Valpar Corporation. (1978). *Valpar #17 prevocational readiness battery.* Tucson, AZ: Author.

Valus, A. (1986). Teacher perceptions of identification criteria emphasized in initial learning disabilities placement. *Learning Disabilities Research, 2,* 21–25.

Van Reusen, A. K., Bos, C. S., Schumaker, J. B., & Deshler, D. D. (1987). *The education planning strategy.* Lawrence, KS: EXCELLent.

Vasa, S. (1981). Alternative procedures for grading handicapped students in the secondary schools. *Education Limited, 3,* 16–23.

Vaughn, S., Bos, C. S., Harrell, J. E., & Lasky, B. A. (1988). Parent participation in the initial placement/IEP conference ten years after mandated involvement. *Journal of Learning Disabilities, 21,* 82–89.

Vogel, S. A. (1982). On developing LD college programs. *Journal of Learning Disabilities, 15,* 518–528.

Vogel, S. A. (1985). Comments on "Are commonly used predictors of college success applicable to the learning disabled?" *Thalamus, 5,* 62–74.

Vogel, S. A. (1987). Issues and concerns in LD college programming. In D. Johnson & J. Blalock (Eds.), *Adults with learning disabilities* (pp. 239–276). Orlando: Grune & Stratton.

Vogel, S. A., & Sattler, J. (1981). *The college student with learning disability: A handbook for university admissions officers, faculty, and administration.* Illinois Council for Learning Disabilities.

von Isser, A., & Kirk, W. (1980). *Prueba Illinois de habilidades psicolingüísticas.* Tucson: University of Arizona.

Wald, B. (1982). On assessing the oral language ability of limited-English-proficient students: The linguistic bases of the noncomparability of different language proficiency assessment measures. In S. S. Seidner (Ed.), *Issues of language assessment* (pp. 117–124). Illinois State Board of Education.

Walker, B. J. (1988). *Diagnostic teaching of reading.* Columbus, OH: Merrill.

Walker, H. M. (1983). *Walker problem behavior identification checklist* (rev.). Los Angeles: Western Psychological Services.

Walker, H. M., & Bull, S. (1970). *Validation of a behavior rating scale for measuring behavior within the classroom setting.* Eugene, OR: Unpublished manuscript, University of Oregon.

Walker, H. M., & Hops, H. (1979). The CLASS program for acting-out children: R & D procedures, program outcomes, and implementation issues. *School Psychologist Digest, 8,* 370–381.

Walker, H. M., & McConnell, S. R. (1988). *Walker-McConnell scale of social competence and school adjustment.* Austin, TX: PRO-ED.

Wallace, G., & Kauffman, J. M. (1986). *Teaching students with learning and behavior problems* (3rd ed.). Columbus, OH: Merrill.

Wallace, G., & Larsen, S. C. (1978). *Educational assessment of learning problems.* Boston: Allyn & Bacon.

Wallace, G., & McLoughlin, J. (1979). *Learning disabilities: Concepts and characteristics* (2nd ed.). Columbus, OH: Merrill.

Wallace, G., & McLoughlin, J. (1988). *Learning disabilities* (3rd ed.). Columbus, OH: Merrill.

Wang, M. C. (1987). Toward achieving educational excellence for all students: Program design and student outcomes. *Remedial and Special Education, 8,* 25–34.

Waugh, R.P. (1973). Relationship between modality preference and performance. *Exceptional Children, 6,* 465–469.

Wechsler, D. (1967). *Wechsler preschool and primary scale of intelligence.* San Antonio, TX: Psychological Corporation.

Wechsler, D. (1974). *Wechsler intelligence scale for children–Revised.* San Antonio, TX: Psychological Corporation.

Wechsler, D. (1981). *Wechsler adult intelligence test–Revised.* San Antonio, TX: Psychological Corporation.

Weiner, E. S. (1980). Diagnostic evaluation of writing skills. *Journal of Learning Disabilities, 13,* 43–53.

Weller, C., & Strawser, S. (1981). *Weller-Strawser scales of adaptive behavior for the learning disabled.* Novato, CA: Academic Therapy Publications.

Wells, C. G. (1981). *Learning through interactions: The study of language development.* Cambridge, England: Cambridge University Press.

Wells, G. (1973). *Coding manual of the description of child speech.* Bristol, England: University of Bristol School of Education.

Wepman, J. M. (1975). *Auditory discrimination test* (rev. 1973). Palm Springs, CA: Research Associates.

Wesson, C. L. (1987). Increasing efficiency. *Teaching Exceptional Children, 20,* 46–47.

White, R., & Calhoun, M. L. (1987). From referral to placement: Teachers' perceptions of their responsibilities. *Exceptional Children, 53,* 460–468.

White, W. J., Deshler, D. D., Schumaker, J. B., Warner, M. M., Alley, G. R., & Clark, F. C. (1983). The effects of learning disabilities on post-school adjustment. *Journal of Rehabilitation, 49,* 46–50.

Wiederholt, J. L. (1986). *Formal reading inventory.* Austin, TX: PRO-ED.

Wiederholt, J. L., & Bryant, B. R. (1986). *Gray oral reading test–Revised.* Austin, TX: PRO-ED.

Wiederholt, J. L., Cronin, M., & Stubbs, V. (1980). Measurement of functional competencies and the handicapped: Constructs, assessments, and recommendations. *Exceptional Education Quarterly, 1*(3), 59–73.

Wiederholt, J. L., & Hammill, D. D. (1971). Use of the Frostig-Horne perception program in the urban school. *Psychology in the Schools, 8,* 268–274.

Wiederholt, J. L., Hammill, D. D., & Brown, V. (1978). *The resource teacher: A guide to effective practices.* Boston: Allyn & Bacon.

Wiederholt, J. L., & Larsen, S. C. (1983). *Test of practical knowledge.* Austin, TX: PRO-ED.

Wiig, E. H. (1982a). Communication disorders. In N. G. Haring (Ed.), *Exceptional children and youth* (3rd ed.) (pp. 81–109). Columbus, OH: Merrill.

Wiig, E. H. (1982b). *Let's talk: Developing prosocial communication skill.* San Antonio, TX: Psychological Corporation.

Wiig, E. H. (1982c). *Let's talk inventory for adolescents.* San Antonio, TX: Psychological Corporation.

Wiig, E. H., & Semel, E. (1984). *Language assessment and intervention for the learning disabled* (2nd ed.). Columbus, OH: Merrill.

Wilkinson, G. S. (1987). *WRAT–R monograph 1.* Wilmington, DE: Jastak Associates.

Williams, R. L. (1972). *The BITCH test (Black intelligence test of cultural homogeneity).* St. Louis: Williams & Associates.

Williams, R. L. (1974). Black pride, academic relevance, and individual achievement. In R. W. Tyler & R. M. Wolf (Eds.), *Crucial issues in testing* (pp. 13–20). Berkeley, CA: McCutchan.

Wimmer, D. (1982). Career education. In E. Meyen (Ed.), *Exceptional children in today's schools* (pp. 151–184). Denver: Love.

WISC–R microcomputer-assisted interpretive report [Computer program]. (1986). San Antonio, TX: Psychological Corporation.

Wisconsin tests of reading skill development: Word attack, study skills and comprehension. (1972, 1977). Developed by the Evaluation and Reading Project Staffs at the Wisconsin Research and Development Center for Cognitive Learning. Madison, WI: Learning Multi-Systems.

Wissink, J., Kass, C., & Ferrell, W. (1975). A Bayesian approach to the identification of children with learning disabilities. *Journal of Learning Disabilities, 8,* 58–66.

Wittenberg, W. (1980). *Diagnostic achievement test in spelling.* Baldwin, NY: Barnell Loft.

Wong, B. Y. L. (1980). Activating the inactive learner: Use of questions/prompts to enhance comprehension and retention of implied information in learning disabled children. *Learning Disability Quarterly, 3*(1), 29–37.

Wood, F. H., Johnson, J. L., & Jenkins, J. R. (1986). The Lora case: Nonbiased referral, assessment, and placement procedures. *Exceptional Children, 52,* 323–331.

Woodcock, R. W. (1973). *Woodcock reading mastery tests.* Circle Pines, MN: American Guidance Service.

Woodcock, R. W. (1978). *Development and standardization of the Woodcock-Johnson Psycho-Educational Battery.* Allen, TX: DLM Teaching Resources.

Woodcock, R. W. (1980). *Woodcock language proficiency battery, English form.* Allen, TX: DLM Teaching Resources.

Woodcock, R. W. (1981). *Woodcock language proficiency battery, Spanish form.* Allen, TX: DLM Teaching Resources.

Woodcock, R. W. (1982). *Woodcock Spanish psycho-educational battery (batería Woodcock psico-educativa en español).* Allen, TX: DLM Teaching Resources.

Woodcock, R. W. (1984). A response to some questions raised about the *Woodcock-Johnson:* The mean score discrepancy issue. *School Psychology Review, 13,* 342–354.

Woodcock, R. W. (1987). *Woodcock reading mastery tests–Revised.* Circle Pines, MN: American Guidance Service.

Woodcock, R. W., & Johnson, M. B. (1977). *Woodcock-Johnson psycho-educational battery.* Allen, TX: DLM Teaching Resources.

Woodcock, R. W., & Johnson, M. B. (1989). *Woodcock-Johnson psycho-educational battery–Revised.* Allen, TX: DLM Teaching Resources.

Woodcock, R. W., & Mather, N. (1989a). WJ–R tests of achievement–Standard and supplemental batteries: Examiner's manual. In R. W. Woodcock & M. B. Johnson, *Woodcock–Johnson psycho-educational battery–Revised.* Allen, TX: DLM Teaching Resources.

Woodcock, R. W., & Mather, N. (1989b). WJ–R tests of cognitive ability–Standard and supplemental batteries: Examiner's manual. In R. W. Woodcock & M. B. Johnson, *Woodcock–Johnson psycho-educational battery–Revised.* Allen, TX: DLM Teaching Resources.

Woods, M. L., & Moe, A. J. (1989). *Analytical reading inventory* (4th ed.). Columbus, OH: Merrill.

Wrenn, C. G. (1941). *Study-habits inventory.* Palo Alto, CA: Consulting Psychologists Press.

Yarrow, M. R. (1963). Problems of methods in parent-child research. *Child Development, 34,* 215–226.

Yoshida, R. K. (1982). Research agenda: Finding ways to create more options for parent involvement. *Exceptional Education Quarterly, 3,* 74–80.

Yoshida, R. K. (1984). Planning for change in pupil evaluation practices. In C. A. Maher, R. J. Illback, & J. E. Zins (Eds.),

Organizational psychology in the schools (pp. 262–282). Springfield, IL: Thomas.

Yoshida, R. K., & Bryne, C. (1979). Mediation in special education: The right idea in the wrong form? *School Administrator, 36,* 18–19.

Yoshida, R., Fenton, K., Kaufman, M., & Maxwell, J. (1978). Parental involvement in special education pupil planning process: The school's perspective. *Exceptional Children, 44,* 531–534.

Ysseldyke, J. E. (1983). Current practices in making psychoeducational decisions about learning disabled students. *Journal of Learning Disabilities, 16,* 226–232.

Ysseldyke, J. E., & Algozzine, B. (1982). *Critical issues in special and remedial education.* Boston: Houghton Mifflin.

Ysseldyke, J. E., Algozzine, B., & Allen, D. (1981). Participation of regular education teachers in special education team decision making: A naturalistic investigation. *Elementary School Journal, 82,* 160–165.

Ysseldyke, J. E., Algozzine, B., & Shinn, M. (1981). Validity of the *Woodcock-Johnson Psycho-Educational Battery* for learning disabled youngsters. *Learning Disability Quarterly, 5,* 37–44.

Ysseldyke, J., Algozzine, B., & Epps, S. (1983). A logical and empirical analysis of current practice in classifying students as handicapped. *Exceptional Children, 50,* 160–166.

Ysseldyke, J. E., Algozzine, B., Regan, R., & McGue, M. (1981). The influence of test scores and naturally occurring pupil characteristics on psychoeducational decision making with children. *Journal of School Psychology, 19,* 167–177.

Ysseldyke, J. E., Algozzine, B., Regan, R. R., Potter, M., Richey, L., & Thurlow, M. (1980). *Psychoeducational assessment and decision-making: A computer-simulated investigation.* (Research Report No. 32). Minneapolis: University of Minnesota Institute for Research on Learning Disabilities.

Ysseldyke, J. E., Algozzine, B., Richey, L., & Graden, J. (1982). Declaring students eligible for learning disability services: Why bother with the data? *Learning Disability Quarterly, 5,* 37–44.

Ysseldyke, J. E., & Christenson, S. L. (1987a). Evaluating students' instructional environments. *Remedial and Special Education, 8,* 17–24.

Ysseldyke, J. E., & Christenson, S. L. (1987b). *The instructional environment scale.* Austin, TX: PRO-ED.

Ysseldyke, J. E., Samuels, S. J., & Christenson, S. L. (1988). *The teacher evaluation rating scales.* Austin, TX: PRO-ED.

Ysseldyke, J. E., Thurlow, M., Graden, J., Wesson, C., Algozzine, B., & Deno, S. (1983). Generalizations from five years of research on assessment and decision-making: The University of Minnesota Institute. *Exceptional Education Quarterly, 4,* 75–95.

Zaner-Bloser evaluation scales. (1984). Columbus, OH: Zaner-Bloser.

Zehrbach, R. R. (1975, 1985). *Comprehensive identification process.* Bensenville, IL: Scholastic Testing Service.

Zigmond, N., Vallecorsa, A., & Leinhardt, G. (1980). Reading instruction for students with learning disabilities. *Topics in Language Disorders, 1*(1), 89–98.

Zigmond, N., Vallecorsa, A., & Silverman, R. (1983). *Assessment for instructional planning in special education.* Englewood Cliffs, NJ: Prentice-Hall.

Zinsser, W. (1983). *Writing with a word processor.* New York: Harper & Row.

Test Index

Author Index

Subject Index

WE VALUE YOUR OPINION—PLEASE SHARE IT WITH US

Merrill Publishing and our authors are most interested in your reactions to this textbook. Did it serve you well in the course? If it did, what aspects of the text were most helpful? If not, what didn't you like about it? Your comments will help us to write and develop better textbooks. We value your opinions and thank you for your help.

Text Title _____ Edition _____

Author(s) _____

Your Name (optional) _____

Address _____

City _____ State _____ Zip _____

School _____

Course Title _____

Instructor's Name _____

Your Major _____

Your Class Rank _____ Freshman _____ Sophomore _____ Junior _____ Senior

_____ Graduate Student

Were you required to take this course? _____ Required _____ Elective

Length of Course? _____ Quarter _____ Semester

1. Overall, how does this text compare to other texts you've used?

_____ Superior _____ Better Than Most _____ Average _____ Poor

2. Please rate the text in the following areas:

	Superior	Better Than Most	Average	Poor
Author's Writing Style	_____	_____	_____	_____
Readability	_____	_____	_____	_____
Organization	_____	_____	_____	_____
Accuracy	_____	_____	_____	_____
Layout and Design	_____	_____	_____	_____
Illustrations/Photos/Tables	_____	_____	_____	_____
Examples	_____	_____	_____	_____
Problems/Exercises	_____	_____	_____	_____
Topic Selection	_____	_____	_____	_____
Currentness of Coverage	_____	_____	_____	_____
Explanation of Difficult Concepts	_____	_____	_____	_____
Match-up with Course Coverage	_____	_____	_____	_____
Applications to Real Life	_____	_____	_____	_____

3. Circle those chapters you especially liked:
   1 2 3 4 5 6 7 8 9 10 11 12 13 14 15 16 17 18 19 20
   What was your favorite chapter? _____
   Comments:

4. Circle those chapters you liked least:
   1 2 3 4 5 6 7 8 9 10 11 12 13 14 15 16 17 18 19 20
   What was your least favorite chapter? _____
   Comments:

5. List any chapters your instructor did not assign. _____

6. What topics did your instructor discuss that were not covered in the text?_____

   _____

7. Were you required to buy this book? _____ Yes _____ No

   Did you buy this book new or used? _____ New _____ Used

   If used, how much did you pay? _____

   Do you plan to keep or sell this book? _____ Keep _____ Sell

   If you plan to sell the book, how much do you expect to receive? _____

   Should the instructor continue to assign this book? _____ Yes _____ No

8. Please list any other learning materials you purchased to help you in this course (e.g., study guide, lab manual).

   _____

9. What did you like most about this text? _____

   _____

10. What did you like least about this text? _____

    _____

11. General comments:

    May we quote you in our advertising? _____ Yes _____ No

    Please mail to: Boyd Lane
                     College Division Research Department
                     P. O. Box 508
                     Columbus, Ohio 43216-0508

    Thank you!